JIM MURRAY'S
WHISKEY
BIBLE
2022

This 2022 edition is respectfully dedicated to
the memory of
Sheila Megeary

This edition first published 2021 by Dram Good Books Ltd

10 9 8 7 6 5 4 3 2 1

The "Jim Murray's" logo and the "Whiskey Bible" logo are trade marks of Jim Murray.

For information regarding using tasting notes from Jim Murray's Whiskey Bible contact:
Dram Good Books Ltd, Unit 2, Barnstones Business Park, Litchborough, U.K., NN12 8JJ
Tel: 44 (0)117 317 9777. Or contact us via www.whiskybible.com

A CIP catalogue record for this book is available from the British Library

ISBN: 978-1-8383207-4-4

Printed in Belgium by Graphius Group.

Written by: Jim Murray
Guest writer: Quentin Letts
Edited by: Matthew S. Stanley, Peter Mayne and David Rankin
Design: Jim Murray, Vincent Flint-Hill and James Murray
Maps: James Murray, Rob-indesign and Vincent Flint-Hill
Office Woke Detox Center Manager: Jane "Carville" Garnett
Sample Research: Vincent Flint-Hill, Julia Nourney, Kelly May
Sales: info@whiskybible.com
PA to Jim Murray: Jane Garnett
European Dictionary: Julie Nourney, Tom Wyss, Mariette Duhr-Merges, Stefan Baumgart,
Erik Molenaar, Jürgen Vromans, Henric Molin and Kalle Valkonen.

Author's Note
I have used the spelling "whiskey" or "whisky" depending on how the individual distillers
prefer. All Scotch is "whisky". So is Canadian. All Irish, these days, is "whiskey", though
that was not always the case. In Kentucky, bourbon and rye are spelt "whiskey", with the
exception of the produce of the early Times/Old Forester Distillery and Maker's Mark which
they bottle as "whisky". In Tennessee, it is a 50-50 split: Dickel is "whisky", while Daniel's is
"whiskey".

JIM MURRAY'S
WHISKEY
BIBLE
2022

DRAM GOOD BOOKS

Contents

Introduction

It is a strange feeling knowing that someone is trying to destroy you. And, not only that, attempt to invalidate by association 30 years of painstaking and dedicated work: an entire professional lifetime.

But, a year ago this week, this is exactly what happened to me when a ludicrous – some have said vile - article appeared accusing me and The Whisky Bible of sexism. It is a day I am hardly ever likely to forget.

It had started in my garden, where I sat marvelling at the dozen or so chiffchaffs which had for the previous few days been using my trees, hedges, bushes and plants as base camp as they fuelled up for their migratory journey south. Their busying around my garden was balm to me: I had just written the 2021 Whisky Bible during Lockdown and had escaped to stay away from my village only once, in order to edit another book. I was physically and mentally drained and in desperate need of a break. But it was while sipping a half pint of Hooky at an ancient hostelry – only the second pub I had visited since the outbreak of Covid – that I received a text from my staff to tell me that Twitter was ablaze with accusations of sexism. By me.

We were baffled and bewildered as neither I, nor the Whisky Bible, is sexist. The situation was surreal. It was a bright, sunny Sunday, a day that had been planned as my first of total rest in six months. Yet elsewhere all hell had broken loose. And when I say bewildering, consider this.... In 17 years of writing the Whisky Bible, with nearly a million copies sold across every continent, there had never been a single complaint. Not from the public, not from distilleries, not even from the drinks companies whose executives told me how much they enjoyed my writing. Nothing. Not a peep...

Suddenly, people were piling in denouncing me, using that ducking stool of present-day witch-hunts, Twitter. The Woke smelt blood and here was their latest victim, whoever he may be. White, tick! Privileged, tick! Male, double tick! Middle-aged, tick! Just perfect for burning at the stake. My crime, it seems, is that I had mentioned sex, often tenuously, in reference to whisky, around 30 times in over 4,500 tasting notes. Even worse, once or twice a woman might be referred to. If I did mention a female, it was usually an ex with whom I still am on very good terms and the notes were sent as a coded message of fun. The only time I did refer to a woman that wasn't someone I knew was a tasting note where I had mentioned Arabella from Thomas Hardy's *Jude The Obscure*. However, mindful that the Bible sells in some 40 different countries, I took out her name and replaced it with "lady". Serves me right for dumbing down...

Bizarrely, I then had members of the gay community defending me, pointing out that my tasting notes containing sexual references were virtually all non-gender specific...so it was not women I might have been referring to, but men.

However, all this indignation, whether real or manufactured, was possible because everything had not only been exaggerated but taken entirely out of context. The Whisky Bible makes a point of shewing that all the tasting notes are written using the Murray Method, which I devised nearly 30 years ago after years of experimentation. That means slowly warming the whisky so its nose and taste continuously changes and grows in the glass. So the entire book is based on **sensuality**. Because the Murray Method magnifies the three senses used to enjoy (or not) a whisky: smell, taste and touch, which is crucial as it highlights the importance of mouth feel, something so often overlooked by whisky drinkers.

On the Monday in the office my staff and I sat in disbelief and dismay as one company after another publicly severed any connections with Jim Murray and the Whisky Bible, usually denouncing me as a sexist or misogynist along the way. And so all week it continued around the world, aided by quite astonishing claims from another party which began circulating on the Internet, and thus damaging lies solidified into "fact" as shall be discussed in my Bible Thumping section. Within a week, my world without warning had collapsed about me. Thanks to a single article by a person I cannot ever remember meeting, I had never heard of and who was not interested in discovering my side of the story: the truth.

Thankfully, many whisky companies also stood by me, their executives as nonplussed and appalled as the massive number of Whisky Bible readers whose warmth and support at times brought a tear to my eye. And I have not, to my knowledge, lost a single female friend (of which I have a great many) and even had to dissuade a couple in the drinks industry not to enter the firestorm on Twitter to defend me, in case they were badly burnt also. Such is the nature of a witch-hunt. My God, there are some deeply unpleasant people in the world today...

Ask any genuine British journalist who the best writer in the country is today, and Quentin Letts is most likely to be the answer. A regular on the front page of The Times with his often hilarious and invariably scalpel-sharp political sketches, he is also a fellow critic – in his case of the theatre. Quentin has become the first person ever given his own page in the Whisky Bible, where he offers a neutral view on the situation. His payment: a personal tutoring in the Murray Method, which you will discover, he clearly is in serious need of...

Jim Murray
A bunker in rural Northamptonshire. September 2021.

How to Read The Bible

The whole point of this book is for the whisky lover – be he or she an experienced connoisseur or, better fun still, simply starting out on the long and joyous path of discovery – to have ready access to easy-to-understand information about as many whiskies as possible. And I mean a lot. Thousands.

This book does not quite include every whiskey on the market... just by far and away the vast majority. And those that have been missed this time round – either through accident, logistics or design – will appear in later editions once we can source a sample.

WHISKEY SCORING

The marking for this book is tailored to the consumer and scores run out just a little higher than I use for my own personal references. But such is the way it has been devised that it has not affected my order of preference.

Each whisky is given a rating out of 100. Twenty-five marks are given to each of four factors: nose (**n**), taste (**t**), finish (**f**), balance and overall complexity (**b**). That means that 50% of the marks are given for flavour alone and 25% for the nose, often an overlooked part of the whisky equation. The area of balance and complexity covers all three previous factors and a usually hidden one besides:

Nose: this is simply the aroma. Often requires more than one inspection as hidden aromas can sometimes reveal themselves after time in the glass, increased contact with air and changes in temperature. The nose very often tells much about a whisky, but – as we shall see – equally can be quite misleading.

Taste: this is the immediate arrival on the palate and involves the flavour profile up to, and including, the time it reaches maximum intensity and complexity.

Finish: often the least understood part of a tasting. This is the tail and flourish of the whisky's signature, often revealing the effects of ageing. The better whiskies tend to finish well and linger without too much oak excess. It is on the finish, also, that certain notes which are detrimental to the whisky may be observed. For instance, a sulphur-tarnished cask may be fully revealed for what it is by a dry, bitter residue on the palate which is hard to shake off. It is often worth waiting a few minutes to get the full picture of the finish before having a second taste of a whisky.

Balance: This is the part it takes a little experience to appreciate but it can be mastered by anyone. For a whisky to work well on the nose and palate, it should not be too one-sided in its character. If you are looking for an older whisky, it should have evidence of oak, but not so much that all other flavours and aromas are drowned out. Likewise, a whisky matured or finished in a sherry butt must offer a lot more than just wine alone and the greatest Islay malts, for instance, revel in depth and complexity beyond the smoky effects of peat.

Each whisky has been analysed by me without adding water or ice. I have taken each whisky as it was poured from the bottle and used no more than warming in an identical glass to extract and discover the character of the whisky. To have added water would have been pointless: it would have been an inconsistent factor as people, when pouring water, add different amounts at varying temperatures. The only constant with the whisky you and I taste will be when it has been poured directly from the bottle.

Even if you and I taste the same whiskies at the same temperature and from identical glasses – and even share the same values in whisky – our scores may still be different. Because a factor that is built into my evaluation is drawn from expectation and experience. When I sample a whisky from a certain distillery at such-and-such an age or from this type of barrel or that, I would expect it to offer me certain qualities. It has taken me 30 years to acquire this knowledge (which I try to add to day by day!) and an enthusiast cannot be expected to learn it overnight. But, hopefully, Jim Murray's Whisky Bible will help...!

SCORE CHART

Within the parentheses () is the overall score out of 100.
0–50.5 Nothing short of absolutely diabolical.
51–64.5 Nasty and well worth avoiding.
65–69.5 Very unimpressive indeed.
70–74.5 Usually drinkable but don't expect the earth to move.
75–79.5 Average and usually pleasant though sometimes flawed.
80–84.5 Good whisky worth trying.
85–89.5 Very good to excellent whiskies definitely worth buying.
90–93.5 Brilliant.
94–97.5 Superstar whiskies that give us all a reason to live.
98–100 Better than anything I've ever tasted!

KEY TO ABBREVIATIONS & SYMBOLS

% Percentage strength of whisky measured as alcohol by volume. **b** Overall balance and complexity. **bott** Date of bottling. **nbc** No bottling code. **db** Distillery bottling. In other words, an expression brought out by the owners of the distillery. **dist** Date of distillation or spirit first put into cask. **f** Finish. **n** Nose. **nc** Non-coloured. **ncf** Non-chill-filtered. **sc** Single cask. **t** Taste. ⬧ New entry for 2021. ⊙ Retasted – no change. ⊙⊙ Retasted and re-evaluated. **v** Variant ⬧ 2022 Category Winner. ⬧ 2022 Category Runner-up.

Finding Your Whisky

Worldwide Malts: Whiskies are listed alphabetically throughout the book. In the case of single malts, the distilleries run A–Z style with distillery bottlings appearing at the top of the list in order of age, starting with youngest first. After age comes vintage. After all the "official" distillery bottlings are listed, next come other bottlings, again in alphabetical order. Single malts without a distillery named (or perhaps named after a dead one) are given their own section, as are vatted malts.

Worldwide Blends: These are simply listed alphabetically, irrespective of which company produces them. So "Black Bottle" appears ahead of "White Horse" and Japanese blends begin with "Ajiwai Kakubin" and end with "Za". In the case of brands being named after companies or individuals the first letter of the brand will dictate where it is listed. So William Grant, for instance, will be found under "W" for William rather "G" for Grant.

Bourbon/Rye: One of the most confusing types of whiskey to list because often the name of the brand bears no relation to the name of the distillery that made it. Also, brands may be sold from one company to another, or shortfalls in stock may see companies buying bourbons from another. For that reason all the brands have been listed alphabetically with the name of the bottling distiller being added at the end.

Irish Whiskey: There are four types of Irish whiskey: (i) pure pot still; (ii) single malt, (iii) single grain and (iv) blended. Some whiskies may have "pure pot still" on the label, but are actually single malts. So check both sections.

Bottle Information

As no labels are included in this book I have tried to include all the relevant information you will find on the label to make identification of the brand straightforward. Where known I have included date of distillation and bottling. Also the cask number for further recognition. At the end of the tasting notes I have included the strength and, if known, number of bottles (sometimes abbreviated to btls) released and in which markets.

PRICE OF WHISKEY

You will notice that Jim Murray's Whisky Bible very rarely refers to the cost of a whisky. This is because the book is a guide to quality and character rather than the price tag attached. Also, the same whiskies are sold in different countries at varying prices due to market forces and variations of tax, so there is a relevance factor to be considered. Equally, much depends on the size of an individual's pocket. What may appear a cheap whisky to one could be an expensive outlay to another. With this in mind prices are rarely given in the Whisky Bible.

Bible Thumping
A Joyless Return to Puritanical Prohibition

⫻My Luve is like a red, red rose..." crooned Scotland's immortal bard Robert Burns.

Well, it was fortunate that he didn't compare her to a whisky, or that would have been him well and truly cancelled. As it happens, Burns' treatment of women 250 years ago has, in recent times, come under the microscope and caused a few furrowed brows and pursed lips among female scholars in particular. Yet no calls for his books to be returned to the publishers. For his name to be removed from polite conversation. Probably because it is in nobody's best interests to do so.

We have, I think I can say without too much contradiction, entered an age of complete and total insanity. And one that is in many ways deeply sinister. The world is now a place few of us recognize from, say, ten or five or even three years ago. Now people are terrified. One innocent word, or a refusal to agree with the Newspeak of the radical left, and they see their careers ended. And it is one where it is now easy to destroy an enemy just by getting that person on the wrong side of the Woke activists who patrol social media with their weaponized critical race and critical feminist theories waiting for their next victim. Make a claim of sexism against someone, whether genuine or not, and then sit back as Twitter does its evil work. Which, in short, is what happened to me last year.

Twitter, incidentally, is something I have never embraced. I have never tweeted (I have no idea how), just as I have never smoked or seen a Harry Potter movie (am I allowed to mention Harry Potter? As I believe the author has been cancelled). Many years ago a PR manager of mine insisted he Tweet in my name to keep me "out there", though I was never happy with that. And whenever anyone asked, I told them it wasn't me. The first time I ever saw Twitter in action – actually, until that moment I'd never heard of it – was when a publisher started sending out a message from a press conference to a wider world. He explained what he was doing...and I shuddered. Unlike most drinks writers, I came from a background of national newspapers, covering murders and other crimes against humanity. Working in an investigations department. taught you much about people and life. Each week we would receive hundreds of letters and on the Monday we would read through them. Probably about 80% were malicious, someone simply setting up someone else usually by making deeply unpleasant accusations that were easily proved to be untrue. Newspapers, for all their bad press, had always been there to prevent the innocent from being smeared; and for those of a certain disposition from making mendacious claims against others. They were the unlikely filter that helped save us from the worst of human nature.

But that changed drastically when social media kicked in, Twitter in particular. The filter had gone. Those 80 vitriolic letters a week would turn into 8,000 and they would be for all to see. Decency and common sense would be eroded. The world would become a much nastier place in which to live and one in which a lie would be harder to tell from the truth.

And so, the witch-hunt began. With Twitter there is no nuance, no debate. Just spittle-flecked demented hatred. And untruth, so long as it served some cause or other.

The claim against me was that because a tiny fraction (around 30 of over 4,500 tasting notes) contained a reference that could be interpreted as sexual, then I and the Whisky Bible were palpably sexist and a disgrace to the industry. Oh, and that I had objectified women (as it happened, they were close friends) by comparing them to a whisky. As Burns had compared his Luve to a rose.

No mention, of course, that I have been a feminist all my life, helped women progress in the industry, stated for years that, in general, the best blenders are women, and long publicly complained about drinks companies using models at whisky shows. No mention, either, the reason why Jim Murray's Whisky Bible has been the world's biggest-selling annual spirits guide for the last decade and a half is because so many people seem to love the fact that I write with a genuine and unmanufactured passion, that I do not use pretentious, flowery tasting notes that people cannot even begin to recognize and that I build the entire book on the sensuality, rather than sexuality, of whisky...though obviously with the better whiskies there is an overlap. Whenever possible, I use humour, too, something the Woke mob have a problem processing. But, also, I get people to look at whisky in a way that is very different from the traditional "bagpipes and water" cliché which, even now, dominates the scene. It is amusing watching people denounce, for example, the Murray Method, without ever having tried it.

The sad fact is that when you have spent three decades at the top of something and produce the world's most influential book in the industry, too, then resentment and hatred builds. Especially from those no-one has heard of or who have failed. It is called jealousy. And jealousy, we all know, brings out the very worst in people.

However, once the call of "sexist" has been made, Twitter melts with radical feminists, most hitherto unaware of the book's existence, pointing their fingers and denouncing me from near and afar – and even "journalists" (and I use the term very loosely), eternal shame on them, trying to get the book banned from sale. Sections of the industry, bitten by a puritanical moral code, then began to denounce me also.

But how about this? The person who had originally denounced me and is now talking about a #MeToo movement in whisky due to my alleged exposure – yes, I was now being compared to the rapist Harvey Weinstein – was someone who, The Times reported, had herself written non-judgmental trade magazine articles about, among other things, a whisky that had been poured over a naked women's breasts before bottling: you could hardly make this up. Then a shopkeeper made a big play of sending back my books...the very same person who a few years earlier my female staff refused to take calls from because of the way he spoke to them: I had had to ring him and ask him to alter his sexist approach; a journalist who, in my kitchen, once admitted that he gave his wife a difficult time because of his drinking; another shopkeeper who had owed my company a four-figure sum for well over a year. And all the time in the background, newspapers celebrated the continuing success of the internationally acclaimed television show The Great British Bake Off, which trades on smutty double entendres, one broadsheet even providing a list of its greatest innuendoes. And while they did this my own staff, male and female, were shell-shocked and traumatized. Frankly, it was impossible to smell the whisky for the stench of hypocrisy.

And my crime? I had sensualised whisky. And, most suspect, I was also guilty of being male and successful.

Privately, I was getting calls from executives within the companies saying they were shocked and appalled. However, one public relations executive sent an unpleasant email in which he claimed: "It has nothing to do with free speech."

Yes it has. And I don't need to be lectured to by some bloke on a fat salary in a plush office about free speech, thanks. As a journalist I twice had a gun shoved into my stomach trying to maintain free speech, one a cocked automatic. I have also worked in a newspaper office in Africa where on the wall above my head were still the bullet holes marking the very spot where a journalist had laid down his life defending free speech.

People seem to have no idea of the value of something that is so blithely being surrendered.

But as well as Twitter, you then have the Internet. And as soon as the sexism claims were made against me, here was a chance for others to crawl out onto social media to inject a few lies and pass them off as established as fact. Here is a taste of some of the outrageous claims made:

The Lie: "Banned from distilleries for pervasive attitude to female staff."

The Truth: Never happened anywhere in the world. Not once. I have been banned from distilleries: once because a photo of their brand appeared in a national newspaper when I was blasting the industry for the use of sulphur sherry butts. Another time a control-freakish PR executive ordered that I must always alert him whenever I was in the area of one of their distilleries – my reply was controlled but colourful.

The Lie: "Turns up drunk at his tastings."

The Truth: In my entire lifetime I've been drunk less than half a dozen times, and probably twice in the last 30 years (both on empty stomachs). I don't allow people to swallow whisky at my events and anyone who turns up the worse for alcohol is not let in.

The Lie: "Banned from many whisky shows around the world because of his sexism".

The Truth: Not banned from any shows around the world. And never once been accused of sexism. Due to work demands, I've only ever been able to attend a fraction of those shows I've been invited to.

A witch-hunt, no...? Well, one major company CEO actually told me he didn't think that my writing was sexist, but I was being cancelled by them because I didn't apologise to my accuser. So here we are with the perfect witch-hunt scenario, where if you survived the ducking stool you were guilty. If you drowned you were innocent. I had to apologise for something I didn't do, thereby admitting guilt... I refused.

Then there was another (female) exec who sent me this message; "Dear Jim. I am without doubt the happiest person on the planet today! Thank you for your incredible quote and beautiful tasting notes...I am sincerely over the moon!" A week after I received that message her company cancelled me.

Despite all this, I have carried out writing this year's Whisky Bible without fear or favour. A company which has stood by me has not received a single extra mark over those who denounced me. I continue to give scores and awards to whiskies, irrespective who the owners are, on merit alone. I will not be cowed. Nor shall I ever lose my sense of natural justice.

Because, at the end of the day, this book is written for the public. Not the industry. It is called independent free speech. And it has, as it happens, served the whisky industry rather well. A lot better, in fact, than it ever served me.

Quentin Letts
Cancel Culture Puts Whisky on the Rocks

Confession: I know nothing about whisky. As a nipper I sipped my gran's Vat 69 and thought it disgusting. As a teenager I visited cousin Nigel in County Cavan and he handed me a full tumbler of Power's. I had lowered it by an inch when Nigel leapt up with the bottle and said 'let me take the air out of that glass!' and filled it all over again. Nowadays, if seeking late-night oblivion, I will glug a few fingers of Bell's with soda water and ice. Such is the level of my barbarianism. Plainly I have nothing useful to say to you about whisky.

But allow me a few words about the man who has written this book.

Jim Murray has had a bad year. Okay, we all have. But in addition to covid, Jim was fed through the cancel-culture mincer. One of his rivals shrieked that Jim, in tasting notes, had occasionally mentioned past girlfriends. He was known to compare a whisky to a beautiful or temperamental or perfumed woman. The rival took to social media – as they do – and created a rumpus about Jim 'objectifying women'.

In an instant the tricoteuses of Twitter found Jim guilty. Down slammed the gavel; off went citoyen Murray on the tumbrils. To the guillotine!

The big distillers and their lackeys, naturally, were delighted. For years Jim Murray has used his remarkable nose and palate to give Bible readers his verdict on the distillers' noxious brews. Often he is complimentary, sometimes he is not. He writes what he thinks. He accepts no bribes. Disgraceful! If small distillers deserve praise, Jim says so. The conglomerates didn't like that, either. They saw a chance to destroy the Whisky Bible and they seized it.

They nearly succeeded. Jim is not a robot. He is a normal bloke, as prey to self-doubt as the rest of us. Not being much good at the internet, he was baffled by the kerfuffle. Hurt, too. He knew it was unfair. But there's no reasoning with the puritans of woke. Jim, distracted from his work, took a hit – even though many whisky people were soon conceding that the row was overblown. After all, Jim's principal accuser had herself in the past referred to women in colourful terms when writing about whisky.

Whisky is a sensual drink. Taste, scent, the tang of power, the lingering, giddying nature of it all: who can deny that love is so different? Push the analogy and you may agree that some love affairs are blended while others are single-malt Speysides. Love can give you a worse hangover than even the most sulphurous Sir John Moore, or it can send you drifting to a blissful horizon like that Abhainn Dearg I see I should try. By the way, I see Jim mentions a Kentucky bourbon called Knob Creek. How have they not yet been cancelled?

By day I write about Britain's parliament and by night I review theatre. Why is this any of my business? Why should I care about the persecution of some whisky guy I have met only once? Well, there is a custom of the high seas, older and nobler than the most ancient Inchgower, that you assist stricken fellow-mariners. No matter how busy you are, no matter how important your passengers, you stop for seafarers in trouble. Because it's right. And because some day it might happen to you.

Critics, in whatever sphere, aim for the truth. The best way to do that is to write from the heart. Once we start trimming our verdicts, fitting them to fashionable concepts of etiquette or political correctness – which is another word for dullness – the truth is impaired. The reason Jim Murray is read widely is that he puts his soul and character into his reviews. He writes about his life. What else can we write about? And amid all his learning – which is enormous - he approaches whisky as an amateur. I mean that in the old sense of the word. It means 'lover'.

Long live fun and colour and romance. Long live the Whisky Bible. And may the cancel-culture numpties be assailed by a veritable hailstorm of rotten cabbages.

Quentin Letts is author of Stop Bloody Bossing Me About (Constable, 2021), Parliamentary sketch wrtiter for The Times and Theatre Critic for the Sunday Times.

How to Taste Whiskey

I t is of little use buying a great whisky, spending a comparative fortune in doing so, if you don't get the most out of it.

So when giving whisky tastings, no matter how knowledgeable the audience may be I take them through a brief training schedule in how to nose and taste as I do for each sample included in the Whiskey Bible.

I am aware that many aspects are contrary to what is being taught by distilleries' whisky ambassadors. And for that we should be truly thankful. However, at the end of the day we all find our own way of doing things. If your old tried and trusted technique suits you best, that's fine by me. But I do ask you try out the instructions below at least once to see if you find your whisky is talking to you with a far broader vocabulary and clearer voice than it once did. I strongly suspect you will be pleasantly surprised – amazed, even - by the results.

Amusingly, someone tried to teach me my own tasting technique some years back in an hotel bar. He was not aware who I was and I didn't let on. It transpired that a friend of his had been to one of my tastings a few years earlier and had passed on my words of "wisdom". I'd be lying if I said I didn't smile when he informed me it was called "The Murray Method." It was the first time I had heard the phrase... though certainly not the last!

"THE MURRAY METHOD"

1. Drink a black, unsweetened, coffee or chew on 90% minimum cocoa chocolate to cleanse the palate, especially of sugars.

2. Find a room free from distracting noises as well as the aromas of cooking, polish, flowers and other things which will affect your understanding and appreciation of the whisky.

3. Make sure you have not recently washed your hands using heavily scented soap or are wearing a strong aftershave or perfume.

4. Use a tulip shaped glass with a stem. This helps contain the alcohols at the bottom yet allows the more delicate whisky aromas you are searching for to escape.

5. Never add ice. This tightens the molecules and prevents flavours and aromas from being released. It also makes your whisky taste bitter. There is no better way to get the least from your whisky than by freezing it.

6. Likewise, ignore any advice given to put the bottle in the fridge before drinking.

7. Don't add water! Whatever anyone tells you. It releases aromas but can mean the whisky falls below 40%... so it is no longer whisky. Also, its ability to release flavours and aromas diminishes quite quickly. Never add ridiculous "whisky rocks" or other supposed tasting aids.

8. Warm the undiluted whisky in the glass to body temperature before nosing or tasting. Hence the stem, so you can cradle in your hand the curve of the thin base. This excites the molecules and unravels the whisky in your glass, maximising its sweetness and complexity.

9. Keep an un-perfumed hand over the glass to keep the aromas in while you warm. Only a minute or two after condensation appears at the top of your glass should you extend your arms, lift your covering hand and slowly bring the glass to your nose, so the alcoholic vapours have been released before the glass reaches your face.

10. Never stick your nose in the glass. Or breathe in deeply. Allow glass to gently touch your top lip, leaving a small space below the nose. Move from nostril to nostril, breathing normally. This allows the aromas to break up in the air, helping you find the more complex notes.

11. Take no notice of your first mouthful. This is a marker for your palate.

12. On second, bigger mouthful, close your eyes to concentrate on the flavour and chew the whisky - moving it continuously around the palate. Keep your mouth slightly open to let air in and alcohol out. It helps if your head is tilted back very slightly.

13. Occasionally spit – if you have the willpower! This helps your senses to remain sharp for the longest period of time.

14. Look for the balance of the whisky. That is, which flavours counter others so none is too dominant. Also, watch carefully how the flavours and aromas change in the glass over time.

15. Assess the "shape" and mouthfeel of the whisky, its weight and how long its finish. And don't forget to concentrate on the first flavours as intensely as you do the last. Look out for the way the sugars, spices and other characteristics form.

16. Never make your final assessment until you have tasted it a third or fourth time.

17. Be honest with your assessment: don't like a whisky because someone (yes, even me!), or the label, has tried to convince you how good it is.

18. When you cannot discriminate between one whisky and another, stop immediately.

Immortal Drams:
The Whiskey Bible
Winners 2004-2020

	World Whiskey of the Year	Second Finest Whiskey of the Year	Third Finest Whiskey of the Year
2004/5	George T Stagg	N/A	N/A
2006	George T Stagg	Glen Moray 1986	N/A
2007	Old Parr Superior 18 Years Old	Buffalo Trace Twice Barreled	N/A
2008	Ardbeg 10 Years Old	The Ileach Single Islay Malt Cask Strength	N/A
2009	Ardbeg Uigedail	Nikka Whisky Single Coffey Malt 12 Years	N/A
2010	Sazerac Rye 18 Years Old (bottled Fall 2008)	Ardbeg Supernova	Amrut Fusion
2011	Ballantine's 17 Years Old	Thomas H Handy Sazerac Rye (129 proof)	Wiliam Larue Weller (134.8 proof)
2012	Old Pulteney Aged 21 Years	George T Stagg	Parker's Heritage Collection Aged 10 Years
2013	Thomas H Handy Sazerac Rye (128.6 proof)	William Larue Weller (133.5 proof)	Ballantine's 17 Years Old
2014	Glenmorangie Ealanta 1993	William Larue Weller (123.4 proof)	Thomas Handy Sazerac Rye (132.4 proof)
2015	Yamazaki Single Malt Sherry 2013	William Larue Weller (68.1 abv)	Sazerac Rye 18 Years Old (bottled Fall 2013)
2016	Crown Royal Northern Harvest Rye	Pikesville 110 Proof Straight Rye	Midleton Dair Ghaelach
2017	Booker's Rye 13 Years, 1 Month, 12 Days	Glen Grant 18 Year Old	William Larue Weller (134.6 proof)
2018	Colonel E.H. Taylor 4 Grain Aged 10 Years	Redbreast Aged 21 Years	Glen Grant 18 Year Old
2019	William Larue Weller (128.2 proof)	Glen Grant Aged 18 Years	Thomas Handy Sazerac Rye (127.2 proof)
2020	1792 Full Proof Kentucky Bourbon	William Larue Weller (125.7 proof)	Thomas Handy Sazerac Rye (128.8 proof)
2021	Alberta Premium Cask Strength Rye	Stagg Jr Barrel Proof	Paul John Mithuna

Who has won this year? You are one page away...

13

Jim Murray's Whiskey Bible Awards 2022

When, all those years ago, I awarded George T Stagg the Whiskey Bible's first-ever World Whiskey of the Year gong it caused consternation. And no little anger. The question was: how could anyone in their right mind not give the award to a Scotch whisky, a single malt especially? The Whiskey Snobs had a major attack of the vapours and one or two enemies north of the border were born.

Apparently, I had done it to be sensationalist and gain publicity. Actually, no. I did something nobody had ever before done: treated all whiskies as equals. Just in the same way through my entire life I had treated both men and women. And in the 18 years since, the whisky-loving public has moved on and now the vast majority I meet think the same way: looking at the whisky for its overall beauty. Which helps explain why in America the once ever growing shelves of Scotch have receded and bourbon has retaken its old ground: people have realised that it is time to stop listening to the hype and instead the whisk(e)y in their glass.

It was with George T Stagg I was able to begin this trend of thinking and for three years it reigned supreme...until its performances wavered a little and other whiskies caught up and won by a nose...or a finish.

But now George T is back. It saw off all comers, only Thomas Handy Rye giving it a run for its money. Three days it took me to separate them. Stagg always had that imperceptible edge, despite being quality being as close to a tie as you might ever find. But the greatest whiskey always has something for which there are no words, no description, nothing you can actually point to and say why it is better. It just has...IT...!

Well, there was another miraculous whisky out there this year: a 72-year-old Glen Grant from Gordon and MacPhail, a single cask. I have no idea its price per bottle – frankly, these days I'd rather not know. But tasting two glasses side by side, one gently warmed, the other at normal room temperature, allowed me to venture back to the year my parents married and seemingly nose and taste every month since. It was a remarkable experience and probably the most complete and finest single cask I have ever encountered. Were it not for George T Stagg's mysterious something, it most probably would have been the first single cask to lift the World Whisky of the Year award.

And on the subject of old age, this year brought out the oldest-ever English, Welsh and Belgium whiskies. And they were all utterly magnificent with many a prize heading in their directions.

Oh, a Canadian 43-year-old also walked off with that country's top prize. So despite the excellence of so many relatively young whiskies out there, for instance the formidable Garrison Brothers Balmorhea this year making it four straight awards, it just shews that us oldies still know a trick or two...

2022 World Whiskey of the Year
George T Stagg

Second Finest Whiskey in the World
Thomas Handy Sazerac Barrel Proof Rye

Third Finest Whiskey in the World
Glen Grant Aged 18 Years

Single Cask of the Year
Gordon & MacPhail Glen Grant 1948

SCOTCH
Scotch Whisky of the Year
Gordon and MacPhail Glen Grant 1948
Single Malt of the Year (Multiple Casks)
Glen Grant Aged 18 Years
Single Malt of the Year (Single Cask)
Gordon and MacPhail Glen Grant 1948
Scotch Blend of the Year
Ballantine's Finest
Scotch Grain of the Year
Whisky-Fässle Invergordon 44 Year Old
Scotch Vatted Malt of the Year
Chapter 7 Williamson 9 Years Old

Single Malt Scotch
No Age Statement
Wolfburn Latitude
10 Years & Under (Multiple Casks)
Glen Grant 10 Year Old
10 Years & Under (Single Cask)
Demijohn Islay 10 Year Old
11-15 Years (Multiple Casks)
Clynelish 14 Year Old
11-15 Years (Single Cask)
Old Malt Cask Laphroaig 14 Year Old
16-21 Years (Multiple Casks)
Glen Grant 18 Year Old
16-21 Years (Single Cask)
Cadenhead's Glenfarclas
22-27 Years (Single Cask)
Old Malt Cask Speyside 25 Years Old
28-34 Years (Single Cask)
Kingsbury Gold Linkwood
35-40 Years (Single Cask)
The Perfect Fifth Glenlivet 40 Year Old

BLENDED SCOTCH
No Age Statement (Standard)
Ballantine's Finest
5-12 Years
Johnnie Walker Black Label Aged 12 Years

IRISH WHISKEY
Irish Whiskey of the Year
Ash Tree 30 Year Old
Irish Single Malt of the Year (Mulitple Cask)
Hinch Ch. De La Ligne
Irish Single Malt of the Year (Single Cask)
Ash Tree 30 Year Old
Irish Blend of the Year
Bushmills Black Bush
Irish Single Cask of the Year
Ash Tree Bushmills 30 Year Old

AMERICAN WHISKEY
Bourbon of the Year
George T Stagg
Rye of the Year
Thomas H. Handy Sazerac
US Micro Whisky of the Year
Garrison Brothers Balmorhea 2021 Release

American Other Style
World Whisky Kentucky Samurai 15 Year Old
Special Award, Bourbon
Knaplund Wheated Bourbon Atlantic Aged

CANADIAN WHISKY
Canadian Whisky of the Year
Canadian Club Chronicles Aged 43
Canadian Under 21 Years Old
Canadian Rockies 17
Canadian Over 22 Years Old
Canadian Club Chronicles Aged 43

JAPANESE WHISKY
Japanese Whisky of the Year
The Kurayoshi 18 Pure Malt
Japanese Single Grain of the Year
Nikka Coffey Grain
Japanese Single Malt of the Year
The Matsui Sakura Cask
Japanese Pure Malt Whisky of the Year
The Kurayoshi 18 Pure Malt
Japanese Blended Whisky of the Year
Suntory Toki

ENGLISH & WELSH WHISKY
English Whisky of the Year
The English Vintage 2010
Welsh Whisky of the Year
Penderyn 15 Year Old

EUROPEAN MAINLAND
Multiple Cask
Kornog St Erwan
Single Cask
Belgium Owl 15 Year Old

ALL EUROPEAN WHISKY (Inc England & Wales
Whisky of the Year
Penderyn 15 Year Old

AUSTRALIAN
Australian Whisky of the Year
Tin Shed Flustercluck

WORLD WHISKIES
Asian Whisky of the Year
Cyprus Whisky Association Paul John
Southern Hemisphere Whisky of the Year
Tin Shed Flustercluck

*Overall age category and/or section winners are presented in **bold**.*

The Whiskey Bible Liquid Gold Awards (97.5-94)

Jim Murray's Whiskey Bible is delighted to again make a point of celebrating the very finest whiskies you can find in the world. So we salute the distillers who have maintained or even furthered the finest traditions of whiskey making and taken their craft to the very highest levels. And the bottlers who have brought some of them to us.

After all, there are over 4,300 different brands and expressions listed in this guide and from every corner of the planet. Those which score 94 and upwards represents only a very small fraction of them. These whiskies are, in my view, the élite: the finest you can currently find on the whiskey shelves of the world. Rare and precious, they are Liquid Gold.

So it is our pleasure to announce that all those scoring 94 and upwards automatically qualify for the Jim Murray's Whiskey Bible Liquid Gold Award. Congratulations!

97.5

Scottish Single Malt
Gordon & MacPhail Speyside Glen Grant 1948
Glenmorangie Ealanta 1993 Vintage
Old Pulteney Aged 21 Years

Scottish Blends
Ballantine's 17 Years Old

Irish Pure Pot Still
Midleton Dair Ghaelach Grinsell's Wood Ballaghtobin Estate

Bourbon
1792 Full Proof Kentucky Straight Bourbon
Colonel E.H. Taylor Four Grain Bottled in Bond Aged 12 Years
George T. Stagg
Stagg Jr Barrel Proof
William Larue Weller 125.7 proof
William Larue Weller 128.2 proof
William Larue Weller 135.4 proof

American Straight Rye
Booker's Rye 13 Years, 1 Month, 12 Days
Pikesville Straight Rye Aged at Least 6 Years
Thomas H. Handy Sazerac Straight Rye

Canadian Blended
Alberta Premium Cask Strength Rye
Crown Royal Northern Harvest Rye

97

Scottish Single Malt
Ardbeg 10 Years Old
Bowmore Aged 19 Years The Feis Ile Collection
Glenfiddich 50 Years Old
Glen Grant Aged 15 Years Batch Strength 1st Edition bott code: LRO/HI16
Glen Grant Aged 18 Years Rare Edition
Glen Grant Aged 18 Years Rare Edition bott code. LRO/EE04
Glen Grant Aged 18 Years Rare Edition bott code: LRO/EE03
Gordon & MacPhail Mr George Centenary Edition Glen Grant 1956
The Macphail 1949 China 70th Anniversary Glen Grant Special Edition 1
The Last Drop Glenrothes 1970

Scottish Grain
The Last Drop Dumbarton 1977

Scottish Blends
Compass Box The Double Single
The Last Drop 1971 Blended Scotch Whisky

Irish Pure Pot Still
Redbreast Aged 21 Years

Bourbon
Elmer T. Lee 100 Year Tribute Kentucky Straight Bourbon Whiskey
Old Forester
William Larue Weller 128 proof

American Straight Rye
Thomas H. Handy Sazerac 125.7 proof

Thomas H. Handy Sazerac 127.2 proof
Thomas H. Handy Sazerac 128.8 proof

Canadian Blended
Canadian Club Chronicles: Issue No. 1 Water of Windsor Aged 41 Years
Crown Royal Northern Harvest Rye

Indian Single Malt
Paul John Mithuna

96.5

Scottish Single Malt
The Perfect Fifth Aberlour 1989
Annandale Man O' Sword Smoulderingly Smoky
Ardbeg 20 Something
Ardbeg 21 Years Old
Berry Bros & Rudd Ardmore 9 Years Old
Bowmore Black 50 Year Old
Octomore Edition 10.3 Aged 6 Years
Dramfool Port Charlotte 2002 16 Years Old
Old Malt Cask Bunnahabhain Aged 27 Years
Caol Ila 30 Year Old
Convalmore 32 Year Old
Glencadam Aged 18 Years
Glenfiddich 30 Years Old
Glen Grant Aged 15 Years Batch Strength 1st Edition bott code: LRO/FG 19
Glen Grant 18 Years-Old Rare Edition
The Glenlivet Cipher
Golden Glen Glenlossie Aged 22 Years
Highland Park 50 Years Old
The Perfect Fifth Highland Park 1987
Gordon & MacPhail Private Collection Inverleven 1985
Berry Bros & Rudd Arran 21 Years Old
Kilchoman Private Cask Release
Knockando Aged 21 Years Master Reserve
AnCnoc Cutter
AnCnoc Rutter
Laphroaig Aged 27 Years
Kingsbury Sar Obair Linkwood 30 Year Old
Loch Lomond Organic Aged 17 Years
The Whisky Agency Lochside 1981
The First Editions Longmorn Aged 21 Years
Port Ellen 39 Years Old
Gleann Mór Port Ellen Aged Over 33 Years
Talisker Aged 25 Years
Tomatin 36 Year Old American & European Oak
Tullibardine 1970
Arcanum Spirits TR21INITY Aged Over 21 Years
Glen Castle Aged 28 Years
Whisky Works 20 Year Old Speyside 2019/WV02./CW

Scottish Grain
Berry Bros & Rudd Cambus 26 Years Old
The Perfect Fifth Cambus 1979
The Whisky Barrel Dumbarton 30 Year Old

Scottish Blends
The Antiquary Aged 35 Years

Dewar's Aged 18 Years The Vintage
Dewar's Double Double Aged 27 Years
Blended Scotch Whisky
Johnnie Walker Blue Label The Casks Edition
The Last Drop 1965
The Last Drop 56 Year Old Blend
Royal Salute 32 Years Old
Teacher's Aged 25 Years

Irish Pure Pot Still
Midleton Barry Crockett Legacy
Redbreast Aged 32 Years Dream Cask

Bourbon
1792 Bottled In Bond Kentucky Straight Bourbon
Blanton's Uncut/Unfiltered
Bulleit Bourbon Blender's Select No. 001
Colonel E.H. Taylor 18 Year Marriage BiB
Colonel E H Taylor Single Barrel BiB
George T. Stagg 116.9 proof
George T. Stagg 129.2 proof
George T. Stagg 144.1 proof
Michter's 20 Year Old Kentucky Straight
Bourbon batch no. 18I1370
Michter's 20 Year Old Kentucky Straight
Bourbon batch no. 19H1439, bott code:
A192421439

American Straight Rye
Knob Creek Cask Strength

American Microdistilleries
Garrison Brothers Balmorhea Texas Straight
Bourbon Whiskey
Garrison Brothers Balmorhea Texas Straight
Bourbon Whiskey dist 2014
Garrison Brothers Balmorhea Texas Straight
Bourbon Whiskey dist 2015
Woodinville Straight Bourbon Whiskey
Private Select

American/Kentucky Whiskey Blends
Michter's Celebration Sour Mash Whiskey
Release No. 3

Whiskey Distilled From Bourbon Mash
Knaplund Straight Bourbon Whiskey Atlantic
Aged

Canadian Blended
Canadian Club Chronicles Aged 42 Years

Japanese Single Malt
Nikka Whisky Single Malt Yoichi Apple
Brandy Wood Finish

English Single Malt
The English Single Malt Aged 11 Years
The Norfolk Farmers Single Grain Whisky
The Norfolk Single Grain Parched

Welsh Single Malt
Penderyn Icons of Wales No 5 Bryn Terfel
Penderyn Rhiannon
Penderyn Single Cask no. 182/2006
Penderyn Single Cask 15-Year-Old
Bourbon Cask

Belgian Single Malt
Belgian Owl 12 Years Vintage No. 07 First Fill
Bourbon Single Cask No 4275925
Belgian Owl Single Malt The Private Angels
60 Months
Braeckman Belgian Single Grain Whiskey
Single Barrel Aged 10 Years

Danish Single Malt
Thy Whisky No. 9 Bøg Single Malt

Italian Single Malt
PUNI Aura Italian Single Malt

Indian Single Malt
Paul John Single Cask Non Peated #4127

Taiwanese Single Malt
Kavalan 40th Anniversary Single Malt
Selected Wine Cask Matured Single Cask

Nantou Distillery Omar Cask Strength

96
Scottish Single Malt
Annandale Vintage Man O'Words 2015
Ardbeg 1977
Ardbeg Provenance 1974
The Balvenie The Week of Peat Aged 14 Years
Octomore 71 5 Years Old
Glenwill Caol Ila 1990
Gordon & MacPhail Connoisseurs Choice
Caol Ila Aged 15 Years
Gordon & MacPhail Private Collection
Dallas Dhu 1969
The Dalmore Candela Aged 50 Years
Gordon & MacPhail Glen Albyn 1976
Cadenhead's Cask Strength Glendronach
Aged 30 Years
Cadenhead's Cask Strength Glenfarclas
Aged 17 Years
Glenfiddich Fire & Cane
Glen Grant Aged 10 Years
Glen Grant Rothes Chronicles Cask Haven
First Fill Casks bott code: LRO/FG 26
Glen Grant Rothes Chronicles Cask Haven
The Macphail 1949 China 70th Anniversary
Glen Grant Special Edition 2
Glen Scotia 45 Year Old
Cadenhead's Cask Strength Glentauchers
Aged 41 Years
The Glenturret Fly's 16 Masters Edition
The Perfect Fifth Glenlivet 40 Year Old
Highland Park Loki Aged 15 Years
Highland Park Aged 25 Years
Highland Park 2002
Highland Park Sigurd
Kilchoman 10 Years Old
Lagavulin Aged 12 Years
Lagavulin 12 Year Old
Cadenhead's Lagavulin 11 Year Old
Laphroaig Lore
Laphroaig PX Cask
Laphroaig Quarter Cask
Loch Lomond 10 Year Old 2009 Alvi's Drift
Muscat de Frontignan Finish
G&M Private Collection Longmorn 1966
Port Ellen 9 Rogue Casks 40 Year Old
Old Pulteney Aged 25 Years
Artful Dodger Springbank 18 Year Old 2000
The Perfect Fifth Springbank 1993
Gordon & MacPhail Private Collection St.
Magdalene 1982
Ledaig Dùsgadh 42 Aged 42 Years
Tomatin Warehouse 6 Collection 1977
Compass Box Myths & Legends I
Glen Castle Islay Single Malt 1989 Vintage
Cask 29 Years Old
Abbey Whisky Anon. Batch 3 Aged 30 Years
Whiskey Bottle Company Cigar Malt Lover
Aged 21 Years

Scottish Vatted Malt
Compass Box The Spice Tree
Glen Castle Blended Malt 1992 Sherry Cask
Glen Castle Blended Malt 1990 Sherry Cask
Matured 28 Years Old

Scottish Grain
SMWS Cask G14.5 31 Year Old
Single Cask Collection Dumbarton 30 Years Old
The Cooper's Choice Garnheath 48 Year Old
Port Dundas 52 Year Old
The Sovereign Blended Grain 28 Years Old

Scottish Blends
Ballantine's Aged 30 Years

Ballantine's Finest
Ballantine's Limited release no. A27380
Dewar's Aged 25 Years The Signature
Grant's Aged 12 Years
Islay Mist Aged 17 Years
Johnnie Walker Blue Label Ghost & Rare
Oishii Wisukii Aged 36 Years
Royal Salute 21 Years Old
Whyte & Mackay Aged 50 Years

Irish Pure Pot Still
Method and Madness Single Pot Still
Powers Aged 12 Years John's Lane Release
Redbreast Aged 12 Years Cask Strength
batch no. B1/18
Redbreast Dream Cask Aged 28 Years

Irish Single Malt
The Whisky Cask Company The Ash Tree 1989

Bourbon
Ancient Ancient Age 10 Years Old
Bib & Tucker Small Batch Aged 6 Years
Cadenhead's World Whiskies Heaven Hill Aged 23 Years
Colonel E.H. Taylor Barrel Proof
Elijah Craig Barrel Proof Kentucky Straight Bourbon Aged 12 Years
Elijah Craig Toasted Barrel Kentucky Straight Bourbon
Michter's Single Barrel 10 Year Old Kentucky Straight Bourbon barrel no. 19D662
Old Grand-Dad Bonded 100 Proof
Pappy Van Winkle 15 Years Old
Pappy Van Winkle Family Reserve Kentucky Straight Bourbon Whiskey 15 Years Old
Stagg Jr
Very Old Barton 100 Proof
William Larue Weller

American Straight Rye
Colonel E.H. Taylor Straight Rye BiB
J Mattingly House Money Small Batch Rye Whiskey Aged 4 Years
Michter's 10 Years Old Single Barrel Kentucky Straight Rye barrel no. 19F965
Sazerac Rye
Sazerac 18 Years Old bott Summer 2018
Sazerac 18 Years Old bott Summer 2019
Smooth Ambler Old Scout Rye Single Barrel 4 Years Aged
Van Winkle Family Reserve Kentucky Straight Rye Whiskey 13 Years Old No. 99A
Wild Turkey Master's Keep Cornerstone Aged a Minimum of 9 Years

American Microdistilleries
Balcones Peated Texas Single Malt Aged 26 Months in American Oak
291 Barrel Proof Aged 2 Years
Garrison Brothers Balmorhea Texas Straight Bourbon Whiskey 2021 Release
Garrison Brothers Cowboy Bourbon Barrel Proof Aged Four Years
Grand Traverse Michigan Wheat 100% Straight Rye Wheat Whiskey Bottled in Bond
Rock Town Single Barrel Rye Whiskey Aged 32 Months
The Notch Single Malt Whisky Aged 15 Years
Woodinville Bottled-in-Bond Straight Bourbon Whiskey Pot Distilled

Canadian Blended
Crown Royal Noble Collection 13 Year Old Bourbon Mash
Crown Royal Special Reserve
Heavens Door The Bootleg Series Canadian Whisky 26 Years Old 2019
J. P. Wiser's 35 Year Old

Lot No. 40 Rye Whisky

Japanese Single Malt
Chichibu 2012 Vintage
The Hakushu Paul Rusch 120th Anniversary
Nikka Coffey Malt Whisky
ePower Komagatake
The Matsui Single Cask Mizunara Cask
The Yamazaki Single Malt Aged 18 Years

English Single Malt
Cotswolds Single Malt Whisky Peated Cask Batch No. 01/2019
The English Single Malt Whisky Small Batch Release Heavily Smoked Vintage 2010
The English Single Malt Triple Distilled

Welsh Single Malt
Penderyn Portwood Single Cask 12 Year Old
Penderyn Single Cask Ex-Bourbon cask no. 195/2007

Australian Single Malt
Adams Distillery Tasmanian Single Malt Whisky Cask Strength
Launceston Distillery Cask Strength Bourbon Cask Tasmanian Single Malt
Tasmanian Heartwood The Angel of Darkness Cask Strength
Iniquity Anomaly Series Flustercluck Single Malt

Belgian Single Malt
Belgian Owl Single Malt 12 Years Vintage No 6 Single First Fill Bourbon Cask No 4018737
Belgian Owl Single Malt 12 Years Single Cask No 14018725
Belgian Owl Single Malt Aged 15 Years First Fill Bourbon cask

Czech Republic Single Malt
Gold Cock Single Malt 2008 Virgin Oak

Danish Single Malt
Copenhagen Single Malt First Edition
Stauning Kaos
Thy Danish Whisky No. 12 Kornmod Aged 3 Years

French Single Malt
Kornog Single Malt Oloroso Finish 2019

German Single Malt
Feller Single Malt Valerie Madeira
Hercynian Willowburn Exceptional Collection Aged 5 Years Single Malt

Swedish Single Malt
Mackmyra Svensk Single Cask Whisky Reserve The Dude of Fucking Everything
Smögen 100 Proof Single Malt Whisky

Swiss Single Malt
Langatun Old Woodpecker Organic

Indian Single Malts
Paul John Kanya
Paul John Single Cask Non Peated #6758
Paul John Single Cask Peated #6355
Paul John Select Cask Peated
Paul John Tula

95.5
Scottish Single Malt
Ardbeg An Oa
Ardbeg Grooves Committee Release
Balblair 2000 2nd Release
Ben Nevis 32 Years Old 1966
The BenRiach Aged 12 Years Matured In Sherry Wood
Benromach 30 Years Old
Benromach Organic 2010
Bowmore 20 Years Old 1997

Octomore Edition 10.4 Aged 3 Years

The First Editions Bruichladdich Aged 28 Years 1991

Caol Ila Aged 25 Years

Fadandel.dk Caol Ila Aged 10 Years

The Dalmore Visitor Centre Exclusive

Abbey Whisky Glendronach 1993

Glenfarclas 105

Glenfarclas The Family Casks 1979 W18

Glenfarclas The Family Casks 1989 W18

Glenfiddich Aged 15 Years Distillery Edition

Glenfiddich Project XX

Glengoyne 25 Year Old

Glen Grant Aged 10 Years bott code: LRO/GE01

Gordon & MacPhail Private Collection Glen Grant 1948

The Glenlivet Archive 21 Years of Age

The Whisk(e)y Company The Spirit of Glenlossie aged 22 Years

Glenmorangie 25 Years Old

Glenmorangie Private Edition 9 Spios

Glen Moray Chardonnay Cask 2003

The Singleton of Glen Ord 14 Year Old

The Singleton Glen Ord Distillery Exclusive

The Last Drop Glenrothes 1970

Whisky Illuminati Glentauchers 2011

G&M Rare Old Glenury Royal 1984

Highland Park Aged 18 Years

Fadandel.dk Orkney Aged 14 Years

AnCnoc 1999

Lagavulin Aged 8 Years

Loch Lomond The Open Special Edition Distiller's Cut

The Macallan Fine Oak 12 Years Old

Cadenhead's Whisky & More Baden Miltonduff 10 Year Old

Old Pulteney Aged 15 Years

Gordon & MacPhail Connoisseurs Choice Pulteney Aged 19 Years

Rosebank 21 Year Old

Springbank 22 Year Old Single Cask

Kingsbury Sar Obair Springbank 28 Year Old

Tomatin Warehouse 6 Collection 1975

Tullibardine The Murray Double Wood Edition

Wolfburn Latitude

Port Askaig Islay Aged 12 Years Spring Edition

Arcanum Spirits Arcanum One 18 Years Old

Compass Box Myths & Legends III

Whisky Illuminati Artis Secretum 2011

Scottish Vatted Malt

Compass Box The Lost Blend

Chapter 7 Williamson 2010 Aged 9 Years

Valour Speyside Blended Malt Aged 27 Years

Wemyss Malts Spice King Batch Strength

Scottish Grain

Whisky-Fässle Invergordon 44 Year Old

Scottish Blends

Artful Dodger Blended Scotch 41 Year Old

Ballantine's Aged 30 Years

The Chivas 18 Ultimate Cask Collection First Fill American Oak

Chivas Regal Aged 25 Years

James Buchanan's Aged 18 Years

Johnnie Walker Black Label 12 Years Old

Royal Salute 21 Year Old The Lost Blend

Royal Salute 62 Gun Salute

Irish Pure Pot Still

Redbreast Aged 12 Years Cask Strength batch no. B2/19

Irish Single Malt

Bushmills Aged 21 Years

Bushmills Port Cask Reserve

The Irishman Aged 17 Years

J. J. Corry The Flintlock No. 1 16 Year Old

Kinahan's The Kasc Project M

Kinahan's Special Release Project 11 Year Old

Bourbon

Blade and Bow 22 Year Old

Buffalo Trace Single Oak Project Barrel #27

Buffalo Trace Single Oak Project Barrel #30

Eagle Rare Aged 10 Years

Elmer T Lee Single Barrel Kentucky Straight Bourbon Whiskey

Frankfort Bourbon Society Elijah Craig Small Batch Serial No 4718833

Knob Creek Aged 9 Years

Michter's 25 Year Old

Michter's Single Barrel 10 Year Old Kentucky Straight Bourbon barrel no. 19D625

Old Forester 1920 Prohibition Style

Pappy Van Winkle Family Reserve Kentucky Straight Bourbon Whiskey 23 Years Old

Parker's Heritage Collection 24 Year Old Bottled in Bond Bourbon

Rock Hill Farms Single Barrel Bourbon

Weller Antique 107

Weller C.Y.P.B Wheated Straight Bourbon

Wild Turkey Rare Breed Barrel Proof

William Larue Weller 135.4 proof

World Whisky Society Reserve Collection Kentucky Straight Bourbon Single Barrel Aged 15 Years

Tennessee Whiskey

Uncle Nearest 1820 Aged 11 Years

American Straight Rye

Knob Creek Rye Single Barrel Select

Michter's US*1 Single Barrel Strength Kentucky Straight Rye

Wild Turkey 101 Kentucky Straight Rye

American Microdistilleries

Horse Soldier Reserve Barrel Strength Bourbon Whiskey

Burns Night Single Malt

Balcones FR.OAK Texas Single Malt Whisky Aged at least 36 Months in Oak

Corsair Dark Rye American Rye Malt Whiskey Aged 8 Months

Garrison Brothers Cowboy Bourbon Barrel Proof Aged Five Years

Garrison Brothers Cowboy Bourbon Texas Straight Bourbon Whiskey 2020 Release

Garrison Brothers Laguna Madre Texas Straight Bourbon Whiskey 2020 Release

Cadenhead's Garrison Brothers 2014

Laws Whiskey House Four Grain Straight Bourbon Whiskey Barrel Select Aged 8 Years

Woodinville Cask Strength Straight Bourbon

Canadian Single Malt

Lohin McKinnon Peated Single Malt Whisky

Forty Creek Copper Pot Reserve

Canadian Rockies 17 Years

Shelter Point Single Cask Virgin Oak Finish

Canadian Blended

Crown Royal Northern Harvest Rye

Gibson's Finest Rare Aged 18 Years

Japanese Single Malt

The Matsui Single Malt Sakura Cask

Mars Komagatake Single Malt Limited Edition 2020

Japanese Vatted Malt

Nikka Taketsuru Pure Malt

The Kurayoshi Pure Malt Whisky Aged 18 Years

Japanese Single Grain

Makoto Single Grain Whisky Aged 23 Years

Nikka Coffey Grain Whisky

English Single Malt
Bimber Distillery Single Malt London
Cotswolds Single Malt Whisky Founder's Choice STR
The English Single Malt Whisky 'Lest We Forget' 1914 - 1918
The English Single Malt Whisky Small Batch Release Triple Distilled

Welsh Single Malt
Penderyn Celt
Penderyn Legend
Penderyn Madeira Finish
Penderyn Myth bott code 200292
Penderyn Rich Oak bott code 200563
Penderyn Single Cask no. 2/2006
Penderyn Single Cask 8-year-Old
Penderyn Ex-Madeira Single Cask no. M524
Penderyn Single Cask 13 Year Old Rich Oak Cask

Australian Single Malt
Bakery Hill Peated Malt Cask Strength Single Malt Whisky
Cadenhead's World Whiskies Cradle Mountain Aged 24 Years
Heartwood Night Thief
Limeburners Western Australia Single Malt Whisky Port Cask Cask Strength

Austrian Single Malt
J.H. Original Rye Whisky 6 Jahre Gelagert

Belgian Single Malt
Belgian Owl Intense Single Malt
Braeckman Belgian Single Grain Whisky Single Barrel Aged 12 Years

Corsican Single Malt
P & M Aged 13 Years Corsican Single Malt

Danish Single Malt
Stauning Peat
Stauning Rye The Master Distiller

French Single Malt
Eddu Gold
Kornog Single Malt Sant Erwan 2021

German Single Malt
Feller New Make Barley Malt Peated

Swedish Single Malt
High Coast Distillery Visitor Center Cask
Mackmyra Brukswhisky art nr. MB-003
Mackmyra Brukswhisky art nr. MB-004
Mackmyra Single Cask 2nd Fill ex-Bourbon Cask Fat Nr 11638
Mackmyra Svensk Rök
Mackmyra Svensk Moment 22
Smögen Primör Revisited Single Malt 2019

Swiss Single Malt
Langatun 10 Year Old Chardonnay
Langatun Cardeira Cask Finish Single Malt
Langatun Single Malt Old Crow

Indian Single Malt
Amrut Greedy Angels Peated Rum Finish Chairman's Reserve 10 Years Old
Amrut Peated Port Pipe Single Cask
Paul John Christmas Edition
The Cyprus Whisky Association Paul John Single Malt

95 (New Entries Only)
Scottish Single Malt
Arcanum Spirits Private Release Ardmore Aged 10 years
Clynelish Aged 14 Years
Cadenhead's Cask Strength Highland Park Aged 28 Years
Talisker Skye
Demijohn Islay 10 Year Old
Kingsbury Sar Obair Mhain Baraille 40 Year Old

Scottish Grain
The Sovereign North British 32 Years Old

Scottish Grain
Ballantine's Finest
Johnnie Walker Black Label Aged 12 Years

Irish Single Malt
Hinch Single Malt Aged 18 Years Château De La Ligne Grande Reserve Finish

Bourbon
1792 Full Proof Kentucky Straight Bourbon
Knaplund Wheated Straight Bourbon Whiskey Atlantic Aged
Lucky Seven The Holiday Toast
Smooth Ambler Old Scout Aged 5 Years Bourbon

Tennessee Whiskey
Jack Daniel's No 6 Edition Master Distiller Series Jimmy Bedford

American Microdistilleries
Pinhook Bourbon War Straight Bourbon Whiskey Aged 5 Years
Copper Fox Peachwood American Single Malt
291 Barrel Proof Single Barrel Colorado Bourbon Whiskey

Canadian Single Malt
SE Eleven Single Grain
Ghleann Dubh Peated Single Malt Whisky Aged 13 Years
Macaloney's Caledonian Skarrabollis Single Cask Ex-Bourbon Peated

Canadian Blended
Canadian Club Chronicles Aged 43 Years
Great Plains Craft Spirits 18-Year-Old Brandy Casks

Japanese Single Malt
The Matsui Single Malt Mizunara Cask
Mars Tsunuki The First

Japanese Blended
Suntory Toki

English Single Malt
Cotswolds Peated Cask Single Malt

Welsh Single Malt
Penderyn Legend bott code 931010
Penderyn Single Cask Ex-Tawny Port Cask

Australian Single Malt
Heartwood Don't @#$%&* It Up, Son

Belgian Single Malt
Belgian Owl Passion Single Malt 40 Months
Belgian Owl Single Malt Aged 7 Years
Belgian Owl Single Malt Aged 13 Years First Fill Champagne 6

French Single Malt
Kornog Single Malt Pedro Ximinez 2020

German Single Malt
Feller Single Malt Torf
Marder Single Malt Black Forest Reserve Aged 10 Years

94.5 (New Entries Only)
Scottish Single Malt
The Whisky Cask Company Allt-A-Bhainne 1992
The Whisky Tasting Club Ardmore 12 Year Old
Benromach Aged 15 Years
Single & Single Bunnahabhain 2002 17 Year Old
Old Malt Cask Glen Moray Aged 24 Years
Old Malt Cask Laphroaig Aged 14 Years
Old Malt Cask Pulteney Aged 18 Years
Gleann Mór Rare Find Teanininch 1975 Aged 46 Years
Chapter 7 Tormore 1990 Aged 31 Years

Bourbon
1792 Small Batch
Bulleit Bourbon Frontier Whiskey
Green River Kentucky Straight Bourbon

American Microdistilleries
291 Bad Guy Colorado Bourbon Whiskey
291 Small Batch Colorado Bourbon Garrison Brothers Single Barrel Texas Straight Bourbon Whiskey Aged 3 Years

Whiskey Distilled From Bourbon Mash
World Whiskey Society Kentucky Samurai Edition Kentucky Straight Bourbon Whiskey Finished In Japanese Mizunara Oak Shochu Barrels Aged 15 Years

Canadian Single Malt
Glen Breton Rare Single Malt Aged 21 Years

Japanese Blended
The Kyoto Kuro-Obi black belt
The San-In Blended Japanese Whisky

English Single Malt
Cotswolds Private STR Cask 140 Single Malt
Cotswolds Sherry Cask Single Malt
The English Single Malt Whisky Aged 11 Years

Welsh Single Malt
Penderyn Legend bott code 203301
Penderyn Madeira Finish bott code 202684
Penderyn Single Cask Ex-Olorosos Cask cask no. S76

Australian
Shene Cognac Release Tasmanian Single Malt
Tasmanian Independent Bottlers The Blend Malt and Oat Sherry x 3 Virgin Oak

Danish Single Malt
Stauning Rye Whisky

Finnish Single Malt
Teerenpeli Kaski Single Malt

French Single Malt
Kornog Single Malt Roc'h Hir 2019

German Single Malt
Slyrs Bavarian Single Malt Madeira Cask Finishing
Mary Read Single Cask Malt Whisky Fassstärke 20 Years Old

Taiwanese Single Malt
Kavalan Single Malt Madeira Cask Solist

94 (New Entries Only)
Scottish Single Malt
Valour Highland Single Malt Ben Nevis Aged 25 Years
Old Malt Cask Bowmore Aged 18 Years
Skene Bunnahabhain 2013 Peated Islay Scotch Single Malt
The Single Cask Caol Ila 2008
The Single Cask Craigellachie 2012
Hepburn's Choice Glenburgie 10 Years Old
Kingbury Sar Obair Glenlivet 30 Year Old
Glenmorangie The Original Aged 10 Years
Kingsbury Gold Miltonduff 21 Year Old
The Single Cask Royal Brackla 2009
The First Editions Speyburn Aged 14 Years
Whisky-Fässle Ledaig 10 Year Old
The First Editions Tomatin Aged 25 Years 1994
Scyfion Choice Tormore 1992
Old Malt Cask Orkney Aged 13 Years
Whisky-Fässle Aged 27 Years
Fadandel.dk Isla Blended Aged 10 Years In Memory of Bessie Williamson

Scottish Blends
Chivas Regal Aged 12 Years
The Famous Grouse Smoky Black
For Peat's Sake
The Woodsman

Irish Blends
Bushmills Black Bush Sherry Cask Reserve

Bourbon
Eagle Rare 17 Years Old
Knaplund Handcrafted Small Batch

Lucky Seven The Proprietor Aged 12 Years
Old Fitzgerald Bottled-in-Bond Aged 14 Years Fall 2020

American Microdistilleries
291 Barrel Proof Colorado Straight Bourbon
291 Barrel Proof Colorado Straight Rye
291 E Colorado Whiskey Blend of Wheat and Malt Barley Whiskey
Iron Smoke Straight Bourbon Whiskey Four Grain Aged a Minimum of 2 Years
Spirit Hound Straight Malt 5 years Old
Boulder Spirits American Single Malt Bottled In Bond

Canadian Single Malt
Macaloney's Caledonian Skarrabollis Single Cask Peated

Canadian Blended
Crown XR Extra Rare

Japanese Single Malt
BS Fuji X The Akkeshi Single Malt Whisky
Mars Komagatake Single Malt Double Cellars Bottled 2019
Mars Komagatake Single Malt Yakushima Aging Bottled 2020

Japanese Vatted Malt
Nikka Taketsuru Pure Malt

English Single Malt
Cotswolds Signature Single Malt
The Lakes Single Malt The Whiskymaker's Editions Colheita
M & S Norfolk Distilled English Whisky

Welsh Single Malt
Penderyn Celt bott code 200503
Penderyn Madeira Finish bott code 203085
Penderyn Madeira Finish bott code 200581
Penderyn Myth bott code 90644

Australian
VI Anthropocene Small Reserve Release 04 Single Malt
Chief's Son 900 Standard
Launceston Distillery Cask Strength Tawny Cask Tasmanian Single Malt
McHenry Singe Malt Whisky
Starward Left-Field Single Malt

Belgian Single Malt
Belgian Owl Intense Single Malt 58 Months
Belgian Owl Intense Single Malt

Czech Single Malt
Svach's Old Well Single Bohemian Whisky Malt Unpeated

Danish Single Malt
Thy Danish Whisky No. 14 Bøg Aged 3 Years

Faroe Island
Batch 5

French Single Malt
Kornog Single Malt Roc'h Hir 2021
Maison Benjamin Kuentz Fin de Partie Single Malt

German Single Malt
Doinich Daal Blackforest Single Malt Erbenwald
Eifel Whisky 746.9 Single Rye 12 Jahre Alt
Eifel Roggen Ahrtaler Reserve Pinot Noir
Whisky Stube Spirit Of The Cask Roggen Whisky
The Nine Springs Single Malt Peated Breeze Edition
Slyrs Single Malt Whisky Fifty One
Slyrs Single Malt Whisky Oroloso Cask Finish
Otto's Uisge Beatha Single Cask Malt Fassstärke

Brazillian Single Malt
Lamas Smoked Single Malt Whisky

American Whiskey

During the early Spring of last year I took a very long drive. It was from Texas to Kentucky, taking me on a route which cut through the Ozark Mountains in both Arkansas and Missouri, where I dropped in on a forest in which oaks had been felled for the making of bourbon barrels. And then stood beside the stumps of departed trees holding in my hands the last acorns they had ever deposited.

I stopped at quite a few liquor stores en-route, also. And found something possibly even more astonishing. Where, once, the whisk(e)y shelves had contained an ever-increasing number of single malt Scotch whiskies, now they contained bourbon and rye.

Kentucky bourbon, Colorado bourbon, Texas bourbon. They were all there. Alongside ryes and Tennessee and various types of whiskeys from the smaller concerns that had mushroomed up around the country since the turn of the century. It seemed that in mid-America at least bourbon and rye had Scotch whisky on the run: a nation had fallen back in love with its national whiskey.

And that can hardly be surprising when the consistency of Kentucky rye and bourbon has been so unrelentingly good. Indeed, Indeed, having won the first three Jim Murray Whisky Bible World Whisky of the Year titles, it has this year, for the 2022 edition, regained its crown for the first time since 2006. Which means that in the 18 years the Whisky Bible has been published, the finest whiskey was claimed by Kentucky 10 times: an extraordinary achievement.

Even more extraordinary is that George T Stagg's success means that that Kentucky has won the top prize for five of the last six years, a brilliant Canadian from Alberta being the only obstacle to a clear run of victories. And it probably hardly needs saying that the only whiskey that was a serious threat to the Stagg among the multiple cask bottlings came from its stablemate, Thomas Handy Rye.

In Texas, so high is the standard of the whiskeys there, I was recently able to travel to the State to carry out a whiskey shootout between 11 of their distilleries there to see which, through blind tasting, the assembled crowd appreciated most. It was Garrison Brothers' Balmorhea. This enormous bourbon this year made it four times in a row of picking up Microdistillery Whisky of the Year with yet another stupendous bottling.

A quarter of a century ago the liquor store owners from New York to San Francisco were telling me that bourbon and rye would soon be a thing of the past as single malts moved in. Bourbon is well and truly back. And, as the top awards of Jim Murray's Whisky Bible underlines, with very good reason.

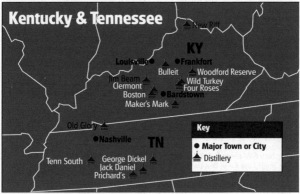

Bourbon Distilleries

Bourbon confuses people. Often they don't even realise it is a whiskey, a situation not helped by leading British pub chains, such as Wetherspoon, whose bar menus list "whiskey" and "bourbon" in separate sections. And if I see the liqueur Southern Comfort listed as a bourbon one more time I may not be responsible for my actions.

Bourbon is a whiskey. It is made from grain and matured in oak, so really it can't be much else. To be legally called bourbon it must have been made with a minimum of 51% corn and matured in virgin oak casks for at least two years. Oh, and no colouring can be added other than that which comes naturally from the barrel.

Where it does differ, from, say Scotch, is that the straight whiskey from the distillery may be called by something other than that distillery name. Indeed, the distillery may change its name which has happened to two this year already and two others in the last three or four. So, to make things easy and reference as quick as possible, I shall list the Kentucky-based distilleries first and then their products in alphabetical order along with their owners and operational status.

Bourbon Distillery List

Bardstown	Lexington	Jim Beam Urban Stillhouse
Barton 1792	Barrel House	Kentucky Peerless
Rebell Yell	Bluegrass	Michter's Fort Nelson
Willett Distillery	James E. Pepper	Michter's Shively
	Town Branch	Old Forester
		Rabbit Hole
	Louisville	Stitzel Weller
Frankfort	Angel's Envy	
Buffalo Trace	Bernheim.	**Shelbyville**
Castle & Key	Evan Williams	Bulleit Distilling Co.
Glenns Creek	Heaven Hill Bernheim	Jeptha Creed

Jim Murray's Whisky Bible 2021 American Whiskies of the Year

Bourbon of the Year	George T Stagg
Rye of the Year	Thomas H. Handy Sazerac
US Micro Whisky of the Year	Garrison Brothers Balmorhea Texas Straight Bourbon Whiskey 2021 Release
American Other Style	World Whisky Kentucky Samurai 15 Year Old
Special Award, Bourbon	Knaplund Wheated Bourbon Atlantic Aged

Jim Murray's Whisky Bible American Whiskey Award Winners

	Overall Winner	Bourbon	Rye	Microdistilleries
2004-2006	George T. Stagg	George T. Stagg	Sazerac Rye 18 Years Old	McCarthy's Oregan Single Malt
2007	Buffalo Trace Experimental	Buffalo Trace Experimental	Rittenhouse Rye 21 Barrel No.28	McCarthy's Oregan Single Malt
2008	George T. Stagg 70.3%	George T. Stagg 70.3%	Old Potrero Hotaling's 11 Essay	Old Potrero Hotaling's 11 Essay
2009	George T. Stagg (144.8 Proof)	George T. Stagg (144.8 Proof)	Rittenhouse Rye 23 Barrel No.8	Stranahan's Colorado 5 Batch 11
2010	Sazerac Rye 18 (Fall 2008)	George T. Stagg (144.8 Proof)	Sazerac Rye 18 (Fall 2008)	N/A
2011	Thomas H. Handy Rye (129 Proof)	William Larue Weller (134.8 Proof)	Thomas H. Handy Rye (129 Proof)	N/A
2012	George T. Stagg (143 Proof)	George T. Stagg (143 Proof)	Thomas H. Handy Rye (126.9 Proof)	N/A
2013	Thomas H. Handy Rye (128.6 Proof)	William Larue Weller (133.5 Proof)	Thomas H. Handy Rye (128.6 Proof)	Balcones Brimstone
2014	William Larue Weller (1234 Proof)	William Larue Weller (1234 Proof)	Thomas H. Handy Rye (132.4 Proof)	Cowboy Bourbon Whiskey
2015	William Larue Weller	William Larue Weller	Sazerac Rye 18 (Fall 2013)	Arkansas Single Barrel Reserve #190
2016	Pikesville Straight Rye (110 Proof)	William Larue Weller	Pikesville Straight Rye (110 Proof)	Notch 12 Year Old
2017	Booker's Rye 13 Years 1 Mo 12 Days	William Larue Weller (1346 Prof)	Booker's Rye 13 Years 1 Mo 12 Days	Garrison Brothers Cowboy 2009
2018	Colonel E.H. Taylor Four Grain	Colonel E.H. Taylor Four Grain	Thomas H. Handy Rye (126.2 Proof)	Balcones Texas Blue Corn
2019	William Larue Weller (128.2 Proof)	William Larue Weller (128.2 Proof)	Thomas H. Handy Rye (127.2 Proof)	Garrison Brothers Balmorhea
2020	1792 Full Proof Bourbon	1792 Full Proof Bourbon	Thomas H. Handy Rye (128.8 Proof)	Garrison Brothers Balmorhea
2021	George T. Stagg	George T. Stagg	Thomas H. Handy Rye	Garrison Brothers Balmorhea

Bourbon

1792 Aged 12 Years Kentucky Straight Bourbon Whiskey nbc db **(94.5)** n24 those busy small grains – a kind of 1792 Distillery trademark– are burbling and bubbling away under the red liquorice, the rye in particular surfacing for a quick stab before vanishing again. Despite the good age, the tannins remain restrained and delicately in keeping with the grains. The softer corn gently offers an enticing bready sweetness; **t24** the delivery is all about the corn oil. So sensual, every nuance just melts into the next. Light acacia and ulmo honey mix for a controlled sweetness; the red liquorice is a meagre nod towards the big age. But, as usual, the star turn is the bubbling grains busily frothing away; **f23** surprisingly quiet. But, as usual below the surface, so much is happening...; **b23.5** the usual 1792 complexity mixed with sleek curves. Nowhere near in the same league as last year's world conquering Full Proof version. But for a gentle perambulation among the unsung small grains, this is as good a route as you can take... *48.3% (96.6 proof).*

1792 Bottled In Bond bott code: L172731504:465 db **(93)** n23 t23.5 f23 b23.5 An unusually salty resonance to this which travels from the nose to the very last moments of the finish. Certainly does a job in sharpening up the flavour profile! *50% (100 proof).*

1792 Bottled In Bond Kentucky Straight Bourbon bott code: L183471505565 **(96.5)** n24 t24 f24 ...b24.5 Well, it's only gone and improved, hasn't it..!!! I just wish this distillery would give a whiskey I could seriously pan..! Just so damn, indecently beautiful...! *50% (100 proof).*

1792 Full Proof Kentucky Straight Bourbon bott code: L18135151:425 **(97.5)** n24 t24.5 f24 b25 Sings on the nose and palate like a wood thrush in a Kentucky forest: melodious, mysterious and slightly exotic. On this evidence Buffalo Trace has a threat to its world supremacy – from a rival distillery...they own! This is a whiskey of stand out, almost stand-alone beauty. Finding fault is not easy with something this intense and magnificently rich. If this is not World Whisky of the Year for 2020, then its master will be something to marvel at. *62.5% (125 proof).*

◈ **1792 Full Proof Kentucky Straight Bourbon** bott code: L0930 db **(95)** n23.5 the trademark fizzing and intertwangling of myriad little aroma combinations, and in a way perhaps only this distillery on the planet can achieve. Particularly outstanding is the fragile hickory element which ensures you know some decent aging has been going on here...; **t24** if you find any bourbon more salivating than this this year, please let me know. I suspect it is the rye section of the mash bill at work here as the juiciness is also met by a crisp, almost brittle succulence...which in turn gives way to an unexpected early milk chocolate softness wending in off the oak. The spices tease rather than attack, while the sugars are a wonderful mix of Demerara and ulmo honey; **f23.5** thankfully the finish simplifies, which is just as well because I'm not sure my brain has the energy to try and work anything that is half as complex as the delivery. Here we are now left with a gentle corn oil and light tannin mix, denser heather honey now replacing the ulmo variety....; **b24** such is the effortless complexity of this whiskey, that when aided by the Murray Method you do not even for a second regard the huge strength: your mind is focussed purely on the delights playing out in tiny detail on your palate. Not quite in the same league as the bottling which won World Whisky of the Year, a year or two back, but certainly good enough to make a great evening perfect. *67.25% (134.5 proof)*

1792 Single Barrel Kentucky Straight Bourbon nbc **(90.5)** n22.5 t22 f23 b23 Typical of a single cask, offering some of what you expect from a distillery though not necessarily all. Delicious and more mouth-filling as it progresses. *44% (88 proof). sc.*

1792 Small Batch bott code: L173111514:395 **(94)** n23 t24 f23.5 b23.5 Yet again a 1792 expression pulls off Whisky Bible Liquid Gold status. Astonishing. *46.85% (93.7 proof).*

1792 Small Batch Kentucky Straight Bourbon bott code: L190461512595 **(94)** n23.5 t24 f23 b23.5 On the lighter side of the 1782 spectrum, though definitely within the distillery's new orbit. Where there is often a rich wave of soft tannins, here it concentrates on the defter vanillas, at times delicate to the point of fragility, though the trademark weight and gravitas is not far behind... *46.85% (93.7 proof).*

◈ **1792 Small Batch** bott code L21070 **(94.5)** n23.5 heather honey and black liquorice intermingle with silky grace. The molasses seems to offer extra weighty depth. Meanwhile the faintest buzz of the small grains furthers the complexity. A little hickory stakes claim, too...; **t24** what a delivery...Almost the perfect combination of intensity and guile. Heather honey is the first point of call, thinning towards acacia but the oak gets in with some sombre vanilla notes enlivened by onrushing, super-busy spices. Red liquorice melts into the mix; **f23.5** corn oils hold their ground and allow the myriad honey and sugar notes to play out without hindrance. And just how many shades of vanilla can you spot...? **b23.5** after tasting one or two surprisingly disappointing bourbons, I was beginning to wonder if my taste buds were out of sync. Then I tasted this...and all is right with the world...and my taste buds. Another wonderful rendition from a distillery which seems to specialise in symphonies... *46.85% (93.8 proof)*

Abraham Bowman Limited Edition Viriginia Sweet XVI Bourbon dist 4-26-02, bott 4-26-18 **(95.5)** n23.5 t24.5 f23.5 b24 Probably the most outrageously complex and full-flavoured Virginia whiskey I have ever encountered in bottled form...Just amazin'! *58% (116 proof).*

American Eagle Tennessee Bourbon Aged 4 Years bott code: L927704 db **(91)** n22.5 such an attractive mix between mildly damp muscovado sugar and drier, powdery hickory; t23 any specialist in Bowmore will immediately recognise an earthy Victory V cough sweet assembly which apes that distillery remarkably from how it was 15 years ago. The hickory really does do a star turn...; f22.5 a light oiling of corn heralds the arrival of the delicate spices; b23 an attractive bourbon very much of the hickory persuasion. Enticing, soft, good corn involvement and well distributed spice. A very sound whiskey. *40%.*

American Eagle Tennessee Bourbon Aged 12 Years bott code: L9053HA12 db **(84.5)** n21 t22 f20 b21.5 When I tasted this earlier in the year, I was quite impressed. This bottling seems to have dropped a notch. The nose warns of an unhappy alliance between the spirit and oak. The unhappy finish confirms it dramatically. *43%.*

American Rockies Small Batch Bourbon Whiskey (76) n19 t22 f17 b18 Sweet, soft, fruity and rounded. But very dull. With an unattractive furry finish to boot. Just not sure what all these fruit notes are doing in a bourbon. *44% (88 proof).*

Ancient Age bott code: 03072163212:09F **(94)** n24 t23.5 f22.5 b24 Though at times a little youthful and proudly possessing a little nip to the delivery, this still exudes Buffalo Trace character and class and a lot more inner oomph than when I first encountered this brand decades ago – indeed, when the distillery was still called Ancient Age. Enough oak to make a comfortable foil for the busy small grain. Salivating, complex and deeply satisfying, especially when the burnt honey begins to make itself heard. A classic name and my word, this bottling shows it in a classic light. *40% (80 proof)*

Ancient Age Kentucky Straight Bourbon bott code: L190240120:254 **(93)** n23 t23 f23.5 b23.5 Very similar to the bottling code above One very slight difference here is just a slight downturn in the intensity of the honey while the spices, perhaps with a fraction less to counter it, have a marginally louder voice. Perhaps not quite the same balance, but the finish goes on so much longer. *40% (80 proof).*

Ancient Age Bonded (92) n23 t24 f23 b23. Unmistakably Buffalo Trace... with balls. *50%*

Ancient Ancient Age 10 Years Old (96) n23.5 t24 f24 b24.5. This whiskey is like shifting sands: same score as last time out, but the shape is quite different again. Somehow underlines the genius of the distillery that a world class whiskey can reach the same point of greatness, but by taking two different routes...However, in this case the bourbon actually finds something a little extra to move it on to a point very few whiskeys very rarely reach... *43%*

Ancient Ancient Age 10 Star (94.5) n23 t24 f23.5 b24. A bourbon which has slipped effortlessly through the gears over the last decade. It is now cruising and offers so many nuggets of pure joy this is now a must have for the serious bourbon devotee. Now a truly great bourbon which positively revels in its newfound complexity: a new 10 Star is born... *45%*

Ancient Age 10 Star Kentucky Straight Bourbon bott code: L182010116 **(94)** n22.5 t23.5 f24 b24 A bourbon which had lost its way slightly in recent years. And though it still splutters about a bit for identity and rhythm on the nose, there is no doubting it is right back on track with some taste-bud catching moments. It is at times, monumental. *45% (90 proof).*

Ancient Age 90 bott code: 03072173209:38W **(88.5)** n22 t22 f22.5 b22 An emboldened bourbon showing little of genteel complexity of the standard Ancient Age. Delicious, though! *45% (90 proof)*

Ancient Age 90 Kentucky Straight Bourbon Whiskey bott code: B1310606 **(93.5)** n23 t23 f23.5 b24 More of the same as above, though now is a lot more vibrant. A little more stark tannin on the nose to this one and an infinitely more lush and bold delivery. If the layering was good before, then now it is excellent with not just an extra layer or two of strata to negotiate but much more Manuka honey coming through at the death. How can two whiskeys be outwardly so similar, yet so different? A bit like having a polished Jaguar XK against a slightly dusty one. *45% (90 proof).*

Baker's Kentucky Straight Bourbon Single Barrel Aged 8 Years, 3 Months dist 10-2011, warehouse CL-Z, serial no. 000289669 db **(93)** n23.5 t23.5 f22.5 b23.5 Just amazing that the distillery that brings you the occasionally pulverising Knob Creek can also caress you so tenderly with a Baker's like this... *53.5% (107 proof). sc.*

Baker's Kentucky Straight Bourbon Single Barrel Aged 8 Years, 6 Months dist 01-2011, warehouse CL-D db **(94)** n23.5 almost a light smokiness to soften the impact of the prevailing tannins. A dusting of hickory and a small pinch of spice compliments the light maple syrup and molasses mix; t24 silky corn oils abound and ensures a sublime counter for the most prickly of spices that try to puncture the sugary frame. So chewy and elegant; f23 just a trace of bitterness follows the hefty liquorice; b23.5 surely Jim Beam's Clermont Distillery has to be the most under-rated in the world: familiarity breeding contempt, I suppose. But this single barrel shows you in no uncertain terms just how high grade and beautifully complex their output can be. *53.5% (107 proof). sc.*

Barrel Bourbon Cask Strength Aged 9.5 Years batch 015 **(88)** n22 t23 f21 b22 An interesting bottling which fits cosily together in places and falls apart slightly in others. Overall, though, enjoyable. *53.8% (1076 proof). Distilled in Tennessee and Kentucky.*

Basil Hayden's Kentucky Straight Bourbon Whiskey bott code L5222 **(87)** n22.5 t22 f21 b21.5. Bigs up the bitter marmalade but a relatively thin bourbon with not enough depth to entirely manage the flattening and slightly unflattering vanilla. The usual rye-based backbone has gone missing. *40% (80 proof)*

Bib and Tucker Small Batch Bourbon Aged 6 Years batch no 018 **(88.5)** n22 t22 f22.5 b22 Bit of a straight up and downer, with the complexity at last formulating towards the finale. About as easy-going and even as it gets. *46% (92 proof).*

Bib & Tucker Small Batch Bourbon Aged 6 Years batch no. 21 **(96)** n24 t24.5 f23.5 b24 A far more intense and captivating bourbon than the last bottling I sampled. This is Tennessee bourbon to put hairs on your chest. I'd love to see this at full strength, I can tell you! A whiskey demanding to be served in a dirty glass. I absolutely love this! *46% (92 proof).*

Blade & Bow batch SW-B1 **(84)** n21.5 t21.5 f20 b21. A simple, if at times massively sweet, offering which minimises on complexity. *45.5%*

Blade and Bow 22 Year Old (95.5) n24 t24 f23.5 b24 This may not be the oldest bourbon brand on the market, but it creaks along as though it is. Every aspect says "Old Timer". But like many an old 'un, has a good story to tell... in this case, exceptional. *46% (92 proof)*

Blade & Bow DeLuxe batch WLCFSS-2 **(88.5)** n22.5 t22.5 f21 b22.5 A steady ship which, initially, is heavy on the honey. *46%*

Blanton's (92) n21.5 t24 f23 b23.5. If it were not for the sluggish nose this would be a Whisky Bible Liquid Gold award winner for sure. On the palate it shows just why little can touch Buffalo Trace for quality at the moment... *40%*

Blanton's dumped 10-10-19 Warehouse H Rick 1 db **(84.5)** n21 t22 f20 b21.5 Well, what do you know? A Blanton's firing off only half its cylinders at most. Both the nose and finish are strangely muffled and muted. And despite a brief moment of juicy brilliance on delivery, the musty, bitter finale confirms all is not well. My God! This bourbon is made by humans after all... *46.5% (93 proof).*

Blanton's Gold Edition Bourbon Whiskey dumped 15 Jan 19, barrel no 131, Warehouse H, Rick 15 **(90)** n22 t23 f22 b23 The last time I tasted a Blanton's Gold, I was stopped in my tracks and knew I had, in my glass, some kind of major Whisky Bible award winner. And so it proved. This time the key honey notes crucial to greatness are thin on the ground. And, lovely whiskey though it may be, this one is no award winner..! *51.5% (103 proof). sc.*

Blanton's The Original Single Barrel Bourbon Whiskey dumped 7 March 19, barrel no 199, Warehouse H Rick 11 **(94)** n24 t23.5 f23 b23.5 Not sure bourbon gets any friendlier and sweeter than this without losing shape. Superb! *46.5% (93 proof). sc.*

Blanton's Single Barrel Kentucky Straight Bourbon dumped 30th April 18, barrel no 126, Warehouse H Rick 52 **(94.5)** n23.5 t24 f23 b24 A very long journey from beginning to end: intriguing as you are never sure what will be happening next. *46.5% (93 proof). sc.*

Blanton's Uncut/Unfiltered (96.5) n25 t24 f23.5 b24. Uncut. Unfiltered. Unbelievable. *65.9%*

Bomberger's Declaration Kentucky Straight Bourbon 2018 Release batch no. 18C317, bott code: A18096317 **(95)** n23.5 t24 f23.5 b24 A breath-taking whiskey which, despite its seemingly soft and inclusive nature, is huge in personality. *54% (108 proof). 1,658 bottles. Bottled by Michter's Distillery.*

Bomberger's Declaration Kentucky Straight Bourbon 2019 Release batch no. 19G1234, bott code: A192071234 **(94)** n23.5 t24 f23 b23.5 Proper bourbon, this. Ticks every box. And there is nothing more dangerous than a Bomberger that ticks... *54% (108 proof). 2,577 bottles. Bottled by Michter's Distillery.*

Bondi Bourbon Whiskey Aged 4 Years (85) n20.5 t21.5 f21.5 b21.5 Rammed full of varied honey notes, the feintiness on both the nose and delivery can't be entirely ignored. Still. Chewy and attractive late on. *40% (80 proof).*

Booker's Kentucky Straight Bourbon Aged 6 Years, 6 Months, 19 Days batch no. 2019-04 db **(95)** n23.5 t24 f23.5 b24 Huge! Not a bourbon to be trifled with. And you will note that despite its enormity there is not a single off-key moment, not a single false step. *63.5%*

Boone County Eighteen 33 Straight Bourbon Aged 12 Years nbc **(94.5)** n23.5 t24 f23 b24 Sits as beautifully on the plate as it does in the glass. Gorgeous! *45.4% (90.8 proof). Distilled at DSP-IN-1 (MGP, Indiana, presumably.).*

Bourbon 30 (91) n22 t23.5 f22.5 b23 A sturdy, highly attractive bourbon making maximum use of the small grains to really ramp up the complexity. Beautifully deft sugars give an extra crispness...while the small grains fizz and nip. Vanilla everywhere! Love the late spice, too. Great stuff...!! *45% (90 proof).*

Bourbon 30 (94) n23.5 t23.5 f23 b24 A little more oily than their 45% bottling with far more corn visible on the nose and, especially, the delivery. Much more roasty, headstrong liquorice forming the meat of the body. In fact, just a little more everything compared to the 45%, chest-beating liquorice especially. The late spices here aren't afraid to pack a punch, either... Truly classic high class bourbon. Delicious. *50% (100 proof).*

Bowman Brothers Small Batch Virginia Straight Bourbon bott code: L183540513 **(93)** n23.5 t23 f23 b23.5 A significant improvement on the last Small Batch I encountered with much more confidence and depth on the finish. The coffee note hangs around wonderfully... *45% (90 proof).*

Bowman Brothers Virginia Small Batch bott code: 71600080ASB08:22 **(88.5)** n22 t23 f21.5 b22 A lovely bourbon, though the sugars are thinly spread. *45% (90 proof).*

Buffalo Trace (92.5) n23 t23 f23.5 b23. Easily one of the lightest BTs I have tasted in a very long while. The rye has not just taken a back seat, but has fallen off the bus. *45%*

Buffalo Trace Kentucky Straight Bourbon bott code: L190400220 **(94)** n23.5 t23.5 f23 b24 A huge whiskey dressed up as something altogether more modest. But get the temperature right on this and watch it open up like a petal in sunlight. A true anywhere, anytime bourbon with hidden sophistication. *45% (90 proof).*

⬦ **Buffalo Trace** bott code L21084 **(92.5)** n23 the least intense BT I have encountered: the light hickory tones and grapefruit peel are both line drawings, rather than broad strokes. The corn oils seem a little reduced... Delicious and enticing, but something odd here...; t23.5 a polite parade of vanilla tones, some sweetened by butterscotch and the slow drawing out of liquorice. The spices arrive almost in slow motion while the Demerara sugar and lightly roasted tannins have a divine duet; f23 a noticeably shorter finish than usual, but now the spices have the bit between their teeth and linger. The vanillas remain delicate and unperturbed; b23 the first thing to hit me about this bottling was how the oils and lingering richer notes were a little duller. So, after nosing I checked the bottle. And sure, enough, the strength had been dropped from 45% to 40%, a whopping drop of 10 proof. That is a significant change and will mean the finishes will never quite linger as they once did due to the oil being broken. However, in the case of this bottling, richness of texture has given way to elegance. *40%*

Buffalo Trace Single Oak Project Barrel #132 (r1yKA1 *see key below*) db **(95)** n24 t23.5 f23.5 b24. This sample struck me for possessing, among the first batch of bottlings, the classic Buffalo Trace personality. Afterwards they revealed that it was of a profile which perhaps most closely matches their standard 8-year-old BT. Therefore it is this one I shall use as the tasting template. *45% (90 Proof)*

Key to Buffalo Trace Single Oak Project Codes

Mash bill type: r = rye; w = wheat
Tree grain: 1 = course; 2 = average; 3 = tight
Tree cut: x = top half; y = bottom half
Warehouse type: K = rick; L = concrete

Entry strength: A = 125; B = 105
Seasoning: 1 = 6 Months; 2 = 12 Months
Char: All #4 except * = #3

Buffalo Trace Single Oak Project Barrel #1 (r3xKA1*) db **(90.5)** n22 t23 f23 b22.5. *45%*
Buffalo Trace Single Oak Project Barrel #2 (r3yKA1*) db **(91.5)** n23 t23 f22.5 b23. *45%*
Buffalo Trace Single Oak Project Barrel #3 (r2xKA1) db **(90.5)** n22.5 t23 f22.5 b22.5. *45%*
Buffalo Trace Single Oak Project Barrel #4 (r2yKA1) db **(92)** n23 t23 f23 b23. *45%*
Buffalo Trace Single Oak Project Barrel #5 (r2xLA1*) db **(89)** n23 t22.5 f21.5 b22. *45%*
Buffalo Trace Single Oak Project Barrel #6 (r3yLA1*) db **(90)** n22.5 t22 f23 b22.5. *45%*
Buffalo Trace Single Oak Project Barrel #7 (r3xLA1) db **(90.5)** n23 t22.5 f22.5 b22.5. *45%*
Buffalo Trace Single Oak Project Barrel #8 (r3yLA1) db **(92.5)** n23 t23 f23.5 b23. *45%*
Buffalo Trace Single Oak Project Barrel #9 (r3xKA2*) db **(90)** n22 t22.5 f23 b22.5. *45%*
Buffalo Trace Single Oak Project Barrel #10 (r3yKA2*) db **(93)** n23.5 t23.5 f22.5 b23.5. *45%*
Buffalo Trace Single Oak Project Barrel #11 (r3xKA2) db **(94.5)** n23 t24 f23.5 b24. *45%.*
Buffalo Trace Single Oak Project Barrel #12 (r3yKA2) db **(92)** n24 t23 f22.5 b22.5. *45%*
Buffalo Trace Single Oak Project Barrel #13 (r3xLA2*) db **(89.5)** n22 t23 f22 b22.5. *45%.*
Buffalo Trace Single Oak Project Barrel #14 (r3yLA2*) db **(95)** n24 t24 f23 b24. *45%*
Buffalo Trace Single Oak Project Barrel #15 (r3xLA2) db **(90.5)** n22.5 t23 f22 b23. *45%.*
Buffalo Trace Single Oak Project Barrel #16 (r3yLA2) db **(91.5)** n22.5 t23.5 f22.5 b23. *45%.*
Buffalo Trace Single Oak Project Barrel #17 (r3xKB1*) db **(88.5)** n21.5 t22.5 f22.5 b22. *45%.*
Buffalo Trace Single Oak Project Barrel #18 (r3yKB1*) db **(92.5)** n23 t23 f23.5 b23. *45%*
Buffalo Trace Single Oak Project Barrel #19 (r3xKB1) db **(90)** n23 t23.5 f23 b23.5. *45%.*
Buffalo Trace Single Oak Project Barrel #20 (r3yKB1) db **(95)** n23.5 t24 f23 b23.5. *45%*
Buffalo Trace Single Oak Project Barrel #21 (r3xLB1*) db **(92)** n23 t23 f23 b23. *45%*

Buffalo Trace Single Oak Project Barrel #22 (r3yLB1*) db **(91)** n22 t23.5 f22.5 b23. *45%.*
Buffalo Trace Single Oak Project Barrel #23 (r3xLB1) db **(89)** n21 t22.5 f22.5 b23. *45%.*
Buffalo Trace Single Oak Project Barrel #24 (r3xLB1) db **(90)** n22 t23 f22.5 b22.5. *45%*
Buffalo Trace Single Oak Project Barrel #25 (r3xKB2*) db **(90.5)** n22.5 t23 f22.5 b22.5. *45%*
Buffalo Trace Single Oak Project Barrel #26 (r3yKB2*) db **(89.5)** n22 t23.5 f22 b22. *45%*
Buffalo Trace Single Oak Project Barrel #27 (r3xKB2) db **(95.5)** n23 t24 f24.5 b24. *45%*
Buffalo Trace Single Oak Project Barrel #28 (r3yKB2) db **(94.5)** n23 t24 f23.5 b24. *45%*
Buffalo Trace Single Oak Project Barrel #29 (r3xLB2*) db **(91)** n23 t22.5 f23 b22.5. *45%*
Buffalo Trace Single Oak Project Barrel #30 (r3yLB2*) db **(95.5)** n23.5 t24 f24 b24. *45%*
Buffalo Trace Single Oak Project Barrel #31 (r3xLB2) db **(87.5)** n22 t22 f21.5 b22. *45%*
Buffalo Trace Single Oak Project Barrel #32 (r3yLB2) db **(90.5)** n23.5 t23 f21.5 b22.5. *45%*
Buffalo Trace Single Oak Project Barrel #33 (w3xKA1*) db **(94.5)** n24 t23.5 f23 b24. *45%*
Buffalo Trace Single Oak Project Barrel #34 (w3yKA1*) db **(90)** n21.5 t23.5 f22.5 b22.5. *45%*
Buffalo Trace Single Oak Project Barrel #35 (w3xKA1) db **(89.5)** n22 t22 f23 b22.5. *45%*
Buffalo Trace Single Oak Project Barrel #36 (w3yKA1) db **(91.5)** n23 t23 f22.5 b23. *45%*
Buffalo Trace Single Oak Project Barrel #37 (w3xLA1*) db **(90)** n21 t23 f22 b22. *45%*
Buffalo Trace Single Oak Project Barrel #38 (w3yLA1*) db **(87.5)** n22 t23.5 f20.5 b21.5. *45%*
Buffalo Trace Single Oak Project Barrel #39 (w3xLA1) db **(87)** n21.5 t22 f21.5 b22. *45%*
Buffalo Trace Single Oak Project Barrel #40 (w3xLA1) db **(93)** n23 t23 f23.5 b23.5. *45%*
Buffalo Trace Single Oak Project Barrel #41 (w3xKA2*) db **(92.5)** n22 t23 f23.5 b24. *45%*
Buffalo Trace Single Oak Project Barrel #42 (w3yKA2*) db **(85.5)** n22 t21.5 f21 b21. *45%*
Buffalo Trace Single Oak Project Barrel #43 (w3xKA2) db **(89)** n22 t23 f22 b22. *45%.*
Buffalo Trace Single Oak Project Barrel #44 (w3yKA2) db **(89)** n23 t23 f21 b22. *45%*
Buffalo Trace Single Oak Project Barrel #45 (w3xLA2*) db **(87)** n23 t22 f21 b21. *45%.*
Buffalo Trace Single Oak Project Barrel #46 (w3yLA2*) db **(88)** n21.5 t22 f22.5 b22. *45%*
Buffalo Trace Single Oak Project Barrel #47 (w3xLA2) db **(88.5)** n22.5 t22 f22 b22. *45%.*
Buffalo Trace Single Oak Project Barrel #48 (w3yLA2) db **(90.5)** n22 t23 f22.5 b23. *45%.*
Buffalo Trace Single Oak Project Barrel #49 (w3xKB1) db **(93)** n24 t23 f23 b23. *45%*
Buffalo Trace Single Oak Project Barrel #50 (w3yKB1*) db **(88)** n21.5 t23 f21.5 b22. *45%*
Buffalo Trace Single Oak Project Barrel #51 (w3xKB1) db **(89.5)** n23 t23 f21.5 b22. *45%*
Buffalo Trace Single Oak Project Barrel #52 (w3yKB1) db **(87.5)** n21.5 t22 f22 b22. *45%*
Buffalo Trace Single Oak Project Barrel #53 (w3xLB1*) db **(91)** n22 t23 f23 b23. *45%*
Buffalo Trace Single Oak Project Barrel #54 (w3yLB1*) db **(89)** n22 t23 f22.5 b22.5. *45%*
Buffalo Trace Single Oak Project Barrel #55 (w3xLB1) db **(89)** n22 t22 f23 b22. *45%.*
Buffalo Trace Single Oak Project Barrel #56 (w3yLB1) db **(91)** n24 t22.5 f22 b22.5. *45%*
Buffalo Trace Single Oak Project Barrel #57 (w3xKB2*) db **(94)** n23 t23.5 f23.5 b24. *45%*
Buffalo Trace Single Oak Project Barrel #58 (w3xKB2*) db **(90.5)** n22.5 t23 f22.5 b22.5. *45%*
Buffalo Trace Single Oak Project Barrel #59 (w3xKB2) db **(92)** n22 t23.5 f23 b23.5. *45%*
Buffalo Trace Single Oak Project Barrel #60 (w3yKB2) db **(87.5)** n22.5 t22.5 f21 b21.5. *45%*
Buffalo Trace Single Oak Project Barrel #61 (w3xLB2*) db **(94.5)** n24 t23 f23.5 b24. *45%*
Buffalo Trace Single Oak Project Barrel #62 (w3yLB2*) db **(88)** n22 t22.5 f21.5 b22. *45%*
Buffalo Trace Single Oak Project Barrel #63 (w3xLB2) db **(95.5)** n24 t23 f24 b24.5. *45%*
Buffalo Trace Single Oak Project Barrel #64 (w3yLB2) db **(91)** n22.5 t23.5 f22.5 b23. *45%*
Buffalo Trace Single Oak Project Barrel #65 (r2xKA1) db **(91)** n23.5 t22 f23 b22.5. *45%*
Buffalo Trace Single Oak Project Barrel #66 (r2yKA1*) db **(88.5)** n22.5 t22.5 f21.5 b22. *45%*
Buffalo Trace Single Oak Project Barrel #67 (r2xKA1) db **(89.5)** n22 t23 f22 b22.5. *45%*
Buffalo Trace Single Oak Project Barrel #68 (r2yKA1) db **(92)** n22.5 t23 f23.5 b23. *45%*
Buffalo Trace Single Oak Project Barrel #69 (r2xLA1*) db **(94.5)** n23 t24 f23.5 b24. *45%*
Buffalo Trace Single Oak Project Barrel #70 (r2yLA1*) db **(91.5)** n22.5 t23 f23 b23. *45%*
Buffalo Trace Single Oak Project Barrel #71 (r2xLA1) db **(92)** n22.5 t23 f23.5 b23. *45%*
Buffalo Trace Single Oak Project Barrel #72 (r2yLA1) db **(89)** n22.5 t23 f21.5 b22. *45%*
Buffalo Trace Single Oak Project Barrel #73 (r2xKA2*) db **(87.5)** n21.5 t22 f22 b22. *45%*
Buffalo Trace Single Oak Project Barrel #74 (r2yKA2*) db **(88)** n22 t22 f22 b22. *45%*
Buffalo Trace Single Oak Project Barrel #75 (r2xKA2) db **(91.5)** n23 t22.5 f23 b23. *45%.*
Buffalo Trace Single Oak Project Barrel #76 (r2yKA2) db **(89)** n22.5 t22.5 f22 b22. *45%.*
Buffalo Trace Single Oak Project Barrel #77 (r2xLA2*) db **(88)** n22 t23 f21 b22. *45%*
Buffalo Trace Single Oak Project Barrel #78 (r2yLA2*) db **(89)** n22.5 t22 f22.5 b22. *45%*
Buffalo Trace Single Oak Project Barrel #79 (r2xLA2) db **(93)** n23 t23.5 f23 b23.5. *45%.*
Buffalo Trace Single Oak Project Barrel #80 (r2yLA2) db **(91.5)** n23 t22.5 f23 b23. *45%*
Buffalo Trace Single Oak Project Barrel #81 (r2yKB1*) db **(94)** n23 t23 f24 b24. *45%*
Buffalo Trace Single Oak Project Barrel #82 (r2yKB1*) db **(91.5)** n22.5 t23.5 f22.5 b23. *45%*
Buffalo Trace Single Oak Project Barrel #83 (r2xKB1) db **(92)** n22.5 t23 f23.5 b23. *45%.*
Buffalo Trace Single Oak Project Barrel #84 (r2yKB1) db **(94)** n23.5 t24 f23 b23.5. *45%.*
Buffalo Trace Single Oak Project Barrel #85 (r2xLB1*) db **(88.5)** n21.5 t22.5 f22 b22.5. *45%*

Buffalo Trace Single Oak Project Barrel #86 (r2yLB1*) db (90) n22.5 t22 f23 b22.5. 45%
Buffalo Trace Single Oak Project Barrel #87 (r2xLB1) db (93.5) n22.5 t23.5 f23.5 b24. 45%.
Buffalo Trace Single Oak Project Barrel #88 (r2yLB1) db (89) n23.5 t22 f21.5 b22. 45%
Buffalo Trace Single Oak Project Barrel #89 (r2xKB2*) db (89.5) n22 t22.5 f22 b22.5. 45%
Buffalo Trace Single Oak Project Barrel #90 (r2yKB2*) db (94) n23.5 t24 f23 b23.5. 45%
Buffalo Trace Single Oak Project Barrel #91 (r2xKB2) db (86.5) n21.5 t22 f21.5 b21.5. 45%
Buffalo Trace Single Oak Project Barrel #92 (r2yKB2) db (91) n22 t23 f23 b23. 45%
Buffalo Trace Single Oak Project Barrel #93 (r2xLB2*) db (89) n22.5 t22 f22 b22.5. 45%
Buffalo Trace Single Oak Project Barrel #94 (r2yLB2*) db (92.5) n22.5 t24 f23 b23. 45%
Buffalo Trace Single Oak Project Barrel #95 (r2xLB2) db (94) n23 t23.5 f23.5 b24. 45%
Buffalo Trace Single Oak Project Barrel #96 (r2yLB2) db (89) n22 t23.5 f21.5 b22. 45%
Buffalo Trace Single Oak Project Barrel #97 (w2xKA1*) db (87) n22.5 t22 f21.5 b21.5. 45%
Buffalo Trace Single Oak Project Barrel #98 (w2yKA1*) db (93) n23 t23.5 f23 b23.5. 45%
Buffalo Trace Single Oak Project Barrel #99 (w2xKA1) db (86.5) n22 t22 f21 b21.5. 45%
Buffalo Trace Single Oak Project Barrel #100 (w2yKA1) db (94) n23 t23.5 f23.5 b24. 45%
Buffalo Trace Single Oak Project Barrel #101 (w2xLA1) db (96) n23.5 t24 f23.5 b25. 45%
Buffalo Trace Single Oak Project Barrel #102 (w2yLA1*) db (88.5) n22 t22 f22.5 b22. 45%
Buffalo Trace Single Oak Project Barrel #103 (w2xLA1) db (89) n22.5 t22 f22 b22.5. 45%
Buffalo Trace Single Oak Project Barrel #104 (w2xLA1) db (91) n23 t23 f22.5 b22.5. 45%
Buffalo Trace Single Oak Project Barrel #105 (w2xKA2*) db (89) n22.5 t22 f22.5 b22. 45%
Buffalo Trace Single Oak Project Barrel #106 (w2yKA2*) db (92.5) n24 t23 f23 b23.5. 45%
Buffalo Trace Single Oak Project Barrel #107 (w2xKA2) db (93.5) n23.5 t23 f23 b24. 45%.
Buffalo Trace Single Oak Project Barrel #108 (w2yKA2) db (94) n22.5 t24 f23.5 b24. 45%
Buffalo Trace Single Oak Project Barrel #109 (w2xLA2*) db (87.5) n21.5 t23.5 f21 b21.5. 45%.
Buffalo Trace Single Oak Project Barrel #110 (w2yLA2*) db (90) n22 t22.5 f22.5 b23. 45%
Buffalo Trace Single Oak Project Barrel #111 (w2xLA2) db (89) n22.5 t22.5 f22 b22. 45%.
Buffalo Trace Single Oak Project Barrel #112 (w2yLA2) db (90) n21.5 t22 f22.5 b23. 45%.
Buffalo Trace Single Oak Project Barrel #113 (w2xKB1*) db (88) n22.5 t22 f22 b21.5. 45%
Buffalo Trace Single Oak Project Barrel #114 (w2yKB1*) db (90) n22 t23 f22 b23. 45%
Buffalo Trace Single Oak Project Barrel #115 (w2xKB1) db (88.5) n22 t22.5 f22 b22. 45%
Buffalo Trace Single Oak Project Barrel #116 (w2yKB1) db (90.5) n22 t22 f23.5 b23. 45%
Buffalo Trace Single Oak Project Barrel #117 (w2xLB1*) db (82.5) n20 t20.5 f22 b20. 45%
Buffalo Trace Single Oak Project Barrel #118 (w2yLB1*) db (86) n20.5 t21.5 f22 b22. 45%
Buffalo Trace Single Oak Project Barrel #119 (w2xLB1) db (93.5) n22.5 t24 f23.5 b23.5. 45%
Buffalo Trace Single Oak Project Barrel #120 (w2xLB1) db (89.5) n23 t22 f22.5 b22. 45%
Buffalo Trace Single Oak Project Barrel #121 (w2xKB2*) db (89) n22.5 t23 f21.5 b22. 45%
Buffalo Trace Single Oak Project Barrel #122 (w2yKB2*) db (93) n22 t23.5 f23.5 b24. 45%
Buffalo Trace Single Oak Project Barrel #123 (w2xKB2) db (85.5) n21 t22 f21 b21.5. 45%
Buffalo Trace Single Oak Project Barrel #124 (w2yKB2) db (90.5) n22.5 t23 f22.5 b22.5. 45%
Buffalo Trace Single Oak Project Barrel #125 (w2xLB2*) db (93) n24 t22 f22.5 b22.5. 45%
Buffalo Trace Single Oak Project Barrel #126 (w2yLB2*) db (90) n22 t23 f22.5 b22.5. 45%
Buffalo Trace Single Oak Project Barrel #127 (w2xLB2) db (85.5) n21.5 t22 f21 b21. 45%.
Buffalo Trace Single Oak Project Barrel #128 (w2yLB2) db (89) n21.5 t22 f22.5 b22.5. 45%
Buffalo Trace Single Oak Project Barrel #129 (r1xKA1*) db (88) n22.5 t22 f22 b22. 45%
Buffalo Trace Single Oak Project Barrel #130 (r1yKA1*) db (92.5) n22 t23.5 f23 b24. 45%
Buffalo Trace Single Oak Project Barrel #131 (r1xKA1) db (92.5) n23 t23 f23.5 b23. 45%
Buffalo Trace Single Oak Project Barrel #132 *See above.*
Buffalo Trace Single Oak Project Barrel #133 (r1xLA1*) db (89) n22.5 t23 f21 b22.5. 45%
Buffalo Trace Single Oak Project barrel #134 (r1yLA1*) db (91.5) n22 t23.5 f23 b23. 45%
Buffalo Trace Single Oak Project Barrel #135 (r1xLA1) db (92.5) n23 t23 f23.5 b23. 45%
Buffalo Trace Single Oak Project Barrel #136 (r1yLA1) db (92) n23.5 t22.5 f23 b23. 45%
Buffalo Trace Single Oak Project Barrel #137 (r1xKA2*) db (90.5) n22 t23.5 f22 b23. 45%
Buffalo Trace Single Oak Project Barrel #138 (r1yKA2*) db (87) n22.5 t21.5 f21.5 b21.5. 45%
Buffalo Trace Single Oak Project Barrel #139 (r1xKA2) db (88) n22.5 t22 f21.5 b22. 45%.
Buffalo Trace Single Oak Project Barrel #140 (r1yKA2) db (93) n23 t24 f23 b23. 45%
Buffalo Trace Single Oak Project Barrel #141 (r1xLA2*) db (90) n22.5 t22 f22.5 b22. 45%.
Buffalo Trace Single Oak Project Barrel #142 (r1yLA2*) db (89.5) n22.5 t22.5 f22 b22.5. 45%.
Buffalo Trace Single Oak Project Barrel #143 (r1xLA2) db (88.5) n22.5 t22.5 f21.5 b22. 45%.
Buffalo Trace Single Oak Project Barrel #144 (r1yLA2) db (91) n23 t23 f22.5 b22.5. 45%.
Buffalo Trace Single Oak Project Barrel #145 (r1xKB1*) db (91) n22.5 t22 f23.5 b23. 45%.
Buffalo Trace Single Oak Project Barrel #146 (r1yKB1*) db (93) n23 t24 f22 b24. 45%
Buffalo Trace Single Oak Project Barrel #147 (r1xKB1) db (93) n23.5 t23 f23.5 b23. 45%.
Buffalo Trace Single Oak Project Barrel #148 (r1yKB1) db (94) n22.5 t24 f23.5 b24. 45%
Buffalo Trace Single Oak Project Barrel #149 (r1xLB1*) db (92) n22.5 t23.5 f23 b23. 45%

Buffalo Trace Single Oak Project Barrel #150 (r1yLB1*) db **(93)** n23 t23.5 f23 b23.5. *45%*
Buffalo Trace Single Oak Project Barrel #151 (r1xLB1) db **(91.5)** n22 t23 f23.5 b23. *45%*.
Buffalo Trace Single Oak Project Barrel #152 (r1yLB1) db **(81.5)** n21 t20.5 f20 b20.5. *45%*
Buffalo Trace Single Oak Project Barrel #153 (r1xKB2*) db **(94)** n23.5 t23.5 f23 b24. *45%*
Buffalo Trace Single Oak Project Barrel #154 (r1yKB2*) db **(92)** n22.5 t23 f23.5 b23.5. *45%*
Buffalo Trace Single Oak Project Barrel #155 (r1xKB2) db **(93)** n23 t24 f22.5 b23.5. *45%*
Buffalo Trace Single Oak Project Barrel #156 (r1yKB2) db **(85.5)** n22 t21 f21.5 b21. *45%*
Buffalo Trace Single Oak Project Barrel #157 (r1xLB2*) db **(84.5)** n21 t21.5 f20.5 b21. *45%*
Buffalo Trace Single Oak Project Barrel #158 (r1yLB2*) db **(88)** n22 t22 f22 b22. *45%*
Buffalo Trace Single Oak Project Barrel #159 (r1xLB2) db **(88)** n20.5 t22.5 f22 b22.5. *45%*
Buffalo Trace Single Oak Project Barrel #160 (r1yLB2) db **(92.5)** n23.5 t23 f22 b23. *45%*
Buffalo Trace Single Oak Project Barrel #161 (w1xKA1*) db **(87)** n21 t22 f22 b22. *45%*
Buffalo Trace Single Oak Project Barrel #162 (w1yKA1*) db **(88.5)** n22 t22 f22.5 b22. *45%*
Buffalo Trace Single Oak Project Barrel #163 (w1xKA1) db **(90)** n22 t22.5 f22 b22.5. *45%*
Buffalo Trace Single Oak Project Barrel #164 (w1yKA1) db **(94.5)** n23.5 t23 f24 b24. *45%*
Buffalo Trace Single oak Project Barrel #165 (w1xLA1*) db **(91.5)** n22.5 t23 f23 b23. *45%*
Buffalo Trace Single Oak Project Barrel #166 (w1yLA1*) db **(91)** n22 t23 f23 b23. *45%*
Buffalo Trace Single Oak Project Barrel #167 (w1yLB1) db **(94)** n23.5 t23.5 f23 b23. *45%*
Buffalo Trace Single Oak Project Barrel #168 (w1xLA1) db **(89.5)** n22 t23 f22 b22.5. *45%*
Buffalo Trace Single Oak Project Barrel #169 (w1xKA2*) db **(94)** n23.5 t23.5 f23 b24. *45%*
Buffalo Trace Single Oak Project Barrel #170 (w1yKA2*) db **(92.5)** n22.5 t23 f23.5 b23.5. *45%*
Buffalo Trace Single Oak Project Barrel #171 (w1xKA2) db **(88.5)** n22 t23 f21.5 b22. *45%*.
Buffalo Trace Single Oak Project Barrel #172 (w1yKA2) db **(90.5)** n22.5 t23 f22.5 b22.5. *45%*
Buffalo Trace Single Oak Project Barrel #173 (w1xLA2*) db **(91)** n23.5 t23 f22 b22.5. *45%*.
Buffalo Trace Single Oak Project Barrel #174 (w1yLA2*) db **(89)** n22 t22.5 f22.5 b22. *45%*
Buffalo Trace Single Oak Project Barrel #175 (w1xLA2) db **(91.5)** n21.5 t23 f24 b23. *45%*.
Buffalo Trace Single Oak Project Barrel #176 (w1yLA2) db **(89)** n21.5 t22.5 f22.5 b22.5. *45%*.
Buffalo Trace Single Oak Project Barrel #177 (w1xKB1*) db **(87)** n21.5 t22 f22 b21.5. *45%*
Buffalo Trace Single Oak Project Barrel #178 (w1yKB1*) db **(88.5)** n22.5 t23 f21.5 b21.5. *45%*
Buffalo Trace Single Oak Project Barrel #179 (w1xKB1) db **(88)** n21 t22 f22.5 b22.5 *45%*.
Buffalo Trace Single Oak Project Barrel #180 (w1yKB1) db **(92)** n22 t23.5 f23 b23.5. *45%*
Buffalo Trace Single Oak Project Barrel #181 (w1xKB1*) db **(94.5)** n22.5 t24.5 f23 b23.5. *45%*
Buffalo Trace Single Oak Project Barrel #182 (w1yLB1*) db **(86)** n21.5 t21.5 f22 b21. *45%*
Buffalo Trace Single Oak Project Barrel #183 (w1xLB1) db **(95.5)** n24 t24 f23.5 b24. *45%*.
Buffalo Trace Single Oak Project Barrel #184 (w1yLA1) db **(93)** n23.5 t23 f23 b23.5. *45%*
Buffalo Trace Single Oak Project Barrel #185 (w1xKB2*) db **(92.5)** n23 t23.5 f23 b23. *45%*
Buffalo Trace Single Oak Project Barrel #186 (w1yKB2*) db **(90)** n23 t22.5 f22 b22.5. *45%*
Buffalo Trace Single Oak Project Barrel #187 (w1xKB2) db **(88)** n22 t22 f22 b22. *45%*
Buffalo Trace Single Oak Project Barrel #188 (w1yKB2) db **(90)** n21.5 t23.5 f22.5 b22.5. *45%*
Buffalo Trace Single Oak Project Barrel #189 (w1xLB2*) db **(88.5)** n24 t22 f21 b21.5. *45%*
Buffalo Trace Single Oak Project Barrel #190 (w1yLB2*) db **(94)** n23.5 t24 f23 b23.5. *45%*
Buffalo Trace Single Oak Project Barrel #191 (w1xLB2) db **(94.5)** n23 t23.5 f24 b24. *45%*
Buffalo Trace Single Oak Project Barrel #192 (w1yLB2) db **(94.5)** n23 t24 f23.5 b24. *45%*
Bulleit Bourbon **(87)** n21.5 t22 f21.5 b22. Vanilla-fashioned on both nose and flavour development. If it was looking to be big and brash, it's missed the target. If it wanted to be genteel and understated with a slightly undercooked feel yet always friendly, then bullseye... *45% (90 proof)*

Bulleit Bourbon Frontier Whiskey bott code: L9197ZB001 **(94)** n23.5 t23.5 f23 b24 In style this has just about become a stand-alone bourbon, with a crisp character all its own: like a rye, but chiselled from corn. It has been fascinating watching the quality of this brand rise quite dramatically in recent years and now enjoys a consistency and dependability which makes it an easy 'go to' bourbon. As for that unique clarity of flavour, have to say I now regularly use this brand to help re-set my taste buds after they have been clattered into submission and disabled by some sulphur-ruined Scotch or Irish. A magnificent every day non-age statement bourbon but boasting a cut-glass rye edge. *45% (90 proof)*.

⟐ **Bulleit Bourbon Frontier Whiskey** bott code: L1166ZB001 **(94.5)** n23.5 t23.5 f23.5 b24 Reading my tasting notes from last year, very little to add or take away. Except this bottling has a subtle extra degree of spice and chocolate, finishing with extra depth and a flourish. Another Bulleit which impressively hits the target. *45%*

Bulleit Bourbon 10 Year Old **(90)** n23 t22.5 f22 b22.5 Not remotely spectacular. But does the simple things deliciously. *45.6% (91.2 proof)*

Bulleit Bourbon Frontier Whiskey Aged 10 Years bott code: L9229R60010249 **(92.5)** n24 t23.5 f22 b23 "But how can a 10-year-old bourbon be not as good as a younger one with no age statement?" I hear you ask. Well, there is nothing wrong with this. It is just less brilliant! Definitely upped in whiskey values since I last encountered it. But that extra tannin, which giving extra intensity depth, does slightly lose the complexity and harmony of the standard Bulleit as the spaces in which the younger bourbon could perform have now been filled in. That said, there are a few moments of whiskey heaven just after delivery as that classic hickory note kicks in with the dark sugars. *45.6% (91.2 proof).*

Bulleit Bourbon Barrel Strength (91.5) n22.5 t22.5 f23.5 b23 The extra oils at full strength make such a huge difference in seeing the fuller picture. *59.6% (119.2 proof)*

Bulleit Bourbon Frontier Whiskey Blender's Select No. 001 bott code: L0023ZB001 **(96.5) n23.5 t24.5 f24** long...could it be anything else? Still the corn oils hold their ground, but the spices are more keen now. The small grain still pulse to their rye-rich beat while the cocoa mingles with the oils...; **b24.5** an extraordinary halfway house between the standard Bulleit and their 10-year-old, with the all the richness and gravitas of the older whiskey married with the vivaciousness of the younger bottling. So much rye to be found...yet never quite has the chance to dominate, such is the labyrinthine complexity of this stunning whiskey. One of the bourbons of 2021, to be sure...and truly world class. *50% (100 proof).*

⋘ **Cadenhead's World Whiskies Heaven Hill Aged 23 Years** dist 1996, bott 2020 **(96) n25** such a glorious marriage of high end, super-rich vanilla, and heather honey. Even the hickory has had its edges rounded by the vanilla-led oak. The liquorice is deft and merges with the natural toffee to complete the caress...; **t24** it is quite astonishing that even after all these years that sharp, metallic lilt of copper comes through loud and clear. Though only after a sumptuous mix of corn oil, ulmo and heather honeys has coated the palate with the friendliest and undemanding of sweetness. The great vintage of the oak is apparent by some toasty interventions. But the structure is never weakened by age. The liquorice is so proud and pure, t seems to be saluting the bourbon flag; **f23** far more simplistic, though now some spicy residue has come into play. But it is the vanillas which dominate; **b24** as the all-consuming fire at Heaven Hill was in November 1996, one can presume that this is one if the last casks of among the very last bourbon made on those unique, truly irreplaceable, and much missed high copper still. For once, absolutely none of this hallowed whiskey from what I always considered probably one of the world's most underestimated distilleries was spat out during tasting... *54.5% 132 bottles*

Clarke's Old Kentucky Straight Sour Mash Whisky Bourbon (88.5) n22.5 t22 f22 b22. Honest and hugely impressive bourbon. The rich colour – and remember straight bourbon cannot be falsely coloured – tells its own tale. *40%. Aldi.*

Clyde May's Straight Bourbon batch CR 079 recipe no 2. **(95) n23.5 t24 f23.5 b24** Though from a Florida company, this busy Kentucky bourbon sings pure Bluegrass. Love it! *46% (92 proof). ncf. Distilled in Kentucky*

Colonel E.H. Taylor 18 Year Marriage Bottled in Bond bott code: L201270114:141 db **(96.5) n24 t24 f24 b24.5** Well this marriage lasted twice as long as mine and was a least twice as good... *50% (100 proof).*

Colonel E.H. Taylor Amaranth Grain of the Gods Bottled in Bond bott code: L191800112:17K db **(91.5) n23 t23 f22.5 b23** Not sure amaranth grain is a true cereal, but if it is good enough for BT, then it is good enough for me. I'm presuming that the amaranth has usurped the rye for this bottling as I can't locate any of the sharp sugary tones normally associated with that grain and the bitterness towards the end is most un Colonel Taylor-ish. Different and thoroughly enjoyable stand-alone bottling, with moments of brilliance, but not a patch of the distillery's usual genius. *50% (100 proof).*

Colonel E.H. Taylor Barrel Proof bott code: B1319909:44M **(93) n23 t23.5 f23 b23.5** It is as though every last trace of natural caramel has been sucked from the barrel... *67.7% (135.4 proof).*

Colonel E.H. Taylor Barrel Proof bott code: L81313910:20M db **(96) n24.5 t24 f23.5 b24** This, amazingly, is the 19,999th whiskey I have tasted for the Jim Murray's Whisky Bible since it first began in 2003. I chose E H Taylor as I have had (very happy) memories going back over 25 years of trying to piece together and discover where his distillery was. And really, if you are going to taste a special bourbon, then it really should be at a strength nature intended. And as for the whiskey itself...? Just another exhibition from this distillery of truly astonishing bourbon making. *67.7% (135.4 proof).*

Colonel E.H. Taylor Four Grain Bottled in Bond Aged 12 Years db **(97.5) n24.5 t24.5 f24 b24.5** Unquestionably one of the greatest whiskeys bottled worldwide in the last 12 months, simply because of the unfathomable depths of its complexity. Every aspect of great whiskey making clears its respective hurdle with yards to spare: brewing, distilling, maturation...the nose and taste confirms that a team of people knew exactly what they were doing...and achieved with rare distinction what they set out to do. Forget about the sheer, undiluted beauty of this bourbon: for me, it is simply a true honour – and thrill - to taste. *50% (100 proof).*

Colonel E.H. Taylor Seasoned Wood db **(93.5)** n25 t24 f21.5 b23 I am sitting in my garden in near darkness tasting and writing this, the near-thousand-year-old church just 75 yards or so behind me clanging out that it is ten of the clock. Although mid-July, it is the first day warm enough in this apology of a British summer where I have been able to work outside. Oddly, it reminded me when I used to write my books and chapters on bourbon in the grounds of Buffalo Trace in the 1990s, the sun also set and a warm breeze kissing my face. No possums here for company, although the bats are already circling me, kindly protecting me from midges. And as I can't read the label of the whiskey, it makes my senses all the more alive. A whiskey, though not perfect, for when the sun sets but your day is really about to begin... *50% (100 proof)*

Colonel E H Taylor Single Barrel Bottled In Bond bott code: L190740114 **(96.5)** n24 t24 f24 b24.5 Absolutely no single cask whiskey, of any type, has the right to be this good. How on earth does it achieve this balance? So many nuances, yet each in league or sympathetic to another? A world single cask of the year contender for certain. Breathtaking. *50% (100 proof). sc.*

Colonel E.H. Taylor Small Batch Bottled in Bond nbc **(94.5)** n23.5 t23.5 f23.5 b24 Just balances out so beautifully. *50% (100 proof).*

Colonel E.H. Taylor Small Batch Bottled in Bond bott code: L190980115:45D **(90)** n23 t23 f22 b22 Well, I'd not have recognised this as a Colonel Taylor offering unless I had opened the bottle and poured it myself. Not a patch on the exquisite single barrel and, for all its caramel softness and other riches, still one for a dirty glass... *50% (100 proof).*

Coopers' Craft Barrel Reserve bott code: SS3501815 db **(92)** n22.5 t23.5 f23 b23 A distinctly different slant to a bourbon with the emphasis placed where it usually isn't, the pace of development slightly skewed. Fascinating. *50% (100 proof). Chiseled & Charred Collection.*

David Nicholson 1843 Kentucky Straight Bourbon Whiskey bott code: LF3936 **(91.5)** n22.5 t23 f23 b23 An engagingly timid bourbon which wins your heart with its polite and well-mannered ways. *50% (100 proof).*

David Nicholson Reserve Kentucky Straight Bourbon Whiskey bott code: LF4223 **(90.5)** n22.5 t23 f22.5b22.5 An example of a little more meaning a little less. Delicious bourbon, for sure, but not quite so well-balanced or teasing as the 1843. *50% (100 proof).*

Eagle Rare Aged 10 Years bott code: L172800119:194 **(95.5)** n23.5 t24 f24 b24 To the British and Europeans Eagle Rare means Crystal Palace not losing a game...very rare indeed. In the US it will probably mean a lot more to those who once hankered after Ancient Age 10, as this is not the Single Barrel incarnation. And while Crystal Palace may be pointless, literally, this striking whiskey most certainly isn't... That's one soaring, beautiful eagle... *45% (90 proof)*

Eagle Rare Aged 10 Years Single Barrel **(89)** n21.5 t23 f22 b22.5 A surprising trip, this, with some dramatic changes en route. *45%*

Eagle Rare 17 Years Old bott Summer 2018 db **(95)** n24 t24 f23 b24 This version goes into cream toffee overload. But, it does it so well... *50.5% (101 proof).*

Eagle Rare 17 Years Old bott Summer 2019 db **(95)** n24 t23.5 f23.5 b24 The rich caramel thread found in this whiskey could so easily become its tomb, as with many bourbons that toffee note strangles the life out of all development. Not here: the hickory and spice in tandem produce some truly wonderful moments. *50.5% (101 proof).*

◈ **Eagle Rare 17 Years Old** bott Summer 2020 db **(94)** n24 blood orange and hickory. Once I remember cream caramel running along on the nose. Not here. This is more angular, a little more sharply spiced. A very slightly different aroma pattern, but same excellence; t23.5 though the caramel may have been missing on the nose, it takes little time to arrive on the palate, linking up with the rich corn oils to form, once the butterscotch and Demerara sugars have completed the formation, a truly delicious delivery. As it thins the delicate liquorice begins to shew and spices nip; f23 an unspectacular finish by Buffalo Trace standards, but one that makes the most of the light cocoa and vanilla on hand. The late bitterness causes a surprise; b23.5 this has to be one of the more evenly weighted Eagle Rares, certainly shewing dexterity early on which was not present four or five years ago. Only the finish, perfectly acceptable by usual standards, fails to stand up to the pedigree. *50.5% (101 proof).*

Early Times Bottled-in-Bond Straight Bourbon bott code: A146171040 3131550 **(94)** n23 t23.5 f23.5 b24 They call this "Old Style", and it really is. A blast from the past bourbon, oozing personality. A bit of a stunner. *50% (100 proof).*

Elijah Craig Barrel Proof Kentucky Straight Bourbon batch no. C917 db **(95)** n23.5 t24 f23.5 b24 A bourbon which is winner just for much for its rich texture as it is the subtle complexities of its nose and delivery. A real honey – in every sense! *65.5% (131 proof).*

Elijah Craig Barrel Proof Kentucky Straight Bourbon batch no. B520 db **(94.5)** n23.5 t24 f23.5 b23.5 Unambiguous quality! *63.6% (1272 proof).*

Elijah Craig Barrel Proof Kentucky Straight Bourbon batch no. C918 db **(94.5)** n23.5 t24 f23 b24 Just classic stuff! All the usual cast members of red liquorice and Manuka honey are trotted out to make their bow, but there is a slight saltiness to this bottling also...something that isn't usually in the script. Intense, yet at the same time restrained; the burnt toast and marmalade towards the finish works rather well and fits the narrative. *65.7% (131.4 proof).*

Elijah Craig Barrel Proof Kentucky Straight Bourbon Aged 12 Years batch no. A119 db **(96) n24 t24.5 f23.5 b24** When you get this degree of toastiness from a bourbon, either there has been one hell of an average temperature rise over the last dozen years in Kentucky. Or this has been plucked from near the top of a warehouse, where it has been cooking happily for over a decade. The result is bourbon that takes no prisoners. It is also a fascinating bourbon, not just because of the intensity of the blood oranges on the nose or the prickle of the splinters on the palate. But it is because it shews an inordinate degree of copper in the flavour profile, the mid-point to the finish in particular. It is as though something was just done to the still, maybe some repair work, just prior to this being distilled. And that to the blindingly busy small grain input and the result is a bourbon of cor blimey richness! *67.6% (135.2 proof).*

Elijah Craig Barrel Proof Kentucky Straight Bourbon Aged 12 Years batch no. B519 db **(90.5) n22.5 t23 f22 b23** One of those quietly delicious bourbons which is saturated in caramel and goes for mouthfeel effect over complexity. Mouth-puckering on delivery, this is sticky whiskey on the palate so thick is that corn oil. But the growth of cocoa and spice is nothing to quibble about. *61.1% (122.2 proof).*

Elijah Craig Barrel Proof Kentucky Straight Bourbon Aged 12 Years batch no. C919 db **(90.5) n23 t23 f22 b22.5** Good grief!!! The original Heaven Hill distillery could never have made a bourbon this uncompromising, this harrowing... The old stills always would have injected extra copper to soften even their most unforgiving grain-led creations. This is as memorable as it is different...and scary! *68.4% (136.8 proof).*

Elijah Craig Small Batch Kentucky Straight Bourbon db **(89.5) n22.5 t22.5 f22 b22.5** About as quiet and understated as Elijah Craig ever gets. *47% (94 proof).*

⋙ **Elijah Craig Toasted Barrel Kentucky Straight Bourbon** finished in toasted new oak barrels, bottle code: A20702146 db **(96) n24** no bourbon this year will be roastier. Or oakier. Well, it just couldn't! Dried blood orange peel adds to the massive presence, along with the nose-nipping spice. Liquorice and manuka honey attack in distilled form. By far the creosote-stained sawdusty oak has the lion's share of the personality. But give it a minimum 10 minutes, this. For the complexity knows no bounds...; **t24** in the total peace and quiet of secluded isolation and free from distraction, I have counted no less than three different honey notes at work. The manuka is obvious. But it is thinned by something less forceful. And look closely and you will find both ulmo and orange blossom honeys also working subtly and diligently at controlling the mammoth tannins. These give a waxy mouth feel which keeps the sugars in check and allows the spices and more cocoa-infused tannins a little extra freedom; **f23.5** waxy liquorice with just a slight bitterness of the oak which the sugars can't man mark. The concentrated vanilla, though, is lush...; **b24.5** this is bourbon squared. Bourbon concentrate. Bourbon max. Bourbon, taken out of bourbon casks and then put back into virgin oak again. It is like shoving a 7-litre engine beside the 5 litre one already in our car. It is for those who think great straight bourbon isn't quite enough. The colour is Mahoney, and the nose and flavour is festooned with splinters. Only at the very death does it slightly come off the rails when the tannins have herded up a few too many bitter notes. But that apart, for those who like to take their bourbon pure.... One of the best things to come from Heaven Hill in my lifetime... *47% (94 proof).*

Elmer T. Lee 100 Year Tribute Kentucky Straight Bourbon Whiskey bott code: L192240121:22K db **(97) n24.5 t24 f24 b24.5** I had the great fortune not only to know Elmer but have him as my mentor as I got to grips with the complex world of bourbon whiskey. I know that this particular barrel would have blown him away as it is choc-a-bloc with all the features and devices he thought sacred within a bourbon. Knowing him so intimately, before tasting I had feared that this tribute would be a bit of a let-down. I really should have known better. As a mark of respect to Elmer, I left this to be the final whiskey tasted for the Jim Murray Whisky Bible 2021, the 1,252nd whisky in all. It is just as well. Because, just like Elmer T Lee, this would have been a very hard, if not impossible, act to follow... *50% (100 proof).*

Elmer T Lee Single Barrel Kentucky Straight Bourbon Whiskey bott code: L18199011025K **(95.5) n24 t24 f23.5 b24** A peach of a single cask. The great man would have celebrated this one... *45% (90 proof). sc.*

Evan Williams 23 Years Old (94) n22 t23.5 f24.5 b24. Struts his stuff, refusing to allow age to slow him or dim the shine from his glowing grains. Now oak has taken its toll. This seems older than its 23 years... Or so I first thought. Then a light shone in my soul and it occurred to me: hang on...I have wines going back to the last century. For the older ones, do I not allow them to breathe? So I let the whiskey breathe. And, behold, it rose from the dead. This Methuselah of a whiskey had come alive once more...and how!! *53.5%*

Ezra Brooks Bourbon Whiskey bott code: A193180914 **(90) n22.5 t22.5 f22 b23** A truly classic young to medium bourbon which celebrates the beautiful arrangement come to between the corn and tannin. An absolutely classic old style of bourbon that the grandfather of whoever distilled this would instantly recognise. *40% (80 proof).*

Falls Church Distillers Church Bourbon Whiskey batch no. 19, American oak barrels **(87.5) n21.5 t22.5 f21.5 b22** Certainly likes to go worship at the Hickory Church of Latter Day Bourbon, boasting all kinds of cough sweet richness, and softer liquorice and vanillas, too. If they could just cut down on some of the superficial oils this really would be very impressive. *40% (80 proof).*

Four Roses Bourbon bott code: 2018/11/20 db **(88) n24 t22.5 f20 b21.5** After a few years with a little extra weight behind it, the standard Four Roses has reverted back to a light and flimsy style recognisable to those of us who encountered it between the 1970s and late 1990s. One of the most fragile Kentucky bourbons in the market place, but profiting from a sublime nose. *40%.*

Four Roses Single Barrel warehouse No. LE, barrel no. 4-25, bott code: 1400 05218 0655 db **(91) n23 t23 f22 b23** A very distinctive style of bourbon: crisp caramelised shell around the house light corn and vanilla. *50%.*

Four Roses Small Batch bott code: 1316 14318 1363 db **(95) n23.5 t24 f23.5 b24** A hugely satisfying, high quality bourbon. Undisputed class. *45%.*

Frankfort Bourbon Society Buffalo Trace Single Barrel Select (86) n21.5 t22 f21. b21.5 A spluttering bourbon in part, haunted by a lactic note visible on both the nose and finish. At least the denser, sugar-spiced high points are truly majestic. *45% (90 proof).*

Frankfort Bourbon Society Elijah Craig Small Batch Serial No 4718833 bott Fall 2018 **(95.5) n24 t24 f23.5 b24**. This gem of a barrel was hand-picked by members of the Frankfort Bourbon Society and I suspect that had they had a hundred stabs at the stocks, they would not have come away with something more alluring and complex than this. *47% (94 proof).*

Frankfort Bourbon Society Knob Creek Single Barrel Reserve Aged 9 Years Barrel No 6225 bott Spring 2018 **(95) n23.5 t24 f23.5 b24** Unusual for a single barrel to so comprehensively typify an entire brand. Bold, bracing and brilliant! *60% (120 proof).*

Frankfort Bourbon Society Weller Antique 107 Single Barrel Select Serial (94) n23 t23.5 f23.5 b24 Despite the relative youth of this bourbon, the effect of the wheat is astonishing, radiating its spicy intent from the very first moment. But only when the honey catches up and mingles with an exquisite feel for balance do things become truly special. Tasting this on a day when Frankfort, Ky, dropped to around minus 15 degrees – one of the coldest days here in many a year – those warming spices came in most welcome...even though the bourbon was not swallowed! *53.5% (107 proof).*

George T. Stagg db **(97) n24 t24.5 f24 b24.5** Funny: I nosed this and I thought: "T-bone steak."Huge whiskey deserving to be the warm-up act for a meal at either RingSide Steakhouse, Portland or Barberian's Steak House in Toronto or even some outdoor parrilla in Uruguay. It is the kind of whiskey that demands something truly special: it just refuses, point-blanc, to do ordinary... *64.6% (129.2 proof).*

George T. Stagg db **(96) n24 t24.5 f23.5 b24.5** As a George T Stagg goes, this is a bit of a wimp: some 20 proof weaker than some of its incarnations. So for those of you of a delicate disposition, you might be able to tackle this tamed monster for once. *62.45% (124.9 proof).*

George T. Stagg db **(96.5) n24 t24 f24.5 b24** On nosing this I did the kind of double take James Finlayson would have been proud of in a Laurel and Hardy film. Stagg...at this strength? I was expecting the usual low 70% abv or high 60s, perhaps. But less than 60%....? A very different George T Stagg to what we have seen over the years. But the pedigree remains... *58.45% (116.9 proof).*

♦ **George T. Stagg** db **(97.5) n24.5** I have just nosed the glass and sunk into my chair, experiencing some kind of nasal bliss. A near perfect aroma with the spices prickling away with challenging intent. The trick, though, is to mentally shut off those spices and search deeper...much deeper. And now we hit something extraordinary. A wall of aroma which you are able to identify brick by brick. The rye is sharp, granite-like and imperious. But giving off a sugary coating. And there is the oak....my God, there is the oak! A near 50/50 cut between liquorice and hickory. Usually corn oils mean that these notes float around the and soften. Not here. The corn is there, but solid. Little oil, but plenty of mass, aligning with a roasted nuttiness which melds with the liquorice in particular...; **t24.5** just.... brilliant! The spices...the oils... But that is just the outline, the blueprint. Get into the nitty gritty and here is something very special. The chocolate ensures respite. But essentially this is bourbon in concentrate. The corn oils, so absent on the nose, now make up for their earlier absence: we now know where they had been hiding; **f24** chocolate...corn oil...spiced marzipan...and repeat...almost ad infinitum...; **b24.5** Stagg hovering around about its ultimate. And we know what that means: one of the greatest whiskey experiences of your life. This is one of those whiskies where it is a case of not whether it is good enough for you? The question is whether is, are you good enough for it...? Staggering. Quite literally. *65.2% (130.4 proof).* ♦

✧ **Green River Kentucky Straight Bourbon Whiskey** aged 3 years 9 months, db (**94.5**) n24 oh...worship at the altar of molasses and liquorice, why don't you? It would almost be a parody, if it wasn't so damned good...; t23.5 the corn oils bathe the taste buds in the most glorious array of red and black liquorice, fully backed up and sweetened by ulmo and manuka honey. There is a creamy vanilla texture coating the persistent liquorice; f23.5 fading spice matches the dying toastiness. The trick, though, is that even in death this manages to harmonise...; b23.5 for a barrel under four years, this is outrageously good. Must have come from the very top story of a warehouse as this has matured way beyond its tender years. Rich and ticks every box under the sun. Plus a few more besides. This is some hell of a barrel pick. (117 proof)

H. Deringer Bourbon Whiskey (88) n21.5 t22 f22 b22.5 Despite the huge, weighty bottle, this is the lighter side of bourbon whiskey with vanilla and sugars in quiet agreement. 40%. Aiko Importers, Inc.

Hancock's President's Reserve Single Barrel bott code: B1710117:26K (**90.5**) n22.5 t23 f22.5 b22.5 A joyous Bourbon that gives the impression that it is performing well within itself. 44.45% (88.9 proof)

Heaven Hill Bottled in Bond 7 Years Old Kentucky Straight Bourbon Whiskey nbc db (**90**) n22.5 t23 f22 b22.5 A satisfying, if at times docile, BIB. 50% (100 proof).

✧ **High West Whiskey American Prairie Bourbon** batch no. 20B11 (**90.5**) n22.5 hickory with a deft honey balance. Quietly attractive...; t23 very impressive entry onto the palate with thick corn oil swishing around and taking hold before the hickory and liquorice begin to form a more solid base. Deposits of molasses are washed up against it; f22 slightly salty and tannic towards the finish as the sugars are played out. Just a little OTT at the death; b23 an usually high corn oil statement gives this bourbon a soft and long tenure. The sweeter tones keep the hickory straight. A little unusual. But satisfying, nonetheless. 46% (92 proof). nc ncf. A blend of straight bourbon whiskies.

I.W. Harper Kentucky Straight Bourbon 15 Year Old (94.5) n23.5 t23.5 f24 b23.5 Class in a glass. 43% (86 proof)

J Mattingly Bobo's Bourbon Small Batch Bourbon Whiskey (95) n23 t24 f24 b24 A brilliant sharpness to the small grains underlines the excellence of both the distillate the high-grade casks. Presumably a rye mashbill, for no other reason than the extraordinary crispness and salivating qualities of the treacle and vanilla mix. That said, some fair spices abound (well within the scope of a wheated mashbill) always balanced within limits...and then the amazing dark chocolate fade...complete with bewildering spice and thick molasses. What amazing balance and complexity...just...wow! If anyone doesn't appreciate this for what it is, they wouldn't know a truly great bourbon if it hit them around the head with a with a 32oz bone-in ribeye steak. (CV) 61.5% (123 proof). Distilled in Kentucky and Indiana

J Mattingly Ripcord Single Barrel Straight Whiskey (83.5) n21 t22 f20 b20.5 You know how amazingly good Bobos Bourbon (above) is. Well, this just isn't...Just way too liquorice dominated, bitter and tart. If this was a real ripcord, you'd end up crashing to the ground... 55% (110 proof).Distilled in Indiana sc.

James E. Pepper 1776 Straight Bourbon Whiskey Aged Over 3 Years (91.5) n23 t23 f22.5 b23 Beautiful old school bourbon. 50% (100 proof). ncf.

Jim Beam Black Double Age Aged 8 Years (93) n23 t24 f22.5 b23.5. Rather than the big, noisy, thrill-seeking JB Black, here it is in quiet, reflective, modest mode. Quite a shift. But no less enjoyable. 43% (86 proof)

Jim Beam Bonded 100 Proof bott code: L8 305 (**90**) n22.5 t23 f22 b22.5 Satisfyingly salivating with lots to chew on here and offers some truly classical moments. That said, thins out late on as a younger style takes control... 50% (100 proof).

Jim Beam Signature Craft Aged 12 Years db (**92.5**) n23 t23.5 f23 b23 Classic Beam: big rye and massive fruit. Quite lovely. 43%.

Jim Beam Repeal Batch Bourbon bott code: L8226FFE222730700 db (**89**) n22 t22.5 f22 b22.5 Good, honest, unspectacular, understated but unerringly delicious and charming bourbon bottled to celebrate the 85th Anniversary of the repeal of Prohibition. On this evidence, I think they should equally celebrate the 86th anniversary... 43% (86 proof). ncf

John E. Fitzgerald Very Special Reserve Aged 20 Years (93) n22.5 t24 f23 b23.5 A bourbon lover's bourbon! 45% (90 proof)

John J Bowman Single Barrel Virginia Straight Bourbon bott code: L172010507:28B (**93**) n23 t23.5 f23 b23.5 This is very high quality bourbon making the most of both its big toastiness and its more intrinsic honey tones. Simple...yet devastatingly complex... 50%

John J Bowman Single Barrel Virginia Straight Bourbon bott code: L190070510 (**94.5**) n23 t24 f23.5 b24 A very different animal to the Small Batch with a greater emphasis on the sugars and just more all round drama and muscularity. Stunning. 50% (100 proof). sc.

Kentucky Owl Bourbon Whiskey batch no. 9 **(90.5)** **n23 t23 f22 b22.5** If, like me, you are a pretty serious birdwatcher then you know just how captivating the sight of an owl in full swoop can be. Trust me: despite those extra oils, this will captivate you... *63.8% (1276 proof). 11,595 bottles.*

Kentucky Owl Confiscated bott code: 3158860834 **(80)** **n19 t22 f19 b20** From the moment the boiled cabbage nose hits you, this is one very disappointing whiskey. Stands up to scrutiny on delivery, where the intense caramels and vanillas combine rather well. But the dirty, buzzy finale is also a let down. Not a bourbon, in this form, I could give two hoots about, to be honest. *48.2% (96.4 proof).*

Kentucky Tavern Straight Kentucky Bourbon bott code: L190081510 **(92)** **n22.5 t23 f23 b23.5** What a great improvement on when I last tasted this several years back. Much more depth, balance and chewability. One of the biggest – and most pleasant - surprises of my tasting day. Delicious! *40% (80 proof).*

⟐ **Knaplund Straight Bourbon Whiskey Atlantic Aged** batch no.B01 **(92.5)** **n22.5** man-size hickory (yeah, I know, I know...)...; a very curious vegetable note, too: boiled stinging nettles. Not often you'll find that in a tasting note...; **t24** as is the house style, a sharp delivery. Here, though, there are industrial lashing of extra vanillas where you'd normally expect the liquorice. So kind of full on...but soft, too. Some early spice, though which fades quite quickly; **f23** as though a white flag has been produced. Much more serene than the delivery promised, still the vanilla controls, though a little butterscotch moves in for the kill. However...along comes the hickory...; **b23** I have found the whiskeys of Knaplund among the most fascinating encountered this year. There is nothing new about sending single malt half way around the world, but giving Bourbon a life at sea is most uncommon. Without doubt, Knaplund have created a truly unique and distinctive style. *45% (90 proof) Distilled in the US, aged at the Atlantic sea and bottled in Denmark by Knaplund Distillery.*

⟐ **Knaplund Wheated Straight Bourbon Whiskey Atlantic Aged** batch no.01 **(95)** **n24** the spiced hickory suggests a lot of small grain involvement despite the telling oak infusion. Complex and dry the layering to this is truly labyrinthine...; **t23.5** forget the dry nose: the sugars burst out on delivery like prisoners from a breeched jail. The wheat content fans the spicy flames, and the midpoint has a magnificent toasted brown bread dripping with heather honey moment or three. Just a tad salty, too...; **f23.5** just how long can this finish go on for...? Just more of the same as the delivery, except now the tannins are starting to take on a deeper, more aged countenance. **b24** quite literally, a winner by a nose. This is a bourbon that just exudes complexity. A 20-minute whiskey...and that's just to sniff at. My god, this is serious stuff...! *50% (100 proof) Distilled in the US, aged at the Atlantic Sea and bottled in Denmark by Knaplund Distillery.* ⚑

⟐ **Knaplund Handcrafted Small Batch Whiskey** blend of American and Danish whiskey, bott 10/6/21 **(94)** **n23.5** a seriously salty, iodine lilt to the sharp red and black liquorice mix and heather honey lead....; **t23.5** sharper than a razer, more juicy than glass of juice. The grains are propelled at the taste buds at the highest velocity: hang on to your seat...this is some ride...; **f23** a huge wave of pure vanilla breaks over all that has gone before. The oak now sets about drying out the sweeter nuances; **b24** if you're looking for complexity, I think you've just found it.... *50% (100 proof) Aged in the Atlantic Sea then blended and bottled in Denmark by Knaplund Distillery*

Knob Creek 100 Proof Small Batch bott code:: L9/55 CLH290 **(89)** **n22.5 t22.5 f21.5 b22.5** "Since 1992" chirps the label. But if you tasted that original Knob Creek against this, you might have a few problems spotting the relationship. This is the lightest of the Knob Creeks I have ever encountered, with a youthful zestiness to where you would normally find heady, rumbling dark sugars and tannin. Enjoyable, drinkable bourbon? Of course. But a chest-hair curling Knob Creek to chew on until your jaw drops, as of old? Nope. *50%.*

Knob Creek 25th Anniversary Single Barrel barrelled 2/25/2004 db **(93)** **n23 t24 f23 b23** A caramel-rich critter, yes-siree! But let it hang around the glass a bit and a rich liquorice edginess will develop... *62% (124 proof). sc.*

Knob Creek Aged 12 Years bott code: L9252CLA db **(93.5)** **n23.5 t23.5 f23 b23.5** Needs the full Murray Method of tasting to really get this engine to fire up. Too cool and the caramels swamp everything. When warmed slightly, the small grains go into complexity overdrive. *50% (100 proof).*

Knob Creek Aged 15 Years release no. KC001, bott code: L0139CLJ db **(92.5)** **n23 t23 f23 b23.5** It is a curious thing that when Knob Creek first came into the market, the style chosen – and from much younger barrels than used here – was intensity married with complexity: Knob Creek was a huge, uncompromising bourbon; but one always celebrating its role as the gentle giant. Here the bourbon is markedly older. But it appears the blender has decided to pick a slightly different type of barrel, those it appears that were lodged in the lower rungs of the warehouse rather than somewhere much higher up, as had previously been the case. So this is a surprise bourbon, not at all expected. Muscle makes way for elegance, baritone for tenor. *50% (100 proof).*

Larceny Barrel Proof batch no. A1200, bott code: A32291246 db **(95) n23.5 t24 f23.5 b24** il you don't track down a bottle of this stunning batch, then you have just committed one hell of a crime...!!! *61.6% (123.2 proof).*

Larceny Barrel Proof batch no. B520 db **(95) n23.5 t24 f23.5 b24** A glorious variation on a theme from batch A1200 but fractionally less complex. But it is like choosing between one Dashiell Hammett novel and another... *60.6% (122.2 proof).*

Liquid Treasures 10th Anniversary Heaven Hill 10 Year Old bourbon barrel, dist 2009, bott 2019 **(88.5) n22 t22 f22.5 b22** Heaven Hickory: the most one-dimensional bourbon I have tasted this year. But is it thoroughly enjoyable? Yep! *50.2%. sc. 161 bottles.*

⬧ **Lucky Seven The Hold Up Aged 12 Years** batch no. 1 **(93.5) n24** the kind of bourbon nose which makes you inwardly purr...A blend of heather and manuka honeys offer both an earthy and toasty sweetness. The house style hickory employs a little spice to give it extra bite and dimension; **t23** didn't expect salivating as the first offering from this 12-year-old. The early freshness dispels fears that the tannins might kick too hard. No less surprising is the busy working of the small grains before, at last the toasty liquorice, hickory and honey begin to weave complex patterns through the middle; **f23** the chocolate and liquorice is such a delight; **b23.5** a big bourbon which never bullies. The chocolate from the midpoint onwards will sate the most voracious of chocoholics. *50% (100 Proof).*

⬧ **Lucky Seven The Holiday Toast** double oak finished in new American oak barrels, batch no.01 **(95) n23.5** not so much toasted mallow, but thrown onto the fire. There is a stand-off between the sharp marmalade and manuka honey mix and more gentle vanillas and hickory, with odd acidic nip of a burnt offering, too...; **t24** double matured bourbon has a tendency to ramp up the dark sugars on delivery...and this is no exception. I expected, from the nose, a tart, scorched feel, too. But this never materialises and instead we enjoy variations on a theme of hickory, ulmo honey and molasses. The sheer brilliance is the waves of intensity and fade; **f23.5** late black cherry, chocolate, and blood orange, but mainly thick vanilla; **b24** when I see that a straight bourbon has been finished in a fresh virgin oak cask, and at full strength for good measure, I strap myself in for the tannin attack that is to follow. And the question I ask, even before nosing: have they overcooked it....? No, they certainly haven't. If anyone else is considering treating their bourbon this way, they could do worse than to use this as a blueprint. *57.5% (115 proof)*

⬧ **Lucky Seven The Jokester Aged 6 Years** batch no. 1, bott code: 19339SS11235 **(89.5) n22.5** full volume hickory; **t22.5** excellent oil and heather honey and molasses mix; **f22** dry, barely sweetened liquorice and light spices; **b22.5** not a bourbon that tries to wow you with a dazzling degree of complexity. Instead, ensures good traditional hickory themed solidity and a subtle change in sugar levels does the trick. *47.5% (95 Proof).*

⬧ **Lucky Seven The Proprietor Aged 12 Years** barrel no. 7, bott code: 19339SS11446 **(94) n23** for a barrel strength bottling, the nose is supine despite its toasty tones...; **t23.5** very little linkage between nose and delivery. The chocolate liquorice which is such a feature at the finale of their Hold Up here arrives early and in huge quantities. Towards the midpoint the spices really start to warm up while the vanillas make their well-balanced mark. A few impressive corn oil moments, too...; **f23.5** salty liquorice lingers with the dried manuka honey; **b24** I have no idea what kind of strange alchemy has been going on here. But this is almost identical to Lucky Seven's Hold Up...except everything is back to front, or the wrong way round...the flavours and development coming in reverse order, the early mouth-watering character apart. Fun and fascinating. In 30 years, I cannot remember this happening before...! You really have to track down both bottlings to see exactly what I mean... Anyway, magnificent, hairs-on-chest bourbon. *59.15% (1173 Proof). sc.*

⬧ **Maker's Mark (Red Wax Seal)** bott code: L1056MMB **(92.5) n23** one of the lighter and sweeter bourbon noses these days with an attractive freshly baked brown loaf quality to it, garnished by spices and sugars found on a bun. Wonderfully alluring...; **t23.5** yes, that sweetness seems to have multiplied in recent years. The tannins are charming and controlled, offering a less than energetic heftier note which refuses to impinge on those lightly dominating Demerara tones. The best point is reached at the halfway stage, by which time the spices have pulled up their sleeves and decided to wade into the mix and start to make things really happen...; **f23** returns to its crusty brown bread roots, but with a little French toast for good measure...with black peppers aplenty; **b23** been a little while since I gave this a thorough going over. And I'm intrigued by the subtleness of the very slight changes. This has now become the sweetest of all Kentucky's bourbons, but the balancing spices ensures the sugars never dominate. A friendly distillery producing the friendliest of bourbons. *45%.*

Maker's 46 (95) n23.5 t24.5 f23 b24 Some people have a problem with oak staves. I don't: whisky, after all, is about the interaction of a grain spirit and oak. This guy is all about the nose and, especially, the delivery. With so much controlled honey on show, it cannot be anything other than a show-stopper. Frankly, magnificent. I think I've met my Maker's... 47% (94 proof).

Maker's 46 barrel finished with oak staves, bott code: L6155MMB 00651 1233 (89) n22.5 t22.5 f22 b22 Maker's at its most surprisingly genteel. 47% (94 proof).

Mayor Pingree Aged 7 Years Straight Bourbon Whiskey batch no. 4 db (94.5) n24 t23.5 f23.5 b23.5 Distilled in Lawrenceburg, Indiana, the label confirms. The announcement had already been made on the nose... Casks almost certainly picked from the higher points of the warehouse. 59% (118 proof). ncf sc.

McAffee's Benchmark Old No 8 Brand Kentucky Straight Bourbon bott code: L190260113 (87.5) n22 t22 f21.5 b22 A good, honest, unspectacular bourbon which ticks all the boxes without for a moment trying to go into superdrive. Lays on the natural caramels thickly, then some low voltage spice to stir things up. The sugars are on a slow build, but get there. 40% (80 proof).

Michter's 20 Year Old Kentucky Straight Bourbon batch no. 18I1370, bott code: A182681370 (96.5) n24 t24 f24 b24.5 When people ask me why I think that bourbon has the edge over Scotch at the moment, perhaps I should point them in the direction of a bottling like this to give them some understanding as to why... One of the best 20+ year-old bourbons I have ever encountered. 57.1% (114.2 proof). 463 bottles.

Michter's 20 Year Old Kentucky Straight Bourbon batch no. 19H1439, bott code: A192421439 (96.5) n24.5 t24 f23.5 b24.5. When this bourbon was distilled, it was unlikely a barrel could reach this degree of antiquity and still taste as wonderfully complete as this. Then, if a bourbon reached its second decade, it was one that had slipped through the net and had not been especially cared for. Meaning, nearly always, they were too old and clogged with oak. Not this fellow. This is an old timer all right. But beautifully manicured and more beautiful now than at any previous time in its life. A privilege to taste. 57.1% (114.2 proof). 440 bottles.

⟡ **Michter's 25 Year Old Kentucky Straight Bourbon** batch no. L20I2076, bott code: A202612076 (95.5) n24 what a clever trick! Huge age apparent...but it has not gone down the burnt oak route of so many super-aged bourbon casks. Instead, it has the crotchetiness of a senior citizen disgusted with the news in that day's paper, spitting out a sharp incentive here and there. But elsewhere is a much more gentle soul, lightened by Demerara and red liquorice and softening hum of hickory. Old it may be, but there is style so much life left in this one....; t24.5 oh, my word! The mouth feel could hardly be created if you tried. It borders on perfection with the corn oils proudly intact and happily baring the weight with the far firmer sugars. You wait for the big oak surge...but it doesn't come. Instead, the most subtle hickory develops before making way to the cocoa notes which gather over the palate like dense, pewter clouds in a storm. While spices seem to be happy to accompany the oils, the chocolate intensifies, sweetened by light maple syrup; f23 now the age really has its say as it dries with a dusty vanilla fade. No bitterness, no aggression. Just a shutting down of the more classic bourbon lines...; b24 it is not only the age which is jaw-dropping: the fact that after all these years a bourbon can offer so many untarnished gems...! The midground is fascinating with wonderful mix of dark chocolate mousse and bourbon, one of my favourite combinations. Here it comes with cobwebs. And they only seem to intensify the experience further. Amazingly, the elegance has not been compromised any way shape or form. Simply majestic! 58.1% (116.2 proof). sc. 348 bottles.

Michter's Single Barrel 10 Year Old Kentucky Straight Bourbon barrel no. 19D625, bott code: A19095625 (95.5) n24.5 t23.5 f23.5 b24 An incredibly beautiful whiskey. A contender for the single barrel of the year, for sure... 47.2% (94.4 proof). sc.

Michter's Single Barrel 10 Year Old Kentucky Straight Bourbon barrel no. 19D662, bott code: A19099662 (96) n24 t24 f23.5 b24.5 A classic top quarter of warehouse 10-year-old (barrel 625, above, was much nearer midpoint) which has seen some heat action and ensures maximum depth and entertainment for its age. Beautifully made, too...! 47.2% (94.4 proof). sc.

Michter's Small Batch Kentucky Straight Bourbon batch no. L18F873, bott code: A8172873 (87.5) n22 t22.5 f21 b22 An attractive, slightly minty and ungainly offering with extra bitterness to the toastiness, especially at the death. Some subtle orange blossom honey aids the sweetness. 45.7% (91.4 proof).

Michter's Small Batch Kentucky Straight Bourbon batch no. 20C430, bott code: A200830430 (92) n23 t23.5 f22.5 b23 A deceptively weighty bourbon which is an essay in genteel understatement. Complex and fascinating, especially in the many guises the cocoa creates. 45.7% (91.4 proof).

Michter's Small Batch Original Sour Mash batch no. L18V1608, bott code: A183041608 (92) n23.5 t23 f22.5 b23 One of the weaker Michter's by strength, but lacks nothing in subtlety. 43% (86 proof).

New Riff Backsetter Bourbon Bottled in Bond db **(87) n22.5 t22 f21 b21.5** One of the sweetest bourbons I've encountered for a little while: the expected liquorice and toasty molasses making way for an infinitely more honeyed style with a heather honey forging ahead of the later maple syrup. Strangely tangy, though: a bit like particularly virile marmalade. *50% (100 proof). ncf.*

New Riff Kentucky Straight Bourbon Aged At Least 4 Years dist Fall 2014, bott Fall 2018 nbc **(91.5) n22 t23.5 f22.5 b23.5** I will have to get to Newport, on the opposite banks of the Ohio to Cincinnati, to see this excellent new Kentucky distillery in action. This is as big and impressive as the river that flows astride the two towns. *50% (100 proof). 65% corn, 30% rye 5% malted barley.*

New Riff Kentucky Straight Bourbon Whiskey Bottled in Bond dist Fall 2015, bott Spring 2020 db **(87) n22 t22.5 f21 b21.5** An oily cove with the odd tell-tale sign of wider cut. The massive natural caramels do al they can to hush it up. *50% (100 proof). ncf.*

New Riff Single Barrel Kentucky Straight Bourbon Whiskey barrel no. 15-6995, dist Fall 2015, bott Fall 2019 db **(89) n22.5 t22.5 f21.5 b22.5** Maybe a little too much extracted from the still by this distillery's usually high standards. *56.75% (113.5 proof). ncf sc.*

New Riff Single Barrel Kentucky Straight Bourbon Whiskey barrel no. 16-7128, dist Spring 2016, bott Spring 2020 db **(92) n22.5 t23.5 f22.5 b23.5** A rich, sweet and satisfying bourbon. *56.6% (113.2 proof). ncf sc.*

Old Charter 8 bott code: B170871 10:094 **(91) n22.5 t22.5 f22.5 b23** A wonderfully oily affair which sticks to the palate like a limpet. From taste alone, appears no longer to be an 8-year-old but has retained the number 8. Probably a mix of years as the layering and complexity is significant. *40% (80 proof)*

Old Charter 8 Kentucky Straight Bourbon bott code: L183420122 **(92) n22.5 t23.5 f22.5 b23.5** Very similar to the bottling above, except here the sugars, up in attack earlier, gleam and sparkle while the later spices bristle a little more aggressively: slightly more polarisation, but more polish, too. Such great stuff! *44% (88 proof).*

Old Carter Straight Bourbon Barrel Strength Batch 1 (91.5) n22 t23.5 f23 b23 The nose may be slightly cumbersome and plodding, like the move on the label, but as soon as it hits the palate you know you are backing a winner. *54.45% (108.8 proof). 1567 bottles.*

Old Ezra Aged 7 Years Kentucky Straight Bourbon bott code: LF4227 **(92) n22.5 t23.5 f23 b23** Essentially, a light and complex bourbon with, presumably, the majority of barrels gleaned from the lower floors. *50.5% (101 proof).*

Old Fitzgerald Bottled-in-Bond Aged 9 Years Fall 2018 Edition made: Fall 2008, bott 05/23/2018 db **(93.5) n23.5 t23.5 f23 b24** Middle aged wheated bourbon at its deliciously complex best. *50% (100 proof).*

◇ **Old Fitzgerald Bottled-in-Bond Aged 9 Years Spring 2020 Edition** made: Spring 2011, bott Spring 2020 db **(91.5) n22.5** the dry, peppery, bready influence of the wheat is unmistakable; **t23** now can't say I expected those Demerara sugars to gain traction quite so fast. But they certainly make an impact with the corn oils. The spices grow more meaningful by the minute; **f23** warming with a lovely layered tannin beginning to show belated signs of roastiness; **b23** as the spices kick in there is the effect of good old fashioned British Bread Pudding. Not as good as that my old mum used to make...nothing ever could be! But one of the things I love about Old Fitz is that you never quite know where this brand will take you next. Also, a very sweet version, too... *50% (100 proof).*

Old Fitzgerald Bottled-in-Bond Aged 13 Years Spring 2019 Edition made: Fall 2005, bott 01/30/2019 db **(95) n23.5 t24 f23.5 b24** A very different animal to their 9-year-old offering, which is tighter and with a more precise game plan. By contrast, this drifts and is less attentive to the wheat...though you never lose sight of it. *50% (100 proof).*

◇ **Old Fitzgerald Bottled-in-Bond Aged 14 Years Fall 2020** Edition made: Fall 2005, bott Fall 2020 db **(94) n23.5** fabulously complex: the ulmo honey and vanilla form one, more gentle side. While a drier red liquorice and hickory fusion certainly leaves you in no doubt of the excellent age here. The spices not only represent the wheat, but now the oak, also...; **t23.5** just brilliant: salivating – reflecting the lighter, more flighty sugary notes but arrives at the same time as the heavyweight oak: an unusual and impressive delivery. It means the midground churns with liquorice and salivating heather honey while the spices go to town with a vengeance...; **f23** drier now as the oak has really staked its claim. Caramels and mocha abound, though the liquorice keeps its under control. Just a few molasses notes keep the sugar levels in syc...: **b24** a serious, weighty bourbon with a sweet tooth. Carries its years effortlessly. *50% (100 proof).*

Old Fitzgerald Bottled-in-Bond Aged 15 Years Fall 2019 Edition made: Fall 2004, bott Fall 2019 db **(89) n23 t22 f22 b22** Old Fitz is feeling his years in this one... *50% (100 proof).*

Old Forester bott code: A083151035 db **(94.5) n23.5 t23.5 f23.5 b24** Solid as a rock: a classic and criminally under-rated bourbon which is wonderfully true to the distillery. *43%.*

Old Forester bott code: A115192109 db **(96.5) n24 t24.5 f23.5 b24.5** Having taken it right through the Murray Method, this is one of those very rare whiskies – maybe one in between 300 and 400 - which can be found at its absolute best at ordinary room temperature. Then the influence of the oils is arrested and the grains become the dominating force. And the degree of layering takes a good half hour to fathom. So far this whiskey has taken me around two hours to tame. It is, unquestionably the best whiskey I have tasted so far this year, either for the Bible, or in general whisky work. And, do you know what else I love. No corks. No wax. You are just a bottle top click away from true bourbon genius... 43% (86 proof).

Old Forester bott code: A115191606 db **(91) n22.5 t22.5 f23 b23** Simplistic – and really goes to town on the hickory! 50% (100 proof).

⬦ **Old Forester** bott code: A2822020 **(89.5) n23** crisp and rich with Demerara sugar, an aromatic salute to the rye recipe, it seems, a little mintyness represents the oak charmingly **t23.5** the demerara and liquorice collides on impact, ensuring an intense start. Vanilla is ladled into the mix quite liberally as spices and liquorice re-emerge at the midpoint; **f21** the roast sugars clash slightly with a degree of bitterness: untidy and a bit tangy; **b22** last year I encountered two different standard Old Foresters: one was merely excellent, the other was stonkingly world class. Which suggests that while the average means this is a brilliant bourbon by any definition, there is no knowing for certain just how good it will be. This bottling is slightly on the less compelling side, though the classic nose and huge delivery are to be thoroughly enjoyed. Just hits the buffers towards the unusually unaligned finale. 43% (86 proof)

Old Forester 1870 Original Batch bott code: F050191128702394 db **(94) n23.5t23.5 f24 b24** Simply glorious bourbon! 45% (90 proof).

Old Forester 1897 Bottled in Bond bott code: L297811823 **(92.5) n22.5 t23.5 f23 b23.5** The toast starts to slowly smoulder in a gorgeous bourbon that creeps up and mugs you. Surprisingly rich and just so lush. 50% (100 proof).

Old Forester 1910 Old Fine Whisky nbc **(92) n23 t23.5 f22.5 b23** The kind of dark, hefty bourbon this distillery has long championed. Substantial and satisfying. 46.5% (93 proof).

Old Forester 1920 Prohibition Style nbc **(95.5) n23.5 t24 f24 b24** Just oozes with classic Old Forester depth and oomph! A classic of its style. 57.5% (115 proof).

Old Forester Statesman bott code: L2337123:49 db **(92.5) n23 t23.5 f23 b23.5** A very laid back and relaxed Forester. 47.5% (95 proof).

Old Grand-Dad (90.5) n22 t23 f23 b23.5. This one's all about the small grains. A busy, lively bourbon, this offers little to remind me of the original Old Grand-Dad whiskey made out at Frankfort. That said, this is a whisk(e)y-lover's whiskey: in other words the excellence of the structure and complexity outweighs any historical misgivings. Enormously improved and now very much at home with its own busy style. 43%

Old Grand-Dad 80 Proof bott code: L7119FFB140640030 **(87) n21.5 t22.5 f21 b22** Steady and pretty light weight. Doesn't have quite the same backbone as the 43%. But who cannot fall for the charm of delicate citrus and chalky vanillas? Just enough liquorice and rye juiciness to lift it into the easy drinking category. 40% (80 proof).

Old Grand-Dad Bonded 100 Proof bott code: 258/17 **(96) n23 t24.5 f24 b24.5** For a bourbon, I have tasted rye less rye-like than this. A bourbon standing erect, proud pretty much top of its game wallowing in its faultless distillation and maturation; indeed, probably the best Grand-Dad Bonded I have yet encountered, which really is saying something over so many years! Glorious. 50% (100 proof).

Old Rip Van Winkle Aged 10 Years bott code: B1705307:267 db **(93.5) n24 t23 f23 b23.5** There is something of the old Ancient Age 10 in this, you know... 53.5% (107 proof).

Old Taylor 6 Kentucky Straight Bourbon bott code: B1631608446 **(90) n22.5 t23 f22 b22.5** Exactly as above. Except we now see a little more corn oil and rye glisten on the finish. What a lovely old-fashioned kind of bourbon this is, especially for Old Timers like me...! 40% (80 proof).

Old Virginia Kentucky Straight Bourbon Aged 6 Years bott code: L833901B **(91.5) n23 t22.5 f23 b23** The kind of old-fashioned style bourbon I fell in love with over 40 years ago... 40%.

Orphan Barrel Rhetoric Aged 24 Years bott code: L8059K1002 **(95) n24 t24 f23.5 b23.5** An unusual bourbon for this kind of great age. Usually they head down a heavy duty tannin route. Instead this one almost drowns in natural creamy caramels. Almost as meek as Theresa May when facing the EU bully boys though, of course, nothing on the planet is that pathetic. 45.4%

Pappy Van Winkle Family Reserve 15 Years Old bott code: L172520110:237 **(96) n24 t23.5 f24 b24.5** Weller Antique fans will possibly find a closer match here structure-wise than the 10-year-old. While those in pursuit of excellent bourbon should just linger here awhile. Anyone other than true bourbon lovers need not sample. But there again... 53.5%

Pappy Van Winkle Family Reserve Kentucky Straight Bourbon Whiskey 15 Years Old bott code: L181340105:017 db **(96) n24 t24.5 f23.5 b24** Usually I spit everything I taste. I accidentally found myself swallowing a drop of this without thinking. A bourbon-lover's bourbon... *53.5% (107 proof).*

Pappy Van Winkle's Family Reserve 20 Years Old bott code: L172640108:18N **(95) n24 t22.5 f24.5 b24** An ancient bourbon, so should be a flavour powerhouse. But this is all about understatement and complexity. *45.2% (90.4 proof).*

Pappy Van Winkle Family Reserve Kentucky Straight Bourbon Whiskey 20 Years Old bott code: L18233C10723N db **(85.5) n21 t22.5 f21 b21** Some profound vanilla and citrus moments on delivery. But the nose tells you things aren't as they should be and the finale confirms it. One or two casks used here that have gone through the top, bringing out some pretty tired notes from the oak. Just never comfortable in its own skin. *45.2% (90.4 proof).*

Pappy Van Winkle's Family Reserve 23 Years Old bott code: L1707013:20N **(94.5) n24.5 t23 f23.5 b23.5** I well remember the first Pappy boasting this kind of age: it was horrifically over-oaked and lacked any form of meaningful structure. Well, this also has the odd moment where the tannins are slightly out of control, especially just after delivery. But the structure to this is sound, the complexity a joy. And as for the nose....wow! *47.8% (95.6 proof).*

Pappy Van Winkle Family Reserve Kentucky Straight Bourbon Whiskey 23 Years Old bott code: L180590111:08N db **(95.5) n24 t24 f23.5 b24** One of the holy grails of bourbon is to produce consistently a 23- to 25-year-old which is still sweet and not tannin dominated: no easy ask. This has certainly moved a little way towards that, shewing some of the character of the last bottling I tasted, although this is unquestionably drier. At least on the nose a decisive sweetness I detected and there are still sugars enough to give some fabulous moments on the palate. The tannins do, though, still have the biggest say. But remember: this whiskey has matured for a very long time. In the glass it takes well over an hour to get the best out of it: the secrets of such an ancient bourbon are always revealed tantalisingly slowly... *47.8% (95.6 proof).*

Parker's Heritage Collection 24 Year Old Bottled in Bond Bourbon dist Fall 90 **(95.5) n24 t24 f23.5 b24** For my 999th whisky for the 2018 Bible, thought I'd take on the oldest commercially bottled Kentucky bourbon I can ever remember seeing. Had no idea how this one would go, as the heat of the Midwest means there is little room for the whiskey to manoeuvre. What we actually have is a bourbon in previously unchartered territory and clearly experiencing new, sometimes mildly bewildering, sensations, having proudly gone where no bourbon has gone before... *50%.*

⬧ **Penelope Barrel Strength Four Grain Straight Bourbon Whiskey Aged a Minimum of 36 Months** in charred new American oak barrels, batch no. 05, bott code: L20268SS10828 **(93) n23** red liquorice aplenty. And tannin-infused spices to ensure it has some decent bite, too...; **t23.5** excellent delivery. The small grains are working their socks off to make the busiest of imprints on the palate. At first ulmo honey leads the sweetness, but this slowly turns into headier heather honey with liquorice and mocha gaining in importance as the bourbon grows; **f23** a lovely small grain and tannin spice buzz...; **b23.5** pretty classic bourbon for the age – that is if it has been housed in the higher compartments of the warehouse. Dangerously drinkable. And Lawrenceburg Indiana at its absolute best... *58% (116 Proof). ncf. Distilled in Lawrenceburg, IN.*

⬧ **Penelope Barrel Strength Four Grain Straight Bourbon Whiskey Aged a Minimum of 44 Months** in new American oak barrels, batch no. 07, bott code: L1154SS116:34 **(87) n22.5 t22 f21 b21.5** Typical temperamental Lawrenceburg bourbon. A hotch-potch of a glass with some sublime honey and chocolate notes battling it out with an undesired bitterness. Elsewhere, the grains sing sweet and the corn oil is sticky...but it never quite seems to come together as hoped. And certainly not like Penelope's exquisite 36-month effort. So close to being brilliant, you could scream! *57.6% (115.2 Proof). ncf. Distilled in Lawrenceburg, IN.*

⬧ **Penelope Four Grain Straight Bourbon Whiskey Aged a Minimum of 24 Months** in charred new American oak barrels, bott code: PB17701240 **(88.5) n22 t22.5 f22 b22** For a two-year-old bourbon, this impresses. The overt simplicity is all you would expect for a whiskey this age. But dig a little deeper by giving it the time it deserves, and far more complexity is there to be cherished., wrapped in a banana and vanilla shield. The Marriage of oil and light molasses also strikes a pleasant chord. (And the Murray Method, of course) "I say, don't you think this is a rather decent bourbon, Parker?" "Yusss, m'Lady" ...! *40% (80 Proof). ncf. Distilled in Lawrenceburg, IN.*

Quarter Horse Kentucky Bourbon Whiskey Aged a Minimum of 1 Year in New Oak (87) n21.5 t23 f21.5 b21.5 An intriguing whiskey which simultaneously shews its youth and the spirit and maturity from the cask. The creamy toffee notes on delivery and follow through are superb. For a Quarter Horse it's not half bad... *46% (92.*

Rebel Yell Kentucky Straight Bourbon Whiskey bott code: A305181406 **(88) n22.5 t22 f21 b22** When, back in 1992 I had set off on my uncertain future as the world's first full time whisky writer, the London underground was festooned with adverts for Rebel Yell, complete with Confederate flag, if memory serves over the passing quarter of a century. It was United Distillers' (now Diageo) great hope of conquering the world with bourbon. They didn't and the company, with their fingers scorched, turned their backs on not only what was actually a very good bourbon, but the entire genre. They had gone in all guns blazing, when in fact what bourbon needed – after so many decades of decline - was a softly softly approach. This doesn't have quite the richness of that defeated Rebel Yell from a previous era, but the delicate nature of the sweetness is very attractive. *40% (80 proof).*

Rebel Yell Small Batch Reserve Kentucky Straight Bourbon Whiskey (94.5) n23.5 t24 f23 b23.5 A full on, toasty bourbon making the most of the ample spices on hand. *45.3% (90.6 proof).*

Redemption Bourbon Aged No Less Than 2 Years batch no. 029, bott code: L9269607:16 **(83.5)** n22 t22.5 f19 b20 Certainly kicks off well enough both on nose and delivery with an attractive mix of vanilla and liquorice. But the finish is curiously bitter: not a trait one normally associates with bourbon. Some decent redeeming muscovado sugars at play. *42% (84 proof).*

Redemption High Rye Bourbon Aged No Less Than 2 Years batch no. 122, bott code: L9262600:23 **(91)** n22.5 t23 f22.5 b23 So much better than the last Redemption High Rye I encountered. Surprisingly well spiced for a bourbon sporting a rye content weighing at a hefty 38% of the mash bill. *46% (92 proof).*

Redwood Empire Pipe Dream Bourbon Whiskey Aged at least 4 Years bott code: L19 1760 **(91.5)** n23 t23 f22.5 b23 For a whiskey of this age, the hickory content is high. And a very sweet hickory at that. Very distinctive bourbon. *45%.*

Rock Hill Farms Single Barrel Bourbon bott code: B1717118:40K **(95)** n24 t24 f23.5 b24 Almost impossible to find fault with this. Anyone who loves whisky, bourbon in particular, will simply groan in pleasure in the same way you might jolt out when the knee is tapped. The only fly in the ointment is that I cannot tell you the barrel or bottling, because it isn't marked on the bottle. This really is bourbon at it sexiest. *50% (100 proof)*

Rock Hill Farms Single Barrel Bourbon bott code: L18102010829K **(95.5)** n24 t24 f23.5 b24 Take a bet on this and you are likely to be a winner. A true bourbon connoisseur's favourite... *50%.*

Russell's Reserve Kentucky Straight Bourbon 10 Years Old bott code: LL/GI210755 db **(92.5)** n23 t23 f23 b23.5 One of the softest decade-old bourbons I have tasted in a very, very long time. *45% (90 proof).*

Russell's Reserve Single Barrel no 17-0208 Rickhouse B Floor 6 17 2 **(95.5)** n23.5 t24 f23.5 b24.5 So understated, this bourbon communicates in gentle whispers. Comes across sweet as honey but thickens into a gentle giant - yet all the time the balance is never threatened, only continually enhanced. Sublime. *55% (110 proof). Selected by the Frankfort Bourbon Society*

Seven Devils Straight Bourbon Whiskey (82.5) n20 t21.5 f20.5 b20.5 Nutty, caramel-laden and sweet, there is a buzz on the palate to this which suggests the distillate has not been quite as well made as it could be. Doesn't sit right, despite (or maybe because of) the praline. *45% (90 proof). Bottled by Koenig Distillery*

Shenk's Homestead Kentucky Sour Mash 2019 Release batch no. 19G1139, bott code: A191861139 **(88)** n22.5 n22.5 t22 f21.5 b22 Exceptionally gentle whiskey boasting modest but important kumquat note on both nose and body and a shimmering, slightly metallic heather honey sweetness. A tad bitter late on. *45.6% (91.2 proof). 2,882 bottles. Bottled by Michter's Distillery.*

The Single Cask Heaven Hill 2009 barrel, cask no. 152724 **(94)** n23.5 t24 f23 b23.5 HH at is busiest, though not quite brightest. The liquorice and brief maple syrup mix are the highlight, just after delivery. But the toastiness is a little aggressive and, ultimately, on the bitter side. Even so, there is much to enjoy elsewhere, especially with the corn oils, spices and, above all, the controlled depth of the Victory V cough sweet-style hickory. Lovely stuff! *62.5%. nc ncf sc.*

Smooth Ambler Contradiction Bourbon a blend of straight bourbons blended in West Virginia, Tennessee and Indiana, batch 273 **(94)** n23.5 t24 f23 b23.5 If this whiskey had a middle name, it would be Complexity...and you would hear no contradictions from me...! *46% (92 proof).*

◈ **Smooth Ambler Contradiction Bourbon** blend of straight bourbon whiskies, batch no. 385 **(89)** n22.5 a genteel vanilla dominates. The tannins are remarkably docile...; t23 it's the excellent complexity and layering on delivery which really hits the spot here: everything is ultra-low-key mode; f21.5 a slightly toasty bitterness exposes the lack of late sweetness; b22 not all singing and all dancing Contradiction I tasted last time out, but far from a white elephant either. All the superstar action crammed int the opening salvo on the palate, which is exceptional. *46% (92 proof) Blended from whiskeys distilled in West Virginia, Tennessee and Indiana.*

◈ **Smooth Ambler Old Scout Aged 5 Years Bourbon** barrel no. 28092 **(95)** n23.5 brilliant liquorice and hickory mix. Prickling spice countering the lightly salted ulmo honey; t24 superb delivery with the trademark corn oils again setting up camp but now the dark sugars arrive early and in force, as does the saline kick advertised on the nose. The best is yet to come as three or four waves of toasted, almost burnt, honeycomb which gives a feeling of both great age and substance; **f23.5** the corn oils have stretched a long way and still have a little more in reserve. The salty, toasted honey also has depth enough to keep the narrative going, complete with some light spices; **b24** a truly wonderful barrel plucked, most likely, from the upper stories of the warehouse, as this has the personality of a standard bourbon twice its age. The secret of its greatness, however, is the balance of its controlled intensity. A bourbon lover's bourbon... *59.1% SC Distilled in Indiana*

Smooth Ambler Old Scout Straight Bourbon batch No 55 distilled in Indiana **(92) n23 t23 f22.5 b23.5** Non-spectacular but thoroughly enjoyable bourbon that wears its excellence well. *49.5% (99 proof).*

❖ **Smooth Ambler Old Scout Straight Bourbon** batch no. 80 **(92) n23.5** that lovely house yeasty style is maintained, though with a soft nuttiness and hickory polished by light heather honey; **t23** silky corn oils help the lightly toasted vanilla to stick around. The heather honey on the nose is apparent here but makes no big fuss; **f22.5** long, quiet vanilla with the spices gathering only as the toastiness intensifies; **b23** an interesting variant on the last batch I tasted with the hickory now restricted to the nose. A very relaxed, high-grade bourbon. *49.5% (99 proof) Distilled in Indiana*

Spirits of French Lick The Wheater Straight Bourbon Whiskey batch no. 4 **(92) n23 t23 f22.5 b23.5** This mixing of two-year-old French Lick and 7-year-old Wyoming Wheated bourbons has to be one of the creamiest of this style I have ever encountered. The nose is fat and friendly with a light brushing of cinnamon on the ginger and over cooked toast. However, the sugars are first on parade on the palate, most of the presenting a toasty Demerara style. However, those corn oils insist on being counted to ensure a lush and lingering mouthfeel. The toastiness increases as the spices mount but red liquorice balances things neatly. Wonderfully flavoursome! (CV) *51% (102 proof).*

Stagg Jr bott code: B1707310457 **(96) n24 t24.5 f23.5 b24** I well remember the first Stagg Junior I encountered. Which though truly excellent, skimped a little too much on the sugars and struggled to find its balance and, thus, full potential. Certainly no such worries with this bottling: indeed, the honey is remarkable for its abundance. Staggering... *64.75% (129.5 proof)*

Stagg Jr Barrel Proof bott code: L192940114.09D db **(97.5) n24 t25 f24 b24.5** It may be called Junior. But it is towering over Daddy these days.... Spectacularly mind-blowing! *64.2% (128.4 proof).*

Ten High Kentucky Bourbon bott code: L172211518053 **(72) n19 t19 f16 b18** Docile, unusually sweet early on but the finish never quite feels right, the flavours jarring badly. Bitter at the death. This is a bourbon...? *40% (80 proof).*

Treaty Oak Distilling Red Handed Bourbon Whiskey db **(90) n22 t23 f22.5 b22.5** As thick cut as a Texas steak....and no less juicy! *47.5% (95 proof).*

Van Winkle Special Reserve 12 Years Old Lot "B" bott code: L172550110:147 **(93.5) n23 t23 f24 b23.5** Those looking for comparisons between certain Weller products and Van Winkle's might find this particular bottling a little better weighted, less forthright and more complex. *45% (90 proof)*

Van Winkle Special Reserve 12 Years Old Lot "B" Batch Bourbon Whiskey bott code: L181300112 **(94.5) n23.5 t23.5 f23 b23.5** Roughly consistent in quality to the bottling above, but better here and takes a slightly different route - by putting its foot on the toastiness and steering by some very impressive waxy Manuka honey. For those who like their bourbon hairy, bristling with spice, honey and big oak interaction. *45.2% (90.4 proof).*

Very Old Barton bott code: L17/60111:104 **(87.5) n22 t22 f21.5 b22** Attractive, brittle and with a delicious slow burn of first delicate, then broader hickory tones. The small grains fizz and dazzle in typical VOB style. If anything, slightly undercooked at this strength, and missing the extra oils, too. *40% (80 proof)*

Very Old Barton 6 bott code: 907:104 **(93) n22 t24 f23.5 b23.5** The VOB 6, when the number stood for the years, has for the last quarter of a century been one of my bourbons of choice: an understated classic. This version has toned down on the nose very slightly and the palate underlines a far less definite oak-to-grain parry and counter-thrust. That said, still a bourbon which mesmerises you with its innate complexity and almost perfect weight and pace on the palate. One that has you instinctively pouring a second glass. *45% (90 proof)*

Very Old Barton 90 Proof Kentucky Straight Bourbon bott code: L181370113 **(92) n22.5 t23.5 f23 b23** Gorgeous whiskey, though not perhaps the tour de force of previous bottlings. *45% (90 proof).*

Very Old Barton 100 Proof bott code: L17/640102:074 **(96) n23.5 t24.5 f23.5 b24.5** Here's a challenge for you: find fault with this whiskey... Brilliant bourbon of the intense yet sophisticated variety. *50% (100 proof)*

Very Old Barton Kentucky Straight Bourbon bott code: 3820123 **(87.5) n22 t22 f21.5 b22** A consistent bourbon (just noticed I have marked it identically to the last bottling!) giving a limited but delightful account of the VIB brand, ensuring the busy small grains keeps on scrambling around the palate and just enough liquorice and hickory meets the onrushing caramel and praline. Deceptively delicious. 40% (80 proof).

Virginia Gentleman (90.5) n22 t23 f23 b23.5. A Gentleman in every sense: and a pretty sophisticated one at that. 40% (80 Proof)

Weller Aged 12 Years bott code: B17081 20:56 **(91)** n22.5 t23 f22.5 b23 Firm, crunchy, sweet bourbon and very warming... 45% (90 proof)

Weller Aged 12 Years Kentucky Straight Bourbon Whiskey bott code: L190790117 **(91.5)** n22.5 t23.5 f22.5 b23 Spookily similar to the bottling above, the only noticeable difference being the degree of waxy honey on delivery. 45% (90 proof).

Weller Antique 107 Kentucky Straight Bourbon bott code: L190170117 **(88)** n22 t23 f21 b22 Enjoyable, but nothing like the Antique 107 I have become used to swooning over. Attractive, but some antiques are more desired than others. 53.5% (107 proof).

Weller C.Y.P.B Wheated Kentucky Straight Bourbon bott code: L18163011042N **(95.5)** n24 t24 f23.5 b24 Has all the chutzpah of a wheated bourbon that knows it's damn good and goes out to shock. Enjoy the myriad little favour and spice explosions. And the deceptive depth.... 47.5% (95 proof).

Weller Full Proof Kentucky Straight Bourbon bott code: L192200103:21B db **(94)** n23 t23.5 f23.5 b24 A thick knife, fork and spoon bourbon that you can make a right meal from. Fabulous balance to the intensity here. And who doesn't love bourbon in their dark chocolate mousse... 57% (114 proof).

Weller Single Barrel Kentucky Straight Bourbon bott code: 30022133321 db **(91.5)** n23.5 t23 f22 b23 A beautifully competent, undemonstrative wheated bourbon which never puts a foot out of place and enjoys a quiet complexity. 48.5% (97 proof). sc.

Weller Special Reserve bott code: L172080115:014 **(93)** n23 t23.5 f23 b23.5 Imperiously excellent, yet somehow given to understatement. 45% (90 proof)

Weller Special Reserve Kentucky Straight Bourbon bott code: L19018 0118 **(94)** n23 t23.5 f24 b24 Almost too soft and easy to drink. A thousand kisses in a glass.. 45% (90 proof).

Western Gold 6 Year Old Bourbon Whiskey (91.5) n22 t23 f22.5 b23 Taken from barrels sitting high in the warehouse, that's for sure. You get a lot for your six years... 40%.

❖ **The Whisky Cask Company Heaven Hill 2009 Kentucky Straight Bourbon Whiskey** American white oak casks, dist Aug 2009, bott Sep 2019 **(87.5)** n22 t22 f21.5 b22 Both nose and delivery are heavy on the hickory. A little golden syrup runs off with the corns oils. A tad bitter on the finish but compensated for by the delicate late vanillas. 58.2% 296 bottles

The Whisky Shop Maker's Mark batch no. 002, oak staves with barrel finish **(94.5)** n23.5 t24 f23 b24 So rare to find Maker's Mark at this strength. The kind of whisky that give wheated bourbon lovers a little stiffy... 54.95%.

Widow Jane Straight Bourbon Whiskey Aged 10 Years barrel no. 1785, bott 2018 **(95)** n23.5 t23.5 f24 b24 This is one very passionate Widow... 45.5% (91 proof). sc.

Wilcox Bourbon Whiskey (73.5) n19 t19 f17.5 b18 When you buy a bourbon whiskey, you have in your mind a clean, complex Kentuckian. Not sure who made this, but far too feinty for its own good with none of the liquorice and honey notes you should rightfully expect. A very poor representation of bourbon, and not remotely in the true Kentucky style. 40% (80 proof). BBC Spirits.

Wild Turkey 81 Proof bott code: LL/DF291109 db **(91.5)** n23 t23 f22.5 b23 A much sweeter, more relaxed bottling than the old 40% version, gathering up honey notes like a wild turkey hoovering up summer berries. 40.5% (81 proof).

Wild Turkey 81 Proof bott code: LL/HA040353 db **(92)** n22.5 t23.5 f22.5 b23 More oak interaction with this feller than any other 81 proof I've encountered. Lays on the hickory with a trowel: delicious! 40.5% (81 proof).

Wild Turkey 101 Proof bott code: LL/HH300747 db **(93)** n23.5 t23.5 f23 b23 The astonishing overall softness on the palate is counterintuitive to the slight aggression on the nose. I've been savouring this whisky for over 30 years. And still it has the ability to surprise. 50.5% (101 proof).

❖ **Wild Turkey 101** bott code LL7JD071129 **(88)** n22 t22.5 f21 b22 Not often I feel that Wild Turkey 101 isn't quite on the ball. But that is certainly the case here. The red liquorice and rye-rich nose, attractive as it is, seems a little off the pace. Further, the corn oil dominated delivery, plus the imprecise hickory is loose in its construction. The prevailing bitterness to the sugary finish almost comes as no surprise. Doubt you'd say no to a second glass offered, as there is still plenty to enjoy. But by WT101 usually very high standards, it's a bit of a turkey. 50.5%

Wild Turkey Kentucky Spirit Single Barrel barrel no. 0401, warehouse A, rick no. 6, bott 01/14/19, bott code: LL/HA152135 db **(89) n22.5 t23 f21.5 b22** A real enjoyable softie if, perhaps, a tad one dimensional. 50.5% (101 proof). sc.

Wild Turkey Longbranch oak and Texas mesquite charcoal refined bott code: LL/GI180207 db **(91.5) n23 t23 f22.5 b23** Mesquite must be America's answer to peat: here there is a just a light touch, barely noticeable until the finish, and emphasised by the very late warmness to the finale itself. 43% (86 proof).

Wild Turkey Longbranch bott code: LL/HD261325 db **(92.5) n23 t23 f23 b23.5** "Mesquite must be America's answer to peat" I thought as I nosed and tasted this. "Have I written that before about this?" I mused. I had. And it is... 43% (86 proof).

Wild Turkey Rare Breed Barrel Proof bott code: LL/HA140731 db **(95.5) n23.5 t24 f24 b24** A clever glass bottle, its roundness reinforcing the mouthfeel and character of the bourbon itself: one of the most rounded in all Kentucky. In some ways this whiskey is the blueprint for bourbon: its characteristics embrace what we mentally define as bourbon. 58.4% (116.8 proof).

Wild Turkey Rare Breed Barrel Proof bott code: LL/HA140731 db **(94.5) n23.5 t24 f23 b24** Hickory is all the rage with Wild Turkey this year: another bottling that is leading with that delightful trait. However, have noticed the honey level has receded slightly. 58.4% (116.8 proof).

Wilderness Trail Single Barrel Kentucky Straight Bourbon BIB Sweet Mash barrel no 14E23 **(83.5) n20.5 t21.5 f21 b20.5** A hot, aggressive bourbon with more bite than spice. The corn element ticks the right boxes and does a great job, but this bourbon struggles to find its rhythm despite an attractive mocha finale. 50% (100 proof). ncf. 245 bottles. 64% corn, 24% wheat 12% malted barley. sc.

William Larue Weller db **(97.5) n24 t25 f24 b24** ...The most delicious lesson in whiskey structure imaginable. This was my 1,263rd and final new whiskey for the Jim Murray Whisky Bible 2019. Did I leave the very best until last....? 64.1% (128.2 proof).

William Larue Weller db **(97.5) n25 t24.5 f23.5 b24.5** I have before me a glass of whiskey. It is pure amber in colour and has won more top honours, including World Whisky of the Year, in Jim Murray's Whisky Bible than any other brand. For that reason the sample before me is, as I nose and taste it on the evening of 26th August 2019, the 20,000th whisky I have specifically tasted for this book since it was first published in 2003. There really could be no other I could possibly bestow this personal honour upon. It is a landmark whiskey in every sense... Oh, once again, I have not been let down. I will have to wait to see if this is World Whisky of the Year once more: on the evidence before me it will be close. But I do know no whiskey will better its truly perfect nose... 62.85% (125.7 proof).

William Larue Weller db **(97) n24.5 t24 f24 b24.5** Has a subtly different approach to last year's William Larue Weller, which was enormous with all its knees and elbows protruding among the massive favour values. This is more reserved, yet no less powerful or complex. Tells a similar story, but in a much quieter voice, seemingly understated. Unless you pay attention... 64% (128 proof).

⬧ **William Larue Weller** db **(96.5) n24** a fat old nose, just brimming with corn and toasted brown bread. An occasional peek at some thick cut marmalade, but this is obscured by the galloping, tannin-thick, wheat-thin spices. As ever the honey has almost magical powers. Is this the one I once picked out some Corsican bruyere? I think it must be, because I am certainly picking it up here – a kind of earthier, slightly more phenolic version of standard heather honey – mingling suggestively with liquorice and manuka: everything is such a tease...; **t24.5** you could almost bet your house that one of the great deliveries of any whisky you will taste in any year will be a Weller. And your house will be safe again for another 12 months. It's one of the few whiskies I find myself actually closing my eyes with sheer pleasure, rather than just following the Murray Method. The corn oils are profound in this bottling, more so than usual, but it is the next phase of vividly intense spice against a blend of corn and varied dark honeys, plus a little extra molasses, that totally swamps your senses. Very few whiskies can even get close to this degree of intensity...and pleasure...; **f24** the spices continue to fizz to the very last toasty embers. Indeed, all now is toasty, especially the liquorice and molasses, bathed as they are in late caramels and vanillas. These all carry on indefinitely on a bed of oily corn...; **b24** another blistering, palate-seducing chunk of whiskey genius from Weller which, perhaps with Glen Grant, is the most consistent whiskey in the universe. Certainly, on this planet. There are always fine lines between each year's bottling. This one is perhaps defined by the determination of the spice and the unrelenting toastiness. Most previous bottlings have had a thin layer of delicate, sweetening sugars which cannot be found here. So, this is more business-like and intense. It sorts out the men from the boys...sorry, I mean the adults from the children. But it remains, unquestionably, whiskey gold of the very purest quality... 67.25% (134.5 proof).

Winchester Bourbon Whiskey Aged a Minimum of 6 Months in New Oak bott code: L219A090024564 **(85.5) n21.5 t22 f21 b21** That is one very curious bourbon with an arrangement of tobacco and leather on the nose and thick corn oil and orange blossom honey on delivery. A little chunky and feinty towards the close, but the spices do a good job. Complex and decidedly idiosyncratic. *45% (90 proof*

Woodford Reserve Distiller's Select Batch 500 (87.5) n21.5 t22 f22 b22 A steady, laid-back bourbon, happy to wallow in its own understatement. The nose is light with a gentle sweet, hickory theme; the taste is no more taxing and relying on a thin-ish spicy sweetness amid the gentle tannins. Attractive and undemanding. 43.2%. (86.4 proof).

⬦ **Woodford Reserve label batch 1153 (92.5) n22.5** attractive chocolate mint. Quite elegant, if not a little docile by Kentucky standards; **t23.5** very light for a straight bourbon, the small grains doing a lot of the donkey work so far as complexity is concerned. A milky-caramel softness attaches to the weak liquorice. Delightful layering to oak, adding to the complexity; **f23** lots of busy-ness to the last, though perhaps a tad bitter off the oak late on. Warming, but that usual liquorice/hickory kick usually associated with Kentucky never quite arrives, though both notes are present in dignified amounts; Unusually oily late on, too...; **b23.5** I have to say that this is probably the first Woodford Reserve which I have thoroughly enjoyed and found without a wobble somewhere along the line or annoyingly too ineffectual. Incredibly delicate in many ways, which is the norm, but now far more complex than was once the case. Absolutely delighted to report this, as my less than over enthusiastic reviews of the past have jarred, seeing how I knew the place intimately and has many happy memories for me before the distillery was rebuilt. This is now a very serious bourbon 43.2%

⬦ **World Whisky Society Reserve Collection Kentucky Straight Bourbon Single Barrel Aged 15 Years** batch no. 257 **(95) n23.5** superb, truly classic bourbon aroma: manuka honey and molasses should make this a heavyweight. But it hasn't. Instead, there is calming vanillas and caramels helping the illuminate the spices a little better; **t23.5** if the nose was classic, then the same goes for the delivery. Much more corn present here than on the nose. But it is that layering which really blows you away. Light mint and chocolate show quite early with a liquorice and molasses spine. Just a little hickory nip in here and there. The spices, though busy, are much quieter than on the nose; **f24** still that corn oil continues, but just look at that praline and liquorice duet! Have to say it: classic...; **b24** a bourbon which is as elegant as it is eloquent. There is a massive mismatch between the enormity and heftiness of the extraordinary bottle and its deceptively subtle and complex contents. The bottle would make a very good murder weapon: the whiskey it contains is gentle, for all its barrel strength, and would bring even the most exhausted back to life. You may have gathered that one word only can satisfactorily sum this bourbon up: classic! *56% (112 Proof).*

Yellowstone Aged 9 Years Kentucky Straight Bourbon Whiskey 2019 Edition bott code: 211 19 **(93.5) n23.5 t23.5 f23 b23.5** Remarkable for its almost unremitting dryness. The delicate sweetness does just the job required. *50.5% (101 proof). Limestone Branch Distillery Co.*

Yellowstone Select Kentucky Straight Bourbon Whiskey bott code: 311 19 **(92.5) n23 t23 f23 b23.5** A good, honest Kentucky bourbon which pulls no punches. Just a little more confident and assertive than the last bottling I found. *46.5% (93 proof). Bottled by Limestone Branch Distillery Co.*

Tennessee Whiskey

Heaven's Door Tennessee Bourbon Whiskey 10 Year Old bott code: 10/25/18 **(85) n21.5 t22.5 f20 b21** I'm knock-knock-knocking this Heaven's Door: far too heavy, I'm afraid. But, wow! What a delivery...!!! *50% (100 proof).*

Heaven's Door Tennessee Bourbon Whiskey Aged for a Minimum of 7 Years bott code: 2019/04/120555 **(94) n23 t24 f23.5 b23.5** Another bewildering whiskey type to contend with in the USA. Now it is Tennessee Bourbon. I presume that is a bourbon whiskey made in Tennessee but without deploying the charcoal mellowing process. Whatever, it is quite Heavenly.... *45% (90 proof).*

Joe Got a Gun batch no. 1, bott code: 10/07/19 **(88.5) n23 t22 f21.5 b22** The nose has star billing here. Such a charming marriage between hickory and citrus. On the palate it proves a little more workaday, but still shewing much to enjoy. The sugars, though toasty are elegantly done. Perhaps a shade too much chalkiness on the finale, though. *40%. BBC Spirits.*

Joe Got a Gun Single Barrel #1 bott code: 10/07/19 **(94) n23.5 t23.5 f23 b24** A far more masculine bottling than their batch no 1. The tannins are not shy and give a delicious account of themselves. A quite superb Tennessee. Joe's gun has hit the bullseye with this one... *45%. sc. 300 bottles. BBC Spirits.*

Obtainium Tennessee Rye db **(83) n21 t21.5 f20 b20.5** Far too dependent on the blood orange core. Sharp, fruity, ultimately bitter and, overall, just awry with the rye... *57.8%.*

 Peg Leg Porker Tennessee Straight Bourbon Whiskey (91.5) n22.5 t23 f22.5 b23.5 Still generally has the awkward gait of youth but is old enough to unveil sufficiently luminous sugar to perfectly match the surprising intensity to the spice. Some enjoyable late cocoa towards the death lifts the whole piece considerably. The lushness of the corn oil is exhibition quality; and unlike the 8- and 12-year-old is hickory free. Incidentally, this is a bourbon which benefits massively by the Murray Method...by over five points, no less. You could say it saves its bacon... *45% (90 Proof)*

 Peg Leg Porker Tennessee Straight Bourbon Whiskey Aged 8 Years (91) n22.5 t23.5 f22 b23 Deeply attractive, straight as a die bourbon with a decidedly hickory-rich bent on the nose and sturdy corn oils to ensure a rich texture and a generous spreading of muscovado sugars. One of those delightful bourbons where the actual mouth feel is as enjoyable of the flavours themselves. The midground to finish is a glorious exhibition of light ulmo honey and deep vanilla, the spice being the flag planted on the top of the pile. *45% (90 Proof)*

 Peg Leg Porker Tennessee Straight Bourbon Whiskey Aged 12 Years (87.5) n22 t22.5 f21 b22 an interesting bourbon, not least because the distillate does not seem to be as such high class as their No Age Statement and 8-year-old versions. This is vaguely fruitier, more meandering and less precise. A kind of bourbon that keeps standing at the edge of a road and is not sure whether to cross or not. This hesitancy is particularly noticeable on the uneven finish. But, again, the corn oils are simply brilliant; the slow leakage of cocoa into the system delightful and, for its obvious weaknesses, the overall experience is enjoyable *45% (90 Proof)*

 Peg Leg Porker Tennessee Straight Bourbon Whiskey Aged 15 Years batch no. 1 **(84.5)** n22 t21.5 f20 b21 This wouldn't have been the finest white dog you would have found in Tennessee when it was made 15 years ago. The years in cask has helped for sure, injecting plenty of sugars from the oak which proffers respectability. But there is no escaping the vegetable tones which point towards a fermentation problem and/or an early lack of copper in the system. *45% (90 Proof). 2,500 bottles*

Uncle Nearest 1820 Premium Whiskey Aged 11 Years barrel no. US.21, bott 11/5/19 **(95.5)** n24 t24 f23.5 b24 I have waited all day to get through the previously scheduled whiskeys to taste this I was so looking forward to it! It was worth the wait as this has not just stayed true to form but improved magnificently on the last excellent bottle of this I encountered. Real, rich chewing whiskey! What a treat! *58.6% (117.1 proof). sc. 126 bottles.*

Uncle Nearest 1820 Premium Whiskey Aged 11 Years Nearest Green Single Barrel barrel no. US-1 **(94.5)** n23 t24 f23.5 b24 A real roller coaster of a ride. Let's get back on again... *57.6%*

Uncle Nearest 1820 Premium Whiskey Aged 11 Years Nearest Green Single Barrel barrel no. US-2 **(92.5)** n23 t23 f23 b23.5 Have to applaud the delicate nature of this whiskey and its superior layering. Just too easy to enjoy. *55.1% (110.2 proof). 146 bottles.*

Uncle Nearest 1856 Premium Whiskey (89.5) n22 t22.5 f22.5 b22.5 No bells and whistles. Just a slow radiating of gentle sugar and tannin tones. Easy sipping. *50% (100 proof).*

Uncle Nearest 1856 Premium Whiskey bott code: 192451651 **(91.5)** n23 t23 f22.5 b23 A busier incarnation than the last bottling of 1856 I encountered. Thoroughly enjoyable. *50%* .

Uncle Nearest 1884 Small Batch Whiskey bott code: 10/29/20191007 **(90.5)** n22.5 t22 f23 b23 Perhaps noticeable for its significant lack of corn oils. Delicate and leans towards a hickory persona. A covertly complex and delightful Tennessee. *46.5% (93 proof).*

 Whisky-Fässle Fine Tennessee Whisky 15 Years Old dist 2003, bott 2018 **(91.5)** n22 t23 f23.5 b23 Not sure I have ever encountered more buttery bourbon from either Tennessee or Kentucky for a very long time. This is partly due to the lightness of the ulmo honey intertwangling with the corn oils, but there is something else besides: a light saltiness catching the mood of the healthy vanillas which have been slowly leached from the barrel over the passing decade and a half. The spices nip and nibble like friendly fish on your feet in a Nantucket rockpool. And the sugars, mainly of a icing sugar disposition, melt into the vanilla to ward off any transgressing bitterness from the oak. As comfortable to your palate as your favourite old shoes are to your feet... *49.6% nc ncf*

GEORGE DICKEL

George Dickel Aged 17 Years bott code: L6154K1001 db **(94)** n24 t24 22.5 b23.5 The oldest George Dickel I have ever encountered has held its own well over the years. A defiant crispness to the piece makes for memorable drinking, though it is the accommodating and comfortable nose which wins the greatest plaudits... *43.5% (87 proof).*

George Dickel Barrel Select (90.5) n21 t23 f23.5 b23 The limited nose makes the heart sink. What happens once it hits the palate is another story entirely. Wonderful! *43%*

George Dickel Distillery Reserve Collection 17 Year Old (91.5) n23.5 t23.5 f21.5 b23 Outside of a warehouse, I'm not sure I've encountered a Tennessee whiskey of this antiquity before. I remember one I tasted some while back, possibly about a year older or two older than this, was black and like tasting eucalyptus concentrate. This is the opposite, showing extraordinary restraint for its age, an almost feminine charm. *43.5%*

George Dickel No. 12 bott code: L7034R60011402 db **(89) n21.5 t23.5 f22 b22** In a way, a classic GD where you feel there is much more still in the tank... *45% (90 proof).*

JACK DANIEL

Jack Daniel's 120th Anniversary of the White Rabbit Saloon (91) n22.5 t23.5 f22 b23 On its best-behaved form. After the delivery, the oils are down a little, so not the usual bombastic offering from JD. Nonetheless, this is pure class and the clever use of sugars simply make you drool... *43%. Brown-Forman.*

Jack Daniel's Gentleman Jack bott code: 141734518B db **(90.5) n22.5 t22.5 f22.5 b23** A Jack that can vary slightly in style. A couple of months back I included one in a tasting which was much fuller bodied and dripping in maple syrup. This one is infinitely more laid back. *40% (80 proof).*

Jack Daniel's Old No.7 Brand (Black Label) (92) n23 t23 f22.5 b23.5. Actually taken aback by this guy. The heavier oils have been stripped and the points here are for complexity...that should shock a few old Hell's Angels I know. *40%*

⬩ **Jack Daniel's Old No 7 Brand** bott code: L214734202 **(92) n22.5** there's plenty of hickory and molasses at work here. The usual oils, though, appear unusually subdued...; **t23** yes, unquestionably lighter on delivery with much more elegance and structure working through from the oak and the oils coming more from the corn than the actual distillation process...wow! Just as on the nose the hickory and sugars are working is delightful unison, not cramped by the usual oily bite-back...; **f23** this is now so soft and gentle, I've had to reach for the bottle just to convince myself this is JD. Well, of course it is. But the way light strands of heather honey working with the hickory and layered tannins.... well, you can forgive me for my slightly puzzled, raised eyebrows...; **b23.5** this is JD wearing its best bib and tucker: rarely have I seen it quite so well behaved. It is as though someone has got that doubler up and working properly, because this is a much cleaner whiskey than when I last tasted it a couple of years back: a kind of a halfway house between Gentleman Jack and the original Ol' No 7. Refined, elegant and pretty classy. *40%.*

Jack Daniel's Master Distiller Series No 1 db **(90.5) n24 t22 f22 b22.5** no mistaking the JD pedigree. Just a few telling extra degrees of fruit. *43%*

⬩ **Jack Daniel's No 6 Edition Master Distiller Series Jimmy Bedford** bott code L204705422: **(94.5) n23.5** liquorice and hickory at full volume, with no shortage of corn oil, either. Love the dried blood orange peel, too. Truly classic JD...; **t24** those oils, lacking slightly in the current No 7, make a huge difference here, clinging to the palate like a mountaineer to the north face of the Eiger. The layering of the hickory is sublime, the oak offering here a more sophisticated dryness than this whiskey is often given credit for, keeping the light molasses in check. Black liquorice is tied into place by the delicate by fizzing spices: beautifully constructed; **f23** excellent length excellent length, those spices still fizzing and a little heather honey now mingling with the liquorice. Impressively, even now the layers come; **b24** that's more like it! Very much the Old No 7 from a decade ago when everything was that bit more intense and "dirty" than is the case now, with liquorice and hickory on steroids. What an underrated treat this whiskey is: underrated because how many people do you know would drink it neat? A truly classic JD which the late Jimmy Bedford, who spent countless hours the best part of 30 years ago teaching me the nuances and secrets of Tennessee whiskey, would absolutely adore. *43%*

Jack Daniel's Single Barrel Select barrel no. 18-7604, rick no. R-18, bott 10 18 18 db **(94) n23 t23.5 f23.5 b24** Outwardly very similar to a standard Jack, only with a few extra waves of honey and a little less fat around the edges. More subtle but incontrovertible evidence that JD is a far better distillery than most connoisseurs give it credit for. *45% (90 proof). sc.*

Jack Daniel's Straight Rye Whiskey bott code: L184601033 db **(87.5) n21.5 t23 f21.5 b21.5** For some reason the rye refuses to take pole position and is lost behind a series of pretty ordinary corn and oak-vanilla notes, though the cool mintiness is a classy touch. Pleasant and plodding without being in any way - well, except minty moments - exciting or stimulating...as a good rye should always be! *45% (90 proof).*

Corn Whiskey

Obtainium Kentucky Corn Whiskey db **(92.5) n23 t23.5 f23 b23** Now that's pretty good corn whiskey! Beautifully made and matured. *63.1% (126.2 proof).*

Straight Rye

Booker's Rye 13 Years, 1 Month, 12 Days batch no. 2016-LE db **(97.5) n25 t24 f24 b24.5** This was a rye made in the last days of when Jim Beam's Yellow Label was at its very peak. Then, it was the best rye commercially available. Today, it is simply a staggering example of a magnificent rye showing exactly what genius in terms of whiskey actually means. If this is not World Whisky of the Year for 2017, it will be only fragments of molecules away... 68.1% (136.2 proof)

Bulleit 95 Rye bott code: L6344R60010848 **(83) n20.5 t22 f20 b20.5** In some 30 years of tasting rye from the great Lawrenceburg, Indiana, distillery, this has to be the weirdest batch I have yet encountered. The highly unusual and mildly disturbing tobacco note on the nose appears to be a theme throughout the tasting experience. A rye which rallies briefly on delivery but ultimately falls flat on its face. 45% (90 proof).

Bulleit 95 Rye Frontier Whiskey bott ode: L9145R60011708 **(86.5) n21.5 t23 f20.5 b21.5** An upgrade on the last bottling, but still that mysterious tobacco note issuing from an Indiana distillery which was once the byword for pristine, super-pure nosing and tasting rye. When the grain does burst through it is sharp, salivating and full of its old Demerara sugar crispness. Lots of chocolate to be had, too, even if there is a strange buzz to the finish. And if you are into tobacco, this Bulleit's got your name on it. 45% (90 proof).

Colonel E.H. Taylor Straight Rye Bottled in Bond bott code: L1728501 **(94.5) n23.5 t24 f23.5 b23.5** Nothing like the big rye lift I found on the previous E. H. Taylor rye: this is happier to play the subtle game with a slow build rather than a naked graininess. A genuine surprise package. 50% (100 proof).

Colonel E.H. Taylor Straight Rye Bottled in Bond bott code: L182130113:007 **(96) n24 t24 f24 b24** hose were the very simplified notes of a long and beautiful story... 50% (100 proof).

Elijah Craig Kentucky Straight Rye Whiskey first to char oak barrels, bott code: A35292135 db **(94.5) n23 t24 f23.5 b24** Superbly made. And as relaxed yet beautifully busy as ol' Earl Scruggs on his banjo. And just as note perfect... 47% (94 proof).

Ezra Brooks Kentucky Straight Rye Whiskey bott code: A129171852 **(91.5) n23 t23.5 f22 b23** Pretty classic rye of the old school. Go back 25 years, pick a rye up off the shelf...and here you go! 45% (90 proof).

Frankfort Bourbon Society Knob Creek Single Barrel Select Rye Barrel No 7540 bott Fall 2018 **(88.5) n22 t23 f21.5 b22** One of the spicier rye whiskeys you are likely to encounter. Pleasant, but the inert nature of the vanilla and the rapid loss of sugars make this a bit of an also ran in Knob Creek terms. 57.5% (115 proof).

Highspire Whiskey 100% Rye Grain Aged 4 Months oak, finished with oak staves, batch no 3 **(73.5) n18.5 t19 f18 b18** Youthful and a rather feinty. Both the rye and tannin are there in spades, but with little integration; some hefty flavours, especially on the oak side which somehow over-dominates the grain. An interesting young whiskey, but the oak seems forced and at no times forms an attractive allegiance with the rye. I think they need to go a little gentler on this one. 40% (80 proof). Distilled by Kindred Distilled Spirits Crestwood, Ky.

◈ **High West Whiskey Double Rye!** batch no. 20B11 **(86) n21 t22.5 f21 b21.5** Mouth filling and chewy, the rye grain doesn't really get into its stride until we are on the second or third major flavour wave, when the bristling fluty, fruitiness catches hold. The fact there is a little tobacco on the nose and distinct oily earthiness on the finish suggests that one of the ryes used came from an undistinguished cut. A pity, as it was obvious there was massive potential otherwise. 46% (92 proof). nc ncf. A blend of straight rye whiskies.

High West Whiskey Rendezvous Rye batch no. 19K12 **(93.5) n23.5 t23.5 f23 b23.5** One of those ryes where you find yourself slapping the back of your head to overcome the eye-watering sharpness of the grain. 46% (92 proof). nc ncf. A blend of straight rye whiskies.

J Mattingly House Money Small Batch Rye Whiskey Aged 4 Years (96) n23.5 t24 f24.5 b24 If you see the magic words "Distilled in Indiana" attached to any rye whiskey, then you know there is a high possibility that you are in for something world class. Only Lawrenceburg Indiana produces a rye that can give Buffalo Trace a run for its money...and here you can see exactly why. The grain itself takes first, second and third position on both nose and delivery before the softer and beautifully balancing chocolate mousse accepts a humble but vital position of second in command. The spices are far more restrained than most ryes, but still make a telling contribution as they represent their tannins in their splendidly refined and elegant pose. Added to this, there is a concentrated rye Demerara sugar crispness to the very end which melds with unbelievable finesse with the mocha. Fantastic rye of the very highest calibre: unquestionably the finest made anywhere in the world outside Kentucky. 57% (114 proof) distilled in Indiana.

James E. Pepper 1776 Straight Rye Whiskey (88.5) n22 t22.5 f21.5 b22.5 Not technically quite on the ball, but the intensity of the rye deserves a standing ovation. 50% (100 proof). ncf

James E. Pepper 1776 Straight Rye Whiskey Barrel Proof (87.5) n22 t22 f21.5 b22 On the nose, delivery and finish there is evidence of a wider than normal cut here, giving the whisky a slightly murky feel. Great rye contribution and spices. But the oils are a bit OTT. 57.8% (115.6 proof). ncf.

Jim Beam Pre-Prohibition Style Rye db **(95) n23 t24.5 f23.5 b24** Very similar to how Jim Bean Yellow Label was over 20 years ago. In other words: simply superb! 45% (90 Proof)

Kentucky Owl Aged 10 Years Kentucky Straight Rye bott Nov 18 **(90.5) n22.5 t23.5 f21.5b23** Unlike their pretty poor bourbon offering, this rye is more Owl than Ow! 57% (114 proof).

◈ **Knaplund Rye Whiskey Atlantic Aged** batch no. R01 **(90) n22.5** barbed hickory, razor-wire rye; **t22** brittle, salivating grains as soon swamped by hickory and vanilla tones, flattening the effect a little; **f23** at last finds some natural complexity, with a fruity, sugary grain note dovetailing with hickory and spice; **b22.5** a good but curious whiskey. When using the Murray Method, the nose and early delivery are best at room temperature, the middle and finish when warmed slightly. Either way, the hickory does detract from the effect of the rye slightly. 45% (90 proof) Distilled in the US, aged at the Atlantic Sea and bottled in Denmark by Knaplund Distillery.

Knob Creek Cask Strength warehouse A, barreled 2009, 2018 release, bott code: L8106CLA **(96.5) n24 t24 f24 b24.5** Knob Creek rye has always been excellent, but having tasted Jim Beam's rye output for some 40 years I always thought it delivered within itself. Now this one is much closer to what I had been expecting. Brilliant! And the first rye to give the great rye of Buffalo Trace a serious run for their money. Indeed; this is going for a head to head... 59.8% (1196 proof).

Knob Creek Cask Strength Rye db **(95) n24 t24 f3.5 b23.5** Another unforgettable rye from Knob Creek, not least for the amount of hairs you'll find on your chest the next day. This is uncompromising in every sense of the word, but scores a little lower than last year's award winner as the tannin just seems a little tighter and less willing to give the grain full scope. The delivery, though...just rye-t on...!!! 63.1% (126.2 proof).

Knob Creek Rye Single Barrel Select barrel no. 7809 **(95.5) n23.5 t24 f23.5 b24.5** A cleverly selected bottle by Kelly May, who appears to have eschewed the usual pile-driver Knob Creek style for a nuanced and satisfying rye where both the barrel and grain appear to have an equal say. Stunning stuff! Just hope you can get to their bar before this little classic runs out! Certainly one of my favourite ryes for 2019 and unquestionably one of the most enigmatic... 57.5% (115 proof). Selected by Kelly May of Bourbon on Main, Frankfort, Ky. sc.

Knob Creek Straight Rye Whiskey **(92.5) n23.5 t23.5 f22.5 b23** a slightly more genteel rye than I expected, if you compare standard Knob Creek to their usual bourbon. 50% (100 proof).

Knob Creek Straight Rye Whiskey batch L5349CLA **(92.5) n23.5 t23.5 f22.5 b23** Curious: just checked: I scored a batch from last year at 92.5 also. Can't say this isn't consistent quality...! 50%

Michter's 10 Years Old Single Barrel Kentucky Straight Rye barrel no. 19F965, bott code: A19156965 **(96) n24.5 t24 f23.5 b24** Interesting how the rye itself takes a back seat and intervenes only when the chocolate richness of the oak becomes slightly too dominant. Doesn't possess the obvious rye-rich traits of their barrel 19H1321, but the whole works far, far better. 46.4% (92.8 proof). sc.

Michter's 10 Years Old Single Barrel Kentucky Straight Rye barrel no. 19H1321, bott code: A192341321 **(93.5) n24 t23.5 f22.5 b23.5** Radiates great age. Wears its vintage well and with great pride. 46.4% (92.8 proof). sc.

◈ **Michter's Single Barrel 10 Year Old Kentucky Straight Rye** barrel no. 20E985, bott code: A201490985 **(92.5) n24** one word: brilliant. Actually, you can't really leave it there. The complexity levels go through the roof on this one. There is a surfeit of small grains all pummelling away at the dried orange peel, black liquorice, and black cherry. The corn oils are in there, too, upping that grains presence. Yet still shews greater age than its ten years, especially when delicate hickory starts poking through...; **t23** considering the flighty complexity of the nose, the lightness of the body comes as no great surprise. That black cherry was no illusion and turns up here to play alongside the crisper, darker sugars. The oils are restrained but carry weight enough to ensure body and chewability. The midground is a lovely meeting of heather honey, vanilla, butterscotch and some rye-confirming red liquorice; **f22.5** much more simplistic with vanillas and buzzing, oily spices; **b23** the crispness and sharpness of the rye is never compromised and adds to the charming fragility of this whiskey. Wonderfully spiced and slightly unusual to see the corn make such a telling contribution to a rye, too. 46.4% (92.8 proof). sc.

Michter's Barrel Strength Kentucky Straight Rye barrel no. 19C467, bott code: A19071467 **(94.5) n23.5 t24 f23 b24** One or two moments here are pure textbook rye. Just savour that amazing sharpness and clarity on delivery! 56% (112 proof). sc.

Michter's Barrel Strength Kentucky Straight Rye barrel no. 19C386, bott code: A19066388 **(94) n24 t23.5 f23 b23.5** A full-bloodied rye that isn't for the squeamish. 55% (110 proof). sc.

Michter's Single Barrel Kentucky Straight Rye barrel no. L18F881, bott code: 8173881 **(88.5) n22 t22 f22 b22.5** A pretty low voltage rye. 42.4% (84.8 proof). sc.

Michter's Single Barrel Kentucky Straight Rye barrel no. 20C549, bott code: A200950549 **(89.5) n22.5** quite a vanilla-rich flourish to this. The grain keeps itself surprisingly low key; **t22.5** sharp – almost eye-wateringly so. As on the nose, the rye doesn't come at you directly, but hides behinds the skirts of the vanillin. The sugars expected are replaced by an almost puckering fruitiness to the rye – very unusual...indeed, intriguing. A little cocoa by the midpoint; **f22** dry and spicy, the rye has now almost vanished altogether; **b22.5** a highly distinctive rye that refuses to keep to the script. Follows no usual set pattern and insists on following its own singular route. *42.4% (84.8 proof). sc.*

◇ **Michter's US*1 Single Barrel Strength Kentucky Straight Rye** charred white oak barrel, barrel no: L21B478, db, **(95.5) n24** truly fascinating: I have spent ten minutes on this aroma and can say that this is the first rye in the world I have encountered with a spice not unlike chicken korma. Indeed, this is making me want to get down to an Indian restaurant now...having abstained for the several months while writing the Bible 2022. Of course, all the usual rye pointers are present, including, of course the rye itself. Though it has eschewed its normal crispness to meld with the muscular oak; **t24** corn oils are to the fore, but intense, salivating spiced black cherry is not far behind. So, the delivery is an oil explosion: the corn is everywhere, but it is brought to rampant fertility by the cherry and molasses which ensure a just-so degree of controlled sweetness. The spices are way beyond denial and pile on the intensity...; **f23.5** calmer now, as it should be. But the butterscotch leaks cherry juice and there are even hints of a sherry trifle at play with the combination of fruitiness and vanilla custard **b24** some rye whiskey seems to bask in a Demerara crispness. Michter's appear to prefer a black cherry countenance. And there are no complaints here, not least because we are up there with the truly great rye whiskeys. *55.6% (111.2% Proof) sc*

New Riff Backsetter Rye Bottled in Bond db **(86) n21 t22.5 f21 b21.5** Well, that was an experience! The nose works you hard to find the rye. The flavours are flowing and full on. But, again, in a very idiosyncratic style. Pleasant enough, but not exactly what I look for in a classic rye style. Still, the acacia honey middle works well with the oaky vanillas. But not a patch on New Riff's straight rye. *50% (100 proof). ncf.*

New Riff Balboa Rye Whiskey Bottled in Bond dist Jun 14, bott Nov 19 db **(94) n24 t23.5 f23 b23.5** A good old-fashioned 4-year-old rye very much in the Kentucky tradition. Quite beautifully distilled – as clean and technically excellent as any outside the Kentucky and Indiana big boys. One of those stunners that is all about crisp grain and molten Demerara. Lip-smacking and enough sweetness and chocolate to make up for the late oils on the finale. *50% (100 proof). ncf.*

New Riff Kentucky Straight Rye Whiskey Bottled in Bond dist Fall 2015, bott Fall 2019 db **(92.5) n22.5 t23.5 f23 b23.5** At times this seems a bit of a bruiser. But for all its chunky oils, the rye itself come through unmolested and clear. *50% (100 proof). ncf.*

New Riff Single Barrel Kentucky Straight Rye Whiskey barrel no. 15-6614, dist Fall 2015, bott Fall 2019 db **(91) n22 t23.5 f22.5 b23** Though the flavour profile keeps you entertained with its big rye presence, it never quite hits a rhythm. *56.15% (112.3 proof). ncf sc.*

New Riff Single Barrel Kentucky Straight Rye Whiskey barrel no. 16-7625, dist Spring 2016, bott Spring 2020 db **(93) n23 t23.5 f23 b23.5** That's much more like it. Better made and better balanced. *55.9% (111.8 proof). ncf sc.*

Old Forester Straight Rye 100 proof bott code A016 191607 **(93) n23 t23.5 f23 b23.5** Beautifully made, beautifully devised...and a beautiful, slightly rugged, experience. *50% (100 proof). 65% rye, 20% malted barley 15% corn*

Peerless Straight Rye Aged 3 Years batch 150812105 **(84.5) n22 t21 f20.5 b21** A new whiskey distilled in Louisville. Peerless might not be quite the way to describe it. A tad feinty, alas, *54.55% (109.1 proof).*

Pikesville Straight Rye Whiskey Aged at Least 6 Years (97.5) n24.5 t24.5 f24 b24.5 The most stunning of ryes and the best from Heaven Hill for some time. *55% (110 Proof)*

Rebel Yell Small Batch Rye Aged 24 Months bott code: A075181421 **(83.5) n21.5 t21.5 f21.5 b19** Normally ryes coming out of Indiana score highly, as they should because with Buffalo Trace the output from there represents, on their day, the best rye in the world. However, this is a classic example of when a whiskey is undercooked; it is way too young in that the grain and tannin are barely on speaking terms. Negligible balance, though the light liquorice note early on in delivery and late spices do salvage something. *45% (90 proof).*

Redemption Riverboat Rye (78) n19 t21 f19 b19. Dry, weirdly off key and oily – and holed below the water line. *40%*

Redemption Rye (85.5) n22 t22.5 f20 b21. The tobacco nose is a bit of a poser: how did that get there? Or the spearmint, which helps as you try to chew things over in your mind. The big rye wave on delivery is supported by mixed dark sugars yet something ashy about the finish. *46%*

Redemption Rye Aged No Less Than 2 Years batch no. 259, bott code: L9169607:27 **(86.5) n22 t23 f20 b21.5** Bright, brittle rye but always with a feintiness lurking in the wings. The delivery, though, is rye at its most beautifully intense and pure. *46% (92 proof).*

Redwood Empire Emerald Giant Rye Whiskey Aged at least 3 Years bott code: L19 1490 **(86) n22 t21.5 f21 b21.5** While the grain may be stark, the tobacco note tends to knock this whiskey sygogglin, as the moonshiners of the south Appalachians might say. Never seems to be on an even keel, thought the odd sharp note is more than attractive. 45%.

Russell's Reserve Kentucky Straight Rye 6 Years Old bott code: LL/GD240744 db **(94) n23.5 t23.5 f23 b24** All incredibly charming and understated – a bit like Jimmy Russell himself... 45% (90 proof).

Sagamore Spirit Straight Rye Whiskey batch no. 7C **(90.5) n23.5 t23 f21.5 b22.5** Very attractive rye, but seems underpowered and slightly lacking in the oils required for the expected rich finish. 41.5% (83 proof).

Sagamore Spirit Straight Rye Whiskey Barrel Select Aged 6 Years barrel no. 2, floor 3, rack 2, new charred oak barrels **(94.5) n23.5 t24 f23 b23** When top form Indiana rye is at work, what's not to like...? Oh, and one of those rare whiskies at its best when at ambient room temperature than slightly warmed. 55% (110 proof). sc. Bottled for Ryeday 13.

Sagamore Spirit Straight Rye Whiskey Cask Strength batch no. 4A **(95) n24 t24 f23.5 b23.5** Wow! What a way to start another Whisky Bible tasting day...!!! 56.1% (112.2 proof).

Sagamore Spirit Straight Rye Whiskey Double Oak batch no. 2C **(91) n24 t23 f21.5 b22.5** Beautiful in part but a little too intense with the oak late on. 48.3% (96.6 proof).

Sagamore Spirit Straight Rye Whiskey Double Oak batch no. 4A, new charred oak barrels **(95) n23 t24 f24 b24** It may sound strange but there is a distinctive bourbon type feel to the rye, perhaps from the ratio of tannin to grain. A serious mouthful just laden with flavours. Superb. 48.3% (96.6 proof).

Sazerac Rye bott code: L172540108: 414 ref 1A 5C VT 15C **(96) n24 t24.5 f23.5 b24** The nose and delivery are just about as good as it gets. Anyone thinking of making a clean and succulent rye whiskey should plant this on a dais and bow to it every morning before heading into the stillroom... 45% (90 proof).

Sazerac 18 Years Old bott Summer 2018 db **(96) n24.5 t24.5 f23 b24** I have chosen this as my 1,250th whisky for the Whisky Bible 2020 (and 20,026th whiskey sample tasted for the book) because, many years ago, I (with my blending hat on) played a part in the development of this whisky – for which I was given the priceless very first bottle off the production line as a token of thanks. Sadly, it was stolen just a few days later in New York at a Whiskey Festival there. But I can still remember vividly as Elmer T Lee and I pieced this whiskey together how it might taste and feel in the mouth. And, you know, some 15 years or so on it really hasn't altered that much, other than in this case the finish perhaps... But someone, somewhere - hopefully with a guilty conscience - might be able to be able to tell me differently... 45% (90 proof).

Sazerac 18 Years Old bott Summer 2019 db **(96) n24.5** the sensuality of the age on this rye is akin to having a lover who has enjoyed many summers and knows exactly how to please. Just effortlessly finding those palate's g spots on your nose and teasing you with a balmy mintiness, then caressing and kissing you with rye-stained sugars that are dark, slightly salty like sweat but, oh, so ridiculously sweet and tender...; **t24** possibly the softest delivery of any of the near 1,250 whiskeys I have tasted so far this year. Lands like a butterfly on the palate and immediately opens up to reveal a slight eucalyptus earthiness to counter the sharper, sweeter grains which abounds with a mix of Demerara sugars, molasses and red liquorice; **f23** not quite as long as some previous Sazerac 18s, but determined to extract every last delicate nuance from the grain to complement the gathering butterscotch; **b24.5** this is simply a whiskey with a greatness all its own. What can you say...? 45% (90 proof).

⟨⟩ **Sazerac 18 Years Old** bott Summer 2020 db **(89.5) n22.5** sharp rye, as one would expect. But another note, not at all usual or consistent: an almost a dull semi-mustiness. Acceptable for many ryes, but a Sazerac...? **t23.5** there go those ryes, crisp and salivating. But that strange lethargy detected on the nose is present here, too. Again, still a lovely rye but this is Sazerac...and that dulling effect just shouldn't be there. Taking that aside, still a lovely light Demerara sugar touch to this, but...; **f21** more spices, chocolate, and oil. But fades out very untidily and lacking anything like its usual aplomb; **b22.5** right. Where do I start? A lovely whiskey with so many characteristics to fully enjoy. But... Both Elmer T Lee and I had a little say in how this whiskey was shaped at its conception. And this wasn't it: this is not what we signed off on. There is dullness here which is in stark contrast to the Sazerac which has been acknowledged across the globe as the blueprint for sensational rye. Many companies would die for a whisky this tasty. But.... 45% (90 proof).

⟨⟩ **Smooth Ambler Old Scout Rye Single Barrel 4 Years Aged** barrel no.16805 **(96) n24** this is dual personality rye on the nose: first comes the rumble, like thunder in the distance, of the deep-rooted grain, enmeshed in the weightier aspect of the tannins. Then there is the sharper, crisper friable aspects to its aroma; **t24** stupendously stupendous. The arrival on the palate is like Concorde booming through the sound barrier. A ride never to be forgotten with salivation levels needing a new type of gauge to measure it...then, almost unbelievably for a four-year-old, a liquorice and manuka honey toasty thickness to absorb the fabulous lustre of the crusty, Demerara sugar-topped grain; **f24** some pretty brazen toasty tannins for a rye so young: toasted mallow and black liquorice. But that extraordinary rye signature is never far from the surface...; **b24** for a little while now, two distilleries have been making the best rye whiskey on the planet: one in Frankfort, Ky, and the other Lawrenceburg, In. This is from the latter. And leaves you in no doubt why I hold this distillery in such high esteem. This single cask is absolutely extraordinary. And for a four-year-old shews all the toasty intensity of a rye that has been bubbling away, cooking in the heat of the buzzard's roost for those few summers...By the way: 462 whiskeys into this Bible, and the best I have tasted yet... *61.5% sc Distilled in Indiana*

Thomas H. Handy Sazerac db **(97) n24.5 t24.5 f24 b24** I am often asked by those unable to track down either Sazerac, or, at best, just one: "what is the difference between these two whiskeys?" The grains are jagged and crisp...shards of rye that cut deep. A light floral edge accompanies the vivid fruit. This is sharp and delectable. Rye with a three dimensional firmness; one of the deliveries of the year. As near as damn it getting a 25 for its intensity and elan. Rich chocolate, black cherry... and yet more and more insistent, relentless, rye...;*62.85% (125.7 proof).*

Thomas H. Handy Sazerac Straight Rye (97.5) n24 t24.5 f24.5 b24.5 This was World Whisky of the Year last year and anyone buying this on the strength of that will not be disappointed. Huge whiskey with not even the glimmer of a hint of an off note. Magnificent: an honour to taste and rye smiles all round... *66.2%. ncf.*

Thomas H. Handy Sazerac Straight Rye (95.5) n24 t24 f23.5 b24 Perhaps because this has become something of a softie, without all those usual jagged and crisp rye notes, it doesn't quite hit the spot with quite the same delicious drama. Still a beauty, though. *64.6%*

Thomas H. Handy Sazerac db **(97) n24 t24.5 f24 b24.5** Just one of those must have whiskeys. Dramatic. And dreamy. All in one. *63.6% (127.2 proof).*

Thomas H. Handy Sazerac db **(97) n24 t24.5 f24 b24.5** Rye whiskey par excellence. How can one grain do so much to the taste buds? As bewildering as it is beautiful. *64.4% (128.8 proof).*

⋙ **Thomas H. Handy Sazerac** db **(97.5) n24.5** pristine rye: it as though the grain is in aspic. The clarity of the rye could hardly be bettered while the Demerara feels as though one punch would shatter it completely **t24.5** go on you spices: fizz away, why don't you! What a delivery! What an attack! What a statement of intent! The marriage of the flame-throwing spice and the insanely salivating Demerara is the perfect union to prevent total conflagration. Chugging behind this show is a much more sanguine vanilla and ulmo honey mix, together producing the chewy element of the wonderful rye...; **f24** now where did all that dark chocolate mousse come from? The demerara and vanilla has no intention of quitting and ensure the crispy rye carries through to the last...; **b24.5** truly breathtaking! What a joy! What a rye! What a winner...!!! *64.5% (129 proof).* 🏆

Treaty Oak Distilling Red Handed Rye Whiskey Aged 10 Years db **(91) n22 t23 f22.5 b23.5** A very odd rye, where the tannins appear half-hearted and happy to allow the grain a bigger say than normal. Different, but delicious. *50% (100 proof).*

Van Winkle Family Reserve Rye 13 Years Old batch Z2221 **(90) n22.5 t23.5 f22 b22** A hard-as-nails, uncompromising rye with a slightly tangy finale. A whiskey to break your teeth on... *478% (95.6 proof)*

Van Winkle Family Reserve Kentucky Straight Rye 13 Years Old No. 99A bott code: L180400107:23N db **(96) n24.5 t24 f23.5 b24** Quite simply, textbook rye whiskey... *478%*

Wild Turkey Master's Keep Cornerstone Aged a Minimum of 9 Years batch no. 21587, bott code: LLJHE301949 db **(96) n23.5 t24 f24 b24.5** Easily the most profound rye whiskey I have ever seen carrying the Wild Turkey name. Easy for the chocolate off the oak to overwhelm the rye and the rye to also for an imbalance with the chocolate. Instead, they support each other magnificently. *54.5% (109 proof).*

Wild Turkey Rye bott code: 194712P22:59 db **(91.5) n23 t23 f22.5 b23** A perfectly graceful, well-made rye. But at this strength a bit like Rolls Royce powered by a lawnmower engine. *40.5% (81 proof).*

Wild Turkey Rye 81 Proof bott code: LL/GE250429:59 db **(92.5) n23.5 t23 f22.5 b23.5** A greatly improved rye than in recent years, here really displaying the grain to excellent effect. The finish has a slight tang, but, that apart, spends its tine moulding the mint to the sugars. One characterful whiskey... *40.5% (81 proof)*

Wild Turkey 101 Kentucky Straight Rye bott code: LL/GH130429 db **(95.5) n23.5 t24 f23.5 b24.5** Simply magnificent. The kind of whiskey, when you spot in the bar, it is almost impossible not to order. *50.5% (101 proof).*

Straight Wheat Whiskey

Bernheim Original 7 Years Aged Kentucky Straight Wheat Whiskey bott code: A33582052 db **(94) n23.5 t23.5 f23 b24** A step up from the last Bernheim I tasted, the spices and sugars this time working in breathtaking tandem. The bass notes even deeper than the lower recesses of Larry Kass's voice, though that seems hardly possible...(hope you are enjoying your retirement, Larry!) What a treat this whiskey is! *45% (90 proof).*

American Microdistilleries
Alabama
JOHN EMERALD DISTILLING COMPANY Opelika, Alabama.

John's Alabama Single Malt Whiskey Aged Less Than 4 Years batch no. 102 db **(86)** n21.5 t22 f21 b21.5 This distillery has the propensity towards going for a wider cut during distillation, ramping up the oils and spices in the process. Makes for an uneven affair, though very much to type the caramels are lush and chewy. *43% (86 proof).*

John's Alabama Single Malt Aged Less Than 4 Years batch no. 103 db **(89)** n22.5 t22.5 f22 b22 A little extra thrust from the delicate smoke makes a huge difference. *43%.*

John's Alabama Single Malt Whiskey Aged Less Than 4 Years batch no. 104 db **(88)** n22 t23 f21 b22 Presumably the horse on the label of this whisky was presented to Troy... Massively oaky but a little feinty, too. *43%*

Alaska
ALASKA DISTILLERY Wasilla, Alaska.

Alaska Proof Bourbon db **(86)** n22 t22.5 f20 b21.5. It must be Alaska and the lack of pollution or something. But how do these guys make their whiskey quite so clean....? For a rugged, wild land, it appears to concentrate on producing a bourbon which is borderline ethereal and all about sugary subtlety. The downside is that such lightness allows any weakness in the wood or distillation to be flagged up, though with nobody saluting. *40% (80 proof)*

Arizona
GRAND CANYON DISTILLERY Williams, Arizona.

❖ **Grand Canyon Star Shine American Single Malt** aged 18 months in new American oak barrels, db **(93)** n23.5 such has been the sugary tannin intake in its relatively short life, you'd be forgiven for initially thinking bourbon, not malt. The heather honey, molasses, Jaffa Cake and black cherry form perfect little constellations and, you fancy, though it needs a telescope to see it, a good pair of binoculars at least, some feint maltiness...; t23.5 what a delivery! Forget about tannins which hurtle at you like an asteroid, look further in at the wonderful mouthfeel: a kind of milky way. For the light oils, beautifully coloured in taste by the vanillas and malt compliments the buttery oils perfectly; f23 drier with late liquorice and b23 forget about the maturation under the twinkling firmament. It is one particular star that has cosmic effect on this, and all of it for the good. This is heavenly whisky *46%*

❖ **Grand Canyon Straight Bourbon Whiskey** aged minimum 24 months, db **(86)** n21 t22 f21.5 b21.5 Of all the whiskies I have tasted from the USA, this is the closest to Indian whisky I was tasting in the 1990s. This is most likely to do with the accelerated maturation in high temperatures. Of course, in India it was single malt, here it is bourbon but the rhythm of the sugars in the tannin is just about identical. Maybe the slightly over generous cut had something to do with it also, as that was not uncommon back in India in those days, either. There is a banana-yeasty kick to this one, which seems to also churn out a dried hay aroma, too...something else unusual for a bourbon. Not unpleasant, but not a patch on their single malt, where in the six months between distillation they have appears to gained a better understanding of their kit. *40% (80 proof)*

HAMILTON DISTILLERS Tuscon, Arizona.

Whiskey Del Bac Dorado Mesquite Smoked Single Malt batch MC16-1, bott 29 Feb 16 db **(94)** n23 t23.5 f24b23.5 Dang! I'd sure like to see a bottle of this come sliding up to me next time I'm-a-drinkin' in the Crystal Palace Saloon Bar in Tombstone, yesiree! And I'd take my own dirty glass — one smoked with mesquite!! *45% (90 proof). ncf.*

SANTAN SPIRITS Chandler, Arizona.

Sacred Stave American Single Malt Whiskey finished in American red wine barrels db **(85.5)** n20.5 t22.5 f21 b21.5 A bit of a wide cut here which has a few problems gelling with a fruit influence so far as harmony is concerned. But plenty to enjoy of the creamy crescendo just after delivery when the malt's sharper, more vivid qualities take on a purer form. *45% (90 proof).*

Sacred Stave American Single Malt Whiskey Cask Strength F.O. Moorvedre barrels, finished in American red wine barrels db **(88)** n22 t23 f21 b22 Impressed that even through the slapped on fruit the malt has its moments to intensify and shine: unusual, that. The house feinty style does ensure a degree of murkiness. But there is also a pleasing toffee-raisin mixing with the malt and spices for the attractive, mildly charismatic middle. *63.9% (1278 proof).*

Butcher Jones American Straight Rye Whiskey Cask Strength char #3 barrels db **(90.5)** **n22.5** one of the most intense, unyielding and truly unambiguous rye noses of the year. A little bit of feint is mixed in, but the sharpness of the grain is superb; **t23.5** hold on tight! The combination of the high strength and the concentrated intensity of the grain appears to drill holes into your taste buds. Again, as on the nose, there is the murky evidence of a wide cut. But it is like making love in the middle of a thunderstorm: forget the off-putting noise around you and concentrate on the highly pleasurable bits; **f22** more off-putting noise...; **b22.5** for those who like rye whiskey with hairs on... *64.7% (129.7 proof).*

Arkansas
ROCK TOWN DISTILLERY Little Rock, Arkansas.

Rock Town Arkansas Barley Straight Bourbon Whiskey Aged 2.8 Years batch no. 3 db **(93) n23** light liquorice amid the chocolate orange; **t23.5** eye-watering juiciness to the grains which are young and vibrant. As in the nose, the liquorice plays a major role adding both a flighty sweetness and depth; **f23** always a great sign when molasses leave it late to emerge; **b23.5** high grade, complex and deeply satisfying bourbon *46% (92 proof).*

Rock Town Arkansas Straight Golden Promise Bourbon Whiskey Aged 2.4 Years batch no. 2 db **(92) n22.5** gentle strains of heather honey; **t23.5** that is huge jump for nose to delivery: on the nose, the honey almost apologetic. Here it intensifies, fortifies itself with rabid spices...and goes for the jugular; **f23** gloriously toasty. Honey has made way for very dry molasses and liquorice; **b23** having previous tasted this at half this age, I can confirm it has moved on very positively in the passing year... *46% (92 proof).*

Rock Town Arkansas Straight Rye Whiskey Aged 2.5 Years batch no. 26 db **(95) n24** classic! Clean, crisp, chiselling. The fruitiness here is set in stone. So intense...! **t23.5** the rye runs amok. Pulsating grain with light tannins and a spicy back up; **f23.5** sensuous brown sugars, a lick of red liquorice...and then still that concentrated rye...; **b24** for unerring consistency, this has to be the brightest star in the Rock Town firmament. Just as beautifully distilled and matured, seemingly extracting every last atom of beauty from each grain. *46% (92 proof).*

Rock Town Bottled-in-Bond Arkansas Straight Bourbon Whiskey Aged 4 Years batch no. 1 db **(91.5) n22.5** clean and softly honeyed enough to be distilled American breakfast cereal...; **t23.5** brilliant display of mixed brown sugars – embedded in heather honey, of course...; **f22.5** bitters out slightly as the oily residue wells up. But now it is the turn of the liquorice and cough sweet hickory to have a big say; **b23** after a run of three RT whiskeys with big feints – something I have never encountered before – it is great to be back tasting a bourbon from them of the type of quality I usually associate with them *50% (100 proof).*

Rock Town Chocolate Malt Straight Bourbon Whiskey Aged 2.4 Years batch no. 2 db **(93) n23.5** some green corn oils work closely with the weightier and noticeable malt; **t23** silky soft oils, again the corn coming up fast, strong, sweet and in very juicy fashion. Then towards the midpoint the chocolate malt hits overdrive; **f23** chocolate lime; **b23.5** a typically big-favour Rock Town. *46% (92 proof).*

Rock Town Four Grain Sour Mash Straight Bourbon Whiskey Aged 2.5 Years batch no. 14 db **(86.5) n21.5 t22.5 f20.5 b22** Another big, oily offering from their Four Grain stable. Lots of maple syrup and liquorice work hard to keep the bourbon on course, but the finale is on the bitter as well as oily side. *46% (92 proof).*

Rock Town Single Barrel Bourbon Whiskey Aged 48 Months 53 gallon cask, cask no. 434 db **(95) n23.5** a little saltiness to the tannins. Dried orange peel, too; **t24** one of the most complex deliveries from Rock Town this year: puckering tannins – and there's that salty disposition, too, seemingly lifting all the vanillas and sugars to far more lurid heights. The liquorice gives the follow through the full bourbon works...wow! Superb molasses at the midpoint; **f23.5** settles for a dry-ish, sophisticated mocha and toast fade; **b24** brilliant. *58.6% (117.2 proof). sc.*

Rock Town Single Barrel Four Grain Sour Mash Bourbon Whiskey Aged 27 Months 25 gallon cask, cask no. 66 db **(87.5) n22 t22.5 f21 b22** Rock Town is one of the few distilleries that could come up with this kind of careless cut and still come away smelling of bourbon... just love the liquorice, slightly overdone toast and then a big dose of manuka honey. *56.7% (113.4 proof). sc.*

Rock Town Single Barrel French Oak Single Malt Whiskey Aged 39 Months 250L cask, cask no. 65 db **(91) n22.5** rolls its sleeves up and means business: oily, but without the feinty threat. Bread pudding and molten Demerara; **t23** boldly gets into its stride. Harnesses the oils thicken up the spiced manuka honey even further; **f22.5** drier, toasty and sensibly spiced; **b23** c'est magnifique! *55.6% (111.2 proof). sc.*

Rock Town Single Barrel Rye Whiskey Aged 30 Months 15 gallon cask, cask no. 160 db **(94.5) n23.5** just fabulous: the grain is dual toned: hard on the outside with a soft rye middle... or is it the other way round? Certainly, a little mocha is in on the act; **t23.5** toasted honeycomb coats the rock-hard shell of the fruity rye. Luxurious and juicy all at once; **f23.5** long, with the oils gathering in typical RT style. Chocolate transforms to mocha; **b24** if anyone goes into the business of making chocolate rye candy, they'll be on a winner... 61% (122 proof). sc.

California
ALCHEMY DISTILLERY Arcata, California.

Boldt Cereal Killer Straight Rye Whiskey Aged 2 Years batch no. 8 **(94.5) n23.5 t24 f23 b24** Don't know about cereal killer: more the Rye Ripper! 62% (124 proof). nc sc.

Boldt Cereal Killer Straight Triticale Whiskey Aged 2 Years batch no. 10 **(94) n23.5 t24 f23 b23.5** In the 20,000 whiskies I have tasted for the Whisky Bible since 2003 this may be the first time I have tasted mash made from Triticale. This is one big-arsed killer and I can see this being a massive whiskey favourite among Star Trek fans...and Tribbles. 62.5% (125 proof). nc sc.

CHARBAY DISTILLERY Napa Valley, California.

⁂ **Charbay Double & Twisted Lot No. 2 Double Alambic Pot Distilled Single malt Whiskey** nbc, db **(83.5) n21.5 t22 f20 b20** I am still dying to see what this whiskey is like when stood in a proper whisky cask for a few years. The hops kill the whiskey side of things stone dead towards the finish, the unnatural bitterness doing damage to the balance the evident charm of the malt. However, after the nougat and beer-laden nose, comes the delivery and that, in itself, is rather attractive as the barley and demerara sugars do have a big input. However, the effect of the hop is simply too overwhelming throughout. Please, next time, let's have bottling from a used bourbon barrel...give us a chance to enjoy you! 45% (90 proof)

GRIFFO DISTILLERY Petaluma, California.

Belgian Hen Single Malt Whiskey db **(83.5) n21 t21.5 f20 b21** Well, that was different. Less single malt. More lightly spiced soft centred orange liqueur chocolate. 46% (92 proof).

Stony Point Whiskey db **(85) n20 t22 f21.5 b21.5** Makes up for the tobacco feinty tones with a rush of muscovado sugars. Good texture and chewability and spice. 47% (94 proof).

Stout Barreled Whiskey db **(84.5) n21 t22 f20 b21.5** Robust, sweet and full bodied. But I must say I have a problem with hops in whisky. Sorry. 45% (90 proof).

LOST SPIRITS DISTILLERY Monterey County, California.

Abomination The Crying of the Puma Heavily Peated Malt **(93) n23.5 t24 f22.5 b23** An utterly baffling experience. This is, for all intents and purposes a Scotch whisky: at least in personality. If this was distilled in the US, then they have cracked it. The thing I particularly couldn't work out was an unrecognisable fruit edge. And after tasting I dug out the bottle and read the small print (so small, the detail was left off the heading by my researchers) that Riesling seasoned oak staves had been used. From the bizarre label and even brand name to the battle on your palate this is a bewildering and nonsensical whisky – if it is whisky at all, as the term is never used. But wholly delicious if raw...and boasting an impact that blows the taste buds' doors down... 54%. nc ncf.

SONOMA DISTILLING COMPANY Rohnert Park, California.

Sonoma Bourbon Whiskey nbc, db **(87.5) n21.5 t23 f21 b22** Big and flavoursome, they just need to get that cut reduced slightly so all the oils belong to the corn and are not from elsewhere. The small grains pulse out a lot of coffee-rich vitality and there are fabulous molasses in midstream. But the finish is slightly undone by the feints. 46% (92 proof). 70% corn (CA & Midwest), 25% wheat (CA & Canada) & 5% Malted Barley (Wyoming).

Sonoma Cherrywood Rye Whiskey lot: CR01AC db **(91) n22.5 t23.5 f22 b23** When the rye pops through, it rips... 47.8% (95.6 proof). 80% rye (California & Canada), 10% wheat (California) & 10% cherrywood smoked malted barley.

Sonoma Rye Whiskey nbc, db **(89.5) n22.5 t23 f21.5 b22.5** A rye that could do with a polish when distilling, but the sheer enormity of the rye wins through in the glass...and your heart. 46.5% (93 proof). 80% rye (California & Canada) & 20% malted rye (United Kingdom).

ST GEORGE SPIRITS Alameda, California.

Baller Single Malt Whiskey Aged 3 Years batch no. BW-5 db **(87) n22.5 t22 f21 b21.5** The nose made me laugh out loud: only one distillery on the planet can produce something that outrageously apple strewn...Elsewhere, though, I'm not so sure. After the initial big malt delivery, it then zips of into European style malt, the type where hops are at play. Certainly there is an imbalance to the marauding light bitterness which undermines what should be, one feels, a fragile and juicy malt. 47% (94 proof).

Breaking & Entering American Whiskey Aged no less than 2.5 Years batch no. 06302018 **(92) n23 t24 f22 b23** The crisp apple aroma wafted through long before I realised this was from St George. Not only breaking and entering, but St George has left his fingerprints everywhere... *47% (94 proof).*

STARK SPIRITS Pasadena, California.

Stark Spirits California Single Malt Whiskey American oak barrels, batch no. 52-13, bott 10-1-19 db **(88) n21.5 t22 f22.5 b22** Well, certainly no shortage of character on this chap! Takes a little time to settle down, and the slight feinty nose explains exactly why. But the barley hits its straps about a third of the way in and the oils from the generous cut helps elongate the growing gristy sugars. The finish has a satisfying degree of banana and custard as well as malt. Certainly grows on you! *46% (92 proof).*

Stark Spirits Peated Single Malt Whiskey American oak barrels, batch no. 4, bott 8-2-19 db **(92) n23.5** a technically sound aroma, seemingly clean off the still with only the beautifully sweet phenols offering their gentle depth. A true delight...; **t23** again the peat is to the fore, but it is as much noticeable for its sleight of hand as it is its smoky quality. Everything understated with toasted mallows sweetening further the smoky grist; the underlying sugars of a crystalised molassed style; **f22** there must have been a wide-ish cut after all, as the hefty oils gang up in force; **b23.5** well, they may have got the nose all wrong for batch 52-13. But here are no complaints here. A far better distillation, helped along further by some pretty decent peat. *46% (92 proof).*

Colorado
10TH MOUNTAIN WHISKEY & SPIRIT COMPANY Vail, Colorado.

10th Mountain Rocky Mountain Bourbon Whiskey Aged 6 Months db **(92) n22 t23 f23.5 b23.5** The youth of the spirit is apparent on the nose where slightly more hostile tannins have not yet had a chance to say howdy to the corn. But once on the palate the entire story changes as the maple syrup and molasses – and, amazingly, even liquorice already – makes a far better attempt to find a happy medium with the grain. Beautifully made and a really sumptuous and spice-ridden offering. *46% (92 proof).*

AXE AND THE OAK Colorado Springs, Colorado.

Axe and the Oak Bourbon Whiskey batch no. 20 db **(86.5) n20.5 t22.5 f21.5 b22** Although this is batch number 20, you still get the feeling this is a work in progress. The nose at times displays some most unbourbon-like traits with far more of the still and/or fermentation room than opened cask. But the whiskey recovers with admirable calm: on the palate the corn oils establish themselves and the rye present kicks in with a firm sweetness while the tannins crank up the light liquorice and spice. The soft chocolate mousse on the finish works well with the molasses. Promising. *46% (92 proof).*

Axe and the Oak Cask Strength Bourbon Whiskey batch no. 1 db **(87.5) n21 t23 f21.5 b22** Big, bustling, no-prisoners whiskey which reveals quite a wide cut. That adds extra weight for sure, but a tanginess interrupts the flow of the excellent liquorice and molasses tones which had made the delivery and immediate aftermath something genuinely to savour. Get the cut right on the run and this will be one hell of a bourbon. *64.4% (128.8 proof).*

BLACK BEAR DISTILLERY Green Mountain Falls, Colorado.

Black Bear Bourbon Irish Style Colorado Whiskey finished in sherry casks db **(88) n21.5 t22.5 f22 b22** Quite a bulky whiskey, with the additional fatness of the grape adding to the oils from the generous cut. Technically, doesn't pull up any trees. But it is impossible not to be drawn towards the delicious mix of blackcurrant pastel candy and mocha. Genuinely tasty whiskey and great fun. Oh, and lip-smackingly salivating to boot. *45% (90 proof).*

BRECKENRIDGE DISTILLERY Breckenridge, Colorado.

Breckenridge Bourbon Whiskey db **(84.5) n21 t21.5 f21 b21** Definitely on the flat side, with a dusty, dry character. *43% (86 proof).*

Breckenridge Colorado Whiskey Powder Hound batch no. 1 db **(91) n22 t23.5 f22 b23.5** Despite a slight blemish at the death, this is probably the most complex and well balanced whiskey I have yet seen from this distillery. *45% (90 proof).*

Breckenridge Dark Arts batch no. 5 db **(87.5) n20 t24 f21 b22.5** I appear to have missed out on batch 4 (apologies) but this appears to have started when batch 3 ended. Some of the sensations on delivery are borderline orgasmic, the golden syrup, praline and barley melding together with the spices with uncanny intuition and balance. But, once more, the very wide cut has a negative effect on both nose and finish. As for the delivery and aftershocks, though: world class! *46% (92 proof). Whiskey distilled from malt mash.*

Breckenridge High Proof Blend Aged a Minimum of at least Two Years db (90) n22.5 t23.5 f21.5 b22.5 Maybe not technically perfect, but some of those honey tones are pure 24 carat... 52.5% (105 proof). A blend of straight bourbon whiskeys.

DEERHAMMER DISTILLING COMPANY Buena Vista, Colorado.

Deerhammer American Single Malt Whiskey virgin oak barrel #2 char, batch no. 32 db (87.5) n21.5 t23.5 f20.5 b22 This, like most Colorado whiskeys, is huge. Had the cut been a little less generous, the oils a little less gripping and tangy, this would have scored exceptionally highly. For there is no doubting the deliciousness of the big toasted malt, the kumquat citrus element, the moreishness of the heavyweight dark fudge and the magnificent Java coffee. All these make a delivery and follow through to remember. I look forward to the next bottling where hopefully the cut is a little more careful: a very significant score awaits as this is borderline brilliant... 46% (92 proof). 870 bottles.

DISTILLERY 291 Colorado Springs, Colorado.

291 Bad Guy Colorado Bourbon Whiskey Aged 324 Days Aspen Stave Finished American oak barrel, batch no. 5 db (94) n23.5 t23.5 f23 b24 Less fruity on character than some previous bottlings, tasting this after their 50%abv Small Batch, below, this Bad Guy is the very much the good guy. And at 123.4 proof, they can still show that making good bourbon is as easy as ABC... 61.6% (123.4 proof). 1,257 bottles.

◈ **291 Bad Guy Colorado Bourbon Whiskey** finished with aspen wood staves, batch no.6, db (94.5) n23 hickory wraps itself around the heather honey like a {Mexican meal} wraps itself around chicken...; t24 piles on the early sugars as if there's no tomorrow...or more likely to balance out the dry, intense toastiness which shews a scary degree of oak activity. The spices are also not slow coming forward and burn with a dim glow for most of the early phases. The creamy texture borders halfway between exotic and erotic...; f23.5 curious that the toasty tannin, normally a given at the death of such whisky has by now burnt out. We are left instead with a civilised fade of vanilla and ulmo honey...; b24 if there was an award for the "Popping Whiskey Cork of the Year" this would win with terrifying ease: fair set off my tinnitus, it did. Have to say that this a corker of a bourbon, too...This is not just a Bad Guy. It's a Big Bad Guy.... 62.7% (125.5 proof) 1014 bottles

◈ **291 Barrel Proof Colorado Straight Bourbon Whiskey** finished with aspen wood staves, batch no.1, db (94) n23.5 when you get a teasing whiff of Java medium roast coffee mingling with the high-grade classic liquorice tannins and elegant molasses, you know you are on a winner t24 a rip-roaring arrival. There is no beating around the bush so far as that coffee note is concerned: it arrived on the nose...and this states that it is staying. The liquorice becomes more intense and toastier as it moves along with pace. The spices mingle with the sugars, but still hammers themselves home; f23 oooh, absolute maximum roastiness here, borderline OTT. Thankfully that Java coffee and a slab of fudge do the job; b23.5 never seen the coffee element quite so high in a 291 before. And that is no complaint...! 66.9% (133.8 proof) 176 bottles

◈ **291 Barrel Proof Colorado Straight Rye Whiskey** finished with aspen wood staves, batch no.1, db (94) n23.5 the rye is clean and resolute. Fruity in that uniquely rye way with the white peppers being slightly usurped by a toasty tannin; t24 brilliant! The delivery is exactly what I want to see from a full-strength rye: the grain is crisp, three dimensional and salivating while the tannins wade in with an exquisite Eucalyptus note. Meanwhile the peppers pound the tastebuds and occasionally flare. The vanilla exudes oak...; f23 a gorgeous first chocolate then praline fade sees us through....; b23.5 now that's much more like it. Have been a little disappointed with some of their rye offerings, which have been far too tobacco oriented and with room for improvement. But this one is absolutely on the money. Just adore the classic crispiness of the grain early on. Reminds me slightly of the very first Old Potreros from 25 years ago.... 64.3% (128.6 proof) 222 bottles

◈ **291 Barrel Proof Single Barrel Colorado Bourbon Whiskey** finished with aspen wood staves, barrel no.577, db (95) n23.5 the depth of colour already has the nose buds on high alert. And straight away they go from gentle reconnaissance mode to intense scrutiny: this bourbon has an extraordinary complexity, from a thin red liquorice and muscovado sugar to slightly overcooked yams. Jamaican Blue Mountain coffee and delicate hickory drift around, too. For a 133-proof whiskey, this is just so remarkably understated and gentle...; t23.5 there is a little reminder of youth on delivery, but this is soon swamped by successive waves of coffee-framed cough syrup and molasses. The corn oil texture is beyond exemplary...; f24 this isn't just long. This is of Biblical in proportions: if he was still alive Charlton Heston would be playing it. I really don't know where to start. Perhaps with the corn oils which act as the base and attracts, or rather dissipates, the stupendous and amazingly beautifully weighted toasty tones, just successive pulses of liquorice and coffee (a kind of blend of Blue Mountain and

Sumatra Coffee) then a slow, almost massaging fade of molasses and vanilla; **b24** this is an insanely coloured bourbon for its age: pure teak. It is also, with not a shadow of doubt, one of the great Colorado bourbon whiskies of nor just this but many years.... If 291 weren't already up there on the highest dais on the world stage, then this bottling alone has planted them there. Had she still been alive, yesterday would have been my mother's 100th birthday. And had I had known the contents of this bottle; I would have toasted her with a glass... *66.5% (133.0 proof) sc 40 bottles*

291 E Colorado Whiskey Aged 578 Days Aspen Stave Finished American oak barrel, finished in cherry and Peach Nine barrels, batch no. 6 db **(93) n23 t23.5 f23 b23.5** A rampant, super-complex whiskey which started life as a bourbon before it lost that status among foreign timbers. The nose is as parched, peppery and prickly as you are likely to find while the delivery compensates with an avalanche of Demerara sugars and heather honey. But it is those spices which take star billing. Though there is nothing wrong with the chocolate toffee finish, either. The finale, however, is as dry as it gets.... *61.3% (122.6 proof). 303 bottles.*

⬩ **291 E Colorado Whiskey Distilled from a Wheat Mash** finished with aspen wood staves, batch no.7, db **(91) n22.5** a real old-fashioned (almost extinct) English bread pudding nose to this, though the spices are well-behaved; **t23** oily and bursting at the seams with myriad dark sugars glistening in manuka honey. The peppers, though playing a part, are surprisingly hesitant; **f22.5** still oily with a light toasted Hovis fade...; **b23** pretty tame it might be said for a wheat whiskey with the usual big, spiced personality missing. But still exudes youthful quality and always deeply attractive and elegant... *60.5% (121 proof) 160 bottles*

⬩ **291 E Colorado Whiskey Blend of Wheat and Malt Barley Whiskey** finished with aspen wood staves, batch no.8, db **(94) n23** such an unusual aroma. A light Fisherman's Friend cough sweet nose mingles with a little Darjeeling tea but much more Bread Pudding...; **t23.5** the texture is unusually thin for a Colorado. Indeed, the delivery is confused and for a moment there is a hiatus, as though unsure the direction to take. But soon it heads towards a gorgeously spiced, playfully oily sugar plane. The tannins build as though one layer arrives after another. The malted barley influence generates an unusual degree of juiciness; **f24**..which means we are for a seriously long and complex finish. The spices buzz but take care not to fizz. The sugars sweeten but take care not to sicken. The tannins dry but take care to never leave you parched. The toast is browned but never burnt...; **b23.5** just fascinating. The oscillating qualities of the whiskey is something else: the peak and troughs have their very own fingerprint. Unlike any other whisky or whiskey tasted this year. But exudes class. *65.4% (130.9 proof) 350 bottles*

291 HR Colorado Bourbon Whiskey Aged at Least 1 Year American oak barrel, batch no. 23 db **(92.5) n23 t23 f23.5 b23** For a bourbon, the rye has a lot to say for itself. A muscular, no-prisoners taken whiskey that is not for the squeamish.... *60.9% (121.9 proof). 458 bottles.*

⬩ **291 HR Colorado Bourbon Whiskey** aspen stave finished, batch no.24, db **(92.5) n23** a huge fruity kick on this suggest that the rye in the mash bill is pretty healthy. Very different from their usual bourbon noses...; **t22.5** Ok, I had to look at the bottle here because the rye flung itself at my tastebuds like a heartbroken lover at an amore about to leave for a rival. "...a high rye content in the mash bill" whispers the back label...they ain 't kidding...; **f24** the finish is long with an increasing toasty oak element displacing the pushy rye. Indeed, the finale is seemingly endless and the complexity levels border on the miraculous. He mocha levels explode off the scale and as the fruit recedes the whole timbre of the whiskey changes...now into a far more bourbon mode; **b23** a fascinating bourbon, quite unlike 291's standard fare. This needs a good map to get you from one side to the other: some journey! *63.4% (126.8 proof) 882 bottles*

⬩ **291 M Colorado Rye Whiskey** finished with aspen wood staves and maple syrup barrels, batch no.1, db **(88) n21.5 t23 f21.5 b22** A slight tobacco note keeps the sweet rye company from nose to finish. The succulent fruitiness of the delivery, juxtaposed by the spice, is a treat, though... *61.7% (123.4 proof) 866 bottles*

291 Small Batch Colorado Bourbon Whiskey Aspen Stave Finished batch no. 1 db **(83.5) n21.5 t21 f20.5 b20.5** Heavy handed and feinty, this is not a patch on their normal high-quality whiskey. There is a brief flirtation with honey early on, but nothing to (bees) wax lyrical about. *50% (100 proof). 1,226 bottles.*

⬩ **291 Small Batch Colorado Bourbon Whiskey** finished with aspen wood staves, batch no.6, db **(94.5) n23** as is the house style, the oak not only takes up pole position with its hairy, chest-beating toasty tannin, but also seems to have its tentacles into a few slower more rumbling back notes, too: for instance, the dried orange peel; **t24** wow! Diced orange peel to the fore; it wasn't just your imagination on the nose. But now the middle goes into a lurid chocolate dessert mode, thick and delightfully oiled. Liquorice, manuka honey and even a dose of slightly overcooked butterscotch tart....; **f23.5** slightly burned toast has never tasted so good...! The corn oils make a rich, satisfying entry...; **b24** another golden nugget of a bourbon from a distillery that inhabits the top echelons of American bourbon makers. You know, if someone asked me to shew them a bourbon which is probably closest in style to the stuff the old timers would have been knocking back in the better western saloons...this might just be it. Rugged...yet refined. *50% (100 proof) 574 bottles*

291 Small Batch Colorado Rye Whiskey Aspen Stave Finished batch no. 1 db **(86) n21 t23 f20.5 b21.5** Astonishingly sweet rye that celebrates concentrated molasses as much as it does the grain. A slightly over-generous cut robs this rye of any chance of greatness, and makes for some hard work on both the nose and finish. But as for that salivating delivery: no complaints there. *50.8% (101.7 proof). 1,185 bottles.*

⬩⬩⬩ **291 Small Batch Colorado Rye Whiskey** finished with aspen wood staves, batch no.6, db **(83) n20.5 t22 f19.5 b21** Tobacco festooned, there is far too much bitterness in the system here. The little honey on shew is thinly stretched and fully tested. Hardly a flagship of the distillery's usual excellence. *50.8% (101.7 proof) 482 bottles*

DOWNSLOPE DISTILLING Centennial, Colorado.

⬩⬩⬩ **Downslope Bourbon Whiskey (91) n23** pretty classic stuff! Ulmo honey, buttery black liquorice, and light hickory; **t23** salivating with a sticky honey delivery backed up by above average corn oils. Chewy, drying as the vanillas get a grip; **f22.5** a more modest fade, a little liquorice towards the end of the fade giving way to the vanilla; **b22.5** a wonderfully vibrant bourbon that clatters about the palate saying all the right things. *52% (104 proof)*

Downslope Double Diamond Rye/Malt Whiskey Aged 3 Years bourbon cask finish, cask no. 326 db **(89) n22 t22.5 f22 b22.5** A blend of 60% rye and 40% malted barley certainly shows the rye, which is tight and fruity. Don't know if it is the word association with Double Diamond, an old British bottled beer of my youth, but I also pick up a vaguely hop-type note to this, too. But it's the rye which runs the show here big time. *45% (90 proof). sc.*

Downslope Double Diamond Straight Rye Whiskey Aged 3 Years cask no. WR-235 db **(87.5) n22 t23 f20.5 b22** Downslope certainly know how to make their rye talk. This is at its fruitiest and most eye-watering. A light vanilla sub-plot is hard to engage with when the grain is being so attention seeking and bolshy. There is still that mysterious house bitterness that is vaguely hoppy in style and slightly unravels some of the earlier good. If they could dispense with that, they would be operating at a different level. *45% (90 proof). sc.*

⬩⬩⬩ **Downslope Double Diamond Whiskey (86) n21.5 t22 f21 b21.5** Quite a non-committal, easy drinking whiskey, packed with silky toffee and vanilla notes. *45% (90 proof)*

⬩⬩⬩ **Downslope Rye Whiskey (88.5) n22 t22 f22.5 b22** Not quite so sharp and precise on the rye notes as I remember their last bottling. Instead, we have wave upon wave of silky vanilla, perhaps helped along by a wider cut than last time. A little light chocolate and dark cherry on the finish. Very pleasant, easy-going rye. *48% (96 proof)*

LAWS WHISKEY HOUSE Denver, Colorado.

Laws Whiskey House Centennial Straight Wheat Whiskey Bonded batch no. 1 db **(87.5) n21.5 t22.5 f21.5 b22** A charming grain that strives for finesse over power. And achieves in it in the most part as the playful sugars join the usual wheat-induced spice to tease and tingle. The trouble with finesse is that any cracks show in double measure, and here cloying oiliness of the feints can be seen clearly. But there is no faulting the delivery where the grain is seen at its very brightest. *50% (100 proof).*

Laws Whiskey House Four Grain Straight Bourbon Whiskey Aged 3 Years batch no. 20 db **(88.5) n22 t23 f21.5 b22** Plucked from the warehouse at not quite the time when it wanted to be. From the nose through to the finale, you get the feel of a bourbon only half cooked. That said, still makes for a very tasty meal with more natural caramel than your average toffee factory. This ensures, along with the sterling corn oil, a soft countenance; the spices and busy grains guarantee a warming one, too... No feints, beautifully made, excellent oak involvement...just needed a bit of extra time... *47.5% (95 proof).*

Laws Whiskey House Four Grain Straight Bourbon Whiskey Barrel Select Aged 8 Years barrel no. 66 db **(95.5) n24 t24.5 f23 b24** This distillery's four grain bourbon is a Laws unto itself...especially when it reaches 8 years, as I believe this has. Monumentally magnificent. *55% (110 proof). sc.*

Laws Whiskey House Henry Road Straight Malt Whiskey Bonded 4 Years Old batch no. 1 db **(93) n23 t23.5 f23 b23.5** If this is Batch One, I can't wait for the next ones. Congratulations to all at Laws for producing such an outstanding malt whiskey first time out. *50% (100 proof).*

Laws Whiskey House San Luis Valley Straight Rye Whiskey Cask Aged 3 Years barrel no. 152 db **(81.5) n20 t22.5 f19 b20** For a while this recovers impressively from an indifferent nose that is technically way off beam. Rye often yields a fruity persona and here we have, quite uniquely, blood orange and kumquat in equal measure. Sadly the finale apes the nose's ungainly feints. *56.8% (113.6 proof). sc.*

Laws Whiskey House San Luis Valley Straight Rye Aged 6 Years Bonded batch 1 db **(86) n21 t23 f20 b22** An historic whiskey by all accounts: the first-ever to be Bottled in Bond in Colorado's rich history. Sadly, the back label also mentions tobacco notes, and that usually spells a problem. Not because I don't smoke – and never have - but a tobacco aroma and taste is, 99 times out of 100, associated with feints. And there is no escaping that the cut on this was as wide as the Colorado River. But, that said, it also relishes its kumquat and ginger main show and simply revels in the massive molasses they melt into. And despite the obvious weakness on nose and finish, there is also no getting away from the mind-boggling intensity of the grain itself. *50% (100 proof).*

LEOPOLD BROS Denver, Colorado.

Leopold Bros Maryland-Style Rye Whiskey barrel no. 174 db **(77.5) n20.5 t19 f19 b19** Because of the vast over generosity of the cut, their bourbon shows more rye character than this actual rye does. Very much in the German mould of whisky making with those feints offering a distinct nougat style. Badly needs a far more disciplined approach to their cut points. Their bourbon shews they have much more to offer than this. *43%. sc. American Small Batch Whiskey Series.*

Leopold Bros Straight Bourbon Cask Select barrel no. 135, bott 11 Mar 19 db **(87.5) n22 t22.5 f21 b22** Really interesting here how the rye plays such a significant role in the flavour personality of this bourbon. The given mash bill reveals 17% malted barley to 15% rye, yet it is that latter grain that can be found in all the highlights. Especially on the nose and eye-watering delivery. Good spice, but just need to get the feints down a little to make the most of the growing honey tones. Seriously promising. *50%. sc.*

SPIRIT HOUND DISTILLERS Lyons, Colorado.

◇ **Spirit Hound Straight Colorado Bourbon** aged 3 years, barrel no: 3, db, **(84) n21 t22 f20 b21** I think we have just found Hickory Central. The nose, oddly, reminds me of a certain breed of Bowmore from about 20 years ago, full of cough sweet promise. Then, on the palate, we go into hickory meltdown with a mix of muscovado sugars and molasses ensuring balance, though even they can't quite muzzle the very late bitterness... A very strange cove and nowhere near as relaxed and confident as their single malts, though always a tasty, chewy experience. An early barrel: doubtless they were still in learning mode... *64.7% sc*

◇ **Spirit Hound Straight Colorado Rye** aged 4 years, barrel no: 3, db **(87) n22 t23 f20 b22** Hickory and rye this time. The grain comes out fighting and refuses to play second fiddle to the oak. To that end it is wonderfully juicy, and the style of grain is never in doubt, some excellent vanilla and acacia honey helping it gain extra heights to warble its crisp notes. The finish, though, is untidy and back down the hickory route again. The arrival, however, is unquestionably a delicious handful. Early days and look forward to watching this brand develop. *45% (90 proof) sc*

◇ **Spirit Hound Straight Malt 2 Years Old** barrel no: 175, db **(89.5) n23** fascinating...really different. I'm sure I can detect just the shyest degree of peat reek here, but it can hardly be heard with the intensity of the malt to contend with and a citrussy vanilla/underripe banana element, too. Where's the tannin...? **t23** this was always going to be mouth-watering prospect, and so it proves. The malt is wonderfully fresh and brings with it no little lemon blossom honey; **f21.5** cuts up a little rougher here as the tannins and grains are no longer quite of the same wavelength...; **b22** really love this. Despite its age it abounds with character. You almost want to put it in a dirty glass. *45% (90 proof) sc*

◇ **Spirit Hound Straight Malt 2 Years Old** barrel no: 196, db **(93) n23** all the tannin missing from the nose of barrel 175 (above) has been found. It is here...; **t24** fabulous...just fabulous. The irrepressible beauty of ulmo honey and toasted honey is ladled out on delivery A few spices attempt to pucker, but the gorgeous butterscotch and buttery oils just continue their sojourn with the brilliant honey ensemble...; **f22.5** much toastier now with mocha hamming up the cocoa side of things in particular. But the ulmo honey seems to last the course, as do the increasing spices; **b23.5** chalk and cheese to barrel 175. This broadcasts its tannins at full volume to give a distinctly bourbony feel...Brilliantly made whiskey pounding with personality. *64.24% sc*

◇ **Spirit Hound Straight Malt 5 years Old** barrel no: 55, db **(94) n23.5** that blend of black and red liquorice that usually spells bourbon. Plenty of molasses, even the outline of hickory.... but precious little malt...! **t24** just imagine if this had corn oil to contend with: how thick would this delivery be? But it is malt only, yet still this must be lusciousness defined in a glass. The molasses moves forward and melds with manuka honey forming a wonderfully rich platform for the malt to finally assemble...and in style matching intensity; **f23** I remember a whiskey from this distillery that was a bit light on copper. Not this time: absolutely saturated with it, this giving a gloriously sharp sheen; **b23.5** a malt it may be. Be this so desperately wants to be a bourbon! This is just magnificent! The mouth feel in particular is worthy of a medal. This distillery is one Hound I am becoming rather fond of.... 68.1% sc

VAPOR DISTILLERY Boulder, Colorado.

⬦ **Boulder Spirits American Single Malt** aged no less than 3yrs, 53 gall level 3 char cask db **(87) n22 t23 f21 b21** Like their bourbon of the same age, sweetness has been compromised very slightly. Certainly, gets off to a storming, malty start on delivery with a sublime toasted honeycomb back up. The finish, though, is a little dry, tangy and out of sorts. 46% (92 proof)

⬦ **Boulder Spirits American Single Malt Bottled In Bond** aged no less than 4yrs, 53 gall level 3 char cask, db **(94) n22.5** gloriously nutty with a toasty maltiness as a back-up. Just a teasing hint of citrus, too...; **t24** one of those adorable bourbon/malt crossbreeds which dovetails liquorice and heather honey with a salivating barley concentrate; **f23.5** what a finish. The honey remains true, though now with a little treacle to give it a toastier hue. The barley and tannins also form the neatest partnership; **b24** damn! This distillery knows how to distil high quality whiskey! This is stunning! 50% (100 proof)

⬦ **Boulder Spirits American Single Malt Port Cask Finish** aged 3yrs 10 mo, 53 gall level 3 char cask, 10 months in port cask db **(88.5) n22 t23.5 f21 b22** While the nose has a controlled, dry, plummy style, the delivery offers something altogether more expansive - not least when the heather honey and muscovado sugars kick in with the bold spices. There is also a plum jam fruitiness. But this retracts slightly on the restrained, dry finale. Some serious flavour on offer here. 46% (92 proof)

⬦ **Boulder Spirits American Single Malt Sherry Cask Finish** aged 3yrs 6 mo, 53 gall level 3 char cask, 6 months in sherry cask db **(87) n22.5 t23 f20 b21.5** Silky and voluptuous to start with, there is more than a hint of sherry trifle on delivery. The finish, however, is a little dry and tangy. 47% (94 proof)

⬦ **Boulder Spirits Straight Bourbon** aged no less than 3yrs, 53 gall level 3 char cask, db **(87.5) n22.5 t21.5 f22 b21.5** From the attractive, honey-ringed nose it drops in sweetness on delivery and, for a bourbon, becomes quite remarkably dry. Readjusts about two thirds of the way in as the vanillas gather and the spices rise. 42% (84 proof)

⬦ **Boulder Spirits Straight Bourbon Bottled In Bond** aged no less than 4yrs, 53 gall level 3 char cask, db **(92.5) n22.5** some bourbons power through on the liquorice, some on honey. The main thrust of this - and by some margin – is the vanilla. Soft and soothing...; **t23.5** excellent delivery thanks to gentle corn oils and muscovado sugars. Made all the sharper by a small dose of copper which give a decidedly attractive metallic feel. A spiced note of liquorice and heather honey; **f23** we're back to the healthy vanillas detected on the nose....and a little prickly spice to stir things up slightly; **b23.5** a much happier bottling than their standard bourbon, a place found for the balancing sugars from first to last. A beautiful fellow, this. 50% (100 proof)

⬦ **Boulder Spirits Straight Bourbon Sherry Cask Finish** aged 3yrs 6 months, 53 gall level 3 char cask, 6 months in sherry cask db **(85.5) n22.5 t23 f19 b21** It is fascinating how the fruit influence of the sherry cask has turned what was originally a straight bourbon into something nosing far more along the lines of a rye! The delivery boasts a real cream sherry feel, despite only a six month stint with the wine cask. Again, the finish is dull, a tad furry and bitter. Up to that point we had been treated to a moist fruitcake with a fair dose of golden syrup. 47% (94 proof)

WOOD'S HIGH MOUNTAIN DISTILLERY Salida, Colorado.

Wood's Alpine Rye Whiskey Aged 2 Years batch no. 16 db **(87) n21 t22 f22 b22** These guys really go for their rye full throttle. The grains thump into the taste buds with purpose and vigour – and make a point of hanging around on the chewy oils. But the nose is a little murkier than the last bottling I sampled, the wider cut making its mark. 49% (98 proof).

Wood's Sawatch American Malt Whiskey Aged 4 Years batch no. 2 db **(87) n22 t22 f21 b22** Just as you spot the rye in their rye, so the barley (well, they say "Malt" but it has a barley-esque quality) leaves nothing to the imagination here, a juicy grassiness dominating. Again, a wide cut makes for a hefty experience, some mocha arriving late on. 49% (98 proof).

Wood's Tenderfoot American Malt Whiskey Aged 18 Months batch no. 66 db **(88) n21.5 t22 f22.5 b22** A cleaner distillate than the 4-year-old means the grain here piles in at its most juicy and grassy. More melt-in-the mouth sugars, too, and though the house cocoa turns up towards the end as expected, there is far more layering from the grain now. 45% (90 proof).

Florida
FISH HAWK SPIRITS Gainesville, Florida.

Sui Generis Conquistador 1513 batch no. 6 db **(68) n21 t20 f12 b15** I had learned the hard way, from tasting their other two whiskies first, to wait until the finish kicked in before even beginning to form a view. And, again, the awful finish makes what goes on before almost irrelevant. 40% (80 proof).

Sui Generis Silver Queen batch no. 2 db **(70)** n17 t18 f17 b18 There are no words. Perhaps other than "fish".... 40% (80 proof).

Sui Generis Siren Song batch no. 6 db **(78)** n21 t22 f17 b18 Where the Silver Queen was dethroned (and hopefully guillotined), at least this Siren Song has some allure. The big salty nose and big sweet delivery make some kind of sense. But this song goes horribly out of tune as the fade beckons. 40% (80 proof).

FLORIDA FARM DISTILLERS Umatilla, Florida.

Palm Ridge Golden Handmade Micro Batch Wheated Florida Whiskey nbc db **(92)** n22.5 full of the vitality of Florida youth, the grain has a jauntiness to its step while the sugars err on the side of golden syrup; t23..... on the subject of golden syrup, that is a close proximity to the mouthfeel of this little beauty. A slightly wide cut is detected, but the marriage of intense wheat and layered muscovado sugars make for an impressive match; f23.5 just love the patient finish, the continuous waves of vanilla of varying hue, the spice-pricked chalkier tannins and, for the most part, those deft balancing sugars; b23 a massive personality and an exhibition of controlled sugars. 45% (90 proof). ncf.

Palm Ridge Rye Handmade Micro Batch Florida Rye Whiskey nbc db **(88)** n21 t23.5 f21.5 b22 A bit of a heavy-handed, clumsy fumble of a rye. Where they got away with a slightly wide cut on their wheat, they were unable to pull off the trick quite so well here with this unforgiving grain. Certainly a delivery to remember with the rye in almost insanely intense form, and is worth finding a bottle of this to experience rye on steroids. However, the finish drops away alarmingly as the over-egged cut moves in with its heavier oils. A genuine Jekyll and Hyde rye. 50% (100 proof). ncf.

MANIFEST DISTILLING Jacksonville, Florida.

Manifest 100% Rye Batch 1 db **(86.5)** n20.5 t21.5 f23 b21.5 A very untidy rye, not least with a bitter-ish tobacco note on the nose and very little structure to the delivery. However, at around the midpoint it throws off its shackles and displays both the grain and a gorgeous chocolate milkshake note off to superb effect, the sparkling Demerara on the finale rounding things off superbly. Worth investigating just for that dreamy finish. 50% (100 proof).

Georgia
ASW DISTILLERY Atlanta, Georgia.

Burns Night Single Malt db **(95.5)** n24 t24 f23.5 b24 I tasted this after their Tire Fire, as this contained the feints from that distillate...so one must assume there was a lot, as Tire Fire is so clean. I suspect this is better quality whiskey than Rabbie Burns ever got his lips around... This will be in the running for micro-distillery whiskey of the year for certain... Magnificent: such a classy, classy act... 46% (92 proof).

Fiddler Unison Bourbon (91.5) n23 t23.5 f22 b23 A thoughtful blend of bourbons which suggests boldness, but always with a touch of elegance not far away... 45% (90 proof).

Maris Otter Single Varietal Single Malt db **(88.5)** n21.5 t23.5 f21.5 b22 A malt that a tasting glass does well to hold, for this is bursting with the most intense barley flavours imaginable. The slightly wide-ish cut means a few oils get in on the act, too, making thing a much heavier whiskey than is best for this grain. That said, the blend of ulmo and heather honeys on delivery really are a joy, as is the waxiness they form. A unique single malt style and, with a tighter cut, one to be seriously reckoned with further down the line. 46% (92 proof).

Resurgent Rye db **(87)** n20.5 t22.5 f22 b22 Thunders out the grain on delivery, both in juicier crisp and drier, oilier, rounded form. A chewing rye, not least because the cut here has been a little on the generous side. But if nothing else that means the spices on the finish are really something to behold. A rye that lets you know it....!! 67.2% (134.4 proof).

Tire Fire Single Malt db **(94)** n23.5 t23.5 f23 b24 Amazing what can be achieved when you get those cuts right! Beautifully made and smoky malt with finesse. The best peated from America I have tasted this year. Superb! 45.5% (91 proof).

SWAMP FOX DISTILLING CO. Buena Vista, Georgia.

Swamp Fox Distilling Co. F. Marion Single Barrel Continental Whiskey Aged 3 Months Minimum nbc db **(62)** n15 t17.5 f14 b15.5 Words fail me. I have no idea what this whiskey is trying to achieve. Or even why it is in a rut. 41% (82 proof). sc.

Swamp Fox Distilling Co. Kettle Creek Malt Whiskey Aged 3 Months Minimum nbc db **(80.5)** n19 t21 f20 b20.5 There is a house pattern here of off-key nose and finish and huge, mind-stunning delivery. But, again, those tobacco notes tend to point towards a distillation where the heart is over enlarged. 50% (100 proof).

Swamp Fox Distilling Co. King's Town Rye Whiskey Aged 3 Months Minimum nbc db **(76.5) n19.5 t20 f18 b19** When a new distillery breezes into town, there is nothing more I like than to taste their whiskey, put my arms around their shoulders and say: "well done, lads". Sadly, I'm not getting much of a chance here. The mixture of mouldy, dank straw and tobacco points towards a number of failures which even a few rounds of sharp rye notes can't repair. *50% (100 proof).*

Swamp Fox Distilling Co. Will O' The Wisp White Whiskey Aged 3 Months Minimum nbc db **(84) n20.5 t21.5 f21 b21** This young whiskey is vibrant and bursting at the seams with busy sugars and complex compound grains. It is undone, though, by the tobacco notes from the distillation which undermines both the nose and finish in particular. *50% (100 proof).*

Illinois
BLAUM BROS Galena, Illinois.

Blaum Bros Bourbon Aged 3 Years db **(81) n19.5 t22 f19 b20.5** A curious bourbon, this. Has the complex spice make up of a cake mix. Exceptionally sweet and leaves the tongue buzzing... *50% (100 proof).*

Blaum Bros Fever River Rye Aged 2 Years new American oak, finished in Port and Madeira barrels db **(86.5) n21.5 t21.5 f22 b21.5** Less bizarre spices at play here, the wine casks making for a friendlier, after experience with an attractive complexity that now makes sense. *40% (80 proof).*

Blaum Bros Straight Rye Whiskey 4 Years Old db **(90.5) n23 t23 f22 b22.5** A sturdy and steady rye with just the right degree of brittleness. *50% (100 proof).*

FEW SPIRITS DISTILLERY Evanston, Illinois.

FEW American Whiskey Aged at Least 1 Year batch no. 18H30, bott code: FS 18297 333 db **(90) n22 t23 f22.5 b22.5** They've cracked it...! *46.5% (93 proof).*

FEW Bourbon Whiskey batch no. 18K14, bott code: 318 347 1555 db **(95) n23.5 t24 f23.5 b24** This distillery has moved a long way in a relatively short space of time. A real force for quality now on the US whiskey scene. *46.5% (93 proof).*

FEW Rye Whiskey batch no. 18E30 db **(94) n23.5 t24 f23 b23.5** The cleanest FEW whisky I have tasted to date, the grain positively sparkles. And the way this whiskey has panned out... regrets? Too FEW to mention...... *46.5% (93 proof).*

KOVAL DISTILLERY Chicago, Illinois.

Koval Single Barrel Bourbon Whiskey cask no. 4Q3P7W db **(94.5) n23.5** I could stick my snout in this glass all day long! Oozing liquorice, but seemingly dipped in thick heather honey; **t24** the corn oils do a blinding job of holding together the sweeter, honeyed elements and the toastier tannins. Big without blustering or bullying; the slow spice build is masterful; **f23** warmly spiced ulmo honey and vanilla. Long and luxuriant; **b24** technically on the money and ticks all the bourbon boxes. Big and rich in honey. *47%. sc.*

Koval Single Barrel Four Grain Whiskey cask no. NB6M34 db **(84.5) n19 t23.5 f21 b21** After finding their Four Grain sporting a wide cut last year, I was expecting service to return to normal this. Sadly not. The feints are even more exaggerated this time out making the nose challenging and the dying embers very untidy. However, the delivery is a different matter, and you feel like forgiving the whiskey's sins simply for the sheer joy of the heather honey and ginger delivery and follow through. That may well be short, but it really is perfectly formed. *47%. sc.*

WHISKEY ACRES DISTILLING CO. DeKalb, Illinois.

Whiskey Acres Distilling Co. Straight Bourbon Whiskey Aged at Least 2 Years db **(91.5) n23.5** chocolate sauce on vanilla ice cream: and I mean thick chocolate...the liquorice and molasses give this a real old-fashioned bourbon feel...; **t22.5** still on the heavy side, the corn oils respond to sweeten while the liquorice delves deep; **f22.5** a little manuka honey battling it out with the various oils; **b22.5** you can see what a difference two extra years of working those stills has made. A much more sympathetic cut. Still plenty of oils to make for a chewathon, but now the tannins really come out to play. *43.5% (87 proof). ncf.*

Whiskey Acres Distilling Co. Straight Bourbon Whiskey Bottled-in-Bond Aged at Least 4 Years db **(87) n22.5 t22 f21 b21.5** Bottled-in-Bond...and Big! The wide cut has meant little too much feint has entered the system here. The nose has a magnificent heather- and manuka honey mix to compensate and enough salivating corn oil on delivery melds with the maple syrup to make for and enjoyable delivery. The finish, though, is not quite so forgiving... *50% (100 proof). ncf.*

Whiskey Acres Distilling Co. Straight Rye Whiskey Aged at Least 2 Years db **(92) n23.5 t23 f22.5 b23** An incredibly tasty rye where the flavours are impossible to tame. Rich and vibrating with rye intensity. Again, a slightly cleaner cut and we'd be talking top drawer whiskey. *43.5% (87 proof). ncf.*

Indiana
SPIRITS OF FRENCH LICK West Baden Springs, Indiana.
Spirits of French Lick Lee W. Sinclair 4 Grain Indiana Straight Bourbon Whiskey db **(89) n22.5** the four grains combine to offer attractive complexity. The oats – as oats often do – have a slightly louder voice than most; **t23** a sweet caress on entry followed by a decent dollop of ulmo honey, spices and polite tannin; **f21.5** the spices keep nagging; there is a late metallic tartness; **b22** silky and soft thanks probably to the oat contingent, the aroma of which is definitely easy to spot. *45% (90 proof).*

Iowa
CAT'S EYE DISTILLERY Bettendorf, Iowa.
Cat's Eye Distillery Essence of Iowa db **(87) n21.5 t22 f21.5 b22** Ah! So this is what Iowa smells like, is it? Well, for those who have never been there, let me tell you it has a distinctive citrus lightness to the aroma, though at times it can come through quite sharply. Strange, as I always though Iowa smelt like cheese. To taste, there is a very sweet vanilla lead, the corn oils filling the palate to generate a lush and friendly mouthfeel. Perhaps a little tangy at the death. But, in essence, Iowa is a very friendly place, indeed. *40% (80 proof).*

CEDAR RIDGE Shwisher, Iowa
◈ **No 9 Slipknot Iowa Corn Whisky Aged 3 Years** db **(91) n22.5** impressive nose. Understated and elegant corn dispersal all helped along but the lightly honeyed oils...; **t23.5** beautiful. I mean really beautiful...! Now that's about an impressive corn oil depth on delivery as I could hope for from a relatively new distillery. And, better still, it sets off the butterscotch and acacia honey. The oaky vanilla plays it low key but offers a biscuity base; **f22** long thanks to the oils, with the spices beginning to burble...; **b23** pretty classic corn oil, not one of the easier American whiskies to get right. No shortage of acacia honey to aid the enjoyment. Iowa is one of the few States in the US I have yet to visit. This distillery gives me reason enough to put that right. *45% (90 proof)*

Kentucky
CASTLE AND KEY Millville, Kentucky
◈ **Pinhook Bourbon Heist Kentucky Straight Bourbon Aged More Than 3 Years** crop 2021 **(90.5) n23** a charming spice throb pulses its way through the delicate red and black liquorice blend: pretty classic stuff for a three-year-old. Some lovely hickory, too...; **t23** there is both an embracing sweetness on delivery, and warmth, too, as the spices kick in early. The corn oils, so often overlooked as a vital part of a bourbon's make up, haven't been here and gives a wonderfully display of deftly sweet lusciousness; **f21.5** although the high vanilla and heather-honey stay to the end, a slightly uneven bitterness crops up also; **b23** this has all the feel of a very good whiskey stirring from its slumber. *49% (98 proof)*

◈ **Pinhook Bourbon War Straight Bourbon Whiskey Aged 5 Years** Crop 2020 **(95) n24** this is a 15-minute nose, and you can double it going through the temperatures in the Murray Method. You'll find toffee apple, spiced red liquorice, manuka honey, a little marzipan with a tangerine tinge...and possibly Uncle Tom Cobley if you hunt hard enough. The epitome of a complex bourbon; **t23.5** the corn oils shew first and massages the taste buds. A blend of buttery golden syrup and molasses piles on the sugars before a spicy liquorice backdrop forms. Both light...yet hefty...and lively enough to give a salivating start to proceedings; **f23.5** to say this is long and languid hardly covers it. The entire whiskey is played out as though in a slow Kentucky drawl and with the finish it appears that time almost stops completely. Again, thank the corn oils for this, which are present in both the continuing sticky texture and the late flavour profile. The vanillas emerge with a light muscovado flourish; **b24** close on 30 years ago I and Cecil Withrow, who owned and lived within the long-closed and gutted Old Taylor Distillery would sit together and try to work out how this historic landmark of early and great Kentucky whiskey making. Sadly, Cecil died before he was ever able to see his dream come true. New owners came in...and made it happen. My old Kentucky home of 20 years was just a short walk from this distillery along McCracken Pike...until a freak storm flattened it. But I still own the two acres of land which I have left as a birdwatching area. And occasionally whisky sipping. And I'd be happy to sip this, my old neighbour's whiskey, any day of the week. Even old Cecil would have been proud of this one... *52% (104 proof)*

◈ **Pinhook Hard Rye Guy Kentucky Straight Rye Whiskey Aged More Than 2 Years** custom Pinhook mash bill, crop 2021 **(89) n22.5** no doubting the grains here and, despite the young age, the tannins have already decided to pack a punch, too. Clean and sharp; **t23** the delivery simply allows the rye to show off: both fruity and sweet with a comfortable, lightly oiled vanilla bed on which it lies; **f21.5** lots of spicy vanilla. But a nagging bitterness, too; **b22** not sure about that late bitterness, but the ride until then was one of a thoroughbred. *49% (98 proof)*

⬩ **Pinhook Tiz Rye Time Straight Rye Whiskey Aged 5 Years** crop 2021 **(92) n23.5** the kind of rye nose that you could cut yourself on if you breathe in too energetically. Sharp, as a great rye should be, with an eclectic mix of varying fruit notes. Sebaceous vanilla notes are found just below the rye; **t24** there can probably no delivery more startling and intense that clean barley and copper off the still. This takes salivating up to Olympic levels as the tastebuds are constantly poked and prodded by the concentrated crisp grain. You have to have a degree in the blending of sugars to understand how this one works. But the best I can work out we have orange blossom and ulmo honey mixed with a dash of molasses, all blended in with butterscotch. That's how I'd try to recreate the underlying charm of this, and I suspect I'd get pretty close. But nothing I do can recreate that rye top note: that is truly unique; **f21.5** a little green tea makes a surprise entrance, the tannins boring into the vanilla; **b23** just like the bourbon, the jump between the younger and older bottlings is significant. This is one deliciously rich rye... And, even more intriguing: use the Murray Method here. Make sure you taste when at room temperature and compare to when slightly warmed. So different: you really are able to change horses in midstream *51.5% (103 proof)*

GLENNS CREEK DISTILLERY Frankfort, Kentucky.

Glenns Creek Café Olé Kentucky Bourbon Barrel No 1 Aged At Least 1 Year (94) n23 t23.5 f23.5 b24 The thing about big David Meier the distiller is that he like to make whiskies more enormous than himself. And, my word...has he succeeded here! Stupendous whisky! *57% (114 proof). sc.*

Glenns Creek OCD#5 (94.5) n23 t24 f23.5 b24 This is one quirky distillery. But, by thunder, it knows how to make truly great bourbon. *57.8 % (115.6 proof).*

Ryskey barrel 4 single barrel double oaked db **(92.5) n23.5 t23.5 f22 b23** The usual excellence from the Lawrenceburg, Indiana, distillery but given a curious twist but the stirring in of some muscular tannin. Attractive and intriguing. *59.3% (118.6 proof) distilled Indiana – oak staves added at Glenns Creek.*

O. Z. TYLER Owensboro, Kentucky.

O.Z. Tyler Kentucky Bourbon Aged a Year and a Day Minimum (83) n20 t21 f21 b21 A tight, nutty bourbon shewing good late chocolate and molasses. But the youth of the whiskey means it has little ability to relax, although decent oils allow the sugars to distribute evenly. No off notes: just green and undercooked. Would love to see this at four or five times this age... *45%*

Maryland
MISCELLANEOUS DISTILLERY Mt Airy, Maryland.

Brill's Batch Bourbon Whiskey Aged 420 Days batch no. 8 db **(88.5) n22 t22.5 f22 b22** Pretty well distilled bourbon with specific emphasis on a maple syrup sweetness allowed to drier tannins. A salivating sharpness works particularly well just after the delivery. A light liquorice fade. *44% (88 proof).*

Gertrude's 100% Rye Whiskey Aged 7 Months batch no. 9 db **(87) n20.5 t23 f21.5 b22** Maryland is one of the original homes of rye whiskey, so it is always engaging to taste the spirit from there. The only fault here is the wide cut which allows more feint in than the grain can handle. But, that said, the type of grain is never in question because the rye announces itself in deliciously muscular fashion, both the fruitiness and crisp sugar quality is very much in evidence and certainly knows how to create a crescendo. One compensation of the extra cut is the richness of the chocolate on the finish. If this could be a bit cleaner this really has potential for excellence. *50% (100 proof).*

OLD LINE SPIRITS Baltimore, Maryland.

⬩ **Old Line American Single Malt Whiskey Cask Strength** aged 3 years **(88.5) n22 t22.5 f21.5 b22.5** Salty and remarkably linear in its development. Caramel abounds, but so do molasses. *56.8%*

⬩ **Old Line American Single Malt Whiskey Double Cask** aged 3.5 years, Port cask, id: 2102ASM.PCF375 **(92.5) n22.5 n22.5** has more plums than a plum pudding. Or even my plum tree. Salty, earthy...but always silky, irredeemably so; **t23.5** this is fabulous. It breaks every rule in the book by being so totally one-sided: this is seemingly to fruit what the BBC definitively is by the Woke: overrun. But here's the rub. Yes, there appears to be too much plummy raisin. But watch the way the salt and muscovado sugars kick in early on...notice the way the oak start to form little rods of toasty tannins, the spices have now rodded their way into a prominent position and then, as you near the finale... **f23** note the amazing creation of a chocolate fade, complete with black cherry...and finally, miraculously, malt...! **b23.5** it is now fair to say that Old Line have developed their own unique stye of whiskey different to anything else on the planet. It is certainly, for me, the most confusing. Because there is an all-consuming silkiness to their whiskies which are always borderline: when fruit takes over and the malt is lost, does it then cease to be a whisky? I think Old Line has given me more cause for lost sleep, more re-visits to my tasting lab than any other distillers for the last year or two because I keep asking myself: do I love this or am I disappointed by its incredibly linear personality? Then you taste a whiskey like this, watch the atom-by-atom development of the chocolate, as though in super slow motion and you conclude: hell! How can you not love this...? *61.8%*

⟜ **Old Line American Single Malt Whiskey Golden Edition (93) n23** brittle toffee. My word, those tannins are thick and confident...; **t23.5** golden syrup and vanilla make for a welcoming delivery followed by a coppery sharpness (new stills?). The dark sugars and toastier tannins make a very pretty couple. Always juicy...until the oils begin to form around the midpoint, then takes a turn for the cocoa...; **f23** an elegant mocha fade, still with a toasty Demerara and spice background; **b23.5** I have noticed a move by some distillers, whether purposely or by accident, towards an almost Jamaican/Fijian rum style whisky with an estery, rich persona. This excellent malt is very good example. Outwardly massive...inwardly a bit of a pussy... *50% (100 proof)*

TOBACCO BARN DISTILLERY Hollywood, Maryland.
Tobacco Barn Distillery Small Batch Straight Bourbon Whiskey Aged More Than 3 Years batch no. 17 A-8 db **(82) n20 t21 f20.5 b20.5** Some of the first American whiskey I ever tasted — way back in 1974 - was made in Maryland, where I was staying at the time. That came from a Seagrams plant, long since closed. It was very different to this, I remember, as this flags up its small distillery credentials with its very wide cut. Ironically, those feints wrap tobacco feel around the whiskey. Whether that was on purpose or not I can't say. But I hope future bottlings will show greater restraint in the still house. *45% (90 proof). 402 bottles.*

Massachusetts
TRIPLE EIGHT DISTILLERY Nantucket, Massachusetts.
Nor' Easter Bourbon Whiskey A Blend nbc db **(73.5) n19 t19.5 f17 b18** Not sure how much of this was distilled in Nantucket: very little or none, I suspect. Doesn't contain their usual classy touch and instead relies on a minty, milky nose and flavour profile which is hardly up to the great name of this distillery. This Nor' easter has sunk this whiskey with all hands lost... *44.4% (88.8 proof).*

The Notch Single Malt Whisky Aged 12 Years batch no. 003, dist 2005, bott 2018 db **(94.5) n23.5 t24 f23 b24** There is a reason why America's good and great gravitate to Nantucket. For the whiskey, of course... *48% (96 proof).*

The Notch Single Malt Whisky Aged 15 Years batch no. 001, dist 2002, bott 2018 db **(96) n24 t23.5 f24 b24.5** Unquestionably one of the great island malt whiskies outside Scotland. Exudes class from first sniff to last, fading salty signal. Truly brilliant. *48% (96 proof).*

The Notch Single Malt Whisky Peated nbc db **(92.5) n23 t23 f23 b23.5** Triple Eight's trademark super-clean malt allows the light smoke far greater licence than a more clumsily distilled malt would allow. The result is an essay of charm and subtlety. Indeed, the peat has the lightest of footprints, but is confident enough to ensure weight is added to the juicy cream toffee malt. Spices give the gentle marmalade notes a little extra zip. *52% (104 proof).*

Michigan
GRAND TRAVERSE DISTILLERY Traverse City, Michigan.
Grand Traverse Distillery Bourbon Aged at Least 4 Years bott code: 192090524 db **(84.5) n21 t21.5 f21 b21** Huge toffee from start to finish. And no shortage of Demerara sugars, too. But there is no escaping the feints from the overly generous cut. *46% (92 proof).*

Grand Traverse Distillery Michigan Wheat 100% Straight Rye Wheat Whiskey Bottled in Bond bott code: 192090514 db **(96) n23.5 t24 f24 b24.5** It is hard to imagine a modestly-sized distillery making a wheat whiskey any better than this. On this evidence, the usage of wheat for bread should be banned and it should all be sent to Grand Traverse... *50% (100 proof).*

Grand Traverse Distillery Ole George 100% Straight Rye Whiskey bott code: 192090320 db **(90.5) n23 t23 f22 b22.5** The sheer force of personality means it escapes censure for any lapse. *46.5% (93 proof).*

Grand Traverse Distillery Ole George Double Barrel 100% Straight Rye Whiskey French white oak finish db **(89.5) n21.5 t23 f22 b23** A very different fingerprint to any rye I have tasted before: the sugar seems natural enough and just keeps on coming – and it transpired that toasted French white oak was used in a finishing process. Which would, indeed, ramp up the natural sugar content... Clever whiskey. *46.5% (93 proof).*

JOURNEYMAN DISTILLERY Three Oaks, Michigan.
Journeyman Buggy Whip Wheat Whiskey batch 38 db **(94.5) n24 t23.5 f23 b24** I'll climb aboard this buggy any day. What a beautiful wheat whiskey this is...cracking, in fact...! *45% (90 proof).*

Journeyman Corsets, Whips and Whiskey 100% Wheat Whiskey batch no. 7 db **(89.5) n22 t23 f22 b22.5** One mouthful of this and I thought: "Oh, yes! The cough syrup distillery!" And sure enough this was one the one whose whiskey, a year or two back, reminded me of pleasant medication I had taken as a child. *64.5% (129 proof).*

Journeyman Featherbone Bourbon Whiskey batch 72 db **(84) n21 t21.5 f20 b21.5** The first mouthful of this flung me back 50 years to when I was a kid tucked up in bed and having to swallow a couple of spoons-worth of cherry-flavoured cough syrup. I can picture their salesmen getting people to gather round and peddling this as Dr Journeyman's Elixir for Coughs and Colds. In truth, though, a forceful corn-rich, oily, muscovado-sugared bag of tricks. *45% (90 proof).*

Journeyman Last Feather Rye Whiskey batch 72 db **(91) n22.5 t23.5 f22 b23** Truly a unique rye whiskey profile and one, that despite the odd fault, literally carries you on a delicious journey. *45% (90 proof).*

Journeyman Silver Cross Whiskey batch 61 db **(86) n22 t22 f20.5 b21.5** I am a fan of this fascinating distillery, that's for sure, and wondering what they are up to next. Not sure if this was designed to ward off vampires, but to be on the safe side I tasted this long after the sun set. A serious mish-mash of a whiskey which celebrated a rich ulmo-honey sweetness, but is ultimately undone by a bitterness which, sadly, no amount of sugar can keep fully under control and gets you in the neck in the end... *45% (90 proof).*

NEW HOLLAND BREWING COMPANY Holland, Michigan.
New Holland Beer Barrel Bourbon bott code: 192201 db **(80.5) n22 t21.5 f18 b19** It was doing so well until that heavy hop kicked in on the finish: the bourbon notes on this are as good as anything I've encountered from this distillery. I want my hops with my beer, not whisky. I just don't even begin to understand the concept of this style of whisk(e)y. Sorry. *40% (80 proof).*

New Holland Beer Barrel Rye American white oak db **(80) n21 t21 f19 b19** Were this from Speyside, I dare-say it would be called hopscotch... The hoppiest whisk(e)y I have tasted anywhere in the world. Apart from a brief chocolate intervention, this is seriously not my kind of thing. I mean: I love whisky and I love beer. But just not together. Less befuddled by it than befuggled... *40% (80 proof).*

Pitchfork Wheat Michigan-Grown Wheat Whiskey aged 14 months, American oak barrels db **(93) n22.5 t23.5 f23.5 b23.5** So love it! Like a digestive biscuit you want to dunk in your coffee...By far and away the best thing I have ever seen from this distillery: this really is top drawer microdistillery whiskey just brimming with flavours and personality. Genuinely impressed. *45% (90 proof).*

Zeppelin Bend Straight Malt Whiskey American oak barrels db **(84.5) n21 t21.5 f21 b21** The Zep is back!! Not seen it for a while and this is a new model. Actually, in some ways barely recognise it from the last one I saw about five years ago. Much more effervescent than before, though that curious hop note I remember not only persists but appears to have been upped slightly. *45% (90 proof).*

VALENTINE DISTILLING CO. Ferndale, Michigan.
Mayor Pingree Small Batch Bourbon Whiskey batch no. 39 db **(89.5) n23.5 t22.5 f21.5 b22** A very different animal, or mayor, and obviously distilled in different stills from their 9- and 10-year-old Mayor Pingree brands. A little confusing for the punter but a very attractive if under-stated micro-bourbon without doubt. *45% (90 proof).*

Montana
MONTGOMERY DISTILLERY Missoula, Montana.
Sudden Wisdom Straight Rye Whiskey Aged 3 Years new American white oak barrels, bott code: 19258 0856 db **(85) n21.5 t21.5 f21 b21** I tasted this unaware of this distillery's dallying with hoppy whiskey, as there is nothing on the label to suggest traditional beer is in any way involved. Yet the first thing I spotted on the nose and on the delivery was a distinct

hoppiness which out-punched the rye. A shame, as this is well distilled and if the grain had been allowed to shine to its fullest extent, this could have been a cracker. *45% (90 proof).*

New England
SONS OF LIBERTY Rhode Island, New England.
Battle Cry American Single Malt Whiskey db **(77.5) n19 t21 f18 b19.5** A sweet, nutty whisky weakened by the butyric-like off notes. *46% (92 proof).*

New York
BLACK BUTTON DISTILLING Rochester, New York.
Empire Rye Whiskey Aged at least 2 Years distilled from New York State rye & malted barley, batch no. 3 db **(85) n20 t23.5 f20.5 b21** The tobacco smoke underlines the wide cut on this. Technically imperfect it may be, but the delivery and immediate follow-through is gripping - and delicious! For a moment it is like distilled mead as the honey takes on a concentrated form you so very rarely see. The tannins are multi-layered and the chocolate tones have a touch of intense Lubek marzipan at work. The finish, as one might suspect, leaves a little to be desired. But this is all about a follow-through that transfixes and, frankly, blows you away! *42% (84 proof). ncf.*

BREUCKELEN DISTILLING Brooklyn, New York.
77 Whiskey Bonded Rye Distilled From 100% Rye Aged 6 Years db **(91) n22.5 t23.5 f22 b23** A beautifully understated rye whiskey. 50% (100 proof).

77 Whiskey Bonded Rye & Corn Aged 4 Years American oak barrels db **(95) n23.5 t24 f23.5 b24** There you go: Breuckleyn back on track with a spot edition of their signature brand. Sings from the glass like a barber-shop quartet. *50% (100 proof).*

77 Whiskey Local Corn 700 Days Old db **(92) n23 t23.5 f22.5 b23** It is as if very single atom of sugar has been sucked out of the oak though, thankfully, baser tannins give balance. Remarkable and delicious! *45% (90 proof).*

77 Whiskey Distilled From 100% Corn 1377 Days Old American oak barrels db **(92) n23 t23.5 f22.5 b23** The mark of a good corn whiskey is the honey hanging off the clean oils. And this has it by the bushel: a corn-ucopia, you might say... *45% (90 proof).*

77 Whiskey Local Rye & Corn 538 Days Old American oak barrels db **(92.5) n22.5 t23.5 f23 b23.5** The 377th whisky tasted for my Bible 2018 just had to be this. I remember last year tasting a younger version of this which was quite astonishing. Here the rye, which was so prominent last time, has been overtaken by the corn which has clipped its brittle wings. Still an astounding experience, nonetheless... *45% (90 proof).*

77 Whiskey Distilled From Local Rye & Corn 655 Days Old American oak barrels db **(87) n22 t22.5 f21 b21.5** An extraordinary degree of citrus on the nose – it is almost like opening up a pack of fruit pastel candy – sends this whiskey into unusual territory and it doesn't end there! The palate is awash with all kinds of dark sugars with an under note of fruit and spice. A little thin. Which doesn't help the finish ward off a slight bitterness. A distinctly idiosyncratic style. *45% (90 proof).*

77 Whiskey Distilled From New York Wheat 624 Days Old American oak barrels db **(89.5) n22 t23 f22 b22.5** Wheat whiskeys tend to be ablaze with spices. This, however, follows the distillery style of succulent sweetness. *45% (90 proof).*

Brownstone Malt Whiskey 6 Years Old batch no. 1 db **(87.5) n21.5 t21 f23 b22** OK. So we accept that the nutty-nougat element on both nose and delivery yells of over-egged feints. But once you get past that...just...wow! As thick, rich and chocolatey as any malt you could hope for, with a superb spiced Jaffa Cake. A finish to be savoured... *50% (100 proof).*

Project No 1: Wheated Straight Bourbon Bottled in Bond Aged 4 Years dist 2013 db **(88) n22 t22.5 f21.5 b22** A bit heavy on the oils, but the wheat and associated spices make their mark. *50% (100 proof).*

Project No 2: Single Malt Whiskey Bottled in Bond Aged 4 Years dist 23 Mar 13, bott 26 Feb 18 db **(84.5) n21 t21 f21.5 b21** Sweet and widely cut. A project still in development, I suspect... *50% (100 proof).*

COOPERSTOWN DISTILLERY Cooperstown, New York.
Cooper's Classic American Whiskey bourbon mash finished in French oak barrels, bott code. 148 10 db **(90.5) n22.5 t22.5 f23 b22.5** Plugs into the sugars and takes full voltage. 45%.

Cooper's Legacy Bourbon Whiskey Grant's Recipe bott code. 147 02 db **(95) n23.5 t24 f23.5 b24** I'd like, with this exceptional bourbon, to raise a toast to my son, James', new (indeed, first) dog: Cooper. Named, naturally, after Dale Cooper of Twin Peaks fame. Dale whippet. Dale bourbon. *50% (100 proof).*

Cooper's Ransom Rye Whiskey db **(86.5) n21 t22 f21.5 b22** If they could just keep the cut points a little more tight, they'd have some rye here. Despite the light feints the rye does at times sparkle with commendable crispness. *51% (102 proof).*

FINGER LAKES DISTILLING Burdett, New York.

McKenzie Wheated Bourbon Whiskey Bottled in Bond Aged a Minimum of 4 Years American oak db **(93) n23 t23.5 f23 b23.5** Rich, full flavoured and well powered. Not a bourbon for the faint of heart. Beautifully constructed and structured. *50% (100 proof). ncf.*

HIGH PEAKS DISTILLING LLC Lake George, New York.

High Peaks Cloudsplitter Aged 2 Years db **(91) n23 t23 f22 b23** Their label is interesting. They are one of the few distilleries that boast of refined cuts...and that is what they had, because the distillate is feint free. But they fall into the trap of saying that sherry sweetens: most actually impart a dryness, which I feel has happened here. No complaints from me, as that has certainly upped the sophistication of this hugely attractive malt. *46%.*

HILLROCK ESTATE DISTILLERY Hudson Valley, New York.

Hillrock Double Cask Rye Whiskey barrel no. OSR DC Rye 1 db **(77) n20 t20.5 f17.5 b19** Tomorrow I have to drastically cut short my time at my home and tasting room on the banks of the Kentucky River to return to England. The President has decreed that no more incoming craft will be allowed to travel from the UK because of the C-19 crisis. I could have stayed here and worked on, but there was a chance my health insurance would have run out before the travel ban was lifted...so I have booked a flight home later today. I have worked all day and into the early hours of the morning, trying to keep away from the wine finishes and hop-fermented whiskeys which would have so drastically slowed down my palate and ability to work. My last whiskey before I leave is this one, simply because I wanted to taste one of the great Dave Pickerell's creations, from a distiller I have known and admired now for a quarter of a century, before heading back. That said, this distillery's track record with finishing leaves a little to be desired, not seeming to understand the damage that sulphur can cause to a whiskey. I picked this one because it said it was double matured in American wood. Even so, the grim finish is one that would have seen me off for the night anyway, as it is unforgiving in its bitterness and furriness. As long as I live, I will never understand why any American distilling company would like to ape the very worst of Scotch whisky, repeating the mistakes that has allowed true bourbon and rye whiskey to sail above most Scotch single malts in quality. *53.6% (107.2 proof). sc.*

IRON SMOKE WHISKEY Fairport, New York.

Iron Smoke Casket Strength Straight Bourbon Whiskey Aged a Minimum of 2 Years batch no. 2, bott 7-11-19 db **(94) n23.5 t24 f23 b23.5** Might be a little less wheat in the mash bill here as the usual smokiness (carried on that one particular grain) is much less evident than usual. It doesn't appear to suffer from that fact, either... *60% (120 proof).*

◇ **Iron Smoke Casket Strength Straight Bourbon Whiskey Aged a Minimum of 2 Years** batch no. 3, bott 9-16-20 db **(92.5) n24** compared to their last batch, there is a slight upping in the applewood smoke. But don't expect this to be a riot of phenols. This wins nose down because of the amazing balance, weight and subtlety: the smoke dances nimbly around the more traditional liquorice and honey straight bourbon signature, this seems to lift a certain saltiness, too. No matter at the cool or warmer end of the Murray Method scale, the results are broadly the same...; **t23** by comparison to the nose, this is a starker, simpler experience, the lack of oils making for a degree of turbulence, too. The sugars are in short supply, and there is just honey enough to counter the more aggressive spices; **f22.5** one of the driest Iron Smoke I've encountered for a while. The vanilla and spices have things pretty much to themselves; **b23** one of the distilleries I always look forward to tasting with relish. This is showing the distillery in a slightly brutalist light, the strength, spices, and lack of oils taking no prisoners. But the subtlety of all the elements makes for brilliant complexity. Slug it down if you wish. But you'll still find yourself thinking deeply about the complex matters being played out on your palate... *60% (120 proof).*

Iron Smoke Special Reserve Single Barrel Straight Bourbon Whiskey Aged a Minimum of 2 Years barrel no. 246, dist 8/19/15 db **(92) n22 t23.5 f23 b23.5** A unique Iron Smoke style here beautifully played out. *45% (90 proof). sc. MAHAN Liquor.*

Iron Smoke Special Reserve Single Barrel Straight Bourbon Whiskey Aged a Minimum of 2 Years barrel no. 515, dist 9/28/16, bott 12-6-19 db **(92) n22.5 t23 f23 b23.5** Iron Smoke in its typically full on demeanour. *45% (90 proof). sc. DW Select Batch no. 2.*

◇ **Iron Smoke Special Reserve Single Barrel Straight Bourbon Whiskey Aged a Minimum of 2 Years** barrel no. 541, bott 11-25-19 db **(89) n21.5** the apple wood-smoked wheat holds court for a little while before a slight salted bacon theme begins to unfurl. The tannins hold back for a while. The fermentation appears to have bestowed a hayrick dried grassiness; **t22** simplistic hickory is about as sweet as it gets; **f22.5** here we go! Brilliant layering now as the hickory forms impressive layers with both red and black liquorice. The manuka honey is placed with precision; **b23** takes a bit of time to get out of the blocks, but once it gets going there is no stopping it. Busy, complex bourbon. *45% (90 proof). sc.*

Iron Smoke Straight Four Grain Bourbon Whiskey Aged a Minimum of 2 Years batch n. 29, bott 11-22-19 db **(87.5) n22 t22.5 f21 b22** I was really looking forward to this bottling as in the past their Four Grain has been a source of delight. And while this isn't bad, it doesn't hit the heights expected due to a slightly over-enthusiastic oiliness. What we used to call "dirty" in the old days isn't exactly that here, but the hefty cut combined with the smoke makes for a complex but testing bourbon. *40% (80 proof).*

⬩ **Iron Smoke Straight Bourbon Whiskey Four Grain Aged a Minimum of 2 Years** batch no. 34, bott 10-1-20 db **(94) n23** though there is the vaguest hint of a generous cut, it is the extraordinary dexterity of the wispy smoke and salted heather honey which concentrates the mind...; **t23.5** the healthy oils confirms that wide-ish cut. But there are none of the bitter tones that accompany spirit taken too far from the heart. Instead, corn oil and hickory combine for a slow build of jam tart and muscovado sugars; **f24** now it reaches a supreme crescendo with vanillas weaving into soften, and a little ulmo honey, too. Meanwhile the traditional liquorice/hickory tannins present the seal of bourbon. The dark chocolate flourish is almost an act of conceit...; **b23.5** I think it was last year's Four Grain that let me down slightly of the Iron Smoke family. Not this time: it has hit back with a bourbon of outstanding complexity...and which just gets better and better as it progresses. Indeed, the finish is as long and delicious as it gets... *40% (80 proof).*

KINGS COUNTY DISTILLERY Brooklyn, New York.
Kings County Distillery Bottled-in-Bond Empire Rye Four Years Old dist Spring 2015, bott Fall 2019 db **(90.5) n22** slightly extra on the cut leaves louder oils to drown out some of the rye intensity; **t23.5** sweet, oily and juicy, the spices take no time in running the show. Brilliant mocha, liquorice and molasses at the midpoint, but it is fleeting; **f22** dry and oily. The vanilla has a dusty quality; **b23** very oily and, spices apart, moderately subdued by comparison to their sublime 51% version. *50% (100 proof).*

Kings County Distillery Peated Rye Aged 2 Years or More batch no. 2 db **(94) n23 t24 f23 b24** From those who brought you Peated Bourbon, Kings Country now offer their Peated Rye version. It takes a while or the palate to adjust to these unusual signals, but once it does it is a joy all the way... Brilliant! *45% (90 proof).*

Kings County Distillery Straight Bourbon Blender's Reserve Aged 5 Years batch no. 1 db **(94.5) n23 t23.5 f24 b24** This distillery is seriously impressing me... Another big experience... *52.5% (105 proof).*

TACONIC DISTILLERY Stanfordville, New York.
Taconic Dutchess Private Reserve Straight Bourbon Whiskey db **(86) n21.5 t22 f21 b21.5.** A pretty bourbon, with the sugars sitting in the right place, if sometimes over enthusiastically. Good spice balance, roastiness and generous oils. Also, some decent rye in that mash bill it seems. *45%*

Taconic Straight Bourbon Whiskey db **(92.5) n23 t23.5 f23 b23** I well remember their bourbon from last year: this appears to have upped a gear...not only in strength but in far better usage of the sugars. *57.5% (115 proof).*

Taconic Straight Rye Whiskey db **(91.5) n22.5 t23.5 f22.5 b23** If memory serves, this is the same distillery which came up with a resounding rye last year. This, though, has a different feel with the oak enclosing in on the grain like a python gets all up close and personal to a lamb. *57.5% (115 proof).*

TOMMYROTTER DISTILLERY Buffalo, New York.
Tommyrotter Triple Barrel American Whiskey batch no. 3 French oak Finish **(88.5) n22 t22.5 f22 b22** Despite using three barrels, it as though the caramel has merged many of the facets to create a continuous flavour stream. Not as a complex as I hoped for, but not a whiskey to turn down a second glass of. *46% (92 proof). nc ncf.*

WIDOW JANE DISTILLERY Brooklyn, New York.
Baby Jane Bourbon Whiskey batch no.1 db **(85.5) n21 t22 f21 b21.5** Jane is a chubby little thing, displaying plenty of baby fat. Sweet, though, with an enjoyable molasses and nougat theme. *45.5% (91 proof).*

North Carolina
BLUE RIDGE DISTILLING CO. Golden Valley, North Carolina.
Defiant American Single Malt 100% malted barley, bott code: 307/18 04:43 L32 db **(81.5)** n18 t22.5 f20.5 b20.5 Wow! I see they have done nothing to reduce the cut since I last tasted this, resulting in a challengingly feinty nose. Must say, though, that the malty, ulmo honey on delivery is a delicious surprise! 41% (81 proof).

Defiant Rye Whisky bott code: 066/18 05:26 L32 db **(86.5)** n21.5 t22 f21.5 b21.5 With the exception of slightly more honey on delivery, the tasting notes (and quality of rye) remains absolutely identical to the last time I tasted this! 46% (92 proof).

Defiant Rye Whisky bott code: 082/19 db **(84.5)** n20.5 t21 f22 b21 A nougat-laden rye which tends to suggest, correctly, that the cut is a lot less disciplined than it ought to be. The grain appears to manifest itself with an attractive honeyed swirl towards the midpoint. 46%

BROAD BRANCH DISTILLERY Winston-Salem, North Carolina.
Broad Branch Rye Fidelity Aged 6 Years charred new oak barrels, barrel no. 37 db **(85)** n21 t22 f20.5 b21.5 There is no doubting the intensity of the rye itself which blends in with the vanillas and butterscotch from the oak to good effect. And the heather honey at the midpoint is truly superb. The spices are also in fine fettle. However, the smokiness claimed on the back label comes from the cut being a little too generous for its own good. Indeed, those minor feints have enough influence to slightly lessen the complexity on the finish and leave an oily residue. It will be interesting to see if future bottlings reflect a correction of this. What we are looking for is High Fidelity... 45% (90 proof). ncf sc.

Ohio
AMERICAN FREEDOM DISTILLERY Columbus, Ohio
Soldier Commanders Select Bourbon Whiskey Aged 12 Years db **(82.5)** n20 t21.5 f21 b20 One of the most yeasty whiskeys I have tasted in many a year. A defiant steak of hickory and liquorice gives it its bourbon stripes. 48.5% (97 proof).

Horse Soldier Premium Straight Bourbon Whiskey Aged a Minimum of 2 Years db **(89.5)** n22 t22.5 f22.5 b22.5 Unerringly pleasant and polite. 43.5% (87 proof). ncf.

Horse Soldier Reserve Barrel Strength Bourbon Whiskey db **(95.5)** n23.5 t24.5 f23.5 b24 Uncannily beautiful. 58.45% (116.9 proof).

Horse Soldier Signature Small Batch Bourbon db **(91)** n22 t23.5 f22.5 b23 This isn't a small batch whiskey: it's a very naughty boy. A bourbon that refuses to behave... 47.5%

MIDDLE WEST SPIRITS Columbus, Ohio
OYO Michelone Reserve Bourbon Whiskey db **(86)** n22.5 t22 f20 b21.5 A mainly attractive, restrained bourbon showing limited age and therefore depth. Lovely small grains to the busy nose and the sugars rise early before the buttery spices begin, but runs out of steam quite soon after. Not too happy with the tangy finish. 45% (90 proof).

Oregon
CLEAR CREEK DISTILLERY Portland, Oregon.
McCarthy's Oregon Single Malt Aged 3 Years batch W16-01, bott 6 May 16 db **(88.5)** n22 t23 f21.5 b22 For the first time since I tasted their first bottlings – in the days when my beard was still black – this whiskey has changed. Appears to have far less copper in the system to give the normal all-round richness; this is quite apparent on the nose and finish in particular. But they appear to have upped the peat ratio to good effect. 42.5% (85 proof)

HOUSE SPIRITS DISTILLERY Portland, Oregon.
Westward American Single Malt Whiskey new American oak barrels, bott code: L9 067 0010 db **(84)** n21.5 t22 f20.5 b20 Well, it is certainly different. Not sure the last time I tasted such a dramatic variance between the sweetness and bitterness. Or such huge but random flavours. The problem is that it never quite resolves itself. Or finds something close to balance. Love the delivery, when the gristy barley sweetness is just budding. But from then after, it is every man for himself: American Pioneer spirit, indeed! 45% (90 proof). ncf.

OREGON SPIRIT DISTILLERS Bend, Oregon.
Oregon Spirit Distillers Straight American Bourbon Aged 4 Years charred new American oak barrels, barrel series no. 150704 db **(88.5)** n22 t23 f21 b22.5 A truly lovely bourbon of the nutty and enigmatically sweet style basting a deeply enjoyable mouthfeel. The finish is perhaps its Achilles heel with a little too much dryness present and even a degree of bitterness. But until then both the nose and delivery rejoice in its hazelnut praline persona and its softness of touch. The strands of Lubeck marzipan are also to be celebrated and admired. (CV) 47% (94 proof).

RANSOM SPIRITS Sheridan, Oregon.

Ransom The Emerald 1865 batch no. 005 db **(86.5) n21 t23 f21 b21.5** "This whiskey rings a bell", thought I. Brilliant delivery, magnificently complex grains at play, but OTT feints. I've tasted this one before, I concluded. And, on checking in a previous Bible, I see I had a couple of years back, though an earlier bottling and then not called The Emerald. Brilliant Irish style mix of malted and unmalted barley. But just need to sort that cut out. *43.8%.*

Ransom Rye, Barley, Wheat Whiskey Aged a Minimum of 2 Years batch no. 003 db **(85.5) n21 t22 f21 b21.5** A little too much earthiness to this for its own good, meaning the wheat has to fight hard to get its sweet and spicy message out there. Needs a tad more copper in the system to get the most out of this whiskey, as a metallic spark appears missing. Just love this distillery's labels, by the way: real class. *63.4%.*

ROGUE SPIRITS Newport, Oregon.

Rogue Dead Guy Whiskey ocean aged in oak barrels at least 1 year db **(86) n22.5 t22 f20.5 b21.** Ah, I remember this guy from a year or two back: I had a bone to pick with him about his finish. Well, not the preferred drink of the Grim Reaper now, and makes good use of its malty, peppery structure. The finish is still a bit tangy and salty. But a big improvement. *40% (80 proof)*

Pennsylvania
DAD'S HAT RYE DISTILLERY Bristol, Pennsylvania.

Dad's Hat Pennsylvania Straight Rye Whiskey Aged Minimum 3 Years db **(91.5) n23 t23.5 f22 b23** The truest rye I have seen from you yet: I take my hat off to you guys...quite literally...! *47.5% (95 proof).*

South Carolina
PALMETTO DISTILLERY Anderson, South Carolina.

Palmetto SC Whiskey bott code: 325 04 db **(85) n21.5 t23 f19.5 b21** Prefer this to the last bottling I sampled. Here the emphasis is on chocolate-caramel with a delicious spiced ulmo honey back up. But the cut here is a little tardy, which damages both the nose and, especially, the finish. But I'm clinging on to the memories of the rousing delivery – and so are my taste buds.... *44.65% (89.3 proof).*

Tennessee
CORSAIR ARTISAN DISTILLERY Nashville, Tennessee.

Corsair Dark Rye American Rye Malt Whiskey Aged 8 Months batch no. 3 db **(95.5) n23.5 t24.5 f23.5 b24** I am assuming that the rye has been roasted into chocolate form in the same way chocolate malt is made from barley (and first used in a whisky by Glenmorangie a good decade or so ago). With rye having a far starker flavour profile than barley, the chocolate effect has to work harder to make an impact. But it certainly does as those sweet cocoa notes filter through at the finale. A whiskey-lover's whisky. *42.5% (85 proof). 385 bottles.*

Corsair Triple Smoke American Single Malt Whiskey Aged 8 Months batch no. 319 db **(92.5) n24 t22.5 f23 b23** Bottled a tad too young, despite the high pleasure value. Even so, a very complex offering. *40% (80 proof). 252 bottles.*

Texas
BALCONES DISTILLERY Waco, Texas.

Balcones 1 Texas Single Malt Aged at Least 26 Months in Oak batch no. SM19-1, bott 3.12.19 db **(84.5) n22 t21.5 f20 b21** Nowhere near Balcone's normal high standard with the cut as wide as a Texas rib eye, even more fatty and thick but with nothing like the taste. Some big natural caramel and lighter molasses...but it isn't enough. This weekend of 20-21 July 2019 I am tasting all my remaining Texas whiskeys for this forthcoming Bible. Because it was 50 years ago this weekend that man first walked on the Moon, an event I remember vividly as a child watching in thrilled awe on our black and white television with my now departed parents. And Texas played a key part in that amazing event, something that will never be forgotten by those who witnessed it. Houston: this whiskey has a slight problem... *53%. nc ncf.*

Balcones FR.OAK Texas Single Malt Whisky Aged at least 36 Months in Oak batch no. FROAK19-1, bott 5/30/19 db **(95.5) n24 t24 f23.5 b24** While I was mightily impressed with their previous French Oak matured malt, this one here really knocked me back in my chair with delight. You get the feeling that they have quickly learned how to better control the more masculine chars of the French tannin and nowhere better does this shew but on the rich but magnificently complex nose. The sugars are pristine and sharp, the liquorice tones mingling and with and controlling the spices. You expect this to fall apart slightly on delivery, but it doesn't. Indeed the early Demerara sugars mutate into molasses while, against the odds, the barley itself can be detected alive and well clinging to the roof the mouth, with a burnt raisin, fruity muscovado sugar accompaniment. Perhaps only Texas can provide us with a malt this mind-bogglingly big....(CV) *61.9% (123.8 proof). nc ncf.*

Balcones Peated Texas Single Malt Whisky Aged at least 36 Months in Oak batch no. PEAT19-1, bott 10.26.19 db **(95) n24 t24.5 f23 b23.5** It is interesting how extra time in cask can subtract as well as add. Their last peated malt was about year younger if I remember correctly. The smoke and tannin fitted like a hand in glove. This is still a significantly stunning malt, on the nose especially, where the peat forms pretty patterns as it dovetails with the tannin. But the extra oak here has slightly nudged the balance – so this is now drier overall and the bigger flavours seemingly weighted towards the overture on the palate. Having said that, the mix of heather and ulmo honeys and the upping of the spice means you are still in for a spectacular treat and, make no mistake, this is one of the great malt whiskeys produced anywhere in the USA during the last year. *65.2% (130.4 proof). nc ncf.*

Balcones Texas Blue Corn Bourbon Aged at least 34 Months in Oak batch no. BCB19-1, bott 6.25.19 db **(94.5) n23 t24 f23.5 b24** After the disappointment of the wheated bourbon, normal service has been resumed....and with interest! All kinds of dark sugars vie for pole position on both nose and delivery. But the hickory and cream toffee mix meet with bold spices so both nose and delivery are treated to a scintillating experience. Wonderful finish, also, with that creaminess increasing as the corn is gather and the ulmo honey adding just the right touch of elegant sweetness to a bourbon so big. (CV) *65% (130 proof). nc ncf.*

Balcones Texas Rye Cask Strength Aged at Least 27 Months in Oak batch no. RCS19-1, bott 1.29.19 db **(95) n23 t24 f23.5 b24.5** Every bit as beautiful and on the money as their 15-month old rye was lacklustre. It is this type of excellence I normally associate with this distillery. *63.3%. nc ncf.*

Balcones Texas Single Malt Rum Cask Finished Aged at Least 27 Months in Oak batch no. SMR19-1, bott 1.15.19 db **(91.5) n22.5 t23.5 f22.5 b23** Rum cask whiskeys have a tendency to be hard as nails. This is one very big nail... *63.5%. nc ncf.*

Balcones Texas Single Malt Single Barrel Aged at Least 24 Months in Oak cask no. 17222, American oak cask, dist 5.3.17, bott 6.13.19 db **(88) n22.5 t22 f21.5 b22** Enjoyable and another that is not quite up the distillery's usual brilliant standard. *64%. nc ncf sc.*

Balcones Texas Single Malt Single Barrel Aged at Least 65 Months in Oak cask no. 2642, American oak cask, dist 1.8.14, bott 6.11.19 db **(95) n23.5 t24 f23.5 b24** So thick and dense, probably has more gravitational pull than that Moon these Texans went out and lassoed 50 years ago... *66.4%. nc ncf sc.*

Balcones Texas Single Malt Single Barrel Aged at Least 60 Months in Oak cask no. 2504, American oak cask, dist 2.17.14, bott 2.20.19 db **(94.5) n23.5 t24 f23 b24** A wonderfully honeyed and metallic malt from when the stills were younger and at times upping the richness dramatically. A five-year-old with an attractive aloofness. *64.8%. nc ncf sc.*

Balcones Texas Wheated Bourbon Aged at least 34 Months in Oak batch no. WHB19-1, bott 9.2.19 db **(83.5) n21 t21.5 f20 b21** Unusually feinty for a Balcones. This is a distillery that has rightly earned its high reputation of getting its cuts right, so when even a relatively marginal off-cut can be noticed, then it sends shock waves. Of the favour profile, after the big vanilla and caramel statement the extra spices certainly point towards the wheat but, overall, this is a pretty coarse experience for a Balcones. (CV) *61.3% (122.6 proof). nc ncf.*

Balcones True Blue Cask Strength Straight Corn Whiskey Aged at least 31 Months in Oak batch no. TCB19-1, bott 6.27.19 db **(95) n23.5 t24 f23.5 b24** Ye Gods...!!! This is so good. Pretty estery on the nose and with mocha on both the aroma and finish there is something of old, high grade Demerara Pot Still rum about this: that is a hell of a compliment, believe me. This is a chewing whiskey of the highest order. Sweet chestnuts are noticeable at almost every point, as is the high quality of the distillate – the cut is clean but has enough corn oils to make the enjoyment last for a very impressive amount of time. Love the controlled spice, too, so as not to distract from the complex whole. Brilliant! (CV) *63.1% (126.2 proof). nc ncf.*

DALLAS DISTILLERIES Garland, Texas.
Herman Marshall Texas Bourbon batch 18/12 **(90.5) n22.5 t23 f22.5 b22.5** A very confident and beautifully-made Texan which never sits still. *46% (92 proof).*

DEVILS RIVER WHISKEY San Antonio, Texas.
Devils River Barrel Strength Texas Bourbon batch SW8325 **(87.5) n22 t21.5 f22 b22** A light, delicate Texan with the emphasis on a vanilla and almost cream soda theme. Busy spices up the salivation levels to a considerable degree, while the light oils from the uncut spirit stretch the icing sugar almost to breaking point. Nothing like so hefty as your average Texas bourbon despite the strength. And as the bottle suggests: "sin responsibly". *48.5% (117 proof).*

FIRESTONE AND ROBERTSON DISTILLING CO LTD Fort Worth, Texas.

TX Texas Straight Bourbon bott code: 20181214B **(91)** n22.5 t23 f22.5 b23 A well-made, satisfying whiskey. Once you get past its unusual firmness on both nose and palate, it becomes pretty easy to start picking out the impressive layering and balance. Another quality bourbon from Texas. *45% (90 proof). Firestone and Robertson Distilling Co Ltd.*

FIVE POINTS DISTILLING Forney, Texas.

Lone Elm Single Barrel Texas Straight Wheat Whiskey barrel no. 100 barreled 9/13 db **(95)** n23.5 t24 f23.5 b24 You could stand a spoon up in a glass of this monster whiskey. This is as thick on the palate as whiskey gets and the world's oak tannins appear to be having their annual congress there. Heavily represented is the maple syrup branch of oaky sugars which dominate both the nose and early delivery. And they need to be there, or this would be a puckering-fest, as the tannins are relentless; this is a whiskey to appeal to the Pappy Van Winkle devotees....and those with a good half hour to spare just to understand what kind of mighty straight wheat they are dealing with here. Plenty of mocha and liquorice concentrate, too, which arrive and disappear in the myriad layers. With this much outrageous oak on show, mind the splinters... (CV) *53.8% (107.6proof).*

Lone Elm Texas Straight Wheat Whiskey db **(87)** n21 t22.5 f21.5 b22 Texas doesn't really do subtle. And there is no evidence of it here, either. The cut is a wide one, without any major problem from feints. This means the extra oils plus the oils off the grain make for a spirit very high in viscosity: this is a chewing, not a sippin' whiskey. Superb initial delivery, with liquorice levels high. The sugars are as thick as the oils, but wilt slightly as the tannins bite and the oils thicken at the death. Not technically perfect for sure, but the sweet-dry ratio makes for a fascinating experience. (CV) *45% (90 proof).*

GARRISON BROTHERS Hye, Texas.

Garrison Brothers Balmorhea Texas Straight Bourbon Whiskey #1 panhandle white corn, corn harvest 2013, dist 2014, bott 2019 db **(96.5)** n24 t24 f24 b24.5 Tasting this just about 50 years ago to the very minute of the first man setting foot on the Moon. He had started his journey in Texas...of course... And the whiskey? Out of this world class... *57.5% (115 proof).*

Garrison Brothers Balmorhea Texas Straight Bourbon Whiskey 2020 Release food grade #1 white corn, dist 2015 db **(96.5)** n24 t24.5 f23.5 b24.5 Almost exactly a year ago today (20th July 2019, today is 19th July 2020) I tasted last year's bottling the exact moment 50 years to the second man first walked on the moon — the crew having been supported by their team in Houston, Texas. Today, I taste this on the final day of tasting for the Jim Murray Whiskey Bible 2021: this is number 1,244 with just eight more to do. So I am ending my own epic journey through a Covid-19 ridden world, by far the hardest assignment of my long whiskey life. But when you encounter a whiskey like this and can help the world to share such beauty, you know that four months of near total isolation was in fact worth it... *57.5% (115 proof).*

◇ **Garrison Brothers Balmorhea Texas Straight Bourbon Whiskey 2021 Release** food grade #1 white corn, dist 2015 db **(96)** n23.5 just breath in those controlled, sweetened black peppers. The corn is everywhere, but so is the oak which seems to intensify in its timber qualities – and timbre - with each sniff without remotely going over the top. That is some trick... Toasty, but no burning. The hickory and liquorice magnificently entwined. It's a nose which states, proudly: "I am bourbon" ....; **t24** it's for moments like this you go through so many thousands of average whiskies. The delivery here makes you purr and salivate at the same time. The dark sugars alone take some time to work out, but there is a fabulous balance to them, so at no time does it begin to overtake the throbbing roastiness of the oak, or the pulsing spices which arrive early but only in perfect tandem with all else about them; **f24** when you are not sure when the finish begins, you know you are on to a winner. There is a just-so creaminess to this finale that is so rare in any whiskey, and the layering of chocolate, black liquorice, and molasses. Don't be in a hurry, though, because this finish ends in its own time...which isn't any time soon...; **b24.5** the last 12 months have been difficult for many of us. But the spirits are first nudged and then shaken by this exceptional bourbon, until your mind and body come alive. You need the Murray Method for best results, because this is one tactile and sensual beast of a bourbon. And it is so intense and complex, don't even start thinking about understanding this whiskey until you have just spat out your third full mouthful. Usually, Balmorhea juts proudly above the stack of great whiskeys from Garrison. This year is a bit different: both their Cowboy bourbon and Laguna Madre stand shoulder to shoulder. If on only a slightly lower dais. I cannot thank the great people of Garrison Brothers enough for raising our spirits and bringing a smile of joy in these difficult times. It is too early to say if any awards have been won. But whether they have or not, I toast you all! *57.5% (115 poof).* 🍷

⬦ **Garrison Brothers Cowboy Bourbon Texas Straight Bourbon Whiskey 2020 Release** food grade #1 white corn db **(95.5) n24** ridiculous nose. On one hand there is a little note suggesting no great age to the spirit and on the other, much bigger one, we have a macho gathering of thumping tannins with lusty liquorice and herculean hickory topping the bill. The spices nip and the molasses ensures it is never too sweet; **t24** just so sensual. The corn oils glide over the palate imparting in equal measure mocha and corn-rich Demerara sugars and ulmo honey. The spices tease and pucker while the ulmo honey and molasses compensate. Everything is about balance, as huge as this bourbon is; **f23.5** settles on the more slightly bitter aspect with the sugars at last running out of steam, while the tannins pile on anyway; **b24** Cowboy...? Beware good people of Garrison Brothers! You'll be cancelled for alleged sexism....! Cowpeople or Cowgirl, surely... And the one thing that doesn't need cancelling in life is a near perfect whiskey such as this. I have spent half an hour searching for a fault...and, other than detecting its comparative youth, failed miserably. Such a huge whiskey. Yet such grace and elegance to accompany it. *66.95% (133.9 poof).*

⬦ **Garrison Brothers Laguna Madre Texas Straight Bourbon Whiskey 2020 Release** finished for four years in Limousin oak. food grade #1 white corn db **(95.5) n24.5** the closest nose I have found yet to certain well-aged Indian single malt: huge yet somehow controlled tannin offering a big roast coffee note (and, if you must know, a blend of very high roast Java/Sumatra/Columbian in that order of high percentage). But that is only the start. There is wafer biscuit. The sweetness again is a blend: Manuka honey, toasted caramel and slightly burned Dundee cake. The spices are incredibly well controlled and defined... This is a borderline 25/25...; **t24** just ridiculously slick. Corn oils first and foremost, carrying with them extraordinary, labyrinthine, layers of honeycomb, marzipan, treacle, thickened corn oil to the point of solidity. As for the roasty sugars...where the hell do you start...???? **f23** just the odd bitter note, as might be expected after so much roastiness coming at you from a single glass. But it is hardly damaging to the bourbon and the spices and sugars continue their cat and mouse games, able accompanied by the thick corn oil; **b24** the definition of a stretch limousin whiskey. Because so few whiskies in the world go on, from first sniff, to last dying ember quite as long as this. Few whiskeys on the planet are quite this profound. Or beautiful. A Texan masterpiece. *50.5% (101 poof).*

⬦ **Garrison Brothers Small Batch Texas Straight Bourbon Whiskey 2020 Release Aged 3 Years** food grade #1 white corn db **(91.5) n23** the lower strength appears to allow some nuttiness to enter the fray. With the oils broken, the sugars are more prone to a drier vanilla backdrop...and that's exactly what happens here. My! This is one very gentle and polite Texan... ; **t23** the sugars, so shy on the nose, need no second invitation here. Quite thin, though, by GB standards, with the early molasses barely shewing their usual viscosity. The balance, though between those sugars and delicate corn oils remains spot on; **f22** dries towards as relatively simplistic vanilla fade out; **b23.5** "food grade corn": now there is one very interesting concept. A bourbon that is good enough to eat, let alone drink. Actually, I'd have to say that there is a politeness to this where the Texan hat is definitely taken off at the meal table. Both delicate and delicious! *47% (94 poof).*

⬦ **Garrison Brothers Single Barrel Texas Straight Bourbon Whiskey Aged 3 Years** food grade #1 white corn, barrel no 9336, dist 2016 db **(94.5) n23.5** the nose all but drags you into the glass. This is butch stuff, complete with droopy moustache and hair chest. The molasses and black liquorice for a fabulous combination, big enough to keep the spices in check; **t24** one of the best corn oil deliveries of the year. Just amazing... This is also quite remarkable for the relaxed way in which such intense characters form happy partnerships: no unseemly jostling for power here. The marriage between the molasses and heather honey was made somewhere around heaven, while even the black liquorice is happy to give way to its more tender red brother. Butterscotch and spices head towards the finale...; **f23** big! **b24** this is obviously a version of their small batch 2020 Release...but without any pesky water bothering it. Such a huge whiskey. But just so beautifully drawn and delivered. *59% (118 poof).*

Garrison Brothers Texas Straight Bourbon Whiskey Single Barrel Aged Three Years #1 panhandle white corn, corn harvest 2011, cask no. 3433, dist 2012 db **(93.5) n23 t23.5 f23.5 b23.5** Delicious, but Garrison's whiskey at this strength always seems a fraction under par. *47% (94 proof). sc.*

Garrison Brothers Texas Straight Bourbon Whiskey 2020 Release #1 panhandle white corn db **(94.5) n24 t23 f23.5 b24** Wanted to finish the day's tasting on a high – and even better still, a Hye!! You see I've just tasted a succession of pretty average American whiskies, and needed my confidence restored. This was earmarked for tomorrow... but great whiskey has long been regarded an excellent restorative. And, trust me, on the evidence of this it certainly is... One of those big whiskies with a gentle but charismatic character that needs you to taste as many times as you need to listen to a Handel cantata before you fully appreciate the intricate accord. *47% (94 proof).*

Cadenhead's Garrison Brothers 2014 cask no. 7117, bott 2020 db **(95.5) n24 t24 f23.5 b24** What a sensational representation of this great distillery. The nose with a purity and surety of intent and intensity is unique to this Texas whisky landmark: the blend of molasses and Manuka honey, an unerring, linear broadcast of muzzled sweetness…the liquorice and vanillas calm those sugars. The spices, also, ensure balance is honoured. And that's just on the nose. On the palate it is less a whiskey and more a rambling story to be told over a campfire. The liquorice doesn't tighten and cramp as it sometimes can, not least because of the lashings of ulmo and heather honey that pitches in to offer both a balancing sweetness but the softest, most yielding mouthfeel. Coffee and hickory abounds, too, drying and softening further. As they say in them thar parts….Yep! 60.1% (120.2 proof). 81 bottles. Selected by Peter Siegenthaler.

Cadenhead's Garrison Brothers 2015 cask no. 9057, bott 2019 db **(93) n23.5 t23.5 f23 b23** An unusually mild Garrison Brothers bourbon which reaches for the toffee within itself rather than the liquorice. And finds it! As soft and even as Garrison gets – almost to the point of docility. But if you love concentrated cream toffee, all polished off with a delightful coating of hickory, then you won't be disappointed. Have to admit I was a little surprised by this. But certainly not disappointed… 47% (92 proof). 63 bottles. Selected by Peter Siegenthaler.

IRONROOT REPUBLIC DISTILLING Denison, Texas.

Ironroot Harbinger Straight Bourbon Whiskey 32 Months Aged H2OA Edition db **(91.5) n23.5 t23 f22 b23** One of the rising stars of Texas whiskey is shining brightly here. Lovely stuff! 57.5% (115 proof). ncf.

Ironroot Hubris Straight Corn Whiskey 31 Months Aged 2020 Edition db **(87.5) n22 t22.5 f21 b22** Yay!! How I love to see straight corn whiskey – nowhere near enough of it made. This one displays above average spice – especially on the husky delivery - but there is a muffled bitterness on both the nose the palate. The sugars are relaxed but of a light mollassed variety. Decent and doesn't stint on entertainment value. But you get the feeling that better will be coming down the line. 58.90% (117.8 proof). ncf.

Ironroot Ichor Straight Bourbon Whiskey 46 Months Aged db **(93) n23.5** hang on tight, ladies and gentlemen. The first message from this aroma is that we're about to be taken on a foot to the floor ride. This is heavy duty bourbon: the aromas are thick and weighty. So hefty that the spices seem crushed just by the intent of the tannin alone…; **t24** just wow….!! A good three minutes of chewing required for this one. The corn oil is in concentrated form, thick and sticky with it. But the burnt toffee works so well with the molasses and peppers. Maybe, though, it is that giant wave of eucalyptus that pounds the taste buds early on that sets the scene and takes the breath away most. Had to say…this layered giant offers a quite incredible delivery and midpoint, which is deliciously cocoa-rich by the way…; **f22** the finish is usually the weak spot of Ironroot and, comparatively, it is here also with a little bitterness digging in; **b23.5** 61.5% (123 proof). ncf. 5th Anniversary.

Ironroot Ichor Straight Bourbon Whiskey Aged 48 Months db **(94.5) n23.5 t24 f23 b24** A bourbon behemoth very much of the hickory kind. Beautiful! 61.5% (123 proof). ncf.

KIEPERSOL DISTILLERY Tyler, Texas.

Jimmy's 100 Texas Straight Bourbon db **(86) n21.5 t22 f22 b20.5** It is not the extra strength of alcohol that is the problem here, but the unforgiving nature of the oak. To carry this amount of tannin in a bourbon there must be balancing sugars, and most have been spent here. That said, for those looking at pure oomph and eye-watering wood, you may have found your perfect mate. 50% (100 proof).

Jimmy's Through Heroes Eyes Texas Straight Bourbon db **(91) n22 t23 t22.5 b22.5** A clean, well-made bourbon with a big spicy depth. From a distance, Jimmy's Second World War goggles look like a pair of peaches on the label…and ironically there is a delicate hint of peach in the whiskey. 45% (90 proof).

RANGER CREEK DISTILLING, San Antonio, Texas.

Ranger Creek .36 Straight Texas Bourbon Aged For a Minimum of 2 Years db **(91) n23 t23 f22 b22.5** Not technically perfect, but the nose and taste profile cannot be faulted, nor the subtle range of honeys at play. 48% (96 proof).

Ranger Creek Rimfire Mesquite Smoked Texas Single Malt batch 1 **(85) n21.5 t22 f20.5 b21.** As I have never tasted anything smoked with mesquite before – especially whiskey – I will have to guess that it is the tree of the semi-desert which is imparting a strange, mildly bitter tang on the finish. Whether it is also responsible for the enormous degree of creamed toffee, I am also not sure. Enjoyable, fascinating even…but something the ol' taste buds need a bit of acclimatising to. 43% (86 proof)

TAHWAHKARO DISTILLERY Grapevine, Texas.

Tahwahkaro TAH Four Grain Bourbon Whiskey Aged Not Less Than 1 Year batch 1 **(79)** n19 t21 f19 b20 A very first effort from a new Texas distillery. Shows some lovely toffee apple touches and certainly not short on sugars and character. But appears to need a little extra copper contact to clean up the nose and finish as well as a slightly more precise cut off the stills. *48% (96 proof).*

TREATY OAK DISTILLING Ranch Drippings Springs, Texas.

Treaty Oak Distilling Ghost Hill Texas Bourbon Whiskey db **(87)** n22 t21 f22 b22 The good folk of Treaty Oak actually let us into the make-up of their mash bill: 57% Texas corn, 32% Texas wheat, 11% American barley (are we to infer that Texas is a separate country from America..?) No doubt some Texans will raise a glass of this to toast that notion...They will enjoy this whiskey, but that is providing they forgive the very slight indiscretions in the distilling itself which results in a sometimes sharp, often jarring but always full-favoured bourbon. Some real cough sweet hickory depth to this, too. *47.5% (95 proof).*

YELLOW ROSE DISTILLING Houston, Texas.

Yellow Rose Outlaw Batch Bourbon batch 16-33, made from 100% corn db **(94)** n24 t23.5 f23 b23.5 Outlaw? This should be made both legal and compulsory. Really high grade corn whiskey, even if they do call it, outlawishly, bourbon. *46% (92 proof).*

Virginia
CATOCTIN CREEK DISTILLERY Loudoun County, Virginia.

Braddock Oak Single Barrel Rye Whisky batch B17K1 db **(90)** n22.5 t23 f22 b22.5 It is heart-warming to see a distillery dedicated to making rye. Still the odd technical off-note but I am sure this will be corrected with time and experience. Plenty here to savour. *46% sc.*

Catoctin Creek Cask Proof Roundstone Rye Whisky batch B17A2, charred new oak barrels db **(88)** n21.5 t22.5 f22 b22 So much flavour. But needs to get those cuts cleaner to maximise the rye profile. *57.8% (115.6 proof). ncf.*

Catoctin Creek Roundstone Cask Proof Edition Rye Whiskey batch no. 18919 db **(87)** n20.5 t23.5 f21 b22 Presumably German stills at work here as that unmistakable light feint note just chips the top off the peak of the higher rye notes. Masses of charm and flavour on delivery, and buckets of spice, too. With a little cleaning up, this could be such a substantial and classy whiskey. *58% (116 proof). ncf sc. 125 bottles.*

Catoctin Creek Roundstone Distillers Edition Rye Whiskey batch no. 18621 db **(87.5)** n21 t22.5 f22 b22 This is cleaner than Cask Proof above. But it just its lacks muscular rye complexity and is much more happy for a dithering grain note to merge with the tannins and lingering oils to form a slightly nutty chocolate theme. *46% (92 proof). ncf sc.*

Catoctin Creek Roundstone Rye Whisky batch B17G1, charred new oak barrels db **(88)** n21.5 t23.5 f21 b22 The brighter end of the distillery's narrow spectrum: the rye here really is deliciously on song! *46% (92 proof). ncf.*

Catoctin Creek Roundstone Single Barrel Virginia Rye Whiskey batch no. 19A01 db **(88)** n19.5 t23 f22.5 b23 Again, the wide cut acts as a bit of a ball and chain around this whiskey. But when it gets rolling, the salivating qualities of the crisp rye and then chocolate and honey notes are really impressive. Most enjoyable. *40% (80 proof). ncf sc.*

COPPER FOX DISTILLERY Sperryville, Virginia.

Copper Fox Original American Single Malt batch no. 159, finished in a second used bourbon barrel db **(93.5)** n22.5 t24 f23 b24 Technically, as good as anything I have seen from this distillery. Superbly distilled and very cleverly engineered in the cask to really pump out the personality. Big stuff! *48% (96 proof). ncf.*

Copper Fox Original Rye batch no. 136, finished in a second used bourbon barrel db **(92)** n22 t24 f22.5 b23.5 A couple of days ago I was out walking in the glorious, lonely countryside around my UK home and, once more, I came face to face with a fox - just how I had done on the day I last tasted this whiskey. Once more we stood eye to eye regarding the other...until finally off he trotted in his own time. On the way back home I pondered this incident and I hoped my research team had come up with Rick Wasmund's latest rye. And what do you know... *45% (90 proof). ncf.*

◈ **Copper Fox Peachwood American Single Malt** finished toasted peach wood and oak, batch no. LIB **(95)** n23.5 the distillery's unique "bonfire" style smokiness is more than evident here – taking me back to my childhood days in Surrey with my father burning all the scraps of wood and leaves on his allotment. Not as acidic as some smoked whiskies with a sub-current of toasted vanilla mallows...; t24 a magnificently distilled malt with a gorgeous light oiliness achieved without recourse to extra feints. Despite the bombardment of tannins, the malt still has a huge say and is the thick, underlying theme. But this is Copper Fox, so the tannin involvement is serious, though noticeably restrained. It is as though the malt has sightly burnt edges. But I suppose it is the delivery which really surprises with an instant dose of molasses, softening the way for the following It...; **f23.5** a deeply attractive finish, still boasting plenty of malt but now with ulmo honey and vanilla taking the lead. That nibbling, burnt tannin note offers the most beautiful counter; **b24** if you want a good dose of controlled tannin, then Rick Wasmund's your man. On this evidence peach wood is lot more forgiving than apple wood and refuses to blast a fruity aspect all over the whisky and appears much more happy to add an extra dimension entirely in keeping with the distillery's style. If your Whiskey Club is thinking of buying a bottle to try...then chip in! For if this distillery has produced anything better than this, then it is escaping my memory.... *48% (96 proof)*

RESERVOIR DISTILLERY Richmond, Virginia.

Reservoir Distillery Bourbon Whiskey year 18, batch no. 1 db **(94.5) n23.5 t23.5 f23.5 b24** They have excelled: a Reservoir that is so damned good... *50% (100 proof).*

Reservoir Distillery Bourbon 100% Corn Aged a Minimum of 2 Years 5 gallon barrels db **(94.5) n23 t24 f23.5 b24** A very well made Corn Whiskey (hang on: they are mysteriously still calling this a bourbon..) which successfully extracts the full oily value from the grain and sets about using its considerable charm to further the cause of the ulmo honey and butterscotch.... not to mention the profound spice. It is all rather beautiful...and technically of a very high standard. *50% (100 proof).*

Reservoir Distillery Grey Ghost Bourbon 2019 100% Corn Aged 4.5 Years 5 gallon barrels db **(83.5) n21 t20 f21.5 b21.5** Nowhere near as well made as the 2-year-old corn, above, and abounds in one too many slightly off-key notes. All rather green, too, despite its age. *50% (100 proof).*

Reservoir Distillery Holland's Milkman Aged a Minimum of 2 Years 5 gallon barrels, aged milk stout beer barrel finish db **(87) n21.5 t23 f22 b20.5** Can't say I'm much a fan of the prevailing hop note, as modest as it is. But there is just enough in there to upset the balance what had previously been an excellent joust between the sharp tannins and the milk chocolate. *53.5% (107 proof).*

Reservoir Distillery Hunter & Scott Bourbon Aged 1.5 Years 5 and 10 gallon barrels db **(91.5) n22 t23.5 f23 b23** Be thankful that the tannins have thrown in some genuinely toasty, almost earthy, elements here. Otherwise those sugars would spin out of control. Rarely have I seen such concentrated forms of Demerara let loose in a whiskey, linking up with the corn oil to not just hit but remain at every taste bud it can find. Those with a sweet tooth will merrily kill for this. Those of us with more moderate tastes will also find themselves seduced. One way or another, you stand no chance: just enjoy... *45% (90 proof).*

Reservoir Distillery Hunter & Scott Rye Aged 1.5 Years 5 and 10 gallon barrels db **(93.5) n23.5 t23.5 f23 b23.5** Although matured in very small barrels, it is still the grain that has star billing on both nose and delivery. Everything about this whiskey is intense and urgent: the rye is piercing, almost shrill, on the nose, the sturdy oak no more than a dais; and so it is on delivery – exactly. There is something of the chocolate liqueur on the finale. One hell of a rye! *45% (90 proof).*

Reservoir Distillery Maison de Cuivre Aged a Minimum of 2 Years 5 gallon barrels, Merlot barrel finish db **(92.5) n23.5 t23 f22.5 b23.5** First thing to report is that the Merlot barrel is free of sulphur. And those of you who have found whisky matured in Merlot elsewhere around the world will know, that has not always been the case....with dire consequences. Some lovely dry pepper notes ingratiate both on nose and delivery into a more robust liquorice note. If there is a fruitiness to be found, it seems more like small grains going about their work rather than any grape. Just-so amounts of maple syrup enter the fray from just before the midpoint and hang around, even blending into a little cocoa late on. An elegant, often brisk but never brusque whisky *50% (100 proof).*

Reservoir Distillery Rye Whiskey year 18, batch no. 1 db **(89) n22.5 t23 f21 b22** An annoying bitter note just takes the edge off what would have been a superb rye. Grrrr! *50% (100 proof).*

Reservoir Distillery Rye Whiskey 100% Rye Aged a Minimum of 2 Years 5 gallon barrels db **(81) n21 t21.5 f19 b19.5** A strange one, this. The nose gives mixed messages, both of lively rye and something very amiss. The delivery initially follows the route of the sharp heartwarming grain. But even as the ulmo honey begins to appear, so do the myriad puckering, tangy faults. A whiskey probably lost somewhere in the fermentation, I suspect. 50% (100 proof).

Reservoir Distillery Wheat Whiskey year 18, batch no. 1 db **(93) n24 t24 f22 b23** A top (reservoir) dog wheat whiskey. A *50% (100 proof).*

Reservoir Distillery Wheat Whiskey 100% Wheat Aged a Minimum of 2 Years 5 gallon barrels db **(89) n21.5 t23 f22 b22.5** All kinds of crispy Demerara sugar on display here and makes for some duet when the spices are unleashed by the wheat. A curious bitter thread runs throughout this. Big stuff, all the same. *50% (100 proof).*

SILVERBACK DISTILLERY Afton, Virginia.

Blackback Straight Bourbon Whiskey Aged 3 Years batch no. 18 db **(89) n22.5** soft and eschews a roasty style for a more relaxed caramel and cod liver oil one...; **t22.5** the house style of molten sugar has its fingerprints all over this from the start. Does finally tart and toast up a little, but then a lovely hazelnut praline depths develops; **f22** lots of nutty vanilla, though thins out quickly; **b22** for those who prefer their bourbons a little nutty... *43% (86 proof). sc.*

Blackback Straight Rye Whiskey Alpha Series Aged 4 Years barrel no. 51 db **(95) n23.5** fruity and crisp as every self-respecting rye whiskey should be. Impressively intense, too. So much so, the nose has the spicy quality of a Grand-cru wine...but without the grape...; **t24.5** I am astounded. This is absolutely sublime rye that gives a master class in how to be both bold and assertive yet yielding enough to allow the tannins to make an impassioned contribution. Like on the nose, one is reminded of a Chateau Lafite, or Margeaux...but without the grape. How!!! It pulls off this amazing trick, I really don't know.... As for the grain input...just bloody wow!!! **f23** OK, just a little too oily at the very death – so this was made by humans after all. But before we get to that point there is a wonderfully glazed molasses moment or three, where the rye appears to be captured in the molten sugars but able to radiate its crisp, slightly chocolatey message...; **b24** not sure if this is a Virginian rye or from Pennsylvania. Surely the latter: after all, it was there that rye whiskey was perfected. And while this may not be perfect, they have had a damn good try in making it so. The impact of the rye is truly thrilling. Make no mistake: this is a stunning rye whiskey. *55% (110 proof). sc.*

Blackback Straight Rye Whiskey Lucky 13 Aged 3 Years batch no. 25 db **(87) n22 t23 f20.5 b21.5** A liquorice-laden rye thumping its chest with personality. But not distilled to the same degree of excellence as their Alpha Series Rye (above), resulting in a tangy finish. Can't fault the second and third flavour-waves after delivery, though – a gorgeous molasses and mocha concoction that is immensely pleasing. *43% (86 proof).*

Christine Single Barrel Virginia Bourbon Whiskey Riggleman Reserve batch no. 1 db **(94) n23.5** both curvaceous and with a playful spicy nip at the same time...intriguing... and classically bourbony; **t23.5** full-bodied and rounded from the off: kind of like the nose, but now with much more flesh on the bone. The spices are launched from every angle and in increasing intensity. Natural caramels. Form a chewy bridge on which the manuka honey and liquorice crosses. This is very serious, beautifully structured bourbon...; **f23** drying, toasty tannins begin to bite deep. A shell of molasses ensures the balance is never breeched; **b24** I have never met Christine Riggleman. But if she is anything like this whiskey, then I'd sure like to. Distinguished and a little classy. *56% (112 proof). sc. 179 bottles.*

VIRGINIA DISTILLERY CO. Lovinston, Virginia.

Virginia Distillery Co. Courage & Conviction Prelude American Single Malt Whisky db **(88) n22 t22.5 f21.5 b22** Everything about this youthful single malt screams "new distillery!". And what a gorgeous distillery this is, located in the stunning highlands of Virginia, close to the Blue Ridge Mountains. Even if the Scotch Whisky Association arrogantly believe that only Scotland possesses such things as highlands and litigiously and ridiculously claim otherwise should any distillery in the world dare mention the fact. Virginia has them also. There's a little feint on the early nose, but this soon burns off with a little Murray Method handling, then an overriding degree of copper and light vanilla. But the nose is ostensibly buttered up new make – and from new stills. The flavour profile is rich from the wide cut but then increasingly, and deliciously, malty. Fascinating! I have seen some of what is coming further down the line. It is ,technically better than this, as you would expect from a fledgling copper pot still distillery, And promising some glorious days ahead. *46% (92 proof).*

VIRGINIA SPIRITS

◈ **Thirty-Six Short Single Malt Aged 2 Years and 2 Months** oak & bourbon barrels **(92) n22.5** the oak has already formed a poker-straight and firm backdrop for the gently spiced marzipan. Though there is a new-make freshness to this, the effect is fleeting; **t23** glorious hotch-potch of salivating and intense barley notes, all brazenly on the young side, perfectly aligning with a much more spiced oak attack. The surprise, though, is the by-product of light heather honey...something I was hardly expecting to see for a whiskey so young...; **f23** top quality vanilla, still with a little honey to sweeten...and, more amazing still, malt easily discernible so late on. A thin hint of very late mocha; **b23.5** it always warms the heart when you see a single malt whisky made this well. And have so much character after such a short time. Technically excellent. Factually delicious. *45%*

Washington
BAINBRIDGE ORGANIC DISTILLERS Bainbridge Island, Washington.
Bainbridge Battle Point Organic Wheat Whiskey db **(87.5) n21.5 t23 f21 b22** A charming if single-paced wheat whiskey with only a modest degree of the usual spice one associates with this grain type. The delivery, with its mix of silky tannins, lightened molasses and caramel is its high point by a distance; the finish has a slightly bitter edge at the death. Very well distilled without doubt. *43% (86 proof).*

Bainbridge Battle Point Two Islands Organic Wheat Whiskey Islay cask db **(95) n23.5 t24 f23.5 b24** Now the Japanese cask (below) may not work quite as had been hoped, but this certainly does! Has to be one of the surprise packages of the year. An exercise in poise and balance: just so effortlessly and gracefully beautiful. *43% (86 proof).*

CHAMBERS BAY DISTILLERY University Place, Washington.
Chambers Bay Captain's Reserve Bottled-in-Bond Bourbon Boathouse-Aged a minimum of Five Years barrel no. 45 db **(87) n22 t22.5 f20.5 b22** Tasting the five- against the three-year-old suggests that in those intervening two years the distillery's fermentation and distilling abilities rose significantly. This has swarths of vanilla, salt and toffee. But underneath all that is a rather heavyweight and clumsy spirit whose weaknesses are evident at the death: there are no similar faults with the three year-old. *50% (100 proof). sc.*

Chambers Bay Greenhorn Bourbon Micro-barrel Aged a minimum of One Year batch no. 15 db **(86) n21.5 t21.5 f21.5 b21.5** Well it certainly is green, the youth apparent with every atom of aroma and flavour. On the subject of the nose, how about that vanilla coffee...? It is like going into a west coast coffee house for the 30-somethings... On the palate juicy and tart but, overall, a significant step up from previous bottlings. *44% (88 proof).*

Chambers Bay Straight Bourbon Whiskey Bourbon Boathouse-Aged a minimum of Three Years batch no. 07 db **(91.5) n22.5 t23 f23 b23** Anchors away for a full-bodied bourbon that gets the liquorice and spice mix pretty ship shape. *47.5% (95 proof).*

COPPERWORKS Seattle, Washington.
Copperworks American Single Malt Whiskey Release No. 017 Aged 25 Months Collaboration Cask new American oak, finished for 6 months in Amaro Amorino, pale malt recipe db **(82.5) n20 t22 f20 b20.5** Well, I didn't expect that! Yes, I was prepared for a subtle orange infusion. But the effects of the liqueur hits you right between the eyes – and on the nose in particular. You look for an aroma, but find a perfume... A malt that will thrill liqueur lovers, but has left a maligne effect on old traditionalists like me. That said, there are a few passing moments when the malt does get a word in edgeways. The bitter finale, after so much early sweetness, was a foregone certainty. *50% (100 proof). 290 bottles.*

Copperworks American Single Malt Whiskey Release No. 019 Aged 34 Months new American oak, cask no. 138, Knutzen Farms Alba Skagit Valley Malting db **(91.5) n23 t23 f22.5 b23** Extracts every last flavour profile from the virgin oak, but still allows the lightening barley to have its say. Impressive. *50% (100 proof). sc. 264 bottles.*

Copperworks American Single Malt Whiskey Release No. 020 Aged 34 Months new American oak, cask no. 142, Knutzen Farms Alba Skagit Valley Malting db **(94) n23 t23.5 f23.5 b24** Such an understated malt, its shyness almost hiding the enormity of the whiskey. Almost... *50% (100 proof). sc. 262 bottles.*

Copperworks American Single Malt Whiskey Release No. 021 Aged 38 Months new American oak, alba, five malt & pale malt recipe db **(89) n22** there's that mystery minor hop note again! Though this is all about cream toffee; **t22.5** one of those sensuous deliveries which starts soft and innocently – and very much staying on the cream toffee threat – then suddenly takes off with a malty-tannin kick...; **f22** ....then quietens for the slightly bitter, vaguely hoppy finish; **b22.5** pretty docile by Copperworks' standards. Wish I knew why the odd bottle of theirs sports a distinct hoppy note. *50% (100 proof). 1,760 bottles.*

Copperworks American Single Malt Whiskey Release No. 022 Aged 29 Months new American oak, pale malt recipe db **(86.5) n21 t22 f21.5 b22** Enjoyable, but pretty one-dimensional by their standards (and overly bitter, too), the caramel always in the ascendancy. If this malt were a colour, it'd be beige.... *51% (102 proof). 1,707 bottles.*

Copperworks American Single Malt Whiskey Release No. 023 Aged 29 Months new American oak, pale malt & five malt recipe db **(86.5) n21.5 t22.5 f21 b21.5** The sharp and awkward nose is countered by super-soft delivery. Creamy textured with thick vanilla and light molasses interference from the tannins. Finally, spicy yet bitter-sweet, then emphasis on the bitter. So, in all, about as well disciplined as a bunch of kids after eating highly coloured candy. *50% (100 proof). 1,329 bottles.*

Copperworks American Single Malt Whiskey Brewery Casks Release No. 024 Aged 29 Months new American oak, finished for 2 months in a Three Magnets Copperworks Tompkins Imperial Stout cask, five malt recipe db **(93) n22.5 t23 f23.5 b24** Creamy-textured and initially well spiced, it at first appears rather monotoned by this distillery's high standards. But a serious dose of the Murray Method soon changes the perspective of things – quite dramatically in the end - and slowly you are able to tease out its extraordinary charm and complexity. Truly a one-off in style and mood for the 2021 Whisky Bible, and not a bad choice for its 900th whisky... *50% (100 proof). 500 bottles.*

Copperworks American Single Malt Whiskey Release No. 025 Aged 43 Months new American oak, cask no. 148, queen's pale & alba recipe db **(94) n23.5 t23.5 f23 b24** The extra months appear to make a telling difference with the honey far more relaxed and settled. Settled in Seattle. Beautifully. *56.1% (112.2 proof). sc. 167 bottles.*

Copperworks American Single Malt Whiskey Release No. 026 Aged 31 Months new American oak, cask no. 200, five malt recipe db **(92) n22** creamy and full of caramels; **t23.5** whoomph! Goes up like a national forest during an illegal barbecue: the spices seer into the taste buds as light maple syrup and liquorice try to douse the flames. Slowly a crescendo of spiced chocolate forms...; at times the oils are something to be believed; **f23** despite a nagging low key bitterness, the mix of chocolate-flavoured molasses and spices continue to melt the heart...; **b23.5** one of the spiciest Copperworks I've ever encountered. But the balancing sugars border on magical. *574% (114.8 proof). sc. 232 bottles.*

Copperworks American Single Malt Whiskey Release No. 027 Aged 31 Months new American oak, cask no. 205, five malt recipe db **(94.5) n23** one of the fattest noses on the malt scene: muscovado sugar, ulmo honey and lashings of vanilla to the fore...; **t23.5** ever licked the remains of a pot of ulmo honey...No? You have now...; **f24** the creamy butterscotch-vanilla blend and ulmo honey embrace the drier, spicier tannins and are easily their match; **b24** malt that is both lush and luscious.... *576% (115.2 proof). sc. 230 bottles.*

Copperworks American Single Malt Whiskey Release No. 028 Aged 30 Months new American oak, cask no. 207, five malt recipe db **(93) n23** a flicker of liquorice here, hickory there...and malt everywhere...; **t23.5** fabulously estery, the malt goes into mouth-watering ecstasy. The barley is rich and topped with no shortage of marzipan; **f23** bitters slightly in the house style, but the spices and hang-on malt go for a superb countering job; **b23.5** another example of the big jump in quality in the mid to late 20s bottling, to the earlier American cask ones. *58.8% (1176 proof). sc. 230 bottles.*

Copperworks American Single Malt Whiskey Aged 33 Months new American oak, cask no. 108, five malt recipe db **(84) n20 t22.5 f20.5 b21** One very strange beast. A great distance away from Releases 19 and 20, this has some technical, feinty flaws on both the nose and finish that cannot easily be overlooked. However, those extra oils certainly boost up both the intensity and sweetness of the huge malt on delivery. *57% (114 proof). sc. 100 bottles. Proof Washington Distillers Festival release.*

Copperworks American Single Malt Whiskey Cask No. 187 Aged 29 Months new American oak, pale malt recipe db **(94.5) n23.5** maybe this is why it;s called Copperworks: there is copper all over this like mint sauce all over a shoulder of lamb. And, my word... it works...! **t24** that slightly metallic sharpness does a great job of offering a spice to the heather-honey that dominates. The barley is profound and juicy; **f23.5** still attractively coppery with a plethora of dark sugars and chocolate...then a nagging bitter note...hmmm; **b23.5** just that little bit of mysterious inherent hop-like bitterness prevents this from going onto a greater score still. But just be thankful for the fabulous. *64% (128 proof). sc. 100 bottles. Proof of Washington Distillers Festival 2019.*

◈ **Copperworks American Single Malt Whiskey Release No.30** aged 34 months in 4 casks new American oak, cognac & oloroso, db **(89.5) n23** if the oloroso was any fresher, you'd feel the grapes had just been peeled...; **t22.5** as per nose, the grape is of rare succulence: salivating over both the fruit and barley is inescapable. The midground fills with light ulmo honey and vanilla; **f21.5** bitters slightly in the house style, but there is a dogged maltiness which will bow to no other element; **b22.5** despite the Cognac, which has little meaningful influence, and oloroso, which has much, it is the barley which stars here. *50% (100 proof) 709 bottles*

◈ **Copperworks American Single Malt Whiskey Release No.31** aged 32 months in 7 casks new American oak, db **(91.5) n23** so much caramel. And so much barley, too. If a nose can be silky, then this is it...; **t23.5** the house rich, sweet caramel delivery, though the layering of barley behind it is complex and far from linear. Spices and ulmo honey arrive more or less within the same flavour beat; **f22** the delicate vanillas battle with the inhouse bitterness and just about keep things neat and tidy. The spices really are amazingly busy...; **b23** very easy to underestimate the complexity of this whisky. *50% (100 proof) 1795 bottles*

⬥ **Copperworks American Single Malt Whiskey Release No.32** aged 41 months in 1 cask new American oak, cask no.206, db **(94) n23.5** such a wonderful display of toffee nut...; **t24** the delivery of dreams: a kind of halfway house between bourbon and malt, with an almost corn oil style oiliness allowing the barley to get the juices flowing while heather honey and red liquorice ramps up the sweetness. Excellent light spice and more toffee-honey; **f23** the usual house bitterness comes into play. But the light manuka honey arrests its development. The spices keep fizzing along...; **b23.5** I'm in love... this is just so good, and the high strength suits the style perfectly. *59.7% (119.4 proof) 230 bottles*

⬥ **Copperworks American Single Malt Whiskey Release No.33** aged 30 months in 1 Fino sherry cask, pale malt recipe, db **(77) n19 t21 f18 b19** An elementary mistake. And those two elements are: copper (which is good) and, alas, sulphur (which very much isn't!). *50% (100 proof) 594 bottles*

⬥ **Copperworks American Single Malt Whiskey Release No.34** aged 49 months in 8 casks new American oak, WA peated malt Skagit valley malting recipe, db **(87) n22.5 t22 f21 b21.5** Bit of a curious customer, this. Love the celebration of caramels on both nose and delivery. There is often an underlying bitterness found to their whiskey and usually the more honeyed aspects are able to counter this as the sugars build up. This time, though, it has fallen just a little short. Not bad. Just not quite what I have become used to: Copperworks have obviously spoiled me in recent years! *52% (104 proof) 1934 bottles*

⬥ **Copperworks American Single Malt Whiskey Release No.35** aged 39 months in 6 casks new American oak, Baronesse & pale malt recipe, db **(86.5) n22 t23 f20 b21.5** The delivery is pure Copperworks: sharp, salivating and immersed in delightful vanilla. However, both the nose and finish ask some bitter questions which the charm of the ulmo honey alone cannot answer. *50.5% (101 proof) 1521 bottles*

⬥ **Copperworks Double Peated American Single Malt Whiskey Release No.36** aged 45 months in 2 casks American oak and 7 months in Ardbeg cask, WA peated malt recipe, db **(92) n23** my memory is running through thousands of whiskies and I'm trying to find a peated one which matches this in style. Nope, not at the moment. Nothing unusual about the slight chocolate lilt to this. But what is different is the structure and type of acid bite that the phenols are kicking up and mingling with a lazy fruitiness...; **t24** a truly faultless delivery. In fact, you could hardly shape it any better if you tried. There is a buttery butterscotch sweetness followed quickly by the most gentle smoke tones. No aggression, the smoke appears to be comforting the tannins and barley. The phenols appear to slowly gather in intensity, forming a drier bite to accompany the spice; **f22** so much caramel. Long phenols and a growing bitterness...; **b23** well, that's different. I suspect I have nosed more different styles of peated whisky from around the world than any other person not only living, but who has gone before me. And here we have something that on the malted whisky front moves into entirely new territory. Even as Ardbeg's former blender I cannot say that I can detect the distillery fingerprint as such, though I can see where it has sculpted both the nose and delivery *49% (98 proof) 386 bottles*

DRY FLY DISTILLING Spokane, Washington.

Dry Fly Straight Bourbon 101 Whiskey Aged 4 Years bott 12/30/19 db **(88.5) n21.5 t23.5 f21.5 b22** A decent bourbon that pitches on the toffee-mocha side of the wicket with the emphasis on subtlety rather than power. Let down slightly by just a fraction too wide of a cut which undermines the finish. Frustrating, as this is on the cusp of excellence. *50.5%*

Dry Fly Straight Triticale Whiskey Aged 4 Years bott 11/15/19 db **(89.5) n23.5 t23 f21 b22** One of those frustrating whiskeys where the nose cannot be matched by what follows after, though that would have been a tall order. Please give this one at least ten minutes nosing before tasting.. *45% (90 proof).*

Dry Fly Straight Wheat Whiskey Aged 3 Years bott 01/20/20 db **(90) n22.5 t23 f22 b22.5** The one thing you must say about this distillery's whiskey is its remarkable consistency of quality. Here again, we have a well-made whiskey with no pretensions of breath-taking greatness, but does what you'd like it to do well. In this case it displays the wheat to good effect, maximising the spices to counter the bready sugars. This one peaks on delivery and displays a languid chewiness to the lightly molassed cream toffee. Impressive. (CV) *45% (90 proof).*

Dry Fly Straight Wheat Whiskey Cask Strength Aged 3 Years bott 12/09/19 db **(95) n23.5 t24 f23.5 b24** No doubt about it: Dry Fly are making a massive statement with this one! Beautifully distilled and very sympathetically matured, they have hit the big time thanks to the understated complexity and even more quietly spoken enormity. Like their 45% version, there is a bread-like quality to this - on the palate especially. But the charm is all in the molten Demerara sugars mixing it with the kind of fiery spices only wheat whiskey can produce, with all this to the backdrop of as clean and intense wheat as you likely to find this year. A deft oiliness makes for a sensual mouthfeel, the grains are still young enough to induce some major salivation. A whiskey which takes this distillery up another notch and one I hope they use as their benchmark for greater things. Not just superb; this is a true classic (CV) *60% (120 proof).*

O'Danaghers Whiskey American Caledonian Single Potstill Aged 5 Years Single Barrel db **(88.5) n22 t22.5 f21.5 b22.5** This offers an interesting variation to their Hibernian version (below). By comparison to this plodder, the Hibs bottling is flighty and lively. This appears to rejoice in its lumbering style though, paradoxically, it shews more fruitiness than its lighter, sweeter twin. The oak is offering a tad more tannin and the spices can do battle with a more molassed sweetness. Yet, for all this, the Pot Still style is less pronounced, even cryptic. A big, dense whiskey that needs chewing - and then chewing some more.... *45% (90 proof). sc.*

O'Danaghers Whiskey American Hibernian Triple Distilled Potstill Aged 5 Years Single Barrel bott 11/23/19 db **(89.5) n22 t23 f22 b22.5** Over a quarter of a century ago, I took on the old guard at Irish Distillers to ensure that the production of Irish Pot Still would not be phased out, or even reduced. It was certainly on their minds. So, it is heart-warming to see, so many years on, a distillery from the Washington State part of Ireland adding to the growing number of pure Pot Still brands. In all honesty, I can't say the not unattractive nose much reminds me of the original stuff. And must also say that the cut has been quite clever here to allow the subtleties of the unmalted grains to shew. The sweet lightly honeyed juiciness on the palate is sheer Dry Fly in style – and for an extended moment or two there is a glimpse of the true Pot Still style, especially when the acacia honey kicks in against a semi-murky, more bitter back drop: a hard trick to pull off. I really hope they keep working at perfecting this. For this is a cracking effort worthy of investigation. "...whiskey in the Celtic tradition from the auld sod" says the label. To be sure. And reviewed by one, an' all... *45% (90 proof). sc.*

WESTLAND DISTILLERY Seattle, Washington.

Westland Distillery Colere Edition Aged 4 Years db **(90) n23 t23 f22 b22** A highly perfumed cedary whisky which is never less than full-flavoured. If you are not into big tannins, you might have problems here as you'll find them smeared in abundance all over the nose and very dry finish. The light acacia honey on delivery is probably the one and only concession to softness. *50% (100 proof).*

Westland Distillery Garryana 3|1 bott 2018 db **(92.5) n23 t23 f23.5 b23** From the rich, honeyed and oily school of malt. The mouthfeel has a gloss which perfectly reflects the dark sugars to be found on the spicy nose. But the spice, though present, is far more restrained on the palate until it accumulates at the strangely sweet and dry finale. Certainly complex. *56% (112 proof).*

Westland Distillery Garryana 4|1 bott 2019 db **(90.5) n22 t22.5 f23 b23** A much slimmer vrsion where, compared to 3/1, they have eschewed the honey and oils for a more dusty, drier tannin and spice take on things. A little molasses thickens the sweetness very late on and helps bring on the even later chocolate. A very subtle whisky. *50% (100 proof).*

Westland Distillery Peat Week 6th Annual Edition db **(93) n23.5 t23 f23 b23.5** A far more youthful nature on both nose and delivery than previous bottlings. And that youth means the peat has a far more solid, chunky persona than before. No stinting on the smoke whatsoever, nor the gristy sugars. Raw and rewarding. *60.4% (120.8 proof).*

Westland Distillery Single Cask Aged 46 Months cask no. 3204 db **(94) n23.5 t23.5 f23 b24** A luxurious whisky which makes no attempt to compromise on its depth and richness. A mix of maple syrup and Demerara sugar helps illuminate a fruity character to the sweetness while the tannins are both huge but always kept under control and in overall context. The fact there is no massive age is always evident. But it doesn't really matter. When all the pieces of the jigsaw fit this comfortably together, age is immaterial... *60% (120 proof). sc*

WOODINVILLE WHISKEY CO. Woodinville, Washington.

Woodinville Bottled-in-Bond Straight Bourbon Whiskey Pot Distilled db **(96) n24 t24.5 f23.5 b24** Happy anniversary to unquestionably one of the greatest bourbon distilleries outside Kentucky. The whiskey used here has a maximum 10-year-old age statement. But it isn't so much the age as the stunning layering of this classic bourbon. As always, a joy to taste. *50% (100 proof). 10 Years Anniversary Edition.*

Woodinville Cask Strength Straight 100% Rye Whiskey db **(94.5) n23.5 t23.5 f23.5 b24** When a rye is crisp, salivatingly fruity and offers an enigmatic sweetness, then you know it has done its job. *59.24% (118.48 proof).*

Woodinville Cask Strength Straight Bourbon Whiskey cask no. 1528, bott 4/22/20 db **(95.5) n23.5 t24 f24 b24** Just so staggeringly well made. *61.91% (123.82 proof). sc.*

Woodinville Straight 100% Rye Whiskey Pot Distilled db **(88) n22.5 t22 f21.5 b22** An attractive rye, though the grain plays second fiddle to a chalky vanilla lead. Very dry despite the odd heather honey cameo appearance. Do really like the rich copper which infiltrates this, though the distillate isn't up to the usual sky-high standard.. *45% (90 proof).*

Woodinville Straight Bourbon Whiskey Pot Distilled db **(92.5) n23.5** such satisfying caramel. A little ulmo honey and hickory adds shape..; **t23.5** the house style volley of muted sugars makes for the most pleasant of deliveries. Slowly the hickory and molasses unfurl to take hold; **f22** a little dry and bitter as the oils gather. The spices now become quite loud...; **b23.5** a charming bourbon that appears to be operating well within its range. I think this is the definition of easy drinking... *45% (90 proof).*

Woodinville Straight Bourbon Whiskey Private Select cask no. 1953 db **(96.5) n24.5 t24 f24 b24** To put it simply: this is fantastic, flawless bourbon. And, I'd so love to see this follow hard on the heels of a 12 ounce ribeye! Probably because it has taken me longer to analyse this bourbon than it would to fight my way through the steak. It is to my great shame that I have been neither to the Woodinville distillery near Seattle (I was going to visit once, unannounced, but after the dreadful experience of driving through the Canadian border - on the Canadian side, as usual - from Vancouver I hadn't quite lost the will to live, but I certainly wasn't in the right frame of mind for congenial discourse) nor Bern's Steak House in Tampa, a restaurant that has been on my must experience list for 30 years but still eluding a tick. There's only the little matter of a 3,000 mile drive between these two establishments. But once it becomes safe to travel again, after being cooped up in the same place for two months on Covid Lockdown....just give me a map! *61.6% (123.20 proof). sc. Bottled for Bern's Steak House 2020.*

Woodinville Triple Barrel Blended Whiskey Pot Distilled bott 9 Feb 20 db **(88.5) n22 t23 f21 b22.5** Sweet and lush, there is almost a maltiness to this whiskey. As much butterscotch as you can imagine and no shortage of dark sugars, too. Spices are in no hurry to arrive but boost the dry finish when they do. Very pleasant, indeed. *45.5% (91 proof).*

West Virginia
SMOOTH AMBLER Greenbrier County, West Virginia.

Smooth Ambler Big Level Wheated Bourbon batch 49 db **(91) n23** have to say that that is one quite brilliant nose: the wheat kicks up a storm of minor spices while the hickory-liquorice spice has a fair bit of muscle attached; **t22** a slightly weaker delivery than nose as there are quite a few oils vying to be top dog here, leaving dusky sugars to carry the load; by the midpoint things are starting to make sense; **f23.5** so it all about the finish, then. For that is where the grains, corn oils and busy tannin hit maximum harmony. Light spice and hickory on the heather honey afterglow....; **b22.5** a really impressive bourbon bursting with depth and personality. *50% (100 proof).*

American/Kentucky Whiskey Blends

Ancient Age Preferred Blended Whiskey bott code: L181271517082 **(70) n18 t19 f16 b17** Remains thin gruel for those looking for the richness of an Ancient Age bourbon. But this is a blend, and a very ordinary one at that. The nose has improved a tad, but the finish falls apart more than it once did. *40% (80 proof).*

Falls Church Distillers Church Whiskey batch no. 3, used American oak bourbon barrels **(86.5) n21 t22 f21.5 b22** Pretty attractive, as American blends go. Thin in part, but no stinting on the fuller-bodied liquorice. *40% (80 proof).*

Heaven's Door Double Barrel Whiskey bott code: 2018/05/121045 **(90) n23.5 t22.5 f22 b22** Does all the right things and with minimum fuss! *50% (100 proof).*

Lewis & Clark American Whiskey bott 30 Aug 18, bott code: L1656 003075 **(85.5) n21 t21 f22 b21.5** A silky Toffee Fest. Thoroughly attractive and enjoyable in its own way, but don't expect any great complexity. *40% (80 proof). BBC Spirits.*

Little Book Chapter 02: Noe Simple Task Blended Straight Whiskey **(91) n22.5 t23 f22.5 b23** Very distinctive Beam-like elements which is taking blended American whiskey into higher, more rarified atmosphere. *60.55% (121.1 proof).*

Michter's Celebration Sour Mash Whiskey Release No. 3 **(96.5) n24 t24.5 f23.5 b24.5** I have tasted some pretty average whisky for the last three or four days, my taste buds being assaulted by one sulphur-ruined sherry butt after another. Then, as you begin to wilt and wonder "what is the point?", you come across a whiskey like this. And then you remember. No wonder American whiskey keeps on winning so many awards when they can come up with releases like this. *57.8% (115.6 proof). 277 bottles.*

Mulholland Distilling American Whiskey (87.5) n21.5 t22.5 f21.5 b22 Fat, exceptionally sweet and a little monotone. That said, has a kick in the right place and a lovely chewing whiskey. Just needs a tidy up at the finish, a change in flavour stance, a bit of complexity... And, dare I say it? A little drive... *50% (100 proof).*

Redwood Empire Lost Monarch A Blend of Straight Whiskies Aged at least 3 Years bott code: L19 1506 (92.5) n24 t23 f22.5 b23 A style of nose I had previously only ever experienced in my own blending lab...for the last 30 years! With the emphasis, inevitably, on the rye, they have done an excellent job of marrying rye and bourbon together to produce a wonderfully emphatic and rich whiskey with no quarter asked or given. Seeing as this whiskey is in honour of the most colossal of the giant redwoods, the hugeness of the whiskey is in perfect keeping, though perhaps a 101 strength might also have added to the controlled enormity. *45%.*

Widow Jane Aged 10 Years batch no. 60, bott 2018 db (94) n23 t24 f23.5 b23.5 This is one widow that has been married beautifully..... *45.5% (91 proof). ncf.*

Whiskey Distilled From Bourbon Mash

Angel's Envy Cask Strength Kentucky Straight Bourbon Whiskey Finished in Port Wine Barrels bott 2019 db (87) n22.5 t22 f21 b21.5 At this strength a grain and grape should be singing from the same hymn sheets, Here they are at war though. I admit I do love the hickory foreground desperately trying to act as peacemaker. An aggressive piece of work, saved by the odd charming moment or two. *61.2% (122.4 proof).*

Angel's Envy Straight Bourbon Whiskey Finished in Port Wine Barrels db (86.5) n22 t22 f21 b21.5 A curious whiskey, though not with serious presence. There are some standard bourbon markers of note, the liquorice in particular. But the whole deal is eclipsed by a strange sultana stranglehold. Not unattractive. But infuriatingly frustrating as a whiskey as it falls between two stools with minimal harmony. *43.3% (86.6 proof).*

Artful Dodger Heaven Hill Bourbon 10 Year Old port pipe (81.5) n20 t21.5 f21 b19 Hard to know how to describe this. The fruit is all over the corn oil, while the tannins, the hickory in particular look ether isolated or lost. Lacks cohesion and balance: a real mess. *59.3%.*

Blood Oath Pact No.5 2019 Release bott 1/17/2019 (87.5) n22 t23.5 f20.5 b21.5 The usual glassy feel to the palate, by no means unusual with rum cask finishes with any spirit, dampens the fun on this whiskey that had been distilled from bourbon mash. So it is principally all about the strikingly wonderful delivery, at once sweet and peppery, and broadened in character with lovely chocolate lime candy, all mixed in with powering liquorice. The thin finish is a disappointment by comparison. *49.3% (98.6 proof). Kentucky straight bourbon whiskey finished in Caribbean rum casks. Lux Row Distillers.*

Cadée Distillery Deceptivus Bourbon Whiskey finished in Portuguese Port barrels (86.5) n21.5 t22 f21 b22 What was once bourbon has been lost in a sea of Demerara sugars and grape. Soft and sweet, it benefits from the volley of spices unleashed at the midway point. *42.5% (85 proof).*

Knaplund Straight Bourbon Whiskey Atlantic Aged batch no. B201 (96.5) n24 t24 f24 b24.5 No, it's not your imagination. This really is a salty bourbon! What started life as a pretty decent bourbon, has become more interesting still. Uniquely so! As an experiment, you could say that this was one hell of a success as this is one of the most complex whiskies of 2021... *50% (100 proof). Distilled in the US, aged at the Atlantic sea and bottled in Denmark by Knaplund Distillery.*

Legent Kentucky Straight Bourbon Partially Finished in Wine and Sherry Casks (88.5) n23 t23.5 f20 b22 "East is east and west is west and never the twain shall meet"... well, so wrote my former fellow Savilian, Rudyard Kipling. And I think in the same poem he gave us "a gift for a gift". Well here there has been a gift for a gift and the twain have met, for this is a joint creation by Fred Noe of Jim Beam and Shinji Fukuyo, chief blender at Suntory, Japan. A highly attractive piece, let down very slightly by a finishing note you will never find at Suntory, but no stranger to sherry or wine casks. It certainly ain't bourbon, but who cares? There are some moments even Kipling might have struggled to find the words for... *47% (94 proof).*

Michter's Toasted Barrel Finish Kentucky Straight Bourbon batch no. 18H1191 (89) n22 t22.5 f22 b22.5 As is so often the case, the extra toasting has resulted in a massive dollop of natural caramels which levels slightly the peaks and troughs. Attractive, but quite restrained. *45.7% (91.4 proof).*

Micther's Toasted Barrel Finish Kentucky Straight Bourbon batch no. 18H1193, bott code: A182751193 (92.5) n23 t23.5 f23 b23 A much perkier and altogether more entertaining bottling than 1191, making far better use of both corn and sugars. *45.7% (91.4 proof).*

Parker's Heritage Collection 12th Edition Aged 7 Years bourbon finished in orange Curacao barrels db (72) n18 t19 f17 b18 Oh, dear. It's whisky, Jim; but not as we know it... *55% (110 proof).*

❦ **Penelope Bourbon Rosé Cask Finish** Aged a Minimum of 24 Months in charred new American oak barrels, finished in French Grenache Rosé Wine Casks, batch no. 01, bott code: L28267SS11818 **(86.5) n21 t22 f22 b21.5** Anyone looking for a bourbon character – let along straight bourbon – is sniffing at the wrong rose... As it happens, the nose is the weak spot as the wine casks tend to neuter any bourbon character...and it appears the bourbon has done a similar job on the wine, leaving a wishy-washy sweetness.... though the odd spice does nip. Better after the quiet delivery when a fruity muscovado sugary note passes through, not unlike boiled candy. Where there is little trace of bourbon on the nose, the same can't be said for the rather lovely delivery. But it is all too short, and what follows is a little too thin and confused. That it is a gentle and pleasant experience, though, there is no denying...and the late chocolate mousse does no harm, either... 47% (94 Proof). ncf.

Rebel Yell Kentucky Straight Bourbon finished in French oak barrels, bott code: A207192107 **(82.5) n21 t22 f20.5 b19** A dull, unbalanced whiskey (not straight bourbon), where the French oak does what French oak does best: dominate. The entirely avoidable result was something that was probably once very good, now becoming weighed down and lop-sided as the tannins first wipe out the charm of the grains and then any hope of subtle oaky layering. Instead we get a straight race between corn oils, molasses, liquorice and tannin. But never, sadly, shall they mix. 45% (90 proof). Lux Row Distillers.

Rock Town Single Barrel Cognac Cask Bourbon Whiskey Aged 21 Months 450L cask, cask no. 759 db **(86.5) n21.5 t22.5 f21.5 b21** Thin and bottled at a time when cask and grain were still struggling to find common ground. At least the delivery has an entertaining tannin surge, accompanied by light cocoa. 57.8% (115.6 proof). sc.

❦ **Wheat Penny 1958 Bourbon** finished with black cherry and toasted oak wood, **(86) n21.5 t22.5 f21 b21** In some ways this comes across almost more of a liqueur than a whiskey. Not just the sweetness – though, thankfully, never cloyingly sweet – but rich, silky mouth feel which one rarely associated with a whiskey working from a mash bill including 45% wheat because then, spices usually come into play. And here, save a slightly discordant buzz, there are none of any note. It isn't the first time I have encountered a whiskey using black cherry wood in the maturation process. But it is the first with this rather soothing and delightful countenance. I must say I thoroughly enjoyed the delivery, though may not have done had I gone to the bar sorely needing a whiskey. Only the finish has problems, not quite sure of its footing 47% (94 proof)

Woodinville Straight Bourbon Whiskey Finished in Port Casks Pot Distilled db **(80.5) n21.5 t21 f19.5 b18.5** Nothing technically wrong with this whiskey, except maybe for a niggardly finish. However, I don't actually understand it. There you have one of the finest bourbon whiskeys made anywhere in the world, and you throw a lush port cover over it. It is like a Klingon Cloaking Device: the whiskey itself has vanished, and now there is fruit from the port and little else besides. I know they say the market demands this. Fine. But all I can see is a total waste of great whiskey. 45% (90 proof).

❦ **World Whiskey Society Classic Collection Bardstown Edition Kentucky Straight Bourbon Whiskey Finished In Japanese Mizunara Oak Shochu Barrels (93.5) n23.5** really surprised by the degree of spice that the Mizunara oak has managed to generate against the calming sugars of the bourbon casks. Have to say this makes a highly attractive combination, especially when the united front of ulmo honey and vanilla begin to topple the early liquorice lead. It is this soft sweetness that takes the sting out of the spice...but spices there most certainly are...! There is another very unusual aspect to this nose is the curvature of the fruit: seemingly rounded, with fat gooseberries but then pinging back at you are more acidic kumquat. Just adore this nose...; **t23.5** mmmm! Those of you who like a serious bit on salivation on delivery will be hogging the bottle. Not soon after a chocolate theme strikes up and intensifies as the strident vanillas pin backs the liquorice notes to really the rich underbelly. This is working better than I suspect those who came up with the idea hoped...; **f22.5** usually you get a great start to a unique whisky, or it fades, or fault lines begin to fracture. Not this time. The vanillas reconfigure the juiciness notes found on delivery and the corn oils are saved to last to ensure the drier vanillas are lubricated; **b24** a world first they rightly claim. Not sure if it is for the type of whiskey or the longest title for any whisky ever bottled! But, yes, this is a first because in the 20,000 plus whiskies I have tasted for the Bible alone, I can confirm I have never before encountered this fascinating combination. When I approach unique whiskies like this, it is my habit to close my eyes and formulate in my mind how I expect the nose and flavours to pan out, given what I understand about the distillation and casks. Well, I admit I was absolutely miles out on the nose: didn't see the muted spices coming, but much, much closer to the mark on the delivery and follow-through (especially the early chocolate, which I treated myself to a little pat on the back about). My guess was that, given the right quality shochu casks and dependent on finishing time (and times of year) this could be an attractively complex whiskey. I was not disappointed. Nor will you be. *60% 1250 bottles*

◈ **World Whiskey Society Kentucky Samurai Edition Kentucky Straight Bourbon Whiskey Finished In Japanese Mizunara Oak Shochu Barrels Aged 15 Years (95)** n24 absolutely 100% unique. Bourbony, yet not. Light praline wafer, red liquorice and even outline hickory. But then an extraordinary barrow load of exotic fruit: it as though someone has picked up some aged bourbon and blended it with a 40-year-old Glen Grant...; **t24** now this is quite fascinating.... and proper. Because the delivery and follow-through almost exactly mirror the nose – by no means a usual occurrence in a whisky. When a top-quality Speyside whisky reaching the age (in whisky years) when bewhiskered Victorian vicars would start shuffling off this mortal coil, the malt would start taking on an exotic fruity quality which, at its very best, could set itself up as a potential World Whisky of the Year in this much slandered publication. And, as we found on the nose, so too it is going all exotic here. Except unlike on the nose there is chocolate truffle kick, too, which fully compliments the fruit and liquorice; **f23** just as with the younger version the corn oils at last come into play, doing a first-class job of continuing the fun. Drier now, even vaguely salty the vanillas have now **b24** not only unique. Brilliantly unique. One of the most enjoyable and fascinating whiskeys of the year. I mean, who doesn't like grasping a samurai sword in both and hands and hacking your way into previously undiscovered whisky territory? Which is exactly what we are doing here... *51% 650 bottles* ⚔

Whiskey Distilled From Malt Mash

Battle Cry American Single Malt Whiskey finished in Sauternes wine barrels db **(71)** n18 t19 f16 b18 When even something as magical as a Sauternes cask fails to deal with the fire on the throat and the persistent weaknesses of the spirit, you know it's back to the drawing board. Less Battle Cry: more hara kiri... *46% (92 proof).*

Battle Cry American Single Malt Whiskey finished in oloroso sherry barrels, batch no. 2 db **(80)** n20 t21 f19 b20 An acceptable malt which does little to entertain other than allow the richer notes of the oloroso to show a sweet, fruit cake intensity. Still a bit of flame-thrower late on, though. *46% (92 proof). 625 bottles.*

Copperworks American Single Malt Whiskey Release No. 018 Aged 32 Months new American oak (90%) and Oloroso sherry (10%), five malt & pale malt recipe db **(89)** n22.5 t23 f21.5 b22 An attractive malt where the flavours arrive in solid, rather than pastel, shades. *48.5% (97 proof). 1,220 bottles.*

Copperworks American Single Malt Whiskey Release No. 029 Aged 31 Months new American oak, cognac & oloroso casks, full pint, five malt & pale malt recipe db **(83)** n21 t21.5 f20 b20.5 A real mess. Drier than the Gobi desert. Just doesn't work unfortunately. *50% (100 proof).*

Downslope Double Diamond Malt Whiskey Aged 4 Years Cognac cask finish, cask no. WR-260 db **(87)** n21.5 t22.5 f21 b22 Rather lacks the finesse that their previous Cognac Cask Finish displayed. But at least the juicy barley on delivery has not been taken out of its stride. The odd bit of chocolate lurks, too. *40% (80 proof). sc.*

New Holland Zeppelin Bend Reserve American Single Malt sherry cask finish db **(87)** n22 t21.5 f22 b21.5 My Panama off to the chaps at Zep Bend for finding some outstanding sherry casks to help infuse the most wonderful, succulent grape note to this mouth-filling malt and slow-burning cocoa. Rich fruit cake at its most moist and spicy, though a slight, off-key hop note somewhat paddles against the style and grain. Otherwise, close to being a stunner. *45% (90 proof).*

Westward American Single Malt Oregon Stout Cask new American oak barrels, bott code: L9 067 0015 db **(86)** n21.5 t22.5 f21 b21 There is a fragmentary moment, just after delivery, when all is right in the world: the malt has blossomed like a rhododendron on steroids, the palate is thick with delightful gristy sugars and light maple syrup....then the darker clouds return. Again, it is in the form of bitterness from the distillate. Technically flawed, but those malty moments, plus some late dark chocolate, which ensures some delicious moments. *45% (90 proof). ncf.*

Westward American Single Malt Whiskey Single Barrel Selection Pinot finish Suzor Wines, barrel no. 1+3, bott code: L9 067 0013 db **(83.5)** n21 t22.5 f19.5 b20.5 If you can't get decent Pinot Noir barrels when based in Oregon, you might as well call it a day. For my money, some of the finest Pinots I've ever encountered came from that State and there is a golden moment on delivery when a charmingly understated fruity richness fills the mouth and thrills the taste buds. However, the Pinot has a bit of a fight on its hands as the base malt stills bears many scars in its distillation, the feints not conceding ground without a fight. *45% (90 proof). ncf.*

Whiskey Distilled From Rye Mash

Angel's Envy Rye Whiskey Finished in Caribbean Rum Casks bott 2019 db **(91.5) n23.5 t22.5 f22.5 b23** The spiciest and most beautifully balanced of all this style of whisky on the planet, It is like tasting distilled Christmas cake. Indeed, a seasonal whiskey seasoned almost to perfection. Don't see this lasting more than a day on the shelves in Germany...! *50% (100 proof).*

Cadée Distillery Cascadia Rye Whiskey finished in Portuguese Port barrels **(75) n19 t23 f15 b18** While the nose doesn't work – the rye and fruit are never on the same wavelength – the same can't be said for the delivery, which strikes like an iron hand in a velvet glove. Sublime bitter-sweet tones soon move towards full-blown spices. Loses its way again on the finish, which is a little harsh, bitter and furry. But that's what happens when you deploy sulphur-treated European casks *43.5% (87 proof).*

Grand Traverse Distillery Ole George Rye Whiskey Finished in Maple Syrup Barrels bott code: 9259 1 438 db **(87) n22 t22.5 f21 b21.5** The maple has far less effect than might be envisaged. Certainly no complaints about the delivery and follow-through profile which abounds in both juicy rye notes and enthusiastic spices. The balance elsewhere, though, doesn't hit quite the same high water mark. *50% (100 proof).*

Grand Traverse Distillery Ole George Rye Whiskey Finished in Sherry Casks db **(77) n20.5 t22.5 f16 b18** Just a word about putting excellent rye into sherry butts. Don't. *50% (100 proof).*

Heaven's Door Straight Rye Whiskey finished in Vosges oak barrels, bott code: 2019/19/11172 **(87.5) n22 t23 f21 b21.5** Not entirely sure what the point was of using these secondary barrels for maturation. The visible rye seems very high class. But there is dumbing down on both nose and palate with more seemingly taken away than added late on. Even so, some attractive moments, especially when the rye goes into super-fruity mode. *46% (92 proof).*

Knaplund Rye Whiskey Atlantic Aged batch no. 02 **(92) n22.5 t22.5 f23.5 b23.5** A whiskey where the whole is bigger than the sum of its parts. Shyly beautiful. *50% (100 proof). Distilled in the US, aged at the Atlantic sea and bottled in Denmark by Knaplund Distillery.*

Laws Whiskey House Experimental Barrel Rye Whiskey Finished in Sauternes Casks dist 16 Jan 16, bott 25 Feb 19 db **(68) n16 t22 f14 b16** Ignore the nose, which is a chaotic mish-mash of aggressive tones hardly on speaking terms. And the finish, which reveals sulphur in its naggingly unattractive and furry form. But if you must taste this, then concentrate on the delivery alone. For you are given ten seconds of brilliance as the sharp rye grain hits like a laser beam into the sweet fruit. But it is all far too brief. If you play with the type of barrels which have done so much to damage Scotch, then expect to be damaged yourself. *50% (100 proof). ncf. 1,450 bottles*

Micther's Toasted Barrel Finish Kentucky Straight Rye batch no. 18H1329, bott code: A182471329 **(89.5) n22 t23 f22 b22.5** Toasted barrel often equates to greater sugar. And that's what we have here – seemingly to the detriment of the rye. Pleasant but, for rye, a little on the dull side. *54.7% (109.4 proof).*

Minor Case Straight Rye Whiskey Sherry Cask Finished Aged 24 Months bott code: 178 19 **(78) n21 t22 f17 b18** Though sherry cask finished, this is dominated on both nose and delivery by all kinds of citrus. Sadly, a bitter and off-key finish (tragically typical of the finishing cask type) undermines the whiskey altogether. *45% (90 proof). Bottled by Limestone Branch Distillery.*

Obtainium Polish Rye Whiskey port barrel finish db **(84.5) n22 t21.5 f21 b20** As far as I can see, this is a well-made whiskey. But why Port has been involved I have no idea as the fruit makes a complete mess of the grain. The balance has been severely compromised. *57.45% (114.9 proof).*

Widow Jane Whiskey Distilled From A Rye Mash Oak & Apple Wood Aged batch no. 13 db **(86) n22 t21.5 f21 b21.5** Sweet, firm, has a few teeth that aren't afraid to nip – and a slight tobacco note on the nose. Plenty to chew on, for sure. *45.5% (91 proof).*

Whiskey Distilled From Wheat Mash

Laws Whiskey House Experimental Barrel Straight Wheat Whiskey Finished in Curaçao Casks dist 22 Apr 15, bott 22 Mar 19 db **(84.5) n20 t22.5 f21 b21** So overwhelming is the orange influence, this is not a nose any whiskey lover can take too seriously. That said, the delivery is another matter entirely with a sublime chocolate orange explosion with a fascinating spice sub-plot. The finish bitters out and wanders hopelessly off course. *47.5% (95 proof). ncf. 390 bottles.*

White Dog

Buffalo Trace White Dog Mash #1 bott code: L181550112 **(94) n23 t24 f23 b24** Almost exactly as above: no change, other than being slightly more salivating. But talk about consistent...! 57%

Buffalo Trace White Dog Rye Mash bott code: L180080113 **(95.5) n23 t24.5 f24 b24** Just so consistent by comparison to the last bottling, though half a mark off for a slight drop in copper contact. If I was ever to be converted to regularly imbibing white spirits, I would drink this – and, for the odd utopian experience, blend of this and the new make from Glen Grant in Scotland. Get those proportions right and this little gin revolution will be a thing of the past... Which reminds me: blending the different Buffalo Trace White Dogs can be a thing of endless fun, and occasional surprises, too...(and something I concocted from those here has already outscored the individual bottlings...!) *57% (114 proof).*

Buffalo Trace White Dog Wheated Mash bott 9065011647M **(94.5) n22.5 t24 f24 b24** An earthier, oilier version with the spices taking their time to arrive but do so at exactly the same moment the sugars begin to open up. A little more chocolate than before, also. *57% (114 proof).*

Other American Whiskey

Breckenridge Colorado Whiskey PX Cask Finish Aged a Minimum of at least Three Years batch no. 2 db **(84.5) n22 t22 f20.5 b20** Some enjoyable early spice amid the fruity, prune-rich soup. But, ultimately, flat as a witch's tit. *45% (90 proof).*

Breckenridge Colorado Whiskey Sauternes Finish Aged a Minimum of at least Three Years batch no.1 db **(82.5) n22 t21.5 f20 b19** Very clean grape with no shortage of over-ripe greengages on display. But it is hard to follow the narrative, as the grape and grain appear to largely cancel the other out. A little furriness at the death? *45% (90 proof).*

Cadée Distillery Medusa American Whiskey Finished in Madeira Wine Barrels db **(92.5) n23.5 t23 f23 b23** An almost infinitely huge improvement on the ugly old hag I had in my glass the last time I tasted this brand. A disarming softness and controlled sweetness, offset by the late buzzing spice, make for a charming whiskey. *40% (80 proof).*

Cascade Blonde American Whiskey bott code: L8081ZX222 1458 **(85.5) n22 t22 f20.5 b21** An exceptionally easy ride, soft and avoiding any big flavours without ever lacking character. The thin finish apart, abounds with tannin and roasty promise. *40% (80 proof).*

Downslope Double Diamond Whiskey Aged 2 Years triple casked, Cabernet Sauvignon finish, cask no. 321 db **(81.5) n22 t20.5 f19 b20** The Cab Sauv is all over nose like a 1970s hairpiece. But the fresh fruitiness fails to materialise on the palate which is at times puckeringly tart and towards the end painfully dry and bitter. *40% (80 proof). sc.*

Early Times Kentucky Whisky bott code: A027161143 3125362 **(89) n22.5 t22.5 f21.5 b22.5** The fact they are using what they term on the label as "reused cooperage" means this is Kentucky Whisky as opposed to Kentucky Bourbon, which requires virgin oak (and before you ask, YES, bourbon is a whisky...!). So, while it may not be a mighty fine Kentucky bourbon, brimming as it is with all kinds of liquorice and molasses this is still mighty fine Kentucky whisky...!! *40% (80 proof).*

Falls Church Distillers Church Burn batch no. 1, finished in habanero porter barrels **(79) n19 t19 f21 b20** Way too many tobacco notes on the nose and delivery. Redeems itself slightly late on as the sugars and spices mount. *46% (92 proof).*

J Mattingly White House 13 Whiskey (88) n22.5 t23.5 f20.5 b21.5 For the most part an agreeable whiskey which runs out of steam long before the end. But the nose and delivery are both charged with deeply attractive classical spiced hickory and liquorice notes impressively sweetened with light molasses. The finish is thin fare by comparison. *68.5% (137 proof).*

Knaplund Barrel Select Port Finished Whiskey barrel no. PFW02, aged 3 years in new American white oak barrels, finished in used 55l port barrels at Knaplund Distillery, Denmark **(89) n22.5** vanilla ice cream with a blackcurrant sauce...; **t22.5** crisp and salivating with the fruit calling every shot. Even a little kiwi fruit at the sharper end of this. Decent, well-weighted, spices make their mark; **f22** back to a butterscotch and blackcurrant tart. A few dark cherries to end the evening...; **b22** I have to say that I really enjoyed this. But there was a nagging feeling in me that the whiskey itself was nowhere to be seen, or had so heavily vanished into the fruit all traces had been lost. Maybe the vanilla and butterscotch were its last remains. But the whisky man inside me always laments at the loss of a whisky within a whisky... *50% (100 proof). sc. 196 bottles.*

Michter's Small Batch Original Sour Mash batch no. 20B203, bott code: A2005800203 **(93) n23** superbly supple as well as subtle spice presence, the major corn attack giving the toastier notes, sugars and spices an oily, rounded feel...; **t23** light heather honey moves towards muscovado sugars. Again the corn surges through and with it comes the toastier notes, though any bitterness is handsomely offset by the healthy honey; **f23.5** very pleasing soft spice sitting comfortably with the corn and light molasses; **b23.5** an exceptionally comfortable ride which goes big on the corn oil. *43% (86 proof).*

Micther's Toasted Barrel Finish Kentucky Sour Mash Whiskey batch no. 19G1244, bott code: A192171244 **(93) n23 t23.5 f23 b23.5** Just such great chewing whisky. Sipping? Forget it! What a great whiskey! And shows batch 1249 just how it should be done. *43% (86 proof).*

Michter's Toasted Barrel Finish Kentucky Sour Mash Whiskey batch no. 19H1249, bott code: A192201249 **(89) n22.5** saturated in caramel, the creamy toffee trumps the delicate and clever spices; **t22** silky soft with thick corn oils mingling with chewy caramel; **f22.5** more complex as the corn dissipates slightly. The spices re-emerge, but it is barely a whisper...; **b22** toasted oak can work with a bourbon, but it is a tough ask to get the balance right. I have yet to encounter such a finish with the natural caramels being raised significantly. And it is here that it is too easy to lose the complexity and the overall direction of the bourbon. Plenty to enjoy, nonetheless. *43% (86 proof).*

Michter's Unblended American Whiskey batch no. 20C371, bott code: A2000760371 **(91) n23** a celebration of all things sugary – and, specifically, all things brown sugary...; a lovely layering of gentle hickory softens matters and gives it a distinctive Kentucky aroma; **t22.5** here we go! It's those brown sugars, crisp and melting in the mouth. The liquorice is little more than a nudge and a hint; **f22** elegant; **b23.5** all low key, yet spick and span. A kind of bourbon, but in miniature... *41.7% (83.4 proof).*

Obtainium Light Whiskey db **(88.5) n21.5 t22.5 f22 b22.5** Curiously, I'm tasting this Light Whiskey entirely in the dark... And I have to say that the fruit-charged delivery is like a blast to the head: massive. A whiskey you can chew until your tongue drops off with a muscovado rich delivery to fair make you wince...in pleasure. Big, brooding...and bloody delicious. Oh, and "light" it most certainly ain't... *67.3% (134.4 proof).*

Sagamore Spirit Brewer's Select Destihl Brewery Imperial Stout Barrel Finish batch no. 1A **(85) n21.5 t22 f21 b21** Well, if you are looking for something very different, I may have found it for you. At times you feel the rye is about to take off, but then it is gagged while the traditional sharper edges of the grain are filed down and rounded off. Many whiskeys are bitter-sweet. This one is very bitter-slightly sharp. Then very bitter-creamy soft. I think odd would be an accurate and not unkind description. *47.5% (95 proof). Straight rye whiskey finished in Imperial Stout beer barrels.*

Sagamore Spirit Brewer's Select Sierra Nevada Rye Ale Barrel Finish batch no. 1A **(89) n22.5 t22.5 f22 b22** Being a massive fan of the Sierra Nevada brewery, I was hoping this would be from a barrel of one of the less hopped beers I sampled there once. And, from the relatively carefree attitude of the rye, it certainly seems to be. Not too much damage to the rye at all. *47.5% (95 proof). Straight rye whiskey finished in rye ale barrels.*

Sagamore Spirit Calvados Finish batch no. 1A **(95) n23.5t24 f23.5 b24** I am probably moved to say that this is the first specially finished bourbon or rye that I have tasted that actually works...ever! The crisp, sharp fruity element of the Calvados seems a very natural fit for the crisp, sharp fruity element of the grain. I so thoroughly enjoyed this! Bravo! This is sheer class. *50.6% (101.2 proof). A blend of straight rye whiskies.*

Sagamore Spirit Cognac Finish batch no. 1A **(86.5) n22.5 t22 f21 b21** The stupendous marzipan on the nose and leather honey delivery apart, too much on the hard, bitter and unyielding side. *52.5% (105 proof).*

Sagamore Spirit Sagamore Reserve Moscatel Barrel Finished Whiskey batch no. 1A **(91.5) n23 t23.5 f22 b23** Pretty well balanced with no flavour cul-de-sacs. *50.6% (101.2 proof).*

Sagamore Spirit Port Finish batch no. 1C **(90.5) n23.5 t23.5 f21 b22.5** Though not the greatest fan of wine finished American whiskies, this one has got it absolutely spot on. And, thankfully, it doesn't call itself a rye, though that is the base spirit. *50.5% (101 proof).*

Sagamore Spirit Sagamore Reserve Vintner's Finish batch no. 1A **(85.5) n22 t22 f20.5 b21** A cumbersome whisky where the fruit strangles the grain but leaves a little too much bitterness hanging around after the super-soft and salivating delivery. *49.2% (98.4 proof).*

Taconic Distillery Mizunara Cask db **(94) n22.5 t24 f23.5 b24** No easy matter to make a subtle whiskey out of a cask such as this. But they have succeeded brilliantly. Of its style, as good as I have ever encountered. *53.5% (107 proof).*

Wild Turkey Master's Keep Revival Aged 12 to 15 Years batch 001, oloroso sherry cask finish, bott code: LL\GD130911 db **(86.5) n22 t23 f20 b21.5** A boxer's nose: flat. And offers no punch whatsoever. That said, not normally a great fan of this whiskey style. However, this is better than most and the delivery itself offers ten seconds of beauty as a Demerara/rye sharpness is caressed by the fruit. But it is too brief and the weakness in the oloroso is visible late on. *50.5% (101 proof).*

Canadian Whisky

The vastness of Canada is legendary. As is the remoteness of much of its land. But anyone who has not yet visited a distillery which sits serenely on the shores of Lake Manitoba more or less bang in the middle of the country and, in early Spring, ventures a few miles out into the wilderness, has really missed a trick.

Because there, just a dozen miles from the remotest distillery of them all, Gimli, you can stand and listen to the ice crack with a clean, primeval crispness unlike any other thing you will have experienced; a sound once heard by the very first hunters who ventured into these uncharted wastes. And hear a distant loon call its lonely, undulating, haunting song, its notes scudding for miles along the ice and vanishing into the snow which surrounds you. Of all the places on the planet, it is the one where you will feel a sensation as close to nature - and your insignificance - as you are likely to find.

It was also a place where I felt that, surely, great whisky should be made. But in the early days of the Gimli distillery there was a feeling of frustration by the blenders who used it. Because they were simply unable to recreate the depth and complexity of the legendary Crown Royal brand it had been built to produce in place of the old, now closed, distilleries to the east. When, in their lab, they tasted the new Crown Royal against the old there were furrowed brows, a slight shaking of heads and an unspoken but unmistakable feeling of hopeless resignation.

To understand why, we have to dispense with the nonsense which appears to have been trotted out by some supposed expert in Canadian whisky or other who has, I have been

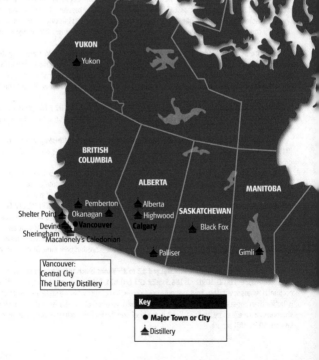

YUKON
⛰ Yukon

BRITISH COLUMBIA

ALBERTA

MANITOBA

⛰ Pemberton   ⛰ Alberta
Shelter Point ⛰ ⛰ Okanagan   ⛰ Highwood   SASKATCHEWAN
Devine ⛰ ⚫ Vancouver   Calgary ⚫   ⛰ Black Fox
Sheringham ⛰ Macalonely's Caledonian
⛰ Palliser   Gimli ⛰

Vancouver:
Central City
The Liberty Distillery

Key
⚫ **Major Town or City**
⛰ Distillery

advised by quite a few people I meet at my tastings, been writing somewhere that Canada has no history of blending from different distilleries. Certainly that is now the perceived view of many in the country. And it is just plain wrong: only a maniac would write such garbage as fact and completely undersell the provenance of Canadian whisky. Crown Royal, when in its pomp, was a meticulous blending of a number of different whiskies from the Seagram empire and by far the most complex whisky Canada had to offer.

The creases in the furrowed brows deepened as the end of the last century approached. Because the key distilleries of LaSalle, Beupre and Waterloo were yielding the very last of their stocks, especially top quality pure rye, and although the much lighter make of Gimli was of a high standard, they had not yet been able to recreate the all- round complexity as when adding the fruits of so many great distilleries together. The amount of experimentation with yeasts and distilling speeds and cutting times was a wonder to behold. But the race was on: could they, before the final stocks ran dry, produce the diversity of flavours to match the old, classic distilleries which were now not just closed but in some cases demolished?

When I had sat in the LaSalle blending lab for several days in the 1990s and worked my way through the near extinct whiskies in stock I recognised in Beupre a distillery which, had it survived, probably might have been capable of producing something as good, if not better, than anything else on this planet. And it was clear just what a vital contribution it made to Crown Royal's all round magnificence.

So I have monitored the Crown Royal brand with interest, especially since Gimli and the brand was acquired by Diageo some 15 years ago. And anyone doubting that this really was a truly great whisky should have accompanied me when I visited the home of my dear friend the late Mike Smith and worked our way through his astonishing Crown Royal collection which showed how the brand's taste profile had evolved through the ages.

And, at last, it appears all that hard work, all those early days of experimentation and fine tuning at Gimli have paid off. For while the standard Crown Royal brand doesn't yet quite live up to its starry past, they have unleashed upon us a whisky which dazzles, startles and engulfs you in its natural beauty like an early spring morning on Lake Manitoba. The whisky is called Crown Royal Northern Harvest Rye. It was Jim Murray's World Whisky of the Year 2016: batch L5085 N3 had redefined a nation's whisky.

The fact it should have achieved this at a time when Canadian whisky was at a nadir, with far too many brands dependent on adding too many unacceptable things as flavouring agents, is providential. It shows that keeping the grains at a maximum to be, with oak, the main source of flavour is the way to define a nation's whisky style: rye whisky by name, rye whisky by nature. So perhaps it is no great surprise that five years on Canada did it again and pulled off the Whisky Bible World Whisky of the Year for a second time with the 2021 edition. The closest whisky in style to Northern Harvest is Alberta Premium. And when they let this astonishing whisky loose at cask strength there was no stopping it. By anything worldwide.

QUEBEC

ONTARIO

Glenora

Caldera **NOVA SCOTIA**

●**Quebec**

Valleyfield ●**Montreal**
Cirka

Still Waters

Canada Mist ●**Toronto**
Forty Creek
Kittling Ridge

Walkerville

Jim Murray's Whisky Bible Canadian Whisky of the Year Winners	
2004/5	Seagram's VO
2006	Alberta Premium
2007	Alberta Premium 25 Years Old
2008	Alberta Premium 25 Years Old
2009	Alberta Premium
2010	Wiser's Red Letter
2011	Crown Royal Special Reserve
2012	Crown Royal Special Reserve
2013	Masterson's 10 Year Old Straight Rye
2014	Masterson's 10 Year Old Straight Rye
2015	Masterson's 10 Year Old Straight Rye
2016	Crown Royal Northern Harvest Rye
2017	Crown Royal Northern Harvest Rye
2018	Crown Royal Northern Harvest Rye
2019	Canadian Club Chronicles: Issue No. 1 41 Year Old
2020	Crown Royal Northern Harvest Rye
2021	Alberta Premium Cask Strength Rye
2022	Canadian Club Chronicles Aged 43

Canadian Distilleries
BLACK FOX FARM AND DISTILLERY Saskatoon, Saskatchewan. 2015.

Black Fox Blended Canadian Whisky (88) n22 t22.5 f21.5 b22 Both complex, especially on the salivating delivery, and tart. Just a little too bitter on the finish but an agreeable sub-plot of molasses throughout the piece does wonders. 47.1%. nc ncf.

Black Fox Cask Finished Canadian Whisky 100% Avena Sativa grain, port finish (89.5) n23 t23 f21.5 b22 A great oat whisky is usually something to savour, as it is unusual to find as it delicious. You get the feeling that less wine influence would have upped the complexity here considerably. An enjoyable dram which is technically flawless. But you also know that this could have been another three or even four points better... 45.7%. nc ncf.

Black Fox Single Grain Canadian Whisky 100% Triticosecale, virgin oak (92) n23 t23.5 f22.5 b23 My interest is always pricked when I see a distillery has chosen this rare grain – a cross between wheat and rye – because when dealt with correctly, it has the propensity to deliver a whisky big in flavour. This doesn't disappoint. 46.3%. nc ncf sc.

◈ **SE Eleven Blended Whisky 2021** Quercus cask, serial no. 00152B, db (86.5) n21.5 t22.5 f21 b21.5 This is one of the most exotically spiced whiskies I have encountered for a very long time. Despite the chocolatey sweetness, it is just too spicy on this occasion and gives just a little bit too much of the traditional English Bread Pudding feel for its own good. 48.2%

◈ **SE Eleven Cask Finish Single Grain** triticosecale grain, oloroso cask, serial no. 00920, db (90) n22 flat juicy, clean grape, save for a few spicy peaks; t22.5 I'm almost thrown back in my chair by the intensity of the raisiny sugars that combust on arrival. Salivating, thick with concentrated fruitcake and lashings of molasses; f23 dries slightly as the warming spices begin to take control. Some vanilla makes a welcome entry. The tannins do control the finale...; b22.5 if you want to compare the difference between the effects of bourbon/virgin oak and sherry casks, here's a great example. The bottling below is one of the most complex whiskies I have tasted this year. This isn't. Pleasant, as this is a decent quality wine cask at work. But the layering and complexity has been massively compromised and the unique qualities of the grain muted. That said...I think you'll rather enjoy it...! 47.5%

◈ **SE Eleven Single Grain** triticosecale grain, Quercus cask, serial no. 01206, db (95) n23.5 wow....! That is a unique nose for this year, one of the most questioning you'll find. The tannins from oak (Quercus), which includes black liquorice, practically throbs while the grain, seems both tight and relaxed offering a half fruit/half vegetable soupiness; t24 truly unique. Loads of bourbony tones with a mix of ulmo and heather honey alongside molasses, but then we cut down into a deeper level where the grains reside, partially spicy, semi-fruity and at once melting in the mouth and yet firm and rigid. The mouth feel. incidentally, is nigh on perfect...; **f23.5** all as before, melded together and fading amid extra molasses; long with a toasty residue **b24** last time I tasted this it was given as virgin oak. Well, Quercus is oak, so I presume they mean this is virgin cask again. If so, they seem to have for the balance working much better this time to make the most of this hugely flavoured grain – a kind of wheat and rye cross - to make for one of the most distinguished Canadians this year. Not just beautiful...amazing, too... **47.6%**

CENTRAL CITY BREWERS & DISTILLERS LTD. Surrey, British Columbia. 2013

Lohin McKinnon Chocolate Malt Single Malt Whisky Sauternes barrels db (80) n19 t23 f17 b21 Chocolate malt and Sauternes Barrels...? Sound like something straight out of the Glenmorangie blending lab. To taste, this is truly amazing: the closest thing to liquid Jaffa Cake biscuits I have ever encountered. So orangey...so chocolatey... Sadly, the nose and finish tell their own tale: if you are going to use wine casks from Europe, make sure they have not been sulphur treated first. *43%.*

Lohin McKinnon Lightly Peated Single Malt Whisky oloroso sherry barrels db (69.5) n17.5 t19 f16 b17 A polite tip to any micro distillery planning on using European wine casks. Just don't. Or you might end up with a sulphur-ruined disaster like this. *43%.*

Lohin McKinnon Muscat Wine Barrel Single Malt Whisky db (78.5) n19 t21.5 f19 b19 A reminder, were it needed, that disappointing wine casks are not just restricted to Spain. *43%.*

Lohin McKinnon Niagara Wine Barrel Single Malt Whisky db (87) n21.5 t22.5 f21 b22 If memory serves, it was these poor chaps who ended up with malt shewing the dangers of maturing whisky in sherry butts. They have wisely gone closer to home for their wine cask this time: Niagara. And this wasn't a barrel that fell over the Falls (well, I don't think so, anyway) but from one of the local vineyards. The result is a full-flavoured but eye-watering experience, certainly sulphur free, but with enough under-ripe gooseberry to keep your eyes watered for quite a while. Just needed an extra year or two in cask maybe for a more meaningful relationship between fruit and oak. Tart but very tasty. *43%.*

Lohin McKinnon Peated Single Malt Whisky db (95.5) n23.5 t24 f23.5 b24.5 This is genuinely top rate, outstandingly distilled and matured peated whisky *43%.*

Lohin McKinnon Tequila Barrel Finished Single Malt Whisky db (92) n23 t23 f22.5 b23.5 A fascinating and salivating addition to the whisky lexicon. *43%.*

Lohin McKinnon Wine Barrel Finished Single Malt Whisky finished in B.C. VQA Okanagan Valley Back Sage Vineyard Pipe wine barrels db (90.5) n22 t23 f22.5 b23 Impressive balance here with the fruit doing enough but not too much. *43%.*

DEVINE SPIRITS Saanichton, British Columbia. 2007.

Glensaanich Single Malt Whisky batch no. 4 db (88) n22.5 t23 f20.5 b22 As the first bottling I encountered of this was superb and the second not so, I was curious to see what a pour from the bottle would bring forth this time. Well, something that sits somewhere between the two but with a character all its own. *45%.*

Glensaanich Quarter Cask Ancient Grains batch no. 1 db (91.5) n23 t23 f22 b23.5 A beautiful little essay in complexity. The varied grains spelt, emmer, einkorn, khorosan and, of course, locally grown organic BC barley have been put together to delicious and fascinating effect. A real entertainer, especially when warmed for a while. *45%.*

FORTY CREEK Grimsby, Ontario. 1992.

Forty Creek Confederation Oak Reserve lot no. 1867-L, finished in Canadian wine barrels (94) n23 t23.5 f23.5 b24 Forty Creek feel relaxed with this brand and seem to know how to pull the strings for near maximum effect. Very clean, too. *40%.*

Forty Creek Confederation Oak Reserve lot no. 1867-M, finished in Canadian wine barrels, bott code: BG/HL12447 (94.5) n23.5 t23.5 f23.5 b24 Just so charming and elegant. It's the quiet ones you have to watch... *40%.*

Forty Creek Copper Pot Reserve bott code: DGIHC12074 (89.5) n22.5 t23 f21 b23 They have remained very true to style since this brand first hit the shelves. The finish could do with a clean-up, though. *43%.*

Forty Creek Copper Pot Reserve bott code: DGIHK01391 (95.5) n23 t24 f24 b24.5 Another stupendous Canadian from a distillery that has re-found its brilliance. This is the cheese to their Confederation oak chalk... And don't ye knock it all back at once... *43%.*

Forty Creek Double Barrel Reserve lot no. 267, finished in once used American bourbon barrels (87) n21.5 t22.5 f21 b22 Incredibly lush, but perhaps a tad too incredibly lush. Those caramel notes dominate with too much of a velvet fist, though it does briefly open out for some enjoyable oaky interplay, though all a little muffled. The finish is somewhat off key, alas. *40%.*

Forty Creek Double Barrel Reserve lot no. 272, finished in once mellowed American bourbon barrels, bott code: DGIIA09007 (**91**) n23 t22 f23 b23 Badly needs the Murray Method to get this one singing in harmony. When it does, just sit back, listen...and be entertained. 40%.

Forty Creek Premium Barrel Select bott code: DGIHC14075 (**81**) n21.5 t22 f18.5 b19 Massively thick on delivery, fruity but, sadly, the sulphur has returned. Decent spice, though. 40%.

Forty Creek Premium Barrel Select bott code: DGIIB11069 (**88.5**) n22 t22.5 f22 b22 A silky soft arrangement which ensures the fruity element always has pride of place and the juicy, marzipan sweetness is controlled. A little dull at the death, spices apart, but this is as friendly as a relatively rich whisky can get. 40%.

GLENORA Glenville, Nova Scotia. 1989.

⟡ **Glen Breton Rare Single Malt Aged 10 Years** nbc db (**93**) n22.5 slightly untidy but there is no escaping the solidity of the malt; t23.5 now...that I didn't expect. A quite stunning intertwangling between thick malt and top notch ulmo honey. The tannins are delicate but still forthright enough to act as a bind for the two varying sweeter elements. Add to that the mouth feel and.... wow! f23 the malt appears to mine new depths: this is so seriously intense. The honey has now moved across to a heavier heather-honey which keeps a lid on the full-on spice which tailgates the balmier sugars. It's Glenora, Jim: but not as we know it.... b24 genuinely delighted to see this whisky in such wonderful shape. Unlikely any other Canadian malt has this degree of honey to enjoy. As good as anything I've ever experienced from this distillery – and trust me: I have tasted probably more than anyone else living... 43%

⟡ **Glen Breton Rare Single Malt Aged 14 Years** nbc db (**86.5**) n21 t22 f21.5 b22 A relaxed, simplistic malt which goes easy on the complexity but is happy to mine the malt for all it is worth. Not as technically on the money as the younger Glen Bretons, it does however make amends with the extraordinary integrity of the malt itself. Only late in the day does the oak decide to make any form of contribution. 43%

⟡ **Glen Breton Rare Single Malt Aged 19 Years** nbc db (**91.5**) n22 malt and caramel make a genteel alliance. The spices try to add a bit of zip... Just a hint of something vaguely coastal as the salt makes a mark...; t23 a superb little volley of gristy sugars, helped along by delicate orange blossom honey ensures this malt never moves away from a style of refined f23 it needs light, busy spices to elongate the experience as the malts and sugars are already packing up, happy with the job they have done...; b23.5 one of the easiest going, least demanding 19-year-olds you'll ever meet. Not even a hint of tiredness or bitterness as the concentrated barley keeps the entire whisky on course. 43%

⟡ **Glen Breton Rare Single Malt Aged 21 Years** nbc db (**94.5**) n23 how subtle does a nose get? Just look at those slivers of marmalade amid the grist. Then how the fragile vanillas from the casks form muscle rather than backbone... So soft...; t23.5 the intensity of the grist is surprising. The juiciness at first appears to be the work of the delicate fruits detected on the nose. But soon it becomes clear that this is the handiwork of the malt, the sugars on the grists melting into a grassy freshness despite the passing two decades. The vanilla and spices, both oak induced, seem inseparable... f24 what a stunning finish. The malt has gathered... and gathered...and gathered. And now it holds together as the main theme eschewing the darker, weightier oak tones to ensure the salivating barley lingers on the lightest of oils for an improbably long time. Just staggering...; b24 had you, 21 years ago, asked me if this distillery would be able to produce a coming-of-age malt of this quality, I might have looked at you as if you'd just floated down from Mars or somewhere. I, for one, am so delighted that Glen Breton was able to salvage some extraordinarily beautiful casks from the wreckage of its earliest days. I think this should be called The Miracle Malt, because I didn't see it happening. Although I knew that their warehouses contained some amazingly fine casks, there was no knowing how they would develop in time. Into a whisky of unmistakable beauty is the answer. 43%

⟡ **Ghleann Dubh Peated Single Malt Whisky Aged 13 Years** nbc db (**95**) n24 if you are one of those people who wants the peat not to dominate but simply (actually, not simply at all!) add a further degree of beguiling complexity to an already charming and high-quality malt, then you have found your Canadian. Where do I start with this? The roast chestnut sweetness? The marriage between spice and grist? The barley sugar? The clever distance the smoke gives all else for it to blossom...? t23.5 the malt hits the bullseye here: enjoys a dual role of both offering a sweeter backdrop and the more intense sugars. The spices ping and sing, while the smoke rumbles like distant thunder...; f23.5 a series of dark sugar notes makes the most of the beautiful, biscuity vanillas. As elsewhere the smoke accompanies with just the right degree of menace. But like everything else before, we are talking shadows and pastel shades; b24 I am absolutely blown away by this. Excellent distillate and faultless cask management. Lucky 13 for Glenora: in this essay of subtlety and understatement, this is World Class...! 43%

HIGHWOOD DISTILLERS High River, Alberta. 1974.

◈ **Highwood Distillers Centennial Canadian Rye Whisky** db (87.5) n21.5 t22 f22 b22
A much more even Canadian than the last time I encountered this. The tangy note which disrupted its natural flow has been replaced by a much more alluring oily-ulmo honey sweetness which sits attractively with the toffee, sultana, and delicate spice. 40%

◈ **Highwood Distillers Highwood Canadian Rye Whisky** db (90) n22 the acacia honey and toffee is jazzed up gently with delicate spice; t23 silky cream toffee with delicate shards of vanilla; f22.5 the lightest sticky toffee pudding; b22.5 a quintessential Canadian rye. More to the point Highwood at its most Highwood... 40%

◈ **Highwood Distillers Liberator Canadian Rye Whisky** db (90) n21.5 dull fruit and toffee; t23 brilliant! The delivery is a joy: an immediate mini explosion of spice perfectly counters the chewy cream toffee and vanilla thrust....; f22.5 a little citrus on the vanilla and toffee fade makes this surprisingly salivating very late on; b23 much more to this than the dull fruit and toffee nose promises. As Canadian as a punch-up at an ice-hockey match. Except here they are hitting each other with feathers... 42%

◈ **Highwood Distillers 'Ninety' 5-Year-Old Canadian Rye Whisky** db (85) n21.5 t22 f20.5 b21 An undemanding Canadian rye where the toffee is ubiquitous. Just let down slightly by a degree of bitterness on the fade. 45%

◈ **Highwood Distillers 'Ninety' 20 Year Old Canadian Rye Whisky** db (91) n22.5 fruity and fulsome, there is a curious salty, almost coastal feel to this...although the distillery is some 600 miles from the sea...; An unusual mix of apple and rhubarb tart, with an extra dollop of vanilla; t22.5 the immediately enveloping fruit is punctured by the strafing of peppers, which themselves seems to kick of a wonderful ulmo honey middle.. with toffee fudge for company. You are not going to find many 20-year-old whiskies this salivating; f22.5 the layering of the oak is polite and understated, while the spices still fizz slightly. A little bread and butter pudding on the finish, helped along by light molasses; b23.5 just had a horrible thought: the last time I visited this distillery, this 20-year-old whisky hadn't even been made. When this Covid nightmare is over is time to get out to the Prairies once more. Would love to see what else they have lurking in their warehouse! 45%

◈ **Canadian Rockies 17 Years** nbc (95.5) n24 where did that mix of ripe and under-ripe gooseberry come from? Mingles with the vanilla and grain as if balancing a 12-inch ruler on your finger...; t24 with that gooseberry nose, the delivery could only be a mouth-watering affair. And now with a mix icing sugar, light butterscotch, and vanilla, all in tune with that singular fruity feature and an almost perfectly proportioned pinch of white pepper, we have a Canadian that is stunningly layered and constantly melting in the mouth; f23 the peppers persist. Though the fruit has vanished now, the vanilla remains unsullied and pure to the end; b24.5 this whisky has made a huge leap in quality since I last encountered it. I tried to count the layers after delivery... and gave up. Shows an elegance to win any heart. Magnificent. 50% ♈

◈ **Canadian Rockies 21 Years** nbc (92) n23 the oak enjoys room for a quiet solo while a fruit pastel sharpness lingers in the background with semi-sleeping spice; t23.5 a lush mouth-feel rather than flavour profile arrives first. But when the flavours do arrive, it is the ulmo honey which leads the way, just ahead of the vanilla which mix deliciously in the light oils; f23 chocolate vanilla wafer, with the vaguest hint of gooseberry; b24 Intriguing. Elegant. Delicious.... 46%

THE LIBERTY DISTILLERY Vancouver, British Columbia. 2013.

◈ **The Liberty Distillery Trust Whiskey Ancient Grains** nbc db (92.5) n23 a very bitty and biting nose as the grains and tannins vie for maximum spiciness...; t23.5 the initial moments of delivery reflect the nose perfectly: complex and pithy allowing a little attitude to mix with the coffee-led tannins. A little toffee begins to seep into the mix; f22.5 pleasant, but very much a 40-watt bulb compared to the brighter nose and delivery. The toffee and vanilla take over just a little too efficiently, though some late cocoa keep the complexity going...; b23.5 a high class, deeply pleasing, complex whisky which with a little extra boldness could be even more pleasing and complex still... 44%

The Liberty Distillery Whiskey Canadian Rye nbc db (84.5) n21 t22 f20.5 b21 Falls into the not uncommon practice in making rye – making the cut too wide. Means the oils are pretty demanding and strangle the grain itself. Not short of spices. 43%.

The Liberty Distillery Trust Whiskey Single Grain nbc db (87) n22 t22 f21.5 b21.5 Light bodied and bordering on thin. All kinds of sugars at play alongside the toffee and drying vanillas. Pleasant and untaxing. 40%.

◈ **The Liberty Distillery Trust Whiskey Single Cask Burgundy** nbc bc (77.5) n19 t20 f19 b19.5 Feinty, musty and way off key. Even the world's greatest ever known Burgundy barrel, had they been able to procure it, would never save this one. 42%

MACALONEY CALEDONIAN DISTILLERY Victoria, British Columbia. 2016.

Macaloney's Caledonian Dunivaig Peated Single Malt matured in Kentucky bourbon, recharred Portuguese, red wine & virgin American casks, db **(93.5) n23** pork scratchings! Wonderful! The peatiness mimics a Dudley delicacy, while elsewhere the malt, still young, parades around confidently...; **t23.5** stunning mouth feel. The most sensual of oils spreads ulmo honey-sweetened vanilla and dates. The smoke, however, plays a complex game, both pricking the oiliness, offering a drier phenol tone and a softening cloudiness, too...; **f23.5** we are now back with the ulmo honey and vanilla, plus a little butterscotch. The smoke has dropped off the pace, save a playful prickling of spice; **b23.5** a rather gorgeous young malt where the mouth feel is perfectly matched by the alure of the unique peaty tones. Should sell well in the Black Country of England, this. As it happens, I have probably tasted better in their warehouse, but not, so far, in bottled form. Superb! *46% nc ncf*

Macaloney's Caledonian Glenloy Single Malt matured in Kentucky ex-bourbon, recharred red wine and sherry casks, batch no.3, bott Jun 2021, db **(90.5) n22.5** the faintest over exuberance on the cut means a couple of half points are lost, but those feints might come in useful further down the line. Elsewhere the sugars are healthy and the oak firm; **t23** genuinely fat and chewy where the malt get maximum game time. Very much how I remember the last batch, complete with the sticky toffee pudding and associated dates. Never less than lively and salivating...; **f22.5** long with a slight nod towards moist date and walnut cake...; **b22.5** further evidence that this distillery is coming along rather well. *46% ncf 1215 bottles*

Macaloney's Caledonian Glenloy Island Single Malt Whisky Whisky Maker's Signature Expression Kentucky bourbon, re-charred red wine & sherry casks, bott Apr 20 db **(90.5) n22 t23 f22.5 b23** When in my Canadian base, Victoria, after a day's tasting I'll settle down at my Club to dine on that prince of fish, the halibut, to allow its tender meat and exquisite flavours to massage my tired taste buds. As I was examining Victorian whisky today, but in Lockdown UK rather than British Columbia, I had a halibut here, instead, perfectly baked in enough tin foil to forge a coat of armour...and not allow a single atom of juice to escape. Tasting this malt both before and after the melt-in-the-mouth fish (but certainly not with) was an experience I can thoroughly recommend. This, is by far and away, the best thing from Macaloney's I have tasted this year. *46%. nc ncf. 1,276 bottles.*

Macaloney's Caledonian Invermallie Single Malt matured in recharred Portuguese red wine barrique, cask no.60, bott Jun 2021, db **(89) n22.5** now that is very, very different. I think the last bottling I saw had all kinds of feint problems. Not this time: beautifully distilled but trying to grasp exactly what it is that is under your nose is quite a challenge. There is a phenolic tone, not as in an Islay-style sense. But more a passing smokiness: unsubstantial, but just enough to give the fruit a rare richness; **t23.5** now comes the almost house style soupiness with the fruit shewing such a chewy intensity...perhaps a style that will be remembered by those who tasted the Glendronach of the early 1990s; **f20.5** just the slightest weakness on the finish with a late niggly note. A little late muscovado sugar helps overcome the worst...; **b22.5** oh my word! This has made a Herculean jump in quality from the last time I tasted it. Shame about that slight furriness. *46% ncf sc 352 bottles*

Macaloney's Caledonian Invernahaven Single Malt matured in oloroso & PX casks, batch no.1, bott Jun 2021, db **(89) n22** thick, sweet, grape; **t22** grape, sweet, thick; **f22.5** sweet, thick, grape. And spice!!!! **b22.5** well, if you ever want to do away with yourself with a sherry overdose, here's your weapon... *46% ncf 421 bottles*

Macaloney's Caledonian Kilarrow Peated Single Malt matured in Kentucky bourbon, recharred Portuguese red wine & sherry casks, db **(83) n20 t22 f20 b21** Flavoursome and chewy. But an overwhelming feeling that the spirit isn't up to the normal high standards. The result is too much bubble gum and an uncomfortable niggle of feints at key moments. A shame. *46% nc ncf*

Macaloney's Peated Mac Na Braiche Island Single Malt Spirit nbc, db **(81.5) n21 t22 f18.5 b20** A head-scratcher of a malt. Whatever happened to the character and personality? It has peat and it comes from a distillery I know, from having sampled from their maturing stock, is not short of characterful and good quality malt. But even allowing for the slightly wide cut, you expect more; instead you appear to get some kind of overwhelming flat-caramel rich fruitiness cancelling out the peat. A bemusing dram. Not unpleasant, save an obvious cask niggle on the finish. Just far, far too dull and ordinary elsewhere. *46%. nc ncf.*

Macaloney's Caledonian Skarrabollis Single Cask Peated matured in virgin American cask, db **(94) n22.5** layered butterscotch offers as much clout as the shy peat...; **t24** the all-round succulence and chewability languidly hits home first, then...Eureka! Out of nowhere the malt hits its straps, the phenols engage with the honeyed tannins and my word! We're in business! Spices arrive, gently at first...then in force. The vanilla re-forms as ulmo honey, the light maltiness turns into concentrated grist...and at last the smoke decides it has a job to do and gently fills the mouth. The complexity is compelling, almost shocking...; **f23.5** a very long finale with the peaty spices buzzing, balancing out the thick, creamy vanillas; **b24** technically, a dream of a malt with faultless distillate merging beautifully with a very fine cask. The amazing thing is, at the beginning so little happens. It is a dropped intro of a dram... *46% nc ncf sc*

◇◇ **Macaloney's Caledonian Skarrabollis Single Cask Ex-Bourbon Peated** matured in Kentucky bourbon cask, db **(95) n23.5** soft and comforting...peak reek carried on the wind from a croft; **t24** the nose had already announced that this is high quality malt. And the clarity of the flavours here reveals far better cuts on the still than had previously been found. The smoke almost oscillates dampened slightly by a fruit pastel sweetness and intensifying maltiness. The midground vanilla explosion almost makes you punch the air with delight; **f23.5** long, light ulmo honey, ultra-intense malt....and still that warming cloud of smoke to accompany the spices...; **b24** I think we can safely say that, on this evidence, Macaloney Caledonian has arrived on the world stage of great distillers. A little bit of mucking about and a few learning curves negotiated to get there. But if they can keep this up then they will be much admir'd and loved across the whisky-loving world. *46% nc ncf sc previously Peated Darach Braiche spirit*

◇◇ **Macaloney's Caledonian Skarrabollis Single Cask Red Wine Peated** matured in recharred Portuguese red wine barrique, db **(89.5) n21.5** next quite gels as the peat struggles to find an ally; **t23** fat, busy, eye-watering grape infusion but calmed by the beautiful peated vanilla. Possesses a degree of harshness, too...; **f22.5** still quite harsh as the fruit gives the peat a decidedly metallic nudge; **b22.5** an interesting drop off in quality from the Skarrabollis Kentucky barrel. Here the wine has managed to skew the balance and make for a much harder malt. Just a little too ragged at certain times. That said, this is big and flavoursome and still loads to get our teeth into. *46% nc ncf sc previously Peated Mac na Braiche spirit*

◇◇ **Macaloney's Caledonian Spirit of Kikinriola Single Cask Spirit** triple distilled pot still, recharred Portuguese red wine barrique, db **(93) n23 t23.5 f23 b23.5** A weighty spirit despite having gone through the still thrice: the fruit offers both a Jammy Dodger biscuit to go with the Custard Creams. Excellent spices, in perfect sync. And the late chocolate and cherry cake is rather wonderful Superbly constructed. Seriously tasty and complex *46% nc ncf sc previously Darach Poitin spirit*

◇◇ **Macaloney's Caledonian Spirit of Kikinriola Single Cask Spirit** triple distilled potstill, virgin American cask, db **(91) n22.5 t23 f22.5 b23** The kind of experience to almost leave you in a trance, so mesmerising is it. Borderline overly sweet to the point of liqueur. But far too complex to fall into that trap. The mouth feel is ridiculously lush without ever falling into the trap of being cloying. And though all kinds of sugars abound – golden syrup particularly - the winning formulae is achieved by the ridiculously complex layering of the virgin oak, taking us from red liquorice to black cherry. *46% nc ncf sc*

PEMBERTON DISTILLERY Pemberton, British Columbia. 2008.

Pemberton Valley Single Malt Whisky cask no. 1, 200 litre Four Roses ex-bourbon barrel, dist 20 Sept 10, bott 13 Mar 20 db **(88) n22 t23 f21 b22** A far slicker malt than their previous expressions over the years. Still a niggling degree of feint. But the barley gives full value for money with a confident and intense performance. Rather like the delicate hickory that flits around the nose and the midpoint. Enjoyable. *44%. nc ncf sc.*

Pemberton Valley Single Malt Whisky 120 litre French oak apple brandy cask, dist 22 Nov 14, bott 9 Mar 20 db **(85) n20.5 t22 f21 b21.5** Doesn't hold back on the flavours. Thick with malty, apple-ey nougat. The last note again underlines the weakness of the cut, but the influence of the oak – and the juicy properties of the barley – are first class. *44%. nc ncf sc.*

Pemberton Valley Single Malt Whisky 200 litre Woodford Reserve ex-bourbon barrel, dist 10 Jun 14, bott 9 Mar 20 db **(90) n21.5 t23.5 f22 b23** A much better, more beautifully balanced and rounded malt from Pemberton. Helped by starting off with a much superior spirit than usual. Not perfect, but the extra chocolate nougat notes from the cut fit in very comfortably with the beautifully intense barley. Chewy and delightfully weighted and paced, this is on a different level altogether to anything I have seen from them before. The extra tannin towards the end not only offers weight, but a charming spiciness and depth, too... *44%. nc ncf sc.*

SHELTER POINT DISTILLERY Campbell River, British Columbia. 2011.

Shelter Point Distillery Artisanal Cask Strength Whisky American oak, finished in French oak db **(91) n22.5 t23.5 f22 b23** Looks as though the law in Canada now says you even have to have the barrels from both English and French language... A beautifully complex and intense malt. *54.8%. 1,200 bottles.*

Shelter Point Artisanal Single Malt Whisky Distiller's Select db **(94.5) n23 t24 f23.5 b24** When I initially tasted this distillery's very first maturing cask quite a little while ago now, the evidence provided by the lightly yellowing spirit left me fully confident that they would, with great care, be capable of producing a very high class malt. They have not let me down. This is truly beautiful. 46%. nc ncf.

Shelter Point Double Barreled Single Malt Whisky finished for 335 days in Quails Gate Pinot Noir cask, bott 2019 db **(89)** n22 t23 f21.5 b22.5 Whisky from one of my favourite Canadian distilleries maturing in a barrel from one of my favourite Pinot Noir winemakers. Quails Gate is usually pretty dry and medium bodied, sometimes a tad heavier. Shelter Point malt is delicate. The balance, as might be expected is patchy. But when it works, it does so beautifully...; 50%. nc ncf.

Shelter Point Double Barreled Whisky finished for 152 days in Quails Gate Old Vines Foch cask, batch no. 4, bott 2019 db **(86)** n22 t21 f22 b21 Nowhere near the usual high standard of Shelter Point. The wine has overwhelmed the malt and seldom is there cohesion. Juicy in part with the odd cocoa note. But not an unqualified success. 50%. nc ncf. 1,644 bottles.

Shelter Point Single Cask Quails Gate Old Vines Foch Reserve Finish bott 2019 db **(84.5)** n22 t22.5 f20 b20 A hard, tight whisky which is unforgiving. The fruit seems detached and the whole metallic and tart. The big, juicy flavour delivery apart, fails to find happiness on the palate. 46%. nc ncf sc. 228 bottles. Single Cask Release no. 2.

Shelter Point Single Cask Virgin Oak Finish db **(95.5)** n23.5 t24 f23.5 b24.5 Stunningly well distilled and matured: an absolute pearl from the distillery on the Oyster River... 56.8%. nc ncf sc. 174 bottles. Edition no. 3.

Shelter Point Smoke Point Whisky peat finished, bott 2019 db **(92.5)** n23 t23 f23 b23.5 Even the healthy dose of peat injected into this with a high-quality finish can't entirely hide away the youthful nature of this malt. But when something is this fresh, mouth-watering and simply alive, then perhaps you don't want it to. Oh, for the vitality of youth... 55%. nc ncf. 1,044 bottles.

SHERINGHAM DISTILLERY Sooke, British Columbia. 2015.

Sheringham Whisky Red Fife grain: Red Fife/barley, ex-bourbon cask, bott 2019 db **(86)** n21.5 t22 f21 b21.5 Not technically a perfect whisky, but the initial produce of new distilleries very seldom are. The usual light feint at work here which adds on the extra oils and slight bitterness on the finish. But provides, also, an attractive chewability to the abundant sweet caramels extracted from an excellent ex-bourbon cask. A work in progress, for sure. But enough good points not to forsake this distillery from Sooke. 45%.

SPIRIT OF YORK Toronto, Ontario. 2015.

Spirit of York 100% Rye db **(93.5)** n24.5 t23.5 f22 b23.5 Whoever engineered this, their first-ever whisky bottling, must have been using the Lawrenceburg, Indiana, rye as its blueprint, including virgin oak casks. Matches its intensity and clarity in so many ways, though perhaps not at the death. For a first whisky from Toronto's famous and historic distilling district, the distillers from the Spirit of York should take a bow: this is memorable and authentic stuff distilled, romantically, in part of the old Gooderham and Worts Building...! Toronto is well and truly back on the whisky distilling map... 46% (92 proof).

STILLWATERS DISTILLERY Concord, Ontario. 2009.

Stalk & Barrel 100% Rye Single Cask Whisky **(86.5)** n20 t23 f21.5 b22 Despite the light feintiness, this really does rack up some big rye notes. Rock hard from nose to finish – save for the oils from the wide cut – the delivery and afterglow offer a stupendous degree of grain and spice. Technically not perfect, but worth discovering just for the uncompromising ride. 60.2%. sc.

Stalk & Barrel Single Malt Whisky **(84)** n19 t22.5 f21.5 b21 Full on malty, chocolate-laden spiced toffee nougat. Once past the so-so nose, becomes pretty enjoyable. 60.2%. sc.

YUKON BREWING Whitehorse, Yukon. 1997.

◈ **Two Brewers Yukon Single Malt Release 19 Peated** db **(91.5)** n22.5 t22.5 f23 b23.5 Not often you find a crisp and flinty peated malt. But here's one with knobs on. The smoke is well structured and firm, allowing it to come across on both nose and palate in bipolar fashion, as there is a secondary floaty softness filling in all the gapes. There appears to be a fruity element to this, too...vaguely plummy, of the under-ripe variety. The spices and soot form late on for a highly satisfying and well balanced finish 43%.

◈ **Two Brewers Yukon Single Malt Release 20 Innovative** db **(93)** n23 t23.5 f23 b23.5 I do love the way this malt keeps things simple. If I'm not mistaken there is some maple cask influence here, as the sugars have a particular roasty tightness to it peculiar to that style. But better still that wood type also lassoes the malt to hold it firmly in place. It's kind of simplistic in a surprisingly complex way once you really start studying its format. The other plus is the overall mouth feel: a combination of rich, oak, dried sugars giving a certain thickness for the malt to infuse into. Once you start adding the buzzing spice, we have a whisky of understated and easily missed complexity. A bit of an easily overlooked gem, this. 43%.

⟨⟩ **Two Brewers Yukon Single Malt Release 21 Classic** db (82) n20.5 t22 f19.5 b20 An untidy malt for this increasingly impressive distillery. There is a bizarre bubblegum and minty chewing gum persona which arrives on the nose and refuses to give any ground, even at the death. Plenty of spice and sugars yinging and yanging but never particularly comfortable or happy with itself. 43%.

⟨⟩ **Two Brewers Yukon Single Malt Release 23 Special Finishes** sherry & port barrels db (91) n22.5 t23 f22.5 b23 Some lovely cask at work here. No off notes, no sulphur. Just beautifully distilled malt allowed to stretch itself about some accommodating oak. The fruit does perhaps simplify some of the personality on show, allowing a silky, toffee-raisin maltiness to spread about the palate. Not expected, though, is the pin-pricking busy spices which offer another dimension entirely. The two styles work wonderfully well together. Even better, the muscovado sugars meld with the grist gorgeously. 46%.

⟨⟩ **Two Brewers Yukon Single Malt Release 25 Peated** db (92.5) n23 t22.5 f23.5 b23.5 Have to admit, I have a soft spot for peaty whiskies which start off light and on the back foot, tricking you into thinking the phenols are not there. But, by the time the malt has finished performing its act, you are left in no doubt of its phenolic capabilities. This is a much saltier cove than Release 19, another attractively peated effort. And buttery, too, so the initially gristy sugars on delivery glide over the light, creamy oils. Indeed, the delivery is a little simplistic, happy for the malty grist to bear the brunt. Slowly, however, a charming complexity evolves, helped along by the smoke which girds its loins and sings lustily to the spicy finish. I am slowly falling in love with this distillery... 43%

Canadian Single Rye
CIRKA DISTILLERIES Montréal, Quebec. 2014.
Cirka Premier Whisky 93/07 Québécois Réserve Paul Cirka 3 years in new American oak #3, 5 weeks in Oloroso sherry casks db (82) n22 t21.5 f19.5 b19 Fantastic to see a new distillery making 100% rye whisky in Canada. It warms the heart! Not so good, though, is to see the grain vanish without trace under an uncompromising blanket of fruit, so the rye's unique qualities cannot be heard and enjoyed. A smattering of sulphur from the oloroso butt does it no favours, either. Still, I look forward to seeing this distillery flourish. It deserves to. 46%. nc ncf.

Canadian Blended Whisky
Alberta Premium (95.5) n24 t25 f22.5 b24 It has just gone 8am and the Vancouver Island sky is one of clear blue. My windows are open to allow in some chilly, early Spring air and, though only the first week of March, an American robin sits in the arbutus tree, resplendent in its now two-toned leaves, calling for a mate, as it has done since 5.15 this morning, his song blending with the lively trill of the house finches and the doleful, maritime anthem of the gull. It seems the natural environment of Alberta Premium, back here to its rye-studded best after a couple I tasted socially in Canada last year appeared comparatively dull and restrained. I am tasting this from Bottle Lott No L93300197 and it is classic, generating all I expect and now demand. A national treasure. 40%

Alberta Premium Aged 20 Years db (72) n19.5 t20.5 f15 b17 Singularly the biggest disappointment of the year. A strange cold tea and tobacco note has infiltrated what is usually the most rock-solid rye in the business. This is my beloved Alberta Premium.... unrecognisable. They have got this so wrong... 42%.

Alberta Premium Cask Strength Rye bott code: L9212ADB013408:16 db (97.5) n24.5 t24.5 f24 b24.5 Truley world-class whisky from possibly the world's most underatted distillery. How can something be so immense yet equally delicate? For any whisky lover on the planet looking for huge but nearly perfectly balanced experience, then here you go. And with rye at its most rampantly beautiful, this is something to truly worship. Daily. 65.1%.

Bearface Aged 7 Years Triple Oak Canadian Single Grain ex-bourbon barrels, finished in French oak red wine barrels & Hungarian oak, bott no. H1418W1MH (88.5) n22 t22.5 f22 b22 About as soft as whisky gets. If they could find a way of tuning out some of the caramel, they'd definitely have a more satisfying whisky. 45.5%.

Bearface One Eleven Series batch no. 1, nbc (89) n22 t23 f22 b22 OK, this is one very weird Canadian whisky. But is it enjoyable? Well, anyone who says it isn't is telling you a Bearfaced lie... 42.5%. Ten parts Bearface cut with one part Agave Espadín.

⟨⟩ **Benjamin Chapman 7 Year Rye** (86.5) n21.5 t23 f20 b22 Once you overcome the nose, which appears almost to possess a hoppy kick, we are on much more enjoyable territory. Incredible molasses and cocoa theme, especially on the glutinous delivery. The strange hop-like bitterness returns at the very death, alas. But such is the glorious richness of the delivery, this is well worth looking out for. 45% (90 proof) imported & bottled by 3Badge.com

Black Velvet (78) n18 t20 f20 b20. A distinctly off-key nose is compensated for by a rich corn and vanilla kick on the palate. But that famous spice flourish is a distant memory. Another big caramel number. 40%

Canadian Club 100 Proof (89) n21 t23 f22 b23. If you are expecting this to be a high-octane version of the standard CC Premium, you'll be in for a shock. This is a much fruitier dram with an oilier body to absorb the extra strength. An entertaining blend. 50%

Canadian Club 100% Rye (92) n23 t23.5 f22.5 b23 Will be interesting to see how this brand develops over the years. Rye is not the easiest grain to get right when blending differing ages and casks with varied histories: it is an art which takes time to perfect. This is a very attractive early bottling, though my money is on it becoming sharper in future vattings as the ability to show the grain above all else becomes more easily understood. Just so wonderful to see another excellent addition to the Canadian whisky lexicon. 40% (80 proof)

Canadian Club 1858 Original Blended Canadian Whisky American oak barrels, bott code: L0042FFB325471529 **(92) n23 t23.5 f22.5 b23** One of those quiet, understated and criminally underrated whiskies which pays back close scrutiny handsomely. 40%

⬥ **Canadian Club 1858 Original** bott code: L1019FFBB **(91) n22** a much more pronounced toffee-raisin effect here than recent bottlings; **t23.5** ah, the highlight: the delivery! Just an adorable transition from pure silk to peppery spices tweaking the taste buds. The midground becomes a lightly oaked and toffee chewathon; **f22.5** thinner than previous years, allowing those peppers to ramp up the heat; **b23** I'm always amused when I hear from single malt connoisseurs that Canadian Club is a neutral whisky. Gosh, if those peppers are neutral, I'd hate to see what they do should they ever go to war... 40%

Canadian Club Chronicles: Issue No. 1 Water of Windsor Aged 41 Years (97) n24.5 t24 f24 b24.5 Have I had this much fun with a sexy 41-year-old Canadian before? Well, yes I have. But it was a few years back now and it wasn't a whisky. Was the fun we had better? Probably not. It is hard to imagine what could be, as this whisky simply seduces you with the lightness and knowledgeable meaning of its touch, butterfly kissing your taste buds, finding time after time your whisky erogenous zone or g spots ... and then surrendering itself with tender and total submission. 45% (90 proof).

Canadian Club Chronicles Aged 42 Years bott code: L19260IW **(96.5) n24 t24 f24 b24.5** I have just tasted one of the top ten whiskies of the year for absolute certain. Simply spellbinding. 45% (90 proof). Issue No. 2.

⬥ **Canadian Club Chronicles Aged 43 Years** bott code: L202311W11:20 **(95) n24.5** where the 42-year-old was delicate, fragile even, this is another matter: what we are talking here is assertive spicy oak. Indeed, the tannins come in varying guises, cedarwood leading the way. While the spices have decided to roll their sleeves up and mean business: this is super-prickly. There is a stark fruitiness to this, too: dried orange peel – old thick-cut marmalade from a jar reopened after a couple of years. The whole nose is now geared towards age and assuredness. So much so that for the first time we're beginning to notice a timbre not unaligned to bourbon. This nose is not just Chronicling: it is making a statement; **t23.5** cometh the age, cometh the toffee. Where I had expected vanillas, I now get caramel: presumably the oak is depositing chewier elements into the mix as the spirit explores deeper. That gorgeous caress to a light, corny, mouth-feel has not deserted us, though, and as the toffee subsides momentarily, at last the vanilla and incorrigible spice rush in to quite different effect: one soothing and bathing, the other nipping an biting...; **f23** after the busy layering and counter attractions through the middle, the finale is relatively simple and supine, though with a light ache of oak bitterness at h death; **b24** this has certainly moved on, even from the 42-year-old and a long way from the 41. To truly understand this Canadian, the Murray Method is not just a suggestion, but essential. It opens up the nose to show one of the most complex and complete in the world this year, involving layering and subtle side plots which eventually mesmerise. By comparison, the experience on the palate is more simplistic, as is always the case when caramels begin to enter the conversation: had it been the equal of the nose, this would have been in the running for World Whisky of the Year... 45%. Issue No. 3 - The Speakeasy. 🏆

Canadian Club Premium (92) n23 t22.5 f23 b23.5. A greatly improved whisky which now finds the fruit fitting into the mix with far more panache than of old. Once a niggardly whisky, often seemingly hell-bent on refusing to enter into any form of complexity: but not now! Great spices in particular. I'm impressed. 40%

Canadian Mist (78) n19 t20.5 f18.5 b20. Much livelier than previous incarnations despite the inherent, lightly fruited softness. 40%

Century Reserve Custom Blend 15 Years Plus (88.5) n21.5 t22 f23 b22. After two days of being ambushed in every direction, or completely steamrollered by Canadian caramel, my tastebuds are in total shock. Caramel kept to an absolute minimum so that it hardly registers at all. Charming and refined drinking. 40%

Century Reserve 21 Years Old (91.5) n23.5 t23 f23 b22. Quite beautiful, but a spirit that is as likely to appeal to rum lovers as whisky ones. *40%*

Crown Royal bott code: 318 B4 2111 **(87.5)** n22 t23 f21 b21.5 Carries on in the same style as above. But at least the finish is a lot happier now with welcome ulmo honey extending further and the spices also working overtime. Still a little residual bitterness shows more work is required but, unquestionably, keep on this course and they'll soon be getting there. *40%*

Crown Royal Black (85) n22 t23 f18.5 b21.5. Not for the squeamish: a Canadian which goes for it with bold strokes from the off which makes it a whisky worth discovering. The finish needs a rethink, though. *45%*

◈ **Crown Royal Black** bott code: L9 337 N9 4:05 db **(87)** n21 t22 f22 b22 Definitely an improvement from the last time I tasted this, which was something akin to being hit over the head by a branch falling from a maple tree. Sill it maintains its muscular façade, and the nose with its peculiar fruity barbs is still a little bit of a challenge; but now it offers something which before eluded it: layering. Chewier and sweet and sugars now seem to enjoy a pleasant toing and froing with the toasty oak and spice. Plenty to grapple with here. *45% (90 proof).*

Crown Royal Blender's Select Bourbon Whiskey db **(91)** n22 t23.5 f22.5 b23 A pretty classic Canadian very much in the Crown Royal mould. *44% (88 proof).*

Crown Royal Bourbon Mash Bill bott code: L8 N04 N7 db **(94.5)** n23.5 t23.5 f23.5 b24 Whiskies like this do so much to up the standing of Canadian whisky. *40% (80 proof).*

Crown Royal Cornerstone Blend (85.5) n21 t22 f21 b21.5. Something of a mish-mash, where a bold spiciness appears to try to come to terms with an, at times, random fruity note. One of the most curious aspects of this quite different whisky is the way in which the weight of the body continues to change. Intriguing. *40.3% (80.6 proof).*

Crown Royal DeLuxe (91.5) n23.5 t23 f22.5 b22.5 Some serious blending went into this. Complex. *40% (80 proof)*

Crown Royal Hand Selected Barrel (94.5) n23.5 t24 f23.5 b23.5 If this is a single barrel, it boasts extraordinary layering and complexity *51.5% (103 proof)*

Crown Royal Limited Edition (87) n22 t22.5 f20.5 b22. A much happier and productive blend than before with an attractive degree of complexity but the more bitter elements of the finish have been accentuated. *40%*

Crown Royal Noble Collection 13 Year Old Bourbon Mash bott code: L8037 2S 00108:06 db **(96)** n24.5 t24 f23.5 b24 It's Canadian, Jim: but not as we know it... Deliciously going places where no other Canadian has gone before... *45% (90 proof).*

◈ **Crown Royal Noble Collection 16-Year-Old Rye** db **(86)** n22 t22 f21 b21 Very curious Canadian, this, nothing in the league of Northern Harvest. Slightly too many dead ends – especially on the finish – and baffling green tea moments. When the rye is let loose it howls loudly and hits with juicy precision, especially on delivery. But the background noise is clumsy and confusing. Just never happily harmonises and also difficult to see what its objective is. Yours, Confused, England... *45% (90 proof).*

◈ **Crown Royal Noble Collection French Oak Cask Finished** bott code: L9 086 2S 001 db **(88.5)** n22.5 t23.5 f20.5 b22 Not quite the same tale of unalloyed joy at the last time I tasted this. This is an altogether tighter version with most of the fun restricted to the delivery which, when combined with a satin mouth-feel, makes for a gorgeous fruit-laced and spicy experience made all the chewer by the generous toffee. However, the finish is bitter, tangy, and completely out of sorts, undoing some of the earlier excellent work. Hopefully, the next bottling will be a little truer to type. *40% (80 proof).*

Crown Royal Northern Harvest Rye bott code L5085 N3 **(97.5)** n25 t24.5 f23.5 b24.5 This is the kind of whisky you dream of dropping into your tasting room. Rye, that most eloquent of grains, not just turning up to charm and enthral but to also take us through a routine which reaches new heights of beauty and complexity. To say this is a masterpiece is barely doing it justice. *45%*

Crown Royal Northern Harvest Rye bott code: 095 B1 0247 db **(95.5)** n24 t24 f23.5 b24 Not quite the same beguiling intensity as the batch which once won the Whisky Bible's World Whisky of the Year, but what an absolute salivating treat of a whisky this remains...as sprightly and fresh as any NHR I have tasted yet. *45% (90 proof).*

Crown Royal Northern Harvest Rye bott code: L8 353 N5 **(97)** n25 t24 f23.5 b24.5 Having spent a little while in Canada over the last year, I have had the pleasure of a few stunning Northern Harvest Ryes in that time. But I admit I did a double-take when this bottling turned up in my lab for the official sample tasting. It was by far the darkest example of this brand I had ever seen – and I admit that I feared the worst, as that can often mean the sharp complexity which is the hallmark of a whisky such as this can be compromised. I need not have worried: the glass is almost shattering from the enormity of vivid delights contained therein. A stunning whisky, as usual, but they will have to ensure that the colour returns to its lighter gold, perhaps with slightly younger casks, to guarantee the fresh style remains, as this could easily have become a dullard. This, though, is anything but. *45% (90 proof).*

◈ **Crown XR Extra Rare** bott code: L9 257 2S 001 db **(94)** n23.5 adorable mix of varied fruit notes: most are of a dried citrus peel variety, including blood orange and lime. But even better is the balance and weight which intertwangles the drier vanillas with the shy sugars beautifully. The oak is constant....and consistent...; **t23.5** allow me a little groan of delight with this one: the weight of the sugars and oils are exemplary. But even better still is the pulsing of the tannins which offers both a slow spice attack and a far weightier depth **f23** dark, chewy toffee with layering of spice and raisin. But always...and I mean always!... the outstanding throbbing of the tannins...; **b24** complex and absolutely first rate. I had feared it would not live up to earlier glories. But the blender must take a bow: this is serious blending..! *40% (80 proof).*

Crown Royal XO (87.5) n22 t21 f22.5 b22. With an XO, one might have hoped for something eXtraOrdinary or at least eXOtic. Instead, we have a Canadian which carried on a little further where their Cask No 16 left off. Always a polite, if rather sweet whisky, it falls into the trap of allowing the Cognac casks a little too much say. Only on the finish, as the spices begin to find channels to flow into, does the character which, for generations, set Crown Royal apart from all other Canadians begin to make itself heard: complexity. *40% WB15/398*

Gibson's Finest Aged 12 Years (77) n18 t20 f19 b20. Unlike the Sterling, going backwards rather than forwards. This is way too syrupy, fruity and toffee impacted. Despite the very good spice, almost closer to a liqueur than a true whisky style. *40%*

Gibson's Finest Rare Aged 18 Years (95.5) n24 t24.5 f23.5 b23.5 So far ahead of both Sterling and the 12, it is hard to believe they are from the same stable. But make no mistake; this is pure thoroughbred: truly world class. *40%*

◈ **Great Plains Craft Spirits 18-Year-Old Brandy Casks** finished in Jerez brandy casks, bond date. 09 01 00, batch no.1 **(95)** n23.5 a whisky that needs studying on the nose for as long as you can spare as this shews rare unification between aged oak and slightly unusual fruit tones. Never aggressive, it is always firm, though gives a slightly misleading softer feel. As fascinating as it is charming...; **t24** silk...and then there we are that crisp, firm undertone, just as can be found on the nose. It is the extraordinary lushness which will equally amaze and seduce...; **f23.5** Fry's Turkish Delight...with a tannin-rich backbone...; **b24** Great Plains it may be. But there is nothing plane, or particularly Canadian, about this one-off blockbusting beauty. This is something completely different...and if you are not careful it will seduce you until you have tracked down every last bottle. Superb cask management married to a very impressive distillate results in a Canadian offering rare cadence. To say I'm impressed doesn't quite cover it... *54.5% (109 proof)*

Heavens Door The Bootleg Series Canadian Whisky 26 Years Old 2019 finished in Japanese Mizunara oak casks **(96)** n24 t24 f23.5 b24.5 It thrills me when I see Canadian whisky take on this advanced form of complexity, rather than rely on the false promises of fruit juice. A standing ovation to those responsible for this delightful and star quality Canadian. *55.75% (111.5 proof). 3,797 bottles.*

the required sharpness. *40%.*

J.P. Wiser's 18 Years Old bott code 54SL24 L16341 **(94)** n23 t24 f23 b24 Some great blending here means this is a slight notch up on the bottling above, though the styles are almost identical. Main differences here concern the fruit aspect: more prolific and spicier on the nose and then added moist date on the delivery. Significantly, there is more honey on the longer finish, also. Remains a deliciously rounded and satisfying whisky. *40%.*

J. P. Wiser's 35 Year Old (96) n23.5 t24 f24 b24.5 Many, many years ago I tasted Canadian older than this in the blending lab. But I have never seen it before at this age as an official bottling. What I had before me on the lab table could not have engineered this style, so this is as fascinating as it is enjoyable. *50%. Ultra-Rare Craft Series.*

J. P. Wiser's Dissertation (89) n22 t22 f22 b22.5 A distinctive and quite different style being handsome, a little rugged but always brooding. *46.1%.*

J.P. Wiser's Double Still Rye (94) n23.5 t23.5 f23.5 b23.5 Big, superb rye: a genuine triumph from Wiser's. *43.4%*

J.P. Wiser's Last Barrels Aged 14 Years (94.5) n24.5 t23.5 f23.5 b23.5 You don't need to be pulsing with rye to ensure a complex Canadian of distinction. *45%*

J. P. Wiser's Rye 15 Year Old (89) n22 t22.5 f22.5 b22 Doesn't do too much. But what it does do, it does big... *40%.*

J. P. Wiser's Rye Triple Barrel bott code L16331 54SL24 **(85.5)** n22 t21.5 f21 b21 Three types of toffee barrel by the looks of it. Pleasant but lacking complexity. *45%.*

J. P. Wiser's Seasoned Oak Aged 19 Years seasoned 48 months, bott code L18114EW0814 **(87.5)** n22.5 t23 ff20.5 b21.5 Some high-octane tannin trumps all, though some rich fruit – moist dates especially - rounds off the peppery oak. Enjoys a glossy, coppery but unravels somewhat at the death with a furry, off-key finale. Some lovely, lilting moments but the balance seems controlled. 48%. Rare Cask Series. Exclusive to the LCBO.

Lot 40 Cask Strength (88.5) n23.5 t24 f20 b22 At last! Lot 40 at full strength! You will not read this anywhere (or anything to do with my many whisky creations over the last 25 years as journalists can sometimes be a pathetically narrow-minded and jealous bunch disinclined to tell the true story if it doesn't suit their own agenda) but when I first created the style for Lot 40 a great many years back the first thing I proposed was that it should be a rye at cask strength. The idea was liked in principle but regarded way too radical for its time and dropped. So I helped come up with a weaker but still excellent rye. This is a different style to what I had in mind as the oak gives a slant I would have avoided. But it gladdens my heart to see it nonetheless. 53%. Ultra-Rare Craft Series.

Lot No. 40 Rye Whisky bott code 54SL24 L16344 **(96) n24 t24 f23.5 b24.5** Now this is very close to the rye I had in mind when first involved in putting this whisky together the best part of a couple of decades ago. Much more complex and satisfying than the previous re-introduced bottling I encountered...which in itself was magnificent. Here, though, the honey I had originally tried to lasso has been brilliantly recaptured. Happy to admit: this is better than my early efforts. There really is a Lot going on... Classic! 43%.

Masterson's 10 Year Old Straight Rye Whiskey batch no. 016 **(94) n23 t23 f24 b24** One of the most beautiful finishes to any whisky on the planet this year. 45% (90 proof).

Pendleton 1910 Aged 12 Years Rye (83) n21 t22 f20 b20. Pleasant enough. But if it wasn't for the small degree of spice pepping up this fruitfest, it would be all rather too predictable. 40%

Pike Creek French, Hungarian & American oak casks **(89) n23 t22.5 f21.5 b22** You know you have a great nose on your hands when a fly drowns in your whisky even before you get a chance to taste it... Decent stuff keeping your taste buds at full stretch. 45%.

Pike Creek 10 Years Old finished in port barrels **(80) n21.5 t22.5 f17 b19.** The delivery is the highlight of the show by far as the fruit takes off backed by delicate spices and spongy softness. The nose needs some persuading to get going but when fully warmed, gives a preview of the delivery. The furry finish is a big disappointment, though.40%

Pike Creek 10 Year Old Rum Barrels Finish bott code 54SL24 L16174 EW07:30 **(86.5) n22 t22.5 f20 b22** A far happier fellow than the Port finish, for sure – even though the slight furriness on the finale is a bit of a bore. Before reaching that point, though, there is a velvet revolution involving much honey. 42%.

Pike Creek 21 Year Old Single Malt Cask Finish (87.5) n21 t23.5 f21.5 b21.5 Pleasant and fruity. As silky as you like with a moist date and spiced theme. But, doubtless, through the cask finish, the age and accompanying complexities seems to have been lost in translation somewhere... 45%. Ultra-Rare Craft Series.

Rich and Rare (79) n20 t20 f20 b19. Simplistic and soft. One for toffee lovers. 40%

Rich and Rare Reserve (86.5) n19.5 t21 f23.5 b22.5. Actually does what it says on the tin, certainly as to regard the "Rich" bit. But takes off when the finish spices up and even offers some ginger cake on the finale. Lovely stuff. 40%

Sam Barton Aged 5 Years bott code: L814502B **(86.5) n21 t22 f21.5 b22** A much improved blend of late with a much studier structure after the clean, now classically Canadian nose. Good spice buzz and lots of easy charm. 40%. La Martiniquaise.

Seagram's Canadian 83 (86.5) n21 t22 f21.5 b22. A vastly improved blend which has drastically cut the caramel to reveal a melt-in-the-mouth, slightly crisp grain. There are some citrusy edges but the buttery vanilla and pleasing bite all go to make for a chic little number. 40%

Seagram's VO (91) n22 t23.5 f22.5 b23. With a heavy heart I have to announce the king of rye-enriched Canadian, VO, is dead. Long live the corn-dominant VO. Over the years I have seen the old traditional character ebb away: now I have let go and have no option other than to embrace this whisky for what it has become: infinitely better than a couple of years back; not in the same league as a decade ago. But just taking it on face value, credit where credit is due. This is an enjoyably playful affair, full of vanilla-led good intention, corn and complexity. There is even assertive spice when needed and the most delicately fruity edge...though not rye-style. Thoughtfully blended and with no little skill, I am impressed. And look forward to seeing how this develops in future years. A treat which needs time to discover. 40%

Signal Hill Whisky bott no. 181560932 **(82) n21.5 t21.5 f19 b20** There is no little irony that a hill which dramatically juts 470 feet out of the sea to present one of Canada's most startling and historical points should be represented by a whisky that is so intransigently flat... 40%. ncf.

Union 52 (90.5) n23 t23 f22.5 b23 A very different type of Canadian which is as busy as it gets. 40%.

Western Gold Canadian Whisky (91) n23 t23 f22.5 b22.5. Clean and absolutely classic Canadian: you can't ask for much more, really. 40%

Scottish Malts

For those of you deciding to take the plunge and head off into the labyrinthine world of Scotch malt whisky, a piece of advice. And that is, be careful who you take your advice from. Because, too often, I hear that you should leave the Islays until you have tackled the featherlight Speysiders and the bolder, weightier Highlanders. This is just complete, patronising nonsense. The only time that rings true is if you are tasting a number of whiskies in one day. Then leave the smoky ones till last, so the lighter chaps get a fair hearing.

I know many people who didn't like whisky until they got a Talisker from Skye inside them, or a Lagavulin to swamp their tastebuds with oily iodine. The fact is, you can take your map of malt whisky, start at any point and head in whichever direction you feel. There are no hard and fast rules. Certainly with over 1,600 tasting notes for Scottish malts here you should have some help in picking where this journey of a lifetime begins.

It is also worth remembering not always to be seduced by age. It is true that many of the highest scores are given to big-aged whiskies. The truth is that the majority of malts, once they have lived beyond 25 years or so, suffer from oak influence rather than benefit. Part of the fun of discovering whiskies is to see how malts from different distilleries perform to age and type of cask. Happy discovering.

Abhainn Dearg

LEWIS

Isle of Harris

SKYE Isle of Raas

Talisker

Torabhaig

Ardnamurc

Tobermory Ncn'ean

MULL

Oban

Isle of Jura

ISLAY

Isle of Arra

Springbank
Glen Scotia
Glengyle

Islay

Bunnahabhain
Ardnahoe
Caol Ila

Kilchoman
Bruichladdich
Bowmore

Port Ellen Ardbeg
Laphroaig Lagavulin

ORKNEY ISLANDS

Highland Park
Scapa

Wolfburn

Pultney

Clynelish
Brora

Dornoch

Balblair
Glenmorangie
Dalmore
Invergordon
Teaninich

Speyside see page 24

Glen Ord
Glenglassaugh
GlenWyris
Royal Brackla
Knockdhu
Banff ✞
Macduff
Inverness
Glen Albyn ✞
Glendronach
Glenugie
Glen Mhor ✞
Tomatin
Ardmore
Millburn ✞
Gien Garioch
The Speyside Distillery
Royal Lochnagar

Dalwhinnie
Aberdeen

✞ Glenury Royal

Fettercairn

Blair Athol
Glencadam
✞ North Port
Glenesk ✞
Fort William
Edradour
Lochside
Ben Nevis
Aberfeldy
Arbikie
Glenlochy ✞

Lindores
Dundee
Strathearn Abbey

Glenturret
Perth
Aberargie
Daftmill
Kingsbarns
Tullibardine
Eden Mill

Deanston
Cameronbridge
InchDairnie

Glengoyne
✞ Rosebank
St. Magdelene
Glenkinchie
Loch Lomond
✞ **Dumbarton**
Starlaw
Edinburgh
✞ Interleven
North British
✞ Littlemill
Glasgow
Auchentoshan
Glasgow
Strathclyde
Port Dundas
Kinclaith ✞

Borders

Girvan
Ailsa Bay
Ladyburn ✞

Annandale

Bladnoch

Key	
●	**Major Town or City**
▲	Single Malt Distillery
▲	(*Italics*) Grain Distillery
✞	Dead Distillery

Speyside

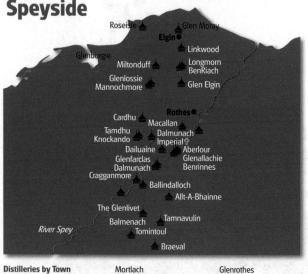

Roseisle
Glen Moray
Elgin
Linkwood
Glenburgie
Miltonduff
Longmorn
BenRiach
Glenlossie
Mannochmore
Glen Elgin
Rothes
Cardhu
Macallan
Tamdhu
Dalmunach
Knockando
Imperial ✚
Dailuaine
Aberlour
Glenfarclas
Glenallachie
Dalmunach
Benrinnes
Cragganmore
Ballindalloch
Allt-A-Bhainne
The Glenlivet
Tamnavulin
Balmenach
River Spey
Tomintoul
Braeval

Distilleries by Town	Mortlach	Glenrothes
Dufftown	Dufftown	Glenspey
Glenfiddich	Pittyvaich	**Keith**
Convalmore	**Rothes**	Aultmore
Balvenie	Speyburn	Strathmill
Kininvie	Glen Grant	Glen Keith
Glendullan	Caperdonich	Strathisla

SINGLE MALTS
ABERFELDY

Highlands (Perthshire), 1898. Bacardi. Working.

Aberfeldy Aged 12 Years bott code: L19032249021553 db **(78.5) n20 t20.5 f19 b19** Reduced to 40% and then rammed with caramel for colouring. And we are talking at this age, when tasted in good bourbon casks, one of Scotland's more delightful and effortlessly complex whiskies. Instead we are still presented with this absolute non-event of a bottling. Bewildering. *40%.*

Aberfeldy Guaranteed 15 Years in Oak finished in red wine casks, batch no. 2919, bott code: L19291ZA8021209 db **(92) n22.5 t23 f23.5 b23** No easy task to create a whisky that is both exceptionally gentle and delicate but without being bland and uninteresting. They have pulled it off here! *43%.*

Aberfeldy Aged 16 Years bott code: L16118ZA805 db **(83.5) n21 t21 f20.5 b21** An astonishingly dull whisky for its age. Sweet and soft for sure, but very little character as it appears to bathe in rich toffee. If you want a safe, pleasant whisky which says very little, here's your dram. *40%.*

Aberfeldy Aged 21 Years bott code: L18092ZA803 db **(88) n22 t22.5 f21.5 b22** Poodles along pleasantly but feels like a Fiat Uno engine in what, for this distillery, should be Jaguar XK... *40%.*

Aberfeldy Aged 25 Years db **(85) n24 t21 f19 b21.** Just doesn't live up to the nose. When Tommy Dewar wrote, "We have a great regard for old age when it is bottled," as quoted on the label, I'm not sure he had as many as 25 years in mind. *40%.*

Gordon & MacPhail Connoisseurs Choice Aberfeldy Aged 25 Years first fill sherry puncheon, cask no. 4054, dist 6 Jun 93, bott 21 Jun 18 **(94.5) n23.5 t24 f23 b24** Don't know about Aberfeldy: almost Aberlour a'bunagh-esque in the intensity of its sherry attack. And make no mistake: this is high grape, faultless oloroso at work here. Except, this presents the fruit in a much more clear, untroubled form, making the power of the personality of the distillery, slowly work its way into the picture which it does thanks to its rich, malty chassis. *58.8%. sc. 444 bottles*

ABERLOUR

Speyside, 1826. Chivas Brothers. Working.

Aberlour 10 Years Old db **(87.5) n22.5 t22 f21 b22.** Remains a lusty fellow though here nothing like as sherry-cask faultless as before, nor displaying its usual honeyed twinkle. *43%*

Aberlour 12 Years Old Double Cask db (89) n22 t23 f21.5 b22.5 A delicately poised malt which makes as much ado about the two different oak types as it does the fruit-malt balancing act. 40%

Aberlour 12 Years Old Double Cask Matured db (88.5) n22 t22.5 f22 b22. Voluptuous and mouth-watering in some areas, firmer and less expansive in others. Pretty tasty in all of them. 43%

Aberlour 12 Years Old Non Chill-Filtered db (87) n22.5 t22 f21 b21.5. There are many excellent facets to this malt, not least the balance between barley and grape and the politeness of the gristy sugars. But a sulphured butt has crept into this one, taking the edge off the excellence and bringing down the score like a cold front drags down the thermometer. 48%. ncf.

Aberlour 12 Years Old Sherry Cask Matured db (88) n23 t22 f21 b22. Could do with some delicate extra sweetness to take it to the next level. Sophisticated nonetheless. 40%

Aberlour 15 Years Cuvee Marie d'Ecosse db (91) n22 t24 f22 b23. This always was a deceptive lightweight, and it's got lighter still. It is sold primarily in France, and one can assume only that this is God's way of making amends for that pretentious, over-rated, caramel-ridden rubbish called Cognac they've had to endure. 43%

Aberlour 15 Year Old Double Cask Matured db (84) n23 t22 f19 b20. Brilliant nose full of vibrant apples and spiced sultana, but then, after a complex, chewy, malt-enriched kick-off, falls surprisingly flat on its face. 40%

Aberlour 15 Year Old Sherry Finish db (91) n24 t22 f23 b22 Quite unique: freaky, even. Really a whisky to be discovered and ridden. Once you acclimatize, you'll adore it. 43%

Aberlour 16 Years Old Double Cask Matured traditional oak & sherry oak casks, bott code: L N2 27 2019/05/14 db (88) n22.5 t22 f21.5 b22 None of the dreaded S word here, so well done sherry butts. But this is underpowered in this day and age for the kind of malt it could be. The lack of oils are crucial. 40%.

Aberlour 18 Years Old db (91) n22 t22 f24 b23 Another high performance distillery age-stated bottling. 43%

Aberlour 100 Proof db (91) n23 t23 f22 b23. Stunning, sensational whisky, the most extraordinary Speysider of them all...which it was when I wrote those official notes for the bottling back in '97, I think. Other malts have superseded it now, but on re-tasting I stand by those original notes, though I disassociate myself entirely with the rubbish: "In order to savour Aberlour 100 at its best add 1/3 to 1/2 pure water." 57.1%

Aberlour A'Bunadh Batch No. 61 Spanish Oloroso sherry butts db (95) n23 t24 f23.5 b24.5 Although matured in 100% sherry butts – and clean, sulphur-free ones at that – one of the most remarkable, and delicious, features of this malt is the bourbon-esque quality of the oak notes mixing in with the grape. Wow! 60.8%. ncf.

Aberlour A'Bunadh Batch No. 63 Spanish Oloroso sherry butts db (93) n23.5 t24 f22 b23.5 Slightly lighter than some A'Bunadhs, which holds out well and seemingly clean until trace bitterness arrives. But so much to savour here. 61%. ncf.

Aberlour Casg Annamh batch no. 0001 db (84.5) n21.5 t22.5 f19 b21.5 The nose is at first promising with nutty sherry tones dominating, then dry but with the most subtle countering muscovado and black cherry sweetness. Then comes the threat of the S word... which is confirmed on the rough, furry finish. The delivery starts with those sugars well into their stride, arriving early and mingling with the spice. Dates and figs represent the fruit with panache. 48%. ncf.

⬦ **Cadenhead's Sherry Cask Aberlour Aged 9 Years** oloroso sherry hogshead, dist 2011, bott 2020 (90) n22 moist cherry cake. No skimping on the malty vanilla, either...; t23 cherry drop candy bursts on to the palate like a firecracker. Profound demerara sugars and playful grist make unusual but compelling bedfellows; f22.5 at last the tannins arrive. But they are soon biffed up be belligerent fruitiness...; b22.5 vibrant, salivating, young and just damned good fun! 55.0%

eSpirits Shop Selection Aberlour 24 Year Old bourbon hogshead, dist 1995, bott 2019 (94.5) n24 t24 f23 b23.5 Proof, were it needed, that the last thing Aberlour requires to underline its credentials are sherry butts. This top quality cask allows the gooseberries and greengages to present something a little special on the nose. And then the creamiest, most intense barley turns into a near foaming tirade of salivating, grassy barley and butterscotch. The finish is pretty quiet by comparison, concentrating on the salty vanillas. What a no-holds-barred experience! 61.3%. sc. 139 bottles. 10 Years of Dailydram.com.

The Perfect Fifth Aberlour 1989 cask no. 11050 (96.5) n24 t24 f24 b24.5 This malt really has pure star quality. Elegant doesn't do it justice. If you find this in a shop, snap their bloody hands off: this is Scotch malt whisky at its very best! 51.5%. nc ncf sc.

ABHAINN DEARG

Highlands (Outer Hebrides), 2008. Marko Tayburn. Working.

Abhainn Dearg New Make db (92.5) n23 t23 f23.5 b23. Exceptionally well made with no feints and no waste, either. Oddly salty – possibly the saltiest new make I have encountered, and can think of no reason why it should be – with excellent weight as some extra copper from the new still takes hold. Given a good cask, no reason this impressive new born son of the Outer Hebrides won't go on to become something significant. *67%*

AILSA BAY
Lowland, 2007. William Grant & Sons. Working.

Ailsa Bay db **(92.5) n23.5 t23.5 f22.5 b23** I remember years back being told they wanted to make an occasional peaty malt at this new distillery different in style to Islay's. They have been only marginally successful: only the finish gives the game away. But they have certainly matched the island when it comes to the average high quality. A resounding success of a first effort, though I'd like to see the finish offer a little more than it currently does. Early days, though. *48.9%*.

ALLT-Á-BHAINNE
Speyside, 1975. Chivas Brothers. Working.

Berry Bros & Rudd Allt-á-Bhainne 23 Year Old cask no. 125314, dist 1995, bott 2019 **(95) n24 t24 f23 b24** I still smile when I think of conversations I held, long before this whisky was ever made, with blenders who preferred to use this distillery's malt at very young ages, especially 3- to 5-years-old because they felt it was a whisky not best suited to great age. This is coming up for nearly 25 years in cask, and there is not a wrinkle, not a single blemish. Superb! *52.7%. nc ncf sc.*

◈ **Chapter 7 Allt-A-Bhainne 2008 Aged 12 Years** Coal Ila finish bourbon barrel, barrel no.169 **(89.5) n22** when served cool diced green apples abound; as it warms light smoke begins to add weight and depth; **t22** oily, increasingly phenolic and chewy. More sharp than sugary, the barley, as usual, picks on the salivation glands...; **f23** takes its time to arrive but the tannins join in the mix. But now the oils have vanished the piece thins out considerably; **b22.5** in many ways typical of this distillery in its fragility. Seen lightly peated A-A-B in the blending lab from time to time. In bottled form, quite a rarity. Limited complexity, but typically charming. *49.7% sc*

Old Malt Cask Allt A'Bhainne Aged 27 Years refill hogshead, cask no. 16942, dist May 92, bott Oct 19 **(94) n23 t23.5 f23.5 b24** Class in a glass. *50%. nc ncf sc. 256 bottles.*

◈ **The Whisky Cask Company Allt-A-Bhainne 1992** bourbon cask, cask no. 1800472, Sep 1992, Jul2020 **(94.5) n23.5** a pretty ancient nose. But the honey is disciplined, firm and holds the toastier elements in shape. Heather honey with careful attendance by a mix of bourbon-stye liquorice, vanilla, and molasses...; **t23.5** you know that bourbon-style sweetness will turn up somewhere along the line on the palate, and you don't have to wait too long. Oddly enough, for a brief moment you can easily mistake the delivery for corn oil. But it is actually the light ulmo honey taking on board the remnants of the malt and the lighter vanillas; **f23.5** if age is going to be the undoing of this malt, then this is the point where the cracks will appear. But none do. A delightful beeswax and honey fade seems to gloss over the toastier elements of the tannins. This is one very elegant finale...; **b24** I have to admit I was pretty dubious as to whether this malt could make it from one end of the tasting experience to the other without disintegrating: this is not a distillery built for great age. But, my word, it made it: taxed by the tannins, but, protected by the distinct, Clynelishesque waxy honey, you still feel there may have been another four or five years to spare with this one with careful handling... *49.2% nc ncf sc 272 bottles*

ANNANDALE
Lowlands, 2014. Annandale Distillery Company Ltd. Working.

Annandale Founders' Collection Man O'Words 2016 American oak hogshead, cask no. 588 db **(80) n20 t21.5 f18.5 b20** Until now they have timed, chosen and balanced their barrels with almost uncanny and certainly unerring brilliance. Not this time. Here the youth has been amplified to slightly ill-effect, giving this a vague belligerence. Add to that casks which are decidedly unhappy and we have a bottling that does this excellent distillery a grave disservice. *61.4%. sc.*

Annandale Founders' Selection Man O'Swords 2016 Spanish oak hogshead, cask no. 544 db **(89) n22 t23 f23 b22.5** Trying to control the goings on between peat and wine cask on a very young malt is like trying to herd cats. Both elements do as they please, whenever they want. However, sometimes they just happen to hit the right pitch at the right time, and a little magic happens. More, though, by luck than judgement... *61.1%. sc.*

Annandale Man O' Sword cask no. 100, dist 2014 db **(92.5) n23.5 t23 f21.5 b23.5** The strangest thing...I nosed this and thought: Jim Swan. This delightful style has the late, great whisky consultant's finger prints all over it. A young malt from a brand new distillery already punching way above its weight age-wise and in terms of complexity. Welcome to the whisky world, Annandale. And what a worthy addition you have already become. Now you just have to keep up this standard: no pressure at all... *61.6%. sc. 256 bottles.*

Annandale Man O' Sword Smoulderingly Smoky once-used ex bourbon cask, cask no. 470, dist 2015 db **(96.5) n24 t24.5 f23.5 b24.5** Make no mistake: new distillery or no, this is fabulously and truly faultlessly made and brilliantly matured whisky which allows every last element of the distillery's personality to be seen. What a genuine treat! What an immense start to such a new distillery! *60.2%. sc. 271 bottles.*

Annandale Man O' Words cask no. 140, dist 2014 db **(89.5) n22.5 t22.5 f22 b22.5** A malty delight. Had been meaning to take in Annan Athletic FC and Annandale Distillery over the last four years but my diary just wouldn't allow it. Somehow I have to make it happen. This distillery promises great things. *61.6%. sc. 273 bottles.*

Annandale Man O' Words once-used ex bourbon cask, cask no. 149, dist 2015 db **(94) n23 t23.5 f23.5 b24** A few months ago I was doing some quality control checks at a warehouse in Scotland and there, much to my surprise, were a whole bunch of newly filled, quietly maturing Annandale casks. You have no idea how much I wanted to take a break from my designated work to sneakily crack open a few of those Lowland barrels to see how they were getting on. I think I should arrange a return visit... Oh, and good people of Annandale, - congratulations and thank you for bottling from ex-bourbon cask. Because we can see the sheer beauty of the malt you are making, something I could not say if it was hidden under (usually faulty) wine casks or obliterated entirely by bloody PX, the scourge of world whisky today. *61%. sc. 268 bottles.*

Annandale Vintage Man O'Words 2015 once used ex-bourbon cask, cask no. 150 db **(96) n24 t24 f23.5 b24.5** Considering this is a 5-y-o whisky only, I think we are going to have to consider the possibility that we have a truly world-class distillery in our midst... So beautifully made and matured, the age seems almost irrelevant. The malt is absolutely immaculate: no malt should be quite this good as this still tender age...! *61.6%. sc.*

The Whisky Chamber Annandale 4 Jahre 2015 bourbon cask **(95) n24 t23.5 f23.5 b24** What can you say about a 4-year-old? Except that you can ask nothing more it than what you get here. Yep, 95 points for a 4-year-old. Ridiculous! Though it is worth every single mark... *59.1%. sc.*

⬧ **The Whisky Chamber Annandale 5 Jahre 2015** PX sherry hogshead **(87.5) n23 t23.5 f22 b19** OK, I admit it. There is nothing wrong with the sherry: no sulphur and clean. However, there is something wrong with the sherry: it is too big for the delicate 5-year-old malt it is smothering the life out of. Imagine a 300lb man's thick woollen overcoat draped over the shoulders of a five-year-old child. The coat still looks as though it is made from beautiful cloth, expertly cut, but its shape is lost as the child buckles and vanishes under its weight. And so we have this whisky. So, yes, the nose and delivery are enjoyable because this is very fine PX, radiating sweet, thick fruit and spices in more than ample quantities. But as the fruit detracts and dries, (and bitters slightly, as is so often the case with PX) where's the malt? Now there's the question... *56.1%. sc.*

ARDBEG

Islay, 1815. Glenmorangie Plc. Working.

Ardbeg 10 Years Old db **(97) n24 t24 f24 b25** Like when you usually come across something that goes down so beautifully and with such a nimble touch and disarming allure, just close your eyes and enjoy... *46%*

Ardbeg 10 bottling mark L10 152 db **(95) n24.5 t23.5 f23.5 b23.5** A bigger than normal version, but still wonderfully delicate. Fabulous and faultless. *46%. Canadian market bottling in English and French dual language label.*

Ardbeg 17 Years Old earlier bottlings db **(92) n23 t22 f23 b24.** OK, I admit I had a big hand in this, creating it with the help of Glenmorangie Plc's John Smith. It was designed to take the weight off the better vintages of Ardbeg whilst ensuring a constant supply around the world. Certainly one of the more subtle expressions you are likely to find, though criticised by some for not being peaty enough. As the whisky's creator, all I can say is they are missing the point. *40%*

Ardbeg 17 Years Old later bottlings db **(90) n22 t23 f22 b23.** The peat has all but vanished and cannot really be compared to the original 17-year-old: it's a bit like tasting a Macallan without the sherry: fascinating to see the naked body underneath, and certainly more of a turn on. Peat or no peat, great whisky by any standards. *40%*

Ardbeg 19 Years Old db **(93) n23 t23 f23.5 b23.5** One of the sensuously understated Ardbegs that could be found in style (though with a different peat imprint) from time to time during the 1960s. *46.2%.*

Ardbeg 19 Years Old 2020 Release db **(89) n21** unusually untidy for Ardbeg. Attractive saline notes but the phenols are uneven to the point of being discordant; **t23** that's much better!

A quite thick set malty-smokiness drifts off towards the toasty sugars. For a moment there is an air of Ardbeg normality as the light vanillas pulse; **f22.5** all understated and full of trickery. Vague minty notes blossom on the light heather-honey phenol. The oak sticks to that salty tang... and tang is the right word...; **b22.5** pretty much OK and enjoyable despite the slight mess on the nose and mildly odd landing. But not sure when it was just OK was acceptable for Ardbeg... *46%.*

Ardbeg 20 Something db **(96.5) n24 t24 f24 b24.5** Such mastery over the phenols...such elegance! It is though the whisky was distilled from gossamer... *46%.*

Ardbeg 21 Years Old db **(96.5) n24 t24 f24 b24.5** Tap into Ardbeg with great care, like someone has done here, and there is no describing what beauty can be unleashed. For much of the time, the smoke performs in brilliant fashion somewhere between the ethereal and profound. *46%*

Ardbeg 23 Year Old db **(93) n22.5 t24 f23 b23.5** A malt forever treading on eggshells, trying not to disturb the tannins. As a dram, makes a nervous wreck of you, as you spend the entire time waiting for the shallow truce to be broken and the oak to declare war and come pouring in. Thankfully, it never quite happens. As all whiskies, not be taken with water. But, in this instance, a tranquilliser might not go amiss... *46.3%.*

Ardbeg 1977 db **(96) n25 t24 f23 b24.** When working through the Ardbeg stocks, I earmarked '77 a special vintage, the sweetest of them all. So it has proved. Only the '74 absorbed that extra oak that gave greater all-round complexity. Either way, the quality of the distillate is beyond measure: simply one of the greatest experiences – whisky or otherwise – of your life. *46%*

Ardbeg 1978 db **(91) n23 t24 f22 b22.** An Ardbeg on the edge of losing it because of encroaching oak, hence the decision made by John Smith and me to bottle this vintage early alongside the 17-year-old. Nearly ten years on, still looks a pretty decent bottling, though slightly under strength! *43%*

Ardbeg An Oa db **(95.5) n24 t24 f23.5 b24** I'd never say "whoa" if someone poured me an Oa... *46%.*

Ardbeg Arrrrrrrdbeg db **(84.5) n21.5 t21.5 f20.5 b21** For me, more aaarrrrgggghhh! than arrrrrrr. For a start, I hardly recognise this as an Ardbeg in style. Since when did that old Bowmore character of Victory V cough sweets hickory been part of its DNA? And what is that weak, lily-livered finish all about. The sugars come and go as they please but without being part of a set plan while the phenols wobble. Yes, of course there are some pleasant (but short-lived) phases. But Ardbeg? Just nowhere near the mark. *51.8%.*

Ardbeg Blaaack db **(92) n22.5 t23 f23.5 b23** Still a different to feel to this than the Ardbegs of old. And though where once upon a time the move through the gears was seamless and this is just a little clunky at times, overall it works rather attractively. *46%.*

Ardbeg Blaaack Committee Release db **(86.5) n22 t22 f21 b21.5** Just way too dull for an Ardbeg. The wine is just a little too busy filing down the edges of the malt and peat to really offer anything constructive. The result is a malt which lurches about the palate with an ungainly countenance. The spices certainly give their all, but the phenols – following an impressive start - are never allowed to make the kind of complex and stunningly balanced contribution that usually sets Ardbeg apart. *50.7%.*

Ardbeg Dark Cove db **(86) n22.5 t22.5 f19.5 b21.5.** For whatever reason, this is a much duller version than the Committee Edition. And strength alone can't explain it, or solely the loss of the essential oils from reduction. There is a slight nagging to this one so perhaps any weakness to the sherry butts has been accentuated by the reduction of oil, if it has been bottled from the same vatting – which I doubt. Otherwise, the tasting notes are along the lines of below, except with just a little less accent on the sugars. *46.5%*

Ardbeg Dark Cove Committee Edition db **(90.5) n23.5 t23 f21.5 b22.5** Big sherry and bigger peat always struggle somewhere along the line. This one does pretty well until we reach the finale when it unravels slightly. But sulphur-free. And challenging. *55%*

Ardbeg Drum db **(92.5) n23 t23.5 f22.5 b23.5** Well! I wasn't expecting that! It is as if this is from some super-fine cut, with 20% of the usual heart each way being sent back re-distillation. No idea if this is the case, but it is the only way I can think of creating a non-chillfiltered Ardbeg this clean and fragile. Quite extraordinary... *46%.*

Ardbeg Grooves db **(95) n24 t23.5 f23.5 b24** Groovy. *46%.*

Ardbeg Grooves Committee Release db **(95.5) n24 t23.5 f24 b24** Even groovier! *51.6%.*

Ardbeg Guaranteed 30 Years Old db **(91) n24 t23 f21 b23.** An unusual beast, one of the last ever bottled by Allied. The charm and complexity early on is enormous, but the fade rate is surprising. That said, still a dram of considerable magnificence. *46%*

Ardbeg Kelpie db **(95) n24 t23.5 f23.5 b24** Beautifully crafted and cleverly – and intriguingly - structured. An understated Ardbeg for true Ardbeg lovers... *46%.*

Ardbeg Kelpie Committee Edition db **(94) n24 t24 f22.5 b23.5** As Burns might have said: I'se no speer nae to anither helpie o' Kelpie... *51.7%.*

Ardbeg Provenance 1974 bott 1999 db **(96)** n24 t25 f23 b24. This is an exercise in subtlety and charisma, the beauty and the beast drawn into one. Until I came across the 25-year-old OMC version during a thunderstorm in Denmark, this was arguably the finest whisky I had ever tasted: I opened this and drank from it to see in the year 2000. When I went through the Ardbeg warehouse stocks in 1997 I earmarked the '74 and '77 vintages as something special. This bottling has done me proud. 55.6%

Ardbeg Uigeadail db **(89)** n25 t22 f20 b22. A curious Ardbeg with a nose to die for. Some tinkering - please guys, as the re-taste is not better - regarding the finish may lift this to being a true classic 54.1%

Ardbeg Supernova 2019 db **(92.5)** n23.5 t23 f23 b23 A kind of sub-Supernova as it has now lost much of its old explosive oomph. 53.9%.

Ardbeg Traigh Bhan db **(94.5)** n24 t23.5 f23.5 b23.5 Ah, Traigh Bhan, the remote Singing Sands beach on Islay, if memory serves. Where back in the very early 1980s, before anyone had heard of Ardbeg – or hardly Islay whisky come to that matter - you could spend a day at the silent, deserted, unknown distillery and then return to Port Ellen. And as the sun thought about setting, but before the midges (teeth freshly sharpened) came out to play, walk past a herd of goats that could win a World Championship for flatulence, and on to the Singing Sands – Traigh Bhan - where I and the lady who was unluckily destined to be, for a short time, Mrs Murray would find a remote spot to try, but only providing we were upwind from the goats, and add to the Murray clan. It as an act that began and ended with a bottle top or two full of Ardbeg 10. Magical.... Maybe I should return to those sands with a bottle of this – which, fittingly, seems, older, softer, less energetic than the elixir Ardbeg I tasted of yore - and see what happens... 46.6%.

Ardbeg Wee Beastie Guaranteed 5 Years Old bott code: L2395911 22/06/2020 **(91)** n24 t23.5 f21.5 b22 A lovely whisky, make no mistake. But for a five-year-old Ardbeg, over 35 years of experience with this distillery had conditioned me to expect just a little more. Starts off with a mesmerically youthful lustiness full of the sunny joys of a blossoming spring. Ends in the grey of a foggy autumnal evening.... 47.4%. ncf.

◆ **Ardbeg Wee Beastie 5 Years Old** bott code: 18/06/2021 db **(89)** n23 t23 f21 b22 Back in the days when no-one had ever heard of Ardbeg, when not a tourist made their way on the downhill path to this sleeping Cathedral of whisky; when the stills were silent and there was more noise from the owners ripping open quotes from companies in how much it would cost to send the old place to the ground then there was in the distillery itself, I would spend an entire day and see nobody, bar the brewer on his daily five minute march around silent grounds. And on certain days I would join him and walk up the stairs in his near condemned offices passing a little framed notice on a wall, dating from the 1920s or '30s which swore that Ardbeg reached perfection at 7 years. When I had managed to help save the distillery from planned destruction and the present owners brought me in as consultant blender, there was a big problem: they wanted a 10-year-old, but there was none around to bottle. Some very old, or very young. One of my suggestions was that we follow the saying of the 1920s and launch a 7-year-old. No, Glenmorangie wanted to make a statement: it had to be at least 10 years-old. So, I created the 17. And the other problem, which I pointed out while suggesting the 7-year-old would be that bring a malt out of that age, there would be less stock available for the 10 when that finally came of age. So the 7-year-old never happened, alas. Now, nearly 25 years later, they are promoting a 5-year-old. Enjoyable enough in its own way. But too tame and disappointing for me, lacking the salivating complexity that is possible at that age. Mind you, had to laugh at the tasting note saying it had the flavour of creosote. I hope whoever wrote that has never tasted that stuff as it is highly carcinogenic. Sadly, I have (when I was in my late teens, a chemist once made up a mixture to cure a very heavy cold I had, basing his prescription on creosote. He was later struck off...!) and can assure you, there is no creosote flavours involved here! 47.4%

ARDMORE
Speyside, 1899. Beam Suntory. Working.
Ardmore 12 Year Old Port Wood Finish db **(90)** n21.5 t23.5 f22 b23 Here we have a lovely fruit-rich malt, but one which has compromised on the very essence of the complexity which sets this distillery apart. Lovely whisky I am delighted to say...but, dammit, by playing to its unique nuances it could have been so much better...I mean absolutely sensational...!46%. ncf.

Ardmore Aged 20 Years 1996 Vintage 1st fill ex-bourbon & ex-Islay casks, bott code: L723657A db **(89.5)** n22 t23 f22 b22.5 Slightly confused by this malt, for all its charm. At 20 years old this distillery projects, through its usual ex-bourbon cask portfolio of varied usages, a quite disarming complexity. To bolster it with extra oak and smoke slightly undermines the inherent subtlety of this malt which sets it apart from all others. Highly enjoyable, nonetheless. 49.3%. ncf.

Ardmore 25 Years Old db **(89.5) n21 t23.5 f22.5 b22.5** A 25-y-o box of chocolates: coffee creams, fudge, orange cream...they are all in there. The nose may be ordinary: what follows is anything but. *51.4%. ncf.*

Ardmore 30 Years Old Cask Strength db **(94) n23.5 t23.5 f23 b24** I remember when the present owners of Ardmore launched their first ever distillery bottling. Over a lunch with the hierarchy there I told them, with a passion, to ease off with the caramel so the world can see just how complex this whisky can be. This brilliant, technically faultless, bottling is far more eloquent and persuasive than I was that or any other day... *53.7%. nc ncf. 1428 bottles.*

Ardmore 1996 db **(87) n22 t22 f21 b22.** Very curious Ardmore, showing little of its usual dexterity. Perhaps slightly more heavily peated than the norm, but there is also much more intense heavy caramel extracted from the wood. Soft, very pleasant and easy drinking it is almost obsequious. *43%.*

Ardmore Legacy bott code: L713757B db **(88) n22.5 t23 f20.5 b22** That's much more like it! The initial bottling of this brand was a travesty to the distillery, seemingly making a point omitting all of the personality which makes it potentially one of the great whiskies of the world. No such problem here: a much more sympathetic rendition, though the finish is perhaps a little sharper than ideally desired. So, a massive improvement but still room for further improvement. *40%.*

⬩⬩⬩ **Ardmore Legacy** bott code: L1 117 SB1 db **(91.5) n23.5** they really have captured the essence of this distillery here: the peat arrives like an echo, rather than a shout. Never even, it is sometimes near, sometimes distant but always alluring, always intriguing....; **t23** the distillery's gentle mouth feel has been enhanced by a little toffee. But the mix of budding peat, light milk chocolate and delicate spices, enriched by semi-gristy barley notes and Walnut-whip vanilla makes for superb arrival and long follow-through; **f22** flattens a little too easily with the toffee seeing off the smoke, but not the spice; **b23** now that's way more like it! I remember how underwhelmed I was when the first bottling of this came out. But year on year they have managed to get far closer to the soul of the distillery, which happens to be one of my favourites in Scotland. Indeed, the present owners have it in their portfolio because of me. But sssssshhhh: don't tell anyone. Still room for improvement, though. Get the colour down and the strength up slightly, and they will have a potential award-winner on their hands. *40%.*

⬩⬩⬩ **Arcanum Spirits Private Release Ardmore Aged 10 years** 1st fill St.Martinique rum barrels **(95) n23.5** the smoke drifts effortlessly, like a red kite on a thermal, so high you can barely just see it. But there it is: graceful, elegant and unique. Only a vague fruitiness is a surprise, obviously an unusual but not unwelcome by-product of the rum cask; **t24** only Ardmore.... The smoke is no less deft here than it is on the nose. But the malt has an old-fashioned bite: a style prized by blenders for unaggressive vitality, but lifting the malt content as well as offering delicate phenols. After a brief, crisp juicy sugar-coating dissolves on entry the effect of the rum cask become negligible...; **f23.5** long, ridiculously delicate smoke lifted by light chocolate...; **b24** even through a rum barrel that totally unique Ardmore persona is unmistakably present. No other distillery in Scotland has such a flourish to its signature phenols. Just....yes! *58.5% nc ncf sc 157 bottles*

Berry Bros & Rudd Ardmore 12 Year Old cask no. 800961, dist 2006, bott 2019 **(90.5) n23 t22.5 f22 b22.5** One of the perennial joys of writing this book is happening across cask-strength bottlings of Ardmore being true to form. This one is slightly young for its age thinner in body than is usual. But still displays a wonderful degree of complexity even when not quite firing on all cylinders. *56.8%. nc ncf sc.*

⬩⬩⬩ **Fadandel.dk Ardmore Aged 11 Year** ex Laphroaig barrel, cask no.709235, dist Dec 2008, bott Dec 2020 **(88.5) n22 t21.5 f23 b22** Now this caught the attention of both the whisky nerd and blender within me. Ardmore is peated to a particular level to do a job. What happens if, as appears to be the case here, you up the phenol content? How does it balance out then? Well, the answer is that, broadly speaking, it doesn't. The smoke on the nose actually has an acidic bite rather than playful nip or caress. And when the unusual hotness of the cask kicks in, the peat has a slightly different, saltier character. So, it is less recognisable as an Ardmore. Is it enjoyable? Of course! But you never feel that the path of the peat is a true one or the balance is quite at home. The finish, though, is enough to forgive 1,000 sins... *59.3% sc 234 bottles*

⬩⬩⬩ **Old Malt Cask Ardmore Aged 12 Years** refill barrel, cask no.HL18700, dist July 2008, bott May 2021 **(87) n21.5 t22.5 f21 b22** A real surprise package. One of the most coastal Ardmores I've encountered for a while, especially on the nose with a pungent saline and seaweed element which transfers on to the delivery. Much to chew on and enjoy, especially when the light praline marks its mark. But always a little bit of attitude and this and drier than most. *50% sc 281 bottles*

⬩⬩⬩ **Single Cask Collection Ardmore 11 Years Old** ex Laphroaig cask, cask no. 707531, dist 2008, bott 2019 **(92.5) n22.5** pungent and salty for an Ardmore; **t23** impressive, sweet oils. But they lose their impact as the spices make their mark. The smoke and malt are a little distracted; **f24** aaah! Here we go. Superb. It has settled brilliantly now with the salt and brown sugars harmonising with more than a touch of malty class..; **b23** Another ex-Laphroaig which initially throws things out of sync momentarily with the extra peat and bite. But then more than amends with a superb and hugely satisfying finish. In an hour's time Scotland will be taking on Croatia, needing a win to stand any chance of qualifying or the last 16 of the European finals. If their forwards can finish as wonderfully as this, they are in with every chance. *61.1%. sc. 245 bottles.*

⟨⟩ **Single & Single Ardmore 2009 10 Year Old** American oak **(91.5) n22.5** well the DNA of an Ardmore is not difficult to sniff out here. The oak plays only lip service while the peat sits back, living it only the lightest touch. What is left is sweet barley with castor sugars aiding the grain; **t23.5** indeed, the peat is only happy to play a genteel role, just as on the nose. The mouth feel, though, is as sexy as it gets...just whispers and caresses all the way with the phenols building into a praline mid-point...; **f22.5** a very simplistic vanilla and phenol fade with just a light spice involvement..; **b23** a totally fascinating bottling. The lack of input from the cask means we are able to see the sweet, malty machinations of the Ardmore up close. For decades I have been telling people that, in whisky, less is often more. Here is a beautiful case in point... *53.9%. sc. 257 bottles.*

Teacher's Highland Single Malt quarter cask finish db **(89) n22.5 t23 f21.5 b22.** This is Ardmore at its very peatiest. And had not the colouring levels been heavily tweaked to meet the flawed perceptions of what some markets believe makes a good whisky, this malt would have been better still. As it is: superb. With the potential of achieving greatness if only they have the confidence and courage... *40%. India/Far East Travel Retail exclusive.*

The Whisky Agency Ardmore 1998 hogshead, bott 2018 **(89) n22 t21.5 f23.5 b22** A very understated Ardmore, offering far less smoke than the norm. Little to write home about on the nose and delivery. But the finish is a different proposition altogether. *51.7%.*

The Whisky Chamber Ardmore 10 Jahre 2009 refill port cask **(94) n23 t23.5 f23.5 b24** / Enjoyable, at times refined and always complex. Certainly, the sum adds up to more than the parts. Quietly brilliant. *57.1%. sc.*

⟨⟩ **The Whisky Chamber Ardmore 10 Jahre 2009** bourbon barrel **(93) n23** just about perfect peat weight so far as Ardmore is concerned; light and young enough to display a little pear alongside the vanilla and delicate peat; **t23** adore the momentary barley sugar explosion of delivery: blink and you miss it. But it perfectly primes the taste buds for the follow through of tingling barley and phenols. Not sure the weight of the oils could be improved upon; **f23** smoked chocolate vanilla; **b24** when it is possible to vat casks together of a certain age at Ardmore, then 10-year-old offers probably the best chance of shewing the distillery at the finest. Not so easy with a single cask, which is just a single fragment of that complex equation. Well, as it happens, this cask has most of the boxes ticked. *56.8%. sc.*

⟨⟩ **The Whisky Tasting Club Ardmore 12 Year Old** bourbon oak first fill, cask no. 70386, dist Jul 2008, bott Dec 2020 **(94.5) n23.5** uniquely Ardmore: no other distillery on the planet gets the sharpness of the grain and understated acidic bite of the peat to harmonise so gorgeously...; **t23** salivating, warming...but never overly aggressive. Outstanding light oils helps the ever-thickening barley to meld with the peat which increasingly displays a minty quality. A crunchy sugary quality fits in well.; **f24** incredibly long. Mixing light liquorice, mocha and chocolate nut together to make for the most complex of peaty fades; **b24** well done, WTC!! This is just like heading into the old Ardmore warehouses and drawing spirit from one of the better condition bourbon barrels. Where it really stars though, is the playful aggression of the spices and spirit, which ensures this is never a simple luxuriant smoothie, but something you have to negotiate. Brilliant! *57.3% 180 bottles*

AUCHENTOSHAN
Lowlands, 1800. Morrison Bowmore. Working.

Auchentoshan 10 Years Old db **(81) n22 t21 f19 b19**. Much better, maltier, cleaner nose than before. But after the initial barley surge on the palate it shows a much thinner character. *40%*

Auchentoshan 12 Years Old db **(91.5) n22.5 t23.5 f22.5 b23** A delicious malt very much happier with itself than it has been for a while. *40%*

Auchentoshan Aged 12 Years bourbon & sherry casks, bott code: L00007SB320081440 db **(86) n22.5 t22.5 f20 b21** Being triple distilled, Auchentoshan is one of Scotland's lightest, most intricate spirits to start with. Therefore, to maximise its character it needs gentle handling and the malts given free reign. This, however, is essentially sherry dominated, except perhaps for on the nose where some attractive acacia honey filters through. The delivery also has moments of complexity and clarity, but they are fleeting before the grape and tannins take command for a surfeit of dryness. The growing furry tones on the finish confirms, as detectable on the nose, that not all the butts escape the dreaded sulphur candle. *40%*.

Auchentoshan 14 Years Old Cooper's Reserve db **(83.5) n20 t21.5 f21 b21.** Malty, a little nutty and juicy in part. 46%. ncf.

Auchentoshan 18 Years Old db **(78) n21 t21.5 f17 b19.** Although matured for 18 years in ex-bourbon casks, as according to the label, this is a surprisingly tight and closed malt in far too many respects. Some heart-warming sugars early on, but the finish is bitter and severely limited in scope. 43%

Auchentoshan 21 Years Old db **(93) n23.5 t23 f23 b23.5** One of the finest Lowland distillery bottlings of our time. A near faultless masterpiece of astonishing complexity to be cherished and discussed with deserved reverence. So delicate, you fear that sniffing too hard will break the poor thing...! 43%.

Auchentoshan 1979 db **(94) n23.5 t24 f23 b23.5** It's amazing what a near faultless sherry butt can do. 50.1%

Auchentoshan American Oak db **(85.5) n21.5 t22 f20.5 b21.5.** Very curious: reminds me very much of Penderyn Welsh whisky before it hits the Madeira casks. Quite creamy with some toasted honeycomb making a brief cameo appearance. 40%

Auchentoshan Blood Oak French red wine db **(76.5) n20.5 t19 f18 b19.** That's funny: always thought blood tasted a little sweet. This is unremittingly bitter. 48%. ncf.

Auchentoshan Classic db **(80) n19 t20 f21 b20.** Classic what exactly...? Some really decent barley, but goes little further. 40%

Auchentoshan Select db **(85) n20 t21.5 f22 b21.5.** Has changed shape of late, if not quality. Much more emphasis on the enjoyable juicy barley sharpness these days. 40%

Auchentoshan Solera db **(88) n23 t22 f22 b21.** Enormous grape input and enjoyable for all its single mindedness. Will benefit when a better balance with the malt is struck. 48%. ncf.

Auchentoshan The Bartender's Malt batch 01, bott code: L172249 db **(94.5) n23.5 t24 f23 b24** Seeing as this was assembled by a dozen bartenders from around the world, namely Messrs Alvarado, Billing, Halsius, Heinrich, Jehli, Klus, Magro, Morgan, Schurmann, Shock, Stern and Wareing surely this is the Bartenders' Malt, not Bartender's Malt. Still, I digress. Good job, boys and (presumably) girls. Some might mark this down as a clever marketing ploy (which it may well be...). I'd rather record it as an exceptionally fine Auchentoshan. And by the way, bartenders, you have proved a point I have been making for the last 25 years: the finest cocktail is a blend of whiskies...even if from the same distillery...Now don't you go ruining this by putting ice, water, or anything else in it... 47%.

Auchentoshan Three Wood db **(76) n20 t18 f20 b18.** Takes you directly into the rough. Refuses to harmonise, except maybe for some late molassed sugar. 43%

Auchentoshan Three Wood bourbon & Oloroso & PX sherry casks, bott code: L9274SB323011209 db **(88) n22 t23 f21 b22** Three woods there may be. But it's the PX that really counts. A semi-syrupy concoction with massive chewiness. The half-expected bitter finish offers a stark contrast. 43%.

Auchentoshan Virgin Oak db **(92) n23.5 t23 f22.5 b23** Not quite how I've seen 'Toshan perform before: but would love to see it again! 46%

⟐ **Chapter 7 Auchentoshan 1998 Aged 22 Years** bourbon barrel, barrel no.100155 **(88) n22.5 t22.5 f21 b22** A nutty version, both on nose and delivery. The clarity of the barley could hardly be in sharper focus but there is not quite enough honey or weight in the system to see off the most excessive elements of the oak. Good lingering spice, though. 51.8% sc

⟐ **Old Malt Cask Auchentoshan Aged 25 Years** refill hogshead, dist Oct 1995, bott Feb 2021 **(89.5) n22.5** a near sherbet-like zest and fruitiness to the barley, giving it zip and vitality; **t23** well, that zing on the nose is accentuated to wonderful effect on delivery, ensuring the barley, despite a covert sweetness, has nip and bite; a mix of melon and passion fruit gives an exotic tang to the sweeter moments; **f21.5** settles down towards a more sombre oakiness; **b22.5** there is a major misconception about whisky 25 years of age that it must be heavy, creaking with more oak than an 18th century frigate and be festooned with cobwebs. This Lowlander clings onto its youthful frame for as long as possible and positively celebrates its malty origins. 50%. nc ncf sc. 152 bottles.

AUCHROISK
Speyside, 1974. Diageo. Working.

Auchroisk Aged 10 Years db **(84) n20 t22 f21 b21.** Tangy orange on the nose, the malt amplified by a curious saltiness on the palate. 43%. Flora and Fauna.

⟐ **Fadandel.dk Auchroisk Aged 9 Years** 1st fill port, cask no. 46, dist Dec 2010, bott Dec 2020 **(86.5) n21.5 t22 f21.5 b21.5** One of those whiskies I'd love to give a high score to just for the bottlers going to such lengths to make it work. However, it appears a very good Port cask has run aground on some intransigent malt which refuses to add much to the fun.

Intrigued by the coastal saltiness which worked well with the raisin. But the actual malty base appears to be a little weak. 59.9%. sc 284 bottles

◇ **Fadandel.dk Auchroisk Aged 10 Years** 1st fill oloroso hogshead, cask no.73, dist Dec 2010, bott Feb 2021 **(87) n23.5 t20.5 f21.5 b21.5** Abounds in spice while the nose enjoys some high-quality Dundee cake moments. Pleasant enough, but the heat is a little too much to bear when so little is offered in malty body. Struggles to find a balance. Like the Port, a shame as the cask is faultless and some hard work gone into this: maybe a case of right cask, wrong distillery... If you do get a bottle, make sure you make the most of the nose; it is terrific! 58.7% sc 256 bottles

◇ **Hepburn's Choice Auchroisk Aged 9 Years** wine hogshead, dist 2011, bott 2020 **(82.5) n21 t21.5 f20 b20** Young and pretty monosyllabic in its utterances. The wine cask has denuded the malt of its sugars at a time it needed them most. No off notes or anything untoward. But the balance isn't quite there, either. 46%. nc ncf 809 bottles.

Hepburn's Choice Auchroisk 10 Years Old rum cask, dist 2009, bott 2019 **(87.5) n22 t22.5 f21 b22** Usually a disappointing malt, it appears that the rum cask has used its sugary influence to hem in the more deliciously malty aspects to wonderful effect. The finish is typically weak, nonetheless. Even so, enjoy the early salivating crispness of the barley tinged with a superb outer coating of lightly spiced heather honey. 46%. nc ncf sc. 182 bottles.

◇ **Old Malt Cask Auchroisk Aged 24 Years** refill hogshead, dist Aug1996, bott Feb 2021 **(88) n22 t22.5 f21.5 b22** Those few extra oils found fattening out the body makes a significant difference when it comes to magnifying the malt. The oak has also waded in here, matching up the mat to the peppery spice. Typically simplistic in the distillery style, but unusually intense early on. 50%. nc ncf sc. 293 bottles.

◇ **The First Editions Auchroisk Aged 23 Years 1997** refill hogshead, cask no. HL17814, bott 2021 **(87.5) n22 t22.5 f21 b22** Seems very settled and comfortable in its malty simplicity. The finish is on the short side of a malt this age, but falls within the Auchroisk remit. The nose and delivery, though, charm – especially thanks to offering just the right degree of semi-gristy sweetness. 54.6%. nc ncf sc. 199 bottles.

◇ **The Whisky Embassy Bonn Auchroisk 8 Year Old** Madeira cask, cask no. 3 **(88) n22 t22.5 f21.5 b22** Impressed with this bottling. It would be only too easy for a Madeira cask to entirely wipe out the malty imprint of a distillery as light a Auchroisk, trampling it underfoot. But this holds back and ensures the fruit adds only weight and a degree of lushness and spice to the party. Not entirely perfectly balanced, but taking the distillery into account, it works rather well. 59.4%. nc ncf sc.

AULTMORE

Speyside, 1896. Bacardi. Working.

Aultmore 12 Year Old db **(85.5) n22 t22 f20 b21.5**. Not quite firing on all cylinders due to the uncomfortably tangy oak. But relish the creamy malt for the barley is the theme of choice and for its sheer intensity alone, it doesn't disappoint; a little ulmo honey and marzipan doff their cap to the kinder vanillas. 46% WB16/028

Aultmore of the Foggie Moss Aged 12 Years bott code: L18135ZA903 db **(92.5) n23.5 t23.5 f22.5 b23** A whisky purist's delight. So delicate you can see the inner workings of this fine malt. 46%. ncf.

Aultmore 18 Year Old db **(88.5) n22.5 t22.5 f22 b21.5** Charming, but could do with having the toffee blended out... 46%

Aultmore of the Foggie Moss Aged 18 Years batch no. 481, bott code: L15244B100 db **(94.5) n23.5 t24 f23 b24** It is so satisfying when the sweetness and spices of a malt combine for near perfect harmony. Flattens towards the finish, but this is high grade malt. 46%. ncf.

Aultmore Aged 21 Years refill hogshead, batch no. 00107, bott code: L18281ZA501 db **(95.5) n24 t24 f23.5 b24** When you get a very decent spirit filled into exceptionally good casks, the result – providing the whisky is disgorged neither too early nor late – is usually a positive one. The refill hoggies here must have been in fine fettle, for this a bit of a stunner. No, make that a classic! Potential gong material. 46%. nc ncf.

Aultmore Exceptional Cask Series 21 Years Old 1996 db **(94.5) n24 t23.5 f23.5 b23.5** There is age creaking from every pore of this whisky. The nose is magnificently sensual with its orange blossom honey theme, spicy toasty tannins lurking at every corner. And those tannins carry on their impressive work, yet at the same time allowing a delicious alloy of malt and sultanas to not only thrive but fully fill the palate. Toward the end we are back to those insistent tannins which, if anything display an age greater than its given years. A malt plucked at the very right time from the warehouse: it would never have made half as good a 25-year-old. 54%. Selected for CWS.

⬦ **Single Cask Collection Aultmore 14 Years Old** 1st fill bourbon cask, cask no. 306878, dist 2006, bott 2020 **(91) n22.5** such a delicate maltiness...; **t23** salivating, clean and shows off the barley in varying moods and modes helped along by a light but ever-gathering oiliness; **f22.5** unashamedly simplistic with the still intense malt and oak-induced vanilla doing little to disturb the peace...; **b23** I have a soft spot for elegantly well-made and matured malts which do not try to show off. Here's classic example. *52.2%. sc. 209 bottles.*

The Whisky Chamber Aultmore 12 Jahre 2006 bourbon cask **(91) n23 t23 f22 b23** Ah! Aultmore in the kind of cask it feels so at home: a reasonably well-used bourbon barrel so it can ramp up the malt content to maximum. Refreshing and delectable. *52.1%. sc.*

Whisky Illuminati Aultmore 2011 Spanish oak sherry butt, cask no. 900367 **(90.5) n22.5 t23.5 f22.5 b22** A sherry butt with NO sulphur whatsoever. But a malt riding this bucking bronco for dear life and making no impression on just where it will be taken. *675%. sc. 120 bottles.*

BALBLAIR
Highlands (Northern), 1872. Inver House Distillers. Working.

Balblair 10 Years Old db **(86) n21 t22 f22 b21.** Such an improved dram away from the clutches of caramel. *40%*

Balblair Aged 12 Years American oak ex-bourbon & double-fired American oak casks, bott code: L18/357 R18/5536 IB db **(87) n21.5 t22 f21.5 b22** There is no escaping a distinct tired cask tang to this. From the nose to the finale the oak pokes around with a little too much meanness of spirit. But it is the wonderful clarity to the barley – including a delicious citrusy freshness – which keeps the malt on course. I suspect the next bottling will be a whole lot better! *46%. nc ncf.*

Balblair Aged 15 Years American oak ex-bourbon casks, followed by first fill Spanish oak butts, bott code: L19 079 R19/5133 IB db **(93) n23 t23.5 f23 b23** Ah, after the relative disappointment of the 12-year-old, so good to see we are right back on track here. Twenty years of very bitter experience has taught me to fear the worst and hope for the best so far as the use of sherry butts are concerned. But my hopes are rewarded here: not 100% perfect, but close enough. *46%. nc ncf.*

Balblair Aged 17 Years American oak ex-bourbon casks, followed by first fill Spanish oak butts, bott code: L19/057 R19/5097 IB db **(94) n23.5 t24.5 f22.5 b23.5** One of the best arrivals on the palate of any Scotch whisky I have tasted this year. *46%. nc ncf. Travel Exclusive.*

Balblair Aged 18 Years American oak ex-bourbon casks, followed by first fill Spanish oak butts, bott code: L19/121 R19/5220 IB db **(83) n22 t23 f18 b20** Balblair's luck has run out on the sherry butts. A heftier expression than the 17-year-old and the sulphur ensures there is nothing like the degree of complexity. *46%. nc ncf.*

Balblair Aged 25 Years American oak ex-bourbon casks, followed by first fill Spanish oak butts, nbc db **(91) n23.5 t23.5 f21 b23** There has been hard work here to harmonise fruit and oak and allow the barley a say, too. But when sherry is this ripe, not the easiest stunt to pull off. Gets pretty close, though! *46%.*

Balblair 1975 db **(94.5) n24.5 t23.5 f23 b23.5.** Essential Balblair. *46%*

Balblair 1989 db **(91) n23 t23 f22.5 b22.5.** Don't expect gymnastics on the palate or the pyrotechnics of the Cadenhead 18: in many ways a simple malt, but one beautifully told. Almost Cardhu-esque in the barley department. *43%*

Balblair 1989 db **(88) n21.5 t22 f22.5 b22.** A clean, pleasing malt, though hardly one that will induce anyone to plan a night raid on any shop stocking it... *46%*

Balblair 1990 db **(92.5) n24 t23.5 f22 b23.** Tangy in the great Balblair tradition. Except here this is warts and all with the complexity and greatness of the distillery left in no doubt. *46%*

Balblair 1991 3rd Release bott 2018, bott code L18/044 R18/5054IB db **(94.5) n23.5 t23.5 f23.5 b24** A malt embracing its passing years and has aged, silver temples and all, with great style and panache. *46%. nc ncf.*

Balblair 1997 2nd Release db **(94) n23.5 t23.5 f23 b24** a very relaxed well-made and matured malt, comfortable in its own skin, bursting with complexity and showing an exemplary barley-oak ratio. A minor classic. *46%. nc ncf.*

Balblair 2000 2nd Release bott 2017, bott code L17/R121 db **(95.5) n24.5 t24 f23 b24** First encountered this malt at a tasting I gave in Corsica earlier in the year. It blew away my audience while equally seducing me. Sampled back in the tasting lab, if anything it is even more stunning. The stock of this under-appreciated distillery rises by the day... *46%. nc ncf.*

Balblair 2001 db **(90.5) n23.5 t23.5 f21.5 b22.5** A typically high quality whisky from this outrageously underestimated distillery. *46%*

The Whisky Barrel Originals Balblair 10 Years Old 1st fill oloroso hogshead, cask no. TWB1008, dist Sept 09, bott 2019 **(91.5) n23 t23 f22.5 b23** The cleanest sherry cask you could ever wish for. And lightest: a butterfly of a sherry cask. *576%. sc. 298 bottles.*

BALMENACH

Speyside, 1824. Inver House Distillers. Working.

Deerstalker Balmenach 12 Years Old Highland Single Malt **(88.5)** n22.5 t22 f22 b22 Attractive, easy going malt, but struggles to get out of second gear. *43%.*

Fadandel.dk Balmenach 7 Year Old 5 months finish in a 1st fill PX Octave, cask no. 430A, dist 17 Oct 12, bott 14 Apr 20 **(90)** n22.5 t22.5 f22.5 b22.5 This is so outrageously ridiculous, it's actually very good. The youthful malt is in mortal combat with a grapey cask of gorilla strength. Bizarre! It is probably just a grape atom away from disaster. ... but so entertaining, too... *55.4%. sc. 75 bottles.*

Fadandel.dk Balmenach 7 Year Old 5 months finish in a 1st fill PX Octave, cask no. 430B, dist 17 Oct 12, bott 16 Apr 20 **(84.5)** n21 t22 f21.5 b20 And I thought cask 430A was dark! For its age, this is borderline opaque! Which is a bit like storm clouds over your feeble summer tent: you know you are in for it! There can be too much of a good thing and where cask 430A miraculously got away with it, this one doesn't... or come even close. Again, no off notes. But PX of this magnitude on a malt as simpering as a Balmenach is like running a fully laden, with each passenger maxing out on their luggage, freshly fuel-filled Jumbo jet over a walnut just to crack it. Hard to give marks for balance, as there simply isn't any. If you like this kind of sticky, overly-sweet, cloying thing, I suggest you buy a bottle of PX, as this is a waste of otherwise good malt. *52.8%. sc. 69 bottles.*

Old Malt Cask Balmenach Aged 14 Years refill barrel, cask no. 16791, dist Dec 04, bott Jun 19 **(94.5)** n23 t24 f23.5 b24 Glories in its complex malty freshness! A joy of a dram. *50%. nc ncf sc. 141 bottles.*

⬧ **Old Malt Cask Balmenach Aged 14 Years** refill hogshead, cask no. HL18196, dist Sept 2006, bott Feb 2021 **(89)** n22.5 still youthful and celebrates a grassy freshness to the delightful barley lead; t22.5 almost pristine clarity to the barley intensity. The middle is skewed slightly more towards the oak as a nutty spiciness begins to develop; f22 very simplistic vanillas; b22 beautifully made and leaves you in no doubt of its Speyside credentials. *50%. nc ncf sc. 301 bottles.*

⬧ **Old Malt Cask Balmenach Aged 14 Years** refill hogshead, cask no. HL18695, dist Mar 2007, bott May 2021 **(91.5)** n22.5 an enjoyable volley of sharp, youngish, quite salty barley tones; t23 such a beautiful collection of crisp, salivating barley tones, accompanied by rich, gristy malt: a kind of double-edged sword...and one that has certainly been sharpened...; f23 a lovely digestive biscuit fade; b23 for whisky of its age, it thoroughly enjoys dishing out lighter, younger sweeter barley notes of a Balmenach some years younger. Malty and refreshing. A more confident, malt intense version than its sister cask. *50% sc 332 bottles*

THE BALVENIE

Speyside, 1892. William Grant & Sons. Working.

The Balvenie Double Wood Aged 12 Years European oak sherry casks, bott code: L8D 7738 2309 db **(82)** n22 t21 f19 b20 Pretty standard but uninspiring fare with sharp fruit pinching the palate until the furry sulphur tang arrives. Oh, how I miss Balvenie in standard bourbon casks at this age or even a little younger which gives you a chance to see how amazingly brilliant this distillery actually is. *40%.*

⬧ **The Balvenie DoubleWood Aged 12 Years** botte code: L34E 4950 **(85.5)** n22 t22.5 f20 b21 Every year I give this whisky (from one of my favourite distilleries) another crack, hoping it will at last heal my broken heart (broken still for the long lost and irreplaceable Balvenie 10). The fact that, at long last, I have found one without a major sulphur nag helps get the score up. That doesn't mean that there isn't sulphur, because, sadly, there is – right at the death. Though, thankfully the sulphur influence peaks at minor, rather than major. The great news is that the nose and delivery can be thoroughly enjoyed, light figs and dates on the aroma, a maltier infusion with toffee tones on delivery. The spices are a Godsend and stir things up which otherwise would have been a touch too linear, as soon as the cherry juicy has vanished. But the sulphur on the finish only moans rather than scolds. But until the sulphur is gone altogether, the distillery will remain underrepresented of its true astonishing capabilities. *40%.*

The Balvenie Single Barrel Sherry Cask Aged 15 Years db cask no 2075 **(58)** n14 t16 f14 b14 Lovely distillery. Shame about this shockingly sulphured cask. *47.8%. sc.*

The Balvenie 16 Year Old Triple Cask db **(84.5)** n22 t22.5 f19 b21 Well, after their single cask and then double wood, who saw this coming...? There is nothing about this whisky you can possibly dislike: no diminishing off notes (OK, well maybe at the very death) and a decent injection of sugar, especially early on. The trouble is, when you mix together sherry butts (even mainly good ones, like here) and first fill bourbon casks, the intense toffee produced tends to make for a monosyllabic, toffeed, dullish experience. And so it proves here. *40%*

The Balvenie Caribbean Cask Aged 14 Years bott code: L8D 7263 1707 db **(91.5)** n23 t23 f22.5 b23 A different kind of rum style from Balvenie to others they have done in the past, this working far better and despite a slight caramel overdose, much more complexity this time round. *43%.*

The Balvenie Double Wood Aged 17 Years db **(84)** n22 t21 f20 b21. Balvenie does like 17 years as an age to show off its malt at its most complex, & understandably so as it is an important stage in its development before its usual premature over maturity: the last years or two when it remains full of zest and vigour. Here, though, the oak from the bourbon cask has offered a little too much of its milkier, older side while the sherry is a fraction overzealous and a shade too tangy. Enjoyable, but like a top of the range Mercedes engine which refuses to run evenly. *43%.*

The Balvenie Double Wood Aged 17 Years European oak sherry casks, bott code: L34D 50322808 db **(95)** n24 t23.5 f23 b24 Just fabulous to see this marriage between bourbon and sherry cask being such a happy one. Both sets of barrels are blemish-free while the weight and balance is exemplary. Luxurious in every degree and a magnificent example of the difference sulphur-free sherry butts can make to a whisky, especially as one as top drawer as The Balvenie...So deserves to be another three percent higher in strength, too... *43%.*

The Balvenie Aged 21 Years Port Wood db **(94.5)** n24 t24 f23 b23.5 What a magnificently improved malt. Last time out I struggled to detect the fruit. Here, there's no escaping. *40%*

The Balvenie PortWood Aged 21 Years finished in PortWood from port casks, bott code: L34D 4498 1204 db **(86)** n23.5 t22.5 f19 b21 The gnawing sulphur fade is an unfortunate ending to a malt which starts so brilliantly well. So much fresh fruit abounding here, much of it of the sugar candy variety. Those incapable of picking up sulphur are in for a treat. *40%.*

The Balvenie The Sweet Toast of American Oak Aged 12 Years finished in Kentucky virgin American oak barrels, bott code: L6D 6404 0603 db **(87.5)** n23 t22 f21.5 b21 Not anything like carefully balanced enough. Virgin oak has to be treated carefully and with respect: that is a lot of tannin being awoken and barley is no corn or rye. Needs rebalancing as this has the potential for greatness. But not in this form. *43%. Story No. 1.*

The Balvenie Tun 1509 Batch No. 6 bott code: L34D 5015 2608 db **(93)** n23.5 t24 b23.5 This must be from Balvenie-by-the-Sea. Amazing salt levels here, especially on the nose and early delivery. Has all the hallmarks of blender David Stewart, one of the top three at layering Scotch whisky in living memory. Just a shame about the late tang, though not too much damage done. *50.4%.*

The Balvenie The Week of Peat Aged 14 Years bott code: L6D 6432 1103 db **(96)** n24 t24 f23.5 b24.5 This could also, I suppose, be called a Weak of Peat as the phenols never really get anything like a head of steam. But, then, it never even attempts to and is quite right to concentrate on a subtlety which demonstrates the greatness of this malt when matured in bourbon casks. One of those rare malts where the delivery and follow through on the palate is a match for a brilliant nose. Make no mistake: we have a true Speyside gem here. *48.3%. ncf. Story No. 2.*

BANFF
Speyside, 1863–1983. Diageo. Demolished.

Gleann Mór Banff Aged Over 42 Years dist 1975 **(91)** n23 t23.5 f22.5 b22 This was distilled in the same year I visited my first distillery in Scotland...and that was a bloody long time ago. Not many casks have made it from then to today, and those that have are in varying states of quality: old age does not always mean an improvement in a whisky's fortunes... often the reverse. This is a classic example of a malt which should have been bottled a little time back. But it is still massively enjoyable, throwing up the odd surprise here and there and keeping to the malty script despite the militant oak. Quite an experience....*41.1%.*

BEN NEVIS
Highlands (Western), 1825. Nikka. Working.

Ben Nevis 10 Years Old 2008 batch no. 1, 1st fill bourbon, sherry and wines casks, dist 21 Apr 08, bott Sept 18 db **(86.5)** n21 t22.5 f21 b22 A robust, no holds barred malt which gets you both with the intensity of fruit and oak as well as the sheer power of the spirit itself! The varied wine casks don't perhaps gel as they might (not helped by a small sulphur note), though the intensity of the delivery may bring a pleasurable bead of sweat to the brow. *62.4%.*

Ben Nevis Synergy 13 Years Old db **(88)** n22 t22 f21.5 b22.5 One of the sweetest Ben Nevises for a long time, but as chewy as ever! A bit of a lady's dram to be honest. *46%*

Ben Nevis 32 Years Old 1966 dist Jun 66, bott Sept 98 db **(95.5)** n24.5 t23.5 f24 b23.5 Way back in 1998 some 1966 Ben Nevis was bottled for the US market as a "101" in 75cl bottles...but for some reason never got there. So for 20 years they slumbered peacefully in a warehouse at the distillery, entirely and blissfully forgotten, about until one day they were rediscovered by chance. That whisky, with a little softening from 20 years in glass, has now been re-consigned to 70cl bottles and at last put up for sale. What we have is a real blast from the past: a window into a Ben Nevis's distilling history, as a 32-year-old whisky bottled now from 1987 stock would certainly have a different feel. This reveals the distillery when it had the type of bite much favoured by blenders and which ensures a single malt with a singular personality. Just magnificent! *50.5%. Forgotten Bottlings Series.*

Cask & Thistle Ben Nevis 1997 Aged 22 Years refill butt, cask no. 126 **(93.5)** n23 t24 f23 **b23.5** A thistle can make your eye water. This cask certainly does for sure... *52.5%. sc.*

◈◈ **Hepburn's Choice Ben Nevis 9 Years Old** bourbon barrel, dist 2011, bott 2020 **(89.5) n22.5** the malt is piled so high on the nose, it positively pulses! The youthfulness is apparent, but the light but balancing strands of oak deserve respect, too...; **t22.5** the nose forecasts the malty soup to come and the oils guarantee a real chewabilty to this; **f22** light cocoa touch gives a certain Malteser candy quality to this; **b22.5** just brilliant to see this distillery unplugged. A really fun ride, shewing just how beautifully distilled this malt was. *46%. nc ncf sc. 251 bottles.*

Kingsbury Gold Ben Nevis 22 Year Old barrel, cask no. 2118, dist 1996 **(93)** n24 t24 f22 **b23** Ben Nevis in very rare island form, with so much salt and heather hanging about it. Great to see the distillery in tip-top form. *57.2%. sc. 514 bottles.*

◈◈ **The Duchess Ben Nevis 10 Years Old** shiraz cask finish, cask no: 1800020, dist 28/10/2010, bott 30/11/2020 **(87) n21.5 t22.5 f21 b22** Well, if it is part of their Game and Wildlife Series, have to mark this down as a barley-eating mole: earthy, dry and keeps you in the dark for quite a while about what direction this is taking. Despite the cask finish, the very young barley bores down into your tastebuds, initially offering grassy sweetness. But the restricting dryness of the finale is a little too tunnel visioned. 56.7%. *sc Game & Wildlife series*

◈◈ **The Single Cask Ben Nevis 2012** PX sherry finish, cask no. 1734 **(86) n21.5 t22 f21 b21.5** Kind of the equivalent of a whisky steamroller coming straight at you, flattening everything in its path...the taster included. The dull sweet grape on the nose is even outperformed on the delivery which is positively cloying and liqueuresque. The sweetness also tends to accentuate the more bitter foibles, particularly noticeable on both the nose and finish. One expects to have a toothache after this at any moment... *60.9% sc*

◈◈ **Valour Highland Single Malt Ben Nevis Aged 25 Years** cognac butt, cask no. 503, dist Oct 1995, bott Mar 2021, **(94)** n23.5 under-ripe gooseberry crushed in the hand. If you can count the layers of tannin, then you are better person than I. Or which is the more astringent: the fruit or the salty oak. The sweetness is cleverly subdued reliant on the fruit and a darker sugar, muscovado, perhaps...; **t23.5** such a clean, well defined landing on the palate softened by a lush fruitiness. There had been a hint of muscovado sugars on the nose. But here they are in abundance, giving crunchy, scrunchy firmness to the salivating malts which ping around the taste buds on a mission. But still it is the fruit in control, always accompanied by an oaky toastiness; **f23** goosberry jam on slightly burnt toast....; **b24** it is not just about the taste. The texture is to die for. For some, this will be the summit of Ben Nevis. *54.9% nc sc 508 bottles*

◈◈ **Whisky-Fässle Ben Nevis 19 Year Old** hogshead, dist 1998, bott 2019 **(89.5)** n23 t22.5 **f21.5 b22.5** Even after nearly 20 years there is a freshness to the barley on both nose and delivery that you might expect from a whisky half its age. Obviously the cask has been around the block once or twice before, which reduces the complexity a little. But, on the plus side, there is a juiciness to this which truly invigorates. The biggest surprise is a far more macho peatiness than you'd ever expect from this distillery which compensates for the AWOL oak and dramatically helps out with the spices, also. *51.5% nc ncf*

BENRIACH
Speyside, 1898. Brown-Forman. Working.

The BenRiach Aged 10 Years Curiositas Peated Malt bourbon, toasted virgin oak & rum casks, bott code: 2018/10/11 LM11452 db **(89.5) n22.5 t22.5 f22 b22.5** Unrecognisable from the original Curiositas and though the strength is back up to 46% abv, somehow the body has become lighter. Enjoyable but a head scratcher. *46%. nc ncf.*

The BenRiach Aged 12 Years Matured In Sherry Wood db **(95.5)** n23.5 t24 f24 **b24** Since previously experiencing this number of instances of sampling a sherry wood whisky and not finding my taste buds caked in sulphur has nosedived dramatically. Therefore, to start my tasting day at 7am with something as honest as this propels one with myriad reasons to continue the day. A celebration of a malt whisky in more ways than you could believe. *46%. nc ncf.*

The BenRiach Aged 21 Years Classic bourbon barrels, virgin oak, PX sherry & red wine casks db **(90) n22.5 t23 f22 b22.5** Rich textured and complex, there is a glorious clarity to the sugars and fondant vanillas. Even the spices seem happy to dovetail into the merry mix without creating too many waves. 46%.

The BenRiach Aged 21 Years Tawny Port Wood Finish db (87.5) n22 t21 f22 b21.5 I'm not sure if the cask finish was designed to impart a specific fruitiness profile or simply repair some tired old oak. In either case, it has been a partial success only. The intemperance of the tannin makes its mark in no small measure both on nose and delivery and it is only in the finish that the sugars bond strongly enough together to form a balance with the woody input. 46%.

The BenRiach Aged 21 Years Temporis Peated bourbon barrels, virgin oak, Pedro Ximenez & oloroso sherry casks db (87.5) n22.5 t22 f21.5 b21.5 Begins nobly with a fanfare of alluring acidic peat, then strange (mainly orangey) fruit notes keeps chipping away at its integrity and ruining the song and balance. And so it also pans out on delivery, though the smoke is soon muzzled. For a flavour wave or two both smoke and fruit are in perfect harmony but it is fleeting and not worth the dull finish which follows. Enjoyable, but kind of irritating, too. 46%. nc ncf.

The BenRiach Aged 22 years Moscatel Wood Finish db (81) n21 t23 f17 b20 Not sure any wine finish I have tasted this year has thrown up so many huge, one might even say challenging, perfumed notes which score so highly for sheer lip-smacking effect. Had this cask not given the impression of being sulphur treated what an enormous score it would have amassed...! 46%.

The BenRiach 25 Years Old db (87.5) n21.5 t23 f21 b22. The tranquillity and excellent balance of the middle is the highlight by far. 50%

The BenRiach Aged 25 Years Authenticus db (91) n23 t23 f22 b23 Every moment feels as old as a Roman senator...who is eventually stabbed in the back by Oakicus. 46%.

BenRiach 35 Year Old db (90) n23 juicy dates and plums are tipped into a weighty fruitcake; t24 sit right back in your armchair (no..? Then go and find one...!!) having dimmed the lights and silenced the room and just let your taste buds run amok: those plums and toasted raisins really do get you salivating, with the spices also whipping up a mid-life storm; f21.5 angular oak dries and bitters at a rate of knots; b22 sexy fruit, but has late oaky bite. 42.5%

BenRiach Cask Strength batch 1 db (93) n22.5 t24 f23 b23.5 If you don't fall in love with this one, you should stick to vodka... 57.2%

The BenRiach Curiositas Aged 10 Years Single Peated Malt db (90.5) n23 t23 f22 b22.5 "Hmmmm. Why have my research team marked this down as a 'new' whisky" I wondered to myself. Then immediately on nosing and tasting I discovered the reason without having to ask: the pulse was weaker, the smoke more apologetic...it had been watered down from the original 46% to 40%. This is excellent malt. But can we have our truly great whisky back, please? As lovely as it is, this is a bit of an imposter. As Emperor Hadrian might once have said: "ifus itus aintus brokus..." 40%

The BenRiach Peated Cask Strength batch 1 db (95) n24 t23 f24 b24 Stunning whisky magnificently distilled and, though relatively young, almost perfectly matured. 56%.

BenRiach Peated Quarter Casks db (93) n23.5 there's a lot of peat in them barrels. The citrus is vital...; t24 a plethora of sugars and caramel leached from the casks make for a safe landing when the smoke and malt – with a slightly new make feel - arrive in intensive form; f22.5 the caramel continues, now with spice; b23 though seemingly youthful in some phases, works a treat! 46%

Birnie Moss Intensely Peated db (90) n22 youthful, full of fresh barley and lively, clean smoke; t23.5 juicy, fabulously smoked, wet-behind the ears gristy sugars; f22 some vanillas try to enter a degree of complexity; b22.5 before Birnie Moss started shaving... or even possibly toddling. Young and stunning. 48%. nc ncf.

Old Malt Cask Benriach Aged 23 Years refill hogshead, cask no. 16005, dist Mar 96, bott Oct 19 (85) n20.5 t22.5 f21 b21 A tad too untidy and tart. The nose lets you into the secret that the malt and oak have not got on too well over the years and despite the attractive malty rally on delivery the tangy finish confirms the nose's warning. 47.6%. nc ncf sc. 310 bottles.

The Whisky Gallery Two of Wands BenRiach Aged 5 Years refill sherry cask, cask no. 291, dist 2013, bott 2019 (85) n21 t21.5 f21.5 b21 Any younger any they called have called this 'Embryo". Virtually colourless, the malt has picked up little from the cask other than a rasping dryness. Some tangy malt and a new-make chocolate edge ensure some pleasure. 49%. sc. 172 bottles.

BENRINNES
Speyside, 1826. Diageo. Working.

Benrinnes 21 Year Old ex-sherry European oak casks, dist 1992 db (83.5) n21 t22 f19 b21.5. Salty and tangy. Some superb cocoa moments mixing with the muscovado sugars as it peaks. But just a little too furry and bitter at the finish. 56.9%. 2,892 bottles. Diageo Special Releases 2014.

The First Editions Benrinnes Aged 14 Years 2005 refill barrel, cask no. 16782, bott 2019 **(88.5) n21.5 t23.5 f21.5 b22** Benrinnes at it most deliciously jaunty. The barley is on overdrive from the moment it hits the palate, making this one of the maltiest malts of the year without question. The thinness on both the nose and finish is a bridge to be crossed, but that's no good reason not to luxuriate in the very maltiest of deliveries. *56.4%. nc ncf sc. 222 bottles.*

◈ **The First Editions Benrinnes Aged 20 Years 2000** bourbon barrel, cask no. 18212, bott 2020 **(82) n21 t21.5 f19.5 b20** The thinness of the malt is revealed in all its glory here, from the sharp acetate nose right through to quickfire finale. A good show of barley early on, but this soon burns out. *49.4%. nc ncf sc. 243 bottles.*

◈ **Hepburn's Choice Benrinnes 9 Years Old** wine hogsheads, dist 2010, bott 2020 **(86.5) n21.5 t21 f22 b22** The lack of muscle from the malt allows the cask to dictate. That means it's fruit pastels all round...though low calorie ones as sugars remain at a premium. Not typically Benrinnes, though, as this has some chewing in it...and spice! *46%. nc ncf. 696 bottles.*

Hepburn's Choice Benrinnes 10 Years Old wine cask, dist 2009, bott 2019 **(83) n20 t21 f21 b21** Not a particularly bad wine cask. But the malt base is so feeble it is just incapable of making any kind of impression, or ensuring any degree of complexity. Not unpleasant, but a malt which goes precisely nowhere. *46%. nc ncf sc. 110 bottles.*

◈ **Old Malt Cask Benrinnes Aged 24 Years** refill hogshead, cask no. 17812, dist Sept 96, bott Dec 20 **(85) n22 t21.5 f20.5 b21** A little extra body than the norm for a Benrinnes allows the malt and spice to congregate into something momentarily weighty, then salivating but ultimately a little stretched and overly simple. *50%. nc ncf sc. 316 bottles.*

Scyfion Choice Benrinnes 2006 pomegranate Armenian wine cask finished, bott 2019 **(91) n22.5 t23 f22.5 b23** This is very weird. I tasted their Bashta cask vatted malt earlier in the day and got pomegranates....!!! I'm assuming this is the same cask type here: if it is, I have just impressed if not amazed myself! Well, my last girlfriend, Judy, was half Armenian: I think I know what to get her for Christmas. Lots of character and personality here. *50%. nc ncf sc. 158 bottles.*

◈ **Single Cask Collection Benrinnes 12 Years Old** rum cask finish, cask no. 303890, dist 2008, bott 2020 **(83) n20.5 t22 f20 b20.5** A very curious choice of cask for this particular distillery: I think I could have written the tasting notes even before nosing it and putting to my lips. Rum casks have a habit of imprisoning the malt with a crunchy sugar shell. It needs good body to pierce this shield...and Benrinnes would never, in a million years have that kind of weight and energy. So it proves. Not that it doesn't have moments to enjoy, especially though, the midpoint where some malt does seep through. But it is very short-lived. *55.7%. sc. 253 bottles.*

Stronachie 18 Years Old (83.5) n21.5 t21 f20 b21 This is so much like the older brother of the Stronachie 12: shows the same hot temper on the palate and even sharper teeth. Also, the same slim-line body. Have to say, though, something strangely irresistible about the intensity of the crisp malt. *46%*

◈ **The Whisky Chamber Benrinnes 20 Jahre 2000** bourbon barrel **(89) n22.5** an excellently balanced affair: the nose and vanilla harmonise delightfully. Didn't expect that...! **t23** and even better on delivery as the malt takes off with eye-wateringly sharp and salivating confidence: so rare to find a Benrinnes with this kind malty punch; **f21.5** just begins to tire slightly. Dry and vaguely bitter; **b22** now this is impressive. A Benrinnes which for once displays a body rich and fit enough to go on a mini malt marathon. *54.9%. sc.*

BENROMACH
Speyside, 1898. Gordon & MacPhail. Working.

Benromach 15 Year Old db **(78) n20 t22 f17 b19.** Some charming early moments, especially when the grape escapes its marker and reveals itself in its full juicy and sweet splendour. But it is too short lived as the sulphur, inevitably takes over. *43%*

◈ **Benromach Aged 15 Years** first-fill casks, bott code: 30/01/20 db **(94.5) n23.5** how can you not love that marriage between cherry drop candy and rich, toasty tannin, abounding with spices and the lightest licks of liquorice...? **t24.5** this is, on delivery, the very definition of a tactile whisky. The light oils coat the palate and kiss and caress. The fruit forms a soothing layer which drapes, naked, across the palate. Light malty tones caress while the tannins create a more forceful rhythm; **f23** long with a return of that bitter cherry candy; the spices nibble and nip and contrive. Just a slight furriness very, very late on suggests one of the sherry butts had a minor brush with the dreaded S word...; **b23.5** the last time I tasted this sulphur ruled, not OK. Not now. Upgrades to serious little charmer status. The extraordinary touch of this whisky on the palate, its kisses and caresses and its most subtle of flavour profiles...never shouting, just hints, whispers, promises and sighs. Apparently whisky isn't sexy. People have tried to, quite literally, destroy my career because I say it is. Well taste this, Murray Method and all, and tell me if you are being seduced or not...43%.

Benromach 21 Years Old db (91.5) n22 t23.5 f23 b23 An entirely different, indeed lost, style of malt from the old, now gone, big stills. The result is an airier whisky which has embraced such good age with a touch of panache and grace. 43%

Benromach 30 Years Old db (95.5) n23.5 t24 f24 b24 You will struggle to find a 30-year-old with fewer wrinkles than this.. Magnificent: one of the outstanding malts of the year. 43%

Benromach 39 Year Old 1977 Vintage db (94) n23.5 t24 f23 b23.5 Just love it when a whisky creaks and complains and lets you know just how old it is...but then produces the magic that keeps alive, well and captivatingly complex after all these years. 56%.

Benromach 1972 cask no. 4471 db (94) n23 t23.5 f23.5 b24 Has turned completely grey, but this is one sprightly malt. 55.7%. sc.

Benromach 1977 cask no. 1269 db (87.5) n22 t21.5 f22 b22 Plucked from the warehouse a little too late with its best days behind it. The oak is overlord here, the tannins aggressive enough to bring water to the eye, as does the grapefruit citrus kick. But by no means is all lost as the malt is proud, robust and rich and puts up a chewy rear-guard action. 49.6%. sc.

Benromach 100° Proof db (94) n23 t23.5 f23.5 b24 For any confused US readers, the strength is based on the old British proof strength, not American! What is not confusing is the undisputed complexity and overall excellence of this malt. 57%

Benromach 20th Anniversary Bottling db (81) n19 t22 f19 b21 Bit of a clumsy whisky never really feeling right on the nose or palate, though has its better moments with a big malt crescendo and a delicate minty-chocolate movement towards the late middle and early finish. 56.2%.

Benromach Cask No. 1 dist 1998, bott 2018 db (89.5) n23 like a bunch of grapes you forgot you had in the bag...; t22 fat, oily slightly off-key start but corrects itself as a tart but attractive gooseberry notes arrives; f22 dry powdery mocha; b22.5 an unusual fingerprint to this and intriguingly haphazard in its development. 60.1%.

Benromach Cask Strength 2001 db (89) n21.5 t23 f22 b22.5. Just fun whisky which has been very well made and matured with total sympathy to the style. Go get. 59.9%

Benromach Cask Strength 2003 db (92) n22.5 t23.5 f23 b23.5 Hats off to the most subtle and sophisticated Benromach I have tasted in a while. 59.4%.

Benromach Cask Strength Batch 1 dist 2008, bott 2019 db (90.5) n23.5 t22.5 f22 b22.5 Some smoky malts terrify people. This, I suspect, will enjoy the direct opposite effect. As friendly a peated malt as you'll ever find. 57.9%.

Benromach Heritage 35 Year Old db (87) n22 t21.5 f22 b21.5. A busy exchange of complex tannin notes, some backed by the most faded spice and caramel. All charming and attractive, but the feeling of decay is never far away. 43%

Benromach Heritage 1974 db (93) n23.5 t23 f23 b23.5 Made in the year I left school to become a writer, this appears to have survived the years in better nick than I... 49.1%

Benromach Heritage 1975 db (89) n22 t22.5 f22 b22.5 A bottling where the malt is hanging on for grim death against the passing of time. But the discreet light honey notes do just the trick. 49.9%.

Benromach Heritage 1976 db (86.5) n21.5 t21 f22.5 b21.5 There are times when you can have a little too much tannin and this has crossed the Rubicon. That said, look closely on the nose for some staggering lime and redcurrant notes which escape the onslaught as well as the gorgeous butterscotch on the finish as the sugars fight back at the death in style. Some moments of genius in the oakiest of frames. 53.5%.

Benromach Organic Special Edition db (85.5) n22 t21 f21.5 b21. The smoky bacon crisp aroma underscores the obvious youth. Also, one of the driest malts of the year. Overall, pretty. But pretty pre-pubescent, too... 43%

Benromach Organic 2010 db (95.5) n24 t24 f23 b24.5 Gentle, refined and exquisitely elegant. 43%.

Benromach Peat Smoke Batch 3 db (90.5) n22 t23 f22.5 b23 An excellent malt that has been beautifully made. Had it been bottled at 46 we would have seen it offer an extra degree of richness. 40%

Benromach Peat Smoke 2008 db (85.5) n22 t22 f20.5 b21 Well, that was certainly different! The nose has the oily hallmark of a Caol Ila, though without the phenol intensity. The palate, those oils apart, is a very different tale. A unique flavour profile for sure: a kind of smoked toffee fudge which actually makes your tongue ache while tasting! And there is a bitterness, also. Normally I can spot exactly from where it originates...this one leaves me baffled...though I'd go from the distillation if pushed. 46%.

Benromach Sherry Cask Matured Peat Smoke dist 2010, bott 2018 db (94.5) n23.5 t24 f23 b24 These type of whiskies so often fall flat on their face. This, by contrast, is a magnificent beast of a malt... 59.9%.

Benromach Triple Distilled db **(88) n23** the firmness to the malt has an almost Irish pot still quality: sharp, yet with a firm, brooding disposition; **t22.5** salivating and ultra-clean. Gristy sugars melt into the mix with vanilla upping the weight; **f21.5** a slight oak-sponsored bitterness from the more antiquated casks makes its mark; **b22** the finish part, a really charming barley character pervades throughout. 50%.

Benromach Vintage 1976 db **(89.5) n23 t23.5 f21 b22** hardly complex and shows all the old age attributes to be expected. That said...a very comfortable and satisfying ride. 46%

Benromach Wood Finish 2007 Sassicaia db **(86.5) n22 t22 f21 b21.5**. Now back to the new distillery. Problem with this wood finish is that even when free from any taint, as this is, it is a harsh taskmaster and keeps a firm grip of any malty development – even on a dram so young. A brave cask choice. 45%

BLADNOCH
Lowlands, 1817. David Prior. Working.

Bladnoch 10 Year Old bourbon barrels, bott code: L18/8829 db **(91) n22.5 t23 f22.5 b23** Just wonderful to see Bladnoch back in the market place again, and this time obviously receiving the kind of attention in warehouse and tasting lab it deserves. The 10-year-old was for years a Lowland staple before a succession of owners saw it all but vanish off the map. This 10-year-old suggests they have the nucleus of what can again become a much-prized dram. Though a ten-year-old, either some of the casks used in this were a lot older, or there has been heavy usage of first-fill bourbon somewhere along the line, because the tannins have an unusually significant say. The result...rather delicious and you get a hell of a lot for a ten-year-old... 46.7%. ncf.

Bladnoch 11 Year Old bourbon & red wine casks, bott code: L19 WB db **(87.5) n21.5 t23 f21 b22** Certainly no escaping the full- on juiciness of the delivery which broadcasts a full on vividness of the fruit. The malt, though, offers the more alluring backbone, though the two styles have problems integrating at the death. Would love to see this without the wine. 46.7%. ncf. First Release.

Bladnoch 15 Year Old Adela oloroso sherry casks, bott code: L18/8083 db **(91) n22 t23 f23 b23** I still feel a bit like Inspector Clouseau's boss, twitching at the mere thought of a sherry butt. But no need for alarm here: faultless oloroso influence here, indeed coming to the aid perhaps of an initial spirit which may not have been originally up to Bladnoch's excellent name. Surprisingly delightful. 46.7%. ncf.

Bladnoch 17 Year Old Californian red wine finish db **(87.5) n22 t23 f21 b21.5** At its zenith on both nose and delivery, both imparting boiled sweet fruitiness and lustre. After that, as well as spice, a non-sulphured bitterness seeps into the proceedings. 46.7%. ncf.

Bladnoch 27 Year Old bourbon cask finish db **(95) n24.5 t23.5 f23 b24** The best nose of a Lowlander I have encountered for a good number of years. A gem of single malt. 43%. ncf

Bladnoch Samsara Californian red wine & bourbon casks, bott code: L18/8081 db **(87) n21.5 t23 f21 b21.5** Wine casks at work and not a sulphur atom in sight. However, there is no escaping a certain unscheduled bitterness or the fact that perhaps some of the malt was technically not the greatest ever distilled in Bladnoch's history. The result is a patchy experience, delicious in part, but bitty and bitter in others. Lush though on delivery and the plusses are big ones. 46.7%. ncf.

Bladnoch Talia 26 Year Old red wine casks nbc db **(89.5) n23.5 t22.5 f21.5 b22** Have to say, knowing Bladnoch as well as I do (and loving it even more intensely!) I was a little frustrated by the heavy-handedness of the grape which carries all before it. There is still a residual juiciness from the barley 44%. ncf. 2020 Release.

Bladnoch Single Cask 2020/01 California red wine hogshead, cask no. 38, dist Jan 08, bott Mar 20 db **(90) n22.5 t23 f22 b22.5** A very bold wine influence tends to wipe out the usual charming malt character offered up by Bladnoch at this age. But the wine cask is clean and clear in its design, ensuring a wonderfully flavoursome experience. Though if blind-tasted, I wouldn't have picked Bladnoch in 50 increasingly desperate guesses... 56%. nc ncf sc. 289 bottles.

BLAIR ATHOL
Highlands (Perthshire), 1798. Diageo. Working.

Blair Athol 23 Year Old ex-bodega European oak butts db **(90.5) n23 t23.5 f21.5 b22.5** Very often you think: "Aha! Here's an un-sulphur-treated sherry-matured malt!" And then find long into the finish that the taint turns up and sticks with you for another 20 minutes. Is there a slight trace on this late on? Yes. But it is one of the lightest and least concerning I have encountered this year. Which leaves you with plenty of luscious grape to enjoy... 58.4%. 5,514 bottles. Diageo Special Releases 2017.

Blair Athol Distillery Exclusive Bottling batch no. 01, refill, rejuvenated & American oak ex-bourbon casks, bott code: L9316DQ002 db **(94) n23 t24 f23.5 b23.5** A distillery that has come so far away from its days as a producer of fodder malt for Bells, when the spirit was thin and inconsequential, it is now a malt to be sought after and savoured rather than snubbed. This expression really underlines not just the high quality that this distillery is now capable of but also its depth of character. Delightful. *48%. 6,000 bottles.*

⬧ **Hepburn's Choice Blair Athol 10 Years Old** bourbon barrel, dist 2010, bott 2020 **(91)** **n22.5** the malt shines, glittering with sugars; **t23** quite beautiful: not just the sublime intensity of the barley and the glorious backdrop of semi-bourbon style tannin and Demerara, but the mouth-feel, too...; **f22.5** much drier with late cocoa powder; **b23** the distillery feels very at home at this age and in excellent bourbon cask. Shews off the old-fashioned Perthshire sweetness to maximum effect. Adorable. *46%. nc ncf sc. 187 bottles.*

⬧ **Hepburn's Choice Blair Athol 11 Years Old** wine hogshead, dist 2009, bott 2020 **(83.5)** **n20 t21.5 f21 b21** A very tight malt which seems to be clamped in leg irons. Very little sweetness escapes the dull fruit, though for one all too brief moment it does open up after delivery and relaxes. *46%. nc ncf sc. 383 bottles.*

Old Malt Cask Blair Athol Aged 24 Years sherry butt, cask no. 17193, dist Jun 95, bott Sept 19 **(88) n21.5 t22.5 f22 b22** Fat and malty, the sherry butt makes no great impression, other than perhaps upping the viscosity slightly. Some lovely spices in action with the vanilla. Busy and satisfying. *50%. nc ncf sc. 294 bottles.*

⬧ **Old Malt Cask Blair Athol Aged 25 Years** sherry butt, cask no. HL18205, dist Mar 1995, bott Feb 2021 **(89.5) n23** when the fruit is this clean an understated and the cask so confident yet naturally modest, the resulting marriage of styles usually charms and entices. This is no different...; **t23** superb mix of salivating barley even now, moistening the lush, though slightly pithy grape. A light butterscotch touch, too...; **f21.5** the cask tires slightly, but the spices keep the flame burning; **b22.5** not the perfect sherry butt but one good enough to cover the quarter century with something to spare and keep the complexity levels high. *50%. nc ncf sc. 293 bottles.*

⬧ **Old Malt Cask Blair Athol Aged 25 Years** sherry butt, cask no.HL18688, dist Nov 1993, bott May 2021 **(90.5) n23** wonderfully complex if you give it ample time to come alive. At first it appears the wine has the exclusive rights on all aromas, but slowly the oak makes its mark and always in barely discernible layers. At the same time some aspects of the grape lightens and just becomes faintly crisper and more juicy; **t23** silky textured and muscovado sugared. The tannins hold medium weight while the dryness of the grape skin grows in importance; **f21.5** just a little bitter as the tiring oak takes a toasty turn; **b23** the Murray Method and 20 minutes of your times will show this in a light to pleasantly surprise you. *50% sc 197 bottles*

⬧ **Skene Blair Athol 2015 Southern Highlands Scotch Single Malt** first-fill Oloroso sherry, cask no: 900093, dist: 2015, bott: 2020, db **(89.5) n21** dull, vaguely off key despite a attendant grapey sugars; **t23** a dull initial delivery...and then...whoomph! It just goes up in a flame of oak-spattered barely, surprising considering its age. But the layering is sublime, taking full advantage of the limited oil available. The malt pulses proudly but the spice and fruit hit the spot...; **f22.5** a lovely spiced fade with outline vanilla. Dries to a warm, chalky, finish; **b23** one of those rare malts where the nose lies. Totally lacking in inspiration when sniffed at, it comes alive in the glass to a delightful degree. *48% ncf, 246 bottles*

⬧ **The First Editions Blair Athol Aged 10 Years 2010** sherry butt, cask no.HL18378, bott 2021 **(89.5) n22** pretty sharp grape; **t23** beautifully mouth-watering, becoming creamy and meaningfully spiced; **f22** a surprisingly weighty late oaky presence; **b22.5** all ship shape and Harvey's Bristol fashion...*50.1% nc ncf sc 604 bottles*

⬧ **The First Editions Blair Athol Aged 23 Years 1997** sherry butt, cask no. HL18206, bott 2021 **(91) n23.5** salty Calvados...? **t23** there we go again! Distinct Calvados on the delivery. The saline attack on the nose is much less pronounced here, though that isn't to say it isn't noticeable. Meanwhile, the vanillas make a big show of their age. The lightest of oily touches adds to the depth. The spices are slow to arrive, burn busily then fade...; **f22** a little tangy from antiquity, but nothing untoward; then the gentlest spice; **b22.5** forget the grape...look for the ancient apple! *55.3%. nc ncf sc. 269 bottles.*

BOWMORE
Islay, 1779. Morrison Bowmore. Working.

Bowmore Aged 10 Years Spanish oak sherry casks & hogsheads, bott code: L172033 db **(92.5) n23.5 t23.5 f22.5 b23** A very happy marriage between some full on peat and decent sherry butts makes for the intense malt promised on the label. *40%.*

Bowmore Aged 12 Years bott code: L182208 db **(86.5) n22 t22 f21 b21.5** This is some surprise package. With the phenol level being markedly down on the last bottle of this I encountered and the oils wearing thin long before the end – not assisted by the 40% abv

– this Bowmore never quite gets going. Perhaps the midpoint has something to latch on to and thoroughly enjoy where the peat and oils do find accord. But it is far too short-lived. *40%.*

Bowmore Aged 15 Years 1st fill bourbon casks, bott code: L172034 031 db **(88)** n23.5 t22 f21 b21.5 This was going swimmingly until the caramel just went nuts. I know first-fill bourbon casks are at work here, but hard to believe that was all natural... *43%.*

Bowmore Aged 15 Years sherry cask finish, bott code: L172073 db **(91) n23 t22.5 f22.5 b23** A sherry influenced whisky outpointing a bourbon cask one....how often will you find that in this book...? *43%.*

Bowmore Aged 15 Years bott code: L9289SB323250923 db **(94) n23.5 t23.5 f23 b24** A joyful experience with the peat in expansive mode and the Victory V cough sweet adding the right kind of toasted sugars. An easily quaffable kind of 15-year-old...not something you normally associate with a whisky of this good age. I just love to see Bowmore in this kind of mood. *43%.*

Bowmore Aged 18 Years Oloroso & Pedro Ximénez casks, bott code: L172067 060 db **(82) n20.5 t22.5 f19 b20** A dirty old nose – and I don't just mean the peat – pre-warns of the furry finish. But there is no denying the sheer joy of the voluptuous grape grappling with the phenols on delivery and in the wonderful moments just after. *43%.*

Bowmore Aged 18 Years bott code: L9172SB322071130 db **(87) n21.5 t22 f21.5 b22** A grouchy, moody dram inclined to bite your head off. The nose is positively snarling with the peat offering no give whatsoever and happy to give you a bit of the old acid. While the delivery likewise gives your what for with a volley of dry, unforgiving, peaty expletives. The finish is no less harsh. Only a few curt molasses and hickory notes offer solace. *43%.*

Bowmore Aged 23 Years Port Matured db **(86) n22 t22 f21 b21.** Have you ever sucked Fisherman's Friends and fruit pastels at the same time, and thrown in the odd Parma Violet for good measure...? *50.8%*

Bowmore Aged 25 Years Small Batch Release db **(85.5) n21 t22 f21 b21.5.** Distilled at the very heart of Bowmore's peculiar and uniquely distinctive Fisherman's Friend cough sweet era. You will never find a more vivid example. *43%*

Bowmore Aged 30 Years db **(94) n23 t24 f23 b24** A Bowmore that no Islay scholar should be without. Shows the distillery at its most intense yet delicate; an essay in balance and how great oak, peat and fruit can combine for those special moments in life. Unquestionably one of the best Bowmores bottled this century. *43%*

Bowmore Black 50 Year Old db **(96.5) n25 t24 f23 b24.5** a little known fact: a long time ago, before the days of the internet and a world of whisky experts who outnumber the stars that puncture the sky on the very darkest of nights, I actually tasted the first Black Bowmore in their very basic blending lab and gave it the required seal of approval before they allowed it to hit the shelves. It wasn't a 50-year-old beast like this one, though. And it proves that though something may have reached half a century, it knows how to give pleasure on at least a par with anything younger ... *41%*

Bowmore Black Rock oak casks db **(87.5) n22.5 t22 f21 b22.** A friendly, full bodied dram whose bark is worse than its bite. Smoked toasted fudge is the main theme. But that would not work too well without the aid of a vague backdrop cinnamon and marmalade. If you are looking for a gentle giant, they don't come more wimpish than this. *40% WB15/336*

Bowmore Devil's Casks III db **(92.5) n23 t23 f23.5 b23.5** a whisky created by Charles Williams, surely. So, at last....I'm in league with the devil...! Hawwww-hhaaaa-haaaaaa!!!! *56.7%*

Bowmore No.1 first fill bourbon casks, bott code: L172026 db **(91.5) n23 t23 f22.5 b23** Bowmore was never the most peaty of Islay's malts. But here the phenols are at their shyest. Delicate and all a rather sexy tease... *40%.*

Bowmore Small Batch "Bourbon Cask Matured" db **(86) n22 t22 f21 b21.** A big improvement on the underwhelming previous Small Batch from this distillery, then called "Reserve", though there appears to be a naivety to the proceeding which both charm and frustrate. The smoke, hanging on the grist, is very low key. *40%.*

◈ **Old Malt Cask Bowmore Aged 18 Years** refill barrel, cask no. 17813, dist Dec 01, bott Dec 20 **(94) n23.5** more than a speck of salt has brought the ultra-light peat into vivid life. The malt remains intact and juicy, the oak an interested bystander..; **t23.5** oh...wow! Just how juicy is that. The nose didn't lie: its subtle message was brought crashing home by the concentrated form of the barley, though the aroma doesn't warn you if the wave of peat which crashes in soon after. All this kept in place by a delicate heather-honey frame; **f23** the peat and spices, so shy early on, linger now...; **b24** you know when you are in the presence of a great Bowmore: you close your eyes and you can hear the waves lapping on Loch Indaal and the herring gull crying overhead...quietly majestic malt. *50%. nc ncf sc. 206 bottles.*

◈ **The First Editions Bowmore Aged 16 Years 2003** refill barrel, cask no. 17811, bott 2020 **(93) n23** some cooling peppermint leaks into the phenols to add a little extra sweetness to the subtle smoke; **t23.5** just about the perfect Bowmore delivery for this age: the peat makes itself known immediately in the uplifting, though controlled, explosion on delivery, but friendly Demerara sugars help bring a juicy maltiness to the fore, too. The midground is more dense with oak upping the spices; **f23** drier, almost chalky now though soe residual oil allows the phenols some extra time; **b23.5** hard to imagine any Islayphile not to swoon at the smoky tones of this intense yet still gentle beauty.... *58.4%. nc ncf sc. 230 bottles.*

⬦ **Valour Islay Single Malt Bowmore Aged 24 Years** 2nd-Fill Sherry hogshead, cask no: 9002100, dist: 16/02/1997, bott: 14/05/2021 **(93.5) t23.5** the flintiness to the peat is almost unBowmore-esque. But, then, the excellence of the sherry is pretty unusual for a cask of its day, too. So this entertaining aroma is far from what I was expecting...; **t24** such a pleasing delivery, with something, like the nose, very unusual for a Bowmore. Despite the peat, the gristiness of the barley positively sparkles a few flavour waves in. Brilliant! Mind you, the delivery isn't lacking, either. Healthy, ripe, not quite toasted raisin, helped along with some early spice. A real humdinger...; **f22.5** just a little dry bitterness creeps in. Nothing to lament, but while the spices buzz the sugars are struggling to retain their feet; **b23.5** sherry influence without the damaging sulphur hit. Wonderful! A beautifully weighted malt shewing the distillery in lively fashion. Far from your standard Bowmore. *54.8% sc*

Wemyss Malts Black Gold Bowmore 1989 30 Years Old hogshead **(82.5) n20 t22.5 f19 b21** This malt technically fails on so many levels. Something over the 30 years or so has happened to this cask that is very odd. All kinds of strange notes (most of them metallic, but also a bit of the swimming pool on the nose) that, as a blender, I'd mark off and keep away from any whisky I'm working with. Yet, despite all that, despite its metallic tang, there is also something irresistibly attractive about this brute. *50%. nc ncf sc. 175 bottles.*

Wemyss Malts Kilning The Malt Bowmore 1996 23 Years Old hogshead **(94) n23.5 t23.5 f23 b24** If this were any more polite a malt, it'd do a curtsy before a-leaping onto your taste buds... *47.9%. nc ncf sc. 218 bottles.*

Woolf/Sung The Lowest Tide Bowmore 26 Year Old 1991 Sauternes cask finish **(95) n24 t23.5 f23.5 b24** From the very first sniff to the last dying peaty ember, this exudes class. I have long argued that high quality Sauternes cask is by far the most sympathetic of all the wine casks – and this does nothing to disprove my theory. The fruit is always around: clean at times adding candied feel. But the peat is always in control -and here, after more than a quarter of a century, the ppm levels must have been way above the usual 25 when this was made. A tactile dram clinging and kissing with maple syrup to add to the grist. What a sensational experience – in every sense! *50.9%. sc.*

BRAEVAL
Speyside, 1974. Chivas Brothers. Working.

⬦ **Skene Braeval American Oak 2014 Speyside Scotch Single Malt** hogshead cask no: 9900153, dist: 30th Sept 2014, bott: Dec 2020, db **(87.5) n21.5 t22.5 f21.5 b22** A skittish, underdeveloped malt of fascinating unpredictability. The thin nose shews a weakness or two and doesn't prepare you for the juicy, malty onslaught that is to come on delivery. The gristy sugars fare melt in our mouth as the spices ramp up the overall depth. The finish is predictably fragile, but still clings to enough malty citrus and spice to make for an enjoyable encounter. High octane, refreshing barley-water... *50% ncf 327 bottles*

BRORA
Highlands (Northern), 1819–1983. Diageo. Closed.

Brora 34 Year Old refill American oak hogsheads db **(88.5) n22.5 t22 f22 b22** The nose kinds of sums things up perfectly: skeletal fingers of age are all over this: citrus offers sinew and a little smoke the flesh...but time is catching up... *51.9%. 3,000 bottles. Diageo Special Releases 2017.*

BRUICHLADDICH
Islay, 1881. Rémy Cointreau. Working.

Bruichladdich 18 Years Old bourbon/cognac cask db **(84.5) n23.5 t21 f20 b20.** Big oak-spice buzz but thin. Sublime grapey nose, for sure, but pays a certain price, ultimately, for associating with such an inferior spirit... *46%*

Bruichladdich 2005 12 Year Old fresh sherry hogshead, cask no. 998, dist 20 Jul 05, bott 2018 db **(92.5) n23.5 t24 f23 b22** There is virtually no balance to this whisky, yet it somehow works. A whisky every home should have: if you receive a bit of a surprise in your life, this will violently shake you back into the world... *60.4%. nc ncf sc. 372 bottles. Bottled for MacAlabur.*

Bruichladdich Black Art 7 Aged 25 Years db **(95) n23.5 t24 f23.5 b24** Have to say I do love this whisky. One of the most complex Bruichladdichs since its conversion back to a peaty distillery with a delivery that gives you something slightly different each time you taste it....as a genuinely great 25-year-old should be. *48.4%.*

Bruichladdich Islay Barley Aged 5 Years db (86) n21 t22.5 f21.5 b21. The nose suggests a trainee has been let loose at the stills. But it makes amends with an almost debauched degree of barley on delivery which lasts the entirety of the experience. Heavens! This is different. But I have to say: it's bloody fun, too! 50%. nc ncf.

Bruichladdich The Laddie Eight Years Old American & European oak, cask no. 16/070 db (83) n21.5 t22 f19 b20.5 Doesn't chime anything like so well as the Classic Laddie, for instance. The sugars surge and soar in impressive manner, the mid-range smokiness benefiting. But there is a tightness which does very few favours. 50%.

Bruichladdich Laddie Classic Edition 1 db (89.5) n23 t23 f21 b22.5. You probably have to be a certain vintage yourself to fully appreciate this one. Hard to believe, but I can remember the days when the most popular malt among those actually living on Islay was the Laddie 10. That was a staunchly unpeated dram offering a breezy complexity. Not sure of the age on this Retroladdich, but the similarities almost bring a lump to the throat... 46%

Bruichladdich Scottish Barley The Classic Laddie db (78.5) n20 t21.5 f18 b19. Not often a Laddie fluffs its lines. But despite some obviously complex and promising moves, the unusual infiltration of some sub-standard casks has undone the good of the local barley. If you manage to tune out of the off-notes, some sublime moments can still be had. 50%. nc ncf sc.

The Laddie Ten American oak db (94.5) n24 t23.5 f23 b24 This, I assume, is the 2012 full strength version of an Islay classic which was the preferred choice of the people of Islay throughout the 70s, 80s and early 90s. And I have to say that this is already a classic in its own right.... 46%. nc ncf.

The Laddie Sixteen American oak db (88) n22 huge natural caramels dipped in brine; t22.5 very even and gentle with a degree of citrus perking it up; f21.5 reverts to caramels before the tannins strike hard; b22 oak 'n' salt all the way... 46%

The Laddie Twenty Two db (90.5) n24 t23 f21.5 b22 Fabulous coastal malt, though the oak is a presence always felt. 46%

Octomore 7.1 5 Years Old ex-bourbon casks, cask no. 16/080 db (96) n23.5 t24.5 f24 b24 Fan-bloody-tastic...!! A kid of a whisky which sorts the men from the boys... 57%.

Octomore 7.2 5 Years Old bourbon & Syrah casks, cask no. 15/058 db (81.5) n21 t23 f18 b19.5 I love the fact that the sample bottles I have been sent under "education." Brilliant! An hilarious first. But here, if anything is to be learned by those who for some reason don't already know, is the fact that you don't piss around with perfection. Five-year-old Octomore in bourbon cask is a joy that has just about proved beyond description for me. Pointlessly add wine casks – and the sulphur which so often accompanies them – and you get a whisky very much reduced in quality and stature. Some superb moments on this, especially round the time of the warts-and-all delivery. But as it settles the faults of the Syrah casks slowly become clear. What a shame. And waste of great whisky. An education, indeed! 58.5%.

Octomore 10 db (95) n24 t24 f23 b24 When I am tasting an Octomore, it means I am in the home straight inside the stadium after running (or should I say nosing and tasting) a marathon. After this, there are barely another 20 more Scotch malts to go and I am closing in on completing my 1,200 new whiskies for the year. So how does this fare? It is Octomore. It is what I expect and demand. It gives me the sustenance and willpower to get to that crossing line. For to tell you guys about a whisky like this is always worth it...whatever the pain and price. Because honesty and doing the right thing is beyond value. Just ask David Archer. 50%.

Octomore Edition 10.1 Aged 5 Years PPM 107 db (95) n23.5 t24 f23.5 b24 We've been here before. Except maybe this one has a bit more vanilla on hand, as well as some sweetening oils.... 59.8%.

Octomore Edition 10.2 Aged 8 Years PPM 96.9 db (94) n23 t24.5 f23 b23.5 It's an interesting debate: is Octomore at its best when very young and peat has full control? Or when matured and the oak has had a chance to create a more nuanced whisky? I'd say from this evidence, and other Octomores I have seen over the years it is at best when a little younger than this, as here the peat, despite the extraordinary complexity on the delivery, has just lost some of the power of its magic. 56.9%.

Octomore Edition 10.3 Aged 6 Years PPM 114 db (96.5) n24 t24 f24 b24.5 Bloody hell...!! What peat...!!! Yes, we have been down this road before but this one has taken us into a sooty-dry cul-de-sac. Have you ever had an enormous whisky? Yes...? Well, that'll be a little minnow you'll need to throw back against this smoke-billowing beast. 61.3%.

Octomore Edition 10.4 Aged 3 Years PPM 88 db (95.5) n24 t24 f23.5 b24 If you take this whisky for what it is: a very young hugely peated monster of a malt then you'll be very happy indeed. This is one crazy, mixed up kid. And one hell of a smoky one, too. More than great fun. It is a right of passage: for both the whisky and its consumer... 63.5%.

Port Charlotte Aged 10 Years db (95) n23.5 t24 f23.5 b24 Very high quality and teasingly complex peated malt. 50%.

Port Charlotte Heavily Peated db (94.5) n23 t24 f23.5 b24 Rearrange the following two words: "giant" and "gentle". *50%*

Port Charlotte Islay Barley 2011 Aged 6 Years db (95) n23.5 t24 f23.5 b24 There is a controlled intensity to this that is borderline frightening. A malt whisky of majestic beauty. *50%.*

Port Charlotte Islay Barley 2012 Aged 6 Years db (92) n23 a pretty abrasive, acidic kick to the phenol; t23.5 a softer body than the norm with more oils, contrasting vividly with the nose; f22.5 the peats have set leaving only an oily and vanilla-rich glow; b23 it has been a privilege, as well as great fun, to line up all three Port Charlottes together and compare their varying merits, their similarities, their divergencies. It has also been an education, because the beauty of whisky is that you learn from every mouthful – or should – no matter how long you have been in the game. *50%.*

Artful Dodger Port Charlotte 8 Year Old Sauternes cask, cask no. 2009001063 (91) n23.5 t24 f21.5 b22 Though one of the world's greatest advocates of the Sauternes cask, there are times when I think it ill advised to be used...and here is one such occasion. Port Charlotte is about peat, not fruit. And though this is a beautiful whisky in its own right, you still instinctively know that there is a neutralising process going on here with the phenols and fruit cancelling the other out. Even so, there is still much to dive into, not least the sugars which try to counter the sootier smokiness. But the finish, one feels, is unnecessarily unkempt and not in keeping with the Port Charlotte spirit or narrative. Having said all that: the delivery will leave you aghast...! *64.2%. sc.*

⬥ **Fadandel.dk Bruichladdich Aged 13 Years** oloroso octave, cask no.956C, dist Jun 2007, bott Jul 2020 (90.5) n22.5 the grape smothers all. Quietly, though. But relents enough to allow the oaky spice a word...; t23 a tactile, juicy dram, the grape sticking to the roof of the mouth to cast a fruity shadow from there. Now those spices are buzzing warmly and with growing intent; f22 the grape and oak combine to form a slightly bitter edge to this, though, as on the nose, the grape does its best to control...; b23 slightly downbeat and shy, this is an essay in peatless subtlety. *54.5% sc 71 bottles*

Fadandel.dk Bruichladdich 15 Year Old fresh sherry hogshead, cask no. 1198, dist 14 Nov 03, bott 6 Nov 19 (94) n23 t23.5 f23.5 b24 The first thing that I must note is the quality of this sherry cask. Another from Fadandel with once more not even the outline of a hint of sulphur. This is so rare, and I'd like to thank the good people of this company for the massive effort they have obviously put in to secure top quality wine casks, even if I have not enjoyed all of them quite as much as I might, though this was more to do with grape to malt ratio.... This however, is a resounding success: so difficult to pull off with a peated malt. A standing ovation to this company is deserved and I hope other whisky companies take their lead. *62.3%. sc. 157 bottles.*

The Finest Malts Port Charlotte 15 Year Old sherry hogshead, cask no. 1217, dist Oct 04, bott Feb 20 (81) n23 t22 f17 b19 A malt whisky denser than the fog that seems to hang permanently over Islay airport whenever I fly there... Huge peat. But not even a smogful of phenols can disguise or hide the sulphur which makes the finish such hard work and unattractive. Before then there had been some lucid peat and grape moments that bordered on delightful insanity. But the nose suggests this will end in tears...which it dutifully does. *52.1%. nc ncf sc.*

The First Editions Bruichladdich Aged 28 Years 1991 refill hogshead, cask no. 16883, bott 2019 (95.5) n24 t24 f23.5 b24 Spectacularly complex. A whisky technician's dream as this is so beautifully made and matured. *50.7%. nc ncf sc. 295 bottles.*

BUNNAHABHAIN
Islay, 1881. Burn Stewart Distillers. Working.

Bunnahabhain Aged 12 Years db (85.5) n20 t23 f21 b21.5. Lovers of Cadbury's Fruit and Nut will adore this. There is, incongruously, a big bourbony kick alongside some smoke, too. A lusty fellow who is perhaps a bit too much of a bruiser for his own good. Some outstanding moments, though. But, as before, still a long way removed from the magnificent Bunna 12 of old... *46.3%. nc ncf.*

Bunnahabhain 12 Years Old bott code: 1903372L512-1116327 db (84) n20.5 t23 f19 b21.5 Remains true to the new style of Bunna with its slightly skewed sherry notes on nose and finish compensated for by the fabulously sweet and rich ultra - grapey delivery. The sulphur does stick slightly at the death. Oh, how I would still Wester Home back to the great Bunnas of the early 1980s.... *46.3%. nc ncf.*

Bunnahabhain Aged 18 Years db (93.5) n24 t24.5 f22 b23 Only an odd cask has dropped this from being a potential award winner to something that is merely magnificent... *46.3%. nc ncf.*

Bunnahabhain XXV Aged 25 Years db (94) n23 t24 f23 b24 No major blemishes here at all. Carefully selected sherry butts of the highest quality (well, except maybe one) and a malt with enough personality to still gets its character across after 25 years. Who could ask for more...? *46.3%. nc ncf.*

Bunnahabhain 46 Year Old db **(91)** n24 t23 f21.5 b22.5 Needs a good half hour in the glass to open up and have justice done to it. Perishes towards the end, but the nose and build up to that are remarkably beautiful for a whisky which normally doesn't age very well... 42.1%.

Bunnahabhain An Cladach bott code: 20010071L512:3719206 db **(90.5)** n23 t23.5 f21.5 b22.5 For those who prefer their island whiskies to be bold and fulsome. Quite an adventure. 50%. ncf. World Traveller Exclusive.

Bunnahabhain Ceòbanach db **(87.5)** n21.5 t22.5 f21.5 b22. An immensely chewable and sweet malt showing little in years but much in character. A charming liquorice and acacia honey lead then a dry smokiness. Great fun. 46.3%

Bunnahabhain Cruach-Mhòna bott code: 2000996L515:2019169 db **(89)** n23.5 t23 f21 b21.5 Hard to concentrate until you have cleared the water from your eyes. It is not the strength: it is the extraordinary tartness! Technically not the greatest: the messy finish underlines that. But the nose and delivery are something else entirely. 50%. nc ncf. Travel Retail Exclusive.

Bunnahabhain Darach Ùr Batch no. 4 db **(95)** n24 t24.5 f23 b23.5 Because of my deep love for this distillery, with my association with it spanning some 30 years, I have been its harshest critic in recent times. This, though, is a stunner.. 46.3%. nc ncf.

Bunnahabhain Eirigh Na Greine bott code: 1979539L512:4919127 db **(89.5)** n23 t23 f21.5 b22 A sweet, spicy, complex Bunna but with a curiously thin shell. 46.3%. nc ncf. Travel Retail Exclusive.

Bunnahabhain Moine 7 Year Old Oloroso Finish db **(85)** n22 t23.5 f18 b21.5 The faults are apparent on both nose and finish especially. But the grape intensity of the delivery is, momentarily, something special. 60.1%.

Bunnahabhain Stiùireadair bott code: 1910838L514:1919015 db **(83.5)** n21 t22 f20 b20.5 Although the sherry influence is clear of any sulphur content, the grape never comes across articulately on this, either on the nose or delivery. There are some brief moments on arrival when the malt goes directly into delicious fruitcake mode but it is all too brief. From then on it never sits comfortably. The stiùireadair, the helmsman, has steered the wrong course... 46.3%. nc ncf.

Bunnahabhain Toiteach A Dhà bott code: 1767068L510:0218253 db **(86)** n22 t22 f21 b21 A heavyweight malt which first thumps you as hard as possible with unreconstructed peat. And after you get up off the floor from that, you are rabbit punched by chunky fruit notes. Eschews subtlety and charm for impact. But have to say it is a great improvement on the earlier Toiteach. Just a slight technical flaw to this, evident on the finish in particular. 46.3%. nc ncf.

Bunnahabhain Toiteach Un-Chillfiltered db **(75.5)** n18 t21 f17.5 b19. A big gristy, peaty confrontation on the palate doesn't hide the technical fault lines of the actual whisky. 46%. ncf.

◇ **Fanandel.dk Staoisha Aged 7 Years** 1st fill oloroso sherry octave, cask no.10443B, dist Oct 2013, bott Oct 2020 **(89)** n23 rather impressive: acidic peat and anthracite meets smouldering raisin...; **t23.5** excellent mouth feel on delivery: the stickiness of the grape and the intensity of the smoke make for a meritorious and surprisingly well integrated combination. The midpoint, when we eventually get there, has a surprising degree of chocolate on show; **f20** just the slightest nibble on the tongue suggests that the sherry influence is not entirely free of the dreaded S, but has not been applied in anything like the quantities as of old. It means the residual peat can almost outrank in terms of catching your attention...; **b22.5** as you can imagine, that initial thickness of texture slows down development slightly, but then elongates and expands the overall length to very impressive effect.. 56.8% 55 bottles

◇ **Fandandel.dk Staoisha Aged 7 Years** ex-bourbon barrel, cask no.13000728, dist Oct 2013, bott Oct 2020 **(92.5)** n23 sings as sweetly from the glass as an evening blackbird from its lofted perch. Though with a smokier voice....; **t23.5** though from a second or maybe third fill barrel, there is enough vanilla complimenting the sugary phenols as you could wish for to complete an amazingly pretty picture; **f23** just a hint of bitterness, as can be the price paid for using an old cask. But on the positive side the phenols, aided by a dab of oil, see themselves through to a surprisingly gristy finale; **b23** once upon a time – a very long time ago – seven years was often considered the best age for a peated Islay. You can certainly see why on this evidence. Great to see Bunna making high quality malt again. 60.7% 244 bottles

Old Malt Cask Bunnahabhain Aged 27 Years refill hogshead, cask no. 17325, dist Nov 91, bott Oct 19 **(96.5)** n24.5 t24 f23.5 b24.5 Old school Bunna at its oldest! Love it! A truly exceptional cask that demands half an hour just to get to know. 50%. nc ncf sc. 209 bottles.

The Perfect Fifth Bunnahabhain 1991 cask no. 5386 **(93)** n23.5 t23.5 f22.5 b23.5 Old school, proper unpeated Bunna – the way it used to be when at its best under Highland Distillers' ownership. However, this has never been a malt that has aged particularly well and has a habit of starting to fall apart by the time it is about 25-y-o. So much to like here, indeed revere: the astonishingly salty nose and, after a faltering start, fabulous concentrated malt, thick and lush, on delivery. But after the midpoint, balance is compromised as the tannin notes fail to find a balancing malty answer. This is probably about four-years past where I'd really like it to be. Occasionally truly outstanding very old Bunnas make it through – but it is a rare phenomenon. This is borderline brilliant. Incidentally, I stayed at the Bunnahabhain distillery on holiday back in 1991: it was truly the last real vacation I ever had. *50.5%. nc ncf sc.*

⟐ **Single & Single Bunnahabhain 2002 17 Year Old** bourbon cask (**94.5**) **n23** an unpeated earthiness trots out biting spice and a bourbon-style leather character in equal measure. A little heather honey appears to take an odd step forwards, but is soon driven back; **t23.5** just magnificent. No stopping the heather honey now which marches out arm-in-arm with lashing of thick malt. This must have been an exceptional bourbon cask as there is not bitterness over over-enthusiasm among the tannins, thus allowing the honey and malt deliciously safe passage; **f24** another outstanding aspect of the delivery was the silky, succulent mouth feel and this has lasted far longer than could be reasonably be asked or expected. As the honey fades and high-quality praline note picks up where it had left off, becoming even slightly sharper as a little salt and spice build...; **b24** a meticulously complex whisky and worthy 500th sample I have tasted this year in very trying circumstances... *54%. sc. 197 bottles.*

⟐ **Skene Bunnahabhain 2013 Peated Islay Scotch Single Malt** hogshead and Staoisha cask, vatting of casks 878 & 879, dist: 2013, bott: 2020, db (**94**) **n23** a regal elegance to this. The peat is gloriously balanced: plenty of it, but no tasteless and tacky flaunting. Instead, a light chocolate and grist sweetness; **t23.5** again...talk about the grist! As on the nose, Bunna's coastal location is missing. But the mix of peat, citrus, warming, oaky spice and gristy sugars are enough to leave you purring...; **f23.5** some delicate oils pick up and extend not just the smoke but also the light cocoa and vanillas; **b24** an excellent cask shewing that a malt doesn't have to reach best age to be deliciously ripe. Taste this and see why a non-wine cask is so often the best friend of a single malt. If so inclined, could drink this all day every day... *48%, ncf, 504 bottles*

The Whisky Barrel Originals Bunnahabhain 10 Years Old 1st fill oloroso hogshead, cask no. TWB1004, dist Sept 09, bott 2019 (**86.5**) **n22 t22 f21 b21.5** A predominantly clean sherry butt at work here (the finish confirms a slight buzz), thankfully. However, the fusion of grape and grain does little in the way of complexity and when the natural caramels arrive from oak it all becomes a bit of bagpipey drone... *57.1%. sc. 292 bottles.*

The Whisky Barrel Originals Bunnahabhain Staoisha 6 Years Old 1st fill bourbon barrel, cask no. TWB1009, dist Oct 13, bott 2019 (**91.5**) **n23 t23 f22.5 b23** Good to see Bunna technically where it should belong. A very well-made malt. *59.1%. sc. 265 bottles*

The Whisky Embassy Bunnahabhain 2014 re-charred hogshead, cask no. 10598, dist 20 Oct 14, bott 24 Jan 19 (**89**) **n23 t22 f22 b22** Probably one of the peatiest Bunnas I have ever encountered. You wait for complexity to kick in, it does, but as simplistic as the peat...probably for phenol maniacs only. *59.9%. nc ncf sc. 212 bottles.*

Wilson & Morgan Barrel Selection Bunnahabhain 1st fill sherry wood, dist 2009, bott 2019 (**81**) **n21.5 t23 f17 b19.5** Decent sherry giving an attractive toffee-candy feel on delivery to this malt. A sulphur influence is foretold on the nose and comes vividly true at the death... *48%.*

Wilson & Morgan Barrel Selection Bunnahabhain 18 Year Old sherry butt, cask no. 1432, dist 2001, bott 2019 (**90**) **n22.5 t23.5 f21.5 b22.5** Bunna's history with sherry butts has not been the best over the last 30 years. So I feared the worst, to be honest. But this is a very decent and honest cask with no discernible off notes. The spices are x-certificate and its only weakness is over-active tannin. Otherwise a superb whisky experience. *59.7%. sc.*

Wilson & Morgan Barrel Selection Bunnahabhain Heavy Peat dist 2014, bott 2019 (**92.5**) **n23 t23 f23 b23.5** Young and not the slightest attempt at subtlety. But when you have an Islay at this age, it isn't subtlety you are looking for.... *48%.*

CAOL ILA
Islay, 1846. Diageo. Working.

Caol Ila Aged 12 Years db (**89**) **n23 t23 f21 b22.** A telling improvement on the old 12-y-o with much greater expression and width. *43%*

Caol Ila Aged 18 Years bott code: L9185CM008 db (**82.5**) **n21.5 t22 f19 b20** Still improving – slightly. Certainly a little more sweetness early on to bolster the weak phenols. But the off kilter finish remains poor. Still one of the great mysteries of Scotch whisky in how they manage to make a bottling so unrepresentative of such a great distillery.... *43%.*

Caol Ila Aged 25 Years bott code: L71860M000 db (**95.5**) **n24 t24 f23.5 b24** Even after all these years this malt can not only lay on its Islay credentials with its eyes closed, but does so with an almost haughty air, cocking a smoky snook at the passing quarter of a century... *43%.*

Caol Ila 30 Year Old refill American oak & European oak casks, dist 1983 db (**96.5**) **n24 t24.5 f24 b24** Indisputably, one of the most complex, well-rounded and complete Caol Ilas I have tasted since they rebuilt the distillery... *55.1%. 7,638 bottles. Diageo Special Releases 2014.*

Caol Ila Moch db (**87**) **n22 t22 f21 b22** I think they mean "Mocha"... *43%.*

⟡ **Caol Ila Moch** bott code: L9234CM009 db **(92.5) n23** light but uses its oils to lock in the ulmo and acacia honey with the sleepy peat; **t23** silky, lightly oiled but the spice lift is stunning. The smoke works in a similar upward projectory; **f23** long, the ulmo honey returns with a little banana. The smoke and vanillas have formed a late double act as the spices still tingle; **b23.5** this has upped its game phenomenally. Nothing like the limp bottling I tasted last time, this one really does grab Caol Ila by the horns. The only complaint: should have been at 46%... *43%.*

Abbey Whisky Caol Ila Aged 11 Years 2008 hogshead **(93) n23.5 t24 f22.5 b23** So what we have here is Caol Ila naked as it were: in the prime of its life and in what it appears to be a Third-fill hogshead. This means you get little colour and only limited interference from the cask, though what is does offer is a beautifully consistent soft vanilla sub plot. This wins because we can see just how sexy this naked body is, with its voluptuous, oily curves and its peaty, scented magnetism. This is beautifully made whisky allowing the grist a free hit on juicy sweetness. This, ladies and gentleman, is Caol Ila exactly as nature intended... *54.2%. sc. 120 bottles.*

Artful Dodger Caol Ila 9 Year Old 2008 (94) n23.5 t23.5 f23 b24 As a 9-year-old, Caol Ila displaying towards the top of its form with an almost improbably degree of gristy sugars on song. Particularly impressive, though, is the laid-back smoke – this distillery can come through a lot peatier than this – and revels in its slightly ashy, drier sub-plot. Makes a mockery of the strength, as this is a real softy. *63.4%. sc.*

Chapter 7 Chronicle Caol Ila Small Batch 8 Year Old 1998 first fill bourbon casks, dist May 11, bott Mar 20 **(93) n23.5 t23 f23 b23.5** A superb example as to why blenders love working with this malt from bourbon cask. Even at a relatively young 8-years-old you can see how the smoke dishes out power and softness in even doses. The house oils ensure a rounded quality but still lets the light mocha and spice notes off the oak have a good hearing. Not a sensational whisky, but simply one with a massive feel good factor. *49.2%. 893 bottles.*

⟡ **Chapter 7 Caol Ila 2011 Aged 9 Years** bourbon barrel, barrel no.157 **(92) n22.5** super soft with the peating levels seeming a little lower than the normal 35ppm. This gives the thin molasses a little extra chance to shine; **t23.5** the youth of the malt works in its favour as this has the energy to fully concentrate all the peat it can find. The sugars displayed on the nose soon join in the action, too; **f23** dry and powdery with a little cocoa and liquorice mixing with the smoke; **b23** for a 9-year-old there is so much complexity and layering! *50.4% sc*

⟡ **Chapter 7 Caol Ila 2011 Aged 9 Years** first fill bourbon barrel, barrel no.160 **(91) n22** a little bubble gum and cream soda intriguingly mix with the smoke; **t23** curious: a silky Caol Ila, yet not overly oil dependent. There is a sublime wave of ulmo honey and malt, quite apart from the phenols; **f23** usually with this distillery the oils would hit a peak here. But, no! The usual oils have vanished, leaving a much more parched feel to the malt and peat...and still this very unusual intense Malteser candy malt and chocolate finale; **b23** as ubiquitous as Caol Ila as independent bottlings may be, casks with this particular shape and personality are virtually unknown. A subtly distinctive and highly enjoyable version. Considering this is only three casks apart from another, quite different bottling, the intrigue can only grow. *52.2% sc*

⟡ **Chapter 7 Caol Ila 2012 Aged 8 Years** bourbon hogshead, barrel no.325862 **(88) n21 t22 f23 b22** Unusually for Chapter 7 cask, doesn't quite blow you away in the way we have now come to expect. The nose is cranky, aggressive and untidy, while the delivery is a shade too tart. However, as the oils mount so, too, do the soothing praline tones which gives the finish a far more distinguished feel than had once seemed possible. *51.4% sc*

⟡ **Fanandel.dk Caol Ila Aged 8 Years** PX octave finish, cask no.301321, dist Feb 2013, bott Apr 2021 **(87) n21 t23 f21 b22** Possibly only a PX cask could overcome and dumb down a full bloodied Islay malt. The nose has a strange creosote kick, though the delivery is rather wonderful. First the taste buds are almost massaged to death by the mesmerising hand of the grape; a little smoky blanket is there to keep you warm. But once the bullish peppers disappear, there is very little else to report, save some late milk chocolate. *54.2% sc 66 bottles*

The Finest Malts City Landmarks Caol Ila Aged 11 Years bourbon barrel, cask no. 024, dist 2007, bott 2018 **(93) n22.5 t23 f23.5 b24** An attractive, no-nonsense Caol Ila that lets the dog see the rabbit. Slightly drier nose than usual, allowing the peat to nip a little while the palate is massaged by a comforting sweetness that balances out the perfectly-weighted phenols. A lovely buttery flourish to the finale, too. Spot on for its age and cask type. *53.2%. nc ncf sc.*

The First Editions Caol Ila Aged 8 Years 2010 refill hogshead, cask no. 16790, bott 2019 **(92) n22.5 t23.5 f22.5 b23.5** The rough edges to this one act in its favour: complex and bitty, it keeps the taste buds guessing and fully entertained. *59.7%. nc ncf sc. 295 bottles.*

⟡ **The First Editions Caol Ila Aged 10 Years 2010** wine cask, cask no. 18211, bott 2020 **(76) n19 t21 f17.5 b18.5** Tight, compressed and never for a moment relaxing into its usual stride, I would never have recognised this as a Caol Ila. I'm sure some will celebrate the punchiness of the peat and love the all-round aggression. And the acerbic dryness at the death. But, sadly, I'm not one of them... *59.3%. nc ncf sc. 282 bottles.*

Glenwill Caol Ila 1990 hogshead, cask no. 1481 (96) n24 t24 f24 b24 Exemplary. 53.9%.

Gordon & MacPhail Connoisseurs Choice Caol Ila Aged 15 Years first fill bourbon barrel, cask no. 302298, dist 10 Sept 03, bott 1 Feb 19 (96) n23.5 a beautiful controlled pungency to the peat with the tannins mingling to more than make up the numbers; salty and sooty, too; t24 the oils missing in the nose are soon apparent and offering a light gloss to the sweet phenols; a light molasses note sweetens the kippers; f24 the light spices which entered the fray early on stay the pace and add flair to the smoky chocolate; b24.5 classic in every sense. This is what you should expect from a Caol Ila at this age and from this type of cask...and wow! Does it deliver! Truly stunning. 55.7%. sc. 210 bottles.

Hepburn's Choice Caol Ila 8 Years Old refill hogshead, dist 2010, bott 2019 (87) n21.5 t21.5 f22 b22 A light rendition with the smoke fleeting and fragmented. Youthful and fresh, it takes a little time to hit its straps. 46%. nc ncf sc. 379 bottles.

⬩⬩⬩ **Hepburn's Choice Caol Ila 10 Years Old** bourbon barrels, dist 2010, bott 2020 (93) n23 gorgeously layered peat which retains a disarming humbleness to the obviously rich smoke. A sprig of mint and light butterscotch ups the complexity; t23.5 such a delight! A quiet magnificence to the delivery, the light oils helping to soften and spread the smoke so there is no aggression or crash landing...; f23 the delicate vanillas attached to the drier tannins mount a challenge while the spices remain polite and in tune...; b23.5 anyone with a love for a true, traditional Islay - when a 10-year-old was the standard age - will adore the timeless simplicity of this: beautifully made and beautifully matured. 46%. nc ncf. 369 bottles.

Kingsbury Gold Caol Ila 7 Year Old Oloroso sherry hogshead, cask no. 5838, dist 2011 (83.5) n22.5 t22 f20 b19 When you take an apple from a tree you do so when it is ripe. When you select a big peated whisky maturing in a wine cask, you pick when it is balanced. This isn't. Got to love that farmyard nose of the year, though...!!! Sheer, unmucked-out cattle byre. 58.7%. sc. 317 bottles.

⬩⬩⬩ **Kingsbury Sar Obair Caol Ila 30 Year Old** hogshead, dist 1989, cask no. Z89/1 (87) n22 t23 f20 b22 If, on the palate, this was any older it'd soon be getting a telegram from the Queen. Definitely has exceeded its best years, but the result makes for a quite a journey. Sadly, there is a trace of something overcooked and burnt – first detected on the nose- which rather detracts from the finish. The real fun here comes on the delivery and chewiest of follow-throughs. An extraordinary mix of children's cough syrup, Melton Hunt Cake on steroids and a forest of tannin. 46.3% sc 88 bottles

⬩⬩⬩ **Scyfion Choice Caol Ila 2010** Moscatel roxo cask finished, bott 2019 (90.5) n21 salty, phenolic...sweaty armpits...t23 the delivery is much more easy to negotiate: the distillery's oils in full spate and trapping the grape at its juiciest. The peat positively swirls...; f23.5 another Caol Ila where the tannins, smoke and grape have fixed up to present a form of chocolate raisin; b23 there will be those out there who will kick down doors to get hold of this and find no fault with it. My view is a little more reserved...perhaps as I had a problem getting past the sweaty armpit nose. But you are rewarded for forsaking the armpits for the body.... 58.9% nc ncf 246 bottles

The Single Cask Caol Ila 2007 ex-bourbon barrel, cask no. 307362 (94) n22.5 t24 f23.5 b24 Lightly spiced, delicately honeyed and very satisfying. So beautiful... 57.8%. nc ncf sc.

⬩⬩⬩ **The Single Cask Caol Ila 2008** PX sherry finish, cask no. 318690B (94) n23 now there's a miracle: the smoke pierces the grape with some ease. Not complex, but by no means unpleasant; t23.5 now I'm even more amazed: a PX cask giving the smoke and spices a free role. The muscovado sugars have plenty of smoke to contend with; the mouth feel lacks the usual oils and both grape and peat take the opportunity to have their sometime belligerent say. Gloriously salivating; f23.5 calms down now and concentrates entirely on the complexity. Close your eyes and spit the layering between the tannins, smoke, chocolate and almost barely discernible grape and you've got ten minutes to savour; b24 one of the true surprise whiskies of the year. I cannot remember the last time a PX cask was so forgiving...and even beneficial to a whisky. Stunning. 60.9% sc

The Single Malts of Scotland Reserve Cask Caol Ila 10 Year Old (92) n23 t22.5 f23 b23.5 Anything but one dimensional as the peat performs circus acts here to entertain: from the high wire with an ethereal gristiness rich in molten sugar, to earthier, head in lion's mouth phenols that rumble a dull roar. And the delivery is a cannonball firing you some distance. The tannins hitch a ride on the malt's natural oils and an apologetic degree of vanilla. Oh, and did I mention the sublime late spices...? 48%.

The Single Malts of Scotland Reserve Cask Caol Ila 11 Year Old (86) n21 t22.5 f21.5 b21 Gristy, oily and fat. The smoke offers anthracite on the nose and little on the palate. Just not enough oak involvement and never quite gets going. 48%. nc ncf.

⬩⬩⬩ **The Whisky Embassy Bonn Caol Ila 11 Year Old** hogshead, cask no. 300058 (93) n23 the oak hasn't bothered to turn up here, not least because this is possibly a third fill cask: it is all about the charm of the sweet peat; **t23.5** all those luscious oil lines, mingling with the peat and acacia honey...; **f23.5** the usual light cocoa slips in with the smoke, but the honey, uninterrupted by tannin, has stayed the course... **b23** there is an unfussy, naked simplicity to this that one can only applaud. Caol Ila seen stripped down to the basic....and it is a very beautiful experience. *58.6%. nc ncf sc.*

CAPERDONICH
Speyside, 1898. Chivas Brothers. Closed.

Gleann Mór Caperdonich Aged Over 23 Years (86) **n22 t22 f20.5 b21.5** Some beautiful banana skins on the nose. But before it slips up on the clumsy finish, the malt and spice do have a few moments of unbridled glory. A slight failing on the cask, though, means the development is limited and always borderline tangy. *59.4%.*

CARDHU
Speyside, 1824. Diageo. Working.

Cardhu 12 Years Old db (83) **n22 t22 f18 b21.** What appears to be a small change in the wood profile has resulted in a big shift in personality. What was once a guaranteed malt love-in is now a drier, oakier, fruitier affair. Sadly, though, with more than a touch of something furry. *40%*

◈ **Cardhu Aged 15 Years** bott code: L9207IX005 db (88) **n22 t22.5 f22 b21.5** Still a bit of a slave to the toffee, which dominates too often in too many places. But a slight notch up from the last bottle I tasted as there is more heather honey at play now, which works well with the underlying, bitty spices. Yes, enjoyable. But the overall cream toffee theme, however, does this malt no favours at all. *40%.*

Cardhu 18 Year Old db (88) **n22.5 t23 f20.5 b22** Very attractive at first. But when you consider what a great distillery Cardhu is and how rare stocks of 18 year old must be, have to say that I am disappointed. The fruit masks the more intricate moments one usually experiences on a Cardhu to ensure an acceptable blandness and accounts for a poor finish. Why, though, it is bottled at a pathetic 40% abv instead of an unchillfiltered 46% – the least this magnificent distillery deserves – is a complete mystery to me.*40%*

Cardhu Amber Rock db (87.5) **n22 t23 f21 b21.5.** Amber is the right colour for this: it appears stuck between green and red, not sure whether to go or not. The delivery, in which the tangerine cream is in full flow reflects the better elements of the nose. But the finish is all about being stuck in neutral. Not helped by the useless 40% abv, you get the feeling that a great whisky is trying to get out. The odd tweak and we'll have a winner. That said, very enjoyable indeed. Just even more frustrating! *40%. Diageo.*

◈ **Cardhu Gold Reserve** bott code L12181X002 db (86) **n21 t22.5 f21 b21.5** The last time I tasted this, maybe two or three years ago, it was a rather pale – or perhaps I should say overly dark – representation of one of Speyside's finest malts. As before, a wonderful flare on delivery as the spices light up the delicate honey tones. Then comes the caramel of doom... I had hoped that the owners, Diageo, had seen the error of their ways. They haven't. *40%*

Game of Thrones Cardhu Gold Reserve House Targaryen db (84) **n20.5 t22 f20.5 b21** Not having a single television set in any of my three abodes dotted around the place, I have never seen Game of Thrones. Not once. I cannot tell you, even roughly, what the story is about. I have had Bibles to write, distilleries to visit, shows to perform, birds to watch. So I can't tell you whether Targaryen is a person, a place or some kind of fictional spice. Which means I cannot compare the whisky to the name to see if they somehow match. Sorry. However, if it means "a little flat with off-key fruit and plenty of toffee to chew on" then, bingo! They've nailed it. *40%.*

CLYNELISH
Highlands (Northern), 1968. Diageo. Working.

Clynelish Aged 14 Years bott code: L7285CM008 db (86.5) **n22 t22.5 f20 b21** Very strange. This is one of the world's true Super Distilleries, in the top five of the most beautifully complex in Scotland. Yet from this very subdued, relatively character-bypassed bottling it would be hard to tell. *46%.*

◈ **Clynelish Aged 14 Years** bott code: L9331CM007 db (95) **n23.5** salt and honey bound, giving a pleasant sharpness to the sugars while the oak plays a weighty role: the base, alongside what seems like a shard of smoke. Both flighty and weighty at the same time...; **t24** now that is a mouth feel to die for. For a moment you don't concentrate on the flavours, as it is the slightly waxy texture that holds you in thrall. Then the honey slowly makes its mark and spreads. First light and of an acacia bent...then thickening towards rich heather honey. Better still, a three-way layering of ulmo honey, vanilla and toasty tannin spread across the palate as if sauntering across a park on a Sunday afternoon perambulation...; **f23.5** I had expected spices at this point. They arrive, but nothing like in the numbers or with the degree of intensity I have encountered from barrels I have tasted privately over the years. Instead with have a mix of toffee and honey; **b24** the last time I tasted a bottle of this it was one of the biggest disappointments of the year. Make no mistake: Clynelish ranks among the best 10 distilleries in the world and is probably second only to Glen Grant on Scotland's mainland. With the supplies they have available, this should be knocking hard and loud on the door of the Whisky Bible's World Whisky of the Year every single Autumn. The fact it doesn't suggests they have taken a more commercial considerations into account than actually allowing Diageo's world-class blenders to fine tune this into the Lamborghini of a malt, seeming content to see it potter around like a top of the range VW Polo. At last, the style and shape is there to be seen...though there is still so much more to reveal... 46%.

Clynelish Distillery Exclusive Bottling batch no. 01, bott code: L9204DQ001 db **(89) n23 t23 f21 b22** The first batch of a distillery exclusive bottling: this should be fun. Not bad, but the finale in particular is a tad tame by Clynelish's incredibly high standards while the honey notes – and this distillery probably does honey better than any other in Scotland – have been blunted a little. Look forward to the next batch hitting the 95 point mark, where this extraordinary distillery deserves to be... 48%. 3,000 bottles.

Game of Thrones Clynelish 12 Year Old House Tyrell db **(89) n23 t23 f21 b22** Undone slightly by the finish, but that delivery...wow! 51.2%.

Acla Selection Summer Edition Clynelish 21 Year Old hogshead, dist 1996, bott 2018 **(89.5) n23 t22.5 f21.5 b22.5** Even by Clynelish standards much of what to be found here is enigmatic, with the lightest ulmo honeys little more than trace elements over vanilla tones that are barely audible themselves. Underdone slight by a bitter note which creeps in from the late middle. But, elsewhere, salivates and caresses at just the right time in the right places. 45.7%.

Artful Dodger Clynelish 20 Year Old ex-bourbon hogshead, cask no. 6526 **(89) n22 t23 f22 b22** Surprisingly inactive on the nose for a Clynelish. But begins to make amends the moment it hits the palate with a startling saltiness to ramp up the barley. A vague phenol note adds some depth but honey, a given trait of this distillery, is conspicuous by its absence. 55.9%. sc.

The Single Malts of Scotland Reserve Cask Clynelish 8 Year Old **(85.5) n22 t22.5 f20. b21** Clynelish ordinaire. Unaccountably bitter in the wrong places. 48%.

⬦ **The Whisky Cask Company Clynelish 1995** sherry butt, cask no 8655, dist Sep 1995, bott Oct 2019 **(91) n23** a peppery nose: a moist fruitcake with attitude...and no shortage of nuts, too...; **t23.5** the extraordinary complexity to the malt comes to the fore here as few distilleries could see the barley at times battle through so much fruit after all these years. The insane salivation levels on entry are the highlight, though, especially when the orange blossom honey arrives so early; **f21.5** just very slightly off-key and bitter, though some compensating chocolate balances well with the toasted raisins...; **b23** nearly but not quite an outstanding butt. But forget that late lingering bitterness. The journey to that point really is the reason why we love great whisky with a passion. 49.6% nc ncf sc 590 bottles

COLEBURN
Speyside, 1897–1985. Diageo. Closed.
Gordon & MacPhail Private Collection Coleburn 1981 refill sherry hogshead, cask no. 476, dist 11 Mar 81, bott 14 Mar 19 **(94) n25 t22.5; f23 b23.5** It is a strange and interesting fact that the reason this distillery closed down was because blenders didn't much care for the whisky. Back in the 1970s and '80s it built up a deserved reputation for producing a dirty "sulphurous" whisky which many blamed on the worm coolers used in the distilling process. It is curious that the degree of sulphur detected by blenders that made it a distillery non grata was a mere infinitesimal fraction of the degree of sulphur which totally screwed up so many scores if not hundreds of thousands of sherry butts. Yet the Scotch Distillers Association, obedient handbag dogs covering the tracks of their employers and baring their teeth and yapping and snarling at anyone who doesn't feed them, passed it off as just another unique flavour for whisky. And the imagination of egotistical troublemakers such as myself. Such nauseating humbug. The fact is, when well matured the Coleburns of this world produced a beautiful malt whisky, such as this. While whisky, from whichever distillery, sitting in sherry casks treated with sulphur candles are ruined and a pox on the industry no matter however long they remain in the warehouse. And no matter what garbage blow-hards like the SWA PR (Pernicious Rot) department tell you. 55.9%. sc. 101 bottles.

CONVALMORE
Speyside, 1894–1985. William Grant & Sons. Closed.
Convalmore 32 Year Old refill American oak hogsheads db **(96.5) n24 t24 f24 b24.5** Being 32 years old and bottled in 2017, these must be casks from among the very last production of the distillery before it was closed for the final time in 1985. The new spirit then, from what I remember, was not the greatest: thin and with an occasional tendency to be on the rough

house side. Time, though, is a great healer. And forgiver. It has passed the last three decades turning from ugly duckling to the most elegant of swans. A sub-species, though, that is on the brink of extinction... *48.2%. 3,972 bottles. Diageo Special Releases 2017.*

Gordon & MacPhail Rare Old Convalmore 1975 (94) n23 t24 f23 b24 The rarest of the rare. And in tasting, the flavour map took me back 30 years, to when I used to buy bottles of this from Gordon and MacPhail as a 10-year-old...probably distilled around 1975. The unique personality and DNA is identical on the palate as it was then; except now, of course, there is far more oak to contend with. Like finding an old lover 30 years further on: a little greyer, not quite in the same lithe shape as three decades earlier...but instantly recognisable and still very beautiful... *46%*

CRAGGANMORE
Speyside, 1870. Diageo. Working.

◈ **Cragganmore 12 Years Old** bott code: L9304CM005 db **(84) n21.5 t21.5 f20.5 b20.5** As Cragganmore darkened over the years its malty guile receded, finally to a speck before vanishing altogether. How I long for the days when this malt was first launched and it abounded with the sophisticated complexity that blenders drooled over; a malt that could link the other malts together with its charm and understated complexity. And, as a singleton, would keep you spellbound as you watched the fragile union between oak and grain plot its delicious, unusually dry course. I suspect that the all-powerful owners of this distillery have surrounded themselves with "experts" who will tell them how great this Classic Malt is. Grovel, grovel. I think they need to listen, instead, to a genuine friend who will tell them what, after a brief juicy delivery, a toffee-laden Classic Bore it has now become. *40%.*

Cragganmore 15 Years Old 150th Anniversary American oak, bott code: L9116DQ004 db **(94) n23.5 t23.5 f23 b24** Cragganmore is, like most distilleries, at its very best in good American oak. Here the natural caramels have joined the tannins to create about as thick and singular a malty intrigue as you are likely to find. A big whisky, but one that is very easy to scale... *48.8%. 1,869 bottles.*

CRAIGELLACHIE
Speyside, 1891. Bacardi. Working.

Craigellachie 13 Year Old db **(78.5) n20 t22 f18 b18.5.** Oily and intense, it shovels on the malt for all it is worth. That said, the sulphur notes are its undoing. *46%*

Craigellachie 17 Year Old db **(88.5) n22 t22.5 f22 b22** Technically falls flat on its face. Yet the whole is way better than the sum of its parts...*46%*

Craigellachie Aged 17 Years bott code: L19011ZA500 db **(94) n23 t23.5 f23.5 b24** This bottling is a great improvement on previous versions I have encountered. What an interesting and delicious dram, shewing the distillery at its best! *46%.*

Craigellachie 23 Year Old db **(91.5) n23.5 t23 f22 b23.5** Expected a little house smoke on this (the malt made here in the early 1990s always had delicate phenol), but didn't show. The honey is nothing like so shy. *46% WB16/035*

Craigellachie Exceptional Cask Series 1994 bott May 18 db **(91.5) n22.5 t23 f23 b23** How fascinating. Yes, a sherry butt and yes: there is sulphur. But this time it is not from the sherry, as the nose reveals a particular character from the condenser which does accentuate a mild sulphur character. Yet the clean wine casks tell a different, at once puckering yet juicy, story. Beautifully structured and a jaw-aching chewing malt with an unusual late salivation point. *54.8%. Bottled for Whisky L! & Fine Spirits Show.*

The First Editions Craigellachie Aged 11 Years 2008 wine cask, cask no. 16647, bott 2019 **(91) n22.5 t23 f22.5 b23** A surprising degree of smokiness to this works quite well here, not least in taming any excesses of the wine cask. Complex and exceptionally pleasing. Probably the most surprising malt I have encountered so far this year. *59.3%. nc ncf sc. 193 bottles.*

Gordon & MacPhail Connoisseurs Choice Craigellachie Aged 13 Years refill bourbon barrels, cask nos. 16600302, 16600303, 16600305 & 16600307, dist 29 Aug 05, bott 26 Jun 19 **(92.5) n23 t23 f23 b23.5** I know quite a few who are no great fans of Craigellachie. But I have always argued that in the right bourbon cask it offers a very characterful Speyside malt of unusual depth to its high quality. Thank you G&M for so eloquently proving my point. *46%. 1,314 bottles.*

Hepburn's Choice Craigellachie 11 Years Old wine cask, dist 2008, bott 2019 **(85.5) n21 t22 f21 b21.5** Tight and brusque, the out of sync tanginess gives you plenty to whine about. There is one fleeting moment just after delivery where the sweetness of both the barley and grape combine charmingly, but it is over far too quickly. *46%. nc ncf sc. 113 bottles.*

◈ **Hepburn's Choice Craigellachie Aged 11 Years** wine hogshead, dist 2008, bott 2020 **(74) n18 t19 f18 b19** The nose warns, the delivery seconds and the finish confirms: this is one for those who prefer the more sulphury bottlings. Drier than a parched rattlesnake. And with a similar bite. *46%. nc ncf. 797 bottles.*

⸭ **Old Malt Cask Craigellachie Aged 14 Years** sherry butt, cask no. HL18202, dist Aug 200, bott Dec 2020 **(88.5) n22 t23 f21.5 b22** Found myself fascinated by this one: on arrival this initially suggests boiled fruit candy. Then, within a few flavour waves, the sugars have dissipated and we are in dry whisky territory. The nose tingles, but those spices take a little time to arrive and stir the finale up when they do. Pleasant, malty and salivating in the exact spots you'd like them to be. *50%. nc ncf sc. 328 botles.*

Scyfion Choice Craigellachie 2007 Saint Daniel wine cask finished, bott 2019 **(81.5) n19 t22 f20 b20.5** The wine and malt are at odds for this thin gruel of an off-key dram. I'm afraid the saints can't be praised on this occasion. *46%. nc ncf sc. 212 bottles.*

⸭ **The Single Cask Craigellachie 2012** oloroso octave finish, cask no. 800622A **(94) n23** the grape has a jelly reserve quality: sweet and acidic. Love the underlying malt and the very first hints at something oaky...and spicy; **t24** mouth-filling and fat on entry, again it is a grape which rises first, delicious blend of sultan and toasted rain. The midpoint makes a big fuss of the malt which has a gristy sweetness, while delicate tannins throb. The mouthfeel of light, jellied oils is genius...; **f23** an outline hint of praline while the spices have altered from a rhythmic throb to a busy, bitty prattling; **b24** faultlessly clean sherry makes the most of a lively young malt and some outstanding oak. Works a treat as this is one very complex malt. Brilliant! *56.8% sc*

Whisky Illuminati Craigellachie 2011 Spanish oak sherry hogshead, cask no. 900328 **(85) n21.5 t22.5 f20 b21** Interesting to compare this with their Glentauchers sherry offering. That sparkles from first moment to last, while this is a stodgier affair, first with a nose shorn of balance and then on the palate, the malt making no impact on the grape whatsoever. Unlike with the 'Tauchers. Good spices and pleasant chewiness plus sugary notes to enjoy. But never even hints at greatness. *67.9%. sc. 100 bottles.*

DAILUAINE
Speyside, 1854. Diageo. Working.

The First Editions Dailuaine Aged 12 Years 2007 sherry butt, cask no. 16641, bott 2019 **(84) n21 t22 f20 b21** Juicy on delivery, but very limited from then on. Too dry and austere, especially in the gagged finish. *57.6%. nc ncf sc. 294 bottles.*

Old Malt Cask Dailuaine Aged 12 Years sherry butt, cask no. 16640, dist May 07, bott Jun 19 **(88) n21.5 t22.5 f22 b22** Makes a laudable attempt to get the into every square inch of your palate. Ignore the slightly restrained nose and celebrate a very above average Dailuaine where malt is not just in the centre ground, but works its way into every other aspect of the experience. A surprise package – for all the right reasons! *50%. nc ncf sc. 271 bottles.*

The Single Cask Dailuaine 1997 ex-bourbon barrel, sherry cask finish, cask no. 15563 **(85.5) n22 t21 f21.5 b21** A sclerotic malt, set in a grapey straight jacket in which it seems unable to move. That said, it's a clean finish, the spices busy and entertaining. But all a little too stiff. Though, as Dailuaines go, I have tasted a lot worse... *52.9%. nc ncf sc.*

⸭ **The Single Cask Dailuaine 2008** 1st fill bourbon barrel, cask no. 301698, dist 13 Feb 08 **(91.5) n22.5** love that little aroma of freshly shaved oak floorboard nestling spicily into the clean barley; **t23** this is luscious! Just so un-Dailuaine! A lightly oiled body displays the sparkling barley to the max while the spices and tannins mingle with confidence. The acacia honey fits in like a dream; **f23** long, wonderful spice pulses and still that unblemished malt rejoicing in its elevation; **b23** this is one of those distilleries where the quality of the cask will make a huge difference in the outcome of the whisky. The structure of this malt is so delicate that it comes under undue influence from any weaknesses. Here, I'm happy to report there are none. Dailuaine at its absolute finest. *57.3%. sc.*

DALLAS DHU
Speyside, 1899–1983. Closed. Now a museum.

Gordon & MacPhail Private Collection Dallas Dhu 1969 refill sherry hogshead, cask no. 1656, dist 10 Jun 69, bott 12 Jun 19 **(96) n24.5 t24 f23.5 b24** even in the early 1980s when I began in earnest my journeys around Scotland seeking out their rarest drams, Dallas Dhu was among the very hardest to secure. You might find the odd one here and there: indeed, if you did locate one you bought it, no questions, as you knew it might be a year or two before another surfaced. By the time I began writing about whisky full time, the distillery had been closed nine years and even then its rare bottlings were commanding high prices, making it harder to sample. So it is for that reason I have chosen this as the 1,250th whisky tasted for the Jim Murray Whisky Bible 2021. It brought a thrill to find a bottle 40 years ago. That feeling has not remotely diminished in the passing four decades. And the hour spent to understand this magnificently complex malt were as enjoyable as any of the last four months I have spent tasting... Please nose and taste with the reverence it deserves... If you open and taste immediately, it scores in the mid 80s. An hour or so employing the Murray Method...and you'll have one of the whisky experiences of your life.... *43.1%. sc. 176 bottles.*

DALMORE
Highands (Northern), 1839. Whyte and Mackay. Working.

The Dalmore Aged 12 Years American white oak and Oloroso sherry casks, bott code: L0029 09 29 P/011096 db (**87**) **n21.5 t23 f20.5 b22** A malt which has changed tack since I last tasted it. Then, as it had been for years, the malt was lost under a blanket of caramel. Now the barley is muzzled by fruit. Attractively at first as the sugars and grape elegantly and decisively make their mark. Sadly, a furry veil, thin but unmistakable, descends to given it a coarse and bitter finish. Glad to see far less toffee in the mix. But if sherry casks must be deployed, then a malt as potentially good as Dalmore deserves clean and faultless ones. *40%.*

The Dalmore Aged 15 Years American white oak and finished in Oloroso sherry casks, bott code: L0034 08 35 P/011099 db (**90.5**) **n22 t23 t22.5 f22 b23** It speaks! Normally a whisky that has very little to say for itself. Like the Dalmore 12, looks like a malt in transformation here, though in this case with far more success. Where once, for all its years, it, like the 12, refused to offer little more than toffee, now the mouthfeel has altered and allowed the whisky itself to say a few lines. Just an odd mildly naughty sherry butt, but I suspect these will be frogmarched out for future bottlings... *40%.*

The Dalmore Aged 18 Years American white oak and Matusalem Oloroso sherry casks, bott code: L0030 04:17 P/011104 db (**88.5**) **n23 t23 f21 b21.5** There is a timelessness to the nose that takes some of us back to our first whisky experiences of the 1970s; and one presumes that it must have been enjoyed long before then, too. The fusion of malt, light kumquat and moist Dundee cake is truly classic. The mouthfeel, with its kissing oils and glistening sugars are also of noble antiquity. But from the mid-point onwards comes a wailing bitterness from the wine casks which would be better if not there. If only those sugars could be extended and the fruits happier, what a malt this would be! *43%.*

The Dalmore 21 Year Old db (**88.5**) **n22 t23 f21.5 b22** fat, unsubtle, but enjoyable. *42%*

The Dalmore 25 db (**88**) **n23.5 t22.5 f20 b22** The kind of neat and tidy, if imperfect, whisky which, were it in human form, would sport a carefully trimmed and possibly darkened little moustache, a pin-striped suit, matching tie and square and shiny black shoes. *42%.*

The Dalmore 30 Year Old db (**94**) **n24 t24 f22.5 b23.5** A malt, quite literally for the discerning whisky lover. Essays in complexity are rarely so well written in the glass as found here... *45%*

The Dalmore Aurora Aged 45 Years db (**90.5**) **n25 t22 f21.5 b22.** Sophisticated for sure. But so huge is the oak on the palate, it cannot hope to match the freakish brilliance of the nose. *45%*

The Dalmore Candela Aged 50 Years db (**96**) **n25 t24 f23.5 b23.5.** Just one of those whiskies which you come across only a handful of times in your life. All because a malt makes it to 50 does not mean it will automatically be great. This, however, is a masterpiece, the end of which seemingly has never been written. *50% (bottled at 45%).*

The Dalmore 1263 King Alexander III db (**86**) **n22 t22.5 f20 b21.5.** Starts brightly with all kinds of barley sugar, fruit and decent age and oak combinations, plus some excellent spice prickle. So far, so good...and obviously thoughtfully and complexly structured. But then vanishes without trace on finish. *40%*

The Dalmore Ceti db (**91.5**) **n24 t23.5 f21.5 b22.5** A Ceti which warbles rather well... *44.7%*

The Dalmore Cigar Malt Reserve Limited Edition db (**73.5**) **n19 t19.5 f17 b18.** One assumes this off key sugarfest is for the cigar that explodes in your face... *44%*

The Dalmore Dominium db (**89.5**) **n22.5 t23 f22 b22** Like so many Dalmores, starts brightly but as the caramels gather it just drifts into a soupy lump. Still, no taint to the fruit and though the finish is dull you can say it is never less than very attractive. *43%. Fortuna Meritas Collection*

The Dalmore Luceo db (**87**) **n22 t22 f21.5 b21.5.** Pleasantly malty, exceptionally easy going and perfect for those of you with a toffeed tooth. *40%. Fortuna Meritas Collection*

The Dalmore Port Wood Reserve American white oak and Tawny port pipes, bott code: L0036 00 25 P/0111 db (**92**) **n22.5 t23.5 f22.5 b23.5** One of the most dry Port Wood bottlings I have ever encountered. If James Bond insisted on a whisky for his Martini, then it would probably be this. *46.5%.*

The Dalmore Regalis db (**86.5**) **n22.5 t21.5 f21 b21.5.** For a brief moment, grassy and busy. Then dulls, other than the spice. The caramel held in the bottling hall is such a great leveller. *40%. Fortuna Meritas Collection*

The Dalmore Valour db (**85.5**) **n21 t22 f21 b21.5.** Not often you get the words "Valour" and "fudge" in the same sentence. *40%. Fortuna Meritas Collection*

The Dalmore Visitor Centre Exclusive db (**95.5**) **n25 t24 f22.5 b24** Not exactly the easiest distillery to find but a bottle of this is worth the journey alone. I have tasted some sumptuous Dalmores over the last 30-odd years. But this one stands among the very finest. *46%*

The Dalmore Quintessence db **(91)** n22 t23.5 f22 b23.5 A late night dram after a hard day. Slump into your favourite chair, dim the lights, pour yourself a glass of this, warm in the hand and then study, quietly, for the next half hour. 45%.

Deer, Bear & Moose Dalmore Aged 14 Years sherry butt, dist Oct 04, bott May 19 **(84.5)** n19 t23 f20.5 b22 While the nose may be tight and unresponsive, the delivery is an orgy of golden syrup and spiced fruit. Pity the sulphur also reveals itself slightly on the finish, too... 57.4%. nc ncf. Flaviar & Friends.

Fadandel.dk Dalmore 11 Year Old 9 months finish in a 1st fill Oloroso octave, cask no. 800153A **(94)** n23.5 t23.5 f23 b24 Classically nutty and adroit. Such a lovely cask at work, the sophisticated style of which is so rarely found today: for those who like their Martinis very dry... 55.2%. sc. 68 bottles.

◈ **Gleann Mór Rare Find Dalmore Aged 11 Years** dist 2007 **(81)** n21 t22 f18 b20 The highly unusual greeny/black tinge to this whisky sets off a few alarm bells: usually a little iron in the system — so look out for an odd finish. The nose is certainly angular, by no means representative of Dalmore at this age and this is matched by the tart and explosive delivery which enjoys a huge wave of muscovado sugars. But as soon as the malt fades the tangy finish grips and offers the most oddly bitter fades outs. 50.4%

DALWHINNIE
Highlands (Central), 1898. Diageo. Working.

Dalwhinnie 15 Years Old db **(95)** n24 t24 f23 b24 A malt it is hard to decide whether to drink or bath in: I suggest you do both. One of the most complete mainland malts of them all. Know anyone who reckons they don't like whisky? Give them a glass of this — that's them cured. Oh, if only the average masterpiece could be this good. 43%

◈ **Dalwhinnie Winter's Gold** bott code: L1135CM db **(85.5)** n21 t23 f21 b20.5 When I opened this I was fully expecting to nose and taste a potential Whisky Bible Award Winner. The last bottling I tasted scored 95 and was a sublime representation of a complex and truly underappreciated distillery. The nose amazed me right enough...though not for the right reasons. I'm all for the use of young whiskies, as they often have a charm, energy and vibrancy which are free from the occasional corruption of oak. This however, doesn't get the nose right at all, with far too many New Makey notes giving this a positively embryonic feel. Not many winters had passed for some of these casks, one felt. We are at least handsomely compensated on the delivery by the euphoria of toffee and heather honey in full embrace with the thick barley. But by the finish we are left with the toffee alone, save for a few dates. all of which passes by so quickly. One if the biggest disappointments of the year. By a long chalk. 40%.

Game of Thrones Dalwhinnie Winter's Frost House Stark db **(87.5)** n22 t22 f21.5 b22 This is my fourth Game of Thrones whisky I have now sampled. And, having never seen the TV series, I am beginning to get the picture: the programme is about toffee, isn't it! Because, again, caramel is the dominating factor here, somehow flattening out the higher peaks from this mountainside distillery, which happens to be one of the world's best. The delightful burst of juicy barley just after the tame delivery is all too brief. 43%.

DEANSTON
Highlands (Perthshire), 1966. Burn Stewart Distillers. Working.

Deanston 10 Years Old Bordeaux Red Wine Cask Finish bott code: 1952859L511:2619164 db **(91)** n22 t22.5 f23 b23.5 A cask type that seems to suit Deanston's singular style. Very attractive. Impressed with this one big time. 46.3%. ncf. Travel Retail Exclusive.

Deanston 10 Year Old PX Finish db **(83.5)** n21 t22.5 f20 b20 Displays the uncompromising sweetness of a whisky liqueur. A must-have malt for those who like their sherry influence to be way over the top. The finish, like the nose, reveals minor a dry, furry element. 57.5%.

Deanston 12 Years Old bourbon casks, bott code: 17242991509:5018106 db **(84)** n21 t22 f20 b21 All the fun is on the impact, where the barley is about as intense as anything else produced in Scotland. However, the weakness on both nose and finish points accusingly at the Deanston character of off-key feintiness. 46.3%. ncf.

Deanston 18 Year Old batch 2 db **(89.5)** n23 t22.5 f22 b22 A soft treat for the palate... 46.3%. nc ncf.

Deanston 18 Years Old 1st fill bourbon casks, bott code: 1911691L511L:2618334 db **(89.5)** n22 t23.5 f21.5 b22.5 An intense, highly enjoyable dram where the malted barley gangs up and gives the other characteristics only bit parts. 46.3%. ncf.

Deanston 20 Year Old db **(61)** n15 t16 f15 b15 Riddled with sulphur. 55.4%. nc ncf.

Deanston 40 Year Old PX Finish db **(87.5)** n22 t23 f21 b21.5 The PX is doubtless in use here to try and give a sugary wrap around the over-aged malt. Some success, though limited. This type of cask has the unfortunate habit of restricting complexity in a whisky by embracing it too tightly with its wealth of syrupy top notes. The aromas and flavours which do escape often seem brittle and clipped, and this is the case here: the whisky has no chance to tell of its 40 years in the cask – the period that counts most now is the time it has spent in PX. Love the spices, though, and the overall mouthfeel. Whatever its limitations, this still does offer a lovely dram. *45.6%*.

Deanston Virgin Oak virgin oak casks, bott code: 1866939L512:4118241 db **(87.5) n22.5 t22.5 f21.5 b21** The overall lightness of Deanston's malt is emphasised by the lingering impact of the tannin towards the finish which knocks the early balance off kilter. An attractively complex nose, though, and the acacia honey on the barley concentrate delivery, followed by zonking spice, is to die for. *46.3%. ncf*

Acla Selection Summer Edition Deanston 18 Year Old sherry hogshead, dist 1999, bott 2018 **(88.5) n22.5 t23 f21 b22** A busy malt, which though stretched towards the finish, underlining the fragile nature of the spirit, early on delights in a glorious mix of spice, barley and complex tannins. The vital citrussy sugars also impress. Enjoyable fayre. *49.3%.*

⟳ **Malt Vault Deanston 24 Year Old** dist 1996 **(87.5) n22.5 t22.5 f22.5 b22** An usually perky Deanston which makes up for its lack of complexity with a distinctly impressive display on the malt front. The fact that the basic spirit lacked much depth is emphasised by the barrel being good enough to generate an attractive degree of bourbon character, on the nose especially. Harsh and hot in part, as one might expect, it is worth hanging on for the attractive, light chocolate conclusion. *51.4% 271 bottles*

Old Malt Cask Deanston Aged 23 Years refill hogshead, cask no. 15954, dist Jan 96, bott Oct 19 **(86.5) n21.5 t22 f21.5 b21.5** Despite the slight butyric on the nose, this offers plenty of juicy barley bite. A bit thin and warm but certainly not lacking in character. *50%. nc ncf sc.*

⟳ **Old Malt Cask Deanston Aged 25 Years** refill hogshead, cask no.HL18697, dist Jan 1996, Bott May 2021 **(82) n21.5 t21.5 f19 b20** Deanston malt was one, a quarter of a century ago, blenders were hardly lining up outside the distillery gates to grab hold of. This disappointing effort gives a few clues as to why: the maltiness never seems firm or confident while the structure seems profoundly unstable. Only about five or six flavour waves in do we see the sugars in action and in harmony with the malt, but it is criminally brief. The bitterness takes over far too early and easily. *50% sc*

⟳ **The Single Cask Deanston 1996** oloroso sherry finish, cask no. 271 **(86.5) n22 t22 f21 b21.5** A very safe malt where an attractive oloroso cask has ironed out the usual cracks in the Deanston armoury. It certainly allows the spices to forage around the taste buds unhindered and even, briefly, a little orange blossom honey to drift about the malt. *52.7% sc*

DUFFTOWN

Speyside, 1898. Diageo. Working.

The Singleton of Dufftown 12 Years Old db **(71) n18 t18 f17 b18.** A roughhouse malt that's finesse-free. For those who like their tastebuds Dufft up a bit... *40%*

⟳ **The Singleton Dufftown Aged 12 Years** European and American oak casks, bott code: L9039DM001 db **(79) n21.5 t21 f17.5 b19** Much improved from the last bottling I tasted. But still whisky ordinaire and my old comment about the taste buds being "Dufft up" still stands for the rough and ready finish. A little dried orange peel on the nose and a few moments of acceptable maltiness on the delivery really isn't good enough, though. *40%.*

The Singleton of Dufftown Aged 15 Years bott code: L7149DM000 db **(84.5) n21.5 t22 f20.5 b20.5** Nutty and rich on delivery. Toffee-weighted, thin and boring elsewhere. *40%.*

The Singleton of Dufftown Aged 18 Years bott code: L7094DM000 db **(86.5) n21 t22 f21.5 b22** To be honest, I was expecting a bit of a dud here, based on some 30-years-experience of this distillery. And though, for an 18-year-old, it can't be said really to hit the heights, it has – as so many less than brilliant distilleries over the years – mellowed enough with age to show a certain malty gentleness worthy of respect. *40%.*

The Singleton Dufftown Malt Master's Selection blend ref. 1106, refill, ex-sherry and bourbon casks, bott code: L9149DM003 db **(83) n20.5 t21 f20.5 b21** The sherry and bourbon casks wipe each other out leaving a soft, occasionally malty sweetness. Absolutely nothing wrong with it, and better than some Dufftowns of times past. But I'm looking for more than flatline malt...and I don't find it. *40%.*

The Singleton of Dufftown Spey Cascade db **(80) n19 t20 f21 b20.** A dull whisky, stodgy and a little dirty on the nose. Improves the longer it stays on the palate thanks mainly to sympathetic sugars and an ingratiating oiliness. But if you are looking for quality, prepare to be disappointed. *40%*

The Singleton of Dufftown "Sunray" db **(77) n20 t20 f18 b19.** One can assume only that the sun has gone in behind a big toffeed cloud. Apparently, according to the label, this is "intense". About as intense as a ham sandwich. Only not as enjoyable. *40%. WB15/121*

The Singleton of Dufftown "Tailfire" db (79) n20 t20 f19 b20. Tailspin, more like. 40%.

◇ **Kingsbury Gold Dufftown 12 Year Old** dist 2008, cask no. 700208 (84.5) n22 t22.5 f20 b20 Even Kingsbury, who seem to conjure up well above average casks, can't get much of a tune out of this distillery. Expectations for this distillery are low at the best of times. Here we can enjoy some rollicking spices on delivery which momentarily have the key to the more attractive and juicy barley notes. But it is too short and let down by the typically off-key, personality-free finale. 56.1% sc 136 bottles

EDRADOUR
Highlands (Perthshire), 1837. Signatory Vintage. Working.

Edradour 13 Year Old 1st fill oloroso sherry butt, dist 4 Dec 95, bott 4 May 18 db (95) n24 t23.5 f23.5 b24 When this whisky was distilled it was made at, then, Scotland's smallest distillery. Well, that may be so, but there is no denying that this is one absolutely huge whisky. And not only that, one where no degree of understated enormity is out step with any other: it is a giant, but a beautifully proportioned one. The spicy, sherry trifle on steroids nose will entrap you. The staggering complexity of the sturdy tannin and muscular fruit will keep you there, spellbound. The chocolate on the finish is almost an arrogant flourish. This really is Edradour from the old school, where its old manager Puss Mitchell had laid down the law on the type of sherry butt the hefty malt had to be filled into. Were he with us now, he'd be purring... 54.2%. 661 bottles. Bottled for Whisky L! & Fine Spirits Show.

FETTERCAIRN
Highland (Eastern), 1824. Whyte and Mackay. Working.

Fettercairn Aged 12 Years bott code: L0044 15 45 P/011012 db (88.5) n22 t22.5 f21.5 b22.5 Well, I have to laugh. The battles with blender and dear friend Richard Richardson I have enjoyed over the last quarter of a century about the quality, or otherwise, of this malt have been ferocious though (usually) good natured. Here I have to doff my hat and give a nod to acknowledge credit where it is due. This exhibits all the distillery's normal languid nuttiness. But instead of then heading off on a tangent and into areas usually best left unexplored, as is normally the case, this actually embraces some very attractive heather honey notes which sits comfortably with both the juicier barley tones and light caramels. It all works rather well. Yes, I really rather enjoyed this one! 40%.

Fettercairn Aged 16 Years 1st Release 2020 bott code: L0124 08:22 P/0121/6 db (91) n21.5t23 f23.5 b23 It's Fettercairn, Jim. But not as we know it. Those chocolate malt notes enter this into an entirely new dimension. The best bottling from this distillery I can remember. Love it! 46.4%.

Liquid Treasures 10th Anniversary Fettercairn 10 Year Old rum barrel, dist 2008, bott 2019 (80.5) n21 t22.5 f17 b19 Malty but hot and aggressive in time-honoured tradition. As is the exceptionally thin and course finale...though that is a disappointment because there is a promising, though brief buttery but malt-rich oiliness early on. A very grim finish, indeed. 57.4%. sc. 136 bottles.

◇ **MacAlabur Fettercairn 12 Year Old** bourbon barrel, cask no.4611, dist Oct 2008, bott Dec 2020 (88) n22 t23 f21 b22 After so many unpleasant and underwhelming encounters with Fettercairn over the last 30 to 40 years, it is almost bringing a tear to my eye to find a 12-year-old I have quite enjoyed. Indeed, blind-tasted I'm not sure I would have recognised this as the beast of Fasque at all: in fact, I'm sure I wouldn't. Certainly the degree of dull nuttiness has been trimmed on both nose and palate, and the clarity of the barley has been notably improved, especially on the delivery which now even has the confidence to indulge in a little muscovado sugar development. The finish bitters and disappoints after such a welcoming start. But, overall, a very decent malt. 57.8% 210 bottles

Old Malt Cask Fettercairn Aged 11 Years refill butt, cask no. 16646, dist Mar 08, bott May 19 (78) n19 t22 f18 b19 The nose is less than enticing, while the intense barley does have its salivating moments. But, as is the wont of Fettercairn, it never seems to gel and the finish is especially bitter and brutal. 50%. nc ncf sc. 606 bottles.

Old Malt Cask Fettercairn Aged 14 Years refill hogshead, cask no. 15537, dist Jun 04, bott Nov 18 (84) n21 t22 f20 b21 No faulting the momentarily juicy malt. But one dimensional beyond belief. 50%. nc ncf sc. 314 bottles.

◇ **The Whisky Chamber Fettercairn 12 Jahre 2008** Amarone finish barrique (85.5) n21.5 t22.5 f20.5 b21 A case of where the finishing barrel style and malt never hit quite the right rhythm to be entirely mutually beneficial. The nose is harsh, despite the best attention of the grape while the initially attractive explosion on the palate – which is a success while there is enough honey to unite both intense barley and fruit – is not built upon in a satisfactory way. The delivery, though, is worth a squint. 55.4%. sc.

GLEN ALBYN
Highlands (Northern) 1846–1983. Diageo. Demolished.

Gordon & MacPhail Rare Vintage Glen Albyn 1976 (96) n22.5 t24.5 f24.5 b24.5 Wow! My eyes nearly popped out of my head when I spotted this in my sample room. Glen Albyns come round as rarely as a Scotsman winning Wimbledon. Well, almost. When I used to buy this (from Gordon and MacPhail in their early Connoisseur's Choice range, as it happens) when the distillery was still alive (just) I always found it an interesting if occasionally aggressive dram. This masterpiece, though, is something else entirely. And the delivery really does take us to places where only the truly great whiskies go... *43%*

GLENALLACHIE
Speyside, 1968. The GlenAllachie Distillers Co Limited. Working.

The GlenAllachie 10 Years Old Cask Strength batch 2 db **(87.5) n21.5 t22.5 f21.5 b22** Never thought I'd say this of a Glenallachie: but I quite enjoyed this. Despite its strength, the distillery's old trademark flamethrower character didn't materialise. The malt remains intact throughout but it is the natural caramels and vanilla from the oak which seriously catches the eye. This has spent ten years in some seriously good oak. I'll even go as far as to say that the malt-dripping delivery is rather gorgeous. *54.8%. The GlenAllachie Distillers Company.*

The GlenAllachie 12 Years Old db **(86.5) n21.5 t22.5 f20.5 b22** Whoever is putting these whiskies for Glenallachie together has certainly learned how to harness the extraordinary malt intensity of this distillery to its ultimate effect. Still a touch thin, at key moments, though, and the bitterness of the finish is purely down to the casks not the distillation. *46%. The GlenAllachie Distillers Company.*

The GlenAllachie 18 Years Old db **(89) n23 t22.5 f20 b22.5** As friendly as it gets from this distillery. *46%. The GlenAllachie Distillers Company.*

The GlenAllachie 25 Years Old db **(91.5) n23 t23.5 f22 b23** Around about the time this whisky was made, distillery manager Puss Mitchell, who then also had Aberlour and Edradour under his auspices, took me from time to time in his office and poured out samples of new make and maturing Glenallachie. The result, usually was a searing sensation to my mouth and a few yelps and cries from me (much to the amusement of Puss): it was then the most unforgiving – and thin - of all Scotland's malts. Indeed, when I wrote Jim Murray's Complete Book of Whisky in 1997, only one distillery in Scotland was missed out: it was Glenallachie. I had written the piece for it. But it just accidentally fell by the wayside during editing and the whisky was so ordinary I simply didn't notice. "It's a filler, Jim," said Puss as I choked on the samples. "This is for blending. It's too hot and basic for a single malt. This is no Aberlour." How extraordinary then, that the distillery now under new and focused ownership, has brought out the whisky from that very time. It is still a little thin, and on arrival it still rips into you. But the passing quarter of a century has mellowed it significantly; astonishingly. So now the sugars from the grist act as balm; the gentle tannins as peacemaker. This is, against all the odds, now a very attractive whisky. Even Puss Mitchell would have been amazed. *48%. The GlenAllachie Distillers Company.*

Abbey Whisky Glenallachie Aged 10 Years 2008 sherry butt **(87) n22 t22.5 f20.5 b22** Really quite like this. The strength takes some believing and definitely works in the whisky's favour, magnificently ramping up the malt contribution. Elsewhere tart and a little aggressive (nothing to do with strength), the threadbare body confirmed on the finish. But there is enough grape and muscular malt to ensure the good moments are occasionally great. *66.2%. sc.*

◈ The Duchess Glenallachie 24 Years Old cask no. 23, dist 12 Dec 95, bott 13 Aug 20 **(84.5) n21 t21.5 f21 b21** When this was distilled, it was a malt blenders would use sparingly if they could because of its thin, harsh tones. A couple of dozen years in a good cask has becalmed it and managed to highlight both the barley and barley sugars. But the thin, glassy texture ensures that its past never completely hidden. *55.1%. Game & Wildlife Series.*

Fadandel.dk Glenallachie 11 Year Old refill sherry butt, cask no. 900784, dist 28 Aug 08, bott 3 Sept 19 **(88) n22 t22.5 f21.5 b22** For a Glenallachie of this age, I have to say it's pretty damn good! A familiar lack of character on the body means that the sherry is not seriously tested from first to last and has by far too easy a match of it. Happily, this is a sound, rich cask with no obvious faults and is pretty creamy, too. A little late spice adds some verve but this is dangerously easy dramming! *62.3%. sc. 555 bottles.*

The Finest Malts Glenallachie 5 Year Old sherry hogshead, cask no. 33, dist Oct 14, bott Jan 20 **(81) n20 t22 f19 b20** I'm all for shewing off the vigour of young malts – always have been. But to make this work it is not a good idea to use a sulphur-treated cask. Decent sultana and spice delivery. But then goes its own furry way. *55.1%. nc ncf sc.*

Old Malt Cask Glenallachie Aged 27 Years refill hogshead, cask no. 16483, dist Jun 92, bott Oct 19 **(84) n21.5 t21.5 f20 b21** Although this is a malt which greatly benefits from old age, there is still some of its puppy glue from its youth, the tenuity of its body making this a fleeting and meagre experience. At least the barley gets a good run out. *50%. nc ncf sc. 296 bottles.*

GLENBURGIE
Speyside, 1810. Chivas Brothers. Working.

Ballantine's The Glenburgie Aged 15 Years Series No. 001 American oak casks, bott code: LKRM1245 2018/04/03 **(86) n21.5 t22 f21 b21.5** Clunking caramels clog up the nose and finish big time. But there are some interesting tannin-laden spice notes in full swing as well. *40%.*

Gordon & MacPhail Connoisseurs Choice Glenburgie Aged 20 Years refill American hogshead, cask no. 4036, dist 22 Jul 98, bott 31 Jan 19 **(92.5) n23.5 t23.5 f22.5 b23** A single malt that will appeal to the bourbon-loving fraternity. Sweet and beautifully paced throughout. *55.3%. sc. 245 bottles.*

◈ **Hepburn's Choice Glenburgie 10 Years Old** rum barrels, dist 2009, bott 2020 **(94) n23.5** so distinctive, I recognised the rum intervention on first sniff and even before looking to see what whisky this was. On the nose, rum cask maturation can be hit and miss. With the molasses mixing so comfortably with the malt, this is a very much a hit...; **t23.5** oh, just brilliant! There is a sugary shield to this, but that soon cracks and melts, letting the barley to gush, juicily into the command position; **f23** how can you just not fall in love with those teasingly stinging spices to the finish...? **b24** the nose is very similar to some experimental casks I worked on years back, using those from Guyana. So many rum casks simply refuse to allow the malt to play. This is a genuine exception where everything falls into place. For a 10-year-old, it is just frothing with personality. A true classic of its type. *46%. nc ncf. 297 bottles.*

Hepburn's Choice Glenburgie 11 Years Old wine cask, dist 2008, bott 2019 **(83.5) n19 t22 f21 b21.5** Predominantly dry and mainly stifled. The busy spices do the malt a great service, though. *46%. nc ncf sc. 173 bottles.*

Old Malt Cask Glenburgie Aged 19 Years refill butt, cask no. 16779, dist Nov 99, bott Apr 19 **(87.5) n21 t22.5 f22 b22** A malt that rewards a little extra time. At first glance it is austere and limited in scope. But a little bit of the Murray Method releases some previously hidden lychee juice to ensure satisfying depth and extra balance. *50%. nc ncf sc. 193 bottles.*

GLENCADAM
Highlands (Eastern), 1825. Angus Dundee. Working.

Glencadam Aged 10 Years db **(95) n24 t24 f23 b24** Sophisticated, sensual, salivating and seemingly serene, this malt is all about juicy barley and balance. Just bristles with character and about as puckeringly elegant as single malt gets...and even thirst-quenching. My God: the guy who put this one together must be a genius, or something... *46%*

Glencadam Aged 10 Years Special Edition batch no. 1, bott code: L1702608 CB2 db **(90.5) n22.5 t23.5 f22 b22.5** A weightier, oakier version of the standard Glencadam 10. Fascinating to see this level of oak involvement, though it further underlines what a delicate creature its spirit is... *48.2%. nc ncf. Special edition for The Whisky Shop.*

Glencadam Aged 13 Years db **(94) n23.5 t24 f23 b23.5** Tasting this within 24 hours of Brechin City, the cheek by jowl neighbours of this distillery winning promotion after a penalty shoot out success in their play off final. This malt, every bit as engrossing and with more twists and turns than their seven-goal-thriller yesterday, is the perfect way to toast their success. *46%. nc ncf. 6,000 bottles.*

Glencadam Aged 15 Years db **(90.5) n22.5 t23 f22 b23** The spices keep the taste buds on full alert but the richness and depth of the barley defies the years. Another exhibition of Glencadam's understated elegance. Some more genius malt creation... *46%*

Glencadam Aged 17 Years Triple Cask Portwood Finish db **(93.5) n23 t24.5 f22 b24** A 17-year-old whisky truffle. A superb late night or after dinner dram, where even the shadowy sulphur cannot spoil its genius. *46%. nc ncf. 1128 bottles.*

Glencadam Aged 18 Years db **(96.5) n24.5 t24 f23.5 b24.5** So, here we go again: head down and plough on with the Whisky Bible 2018. This is the first whisky tasted in anger for the new edition and I select Glencadam for the strangest of reasons: it is the closest distillery to a football ground (North British, apart) I can think of, being a drop kick from Brechin City's pretty Glebe Park ground. And why is that relevant? Well today is a Saturday and I should really be at a game but decided to start off a weekend when there are fewest interruptions and I can get back into the swing of things before settling into the rhythm of a six day tasting week. Also, Glencadam, though criminally little known beyond readers of the Whisky Bible, is among the world's greatest distilleries producing one of the most charming whiskies of them all. So, hopefully, it will be a little reward for me. And offering the bourbon cask induced natural, light gold - which perfectly matches the buzzard which has just drifted on the winds into my garden

- this enticingly fills the gap between their 17- and 19- years old. Strikes me there is a fraction more first fill cask at play here than usual, ensuring not just a distinctively honeyed, bourbony edge but a drier element also. Distinguished and elegant this is a fabulous, almost unbelievable way to start the new Bible as it has the hallmarks of a malt likely to end up winning some kind of major award. Somehow I think the bar set here, one fashioned from gold, will be far too high for the vast majority that will follow over the next five months... 46%. nc ncf.

Glencadam Aged 19 Years Oloroso Sherry Cask Finish db (84) n21.5 t22 f19.5 b21. Mainly, though not quite, free of sulphur so the whisky after 19 years gets a good chance to speak relatively ungagged, though somewhat muffled. 46%. nc ncf. 6,000 bottles.

Glencadam Aged 25 Years db (95) n25 t24 f22 b24 Imagine the best-balanced team Mourinho ever produced for Chelsea. Well, it was never as good as this nose... 46%. nc ncf.

Glencadam Reserva Andalucia Oloroso Sherry Cask Finish sherry and bourbon casks, bott code: L20 06138 CB2 db (91) n22.5 t23 f22.5 b23 Glencadam is such a charming and fragile malt, it is to be seen at its best in bourbon cask. So I was intrigued to see how they would tackle a sherry cask finish on this. First the all clear: no sulphur. Secondly, they have done justice to the malt as they have not allowed the grape to grip too tightly. Not the same charisma as the bourbon bottlings. But hugely enjoyable still, at least because the young barley continues to hold the upper hand. 46%. nc ncf.

GLENCRAIG
Speyside, 1958. Chivas Brothers. Silent.
Cadenhead's Single Malt Glencraig 31 Years Old (92) n22.5 t23.5 f23 b23 Well done Cadenhead in coming up with one of the last surviving Glencraig casks on the planet. The feintiness shows why it was eventually done away with. But this is a malt with great distinction, too. 50.8%

GLENDRONACH
Highlands, 1826. Brown-Forman. Working.
GlenDronach 8 Year Old The Hielan db (82) n20 t22 f20 b20. Intense malt. But doesn't quite feel as happy with the oil on show as it might. 46%

The GlenDronach Aged 12 Years "Original" db (86.5) n21 t22 f22 b21.5. One of the more bizarre moments of the year: thought I'd got this one mixed up with a German malt whisky I had tasted earlier in the day. There is a light drying tobacco feel to this and the exact same corresponding delivery on the palate. That German version is distilled in a different type of still; this is made in probably the most classic stillhouse on mainland Scotland. Good, enjoyable whisky. But I see a long debate with distillery owner Billy Walker on the near horizon, though it was in Allied's hands when this was produced. 43%

The GlenDronach Aged 18 Years "Allardice" db (83.5) n19 t22 f21 b21.5. Huge fruit. But a long-running bitter edge to the toffee and raisin sits awkwardly on the palate. 46%

The GlenDronach Aged 18 Years Tawny Port Wood Finish db (94.5) n23.5 t24 f23 b24 A malt with not just an excellent flavour profile but sits on the palate as comfortably as you might snuggle into an old Jag. 46%.

The GlenDronach Aged 21 Years Parliament db (76) n23 t21.5 f15 b16.5 Red-hued, myopically one dimensional, rambles on and on, sulphur-tongued, bitter and does its best to leave a bad taste in the mouth while misrepresenting its magnificent land. Now, who does that remind me of...? 48%.

The GlenDronach 25 Years Old oloroso cask, cask no. GD#7434, dist 9 Jul 93 db (94.5) n23.5 t24 f23 b24 Had I any fireworks I would be setting them off outside now in celebration. I'm currently on my 1,058th whisky for the 2020 Bible and this is the first time I have tasted three sherry casks on the trot under 30-years-old that did not have a sulphur problem.... and all Glendronach's. At least I don't think this has, though there is a very late, tantalising niggle. But I can forgive that because this is your archetypal fruitcake single malt, complete with burnt raisins and glazed cherries. Toasty, tingly and just wonderful... 54.2%. sc. Bottled for The Whisky Shop.

The GlenDronach 25 Years Old Pedro Ximénez cask, cask no. GD#5957, dist 21 May 93 db (88.5) n22 t22 f22.5 b22 I thought this may have been bottled for the Flat Earth Society. Because the PX, as PX has a very annoying tendency of doing, has made this very flat, indeed. Pleasant, for sure. But the usual peaks and troughs have been obliterated by the unforgiving thick sherry, though the busy spices shews there is still plenty of signs of life. Also some attractive sticky dates at the very finish. Oh, 100% sulphur-free, too! 55.6%. sc. Bottled for The Whisky Shop.

The GlenDronach 26 Years Old oloroso cask, cask no. GD#77, dist 15 May 92 db (81) n19 t22.5 f19 b20.5 Strangely musty, dull and, late on, tangy. 50.3%. sc. The Whisky Shop.

The GlenDronach Traditionally Peated db **(89.5) n**21.5 **t**23 **f**23 **b**22 A curiously untidy whisky that somehow works. Maybe by the force of will of the intense peat alone. One of those curious drams where the whole is better than the individual parts. 48%.

GlenDronach Peated db **(93.5) n**23.5 **t**23.5 **f**23 **b**23.5 I rarely mark the smoky whisky from a distillery which makes peat as an afterthought higher than its standard distillate. But here it is hard not to give massive marks. Only a failing cask at the very death docks a point or so... 46%

Abbey Whisky Glendronach Aged 24 Years 1993 sherry butt, cask no. 652 **(95.5) n**24 classic old British Christmas cake drowning in rich fruit, molasses and brandy: simply sublime...; **t**24 oh, the layering! From the first moment there is a surprising hint of chocolate – though this soon falls prey to the re-emerging sultanas and plums; **f**23.5 long, increasingly toasty, with a burnt Dundee cake feel before that cocoa makes a gentle reappearance; **b**24 it would be only too easy to mistake this as a duplicate of the 27-year-old below. But it isn't: here the fruit and oak is far more measured and sophisticated. Exemplary... 60.6%. sc.

Abbey Whisky Glendronach Aged 27 Years 1992 PX puncheon, cask no. 5850 **(92.5) n**22.5 **t**23.5 **f**23 **b**23.5 I actually laughed out loud when I nosed this. It was like being back in my reporting days in Fleet Street again at El Vino's in the 1980s and tasting their Glendronach sherry matured malt: a massive, six-foot grapey overcoat drowning the apologetic frame of a five foot man. Once upon a time I used to dislike this whisky style because of its brash fruitiness without a trace a sympathy for the malt. Nearly 30 years on and I could almost dab at a damp eye of fondness. For this is a sherry cask without a blemish, to which sulphur is a stranger. So deep are the scars of the vile, unforgiving sulphur butts we have been forced to endure over the last three decades, today this is a whisky to be revered rather than, as it once was, mocked... 54.5%. sc.

◈ **Cadenhead's Cask Strength Glendronach Aged 30 Years** fresh sherry hogshead since 2013, dist 1990, bott 2020 **(96) n**24.5 complexity doesn't even begin to tell the story here. The cask is a faultless one, free of sulphurous damage. It means the grape has all the muscovado sugars and toasted raisins needed to make its mark in the most impressive way possible...; **t**24 this is olde worlde whisky: pre-sulphur-ruined Highland malt at its most compelling. The slightly burned Dundee cake and molasses combine with an assured sub strata of malt and lashing of vanilla. The mix of dry cotton wool oak and spiced fruit and barley is something to savour...and savour again; **f**23.5 wonderful spices and an almost latent smokiness to that spice allows the malt to mingle with the last strands of the fruit to gain maximum complexity; **b**24 a malt hanging on by a threat. Another summer and the amazing loquaciousness if the barley-grape mix would be compromised The oak has really started to call the shots. But this remarkable distillery has something in reserve if the cask is good enough. And this is. Not a single sulphur note: it represents this distillery at this landmark age at its very best. One of the truly great bottlings of the year. And for a distillery as complex and hard to understand as Glendronach, one if the great bottlings of the last decade... 45.4% Specially bottled for Cadenhead's Whisky Shop Vienna

GLENDULLAN
Speyside, 1972. Diageo. Working.

Singleton of Glendullan 12 Years Old db **(87) n**22 **t**22 **f**21 **b**22. Much more age than is comfortable for a 12-y-o. 40%

The Singleton of Glendullan 15 Years of Age bott code: L7228DM001 db **(89.5) n**22 **t**23 **f**22.5 **b**22 Mixed feelings. Designed for a very specific market, I suspect, and really impossible not to like. But would the real Glendullan with all its intrinsic Speyside characteristics please stand up. 40%.

The Singleton of Glendullan 18 Years of Age bott code: L6186DM000 db **(89) n**23 **t**22.5 **f**21.5 **b**22 A very pleasant if safe whisky where the real character of the malt is hard to unearth. 40%.

The Singleton Glendullan Classic bott code: L5288DM000 db **(91.5) n**23 **t**23 **f**22.5 **b**23 Such an attractive freshness to this, the whole being a cross between barley sugar and fruit candy. 40%. Exclusive to Travel Retail.

Singleton of Glendullan Liberty db **(73) n**17 **t**19 **f**18 **b**19. For showing such a really unforgiving off key bitter furriness, it should be clamped in irons... 40% WB16/036

Singleton of Glendullan Trinity db **(92.5) n**24 **t**23 **f**22.5 **b**23 Designed for airports, this complex little beauty deserves to fly off the shelves... 40% WB16/037

GLEN ELGIN
Speyside, 1900. Diageo. Working.

Glen Elgin Aged 12 Years db **(89) n**23 **t**24 **f**20 **b**22. Absolutely murders Cragganmore as Diageo's top dog bottled Speysider. The marks would be several points further north if one didn't get the feeling that some caramel was weaving a derogatory spell. Brilliant stuff nonetheless. States Pot Still on label – not to be confused with Irish Pot Still. This is 100% malt... and it shows! *43%*

⁂ **Glen Elgin Aged 12 Years** bott code: L007ICM002 db **(91)** n22.5 the oak pounds rather beautifully on the nose, bringing with it some dried orange peel: the bitter-sweet/sharp-dry interactions are superb. Some dulling toffee does it few favours; **t23** a gorgeous texture, helped along by a mix of dark sugars and fizzing spices. The mid-ground is intense malt, but again the toffee tones just take the edge off the more expansive and complex moments. Just beyond the midway point a little bitter chocolate arrives with the dried orange peel...; **f22.5** fabulous spices add a little varoom to late honeycomb; **b23** I had long argued that Glen Elgin was so far ahead of Cragganmore that it should be considered Diageo's Speyside Classic Malt. Having just tasted the two side-by-side in my lab, the Glen Elgin is so far ahead of its once excellent sister brand it is almost to lap it... *43%*.

⁂ **The Whisky Chamber Glen Elgin 10 Jahre 2010** port quarter cask **(93)** n23 black cherry is strangely thinned, then bolstered, by grapefruit. A little pile of malt sweetens the pepper...; **t23** whooomph! In piles the fruit like people bursting through the doors of a Department Store on the first day of sales. Crash! The taste buds shudder then shatter as the tartness of the grape bites deep. Oak is not far behind to patch up any damage done...; **f23.5** some semblance of sanity is restored as the malt finds its voice to help settle the layers of plums and slightly nutty fruitcake. Even a layer of marzipan to be had...; **b23.5** quarter casks have a propensity, when on form, to blast your poor old taste buds to kingdom come. Here is an example how, but this is such excellent Port influence it is bang on form... *58%. sc.*

GLENESK
Highlands (Eastern), 1897–1985. Diageo. Demolished.

Gordon & MacPhail Rare Old Glenesk 1980 (95) n23.5 t24 f23.5 b24 What a charmer: better dead than when alive, some might argue. But this has weathered the passing three and half decades with ease and really does have something of an ice cream feel to it from beginning to the end...well I suppose the distillery was located close to the seaside...One of the most understated but beautiful lost distillery bottlings of the year. *46%.*

GLENFARCLAS
Speyside, 1836. J&G Grant. Working.

Glenfarclas 10 Years Old db **(80)** n19 t20 f22 b19. Always an enjoyable malt, but for some reason this version never seems to fire on all cylinders. There is a vague honey sheen which works well with the barley, but struggles for balance and the nose is a bit sweaty. Still has distinctly impressive elements but an odd fish. *40%*

Glenfarclas 12 Years Old db **(94)** n23.5 t24 f23 b23.5 A superb re-working of an always trustworthy malt. This dramatic change in shape works a treat and suits the malt perfectly. What a sensational success!! *43%*

Glenfarclas 15 Years Old db **(85.5)** n21.5 t23 f20 b21. One thing is for certain: working with sherry butts these days is a bit like working with ACME dynamite... you are never sure when it is about to blow up in your face. There is only minimal sulphur here, but enough to take the edge off a normally magnificent whisky, at the death. Instead it is now merely, in part, quite lovely. The talent at Glenfarclas is unquestionably among the highest in the industry: I'll be surprised to see the same weaknesses with the next bottling. *46%*

Glenfarclas 17 Years Old db **(94.5)** n23.5 t24 f23 b24 When a malt is this delicate, it is surprising the difference that just 3% can make to the oils and keeping the structure together. A dram for those with a patient disposition. *43%*.

Glenfarclas 18 Years Old db **(84)** n21 t22 f20 b21. Tight, nutty and full of crisp muscovado sugar. *43%. Travel Retail Exclusive.*

Glenfarclas 21 Years Old db **(83)** n20 t23 f19 b21. A chorus of sweet, honied malt and mildly spiced, teasing fruit on the fabulous mouth arrival and middle compensates for the few blips. *43%*

Glenfarclas 25 Years Old db **(84)** n20 t22 f20 b22. A curious old bat: by no means free from imperfect sherry but compensating with some staggering age – seemingly way beyond the 25-year statement. Enjoys the deportment of a doddering old classics master from a family of good means and breeding. *43%*

Glenfarclas 30 Years Old db **(85)** n20 t22 f21 b22. Flawed yet juicy. *43%*

Glenfarclas 40 Years Old db **(95)** n24.5 t23.5 f23 b24 A few moments ago an RAF plane flew low over my usually quiet cottage, violently shaking the windows, silencing my parrot and turning a great spotted woodpecker feeding in my garden to stone: it was too shocked to know whether to stay or fly. And I thought, immediately: Glenfarclas 40! For when, a long time ago now, John Grant paid me the extraordinary compliment of opening his very first bottle of

Glenfarclas 40 so we could taste it together, a pair of RAF fighters chose that exact moment to roar feet above his distillery forcing the opened bottle from John's startled hands and onto the lush carpet...into which the initial measures galloopingly poured, rather than our waiting glasses. And it so happened I had a new sample to hand. So, with this whisky I made a fond toast: to John. And to the RAF. *43%.*

Glenfarclas 40 Years Old db **(94) n23 t23 f24 b24** Couldn't help but laugh: this sample was sent by the guys at Glenfarclas after they spotted that I had last year called their disappointing 40-year-old a "freak". I think we have both proved a point... *46%*

Glenfarclas 50 Years Old db **(92) n24 t23 f22 b23** Most whiskies cannot survive such great age. This one really does bloom in the glass and the earthy, peaty aspect makes it all the more memorable. It has taken 50 years to reach this state. Give a glass of this at least an hour's inspection, as I have. Your patience will be rewarded many times over. *44.4%*

Glenfarclas 50 Years Old III ex-Oloroso sherry casks db **(88.5) n23.5 t21 f22 b22** You can actually hear it wheezing as it has run out of puff. But it is easy to recognise the mark of an old champion... *41.1%. ncf. 937 bottles.*

Glenfarclas 105 db **(95.5) n23.5 t24 f24 b24** I doubt if any restorative on the planet works quite as well as this one does. Or if any sherry cask whisky is so clean and full of the joys of Jerez. A classic malt which has upped a gear or two and has become exactly what it is: a whisky of pure brilliance... *60%*

Glenfarclas £511.19s.0d Family Reserve db **(88) n22.5 t22.5 f21 b22** Not the best, but this still ain't no two bob whisky, mister, and make no mistake... *43%*

◈ **Cadenhead's Cask Strength Glenfarclas Aged 17 Years** fresh sherry hogshead since 2017, dist 2003, bott 2020 **(96) n24** now this sets a poser: are we talking Chelsea buns or Danish pastry? Whichever, the moist raisin will tempt you to death: this is fruity perfection...; **t24** mouthfeel and fruity intent can't be bettered: salivation levels are just about manageable as the black cherry and muscovado sugars strike in cahoots with the spice. Oh, that spice... Then we have the layering oak, almost too labyrinthine to begin to full appreciate. But when you get an amazing marriage of French toast with Melton Hunt Cake, I knew we are onto something a little special. Did I mention the spices....? My God...!! The spices...!!! **f23.5** sulphur...? No. Bitterness....? No. Tiredness...? No. Just more bloody near perfect marriage between ridiculously nubile grape and top rate malt, with God knows how many layers of near perfect tannin...? Yes... **b24.5** exquisite. Absolutely, disgustingly, ridiculously exquisite... *52.3% Specially bottled for Cadenhead's Whisky Shop Campbeltown* 🍷

GLENFIDDICH
Speyside, 1887. William Grant & Sons. Working.

Glenfiddich Our Original Twelve 12 Years Old Oloroso sherry & bourbon casks, bott code: L8D 8260 2611 db **(82) n22 t22.5 f18 b19.5** Although they call this their "Original Twelve", I can clearly remember when Glenfiddich dispensed with their flagship unaged bottling, the celebrated fresh and juicy one that after a lifetime in ex-bourbon casks had conquered so many uncharted seas, and replaced it with a 12-year-old. And the original didn't have this degree of sherry involvement by any stretch of the imagination. The nose is attractively infused with fruit and the barley glides over the palate on delivery. It is the scratchy, bitter-ish, furry and off-key finish, revealing more of the olosoro influence than we'd really like to know, that brings the side down. *40%.*

Glenfiddich Caoran Reserve Aged 12 Years db **(89) n22.5 t22 f21.5 b23.** Has fizzed up a little in the last year or so with some salivating charm from the barley and a touch of cocoa from the oak. A complex little number. *40%*

Glenfiddich Rich Oak Over 14 Years Old new American & new Spanish oak finish db **(90.5) n23 t22 f23.5 b22.** Delicious, thoughtful whisky and one to tick off on your journey of malt whisky discovery. Though a pity we don't see it at 46% and in full voluptuous nudity: you get the feeling that this would have been something really exceptional to conjure with. *40%.*

Glenfiddich 15 Years Old db **(94.5) n23 t23 f24.5 b24** If an award were to be given for the most consistently beautiful dram in Scotland, this would win more often than not. This under-rated distillery has won more friends with this masterpiece than probably any other brand. *40%*

Glenfiddich Aged 15 Years Cask Strength db **(85.5) n20 t23 f21 b21.5.** Improved upon the surprisingly bland bottlings of old, especially on the fabulously juicy delivery. Still off the pace due to an annoying toffee-ness towards the middle and at the death. *51%*

Glenfiddich Aged 15 Years Distillery Edition American & European oak casks, bott code: L32C 4704 0908 db **(95.5) n24 t24 f23.5 b24** A rumbustious malt which comes at you at full throttle. Big, muscular...but, deep down, a bit of a pussycat, too...Brilliant! *51%. ncf.*

Glenfiddich 15 Years Old Solera bourbon, new oak and sherry casks, Solera vat finish, bott code: L8D 6980 2106 db **(87) n22 t22.5 f20.5 b22** Have to say that this particular batch is pretty unrecognisable from the 15-year-old Solera I tasted (and helped in creating) in its first-ever form the best part of 30 years ago. The fault lines in the sherry can be detected, especially on the mildly furry finish. But this is thinner of body, too, which means the spices are a little too loud on the nose and struggling to find a counteracting partner on the palate. I do still love the oily drollness of the bitter-sweet delivery. But the middle empties rather than fills. The finish is out of sync and quarrelsome, leaving a disappointing finish to a whisky which once never disappointed. 40%.

Glenfiddich Aged 18 Years Small Batch Reserve Oloroso sherry & bourbon casks, batch no. 3231, bott code: L32D 4706 0606 db **(91.5) n23 t23 f22 b23.5** One of those malts which, cleverly, is as much about the experience of the mouthfeel and texture as it is the flavour itself. A vague weakness on the finish but, otherwise, a celebration of lustre... 40%.

Glenfiddich Age Of Discovery Aged 19 Years Bourbon Cask Reserve db **(92) n23.5t24 f22 b22.5.** For my money Glenfiddich turns from something quite workaday to a malt extraordinaire between the ages of 15 and 18. So, depending on the casks chosen, a year the other side of that golden age shouldn't make too much difference. The jury is still out on whether it was helped by being at 40%, which means the natural oils have been broken down somewhat, allowing the intensity and richness only an outside chance of fully forming. 40%

Glenfiddich Age Of Discovery Aged 19 Years Madeira Cask Finish db **(88.5) n22.5 t22.5 f21 b22.5.** Oddly enough, almost a breakfast malt: it is uncommonly soft and light yet carries a real jam and marmalade character. 40%

Glenfiddich 21 Years Old db **(86) n21 t23 f21 b21.** A much more uninhibited bottling with loads of fun as the mouth-watering barley comes rolling in. But still falls short on taking the hair-raisingly rich delivery forward and simply peters out. 40%

Glenfiddich 30 Years Old db **(93.5) n23 t23.5 f23.5 b23.5** a 'Fiddich which has changed its spots. Much more voluptuous than of old and happy to mine a grapey seam while digging at the sweeter bourbon elements for all it is worth. Just one less than magnificent butt away from near perfection and a certain Bible Award... 40%

Glenfiddich 30 Years Old European Oloroso sherry & American bourbon casks, cask selection no. 00049, bott code: L34D 4828120710 db **(96.5) n24 t24.5 f24 b24** The move from 40% abv to 43% has made a huge difference, as little as it sounds. Taking that further step up to 46% could be a game changer for the distillery itself. Glenfiddich, 30 years ago the champion of the younger Speysider, has always been at its very best, and at its natural limit at the 18 to 21-year-old mark. This bottling reveals that things have fundamentally changed. For the better... 43%.

Glenfiddich 50 Years Old db **(97) n25 t24 f24 b24** William Grant blender David Stewart, whom I rank above all other blenders on this planet, has known me long and well enough to realise that the surrounding hype, with this being the most expensive whisky ever bottled at £10,000 a go or a sobering £360 a pour, would bounce off me like a pebble from a boulder. "Honestly, David," he told my chief researcher with a timorous insistence, "please tell Jim I really think this isn't too oaky." He offered almost an apology for bringing into the world this 50-year-old babe. Well, as usual David Stewart, doyen of the blending lab and Ayr United season ticket holders, was absolutely spot on. And, as is his wont, he was rather understating his case. For the record, David, next time someone asks you how good this whisky is, just for once do away with the Ayeshire niceness instilled by generations of very nice members of the Stewart family and tell them: "Actually, it's bloody brilliant if I say so myself! And I don't give a rat's bollocks what Murray thinks." 46.1%

Glenfiddich Fire & Cane finished in sweet rum casks, bott code: L32D 4985 2608 db **(96) n24 t24 f23.5 b24.5** I think those of us in the industry who can now be described in the "veteran" category can only smile at the prospect of tasting a full blown peaty Glenfiddich: the distillery that once stood for the cleanest, least peat influenced malt in the whole of Scotland. But when you nose and taste this, you wonder why they didn't take this route from day one, for rarely do you find a distillery that creates a peaty malt so naturally to the phenolic manor born. This is not a gimmicky whisky. No, this is something to be respected and cherished for thing of beauty it actually is. 43%. Experimental Series #4.

Glenfiddich Grand Cru Aged 23 Years Cuvée cask finish, bott code: LA4D 9012 0210 db **(90) n22.5 t23 f23 b22.5** Cuvee, but not curvy. Even so, attractive and delightfully salivating in so many ways... 40%.

Glenfiddich IPA Experiment Experimental Series No 1 bott code: L34A4972141211 db **(86) n21.5 t22.5 f21 b21** IPA and XX...all very Greene King brewery of the early 1980s... An IPA is, by definition, extra hopped in order to preserve the beer on a long journey (to India, originally). I can't say I am picking out hop here, exactly, unless it is responsible for the off-key bitter finale. Something is interfering with the navigation and after an attractive early malty blast on delivery everything goes a little bland. 43%.

Glenfiddich Project XX Experimental Series No 2 bott code: L34B4041170207 db **(95.5)** n24 t24 f23.5 b24 "20 minds, one unexpected whisky" goes the blurb on the label. And, in fairness, they have a point. It has been a long time since I have encountered a distillery-produced malt this exceptionally well rounded and balanced. All 20 involved should take a bow: this is Glenfiddich as it should be...xxellent, in fact! 47%.

Glenfiddich Project XX bott code: L34D 4210 2102 db **(90)** n22 t24 f21 b23 A flawed malt thanks to some unsound wine casks. But, that said, the overall composition is viscous, chewy and at times wickedly delicious. Impure gold... And, if finding kinder casks, a potential major award winner. 47%. ncf. Experimental Series #2.

Glenfiddich Reserve Cask sherry casks, Solera vat no. 2, bott code: L2D 6784 2904 db **(88.5)** n21.5 t23 f21.5 b22.5 Glenfiddich, when on song, is one of my favourite distilleries: its malt can offer a clarity of flavour and effervescence that few distilleries in Scotland can match. Sherry influence has a tendency to negate that natural brilliance. However, the delivery reveals a delicious degree of that gorgeous house vitality, an effect which tapers as the grape and other influences slowly takes control. A rather delightful malt with stupendous malty sweetness on delivery and an attractive softness which is entirely in keeping with the pace of the flavour development. A lovely malt, indeed. 40%. Travel Retail Exclusive.

Glenfiddich Select Cask bourbon, European oak and red wine casks, Solera vat no. 1, bott code: L2D 6836 0505 db **(85.5)** n21 t21.5 f21.5 b21.5 With its heavy leaning on a safe, linear toffee-raisin simplicity, some people will call this smooth. Others, like me, will call it a bit of a dullard. 40%. Travel Retail Exclusive.

Glenfiddich Winter Storm Aged 21 Years Icewine Cask Finish Experiment bott code: LA3 C9009 2510 db **(95)** n24 t24 f23 b24 With Storm Dennis on the warpath outside causing widespread flooding and mayhem to much of Britain, never is a whisky needed more than now. And how can you find one more fitting...? What better than to find Glenfiddich at its more juicy, crisp and alluring. Absolutely love it! Almost makes you look forward to the next storm to batter Britain... 43%. Experimental Series #3.

GLEN GARIOCH
Highlands (Eastern), 1798. Morrison Bowmore. Working.

Glen Garioch 8 Years Old db **(85.5)** n21 t22 f21 b21.5. A soft, gummy, malt – not something one would often write about a dram of this or any age from Geary! However, this may have something to do with the copious toffee which swamps the light fruits which try to emerge. 40%

Glen Garioch 10 Years Old db **(80)** n19 t22 f19 b20. Chunky and charming, this is a malt that once would have ripped your tonsils out. Much more sedate and even a touch of honey to the rich body. Toffeed at the finish. 40%

Glen Garioch 12 Years Old db **(88.5)** n22 t23 f21.5 b22.A significant improvement on the complexity front. The return of the smoke after a while away was a surprise and treat. 43%

Glen Garioch 12 Years Old db **(88)** n22.5 t22.5 f21.5 b22. Sticks, broadly, to the winning course of the original 43% version, though here there is a fraction more toffee at the expense of the smoke. 48%. ncf.

Glen Garioch 15 Years Old db **(86.5)** n20.5 t22 f22 b22. In the bottling I sampled last year the peat definitely vanished. Now it's back again, though in tiny, if entertaining, amounts. 43%

Glen Garioch Aged 16 Years The Renaissance 2nd Chapter bott code: L162292 db **(81)** n21 t23 f18 b19 For a wonderful moment, actually two: once on the nose and then again on the delivery, you think you are heading towards some kind of Sauternes-type magnificence... then it all goes wrong. Yes, there are fleeting moments of borderline perfection. But those dull, bitter notes have by far the bigger and longer say. Perhaps the biggest disappointment of the year... 51.4%.

Glen Garioch 21 Years Old db **(91)** n21 t23 f24 b23 An entirely re-worked, now smokeless, malt that has little in common with its predecessors. Quite lovely, though. 43%

Glen Garioch 30 Years Old No. 503 dist 1987, bott 2017 db **(89)** n22.5 t23 f21.5 b22 This is from the exotic fruit school of ancient whiskies, the oak's tannin now out-manoeuvering the fruit. Perhaps moved on a little too far down a chalky, tannin-rich route though a little smoke does cushion the blow. Ancient, but still very attractive. 47.1%. Selected for CWS.

Glen Garioch 1797 Founders Reserve db **(87.5)** n21 t22 f22.5 b22. Impressively fruity and chewy: some serious flavour profiles in there. 48%

Glen Garioch 1958 db **(90)** n24 t21 f23 b22. The distillery in its old smoky clothes: and quite splendid it looks! 43%. 328 bottles.

Glen Garioch 1995 db **(86)** n21 t22 f21.5 b21.5. Typically noisy on the palate, even though the malty core is quite thin. Some big natural caramels, though. 55.3%. ncf.

Glen Garioch 1997 db (89) n22 t22.5 f22 b22.5 had you tasted this malt as a 15-year-old back in 1997, you would have tasted something far removed from this, with a peaty kite ripping into the palate. To say this malt has evolved is an understatement. *56.5%. Whisky Shop Exclusive.*

Glen Garioch 1997 db (89.5) n22 t23 f22 b22.5. I have to say: I have long been a bit of a voice in the wilderness among whisky professionals as regards this distillery. This not so subtly muscled malt does my case no harm whatsoever. *56.7%. ncf.*

Glen Garioch 2000 Bourbon Cask db (93.5) n23 t24 f23 b23.5 The distance this malt has travelled from the days when it was lightly peated firewater is almost beyond measure. A bourbony delight of a Highland malt. *57.3%. ncf.*

Liquid Treasures 10th Anniversary Glen Garioch 8 Year Old bourbon barrel, dist 2011, bott 2019 (87.5) n22 t22 f21.5 b22 Interesting how the old heat that used to be found on this malt back in the 1970s and '80s has returned, but the smoke which used to accompany it those days hasn't....which is a shame. Really makes a big speech on delivery and it is the malt writing the script, with the odd contribution by Demerara sugar, vanilla and natural caramels. But still pretty gruff stuff. *59.9%. sc. 132 bottles.*

GLENGLASSAUGH

Speyside, 1875. Brown-Forman. Working.

Glenglassaugh 30 Year Old db (87) n22.5 t23 f20 b21.5. A gentle perambulation around soft fruitcake. Moist and nutty it still has a major job on its hands overcoming the enormity of the oak. The buzzing spices underline the oak involvement. Meek, charming though a touch furry on the finish. *44.8%.*

Glenglassaugh 40 Years Old Pedro Ximénez cask, cask no. GG#3060, dist 8 Dec 78 db (88.5) n22.5 t22 f22 b22 Despite the best efforts of the molasses and life-giving PX cask, you can't help getting away from the feeling that here is one pretty exhausted malt. Both the nose and delivery in particular reveal oak tones more associated with a spent whisky. Yet it is still breathing and has energy enough to reveal a delicate complexity and grapey charm unbothered by sulphur. Then the late spices arrive like the 8th cavalry when all seems lost. It has hung on in there. Just! *46%. sc. Bottled for The Whisky Shop.*

Glenglassaugh Evolution db (85) n21 t22 f21 b21. Cumbersome, oily and sweet, this youngster is still evolving. *50%.*

Glenglassaugh Nauticus 1st Anniversary 8 Years Old cask no. 288 db (91) n22.5 t23 f22.5 b23 Nauticus. But nice. *56.1%. sc.*

Glenglassaugh Revival new, refill and Oloroso sherry casks db (75) n19 t20 f17 b19. Rule number one: if you are going to spend a lot of money to rebuild a distillery and make great whisky, then ensure you put the spirit into excellent oak. Which is why it is best avoiding present day sherry butts at all costs as the chances of running into sulphur is high. There is some stonkingly good malt included in this bottling, and the fabulous chocolate raisin is there to see. But I look forward to seeing a bottling from 100% ex-bourbon. *46%. nc ncf.*

Glenglassaugh Torfa db (90) n23.5 t22.5 f22 b22 Appears happy and well suited in its new smoky incarnation. *50%.*

Abbey Whisky Glenglassaugh Aged 7 Years 2012 Oloroso hogshead, cask no. 563 (86.5) n21.5 t21.5 f22 b21.5 Some enjoyable phases but this is a wild dog barking in the night. A beautiful creature, I'm sure, but with too many annoying traits and a distinctly mongrel feel with a vague smokiness and a vivid fruit. And with all that spice it bites, too.... *58.7%. sc.*

Woolf/Sung The Hunter Glenglassaugh 40 Year Old 1972 sherry cask (90) n22 t24 f21.5 b22.5 Presumably came out of cask in 2012 and only just been bottled. Probably on the way its strength was heading south. Well, the well-founded fears I had of this being a Glenglassaugh sherried have been alleviated: this has not been topped up in a recent sulphurous sub-standard sherry butt, as is too often the case, but this appears to have lived in only the one wood – filled long before sherry butts and the whisky within them were ruined. That said, this a bit of a thin knave, though patience while holding on the palate will reward handsomely as both the complexity of the grape and the myriad tannin tones interplay with a something approaching an art form. The finish is nowhere near so accomplished but, overall, this is a malt which makes impressive play of its great age. *42.9%. sc.*

GLENGOYNE

Highlands (Southwest), 1833. Ian Macleod Distillers. Working.

Glengoyne 10 Years Old db (90) n22 t23 f22 b23 Proof that to create balance you do not have to have peat at work. The secret is the intensity of barley intertwangling with oak. Not a single negative note from first to last and now a touch of oil and coffee has upped the intensity further. *40%*

Glengoyne 12 Years Old db **(91.5)** n22.5 t23 f23 b23 The nose has a curiously intimate feel but the tasting experience is a wonderful surprise. 43%

Glengoyne 12 Years Old Cask Strength db **(79)** n18 t22 f19 b20. Not quite the happiest Glengoyne I've ever come across with the better notes compromised. 57.2%. nc ncf.

Glengoyne 15 Years sherry casks db **(81)** n19 t20 f21 b21. Brain-numbingly dull and heavily toffeed in style. Just don't get what is trying to be created here. Some late spices remind me I'm awake, but still the perfect dram to have before bed – simply to send you to sleep. Or maybe I just need to see a Doctor... 43%. nc. Ian Macleod Distillers.

Glengoyne 17 Years Old db **(86)** n21 t23 f21 b21. Some of the guys at Glengoyne think I'm nuts. They couldn't get their head around the 79 I gave it last time. And they will be shaking my neck not my hand when they see the score here...Vastly improved but there is an off sherry tang which points to a naughty butt or two somewhere. Elsewhere mouth-watering and at times fabulously intense. 43%

Glengoyne 18 Years first-fill sherry casks db **(82)** n22 t22 f18 b20. Bunches of lush grape on nose and delivery, where there is no shortage of caramel. But things go downhill once the dreaded "s" word kicks in. 43%. nc. Ian Macleod Distillers.

Glengoyne 21 Years Old db **(90)** n21 t22 f24 b23 A vastly improved dram where the caramel has vanished and the tastebuds are constantly assailed and questioned. A malt which builds in pace and passion to delivery a final, wonderful coup-de-grace. Moments of being quite cerebral stuff. 43%

Glengoyne 25 Year Old db **(95.5)** n24 t24.5 f22.5 b23.5 A beautiful sherry-matured malt from the pre-cock up sulphur days. Not a single off note of note and a reminder of what a sherry cask malt meant to those of us who were involved in whisky a quarter of a century ago... 48%

GLEN GRANT
Speyside, 1840. Campari. Working.

Glen Grant 5 Years Old db **(89)** n22.5 t22 f21.5 b23. Elegant malt which has noticeably grown in stature and complexity of late. 40%

Glen Grant Aged 10 Years db **(96)** n23.5 t24 f23.5 b24 Unquestionably the best official 10-y-o distillery bottling I have tasted from this distillery. Absolutely nails it! Oh, and had they bottled this at 46% abv and without the trimmings...my word! Might well have been a contender for Scotch of the Year. It won't be long before word finally gets around about just how bloody good this distillery is. 40%

Glen Grant Aged 10 Years db **(96)** n24.5 t24 f23.5 b24 This is the new bottling purely for the UK market without, alas for a traditionalist like me, the famous, magnificent white label. The bottle design may not be a patch on the beautifully elegant one that had served the distillery with distinction for so long, but the malt effortlessly stands up to all scrutiny. The only difference between this and the original bottling available world-wide is a slight reduction in the work of the sugars, the muscovado ones in particular, and an upping in the green, grassy, sharper barley. Overall, this is a little drier yet slightly tarter, more reserved and stylish. My one and only regret is that it is not yet upped to 46% so the people of Britain could see a whisky, as I have so many times in the private and privileged enclave of my blending lab, as close to perfection as it comes... 40%.

Glen Grant Aged 10 Years bott code: LRO/GE01 db **(95.5)** n24.5 t24 f23 b24 Perhaps slightly fatter than one or two other bottlings of GG10. But still bang on course with my previous observations, other than the finish not having quite the same sparkle. One of those whiskies which seems delicate and fragile, but at the same time big and robust. Just how does it do that....? 40%.

Glen Grant Aged 10 Years bott code: LRO/GD26 db **(94)** n23.5 t23.5 f23.5 b23.5 A malt which wears its heart on its sleeve. So delicate, so fragile and easily fractured that it has to be treated with extraordinary care. Just how delicate and fragile this whisky is, just how under threat unique and beautiful malts like these are, is revealed on both nose and delivery... 40%.

◆ **Glen Grant Aged 10 Years** bott code: LRO/JC17 db **(96)** n24.5 one of the noses of the year: the layering of kumquats, grapefruit and melon suggests a Speysider double its years. But it is not as simple as that: with Glen Grant, it rarely is. This is exceptional because of the detail: it has the complexity of a mosaic, the fineness of a D'Angelo brush stroke and the fragility of the finest porcelain. Rarely do malt and oak harmonise so flawlessly after just ten years....; t24 so soft and salivating on entry. The greeting is one of lightly zesty citrus, grist and acacia honey: the result is profound salvation. You await the layering...and here it comes. The malt is rich. The vanillas are uncluttered and precise. Which all sounds simple, except for the countless layers and hints of fruits, honeys of varied hue and oak-laced spices; f23.5 maybe a hint of light toffee amid the butterscotch and spiced exotic fruit crumble. Even the thinnest layering of praline... b24 last year I had worried that some of the sparkle had been drained from this classic Speysider as a 10-year-old. The fact it took me half an hour just to get through the nose tells you all you need to know. I have just looked at the label for the first time and smiled where it says that you will find "orchard fruits". Maybe. But certainly not any orchard found in Scotland. At this ridiculously young age it has taken on exotic fruit status, usually the domain of the great Speysiders of significant vintage. A whisky for those in search of perfection... 40%. 🌱

Glen Grant Aged 12 Years db **(95)** n23.5 t24 f23.5 b24 Beautifully distilled, thoughtfully matured and deeply satisfying malt. 43%.

Glen Grant Aged 12 Years bott LRO/FE 03 db **(95)** n24 t24 f23 b24 A slightly different slant to previous 12-year-old, but still within the expected and brilliant spectrum. Fabulous. 43%.

Glen Grant Aged 12 Years bott code: LRO/FK06 db **(94)** n24 t23.5 f23 b23.5 Very similar to previous bottling, with no shortage of intensity. The only difference is a little less sweetness through the mid-range between delivery and finish and a slightly bigger caramel note, instead. 43%.

Glen Grant Aged 12 Years bott code: LRO/GE07 db **(92)** n23.5 t23.5 f22 b23 A small step sideways from previous bottlings, not least because of the intensity of the malt and its relaxed attitude with the oaky vanillas then gives way to an surfeit of uncharacteristically dull toffee. Get the distinct feeling that this malt is performing well within its capabilities... 43%.

Glen Grant Aged 12 Years Non Chill-Filtered db **(91.5)** n23 t23 f22.5 b23 In so many ways speaks volumes about what non-filtration can do to one of the world's truly great distilleries... 48%. Exclusive to travel retail.

Glen Grant Aged 12 Years bott code: LRO/GC19 db **(94.5)** n23.5 light lychee and the most delicate barley grist; t24 fizzes on delivery as the barley goes into salivation orbit. The vanillas and butterscotch arrive early, but so to the spices to ensure there is so much life! f23 the spices still rumble, but, as you would expect from GG, the delicate nature of the barley, the mild honey notes and the kissing vanilla just makes you sigh...; b24 that's much more like it: such balance, such dexterity...! The last time I sampled this, though delightful, it didn't quite yield the complexity I was expecting. This one is nearer expectation! 48%. ncf.

Glen Grant Aged 12 Years bott code: LRO/HI18 db **(94.5)** n23.5 t24 f23 b24 My rule is to never look at the previous year's scores and notes and judge the whisky at it comes. So, interesting it matches the last bottling I tasted even, I now see, down to the sectional scoring. Can't quibble with the tasting notes, either, which are pretty much identical. 48%. ncf.

Glen Grant Aged 15 Years Batch Strength 1st Edition bott code: LRO/FG 19 db **(96.5)** n23.5 t24.5 f24 b24.5 When I saw this was also 1st Edition, I thought it was the same whisky as I tasted last time. Except with a different bottling code. However, although the early personality is near identical, it really does change on the finish where the bitterness has now been eradicated. This not only improves the score to the finish, but the overall balance and performance. The entire journey is now faultless; and journeys don't often come better than this. 50%.

Glen Grant Aged 15 Years Batch Strength 1st Edition bott code. LRO/FG 21 db **(94)** n23.5 t24 f23 b23.5 One of the maltiest malts of the year! Just a joy! 50%.

Glen Grant Aged 15 Years Batch Strength 1st Edition bott code: LRO/HI16 db **(97)** n24.5 t24 f24 b24.5 What a malt this has now become! The fact that for two successive bottlings they have blown me off my tasting desk means they appear to have nailed the personality of this malt, and in so doing extracting and then displaying the extraordinary and unique charm of this distillery. 50%.

Glen Grant Aged 18 Years Rare Edition db **(97)** n24.5 t24.5 f23.5 b24.5 The most crystalline, technically sublime Speysider I have tasted in a very long time... I didn't expect to find a better distillery bottled Glen Grant than their superlative 10-year-old. I was wrong... 43%.

Glen Grant Aged 18 Years Rare Edition bott code. LRO/EE04 db **(97)** n24.5 t24.5 f23.5 b24.5 See tasting notes to the Glen Grant 18 above. A different bottling, but not a single alteration in character, other than maybe just a fraction extra spice at the very end. Another Glen Grant knocking on the door of perfection. 43%.

Glen Grant Aged 18 Years Rare Edition bott code: LRO/EE03 db **(97)** n24.5 t24.5 f23.5 b24.5 So, I have chosen this as my 1,200th whisky of the 2020 Bible...which means I have tasted the last 1,000 whiskies on average at 15 samples a day, day in day out – analysing, re-analysing and describing - from morning to late evening virtually every single day without a break. Here I look for faults and weaknesses; changes, shifts of emphasis, a variation of pace as the flavours come through. And can find none. Well, maybe the vaguest hint of bitterness at the death. But this, as usual, is sublime. Though perhaps it does have two new challengers now: the Glen Grant 15 and the Glen Grant Chronicles. Didn't think it possible. But this distillery has just upped its game... 43%.

Glen Grant Aged 18 Years Rare Edition bott code: LRO/GB15 db **(92)** n23 t23.5 f22.5 b23 A surprise bottling, this. Very unlike the Glen Grant 18s I tasted earlier in the year which were their usual bright, dazzling, mesmerising and heart-stopping selves. This is darker in colour, dimmer in flavour, full of malty riches but extra toffee, also, which appears to up the body but compromises the complexity, especially at the death. 43%.

⬧ **Glen Grant 18 Years-Old Rare Edition** db **(96.5) n25** as near as damn it perfection. I have been nosing this for just coming up to 30 minutes now, and still not entirely sure where to start. The nose is a like a chorus trained not just pitch perfect but in precision timing, the breathing patterns inaudible. Even by Glen Grant's extraordinary standards this is exceptional, with the sharpness of the barley a beautiful – and almost impertinent – constant considering we are talking a malt aged 18 years. However, so many other delicate forces are at work here, almost imperceptibly, that that sharpness cannot dominate – it becomes just a factor. Warm slightly and release just the most teasing atom or two of smoke, though against such a flighty background it acts as a balance; it is the base. It is joined by the oak which plays many roles, from a weightier, vaguely bourbon red liquorice depth (just a hint, mind), to more purring, gentle ulmo honey sweetness, a little vanilla dabbing the honey dry here and there. Amazingly there are spices, tiny ones like houses for a model village. Everything is small scale. Intrinsic. But when added together becomes understatedly huge...and a thing of exquisite beauty...; **t24** you can safely say that what goes for the nose applies to the delivery and follow through. This is salivating, as the sharpness on the nose foretells but soon this is met by a slightly unexpected creaminess, the deft oils coating the palate to pleasing effect, allowing the vanillas and butterscotch to tumble around the mouth and stick.. The surprise, however, and the aspect which takes a massive leap from the nose is the energy of the spice; **f23.5** a whisky of such fragility cannot go too long without burning out the more complex aspects, leaving behind the more durable elements. This includes a very slight bitterness gleaned from the oak, though the now fragmenting honey does its best to counter. The spices now gently simmer...; **b24** you know that moment when the last notes fade of Vaughan-Williams' A Lark Ascending, or you are in a hilltop meadow and a real lark sings sweetly above your head for its mate before fluttering and parachuting back to its grassy home, and you sit there quietly pondering what you have just experienced. And so the nose, the best I have experienced all year, has the same effect here. Just as there is sometimes a trill of urgency to the lark, so there is a corresponding sharpness to the call of this Glen Grant nose. But, of course, being Gen Grant that sharpness would never be allowed to be the defining character: there are multiple layers at work to ensure that. It is the thinness and fragility of those layers which sets this distillery apart. Take this magnificent malt through the Murray Method for an almost kaleidoscopic view of this whisky, with it changing from one brilliant nose and flavour formation to the next. There just isn't really time enough in the world to do justice to this malt. But it is worth trying to create it. 43%. 🍷

Glen Grant 40 Year Old db **(83.5) n22.5 t21 f20 b20.** Probably about ten summers too many. The nose threatens an oakfest, though there are enough peripheral sugars for balance and hope. Sadly, on the palate the cavalry never quite gets there.40%.

Glen Grant 170th Anniversary db **(89) n23.5 t23.5 f20 b22.** The odd mildly sulphured cask has slipped through the net here to reduce what was shaping to be something magnificent. Still enjoyable, though. 46%

The Glen Grant Arboralis bott code: LRO/HK 27 db **(90.5) n23 t22.5 f22 b23** For a Glen Grant, this is dense stuff. One of the heaviest noses ever from the distillery I have encountered matched by a personality and flavour profile which is dark, tight, almost filled with angst. GG as I have never quite seen it before in the last 40 years. Enjoyable and stylistic but lacking that elegance, complexity and all-round finesse which sets the distillery apart from all others in Scotland and, indeed, the world. 40%.

Glen Grant Five Decades bott 2013 db **(92) n24 t23.5 f21.5 b23** A nose and delivery of astonishing complexity. Hardly surprising the fade cannot keep up the pace. 46%

Glen Grant Rothes Chronicles Cask Haven first fill casks, bott code: LRO/HI23 db **(96) n24 t24.5 f23.5 b24** Remains, as last year, one of the most significant and alluring of all Scotland's malts. Beautiful. 46%.

Gordon & MacPhail Mr George Centenary Edition Glen Grant 1956 first fill sherry butt, cask no. 4455, dist 13 Dec 56, bott 27 Jun 19 **(97) n24 t25 f23.5 b24.5** In the home stretch for the Whisky Bible 2021 and, as is my long-standing tradition, I now taste the whiskies which have a special place of honour; or from previous bottlings might well be expected to be up amongst the leading lights of the all the whiskies I will have sampled in the last year. This bottling has a special place in my heart for being the only whisky older than me...And from the greatest distillery in Scotland in terms of annually producing malt of the very highest calibre. So I have chosen this as sample number 1,225 (with just 27 more to do). This was a two hour whisky to taste. A malt which opens, closes and opens again. The Murray Method seems to take you on a journey which never ends and different temperatures will give you a different storyline each time, though the outcome is always the same. Oak.

This malt is, as one might expect from such a distillery, one of the great whisky journeys. *51.7%. sc. 235 bottles.*

◈ **Gordon & MacPhail Speyside Glen Grant 1948** 1st fill sherry butt, cask no: 440 (**97.5**) **n25** I really am not sure the nose of a Scotch whisky can be better than this. It has everything you can wish for... and so much more. Indeed, where does one start? Well, I suppose it has to be the peat, the smoke, subtle but telling, reminding us that Speyside whisky was, on a daily basis made to a peatier theme than is the case in most our lifetimes. But it is the way it acts as a curtain to the play: pulling back so the scene is set for a dramatic lead by taught heather honey and the mystery of the spice offering countless levels of warmth and intensity, but all of them – miraculously – in sync with the other players. There is welcoming moist gingerbread where I had expected those tell-tale signs of great age: eucalyptus and menthol. The only nudge in that direction comes from discreet mint, but even that is eclipsed by crisp sugars. There is no severity to the tannins whatsoever and the residual fruit from the sherry has crystalised into a mix of Demerara sugar and, when warmed, a much drier grape skin intensity; **t24** after 72 years, you'd be half expecting the oak to have routed all before it, taking no prisoners. When served cool, the oak remains withdrawn, happy to rumble in its infinite shade of complexity in the background, noticeable only if you concentrate your mind upon it. Only when warmed a little does the oak agitate and demand top billing. In either style (though particularly with the MM) the heather honey blossoms and when warmed offers a waxy texture which works rather brilliantly with the oak **f24** with oak barrels these days not being what they once were, by now, you'd be expecting a bitterness to be biting into the finish. Well, you'll have a long wait: there is a not an atom of an off note to be found. This is an incredibly rare case of an impeccable malt filed into an impeccable cask finished in true harmony. The oils have been measured throughout, but here, no, they begin to collect... and that means a lengthy, tapering finale. The spices also build. But, intriguingly, we can see that this warming is a marriage of oak and the lightest smoke together. So even late on there is weight and complexity. But there needs to be sweetness, too. And here it comes... improbably, through late malt; **b24.5** my lovely old father was 72 when we lost him way back in 1989. If only he had worn as well as this improbably magnificent malt, I think he would have been with us for many more years. This cask could have been kept on for a few more summers yet. But it has been plucked probably at the right time, when the smoke still plays an important role and the oak offers no admonishment, just complexity and joy. I tasted this whisky with two glasses side by side: one was at normal room temperature, the other warmed as in the Murray Method. And here we have a case of a whisky best left undisturbed and allowed to quietly go about its business. Too much excitement and it has a bit of a heart attack... or, rather, oak attack. Though a compensation is that it brings alive the fruit which, at a cooler temperature, had taken a far more sedate position and the honey which alters not only its countenance but texture. Really, to understand the true complexity of this malt may take another 72 years. I left this as the final whisky to taste for the 2022 Whisky Bible. Well, they do they say leave the best 'til last.... *52.5%* ♉

GLENGYLE

Campbeltown, 2004. J&A Mitchell & Co. Working.

Kilkerran 12 Year Old db (**90.5**) **n22.5 t23 f22.5 b22.5** A malt far more comfortable at this age than some of the previous, younger, bottlings from a few years back. Has a fragile feel to it and the air of a malt which must be treated gently and with respect. *46%*

◈ **Cadenhead's Authentic Collection Cask Strength Kilkerran Aged 11 Years** bourbon barrel, dist 2009, bott 2021 (**89.5**) **n23** a delightful mixture of nutty malt and delicate citrus. Possibly one of the most genteel noses I have encountered from Campbeltown. There is a curious, distant, smokiness to this, also, a kind of semi-weighty afterthought... making it softer still, though that hardly seemed possible...; **t23** outstanding structure. There is a firmness to the milt missing on the nose, but this soon melts and the malt comes through in concentrated form with full on salivation; **f21** a little bitterness is captured from the cask; **b22.5** would have scored very high had it not been for the finish. Even so, the nose and delivery deserves mentioning in dispatches as this is a wonderful example of lots of not very much happening combining to make a whole lot... *56.5% 204 bottles*

GLEN KEITH

Speyside, 1957. Chivas Brothers. Working (re-opened 14th June 2013).

Glen Keith 10 Years Old db (**80**) **n22 t21 f18 b19.** A malty if thin dram that finishes with a whimper after an impressively refreshing, grassy start. *43%*

◈ **Glen Keith Distillery Edition** bott code: db (**87.5**) **n22 t22.5 f21 b22** The nose offers flighty malt in the company of weightier caramels. While on the palate excellent sweet/spice arrival on the palate, then a blossoming of barley. Simple vanillas and light tannin through the mid-ground. However, perhaps too toffee dependent on the finish, though the spices buzz contently. So, a malt which keeps true to Glen Keith's ability to remain on the more delicate side of the Speysiders, ensuring a gentle persuasion of malty tones rather than forcing itself upon the drinker. But could benefit from a little less caramel. 40%

The First Editions Glen Keith Aged 26 Years 1993 refill barrel, cask no. 16784, bott 2019 **(93) n23 t24 f22.5 b23.5** For an unfashionable distillery, this can sometimes come up with the odd cracker. And here is one! 56.7%. nc ncf sc. 162 bottles.

◆ **The First Editions Glen Keith Aged 28 Years 1993** refill barrel, cask no. HL18214, bott 2021 **(88.5) n22 t22.5 f22 b22** Great to see a Glen Keith in fine fettle. Always on the lighter side of the Speysiders, this still has enough malty richness to absorb the oak without too much damage. Indeed, the slow arrival and burn of the oaky spice is a very attractive feature. Salivating and tart, blenders would have loved this in a 25-year-old blend to really give the malt section almost a third dimension. A light creamy cocoa signs off the experience attractively. 56.4%. nc ncf sc. 149 bottles.

Liquid Treasures From Miles Away Glen Keith 27 Year Old bourbon barrel, dist Jan 93, bott Feb 20 **(88.5) n22 t22.5 f22 b22** The buyer for Liquid Treasures seems to have a thing for thin and malty malts. Just be thankful this is in a bourbon barrel for the barley can sparkles to maximum effect. In any other cask this would have vanished out of sight. But here, at least, we have some charming citrus notes which lifts the malt both on the nose and on delivery. Little meat but a lovely shape nonetheless. 58.4%. sc. 146 bottles.

GLENKINCHIE
Lowlands, 1837. Diageo. Working.
Glenkinchie 12 Years Old db **(85) n19 t22.5 f21.5 b22.** The last 'Kinchie 12 I encountered was beyond woeful. This is anything but. Still not firing on all cylinders and can definitely do better. But there is a fabulous vibrancy to this which nearly all the bottlings I have tasted in the last few years have sadly lacked. Impressive. 43%

◆ **Glenkinchie 12 Years Old** bott code: L0016CM002 db **(88.5) n21.5 t22.5 f22 b22.5** A definite upgrade on the last 'Kinchie I sat down to properly study. Actually taken aback by the sharp nose which has more in common with new make than a 12-year-old. But soon relaxed into the malt and milky chocolate which makes for a pleasing if simplistic theme. Salivating in part, too, and seems to eke out as much honey as it can find. A tad too much toffee, but pleasant, nonetheless. 43%.

Glenkinchie The Distillers Edition Amontillado cask-wood, dist 2005, bott 2017, bott code: L7222CM000 db **(91.5) n23 t23.5 f21.5 b23** Now that is one very elegant whisky. 43%.

Glenkinchie The Royal Edinburgh Military Tattoo bott code: L9186CM005 db **(93.5) n23 t24 f23 b23.5** One of the most flavoursome Glenkinchies I've ever encountered, really making the most of its malty disposition. Many a Glenkinchie lover will have the name of expression of this tattooed somewhere about their person... Gorgeous! 46%.

THE GLENLIVET
Speyside, 1824. Chivas Brothers. Working.
The Glenlivet 12 Years of Age bott 2017/03/30 db **(92.5) n23 t23 f23 b23.5** Probably the best Glenlivet 12 I have tasted for quite a while...lucky Americans! An extra few percentage points of first fill bourbon cask has gone a long way here. Excellent and satisfying. 40% (80 proof)

The Glenlivet Excellence 12 Year Old db **(87) n22 t21.5 f22 b21.5.** Low key but very clean. The emphasis is on delicate. 40%. Visitor Centre and Asian exclusive.

The Glenlivet 18 Years of Age bott code: 2017/02/02 LKPL0386 db **(83.5) n22 t22 f19 b20.5** This is a rather flat version of a usually rich malt. Has the odd honey-charmed moment and the spices aren't hiding, either. But way too much caramel has turned the usual undulations on the palate to something of pancake proportions. A little furry at the death, also. 43%.

The Glenlivet Alpha db **(92) n23.5 t24 f21.5 b23.** You get the feeling some people have worked very hard at creating a multi-toned, complex creature celebrating the distillery's position at the centre of Speyside. They have succeeded. Just a cask selection or two away from a potential major Bible award. Maybe for the next bottling.... 50%

The Glenlivet Archive 21 Years of Age batch no. 0513M db **(95.5) n24 t24 f23.5 b24** Less archive and more achieve. For getting so many honey tones to work together without it getting overly sweet or syrupy really is a major achievement. 43%

The Glenlivet Captain's Reserve finished in Cognac casks db **(89.5) n22 t23 f22 b22.5** A laid-back malt playing games being simultaneously spicy and super-soft. 40%.

The Glenlivet Cipher db **(96.5) n24.5 t24 f23.5 b24.5** It has taken over half an hour to distil these tasting notes into something that will fit the book: we have more new entries than normal and I'm running out of room. Few whiskies I taste this year, however, will compare to this. 48%

The Glenlivet Conglass 14 db **(92.5)** n22 t23 f23.5 b24 High quality. *59.8%*

The Glenlivet Distiller's Reserve bott code: 2019/04/01 db **(87)** n21.5 t22 f21.5 b22 A soft, rotund malt designed to give minimum offence... and succeeds. Unless you are offended by the overstating of the caramels. *40%.*

The Glenlivet Founder's Reserve bott code: 2017/04/04 LCPL 0591 db **(88.5)** n23 t22 f21.5 **b22** Anyone who can remember the less than impressive start to this brand will be pretty amazed at just how deliciously approachable it is now. *40%.*

⟪⟫ **The Glenlivet Founder's Reserve American Oak Selection** bott code: 2020/11/24 db **(83)** n22 t21.5 f19 b20.5 One of those malts where you aren't always quite sure what you'll be getting. This one is at the lower end of the spectrum hampered by a little too much toffee flatness through the middle and then the double whammy of an untidy fuzzy dullness on the finish. Early on in the delivery the barley positively sparkles. But it is not enough from a distillery as good as this one *40%.*

The Glenlivet 15 Years of Age French Oak Reserve bott code: 2016/12/19 LCPK 2465 db **(93)** n23.5 t23 f23 b23.5 Many years ago when this first came out it wasn't very good, to be honest. Then it was re-shaped, upped a gear and became a very enjoyable dram, indeed. Now, having apparently been steered on a slightly different course again, it is just excellent... An expression that has evolved slowly but quite beautifully. *40%.*

The Glenlivet The Master Distiller's Reserve bott code: 2016/10/04 LCPK 1866 db **(86.5)** n22.5 t22 f20.5 b21 It is a shame the malty sparkle on the nose and delivery isn't matched by what follows. A pleasant, safe dram. But too toffee-rich and doesn't develop as this great distillery should. *40%.*

The Glenlivet The Master Distiller's Reserve Solera Vatted bott code: 2017/03/01 LCPL 0371 db **(89.5)** n22.5 t23 f22 b22 Pretty much in line with the 2015 bottling above, except there is slightly more caramel here shaving the top off the higher notes. *40%.*

The Glenlivet White Oak Reserve bott code: 2019/03/01 db **(89)** n23 t23 f21 b22 Starts promisingly but fades dramatically on the toffee. *40%.*

Gordon & MacPhail Connoisseurs Choice Glenlivet Aged 14 Years refill bourbon barrel, cask no. 800670, dist 10 Nov 04, bott 15 Jul 19 **(94.5)** n23.5 t24 f23 b24 The Glenlivet in maximum honey mode. Brilliant! *64%. sc. 162 bottles.*

⟪⟫ **Kingbury Sar Obair Glenlivet 30 Year Old** hogshead, dist 1990, cask no. 17145 **(94)** **n23** sometimes with a Glenlivet you can pick the strands of barley on the nose and measure the intensity of the varying malty pathways. Here it is the oak The tannins are in control and it will not be relinquished. The question: can enough sweetness be found still to make the aroma work. At first you think maybe not: room temperature gives a very closed shop with an oaky portcullis coming down and allowing nothing to enter or leave. But the Murray Method helps here as it releases some magnificent bitter orange...; **t23.5** again, tasted cold and we come up against a wall of oak. However, warmed and the oils gather and sooth and now we get a muscovado and molasses sugar blend to hold in the tangy ancient tannins; **f23.5** long... just so long! Again the tannins are toasty and straining at the leash but, miraculously, even this late in the day and some barley turns up to a give a brief, sweet glow before disappearing under the vanilla and roast Java coffee...; **b24** someone was either very lucky, or had nerves of reinforced steel. Because this is brinkmanship taken to the max! I would bet a large sum of money that just one more slightly above average warm summer would have taken this over the edge because at times the honey and barley appear to be clinging on by their fingernails, ready to fall off the oaky cliff at any moment. Without the Murray Method, this would be a whisky struggling to impress. With it, and it absolutely amazes. But even the MM probably couldn't save it from another six months to a year in oak... *44.6% sc 246 bottles*

⟪⟫ **The Perfect Fifth Glenlivet 40 Year Old** cask no. 13523 **(96)** n24 something almost like an old cognac about this one as there is a near ethereal lightness to this aroma. Gooseberries bursting in the sun, dates pepped up some white pepper and even a hint of cinnamon, yet among all the essences of old age comes slightly green banana, too. And who can't spot the sugary, zesty bite of sherbet lemons in the sweet shop jar...? **t24** the low abv ensures the delivery is a softy in every sense: this is a glistening, malty caress, though soon some toasty tannins are in play to warm up proceedings. A burnt fudge midpoint leads into the heather honey which spreads, almost grittily, across the roof of the mouth to give a strange but attractive coarseness to the sweetness; **f23.5** the problem, almost invariably, with low strength is a quicker than usual finish. But not here! A little honey lingers and there is even a late surge of barley to match the vanilla; **b24.5** an absolutely top-range malt which has used its 40 years in barrel to excellent, almost near perfect, effect. Not a single off note, no tang from the wood or any other disappointments. Just lots of elegance. And, using the Murray Method, more complexity and surprises than you might believe possible. One of the best Scotch malts released in the last 12 months. *41.7% sc ncf nc* ⚲

GLENLOCHY

Highlands (Western), 1898–1983. Diageo. Closed.

Gordon & MacPhail Rare Old Glenlochy 1979 (95) n23.5 t24 f23.5 b24 It has been many years since a bottle from this long lost distillery turned up and that was such a classic, I can remember every nuance of it even now. This shows far greater age, but the way with which the malt takes it in its stride will become the stuff of legend. I held back on tasting this until today, August 2nd 2013, because my lad David this afternoon moved into the first home he has bought, with new wife Rachael and little Abi. It is near Fort William, the remote west coast Highland town in which this whisky was made, and where David will be teaching next year. His first job after moving in, though, will be to continue editing this book, for he worked on the Whisky Bible for a number of editions as researcher and editor over the years. So I can think of no better way of wishing David a happy life in his new home than by toasting him with what turned out to be a stunningly beautiful malt from one of the rarest of all the lost distilleries which, by strange coincidence, was first put up for sale exactly 100 years ago. So, to David, Rachael & little Abigail... your new home! And this time I swallowed..46%. ncf.

GLENLOSSIE

Speyside, 1876. Diageo. Working.

⬥ **Chapter 7 Glenlossie 2008 Aged 12 Years** bourbon hogshead, barrel no.9603 **(91)** n22 a little spicy celery amid the malt and vanilla; t22.5 gorgeously silky arrival with acacia honey and barley in deep conversation; f23.5 the honey has receded slightly leaving a sawdusty dryness, but the waxiness returns with a little cocoa and liquorice in tow. Very refined, elegant and magnificently complex on the fade; b23 a glossy 'Lossie... 51.1% sc

⬥ **Golden Glen Glenlossie Aged 22 Years** hogshead, cask no. 7108, dist 26 Nov 97, bott 27 Nov 19 **(96.5)** n24 t24 f24 b24.5 A fabulously complex individual, always popping up with the odd surprise each time you taste it. Even if you live by the Murray Method, as you should, you will be entirely forgiven for not spitting this one out. One of those whiskies that demands a leather chair on the spot for you to sink into, subdued lighting, peace and quiet, a clean atmosphere...and all the time in the world. If I were able, I'd mark this down as a 96.75...it is so closely pushing the magical 97 mark! 53.9%. 222 bottles. Bottled by The Last Drop for No. 23.

⬥ **The Single Cask Glenlossie 2008** oloroso octave finish, cask no 12477A **(89)** n22 an attractive fudge and raisin lead with busy spices; t23 lots of toffee before a burst of barley – hard to keep it down at this distillery! – though that soon vanishes as a weightier oaky mocha theme moves in; f21.5 an annoying bit of bitterness at the end; b22.5 some late arriving S off the oloroso rocks the boat slightly at the very death. Which was annoying, as I thought we'd got away with it. The journey up until that point was a delightfully pleasant one... 56.5% sc

The Whisk(e)y Company The Spirit of Glenlossie Aged 22 Years hogshead, cask no. 7107, bott 2019 **(95.5)** n24 t24 f23.5 b24 Keen-eyed observers will notice that this is the sister cask to the monumental Golden Glen bottling. This is also an essay in charm and sophistication, though lacking that almost unidentifiable charisma, that sheer magic, of its sister cask. Truly brilliant, nonetheless... 55.5%. sc. 234 bottles.

GLEN MHOR

Highlands (Northern), 1892–1983. Diageo. Demolished.

Glen Mhor 1976 Rare Malt db **(92.5)** n23 t24 f22 b23.5. You just dream of truly great whisky sitting in your glass from time to time. But you don't expect it, especially from such an old cask. This was the best example from this distillery I've tasted in 30 years...until the Glenkeir version was unleashed! If you ever want to see a scotch that has stretched the use of oak as far it will go without detriment, here it is. What a pity the distillery has gone because the Mhor the merrier... 52.2%

GLENMORANGIE

Highlands (Northern), 1843. Glenmorangie Plc. Working.

⬥ **Glenmorangie The Original Aged 10 Years** bott code: 09/11/2020 db **(94)** n23.5 a beautiful nose marrying a nutty dryness with a sharper, citrussy bite. Oaky vanilla and light spice is all over this...; t24 fabulous. A delivery straight from the school of surprisingly complex whiskies. And ones which go into major salivation mode on arrival. Ticks every classic Glenmorangie box but with the welcome surprise of a little praline developing about a third of the way in, something which you cannot always guarantee to happen. The mix of Demerara sugars and light spices, alongside the intense barley, though, is to be fully worshipped...as usual; f23 the spices really do have a lot to say here, more than usual. The oils are pretty full on by 'Morangie standards, too. Just so deeply satisfying for an essentially light finish...; **b23.5** over the last decade Glenmorangie 10 really has become a byword for consistency and elegance. *40%.*

Glenmorangie 15 Years Old db **(90.5) n23 t23 f22 b22.5** Exudes quality. *43%*

Glenmorangie 15 Years Old Sauternes Wood Finish db **(68) n16 t18 f17 b17.** I had hoped – and expected – an improvement on the sulphured version I came across last time. Oh, whisky! Why are you such a cruel mistress...? *46%*

Glenmorangie 18 Years Old db **(91) n22 t23 f23 b23** Having thrown off some previous gremlins, now a perfect start to the day whisky... *43%*

Glenmorangie 19 Year Old db **(94) n24 t23.5 f22.5 b24** Fruity or malty...? I can't decide...but then I don't think for a moment that you're supposed to be able to... *43%.*

Glenmorangie 25 Years Old db **(95.5) n24 t24 f23.5 b24** Every bit as statesmanlike and elegant as a whisky of this age from such a blinding distillery should be. Ticks every single box for a 25-year-old and is Morangie's most improved malt by the distance of Tain to Wellingborough. There is a hint of genius with each unfolding wave of flavours with this one: a whisky that will go in 99/100 whisky lover's top 50 malts of all time. And that includes the Peatheads. *43%*

Glenmorangie 30 Years Old db **(72) n17 t18 f19 b18.** From the evidence in the glass the jury is out on whether it has been spruced up a little in a poor sherry cask – and spruce is the operative word: lots of pine on this wrinkly. *44.1%*

Glenmorangie Allta db **(89) n22.5 t23 f21.5 b22** This is a very different 'Morangie: the Allta, could well be for Alternative. Because while the distillery is rightly famed for its cask innovation, there is no barrel style I can think of on the planet which can shape the malt in this unique way. So either grain or yeast is the deciding factor here – perhaps a mixture of both (and you can rule out water!). My money is on yeast, as the only ever time I've come across something quite like this was in a lab in Kentucky with some experimental stuff. The perfect Glenmorangie to confuse your friends by... *51.2%.*

Glenmorangie Astar db **(93) n24 t23.5 f22 b23.5** Astar has moved a long way from the first bottling which left me scratching my head. This is one of the maltiest of all their range, though the lightness of touch means that any bitterness can be too easily detected. *52.5%.*

Glenmorangie Bacalta db **(87) n22 t22.5 f21 b21.5.** Unusually for a Glenmorangie the narrative is muffled and indistinct. Has some lovely moments, but a bit sharp and lacking in places. *46%*

Glenmorangie Cadboll db **(86.5) n21 t23.5 f20.5 b21.5** Every year a challenging new breed of Glenmorangie appears to be thrown into the mix, as though to tally the taste buds. This is this year's offering: different again, with neither the nose nor finish quite up to par with the outstanding delivery – indeed, the finale is pretty bitter, indeed. But the texture and intensity of the barley on arrival is borderline brilliant, as is the most wonderful caramel which frames it with a buttery sweetness. *43.1%.*

Glenmorangie Dornoch db **(94) n23.5 t23 f23.5 b24** A rare Glenmorangie which this time does not put the emphasis on fruit or oak influence. But this appears to concentrate on the malt itself, taking it through a routine which reveals as many angles and facets as it can possibly conjure. Even if the casks are from a central warehouse, at times a seascape has been created by a light salty influence – so befitting the whisky's name. A real treat. *43%*

Glenmorangie Ealanta 1993 Vintage db **(97.5) n24 t24 f24.5 b25** When is a bourbon not a bourbon? When it is a Scotch single malt...And here we have potentially the World Whisky of the Year. Free from the embarrassing nonsense which passes for today's sherry butt, and undamaged by less than careful after use care of second-hand bourbon casks, we see what happens when the more telling aspects of oak, the business end which gives bourbon that extra edge, blends with the some of the very finest malt made in Scotland. Something approaching one of the best whiskies of my lifetime is the result... *46%*

Glenmorangie Global Travel Retail 12 Year Old db **(89.5) n22 t23 f22 b22.5** Heavy duty Morangie with subtlety and dexterity giving way to full on flavour with a cream toffee mouthfeel. *43%.*

Glenmorangie Global Travel Retail 14 Year Old db **(84) n22 t22 f19 b21** A pretty straightforward offering by Morangie's normally complex standards but let down by the late furry bitterness on the finish. *43%.*

Glenmorangie Global Travel Retail 16 Year Old db **(94.5) n23.5 t23.5 f23.5 b24** I particularly love this as the distillery in question is never in doubt: had "Glenmorangie" running through it like a stick of Blackpool rock. Despite the light phenols... *43%.*

Glenmorangie Grand Vintage 1995 db **(89) n23 t23 f21 b22** Some 40 years ago Glenmorangie was never considered a candidate for whiskies aged 21 and over. Not now. This holds together well...until the dying moments. *43%.*

Glenmorangie Grand Vintage 1996 db **(95) n23.5 t24 f23.5 b24** Principally has a firm, glazed feel to this. But he intensity of the malt takes the breath away. Too beautiful... *43%.*

Glenmorangie Grand Vintage 1997 db **(95) n23.5 t24 f23.5 b24** Such glorious weight and counterweight: a lesson in cask understanding. A classy vintage, indeed. *43%.*

Glenmorangie Lasanta sherry casks db **(68.5) n16 t19 f16 b17.5.** The sherry problem has increased dramatically rather than being solved. *46%*

Glenmorangie Lasanta Aged 12 Years sherry cask finish db **(93) n23.5 t24 f22 b23.5** A delightful surprise: every bottling of Lasanta I'd ever tasted had been sulphur ruined. But this new 12-y-o incarnation has got off to a flying start. Although a little bit of a niggle on the finish, I can live with that in the present climate. Here's to a faultless second bottling... *43%*

Glenmorangie Legends The Duthac db **(91.5) n23.5 t23.5 f21.5 b23** Not spoken to their blender, Bill Lumsden, about this one. But he's been busy on this, though not so busy as to get rid of the unwelcome you-know-what from the wine casks. Educated guess: some kind of finish involving virgin oak, or at least first fill bourbon, and sherry, probably PX on account of the intensity of the crisp sugar. *43%. ncf.*

Glenmorangie Milsean db **(94) n23 t23.5 f23.5 b24** A quite beautiful malt which goes out of its way to put the orangey in 'Morangie... *46%*

Glenmorangie Nectar D'Or db **(94.5) n23.5 t24 f23 b24** I was told that this was different to the last Nectar D'or as it has no age statement. To be honest, I was never aware that it had! But it doesn't matter: it is always about the blending of the malt styles from the distillery and the pursuit of balance. And what I have said about this whisky before still perfectly sums it up: an exercise in outrageously good sweet-dry balancing... *46%.*

Glenmorangie Private Edition 9 Spios db **(95.5) n23 t24.5 f23.5 b24.5** Glenmorangie displaying countless layers of brilliance. Breathtakingly beautiful. *46%.*

Glenmorangie Quinta Ruban 14 Year Old db **(87) n22 t22 f21 b22** Something of the sweet shop about this with the sugary fruitiness. But doesn't quite develop in structure beyond its simple – though thoroughly attractive – early confines. *46%.*

Glenmorangie Signet db **(80.5) n20 t21.5 f19 b20.** A great whisky holed below the waterline by oak of unsatisfactory quality. Tragic. *46%. Travel Retail Exclusive.*

Glenmorangie Signet db **(94) n23.5 t24 f23 b23.5** Ah, that's better! Faith and excellence has been restored! *46%.*

Glenmorangie Signet Ristretto db **(86.5) n22 t22.5 f21 b21** Not so sure about this one. Think I prefer my Signets non-Ristrettoed. Flies way too far towards unconstrained sweetness on delivery, but big sweetness on delivery often leaves a bit of a mess in its wake. And I have to admit I am no fan of the dishevelled, tangy finish. *46%.*

Glenmorangie Taghta db **(92) n23 t23 f23 b23** A curious Glenmorangie which, unusually, appears not to be trying to make a statement or force a point. This is an old Sunday afternoon film of a dram: an old-fashioned black and whitie, (home grown and not an Ealing, or Bogie or Edward G Robinson) where, whether we have seen it before or not, we know pretty much what is going to happen, in a reassuring kind of a way... *46%*

Glenmorangie A Tale of Cake db **(87) n22 t23 f20 b22** So rare for acacia honey to show so early on a 'Morangie, but there it is and does a great job in offering the delicate touch to the busier spices. Sadly, there is the dull throb of an off-key cask which gets a little too loud for comfort on the finish. There are those who won't spot it, but more who will and it is a distraction from an otherwise genteel dram. *46%.*

Glenmorangie Tarlogan db **(95) n24 t24 f22.5 b23.5** Interesting. I have just tasted three new Dalmore. Identical colour and some very similar toffeed characteristics. I allowed a whisky-loving visitor to taste them, without telling him what they were. He could barely tell them apart. Here, I have three new Glenmorangies. All of a different hue. I may not like them all; we will see. But at least I know there will be remarkable differences between them. This fabulous malt radiates the countryside in a way few drams have done before. As refreshing as an early morning dip in a Scottish pond... *43%*

Glenmorangie Tayne db **(87.5) n21 t22.5 f22 b22.** Tangy back story. But also a curious early combination between butterscotch and Werther's Original candy. The malt – topped with a splash of double cream - in the centre ground, though, is the star showing. *43%. Travel Retail Exclusive.*

Glenmorangie Tùsail Private Edition db **(92) n24.5 t23 f21.5 b23** Doesn't quite live up to the nose. But that would have been a big ask! From the Understated School of Glenmorangie. *46%. ncf.*

GLEN MORAY
Speyside, 1897. La Martiniquaise. Working.

Glen Moray Classic 8 Years Old db **(86) n20 t22 f21 b23.** A vast improvement on previous bottlings with the sluggish fatness replaced by a thinner, barley-rich, slightly sweeter and more precise mouthfeel. *40%*

Glen Moray 10 Years Old Chardonnay Matured db **(73.5) n18.5 t19 f18 b18.** Tighter than a wine cork. *40%*

Glen Moray 12 Years Old db **(90) n22.5 t22 f23 b22.5** I have always regarded this as the measuring stick by which all other malty and clean Speysiders should be tried and tested. It is still a fabulous whisky, full of malty intricacies. Something has fallen off the edge, perhaps, but minutely so. Still think a trick or two is being missed by bottling this at 40%: the natural timbre of this malt demands 46% and no less.... *40%*

Glen Moray 16 Years Old db **(74) n19 t19 f18 b19.** A serious dip in form. Drab. *40%*

Glen Moray 20 Years Old db **(80) n22 t22 f18 b18.** With so much natural cream toffee, it is hard to believe that this has so many years on it. After a quick, refreshing start it pans out, if anything, a little dull. *40%*

Glen Moray Aged 21 Years Portwood Finish db **(95) n23.5 t23.5 f24 b24** As soft and yielding on the palate as any malt you'll ever find. But not short on the complexity front, either. A true entertainer. *46.3%. ncf.*

Glen Moray Aged 25 Years Port Cask Finish dist 1988 db **(88) n23 t22.5 f20.5 b22** Thought I'd celebrate Andy Murray's second Wimbledon victory, which he completed just a few minutes ago, by having another go at a Glen Moray 25-year-old (Moray is pronounced Murray). I remember last time being slightly disappointed with this expression. Well this later bottling is a little better, but nowhere near the brilliance Murray displayed in gaining revenge for Canada last year getting World Whisky of the Year. Curiously, if this is a 25-year-old and was distilled in 1988, then presumably it was bottled in 2013...the first time Murray won Wimbledon! *43%*

Glen Moray Aged 25 Years Port Cask Finish bourbon casks, dist 1994, bott code: L933659A db **(93) n24 t23.5 f22 b23.5** An exhibition of mind-blowing layering. The nose and delivery are a malt-lover's dream come true. *43%.*

Glen Moray 25 Year Old Port Cask Finish batch 2 db **(95) n23.5 t23.5 f24 b24** Some quite first rate port pipes are involved here. Absolutely clean as a whistle and without any form of off-note. A distillery I have a very soft spot for showing very unusual depth – and age. Brilliant. *43%. 3295 bottles.*

Glen Moray Aged 25 Years Port Cask Finish dist 1988, bott code L709759A 2017/04/07 db **(94) n23 t23.5 f23.5 b24** A lovely intense malt where the Port casks leave big fruity fingerprints at every turn. *43%.*

Glen Moray 30 Years Old db **(92.5) n23.5 t23.5 f22.5 b23** For all its years, this is comfortable malt, untroubled by time. There is no mistaking quality. *43%*

Glen Moray 1984 db **(83) n20 t22 f20 b21.** Mouthwatering and incredibly refreshing malt for its age. *40%*

Glen Moray 1989 db **(86) n23 t22 f20 b21.** Doesn't quite live up to the fruit smoothie nose but I'm being a little picky here. *40%*

Glen Moray Bourbon Cask 1994 cask no. 42/0, bott code. 25/04/17 170635 db **(93.5) n23.5 t23.5 f23 b23.5** For most people in England Glen Moray is a highly productive goalscorer for Brighton. But it would be great if the world woke up to just what lovely whisky can come from this much under-rated distillery. *56.4%. sc.*

Glen Moray Burgundy Cask 2004 Distillery Edition cask no. 213, bott code: L012257A 2020/05/01 db **(93) n23 t23.5 f23 b23.5** Curiously, the last few Burgundy casks I had tasted from distilleries around the world, if unmolested by candles, had shewn much more breast-beating spice at work than this relatively sedate chap. But don't get me wrong, this still has plenty of fizz and much to say...all of it worth listening to. *60.1%. sc.*

Glen Moray Chardonnay Cask 2003 Distillery Edition cask no. 7670, bott code: L012257A 2020/05/01 db **(95.5) n24 t24 f23.5 b24** If your thing is burnt fruitcake: smouldering, blackened raisins in particular, then I think I have just unearthed a single malt whisky just for you. A wine cask matured malt with no damaging sulphur whatsoever, which has been a rare thing this year and makes me want to cheer this bottling from the rooftops. However, there is no escaping the fact that this a form of trial by fire...or toasting to be specific. From the eye-watering, spicy and acidic nose to the honeyed finish you are offered something very different and bordering on genius. *58.9%. sc.*

Glen Moray Chenin Blanc Cask 2004 Distillery Edition cask no. 341, bott code: L012257A 2020/05/01 db **(75) n18 t23 f16 b18** If any wine industry was worse for sulphur-treating their casks than the Spanish, it was the French. Alas, in this case. Because the sweet and voluptuous beauty of the delivery is there for all to see. *60.3%. sc.*

Glen Moray Classic db **(86.5) n22 t21.5 f21.5 b21.5.** The nose is the star with a wonderful, clean barley-fruit tandem, but what follows cannot quite match its sure-footed wit. *40%*

Glen Moray Elgin Classic bott code: L929657A 2019/10/23 db **(89) n23 t23 f21 b22** An Elgin Classic ....brushed with peat! Never thought I'd see the day. A delightful aroma of the gentlest nature. The finish, though, could do with a little less toffee. I say this as I am more than aware what a true Elgin Classic is: when my son was born in 1986 I took him to this distillery while he was just a few months old. And I had also bought him a Glen Moray 12 to open on his 21st birthday. Its colour was natural pale straw, as Glen Moray always, classically was. Some 35 years ago Gen Moray was synonymous with light natural colour and a full malty flavour. Wouldn't it be wonderful if it could be again... 40%.

Glen Moray Elgin Classic bott code: 2021/07/07 db **(87) n22 t22.5 f20.5 b22** Have to admit that a greying eyebrow was raised when I nosed this: "bit young for an 8-year-old," thought I. But when I inspected the bottle, no sign of a number eight. Thankfully, youth serves this distillery well. This is a malty cove at the best of times. And when this young it is though you have a ripening barley field right there in your glass. Green, clean and refreshing nose and a startlingly new-makey, freshly cut grass delivery. Sadly, a big toffee effect starts to take hold, slightly bittering and dulling the finale. 40%

Glen Moray Classic Port Cask Finish db **(89.5) n21 t21.5 f23.5 b23.5** A malt which has to somehow work its way to the exit...and finally does so with supreme confidence and a touch of class along the way... 40%

Glen Moray Elgin Classic Cabernet Cask Finish bott code: L820057B 2018/07/19 db **(88) n22 t23 f21 b22** Not normally a great fan of malt with this degree of dryness on the finish. But must say I enjoyed the sophisticated pathway to the finish, if not the eye-wateringly tight finale itself. But enjoy the seasoned moist fruitcake nose and the angular, juicy berry fruits – under-ripe gooseberries in particular on delivery. Then hold on tight... 40%.

Glen Moray Elgin Classic Chardonnay Cask Finish db **(73) n19 t19 f17 b18.** Juicy. But sulphur-dulled. 40%

Glen Moray Elgin Classic Chardonnay Cask Finish bott code: L822667C 2018/08/14 db **(83) n21 t22 f20 b20** You know when you have a date with a rather attractive looker you have only just met. And make a reservation at a special restaurant where, with a sinking feeling of the heart, you find out over dinner that, no matter how well you prompt and cajole, how tightly you hang on to their every dull word, that person has nothing whatsoever of interest to say; and you have so little in common that you cannot wait for the evening to end as boredom sets in. Well, that, I'm afraid, was just like tasting this malt... 40%.

Glen Moray Elgin Classic Peated Single Malt bott code: L912557E 2019/05/06 db **(88.5) n22 t23.5 f21 b22** Definitely a much better all-rounder than the last bottling of this I tasted. But still palpably at the wrong strength, allowing far too much chalky vanilla given free entrance to undo the great work of the peat and the outstanding distillate. Mesmerically soft on delivery and the house mega-maltiness is soon evident, to wholly delicious effect. But the way it crumbles away on the finish is a bit of a shame. This has the potential for a malt in the 93-94 range. As it is: quite lovely...but soooo frustratingly underpowered! 40%.

Glen Moray Elgin Classic Port Cask Finish bott code: L922067B 2019/08/08 db **(92.5) n22.5 t23.5f23 b23.5** Another slightly underpowered malt, but it has to be said that the quality of these Port casks is exceptionally high. This is gorgeous malt at any strength. 40%.

Glen Moray Elgin Classic Sherry Cask Finish db **(85) n21 t22 f20.5 b21.5.** Must be a cream sherry, because this is one exceptionally creamy malt. A bit of a late sulphur tang wipes off a few marks, but the delicious grapey positives outweigh the negatives. 40%

Glen Moray Elgin Classic Sherry Cask Finish bott code: L9150570 2019/08/30 db **(88) n22 t23 f20 b22.5** When the fruit gets into full stride it becomes quite a joy. The dangers of sherry butts though are always there as a reminder. 40%.

Glen Moray Elgin Heritage Aged 15 Years Oloroso sherry casks & ex bourbon American oak, bott code: L890127B 2019/08/14 db **(90.5) n23.5 t23 f21.5 b22.5** Very curious how even though this is weaker than Signature, the characteristics of the casks comes through so much more brightly, mainly thanks to less toffee apparent. The off-key sherry finale, excepted, of course. 40%.

Glen Moray Elgin Heritage Aged 18 Years db **(94) n23.5 t24 f23 b23.5** Absolutely true to the Glen Moray style. Superb. 47%

Glen Moray Elgin Signature Aged 12 Years American oak, bott code: L831157B 2018/11/07 db **(86) n23.5 t22.5 f19.5 b21** Now here's a mystery. Bourbon casks...yet a dull fruity furriness on the finish. Until that point is blazed away with that stunning malty intensity that makes Glen Moray in bourbon cask a little bit special. 48%. ncf. Cask Collection Exclusive.

Glen Moray Elgin Signature Aged 15 Years American & sherry casks, bott code: L821157C 2018/11/07 db **(89) n22.5 t22.5 f22 b22** Another Glen Moray cut off in its prime. Pleasant but goes for impact rather than complexity. 48%. ncf. Cask Collection Exclusive.

Glen Moray Elgin Signature Elgin Classic first fill American oak, bott code: L924157A 2019/09/23 db **(90) n23 t23 f22 b22** Hmmm! Lovely malt from this brilliant distillery. Not sure about the finish, though, where toffee abruptly ends what had been such a satisfying experience. 48%. ncf. Cask Collection Exclusive.

Glen Moray Fired Oak Aged 10 Years db **(90) n22.5 t23 f22 b22.5** Very attractive. But missing a trick at 40%: it is needing the extra oils to ramp up intensity and take into another dimension. *40%.*

Glen Moray Madeira Cask Project 13 Years Old dist 26 May 06, bott code: L012557A 2020/05/04 db **(90.5) n23 t23.5 f21.5 b22.5** Even with a cask offering just a light sulphur touch, the bountiful and slightly unusual delights of the nose and delivery in particular make its sins very easy to forgive. *46.3%. nc ncf. UK Exclusive.*

Glen Moray Mastery db **(89.5) n23.5 t22.5 f21.5 b22** Has an expensive feel to this, to be honest. But, though a huge GM fan, have to say that for all its very clean, attractive, unblemished fruit; for all its juiciness I'm afraid it's just a little bit too one-dimensional. No doubting its charm and elegance, however. *52.3%.*

Glen Moray Peated Classic db **(87.5) n21.5 t22.5 f21.5 b22**. Really never thought I'd see this distillery, once the quintessential Speyside unpeated dram, gone all smoky... A little bit of a work in progress. And a minor word to the wise to their blenders: by reducing to 40% you've broken up the oils a shade – but tellingly - too much, which can be crucial in peaty whiskies. Up to 46% next bottling and I think you'll find things fall into place – and not apart... Some minor erotic moments, though, especially on the fourth or fifth beats, when the sugars and smoked vanilla do work well together. Too fleeting, though. *40%*

Glen Moray Rhum Agricole Cask Finish Project Oloroso sherry casks & ex bourbon American oak, bott code: L921058A 2019/07/29 db **(94.5) n24 t23.5 f23 b24** A beautifully weighted malt that melts on the tongue. A highly unusual flavour profile and one that benefits from some top class blending. What a treat of a dram. *46.3%. ncf. UK Exclusive.*

Glen Moray Sherry Cask Finish 1994 cask no. 904/57, bott code. 25/04/17 170636 db **(92) n23.5 t23 f22 b23.5** Old-fashioned, traditional dry oloroso influence in its most resounding form. A must find malt for those looking to broaden their positive whisky experiences.*56.7%. sc.*

Acla Selection Summer Edition Glen Moray 28 Year Old barrel, dist 1990, bott 2018 **(91.5) n23 t22 f23.5 b23** A very similar experience to the OMC 28-year-old below. Except here the oak has a firmer grip, making the honey play an even more crucial role. *50.9%.*

⬩ **Fananddel.dk Glen Moray Aged 12 Years** 1st fill oloroso quarter cask, cask no.28B, dist Jan 2008, bott Oct 2020 **(89.5) n22.5** healthy moist fruitcake territory; **t23** a Glen Moray without intense malt being at the heart of the delivery is always a shock to the system. Eventually the probity of the sherry wins through and the midpoint offers a delightful Garibaldi biscuit countenance; **f21.5** more toasted raisin and late bitterness...; **b22.5** it is always a bit of a shock to see Glen Moray in anything but a bourbon cask: that is what blenders demanded it to be in as this distillery was guaranteed to considerably multiply the pure barley feel. Thankfully the oloroso cask is essentially blemish free...but the malt struggles to make its normal impact. An enjoyably fruity experience, though the identity of the distillery is lost. *49.5% sc 135 bottles*

⬩ **The First Editions Glen Moray Aged 23 Years 1996** refill barrel, cask no. 18217, bott 2020 **(92.5) n23** seemingly simplistic malt at first. But slowly your nose acclimatises, and the oak comes into focus, forming wonderful patterns with the barley. Charming...; **t23** so, so wonderful! The malt is a tapestry of delicate honeys and sugars – none heavier than Demerara and heather honey – melting and then reinventing themselves in continuously delightful waves....; **f23** just adore the late grapefruit on the finish, ensuring there is more to this than implied by the malt and oak love in...; **b23.5** so wonderful when whisky gives all the outward appearance of something light and inconsequential, but on closer inspection offers so much.... *55.9%. nc ncf sc. 135 bottles.*

The First Editions Glen Moray Aged 25 Years 1994 refill hogshead, cask no. 16609, bott 2019 **(94) n23.5 t24 f23 b23.5** Another first class offering from the First Editions portfolio. *54.6%. nc ncf sc. 339 bottles.*

⬩ **Old Malt Cask Glen Moray Aged 16 Years** refill barrel, cask no. HL18197, dist Aug 2004, bott Feb 2021 **(87.5) n21.5 t22.5 f21.5 b22** Although the slightly sharp nose promises little, the delivery is an eye-opener...literally! Glen Moray is one of the maltiest whiskies in all Scotland and here it has it in shiels. Magnificently lucid on the palate, though after the brief injection of oils, the finish mirrors the thinness of the nose. *50%. nc ncf sc. 260 bottles.*

⬩ **Old Malt Cask Glen Moray Aged 16 Years** refill barrel, cask no. HL18663, dist May 2005, bott May 2021 **(93) n23** malt breakfast cereal with a little molasses sprinkled on...; **t23.5** silky malt...then the sugars and spices arrive at the same instant to give everything a fabulous, mouth-watering jolt and surge; **f23** heather honey on toast. Has someone peppered it...? **b23.5** a model of malty Speyside respectability. Understated in its excellence. *50% sc 322 bottles*

⬩ **Old Malt Cask Glen Moray Aged 24 Years** refill barrel, cask no. 18200, dist Feb 96, bott Dec 20 **(94.5) n23.5** this is brinkmanship: oak offering as much structure and weight as possible without tipping the scales and no longer allowing the malt to hold sway. A lovely grassiness pervades, sharpened further by a hint of lemon drops; **t23.5** the perfect translation on delivery from the story told on the nose. Lemon drops and concentrated barley hit an exact balance with the oaky spices which buzz from the first moment....and remind you of the vintage. So juicy and fresh despite the passing years; **f23.5** understated but effective oils stretch the barley and the profound juiciness to improbable lengths....; **b24** hard to find a more archetypal Glen Moray at this age than this cask. One of my favourite Speyside distilleries at its most delightful. *50%. nc ncf sc. 185 bottles.*

Old Malt Cask Glen Moray Aged 28 Years refill hogshead, cask no. 16610, dist Oct 91, bott Oct 19 **(90) n22.5 t22 f23 b22.5** Has all the marks of an old timer just about on its last legs, but still capable of one final, elegant hurrah! *50%. nc ncf sc. 270 bottles.*

Scyfion Choice Glen Moray 2007 Areni Noir wine cask finished, bott 2019 **(85) n22 t23.5 f18.5 b21** A malt boasting a sublime delivery as the ripe fruits and spices gang together to let rip. Likewise, the follow-through is an outstanding display of layered fruit candy leading down to a small reservoir of malt. Just a little furry tang on the finale though that turns into gnawing sulphur. *50%. nc ncf sc. 132 bottles.*

Scyfion Choice Glen Moray 2007 Foursquare rum cask finished, bott 2019 **(91.5) n23.5 t23 f22 b23** It is perhaps ironic that the owner of the Foursquare distillery in Barbados shares my slight weariness of cask finishes (in my case because over 25 years I have tasted a disproportionately high number of unimpressive ones) yet here is one of his casks being used to finish a single malt. And, I have to say, doing a good job of it. *46%. nc ncf sc. 97 bottles.*

⬦ **The Whisky Chamber Glen Moray 13 Jahre 2007** bourbon cask **(86.5) n22.5 t22 f20.5 b21.5** By no means a normal Glen Moray: much more burn and attitude to this fella, resulting in sharpness which is almost alien to the distillery. The usual high grade, concentrated malt is there. But hard to find among the foreground noise. *58.3%. sc.*

GLEN ORD
Highlands (Northern), 1838. Diageo. Working.

Glen Ord Aged 12 Years db **(81) n20 t23 f18 b20.** Just when you thought it safe to go back...for a while Diageo ditched the sherry-style Ord. It has returned. Better than some years ago, when it was an unhappy shadow of its once-great self, but without the sparkle of the vaguely-smoked bottling of a year or two back. Nothing wrong with the rich arrival, but the finish is a mess. I'll open the next bottling with trepidation... *43%*

Singleton of Glen Ord 12 Years Old db **(89) n22.5 t22.5 f22 b22** A fabulous improvement on the last bottling I encountered. Still possesses blood oranges to die for, but greatly enhanced by some sublime spices and a magnificent juiciness. *40%*

The Singleton of Glen Ord Aged 15 Years European & American oak casks, bott code: L8038DM003 db **(90.5) n23 t23.5 f21.5 b22.5** The fun of the label on many a bottle of whisky is just how far removed the described tasting notes are to what is actually poured from the bottle. Here, there are no quibbles from me: the promised ginger and chocolate come true! *40%.*

Singleton of Glen Ord 32 Year Old db **(91) n23.5 t23 f22 b22.5.** Delicious. But if ever a malt has screamed out to be at 46%, this is it. *40%*

The Singleton Glen Ord Distillery Exclusive batch no. 01, bott 2019, bott code: L9193DQ0002 db **(95.5) n24.5 t23.5 f23.5 b24** It is unfortunate that the Glen Ord distillery is not the easiest in Scotland to get to. But while they have this bottle in their shops, get plane, boat, go-cart, train, pushbike, helicopter, space hopper, parachute, pogo stick, glider, Harley-Davidson, horse, foot-scooter, paraglider, huskies, jet ski, cannon, roller skates, bobsleigh, canoe, Penny Farthing, Zeppelin, windsurf, camel, sedan, jet propulsion pack, elephant, raft, auto-rickshaw, lawnmower, crutches....absolutely bloody ANYTHING to get you there. Because this is the great Gen Ord unplugged, naked and as beautiful as you'll ever find it. *48%. 6,000 bottles.*

GLENROTHES
Speyside, 1878. Edrington. Working.

The Glenrothes 10 Years Old sherry seasoned oak casks db **(80.5) n19 t22.5 f19 b20** Neither a nose or finish I much care for: tight, a little tangy and out of sync. But I certainly approve the delivery which shows no such constraints and celebrates the voluptuousness of its maltiness. *40%. nc. The Soleo Collection.*

The Glenrothes 12 Years Old sherry seasoned oak casks db **(68) n17 t19 f15 b17** Sulphur addled. *40%. nc. The Soleo Collection.*

The Glenrothes 18 Years Old sherry seasoned oak casks db **(87) n22 t22.5 f21 b21.5** Nutty and hefty, there is always a slight tang to this which slightly reduces the intricate nature of the barley. The off-key finish confirms not all is well, but this being the truly brilliant distillery it is, an inner depth of barley and ulmo honey ensures there always something to treasure from this dram. *43%. nc. The Soleo Collection.*

The Glenrothes 25 Years Old sherry seasoned oak casks db **(86) n23 t22 f19.5 b21.5** The nose is the star turn here, shewing some of the complexity you might demand of a 25-year-old malt. The adroitness of the barley ripe Chinese gooseberry is particularly alluring. But after a surprisingly malt delivery and a volley of pleasant sultana, it is the finish (again) which reveals a furry weak link. *43%. nc. The Soleo Collection.*

The Glenrothes Whisky Maker's Cut first fill sherry seasoned oak casks db **(95) n23.5 t23.5 f24 b24** Unspoiled casks at work. An absolute must for sherry cask lovers. *48.8%. nc. The Soleo Collection.*

Cadenhead's Glenrothes 18 Year Old port cask, dist 2001 **(87.5) n21 t23.5 f21 b22** Having spent the last couple of decades running away from any Glenrothes matured in a wine cask, have to admit I took this whisky on with more than a degree of trepidation. The dry, penurious nose makes you start looking for the hills...when suddenly you are stopped in your tracks by the sheer voluptuousness, the honey-laden generosity of the delivery that makes delicious celebration of the stunning grape. There is little else to cling on to with any warmth after that – perhaps a little salty chocolate and spice maybe. But that delivery...just wow! *53.6%. 246 bottles. Cadenhead Shop Cask Series 2019 Baden.*

Liquid Treasures 10th Anniversary Glenrothes 22 Year Old ex rum barrel, dist 1997, bott 2019 **(90.5) n22 t23 f22.5 b23** A deeply satisfying Glenrothes where the malt, so prevalent on the nose, after the hesitation of a half-a-beat on delivery builds rapidly and in almost bewildering intensity. The rum's contribution is easily recognised by a tightening of the sugars. But the profound juiciness of the malt makes for a dram of sheer fun and the spices ensure a rigorous subtext befitting the richness of the malt itself. Lovely! *59%. sc. 109 bottles.*

◇◇ **Skene Glenrothes 2009 Speyside Scotch Single Malt** American Oak, cask no: 7711, dist: 2009, bott: 2021, db **(92.5) n22.5** grape...grape???? A vaguely oloroso bent to the muscovado sugars and malt; **t23.5** fat, oily cream sherry stye mouth feel. But the tannins burn through with both eloquence and elegance; **f23** just love those warming spices which punch through the oils effortlessly. Toffee raisin and nuts sit beautifully with the elasticated malt; **b23.5** have to say I'm bewildered by this one. For American oak, it certainly enjoys a lot of grapey tones with colouring to match. Either way, rather beautiful whisky to be savoured. *48%, ncf, 388 bottles*

◇◇ **Whisky-Fässle Glenrothes 20 Year Old** sherry butt, dist 1997, bott 2018 **(89.5) n23** both concentrated grape and concentrated oak seemingly diluted by barley sugar. The balance is first-class while the intensity somehow never goes into bullying mode. Once common, a very rare aroma these days days...; **t23** pure silk. Despite the close attention of grape and tannin, still there is barley enough to make for a sweet and juicy lead. The raisin is ripe, but no more than kisses while the oils coat the palate with the drier, oakier tones; **f21** a slight bitterness moves int the picture but the playfulness between the tannins and grape remain; **b22.5** very old school Glenrothes. A wonderful oloroso cask, not quite untainted but far better than most and offers a gloss to the malt that was common when I first tasted Glenrothes over 40 years ago... *48.2% nc ncf*

GLEN SCOTIA
Campbeltown, 1832. Loch Lomond Distillers. Working

Glen Scotia Aged 10 Years Peated first fill bourbon barrels db **(94.5) n24 t23 f23.5 b24** This entire whisky style is a throwback to the very first peated whiskies I tasted 40 years ago. Indeed, anyone still alive and able to remember Glen Garioch when it was heavily peated through its own kilns will raise an eyebrow of happy recognition... One of the greatest Glen Scotias of all time. *46%. nc ncf.*

Glen Scotia 11 Years Old 2006 cask no. 532, dist Dec 06, bott Apr 18 db **(92.5) n22.5 t23.5 f23 b23.5** Absolutely typical Glen Scotia, proudly displaying its rugged charm. *55.6%. sc. 212 bottles. Bottled for The Whisky Shop.*

Glen Scotia Aged 15 Years American oak barrels db **(91.5) n22.5 t23 f23 b23** Great to see this rather special little distillery produce something quite so confident and complete. *46%. ncf.*

Glen Scotia 18 Year Old American oak casks & first fill oloroso casks, bott code: L2/221/17 db **(95) n24 t24 f23 b24** ,y Panama is doffed in grateful thanks for the excellent use of un-sulphured clean sherry butts which give this malt a genuine lustre. And as three dimensional as its sister PX bottling is just one... *51.3%. ncf.*

Glen Scotia Aged 25 Years American oak barrels, bott 2017, bott code: L8/187/17 db **(94) n23.5 t24 f23 b23.5** So beautiful! Truly adorable – and probably a Scotia as you have never quite seen it before. Incredibly rare to find a Scotch single malt so under the thumb of a bourbon character: this must have been filled into very fresh first-fill bourbon barrels to come up with this highly American effect. Trump that! *48.8%. ncf.*

Glen Scotia 45 Year Old db **(96) n24** one of those remarkable whiskies where the oak, revealing the odd grey hair (or is that revelling in...?), appears to be holding off to ensure the salty, exotic (or do I mean erotic...?) fruits are allowed the clearest run...; **t24** immediate oak impact on delivery now. But a little maple syrup mingles with butterscotch and salted butter to ensure special things happen. Towards the mid-point orange blossom honey lands, and then melts in the mouth...; **f23.5** light walnut cake complete with crème fondant; lots of intact barley and lighter red liquorice; **b24.5** outrageously beautiful for its age with not even the hint of a beginning of a crack. Stupendous. 43.8%.

Glen Scotia 1999 refill bourbon barrel, cask no. 455 db **(89) n22.5** a slight salty, grassy note; toffee apple; **t22.5** eye-wateringly fresh barley, but the midground fills with fudge; **f22** soft, linear caramels **b22.5** really extracts every last caramel molecule out of the cask! 60.5%. sc. *Bottled for Glenkeir Whiskies.*

Glen Scotia 2008 Second Shop Bottling db **(84) n22 t21 f21 b20** Too salty and bitter for its own good 56.3%. sc.

Glen Scotia Campbeltown 1832 American oak barrels, finished in Pedro Ximenez sherry casks, bott code: L2 087 18 db **(85.5) n22.5 t22 f20 b21** Yes, pleasant enough I suppose...but so dull! As usual there is a bitterness to a PX finish as any foibles in the oak is exaggerated massively by the sweetness of the grape, which in turn fills in all the natural ridge and furrows of the malt and leaves the flattest of whiskies. The sooner distillers and bottlers get over this PX fad the better... 46%. nc ncf.

Glen Scotia Campbeltown 1832 American oak & Pedro Ximenez sherry casks, bott code: L2.186 19 db **(92.5) n23** suet pudding with extra dose of maple syrup; **t23.5** my word, that PX makes its mark early. But, such a rare thing to find, the malt is brought into play early on, thereby arresting the sweetness but allowing a magnificently beautiful duet to be played by the two main characters; **f23** balances out beautifully as the spices kick start late; **b23** one of the best malts using PX casks on the market today. Elegant and adorable. 46%. ncf.

Glen Scotia Campbeltown Harbour first fill bourbon casks, bott code: 23 10 2018 db **(87) n22 t22 f21.5 b21.5** The best description of Campbeltown and its harbour was provided by 19th century whisky explorer Alfred Barnard. This malt hardly matches the whiskies you would have found of that time, and it doesn't quite match up to how you picture Campbeltown whiskies today, either. For this is very flat and far too caramel dependent, though the mix of saltiness and gentle sweetness is high attractive. The smoke unfurls at the very finish...but for all its easy attractiveness, it is still all a little too docile and tame. 40%.

Glen Scotia Campbeltown Harbour first fill bourbon barrels, bott code: L20.111.20 db **(89.5) n22.5** a thin layer of peat smoke breaks up the monopoly of the citrussy tannin; **t22.5** lovely mouthfeel: soft with a few firming ribs. The malt shines briefly before the lightly spiced tannins take over; **f22** just a little bitterness; **b22.5** it is a very brave move to limit a malt to 100% first-fill bourbon cask, as this appears to have done, and reduce to 40% abv, because building structure and layering is almost next to impossible. Instead you are left with a take it or leave it type malt – though this does have plenty to take! Actually, I am being a little unfair because a degree of depth is supplied by the most delicate smokiness. But the scope remains restricted. 40%.

Glen Scotia Campbeltown Malts Festival 2019 rum cask finish db **(94) n23.5 t23.5 f23 b24** Too often rum casks can tighten a malt to the point of strangulation. Not here. Lively and outstandingly well balanced. 51.3%.

Glen Scotia Campbeltown Malts Festival 2020 Tawny Port Finish Aged 14 Years Peated bott code: L4.078 20 db **(93) n23.5 t23 f23 b23.5** Such fun when a distillery employs cask that are 100% clean and sulphur free. Only then can you create a malt like this with so many hidden doors to discover... 52.8%. nc ncf.

Glen Scotia Double Cask finished in American oak & Pedro Ximenez sherry casks db **(85.5) n22 t22 f20.5 b21.** When blending, I do not like to get too involved with PX casks, unless I know for certain I can shape the effect to further or enrich the storyline on the palate. The reason is that PX means the complexity of a malt can easily come to a sticky end. That has happened here with both the malt and grape cancelling each other out. Soft and easy drinking with an excellent early delivery spike of intensity. But a dull middle and finish. And dull has never been a word I have associated with this distillery. Ever. 46%. ncf.

Glen Scotia Double Cask American oak barrels & PX sherry casks, bott code: L2.092.19 db **(88) n22.5 t23 f20.5 b22** "Rich and Spicy" pronounces the label...and they are not wrong. About as succulent as it gets on delivery and there is a golden magic moment as that spice crashes into the heather honey. Undone slightly, though, by a disappointing finish. 46%. ncf.

Glen Scotia Distillery Edition No. 6 19 Years Old first fill bourbon cask, dist Jul 99, bott Aug 18 db **(95.5) n23.5 t24 f24 b24** One of the most charmingly, disarmingly beautiful single cask malts I have tasted this year. 57.9%. sc. 195 bottles.

Glen Scotia Warehouse Edition 2005 13 Years Old recharred American oak, first fill oloroso sherry finish, dist Sept 05, bott Aug 18 db **(87.5) n21.5 t23 f21 b21.5** Another salty offering which peaks on delivery with a huge malt and muscovado sugar burst. Flattens out thereafter and bitters out, too. 56.2%. sc.

Glen Scotia Victoriana db **(89.5) n23 t23 f21.5 b22** An unusual malt for a cask strength. Beyond the nose there is limited layering, instead concentrating on the malt-toffee intertwangling. 51.5%

Glen Scotia Victoriana Cask Strength bott code: L4.053.19 db **(94.5) n23.5** this has come out as gung-ho crushed hazelnut and barley. The subtlest hint of smoke makes you do a nasal double-take: is it there or not? It is...; **t24** a fizzing display of ultra-lively, salivating tannins – a malt revelling in some sublime American oak. And if that isn't juicy enough, the barley pitches in to up the salivation score even further; **f23** an elegant climb down. Drier, a little spice but some sexy cocoa notes moving towards praline; **b24** as cheerfully bright and breezy a malt as you are likely to find and one bursting with deceptive complexity. If this is trying to depict your average bottle of whisky from Victorian Campbeltown, then it has failed miserably: it was never this good...! 54.2%. nc ncf.

Glen Scotia Vintage 1991 American oak barrels, bott code: L8 092 19 db **(94) n23.5 t24.5 f22.5 b23.5** A very honest malt, brimming with the distillery's endearing character. Whilst tasting this whisky I was deeply saddened to learn of the death of a friend and Whisky Bible devotee, Fran Budd, a warm and charming lady who left us long before she should have done. I raise a glass of this excellent malt and toast your memory, Fran: I suspect you would have approved. 46.7%. nc ncf. Traveller Exclusive.

The Cyprus Whisky Association Glen Scotia 10 Years Old bourbon cask, cask no. 467, dist Sept 08, bott Apr 19 db **(90) n21.5** has this cask been submerged under the ocean waves for the last decade? There are lobster pots with less of a marine aroma...; **t22.5** an early saltiness but, thankfully, not on the same page as the aroma. Soon a well weighted dose of ulmo honey is on hand to give the healthy malt a certain sweet lustre; there is even a degree of juiciness at the midpoint; **f23** long, with the saline content on the rise as the sugars degrees. But still well within bounds, and a little citrus preludes the introduction of the sturdier tannins; **b23** not what I was expecting at all. The saltiest nose of the year by a country mile, or perhaps I should say by many a fathom. But that early coastal feel is tempered on delivery. 53.6%. sc. 240 bottles.

The Perfect Fifth Glen Scotia 1992 cask no. 05917, dist 22 Jan 92 **(94) n23** playful, teasing smoke offers an unlikely sharpness to the already busy barley. For its big age, this malt is alive and kicking; **t23.5** brilliant! Sublime depth to the barley which is at its juiciest and glows as the cocoa notes bring out the best of the light smoke; **f23.5** a bitter-sweet finale with the phenols swirling around and spices a-buzzing. No signs of tiredness at all as the barley still plays a big part while the oak offers both cocoa and a proud skeleton on which all else hangs; **b24** just adore that chocolate and light peat mix. Superb! 45.9%. sc.

GLEN SPEY
Speyside, 1885. Diageo. Working.
Glen Spey Aged 12 Years db **(90) n23 t22 f22 b23** Very similar to the first Glen Spey I can remember in this range, the one before the over-toffeed effort of two years ago. Great to see it back to its more natural, stunningly beautiful self. 43%

◈ **Old Malt Cask Glen Spey Aged 24 Years** refill barrel, cask no. 18198, dist Sept 96, bott Dec 20 **(89.5) n23** almost a fizziness to the lemon-lime coating of the barley. Clean and still a little sharp. Hardly seems possible this is nearly a quarter of a century old, but the oak has worn the sharper edges down just enough; **t23.5** one of those drams which makes you sigh with pleasure as it hits the palate. The weight of the oils and barley are improbably on the money; **f21** a light lemon-sherbet fade, but a little bitterness from the oak undoes a little of the stitching; **b22** rarely found these days, Glen Spey was, a century ago, one of the first malts sold internationally as a singleton to promote the lighter Speyside style. Just the slightest tang on the finale apart, this is a wonderful example of a much underappreciated malt. 46.1%. nc ncf sc. 207 bottles.

GLENTAUCHERS
Speyside, 1898. Chivas Brothers. Working.
Ballantine's The Glentauchers Aged 15 Years Series No.003 traditional oak casks, bott code: LKRM0071 2018/02/13 **(86) n22 t22 f21 b21** Alarm bells ring when confronted by the dull nose with a neutral fruit and caramel edge. When the palate offers something fat and glossy (that's a new one for 'Tauchers) with a dull spice development to accompany the vague fruit and caramel, the heart sinks and flashing lights join the ringing alarm. The big, boring caramel finish drives you to distraction.... If anyone on this planet has championed

Glentauchers longer or louder than me, or with more heart-felt gusto, then I would like to meet them. For well over 20 years I have been telling anyone who cares to listen – and many who don't – that this is one of Scotland's finest distilleries worthy of its own proprietory bottling. It finally arrives, and instead of a malt which scores in the mid-90s, as it should (and so often has done with independent bottlings in Whisky Bibles past), we have before us something pleasant, bland and not instantly recognisable as a 'Tauchers. Frankly, it could be from any Scottish distillery as the blueprint for the nose and flavour profile is shared by many: too many. As I say, pleasant whisky. But, knowing just how good this whisky really is (using 100% bourbon cask, no colour, no chill-filtration) what a huge and crushing disappointment. A bit like going to see the Sistine Chapel and finding someone had whitewashed over it.... 40%.

Deer, Bear & Moose Glentauchers 1996 Aged 20 Years bott 2017 **(89)** n22.5 t22.5 f22 **b22** 'Tauchers in slightly uncharacteristic fizzy mode. The delivery virtually bubbles on arrival, despite the oily carpet of malt which helps set the scene. Indeed, this is the distillery at its most thickset, too, so the taste buds are as much assessing the mouthfeel as the flavour structure which is an unusual place to be with this distillery. Very different! 53.1%. nc ncf. 389 bottles. Flaviar & Friends.

The Great Drams Glentauchers 10 Years Old cask no. 700435, dist 24 Jun 09, bott 1 Oct 19 **(94)** n23.5 a delicious cross between a banana sandwich and egg custard tart; t23.5 it's the enigmatic sweetness on delivery that wins you over: just a light brushing of gristy sugars to help facilitate the drier, spicier tannins that hint of chocolate mint; f23 almost sawdusty as a delicate mocha and vanilla theme lasts longer than might be expected; **b24** comes across as one of those whiskies where the distillery doesn't even seem to try, yet effortlessly conjures up something disarmingly stylish and complex. 48.2%. nc ncf sc.

⬧ **Hepburn's Choice Glentauchers 10 Years Old** wine hogsheads, dist 2010, bott 2020 **(81)** n19.5 t21 f20 **b20.5** Such a shame. 'Tauchers is one of my top three Speyside distilleries. But here its personality has been contorted out of recognition by the bitter, strong-arm tactics of a cask that is ill-suited to the manifest complexities of this distillery. 46%. nc ncf. 581 bottles.

Signatory Vintage Glentauchers 22 Year Old bourbon barrel, cask no. 1404, dist 1996, bott 2018 **(94.5)** n23.5 a whispering nose, lime blossom honey just as delicate as the fragile barley. The tannins show exemplary deportment; t23.5 light strands of ulmo honey break up the far firmer oak. A drier element comes into play quite early on, but the honey always ensures the balance and mouthfeel are top drawer; f23.5 long, distinguished, doggedly malty and with a wonderful caramelised biscuit fade; **b24** a great distillery in here in magnificent shape. 50.7%. sc. Handpicked by Acla da Fans.

⬧ **The Single Cask Glentauchers 2013** oloroso octave finish, cask no. 800465A **(90.5)** n22.5 slightly more tannin available than either of the two PX bottlings. A nipping spice kick and attractive toffee apple; t23 no sooner has the thick grape come flooding over the taste buds but the spices go in for the kill; excellent malty-vanilla subtext; f22.5 anyone with a positive memory of 1970s sherry trifle will remember these fading notes fondly...though not sure if it was this well spiced.; **b22.5** for this malt, spice appears to be the variety of life... 55.2% sc

⬧ **The Single Cask Glentauchers 2013** PX octave finish, cask no. 800465B **(88.5)** n22 t22.5 f22 **b22** Glentauchers in unaccustomed sticky form. The sugars and spices run riot at the kick off after a pleasant if slightly muted 'Tauchers nose. Huge dollops of toffee cling to the roof of the mouth to make for an easy going finale. The best point is the delivery when, for a brief moment, the malt explodes to the fore. 55.7% sc

⬧ **The Single Cask Glentauchers 2013** PX octave finish, cask no. 800465C **(92)** n23 a subtly more forthright nose than its sister bottling with both the sugars and the malts having a far more busy and integrated arrangement: deeply attractive; t23 lively and fresh, perfectly representing the youth of the whisky. The malt takes on a biscuity dimension, which transforms into one dipped into golden syrup...; f22.5 spices make just the right noises to ensure the sugary fruits don't become too complacent; **b23.5** a rather wonderful controlled aggression to this. Sticky with sugars, but big enough barley to ensure balance. 59.4% sc

Whisky Illuminati Glentauchers 2011 Spanish oak sherry butt, cask no. 900364 **(95.5)** n23.5 plum pudding concentrate. The 'Tauchers has vanished under a sea of delectable grape. Spicy, too...; t24 oh, wow...!!! Stupendous oloroso intervention bringing those spices in early to complement the juiciest of molasses tones. At first the malt seems lost, but like the flotsam from an overwhelmed yacht, it floats up again, hanging onto the vanilla from the oak; the mouthfeel is lush throughout and never less than perfection; f24 a brilliant, slow waltz played to the tune of fresh fruit and compliant spices; **b24** just so good to taste the fruits of an unspoiled sherry butt once again...it has happened so rarely in the last 20 years. And housing one of the few distilleries in Speyside that has depth enough to add subtle complexity. 63.4%. sc. 150 bottles.

GLENTURRET

Highlands (Perthshire), 1775. Edrington. Working.

Glenturret Aged 8 Years db **(88)** n21 t22 f23 b22. Technically no prizewinner. But the dexterity of the honey is charming, as this distillery has a tendency sometimes to be. *40%*

The Glenturret Aged 10 Years db **(76)** n19 t18 f20 b19. Lots of trademark honey but some less than impressive contributions from both cask and the stillman. *40%*

The Glenturret Aged 15 Years db **(87)** n21 t22 f22 b22. A beautifully clean, small-still style dram that would have benefitted from being bottled at a fuller strength. A discontinued bottling now: if you see it, it is worth the small investment. *40%*

The Glenturret Fly's 16 Masters Edition db **(96)** n24.5 t24 f23.5 b24.5 When I first found Glenturret some 30 years so ago, their whisky was exceptionally rare – on account of their size and having been closed for a very long time – but the few bottlings they produced had a very distinctive, indeed unique, feel. Then it changed as they used more Highland Distillers sherry butts which were, frankly, the kiss of death. Here, though, we appear to have reverted back to exactly how it tasted half a lifetime ago. Rich, kissed with copper and stirred with honey. It is, as is fitting to old Fly, the dog's bollocks... *44%. 1,740 bottles.*

Glenturret 30 Year Old db **(94)** n23 t24 f23 b24 The ultimate exhibition of brinkmanship, surely: hangs on to its integrity by a cat's whisker... *43.4%.*

Glenturret Peated Drummond db **(87)** n21 t23.5 f21 b21.5 The wide cut from the small still means the odd feint creeps into this one; the peat is too much on the sparse side to paper over the cracks. However, the delivery is something that has to be experienced. A new make freshness can be found all over the show, but even that gives way as the golden syrup and smoke mingle for one of the briefest yet most beautiful star quality moments of the whisky year. *58.9%*

The Glenturret Peated Edition db **(86)** n20.5 t22 f21.5 b22. Pleasant enough, for sure, even if the nose is a bit rough. But in the grand scheme of things, just another peated malt and one of no special distinction. Surely they should concentrate on being Glenturret: there is only one of those.... *43%*

The Glenturret Sherry Edition db **(78)** n19 t21 f19 b19. Not sure if this sherry lark is the best direction for this great distillery to take. *43%*

The Glenturret Triple Wood Edition db **(84)** n20 t22.5 f20 b21.5. Not the happiest of whiskies, but recovers from its obvious wounds by concentrating on the juicy grain, rather than the grape. *43%*

⬧ **Fanandel.dk Ruadh Maor Aged 10 Years Moscatel Quarter Cask** cask no.156A, dist Dec 2009, bott Jul 2020 **(92.5)** n23 the smoke positively billows from the glass and with such a salty nip hat you might be forgiven for mistaking this for passing second world war battleship. The fruit has its place, but is kept is phenolic subservience; t24 battleship did I say...? Make that a destroyer! The delivery goes in all guns blazing and gives you about as much a broadside as can be expected from any 10-year-old. The phenols are not quite uncompromising, but have a huge say in the course this malt takes. But it does allow delightful heather honey and toasted raisin to make a excellent contribution and ramp up the complexity; f22.5 the oils appear to have skuttled ship, meaning the sugars have worn thin and we are left with buzzing spice, distant echoes of peat and relatively little else; b23 just brilliant! A great example of a wine cask genuinely adding rather than subtracting from a peaty encounter. A minor classic, especially for this distillery which appears to be coming back to life quite impressively. *53.8% 178 bottles*

⬧ **The Whisky Chamber Ruadh Maor 9 Jahre 2010** refill PX sherry cask **(89.5)** n23 just brilliant. Really old-fashioned single malt of the age more likely to be seen 30 years ago and with a nip and bite to match. The malts tumbles around while the sherry offers a raged grapiness: this is not slick or sophisticated. Just fabulous, raw fun...; t23.5 ...and this translates immediately onto the palate where there is just the right degree of taciturn nibble to keep the taste buds on their toes; f20.5 a few pigeons – or maybe seagulls – coming home to roost. Evidence of a little sulphur here, which cuts across the late sugars. Busy, but untidy; b22.5 for years the sherry butts at Glenturret meant one thing: sulphur. Having been bought in under the Highland Distillers regime, the sherry bottlings stood no chance. This, however, is another story. Is it a perfect cask? Well, no it does have a little echo at the finish it could do without. But where this malt wins is in its rumbustious nature which old timers like me appreciate. Finish apart, this is old school. And very beautifully made, too. *56.2%. sc.*

GLENUGIE

Highlands (Eastern). 1834–1983. Whitbread. Closed.

Deoch an Doras Glenugie 30 Years Old dist 1980, bott 2011 db **(87)** n22 t23.5 f19.5 b22. It is now 2017 and it has been six long years since this arrived in my tasting room - something I didn't expect to see again: a distillery bottling of Glenugie. Well, technically, anyway, as

Glenugie was part of the Chivas group when it died in the 1980s. As far as I can remember they only brought it out once, either as a seven- or five-year-old. I think that went to Italy, so when I walked around the old site just after it closed, it was a Gordon and MacPhail bottling I drank from and it tasted nothing like this! Just a shame there is a very slight flaw in the sherry butt, but just great to see it in bottle again. *52.13%. nc ncf.*

GLENURY ROYAL
Highlands (Eastern), 1868–1985. Diageo. Demolished.

Glenury Royal 36 Years Old db (89) n21 t23 f22 b23. An undulating dram, hitting highs and lows. The finish, in particular, is impressive: just when it looks on its last legs, it revives delightfully. The whole package, though far from perfect, is pretty astounding. *50.2%*

Gordon & MacPhail Rare Old Glenury Royal 1984 (95.5) n23 t24 f23.5 b25 In the rare instances of the early 1980s I tasted a young Glenury, it was never this good and hardly looked up for 30 years in the cask. But this incredibly rare bottling of the malt, the best I have ever encountered from Glenury and distilled in the final days of its 117 year existence, stands its ground proudly and performs, unforgettably, the Last Post with magical honeyed notes... *46%.*

HAZELBURN *(see Springbank)*

HIGHLAND PARK
Highlands (Island–Orkney), 1795. Edrington. Working.

Highland Park 8 Years Old db (87) n22 t22 f22 b21. A journey back in time for some of us: this is the original distillery bottling of the 70s and 80s, bottles of which are still doing the rounds in obscure Japanese bars and specialist outlets such as the Whisky Exchange. *46%*

Highland Park 10 Year Old Ambassador's Choice db (74) n17.5 t20 f17.5 b19. Some of the casks are so badly sulphured, I'm surprised there hasn't been a diplomatic incident...*46%*

Highland Park Aged 12 Years db (78) n19 t21 f19 b19. Let's just hope that the choice of casks for this bottling was a freak. To be honest, this was one of my favourite whiskies of all time, one of my desert island drams, and I could weep. *40% WB16/048*

Highland Park Aged 15 Years db (85) n21 t22 f21 b21. Had to re-taste this several times, surprised as I was by just how relatively flat this was. A hill of honey forms the early delivery, but then... *40%*

Highland Park Earl Magnus Aged 15 Years 1st edition db (76.5) n20 t21 f17.5 b18. Tight and bitter. *52.6%. 5976 bottles.*

Highland Park Loki Aged 15 Years db (96) n24 t24 f23.5 b24.5 the weirdness of the heather apart, a bit of a trip back in time. A higher smoke ratio than the bottlings of more recent years which new converts to the distillery will be unfamiliar with, but reverting to the levels regularly found in the 1970s and 80s, probably right through to about 1993/94. Which is a very good thing because the secret of the peat at HP was that, as puffed out as it could be in the old days, it never interfered with the overall complexity, other than adding to it. Which is exactly the case here. Beyond excellent! *48.7%. Edrington.*

Highland Park 16 Years Old db (88) n23 t23 f23 f20 b22. I tasted this the day it first came out at one of the Heathrow whisky shops. I thought it a bit flat and uninspiring. This sample, maybe from another bottling, is more impressive and showing true Highland Park colours, the finish apart. *40%. Exclusively available in Duty Free/Travel Retail.*

Highland Park Thor Aged 16 Years db (87.5) n22.5 t23.5 f19 b22.5. Now, from what I remember of my Norse gods, Thor was the God of Thunder. Which is a bit spooky seeing as hailstones are crashing down outside as I write this and lightning is striking overhead. Certainly a whisky built on power. Even taking into account the glitch in one or two of the casks, a dram to be savoured on delivery. *52.1%. 23,000 bottles.*

Highland Park Ice Edition Aged 17 Years db (87) n22 t23 f21 b21. The smoke drifts around until it finds some spices. Frustrating: you expect it to kick on but it stubbornly refuses to. Caramel and vanilla up front, then bitters out. *53.9%.*

Highland Park Aged 18 Years db (95.5) n23.5 t24 f24 b24 If familiarity breeds contempt, then it has yet to happen between myself and HP 18. This is a must-have dram. I show it to ladies the world over to win their hearts, minds and tastebuds when it comes to whisky. And the more time I spend with it, the more I become aware and appreciative of its extraordinary consistency. The very latest bottlings have been astonishing, possibly because colouring has now been dropped, and wisely so. Why in any way reduce what is one of the world's great whisky experiences? Such has been the staggering consistency of this dram I have thought of late of promoting the distillery into the world's top three: only Ardbeg and Buffalo Trace have been bottling whisk(e)y of such quality over a wide range of ages in such metronomic fashion. Anyway, enough: a glass of something honeyed and dazzling calls... *43%*

Highland Park Aged 21 Years db **(82.5)** n20.5 t22 f19 b21. Good news and bad news. The good news is that they appear to have done away with the insane notion of reducing this to 40% abv. The bad news: a sulphured sherry butt has found its way into this bottling. 47.5%

Highland Park Aged 25 Years db **(96)** n24 t24 f24 b24 I am a relieved man: the finest HP 25 for a number of years which displays the distillery's unmistakable fingerprints with a pride bordering on arrogance. One of the most improved bottlings of the year: an emperor of a dram. 48.1%

Highland Park Aged 30 Years db **(90)** n22 t22.5 f23 b22.5 A very dramatic shift from the last bottling I tasted; this has taken a fruitier route. Sheer quality, though. 48.1%

Highland Park 40 Years Old db **(90.5)** n20.5 t22.5 f24 b23.5 Picking splinters from my nose with this one. Some of the casks used here have obviously choked on oak, and I feared the worst. But such is the brilliance of the resilience by being on the money with the honey, you can say only that it has pulled off an amazing feat with the peat. Sheer poetry... 48.3%

Highland Park 50 Years Old dist Jan 60 db **(96.5)** n24.5 t24 f24 b24 Old whiskies tend to react to uncharted territory as far as time in the oak is concerned in quite different ways. This grey beard has certainly given us a new slant. Nothing unique about the nose. But when one is usually confronted with those characteristics on the nose, what follows on the palate moves towards a reasonably predictable path. Not here. Truly unique – as it should be after all this time. 44.8%. sc. 275 bottles.

Highland Park 2002 cask no. 3374-HCF064 db **(96)** n23 t24.5 f24 b24.5 I have always through HP peaked at around 18 in mixed casks rather than 25. This is breathtaking to the point of whisky life changing and revels in its refined, complex sweetness to make a mockery of my theory. The nose apart, this has all the things that makes HP one of the world's great distilleries, and piles it on to an extent it has rarely been witnessed before. Such awesome beauty... 58.4%. sc. Bottled for Loch Fyne Whiskies.

Highland Park 2006 cask no. 2132-HCF067 db **(91)** n22.5 t23 f23 b22.5 You'd be hard pushed to recognise this as an HP unless you were told. Has many of the signature traits, but they don't click into place to create that unique style. An atypical HP, but typically delicious. 67%. sc. Bottled for The W Club.

Highland Park Dark Origins db **(80)** n19 t23 f18 b20. Part of that Dark Origin must be cocoa, as there is an abundance of delicious high grade chocolate here. But the other part is not so much dark as yellow, as sulphur is around on the nose and finish in particular - and does plenty of damage. Genuinely disappointing to see one of the world's greatest distilleries refusing to play to its strengths and putting so much of its weight on its Achilles heel. 46.8%. ncf.

Highland Park Earl Haakon db **(92)** n22.5 t24 f22.5 b23. A fabulous malt offering some of the best individual moments of the year. But appears to run out of steam about two thirds in. 54.9%. 3,300 bottles.

Highland Park Einar db **(90.5)** n23 t23 f22 b22.5 A curious style of HP which shows most of its usual traits but possesses an extra sharpness. 40% WB15/328

Highland Park Freya 1st fill ex-bourbon casks db **(88.5)** n22 t23 f21.5 b22. The majestic honey on delivery makes up for some of the untidier moments. 52.10%.

Highland Park King Christian db **(83.5)** n22.5 t18.5 b20.5. A hefty malt with a massive fruit influence. But struggles for balance and to keep full control of the, ultimately, off-key grapey input. Despite the sub-standard finale, there is much to enjoy with the early malt-fruit battles on delivery that offer a weighty and buttery introduction to the diffused molasses and vanilla. But with the spice arrives the Achilles heel... 46.8%

Highland Park Leif Eriksson bourbon and American oak db **(86)** n22 t22 f21 b21. The usual distillery traits have gone AWOL while all kinds of caramel notes have usurped them. That said, this has to be one of the softest drams you'll find. 40%. Edrington.

Highland Park Ragnavald db **(87.5)** n21.5 t22 f22 b22. Thickest and muscular, this malt offers a slightly different type of earthiness to the usual HP. Even the malt has its moment in the sun. But the overall portrait hangs from the wall at a slight tilt... 45.05%

Highland Park Sigurd db **(96)** n23.5 t24.5 f23.5 b24.5 Breathtaking, star-studded and ridiculously complex reminder that this distillery is capable of serving up some of the best whisky the world can enjoy. 43%

Highland Park Svein db **(87)** n22 t22 f21.5 b21.5. A soft, friendly dram with good spice pick up. But rather too dependent on a tannin-toffee theme. 40% WB15/318

Highland Park Viking Soul Cask 13.5 Years Old 18 month sherry seasoned quarter cask finish, cask no. 700066, bott 2019 db **(88.5)** n22 t23.5 f21 b22 The quarter cask finish is a brave move to make after over 13 years of normality. And the extra oak really does punch through, and not always in a way that feels particularly relaxed or natural. The fruitiness arrives in sugary waves and enjoys a delightful spice flourish. But for an HP, the most rounded of all Scotland's malts, it feels a tad frantic. No faulting the fabulous delivery, though, which appears to have had the cocoa rammed forward with the grape ahead of time... 55.4%. nc ncf sc. 159 bottles. Bottled for MacAlabur.

Artful Dodger Orkney Highland Park 14 Year Old 2004 ex-sherry butt, cask no. 18 **(86.5) n22 t23 f20 b21.5** Less Artful Dodger than Jammy Dodger. The fruit envelops all aspects of this malt – on nose and delivery in particular. Deep vanilla tones hit back, as do the spices, but the dull finish brings an end to an intriguing passage of development. Perhaps by no means the worst sherry butt, but not the best, either. 58.8%. sc.

⁂ **Cadenhead's Cask Strength Highland Park Aged 28 Years** refill butt, dist 1992, bott 2020 **(95) n23.5** by now, after 28 years, the light pettiness of this whisky should be hanging on by a thread. But such is this malt's fragile nature, it is the phenols leading the way. And they have picked up a little eucalyptus along the way to ensure the age is by no means overlooked. The honey of younger casks is missing, though, but compensated for by residual grist. Just so elegant...; **t24.5** ridiculous! Heading for 30-years old and the delivery is salivating. And here's the bonus. That grist apparent on the nose is the first flavour to burst all over the taste buds. Soon followed by a light smearing of honey that was absent from the aroma. By the time you come to terms with the spices you realise it has the lightest touch of peat in its midst; **f23** this is an old school sherry butt with minimum creaking and zero sulphur. The fade has none of the complexity of the delivery and follow-thorough. But, with plenty of vanilla apparent and still the softest peat breeze, it fades in style...; **b24** when you get an HP of this vintage, you hope it will be a used sherry butt at work rather than first fill. It is, and you will be rewarded by seeing HP in its undiluted magnificence. 58.7% Specially bottled for Cadenhead's Whisky Shop Milan

Gordon & MacPhail Connoisseurs Choice Highland Park Aged 30 Years refill sherry butt, cask no. 1089, dist 7 Mar 89, bott 20 Mar 19 **(86) n22 t22.5 f20.5 b21.5** Curious by HP standards – and probably even more curious by G&M's. When this sherry butt was first put into operation it came from a time when the quality of European oak was still very high. But, after the early, attractive vanillas peak, there is an untidy rumble to this, especially on the finish, which when accompanied by the lack of development suggests not all is well with the oak. There is a glossy feel, too, which first works in its favour, seemingly enveloping the lazy honey and vanilla. But then things go slightly askew, the same gloss acts like a shackle, refusing to allow the malt to find an escape route. A very curious HP, indeed. 51.1%. sc. 489 bottles.

The Perfect Fifth Highland Park 1987 cask no. 1531 **(96.5) n24** pretty near perfect HP for its age, and one of the best examples of the distillery of that era I have nosed for a very long time. Slightly above average peat for a HP, which works perfectly in its favour. The usual heather honey has been skewed slightly by the heady mix of tannins and peat. The saltiness is profound, the oak a rich, spicy backbone. The sweetness is subtle and still honeyed, but more now a blend of Manuka and orange blossom. Truly magnificent! **t24** Scotland's silkiest malt at its most silky. The bold smoke on arrival is caught in the velvet gloves of the lightly oiled barley sugar, a dark liquorice sweetness spreading as the oak makes its mark. The spices are prim, proper and just so, never moving out of their set orbit while the honey starts to make its long-awaited mark, bringing with it the light smoke; a quick surge of exotic fruit underlines the antiquity with aplomb; **f24** long, increasingly smoky with the spices still teasing and forging a beautiful duet with the molassed sugars; the oak beats out an aged pulse but the phenols return to soften as well and entertain; **b24.5** this is a malt whisky coming to the end of its life, like a star becomes a white dwarf before the end of its existence. In density is huge...and I mean gigantic. The oaks are about to explode...but the cask has been bottled in the nick of time where the balance is still near perfect. Fine margins...for a very fine whisky... 47.1%. sc.

⁂ **Whisky-Fässle Highland Park 15 Year Old** hogshead, dist 2003, bott 2018 **(90) n23 t22.5 f22 b22.5** One of those rare drams which repays the nosing more than it does to taste. The leaking of the smoke on the aroma is truly sexy...a caress and nibble of your nose buds ahead of bigger, more oafish oakiness. The light honey arrives early on delivery but is always stretched against the tannin. Delicate phenols drift and mend from first to last while the spices giddily hum. 53.3% nc ncf

IMPERIAL

Speyside, 1897. Chivas Brothers. Silent.

Imperial Aged 15 Years "Special Distillery Bottling" db **(69) n17 t18 f17 b17.** At least one very poor cask, hot spirit and overly sweet. Apart from that it's wonderful. 46%

⁂ **Chapter 7 Imperial 1998 Aged 22 Years** bourbon barrel, barrel no.104355 **(88.5) n22 t22 f22.5 b22** Along with Littlemill and others, Imperial holds the distinction of being a malt that was very poor when young, but one that holds a certain elegance in old age. Here we see Imperial at its glassy best: that glassy sheen to the body that, again, Littlemill boasts...

though there is always a little resiny feel to it. With Littlemill that invariably arrives at the end. With Imperial it may arrive at any time. Here it is early. But as that light gluey element dissipates, then the sharp barley intensity becomes deeply attractive. Pretty one dimensional, admittedly – but that's one more than it had in its earlier life... 52.1% sc

◆ **Single & Single Imperial 1995 24 Year Old** American oak (87) n22.5 t22.5 f20 b22 Very typically Imperial in a fine bourbon cask, the oak has laid a excellent foundation for the malt to free itself from the distillery's shackles and really let rip. Sadly, the poor original distillate catches up for a thin, gluey finish. 49.9%. sc. 204 bottles.

The Single Malts of Scotland Marriage Imperial 28 Year Old (80.5) n20.5 t21 f19 b20 For me, this is one of the most fascinating malts I will taste this year, 2020. Because 28 years ago I visited the chilly confines of this distillery quite often – and rarely found a new make that augured well for the future. The fact the distillery closed disappointed but didn't exactly surprise me. Here you can see why. The gluey nose is reminiscent of Littlemill in its last days, the delivery thin and tart. The finish, after it passes through some decent milk chocolate notes, is simply a wreck. This whisky may have soul, but there is no body...and that is why the blenders decided enough was enough. Usually the passing of three decades – or thereabouts – brings redemption to a failed distillery, Littlemill again being a case in point. Not here though. To be sampled simply as a whisky life experience rather than the expectation of great, or even particularly good, whisky. 40.88%.

INCHGOWER

Speyside, 1872. Diageo. Working.

Inchgower 27 Year Old db (93) n22.5 t24 f23 b23.5 Delicious and entertaining. Doesn't try to play the elegant old malt card. Instead gets stuck in with a rip-roaring attack on delivery, the fizzing spices burning deep and making the most of the light liquorice and molasses which has formed a thick-set partnership with the intense malt. The only hint of subtlety arrives towards the death as a little butterscotch tart allows a late juiciness from the barley free reign. Just love it! 43%. 8,544 bottles. Diageo Special Releases 2018.

Deer, Bear & Moose Inchgower Aged 22 Years dist Sept 95, bott Dec 17 (94.5) n23 t24 f23.5 b24 Inchgower in prime Jekyll and Hyde mode, at first the juicy, swashbuckling fruit pointing towards a malt half its age. Then, fascinatingly, a wave of tannins sweeps in bringing with it a salty, mildly earthy depth, as well as major spices... and suddenly the malt looks every bit its years. The layering on delivery is worth savouring, as it really relishes the old school griminess for a minute or two before moving into a sweeter marzipan richness with a seasidey saltiness burning into the piece. You never know what you are going to get from this distillery. But this is one of the most complete and complex versions for quite a while. A wonderful surprise. 52.1%. nc ncf sc. Flaviar & Friends.

◆ **The First Editions Inchgower Aged 23 Years 1997** sherry butt, cask no. 18208, bott 2020 (89.5) n22.5 the molasses which could be picked up on its sister cask 18203 here makes its mark much earlier, this time on the nose. Indeed, there is almost a touch if rum to this one...; t22.5 fat, chewy and just a slight rumbling of something grapey to keep the spices company; just enough malt to fire up the salivation levels; f22 the oak leaks though to give you a sense of decent age for the first time; b22.5 a fuller, more characterful version of cask 18203...dare I say it: a little more like the old, traditional style! 55.6%. nc ncf sc. 264 bottles.

◆ **Kingbury Gold Inchgower 20 Year Old** hogshead, dist 2000, cask no. 2 (92.5) n23 the peppers and no less tingling crisp barley offers great balance. The light puff of anthracite is just so right...; t23 for a 20-year-old malt, this still offers wonderful energy and vivacity to the barley in particular. There is also a light apple and muscovado chirrup to this, the weight increasing exponentially as the oak gets a toehold; f23 a lovely biscuity dryness is met my light mocha; b23.5 Inchgower making a point of showing its considerable character. A must try bottling. 47.8% sc 209 bottles

Old Malt Cask Inchgower Aged 11 Years Firkin cask, cask no. 16749, dist Jan 08, bott Mar 19 (90.5) n22.5 the usual distillery heft and trademark untidiness, but with a dab of liquorice and chicory to beguile; t23 huge! The weight is considerable and the molasses profound. A chewing whisky of the highest order: lush, oily, and with ever deepening degrees of vanilla and dark sugars; f22 slightly tangy, but a dollop of chocolate goes a long way to make amends; b23 Firkin unbelievable: Inchgower at its most intense and startling. 50%. nc ncf sc. 59 bottles.

◆ **Old Malt Cask Inchgower Aged 23 Years** sherry butt, cask no. 18203, dist Aug 97, bott Nov 20 (88.5) n22 t22 f22 b22.5 For an Inchgower, this is a remarkably straightforward cove. Had I been tasting a 23-year-old Inchgower 23 years ago, my tastebuds would have been led merry dance as the oilier notes build up and thickened. A generation on, so to speak, we have a lighter, cleaner malt now, still with a little grime for old time's sake on the nose. But the clarity of the malt on the palate here, aided and abetted by the molasses through the middle keeps a little of the weight but a far brighter, enjoyable, better-balanced experience than of old. *50%. nc ncf sc. 294 bottles.*

INVERLEVEN
Lowland, 1938–1991. Demolished.

Deoch an Doras Inverleven 36 Years Old dist 1973 **(94.5) n24 t23.5 f23 b24** As light on the palate as a morning mist. This distillery just wasn't designed to make a malt of this antiquity, yet this is to the manor born. *48.85%. nc ncf. Chivas Brothers. 500 bottles.*

Gordon & MacPhail Private Collection Inverleven 1985 refill bourbon barrel, cask no. 562, bott 2018 **(96.5) n24 t24.5 f23.5 b24.5** I am still haunted by the day Inverleven distilled for the very last time, their manager telling me: "That's it, Jim. We're done." It was another shocking event: a great Lowland distillery which made a very consistent, malty, mildly fragile make and was absolutely excellent for blenders at about 5 years in decent second fill bourbons, and even better in firsts; and quite magnificent at about 8 years in both. Of course, the demise of Inverleven was the foretelling of the eventual closure of the unbettered Dumbarton grain distillery in which the malt complex was housed. But these were acts of whisky vandalism by a company, Allied Domecq, which never could get it right with the management of their single malts. This delicate and noble malt is a rare testimony to a distillery lost for all the wrong reasons. There is not a bum note, not a blemish. It is Lowland perfection and a whisky tragedy all rolled into one. *57.4%. 130 bottles.*

ISLE OF ARRAN
Highlands (Island–Arran), 1995. Isle of Arran Distillers. Working.

Isle of Arran Machrie Moor 5ᵗʰ Edition bott 2014 db **(91.5) n22.5 t24 f22 b23** A few tired old bourbon barrels have taken the score down slightly on last year. But the spirit itself is nothing short of brilliant. *46% WB16/049*

The Arran Malt 10 Year Old db **(87) n22.5 t22.5 f20 b22.** It has been a while since I last officially tasted this. If they are wiling to accept some friendly advice, I think the blenders should tone down on raising any fruit profile and concentrate on the malt, which is amongst the best in the business. *46%. nc ncf.*

The Arran Malt 12 Years Old db **(85) n21.5 t22 f20.5 b21** Hmmmm. Surprise one, this. There must be more than one bottling already of this. The first I tasted was perhaps slightly on the oaky side but otherwise intact and salt-honeyed where need be. This one has a bit of a tang: very drinkable, but definitely a less than brilliant cask around. *46%*

The Arran Malt Aged 14 Years db **(89.5) n22 t23.5 f21.5 b22.5.** A superb whisky, but the evidence that there has been a subtle shift in emphasis, with the oak now taking too keen an interest, is easily attained. *46%. ncf.*

The Arran Malt Aged 17 Years db **(91.5) n23.5 t23.5 f21.5 b23** "Matured in the finest ex-Sherry casks" trills the back label. And, by and large, they are right. Maybe a single less than finest imparts the light furriness to the finish. But by present day sherry butt standards, a pretty outstanding effort. *46%. nc ncf. 9000 bottles. WB15/152*

The Arran Malt Fino Sherry Cask Finish db **(82.5) n21 t20 f21 b20.5.** Pretty tight with the bitterness not being properly compensated for. *50%*

Acla Selection Island Edition Isle of Arran 22 Year Old hogshead, dist 1996, bott 2019 **(86.5) n22 t22 f21 b21.5** Punches slightly heavier than its strength and while the light heather honey tones impress, a dry, vaguely bitter, flourish to the oak detracts somewhat and closes down the conversation. *48.3%.*

Berry Bros & Rudd Arran 21 Years Old cask no. 370, dist 1996, bott 2018 **(96.5) n24 t24 f24 b24.5.** When my dear old friend Harold Currie built this distillery in the mid-1990s he wanted the spirit to be as close in style to Macallan as he could get it. So, when I selected the very first cuts for the very first distillation, it was Harold's wish I had I mind. This bottling was almost certainly made to the cutting points I chose and my only sadness is that Harold is no longer with us to enjoy his malt whisky coming of age. Though this is probably not from oloroso (or if it was, it was so old that very restrained fruit is imparted) – and that is just as well, as most early oloroso butts from the distillery are poor quality – it certainly matches the profile of Macallan of the same age matured in top end second fill bourbon. This is, unquestionably one of the single malt bottlings of the year. *46.4%. nc ncf sc.*

Cask 88 Isle of Arran 22 Year Old dist 1997 **(73) n19 t20 f16 b18** When a whisky turns up this colour (brown with a green tinge) in the lab you usually give it a very suspicious once-over. And here you'd have done it with good reason. *42.4%.*

Golden Cask Arran Aged 21 Years cask no. CM240, dist 1996, bott 2017 **(94.5) n23.5 t24 f23 b24** Impeccable Arran. *51.6%. sc. 254 bottles.*

◇◇ **MacAlabur Isle of Arran 10 Year Old** peated, first fill bourbon barrel, cask no.09/060, dist Sep 2009, bott Jan 2020 **(94) n23.5** the light drift of mint accompanies the peat like a private eye might shadow his quarry. The barley nips and snaps occasionally; **t24** near perfect weight and mouth feel, the barley still having big thrust that salivates wonderfully. The sugars are initially a succession of crisp muscovado notes, helped long with warmer heather honey. The smoke caresses rather than consumes; **f23** excellent length with now spot on tannin presence giving a controlled, biscuity dryness to accompany the long oils and delicate, very lightly spiced smoke; **b23.5** when you get near distilled malt in a very fine cask there can be only one outcome. Curiously, exactly 25 years ago this week I sat Wembley Stadium with Arran's first-ever distillery manager Gordon Mitchell in the seat beside me, as we watched England beat Scotland 2-0 in the European Championships and, together, marvelled at Paul Gascoigne's legendary goal, our feelings at opposing poles. A few days ago an England team which performs better on its knees than its feet met at the same (updated) venue in the same competition for a joyless 0-0 bore draw. A quarter of a century ago Arran's then Chairman and founder, Harold Currie, also had huge football connections, having once been Scottish League St Mirran's Chairman and gave Alex Ferguson his first-ever senior managing position. When the distillery was being built, I suggested to Harold that he might want to take a peaty route, but his mind was set: "I want it to be as close to Macallan as we can get it. I really don't want it to be Islay style, even if we are on an island." And that was that. I know Gordon wouldn't have minded it being, for at least a few mashes a year, a peated malt. Instead he said. "Well, Jim we'll just have to be content that we get a little bit of peat off the water that runs off Loch na Davy" It is curious that as I watched England pathetic, passionless attempt against Scotland, my mind wondered back to those conversations, not least because neither Gordon Mitchell or Harold Currie are with us now. And then, just a day or two later, I found this waiting for me in my tasting lab. It is excellent. As a 10-year-old I think even the great Harold Currie would be impressed with the elegant touch of the peat. *55.8% 241 bottles*

Single Cask Collection Arran 21 Years Old Platin Edition sherry edition **(88.5) n22.5 t22.5 f21.5 b22** A mainly clean sherry butt doles out the fruit. *51%. sc.*

W.W. Club AR.1 Arran Aged 11 Years American oak cask, cask no. 19, dist Oct 05, bott Feb 17 **(86.5) n21.5 t22.5 f21 b21.5** Plenty of rich, creamy honey on delivery. And no little succulent malt, too. But a little too much tang towards the finish, confirming a quaver on the nose. *57.7%. sc. 321 bottles. William & Co. Spirits.*

ISLE OF JURA
Highlands (Island–Jura), 1810. Whyte and Mackay. Working.

Isle Of Jura Aged 10 Years db **(79.5) n19 t22 f19 b19.5.** Perhaps a little livelier than before, but still miles short of where you might hope it to be. *40%*

Jura Aged 10 Years American white oak bourbon barrels, aged Oloroso sherry butts, bott code: L0143 07 59 P/012028 db **(89.5) n22.5** soft malt, sweet and a little lemon sherbet; **t22** follows the nose by taking the softie route...only here goes into ultra-soft mode. Perhaps a little too much sweetness and caramel early on, but as that clears a light vanilla and raisin combination filters through; **f22.5** decidedly toasty and dry. A little light molasses helps balance things; **b22.5** the best part of 40 years ago I used to travel annually to Jura and stop at the hotel, the owner of which also being a director of the distillery next door. And every year I would bring back one of his hotel bottlings, complete with its label portraying a stag, usually ex-bourbon and sweet as a nut. It would be great if they could revert more towards a bottling which shewed the character of the distillery as starkly as that old hotel bottling did, as this appears to be hiding a great many things. That said, a more enjoyable Jura 10 than in the recent past: definitely on the up and worth watching. *40%*

Jura Aged 12 Years American white oak ex-bourbon barrels, aged Oloroso sherry cask finish, bott code: L80205 00:43 P/005956 db **(87.5) n22.5 t23 f20.5 b21.5** For the most part, this is an artful malt proudly portraying its coastal origins, with a sharp, malty saltiness creeping onto the nose and delivery in very respectable proportions. The mouthfeel is also a delight on entry, as is the rich chocolate fruit and nut middle. Just a shame that a rogue sherry cask has leaked some of the dreaded S element into the mix, which builds into a furry bitterness at the death. Mid Europeans devoid of the sulphur gene will devour this with joy. So much else to enjoy, though, especially that juicy delivery. I look forward to seeing the next bottling... *40%*

Isle Of Jura Aged 16 Years db **(90.5) n21.5 t23.5 f23 b23** A massive improvement, this time celebrating its salty, earthy heritage to good effect. The odd strange, less than harmonious note. But by far and away the most improved Jura for a long, long while. *40%*

Jura Aged 18 Years American white oak ex-bourbon barrels and red wine casks, bott code: L0006 13:36 P/011235 db **(85.5) n21.5 t23.5 f19 b21.5** Although the nose is tight, almost mean, in its persona you are let half-fearing the worst, but wondering for the best. There is an outlandish outbreak of massive flavour on delivery, both the malt and fruit almost shrill in their proclamations of their intent. This is high juiciness in excelsis, the sugars crisp and full of grist and

Demerara. And on the finish a slight chocolate note hovers, but then a degree of sulphur drifts in...as threatened by the nose. It is so frustrating when wine casks have needlessly and fatally been given the sulphur candle treatment. This has so many beautiful moments. But... 44%.

Jura Aged 21 Years Tide American white oak ex-bourbon barrels & virgin American oak casks db (**94**) n23 t23.5 f23.5 b24 Not for the first time, caramel plays a big part in a Jura. But here to appears to be better weighted and structured thanks to greater tannin involvement. Pleasingly and impressively complex. 46.7%.

Jura Aged 21 Years Time American white oak ex-bourbon barrels & ex-peated malt casks db (**92**) n23.5 the playful spice tweaks both your nose and that of the chunky tannin; the phenols offer an attractive deep base note; t23.5 crystalised brown sugars formulate from the off, the tannins having a big say in matters. But it is those wisps of smoke that add structure and balance, seemingly tying together the crisper sweet notes and the earthier oakiness. Spices ping around with abandon; f22 digestive biscuit dipped in mocha; b23 alongside Tide, great to see Jura back offering us something that intrigues: a bit like the first Jura I ever tasted – on the island's hotel - nearly 40 years ago... 47.2%.

Jura 1988 bott 2019 db (**91.5**) n22 t23 f23 b23.5 So unusually clean I wondered if this was a wine cask, almost certainly port, at work or just Demerara sugars off the oak working at their ultimate fruitiness. Or, most likely, both! 52.8%. nc ncf. 1,500 bottles.

Jura 1989 American white oak ex-bourbon barrels, bott 2019 db (**83.5**) n21 t22.5 f19 b21 None of the glitz and little of the balance displayed by the Two-One-Two, below. Not the most enticing of noses , though the piece rallies briefly on delivery as the intense malt is steered into position by excellent spice. Then it all unravels... 53.5%. nc ncf.

Jura One and All Aged 20 Years db (**83.5**) n21 t22 f19.5 b21 A metallic tang to this. Nutty with tart, fruity borders but nothing to get excited about. Doesn't quite add up. 51%. nc ncf.

Jura One For The Road Aged 22 Years Pinot Noir finish db (**89**) n23 t23 f21 b22 Enjoyable though ultimately a bit too straight and, just like the single road on Jura, goes nowhere... 47%. nc ncf.

Jura One For You db (**87.5**) n22 t22.5 f21.5 b21.5 A straight up and down maltfest with a vaguely salty edge. Very pleasant in its own limited way, but don't spend too much time looking for complexity. 52.5%. nc ncf.

Jura Prophecy profoundly peated db (**90.5**) n23.5 t23 f22 b22 Youthful, well made and I prophesy this will be one of Jura's top scorers of 2011... 46%

Jura Special Wood Series French Oak American white oak bourbon barrels, French oak cask finish, bott code: L9108 02:36 P/008522 db (**89**) n22.5 the French oak appears to have brought with it French heather honey – Bruyère – to smarten this up and give the spices something to bounce against; t23 soft delivery with an immediate malty charge. The honey also slowly materialises, though the tannins appear to have a little of the devil about them; f21.5 just a tad untidy here and bitter. But the honey has made way for molasses; b22 so much to enjoy here, but feel this is understrength for what it is trying to achieve, the oils breaking down too quickly and making the transition at the end a little too rugged. But a full-flavoured Jura as you have never quite seen her before! 42%.

Jura Superstition db (**73.5**) n17 t19 f18 b18.5. I thought this could only improve. I was wrong. One to superstitiously avoid. 43%

Jura Turas-Mara db (**82.5**) n20.5 t22 f19 b21. Some irresistible Jaffa Cake moments. 42%.

Jura Two-One-Two American white oak ex-bourbon barrels db (**90.5**) n23 the tannins are embroidered neatly into the lush, citrus-tinged barley; t22.5 busy on delivery – and even busier as the spices make their mark; again the oak holds all the cards and dictates, but the hickory and muscovado sugars work well together; f22 just bitters vaguely on the fade; b23 lets the tannins do the talking. And if anyone is buying this from a bar, say you'll have one, too... 47.5%. 6,000 bottles.

Chapter 7 Jura 21 Year Old 1998 bourbon hogshead, cask no. 2144, dist Sept 98, bott Mar 20 (**87**) n22 t22.5 f21 b21.5 A first-rate bourbon cask goes a long way to seriously upping the complexity levels on this and ensuring a glorious honey theme throughout. The malt possesses a distinct nutty note from a distillate that isn't technically where it should be. 55.1%. sc. 284 bottles.

◈ **The First Editions Jura Aged 14 Years 2007** sherry butt, cask no.HL18376, bott 2021 (**93**) n23.5 underripe gooseberry topped by a little spiced custard; t23.5 forget the sherry butt: it is the malt which gathers in force for the most wonderful butterscotch tart...again with gooseberry topping. Better still is the mouth feel which is lush and quite faultless. The spices build up a head of steam...; f23 ....which continue to the sweet end. A little mocha and vanilla towards the finish as the fruit vanishes; b24 a pleasing, beautifully rounded bottling with a surprise gooseberry kick. Highly attractive and about as good as one might expect from this distillery. I'd say that this is as marvellous and inspirational as the very Paps of Jura, but I'd probably be denounced as sexist by some Woke thickie... 50.1% nc ncf sc 495 bottles

◇◇ **The First Editions Isle of Jura Aged 22 Years 1998** refill barrel, cask no. 18216, bott 2020 **(88) n22 t22.5 f21.5 b22** Jura at its most malty, even going flat out on the barley sugar front until the bitterish oak brings a halt to the sweetness. The midground is distinctly buttery. Late spice props up a slightly disappointing finish. But, overall, a very pleasant experience and rare to find Jura this malt intense. *56.3%. nc ncf sc. 166 bottles.*

◇◇ **Valour Highland Single Malt Jura Aged 30 Years** bourbon hogshead, cask no. 5278, dist Oct 1990, bott Dec 2020 **(92) n23.5** a surprising if barely detectable waft of peat flits over the honey-sharpened, lightly grassy malt for a memorable hello. For a Jura, this is slightly out of its normal territory, especially from ex-bourbon. This is crisp and means business: the usual wishy-washy self-doubt that is the norm from this distillery is markedly absent...; **t23** such crispness on the nose is short-hand for a salivating delivery. And, guess what....? However, once that mix of granular acacia honey and intense barley has done its thing, the encroaching vanilla-rich tannins are unable to match their assuredness..; **f22** a little bit of an untidy finish at first. But as the light molasses stirs and a hint of heather honey drops in, the spices are back in harness and the gathering bitterness is kept in check. Still, there is a tang at the finish, which I had more than half expected before starting...; **b23** now this took a hell of a long time to taste. Nearly an hour. Which shews that this is a malt of astonishing character. Not all of it great, admittedly. But most of it both beguiling and quietly wonderful. *43.3% nc sc 211 bottles*

KILCHOMAN

Islay, 2005. Kilchoman Distillery Co. Working.

Kilchoman 10 Years Old cask no. 150/2007, dist 20 Jul 07, bott 11 Jun 18 db **(96) n24 t24 f23.5 b24.5** Has controlled the oils beautifully. Class in a glass. *56.5%. sc. 238 bottles. Bottled for The Whisky Shop.*

Kilchoman 10 Years Old 100% Islay cask no. 84/2008, dist 6 Mar 08, bott 19 Mar 18 db **(91) n23.5 t23 f22 b22.5** Such is the high class of Kilchomen, even an exceptionally good malt on the whisky stage is not quite up to the distillery's normal performance. Not a bad place to be... *53.2%. sc. 239 bottles. Bottled for Loch Fyne Whiskies.*

Kilchoman 12 Years Old bourbon cask, cask no. 36/2006, dist 4 May 06, bott 21 Jun 18 db **(93.5) n23.5 t23.5 f23 b23.5** High grade malt taking a slightly different course from this distillery's normal style. *56.9%. sc. 228 bottles. Bottled for Loch Fyne Whiskies.*

Kilchoman Private Cask Release bourbon cask, cask no. 431/2007, dist 13 Dec 07, bott 26 Feb 18 db **(96.5) n24.5 t24 f24 b24.5** Someone fell on their feet when they bought this cask: holy crap, this is seriously good whisky! *57.2%. sc. Bottled exclusively for The Whisky Club.*

KINCLAITH

Lowlands, 1957–1975. Closed. Dismantled.

Mo Ôr Collection Kinclaith 1969 41 Years Old first fill bourbon hogshead, cask no. 301453A, dist 28 May 69, bott 29 Oct 10 **(85.5) n22 t22 f20.5 b21.** Hangs on gamely to the last vestiges of life, though the oak, without being overtly aggressive, is squeezing all the breath of out of it. *46%. nc ncf sc. Release No. 2. The Whisky Talker. 164 bottles.*

KINGSBARNS

Lowland, 2014. Wemyss. Working.

Kingsbarns Dream to Dram db **(94) n23.5** a mix of youthful charm and more relaxed maturity gives the malt a nuanced appeal. But the barley is so rich, you feel that you have just picked it from a field, dank after a late summer rain, and crushed it in your hands, even before malting. Green and clean; **t24** salivating, but not in the sharp way I was expecting from the nose. Instead a mashing of icing sugars and fresh barley mix with the light oils from the distillate to provide a seemingly simple and beautifully effacing feal. But as you concentrate, you realise so much good is happening in there; **f23** just a little tanginess as the casks and grain have not quite managed to align quite to perfection. But still no faulting the vanilla and barley fade; **b23.5** just too ridiculously good for a new distillery. The malt really does make this a Dram of Dreams, too. And if this were not a single malt, blenders would be falling over themselves to use as top dressing in a blend. So simple. Yet sublime. *46%.*

Kingsbarns Founder's Reserve #1 American oak bourbon barrel, dist 2015, bott 2018 db **(93.5) n23.5** no age. But, my word! The intensity of the barley is startling and there is tannin enough to ensure this is no one horse race; **t23.5** only excellent American oak can galvanise malt in this way, helping it to really ratchet up the intensity, so there is a stunning purity to help settle the semi-hidden sharp, metallic notes of a new still at work, **f23** long with very beautifully judged oils from an excellent cut. The oak has grace enough to add a little vanilla and custard without taking away from the naked charm of the barley itself; **b23.5** you really can't ask for much more from a three-year-old malt. There are no new makey signs here, though there is always the feel of a little youthful exuberance. Superbly distilled and excellently matured. And enough muscle around the spice to suggest this could have matured for a great many more years. A fledgling distillery heading in the right direction and certainly one to watch. And a perfect choice for the Whisky Bible 2021's 1,200th whisky of the year... 62.1%.

Kingsbarns Founder's Reserve #2 STR barriques, dist 2016, bott 2019 db (**93**) **n23.5** there is a buzz from the barrique: a nose-pinching, fruit-clipped spice which for a while distracts you from the beautifully distilled firmness of the malt. Even the lightest phenol drifts around...; **t23.5** eye-wateringly sharp work from the STRs which gang up and punch your taste buds into submission. The barley then flies forth with a volley of its own, but can't entirely make itself heard above the impact of the barriques; **f23** fruit chocolate with barley sugar and vanilla; **b23** as usual the STRs force their somewhat inelegant, abrasive but mouth-filling will on the whisky. Never match a great bourbon cask for sheer panache and heart-winning charm, but sometimes, like here, for eye-watering effect they have no equal. Oh, here's a little trick for you I have been carrying out for the last decade or so: to get the full flavour from STR-matured malt, leave in a tasting glass for three or four days with a watch lid over the top. This softens the whisky into a much more sensual dram and the malt – and therefore the base characteristic of the distillate - has a far bigger say in proceedings. If you add water very slightly to reduce strength and leave, you don't get anything like the same results or complexity. Try it. But as for this bottling... Wow! What fun! And such high class, too... 61.1%.

KNOCKANDO
Speyside, 1898. Diageo. Working.

Knockando Aged 12 Years bott code: L7229CM000 db (**82**) **n20 t22.5 f19 b20.5** My dear, late friend and mentor Jim Milne was for a very long time J&B blender and for decades this malt came under his clever jurisdiction. It was Jim who persuaded me, over a quarter of a century ago now, to publish my views on whisky, something I felt I was underqualified to do. He vehemently disagreed, so I took his advice and the rest, as they say, is history. I knew Jim's work intimately, so I know he would not be happy with his beloved Knockando in this incarnation. His Knockando was dry, making the most of the interaction between bourbon cask and delicate malt. This is sweet and, worse still, sulphur tarnished by the sherry: I doubt he would ever let grape get this kind of grip, thus negating the distillery's fragile style. Some lovely moments here for sure. But just too fleeting. 43%.

Knockando Aged 18 Years dist 1998, bott code: L9038CM001 db (**94**) **n23.5** malt. To the power of malt...; **t24** this barley boasts a malty intensity that is rare to match in pure atomic mass. Dense, intense, sharp, full...just sheer barley...concentrated...; **f23** still juicy to the end. Malty and spicy fade...; **b23.5** nowhere near the charm and complexity of the 21-year-old. But, my word! This has a malt intensity that is hard to match elsewhere. However, at this age you expect the casks to making a difference. But, no. The malt is in total control. Beautiful for sure. But nowhere near the overall complexity and joy of the 21-y-o... 43%.

Knockando Aged 21 Years Master Reserve dist 1994, bott code: L9081CM001 db (**96.5**) **n24** this is how a Speyside at this age should be: the malt is firm yet lively enough to allow the sugars a controlled, crystalline attachment; **t24** almost beautiful enough to bring a tear to my eye. My mentor, longtime Knockando blender Jim Milne, adored fresh, juicy barley at full salivation (a la...Glen Spey) ...and he particularly appreciated the solemnity and gravitas of the Knockando malt. This appears to have both. The salivation levels are something to be almost astonished at; **f24** the malt rumbles on with a high degree of class and continued salivation in the way that it attaches to the oaky vanillas without demur. But then moves into a richer, more chocolate infested world, the barley never for a moment straying from the path, the spices never for amount raising a voice above a soft grrrr...; **b24.5** some 30 years ago I was on the original J&B training team and Knockando (I think as a 12-year-old) was used in the programme, where I would compare this against the peated malts of Islay. The Knockando I had known and worked with for many years was a bone-crushingly dry dram. Though older, this is alive and fresh. And, frankly, a delightful surprise. The 25-year-old, those three decades ago, had far more tannin per annum spent in cask in its make up and even drier...though I remember marching my students from the Craigellachie Hotel to the River Spey as the mid-summer solstice sun was rising to drink the whisky beside the fast-running waters with which it was rightfully associated. I still get letters and emails from those who experience that spectacular awakening of the whisky spirit in our souls to this very day... This is a much fresher incarnation of that reverential aged malt of the late 1980s and early '90s. And, I have to say...a little bit better,... Indeed, I am soon to embark on my 1,100th whisky of the 2021 Bible. And I cannot think of a better, more complete, single malt so far... 100% sulphur free..100% barley rich... 100% a treasure... 43%.

Knockando 1990 db (**83**) **n21 t22 f20 b20.** The most fruity Knockando I've come across with some attractive salty notes. Dry, but a little extra malty sweetness these days. 40%

KNOCKDHU
Speyside, 1894. Inver House Distillers. Working.

AnCnoc 12 Year Old db **(94.5) n24 t23 f23.5 b24.5** A more complete or confident Speyside-style malt you are unlikely to find. Shimmers with everything that is great about Scotch whisky... always a reliable dram, but this is stupendous. 40%

anCnoc 12 Years Old bott code: L19/051 R19/5082 IB db **(94) n23.5** green banana and lucid barley. Spices flicker and glimmer...; **t23.5** teeming barley, layered in both sweetness and intensity: there is a chewy fatness containing the juicier sugars, then a more gristy side mingling with the spice; **f23** malty to a fault, just a little duller than of yore. Heavier caramels mingle with the slightly bitter tannins; **b24** remains one of the truly beautiful, largely undiscovered great malts of Scotland. At 46% and with other minor technical adjustments, this could be a major award winner... 40%.

AnCnoc 16 Years Old db **(91.5) n22 t23.5 f23 b23** Unquestionably the spiciest AnCnoc of all time. Has this distillery been moved to the coast..? 46%

AnCnoc 18 Years Old db **(88.5) n22.5 t23 f21 b22** Cleaner sherry at work here. But again, the contours of the malt have been flattened out badly. 46%. nc ncf.

anCnoc 18 Years Old bott code: L19/052 R19/5084 IB db **(85) n22 t22 f20 b21** Even one sherry butt containing sulphur in a malt as delicate as anCnoc has consequences. And these can be found on the light furry nibble on the tongue towards the end. A shame, as I had selected this as sample number 1,100 on my home-straight for the 2021 Bible. Has plenty of its old zest and brilliance, for those biologically unable to detect sulphur. 46%

AnCnoc 22 Year Old db **(87) n22 t21.5 f22 b21.5.** Often a malt which blossoms before being a teenager, as does the fruits of Knockdhu; struggles to cope comfortably with the inevitable oakiness of old age. Here is such a case. 46%. Inverhouse Distillers.

AnCnoc 24 Years Old db **(94) n23 t24.5 f22.5 b24** Big, broad-shouldered malt which carries a lot of weight but hardly veers away from the massively fruity path. For sherry loving whisky drinkers everywhere... 46%. nc ncf.

AnCnoc 30 Years Old db **(85) n21 t23 f19 b22.** Seat-of-the-pants whisky that is just on the turn. Still has a twinkle in the eye, though. 49%

AnCnoc 35 Years Old bourbon and sherry casks db **(88) n22.5t22 f21.5 b22.** The usual big barley sheen has dulled with time here. Some attractive cocoa notes do compensate. 44.3%. nc ncf.

AnCnoc 1999 db **(95.5) n24 t24 f23.5 b24** I noticed as I was putting the bottle away that on their back label their description includes "Colour: soft, very aromatic with a hint of honey and lemon in the foreground" and "Nose: amber with a slight yellow hue." Which would make this malt pretty unique. But this is worth getting for far more than just the collectors' item typo: this is brilliant whisky – one of their best vintage malts for a very long time. In fact, one of their best ever bottlings...period.46%. nc ncf. WB15/160

AnCnoc 2002 bott Mar 17, bott code: L17/089 R17/5104 IB db **(86) n21.5 t23 f20.5 b21** Overall, it is enjoyable and well spiced, but a mushy, tangy, untidy finish shows up the failings of the odd cask used. This is a distillery whose spirit yearns for ex-bourbon so its stunning naked form can be worshipped, loved and salivated over. 46%.

AnCnoc Barrow 13.5 ppm phenols db **(88) n22 t21 f23 b22** A quite peculiar Knockdhu. The usual subtle richness of texture is curiously absent. As are friendly sugars. The strange angles of the phenols fascinate, however. 46%. nc ncf. Exclusive to travel retail.

AnCnoc Blas db **(67) n16 t18 f16 b17.** Blast! Great chocolate. Shame about the sulphur.... 54%. nc ncf.

AnCnoc Black Hill Reserve db **(81) n20 t22 f19 b20.** The furriness threatened on the nose and realised at the finish does this great distillery no favours at all. 46%. nc ncf.

AnCnoc Cutter 20.5 ppm phenols db **(96.5) n24 t24 f24 b24.5** Brilliant! An adjective I am far more used to associating with anCnoc than some of the others I have had to use this year. The most Ardbeg-esque mainland malt I have ever encountered. 46%. nc ncf.

AnCnoc Peatheart batch no. 1, 40ppm, bott code: L17/301 R17/5394 db **(91.5) n22 t23.5 f23 b23** Won't be long before Peatheart becomes the peataholics' sweetheart. Curiously underperforming nose, but makes amends in style on the palate. 46%

AnCnoc Rùdhan bott code: L16/273 R16/5391 db **(94.5) n24 t23.5 f23.5 b24** Hard to imagine a mainland Scottish distillery producing a more complex, elegant and wholly ingratiating peated malt... What a gem this is! 46%.

AnCnoc Rutter 11 ppm phenols db **(96.5) n24.5 t24.5 f23.5 b24** I remember vividly, at this great distillery's Centenary party exactly 20 years ago this summer, mentioning to the then distillery manager that I thought that the style of the malt produced at Knockdhu was perfectly geared to make a lightly malted peat along the lines of its neighbour, Ardmore. Only for a few weeks of the year I ventured. I'm pretty certain this malt was not a result of that observation, but it is heartening to see that my instincts were right: it's a sensation! *46%. ncf nc. WB15/320*

LADYBURN
Lowlands, 1966–2000. William Grant & Sons. Closed.
Mo Òr Collection Rare Ayrshire 1974 36 Years Old first fill bourbon barrel, cask no. 2608, dist 10 May 74, bott 1 Nov 11 (89.5) n22 t23.5 f22 b22.5. I had a feeling it'd be this distillery when I saw the title on the label... it couldn't be much else! Fascinating to think that I was in final countdown for my 'O' levels when this was made. It appears to have dealt with the passing years better than I have. Even so, I had not been prepared for this. For years during the very early 1990s Grant's blender David Stewart sent me samples of this stuff and it was, to put it mildly, not great. Some were the oakiest malt I ever tasted in my life. And, to compound matters further, the distillery's own bottling was truly awful. But this cask has re-written history. *46%. nc ncf sc. Release No. 4. The Whisky Talker. 261 bottles.*

LAGAVULIN
Islay, 1816. Diageo. Working.
Lagavulin Aged 8 Years bott code: L7285CM013 db (95.5) n25 t23.5 f23 b24.5 Having gone from the colouring-spoiled Cardhu to this chardonnay-hued Lagavulin in all its bourbon cask nakedness, you have to wonder: why don't they do this for all their whiskies. This was the age I first tasted Lagavulin possibly the best part of 40 years ago. It was love at first flight, and my passions – with the whisky in this beautifully natural form, though not as heavily peated now as then – have not been remotely doused. *48%.*

Lagavulin Aged 12 Years bott 2017, bott code: L7089CM000 db (94) n23.5 t23.5 f23 b24 When I first tasted Lagavulin at this age, the phenol levels were around the 50ppm mark and not the present day 35. That meant the finish offered just a little extra Islay. Even so, I challenge you not to adore this. *56.5%.*

Lagavulin Aged 12 Years bott 2018, bott code: L8072CM008 db (96) n24 t24 f23.5 b24.5 Technically, from a distilling perspective, borderline perfection. From a maturation one, slightly weaker for, although the bourbon casks give you the clearest view possible of the brilliance of the spirit, a very slight late bitterness just breaks the spell. Even so, we are talking Islay at its most truly classic. *57.8%.*

Lagavulin 12 Year Old refill American oak hogsheads db (96) n24.5 t24 f23.5 b24 I think whisky like this was invented by the whisky gods to be experienced at this full strength. Even people who do not regard themselves as peat lovers are likely to be seduced by this one. Talk about controlled power.... *56.5%. Diageo Special Releases 2017.*

Lagavulin 16 Years Old db (95) n24 t24 f23 b24 Although I have enjoyed this whisky countless times socially, it is the first time for a while I have dragged it into the Tasting Room for professional analysis for the Bible. If anyone has noticed a slight change in Lagavulin, they would be right. The peat remains profound but much more delicate than before, while the oils appear to have receded. A different shape and weight dispersal for sure. But the sky-high quality remains just the same. *43%*

Game of Thrones Lagavulin 9 Year Old House Lannister db (89.5) n22 t23.5 f21.5 b22.5 Lagavulin as I have never seen it before, the phenols being kept on a tight leash. *46%.*

Cadenhead's Lagavulin 11 Year Old dist 2007 (96) n24 t24 f23.5 b24.5 If you are going to celebrate an anniversary, then why not pick one of the greatest distilleries in the world, choose a cask from one of its optimum ages and then make sure it is about as honest and accurate a picture of that distillery that a blender could hope for? Well, that's what's happened here. Just look at that grist on that nose, yet as the phenols swirl around there is no mistaking the barley, either. Then, on the palate, the way in which the peat radiates around the mouth as though in slow motion, a burst of barley juice here, light liquorice there. And smoke, so stunningly controlled, everywhere. Congratulations on your anniversary. And also on this glorious, to-die-for Lagavulin. *45%. 348 bottles. 10th Anniversary of Cadenhead Switzerland bottling.*

LAPHROAIG
Islay, 1815. Beam Suntory. Working.
Laphroaig 10 Years Old db (90) n24 t23 f20.5 b22.5 Has reverted back slightly towards a heavier style in more recent bottling, though I would like to see that old oomph at the very death. Even so, this is, indisputably, a classic whisky. The favourite of Prince Charles apparently: he will make a wise king... *40%*

Laphroaig 10 Year Old bott code: L80099MB1 db (94) n23.5 t23.5 f23.5 b24 An essay in voluptuousness. The oils speak volumes here, gathering the two-toned phenols and landing them in all corners of the palate and ensuring they stick there. The iodine kick off on the nose is like a salty trademark, the balance between the sootier phenols and juicer Demera notes a joy to experience. The finish is not so much enormous as controlled and long, with a sublime degree of mocha moving in for the last blissful moments. Glorious. Still, after all these years... 40%.

Laphroaig 10 Year Old bott code: L8 831 SB1 db **(95) n24 t23.5 f23.5 b24** So consistent is the Laphroaig 10, that this is one of the whiskies I test myself each day with to check that my nose and palate are on song. Having done this for the last 15 years or so, I think I can recognise whether a particular bottling from this distillery is up to scratch or not. Just a word of caution: their back label recommends that you add a splash of cool water to this whisky. I thoroughly recommend you do absolutely nothing of the sort. Laphroaig is served best by the Murray Method when its untold brilliance can be seen in its myriad layers. As an experiment, I have added cool water as they suggest – and it shrinks the whisky dramatically and breaks up the oils and sugars which are then lost to us. Please, never murder this fabulous whisky so cold-bloodedly. Oh, and having tasted a few score of Laphroaig 10s over the last 40 years or so, have to say this is bang up there with the very best: it is certainly among the most complex. 40%.

Laphroaig 10 Years Old Original Cask Strength db **(92) n22 t24 f23 b23** Caramel apart, this is much truer to form than one or two or more recent bottlings, aided by the fresh, gristy sweetness and explosive spices. Wonderful! 55.7%

Laphroaig 12 Year Old 2005 bott 2017 db **(91.5) n21.5 t23.5 f23 b23.5** Here we go: one of the exceptions in whisky that proves the rule. I have long wailed about the usage of PX cask and peaty malt together. And from the nose, you think your case will be won again, for here is another example of one giant nullifying another: both the smoke and fruit cancelling the other out. Yet, confound it, the delivery shows signs of proving me wrong and the finish continues in the same fashion. For once a PX cask is allowing the peat to breathe and sing. And what's more itself kick up a juicy encore. Beyond the nose a PX and smoky giant that walks tall. Who would have thought...? 55.3%. Selected for CWS.

Laphroaig 18 Years Old db **(94) n24 t23.5 f23 b23.5** This is Laphroaig's replacement to the woefully inadequate and gutless 15-year-old. And talk about taking a giant step in the right direction. Absolutely brimming with character and panache, from the first molecules escaping the bottle as you pour to the very final ember dying on the middle of your tongue. 48%

Laphroaig Aged 27 Years dist Oct 88 to Nov 89, bott Mar 17, bott code: L7062VB1 db **(96.5) n24.5 t24 f23.5 b24.5** The 27 passing years and the added interference of fresh ex-bourbon barrels and quarter casks has taken its toll on the potency of the peat. Instead of Laphroaig pulsing with its renowned style of sea-soaked phenols, we are now faced with a dram which is more than content to allow age and gentility to be the guiding hand; so now less febrile and more cerebral. Such an honour to taste whiskies of this extraordinary yet understated magnitude. I can think of no other presently available whisky which so eloquently demonstrates that you don't have to stand a spoon up in the peat for the phenols to have such a vital input. 41.7%. ncf.

Laphroaig Aged 30 Years db **(94) n24 t23 f23 b24.** The best Laphroaig of all time? Nope, because the 40-y-o is perhaps better still... just. However, Laphroaig of this subtlety and charm gives even the very finest Ardbeg a run for its money. A sheer treat that should be bottled at greater strength. 43%

Laphroaig Aged 40 Years db **(94) n23 t24 f23 b24.** Mind-blowing. A malt that defies all logic and theory to be in this kind of shape at such age. The Jane Fonda of Islay whisky. 43%

Laphroaig The 1815 Legacy Edition bott code: L7059VB1 2070 db **(92.5) n24 t24 f21 b23.5** a sherry butt away from one of the best new whiskies of the year. 48%. Travel Retail Exclusive.

Laphroaig Au Cuan Mòr db **(95) n24 t24 f23 b24** You don't need to squint at the back label to be told that first fill bourbon barrels are at work here: this is where Kentucky, Jerez and Islay merges with breath-taking ease and harmony. 48%. Travel retail exclusive.

Laphroaig Brodir Port Wood Finish bott code: L6157MB1 db **(91.5) n24** probably one of the most old-fashioned Islay warehouse aromas I have ever encountered: that incomparable mix of smoke, oak and grape hanging thickly in a moist, salty air...; **t22** the usual gristy sugars have been silenced by the intense, moody fruit; **f23** much better balance late on as a little liquorice and treacle joins the clouds of phenols to ensure complexity; **b22.5** this is a big Laphroaig at its most brooding and taciturn. Not for when you are at your most frivolous. 48%.

Laphroaig Four Oak bott code: L6327VB1 2359 db **(88) n22 t22.5 f21.5 b22** Attractive, but the smoke seems a little in awe of the oak as it is unusually quiet. 40%. Travel Retail Exclusive.

Laphroaig Lore db **(94) n23.5 t24 f23 b23.5** Seeing how much I adore this distillery – and treasure my near 40 years of tasting its exceptional malt and visiting its astonishing time – I left this to become my 750th new whisky for the 2016 Whisky Bible. "Our richest expression ever" the label promised. It isn't. Big, fat and chunky? Tick. Bounding with phenols? Yep. Enjoyable? Aye! Richest expression ever. Nah. Not quite. Still, a friendly beast worth cuddling up with. And, whatever they say on the label, this is a stunner! 48%. ncf.

Laphroaig Lore bott code: L7229VB1 db **(96) n23.5 t24 f24 b24.5** Laphroaig how I've never quite seen it before – and we are talking some 40 years of intimately studying this malt: truly a lore unto itself... 48%.

Laphroaig PX Cask bourbon, quarter and Pedro Ximenez casks db **(96) n23.5 t24.5 f24 b24.** I get the feeling that this is a breathtaking success despite the inclusion of Pedro Ximenez casks. This ultra sweet wine is often paired with smoky malt, often with disastrous consequences. Here it has worked, but only because the PX has been controlled itself by absolutely outstanding oak. And the ability of the smoke to take on several roles and personas simultaneously. A quite beautiful whisky and unquestionably one of the great malts of the year...in spite of itself. 48%. Travel Retail exclusive.

Laphroaig Quarter Cask db **(96) n23 t24 f24 b25** A great distillery back to its awesome, if a little sweet, self. Layer upon layer of sexed-up peatiness. The previous bottling just needed a little extra complexity on the nose for this to hit mega malt status. Now it has been achieved... 48%

Laphroaig Quarter Cask bott code: L8268 db **(93) n23 t23.5 f23 b23.5** Laphroaig Quarter Cask: where is thy sting? Easily the most strangely subdued bottlings of this great malt I have ever encountered. Make no mistake: this is still a lovely dram in its own right, but just not what I expected – or now demand – from this Islay classic. 48%. ncf.

⬥ **Laphroaig Select** bott code: L1162SB1 db **(94) n23.5** quite literally reeks of Laphroaig: an unmistakable aroma high on iodine and a sharp saltiness. With unusual mixed messages of young whisky and big, layered "red" oak; **t23.5** ah, I remember: this is the Laphroaig where a degree virgin American oak is deployed in maturation. That immediately makes sense of the follow through which is in contrast to the sublime young Laphroaig which pounds the taste buds with its unrelenting phenolic output. Despite being just 40%abv, the oils are excellent and help meld the smoke and ever-growing tannins into a glorious unit. The sugars are restrained but vital in keeping he balance intact; **f23** once the smoke begins to dissipate slightly, the effect of the oak helps raise the cocoa profile, sweetened by residual Demerara sugars. The spices are far more telling at the death as the smoke collects for a weighty and warming finale; **b24** this is a far better bottling than the last Select I tasted, which was among their earliest. They have obviously come to understand the whisky and the balance between young, vivacious peat and virgin oak that little bit better: the result is a substantial step upwards. Better use of young whisky here than Ardbeg's overly tame 5-year-old and if they could get the strength up six percentage points, this would probably sweep quite a lot of awards – in the Whisky Bible, also. Absolutely delightful and a peat worshipper's wet dream.... 40%. nc

⬥ **Old Malt Cask Laphroaig Aged 14 Years** sherry butt, cask no. 18204, dist Mar 06, bott Dec 20 **(94.5) n23.5** so rare to find so much grist on a sherry butt. The phenols, though gently floating about, are remarkably low for a Laphroaig...; **t23.5** malty with the smoke sauntering about without a care in the world. As on the nose, the malt takes on its own, mouth-watering gristiness. There is perhaps a nip of grape, very early on, helping the overall juiciness; **f23.5** rather lovely, understated chocolate, sweetened by light molasses, weighted by smoke; **b24** it's Laphroaig, Jim. But not as we know it. Just so unexpected and, in it's own, unique way, quite brilliant,. A south coast Islay for the most delicate of souls... 50%. nc ncf sc. 347 bottles. 🍷

LINKWOOD

Speyside, 1820. Diageo. Working.

Linkwood 12 Years Old db **(94.5) n23.5 t24 f23 b24** Possibly the most improved distillery bottling in recent times. Having gone through a period of dreadful casks, it appears to have come through to the other side very much on top and close to how some of us remember it a quarter of a century ago. Sublime malt: one of the most glittering gems in the Diageo crown. 43%

Berry Bros & Rudd Linkwood 12 Years Old cask no. 102, dist 2006, bott 2018 **(91) n22.5 t22.5 f23 b23** Crumbs!! Plays the austere Speysider with panache. 46%. nc ncf sc.

Fadandel.dk Linkwood 10 Year Old hogshead, cask no. 306465, dist 18 Nov 08, bott 5 Jun 19 **(91) n22.5 t23 f22.5 b23** The sharpness on the nose could cut; the bite on the palate could leave some serious marks. This is Linkwood unleashed, maturing in a cask which allows the malt free reign and ensures it is gilded in chocolate from the midpoints onwards. Younger than its years, the grist dishes out some delightful icing sugar notes as well a delicate ulmo honey ones. The oak moves in with the cocoa and the barley does nothing to prevent it. Simple. But often simplicity works.... 594%. sc. 34 bottles.

Fadandel.dk Linkwood 11 Year Old 8 months finish in a 1st fill Oloroso sherry octave, cask no. 306465A **(88.5) n22 t22.5 f22 b22** A perfectly sound cask with no off notes and even offering cherry blossom on the nose. Perhaps, though, the oloroso is just a little too demanding of the malt which is unable to match its bravado. The result is an enjoyable but slightly one-dimensional sherry-heavy offering, full of peppers and pep. Just not quite nuanced enough for greatness. Oh! How about that! Just as I was about push the button to send this to my Editor I noticed that the cask above is this but without the sherry. Well, as I have repeatedly said in these pages over the last 17 years: in whisky less can so often mean so much more... *578%. sc. 69 bottles.*

◇ **Kingsbury Sar Obair Linkwood 30 Year Old** sherry hogshead, dist 1989, cask no. 6617 **(96.5) n24** nose this is like inspecting the rungs in an oak tree: this exhibits age, and increasing amounts of it, with each sniff. Unlikely you will find a Scotch this year where the oak is so intense, yet unfurls like a flower in the sun as it oxidises and warms. How many types of spice? I have no idea... I truly lost count. And the fruit? To say "fruitcake" or "raisin" is simply too simple... This is far more nuanced than that...; **t24.5** mouth feel...? Flavour profile...? In which direction should your brain go? Because something is happening here so special, of such rare quality that it is hard to focus. The mouth feel almost has that of a bourbon, with the oily corn coating the mouth, except here, most probably, it is the ancient sherry, free from any tainting, going about its task of thickening and enriching.... Next come the flavours...and here every sense is stretched. The very first sensation is a sharp, juicy, salivating sweetness: a blend of seemingly still young malt allowing the sugars to get to work. But this is an illusion. There is, of course, age to this but it is the depth – and pointers towards antiquity elsewhere – that makes that segment still seem young. We are now getting into the heart of the whisky and here the oak comes back into play with easily the best display of layering of any whisky I have so far tasted this year. The tongue is investigating the roof of the mouth and discovering tannins of ever thickening intensity, and increasingly warming spice. Yet...never any burn...never any feel of tired tannin. Slowly a chocolate note begins to form, of mousse-like quality, perfectly in sync with the fruit. Miraculous. This is immaculate: the dram of dreams...; **f24** the finish, when you can finally work out which is the finish and not the extension if that extraordinary middle, is like the last mouthful of a classically vintaged Ch Latour: the grape remains intense, though not as muscular as before as the oxidising kicks in a little thinning acidity. The similarity is astonishing....; **b24** one fears that at any given moment this malt will crash and disintegrate as the age catches up with it, as the nose has already told you the oak is playing a blinding game and doing extraordinary things. Miraculously, it seems, this Linkwood keeps its shape throughout and never does drop over the end of a cliff. It is one of those old casks which leaves you not just satisfied but in complete awe... This, incidentally, will be an award winner of some type. If not, there really is no justice in this cruel world... *534% sc 242 bottles* ♈

The Single Malts of Scotland Reserve Cask Linkwood 12 Year Old (92.5) n23 t23 f23 b23.5 Linkwood at its fruitiest and flightiest, concentrating on a lightness of touch that sets out to charm – and does! Lime blossom honey abounds, mixing liberally with the grassy barley to accentuate the malt while giving the limited oakiness an extra boost, too. It is so light you can even pick a molecule or two of peat here and there, though to say weight is added is stretching the imagination. The salivating never lets up from first mouthful to finish, making this joyous malt perfect for summer evenings. A minor little classic, this. *48%.*

◇ **The Whisky Embassy Bonn Linkwood 9 Year Old** charred wine hogshead, cask no. 306191 **(89) n22.5** sharp and angular on the nose, the fruit has taken to attack mode; **t23** the kind of malt which simultaneously cleans both the palate and sinuses. The early alliance of malt and raisin is hair-rising...and wholly delicious; **f21.5** a little thin and vaguely bitter; **b22** hardly a malt for the feint hearted. The wine influence is not playing games here: it puts you to the test from the first moment. Lacks a little perhaps in complexity. But makes up for it is sheer chutzpah. *56.8%. nc ncf sc.*

LITTLEMILL
Lowland, 1772. Loch Lomond Distillers. Demolished.

Littlemill 21 Year Old 2nd Release bourbon cask db **(87) n22 t21.5 f21.5 b22.** So thin you expect it to fragment into a zillion pieces on the palate. But the improvement on this as a new make almost defies belief. The sugars are crisp enough to shatter on your teeth, the malt is stone hard and fractured and, on the finish, does show some definite charm before showing its less attractive teeth...and its roots... Overall, though, more than enjoyable. *47%. nc ncf.*

Littlemill 25 Year Old db **(92.5) n22 t24 f23 b23.5** Another example of a malt which was practically undrinkable in its youth but that is now a reformed, gentle character in older age. *52%*

Littlemill 40 Year Old Celestial Edition db **(90.5) n23.5 t23 f22 b22.5** As we all know, when this was distilled four decades back, the new make sprang from the stills as fire water. And for the first few years in the cask it roared at and incinerated the palate of any blender foolhardy enough to try it. And so, inevitably, the distillery died. In later years it is making up for its violent youth and here offers a serene maltiness about as far removed from its original character as is possible. Enjoy the dying rays of this once vituperative spirit, now so charming in its dotage. *46.8%. 250 bottles.*

Littlemill 1964 db (82) n21 t20 f21 b20. A soft-natured, bourbony chap that shows little of the manic tendencies that made this one of Scotland's most-feared malts. Talk about mellowing with age... 40%

Littlemill 2017 Private Cellar 27 Year Old db (93) n23 t23.5 f23 b23.5 How ironic and sad that the last casks of what were unloved – and unusable - firewater when distilled have now, after nearly three decades, calmed into a malt which is the matured embodiment of grace and finesse. 51.3%.

Master of Malt Single Cask Littlemill 27 Year Old dist 1991 (94.5) n23 t24 f23.5 b24 Another old Littlemill shewing genuine elegance in its twilight years. Kind of Malteser candy with benefits from the moment it hits the palate right through to the finale. A little bourbon-style tannin on the nose doesn't quite prepare you for the chocolatey maltfest which follows... Truly delicious. I promise you: no-one, and I mean no-one, could envision it would be this good in the days when it was working.... 47.2%. sc.

LOCH LOMOND
Highlands (Southwestern), 1966. Loch Lomond Distillers. Working.
Loch Lomond Aged 10 Years Lightly Peated bott code: 10 01 2019 db (86) n20.5 t22 f21.5 b22 Maybe I'm wrong, but this strikes me as being a vatting of distillation types (Inchmoan, Croftengea etc.) with their usual designated Loch Lomond straight and clean style. The result is a feinty beast, much heavier than any "Loch Lomond" I have before encountered, but buttressed with some major fudge and phenols: the Loch Lomond Monster... 40%.

Loch Lomond 10 Year Old 2009 Alvi's Drift Muscat de Frontignan Finish db (96) n23.5 t24.5 f23.5 b24.5 One of those rare whiskies which is every bit as remarkable for its mouthfeel than it is for its flavour personality, which in itself borders on the unique. No, what the hell! This IS unique! A malt whose beauty you can only marvel at....I am truly blown away... 53.2%. Selected by Slijterij Frans Muthert & Dramtime.nl.

Loch Lomond Aged 12 Years db (93.5) n22.5 t23.5 f23.5 b24 Great to see they now have the stocks to allow this malt to really flex its muscles... 46%. ncf.

Loch Lomond 12 Year Old The Open Special Edition 2020 db (92.5) n24 t23.5 f22 b23 If anyone needs proof that superb whisky can be got from a relatively young malt (old when I started this game of writing about whisky in the 1980s!) just by the clever use of bourbon casks in particular, then here it is. 46%.

Loch Lomond Aged 14 Years Inchmoan American oak casks, bott code: L2.080.20 db (88.5) n21.5 t23 f21.5 b22.5 This is like watching Charlie Chaplin sloshing paint onto a wall, or glue onto wallpaper. Slap, slap! Here everything is slapped on: the feints, the barley, the sugars, the oak. Slap, slap, slap! Love it, but don't expect subtlety, 46%. ncf. Traveller Exclusive.

Loch Lomond 15 Year Old db (87.5) n21.5 t22 f22 b22 Spends a lot of its time waving its malty flag. But a slight tartness on both nose and on palate means it never quite settles into a comfortable narrative 46%.

Loch Lomond Organic Aged 17 Years bott code: L2 120 18 db (96.5) n24 t24.5 f23.5 b24.5 Organic...? Orgasmic, more like! A dram which will win the hearts, minds and souls of both bourbon and scotch whisky lovers. In fact, if you don't like this, whatever the cut of your jib, you might as well give up now... 54.9%. nc ncf.

Loch Lomond Aged 18 Years American oak casks, bott code: L2.234.18 db (95) n23 t24 f23.5 b24.5 Tasting the Loch Lomond whiskies this year has been such a pleasure. It is always heart-warming to find a distillery that uses American oak casks to best advantage and other types sparingly and with the distillery style in mind. Here is another case in point: the bourbon casks have been shaped to extract every last jot of honey out this expression, as well as complexity. I doff my Panama... 46%. ncf.

Loch Lomond The Open 18 Year Old Course Collection Carnoustie 1999 db (92) n23 t23.5 f22 b23.5 Decided to wait until the 2018 Open at Carnoustie was in full swing before checking to see if this is up to par. Well, it is beyond that: a true double birdie as rarely is Loch Lomond this clean and malt rich. Would grace any 19th hole... 47.2%.

Loch Lomond Aged 18 Years Inchmurrin American oak casks, bott code: L2.083.20 db (95) n23.5 t24 f23.5 b24 Have to say: this is Inchmurrin revealing all its pure naked beauty. And it's some sight to behold, believe me. At this age always a good dram. Now truly a great one. 46%. ncf. Traveller Exclusive.

Loch Lomond 21 Year Old db (89.5) n22.5 t22.5 f22 b22.5 Not sure if the oily style of the spirit made 21 years ago is quite as accommodating so far as complexity is concerned as most of the spirit which has come since. 46%.

Loch Lomond 25 Year Old Three Wood Matured Colin Montgomerie db (95) n24 t23.5 f23.5 b24 I have never met Colin Montgomery, though his car and my car once parked simultaneously nose to tail in Mayfair, London, our respective personalised number plates almost touching. Mr Montgomery, I noted, was quite a large individual so was not surprised that he could persuade a small rubber ball to travel a great distance with one well-timed thwack. This whisky, then, being of a delicate and fragile nature is very much, physically, his antithesis. No doubt Colin Montgomery found the rough a few times in his long career; he certainly won't with this. *46.3%.*

Loch Lomond 30 Year Old db **(86) n23.5 t23 f19 b20.5** When nosing, just sit there and contemplate the spices on that fruit pudding. Wow..! But on delivery, unusually for a malt this age it is the sugars which gets the first word in, a light golden syrup number moving serenely into position with the duskier plummy tones. The spices build as advertised. But then it all starts going Pete Tong as some major furriness grows on the finish. What a shame! Until the treatment of the sherry butts kick in from three decades back, we had been on a delightful journey of unusually polished balance. But, for better or worse, it is a whisky of its times... *47%.*

Loch Lomond Classic American oak casks, bott code: 17 12 2018 db **(84.5) n21 t22.5 f20 b21** Though called "Classic", the flat, chewy toffee middle and finish makes this pleasant but very un-Lomond like in character. Fudged in every sense... *40%.*

Loch Lomond Cristie Kerr Vintage 2002 db **(94) n23** the vaguest hint of smoky bacon adds what little weight there is to this gentle celebration of barley; **t23.5** such a beautiful presentation of barley in all its heather-honeyed finery. Salivating, lightly oaked and perfectly spiced; **f23.5** continues in the same form, but late on a little nuttiness appears, which moves towards praline; **b24** Lomond at is malty best and cleanest. Someone in Toronto this year told me he had never found a Loch Lomond he'd ever enjoyed. I hope he discovers this minor classic... *48.1%.*

Loch Lomond The Open Special Edition Distiller's Cut first fill bourbon and refill American oak casks, bott code: 12 03 2019 db **(95.5) n23.5 t25 f23 b24** One of the finest Loch Lomonds I have ever encountered. No: the finest. The distillery will go up several notches above par for anyone lucky enough to encounter this one.... *46%. ncf.* Chosen for Royal Portrush.

Loch Lomond Original American oak casks, bott code: L2.042 20 db **(90) n22.5 t23 f22 b22.5** I think this was the malt a few years back I nearly fainted from because of the feints. Many... I pause at this point because after 21,000 different samples, that's well over 100,000 mouthfuls of whisky and over 100,000 times of picking up a glass and putting it down again to write over the last 17 years, I finally knocked a charged tasting glass over the computer, thereby killing it. Death by malt. Or, rather, it was at this point it died as it had happened two samples ago. A brand new Apple Mac bought just for the Whisky Bible 2021 edition dying in its line of duty. So now an old one – with the letters e r t o a h and n obliterated by a few years' pounding has been brought out of retirement to complete the last couple of hundred whiskies (this is number 969)... Anyway, back to the Loch Lomond Original. This now a feint-free maltfest which goes easy on complexity but is big on charm. *40%.*

Glengarry 12 Year Old db **(92.5) n22.5 t23.5 f23 b23.5** Probably the most intense malt on the market today. Astonishing. And stunning. *46%. ncf.*

Inchmoan Aged 12 Years Peated recharred American oak and refill bourbon American oak casks, bott code: L4.295.19 db **(85.5) n20 t22.5 f21.5 b21.5** Seems as though the whole world has gone slightly mad and changed beyond recognition since I last opened a bottle of this. The only thing that hasn't changed, it seems, is the feintiness on Inchmoan. A little sweeter now, maybe. And the peat now has the distinctively chocolate mint quality of the old Merlin's Brew ice lolly. Though that lost old classic would have this licked... *46%. ncf. Loch Lomond Island Collection.*

Inchmoan 1992 Peated refill bourbon barrels db **(95) n23 t24.5 f23.5 b24** I do believe I was at Loch Lomond distillery in 1992 while they were producing the Inchmoan strand of their output. So to see it after all this time is astonishing. No less astonishing is the sheer excellence of the malt, which here is almost a cross between a light rye-recipe bourbon and a smoky island scotch. This is a true Loch Lomond classic *48.6%. ncf. Loch Lomond Island Collection.*

Inchmurrin Aged 12 Years bourbon, refill and recharred casks, bott code: L2.248.18 db **(88.5) n21.5 t23 f22 b22** Best Inchmurrin I have tasted in a good number of years. The calibre of the malt is top-notch, allowing the barley a fabulously lively, intense yet even run. Well spiced, too. Inch by Inch, it is getting there. At this rate the next bottling will be hitting the 90-mark for the Bible, once an unlikely proposition. A little cleaner on the nose and it'll be there. A bit like the distillery: a real character. *46%. ncf. Loch Lomond Island Collection.*

Inchmurrin Madeira Wood Finish bott code: L2.185.18 db **(93) n23 t23.5 f23b23.5** Well, a lush and beautifully clean Madeira cask is one way of negating any weakness on the nose. Trouble is, that fruit becomes a little too bossy....though this can be forgiven when the quality of the casks are this high. A real lip-smacking crowd pleaser. *46%. ncf.*

The First Editions Inchfad Aged 14 Years 2005 refill hogshead, cask no. 16785, bott 2019 **(89) n22 t23 f21.5 b22.5** A brilliant example of Inchfad's truly esoteric style. *56.3%. nc ncf sc.* 293 bottles.

Liquid Treasures 10th Anniversary Inchfad 14 Year Old heavily peated hogsheads, dist 2005, bott 2019 **(94.5) n23.5 t23.5 f23.5 b24** Rarely does an Inchfad turn up in the bottle as clean and well-made as this, with the phenols at their most intense. Not an easy edition of Loch Lomond's output to find anyway, usually the feints makes for a challenging dram. Not this time, though. And while it is not quite technically perfect (not sure I've ever found an Inchfad that really is), this cask comes together in a way that is leaves you cooing like a randy woodpigeon. Just love the mintiness that attaches to the smoke and then the later praline as the nuttiness grows. Perhaps best of all, though, is the mouthfeel which varies between oily and a cocoa dryness, neither gaining control. If you see this bottle, just get it. It's a bit of a one off. *50%. sc. 144 bottles.*

◈ **Old Malt Cask Inchmurrin Aged 24 Years** refill hogshead, cask no.HL18693, dist Aug 1996, bott May 2021 **(92.5) n22.5** agreeably bitty and complex: the tannins appear like weighty flecks on the lighter malt; sometimes the sharper barley notes are like flecks on the tannins. Entertaining...; **t23.5** a magnificent arrival on the palate. Bold, beautifully made and with a just about perfect oiliness and weight to the piece, for the odd flavour wave or two there is a momentarily feel of very young malt...and then it flicks into oaky mode to underline the age; **f23** long with a magnificent malt and barley duet taking turns to lead; **b23.5** memorable for being complex despite the simplicity of the basic elements at works. The secret is in their interplay: a malt that never sits still long enough for either the barley or oak to dominate. Of all Loch Lomond's output, Inchmurrin really knows how to intrigue. *50% sc*

The Single Cask Croftengea 2007 ex-wine cask, cask no. 71 **(81.5) n18 t21.5 f21 b21** Even at the best of times, sampling a Croftengea can be like trying to break in a particularly bloody-minded horse: you get thrown everywhere and can take one hell of a kicking. The fact that your saddle has been loosed by an unimpressive wine cask makes the job even more difficult. Hard to find a single positive about the nose but I suspect the inner masochist in me has a grudging respect for the wildness on the palate. *55.7%. nc ncf sc.*

LOCHSIDE
Highlands (Eastern), 1957–1992. Chivas Brothers. Demolished.
The Whisky Agency Lochside 1981 butt, bott 2018 **(96.5) n24 t25 f23.5 b24** I suspect I must be one of the very last people still working in the whisky industry who visited this distillery in the days when it was at full throttle. I was horrified by its closure way back in 1992 and thinking back on it now still fills me with great sadness. Some distilleries were awful and deserved their fate. This never for a moment did. I remember once going to see Montrose play a home game and afterwards popped into the distillery to have a word with the staff on duty. The new make then, as every time I visited, was spot on (and very warming after perishing in the main stand). And here is a magnificent example of its stunning make spending the best part of 40 years in faultless sherry oak. The result, as I expected (and the reason I left this for among the final five whiskies for the 2021 Whisky Bible) is a study of single malt Scotch: a malt of astonishing and beguiling beauty. *48.6%.*

LONGMORN
Speyside, 1895. Chivas Brothers. Working.
Longmorn 15 Years Old db **(93) n23 t24 f22 b24** These latest bottlings are the best yet: previous ones had shown just a little too much oak but this has hit a perfect compromise. An all-time Speyside great. *45%*

Longmorn 16 Years Old db **(84.5) n20.5 t22 f21 b21.** This was one of the disappointments of the 2008 edition, thanks to the lacklustre nose and finish. This time we see a cautious nudge in the right direction: the colour has been dropped fractionally and the nose celebrates with a sharper barley kick with a peppery accompaniment. The non-existent (caramel apart) finale of yore now offers a distinct wave of butterscotch and thinned honey...and still some spice. Only the delivery has dropped a tad...but a price worth paying for the overall improvement. Still a way to go before the real Longmorn 16 shines in our glasses for all to see and fall deeply in love with. Come on lads in the Chivas lab: we know you can do it... *48%*

Longmorn 23 Year Old db **(93) n23 t24 f23 b23.5** I can just imagine how this would be such rich top dressing for the finest blend I could concoct: as a single malt it is no less a delight. *48%. ncf.*

The First Editions Longmorn Aged 21 Years 1998 refill barrel, cask no. 17324, bott 2019 **(96.5) n25 t24 f23 b24.5** Longmorn is a malt greatly prized by the better blenders. This bottling leaves you in no doubt why...one of the single casks of the year, for sure. *56.3%. nc ncf sc. 186 bottles.*

Gordon & MacPhail Private Collection Longmorn 1966 first fill sherry butt, cask no. 610, dist 1 Feb 66, bott 22 Mar 19 **(96) n25 t24 f23 b24** The colour of a greatly aged tawny port and enough oak for Henry VIII to build the biggest ship ever to set sail for Jerez and plunder as many sherry butts as he wished. Like a great wine, needs a good half hour minimum to breathe in the glass to open for best results and maximum complexity. *46%. sc. 398 bottles.*

THE MACALLAN
Speyside, 1824. Edrington. Working.

The Macallan 10 Years Old db **(91) n23 t23 f21.5 b23.5** For a great many of us, it is with the Mac 10 our great Speyside odyssey began. It has to be said that in recent years it has been something of a shadow of its former great self. However, this is the best version I have come across for a while. Not perhaps in the same league as those bottlings in the 1970s which made us re-evaluate the possibilities of single malt. But fine enough to show just how great this whisky can be when the butts have not been tainted and, towards the end, the balance between barley and grape is a relatively equal one. *40%*

The Macallan Fine Oak 10 Years Old db **(90) n23 t23 t22.5 f21.5 b22** Much more on the ball than the last bottling of this I came across. Malts rarely come as understated or as clever than this. *40%*

Macallan 12 Year Old db **(61) n15 t16 f15 b15** An uncompromising and comprehensive essay in the present day sulphured sherry butt problem. *43% US tag CP981113*

The Macallan Sherry Oak 12 Years Old db **(93) n24 t23.5 f22.5 b23** I have to say that some Macallan 12 I have tasted on the road has let me down in the last year or so. This is virtually faultless. Virtually a time machine back to another era... *40%*

The Macallan 12 Years Old Sherry Oak Elegancia db **(86) n23 t22 f20 b21.** Promises, but delivers only to an extent. *40%*

The Macallan Fine Oak 12 Years Old db **(95.5) n24 t24 f23.5 b24** A whisky whose quality has hit the stratosphere since I last tasted it. I encountered a disappointing one early in the year. This has restored my faith to the point of being a disciple... *40%*

The Macallan Fine Oak 15 Years Old db **(79.5) n19 t21.5 f19 b20.** As the stock of the Fine oak 12 rises, so its 15-y-o brother, once one of my favourite drams, falls. Plenty to enjoy, but a few sulphur stains remove the gloss. *43%*

The Macallan Fine Oak 17 Years Old db **(82) n19.5 t22 f19.5 b21.** Where once it couldn't quite make up its mind on just where to sit, it has now gone across to the sherry benches. Sadly, there are a few dissenters. *43%*

The Macallan Sherry Oak 18 Years Old db **(87) n24 t22 f20 b21.** Underpowered. The body doesn't even come close to matching the nose which builds up the expectancy to enormous levels and, by comparison to the Independents, this at 43% appears weak and unrepresentative. Why this isn't at 46% at the very least and unambiguously uncoloured, I have no idea. *43%*

The Macallan Fine Oak 18 Years Old db **(94.5) n23.5 t24 f23 b24** Is this the new Fine Oak 15 in terms of complexity? That original bottling thrived on the balance between casks types. This is much more accentuated on a cream sherry persona. But this sample is sulphur-free and quite fabulous. *43%*

The Macallan Fine Oak 21 Years Old db **(84) n21 t22 f20 b21.** An improvement on the characterless dullard I last encountered. But the peaks aren't quite high enough to counter the sulphur notes and make this a great malt. *43%*

The Macallan 25 Years Old db **(84.5) n22 t21 f20.5 b21.** Dry with an even drier oloroso residue; blood orange adds to the fruity mix. Something, though, is not entirely right about this and one fears from the bitter tang at the death that a rogue butt has gained entry to what should be the most hallowed of dumping troughs. *43%*

The Macallan Fine Oak 25 Years Old db **(90) n22 t23.5 f22 b22.5** The first time I tasted this brand a few years back I was knocked off my perch by the peat reek which wafted about with cheerful abandon. Here the smoke is tighter, more shy and of a distinctly more anthracitic quality. Even so, the sweet juiciness of the grape juxtaposes gamely with the obvious age to create a malt of obvious class. *43%*

The Macallan Fine Oak 25 Years Old db **(89) n23 t23 f21 b22.** Very similar to the Fine Oak 18. However, the signature smoke has vanished, as I suppose over time it must. Not entirely clean sherry, but much remains to enjoy. *43%*

The Macallan Fine Oak 30 Years Old db **(81.5) n22 t22 f18 b19.5.** For all its many riches on delivery, especially those moments of great bourbon-honey glory, it has been comprehensively bowled middle stump by the sherry. Gutted. *43%*

The Macallan Millennium 50 Years Old (1949) db **(90) n23 t22 f22 b23.** Magnificent finesse and charm despite some big oak makes this another Macallan to die for. *40%*

The Macallan Lalique III 57 Years Old db **(95) n24.5 t23 f23.5 b24** No experience with this whisky under an hour pays sufficient tribute to what it is all about. Checking my watch,

I am writing this just two minutes under two hours after first nosing this malt. The score started at 88.5. With time, warmth, oxidation and understanding that score has risen to 95. It has spent 57 years in the cask; it deserves two hours to be heard. It takes that time, at least, not just to hear what it has to say to interpret it, but to put it into context. And for certain notes, once locked away and forgotten, to be slowly released. The last Lalique was good. But simply not this good. *48.5%*

The Macallan 1824 db **(88)** n24 t23.5 f19 b21.5. Absolutely magnificent whisky, in part. But there are times my job is depressing...and this is one of them.. *48%*

The Macallan 1824 Estate Reserve db **(90.5)** n22 t23 f22.5 b23 Don't know about Reserve: definitely good enough for the First Team. *45.7%*

The Macallan 1824 Select Oak db **(82)** n19 t22 f20 b21. Soft, silky, sometimes sugary... and tangy. Not convinced every oak selected was quite the right one. *40%*

The Macallan Fine Oak Master's Edition db **(91)** n23 t23 f22 b23 Adorable. *42.8%*

The Macallan Fine Oak Whisky Maker's Selection db **(92)** n22 t23 f23 b24. This is a dram of exquisite sophistication. Coy, mildly cocoaed dryness, set against just enough barley and fruit sweetness here and there to see off any hints of austerity. Some great work has gone on in the lab to make this happen: fabulous stuff! *42.8%. Duty Free.*

The Macallan Gold sherry oak cask db **(89.5)** n22 t23.5 f21.5 b22.5. No Macallan I have tasted since my first in 1975 has been sculpted to show the distillery in such delicate form. *40%*

The Macallan Ruby sherry oak cask db **(92.5)** n23 t24 f22 b23.5. Those longer in the tooth who remember the Macallan 10 of 30 years ago will nod approvingly at this chap. Perhaps one butt away from a gong! *43%.*

The Macallan Sienna sherry cask db **(94.5)** n23 t24 f23.5 b24. The pre-bottling sample presented to me was much more vibrant than this early on, but lacked the overall easy charm and readily flowing general complexity of the finished article. A huge and pleasing improvement. *43%.*

The Macallan Rare Cask Black db **(83.5)** n21.5 t22 f19 b21. Pretty rich and some intense, molasses, black cherry and liquorice notes to die for. But some pretty off-key ones, too. Overall, average fare. *48%*

The Macallan Select Oak db **(83)** n23 t21 f19 b20. Exceptionally dry and tight; and a little furry despite the early fruitiness. *40%*

The Macallan Whisky Makers Edition db **(76)** n19 t20 f18 b19. Distorted and embittered by the horrific "S" element... *42.8%*

Heiko Thieme's 1974 Macallan 65th Birthday Bottling cask no. 16807 dist 25 Nov 74 bott Jul 08 **(94)** n23 t23 f24 b24 This is not whisky because it is 38%abv. It is Scottish spirit. However, this is more of a whisky than a great many samples I have tasted this year. Ageism is outlawed. So is sexism. But alcoholism isn't....!! Try and become a friend of Herr Thieme and grab hold of something a little special. *38% 238 bottles.*

Skene Reserve Macallan 1989 30 Year Old 1st fill Oloroso, cask no. 152034 **(76)** n20 t20 f18 b18 This is a distinctly odd malt. At first I thought it was only because it was from the earliest days of when sulphur sticks were used in sherry butts like so much fertiliser was used on a crop of beans. And though I am 100% certain there are very old sulphur effects here (we are probably entering new ground in seeing the effect of candle treatment on casks over such a long period) you also get the feeling there is something else at work here stopping the development of the complexity that, had this been a 30-year-old Macallan I was tasting either from bottle or in their warehouses 30-years-ago, would have given you a result so much more different – and infinitely more beautiful and complex – than this. *43.2%. sc.*

MACDUFF

Speyside, 1963. Bacardi. Working.

The Deveron Aged 10 Years bott code: L17 284ZAB03 2327 db **(94)** n23.5 t23.5 f23 b24 Does the heart good to see a distillery bring their malt out as a ten-year- old – when so many think that such an age is beneath them. This shews the distillery at its most vivid and fresh, when the oak has had time to work its magic but not overstay its welcome; when the barley is still king. And, my word, its crown positively glitters gold here... *40%.*

The Deveron 12 Year Old db **(87.5)** n22 t22 f21.5 b22. Buttery and pleasant. But feels like driving a Ferrari with a Fiat Uno engine. Woefully underpowered and slightly too flat in too many places where it should be soaring. The trademark honey notes cannot be entirely defied, however. *40%*

The Deveron Aged 12 Years bott code: L172018700 db **(94.5)** n23.5 retains its big malt personality, though there is far more citrus about now, the oak is weightier and brings into play delicate layers of acacia honey..; t23.5 ...and it is the honey which lays the foundations for the dropped malty intro.. The mouthfeel is sexy and succulent, a light butterscotch note representing the oak; again, a citrus note hangs about, mainly lime; **f23** at last a little spice comes into play. But the continued complexity...just, wow! **b24** hi honey! I've homed in...! 40%.

The Deveron Aged 18 Years bott code: L181168700 db **(93) n23 t24 f22.5 b23.5** Someone has started not to just fully understand this always badly underrated distillery, but put it on the map. 40%.

Fadandel.dk Macduff 13 Year Old barrel, cask no. 8102355, dist 27 Nov 06, bott 28 Nov 19 **(92) n23 t23.5 f22.5 b23** Oh, thank god!! After a day of one sherry butt or wine cask finish after another at last I can taste malt...as in MALT whisky. How amazing is that! Just like the old days. And you know what...? Not only does it have personality, but it's bloody delicious! 54.2%. sc. 191 bottles.

⟐ **Hepburn's Choice Macduff 13 Years Old** wine barrels, dist 2007, bott 2020 **(84.5) n21 t22.5 f20 b21** The usual honey notes I expect from Macduff at this age are conspicuous by the absence. This is dry to the point of austerity, perhaps the only hint of a sparkle coming at the point of delivery on the palate when the malt bursts out like a firework on a rainy night, soon to be extinguished by bitter grape. 46%. nc ncf. 715 bottles.

⟐ **Old Malt Cask Macduff Aged 14 Years** refill hogshead, cask no.HL18702, dist Apr 2007, bott May 2021 **(88.5) n22 t23 f21 b22.5** Great to see a MacDuff where both the nose and delivery trot out an impressive light honey barley theme which shows the malt in a golden light. However, this was filled into a slightly tired cask and the delicate nature of the malt doesn't have quite enough muscle to fully overcome the late bitter notes. The intensity of the delivery, though, is magnificent. 50% sc 282 bottles

Old Malt Cask Macduff Aged 21 Years refill hogshead, cask no. 15147, dist May 97, bott May 18 **(78) n20 t20 f18 b20** Sticks out like a sore thumb for the other Macduffs in this family, presumably a poor cask undoing the good of the spirit. A duff Macduff... 50%. nc ncf sc.

Scyfion Choice Macduff 2007 Pinot Noir cask finished, bott 2019 **(90.5) n22.5 t23 f22.5 b22.5** Anyone who loves eye-wateringly sharp boiled sweets should hunt this bottling down now..! 46%. nc ncf sc. 160 bottles.

⟐ **Single Cask Collection Macduff 12 Years Old** cask no. 11270, dist 2007, bott 2019 **(87.5) n22 t23 f20.5 b22** A placid Macduff which allows the full-blown malt only so much scope. There is a light fruit note to accompany the barley on the nose. The mouth feel is a much fatter affair and the malt takes off in an attractive if simplistic manner, a little ulmo honey adding to the sweetness and luxuriating effect. The finish is dull and tangy by comparison, however. 47%. sc. 374 bottles.

⟐ **The Single Cask Macduff 1997** oloroso sherry finish, cask no. 5233 **(93) n23** just adore the spices which mingle so noncoherently with the delicate moist fruitcake; **t23.5** first the salivating fruity barley...then a thundering whumph of spices: what a delivery! Not sure the mouth feel could be any more attractive, the rich, lightly oiled contours offering excellent depth; **f23** a little vanilla and cocoa sits perfectly with the lingering toasted raisins; **b23.5** a malt finished in an outstanding sherry butt. 51% sc

The Whisky Gallery High Priestess Macduff Aged 8 Years second fill bourbon barrel, cask no. 800020, dist 2011, bott 2019 **(89.5) n22.5 t22.5 f22 b22.5** Spellbindingly youthful, but technically on the money. 49%. sc. 229 bottles.

Wilson & Morgan Barrel Selection Macduff 1st fill sherry wood, dist 2006, bott 2019 **(95) n24 t24 f23 b24** Well done Wilson & Morgan for again finding an untainted sherry butt. This is big whisky that is so beautifully controlled and balanced it doesn't actually seem like it! An easy to miss stunner. 57.1%.

MANNOCHMORE
Speyside, 1971. Diageo. Working.

Mannochmore Aged 12 Years db **(84) n22 t21 f20 b21.** As usual the mouth arrival fails to live up to the great nose. Quite a greasy dram with sweet malt and bitter oak. 43%.

⟐ **Chapter 7 Mannochmore 2008 Aged 12 Years** bourbon hogshead, barrel no.16612 **(90.5) n22.5** such a freshness of the barley it is almost showing off...; **t23.5** such a clean malt on delivery, but never less than full of fizz and prime juicy barley. Mouth-watering and obviously beautifully made; **f22** surprisingly long, given the limitations of complexity. But the oaky vanilla notes do blend well with the barley; **b22.5** the majority of Mannochmores I have tasted over the years have failed to do justice to a distillery which blenders often enjoy for the lovely clarity of the barley. This is a rare example of its full effervescent quality on show, starting with a hint of it on the three-dimensional nose and really taking off on the juiciest of deliveries. Mannochmore is essentially a light spirit, and again this is true to type which means the cask does leave a few footprints at the finish. A superb dram and, in this form, a fine portrait of the distillery. 52.5% sc

MILLBURN

Highlands (Northern), 1807–1985. Diageo. Demolished.

Millburn 1969 Rare Malt db (77) n19 t21 f18 b19. Some lovely bourbon-honey touches but sadly over the hill and declining fast. Nothing like as interesting or entertaining as the massage parlour that was firebombed a few yards from my office twenty minutes ago. Or as smoky... 51.3%

MILTONDUFF

Speyside, 1824. Chivas Brothers. Working.

Ballantine's The Miltonduff Aged 15 Years Series No.002 American oak casks, bott code: LKRM1193 2018/03/27 (88.5) n23 t22 f21.5 b22 Soft, spicy, attractive but far too much one-dimensional caramel for complexity or greatness. Some decent bourbon notes filter through, though. (The Murray Method brings out the caramels further – best enjoyed at cool bottle temperature). 40%.

Cadenhead's Whisky & More Baden Miltonduff 10 Year Old firkin cask (95.5) n23.5 t24 f24 b24 Firkin hell...!! This really isn't much interested in taking prisoners.! Instead it just wallows in its own swamp of spicy fruitiness and adds chocolate when required. The mouthfeel is as soft, chewy and rounded as any you'll find this year, with the accent on fat dates. As you know, I make no secret that there are some awful fruity whiskies about. This is the antithesis: a huge malt simply brimming with a fruity intensity and clarity to die for. The late mix of Venezuelan cocoa and spiced papaya is almost taking the piss. Magnificent hardly does this justice... 54.5%. sc.

Chapter 7 Miltonduff 21 Year Old 1998 bourbon hogshead, cask no. 10142, dist Oct 98, bott Mar 20 (94) n24 t23.5 f23 b23.5 Looking at this year's scores for, what for me, is one of the most overlooked and underrated of all the Speyside distilleries, you get the feeling that the marketing department for Miltonduff's owners should give very serious consideration into launching a cask strength, uncoloured version at their earliest opportunity. Here the malts seemingly fizz into the nose, sharp and virile despite the passing years. And there is no less malty energy on delivery, also, though a little salty seasoning appears to up the part played in the oaky incursion. Full flavoured, majorly malty and, when those gentle spices start adding their two-penn'orth things are just about complete. 49.7%. sc. 238 bottles.

The First Editions Miltonduff Aged 29 Years 1990 refill hogshead, cask no. 16248, bott 2019 (94) n23.5 ridiculously seductive: the involvement of the tannin is precise, measured and delightful; t24 one of the most viscous mouthfeels I have ever encountered: actually needed to check the bottle to ensure this wasn't a liqueur...! The initial heather honey sweetness on delivery adds to the effect. But soon those tannins so clearly defined on the nose are making their presence felt from about the fourth flavour wave onwards; f23 teasing spices as the oak plays out its wonderfully orchestrated tune; b23.5 a belting malt which will appeal especially to those with a very sweet tooth. But it isn't all one way traffic and some outstanding oak ensures balance. 57.2%. nc ncf sc. 287 bottles.

◈ **Kingsbury Gold Miltonduff 21 Year Old** hogshead, dist 1998, cask no. 10143 (94) n23 even at 21 years, the grassiness to the malt is endearing. The spices and vanillas seem perfectly matched; t24 a dangerous delivery: not one you can be content with just the one! This is the definition of malty complexity: the barley is multi-toned, ranging from almost eye wateringly sharp freshness through digestive biscuit and barley sugar; f23.5 not all the hogsheads Allied filled into were quite as healthy as this: no hidden bitterness, just more and more malt drifting on varied layers of intensity and sometimes spice; b23.5 when you taste one of the older Ballantine blends and wonder why there is such a rich and sturdy composition to the malt, now you know. A sublime example from a sublime distillery. 52.5% scz 233 bottles

Old Malt Cask Miltonduff Aged 25 Years refill hogshead, cask no. 16644, dist Apr 94, bott May 19 (95) n23.5 t24 f23.5 b24 Truly classy, as the finest Miltonduffs invariably are. Impeccable. 50%. nc ncf sc. 228 bottles.

Old Malt Cask Miltonduff Aged 29 Years refill hogshead, cask no. 16260, dist Mar 90, bott Oct 19 (85.5) n22 t22.5 f20 b21 A sister cask to the First Editions Miltonduff (above). But this one is missing most of the lush, sweet genes and after an austere, tannin-infused start buckles somewhat under a degree of late bitterness. 50%. nc ncf sc. 277 bottles.

◈ **Scyfion Choice Miltonduff** rara Neagra wine cask finished, dist 2011, bott 2020 (88) n22 t23 f21.5 b21.5 A perfectly enjoyable and acceptable wine cask influenced malt. The trouble is, the influence is a little too much, therefore, after the spicey crescendo about five or six flavours waves in, we have a pretty monosyllabic grapiness taking us through to the bittering finish. Is this an improvement on Miltonduff left in its natural state? Almost certainly not. Too much is not always a good thing. 46% nc ncf 248 bottles

◈ **The Single Cask Miltonduff** 1st fill bourbon barrel, cask no. 700988, dist 25 Jul 08 (93) n23 the crisp barley strikes against the nose like a wooden hammer on a piano string..;

t24 just about faultless, as you might expect from this distillery. The slow build of barley intensity is magnificent enough as it is. Then add that spice in close on exact quantities and the complexity starts heading through the roof. So mouth-watering.... just so beautifully made...; **f23** light chocolate layering, though the mild late bitterness is not intended; **b23** another superb bottling from this entirely underrated distillery. I have at times argued that this distillery provides the world's most mouth-watering malt. This bottling does little to detract from my point. *59%. sc.*

The Single Cask Miltonduff 2009 sherry butt, cask no. 90030 **(88.5) n22 t22.5 f22 b22** As sherry butts go, not too bad. Perhaps a little tight towards the finish, but forgivably so. Its strength is the intensity of the grape, which is uncompromising, making the integration of the spice and move towards cocoa much more interesting than usual....quite fascinating, even. Its weakness: the uncompromising intensity of the grape.... *64.5%. nc ncf sc.*

The Whisky Barrel Originals Miltonduff 10 Years Old 1st fill oloroso hogshead, cask no. TWB1007, dist Jul 09, bott 2019 **(91.5) n22.5 t23 f23 b23** A rare sulphur-free experience from a sherry butt of this vintage. Technically, a little one dimensional with the fruit filling most of the gaps. But the grape-malt combination works pretty well, though its beating heart is the spice. *63.4%. sc. 254 bottles.*

MORTLACH
Speyside, 1824. Diageo. Working.

Mortlach Aged 12 Years The Wee Witchie sherry & bourbon casks, bott code: L8284DM001 db **(92.5) n23** a lovely toffee and raisin theme with the barley lively enough to have a nibble at it; **t23** mouth-watering, fresh and sharp on delivery. Far more life on this than expected from the colour with the plum notes offering both depth and more salivating qualities; **f23.5** a pleasing spiciness amid the drier vanillas; **b23** clean, untainted sherry casks at work: rather lovely. *43.4%.*

◈ **Mortlach Aged 12 Years The Wee Witchie** bott code: L9176DM006 db **(86.5) n21.5 t22 f21.5 b21.5** A competent full-bodied single malt but overladen and eventually overcome by too much toffee. The tannins cast an attractive spell and the malt stirs the cauldron impressively on delivery. But this is simplistic whisky and lacking in the complexity one feels it could so easily attain. *43.4%*

Mortlach Aged 16 Years db **(87) n20 t23 f22 b22.** Once it gets past the bold if very mildly sulphured nose, the rest of the journey is superb. Earlier Mortlachs in this range had a slightly unclean feel to them and the nose here doesn't inspire confidence. But from arrival on the palate onwards, it's sure-footed, fruity and even refreshing... and always delicious. *43%*

Mortlach Aged 16 Years Distiller's Dram ex-sherry casks, bott code: L8330DM004 db **(93.5) n23.5 t23.5 f23** soft vanilla and barley sugars – as well as a dry, pulsing spiciness representing age; **b23.5** after quite a long period in the doldrums, this distillery really does have the wind in its sails once more. Excellent whisky. *43.4%.*

Mortlach 18 Year Old db **(75) n19 t19 f18 b19.** When I first tasted Mortlach, probably over 30 years ago now, it really wasn't even close to this. Something went very wrong in the late '80s, I can tell you...*43.4%. Diageo.*

Mortlach 20 Year Old Cowie's Blue Seal db **(87) n22 t22 f21.5 b21.5** Pleasant, but apart from a little oak on the nose never gets round to displaying its age. The odd orange blossom honey money opens it up slightly but a shade too tame and predictable. *43.4%.*

Mortlach 25 Year Old db **(91.5) n23** just love the lemon grass alongside the liquorice and hickory; **t23.5** thick and palate-encompassing. The sugars are pretty toasty with a light mocha element in play; **f22.5** crisp finale with a return of the citrus, sitting confidently with the late spice; **b22.5** much more like it. The sugars may be pretty full on, but there is enough depth and complexity for a narrative to be told. Very much a better Mortlach on so many levels. *43.4%.*

Mortlach Rare Old db **(79) n20 t21 f19 b19.** Not rare enough... *43.4%. Diageo.*

Mortlach Special Strength db **(79.5) n20 t21.5 f19 b19.** Does whisky come any more cloyingly sweet than Mortlach...? Not in my experience.... *49%. Diageo.*

◈ **The First Editions Mortlach Aged 13 Years 2007** wine barrel, cask no.18375, bott 2021 **(93) n23 t23.5 f23 b23.5** Now and again a Mortlach appears that tends to surprise you with a puff of smoke. And here is one with the phenols most at home on the nose...mixed in with some acidic (or is it alkaline?) anthracite.... Thankfully that wine cask has left enough room for the malt to stretch its legs, especially on the nose. Though the grape arrives early on in delivery, alongside the reinforcing smoke. As the phenols tail off, the barley becomes cleaner and more dominant forming a superb team with the growing spices. First rate stuff: Mortlach at its absolute best! *50.2%. nc ncf sc 118 bottles*

◈ **The First Editions Mortlach Aged 13 Years 2007** wine barrel, cask no.HL18664, bott 2021 **(84) n22.5 t22.5 f19 b20** One of those casks I find quite fascinating because of the polarisation in its personality. The nose is a tapestry of malt and spicy notes, reinforced with a thread of raisin. Likewise the delivery stops you in your tracks as your taste buds are given a delicious working over of light ulmo honey, muscovado sugars and salivating barley. The finish by comparison is harsh, dry and uncompromising: the exact opposite of the earlier, subtly sweet complexity. Mind you: that can be wine casks for you... 54.5% nc ncf sc 286 bottles

Hepburn's Choice Mortlach 10 Years Old wine cask, dist 2009, bott 2019 **(90.5)** n23 t22.5 f22 b23 Youthfully fresh and malty. But it is the low rumble of smoke on the nose, delivery and finish in particular that genuinely intrigues! Refreshing and crisp, all the same. 46%. nc ncf sc. 375 bottles.

◈ **Hepburn's Choice Mortlach 11 Years Old** wine hogsheads, dist 2009, bott 2020 **(77)** n19 t20 f19 b19 Not sure the wine cask has done this whisky any great favours. A distinctly sulphury hue abounds. 46%. nc ncf. 715 bottles.

◈ **Hepburn's Choice Mortlach 13 Years Old** wine hogsheads, dist 2007, bott 2020 **(78.5)** n20.5 t20.5 f18.5 b19 Overall, a dull and bitter dram which enjoys an all too brief malty surge on delivery. 46%. nc ncf. 512 bottles.

◈ **Old Malt Cask Mortlach Aged 13 Years** wine cask, cask no.HL18667, dist Jun 2007, bott May 2021 **(91)** n23 t23 f22 b23 Few whiskies in Scotland when confronted by the grape thickens up quite like a Mortlach. It is as if the DNA of the malt is predisposed towards gathering together and clotting the very moment a fruit molecule appears. This works both in its favour and against...and here is a classic case of it doing exactly that. When the delivery contracts on the palate we are face to face with a blinding malt intensity, something hinted at by the crushed green grape and gristy nose. The finish is long but limited in complexity, but keeps things simple. Again, in a perfect world, it would have opened up further here...but Mortlach is Mortlach. A superb wine cask....not a single off note or weakness and a chance to watch this distillery do its thing. 50% sc 262 bottles

MOSSTOWIE
Speyside, 1964–1981. Chivas Brothers. Closed.
Rare Old Mosstowie 1979 (84.5) n21.5 t21 f21 b21. Edging inextricably well beyond its sell by date. But there is a lovely walnut cream cake (topped off with brown sugar and spices) to this which warms the cockles. Bless... 43%. Gordon & MacPhail.

NORTH PORT
Highlands (Eastern), 1820–1983. Diageo. Demolished.
Brechin 1977 db **(78)** n19 t21 f18 b20. Fire and brimstone was never an unknown quantity with the whisky from this doomed distillery. Some soothing oils are poured on this troubled – and sometimes attractively honeyed – water of life. 54.2%

OBAN
Highlands (Western), 1794. Diageo. Working.
Oban 14 Years Old db **(79)** n19 t22 f18 b20. Absolutely all over the place. The cask selection sits very uncomfortably with the malt. I look forward to the resumption of normality to this great but ill-served distillery. 43%

◈ **Oban Aged 14 Years** bott code: L9337CM005 db **(88)** n23 t22.5 f20.5 b22 So much better than the last Oban 14 I tasted, which had lost its identity totally. Here it now has a far more bright and shimmering attitude on the nose, as was the case back in the day. Still heavier than of old with less fretwork to admire, but at least we are now blessed with honey and blood oranges, as well as pretty rounded maltiness. Likewise, the delivery is alive and salivating as the heather-honey kissed malt shews little inhibition...well, at first. However, the dull bitterness that creeps in at the midpoint is determined to last the course, alas. A long way from the magnificent Obans of its heyday, but this is much nearer the mark than in recent years. 43%.

Oban The Distillers Edition special release OD 162.FX, dist 1998, bott 2013 db **(87.5)** n22.5 t22.5 f21 b21.5. Some attractive kumquat and blood orange makes for a fruity and rich malt, though just a little furry towards the finish. Decent Demerara early on, too. 43%

Oban Distillery Exclusive Bottling batch no. 02, refill, ex-bourbon and rejuvenated casks, bott code: L9337CM008 db **(91.5)** n23 t23.5 f22 b23 Who knew that one day they'd bring out an Oban this sweet? Usually a malt with an absent-minded, salty dryness that never did anything with great intention or seemingly with a game plan. Here, though, this has been set out to be as friendly as possible. And it has most certainly succeeded! 48%. 7,500 bottles.

Oban Little Bay db **(87.5)** n21 t23 f21.5 b22. A pleasant, refreshing simple dram. Clean and juicy in part and some wonderful oak-laden spice to stir things up a little. Just a little too much chewy toffee near the end, though. 43%

Game of Thrones Oban Bay Reserve The Night's Watch db (87.5) n22 t23 f21 b21.5 Starts promisingly, even offering a saltiness you tend not to see from this distillery these days. The intense grist on the malt makes for a beautiful delivery. But flattens fast and furiously as the caramels kick in. *43%.*

PITTYVAICH
Speyside, 1975–1993. Diageo. Demolished.
Pittyvaich 28 Year Old db (86.5) n22.5 t22 f20.5 b21.5 The nose is an attractive blend of malt and hazelnut. The delivery is sweet, gristy and promising. But it thins out fast and dramatically. So limited in scope, but pleasant in the early phases. *52.1%. 4,680 bottles. Diageo Special Releases 2018.*

PORT ELLEN
Islay, 1825–1983. Diageo. Closed.
Port Ellen 9 Rogue Casks 40 Year Old db (96) n24 t24 f23.5 b24.5 One of the great surprise whiskies of this any many years. I didn't expect this bottling to display such astounding elegance and balance, but it does from the first moment to the last. It has taken me close on three hours to analyse this malt. Had I the space, my notes could probably take up a page of this book. But here I have simplified it over many temperatures and varying oxidisation levels. Those nine rogue casks must have been as beautifully seasoned as they come. Stunning. *50.9%.*

Port Ellen Aged 37 Years dist 1978 db (91) n24.5 t22.5 f22 b22 The bark is far better than the bite: one of the great noses of the year cannot be backed up on the palate as the oak is simply too demanding. An historical experience, but ensure you spend as much time nosing as you do tasting... *55.2%. 2,940 bottles. Diageo Special Releases 2016.*

Port Ellen 37 Year Old refill American oak hogsheads & refill American oak butts db (88) n23 t21.5 f22 b21.5 The oak scars the overall beauty of the malt. *51%. 2,988 bottles.*

Port Ellen 39 Years Old db (96.5) n24 t24 f24 b24.5 A malt which defies time and logic, and the short-sighted individuals who closed down this distillery and later, unforgivably, ripped out its innards (despite my one-kneed imploring). Tragically beautiful. *50.9%.*

PULTENEY
Highlands (Northern), 1826. Inver House Distillers. Working.
Old Pulteney Aged 12 Years db (90.5) n22 t23 f22.5 b23 A cleaner, zestier more joyous composition than the old 43%, though that has less to do with strength than overall construction. A dramatic whisky which, with further care, could get even closer to the truth of this distillery. *40%*

Old Pulteney Aged 12 Years bott code L15/030 R15/5046 IB db (91) n22.5 t23 f22.5 b23 Remarkably consistent from the bottling above. The salt continues to ensure lustre, though this bottling has a little extra – and welcome – barley gristiness. *40%. ncf.*

Old Pulteney Aged 15 Years db (95.5) n24 t24 f23.5 b24 More than a night cap. One you should definitely take to bed with you... *46%.*

Old Pulteney Aged 17 Years bott code: L15/329 R15/5530 IB db (82) n20.5 t22.5 f19 b20 This is usually one of the greatest whiskies bottled anywhere in the world. But not even something of Pulteney 17's usually unfathomable excellence and charisma can withstand this degree of sulphur. Much greater care has to be taken in the bottling hall to preserve the integrity of what should be one of Scotland's most beautiful offerings to the world. *46%. ncf.*

Old Pulteney Aged 18 Years db (81) n19 t21.5 f20 b20.5 If you are going to work with sherry butts you have to be very careful. And here we see a whisky that is not careful enough as the sulphur does its usual damage. For those in central Europe without the "sulphur gene", then no problem as the fruit is still intact. *46%.*

Old Pulteney Aged 21 Years db (97.5) n25 t24 f24 b24.5 By far and away one of the great whiskies of 2012, absolutely exploding from the glass with vitality, charisma and class. One of Scotland's great undiscovered distilleries about to become discovered, I think... and rightly so! *46%*

Old Pulteney Aged 25 Years American & Spanish oak casks, bott code: L17/282 R17/5353 IB db (96) n25 t23.5 f23.5 b24 A quiet but incredibly complex reminder why this distillery is capable of producing World Whisky of the Year. Age is all around you, but degradation there is none. *46%.*

Old Pulteney 35 Year Old db (89) n23 t21.5 f22.5 b22 A malt on the perimeter of its comfort zone. But there are enough gold nuggets included to make this work. Just. *46%.*

Old Pulteney Aged 40 Years db (95) n23.5 t23.5 f24 b24 This malt still flies as close to the sun as possible. But some extra fruit, honey and spice now grasps the tannins by the throat to ensure a whisky of enormous magnitude and complexity *51.3%*

Old Pulteney 1990 Vintage American & Spanish casks db **(85) n21 t23 f21 b20.** As you know, anything which mentions sherry butts gets me nervous – and for good reason. Even with a World Great distillery like Pulteney. Oddly enough, this bottling is, as near a dammit, free of sulphur. Yee-hah! The bad news, though, is that it is also untroubled by complexity as well. It reminded me of some heavily sherried peaty jobs...and then I learned that ex Islay casks were involved. That may or may not be it. But have to say, beyond the first big, salivating, lightly spiced moments on delivery you wait for the story to unfurl...and it all turns out to be dull rumours. *46%*.

Old Pulteney 2006 Vintage first fill ex-bourbon casks, bott 2017, bott code: L17/279 R17/5452 IB db **(93) n23 t23.5 f23 b23.5** A beautiful, lightly salted ceremony of malt with the glycerine feel of raspberry and cream Swiss rolls. Just so love it! *46%*.

Old Pulteney Dunnet Head Lighthouse bourbon & sherry casks db **(90.5) n22 t23.5 f22 b23** Loads to chew over with this heavyweight.*46%. nc ncf. Exclusive to travel retail.*

Old Pulteney Huddart db **(88.5) n22 t22.5 f22 b22** Hopefully not named after my erstwhile physics teacher of 45 years ago, Ernie Huddart, who, annoyingly, for an entire year insisted on calling me Murphy rather than Murray, despite my constant correcting his mistake. One day he told me off for my not remembering some or other Law of Physics. When he finished berating me quite unpleasantly at high volume before my fellow classmates, I simply said: "Well, sir, that's fine coming from you. You've had a year to learn that my name is Murray and not Murphy, and still you failed!" He was so lost for words at this impudence I got away with it, though if his glare could have killed... Anyway, back to the whisky: this seemingly young, lightly smoked version shows all the hallmarks of being finished in peaty casks, as opposed to being distilled from phenolic malt, hence the slightly mottled and uneven feel to this. Odd, but attractive. Oh, and Huddart...? I think that's actually the name of the nondescript old street on which the distillery sits *46%*.

Old Pulteney Navigator bourbon & sherry casks db **(80) n19 t23 f18 b20.** Sherry butts have clearly been added to this. Not sure why, as the sulphur only detracts from the early honey riches. The compass is working when the honey and cocoa notes briefly harmonise in beautiful tandem. But otherwise, badly off course. *46%. nc ncf.*

Old Pulteney Noss Head Lighthouse bourbon casks db **(84) n22.5 t22 f19 b20.5.** If Noss Head was as light as this dram, it'd be gone half way through its first half decent storm. An apparent slight overuse of third and less sturdy second fill casks means the finale bitters out considerably. A shame, as the nose and delivery is about as fine a display of citrus maltiness as you'll find. *46%. Travel retail exclusive. WB15/327*

Old Pulteney Pentland Skerries Lighthouse db **(85) n21 t22 f20.5 b21.5.** A chewy dram with an emphasis on the fruit. Sound, evens enjoys the odd chocolate-toffee moment. But a little sulphur, apparent on the nose, creeps in to take the gloss off. *46%. WB15/323*

Gordon & MacPhail Connoisseurs Choice Pulteney Aged 19 Years first fill bourbon barrel, cask no. 1071, dist 26 Aug 98, bott 21 Jun 18 **(95.5) n23.5 t24 f24 b24** Malt from one of the world's very finest distilleries matured in a first- class cask. The result is inevitable. The interplay between oak and malt starts on the first molecules to hit the nose and ends only when the story is told. Can't ask any more of the spices, or their interaction with the liquorice and Manuka honey mix. Everything is perfectly paced and weighted, even the natural caramels that could so easily have tipped this towards a blander bottling. Toasty, sublimely complex and breath-taking. *57.5%. sc. 192 bottles.*

⬥ **Old Malt Cask Pulteney Aged 18 Years** bourbon barrel, cask no.18699, dist Sept 2002, bott May 2021 **(94.5) n24** a salty serenade on the nose. Traces of honey threading though the still fertile malt. Delicate slices of Brazil nut as it winds towards a biscuit and light golden syrup thread. All the time the tannins offer a deeper note unique to slightly older whiskies... Finally, when you thought you had perhaps worked it all out...the vaguest hint of smoke... Just wow...! **t23.5** that golden syrup/heather honey blend arrives early on delivery and with a wonderful vanilla escort...then we have the slow evolving of myriad complex notes, playing between the deepening tanning and the still intense malt itself. And all in slow motion.. The saltiness on the nose has been replaced by a creamy subtext which binds the more flaky notes to the main theme; **f23** just more of the same...though now with delicate spice and the gentlest hint of milk chocolate to remind you that the oak has been working to great effect over the last 18 years...; **b24** from a truly great distillery comes a cracking cask at a wonderful age. Pure, gorgeously complex enjoyment from a whisky that is in no hurry to reveal its secrets. *50% sc 182 bottles*

ROSEBANK
Lowlands, 1840–1993. Ian Macleod. Closed- soon to re-open. (The gods have answered!)

Rosebank 21 Year Old refill American oak casks, dist 1992 db **(95.5) n23.5 t24 f24 b24** Rosebank is at its very best at eight-years-old. Well, that won't happen again, so great to see it has proven successful at 21... *55.3%. 4,530 bottles. Diageo Special Releases 2014.*

ROYAL BRACKLA

Speyside, 1812. Bacardi. Working.

Royal Brackla Aged 12 Years bott code: L18192B700 db **(85)** n22 t22 f20 b21 A definite improvement on previous bottlings but, coming from Bacardi's formidable stable, I had expected more. The finish is still dull as ditch water, with nothing other than toffee to find but there is an upping of fresh fruit on both nose and delivery. 40%.

Royal Brackla Aged 16 Years bott code: L18158B700 db **(88)** n22.5 light and zesty, a little spice flickers around the caramel; t22.5 soft, bordering luxuriant, there is a big malt and caramel hook up. But it is the all too brief, refreshing, zingy delivery which stars; f21 still a little too much on the dull-ish caramel side; b22 a very pleasant malt, but you get the feeling it is being driven with the handbrake on... 40%.

Royal Brackla Aged 21 Years bott code: L18297B701 db **(91.5)** n23 maintains its unusual but delightful lychee sweetness, that sweetness now extending to maple syrup and fudge; t23 delicate and salivating, initially shewing little sign of great age. It takes a while but the toastier tannins finally arrive; f22.5 salty, with a chocolate fudge finale; b23 where both the 12- and 16-years olds appear both to be tied to a vat of toffee, this beauty has been given its wings. Also, I remember this for being a malt with a curious lychee note, hence tasting it today. For yesterday I tasted a malt matured in a lychee liqueur barrel. Pleased to report no shortage of lychees here, either. 40%.

Scyfion Choice Royal Brackla 2007 Banyuls wine cask finished, bott 2019 **(82)** n20 t21.5 f20.5 b20 Malty, lightly spiced, tart and never, for a moment, properly at home with itself or balanced. 46%. nc ncf sc. 150 bottles.

⋄ **Scyfion Choice Royal Brackla 2007** moscatel naranja cask finish, dist 2007, bott 2021 **(88.5)** n20.5 t23.5 f22 b22.5 Really fascinating malt, this. This nose is disjointed with the grape hardly on speaking terms with either the barley or tannins. And you fear the worst. But this hits the palate running: the usual Brackla malty thrust, but being covered by a sharp fruitiness, like a jam covers the pastry in a jam tart. A whirlwind attack of pepper soon fades out of the equation, allowing a surprisingly soft finish where now the fruit has taken complete control, allowing the tannins only brief incursions. 48% nc ncf 91 bottles

⋄ **The Single Cask Royal Brackla 2009** barrel, cask no. 304159, dist 24 Mar 09 **(94)** n23 clean, gorgeously structured barley. The spices are a side dish: the vanilla and malt is served on a platter; t24 oh...! You hear yourself inwardly groan with delight as the boisterous barley makes its entry, still fresh and intact and helped along by the thinnest strand of ulmo honey. But this has a degree of bite, too, though the amazing salivating qualities tends to take your mind off this side of things; f23.5 buttery butterscotch and vanilla outwardly...look closer and the barley and light tannin still dazzles...; b23.5 one of my greatest disappointments on the scotch scene in recent years has been the lack of excellent bourbon cask bottlings to show distilleries at their very best. One of those which has suffered has been Royal Brackla. From this, you can see why I am a fan of this distillery presented in an oak which showcases its considerable charm. 57.2%. sc.

Whisky Illuminati Royal Brackla 2011 Spanish oak sherry butt, cask no. 900077 **(93)** n23 a real nuttiness to this grape – all guns are blazing; t23.5 lush and chewy with the sherry pounding the taste buds in the same way waves are pounding the British coast at this moment thanks to Storm Ciara, which is presently battering all parts of the British coastline: certainly a dram for the moment...; f23 only toward the finish does the sweetness settle towards a relaxed ulmo honey and plummy interplay. Delightful...; b23.5 every bit as punchy as the strength suggests, with the sherry influence piling in at full tilt and refusing to hold back. 68%. sc. 150 bottles.

ROYAL LOCHNAGAR

Highlands (Eastern), 1826. Diageo. Working.

Royal Lochnagar Aged 12 Years db **(84)** n21 t22 f20 b21. More care has been taken with this than some other bottlings from this wonderful distillery. But I still can't understand why it never quite manages to get out of third gear...or is the caramel on the finish the giveaway...? 40%

⋄ **Royal Lochnagar Aged 12 Years** bott code: L9214CM003 db **(93)** n23.5 superb! A sharp, copper-rich aroma going heavy on the esters. The malt forms a lovely outer shield. But it cannot entirely keep in all the exotic fruit, including pineapple and jackfruit which gives the core a delightful sharpness...; t23 a succulent, salivating delivery, soft on arrival with the barley and light caramels melting first. Slowly that distinctive metallic tang builds, and with it the fruit – though now less from tropical climes but of a more prosaic grapiness; f23 a pleasant farewell of vanilla, toffee, light ulmo honey, barley, Garibaldi biscuit and the very lightest liquorice: complex....; b23.5 for the first time in some little while I have found a Lochnagar 12 which manages to underline the small still properties of this distillery with rich and intense dram true to its traditional style. For too long bottlings had been flat and lifeless

195

and could have been mistaken as the ill-treated malts from anywhere. Not this time. This projects a delightful richness unique to Royal Lochnagar. It is like welcoming back a long lost friend. Queen Victoria, once this distillery's patron, would have been amused.... 40%.

Royal Lochnagar Distillery Exclusive batch no. 01, first-fill European oak and refill casks, bott code: L9302DQ0001 db **(82)** n22 t23 f17.5 b19.5 Ultimately a dull, monotonous whisky after a promising and lively start. Love the fresh, salivating delivery and with some great spices, too. But the story ends by the midpoint. The European oak has done this no favours whatsoever, ensuring a furry, off-key finale. 48%. 5,004 bottles.

Game of Thrones Royal Lochnagar 12 Year Old House Baratheon db **(89)** n22 t22.5 f22 b22.5 Not sure when I last encountered a Lochnager of such simplicity. Friendly and impossible not to like. 40%.

The First Editions Royal Lochnagar Aged 19 Years 2000 refill hogshead, cask no. 16350, bott 2019 **(91.5)** n23 t23 f22.5 b23 There is no getting away from the effect of the small stills here: every sensation is in concentrate form. A kind of a head-shaking, wow! of a malt... 55.5%. nc ncf sc. 384 bottles.

ST. MAGDALENE
Lowlands, 1798–1983. Diageo. Demolished.

Linlithgow 30 Years Old dist 1973 db **(70)** n18 t18 f16 b18. A brave but ultimately futile effort from a malt that is way past its sell-by date. 59.6%

Gordon & MacPhail Private Collection St. Magdalene 1982 refill American hogshead, cask no. 2092, dist 1 Jul 82, bott 21 Mar 19 **(96)** n24 t24 f23.5 b24.5 It has been eight long years since a new St Magdalene turned up in my tasting room and that, like this, was distilled just a year before the closure of the distillery itself. And I can tell you for nothing, when it was made never in a million years did any of those within the distillery believe for a second that it would finally be tasted nearly 40 years after the spirit was filled into a very good American oak barrel. For a start, this was a Lowland malt that, in its lifetime, was used exclusively for blending, most of it at three and five years old. It is light in structure and flavour and conversations I had with blenders in the 1980s confirmed that they didn't trust this malt to add sufficient body to the malt content for it to be used for older blends, though that didn't stop Diageo once bringing it out as a 23-year-old. Of all the St. Mag distillates I tasted from about 1970 through to 1983, I thought 1982 the finest of the bunch, so no surprise that it has held its head high and proud here, even displaying the same citrusy undercurrent that I thought made the 10-year-old so charming way back in 1992. I have in here, not just a throwback but a little whisky miracle in my glass. This malt has no right to be this good. But, my god it is...!! 53%. sc. 161 bottles.

SCAPA
Highlands (Island–Orkney), 1885. Chivas Brothers. Working.

Scapa 12 Years Old db **(88)** n23 t22 f21 b22. Always a joy. 40%

Scapa 16 Years Old db **(81)** n21 t20.5 f19.5 b20. For it to be so tamed and toothless is a crime against a truly great whisky which, handled correctly, would be easily among the finest the world has to offer. 40%

Scapa Glansa peated whisky cask finish, batch no. GL05, bott Jul 18 db **(91)** n22 t23.5 f22.5 b23 A delightful whisky which could be raised several notches in quality if the influence of the caramel is diminished. 40%.

Scapa Skiren db **(89.5)** n22.5 t22.5 f22 b22.5 Chaps who created this: lovely, you really have to power this one up a bit... 40%

Gordon & MacPhail Connoisseurs Choice Scapa Aged 30 Years refill bourbon barrel, cask no. 10585, dist 2 Sept 88, bott 13 Sept 18 **(94)** n22.5 t24 f23.5 b24 One of those exceptionally rare occasions when the threatening tannins on the nose fail to materialise on the palate. Instead we have glorious display of varied honey tones far more usually associated with its neighbouring Orkney distillery. Stunning displays of light saltiness mixes brilliantly with the lime blossom honey before the spices and tannins set. A thing of beauty. 53.8%. sc. 148 bottles.

SPEYBURN
Speyside, 1897. Inver House Distillers. Working.

Speyburn Aged 10 Years bott code: L16/303 R165434 IB db **(84.5)** n21 t21.5 f21 b21 Appears to celebrate and even emphasises its remarkable thinness of body. As usual, juicy with a dominant toffee character. 40%.

Speyburn Aged 10 Years Travel Exclusive American oak ex-bourbon & ex-sherry casks, bott code L18/055 R18/5069 IB db **(89.5)** n21.5 t22.5 f22.5 b23 Really imaginative use of excellent sherry butts. An understatedly complex and delicious malt. 46%. ncf.

Speyburn Aged 15 Years American oak & Spanish oak casks, bott code L1717/253 R17/5323 IB db **(91)** n22 t23.5 f22 b23.5 Well done: not an off sherry butt in sight, helping to make this an enjoyably rich and fulsome malt. One of the most inventive and sympathetic Speyburns of all time. 46%.

Speyburn Aged 18 Years db **(86)** n22 t22.5 f20 b21.5 Nutty, malty and displaying a cocoa tendency. But the finish is a bit on the bitter side. 46%.

Speyburn Aged 25 Years db **(92)** n22 t24 f23 b23. Either they have re-bottled very quickly or I got the diagnosis dreadfully wrong first time round. Previously I wasn't overly impressed; now I'm taken aback by its beauty. Some change. 46%

Speyburn Arranta Casks first fill ex-bourbon casks bott code: L16/097 R16/5130 IB db **(90)** n22 t23 f22 b23 Speyburn at its most vocal and interesting: rather beautifully constructed. 46%.

Speyburn Bradon Orach bott code: L17/039 R17/5048 IB db **(75)** n19 t19 f18.5 b18.5 Remains one of the most curious distillery bottlings on Speyside and one still unable to find either its balance or a coherent dialogue. 40%.

Speyburn Hopkins Reserve Travel Exclusive bott code R18/5066 IB db **(92)** n23 t23 f22.5 b23.5 The kind of ultra-simplistic raw, smoky Speysider that the distillery's founder John Hopkins would have recognised – and drooled over - over a century ago... 46%. ncf.

⬧ **The First Editions Speyburn Aged 14 Years 2007** sherry butt, cask no.HL18373, bott 2021 **(94)** n23 the Dundee cake's toasted raisin compliment runneth over. Those spices are more or less perfection for the weight of the fruit and oak overture...; t23.5 that is rather charming. Speyburn is hardly the most robust of malts and I feared total annihilation by the grape. But it is not so. The retaining walls may be intense fruitiness but the ceilings are certainly plastered in sufficient barley for complexity to be disarming. Indeed, vanilla tones from the oak join forces to keep a dignified dryness to the jammy, plumy tones....; f23.5 excellent spices and now reverting back to the nose with those toasted raisins; b23.5 not only could I easily drink this whisky....I could kiss it. Today I have suffered disappointment with three malts ruined or at least damaged by sulphur casks. This being a sherry butt, I was wary, to put it mildly. There was no need! Speyburn presented in a manner very rarely seen. And beautifully so. 50.2% nc ncf sc 32 bottles

THE SPEYSIDE DISTILLERY
Speyside, 1990. Speyside Distillers. Working.

Spey 10 Year Old port casks db **(87)** n22 t22.5 f20.5 b22 Soft and nutty, there is an attractive easiness to the fruit as it makes its salivating, bitter-sweet way around the palate. Just a little bit of a tang on the finish, though. 46%. nc ncf. 3,000 bottles.

Spey 12 Years Old limited edition, finished in new oak casks db **(85.5)** n21.5 t23 f19.5 b21.5. One of the hardest whiskies I have had to define this year: it is a curious mixture of niggling faults and charming positives which come together to create a truly unique scotch. The crescendo is reached early after the delivery with an amalgamation of acacia honey, barley sugar and butter notes interlocking with something bordering classicism. However, the nose and finish, despite the chalky oak, reveals that something was lacking in the original distillate or, to be more precise, was rather more than it should have been. Still, some hard work has obviously gone into maximising the strengths of a distillery that had hitherto failed to raise the pulse and impresses for that alone. 40%. nc. 8,000 bottles.

Spey 18 Years Old ltd edition, fresh sherry casks db **(82.5)** n19 t23.5 f19 b21. What a shame this malt has been brushed with sulphur. Apparent on nose and finish, it still can't diminish ir detract from the joy of the juicy grape on delivery and the excellent weight as the liquorice and treacle add their gentle treasures and pleasures. So close to a true classic. 46%. nc.

Spey Chairman's Choice db **(77)** n19 t21 f18 b19. Their Chairman's Choice, maybe. But not mine... 40%

Spey Fumare db **(90.5)** n22 t23.5 f22 b23 A very different type of peaty malt with some surprising twists and turns. As fascinating as it is quietly delicious. I am looking at Speyside distillery in a new light...46%. nc ncf.

Spey Fumare Cask Strength db **(93)** n23 t23.5 f23 b23.5 Unquestionably The Speyside Distillery in its prettiest pose. And this strength ensures perfect lighting... 59.3%. nc ncf.

Spey Royal Choice db **(87)** n21 t23 f21 b22. "I'll have the slightly feinty one, Fortescue." "Of course, Your Highness. Would that be the slightly feinty one which has a surprising softness on the palate, a bit like a moist date and walnut cake? But with a touch too much oil on the finish?" "That's the blighter! No ice, Fortescue!" "Perish the thought, Sir." "Or water, Forters. One must drink according to the Murray Method, don't you know!" "Very wise, Sir." 46%

Spey Tenné finished in Tawny Port casks db **(90)** n22.5 t23 f22 b22.5 Upon pouring, the handsome pink blush tells you one of three things: i) someone has swiped the whisky and filled the bottle with Mateus Rosé instead; ii) I have just located where I put the pink paraffin or iii) this whisky has been matured in brand spanking new port casks. Far from a technical paragon of virtue so far as distilling is concerned. But those Tawny Port casks have brought something rather magical to the table. And glass. *46%. nc. 18,000 bottles.*

Spey Tenné Cask Strength db (88) n22.5 t22 f21.5 b22 Plenty of weirdness to this – and spicy fun, too! What magnificent (port?) casks they must have used for this....!! *59.5%. nc ncf. 1,500 bottles.*

Spey Trutina bourbon casks db (90) n22.5 t23 f22 b22.5 The best Speyside Distillery bottling I have encountered for a very long time. Entirely feint free and beautifully made. *46%. nc ncf.*

Spey Trutina Cask Strength db (93) n22.5 t24 f23 b23.5 Feint free and fabulous! *59.1%. nc ncf. 1,500 bottles.*

Beinn Dubh db (82) n20 t21 f21 b20. Mountains. Dogs. Who can tell the difference...? I suppose to a degree I can, as this has for more rummy undertones and is slightly less inclined to layering than the old Danish version. *43%*

◇ **Old Malt Cask Speyside Aged 25 Years** refill hogshead, cask no.HL18698, dist Sept 1995, bott May 2021 (86.5) n22.5 t23 f20 b21 It is quite frightening to think that on a cold Sunday morning in a Glasgow warehouse I opened up the first-ever filled cask of Speyside to taste it on its 3rd birthday. The day Speyside distillery could claim that it made whisky, not just new make or malt spirit. Now here I am tasting it as a 25-years-old...so sobering amid all this alcohol. It would take a little bit of artistic licence to describe this as a great 25-year-old malt. It is certainly pretty good, especially if intense barley is your thing. But there is a bite and thinness to this which suggests the stills were a bit fierce the day the spirit safe was flowing. After a quite beautiful crescendo of concentrated barley and acacia honey, it moves towards an ever-bittering fade and there is not enough body to the malt to see off the excesses of the cask. Such a fascinating experience, though... *50% sc* 🍷

SPRINGBANK

Campbeltown, 1828. J&A Mitchell & Co. Working.

Springbank Aged 10 Years db (89.5) n22 t23 f22 b22.5. Although the inherent youthfulness of the 10-y-o has not changed, the depth of body around it has. Keeps the taste buds on full alert. *46%*

Springbank Aged 15 Years db (88.5) n22.5 t22 f22 b22. Last time I had one of these, sulphur spoiled the party. Not this time. But the combination of oil and caramel does detract from the complexity a little. *46%*

Springbank Aged 18 Years db (90.5) n23 busy in the wonderful Springbank way; delicate greengage and date; nippy; t23 yummy, mouthwatering barley and green banana. Fresh with excellent light acacia honey; f21.5 fabulous oak layering, including chocolate. A little off-key furriness from a sherry butt late on; b23 just one so-so butt away from bliss... *46%*

Springbank Aged 21 Years db (90) n22 t23 f22.5 b22.5 A few years ago I was at Springbank when they were bottling a very dark, old-fashioned style 21-year-old. I asked if I could take a 10cl sample with me for inclusion in the Bible; they said they would send it on, though I tasted a glass there and then just for enjoyment's sake. They never did send it, which was a shame. For had they, they most probably would have carried off World Whisky of the Year. This, though very good, is not quite in the same class. But just to mark how special this brand has always been to me, I have made this the 500th new single malt scotch and 700th new whisky in all of the 2015 Whisky Bible. *46%. WB15/096*

Springbank 22 Year Old Single Cask hogshead, cask no. 582, dist May 97, bott Jan 20 db (95.5) n24 t24 f23.5 b24 It is rare these days for me to be genuinely taken aback by a whisky. But this managed it. The malt is pleasingly light in colour for its age, and certainly for a Springbank of this age. So second fill ex-bourbon, even third, possibly. Which when the tannins fire their broadside on the very first sniff...yes, there is reason to be taken aback. Of course, the trademark of this distillery is labyrinthine complexity. And though labyrinthine may be taking it a bit far here, you can still descend very deeply into this malt and have plenty of passages to explore. Certainly, I love to take the saline route here, which gives a delightful piquancy to tannin and sharpens the barley tones that float around it. So it is pleasing to see that this route can be followed on the beautifully soft delivery which just abounds in vanilla. But there is just as much thickset barley, too. This is magnificent malt which repays using the Murray Method for best results. But, as you will see, the nose is at its best at one temperature (relatively cool and the experience on the palate is at its zenith when warmed a little. Oh, and before I forget...look out for the fascinating strata of peat. Fair took me aback, it did... *55.4%. Bottled for HMMJ collection.*

Hazelburn Aged 8 Years bourbon cask, bott 2011 db (94.5) n23 t24 f23.5 b24 A very curious coppery sheen adds extra lustre and does no harm to a very well made spirit filled into top grade oak. For an eight year old malt, something extra special. *46%*

Longrow Aged 10 Years db (78) n19 t20 f19 b20. This has completely bemused me: bereft not only of the usual to-die-for smoke, its warts are exposed badly, as this is way too young. Sweet and malty, perhaps, and technically better than the marks I'm giving it – but this is Longrow, dammit! I am astonished. 46%

Longrow 14 Years Old refill bourbon and sherry casks db (89) n24 t23.5 f19 b22.5. Again, a sherry butt proves the Achilles heel. But until then, a charmer. 46%

Longrow Aged 18 Years (94.5) n25 t23 f23 b23.5 If you gently peat a blend of ulmo, manuka and heather honey you might end up with something as breathtakingly stunning as this. But you probably won't... 46%. WB15/103

Artful Dodger Springbank 18 Year Old 2000 1st fill sherry hogshead, cask no. 646 (96) n24 t24 f24 b24 For an 18-year-old Springbank has all the creaks and grey hairs of something a lot more than twice its age... The oak seems to date back to Robin Hood, the grape could have been from a wine shared by the disciples. This malt (some of them shewing the odd partiality to peat) bends and bows like a medieval inn. But even so you have to say this: the balance and interplay between the delicate factions is a work of art to behold, The palate is not for a single moment molested as the tannins and gentle juices go about their business. This is a malt for that special occasion. A parent's 90th birthday perhaps; your own 60th. Your child's 30th. This is all to do with time and wisdom. And on the subject of time, less than an hour at the glass with this whisky will not do it any justice at all. The next time I taste this, it will be to celebrate the lockdown that keeps me imprisoned in the UK being lifted. It is a whisky for extraordinary moments in one's life. 45.9%. sc.

⬩ **Kingsbury Sar Obair Springbank 28 Year Old** oloroso sherry butt, dist 1991, cask no. 323 (95.5) n24 exudes Springbank: unmistakable, even when the sherry is standing on a little dais and has more to say for itself than all else around. Salty, too. But it is that labyrinthine fruit starting with lightly salted Cape gooseberry and working through pear and onto deeper raisin/date/sultana mix which keeps you quiet for a good while...; t24 wow! That really is salty! A puckering arriving which shrivels your taste buds and waters the eyes for a second or two, malt cascading down the cracks in the way only Springbank can. There is, like on the nose, a fruit salad to enjoy, though this one is now of the exotic variety, which one tends to find only in the very finest old malts. Then the grip is loosened and, the juicy malt has finished its outpouring...and we are on to immense chocolate and raisin territory...; f23.5 slightly lazier now. I have tasted many a Springbank of this kind of age where the oak really does pile in towards the finish bringing with it eucalyptus and such like. Not here. This has settled on its elegant cocoa finish with only a polite degree of spice: this is astonishingly well behaved...; b24 an incredibly salty dram. But just a little too good to sprinkle on your fish 'n' chips. Not sure that fabulous array of pastel-shaded fruit would go with it either. Come to think of it, this Springbank is a meal of its very own... 54.7% sc 185 bottles

The Perfect Fifth Springbank 1993 cask no. 315, dist 28 May 93 (96) n24 t24 f24 b24 A real return to the past here with Springbank in its most full-bodied, uncompromising and complex style which those of us who discovered the distillery in the 1980s remember with great affection. 52.3%. sc.

The Whisky Agency Springbank 1991 hogshead, bott 2018 (95) n24 t23.5 f23.5 b24 There are many days I'm exhausted because I have tasted nothing but poor or second-rate whisky. Then there are others, like today, when both my brain and taste buds are beaten into submission by a relentless procession of excellent to outstanding drams. Today is the latter, and my day, thankfully, is coming to an end as I head towards my 800th whisky of the year (this is number 799). This malt positively crawls of Springbankian messages: the mix of sturdy oak and varied citrus – lime marmalade leading the way – but also of an antique nature as in the aroma of ancient polished furniture. Can the delivery be quite so good? Surely not! Well, actually it isn't, but only by whisker. The fruit is stubbornly there, though more down the lime pastels this time. Then a massive injection of oaky caramel. The finish maybe a pretty routine round-up of spices and vanillas, but you are thankful for the delicate normality. And, like so many Springbanks of that era you are only afterwards left thinking: actually, there's a little peat doing the rounds, as well. Frankly if all the 1,000 plus whiskies I had to taste for the Bible were like this, I'd never get finished... 46.4%.

STRATHISLA
Speyside, 1786. Chivas Brothers. Working.
Strathisla 12 Years Old db (85.5) n21.5 t22 f21 b21. A slight reduction in strength from the old bottling and a significant ramping up of toffee notes means this is a malt which will do little to exert your taste buds. Only a profusion of spice is able to cut through the monotonous style. Always sad to see such a lovely distillery so comprehensively gagged. 40%.

Hidden Spirits Strathisla 15 Year Old dist 2002, bott 2018 **(89) n21.5 t23 f22 b22.5** At times simplistic, at others attractively complex. *51.2%.*

STRATHMILL
Speyside, 1891. Diageo. Working.

Strathmill 25 Year Old refill American oak casks, dist 1988 Old **(89) n23 t22 f22 b22** A blending malt which reveals the kind of big malty deal it offers older brands. *52.4%. 2,700 bottles. Diageo Special Releases 2014.*

⬦ **The Whisky Chamber Strathmill 13 Jahre 2007** refill Oloroso hogshead **(87) n23 t22 f20.5 b21.5** One of those malts which starts off immaculately smart and in Jermyn Street togs, but once you take the waistcoat off you'll see it is wearing disposable collars and cuffs. Impossible other than to adore the nose which shimmers like a barrow-load of Cape gooseberries and spicy, sweating dates. And at first the succulence, packed with delightful heather honey and sultana kicks off like a dessert wine. But the dryness and bitterness kicks in halfway through and remains. Never mind. Plenty of the delivery to enjoy. *55.5%. sc.*

TALISKER
Highlands (Island–Skye), 1832. Diageo. Working.

Talisker Aged 10 Years bott code: L0045CM001 db **(84.5) n22.5 t22.5 f19 b20.5** There is a more youthful stirring to the nose than the original old 8-year-old used to possess. Decent smoke and a vague spice prickle. A kind of caramelised version of a trusty old friend. Conversely, the attractive, silky delivery sees the smoke taking its time to make its mark though the barley is much livelier, at first offering a juicy start before the caramels take hold. But it's downhill rapidly for the finish which really dishes out the caramel before an untidy light furry touch. So, sadly, still nothing like the dashing Talisker of old (when they purposefully used only ex-bourbon casks for sharper impact and clarity), the one where as a party piece amongst friends I would buy them a double hit of this and then, after carefully nosing, taking the whole lot in one go, chewing slowly, and then let the insane spices do the rest. Just tried it: next to nothing. Just a polite buzz on delivery where once there was a nuclear explosion. Humungous amounts of toffee, though...and the later, irritating, buzz is not, alas, spice at all... *45.8%.*

Talisker Aged 18 Years bott code: L0023CM001 db **(86.5) n23 t22 f20 b21.5** Like the 10-year-old, not up to the same high standards of the last bottling I tasted. Starts promisingly as a deft smokiness drifts in and out a light heather honey and lightly-salted cucumber semi-freshness. But the delivery feels weighed down by far too much toffee while the finish is bitter and uneven. Some OK moments early on. But Talisker should be so much better than this. *45.8%.*

Talisker Aged 25 Years bott 2017, bott code: L7023CM000 db **(96.5) n24 t24 f24 b24.5** A malt of magnificent complexity that generously rewards time and concentration. So for some, it may not be easy to get through the forests of oak early on, but switching your senses on to full alert not only pays dividends, but is no less than this great old malt deserves or demands. *45.8%. 21,498 bottles.*

Talisker 30 Years Old db **(93.5) n23 t24 f23 b23.5** Much fresher and more infinitely entertaining than the 25 year old...!!! *45.8%*

Talisker 30 Years Old db **(84.5) n21 t21.5 f21 b21.** Toffee-rich and pretty one dimensional. Did I ever expect to say that about a Talisker at 30...? *53.1%*

Talisker 57 Degrees North db **(95) n24 t24.5 f23 b23.5** A glowing tribute, I hope, for a glowing whisky... *57%*

Talisker Dark Storm charred oak db **(92) n22 t23.5 f23 b23.5** Much more like it! Unlike the Storm, which appeared to labour under some indifferent American oak, this is just brimming with vitality and purpose. *45.8%.*

Talisker Neist Point bott code: L6067CM000 db **(87) n22 t21.5 f22 b21.5** Not exactly Nil Points, but for people like me who adore Talisker (indeed, it was a visit to this distillery 43 years ago that turned my appreciation of whisky into a passionate love affair), it tastes like the malt has barely got out of second gear. Where is the fizz and bite of the peppery phenols on impact? The journey through myriad styles of smoke? The breath-taking and life-giving oomph? Not to be found in this pleasantly tame and overly sweet version, though the spices do mount to something towards the very end. It is like observing a lion that has had its teeth forcibly removed. *45.8%.*

Talisker Port Ruighe db **(88) n22 t22 f22 b22.** Sails into port without changing course *45.8%.*

Talisker Skye (85) n21 t22 f21 b21. The sweetest, most docile Talisker I can ever remember with the spices working hard in the background but weirdly shackled. More Toffee Sky than Vanilla... *45.8% WB16/051*

Talisker Skye bott code L1215CM011 db **(95) n24** the smoke dazzles: sweet, minty and full on, it also digs out some hickory for good measure. The smokiest Talisker I have nosed possibly this century: one that means business, but never loses its taut elegance, either...; **t24** I am almost in disbelief here. How long has it been since I tasted a Talisker and spices burned though with such a peppery intensity? Not like of 40 years ago, admittedly, or even 30. But certainly with more intent than we have seen in the last quarter of a century. The demerara sugars and gristy young malt also make a delightful mark in whisky which oozes quality from every poore; **f23** the oils which had done such a magnificent job early on really build now and with the light caramels smother all but the soft, velvety vanilla and the jagged spice. Cut the caramel further this would be simply astonishing whisky...; **b24** I had to smile how the label boasts that the distillery is the "oldest" on the island, now that it at last has company. So I was curious to see how they would they respond. Of all island whiskies of Scotland, this is the one that has perhaps disappointed most in recent years, having lost the innate fire and zest that set it apart from not just any other distillery in Scotland, but the world. In other words, it had lost its way. But, my word....this is so much like Talisker of old, warming and comforting in equal measures. Talisker, in 1975, was the first distillery I ever visited and was introduced there to its secrets direct from the cask: a true life-changing moment. I, also, have spent a lifetime encouraging people to spit their whisky rather than swallow...but with one exception: Talisker. Indeed, nearly 30 years ago I had the fun of introducing Sir Michael Palin (oh, congrats on the "Sir", Mike!) to cask strength Talisker in my kitchen, the effect of which was not unlike me strapping him into an electric chair: the greatest experience of his drinking life, he called it as he staggered slightly, in shock, towards my front door... Since then, Talisker has declined to the point of insignificance: a flat whisky with a bit of smoke but too much caramel. Not now; not with this: at that younger age which always suited this distillery better than most. This great distillery, perhaps spurred on by local competition, has with Lazarus qualities returned to life. Don't spit. Don't sip. Gargle and swallow. At last here is a Talisker worthy of that most ancient tradition. 45.8%

Talisker Storm db **(85.5) n20 t23 f21 b21.5** The nose didn't exactly go down a storm in my tasting room. There are some deft seashore touches, but the odd poor cask −evident on the finish, also - has undone the good. But it does recover on the palate early on with an even, undemanding and attractively sweet display showing malt to a higher degree than I have seen any Talisker before. 45.8%.

Talisker Storm bott code: L9249CM003 db **(89.5) n23** much more salient peat than in earlier bottlings and though the normal bite of spice is now a gentle peck, the layering of the phenols, aided by light milk chocolate, is rather lovely; **t21.5** there is a youthful attack to the arrival which is hinted at on the nose, but nothing like so obviously as can be found here. The midground gets lost in just little too much caramel; **f22.5** the peat and cocoa reasserts itself just in the nick of time and the malt grows dramatically in quality from their involvement. The spices certainly begin to kick in as the light oils vanish; **b22.5** what an improvement. Still none of the old Talisker fizz and more of a gentle breeze than the storm that was once guaranteed from any distillery bottling from this distillery. And though naggingly young, there is an attractive character and structure to this, especially on the nose and finish. 45.8%.

Hepburn's Choice Talisker 9 Years Old sherry butt, dist 2011, bott 2020 **(91.5) n22.5** confident, clean, gently peated and a light hint of creamy chocolate mint; **t23** brilliant mouth feel: the oils have gathered just the right degree of viscosity to give both weight and depth but without overwhelming the fragile phenols; **f23** the spices arrive in lacklustre fashion. But the quiet integration of malt, peat and oaky caramels is superb; **b23** one of the those sherry butts that adds not an atom of fruit. And probably just as well, because this will charm you to death in is present form. Just lacking a more intense spiciness to give this more Taliskerness. 46%. nc ncf sc. 903 bottles.

Old Malt Cask Talisker Aged 9 Years sherry butt, cask no. 17806, dist Dec 10, bott Dec 20 **(87.5) n22.5 t21.5 f22 b21.5** Insanely saline on the nose with the peat having to battle its way through alongside the young grist. The sherry butt offers no negative connotations but the peat and spice − the usual foundation stone for this distillery − has gone AWOL. 50%. nc ncf sc. 411 bottles.

Old Man Cask Talisker Aged 12 Years bourbon barrel, cask no.HL18665, dist Dec 2008, bott May 2021 **(90) n23** the peat takes some finding, but it is there. Just as telling is a citrussy maltiness. Understated and elegant; **t22.5** even after a dozen years there is an alluring youthful gristiness to this which helps build the smoke levels. The spices are in no hurry to arrive but once ensconced on your taste buds, decidedly ramp up the amps; **f22** good Lord! This has to be one of the shortest Talisker finishes ever with the spices suddenly vanishing, replaced by some pretty simple vanilla; **b22.5** with such a good bourbon cask in play you'd expect the peat to come out flying, angular and full of attacking intent. Instead, the phenols play a remarkably docile part in the malt and are happy to give the piece an air of sophistication and contentment. *50% sc 298 bottles*

TAMDHU
Speyside, 1897. Ian Macleod Distillers. Working (re-opened 3rd March 2013).

Tamdhu db (84.5) n20 t22.5 f21 b21. So-so nose, but there is no disputing the fabulous, stylistic honey on delivery. The silkiest Speyside delivery of them all. *40%*

Tamdhu Aged 10 Years oak sherry cask db (69.5) n17 t18.5 f17 b17. A much better malt when they stick exclusively to ex-bourbon casks, as used to be the case. *40%*

Tamdhu Aged 18 Years bott code L0602G L12 20/08 db (74.5) n19 t19 f18 b18.5. Bitterly disappointing. Literally. *43%*

Tamdhu 25 Years Old db (88) n22 t22 f21 b23. Radiates quality. *43%*

⟐ **The Whisky Chamber Tamdhu 13 Jahre 2007** port cask (88) n22 t22.5 f21.5 b22 Visually, hard to tell if this has come from a whisky cask or the local blood transfusion unit...I haven't spat out anything of this colour since I was last at the dentist's...This is one very different whisky! Nearer red in colour to the subtle pink many Port Cask whiskies become, it also has an incredible firmness to the palate: the red wall. Sometimes that can result in a brittle whisky; here it is solid. Even the nose offers no yield whatsoever with a piledriving brusqueness to the fruit. Sugars about early on, mainly of the muscovado variety found in Dundee cake. But then it solidifies once more, so both fruit and barley have a crunchiness. Salivating early on, you have to take your hat off an admit that this is something very different, indeed. *57.3%. sc.*

TAMNAVULIN
Speyside. 1966. Whyte and Mackay. Working.

Tamnavulin Double Cask batch no. 0308 db (87.5) n22.5 t22.5 f21 b21.5 A bottling which deserves – and perhaps needs – to be at 46% at least. Reduced down to this strength it is levelled to a much chalkier, drier plane than it requires to fully project the oils, sugars and obvious intricacies. Entirely pleasant as it is, with an attractive clean maltiness to the thinned golden syrup as well as well-mannered spicing. But, overall, refuses to open out and develop as you might hope or expect. A 92-plus whisky just waiting to happen... *40%*.

Tamnavulin Red Wine Cask Edition No. 01 American white barrels and finished in French Cabernet Sauvignon red wine casks, batch no. 001243, bott code: L0064 22 28 P/011888 db (94) n23 t23.5 f24 b23.5 It's like a thriller you can't put down: just gets better and more absorbing as you go along! *40%*.

Tamnavulin Red Wine Cask Edition No. 02 American white barrels and finished in Spanish Grenache red wine casks, batch no. 001075, bott code: L0139 23 10 P/012168 db (88) n22 t22 f21.5 b22.5 Pleased to report that, again, the wine casks are clean and sulphur free. But, unlike, the French Cab Sauv' bottling, this is pretty limited in overall development. A Steady Eddie dram, fat and comfortable in its fruity skin. Good spices late on. But here the bitterness does stand out a little and though enjoyable, it feels like a high-quality sports car underpowered and you are crushing the pedal to the floor for extra power and performance that just isn't forthcoming. *40%*.

Tamnavulin Sherry Cask Edition No. 02 American oak and three types of sherry casks, batch no. 30502, bott code: 23:50 L9290 P/010478 db (91) n23 t23.5 f22 b22.5 I'm presuming PX is one of the sherry types here because there is a dominant stickiness to this bottling. Superb delivery, I must say! *40%*.

Old Malt Cask Tamnavulin Aged 27 Years refill hogshead, cask no. 16113, dist Dec 91, bott Oct 19 (83.5) n21.5 t21.5 f20 b21 The dank hay aroma is attractive, if not entirely technically where you want it to be, but forewarns of an off-kilter sharpness for further down the line... which duly arrives. *46.8%. nc ncf sc. 308 bottles.*

TEANINICH
Highlands (Northern), 1817. Diageo. Working.

Teaninich 17 Year Old refill American oak hogsheads & refill American oak barrels db (90) n22 t23 f22 b23 A distillery rarely celebrated in bottle by its owners. Here they have selected an age and cask profile which gets the mix between simple barley and far from taxing oak just about right. *55.9%. Diageo Special Releases 2017.*

⟐ **Fandandel.dk Teaninich Aged 11 Years** 1st fill oloroso quarter cask, cask no.700799B, dist Jan 2009, bott Aug 2020 (91.5) n22.5 the fruit has a curious punchy brevity to it: concentrated and tight, even after being stretched by the Murray Method. But it is constructed with intricacy and free from faults. The plum jam is mercifully under sugared; t23.5 much fatter than the nose, with the fruit unfurling with a salivating sharpness. This gives a glorious two-tone feel on the palate with a marked contrast between the earlier thick oils and the runny grape juice; **f22.5** impressive late spice and vanilla; **b23** quarter casks have a propensity to intensify everything...and this is no exception. Entirely sulphur free, the fruit is allowed to get on and do its job. And the way it handles both the oak and barley-rich honey and spice (from one of Scotland's heavier malts) it is certainly doing that! *56% 152 bottles*

⬦ **Gleann Mór Rare Find Teanininch 1975 Aged 46 Years (94.5) n24** certainly the oak walks with a limp, has grey hair and when it sits down finds a rocking chair and something to knit. But in this case it is still knitting an intense malty theme into the tannins so we are mesmerised by the deftness of the light banana and butterscotch; **t23.5** a crème brulee for starters, then a salivating layer of slightly tangy malt. Of course it is the oak pulling the strings and soon that is back in the cockpit generating countless layers of the most vaguely spiced vanilla; **f23** even after all these years, no off notes, no bitterness. Just quiet but active old age with the most gentle of vanilla-led farewells; **b24** when you consider that this whisky was made in the very first year I began my journey around the world's distilleries, all I can is that this amazing malt has negotiated the passing 46 years with less scars than I. This is hardly a distillery renowned for reaching great ages. But the oak was so much more reliant then than now and the malt has taken full advantage of that to stun us all. *45.1%*

TOBERMORY
Highlands (Island—Mull), 1795. Burn Stewart Distillers. Working.

Tobermory 10 Years Old db **(73.5) n17.5 t19 f18 b19.** The last time I tasted an official Tobermory 10 for the Bible, I was aghast with what I found. So I prodded this sample I had before me of the new 46.3% version with all the confidence Wile E Coyote might have with a failed stick of Acme dynamite. No explosions in the glass or on my palate to report. And though this is still a long way short, and I'm talking light years here, of the technical excellence of the old days, the uncomplicated sweet maltiness has a very basic charm. The nose and finish, though, are still very hard going. *46.3%*

Tobermory Aged 15 Years db **(93) n23.5 t23.5 f23 b23** A tang to the oils on both nose and finish suggests an over widened middle. But such is the quality of the sherry butts and the intensity of the salt-stained malt, all is forgiven. *46.3%. nc ncf.*

Tobermory 42 Year Old db **(94.5) n23.5 t23.5 f23.5 b24** A real journey back in time. Wonderful. *47.7%*

Ledaig 18 Year Old batch 2 db **(71) n16 t20 f17 b18.** There are many ways to describe this whisky. Well made, alas, is not one of them. The nose sets off many alarms, especially on the feinty front. And though some exceptional oak repairs some of the damage, it cannot quite do enough. Sugary, too – and occasionally cloyingly so. *46.3%. nc ncf.*

Ledaig 19 Year Old Marsala Finish db **(92) n23.5 t23 f22.5 b23** Hardly textbook malt but a real gung-ho adventure story on the palate. *51%.*

Ledaig Dùsgadh 42 Aged 42 Years db **(96) n25 t24.5 f22.5 b24** It has to be about 30 years ago I tasted my first-ever Ledaig – as a 12 year old peated malt. This must be from the same stocks, only this has been housed in exceptional casks. Who would have thought, three decades on, that it would turn into some of the best malt bottled in a very long time. A smoky experience unlikely to be forgotten. *46.3%*

Acla Selection Island Edition Tobermory 23 Year Old hogshead, dist 1995, bott 2019 **(94) n24 t23.5 f23 b23.5** One of the most gentle and elegant malts to comes from this island in a very long time. *49%.*

Acla Selection Island Edition Ledaig 11 Year Old hogshead, dist 2007, bott 2018 **(88.5) n22.5 t22.5 f21.5 b22** The smoke offers a light, acidic fug on both nose and palate, though all the sweetness is confined to the delivery where the grist goes into overdrive. Spices are sprinkled evenly and the youth ensures the sharpness is very, very sharp! *52.6%.*

Cadenhead's Authentic Collection Cask Strength Ledaig 11 Year Old ex-bourbon cask, dist 2008, bott Sept 19 **(90.5) n22 t23 f22.5 b23** If this malt was handed in as homework, it would probably be docked a few marks for being technically off the pace. But it would soon make them up again, as the oak this has been housed in perfectly matches the distillery's style, allowing a nuanced depth to the smoke and an impressive degree of barley to be seen. The nose hints at a lack of copper, and there is some evidence that the stills might have been operating slightly faster than they were comfortable with. But the nutty smokiness compensates for the thinness of body; the barley applauded for its salivating qualities. What great fun! *55.2%. sc.*

Chapter 7 Ledaig 10 Year Old 2009 bourbon hogshead, cask no. 700493, dist May 09, bott Mar 20 **(92.5) n23.5 t23.5 f22.5 b23** Can't remember the last time I tasted a Ledaig so technically on the money as this. I've worked with many a cask of this over the years, in the blending lab as well as in the tasting room for The Bible. The nose is pure grist, the phenols reeking from the malt as though it had just come off the mill. Consequently, the malt simply melts in the mouth with a freshness that fair brings a tear to the eye. Slowly the tannins offer a vanilla alternative...Just beautiful. *51%. sc. 351 bottles.*

Chapter 7 Ledaig 24 Year Old 1995 bourbon hogshead, cask no. 189, dist Sept 95, bott Mar 20 **(91.5) n23.5 t23.5 f22 b22.5** One of those peated whiskies where you aren't quite sure if the lightness of smoke is due to a lower phenol level or the passing of years. Here it is probably both. The lightly smoked butterscotch nose is a treat, the delivery an exhibition of how mouthfeel plays such a vital role. Here it is fat, chewing malt...the longer you chew the slightly peatier it gets. Only a very late bitterness can be found in the deficit column... *51.6%. sc. 242 bottles.*

Gordon & MacPhail Connoisseurs Choice Ledaig Aged 12 Years first fill sherry hogshead, cask no. 16603709, dist 13 Dec 06, bott 1 Feb 19 **(87.5) n22.5 t23 f20 b22** It has taken a while to taste this. You know there's a problem but, like a slow-punctured tyre, it takes time for it to be revealed. Yes, noted a slight off-sulphur note on the nose but, thanks to the peat, it comes through on the finish very late on...actually, so late it is after you have finished the tasting. Crafty, these sulphur cask chaps. Anyway, that apart, the peat is superb and about as hairy-chested and full-on as I've seen from this distillery for a while. And the accompanying milky-marzipan demi-sweetness charms the pants off you. Just such a shame about that slow puncture. Boo....hisssssssssss.... *58.2%. sc. 329 bottles.*

Liquid Treasures From Miles Away Ledaig 13 Year Old PX sherry butt, dist Feb 07, bott Mar 20 **(94) n23.5 t24 f23 b23.5** Delighted and greatly relieved to say to say the PX cask has not interfered with this malt and dragged it down to its excruciatingly dull level. Instead, we see the Ledaig in full vitality with a higher phenol content than normal, dishing out spices and peat reek with happy abandon. Clean, full bodied and superbly layered with what little grape there is to be found in docile mood and the sugars very much under control. Quite impossible not to love. *52.9%. sc. 252 bottles.*

Single & Single Ledaig 2005 13 Years Old (94) n23.5 t24 f23 b23.5 This is Ledaig in very impressive form. And with the peat levels spot on. A heart winner. *58.1%. sc. 624 bottles.*

The Single Cask Tobermory 1995 ex-bourbon barrel, cask no. 1201 **(88) n23 t22.5 f20.5 b22** This malt offers a superstar, nutty nose full of intriguing light tannin-induced sugars – and is about as floral as an island whisky ever gets. But as after the initial attractive gristiness on delivery, it loses its way slightly as the oak gets a little bit to much of the upper hand, leading to a nagging bitterness. However, the better moments are very good, indeed. *54.2%. nc ncf sc.*

The Whisky Barrel Originals Ledaig 11 Years Old 1st fill oloroso hogshead, cask no. TWB1006, dist Feb 08, bott 2019 **(92.5) n23 t23.5 f23 b23** Bizarrely light for a first-fill oloroso: indeed, one of the lightest I have ever seen. But make no mistake: this is a heavyweight and there is no denying its smoky scrumminess. *63.4%. sc. 298 bottles.*

⬦ **The Whisky Cask Company Ledaig 1997** sherry hogshead, dist Sep 1997, bott Oct 2019 **(84.5) n23 t22.5 f19 b20** A very different Ledaig, even taking into account the substantial fruit input thanks to the sherry cask. This is hard whisky, as though distilled from marble rather than malt. Even the nose makes little attempt to befriend, let alone seduce. The acidity levels from the peat is way above the norm, as much sniffing burning anthracite, rather than the usual soothing phenols of the turf. However on the palate things actually become testing: there is a few moments where grape and smoke unite, but the remainder is a battle. Full of flavour, though never harmony. *55.6% nc ncf 264 bottles*

⬦ **The Whisky Embassy Bonn Ledaig 8 Year Old** Bordeaux no. 16 **(91.5) n23 t23 f22.5 b23** A disarmingly beautiful malt which makes the most of its tender years. *60%. nc ncf sc.*

⬦ **Whisky-Fässle Ledaig 10 Year Old** hogshead, dist 2008, bott 2018 **(94) n23.5** an exceptionally highly peated version, cleaner than in past years and positively exulting in its salty, kippery coastalness; **t23.5** here we go again: huge phenol kick but wonderfully in tune with the rich oils. The vanilla and butterscotch involvement from the cask acts as a lovely balancing act rather than a distraction. Despite all this, grist abounds everywhere, so the juiciness is always at maximum levels; **f23** further confirmation of the high quality distillate and top quality cask. Quite literally comes to a sticky end with smoke and ulmo honey travelling a long way...; **b24** just breath-taking. Had I tasted this blind, I might have marked it down as a vatting of Caol Ila and young Ardbeg. Can't see this lasting long on the shelves...or in the home cabinet.. *52.7% nc ncf*

TOMATIN

Speyside. 1897. Takara, Shuzo and Okura & Co. Working.

Tomatin 8 Years Old bourbon & sherry casks db **(89) n22 t23 f21.5 b22.5** A malt very proud of its youth. *40%. Travel Retail Exclusive.*

Tomatin 12 Year Old finished in Spanish sherry casks db **(91.5)** n23 t23.5 f21.5 b23.5 For a great many years, Tomatin operated under severe financial restrictions. This meant that some of the wood brought to the distillery during this period was hardly of top-notch quality. This has made life difficult for those charged with moulding the stocks into workable expressions. I take my hat off to the creator of this: some great work is evident, despite the finish. *43%*

Tomatin 14 Year Old Port Finish db **(92.5)** n23 t24 f22.5 b23 Allows the top notch port a clear road. *46%. ncf.*

Tomatin 15 Years Old American oak casks db **(89.5)** n22.5 t22.5 f22 b22.5 A delicious exhibition of malt. *46%. Travel Retail Exclusive.*

Tomatin Aged 15 Years ex bourbon cask, bott 2010 db **(86)** n21 t22 f21.5 b21.5. One of the most malty drams on the market today. Perhaps suffers a little from the 43% strength as some of the lesser oak notes get a slightly disruptive foothold. But the intense, juicy barley trademark remains clear and delicious. *43% Tomatin Distillery*

Tomatin 15 Years Old bourbon barrels and Spanish Tempranillo wine casks db **(88.5)** n22 t23 f21 b22.5. Not free from the odd problem with the Spanish wine casks but gets away with it as the overall complexity and enjoyment levels are high. *52%*

Tomatin 18 Year Old db **(82)** n21.5 t22 f19 b20 Sadly some sulphur on the casks which makes the finish just too dry and off key. Underneath are hints of greatness, but the sherry butt doesn't give it a chance. *46%.*

Tomatin 21 Year Old db **(94.5)** n24 t23.5 f23 b24 One of those malts which looks as though It's not even trying, but just nonchalantly produces something rather delightful and of very high class. *46%. Global Travel Retail Exclusive.*

Tomatin 25 Years Old db **(89)** n22 t23 f21.5 b22.5. Not a nasty bone in its body: understated but significant. *43%*

Tomatin 30 Year Old European & American oak casks db **(85.5)** n21 t21 f22.5 b21. Unusually for an ancient malt, the whisky becomes more comfortable as it wears its aged shoes. The delivery is just a bit too enthusiastic on the oaky front, but the natural caramels soften the journey rather delightfully. *46%. ncf.*

Tomatin 30 Years Old bott 2018 db **(93)** n23 t22.5 f24 b23.5 Puts me in mind of a 29-year-old Springbank I have tasted for this Bible, which showed similar initial signs of wear and tear. But as the whisky warmed and oxidised, then so it grew in the glass and began to reveal previously hidden brilliance. This is not, perhaps, up to those gargantuan standards but what is achieved here shews the rewards for both patience and the use of the Murray Method. Patience and care are most certainly rewarded *46%.*

Tomatin 36 Year Old American & European oak db **(96.5)** n24 t24.5 f23.5 b24.5 The difference between old oak and the newer stuff is brilliantly displayed here. Make no mistake: this is a masterpiece of a malt. *46%*

Tomatin 40 Years Old Oloroso sherry casks db **(87.5)** n21.5 t23 f21 b22 One of those malts which offers a graceful peep at the past, when sherry butts were clean and offered nothing to fear. But no matter how good the cask time takes its toll and the intense chalkiness reveals tannins that have got slightly the better of the barley. Thankfully the grape is still intact and brings us a beautiful raisin and date depth before the chalk returns a little more determined than before. *43%. Travel Retail Exclusive.*

Tomatin 1995 Olorosso Sherry db **(82)** n21 t22 f19 b20 You can peel the grape off the malt. But one of the sherry butts wasn't quite as spotless as one might hope for. The inevitable tang arrives towards the finish. *46%.*

Tomatin Amontillado Sherry 2006 Aged 12 Years Old db **(82)** n21 t22 f19 b20 You'd think from the score that sulphur plays a part here. And you'd probably be right. Just bitter and dull in all the places it shouldn't be. Those incapable of detecting sulphur will love the rich sultana delivery. *46%.*

Tomatin Cabernet Sauvignon 2002 Edition db **(82)** n21 t22 f18 b21 Surprising degree of weight to this one. The fruit is not quite flawless with a little bit of a buzz on the nose and finish especially. But the rich mouthfeel and a pleasant, lush Garibaldi biscuit effect does ensure some very satisfying phases. *46%.*

Tomatin Caribbean Rum 2007 Edition db **(89.5)** n22 t23 f22 b22.5 Beautifully clean malt though, as is their wont, the rum casks keep everything tight. *46%.*

Tomatin Caribbean Rum 2009 Aged 10 Years Old db **(90.5)** n22.5 clean barley with a light liquorice and Demerara sugar outer casing; t23.5 I think the old term: "pure malt" would be the perfect description for this; f22 the rum casks do their job and lock in the sugars for a slightly fast finish; b22.5 as is so often the case, the rum cask has encased the malt in crisp sugar, limiting development slightly. But it also ensures the malts are at their maximum intensity. *46%.*

Tomatin Cask Strength db **(80)** n19 t22 f19 b20 Stunning malt climax on delivery. But always undone by a dull, persistent off note from the cask. *57.5%.*

Tomatin Decades II db **(91.5)** n23 t23 f22.5 b23 Tomatin does intense malt as well as any distillery in the world. And here they give an object lesson. *46%.*

Tomatin Five Virtues Series Earth Peated Malt refill hogshead oak casks db **(88)** n22 t22.5 f21.5 b22 Can honestly say I have never seen Tomatin in this kind of shape before: enjoyable once you acclimatise... *46%.*

Tomatin Five Virtues Series Fire Heavily Charred Oak de-charred/re-charred oak fired casks db **(94)** n23.5 t24 f23 b23.5 High class malt with a sweet bourbon drizzle. *46%.*

Tomatin Five Virtues Series Metal Bourbon Barrels first fill bourbon barrels db **(95)** n24 t24 f23 b24 There's metal enough in the "Earth" bottling. Was wondering where the metal comes into things here. As these are first fill bourbon casks, wonder if it was the type of warehouse they came from in Kentucky... Anyway, talking metal: this is pure gold... *46%.*

Tomatin Five Virtues Series Water Winter Distillation sherry butts & bourbon barrels db **(72)** n18 t20 f16 b18 A small degree of molassed chocolate escapes the grim sulphured tightness of the sherry. *46%.*

Tomatin Five Virtues Series Wood Selected Oak Casks French, American & Hungarian oak casks db **(90)** n22.5 t23 f21.5 b23 A Franco-Hungarian truce means the malt and bourbon casks can work their magic...Some truly brilliant and unique phrases here. *46%.*

Tomatin Highland Legacy db **(88)** n22 t22.5 f21.5 b22 Clean, nutty malt but beyond that unremarkable. *43%.*

Tomatin Warehouse 6 Collection 1977 db **(96)** n24.5 t24 f23.5 b24 A tale of exotic fruit. Which in turns means a story of great antiquity. Truly old school. And truly magnificent. Do not open the bottle unless you have a good half hour to study this work of art. And the Murray Method will reward you handsomely... *49%.*

Cù Bòcan Signature bourbon, oloroso sherry & virgin oak casks db **(82)** n21.5 t21 f20 b20.5 A virgin defiled amid brimstone. *46%.*

Artful Dodger Tomatin 11 Year Old 2008 ex-bourbon hogshead, cask no. 453 **(88)** n21 t23 f22 b22 A malt not overly troubled by tannin and still a little wet behind the ears after all this time. But this means the famous Tomatin maltiness is seen to optimum effect, like stars in a clear night sky. And that is always a delicious spectacle. *56.1%. sc.*

Fadandel.dk Tomatin 10 Year Old 3 months finish in a 2nd fill Oloroso octave, cask no. 1837A **(94.5)** n23 adorably intense malt with just a little delicate fruitcake on the side. A molecule or two of smoke peels off from the pack, but your nose has to be on full alert to spot it; t24 such a fabulous delivery! The malt is explosive and super salivating – Tomatin at its very best! It is weighed down slightly by a toffee-raisin jacket which slips comfortably over the barley....; f23.5 perfectly judged spice, then those layers of malt. Talk about a nuanced finale...! b24 thankfully second fill oloroso at work, which means the distillery's trademark concentrated malt character still has plenty of room in which to operate and is there to be savoured! A minor masterpiece. *59.9%. sc. 75 bottles.*

◇ **Fadandel.dk Tomatin Aged 10 Years** 2nd fill oloroso octave finish, cask no.1837B, dist Apr 2009, bott Feb 2021 **(88.5)** n22 t22.5 f22 b22 An impressively neat and tidy dram with the required sugars spic and span. Only briefly do those many sugars find enough depth and confidence to speak up loudly enough to be heard. Otherwise it is a series of excellent spice and dry cocoa notes interrupted by a hint of dried grape skin here and there, the tannins never for a moment out of place. For once with this distillery the barley is notably subdued. Elegant enough to be one for the Martini set. *59.9% 69 bottles*

◇ **The First Editions Tomatin Aged 25 Years 1994** sherry butt, cask no. 18213, bott 2020 **(94)** n23.5 something of the bakery about this: a freshly created Chelsea bun with a gorgeous mix of raisin and icing sugar. Of course, after 25 years there is more: the oak opens up different, deeper channels with the vanilla also enjoying a delicate toast chestnut sweetness, too...; t23.5 just a brilliant entry, as still salivating after all these years. The softness of the oils do not detract from the crisper elements of the barley itself, though the midground luxuriates in a mix of spice and very lightest sultana touch. Below all this rumbles the aged oak....; f23 long, thanks to those delicate oils, and the pastry sugars seem to linger with the vanilla; b24 for a Tomatin the barley refuses to dominate like usual and even the sherry butt play an understated game. Instead we have a malt of exquisite balance and charm. Unalloyed beauty. *47.9%. nc ncf sc. 402 bottles.*

The Single Cask Tomatin 2006 ex-bourbon barrel, PX sherry octave finish, cask no. 5777B **(87)** n22 t22.5 f21.5 b21 An even malt where the PX has a surprising degree of influence. As the problem can often be with PX involvement, any bitterness present is amplified by the sugary wine. Some spices relieve the slightly one-dimensional feel. Pleasant enough, but never quite feels comfortable. *53.7%. nc ncf sc.*

The Whisky Chamber Tomatin 11 Jahre 2008 sherry cask **(85.5) n22.5 t22 f20 b21** Eye-wateringly tart, especially at the death. Some attractive chocolate notes mixes in with the burnt raisin. But this is a malt where balance is at a premium and the tightness on the finish doesn't help the cause, either. The masochist in me does kind of enjoy the delivery, though... *56.3%. sc.*

TOMINTOUL

Speyside, 1965. Angus Dundee. Working.

Tomintoul Aged 10 Years bott code: L16 02149 CB2 db **(84.5) n20.5 t22 f21 b21** A very consistent dram but far too much emphasis of the chocolate toffee rather than the big malt you feel is bursting to break free. *40%.*

Tomintoul Aged 12 Years Oloroso Sherry Cask Finish db **(73.5) n18.5 t19 f18 b18.** Tomintoul, with good reason, styles itself as "The Gentle Dram" and you'll hear no argument from me about that one. However, the sherry influence here offers a rough ride. *40%*

Tomintoul Aged 12 Years Oloroso Sherry Cask Finish bott code: L17 02772 CB2 db **(74.5) n20 t19 f17.5 b18** A slightly cleaner sherry influence than the last of these I tasted, but the ungentle sulphur makes short work of the "gentle dram". *40%.*

Tomintoul Aged 14 Years db **(91) n23.5 t23 f21.5 b23** This guy has shortened its breath somewhat: with the distinct thinness to the barley and oak arriving a little flustered and half-hearted rather than with a confident stride; remains a beautiful whisky full of vitality and displaying the malt in its most naked and vulnerable state. But I get the feeling that perhaps a few too many third fills, or under-performing seconds, has resulted in the intensity and hair-raising harmony of the truly great previous bottlings just being slightly undercooked. That said, still a worthy and delicious dram! *46%. nc ncf.*

Tomintoul Aged 15 Years Portwood Finish db **(94) n23 t23.5 f23.5 b24** So rare to find a wine finish which maximises the fruit to the full without allowing it to dominate. Charming. And so clean. Probably a brilliant whisky to help repair my damaged palate after tasting yet another s******ed sherry butt. I'll keep this one handy...*46%. nc ncf. 5,820 bottles.*

Tomintoul Aged 15 Years With A Peaty Tang bott code: L17 02975 CB2 db **(89.5) n23 t23 f21.5 b22** Being a bit older than their original Peaty Tang, the phenols here are less forward. But, then, it calls itself "The Gentle Dram" and on this evidence with good reason. *40%.*

Tomintoul Aged 16 Years db **(94.5) n24.5 t23.5 f23 b23.5** Confirms Tomintoul's ability to dice with greatness. *40%*

Tomintoul Aged 21 Years db **(94) n24 t24 f22.5 b23.5** Just how good this whisky would have been at cask strength or even at 46 absolutely terrifies me. *40%.*

Tomintoul Aged 25 Years db **(95) n25 t24 f23 b23.5** A quiet masterpiece from one of Scotland's criminally under appreciated great distilleries. *43%*

Tomintoul Aged 40 Years db **(86) n22 t21 f21.5 b21.5.** Groans every single one of its 40 years. Some lovely malty moments still, as well as butterscotch. But the oak has just jogged on past the sign that said 'Greatness' and carried straight on into the woods... *43.1%. nc ncf.*

◇ **Tomintoul Cigar Malt** Oloroso sherry casks, bott. code: L20 07917 CB2 db **(92) n23** a dry sherry outline of the old school...and not a sulphur molecule in sight. Not many sugar ones, either...; **t23** so soft. The palate is no more than gently kissed by the passing raisin and then stroked by a biscuity maltiness possessing light Demerara sugar. A weak front of ulmo honey is brushed aside as the spices gain dominance while the fruity notes – all of a wine must quality – begin to take hold; **f22.5** returns willingly to an austere mode, spicey and with the vague cocoa-led dryness from the vanilla seemingly taking on a Dickensian degree of umbrage; **b23.5** as someone who has never smoked so much as a cigarette, let alone a cigar, in my entire life, perhaps I am the last person who can judge this whisky or the purpose it was intended. However, as a judge of the whisky as...well, as whisky, then I have no problems. Perhaps most noticeable is an overwhelming impact of the under-ripe fruit, flattening out and filling in the nooks and crannies. The combined imprint of the grape skin and the vanillas make for a malt in search of its sweet spot, which is finally extinguished when the light trace of ulmo honey alongside the grist gutters and vanishes after too brief a life. A serious whisky...to be taken seriously.... *40%.*

Tomintoul Seiridh Oloroso Sherry Cask first fill Oloroso sherry butts, batch one, bott code: L19 05556 CB2 db **(87) n22 t23 f20.5 b21.5** A right old softy of a malt, the sherry ironing out any creases with the gentlest of fruity caresses. A little sulphur niggle at the end, alas. *40%.*

Tomintoul With A Peaty Tang db **(94) n23 t24 f23 b24.** A bit more than a tang, believe me! Faultlessly clean distillate that revels in its unaccustomed peaty role. The age is confusing and appears mixed, with both young and older traits being evident. *40%*

Old Ballantruan db **(89.5) n23.5 t23 f21 b22** Profound young malt which could easily be taken for an Islay. *50%. ncf.*

Old Ballantruan Aged 15 Years bott code: CBSC4 02976 db **(95)** n23.5 t24 f23.5 b24 A Tomintoul classic. *50%. ncf.*

TORABHAIG
Isle of Skye, 2017. Mossburn Distilleries. Working.

<> **Torabhaig Legacy** first-fill bourbon cask, cask no. 307, dist Jan 17, bott 9 Nov 20 db **(92.5)** **n23** the youthful phenols cling with marvellous freshness to the light oils. A crofter's peat reek carried on the winds from the sea, and the faintest hint of marmalade on toast to greet you from your walk. No great age, but some very serious charm...; **t23.5** now that far exceeds my expectations. The delivery is near perfect as we are gifted the sublime combination of peaty grist melting on the tongue, beautifully wrapped in the lightest oils possible with the first overtures of an oakiness sufficient enough to carry the weight...but enough to ensure the more complex notes are allowed to hang around for a long time. The sugars are slightly more complex than first appears with the gristy barley dying out to be replaced by a strand or two of ulmo honey and Demerara. By now the smoke has found some volume and spices have added a busying accompaniment...; **f22.5** thanks to those oils the sugars and smoke persist, even as the vanilla starts taking control. Just a touch of cocoa to the very death; **b23.5** a marvellous moment. My first visit to a whisky distillery came 46 years ago when I visited the Talisker distillery. And now the Island of Skye boasts a second single malt whisky. At Talisker back in 1975 I was given whisky direct from the cask, truly a life-changing experience. Nearly half a century on, I can still taste it today and remember those sensations, as though it were yesterday.... This beautifully made malt, exceptionally fine for 3-year-old - is a different character: then Talisker was wild, a far more explosive dram than is being made at the same distillery today. This, for all its pleasing smoke and full-on spice does not match the Talisker of yore. But why should it? This is a distillery in its own right, doing its very own thing with its very own personality. And though it maintains the island tradition, its lightness of touch really is something to be admired...and fully savoured. Back in 1975 I had to take an aged, barnacle-clad old puffer across to the distillery. Today I can drive there over a bridge. I genuinely look forward to doing so: some people need congratulating for this excellent addition to the Scotch Malt Whisky lexicon... *61.67%. sc.*

<> **Torabhaig Legacy** first-fill bourbon cask, cask no. 300-600, dist Jan 17, bott 9 Nov 20 db **(89.5) n22.5** a charming youngster with a peaty embrace...but carrying no weight at all. Has lost most of its new make teeth and instead we have a lightly phenolic presence with an outline of citrus and a powdering of vanilla; **t22.5** the nose promised melt-in-the mouth malt...and that's exactly what you end up with. The smoke takes its time to assemble but by the midpoint it has been joined by the politest spices imaginable. Just the faintest echo of ulmo honey and vanilla sweetens; **f22** the very limited oils on this means the sugars run out early, leaving behind light, slightly buzzing peat and dry vanilla. A slight bitterness sails in off the oak; **b22.5** such an attractive whisky for a malt so young. This is all about elegance and fragility which is carried off with panache. *46%. sc.*

TORMORE
Speyside, 1960. Chivas Brothers. Working.

Tormore 12 Years Old db **(75)** n19 t19 f19 b18. For those who like whisky in their caramel. *40%*

<> **Chapter 7 Tormore 1990 Aged 31 Years** bourbon barrel, barrel no.325862 **(94.5) n24.5** one of the great Scotch noses of the year: just the right levels of everything. The sugars are lightly sprinkled, the honey thinly spread; the vanilla build but, aware of the neighbourhood, not too high; the butterscotch is freshly baked; the malt boasting a gristy clarity after such an improbably period of time; the nuttiness is so lightly salted. Nosed this three times, and slightly different in levels each time. So complex...; **t24** brilliant. This is all about the malt. Well, the malt and its interaction with the top grade vanillas: this must have been an exhibition quality Kentucky cask. The sugars are stand out in their elegance...a light brushing of Demerara alongside ulmo honey. The midpoint hints at some kind of malt-bourbon hybrid as the light red liquorice begins to form. All the time it threatens to burst into wrinkled old age yet holds off with amazing control...; **f22** this is where we see the weakness of the distillery come into play: a certain thinness of structure means the finish is a lot more fragile than both nose and delivery and has strength enough only to carry the vanilla; **b24** Tormore, as a standard malt, is a plain Jane. Oops being "sexist"! Let's put a few more of my staff out of work as punishment. Sorry, I meant an inert Bert, a grim Jim, an ordinary Joe. But after three decades we see Tormore produce a nose that it would be hard to believe possible. Jane or Jim, Bert or Bertha, Joe or Jo.... it is quite stunning, an experience of rare beauty. And the most teasing experience on the palate for threatening to go over the age edge, but always coming back to safety. *50.2% sc*

Old Malt Cask Tormore Aged 26 Years refill hogshead, cask no. 16492, dist Nov 92, bott Oct 19 **(88)** n22 t22.5 f21.5 b22 Perhaps one of the most malty and gristy whiskies of such antiquity you will find this and any other year. Belies its age on so many fronts, but there is plenty to enjoy from the concentrated barley sugar delivery. Fades towards a little bitterness late on. *47.3%. nc ncf sc. 285 bottles.*

⋄ **Scyfion Choice Tormore 1992** Shustoff Golden Dyke cask finished, bott 2020 **(94)** n23.5 had I had this placed in front of me as a sample of decently aged Long Pond rum from Jamaica, I may not have been able to tell the difference. The esters on this for a Tormore are off the scale, as is the golden syrup influence. Fabulous! t23.5 Long Pond again!!!! This is amazing. After those first rummy notes wear off, the malt powers through in grand Speyside fashion, just reassuring you of your bearings. Again there is a magnificent golden syrup/ heather honey backdrop, that at the midpoint even moves towards a spiced molasses...; f23 thins out in true Tormore fashion, leaving the vanillas and light spices to carry the flag. Still impressive, though...; b24 it's been a classic year for Tormores. Two bottlings of a style absolutely alien to me for this distillery, despite nearly 40 years of sampling the stuff! This is nigh on faultless. *49.1% nc ncf 106 bottles*

TULLIBARDINE

Highlands (Perthshire), 1949. Tullibardine Ltd. Working.

⋄ **Tullibardine Aged 12 Years** first fill bourbon casks, bott code: 21/0016 db **(92.5)** n23.5 just a single sniff and you know you are dealing with B1s: first-fill bourbons. The peppery spices are bit of a giveaway; the buttery layering over the slightly burnt toast confirms it. The sugars are strictly on the dark side, the honey a gorgeous blend of heather- and orange blossom. Here and there the malt, seemingly frustrated at being ignored, punches through, too...; t23 Tulli being fulsome, but not quite at its fattest: the speaks first, before the tannins quickly nudge it off the stage to go back into burnt toast mode...just as on the nose. The spices form the backing. But the layering of vanilla against thin molasses and still active malt means this is both juicy and drier and toasty at the same time...some trick...; f23 even before tasting this I suspected that the finish would be a long rumble of warming spiciness... and so it proves...; b23 really quite excellent. Should definitely be out at 46% to let the extra oils stretch the tannins and sugars even further. Some malts cannot handle 100% ex-first fill bourbon and lose their personality. This appears to be one which thrives, deliciously, in an oaky climate. *40%*

Tullibardine 15 Year Old db **(87.5)** n22 t23 f21 b21.5 Starts quite beautifully but stubbornly refuses to kick on. Just adore the nuttiness on both the nose and delivery, as well as the lilting malt in the early stages which is both juicy and barley intense. There is even a light orange blossom honey note soon after...then just fades under a welter of dulling vanilla and caramel tones. Not far off being a little beauty. *43%.*

Tullibardine Aged 20 Years db **(92.5)** n22.5 t24 f22.5 b23.5 While there are whiskies like this in the world, there is a point to this book...*43%*

Tullibardine Aged 25 Years db **(86.5)** n22 t22 f21 b21.5. There can be too much of a good thing. And although the intricacies of the honey makes you sigh inwardly with pleasure, the overall rigidity and fundamentalism of the oak goes a little too far. *43%*

Tullibardine 1970 db **(96.5)** n25 t24.5 f23 b24s I am a professional wordsmith with a very long time in whisky. Yet words, any words, can barely do justice... *40.5%.*

Tullibardine 225 sauternes cask finish db **(85)** n20 t22.5 f21 b21.5. Hits the heights early on in the delivery when the honey and Lubeck marzipan are at full throttle. *43%*

Tullibardine 228 Burgundy cask finish db **(82)** n21 t22 f18 b21. No shortage of bitter chocolate. Flawed but a wow for those looking for mega dry malt. *43%*

Tullibardine 500 sherry cask finish db **(79.5)** n19 t21 f19 b20.5. The usual problems from Jerez, but the grape ensures maximum chewability. *43%*

Tullibardine Custodians Collection 1962 52 Years Old db **(87.5)** n22 t22 f21.5 b22 This oldie has gallantly fought in the great oak wars of 1987 to 2014 and shows some serious scars. Thankfully a little exotic fruit and citrus makes some impact on the austere tannins on the nose, but they aren't around to reduce the excesses of the finale, though a little chocolate does go a long way. The silky delivery doesn't quite hide the mildly puckering, eye-watering aggression of the tannin but butterscotch does its best to add a limp sweetness, as does the unexpected wave of juicy barley. Some fascinating old timer moments but, ultimately, a tad too ancient for its own good. *40.1%.*

Tullibardine The Murray Cask Strength dist 2007, bott 2019, bott code: 19/0067 db **(94.5)** n23.5 t24 f23 b24 while touring China at the back end of 2019, I met a couple of people who told me they had bought previous bottles of this brand thinking that it was related to me, and therefore must have my seal of approval. Please let me reiterate: this whisky has nothing to do with Jim Murray, a name which is itself Trademarked. I make no financial gain from this whisky, nor do I allow any whisky in the world to be named after me. I make no profit from the individual sales of whisky and, though I am a consultant blender, do not make money from the sales of any brand; nor do I have any shares in any whisky company. The only recommendation I can make for this brand is confined to my independent review of it here. *56.6%. The Marquess Collection. Sixth edition.*

❖ **Tullibardine The Murray Double Wood Edition** matured in bourbon and sherry casks, dist 2005, bott 2020, bott code: 21/007 **(95.5) n24.5** spellbinding. You are pretty convinced that you have sat on some Jaffa cakes which melted beneath you but then you notice the Chinese gooseberry and guava, There is also passion fruit, but that appears to have absorbed the fresh, gristy tones of the barley, too....And don't think this is all fruity and accommodating: there is white pepper and blueberry, too....One of the noses of the year...; **t24** mainly passion fruit on delivery but a sharp, acidic path across the intense, almost concentrated malt and vanilla. So, salivating of course, increasingly malty and growing inexorably in spice...; **f23** the tannins kick in here alongside the fruit skin to present a slight bitterness where all before had been fruity sweetness and light. The malt, though, holds much of its ground admirably; **b24** the finest example of The Murray I have tasted yet. The balance on the layering is simply exquisite. If you haven't done all your chores for the night: chickens fox-proofed, dog taken for walk, kids in bed, partner safely watching something on tv/reading book/out for the night... then don't bother cracking open this bottle. This is a malt that needs a good hour's peace and quiet...time to concentrate without interruption. The nose alone will eat into half an hour at least.... Don't say you haven't been warned...Oh, and I refer my honourable readers to the appendage of the tasting notes for this brand I did last year... *46%*

Tullibardine The Murray Marsala Cask Finish dist 2006, bott 2018, bott code: 18/0167 db **(86) n22 t22 f20.5 b21.5** A dry and heavy dram, very much the opposite of the standard sweet, gristy, malty affair from bourbon cask. Lots of frisky bite and nibble of delivery as the plummy fruit gets into full swing. But the tightness of the cask arrests further meaningful development. *46%. The Marquess Collection.*

Tullibardine Sovereign bourbon barrel db **(89.5) n22.5 t23 f21.5 b22.5** Beautifully salivating despite the intricate oak notes. *43%*

The First Editions Tullibardine Aged 27 Years 1992 refill hogshead, cask no. 16917, bott 2019 **(86.5) n22 t22 f21.5 b21** There are almost as many bourbon notes to this one as there are malt ones. The kumquats on the nose suggests Kentucky, but the sweetness you hope is going to arrive on the palate never quite materialises. Busy in part and not short of some pleasant, chewy caramel tones. But never quite nails either the rhythm or the balance. *41.1%. nc ncf sc. 81 bottles.*

Old Malt Cask Tullibardine Aged 28 Years refill hogshead, cask no. 16100, dist Sept 91, bott Oct 19 **(81) n20.5 t21.5 f19 b20** Some definite weirdness to this one – perhaps a result of the fermentation process all those long years ago. The malt is in evidence, but feels uncomfortable and incomplete. The bitterness from the cask doesn't help, either. *46.5%. nc ncf sc. 284 bottles.*

WOLFBURN
Highlands (Thurso), 2012. Aurora Brewing Ltd. Working.

Wolfburn Aurora sherry oak casks db **(91.5) n22.5 t24 f22 b23** Early days at a distillery and still finding their feet with the still. The cut on this was wider than on the previous bottling I sampled, but there is no faulting the use of the 100% sulphur-free sherry butt. There is the odd aspect of genius attached to this dram, for sure. For the record: just vatted this with some OTT oak-hit sherry-cask 1954 malt in need of the kiss of life, or like a vampire in need of a virgin's blood: I suspect the first time a Wolfburn has been mixed with a 60-year-old Speysider. Result? One of the most complex and complete experiences of the last couple of months – a would-be award winner, were it commercially available! Stunning! *46%. nc ncf.*

Wolfburn Langskip bott 27 May 19 db **(94) n23 t24 f23 b24** Rich, full bodied, intense, unforgiving. A whisky that doesn't just dip its toe in the outgoing surf... *58%. nc ncf.*

❖ **Wolfburn Latitude** bott code: LATITUDE-0001 db **(95.5) n24** Unusual though it may be. But it more than makes up for it by striking an almost perfect peat note: not one full of muscle and bravado but instead a genteel smokiness that doesn't so much billow as melt on contact with the nose. These playful, purring phenols harmonise perfectly with a more standard fresh maltiness and the first light undercurrents of vanilla and even the occasional hint of a more formal bourbon tannin character. "Elegant" doesn't quite do this justice...; **t23.5** now, on top of all the extraordinary daintiness of the nose another factor comes into play: mouth-feel. And here is could hardly be bettered. The oils have just enough viscosity to cling to the palate without becoming the dominating sensation. Instead it allows the custard-sweet vanillas and first traces of butterscotch to mingle freely with the peat, which starts coquettishly - a taste bud teaser – but slowly grows in weight and spice; **f23** slightly more simplistic. Vaguely buttery but also benefits from a light dab of lemon blossom honey; **b24** Lattitude has put Wolfburn well on course for whisky greatness. From their earlier bottlings I had hoped that they would be slowly building towards a whisky of such excellence. Even more remarkable considering that age plays no part other than to perpetuate the freshness. But age doesn't always matter if you get the balance right. And that they have certainly achieved here. Just imagine a malt like this, this well balanced and in tune, with time on its side. My taste buds quiver in anticipation.... 46%. nc ncf. ♀

Wolfburn Morven db **(91.5) n23 t23 f22.5 b23** Confirmation, were it needed, that lightly peated malt is a brilliant way of getting a distillery's whiskies out at a young age without the lack of development becoming too clear. This is a delicious and refined amble on the taste buds. 46%. nc ncf.

Wolfburn Northland db **(88.5) n22.5 t22 f22 b22** Limited complexity but maximum charm for one so young. 46%. nc ncf.

Wolfburn Single Malt Scotch Whisky db **(91.5) n23 t23 f22.5 b23** This is a very young malt showing an intriguing wispy smokiness, its evenness more in line with having been matured in ex-Islay casks than using low phenol barley. Still, it might have been, and, if so, perhaps reveals a style that would not have been entirely unknown to the people of Thurso when they last drank this during Victorian times. It is probably 30 years ago I was shown to a spot in the town where I was told the original distillery had been. Now it is back, and eclipses Pulteney as the producers of the most northerly mainland Scottish whisky. For all its youth, its excellence of quality glimmers from the glass: a malt as beautifully flighted as a cricket ball delivered by the most crafted of spinners. And offers a delightful turn on the palate, too. The building of a new distillery, no matter how romantic its location or story, does not guarantee good whisky. So I am delighted for those involved in a project as exhausting as this that a very good whisky is exactly what they have on their hands. 46%. nc ncf.

Wolfburn Small Batch Release No. 155 first fill ex-bourbon barrels, finished for six months in fresh port hogsheads db **(93) n23 t23.5 f23 b23.5** My word! This may be a new distillery. But they don't half produce some serious whisky... 46%. nc ncf. 5,300 bottles.

◈ **Wolfburn Small Batch Release No. 204** first fill ex-bourbon barrels, finished for six months in Madeira hogsheads db **(90) n23** such an attractive nose: something of the old-fashioned sweet shop about this with a boiled candy fruitiness giving a crisp sugary countenance. The tannins are only half baked, suggesting there is plenty of youth to this; **t23** there is certainly no doubts about age once the malt this strikes the palate. There is still a slight accent of new makey malt, but this is thoroughly compensated for by a glorious vanilla and butterscotch middle, assisted by an attractive built-up of oils. Rather beautifully structured and deeply satisfying; **f21.5** just a little tangy and flaky as the fruit now takes us towards lime jelly babies. Slightly bitty towards the finish...; **b22.5** a young malt which takes full advantage of the elegance provided by the Madeira casks. 46%. nc ncf. 5,800 bottles.

Wolfburn Small Batch Release No. 270 half-sized first fill ex-bourbon barrels db **(92) n23.5 t22.5 f22.5 b23.5** You'd think from the lighter colour to Wolfburn 128 this would be less developed and offering fewer flavour options. Curiously, the reverse is true, the flavours more even, satisfying and elegant. 46%. nc ncf. 6,000 bottles.

UNSPECIFIED SINGLE MALTS (CAMPBELTOWN)

Cadenhead's Campbeltown Malt (92) n22 t24 f23 b23. On their home turf you'd expect them to get it right... and, my word, so they do!! 59.5%

UNSPECIFIED SINGLE MALTS (HIGHLAND)

◈ **Arcanum Spirits Avalon 12 Year Old Whisky Edition No.4** 1st fill ex-bourbon barrel, dist Nov 2008, bott Nov 2020 **(92) n22** lemon grass, honeysuckle and toffee vanilla combine charmingly; **t23.5** already, from the very first delivery, the malt and tannin are in cahoots to provide something simplistic but absolutely gorgeous; an almost playful acacia honey note fills in the gaps; **f23.5** a celebration of concentrated malt and faultless tannin; **b23** reaps the benefit of an excellent 1st fill bourbon cask, upping the delicate honey notes magnificently. Beautiful malt. 58.9% sc 111 bottles

Asda Extra Special Highland Single Malt bott code: L6B 8127 1511 **(84.5) n21.5 t22 f20 b21** Nutty and lush. But the degree of toffee on show makes this almost closer to being a candy liqueur than a Highland malt. Perfect...if you like toffee! 40%.

Compass Box Myths & Legends I (96) n24.5 t24 f23.5 b24 I quite literally have no idea which distillery this is from. But those who are slightly in love with Clynelish in bourbon cask – one of the greatest experiences available in Scotch single malt whisky – will appreciate this.

It may not be Clynelish, but the apples and honey make for a very creditable impersonation. By the way, I think Compass Box founder John Glaser suggests you can take ice with your whisky. Anyone adding ice or water to this deserves never to taste spectacularly great whisky again. Murray Method all the way for astonishing results... 46%.

Glen Marnoch Highland Single Malt bott code: L12 12 18 **(91)** n22 t23 f23 b23 A beautifully even and satisfying Highlander. No great age, but so much charisma. 40%. *Produced for Aldi.*

Glen Turner Cask Collection Rum Cask Finish bott code: L907357A **(90.5)** n23 t22 f23 b22.5 A very well-manicured malt. 40%. *La Martiniquaise.*

Glen Turner Heritage Double Cask Port Cask Finish bott code: L834657A **(94)** n23.5 t24 f23 b23.5 An impressive piece of cask finishing where the speech by the port is pretty and important, but the microphone has not been turned up too loudly. 40%. *La Martiniquaise.*

Glen Turner Malt Legend Aged 12 Years bott code: L832557C **(87)** n21 t23.5 f21 b21.5 A fat, velvety malt with an attractive, lush fruitiness but just a little too much sharpness out of the oak. Plenty to enjoy. 40%. *La Martiniquaise.*

Glenwill Highland Single Malt rum cask finish **(88)** n22 t22 f21.5 b22.5 An easy malt where the sugary shell of the rum comes into play infrequently. 40%. *Matisse Spirits Company.*

Glenwill RV rum cask finish **(80)** n21 t21 f19 b19 Mainly toffeed, characterless and just zzzzzzzzzzz..... 40%. *Quality Spirits International.*

Glenwill S = 1 sherry butt finish **(73)** n19 t21.5 f16 b17.5 S = Sulphur. 40%. *Quality Spirits International.*

◈ **Highland Queen Majesty Classic** bott code: 21/0043 **(86)** n21.5 t22 f21.5 b21 Her Majesty has turned from Highland Queen to Highland Princess. Notably younger than the last time I looked, the nose makes an exhibition of its new makeyness. Harsh if nosed cool, soft and gristy when slightly warmed. The mouth feel may be silky but the firmness of the young malt itself is striking. Calmed by a little toffee. 40% *Tullibardine Ltd*

◈ **Highland Queen Majesty Aged 12 Years** bott code: 21/0044 **(89)** n22.5 young for its dozen years. But there is a charm to this malty lightness of touch. Gently zesty and always lively; t22 the creamy delivery hardly reflects the nose. Some semi-salivation kicks off from the barley which is green and fresh grass; f22 malty vanilla toffee. Even some late spice off the oak...; b22.5 a better balanced malt than of before: the Queen wears her crown just a little more carefully. There is still a little toffee lurking round, but doesn't play the court jester as it once did. 40% *Tullibardine Ltd*

◈ **Highland Queen Majesty Aged 14 Years Sherry Cask Finish** bott code: 21/0045 **(90.5)** n22 very pleasant, though the plummy fruit leaves it feeling a little flat; t22.5 a curious delivery. Although 14, and despite a hefty touch from the sherry cask, the delivery is a little thin, young in character and salivating thanks to the abundant rich malt: far from what I was expecting. But there is no doubting its alure on the palate as the tannins and spices kick down the doors to make their dramatic entry; f23 long, spicy, silky fruits – mainly blueberries – drift on the palate to unite some time; b23 takes a little while to get the measure of this. But persistence pays off. More complex and rewarding that it first seems. That mix of fruit and spice is rather lovely while the understated malt is heroically brilliant. 40% *Tullibardine Ltd*

Liquid Treasures From Miles Away Highland Malt 19 Year Old bourbon hogshead, dist Aug 20, bott Feb 20 **(80)** n19 t22 f19 b20 A malt from miles away...but not quite far enough. Very flimsy fare, despite the occasional intense barley. 55.6%. sc. 325 bottles.

Master of Malt Highland Single Malt **(86.5)** n21.5 t22 f21.5 b21.5 Pleasant, absolutely middle of the road malt with a juicy, nutty and toffee-rich character. 40%.

The Single Malts of Scotland Orkney 12 Year Old Reserve Cask **(88)** n21.5 t23 f21.5 b22 A slightly tired cask does not make full use of what appears to be an attractively rich spirit. Both the nose and finish reveal a slight weakness to the wood. But the delivery likewise underlines an excellent malt trying to ramp up the honey tones but getting little help from the oak. A temperamental dram but when it sparkles it's pure gold... 48%. nc ncf.

Tesco Finest Aged 12 Years Highland Single Malt bott code L63353 **(80.5)** n20 t21 f19 b20.5 Quite possibly one of the most boring single malts of all time: not recommended as a night cap as you'll doze off by the time you reach the third step on your stairs, and it won't be the effect of the alcohol. Bland barely covers it. With the amount of cream toffee found on the nose and palate not sure if this should be stocked in the Spirits or Sweets aisles. Do I like it? No. Do I dislike it? No. But if I am putting 12-year-old malt into my body, I'd like it to have some semblance of character. I suppose it was designed to offend nobody: a mute hardly can. Trouble is, it is hardly likely to get new drinkers wanting to come back and discover more about single malt, either. Oh well, I suppose that buggers up any chance of getting The Bible stocked and sold by Tesco this year. But I'm afraid they need to hear the truth. 40%.

UNSPECIFIED SINGLE MALTS (ISLAND)

The First Editions Director's Highbrow Selection Aged 13 Years 2006 refill hogshead, cask no. 16651, bott 2019 **(93) n23 t23.5 f23 b23.5** With so much beeswax, a polished malt as you'd expect. *61%. nc ncf sc. 339 bottles.*

◈ **The First Editions Orkney Aged 15 Years 2006** refill hogshead, cask no.HL18701, bott 2021 **(92) n22.5** just the lightest drift of smoke adds a spiced weightiness to the noisy tannin. The malt is restrained, but a few honey tones mingle; **t23.5** now the honey arrives in force: a heather honey dominance with some biting peppers and melting grist; **f23** beautiful smoke and spice interplay. Still the honey lingers. Stylish... **b23** understated complexity. What a treat! *62.8% nc ncf sc 309 bottles*

◈ **Old Malt Cask Orkney Aged 13 Years** sherry butt, cask no. 18195, dist Mar 07, bott Dec 20 **(94) n23.5** the gossamer thin smoke is almost too alluring: what high-quality, beautifully made malt this is...; **t23.5** the caress of the palate by the oils, the kisses by the light acacia honey tones...just wow...; **f23** vanillas and an ever-increasing spice now take over where the honey and smoke have left off...; **b24** forget the sherry cask. The effect has been worn away by the passage of time and here have a story of excellent sexy distillate and a cask which allows it to do as it wishes and be whatever it wants to be. Simply stunning... *50%. nc ncf sc. 257 bottles.*

◈ **Whisky-Fässle Orkney 17 Years Old** butt, dist 2002, bott 2019 **(89.5) n23 t23 f21.5 b22** The oils and fruit on this ensure a long, increasingly toasty and bitter finish. But the nose is an essay of age, charm and balance with the vanilla and barley in harmony with the spiced spotted dog pudding. The delivery, meanwhile, is a festival of varied sugar and honey tones – and malty ones at that – missing on the nose and finish. *49.1%. sc.*

◈ **Whisky-Fässle Orkney 12 Years Old** hogshead, dist 2007, bott 2020 **(89) n22 t23 f22 b22** An exceptionally dry malt, the salt adding to the eye-watering qualities. It's a HP, devoid of both trademark smoke and honey. But still beautifully made and the deft barley interacts with the tannins and spice with a relaxed countenance. Quietly elegant and refined. *51.3%. sc.*

UNSPECIFIED SINGLE MALTS (ISLAY)

Aerolite Lyndsay Aged 10 Years bott code: #4877 **(91) n22.5 t23 f22.5 b23** A classic Islay unchanged in style from 30 years ago. A very pleasing experience. *46%. Atom Brands.*

Angel's Nectar Single Malt Scotch Whisky Islay Edition (91.5) n22 t23.5 f23 b23 A young Islay, but no shame in that when this well made and so beautifully matured. The peat both on nose and palate has an evenness of weight which allows the light saline edge mix with the delicate citrus without too much interruption. Fresh, salivating and incorrigibly gristy. *47%.*

Arcanum Spirits Peaty Little Secret 9 Years Old aged over 8 years in ex-bourbon hogshead, finished a full year in 1st fill Oloroso hogshead, dist 12 Jun 08, bott 19 Oct 17 **(85.5) n22 t22 f20.5 b21** Where there 18-year-old can be held up and worshipped as an extraordinary example of balance and charm at its finest, this takes another route altogether. Finishing is an art form - and a dangerous expedition for any whisky to undertake. As you are always entering uncharted lands and there is no way of knowing when you have found the land you are looking for. Even more dangerous is introducing sherry casks. And I'm afraid that, for one reason or another, this isn't the finest quality and nor has an understanding been achieved between the two parties. (It is 8pm on a Thursday here in England – so pause here for a minute's applause for the brave and wonderful British National Health Service staff who are fighting Covid-19 head on...) What I do adore, though, is the proud cattle byre nose and delivery. Pure farmyard. *58.4%. ncf sc. 439 bottles.*

Asda Extra Special Islay Single Malt bott code: L6C 7619 1109 **(88.5) n22 t22.5 f22 b22** Does exactly what it says on the tin...except for the alleged fruity tones which never materialise... *40%.*

◈ **Bruadaradh Lochindaal 9 Years Old** dist 1 Sept 09, bott 6 Nov 18 **(86.5) n22.5 t22.5 f20.5 b21** The saltiness of the nose, combined with peat reek on the breeze talks Islay to you. But there is a nip on the nose, too, which suggests the cask has a little issue. Thankfully, this doesn't fully arrive until the finish when the burn and bitterness fair grabs you. But until then, enjoy the vanilla, natural caramel, heather honey and ultra-light phenol serenade... *63.4%. nc ncf sc.*

◈ **Bruadaradh Lochindaal 9 Years Old** dist 1 Sept 09, bott 17 Nov 18 **(90.5) n22.5 t23 f22 b23** A much more docile bottling than their other one (above) with far fewer stumbling blocks. The mintiness to the peat on the nose tends to give a feeling of greater age - though they are twins. As before the smoke is shy and happy to hide behind the more militant elements. Though little is particularly militant here with the ulmo honey and light spice really making a wonderful pairing. There is still a little bitterness to negotiate at the end here, but the malt and smoke do some great repair work. *50%. nc ncf sc.*

⟡ **Demijohn Islay 10 Year Old (95) n23.5** a halfway house between sooty, semi-acrid peat and billowing smoke. Better still, both the malt and the oaky vanilla are able to jut out slightly and get noticed, too...; **t24** pure balm for the taste buds. The sugars cling round an ulmo honey centre. From there polite spices and slowly thickening smoke begin to seep...; **f23.5** the lightest liquorice and chocolate fade works beautifully with the light smoke. Still, again – and unusually for an Islay – the barley itself is distinguishable late on...; **b24** a faultless Islay: beautifully distilled and matured just the right number of years in an absolutely brilliant bourbon cask. Whoever selected this cask should take a bow. Hebridean nectar... 58.1% 🍷

The Finest Malts Secret Islay Distillery Aged 6 Years sherry butt, dist Oct 13, bott Jan 20 **(89) n22 t22.5 f22 b22.5** Well, there's something for the diary: the first Islay whisky which, perhaps in conjunction with the sherry butt, offers a smokiness slightly closer to Mesquite thanks to a pretty off the wall acidity biting deep. The sherry but is clean with no sulphur, thank heavens. But, even so, the youthfulness of the malt means the two very different – and egotistical – flavour codes have had little time to strike up much of an understanding. That said, hugely enjoyable if at times a little raucous....as any self-respecting 6-year-old Islay has every right to be. 51.6%. nc ncf sc. 72 bottles.

Finlaggan Cask Strength Islay Single Malt (88) n22.5 t23 f21.5 b21 A massive peated malt which that phenolphiles will lap up. But for its all its big Islay muscle, struggles to come together and balance out as even as might be hoped. 58%. The Vintage Malt Whisky Company.

Finlaggan Eilean Mor Islay Single Malt (88.50) n22 t22.5 f22 b22 Oily Islay with a pleasant if limited disposition. 46%. The Vintage Malt Whisky Company.

Finlaggan Old Reserve Islay Single Malt (91) n23 t23f22.5 b23 No great age I suspect. But the intensity and charm are profound. Unmistakably Islay! 40%.

Finlaggan Port Finish Islay Single Malt (92.5) n23 t23.5 f23 b23.5 Huge peat at work, dry and almost coal dust-like. But its wings are initially clipped by the port before it takes off once more...to profound effect. 46%. The Vintage Malt Whisky Company.

⟡ **Gleann Mór Rare Find Islay Aged 15 Years** dist 2006 **(88.5) n22 t23 f21.5 b22** Was doing so well until the bourbon cask began to bitter out at the end, though the nose did forewarn. However, this is beautifully peated and rounded – true classic Islay style. A little Granny Smith apple gives it a degree of tartness, too. 52.1%

Peat's Beast bott code: L 07 08 17 **(92) n22.5 t23 f23.5 b23** Nosing this whizzed me back to the late 1980s and my old office in a national newspaper in Fleet Street where, by night, I was taking my first tentative steps into the then unknown and practically non-existent medium of whisky writing. And I remember opening up a Bowmore 5-years-old bottled by Oddbins. I'm not saying this is a Bowmore, but so many features on display in that landmark bottling 30 years ago are also to be found here... 46%. ncf.

Peat's Beast Twenty Five bott code: L1 1409-2017 11 **(88.5) n23 t23 f20 b22.5** There are far more beastly Islay whiskies than this out there – a quarter of a century in the cask means the teeth have been blunted, the claws clipped. And if you must "tame it" further, for God's sake ignore the daft advice on the label about adding water. Please use the Murray Method described on page 9. That will keep the thing alive while making it purr at full decibels... And this is so lovely (well, finish apart), it is worth listening to at full volume...which isn't very loud. 52.2%. ncf.

Port Askaig Islay Aged 12 Years Spring Edition ex-bourbon hogsheads, dist 2006 & 2007 **(95.5) n24 t24 f23.5 b24** Only a bourbon cask can allow the phenols to play and galivant with such fun and abandon. You get the feeling that the casks were plucked from the warehouse at exactly the right time. Fabulous! 45.8%. nc ncf. 5,000 bottles.

Port Askaig 14 Year Old Bourbon Cask dist 2004 **(95) n24 t23.5 f23.5 b24** For those who prefer their peat to caress rather than kick. Elegant and so beautifully sensual. 45.8%.

Port Askaig 15 Years Old sherry cask **(87.5) n22.5 t22 f21.5 b21.5** I know, I know: I have a blind spot for this kind of whisky. Rather, not blind, but not an over developed appreciation of the big smoke notes slugging it out with and then being neutralised by equally big, occasionally eye-wateringly sharp, fruit ones. At least the sherry is clean and extra marks for that. But, for me, this is just too much of a tit-for-tat malt leaving a neutral toffee fruitiness to claim the big prize. Pleasant, I grant you. But I want it to be so much more.... 45.8%.

Port Askaig 25 Years Old (91) n23 t23.5 f21 b22.5 Bottled at the right time – another year or two would have seen a dramatic slide. But as it is, so much to quietly savour. 45.8%.

Port Askaig 28 Years Old (92.5) n23.5 t23.5 f22 b23.5 Classically understated. 45.8%.

Port Askaig 33 Years Old Single Cask (95) n23.5 t24.5 f23 b24 Islay at its most coastal. Shews its age with rare elegance. Sublime. 50.3%. ncf.

Port Askaig 45 Years Old (90.5) n23 t23 f22 b22.5 Even in my scaringly long career, I can probably count the number of peated malts that made it to this kind of age and then into a commercial bottling on one hand. Certainly by the end it is showing every year that has passed, but for an unexpected period the malt hangs together...sometimes surprisingly deliciously. 40.8%.

Port Askaig 100 Proof (96.5) **n**24 **t**24 **f**24 **b**24.5 Just exemplary, high quality Islay: a must experience malt. If you find a more beautifully paced, weighted and elegant Islay this year, I'd like to hear about it... *57.1%.*

Port Askaig 110 Proof (91.5) **n**23 **t**23 **f**22.5 **b**23 Beautifully made and elegantly matured. An excellent Islay. *55%.*

The Whisky Chamber Buair an Diabhail Vol. XVIII bourbon cask (86.5) **n**22 **t**22 **f**21 **b**21.5 It may be swamped in more smoke than a 1950s London pub, but there is something unmercifully metallic about this malt. Especially on the rigid finish. Plenty of molasses to sweeten the impact, but a whisky that is hard to embrace. *57.4%. sc.*

⟫ **The Whisky Chamber Teagmháil Leis an Diabhail Vol. II 10 Jahre 2009** bourbon cask (92.5) **n**23.5 any more Scottish coastal and you'd half expect to see HMS Britannia floating around the glass... the peat is docile and sharpened by a citrussy, salty edge. A real tide out charm...; **t**23.5 lovely oils ensure the softest of landings before the peat and spice gang together. The marriage of ulmo and heather honeys woks magnificently and harmonise with the phenols perfectly; **f**22.5 even a slight tiredness to the cask can't take away from the joys of the lightly smoked spice and butterscotch fade; **b**23 if Covid means you can't get to a Scottish beach this year, here's a chance to let it come to you... *58.2%. sc.*

UNSPECIFIED SINGLE MALTS (LOWLAND)

Tweeddale Single Lowland Malt Scotch Whisky 14 Years db (89) **n**21.5 **t**23.5 **f**22 **b**22 busy, bustling, elegant and old-fashioned...like a small borders town. *62%. nc ncf sc.*

UNSPECIFIED SINGLE MALTS (SPEYSIDE)

Abbey Whisky Anon. Batch 3 Aged 30 Years 1988 sherry cask (96) **n**24 **t**24 **f**23.5 **b**24.5 Those who adore Glenfarclas will find a soft spot in their hearts for this as the oaky tannin and aged-dulled fruit apes that distillery's style amazingly uncannily. This is one of the finest sherry butts I have found in action this year. Not an atom of sulphur to be seen: this is 30 year-old whisky as I tasted 30 years ago... *46.6%. sc. 153 bottles.*

A.D. Rattray Cask Speyside 10 Year Old (89) **n**22 **t**22.5 **f**22 **b**22.5 An elegant and lightly smoked malt which would double as either a pre-prandial dram, or one for the wooden hill... *46%.*

⟫ **Angels' Nectar Aged 11 Years Cairngorms Edition** (88.5) **n**22 **t**23 **f**21.5 **b**22 One of those very pleasant, delicate malty drams, slightly pepped-up by spice, sandalwood and such like on the nose which is juicy on the palate...but otherwise happy to play it safe. *46%. sc. 263 bottles.*

⟫ **Angels' Nectar Aged 11 Years Cairngorms 2nd Edition** (92) **n**22.5 coarser grained wood shaving than te previous edition, upping the spices without losing the complexity or depth; **t**23 such a beautiful delivery! That wonderful mix of ulmo and heather honey which always wins (as against light acacia on the First Edition); the midpoint fills with waxy layerings of vanilla and malt; **f**23.5 such impressive oils carry not only elements of the honey, but now far more spice and late cocoa; **b**23 though a collector of First Editions, I tend to think that this 2nd has some slight amendments to ensure extra depth and entertainment. Having said that, there will be times when my mood would take me to the more flighty and fragile First edition. Two very impressive Angels. *46%. sc. 146 bottles.*

Arcanum Spirits Arcanum One 18 Years Old dist 26 Feb 99, bott 8 Jun 17 (95.5) **n**24 **t**24 **f**23.5 **b**24 Classy, classy malt deserving the patronage of any Speysider lover. The way it maintains a degree of youthfulness and then reminds you of its decent age is such fun. Marvellous and deeply desirable whisky. *54%. ncf sc. 396 bottles.*

Arcanum Spirits TR21INITY Aged Over 21 Years refill ex-bourbon barrel, dist 16 Jul 97, bott 24 Aug 18 db (96.5) **n**24.5 **t**24 **f**23.5 **b**24.5 TR21 reminds me, touchingly, of a magazine my old dad used to bring home from work for me in the mid 1960s: TV21...never could get enough Daleks or Thunderbirds... Well this is Thunderbird 5: out of this world...and complexity like this, such utter, almost moving beauty, can only ever be achieved with a bourbon cask where all is laid bare. *52.1%. ncf sc. 222 bottles. Whisky Edition No. 3.*

Asda Extra Special Speyside Single Malt bott code: L6A 8226 1412 (81) **n**20 **t**21.5 **f**19 **b**20.5 Pleasant, soft and sweet and briefly delicious on delivery...but entirely linear. As it develops, devoid of character or personality as the big dollop of caramel and tired casks has taken its toll. *40%.*

Compass Box Myths & Legends II (95) **n**24 **t**23.5 **f**23.5 **b**24 Incredibly lively malt on the palate. The delivery is one of the most memorable this year, aided and abetted by sublime bourbon casks allowing the malt to reveal all its naked beauty.. *46%.*

⟫ **Creag Dhu Speyside** aged in sherry casks, bott code: L151220 (92) **n**23 the clarity to the grape is matched only by an elegance of the drier nuttiness. The low abv means the tannins have a little more chalkiness than might normally be the case and the sweetness of the grape is slightly diluted and compromised. But that's being picky: this is hugely attractive and well-balanced...; **t23.5** the sugars that have gone AWOL on the nose have been rounded up and captured for the delivery. A lovely blend of muscovado and demerara sugars give the fruit a real polished and clean. Lightly salivating in all the right places...; **f22.5** not quite the perfect finale, with its odd rough edge and all, but the dryness is in keeping with the quiet elegance that this malt seems all about...; **b23** malts like this help point towards a recovery from the sulphur problem to hit Scotland's sherry casks. This is almost faultless and the only complaint is that, at barely over 40%abv, too much body has been lost by reduction: this screams out to be cask strength. *40.2%*

The Finest Malts City Landmarks Secret Speyside Aged 24 Years bourbon barrel, cask no. 408895, dist 1994, bott 2019 **(92.5) n22.5 t24 f22.5 b23.5** A lightly honeyed offering here which, even after 24 years, is not frightened of allowing the barley to let rip. The age has crept up quietly and politely, never seemingly wanting to over-interfere. But there is a particular excellence to the saltiness which livens up the heather-honey especially early on before marzipan and caramel starts to intensify....though gently, of course. The vanillas are treading water towards the end as the malt tires. But charm and elegance are always the guiding lights here. Some whiskies wear their years well. This is one with just a little grey around the temples and never less than dapper. A great malt for long study. *49.3%. nc ncf sc.*

◇◇ **Scyfion Carron Burns** griot wine cask finished, dist 2008, bott 2019 **(84) n21.5 t21.5 f20 b21** Well, that's rather different! Normally a bubble gum nose like that would be marked down by me - but here there is an unusual polish to the malt, too. And though that malt pounds through on delivery and for a few beats more, it becomes all a little glassy, bitter.... and a little bit strange. *50% nc ncf sc 228 bottles*

◇◇ **Scyfion Carron Burns** staraya Shalanda cask finished, dist 2008, bott 2019 **(78.5) n19 t21 f19.5 b19** Some whisky finishes work, some don't. This don't. *50% nc ncf sc 172 bottles*

◇◇ **Whisky-Fässle Aged 25 Years** sherry cask, dist 1993, bott 2018 **(92.5) n23 t23 f23.5 b23** They have done well. Somehow they have found a sherry butt from a quarter of a century back not ruined, or even undermined, by sulphur. Instead the grape takes a very firm hand on the nose and refuses to release its grip until the last spicy moment. Although this isn't one of those world-shattering sherry butts of old, where the complexity levels explode off the graph, neither is it a cask where you find yourself discovering the sulphur five minutes later as it nags at your palate. Instead it is content to back up some robust peppers with a juicy cherry moment or two and a little sultana. Yet still the malt comes through loud and clear, plus a little late custard, too. Most impressive, though, is the salivating qualities if both barley and raisin which sets up the late chocolate with aplomb. A round of applause for this minor gem. Well done Whisky-Fassle yet again! *51.7% nc ncf*

◇◇ **Whisky-Fässle Aged 27 Years** hogshead, dist 1991, bott 2018 **(94) n23.5 t23 f23.5 b24** Superb cask which has lasted the near three decades with something to spare. No tiredness. Just a malt that is willing to give, from the first spiced heather honey nose right through to the slightly rugged though still intensely malty finish. The fact, however, that is still a salivating dram after all these years, with the malt veering from grassy to gristy, really takes some doing. As does the management of the oak which ensures the grains carry the necessary depth to impress as a vintage whisky. Just wonderful stuff... *48.8% nc ncf*

Whisky Illuminati Artis Secretum 2011 Spanish oak sherry butt, cask no. 900284 **(95.5) n24 t24.5 f23 b24** A Speyside sherry butt in its finest fettle. What a complete delight... *67.1%. sc. 150 bottles.*

Whisky Works 20 Year Old Speyside 2019/WV02./CW finished in 20 year old Cognac casks, bott code: L9262 13:21 P/010452 **(96.5) n24 t24 f24 b24.5** On the label this whisky states: "Flavour Profile: Like an afternoon in a country garden". Well, I abandoned my tasting lab in order to taste this one afternoon in my garden, which is the quintessential country garden affording an ancient space around a 300-year-old cottage backing onto wild fields. Can't say the whisky is exactly like the world in which I live and relax. I mean, there is none of the speedwell or bird-foot trefoil; the wild rose and foxglove; the lavender or wild poppy. Nor have they managed to distil the song of the dunnock, the chiffchaff, the blackbird, the wren, the blackcap or the chaffinch; nor, as the afternoon wears on, the excitable screech of the swifts overhead or the churr of the whitethroat. But, allowing for a little poetic licence, I think I know what they are getting at... Because my garden is a little corner of Eden. And this natural, untainted whisky feels right at home in it... *47.1%. nc ncf. 1,593 bottles.*

UNSPECIFIED SINGLE MALTS (GENERAL)

Burns Nectar Single Malt bott code: L17/8183 **(77) n20 t19 f19 b19** An ode to toffee. *40%.*

Compass Box Myths & Legends III (95.5) n23.5 t24 f24 b24 It is noticeable that Compass Box have, by and large, reigned back on the over oaking and are back to allowing the whiskies themselves to do the talking. Another exceptionally beautiful malt from them using bourbon casks that allows the personality of the malt to come through in all its gentle but complex beauty. I just wish more blenders would take note of this. *46%*.

Darkness Aged 8 Years sherry cask finished, bott code: #4635 **(92) n23 t23.5 f22 b23.5** ...Being the unreconstructed romantic I am, I tasted this outside in my near silent and perfectly still garden (so silent and still I can hear a train scurrying through a cutting some five miles away – only the second time I have done so in six years) without a breath of wind on the warm summer air as, long after sunset, darkness fell... And the whisky was, I must admit, as gentle as the night which had stealthily crept up and enveloped me... *47.8%. Atom Brands.*

Eternity Single Malt American Oak Matured (82.5) n21 t21 f20 b20.5 Nutty with a vague smokiness adding weight. But the early cloying malty sweetness gives way to a dogged bitterness. *40%*.

Eternity Single Malt 12 Years Old (84) n21.5 t21.5 f20 b21 Full bodied and malty, there is plenty to chew on here including a degree of toffee. Some redeeming spice on the bitter finish, but never quite finds a comfortable rhythm either on nose or palate. *46%*.

Kingsbury Gold Auchindoun 22 Year Old hogshead, cask no. 187, dist 1997 **(86) n23 t21.5 f20.5 b21** After such a charming, citrus-laced nose with its delicate strands of malt and almost imperceptible traces of mint, what follows on the taste buds has a far bigger oaky resonance than might reasonably be expected. A bit like what appears to be a tender steak which turns out to be a little tough and gristly. *48.9%. sc. 282 bottles.*

Kingsbury Gold Culloden 15 Year Old hogshead, cask no. 600044, dist 2004 **(92) n23 t23 f22.5 b23.5** One of those quiet, understated drams which could be easily overlooked. Worth giving a lot of extra time to in order to fully explore. *62.7%. sc. 174 bottles.*

Kingsbury Gold Kilbride 13 Year Old barrel, cask no. 800217, dist 2006 **(94) n23.5 t23.5 f23 b24** Very high class peated malt benefitting from 13 years in excellent oak. A peat-lover's dream! *56%. sc. 220 bottles.*

Kingsbury Gold Ruine 27 Year Old barrel, cask no. 4406046, dist 1992 **(90) n23 t22.5 f22 b22.5** A malt on the cusp of exhaustion but has enough life not to give up the ghost. Overall, as fascinating as it is delicious. *46.3%. sc. 257 bottles.*

M&S Speyside Aged 12 Years bott code: L031220 **(81.5) n22 t21 f18.5 b20** For its age lacks complexity, other than a brief spell on the nose where the malt and oak appear to be gently cajoling the other. But the performance on the palate, if initially pleasant and malty, flattens alarmingly before finishing in overly bitter fashion. *40%*

Matisse Single Malt Aged 19 Years (91) n23 t22.5 f22.5 b23 A malt that operates by stealth, seemingly wanting to go unnoticed. However, perseverance will pay off for the taster. *40%. Matisse Spirits Company.*

Peat's Beast bott code: L 20 02 19 **(89) n22 t23 f22 b22** A very safe malt by heavily peated standards, determined not to offend. *46%. ncf.*

Peat's Beast Batch Strength Pedro Ximenez sherry wood finish, bott code: L 18 10 19 **(89.5) n22.5 t23 f22 b22** If this whisky was comedy it would be pure slapstick. *54.1%. ncf.*

Scottish Vatted Malts
(also Pure Malts/Blended Malt Scotch)

Angels' Nectar (81) n21 t21 f19 b20. This angel has a bitter tooth... *40%*

Angel's Nectar Blended Malt Rich Peat Edition (90.5) n22.5 t23 f22.5 b22.5 Excellently-made malt: sticks unerringly to the script. *46%*

Ben Bracken Blended Malt Aged 12 Years (85.5) n22.5 t21 f21 b21. Quite a tight malt with a predominantly toffee theme. *40%*

Berry Bros & Rudd Islay Blended Malt bott code: L18/8215 **(90.5) n22 t23 f22.5 b23** An endearing vatting which sums up the island's whiskies without any drama but still highly attractively and with no wrong turns. *44.2%. The Classic Range.*

Berry Bros & Rudd Sherry Cask Matured Blended Malt Whisky bott code: P/001036 **(84) n22 t21.5 f20 b20.5** Despite the early muscovado sugars which ooze all over the delivery, this turns into one of the most strangely bitter malts I have tasted in a very long time. Like a fruitcake that has been incinerated in the oven and syrup poured over it so no-one might notice... Odd! Though I'm certain there are types who will fight to the death for a bottle of this. A whisky, let us say, to divide opinion. *44.2%.*

Berry Bros & Rudd Peated Cask Matured Blended Malt bott code: L18/8214 **(92) n22 t23 f23.5 b23.5** Gentle and evenly paced. *44.2%. The Classic Range.*

Berry Bros & Rudd Speyside Blended Malt (85) n20 t22.5 f21 b21.5 A lot of malt to get your teeth into. The oak isn't exactly sympathetic but the big wave of vanilla at the midpoint carries some attractive maple syrup. *44.2%. The Classic Range.*

Black Tartan 88 31 Year Old hogshead, cask no. 00016 **(94) n23 t23.5 f23.5 b24** The nose suggests you might be in for an overly oaky ride. It lies! This is an old dram which retains a marvellous zest for life but piles on the malt in spades. 48%. sc.

◇ **Black Tartan Batch 21 Blended Malt** bott: 2021 **(86) n21.5 t22 f21 b21.5** A very young vatted malt which very much keeps its eye on projecting a clean, malty image. Pleasant, if a little uninspiring. 40% nc. Ncf, 2990 bottles

Chapter 7 Anecdote Blended Malt 24 Year Old 2 bourbon hogsheads, dist Jul 95, bott Mar 20 **(93.5) n23 t23.5 f23.5 b23.5** Tells a quietly delicious tale. 479%. 424 bottles.

◇ **Chapter 7 Williamson 2010 Aged 9 Years** bourbon barrel, barrel no.907 **(95.5) n24** the varying personality between the acidic phenols and the more delicate smokiness quite literally takes the breath away. The same goes for the clever interplay between lighter and roastier sugars; **t24** faultless. This is why it is so good to see a perfectly distilled Islay at a younger age, free from the usual oaky luggage: here you get just how complex the peat structures can be in their own right, how they involve the remaining pure malt characteristics, and how the sugars are neatly spread. Just take as much time as you can chewing this one; **f23.5** at last the tannins arrive, also with a light sprinkling of cocoa. But the spices no more than tingle now while the peat just carries on with its unremitting complexity; **b24** Magnificent: there is no other word. 53.9% ☙

Chivas Regal Ultis bott code LPNK1759 2016/09/16 **(89.5) n22.5 t23 f21.5 b22.5** This vatted malt is the legacy of Chivas' five master blenders. But to pay real respect to them, just remove the caramel from the bottling hall. The whisky will be light coloured, for sure, but I suspect the flavour profile will blow us all away... 40%. Chivas Brothers Ltd.

Compass Box The Circle bott May 19 **(94.5) n23.5 t24 f23 b24** If a malt whisky this year proves no great age is required to create something of great beauty, then here it is. A wonderful crossover between lemon blossom honey and pear drops on the nose helps focus the attention on the clarity of the malt. Such a nose demands a delivery of great malty complexity...and you won't be disappointed. The bourbon casks add their own magic spell to proceedings, intertwangling both vanilla and butterscotch with pipette-measured exactitude and ensuring the spices play an important but never over-dominant role. Simple. Yet not. A real treat of a dram. 46%. nc ncf. 6,151 bottles.

Compass Box No Name bott Sept 17 **(92.5) n23 t23 f23 b23.5** I'll give it a name: Compass Box Bleedin' Delicious! 48.9%. nc ncf. 15,000 bottles.

Compass Box No Name, No. 2 bott Feb 19 **(93.5) n23 t23.5 f23.5 b23.5** Think a lightly oiled Islay whisky where the peat is powering, but totally in sync with the overall balance of the piece. And where a light heather honey note ensures there is no bitterness and the phenols never get too acrid or sooty. Spot on wood management with this fella. 48.9%. nc ncf. 8,802 bottles.

Compass Box The Peat Monster bott code: L 11 12 18 **(94.5) n23.5 t23.5 f23.5 b24** This is the most complete Peat Monster I've encountered for a little while. It's all about the balance and here it manages to allow sheer enormity to come through loud and clear, but not at the expense of tact and complexity. 46%. nc ncf.

Compass Box The Peat Monster Cask Strength (89) n23.5 t23 f20.5 b22 Plenty of peat between your teeth but deserving of some better oak. 573%

Compass Box The Peat Monster Reserve (92) n23 t23.5 f22.5 b23. At times a bit of a Sweet Monster...beautiful stuff! 48.9%

Compass Box The Spice Tree French oak head & American oak body hybrid casks, bott code: L 28 11 18 **(96) n23.5 t25 f23.5 b24** Don't know about The Spice Tree...Honey Tree more like.. So strikingly beautiful! 46%.

Compass Box The Story of The Spaniard 48% aged in Spanish wine casks, bott Jun 18 **(90.5) n23 t23 f22 b22.5** Often Compass Box lets the oak do the talking, occasionally too loudly. Here the tannin has a dry edge, but fits into the scenario perfectly. 43%. nc ncf.

Compass Box The Story of The Spaniard Spanish fortified wine casks, American and French oak barrels, batch no. TS 2019-A **(83.5) n22 t23 f18.5 b20** I have had Spanish lovers: so beautiful, so passionate words alone are inadequate to describe. Close Spanish friends, their humour, sincerity, choice of great food and wine as well as good nature a man of the world only can recognise as truly priceless. Reported on Spanish football played out in front of 120,000 crowds. All exciting; always entertaining, always stretching something within you and taking you to places you have never quite been before.... This, though, doesn't. A dull nagging note keeps the whisky in check despite the sublime natural juiciness of the malt. But just too many things are off key late on. Not the kind of Spaniard I usually cosset. 43%. nc ncf.

Copper Dog batch no. 16/0673, bott code: L8127IY001 **(89) n22 t23.5 f21.5 b22** A whisky which first saw the light of day at the fabulous Craigellachie Hotel in Speyside, where I gave my first whisky lectures over a quarter of a century ago and in the 1990s wrote many chapters of my various books. The number of vatted malts we created from the whiskies in the bar... far too many to mention, though none then capable of shewing this kind of finale. 40%.

Cutty Sark Blended Malt (92.5) n22 t24 f23 b23.5. Sheer quality: as if two styles have been placed in the bottle and told to fight it out between them. What a treat! 40%.

Deerstalker Blended Malt Highland Edition (94) n23.5 t23.5 f23 b24 A quite beautiful whisky by any standards. 43%

⬩⬩⬩ **The Double Peat** bott code: L20 07999 CB3 **(88.5) n22.5 t23 f21 b22** A very youthful, vatted malt which is muscular and full of vitality. Yet, oddly, this isn't in the same League balance-wise with Angus Dundee's peaty blend, For Peat's Sake, so far as balance and complexity is concerned. Still a massively intense peatathon for the Islayphiles of the world to savour. But the thinness on the finish underlines how overall balance is not quite there. That said, the eye-watering delivery is worth investing in a bottle alone...! 46% Angus Dundee ncf

⬩⬩⬩ **Fadandel.dk Isla Blended Aged 10 Years In Memory of Bessie Williamson** hogshead barrel, cask no.LAP224, dist May 2011, bott May 2021 **(94) n23.5** the oak involvement is muted. Which leaves the smoke, the delicate spice and the malt to come to an amicable, slightly citrussy arrangement; **t23.5** ohhhh...! Just love those oils. Wow...whoever was running the stills that day knew exactly what they were doing: this is THE perfect cut: a blender's dream. The creaminess to the palate is genuinely a one in a hundred event, especially when it managed to capture the sugars off the grist, the smoke and the intricacies of the cask all within its grasp...; **f23** long, still improbably gristy...and still sweetly smoked with a gentlest hint of Demerara sugars to merge with the lightest tannins; **b24** trying to think why this reminds me so much of a very decent standard barrel of 10-year-old Laphroaig. Answers on a postcard, please. By the way, if you want to experience malt whisky being perfectly made, then here's your bottle... 58.4% sc 323 bottles

Fadandel.dk MacRothes 25 Year Old 1st fill Oloroso sherry butt, cask no. 3, dist 20 Jan 94, bott 21 Oct 19 **(89.5) n23.5 t24 f20 b22** If you see a bottle of this, please be gentle with other customers and staff. But don't let anyone else get their hands on it. Mild violence is permissible and entirely understandable if provoked. However, this applies only for those lucky enough not to be able to taste sulphur which turns up here very late to the party... and then in quite an insidious manner. 56.6%. sc. 676 bottles.

The Finest Malts Blended Malt Aged 18 Years sherry butt, dist 2001, bott 2019 **(91) n23 t24 f21 b23** Always a relief when you find the advertised sherry butt is, though not quite clean as a whistle, for this day and age not far off. And even more so when the grape doesn't dominate at all costs and spices give a much more incisive than is the norm. This is a vatted malt with huge character. And at the heart, for all the fruit, for all the spice, comes the malt which is thick, lush and true. Then there is a maple syrup running off the oak. All beautifully paced, all wonderfully integrated. Just a shame about that little late blemish. 46.1%. nc ncf sc. 72 bottles.

The Finest Malts City Landmarks Blended Malt Aged 25 Years sherry hogs-head, cask no. 431, dist 1993, bott 2018 **(90) n23 t23 f21.5 b22.5** A surprising low key malt. The nose suggests we are in the land of untainted sherry casks here and celebrates with delicate oloroso and glazed cherry to join the spices and vanilla on the well set nose. And though the delivery is lush on the palate and the peppers now warming to their task, waves of natural caramels tend to ensure that development is modest after those first gorgeous spasms on entry. Subtle and satisfying, a malt that sets off like a train and then thinks better of it. There is a light buzz off the sherry butt late on, but nothing to worry about. A delightful late night dram. 52.1%. nc ncf sc.

The First Editions Hector Macbeth Aged 22 Years 1997 refill hogshead, cask no. 16650, bott 2019 **(93) n23.5 t24 f22 b23.5** Whoever Hector Macbeth was, one assumes he kept bees... 53.6%. nc ncf sc. 326 bottles.

⬩⬩⬩ **The First Editions Hector Macbeth Aged 24 Years 1997** bourbon barrel, cask no.HL18662 **(92.5) n23.5** superb nose! Heather honey swarms all over this like bees on err... heather! Some gentle salty tones lightly season both the honey and butterscotch; **t24** spot on delivery. Even the mouth feel has an early waxiness to match the honey. Toasty liquorice begins to make a weighty mark. Sublime layering and depth; **f22** just a tad bitter as the sugars go roasty; **b23** those for a penchant for whisky distilled by bees had better buzz off and find a bottle... 51% nc ncf sc 333 bottles

The First Editions John McCrae Aged 23 Years 1995 refill hogshead, cask no. 16643, bott 2019 **(86.5) n22 t22.5 f20.5 b21.5** A decent enough vatting in part. But there is perhaps a little too much tang, to reveal tiring oak. 44%. nc ncf sc. 246 bottles.

⬩⬩⬩ **The Gladstone Axe American Oak** bott code: B2061099 **(91.5) n22** it's the layering which works so well: the varying degrees of sweetness. Always with a vanilla edge, but the demerara sharpens it...; **t23** this is clean whisky: both the grains and malts used concentrate on their ability first sharpen, crystalise and then salivate. After that, it's every little spice attack for itself...; **f23.5** a glorious glow of spice and tannin-ripened vanilla. Light buttery toffee elongates and softens furthers, especially when the spiced milk chocolate kicks in; **b23** a deeply pleasing blend. It does what a blend should do: offer succulence and complexity in a way you can barely notice...unless you really look. Unostentatious, but highly impressive. *41%*

⬩ **The Gladstone Axe The Black Axe** peated malts with touch of smoke, bott code: B2031092 **(88.5) n22.5 t22 f22 b22** Pleasant whisky but with a much duller and less tantalising persona than its sister blend, American Oak. Slightly too much emphasis on the spice this time round which seems to make up for the lack of smoke I had been expecting. The nose apart, much drier, less emphasis on the sugars but still with a late satisfying sweep of milky chocolate. Rich toffee, though, can be found in every crevice. *41%*

Glen Castle Blended Malt 1990 Sherry Cask Matured 28 Years Old bott code: LHB 1479-2018 **(96) n24 t24 f24 b24** Anyone who wants to know the difference between ye olde great, untainted sherry butts and the poor and unacceptable offerings we have been subjected to for the last 25 years should grab a bottle of this. Old school brilliance. And beauty. Just...wow! Old Time sherry at its most accessible....and mind-blowing. *55.2%. nc ncf.*

Glen Castle Blended Malt 1992 Sherry Cask Matured bott code: L7 9595-2017 12 **(95.5) n24 t24 f23.5 b24** Just brilliant whisky to be savoured and cherished, restoring my faith in sherry – very few butts from this era survived the sulphury onslaught – and the perfect after dinner or very late night dram. *46.8%.*

Glen Turner Heritage Double Wood Bourbon & Madeira casks, bott code. L311657A **(85.5) n21.5 t22 f21 b21.** A very curious amalgamation of flavours. The oak appears to be in shock with the way the fruit is coming on to it and offers a bitter backlash. No faulting the crisp delivery with busy sugar and spice for a few moments brightening the palate. *40%.*

Glen Turner Pure Malt Aged 8 Years L525956A **(84) n20 t22 f22 b20.** A lush and lively vatting annoyingly over dependent on thick toffee but simply brimming with fabulously mouth-watering barley and over-ripe blood oranges. To those who bottle this, I say: let me into your lab. I can help you bring out something sublime!! *40%*

Hogwash Blended Malt Scotch Whisky Blend No. 08 bott code: LBB 3C 4353 **(85.5) n21.5 t22 f21 b21** Juicy in part. And if you are looking for a gentle, soft, refined, complex, gentleman of a vatted malt...this isn't it. *40%. Produced for Aldi.*

Johnnie Walker Green Label 15 Years Old (95) n24 t23.5f23.5 b24. God, I love this stuff... this is exactly how a vatted malt should be and one of the best samples I've come across since its launch. *43%. Diageo.*

Johnnie Walker Green Label Aged 15 Years bott code: L9076DN002 **(91) n23 t23.5 f22 b22.5** Really lovely malt, but would dearly like to see the degree of toffee reduced on this as you expect there is so much going on that can't quite be heard. *43%.*

⬩ **Kingsbury Sar Obair Mhain Baraille 40 Year Old** hogshead, dist 1979, cask no. 57 **(95) n23.5** sometimes a nose leaves you wondering about the age of a whisky: this doesn't. Oak is practically throbbing from the glass but softened and polished in a way only the passing of time can produce. Dried orange peel mingles with discreet clove and a succession of high-class bourbon notes...; **t24** though time has polished the nose, it hasn't made any attempt to soften the blow of the delivery. This is powering and confident, momentarily offering a phrase or two of phenol but simply alive and writhing with white peppers. There is crystalised heather honey, too, very subtly infused. The midpoint sees the oak serve up a thick dollop of impressively aged vanilla; **f23.5** long with a sublime chocolate mint finale; **b24** age pours off this whisky like sweat from a long distance runner. And this really has come a long way over 40 years, impressively notching up more and more complexity as each year passes. Truly great whisky. *56.4% sc 173 bottles*

Le Gus't Selection X Speyside Blended Malt 39 Years Old sherry cask, cask no. 4 **(94.5) n23.5 t24 f23 b24** Truly Xcellent. *60.4%. sc. 109 bottles.*

Le Gus't Selection XI Speyside Blended Malt hogshead, cask no. 403 **(91) n22.5 t23 f22.5 b23** Appears to have good age to this and a little bit of class. *49.7%. sc. 262 bottles.*

MacNair's Lum Reek 12 Years Old (89) n22 t22.5 f22 b22.5 Interesting chimneys they have in this part of Scotland, which appears to reek marzipan and apple blossom where you might expect, coal, peat or wood...! *46%. The GlenAllachie Distillers Company.*

MacNair's Lum Reek 21 Years Old (91) n22.5 t23 f22.5 b23 A wild malt tamed it seems to me and certainly not lacking in personality *48%. The GlenAllachie Distillers Company.*

MacNair's Lum Reek Peated (88.5) n22 t22 f22 b22.5 Has the consistency of a nail file wrapped in velvet. Enough edges to this to draw blood. But the modest smoke soothes and kisses better. The salivating maltiness is another surprise. Not quite like any other vatted malt I have before encountered. And have to admit: I kind of begrudgingly like it, though McNair's appear to always include a malt that can pick a fight with itself in a 5cl miniature...! *46%. The GlenAllachie Distillers Company.*

Matisse 12 Year Old Blended Malt (93) n23.5 t23 f22.5 b23. Succulent, clean-as-a-whistle mixture of malts with zero bitterness and not even a whisper of an off note: easily the best form I have ever seen this brand in. Superb. 40%. *Matisse Spirits Co Ltd.*

Mo'land (82) n21 t22 f19 b20. Extra malty but lumbering and on the bitter side. 40%.

Monkey Shoulder batch 27 **(79.5)** n21 t21.5 f18 b19. Been a while since I lasted tasted this one. Though its claims to be Batch 27, I assume all bottlings are Batch 27 seeing as they are from 27 casks. This one, whichever it is, has a distinctive fault found especially at the finale, which is disappointing. Even before hitting that point a big toffeed personality makes for a pleasant if limited experience. 40%. *William Grant & Sons.*

Old Perth Blended Malt 23 Years Old dist 1994, bott code: 18/182 **(95)** n24 t23.5 f23.5 b24 Creakier than a haunted mansion. But full of much more welcoming spirits. This shows its oaky age with the same pride a veteran might display his war wounds. Not even a hint of a single off note: amazing! 44.9%. *nc ncf.*

Old St. Andrews Aged 10 Years Twilight batch no. L3017 G2716 **(91)** n22 t23.5 f22.5 b23 Takes a different course from the previous batch, eschewing the sharper tones for a more rumbling, deeper and earthier character. Very much above par. 40%.

Old St. Andrews Aged 12 Years Fireside batch no. L2927 G2716 **(93)** n23 t23 f23.5 b23.5 Returns to its usual high quality brand which usually makes the cut. 40%.

Old St. Andrews Aged 15 Years Nightcap batch no. L2976 G2716 **(86)** n22 t21.5 f21 b21.5 Well, this certainly is a nightcap: I fell asleep waiting for something to happen. Pleasant honey at times and chewy toffee but a bit short on the charisma front. 40%.

Poit Dhubh 8 Bliadhna (90) n22.5 t23.5 f21.5 b22.5. Though the smoke which marked this vatting has vanished, it has more than compensated with a complex beefing up of the core barley tones. Cracking whisky. 43%. *ncf. Pràban na Linne.*

Poit Dhubh 12 Bliadhna (77) n20 t20 f18 b19. Toffee-apples. Without the apples. 43%. *ncf. Pràban na Linne.*

Poit Dhubh 21 Bliadhna (86) n22 t22.5 f21 b20.5. Over generous toffee has robbed us of what would have been a very classy malt. 43%. *ncf. Pràban na Linne.*

Royal Salute 21 Year Old Blended Malt (88.5) n23 t22 f21.5 b22 Malt and caramel-themed throughout. 40%.

Scyfion Choice Westport 1996 Argaman Jezreel cask finished, bott 2019 **(94.5)** n23.5 t24 f23 b24 Now, having a lot of close Jewish friends I certainly know where these casks come from. And as they have not been sulphur treated (probably not Kosher, thankfully) I'm not at all surprised this very high quality wine produces casks which can certainly add a degree of sophistication to a malt. 49.1%. *nc ncf sc. 102 bottles.*

Scyfion Choice Westport 1996 Bashta cask finished, bott 2019 **(94.5)** n23.5 t24 f23 b24 I'd be lying if I said I knew what the hell a Bashta cask was. But all I can say is, if this is an example of it then the Scots should drop sherry (please, God!), PX in particular, and get this in its place. One of the real surprises of the year and one of my favourites for sure for offering something very different, yet still managing to keep the signature of the distillery burnishing brightly. 50%. *nc ncf sc. 77 bottles.*

◇ **Scyfion Choice Williamson 2005 Marsala Cask Finished** bott 2021 **(87)** n22 t23 f20.5 b21.5 Instead of the normal heavenly integration between oak, malt and smoke, we have a slightly aggressive standoff between the now acidic phenols and the grape. When you add the slightly tight and bitter finish, you know that, for this distillery (whichever it may beg, ahemmmm), all is not pucker. Thoroughly enjoyable in certain base ways. But is it an improvement on what the whisky was before it was tipped into the Marsala cask? I am to be convinced. 50% nc ncf 147 bottles

Shackleton Blended Malt bott code: L8123 11:52 P/004904 **(85.5)** n22.5 t22 f20 b21 An old-fashioned dusting of smoke plus a layering of Demerara ensures a certain gravitas is maintained through this vatted malt, starting at the come-to-me nose and continuing throughout the broad body on the palate. Falls away at the end, though, when too much bitterness sneaks in. 40%.

Shetland Reel Finished in Shetland Blended Malt Whisky ex-sherry casks, bott code: 248/19 **(79)** n20 t20 f19 b20 Tight, dry and doesn't sit very prettily... 47%.

Son of a Peat batch no. 01 **(91)** n23.5 t23 f22 b23 Peaty, but not just for peat's sake... 48.3%. *nc ncf. Flaviar.*

◇ **Valour Speyside Blended Malt Aged 27 Years** sherry butt, dist Jan 1994, bott Mar 2021 **(95.5)** n24 the nose drips with both fruit (actually more First Growth St Emilion than Sherry) and age in roughly equal proportions. There is a salty quality to this, also: one closes one's eyes and sees a cask sitting motionless in a corner of a warehouse for a very long time. And for those of us who have been around the industry for many years, the aroma takes you back to a cask being opened back in the '70s, when the wine seemed to have cobwebs sewn into the light sugars...Truly timeless...; **t24** a delivery like this has, cruelly, been far too rare in my life considering the tens of thousands of whiskies I have tasted in recent years. The actual delivery itself and first three or four flavour waves are true perfection. Not a hint of weakness: wine cask in faultless mode allowing perfect proportions of honey and oak-intensified jam; this is almost ridiculously juicy, so though it celebrates its antiquity it is determined to shew this is still alive, well and had many more years left to give. Spices begin to rise as the ok cranks up the driers notes; **f23.5** long with soft oils and chocolate raisin dipped in vanilla **b24** this is brilliantly distilled whisky that has spent 27 years in an unspoiled, top-end sherry butt. The fact that it was distilled on the same date, comes in one cask and yet still is a blended malt should put the Whisky Sherlock Holmes out there on the trail of what this whisky actually is. Single malt or blend, from sherry cask and from 1994...well, it just doesn't come any better.... It will take one hell of a whisky to see this off as Vatted malt of the year. A glorious whisky to hunt down and savour... not least because you are slipping back in style and quality to 25-30 years old sherry cask whiskies found 30 years ago. 55.2% nc 628 bottles

Water Proof batch no. 001 **(86) n21.5 t22.5 f20.5 b21.5** A toffee and raisin style malt which certainly hits a crescendo with the caramel and the sugars have a distinctively grapey quality. But, as pleasant as it is, it is just a little too one-paced and single threaded in style. Also a slight niggle on the finish which matches the bright yellow label... 45.8%. Macduff International.

Wemyss Malts Family Collection Blooming Gorse Blended Malt batch no. 2018/03 **(89.5) n22.5 t23 f22 b22** The gorse is probably my favourite plant. It reminds me of Dartford Warblers, great grey shrikes and stonechats. All of which I have often found around this stunning evergreen of vibrant yellow flower. It also has a sting to its tail, being an unmercifully prickly cove, and woe betide anyone daft enough to fall into it. So I was expecting a malt of beauty and bite. Well this one's a pretty thorn-less gorse with not quite enough polish to match the vividness of the flower. Except perhaps on the delivery, when the frail honey notes grow into something of a crescendo; and though spices do happen along they have none of the spite of the real thing... But if you are looking for a charmingly malty and delicately sweet offering, then you won't be disappointed. 46%. nc ncf. 6,900 bottles.

Wemyss Malts Family Collection Flaming Feast Blended Malt batch no. 2018/04 **(87) n21.5 t23 f21 b21.5** Pleasant enough. Juicy in part, malty and spicy. But from the mid-point onwards, just too flaming dull. 46%. nc ncf. 6,000 bottles.

Wemyss Malts The Hive Blended Malt Whisky batch no. 002 **(91.5) n23 t23.5 f22 b23** A malt greatly bolstered by the upping of the strength since its last bottling, which makes the honey positively buzz... 55.5%. ncf. 9,000 bottles.

Wemyss Malts Nectar Grove Blended Malt Madeira wine cask finished, batch no. 001 **(95) n23 t24.5 f23.5 b24** Just blown away by this. Nectar, indeed...! 54%. nc ncf.

Wemyss Malts Spice King Blended Malt batch no. 002 **(89) n21.5t23 f22 b22.5** I remember last time out with this vatted malt I felt a little swizzed by the lack of spice. No such complaints this time: a real rip-roaring malt! 58%. ncf. 9,000 bottles.

Wemyss Malts Velvet Fig Aged 25 Years Blended Malt sherry casks **(87) n22.5 t22.5 f21 b21** No off notes. Sadly, just one of those occasions when the casks married together here have not gelled quite as one might have hoped. Attractively soft delivery and for a few moments the fruit apparent has a genuinely complex moment or two. But then it falls apart slightly as various strands fail to tie or simply find dead ends. I do love the mouthfeel on delivery, though. 42.3%. nc ncf. 5,000 bottles.

Whisky-Fässle Fine Blended Malt Whisky Aged 17 Years sherry cask, dist 2001, bott 2018 **(91) n22.5 t23.5 f22 b23** This is rich, sensual malt helped along by a faultless sherry cask the emits an air of luxury. The fruit is subdued, perhaps more helpful in its mouth feel that overall flavour as the malt is still dense here. But there is a cream sherry chewability, too, the sultanas turning to toasted raisins as the experience progresses. Love the dry main theme and battle with the more honeyed elements. Perhaps a little too burnt on finish, though...; 46.2% nc ncf

Whisky-Fässle Fine Blended Malt Whisky Aged 24 Years sherry hogshead, dist 1993, bott 2018 **(95.5) n23.5** the oak has ramped up the spices into peppery form, which works surprisingly well with the ancient Melton Hunt Cake; **t24** just extraordinary. Dark cherries abound, mingling with the molasses and heather honey early on before we return to the Melton Hunt Cake, sans icing. Amazingly, in the midst of the this, a thick projecting of rich barley comes through.... how on Earth did they manage that...? **f24** one of the great finishes of the year. Drifts from chocolate raisin to chocolate and Turkish delight with shimmering grace and wonderful spice; **b24** how have they done this? A sherry cask from an era when nearly all were faulty, yet there is not a trace of sulphur to spoil the experience. This is truly wondrous. I thought The Valour Speyside was going to walk the Vatted section: there is a major battle now... *46.2% nc ncf*

⬥ **The Whisky Cask Company Burnside 1994** bourbon cask, cask no. 5114, Oct 1994, Nov 2019 **(91.5) n23** a nose which is a bit out of puff. The oak has taken its toll and it is mustering every last malty nuance to stay on track. The result is an over-ripe banana and lemon curd tart. Most curious, though, is that give it the full Murray Method and, late on, a few embers of peat can be detected...; **t23** a silky countenance. A malty intensity. And an oaky backbone. Plus, a little heather honey to battle against the more spent and hostile tannins; **f22.5** spices nibble while the oak considers spoiling the party but thinks better of it and holds back. Even a reprise of malt makes for a surprising redemption; **b23** enjoys all the usual outstanding Balvenie qualities, except what is so unusual about this is that it is a distillery which really struggles in older age. And for the produce of Balvenie, this is very old. However, on this occasion, though oak scarred and creaking loudly, it has stood up to the tannins manfully and come through the other side with so much class and elegance still intact. *51.1% nc ncf sc 246 bottles*

Wilson & Morgan Barrel Selection Westport 15 Year Old Marsala finish, dist 2004, bott 2019 **(86) n22 t22 f21 b21** Westport at this age when in its usual ex-bourbon garb can be a delightful fellow, abounding with all kinds of lively barley tones. The Marsala intervention has stripped that away, alas. Instead we have sulphur traces making this a very uncomfortable fit, especially at the death when everything is squeezed eye-wateringly tight. Hard as nails and sharp, with that nagging off-key finale despite a late hint of cocoa. A shame. *59.5%.*

SCOTTISH RYE
ARBIKIE
Highlands, 2013. Working.

Arbikie Highland Rye Aged 3 Years Single Grain Scotch charred American oak, Pedro Ximenez barrels, cask nos. 9, 11 & 16, dist 2015 db **(86.5) n21 t22 f21.5 b22** And finally...now for something completely different. The final whisky I shall taste for the Jim Murray Whisky Bible 2020, the 1,252st, is Scotland's first commercially bottled rye whisky. It is being sampled here straight after tasting the world's ultimate ryes, Sazerac and Handy from Buffalo Trace, but I was so impressed with this distillery trying something so different, I wanted them to bring the curtain down on this year's Whisky Bible. After tasting 20,027 whiskies for this book since 2003 you would have thought that amongst them would have been the odd Scottish rye or two. But no: no such thing existed. Until now. Is it a classic? No. Is it historic? Most certainly. Is it any good? Well, it isn't bad, but could be a lot better, especially if they got away from this hysteria sweeping the industry in which PX casks have to be used for everything. Had they asked me the very last cask they should use, I would have told them PX...simply because it smothers a distillery's character to death. And here even the rye, the most toothsome grain of them all, vanishes under a welter of moist dates; though a tobacco character (of concern) on the nose is not extinguished. Am I disappointed? No. Because getting rye right is not at all easy and for a new distillery it is even harder. But they would help themselves by ditching the PX and giving the grain a chance to speak. I look forward to visiting them before the 2021 Bible is published and see what they are up to. In the meantime, congratulations. And here's to reaching for the stars... and touching them. *46%. nc ncf. 998 bottles.*

Arbikie Highland Rye Aged 4 Years Cask Selection Single Grain Scotch charred American oak, Armagnac barrels, cask nos. 3, 5, 13 & 14, dist 2015 db **(89) n21.5 t23.5 f21.5 b22.5** A massive lurch upwards in character and quality from their initial bottling, this time the grain is given a platform to perform and entertain. And doesn't it take the opportunity with both hands! A dense rye, still slightly thick from the wide cut. But the sugars are profound and delicious. So much personality – and still room for improvement as their experience increases. Exciting times! *46%. nc ncf. 1,220 bottles.*

⬥ **Arbikie Highland Rye 1794 Edition Single Grain Scotch** new charred American oak db **(88) n21** a really hefty tobacco note on this from that ultra-generous cut should destroy any hope of a comeback. But the rye is in there in firm, sweet and determined mood; **t22.5** there you go! The intensity of the rye is borderline brutal....and just so beautiful. For a moment those feints attack with gusto. But such is the crispness and classic lines of the pitch-perfect rye, the grain wins in the most impressively salivating manner...; **f22.5** long, with the oils nibbling away. But a wonderful chocolate-toffee note determined to dominate; **b22** now here is a whisky which probably doesn't benefit from the Murray Method, which kicks up more of the heftier feints on show. This is best served at room temperature where the rye retains a charming crispness which salivates the taste buds as a truly great rye should. You know, had the cut been better than this, this would have been one of the top ryes I had tasted this year. This is so close to being a little bit special. Talk about the Beauty and the Beast... *48%.*

Scottish Grain

It's a bit weird, really. Many whisky lovers stay clear of blended Scotch, preferring instead single malts. The reason, I am often told, is that the grain included in a blend makes it rough and ready. Yet I wish I had a twenty pound note for each time I have been told in recent years how much someone enjoys a single grain. The ones that the connoisseurs die for are the older versions, usually special independent bottlings displaying great age and more often than not brandishing a lavish Canadian or bourbon style.

Like single malts, grain distilleries produce whisky bearing their own style and signature. And, also, some display characteristics and a richness that can surprise and delight. Most of the grains available in (usually specialist) whisky outlets are pretty elderly. Being made from either maize or wheat helps give them either that Canadian or, depending on the freshness of the cask, an unmistakable bourbony style. So older grains display far greater body than is anticipated.

That was certainly underlined in most beautiful and emphatic style by last year's Scotch Grain Whisky of the Year. The Last Drop Dumbarton 1977 had all that you should demand from a magnificent grain and more.

The fact that it was from Dumbarton was significant. For years, right up until its tragic and unnecessary closure in 2002, this distillery made the core grain for the Ballantine's blends and it was, following the closure of Cambus, without question the producer of the highest quality grain in Scotland. I had worked with it many times in the blending lab and it was as though I had the finest marble to sculpt from.

Dumbarton and Cambus have long been my two favourite grain distilleries, not least because both are thick with character. So no great surprise, then, that the Jim Murray Whisky Bible 2021 Single Grain of the Year was from Cambus.

Again, a single cask, this time from the American bottlers Perfect Fifth. And not only was this the most compelling grain I encountered in the market place last year, but also within the blending lab where I also tasted many a grain of varying ages. What worries me, though, is how many Cambuses are left out there of this quality still to be unearthed. Very few, I suspect.

Jim Murray's Whisky Bible Scottish Grain of the Year Winners	
2008	Duncan Taylor Port Dundas 1973
2009	The Clan Denny Dumbarton Aged 43 Years
2010	Duncan Taylor North British 1978
2011	The Clan Denny Dumbarton Aged 40 Years
2012	The Clan Denny Cambus 47 Years Old
2013	SMWS G5.3 Aged 18 Years (Invergordon)
2014	The Clan Denny Dumbarton 48 Years Old
2015	The Sovereign Single Cask Port Dundas 1978
2016	The Clan Deny Cambus 25 Years Old
2017	Whiskyjace Invergordon 24 Year Old
2018	Cambus Aged 40 Years
2019	Berry Bros & Rudd Cambus 26 Years Old
2020	The Last Drop Dumbarton 1977
2021	The Perfect Fifth Cambus 1979
2022	Whisky-Fässle Invergordon 44 Year Old

Single Grain Scotch
CALEDONIAN Lowland, 1885. Diageo. Demolished.

The Cally 40 Year Old refill American oak hogsheads, dist 1974 db **(88.5) n**23.5 **t**23 **f**20 **b**22 This poor old sod is tiring before your nose and taste buds. But it hangs on grimly to give the best show it can. Quite touching, really...we are witnessing first hand the slow death of a once great distillery. 53.3%. 5,060 bottles. Diageo Special Releases 2015.

The Sovereign Caledonian 35 Years Old refill hogshead, cask no. 14271, dist Feb 82, bott Oct 17 **(87) n**22 **t**22 **f**21 **b**22 Caledonian MacBrayn? Caledonian Canal? Caledonian Sea? Amazingly salty and coastal, more so than any grain I have encountered before. Has its unique and oddly delicious charm,but runs out of legs well before the finale. 46.9%. nc ncf sc. 154 bottles.

CAMBUS Lowland, 1836. Diageo. Closed.

Cambus Aged 40 Years dist 1975 db **(97) n**24.5 **t**24 **f**23.5 **b**25 I chose this as my 600th whisky for Bible 2018: a tragically lost distillery capable of making the finest whisky you might expect to find at 40 years of age. And my hunch was correct: this is flawless. 52.7%. 1,812 bottles. Diageo Special Releases 2016.

Berry Bros & Rudd Cambus 26 Years Old cask no. 61972, dist 1991, bott 2018 **(96.5) n**24 **t**24 **f**24 **b**24.5 Few whiskies this year have displayed so many beguiling twists and turns: a true gem of a grain, though always a bit of a rum do. I can imagine my dear friend of nearly three decades, Doug McIvor, leaping from his seat when he unearthed this sample.... something as rare as any kind of satisfying Charlton Athletic experience... 55.1%. nc ncf sc.

The Cooper's Choice Cambus 1991 refill sherry butt, cask no. 61982, bott 2018 **(90) n**23.5 **t**24 **f**20.5 **b**22 A very good whisky from the Swedish Whisky Fed which will probably make it to the quarter finals of any whisky competition – and then lose to an English malt... 58.5%. sc. Bottled for the Swedish Whisky Federation.

The Perfect Fifth Cambus 1976 cask no. 05916, dist 27 Oct 76 **(93) n**23.5 **t**24 **f**22 **b**23.5 An impressive example of the what then was arguably the finest grain distillery in Scotland. The structure is sound and the Canadian style of whisky is exactly what should be expected of a fine corn Cambus of this age. There is a slightly nagging bitterness caused by the tiring oak, but the inherent sweetness controls this well. The sugar-spice balance is pretty near perfection. Has the odd fault, but the complexity of the sweet riches outweigh those slightly bitter failings. 57.6%. sc.

The Perfect Fifth Cambus 1979 cask no. 900003 **(96.5) n**23.5 just classic. The corn oils and ulmo honey are in a love clinch....; **t**24.5 now I'm in one...with the glass...! The ulmo honey spreads around your palate like your lover on a rug before a log fire... And now the oak is gorgeously embedded into the corn. So the mouthfeel plays an equal role to the flavours...and they are luxurious and delicate in the extreme. A fragile blend of acacia and heather honey on one higher pitch, ulmo honey on a deeper, and here even with a light coconut touch...; **f**24 no bitter notes, which so often happens at this age and after so much honey on display. Just a slow sunset of corn oils, still the ulmo honey and now a wonderful but measured degree of pattering spice...; **b**24.5 given the right cask and the right time, Cambus is as good as anything distilled in Scotland. Here we see it in sublime form: no major faults from the cask... and certainly not the distillate. How many varying forms and densities of sweetness can you find on one whisky? Well here's your chance to find out...get counting...! 53.2%. nc ncf sc.

Sansibar Whisky Cambus 1991 bott 2019 **(88) n**22 almost rum-like with sweet estery qualities; **t**23 incredibly sweet delivery, but spices arrive early to harmonise. No shortage of golden syrup; **f**21 bitters out as the cask gives way...; **b**22 a rather weak bourbon cask has done this no favours. Some superb moments. 47.7%.

The Sovereign Cambus 29 Years Old refill hogshead, cask no. 15010, dist Sept 88, bott Apr 18 **(86) n**22 **t**22.5 **f**20.5 **b**21 Lots of fat and bubble gum at play here. Some superb moments on the corn, but never feels entirely at ease with itself, thanks to some stuttering oak. 45.6%. nc ncf sc. 299 bottles.

The Sovereign Cambus 30 Years Old refill hogshead, cask no. 14857, dist 1988 **(94) n**23.5 **t**24 **f**23 **b**23.5 A good hundred years ago, this grain was bottled and marketed as an equal to a single malt. If the distillery was still alive today a similar campaign would not bring in many complaints. A beauty! 45.2%. nc ncf sc. 313 bottles. Exclusive to The Whisky Barrel.

The Whisky Cask Company Cambus 27 Years Old bourbon barrel, cask no. 286, dist 24 Sept 91, bott 29 Nov 18 **(95.5) n**24 **t**24 **f**23.5 **b**24 ridiculously beautiful. 57.6%. sc. 286 bottles.

CAMERONBRIDGE Lowland, 1824. Diageo. Working.

Artful Dodger Cameronbridge 35 Year Old bourbon barrel **(94.5) n**23.5 **t**24 **f**23 **b**24 Soft and succulent all the way, this is a masterclass in how to ramp up the natural caramels without losing shape or interest. Light traces of ulmo honey also generate controlled sweetness but it is what feels like corn oil that makes a huge difference, stretching the narrative further than originally seemed possible and allowing the delicate spices and sweeter vanillas plenty of room and time interact. Burnt fudge towards the finish underscores the age. Ridiculously charming. 52.2%.

Liquid Treasures From Miles Away Cameronbridge 38 Year Old bourbon barrel, dist Feb 82, bott Feb 20 **(94.5) n23.5 t23.5 f23.5 b24** Textbook grain whisky seemingly made from corn as there is a Canadian-style corn oil and vanilla richness to this which really extracts the last nuance out from the syrupy sugars. Lush, lengthy and benefitting from a sublime bourbon barrel which ensures a perfect measure of sugars adds to the depth. When these older Cameronbridges are on form they are really something to behold. And this is a faultless stunner. 48.6%. sc. 140 bottles.

Old Particular Cameronbridge 26 Years Old refill hogshead, cask no. 12233, dist Oct 91, bott Dec 17 **(93) n23 t23.5 f23 b23.5** A Scotch that wanted to be a bourbon when it grew up... 51.5%. nc ncf sc. 569 bottles.

The Sovereign Cameronbridge 26 Years Old refill butt, cask no. 14752, dist Oct 91, bott Feb 18 **(79) n19 t22 f18 b20** Sweet and fruity but curiously tight on the nose and finish. 56.9%. nc ncf sc. 481 bottles.

The Whisky Barrel Originals Cameronbridge 37 Years Old refill bourbon barrel, cask no. TWB1005, dist Feb 82, bott 2019 **(86.5) n22 t23.5 f20 b21** As you'd expect from a C'Bridge of this vintage, there is plenty to involve your taste buds and enjoy. But, equally, there is a little frustration of the dustiness on the nose and emaciated body towards the finish – something not normally expected. That essentially leaves the delivery and follow through to enjoy – and it doesn't let you down, the ulmo honey and spices forming a delightful partnership and not without a Canadian feel. The remainder disappoints. 51%. sc. 164 bottles.

World of Orchids Cameron Brig 1991 26 Years Old bourbon cask, cask no. 031 **(94.5) n23.5 t23.5 f23.5 b24** Truly faultless. Cameron Bridge must have had a hell of a bee invasion back in 1991...! 56.4%. sc.

CARSEBRIDGE Lowland, 1799. Diageo. Demolished.

The Sovereign Carsebridge 44 Years Old refill hogshead, cask no. 14189, dist May 87, bott Sept 17 **(90) n22.5 t23 f22 b22.5** Very attractive, but about as sweet as you'd like a whisky to go. 50.9%. nc ncf sc. 150 bottles. The Whisky Barrel 10th Anniversary bottling #7.

DUMBARTON Lowland, 1938. Pernod Ricard. Demolished.

Fadandel.dk Dumbarton 30 Years Old cask no. 25241, dist 18 Mar 87, bott 27 Mar 17 **(86) n22 t22.5 f20 b21.5** A clumsy grain festooned with honey and spice, but little ability to bring them happily together. Delicious early on but bitters out as the oak finally cracks. 57.2%. sc. 168 bottles.

The Last Drop Dumbarton 1977 cask no. 140000004 **(97) n24.5 t24.5 f23.5 b24.5** Last Drop have been and done it again. They've only gone and found a near faultless barrel from what was once, before it was needlessly destroyed, a near faultless grain distillery. Nothing unusual you'd say, except that this spent 42 years in oak, giving it plenty of time to go wrong. Nothing did, so you have a pristine example of a grain distilled in the year I returned to the UK having hitch-hiked through Africa. And in my flat in Melton Mowbray, which also housed my Press Agency, would always sit a bottle of Chivas Regal...a very different, lighter and more delicate blend than you see today. And this barrel, most likely, was filled to be added to another bottling of Chivas, 12 years on. Instead, it remained in a warehouse seeking perfection...and as near as damn it finding it. 48.7%. sc.

Scotch Malt Whisky Society Cask G14.5 31 Year Old 2nd fill ex-bourbon barrel, dist 1 Oct 86 **(96) n24 t24 f23.5 b24.5** The confident solidity of this grain stands out like Dumbarton Rock...one of the great whiskies of the year, anywhere in the world. 50.6%. sc.

Single Cask Collection Dumbarton 30 Years Old bourbon barrel **(96) n24 t24.5 f23.5 b24** Taste a whisky like this and you'll fully understand why I regard the destruction of this distillery as one of the greatest criminal acts ever perpetrated against the Scotch whisky industry by the Scotch whisky industry. 52.1%. sc.

The Sovereign Dumbarton 30 Years Old refill barrel, cask no. 14247, dist Mar 87, bott Sept 17 **(92) n23 t23.5 f22.5 b23** Beautiful stuff and those who appreciate Canadian will particularly benefit. But a little tiredness to the oak reminds you of its great age. 55.3%. nc ncf sc. 160 bottles. The Whisky Barrel 10th Anniversary bottling #6.

The Sovereign Dumbarton 30 Years Old refill barrel, cask no. 14327, dist Mar 87, bott Oct 17 **(94) n23.5 t24 f23 b23.5** Practically a re-run of the Single Cask Dumbarton 30, except not all the dots on the sugars are joined. That said, still a whisky work of art. 50.2%. nc ncf sc. 135 bottles.

The Sovereign Dumbarton 31 Years Old refill hogshead, cask no. 15477, dist 1987 **(92) n22.5** a light lavender note introduces a bourbon weightiness; **t23.5** ah...the trademark stiff spine delivery. Rock hard sugars are surrounded by more forgiving corn notes. A slight oiliness to fill the mouth, but the spice-sugar battle is the main attraction through to the finish...; **f23** ....and more of the same...! **b23** Dumbarton's style stood alone among Scotland's grain distilleries: its idiosyncratic style is in full spate here. *50.5%. nc ncf sc. 207 bottles. Exclusive to The Whisky Barrel.*

The Sovereign Dumbarton 31 Years Old bourbon barrel, cask no. 15801, dist Mar 87, bott Feb 19 **(86.5) n22 t22.5 f20.5 b21.5** Unusually grassy and fresh for a Dumbarton. The firmness arrives later than normal, though with it an unfortunate bitterness from the cask. *43.5%. nc ncf sc. 186 bottles.*

The Whisky Barrel Dumbarton 30 Year Old barrel, cask no. 13436, dist 1987 **(96.5) n24 t24.5 f24 b24** Dumbarton at anything from 21to 30 is about as good as grain whisky gets (hence why Ballantine's can be sensational), providing it has lived in the right cask. And this is the right cask...*56.7%. sc. 197 bottles.*

GARNHEATH Lowland, 1964. Inver House Distillers. Demolished.

The Cooper's Choice Garnheath 48 Year Old dist 1967, bott 2016 **(96) n24 t24 f24 b24** It is an honour to experience a whisky both so rare and gorgeous. Perhaps not the most complex, but what it does do is carried out close to perfection. A must find grain. *41.5%. nc ncf sc. The Vintage Malt Whisky Co.*

GIRVAN Lowland, 1963. William Grant & Sons. Working.

The Girvan Patent Still Over 25 Years Old db **(84.5) n21.5 t21.5 f20.5 b21.** A pretty accurate representation of the character these stills were sometimes quietly known for at this time, complete with some trademark sulphury notes – presumably from the still, not cask, as I do pick up some balancing American white oak character. *42%. nc.*

The Girvan Patent Still No. 4 Apps db **(87) n21.5 t22 f21.5 b22.** A first look at probably the lightest of all Scotland grain whiskies. A little cream soda sweetens a soft, rather sweet, but spineless affair. The vanillas get a good, unmolested outing too. *42% WB15/369*

Berry Bros & Rudd Girvan 12 Years Old cask no. 532388/9, dist 2006, bott 2018 **(94) n23 t24 f23 b24** If you wondered why Grant's blends have been so good for so many years, then try out this straight down the line example of their 12-year-old grain. If I were asked in a tasting to describe what I should expect from this distillery at this age, then really this bottling has completely nutshelled it! This is when average equals excellence. *46%. nc ncf sc.*

⬦ **Chapter 7 Girvan 1991 Aged 30 Years** bourbon barrels, barrels nos 54689 & 54969 **(93) n23** the grain and oaky vanilla make for a lush partnership. A little golden syrup makes it friendlier still; **t23.5** unsurprisingly, a honey tone makes the first move – both in terms of texture and flavour. This is a heather- and ulmo honey mix, supplemented by a light build of warming spice. Slowly the oils from the grain get a foothold, and with it comes the layered vanilla; **f23** a little bitterness tries to make a case, but those honey notes are in no mood to give way; **b23.5** slick and sweet, this is Girvan in overdrive. Few whiskies enter their fourth decade with so many sugars still in pristine nick: this could almost do as a dessert whisky.... Delicious. And remarkable. *49.6%*

Fadandel.dk Girvan 13 Year Old barrel, cask no. 532404, dist 11 Jul 06, bott 30 Aug 19 **(86.5) n22.5 t23 f20 b21** Characteristic fatness surrounded by friendly sugars and marzipan makes for a delicious nose and opening. Sexy spices, too. But not the best finish I've seen from this distillery, being a tad bitter and generally askew. *61.2%. sc. 203 bottles.*

The First Editions Girvan Aged 38 Years refill hogshead, cask no. 14749, bott 2018 **(95) n23.5 t24 f23.5 b24** Wears its age and gravity lightly: this is wonderful grain whisky. *50.3%. nc ncf sc. 302 bottles.*

The Great Drams Girvan 11 Years Old cask no. 300609, dist 27 Jun 07, bott 27 Feb19 **(91.5) n22.5 t23.5 f22.5 b23** Any softer or more shy and this grain would barely escape from your glass. But with some cajoling you end up with a very accurate representation of this distillery for its age. *46.2%. nc ncf sc.*

Lady of the Glen Girvan 1991 cask no. 54459 **(89.5) n22.5 t23 f22 b22.5** Though seemingly soft and yielding, the sturdy subplot maximises the otherwise limited oak influence. Good spice prickle while late sugars are able to counter the encroaching bitterness. *43.2%. sc.*

Liquid Treasures Entomology Girvan Over 28 Years Old ex-bourbon barrel, dist 1989, bott 2018 **(86.5) n23 t22 f20.5 b21** A typical pea-souper of a Girvan, thick on the nose with sugary promise and no shortage of oak-encouraged vanilla depth then eye-smartingly sweet delivery with golden syrup mixing in with the oils. A warming sub plot as the spices build but a little disappointing as the oak gives way to bitterness. *52.7%.*

Old Particular Girvan 27 Years Old refill hogshead, cask no. 12191, dist Dec 89, bott Nov 17 **(91) n24 t22.5 f22 b22.5** It's all about the amazing nose, yesiree...! *51.5%. nc ncf sc. 148 bottles.*

Scyfion Choice Girvan 2006 Islay whisky cask finished, bott 2018 **(92) n23 t23.5 f22.5 b23.5** An intriguing concept brilliantly executed! *46%. nc ncf sc. 90 bottles.*

INVERGORDON Highland, 1959. Emperador Distillers Inc. Working.

Cave Aquila A Knight's Dram Invergordon 44 Years Old cask no. 20, dist Dec 72, bott Mar 17 (95) n24 t24 f23.5 b23.5 You almost want to give the spices a standing ovation... 46.7%. sc.

The Cooper's Choice Invergordon 1974 43 Years Old (91) n24 t23 f21.5 b22.5 If the delivery and finish can't quite live up to the nose, that is hardly surprising. This is the aroma of all talents, offering a small grain bourbon type leathery sweetness together with a more genteel vanilla-clad Canadian of high quality. The immediate delivery has a good stab at matching that, and at first succeeds, especially with the depth of the maple syrup and honeycomb. But it understandably fades, then tires late on as the bitterness evolves. 46.5%. nc ncf sc.

The Finest Malts City Landmarks Invergordon Aged 46 Years bourbon barrel, cask no. 32, dist 1972, bott 2018 (93.5) n23.5 gentle vanilla and corn oil. Uncomplicated but very alluring and effective...; t23.5 simplistic white sugars dissolve on impact forming a juicy frame in which gentle layers of vanilla form and intertwine. Plenty of natural caramels; f23 Curiously for a grain, there is almost a profound maltiness to this; a very slight bitterness of the oak, but nothing drastic; b23.5 time appears to be lost on this one. No great bowing and scraping to the oak. Good age is apparent, but only if you really think about it...Such elegance. 49.9%. nc ncf sc.

The First Editions Invergordon Aged 45 Years refill barrel, cask no. 14772, bott 2018 (94) n23.5 t24 f23 b23.5 Almost a halfway house between ancient grain and a simplistic liqueur. But not so sweet as to be beyond a thing of beauty. 49.6%. nc ncf sc. 230 bottles.

◆◆ **MacAlabur Invergordon 28 Year Old** hogshead, cask no.77737, dist Jul 1991, bott Nov 2019 (91.5) n23.5 Invergordon at its most relaxed: allows the lightly sweetened vanilla a free hand. Curiously spiceless and docile; t23 excellent vanillas coat the palate, even offering a degree of ever-ripe banana. Perhaps even a little moist marzipan, too; f22 very slightly overdoes the bitterness as the oak gives way slightly. A little demerara sugar helps compensate, as do the oils; b23 buckles a little late on under the strain of age. But the nose and delivery are absolutely top notch. 57.0% 220 bottles

Single & Single Invergordon 1974 45 Years Old (94.5) n23 t23.5 f24 b24 Just how you want an old grain to be. Still full of life after all these years... 46.6%. sc. 156 bottles.

Single Cask Collection Invergordon 26 Years Old rum barrel finish (87) n22 t22.5 f21 b21.5 Soft and sweet in the time-honoured Invergordon tradition. But with this amount of sugar at work, it needs to breathe and evolve. Rum casks have a tendency to clip a whisky's wings so, though a very decent and soothing grain, the fun comes to a slightly premature and bitter end. 57.4%. sc.

◆◆ **The Sovereign Invergordon Aged 25 Years** refill barrel, cask no. 18167, dist May 1995, bott Mar 2021 (92.5) n23 just wonderful when a whisky shews not just very good age but a lemon sherbet fizz to underline that this grain is still green and blossoming; t23 a beautiful, if simplistic, mix of salivating lime-blossom honey and sturdy vanilla; f23 a little cocoa powder envelops any lingering sweetness; b23.5 a beautiful cask at work has ensured a charming evenness. Delightful. 42.0%. nc ncf sc. 63 bottles.

The Sovereign Invergordon 30 Years Old refill hogshead, cask no. 15012, dist May 87, bott Apr 18 (88) n23 t23 f20.5 b21.5 Promises so much, but the oak can't quite match the deal. 51.6%. nc ncf sc. 314 bottles.

◆◆ **Whisky-Fässle Invergordon 44 Year Old** bourbon barrel, dist 1972, bott 2017 (95.5) n24.5 where scotch meets Kentucky: the influence of the oak married to the corn offers a distinctive soft bourbon burr with matching delicate spice. But we are talking very well-aged bourbon here where the heather honey has made its mark and the lightest liquorice add colour. A ten minute nose minimum....no, make that 15...Unquestionably one of the greatest noses I'll encounter this year; t24 this, as the nose promises, melts on the tongue allowing the slow dispersal of honey and praline. Strands of red liquorice act as a further bind as the sugars and tannins dovetail gloriously, the spices pricking and soothing, pricking and soothing again; f23 dries and rumbles its spices more quietly as the praline divests itself of its sugars and nuts but retains the cocoas; b24 a potential grain of the year for sure. A faultless cask offering a bourbon style grain...but a bourbon that cannot presently be offered from Kentucky. Because at the moment no 44-year-old bourbon has matured this slowly to allow the very softest of integrations. It doesn't just nose and taste brilliantly, but the entire feel is something that has to be experienced. Truly great whisky that would be admired both sides of the pond. 46.9% nc ncf 🏆

LOCH LOMOND Highland, 1966. Loch Lomond Group. Working.

Loch Lomond Single Grain db (93) n23 crisp sugars are willing to absorb the vanilla; t23.5 indeed, the sugars on the nose are indicative of a sweet grain, for the delivery centres around the maple syrup lead. The oak is something like most anchors at work: barely visible to invisible; f23 the oaks do have a say, though you have to wait a while on the long finale. A little spice arrives, too; b23.5 elegant grain; keeps the sweetness controlled. 46%

Loch Lomond Single Grain Peated db **(91)** n22 more like bonfire smoke, rather than peat. But smoky it is and with a real acidic nip to it, too...; **t23.5** surprisingly, the delivery isn't as soft and oily as their usual mouthfeel for LL Grain. This has a more clipped personality and that includes the Demerara sugars. But just love that flavour explosion shock waves in when the smoke and spices suddenly seem to wake to the fact they are there – and really let you know about it....! **f22.5** settles down a smoky rumble with a light vanilla and muscovado sugar accompaniment; **b23** different, intriguing...and beautifully weighted. Love it! 46%.

LOCHSIDE Highland, 1957. Pernod Ricard. Demolished.

The Cooper's Choice Lochside 44 Year Old dist 1964, bott 2015 **(92.5) n23.5** not unlike a bourbon-Canadian blend (yes, I have encountered such a thing) where a muscular coconut-honey candy theme dominates the subservient vanilla; **t24** salivating and soft, corn oils drift among the obliging sugars without a care in the world; you can hear the tannins knocking, but only the spices gain entry; **f22** back to a coconut toffee thread; bitters late on; **b23** it's hangs on in there, giving in to its age only in the final moments... 41.2%. nc ncf sc. The Vintage Malt Whisky Co.

NORTH BRITISH Lowland, 1885. Diageo & Edrington. Working.

Gordon & MacPhail Connoisseurs Choice North British Aged 28 Years first fill sherry puncheon, cask no. 73847, dist 23 Oct 90, bott 29 Nov 18 **(82.5) n21 t21.5 f21 b19** Huge grape, under which the distillery and grain vanishes entirely. Simply too one-dimensional. Delicious as in part it may be, you might as well get a bottle of sherry. 61%. sc. 181 bottles.

The Sovereign North British 21 Years Old refill hogshead, cask no. 14409, dist Oct 96, bott Nov 17 **(87) n22.5 t22 f21 b21.5** A workmanlike grain keeping true to its age and type so far as a blender is concerned, the sharp clarity of the vanilla-tinged icing sugar more than useful. Likewise, the both lush yet underlyingly firm body would be of great use, especially with the marshmallow sweetness. The slight bitterness on the fade can be compensated for in a blend, though harder when a singleton like this. 54.8%. nc ncf sc. 219 bottles.

⬦ **The Sovereign North British 32 Years Old** refill hogshead, cask no. 18166, dist 1988 **(95) n23.5** such a gorgeous buttery edge to this: reminds me of my old mum's bowl in which she used to make the cakes...and I would help myself to when she'd finished with it so I could dutifully lick it clean as any self-respecting 8-year-old lad would...; **t24** oh, good Lord! That is ridiculous. Near perfect weight on the corn oil, rendering this halfway between Canadian and Bourbon. Then such delicate layers of lime blossom honey, harmonising with the softest vanillas imaginable; **f23.5** just a slight bitterness off the cask, but gentle fruits compensate; **b24** North British at its very finest: this is faultless grain whisky. Amazingly, so gentle it is spice free... 51.1%. nc ncf sc. 199 bottles.

⬦ **Single Cask Collection North British 28 Years Old** cask no. 20013, dist 1991, bott 2019 **(92.5) n22.5** one of those brilliant noses that reminds you more of the actual warehouse than the spirit contained in the barrel. A little saltiness sharpens the nose buds...; **t23** mouth-filling with soft oils and a slight banana take on the vanilla. The spices are in fast, peppery and warmer than an irritated wife's ear lashing....; **f23.5** now the sugars take on a beautiful blend of ulmo and heather honey as the vanillas add depth and slightly dry proceedings; **b23.5** actually spilling over with flavour. "Neutral whisky"? Pull the other one. 50.1%. sc. 180 bottles.

The Whisky Gallery The Magician North British Aged 5 Years oak barrel, cask no. 291, dist 2006, bott 2019 **(94) n22.5 t24 f23.5 b24** Beautifully distilled and really well matured in a barrel which allows the grain to reveal its full character: with North British, that means a lot. Though young there is still marzipan on the nose and sublime heather honey on delivery. A little grassy, too, while the late spices are superb. Any blender would give his right arm to work with a grain of this quality in a 5-year-old blend. Indeed, good enough to mix in with some of your better non-sherried malts up to the age of about 15-year-old as you could create something very interesting with this chap, especially with that light oiliness which means a little of this goes a long way. 49%. sc. 242 bottles.

Whisky Krüger North British 26 Years Old 1991 bott 2017 **(88) n22** a faint spice fizz. But its ultra-friendly vanilla all the way; **t23** juicy, sugar coated corn; **f21** oily vanilla; **b22** despite the sugars a curiously flat grain, but sweet in all the right places. 48.6%. sc.

NORTH OF SCOTLAND Lowland, 1957. North of Scotland Distilling Co. Silent.

The Pearls of Scotland North of Scotland 1971 dist Dec 71, bott Apr 15 **(95.5) n25 t23.5 f23 b24** What a beautifully elegant old lady...and one with virtually no wrinkles... 43.6%

PORT DUNDAS Lowland, 1811. Diageo. Demolished.

The Cooper's Choice Port Dundas 1999 18 Years Old Marsala finish **(87) n21.5 t22.5 f21 b22** Pleasant enough, especially on delivery with the big grape and delicate spice interplay.

But otherwise I don't get it. Grain whisky isn't full-bodied enough to react with wine casks and offer any serous complexity. And this is a lost distillery here being overwhelmed so its unique character is lost. That said, if you are looking simply for delicious, muscular spiced fruit, here's your dram! *53%. nc ncf sc.*

The Great Drams Port Dundas 10 Years Old cask no. 800202, dist 13 Oct 09, bott Feb 20 **(92.5) n23 t23.5 f23 b23** Wonderful to see a grain whisky marketed at an age us blenders tend to thoroughly enjoy using it at. A grain like this will be found in virtually all top blending labs and this sample has the benefit of coming from cask that hadn't at some stage been sulphur treated. So this Port Dundas at 10 is pretty typical as to how I was tasting it 30 years ago at the same age. Timeless. *48.2%. nc ncf sc.*

◈ **The Sovereign Port Dundas Aged 31 Years** refill hogshead, cask no. HL18165, dist Feb1990, bott Mar 2021 **(93) n23** superb density to this: not dissimilar to melted demerara sugar atop a bowl of porridge. The oak ensures an excellent tingle factor with the subtlest spice; **t23.5** immediately mouth-filling and soft, again with the oils on early duty. There is even room for an early juiciness. The vanillas open gently but with no little confidence and slowly soak up the sweeter elements; **f23** dries and spices as the age begins to shew its toasty credentials; **b23.5** pretty much spot on Port Dundas. Not at its most complex, but wonderfully intact and coming through here at the creamier end of its normal spectrum. A chewy, three-course meal of a grain... *48.2%. nc ncf sc. 239 bottles.*

STRATHCLYDE Lowland, 1927. Pernod Ricard. Working.

Artful Dodger Strathclyde 27 Year Old bourbon barrel, cask no. 110035 **(89.5) n22 t23 f22 b22.5** Old school Strathclyde before a small fortune was spent cleaning the place up. This has its traditional "dirty" feel, which over the years has given so many blends a particular character. At 27 years some of the natural blemishes have transformed into a chewy heather-honey tone, with a little manuka and Marmite thrown in. The firmness on the finish is its signature. *51.8%. sc.*

Glasgow Gardens Festival 30th Anniversary Strathclyde 30 Year Old 1988 cask no. 62125, dist 9 Jun 88, bott 10 Jun 18 **(87) n22 t23 f20.5 b21.5** I think I remember Hunter Laing bringing out a 30-year-old Strathclyde last year which surprised me with its gentle good manners. This is probably much closer to what I was expecting, with the rough edges of the distillery at that time clearly on display here, despite a flurry of superb golden syrup notes on delivery. *54.3%. sc. Exclusive to The Whisky Barrel. 138 bottles.*

Old Particular Strathclyde 11 Years Old sherry butt, cask no. 11952, dist Nov 05, bott Jul 17 **(91) n22 t23.5 f22 b23.5** Not just a sherry butt! But a clean, 100% untainted, entirely sulphur-free sherry butt! Fabulous! *55.5%. nc ncf sc. 638 bottles.*

The Sovereign Strathclyde 28 Years Old refill barrel, cask no. 15804, dist Aug 90, bott Feb 19 **(90) n22.5 t23 f22 b22.5** Looks like Strathclyde were still going through a corn mash at this time, so soft, sweet and oily is this. Very un-Strathclyde for the era in its untroubled shifting through the gears. *51.1%. nc ncf sc. 198 bottles.*

The Sovereign Strathclyde 30 Years Old refill hogshead, cask no. 14448, dist Sept 87, bott Nov 17 **(90) n22 t22 f23.5 b22.5** It is as though the grain has fallen asleep after 30 years and finally wakes up late in the day. *50.7%. nc ncf sc. 175 bottles.*

That Boutique-y Whisky Company Strathclyde 30 Year Old batch 1 **(87.5) n22 t22.5 f21 b22** A grain that gives you a right punch in the throat on delivery. The sugars are profound but without structure and of very limited complexity. *53.1%. 228 bottles.*

UNSPECIFIED SINGLE GRAIN

Borders finished in Oloroso sherry casks **(66) n15 t18 f15 b18.** Finished being the operative word. Has no-one been listening regarding the total mess sherry butts are in. I wonder why I bother sometimes. Jeez... *51.7%. nc ncf. R&B Distillers.*

Haig Club toasted oak casks **(89) n21.5 t23 f22.5 b22** When I first saw this, I wasn't quite sure whether to laugh or cry. Because 25 years ago bottles of single grain whisky were the unique domain of the flat cap brigade, the miners and other working class in the Kirkcaldy area of Scotland. Their grain, Cameron Brig, would be drunk with a splash, mixed with Coke or ginger, even occasionally with Irn Bru, or straight and unmolested as a chaser to the ubiquitous kegged heavy, McEwan's lager or a bottle of Sweetheart stout. When I suggested to the hierarchy at United Distillers, the forerunners of Diageo, that in their finer grains they had a product which could conquer the world, the looks I got ranged from sympathy for my lack of understanding in matters whisky to downright concern about my mental well being. I had suggested the exquisite Cambus, now lost to us like so many other grain distilleries in those passing years, should be brought out as a high class singleton. It was pointed out to me that single grain was, always had been and always will be, the preferred choice of the less sophisticated; those not wishing to pay too much for their dram. Fast forward a quarter of a century and here sits a gorgeously expensive bottle in a deep cobalt blue normally associated with Ballantine's and a very classy, heavyweight stopper. In it is a grain which, if the advertising is to be believed, is the preferred choice not of the back street bar room idlers carefully counting their pennies but its major ambassador David Beckham: it is the drop to be savoured by the moneyed, jet-set sophisticates. My, oh my. Let's not call this hype. Let's just say it has taken some genius exec in a suit half a lifetime – and probably most of his or hers - to come around to my way of thinking and convince those in the offices on the floor above to go for it. Wonder if I qualify for 10 percent of profit for suggesting it all those years back...or, preferably, five percent of their advertising budget. Meanwhile, I look forward to watching David pouring this into some of his Clynelish and Talisker. After all, no-one can Blend it like Beckham... *40%. WB15/408*

Haig Club Clubman (87.5) n22 t22 f21.5 b22 A yieldingly soft and easy-as-you-like and at times juicy grain with a pleasant degree of light acacia honey to make friendlier still. *40%.*

Haig Club Clubman bourbon casks, bott code: L90860U002 **(87.5) n21 t22.5 f21.5 b22** Once you get past the caramel on both nose and finish it is easy to be drawn into enjoying this sweet grain which seems to glisten with acacia honey influence. *40%.*

The Tweeddale Grain of Truth Highland Single Grain bott code: L2.282.19 09.10.2019 **(92.5) n23 t23.5 f23 b23** You could imagine some dour Victorian minister of the kirk, lashing his congregation for being the sinners, without a single hope of salvation, he believes them to be over a miserable two hours on a relentlessly grey, rain-sodden, windswept Sunday morning somewhere up in the bleakest Highlands. And when he says there can be no drinking on the Sabbath, he means all alcoholic drink...with the exception of a dram or two of Tweeddale's Grain of Truth... Aye, that should finish them off, he'd be thinking...This is distilled from a mash bill of half wheat and half peated malt. The result is uniquely sombre and austere grain which, it has to be said, is captivating in its unique and fascinating, smoky bleakness. Love it! *50%. nc ncf.*

The Whisky Works Glaswegian 29 Year Old Single Grain (92) n23.5 t23.5 f22 b23 Not often you get ginger on the nose of a grain whisky, butW this one obliges. Signs of a mis-spent youth here, as this shows all the classic signs of a roughhouse whisky when young, a bit of the Gorbals, and though still shewing the odd scar or two, now has a real touch of polished old school, debonair recalcitrance about it. *54.2%. nc ncf. 1,642 bottles.*

WoodWinters The Five Distinguished and Rare Aged 39 Years (93) n22.5 t24 f23 b23.5 A grain of marvellous pedigree and integrity, at least equal to the vast majority of single malts whiskies you will find...*51%. sc. 330 bottles.*

Vatted Grain

Angus Dundee Distillers Blended Grain 50 Year Old (91.5) n23 t23.5 f22 b23 Just champion...! *40.1%.*

Compass Box Hedonism first fill American oak casks, batch no. MMXIX-A, bott 28 Feb 19 **(91) n23 t23 f22.5 b22.5** After suffering at the hands of so many sulphurous sherry casks over the last month, I have sought sanctuary in John Glaser's Hedonism, a safe wine cask-free zone. It was a sensible choice... *43%. nc ncf.*

Compass Box Hedonism Maximus (93.5) n25 t22.5 f23 b23. Bourbon Maximus... *46%*

Compass Box Hedonism The Muse bott Feb 18 **(89) n23 t23 f21 b22** A fruit fly landing in a whisky while it is waiting to be tasted is always a good sign: these things know where to find sweetness. *53.3%. nc ncf.*

Compass Box Hedonism Quindecimus (88.5) n22.5 t22 f22 b22 Sweet and refreshingly ordinary grain. Well made and unspectacularly delicious. *46%*

Count Cristo bott code: L7117HA8 **(89) n22.5 t22.5 f22 b22** "Learning does not make one learned: there are those who have knowledge and those who have understanding. The first requires memory and the second philosophy." This is a whisky worth trying to understand. *40%.*

The Sovereign Blended Grain 28 Years Old bourbon barrel, cask no. 13327, dist Dec 64, bott Mar 17 **(96) n24.5 t24 f23.5 b24** May be completely wrong, but a theory. There is a dryness here which suggests big age, maybe so big that the strength of a barrel fell below 40%abv... so had to be added to another to restore it back to whisky again. As I say: just a theory. But it'd fit the structure of this beautifully fragile old grain perfectly. *47.9%. nc ncf sc. 221 bottles.*

William Grant & Sons Rare Cask Reserves 25 Years Old Blended Grain Scotch Whisky (92.5) n23 t23.5 f23 b23. A really interesting one, this. In the old days, blenders always spent as much time vatting the grains together as they did the malts, for if they did not work well as a unit it was unlikely harmony would be found in their blend. A long time ago I was taught to, whenever possible, use a soft grain to counter a firmer one, and vice versa. Today, there are far fewer blends to choose from, though 25 years ago the choice was wider. So interesting to see that this grain is soft-dominated with very little backbone at all. Delicious. But screams for some backbone. *47%. Exclusive to The Whisky Shop.*

Scottish Blends

If any whisky is suffering an identity crisis just now, it must be the good old Scottish blend.

Once the staple, the absolute mainstay, of the Scotch whisky industry it has seen its market share increasingly buried under the inexorable, incoming tide that is single malt. But worse, the present-day blender has his hands tied in a way no previous generation of blenders has had before.

Now stocks must be monitored with a third eye, one that can judge the demand on their single malt casks and at increasingly varied ages. Worse, the blender cannot now, as once was the case, create blends with subtly shifting textures - the result of carefully using different types of grain. So many grain distilleries have closed in the last quarter of a century that now most blends seem remarkably similar to others. And there is, of course, the problem of sherry butts which has been fully documented over the years in the Whisky Bible.

For Jim Murray's Whisky Bible 2018 I tasted or re-tasted 128 blends in total, a quite significant number. And there is no doubt that the lack of choice of grain for blenders is beginning to pose a problem for the industry. What was particularly noticeable was the number of blends which now lack a crisp backbone and have softened their stance, making them chewy and pliable on the palate but often lacking the crispness which can maximise the complexity of the malts on display. By the time you add in the caramel, the results can sometimes be just a little too cloying.

Naturally, it was the bigger blenders - those possessing by far the largest stocks - who best escaped this narrowing down of style among the younger blends in particular, and last year it was that thoroughbred blend known even by our grand-parents and great-grandparents, White Horse, which really caught the eye...and palate.

But, not for the first time, it has been Ballantine's which this year gave me most pleasure. Blended Scotch of the Year went to their remarkable Ballantine's Finest, one of the few no-age statement blends I found out there this year which was neither dominated in character by either caramel or sulphur...or both. Since they increased the peat levels of this blend, Ballantine's Finest has upped its game year on year with complexity, making this now one of my regular off duty drams. The random bottling acquired for this year's Bible really did hit peak form. And, consequently, the top award...

Jim Murray's Whisky Bible Scottish Blend of the Year Winners	
2004/5	William Grant's 21 Year Old
2006	William Lawson Aged 18 Years
2007/8	Old Parr Superior 18 Years Old
2009	The Last Drop
2010	Ballantine's 17 Years Old
2011	Ballantine's 17 Years Old
2012	Ballantine's 17 Years Old
2013	Ballantine's 17 Years Old
2014	Ballantine's 17 Years Old
2015	The Last Drop 1965
2016	The Last Drop 50 Years Old
2017	The Last Drop 1971
2018	Compass Box The Double Single
2019	Ballantine's 17 Years Old
2020	Ballantine's 17 Years Old
2021	Ballantine's 30 Years Old
2022	Ballantine's Finest

Scottish Blends

100 Pipers bott code LKVK2677 2016/07/01 **(74)** n18 t19 f19 b18 These 100 Pipers deserve an award. How can they have played for so many years and still be so off key and out of tune? It is an art form, I swear. I feel like giving the blend a special gong for so many years of consistent awfulness. *40%. Chivas Brothers Ltd.*

⬩⬩ **Aberdour Finest Piper Blend Scotch Whisky** bott code: L18024 **(86.5)** n21.5 t22 f21.5 b21.5 An attractive, grain-led blend with just the right sweetness at just the right moments. The very lightest of toffee and vanilla finishes, though it is the spice which excels late on. *40%*

Artful Dodger Blended Scotch 41 Year Old ex-bourbon hogshead **(95.5)** n24 t24 f23.5 b24 Now and again, one of those ultra-sensuous whiskies turns up in my tasting room...and you melt into the glass as you sample it. Here's one such occasion where the blender, either 41-years-ago, or now, has understood how the grains can layer and structure a blend, and how the malt can fuse with the tannins and more caramelised elements. The result is a blend that you would chew, except it dissolves before you get the chance. The grain-malt ratio looks to be pretty spot on, as is the spice which nibbles and harries warmly, but without a hint of aggression. Just ahhhhhh.... *494%. sc.*

The Antiquary bott code L 02 08 16 **(86)** n20 t22 f22 b21 Appears to be going along the present day trend of spongy, super soft grain which doesn't always do the best of favours to the obviously high quality malt in here. Pleasantly sweet and chewy with an attractive base note. *40%. Tomatin Distillery.*

The Antiquary Aged 12 Years bott code L 17 12 15 **(87.5)** n21.5 t22 f22 b22 The smoke I so well remember from previous bottlings appears to have dispersed. Instead we have an ultra-lush blend dependent on molasses and spice to punch through the major toffee. *40%.*

The Antiquary Aged 21 Years bott code 2016/02/29 LK30215 **(92.5)** n23 t23.5 f23 b23 If you are not sure what I mean by a beautifully paced whisky, try this and find out. *43%.*

The Antiquary Aged 35 Years bott code L 24 08 15 **(96.5)** n24 t24 f24 b24.5 Enjoy some of the grains involved in this beauty: their type and ability to add to the complexity is, tragically, a dying breed: the hardest whisky I have found so far to spit out...and I'm on dram number 530....! Antiquary's late, great blender, Jim Milne, would shed a tear of joy for this creation of unreconstructed beauty and brilliance, as this was just out of his school of elegance. *46%.*

Ballaglass Blended Scotch Whisky **(85)** n21 t22 f21 b21. Perfectly enjoyable, chewy – but clean – blend full of toffee and fudge. Very good weight and impressive, oily body. *40%.*

Ballantine's 12 Years Old **(87)** n21 t22 f21 b23. The kind of old-fashioned, mildly moody blend Colonel Farquharson-Smythe (retired) might have recognised when relaxing at the 19th hole back in the early '50s. Too good for a squirt of soda, mind. *40%. Chivas Bros.*

Ballantine's 17 Years Old **(97.5)** n24.5 t24 f24 b25 Now only slightly less weighty than of old. After a change of style it has comfortably reverted back to its sophisticated, mildly erotic old self. One of the most beautiful, complex and stunningly structured whiskies ever created. Truly the epitome of great Scotch. *43%.*

Ballantine's Aged 21 Years **(94)** n23.5 t24 f23.5 b24 Even though the strength has been reduced, presumably to eke out rare stocks, the beauty of this blend hasn't. *40%*

Ballantine's Aged 30 Years **(95.5)** n24.5 t24 f23 b24 A fascinating malt, slightly underpowered perhaps, which I have had to put to one side and keep coming back to see what it will say and do next... *40%.*

Ballantine's Aged 30 Years bott code LKRK1934 2016/05/16 **(96)** n24.5 t24 f22.5 b24 Practically a replay of the bottle I tasted last year, right down to that very late, barely perceptible furriness. Simply one of the world's most sensual drams... *40%. Chivas Brothers Ltd.*

Ballantine's Barrel Smooth finished in double charred barrels, bott code: 2018/11/08 **(87.5)** n22 t22 f21.5 b22 A cream toffee-rich blend concentrating on molasses and caramel. A real super-soft member of the Ballantine's family, but possessing only a fraction of the age-statement bottlings' complexity. *40%.*

Ballantine's Finest bott code LKEK4068 2016/10/04 **(96)** n23.5 t24 f24 b24.5 The consistency and enormity of this blend fair staggers me. It is often my go to blend when travelling the world as I pretty much know what I'll get, within its normal parameters. This bottling has a little extra sweetness on the smoke but exceeds expectation on the finish with a slightly more clever use of the spices and Demerara sugars as they merge with the peat. Just such a big and satisfying experience. *40%. Chivas Brothers Ltd*

⬩⬩ **Ballantine's Finest** bott code: 2021/08/03 **(95)** n24 t24 f23 b24 Very much on course to meet last year's bottling in quality. Still a blend which just seems to marry its smoky credentials with the grains and tannins with consummate ease – though I know the truth will be very different: what magnificent mixing this is. One of those whiskies which is just too easy to dismiss as just another blend. Try the Murray Method and just watch this grow in the glass...and count the flavour layers and cleverness of the smoke: for a no-age statement blend, you can ask for little more. Remains one of my preferred whiskies when relaxing. Brilliant. 40% 🏆

Ballantine's Hard Fired (86.5) n22 t22 f21 b21.5. Despite the smoky and toasty elements to this, you're left waiting for it to take off....or even go somewhere. Perhaps just a little too soft, friendly and grain indulgent. Decent, enjoyable blend, of course, but a little out of the Ballantine's usual circle of high class friends. 40%

Ballantine's Limited release no. A27380 (96) n24 t24.5 f23.5 b24 Each Limited release has a slightly different stance and this one holds its posture with more debonair, lighter-on-foot poise. The vague furry note of recent bottlings is missing here or, rather, is of the least consequence. The fruit, also, is more of a sheen than a statement more room for the malt and vanilla to play and the spices to impart age. It may be soft on both nose and palate – especially the delivery – as the grains have obviously been vatted to create minimum traction, but it is a blend of quiet substance. Another Ballantine's brand this year hitting the 96 or more mark. Astonishing, absolutely astonishing...more a case of Ballantine's Unlimited... 40%

Bell's Original (91) n23 t22.5 f22.5 b23 Your whisky sleuth came across the new version for the first time in the bar of a London theatre back in December 2009 during the interval of "The 39 Steps". To say I was impressed and pleasantly surprised is putting it mildly. And with the whisky, too, which is a massive improvement on the relatively stagnant 8-year-old especially with the subtle extra smoky weight. If the blender asks me: "Did I get it right, Sir?" then the answer has to be a resounding "yes". 40%

◈ **Bells Original bott code: L1109CK012 (84) n21 t22 f20.5 b20.5** Having casually tasted Bell's from time to time, it dawned on me that its character was changing. And that I hadn't given it a full review for some little while. The most significant thing I had noticed, and fully confirmed here with this bottle before me, is that the smoke which had been brought back a decade ago to breathe the extra life and weight into the bend had now completely vanished. Also, the grains have a different mouth feel and are far more prominent. If you are looking for a silky blend with a strong grain character, here you go. The old complexity has simply disappeared. The old Bell's just doesn't ring as sweetly as it once did. 40%

Bells 8 Years Old (85) n21.5 t22.5 f20 b21. Some mixed messages here: on one hand it is telling me that it has been faithful to some of the old Bells distilleries – hence a slight dirty note, especially on the finish. On the other, there are some sublime specks of complexity and weight. Quite literally the rough and the smooth. 40%. Diageo.

Berry Bros & Rudd The Perspective Series No.1 21 Year Old bott 2019 **(90) n22.5 t22.5 f22 b23** One of those highly unusual blends where the influence of the grain takes a back seat. 43%. 6,300 bottles.

Black & White (91) n22 t23 f22.5 b23.5 This one hasn't gone to the dogs: quite the opposite. I always go a bit misty-eyed when I taste something this traditional: the crisp grains work to maximum effect in reflecting the malts. A classic of its type. 40%. Diageo.

Black Bottle (74.5) n18 t20.5 f17 b18. Barely a shadow of its once masterful, great self. 40%.

Black Bottle bott code 2038310 L3 16165 **(94.5) n23.5 t23.5 f23.5 b24** Not the byword for macho complexity it was 15 years ago but after a lull in its fortunes it is back to something that can rightfully boast excellence. Brilliant. 40%.

Black Bottle 10 Years Old (89) n22 t23 f22 b23 A stupendous blend of weight and poise, but possessing little of the all-round steaming, rampaging sexuality of the younger version... but like the younger version showing a degree less peat: here perhaps even two. Not, I hope, the start of a new trend under the new owners. 40%

Black Dog 12 Years Old (92) n21 t23 f24 b24. Offering genuine sophistication and élan. This minor classic will probably require two or three glass-fulls before you take the bait... 42.8%

Black Grouse (94) n23 t24 f23 b24. A superb return to a peaty blend for Edrington for the first time since they sold Black Bottle. Not entirely different from that brand, either, from the Highland Distillers days with the smokiness being superbly couched by sweet malts. 40%

The Black Grouse Alpha Edition (72.5) n17 t19.5 f17 b18. Dreadfully sulphured. 40%

Black Hound (83) n21 t21.5 f21 b20.5 Here's to Max! Max grain in this but no complaints here as the relatively limited caramel doesn't spoil the enjoyment of what feels like (though obviously isn't) a single distillery output. Crisp at first, then succulent, chewy cream toffee. 40%. Quality Spirits International.

Black Scott 3 Years Old bott code: 3L08460154 **(85.5) n20.5 t22 f21.5 b21.5** Pretty standard, though not unattractive fare. The nose is a bit of a struggle but relaxes on delivery and even entertains with a spicy blitz. 40%. Toorank Productions BV.

Black Stripe (77) n19 t20 f19 b19 Untidy without character. 40%.

Blend No. 888 bott code L15/8185 **(84.5) n21 t22 f20.5 b21** Light, breezy and sweet, this is grain dominant and makes no effort to be otherwise. Soft, untaxing and pleasant. 40%. House of MacDuff.

Boxes Blend (90) n22.5 t23.5 f21 b23. A box which gets plenty of ticks. 40.9%. ncf.

Buchanan's De Luxe 12 Years Old (82) n18 t21 f22 b21. The nose shows more than just a single fault and the character simply refuses to get out of second gear. Certainly pleasant, and some of the chocolate notes towards the end are gorgeous. But just not the normal brilliant show-stopper! 40%. Diageo.

Buchanan's Master bott code: L7313CE001 **(94.5)** n24 t23.5 f23 b24 Some 40-odd years ago I was in love with Buchanans: it was one of the truly sophisticated blends from which I learned so much and this pays homage to the legacy. On the down side the grains are nowhere near so complex and the vague furry bitterness at the end tells its own tale. But I doff my Panama to blender Keith Law in genuine respect: works like this don't just happen and this is a blended Scotch worthy of the name. 40%.

Castle Rock (81) n20 t20.5 f20 b20.5. Clean and juicy entertainment. 40%

Catto's Aged 25 Years bott code RV9499 **(94.5)** n23 t24 f23 b24.5 A far better experience than the last time I officially tasted a Catto's 25 seven or eight years ago. Both malts and grains are of the charming style once associated with Catto's Rare : so jaw-droppingly elegant... 40%. International Beverage Holdings Ltd.

Catto's Deluxe 12 Years Old bott code L 18 03 16 **(86.5)** n21.5 t22 f21.5 b21.5 A safe, sweet and sumptuous blend which places major emphasis to the molasses. Won't win any beauty contests but there is a weighty earthiness, also. 40%. International Beverage Holdings Ltd.

Catto's Rare Old Scottish bott code L 25 01 16 **(83)** n20.5 t21 f20.5 b21 Once fresh as dew on morning grass, this has changed in recent years with a different grain profile which no longer magnifies the malt. Adopted a rougher, more toffeed approach from its once clean cut personality: not even a close approximation of the minor classic it once was. 40%. International Beverage Holdings Ltd.

Chapter 7 Blended Scotch 26 Year Old 1993 sherry butt, dist Dec 93, bott Mar 20 **(77)** n22 t22 f16 b17 A blend, by definition, should be about layering and complexity and, if desired, not allowing any single trait dictate to the rest. So this blend fails because although the sherry cask is rich and sweet but, sadly, nowhere near sulphur free, the story is fruit and grain. And then sulphur. A lot of sulphur, in fact... Which after the malts have matured for 26 years minimum is a bit sad. A Chapter that needs serious re-writing. 44.9%. sc. 618 bottles.

The Chivas 18 Ultimate Cask Collection First Fill American Oak (95.5) n24 t23.5 f24 b24 Immeasurably superior to any Chivas 18 I have tasted before. A true whisky lover's whisky... 48%. ncf.

Chivas Regal Aged 12 Years bott code 2017/01/31 LPAL 0162 **(93)** n23 t23.5 f22.5 b24 Last year I was in a British Airways Business Lounge somewhere in the world and spotted at the bar two different Chivas Regal 12s: the labels had differing designs. I asked for a glass of each and tried them side by side. The first one, from the older label, was the pleasant but forgettable blend I expected and knew so well. The newer version wasn't: had it not been time to get my flight I would have ordered a second glass of it....and I can't remember the last time I did that. What I have here is something very much like that surprise Chivas I discovered. This is, unquestionably, the best Chivas 12 I've encountered for a very long time (and I'm talking at least 20 years): pretty impressive use of the understated smoke, especially on the nose, which works well with that date and walnut toffee. I really could enjoy a second glass of this, though still a very different, delicate animal to the one I grew up with in the mid-70s. Actually, I just have had a second glass of this: delicious....! 40%. Chivas Brothers Ltd.

◈ **Chivas Regal Aged 12 Years** bott code 2021/07/21 LKX R3996 **(94)** n23.5 beautiful fluty, fruity tones drift from the glass on a wave of malt. Indeed, there is a distinctive Speyside grassiness, too, making for a wonderfully mouth-watering effect, even before it reaches the lips. The grains latch onto the malty sugars, softening and rounding their contours. Charming...; t23.5 that roundness evident on the nose is the first thing to make its mark on delivery. These are caresses and kisses: soft and beautifully weighted by an alignment of malt and grain which harmonise to maximise the sugars without for a second the effect becoming over-sweet or cloying. Sublime layering, especially when the vanillas from the oak begin to be laid down. And if the nose didn't get you salivating, then the crispness of the delivery certainly will...; f23 an attractive finale, perhaps flattened slightly as the caramels begin to add up. But the light spices ensure this never becomes too dull..; b24 does the heart good to see that Chivas have kept the standard of their 12 high, after too long in the doldrums. This is a complex, magnificently structured blend. Sill not with the finesse which put it in a league of its own during the 1970s. But way, way better than it had been for far too long. In a period when standard blends up to 12-years-old are going through a rough patch, Chivas 12-year-old is exactly what it says on the tin: Regal. 40%

◈ **Chivas Regal Extra Aged 13 Years** bott code: 2021/05/24 **(89)** n23 despite the promise on the label of a bigger sherry influence, the nose is shaped a trim graininess, though the malts, of a decidedly Speyside grassy nature do flit around with the delicate grape; t23.5 ah, now that is some delivery! The texture of the piece is even more alluring that the taste: the velvety caress ushers (am I allowed to use that term for a Chivas blend?) in a big toffee-raisin theme, bolstered by light spice. Again, the malt flits around, but not so significantly as on the nose; **f20.5** just a little untidy towards the death and a hint of a (very!) mildly off-key cask. Ah, such are the dangers of playing around with sherry casks. Nothing overly serious, but noticeable after so much earlier harmony. The toffee comes up a little heavy, too...: **b22** one of those frustrating whiskies which starts rather well but tapers off a little. 40%.

Chivas Regal Aged 15 Years finished in Grande Champagne Cognac casks, bott code: 2018/07/19 **(89) n23 t22.5 f22 b22.5** Can't quite escape the over-zealous caramel. But there is an undoubted charm to this and extra clever use of the sweeter elements to good effect. Probably one of the softest and most moreish whiskies launched in the last year or so. 40%.

Chivas Regal Aged 18 Years bott code LKRL0346 2017/01/30 **(86) n22 t22 f21 b21** A great improvement on the last bottling I encountered with a pleasing chewiness and understated spiciness. But this remains far too dependent on a big caramel surge for both taste and structure. 40%. Chivas Brothers Ltd.

Chivas Regal Aged 25 Years bott code 2017/03/01 LPML0373 **(95.5) n24.5 t24.5 f22.5 b24** This is quite brilliant whisky. Maybe just one sherry butt away from what would almost certainly have been among the top three whiskies of the year... 40%. Chivas Brothers Ltd.

Chivas Regal Extra (86) n20 t24 f20.5 b21.5. Chivas, but seemingly from the Whyte and MacKay school of thick, impenetrable blends. The nose may have the odd undesirable element and the finish reflects those same trace failings. But if chewy date and walnuts in a sea of creamy toffee is your thing, then this malt is for you. This, though, does show genuine complexity, so I have to admit to adoring the lush delivery and early middle section: the mouthfeel is truly magnificent. Good spice, too. Flawed genius comes to mind. 40%

Chivas Regal The Chivas Brother's Blend Aged 12 Years bott code 2016/04/12 LPEK0613 **(81.5) n21 t21.5 f19 b20** Oh, brother! Fabulous texture but a furry finish... 40%.

Chivas Regal Mizunara bott code: LPBM0253 2018/02/06 **(89.5) n22.5 t23 f22 b22** For years the Japanese copied everything the Scotch whisky industry did, not quite realising – or perhaps willing to believe – that many of their indigenous whiskies were of world class standard deserving respect and discovery in their own right. Now the Scots have, for the first time I'm aware of, openly copied the Japanese– and celebrated the fact. The Japanese oak used within the marrying process does appear to have given an extra impetus and depth to this blend. Definitely offers an extra dimension to what you'd expect from a Chivas. 40%.

Clan Campbell bott code LR3 1047 13/09/05 **(89) n21.5 t23 f22 b22.5** Amazing what happens when you reduce the colouring Last time I tasted this I could barely find the whisky for all the toffee. Now it positively shines in the glass. Love it! 40%. Chivas Brothers Ltd.

Clan Campbell rum barrel finish, bott code: 2018/04/04 **(90.5) n22 t23.5 f22 b23** This blend is all about impact and staying power. All kinds of rum and caramel incursions, but a really lovely broadside on the palate. 40%.

Clan Campbell Dark rum barrel finish, bott code 2017/03/29 LPHL 0570 **(89.5) n22 t23 f22 b22.5** Putting my rum blender's hat on here, can't think which barrels they used to get this degree of colour and sweetness. Still, I'm not arguing; it's a really lovely, accommodating dram. 40%. Chivas Brothers Ltd.

Clan Gold 3 Year Old (95) n23.5 t24 f23.5 b24. A blend-drinkers blend which will also slay the hearts of Speyside single malt lovers. For me, this is love at first sip... 40%

Clan Gold Blended 15 Years Old (91) n21.5 t23 f23.5 b23 An unusual blend for the 21st century, which steadfastly refuses to blast you away with over the top flavour and/or aroma profiles and instead depends on subtlety and poise despite the obvious richness of flavour. The grains make an impact but only by creating the frame in which the more complex notes can be admired. 40%

Clan Gold 18 Years of Age bott code L6X 7616 0611 **(95) n24 t24 f23 b24** Nothing like as juicy and cleverly fruity as it once was, yet marriage between malt and grain seldom comes more happy than this... 40%. Quality Spirits International.

Clan Gold Finest bott code L10Z 6253 1902 **(83) n20 t21 f21 b21** Sweet, silky, soft and caramel heavy. Decent late spice. 40%. Quality Spirits International.

Clan MacGregor (92) n22 t24 f23 b23 Just gets better and better. Now a true classic and getting up there with Grant's. 43%

Clan Murray bott code L9X 7694 1411 **(86) n20 t22.5 f21.5 b22** For the avoidance of doubt: no, this not my blend. No, I am not the blender. No, I do not get a royalty from sales. If I could have had a tenner for each time I've had to answer that over the last decade or so I could have bought my own island somewhere, or Millwall FC... Anyway, back to the whisky. Far better nose than it has shown in the past and the delivery has an eye-watering bite, the finish a roguish spice. Rough-ish but very ready... 40%. The BenRiach Distillery Co. Ltd.

Clansman (80.5) n20.5 t21 f19 b20. Sweet, grainy and soft. 40%. Loch Lomond.

Clansman bott code L3/170/15 **(84) n21 t22 f20 b21** More to it than of old, though still very soft, the dark sugars and spice have a very pleasant input. *40%. Loch Lomond Group.*

The Claymore (85) n19 t22 f22 b22. These days you are run through by spices. The blend is pure Paterson in style with guts etc, which is not something you always like to associate with a Claymore; some delightful muscovado sugar at the death. Get the nose sorted and a very decent and complex whisky is there to be had. *40%. Whyte & Mackay Distillers Ltd.*

⟜ **Claymore** bott code: L90049/007412 **(89.5) n22.5** the nose in deserves attention from the drinker as there is a gorgeous fruit pout to this: zesty with lemons and limes: very different to how it used to be. The malt really is beautifully visible..; **t22.5** no surprises then that the delivery is exceptionally juicy for a blend, the malts whipping up all kinds of light, vaguely honeyed sugar, and always in sync with the gain which rumbles along softly; **f21.5** the grains do amalgamate late on. But the spices do their job...; **b23** no longer called The Claymore, it seems. And in losing the "The" it appears to have lost a lot of weight, too. This is a much more elegant version than yore, which was a bit of a weighty beast and overly dependent on caramel. This, is without so much caramel in the mix to flatten the content, which I much prefer. Lots of very attractive personality to enjoy. And the perfect whisky for soccer lovers with a touch of romance in their souls. The Claymore was a whisky brand which advertised extensively in London football grounds, such as Millwall and West Ham during the 1910s and 1920s and if you find old film of London-based games during that period on Youtube, watch out for their ubiquitous adverts. Indeed, in the Millwall programme of 100 years ago, there was always a Claymore ad next to the team line-ups. My preferred dram for when watching football...before diving and ridiculous football kits became the fashion. *40%*

Cliff Allen bott 20 07 18, bott code: L1524 015503 **(87) n21.5 t22 f21.5 b22** Though grain heavy, there is a pleasing sweetness to accompany the enveloping softness. Attractive spice prickle, too, as well as decent balance. *40%. BBC Spirits.*

⟜ **Co-op Aged 3 Years** bott code: LL1147P/015640 **(84) n19.5 t22 f21 b21.5** A sweet, chewy, caramel-rich blend which keeps simplicity to a fine art. The nose is a bit of a mess. And the inevitable bitter burn notes of the caramel is detectable at the finish. But pleasant enough its own undemanding way. *40%*

Compass Box Delilah's Limited Release Small Batch American oak **(92.5) n23 t23.5 f23 b23** blends rarely come more honeyed, or even sweeter, than this with every last sugary element seemingly extracted from the oak. My only sorrow for this whisky, given its American theme, was that it wasn't bottled as a 101 (ie 50.5% abv) instead of the rather underpowered 80 proof – because you have the feeling this would have become pretty three dimensional and leapt from the glass. And then down your throat with serious effect. *40%. nc ncf. WB15/171*

Compass Box Delilah's XXV American oak & sherry casks **(82) n20.5 t22.5 f18 b21** A blend with an astonishing degree of natural caramels in play, giving the whole piece a soft, chewy feel with both sugars and spices coming off at a tangent. Sadly, the sherry input is distracting on the nose and distinctly tangy and furry towards the end. *46%. nc ncf.*

Compass Box The Double Single bott Mar 17 **(97) n24.5 t25 f23.5 b24** By no means the first time I have encountered a single malt and grain in the same bottle. But I am hard pressed to remember one that was even close to being this wonderful...This is Compass Box's finest moment... *46%. nc ncf. 5,838 bottles.*

Compass Box Great King St. Artist's Blend (93) n24 t23 f22.5 b23.5. The nose of this uncoloured and non-chill filtered whisky is not dissimilar to some better known blends before they have colouring added to do its worst. A beautiful young thing this blend: nubile, naked and dangerously come hither. Compass Box's founder John Glaser has done some memorable work in recent years, though one has always had the feeling that he has still been learning his trade, sometimes forcing the issue a little too enthusiastically. Here, there is absolutely no doubting that he has come of age as a blender. *43%. nc ncf.*

Compass Box Great King Street Experimental Batch #00-V4 bott Sept 13 **(93) n22.5 t24 f23 b23.5.** A blend combining astonishing vibrancy with oaky Russian roulette. Not a dram to do things by halves... *43%. 3,439 bottles.*

Compass Box Great King Street Experimental Batch #TR-06 bott Sept 13 **(92) n22 t23.5; f23 b23.5** I think this one's been rumbled... *43%.*

Compass Box Great King Street Glasgow Blend (88.5) n22 t23.5 f21 b22 Just the odd note seems out of place here and there: delicious but not the usual Compass Box precision. *43%*

Compass Box Great King St Glasgow Blend batch no. GB 209, bott 8 Aug 19 **(89) n23 t23.5 f20.5 b22** Perhaps a rogue cask away from an award. *43%. nc ncf.*

Compass Box The Circus bott Mar 16 **(93) n23 t23.5 f23 b23.5** Scotland's very own Clown Royal... *49%. nc ncf. 2,490 bottles.*

Compass Box This Is Not A Luxury Whisky bott Aug 15 **(81) n20 t21.5 f19.5 b20.** Correct. *53.1%. nc ncf. 4,992 bottles.*

Compass Box Rogue's Banquet (94.5) n23.5 t23.5 f23.5 b24 Quite a different tack from Compass Box, really concentrating on the daintiness a blend might reveal despite the sometimes voluptuous body. Helped along by sublime cask selection. Gorgeous. *46%.*

Consulate (87) n21.5 t22 f22 b21.5 I assume this weighty and pleasant dram was designed to accompany Passport (whose chewiness it now resembles) in the drinks cabinet. I suggest, if buying them, use Visa. *40%. Quality Spirits International.*

Crawford's (83.5) n19 t21 f22 b21.5. A lovely spice display helps overcome the caramel. *40%.*

❖ **Crag and Glen Aged 3 Years** bott code: L1175P/016087 **(85.5) n21 t21.5 f21.5 b21.5** Even deploying the Murray Method, the uneven grain and toffee mix on the nose won't trouble the drinker for long. Though there is a fair decent marriage of the two styles on the palate, to give a sweet, silky and long ride, though complexity never quite enters the equation. The sweetness to the whisky is never lost. *40% Sainsbury's*

Cutty Black (83) n20 t23 f19 b21. Both nose and finish are dwarfed and flung into the realms of ordinariness by the magnificently substantial delivery. Whilst there is a taint to the nose, its richness augers well for what is to follow; and you won't be disappointed. At times it behaves like a Highland Park with a toffeed spine, such is the richness and depth of the honey and dates and complexity of the grain-vanilla background. But those warning notes on the nose are there for good reason and the finish tells you why. Would not be surprised to see this score into the 90s on a different bottling day. *40%. Edrington.*

Cutty Sark (78) n19 t21 f19 b19. Crisp and juicy. But a nipping furriness, too. *40%*

Cutty Sark bott code L60355 L7 **(84.5) n21 t22 f20 b21.5** To some extent an improvement on a couple of years back when this blend was vanishing in character. But could still do with some urgent extra restorative work. For as long I can remember the grain on this was crisp and brought the sharpest, juiciest notes imaginable from the Speyside malts: indeed, that was its trademark character. Now, like so many standard blends, it is bubble gum soft and spreads the sugars evenly with the malts fighting to be heard. Only very mild sulphur tones to the crippling ones I had previously found. But it really does need to re-work the grain...if it can find it. *40%.*

Cutty Sark Aged 12 Years (92) n22 t24 f23 b23 At last! Cutty 12 at full sail...and blended whisky rarely looks any more beautiful! *40%. Edrington.*

Cutty Sark Aged 15 Years (82) n19 t22 f20 b21. Attempts to take the honey route. But seriously dulled by toffee and the odd sulphured cask. *40%. Edrington.*

Cutty Sark Aged 18 Years (88) n22 t22 f22 b22 Lost the subtle fruitiness which worked so well. Easy-going and attractive. *43%*

Cutty Sark Aged 25 Years (91) n21 t23.5 f22.5 b23 Magnificent, though not quite flawless, this whisky is as elegant and effortlessly powerful as the ship after which the brand was named... *45.7%. Berry Bros & Rudd.*

Cutty Sark Prohibition Edition American oak, bott code L0401W L4 11/18 **(91) n21.5 t25 f20 b24.5** Probably the best label and presentation of any whisky in the world this year: sheer class. On the back label they use the word authentic. Which is a very interesting concept. Except authentic whisky sent to the USA back in the 1920s wouldn't have that annoying and debilitating rumble of sulphur, detectable on both nose and finish. And I suspect the malt content would have been higher – and the grain used showing far more of a corn-oily character. That all said, I doubt the blender of the day would have achieved better delivery or balance: indeed, this delivery has to be one of the highlights of the whisky year. You will not be surprised to discover my resolve cracked, and I swallowed a full mouthful of this special blend. And, gee: it was swell, bud... *50%. Edrington.*

Cutty Sark Storm (81.5) n18 t23.5 f19.5 b20.5. When the wind is set fair, which is mainly on delivery and for the first six or seven flavour waves which follow, we really do have an astonishingly beautiful blend, seemingly high in malt content and really putting the accent on ulmo honey and marzipan: a breath-taking combination. This is assisted by a gorgeous weight to the silky body and a light raspberry jam moment to the late arriving Ecuadorian cocoa. All magnificent. However, as Cutty sadly tends to, sails into sulphurous seas. *40%. Edrington.*

Demijohn Finest Blended Scotch Whisky (88) n21 t22 f23 b22 OK, now that's spooky. You really don't expect tasting notes written ten years ago to exactly fit the bill today. But that is exactly what happens here: well maybe not quite exactly. Ten years ago I wrote of the "wonderful firmness of the grain" where today, like 90% of all blends, it is much more yielding and soft than before. Thankfully, it hasn't detracted from the enjoyment. *40%.*

❖ **Demijohn Finest Blended Scotch Whisky (86) n22 t21 f21.5 b21.5** Soft, undemanding blended with a light juiciness. Big on the toffee, though. *40% Specially blended by Adelphi*

Dew of Ben Nevis Supreme Selection (77) n18 t20 f20 b19. Some lovely raspberry jam Swiss roll moments here. But the grain could be friendlier, especially on the nose. *40%*

Dewar's Aged 12 Years The Ancestor bott code: L17338ZA80109:20 **(87) n21.5 t22 f21.5 b22** A welcoming blend, relying mainly on softer grains which suck you in and caress you.

A little orange peel and tart tannin helps give the blend vibrancy, but there is always a slight murkiness hanging around, too, which becomes more apparent at the death. 40%.

Dewar's Aged 15 Years The Monarch bott code: L18340ZA800 1326 **(81) n21 t21.5 f18 b20.5** Sweet and chewy in part, but the fuzzy finish abdicates. 40%.

Dewar's Aged 18 Years The Vintage bott code: L19030ZA8051642 **(96.5) n24 t24.5 f23.5 b24.5** This is how an 18-year-old blend should be: complex, noble and both keeping you on the edge of your seat as you wonder next what will happen, and falling back into its furthest recesses so you can drift away on its beauty... A blend that upholds the very finest traditions of the great Dewar's name. 40%.

Dewar's Aged 25 Years The Signature bott code: L18081ZA8011034 **(96) n24 t24 f24 b24** A 25-year-old blend truly worthy of that mantle. Always an honour to experience a whisky that has been very cleverly sculpted, not haphazardly slung together: a blender's blend. I doff my Panama to the blender. 40%.

Dewar's Double Double Aged 21 Years Blended Scotch Whisky finished in oloroso sherry casks, bott code: L19106ZA500 **(88) n23.5 t23.5 f18.5 b22.5** Another blender's blend. Or would have been 30 years ago. But doesn't seem to quite take into account the Russian roulette decision to add extra oloroso into the mix – Russian roulette with only one empty chamber that is... 46%.

Dewar's Double Double Aged 27 Years Blended Scotch Whisky finished in Palo Cortado sherry casks, bott code: L19106ZA501 **(96.5) n24 t24 f24 b24.5** A blend not scared to embrace its peaty side. And sherry butts free from sulphur. A double miracle at work. And one of the best new blends I have tasted for a year or two. Superb. 46%.

Dewar's Double Double Aged 32 Years Blended Scotch Whisky finished in PX sherry casks, bott code: L19107ZA501 **(86.5) n21.5 t24 f20.5 b20.5** I clocked the PX influence before I was aware it was officially finished in that cask type. After the staggeringly beautiful and vivid 27-year-old, this is very much a case of following the Lord Mayor's show. Yes, the sherry influence is pristine and untainted by sulphur, and the spices do a grand job. But to put a 30 year old blend into PX is like restoring an Old Master with a nine inch brush dipped into a gloss finish. Lovely in places (the astonishing delivery shews just how much sublime complexity was originally around)...but could have been so much more... 46%.

Dewar's Illegal Smooth Mezcal Cask Finish Aged 8 Years bott code: L20027ZA8002254 **(88) n23 t23 f20 b22** There is not the remotest doubt in my mind that of all the blending companies of Scotland, it is Dewar's that in recent years have upped their game most and returned to their once given place amongst the greats. This is probably just a cask away from adding to their rich tapestry of sublime blends. But, sadly, a little sulphur has entered the fray here – not a massive amount, but enough to dull the glitter from a potentially 24 carat blend. With the muscular grape sparring with the crisp grain and fulsome malt, at first this was going rather well, especially with the lightly spiced undertone. Look forward to seeing the next bottling... 40%.

Dewar's White Label bott code: L18241ZA204 2203 **(82) n20 t21 f20 b21** A great improvement on the last White Label I tasted (though nowhere near my great love of the 1970s!) but some murky grain still apparent. Definite layering and structure here, though. 40%.

Dhoon Glen (86) n21 t22 f21.5 b21.5 Full of big flavours, broad grainy strokes and copious amounts of dark sugars including chocolate fudge and now a little extra spice, too. Goes dhoon a treat... 40%. Lombard Scotch Whisky Ltd.

Dimple 12 Years Old (86.5) n22 t22 f21.5 b21. Lots of sultana; the spice adds aggression. 40%.

Dimple 15 Years Old (87.5) n20 t21 f24 b22.5. Only on the late middle and finish does this particular flower unfurl and to magnificently complex effect. The texture of the grains in particular delight while the strands of barley entwine. A type of treat for the more technically minded of the serious blend drinkers among you. 40%. Diageo.

Dimple Golden Selection (84.5) n21 t22 f20.5 b21 A clumsy, untidy bottling with a little too much bitterness on both nose and finish. The odd heather honey note drifts about and some saving busy spice, too. But too easily the honey turns to burnt honeycomb, especially noticeable on the dry finale. Certainly the caramels add to the ungainly narrative. 40%.

Eternity Diamond Reserve Old Premium Blend Oloroso sherry cask finish **(86) n21 t22 f21.5 b21.5** Enjoy the chocolate notes which pop up at regular intervals and the chewy mouthfeel which accommodates them perfectly. Just not sure about those gin notes which appear to pepper this blend...and have cost points. 40%.

Eternity Royal Reserve Noble Blend ex-bourbon casks **(89) n22.5 t22 f22.5 b22** Determined to stay on the delicate side of the tracks, has both a pleasing sweetness, weight and mouthfeel throughout. Sometimes, though, it reminds me of a Geneve... 40%.

The Famous Grouse bott code L4812TL1 25/08 **(88.5) n22.5 t23 f21 b22** Changed its stance a few years back from light blend to a middle-weighted one and has worked hard to keep that position with thoughtful use of the phenols. Unlike many other brands it has not gone colouring mad and the little toffee apparent does nothing to spoil the narrative and complexity: I doff my hat. *40%*.

⬙ **The Famous Grouse** bott code: L4001DL13 **(87.5)** n22 t23 f20.5 b22 I had held back a year or two from re-tasting this as I wanted to see if they had managed to get the sulphur out of their system. Not quite, but there is definitely a vast improvement from some Grouse I tasted on the road (not in the lab) before Covid hit. Still pretty tight on both nose and finish, although at least the aroma does contain a degree of malt sparkle. But I have to say the delivery is a sheer joy and one of the few blends where the layering is at times quite dazzling with the malts having an input big enough that you can actually pick them out, having their own debate, amid the firm grains. An unusually crisp blend for these days. Just need to get that last sulphur out of the mix...and perhaps re-instate a little smoke, which appears to have been lost: not entirely, but significantly. *40%*

The Famous Grouse Gold Reserve (90) n23.5 t23 f21.5 b22 Great to know the value of the Gold Reserve is going up...as should the strength of this blend. The old-fashioned 40% just ain't enough carats. *40%. Edrington Group.*

The Famous Grouse Married Strength (82.5) n19 t22 f20 b21.5. The nose is nutty and toffeed. But despite the delightful, silky sweetness and gentle Speyside-style maltiness which forms the main markers for this soft blend, the nose, like the finish, also shows a little bitter furriness has, sadly, entered into the mix. Not a patch on the standard Grouse of a decade ago. *45.9% WB16/019*

The Famous Grouse Mellow Gold sherry & bourbon casks **(85)** n20 t23.5 f20 b21.5. While the nose and finish tell us a little too much about the state of the sherry butts used, there is no harm tuning into the delivery and follow though which are, unquestionably, beautiful. The texture is silk normally found on the most expensive lingerie, and as sexy as who you might find inside it; while the honey is a fabulous mix of ulmo and orange blossom. *40%*

The Famous Grouse Smoky Black (87) n22 t22 f21 b22. Black Grouse by any other name. Flawed in the usual tangy, furry Grouse fashion. But have to say there is a certain roughness and randomness about the sugars that I find very appealing. A smoky style that Bowmore lovers might enjoy. A genuinely beautiful, smoky, ugly, black duckling. Sorry, I mean Grouse. *40%*

⬙ **The Famous Grouse Smoky Black** bott code: L02860 **(94)** n23 a strange nose: smothered in peat, though the grains dominate....; **t23.5** now that is rather lovely: the delivery is a sweet, Bowmore-style smokiness drifting amid more Speyside-style malt before the grains begin to get amongst them. Salivating and lively....; **f23.5** long, with the oils bathed in smoke and even late on barley gets in on the act, nestling amid the light tannins and toffee... and late arriving spice; **b24** what a transformation, Last time I tasted this, sulphur was in the system and undermined what looked like a potentially excellent blend. Here, we are talking 100% sulphur-free blended whisky... and the result is glorious. A little on the sweet side, perhaps. But forgivable with such an elastic mouth feel and a smoky disposition to keep you warm and contented on the coldest night...or on the chilliest grouse moors... *40%*.

Firean blend no. 005, bottling line. 003, bott code. L17066 **(91.5)** n23 t23.5 f22 b23 Does the heart good encounter to encounter a blend so happy to embrace its smokier self. Deliciously impressive. *40%. Burlington Drinks.*

⬙ **Firean Lightly Peated Old Reserve Small Batch Blend No 5** L10123 **(91.5)** n23 subtle, smoking embers of peat darting around the nose like flies over a lake; gentle fronds of lemon drizzle cake wave on the smoky breeze; **t23.5** just brilliant! Smoked acacia honey...; **f22** the grains begin to move into view...and so do the lightly smoked spices; **b23** high class blending with top rate layering. Amazingly well structured and silky towards the end. *43%*

⬙ **For Peat's Sake** bott code: L20 07581 CB2 **(94)** n23.5 a superb nose thanks to the layering of the phenols, giving it a bitty, complex persona. Slightly salty and dry, the sweetness arrives in balancing blasts....; **t24** the sugars missing on the nose take no time to accumulate on delivery. They are the perfect accompaniment to the two-toned phenols which offer both a dusty dryness and a far more chewy depth, too. The grains begin to make their mark at the halfway point, just thinning matters slightly; **f23** adorable prickly spices attach to the dying embers of the peat...; **b23.5** anyone can add peat to a whisky. It doesn't guarantee balance or success. But this is a triumph simply because the blend has been careful to keep a shape and structure beyond peat. This is magnificently complex and skilfully weighted. What an absolute treat of a blend. A dram which just doesn't Peater out... *40%*

Fort Glen The Blender's Reserve Aged 12 Years (88.5) n21.5 t23 f21.5 b22.5 An entirely enjoyable blend which is clean and boasting decent complexity and weight. *40%*

Fort Glen The Distiller's Reserve (78) n18 t22 f19 b19. Juicy, salivating delivery as it storms the ramparts. Draws down the portcullis elsewhere. *40%. The Fort Glen Whisky Company.*

Fraser MacDonald (85) n21 t21.5 f21 b21.5. Some fudge towards the middle and end but the journey there is an enjoyable one. *40%. Loch Lomond Distillers.*

Gleann Mór Blended Whisky 18 Year Old (87) n21.5 t23 f20.5 b22. A few passages in this are outstanding, especially when the delicate honey appears to collide with the softest smoke. A slight bitterness does jar somewhat, though the softness of the grain is quite seriously seductive 43.9%

Gleann Mór 40 Year Old Blend (94) n23 t23.5 f23.5 b24 Some 52-year-old Carsebridge makes up about a fifth of this blend, but I suspect the big oak comes from one of the malts. A supreme old whisky which cherishes its age. 44.6%.

Glen Brynth (70.5) n18 t19 f16 b17.5. Bitter and awkward. 43%

Glenbrynth Premium Three Year Old (82) n19 t21 f21 b21 An enormously improved, salivating, toasty blend making full use of the rich muscovado sugars on display. Good late spice, too. 43%. OTI Africa.

Glenbrynth 8 Year Old (88) n21.5 t22 f22.5 b22. An impressive blend which improves second by second on the palate. 40%. OTI Africa.

Glenbrynth Pearl 30 Year Old Limited Edition (90.5) n22.5 t23.5 f21.5 b23 Attractive, beautifully weighted, no off notes...though perhaps quietened by toffee. Still a treat of a blend. 43%. OTI Africa.

Glenbrynth Pearl 30 Year Old bott code L8V 7410 28/11/11 **(88)** n22.5 t22.5 f21 b22 A genuinely strange blend. Not sure how this whisky was mapped out in the creator's mind. A hit and miss hotchpotch but when it is good, it is very good.. 43%. OTI Africa.

The Glengarry bott code L3/301/15 **(80)** n19 t21 f20 b20 A brand that would once make me wince has upped its game beyond recognition. Even has the nerve to now possess an attractively salivating as well as silky disposition. 40%. Loch Lomond Group.

Glen Lyon (85) n19 t22.5 f22 b21.5. Works a lot better than the nose suggests: seriously chewy with a rabid spice attack and lots of juices. For those who have just retired as dynamite testers. Unpretentious fun. 43%. Diageo.

Glen Talloch Choice Rare & Old (85.5) n20.5 t22.5 f21 b21.5. A very pleasing sharpness to the delivery reveals the barley in all its Speyside-style finery, The grain itself is soothing, especially when the caramel notes kick in. 40%. ncf.

Glen Talloch Gold Aged 12 Years (85) n21 t22 f21 b21. Impressive grain at work insuring a deft, velvety caress to the palate. Mainly caramel speaking, despite the age, though there is an attractive spice buzz towards the thin-ish finish. 40%

Glen Talloch Peated (77) n18 t20 f20 b19 The awful tobacco nose needs some serious work on it. The taste is overly sweet, mushy and shapeless, like far too many blends these days. Requires a complete refit. 40%. Boomsma Distillery.

Glory Leading Aged 32 Years (88.5) n22.5 t22.5 f21.5 b22 At times a little heavy handed and out of sync. But the overall experience is one of stunningly spiced enjoyment. 43%

Glory Leading Blended Scotch Whisky 30 Years Old (93) n22.5 t23 f23.5 b24 a big, clever, satisfying blend which just gets better and better... though not too sure about the Crystal Palace style eagle on the label. Even so, love it! 43%

Golden Piper (86.5) n22 t21 f22 b21.5. A firm, clean blend with a steady flush through of diverse sugars. The grain does all the steering and therefore complexity is limited. But the overall freshness is a delight. 43%. Whisky Shack.

Goldfield bott code: L17 02796 CB1 **(86)** n21 t21.5 f21.5 b22 These days I am minded to give an extra mark to any blend that is not carrying a sulphur trace from the grain receptacles. So an extra mark here, for sure, for this fat and full-flavoured blend which, despite its unashamed cream toffee roundness, enjoys enough spice to punch through for bite, as well as some late hickory. 40%.

⬥ **Goldfield** bott code: L1805078CB2 **(87)** n22 t22 f21 b22 High grain on show it may be, but when the grain is this good – and this firm, something of a collectors' item in itself – all can be forgiven. Above average icing sugar involvement, too, to keep you going to the late spice. Forget about malt complexity and all that stuff. Brilliant, unsullied young scotch grain at its best. 40%

The Gordon Highlanders (86) n21 t22 f21 b22. Lush and juicy, there is a distinctive Speysidey feel to this one with the grains doing their best to accentuate the developing spice. Plenty of feel good factor here. 40%. William Grant & Sons.

Grand Macnish bott code L16/8404 **(85.5)** n21.5 t22 f21 b21 Never a blend for the lily-livered this brand has always been a byword for a whisky with big character. It can still claim that, except now we have a much more absorbing grain at play which undermines the blend's former maltiness. 40%. MacDuff International Ltd.

Grand Macnish 12 Years Old (86) n21 t22 f21.5 b21.5. A grander Grand Macnich than of old with the wonderful feather pillow delivery maintained and a greater harmonisation of the malt, especially those which contain a honey-copper sheen. 40%. MacDuff.

Grand Macnish Black Edition charred Bourbon casks, bott code L15 8863 **(94.5)** n24 t23.5 f23 b24 A blended whisky classic. 40%. MacDuff International Ltd.

Grand Macnish Double Matured Aged 15 Years Sherry Cask Edition ex-bourbon barrels, Jerez Oloroso sherry butt finish, batch no. 002, bott code: P/000837 (**94**) **n23.5 t23.5 f23 b24** Delighted to report that the sherry involvement is without blemish. This Grand Macnish is very grand, indeed. 43%. Macduff International.

Grant's Aged 12 Years bott code: L6X 6682 1305 (**96**) **n24 t24 f23.5 b24.5** There is no doubting that their 12-year-old has improved dramatically in recent years. Doubtless better grain than their standard blend, but also a slightly braver use of phenols has paid handsome dividends. Sits proudly alongside Johnny Walker Black as one of the world's must have 12-year-old blends. For me, the perfect daily dram. 40%.

Grant's Cask Editions No. 1 Ale Cask Finish bott code: L1X 7354 1809 (**91**) **n22.5** attractive Demerara firmness and even a malty swirl; the green, youthful freshness charms; **t23** juicy delivery and firmer than the Family Reserve with much more sharpness and clarity; big sugars build; **f22.5** a pleasing spiced mocha fade; **b23** a much cleaner, more precise blend than when this was first launched, with less noticeable beer character: impressive. 40%.

Grant's Cask Editions No. 2 Sherry Cask Finish bott code: L3Z 7760 0211 (**84.5**) **n21.5 t22 f20 b21** A lovely fresh, fruity and salivating edge to this even boasting an early honeyed sheen. Complexity has been sacrificed for effect, however. 40%.

Grant's The Family Reserve bott code: L3A 8017 1711 (**85**) **n21 t22 f21 b21** What was once the very finest, most complex nose in the entire Scotch whisky lexicon is now, on this evidence, a mushy shadow of its former self. Where once there was a judicious mix of softer and firmer grain to ensure the malts could make the most eloquent of speeches, now there is just a spongy sweetness which shouts loud enough to silence the poetry. If you like your blend fat, sweet, chewy, softer than quicksand and boasting a bitter, vaguely off-key finale here you go. But for those of us who once revered Grant's as the greatest of all standard blends, a whisky whose artistry once gilt-framed the very finest Scotland had to offer, this will not be a glass of cheer. I cannot blame the blender: he can work only with what he has available. And today, after a succession of nonsensical grain distillery closures (nonsensical to anyone who understands whisky, but not the soul-less bean counters who haven't the first clue) the choice in his lab is limited. It would be like blaming the manager of Bradford City for being a third tier football club because they won the FA Cup in 1910. Times change. And not, sadly, always for the better... 40%.

Grant's Signature bott code: L1Z 7468 1609 (**79**) **n19 t22 f18 b20** Smudged. 40%.

◈ **Grant's Stand Fast Triple Wood** bott code: L3F 6365 28022124 (**86.5**) **n21.5 t22.5 f20.5 b22** For years one of the great things about Grant's blends was how beautifully integrated the grains and the malts were, making them usually among the most complex all Scotland had to offer. Here you get the feeling that the grains want far too much say, though the malts do dissolve into the mix with a delightful grassy, Speyside touch making the middle ground a delight. You also fear that the grain had been held in once sulphured sherry butts, because the finish is weakened by a distinctive, nagging furriness. The Murray Method does up the oils significantly and help reduce the negative effects. Pleasant enough. 40%

The Great Drams Blended Cask Series 7 Years Old batch no. 2, bott Feb 20 (**89.5**) **n22.5 t23 f22 b22** An exceptionally bright and clean blend to be applauded. But it was like listening to the violins without a single cello to be had. 46.2%.

Green Isle Deluxe bott code: #4878 (**91.5**) **n22.5 t23. f23 b23** For those who like their blends sending out unambiguous smoke signals. A deep, simplistic but satisfying blend. 40%. Atom Brands.

Green Plaid 12 Years Old (**89**) **n22 t23 f22 b22** Beautifully constructed; juicy. 40%.

Guneagal Aged 12 Years (**85.5**) **n21 t22.5 f20.5 b21.5.** The salty, sweaty armpit nose gives way to an even saltier delivery, helped along by sweet glycerine and a boiled candy fruity sweetness. The finish is a little roughhouse by comparison. 40%. William Grant & Sons.

Haddington House (**81**) **n20 t21 f20 b20** Good grief! This has changed since I last tasted it over a decade ago. Gone is its light, bright juicy character and in its place a singularly sweet, cloying blend due, I suspect, to a very different grain input. 40%. Quality Spirits International.

Haig Gold Label (**88**) **n21 t23 f22 b22** What had before been pretty standard stuff has upped the complexity by an impressive distance. 40%. Diageo.

The Half Century Blend batch no. 4 (**95**) **n24 t24 f23 b24** A rich malt making an absolute nonsense of its age statement. A fruitcake theme then moves into far maltier territory, but it is the sheer beauty of the lush mouthfeel which blows you away. Dark summer cherries and chocolate Maltesers melt into the other while light spices offer a third dimension. The is even a Farley's Rusk moment, though totally in keeping with the narrative... Oh, and look out for the flawless, teasingly understated seem of ulmo honey, too. Stunning. For its age: breathtaking. 45.6%. The Blended Whisky Company.

Hankey Bannister (**84.5**) **n20.5 t22 f21 b21.** Lots of early life and even a malt kick early on. Toffee later. 40%. Inverhouse Distillers.

Hankey Bannister 12 Years Old (86.5) n22 t21.5 f21 b22. A much improved blend with a nose and early delivery which makes full play of the blending company's Speyside malts. Plenty of toffee on the finish. *40%. Inverhouse Distillers.*

Hankey Bannister 21 Years Old (95) n23.5 t24 f23.5 b24 With top dressing like this and some obviously complex secondary malts, too, how can it fail? *43%.*

Hankey Bannister 25 Years Old (91) n22.5 t24 f21.5 b23 Follows on in style and quality to 21-year-old. Gorgeous. *40%*

Hankey Bannister 40 Years Old (89) n22 t23 f22 b22. This blend has been put together to mark the 250th anniversary of the forging of the business relations between Messrs. Hankey and Bannister. And although the oak creaks like a ship of its day, there is enough verve and viscosity to ensure a rather delicious toast to the gentlemen. Love it! *44%. Inverhouse.*

Hankey Bannister 40 Year Old (94) n23.5 t23.5 f23 b24. Pure quality. The attention to detail is sublime. *44.3%. Inverhouse Distillers.*

Hankey Bannister Heritage Blend (92) n23 t24 f22 b23 Just so soft and sensual...*46%.*

Harveys Lewes Blend Eight Year Old batch 4 **(93) n23.5 t23 f23 b23.5** First tasted this in the front parlour of legendary Harvey's brewer Miles Jenner's home just after Christmas. It tasted quite different from their previous bottlings – and quite superb. Nosed and tasted now several months on in the cold analytical light of a tasting room...helped along with that deft addition of subtle peat, it still does. Superb! *40%*

Hazelwood 18 Year Old (88) n23.5 t22.5 f20.5 b22 Until the final furry moments, a genuine little, understated, charmer. *40%. William Grant & Sons.*

Hazelwood 21 Year Old (74) n19 t20 f17 b18. Some decent acacia honey tries to battle against the bitter imbalance. *40%. William Grant & Sons.*

Hazelwood 25 Year Old (89.5) n22 t23 f22 b22.5 Distinctly chunky. *40%. WG & Sons.*

High Commissioner bott code L2/305/16 **(87.5) n21.5 t22.5 f21.5 b22** Boasts an unusually well balanced disposition for a young blend, not at all cowered into being a one trick caramelled pony. Instead, we are treated to a fulsome array of huskier and duskier notes, especially the molasses mixing with a hint of phenol. Delicious. *40%. Loch Lomond Group.*

⬡ **High Commissioner** bott code: L111021 **(91) n22** there is a sweet malty, almost fruity, signature to this which cuts delightfully into the soft grain. Deft smoke ensure weight and further, pleasing complexity; **t23** superb mouth feel. Those delicate embers of peat work as planned and gaurantee the depth found on the nose is amplified here. The grain acts only as a slightly sweeter receiving station for the obvious malt; **f22.5** superb light oils work wonders with the faint cocoa, light vanilla and now fuller spices; **b23.5** an attractively complex blend, one of the few these days where the malt (and I think even a certain distillery) can be detected. The grain used for this blend is especially lush, but that doesn't prevent some delightful barley notes push the salivation button. Superb layering with outline vanilla and tannins ensuring an excellent chewiness. Rare to find such top notch layering in such a relatively low budget brand. Deserves better recognition for its excellence. *40%*

High Commissioner Aged 7 Years Lightly Peated bott code: 22 06 2018 **(89) n22.5 t22 f22 b22.5** A seemingly simple malt with a lot of complexity if you want to find it. *40%.*

Highland Baron (88.5) n22 t22.5 f22 b22 Has seriously upped the smoke and honey ratio in recent years. Deserves its Baronetcy. *40%. Lombard Scotch Whisky Ltd.*

Highland Bird bott code L9Z 6253 2302 **(83.5) n21 t21 f20.5 b21** I've had a few of these over the years, I can tell you. Glasses of this whisky, as well. As for the blend, this is by far and away the cleanest, enjoyable and most well-balanced yet: a dram on the up. *40%. QSI.*

Highland Harvest Organic Scotch Whisky (76) n18 t21 f19 b18. A very interesting blend. Great try, but a little bit of a lost opportunity here as I don't think the balance is quite right. But at least I now know what organic caramel tastes like... *40%*

Highland Mist (88.5) n20.5 t23 f22.5 b22.5 Fabulously fun whisky bursting from the bottle with character and mischief. Had to admit, broke all my own rules and just had to have a glass of this after doing the notes... *40%. Loch Lomond Distillers.*

Highland Piper (79) n20 t20 f19 b20. Good quaffing blend – if sweet - of sticky toffee and dates. Some gin on the nose – and finish. *40%*

Highland Pride (86) n21 t22 f21.5 b21.5. A beefy, weighty thick dram with plenty to chew on. The developing sweetness is a joy. *40%. Whyte & Mackay Distillers Ltd.*

Highland Queen bott code L12 356 **(87) n22.5 t22.5 f20.5 b21.5** If the caramels on this could be reduced slightly what a brilliant blend we'd have on our hands here. As it is, the nose is a hotbed of complex intrigue with earthier and lighter honeyed notes combining sublimely while the delivery allows the sugars, vanillas and spices room to make their cases. Bar the spices, just all dies off a little too soon. *40%. Tullibardine Ltd.*

Highland Queen Aged 8 Years bott code L15 071 **(89.5) n23 t22.5 f21.5 b22.5** A classy blend showing great character and entertainment value. *40%. Tullibardine Ltd.*

Highland Queen Aged 12 Years Blended Scotch Whisky (87) n22 t22 f21 b22. A polite, slightly more sophisticated version of the 8-year-old...but without the passion and drama! 40%

Highland Queen Aged 12 Years bott code L15 071 (90) n23 t22.5 f22 b22.5 A much weightier blend than it used to be, displaying excellent pace of flavour development on the palate. Decent stuff! 40%. *Tullibardine Ltd.*

Highland Queen Sherry Cask Finish bott code L16 201 (81.5) n19 t22 f19 b21.5 The sherry isn't exactly free from sin, and the grape easily overpowers the nuances of the blend itself. So, attractive to a degree, but... 40%. *Tullibardine Ltd.*

Highland Queen 1561 bott code L16/80 28.01.16 (94) n23.5 t23.5 f23 b24. As it happens, I have a home where on a living room wall is an oil painting of Fotheringhay, where the life of Mary Queen of Scots, the Highland Queen, ended on an executioners' block in 1561. Indeed, the house is quite close by and sits near the River Nene which passes through Fotheringhay. The village itself is quiet, particularly fragrant during Spring and Summer and with an unmistakable feel of history and elegance. Not at all unlike this excellent and most distinguished blend. 40%. *Tullibardine Ltd.*

Highland Queen 1561 30 Years Old bott code LF13017261 261 (88.5) n23.5 t23.5 f19.5 b22 Shame about the finish. Until then we had one of the sweetest yet gentle blends of the year. 40%.

Highland Reserve bott code B154 (80) n19 t21.5 f19.5 b20 An easy quaffing, silky and profoundly grained, toffee-enriched blend. 43%. *Quality Spirits International.*

Highland Warriors (82) n20 t21 f20.5 b20.5 This warrior must be wanting to raid a few grain stores... 40%. *Quality Spirits International.*

The Highland Way (82.5) n20 t21 f21 b20.5 Grainy, with a big sweet toffee middle which makes for a slightly juicy dram of a class barely distinguishable from so many other standard blends. 40%. *Quality Spirits International.*

The Highland Way bott code B445 (83.5) n20 t21.5 f21 b21 More Milky Way than Highland Way... Very similar to the 40% version, except some extra milk chocolate at the finish. 43%.

HM The King (89.5) n23 t22 f22 b22.5 So majestic to find a blend these days not swamped by artificial colouring. Royalty, indeed! 40%. *Branded Spirits USA.*

Islay Mist Aged 8 Years bott code: L20 06871 CB2 (93.5) n23.5 t23.5 f22.5 b24 Too often their 8-year-old versions have been more a case of Islay Missed than Mist. Not this time: bullseye! I could enjoy that any evening! 40%. *Macduff International.*

Islay Mist Aged 8 Years Amontillado Napoleon Cask Finish bott code L16/8826 (76) n19 t20 f18 b19 For those of you not carrying the sulphur recognition gene, I suspect this will be a delight. For those of us that do, well sorry: but not tonight, Napoleon. And this sulphur is a bit of a carry on, MacDuff... 43%. *MacDuff International Ltd.*

Islay Mist Aged 8 Years Manzanilla La Gitana Cask Finish bott code L15/8293 (85) n21.5 t22 f20 b21.5 Lots of phenolic cough sweet properties but the fruit and smoke form a tight, enclosed union with little room for scope. The finish is rather too bitter. 40%.

Islay Mist Aged 8 Years Palo Cortado Wellington Finish bott code: CBSC4 06075 05.08.19 (81) n20 t22 f19 b20 Tight, eye-wateringly sharp and fights against friendly integration despite the big marmalade theme. The niggling sulphur doesn't help at all. This Wellington has met a Napoleonic-type Waterloo... 43%. *Macduff International.*

Islay Mist Aged 10 Years bott code: L20 07001 CB2 (94) n23.5 t23.5 f23 b24 A rare blend where the emphasis is squarely in the malt. One glass of this is a near impossibility.... 40%. *Macduff International.*

Islay Mist Aged 12 Years bott code: L19 06053 CB2 (86.5) n21.5 t22.5 f20.5 b22 The grains are far more prevalent here than the 10-year-old, giving the blend an attractive softness at the price of complexity. Love the salivating delivery which makes up for the dull, slightly nagging finale. 40%. *Macduff International.*

Islay Mist Aged 17 Years bott code L15/8826 (96) n24 t24 f23.5 b24.5 A truly brilliant blend that should have no water added and be spared as much time as you can afford. 40%. *MacDuff International Ltd.*

Islay Mist Aged 21 Years bott code: L20 07315 CB2 (94.5) n24 t23.5 f23 b24 The blender should take a bow. Jolly well played: this is quite superb! 40%. *Macduff International.*

Islay Mist Deluxe bott code L16/8283 (87) n22 t22 f21.5 b21.5 A charmingly brazen blend, offering young peat to you with far less reserve than it once did. More an Islay Fog than Mist... 40%. *MacDuff International Ltd.*

Islay Mist Peated Reserve bott code L15 9:67 (92.5) n23.5 t23 f22.5 b23.5 The accent is on subtlety and balance: a very classy piece of whisky engineering. 40%. *MacDuff International Ltd.*

Isle of Skye 8 Years Old (94) n23 t24 f23.5 b23.5. Where once peat ruled and with its grain ally formed a smoky iron fist, now honey and subtlety reigns. A change of character and pace which may disappoint gung-ho peat freaks but will intrigue and delight those looking for a more sophisticated dram. 40%. *Ian Macleod.*

Isle of Skye 21 years Old (91) n21 t23.5 f23 b23.5 What an absolute charmer! The malt content appears pretty high, but the overall balance is wonderful. *40%. Ian Macleod.*

Isle of Skye 50 Years Old (82.5) n21.5 t21 f20 b20. Drier incarnation than the 50% version. But still the age has yet to be balanced out, towards the end in particular. Early on some distinguished moments involving something vaguely smoked and a sweetened spice. *41.6%*

The Jacobite (78.5) n18 t18.5 f22 b20. Neither the nose nor delivery are of the cleanest style. But comes into its own towards the finish when the thick soup of a whisky thins to allow an attractive degree of complexity. Not for those with catholic tastes. *40%. Booker.*

James Alexander (85.5) n21 t21.5 f21.5 b21.5. Some lovely spices link the grassier Speysiders to the earthier elements. *40%. Quality Spirits International.*

James Buchanan's Special Reserve Aged 18 Years bott code: L7237CE001 **(89)** n22.5 t24 f20.5 b22 A blend I have known and admired a very long time. Since indeed, my beard was black and I carried not an extra ounce of weight. And I am still, I admit, very much in love with, though she has betrayed me with a Spanish interloper... *40%.*

James Buchanan's Special Reserve Aged 18 Years bott code: L0003CE001 **(95.5)** n24 t24 f23.5 b24 So understatedly complex and as always when free from any off-key sherry casks – as this is – sheer class...!!! *40%.*

James King (81) n20 t19.5 f21 b20.5 A slightly more well balanced and equally weighted blend than it once was with better use of spice and cocoa. *43%. Quality Spirits International.*

James King Aged 5 Years (84) n19.5 t21 f21.5 b21.5 While the nose never quite gets going, things are quite different on the palate. And if you find a more agreeable chocolate fudge blend this year, please let me know. *43%. Quality Spirits International.*

James King Aged 8 Years (86) n21 t21 f22 b22 A far better constructed blend than of old, with the grains far more able to deal with the demands of the caramel. Fresh and salivating early on, despite the lushness, one can even fancy spotting the odd malt note before the spiced fudge takes command. *43%. Quality Spirits International.*

James King 12 Years Old (81) n19 t23 f19 b20. Caramel dulls the nose and finish. But for some time a quite beautiful blend soars about the taste buds offering exemplary complexity and weight. *40%. Quality Spirits International.*

James King Aged 12 Years bott code B289 **(84.5)** n21 t22 f20.5 b21 The malt has a far grander say than the 40% version, chipping in with an elementary Speyside note on both nose and delivery. It doesn't take long for the fudge-rich grain to take command, though. Easy, un-taxing whisky. *43%. Quality Spirits International.*

J&B Jet (79.5) n19 t20 f20.5 b20. Never quite gets off the ground due to carrying too heavy a load. Unrecognisable to its pomp in the old J&B days: this one is far too weighty and never properly finds either balance or thrust. *40%. Diageo.*

J&B Reserve Aged 15 Years (78) n23 t19 f18 b18. What a crying shame. The sophisticated and demure nose is just so wonderfully seductive but what follows is an open-eyed, passionless embrace. Coarsely grain-dominant and unbalanced, this is frustrating beyond words and not worthy to be mentioned in the same breath as the old, original J&B 15 which, by vivid contrast, was a malty, salivating fruit-fest and minor classic. *40%. Diageo.*

J&B Rare (88.5) n21.5 t22.5 f22 b22.5 I have been drinking a lot of J&B from a previous time of late, due to the death of their former blender Jim Milne. I think he would have been pretty taken aback by the youthful zip offered here: whether it is down to a decrease in age or the use of slightly more tired casks – or both – is hard to say. *40%. Diageo.*

❖ **Jock MacDonald Blended Whisky** bott code: L20 Cb3 07469 **(88)** n22 t22.5 f21.5 b22 A charming, sweet, surprisingly malty (well, early on) blend which sets its stall out to offer the gentlest of rides. High grade grain and a light smattering of lemon blossom honey at the start makes up for the thinner, but spicier finale. Limited in scope, but enjoyable. *43%.*

John Barr Reserve Blend bott code: L9287 09:38 P/010214 **(84)** n21 t22 f20 b21 Never quite gels in the way I am now coming to expect from Whyte and Mackay blends. Lurches about both nose and palate as though unsure of which direction to take. The nose is a little raw, the finish bitter and lightly furry. The nuttiness between does have some attraction, though. *40%.*

Johnnie Walker Aged 18 Years bott code: L7276DN001 **(92)** n23 t23.5 f22 b23.5 "The Pursuit of the Ultimate 18 year old Blend," says the label under the striding man. Well, they haven't reached their goal yet as, for all its deliciousness, this falls short of true Johnnie Walker brilliance thanks to an overly soft grain usage, when it was crying out for a variation which included a firmer, ramrod straight grain for extra mouthfeel complexity, and give something for the malts to bounce off. That said, the extra but by no means over enthusiastic use of phenols ensures impressive depth to a genuinely lovely whisky. *40%.*

Johnnie Walker Black Label 12 Years Old bott code: L8217CA003 **(95)** n23.5 n24 f23.5 b24 Just another example of this blend being in tip-top form and showing a consistency which could almost make you weep with delight. The teasing phenols coupled with its salivating properties make for something rather special. *40%*.

⬧ **Johnnie Walker Black Label Aged 12 Years** bott code L1198CA003 **(95) n23** for the first time I can remember, Chivas 12 has out-nosed Black label 12 in a straight, literal, head to head. The subtlest apple note, one of the great features of this astonishing blend – almost a signature trait in fact - has gone missing here and instead we have just an extra rung of smokiness. **t24** the usual quite astonishing weight on delivery and then the breath-taking layering. Again the smoke arrives early and the malts play dizzying tune here: the sugars are honeyed and rich, moving between acacia and heather with ease....; **f24** one of the best finishes to any blend for such a long time. With the colour one naturally fears the caramels will reduce the complexity levels. But, nope! The smoke billows through in perfect unison with the pinging, bitty spices. And here the grains do a magnificent job as they are both crisp and soft, so at times sharpening the malt effect, at other times rounding it, especially when some liquorice tones begin to kick in...; **b24** as I have mentioned elsewhere, blended whisky isn't quite where it should be quality-wise. However, Black Label 12 has made no compromise in quality. And although, for the first time since I first wrote the Whisky Bible in 2003 Chivas 12 has come close to matching it for sheer elegance and élan, still the long stride of Johnnie Walker was able to see it over the finishing line. *40%* 🏆

Johnnie Walker Black Label Triple Cask Edition bott code: L8327CB009 **(92.5) n23 t23.5 f22.5 b23.5** Strange this should be in under the Black Label banner as it lacks the associated weight and delicate smokiness. Still silky and seductive, but much more naked grain on show. *40%*.

Johnnie Walker Blue Label (88) n21 t24 f21 b22 What a frustrating blend! Just so close to brilliance but the nose and finish are slightly out of kilter. Worth the experience of the mouth arrival alone. *43%*. Diageo.

Johnnie Walker Blue Label bott code: L0010DN007 **(86) n21.5 t23 f20 b21.5** The nose tells the story of this malt even without tasting: tune out of the sulphur-tainted fruit influence and the layering of the honey, vanillas, and lightly-peated malts is a masterpiece. And for a short while you can detect the same genius on the palate. But all that counts for little when the wine influence is so off key. Spotted a thinning of the oils, too, which does little to help the finish – and upon investigation see they have dropped the strength. Remains probably the most frustrating whisky in the world! *40%*.

Johnnie Walker Blue Label The Casks Edition (97) n24.5 t24.5 f23.5 b24.5. This is a triumph of scotch whisky blending. With not as much as a hint of a single off note to be traced from the tip of the nose to tail, this shameless exhibition of complexity and brilliance is the star turn in the Diageo portfolio right now. Indeed, it is the type of blend that every person who genuinely adores whisky must experience for the good of their soul....if only once in their life. *55.8%*.

Johnnie Walker Blue Label Ghost & Rare bott code: L8277DN006 **(96) n24 t24 f23.5 b24.5** There is nothing new about using dead distilleries within a blend. However, finding them in one as good as this is a pretty rare occurrence. This just creaks of old whiskies all over the show. And what a marvellous show this is...for me, far more entertaining than the standard Blue Label thanks to less sherry influence, allowing the whiskies themselves to show their talents fully. *43.8%*.

Johnnie Walker Double Black (94.5) n23 t23.5 f24 b24. Double tops! Rolling along the taste buds like distant thunder, this is a welcome and impressive addition to the Johnnie Walker stable. Perhaps not as complete and rounded as the original Johnnie Walker Black... but, then, what is? *40%*.

Johnnie Walker Double Black bott code: L9320CA008 **(94) n23.5 t23 f23.5 b24** A kiss-and-tell blend with the softness of the grains making this among the most gentle of the blend on the market today, with all its attributes, even the peat, no more than a caress... *40%*.

Johnnie Walker Explorers' Club Collection The Gold Route (89) n23.5 t24 f19.5 b22. Much of this blend is truly the stuff of golden dreams. Like its Explorer's Club stable mate, some attention has to be paid to the disappointing finish. Worth sending out an expedition, though, just for the beautiful nose and delivery... *40%*. Diageo.

Johnnie Walker Explorer's Club Collection 'The Royal Route' (93) n24.5 t24 f21.5 b23 A fabulous journey, travelling first Class most of the way. But to have discovered more, could have been bottled at 46% for a much more panoramic view of the great whiskies on show. *40%*. Diageo

Johnnie Walker Gold Label Reserve (91.5) n23 t24 f22 b23. Moments of true star quality here, but the finish could do with a polish. *40%*. Diageo.

Johnnie Walker Gold Label Reserve bott code: L9214DN005 **(91) n23 t24.5 f21.5 b22** A mixed bag of a bottling, with far more highs and lows than you'd normally find. Even so, the highs are of Everest proportions; *40%*.

Johnnie Walker King George V db **(88) n23 t22 f21 b22** One assumes that King George V is no relation to George IV. This has genuine style and breeding, if a tad too much caramel. *43%*

Johnnie Walker Platinum Label Aged 18 Years (88) n22 t23 f21 b22. This blend might sound like some kind of Airmiles card. Which wouldn't be too inappropriate, though this is more Business than First... *40%. Diageo.*

Johnnie Walker Red Label (87.5) n22 t22 f21.5 b22. The ongoing move through the scales quality-wise appears to suggest we have a work still in progress here. This sample has skimped on the smoke, though not quality. Yet a few months back when I was in the BA Business Lounge at Heathrow's new Terminal Five, I nearly keeled from almost being overcome by peat in the earthiest JW Red I had tasted in decades. I found another bottle and I'm still not sure which represents the real Striding Man. *40%. Diageo.*

Johnnie Walker Red Label bott code: L8329T5001 **(86) n21.5 t22 f21 b21.5** Seeing as I spend half my life travelling around the globe – or at least did until Covid-19 happened along – I probably get to taste Johnnie Walker Red more than any other blend as it is a staple of the world's Airline Lounges. And I must say it is rare to find two the same as the smoke levels can differ dramatically from one bottle to the next, sometimes peat-less, at other times seemingly not far off a thinned out Caol Ila. So I must say the Striding Man has become a bit of a friend and travelling companion to me. Which makes it all the more odd and ironic that the first time I actually sit down with a bottle of Red for the Whisky Bible for a year or two this is the first to display a furry note and tang. I have noticed that for the last year it had improved impressively, more often than not with a pleasing smoky rumble and on average from the dozen or so different bottles I've sampled from around the globe, a score something like an 89 world be nearer the mark. Only moderate peating to this and the caramels are just a little too enthusiastic: it is reminiscent of when the blend went through a wobble a couple of years back.... Bet you when I'm back travelling again, the first JW Red will be a belter....! *40%.*

Johnnie Walker Select Casks Aged 10 Years Rye Cask Finish (90) n22.5 t23 f21.5 b23 With the use of first fill bourbon casks and ex-rye barrels for finishing, hardly surprising this is the JW with the most Kentuckian feel of them all. Yet it's even more Canadian, still. *46% (92 proof).*

Johnnie Walker X.R Aged 21 Years (94) n23.5 t24 f23 b23.5. How weird: I nosed this blind before seeing what the brand was. My first thought was: "mmm, same structure of Crown Royal XR. Canadian??? No, there's smoke!" Then looked at what was before me and spotted it was its sister whisky from the Johnnie Walker stable. A coincidence? I don't think so... *40%.*

Kenmore Special Reserve Aged 5 Years bott code L07285 **(75) n18 t20 f19 b18.** Recovers to a degree from the poor nose. For those who prefer their Scotch big-flavoured and gawky. *40%*

Label 5 Aged 12 Years bott code L515467C **(90) n23 t22.5 f22 b22.5** One of the easiest drams you'll find this year with just enough complexity to lift it into the higher echelons. *40%.*

Label 5 Extra Rare Aged 18 Years bott code L5301576 **(87.5) n21.5 t22.5 f22 b21.5** You have to say this is pleasant. But from an 18-year-old blend you should be saying so much more. Salivating and at times fresh and juicy, other than the late spice little gets the pulses racing in the vanilla and sugar morass. A tad too much toffee, alas. *40%.*

Label 5 Classic Black bott code L403055D **(87) n22 t22 f21 b22** A malt famed for its indifferent nose now boasts an aroma boasting complexity, layering and spice. The mix of spice and muscovado sugars elsewhere is no less appealing, though the mouthfeel is a little too fat and yielding. But what an improvement! *40%. La Martiniquaise.*

Label 5 Gold Heritage (92) n22.5 t23.5 f22 b24 A very classy blend very skilfully constructed. A stunningly lovely texture, one of the very best I have encountered for a while, and no shortage of complexity ensures this is a rather special blend. I'll even forgive the dulling by caramel and light milkiness from the tired bourbon barrel. The overall excellence outweighs the odd blemish. *40%*

Label 5 Premium Black bott code: L720856A **(84.5) n21 t22 f20.5 b21** An, at first, luscious, then later on ultra-firm blend with the accent decidedly on the grain and caramels. *40%.*

Langs Full & Smoky (89) n22.5 t22.5 f21.5 b22.5 Light and smoky would be a more apt description. But a pleasant peaty blend all the same. *43%. Ian Macleod Distillers.*

Langs Rich & Refined (90) n23 beautiful structure to this: nutty and warming, vaguely spiced vanillas – offering both weight and lightness of touch simultaneously; **t22.5** the grains perhaps have the braver say even on delivery, but they are assisted by a glossy oiliness which bigs up the light thread of acacia honey. The midpoint has a distinctly Mars Bar feel of nougat, chocolate and caramel working in unison; **f22** mainly spices carried on the oils; **b22.5** a thoughtfully crafted, quietly complex blend. *46%. Ian Macleod Distillers.*

Langs Smooth & Mellow (88.5) n22.5 t22.5 f21.5 b22 No quibbling with the name of this brand! Most of the action is on the graceful nose and honey-flecked delivery which is briefly chewy. The dry and slightly bitter finish, though, doesn't try to compensate for the obvious lack in weight. That apart, agreeably easy going. *43%. Ian Macleod Distillers.*

The Last Drop 1965 American Standard Barrel **(96.5) n24 t24.5 f23.5 b24.5** Almost impossible to imagine a blended whisky to be better balanced than this. If there is a cleverer use of honey or less intrusive oak in any blended whisky bottled in the last year, I have yet to taste it. An award winner if ever I tasted one. Magnificent doesn't quite cover it... 48.6%. *Morrison Bowmore. The Last Drop Distillers Ltd.*

The Last Drop 1971 Blended Scotch Whisky 45 Years Old (97) n24.5 t24 f24 b24.5 Even though I now know many of the people involved in the Last Drop, I am still not entirely sure how they keep doing it. Just how do they continue to unearth whiskies which are truly staggering; absolute marvels of their type? This one is astonishing because the grain used is just about faultless. And the peating levels can be found around about the perfect mark on the dial. Like an old Ballantine's which has sat and waited in a cask over four decades to be discovered and tell its wonderful, spellbinding and never-ending tale. Just mesmerically beautiful. 47%.

The Last Drop 50 Year Old Sherry Wood (97) n24 t24.5 f24 b24.5 You'd expect, after half a century in the cask, that this would be a quiet dram, just enjoying its final years with its feet up and arms behind its head. Instead we have a fairly aggressive blend determined to drive the abundant fruitiness it still possesses to the very hilt. It is backed up all the way by a surprising degree of warming, busy spice. There is a hell of a lot of life in this beautiful ol' dog... 51.2%.

The Last Drop 56 Year Old Blended Scotch Whisky (96.5) n24.5 t24.5 f23.5 b24 Just one of those whiskies there is not enough time in the day for. One to share with your partner... when the lights are low and you are on your own... 47%.

Lauder's bott code L 08 10 14 4 BB (78.5) n19 t20 f19.5 b20 For those who like whisky with their cream toffee. Decent spice fizz, though. 40%. *MacDuff International Ltd.*

Lauder's Aged 15 Years bott code L16/8189 (93) n23 t23.5 f22.5 b24 Not the big fat sherry influence of a decade ago...thank heavens...!! This is a gorgeous blend for dark, stormy nights. Well, any night really... 40%. *MacDuff International Ltd.*

Lauder's Aged 25 Years bott code: P001434 2020/03/18 (91) n23 t23 f22 b23 After two months of incarceration in my British cottage, I moved my tasting room into the garden where the air was still and the whiskies seemed to be more at home: at one with nature. In the cloudless sky a pair of swifts danced for their prey above my garden, one, its head bleached white as it faced the setting sun; the other, as it twisted and turned, reflected the powerful, dying rays off its coal-black wings. To my left a pair of great tits flew to and from their secret chamber in "Mum's" ancient apple tree on their thankless task of feeding their brood. While, just 30 feet away, a crow sat atop a fir, bellowing his mastery over all he surveyed. Meanwhile, a blackbird chinked its evening alarm, much in the way robins do at home in Frankfort. So it was when Archibald Lauder created his first blend in the first half of the 19th century; and so it is now. The finest things in life never change... 42%. *Macduff International.*

Lauder's Oloroso Cask bott code L 25 01 16 4 BB (86.5) n21.5 t24 f19 b22 A magnificent blend for those unable to nose or taste sulphur. For those who can, a nearly whisky as this is borderline brilliant. Yes, both nose and finish especially have their weakness, but the narrative of the delivery, not to mention the brilliance of the mouthfeel and overall weight and pace of the dram is sublime. Before the sulphur hits we are treated to a truly glorious Jaffa cake mix of controlled fruity sweetness as good as any blend I have tasted this year. 40%. *MacDuff International Ltd.*

Lauder's Queen Mary bott code L 04 11 14 4 BB (86.5) n22.5 t21.5 f21 b21.5 The sweet oily aroma of Angel Cake and even some roast chestnut: the nose is certainly highly attractive. This almost translates through the body of blend when the caramel allows, the grains showing an oily strain and a slightly malty kick here and there. 40%. *MacDuff International Ltd.*

Liquid Treasures From Miles Away Taraansay 12 Year Old bourbon barrel, dist Apr 07, bott Feb 20 (92) n22.5 t23 f23 b23.5 A very pretty, flawlessly structured blend which milks every last degree of juiciness from mix of ulmo honey and light maple syrup which have been liberally sprinkled with spice. Not big on complexity, but knows how to maximise on effect, using the full body and delicate oils with aplomb. So lovely. 59.5%. sc. 249 bottles.

The Loch Fyne (89.5) n22 t23 f21.5 b23. This is an adorable old-style blend....a bit of a throwback. But no ruinous sherry notes...just clean and delicious. Well, mainly... 40%

Loch Lomond Reserve db (86.5) n21.5 t22 f21.5 b21.5. A spongy, sweet, chewy, pleasant blend which is more of a take as you find statement than a layering of flavour. 40%

Loch Lomond Signature bott code L3/306/15 (86) n22 t21.5 f21 b21.5 Not quite the malty force it can be, though the sugar almonds are a treat. Succulent and gently spiced though the caramel has just a little too much force towards the end. 40%. *Loch Lomond Group.*

Lombard Gold Label (88) n22 t22 f22 b22 after evaluating this I read the tasting notes on the back of the label and for about the first time this year thought: "actually, the bottlers have the description pretty spot on. So tasted it again, this time while reading the notes and found myself agreeing with every word: a first. Then I discovered why: they are my tasting notes from the 2007 Whisky Bible, though neither my name nor book have been credited... A gold label, indeed... 40%.

Long John Special Reserve bott code: 2017/08/10 **(87.5) n21.5 t22.5 f21.5 b22** An honest, non-fussy blend which makes a point of stacking the bigger flavours up front so it hits the ground running. The grains and toffee shape all aspects, other than this rich delivery where the malt offers both weight and a lighter, salivating quality also; an even a gentle thread of honey. The type of blend that an offer for a refill will be seldom refused. *40%.*

Lord Elcho (83.5) n20 t22 f21 b20.5 Such a vast improvement on the last bottling I encountered: this has lush grain at the front, middle and rear that entertains throughout, if a little one dimensionally. A little bit of a tweak and could be a high class blend. *40%. Wemyss Malts.*

Lord Elcho Aged 15 Years (89.5) n23.5 t22.5 f21.5 b22 Three or four years ago this was a 15-year-old version of the Lord Elcho standard blend today. So, small mercies, this has moved on somewhat and now offers up a genuinely charming and complex nose and delivery. One is therefore surprised to be disappointed by the denouement, taking into account the blend's history. Some more clever and attentive work on the middle and finish would have moved this into seriously high quality blend territory. But so much to enjoy as it is. *40%. Wemyss Malts.*

Lord Scot (77.5) n18.5 t20 f19.5 b19.5. A touch cloying but the mocha fudge ensures a friendly enough ride. *40%. Loch Lomond Distillers.*

The Lost Distilleries Blend batch 9 **(91) n23 t23.5 f22.5 b23** The distilleries may be lost to us, but on the palate they are especially at home. *52.1%. 476 bottles.*

Mac Na Mara bott code L 25 08 14 2 07 48 BB **(84) n21.5 t22 f19.5 b21** As usual, a glass of tricks as the flavours come tumbling at you from every direction. Few blends come saltier and the dry vanilla forges a fascinating balance with the rampant caramel. A fraction furry at the death. *40%. Pràban na Linne Ltd.*

Mac Na Mara Rum Cask Finish bott code L 23 05 16 3 BB **(86) n22.5 t22 f21 b21.5** Lost a degree of the sugary crispness normally associated with this brand and after the initial rum embrace resorts far too quickly to a caramel-rich game-plan. *40%. ncf. Pràban na Linne Ltd.*

Mac's Reserve bott code: L9C 7908 0711 **(84) n21 t21.5 f21 b20.5** Perfectly acceptable, easy going soft and sweet whisky. But if they really want to pay tribute to cooper Jimmy Mackie, the Mac in question, then they should drop the toffee and let the oak do the talking. *40%.*

MacArthur's bott code L16/L31 R16/5192 IB 1735 **(87.5) n21.5 t22 f21.5 b22.5** Not quite the tricky and cleverly smoked blend of a few years back. But still a weightier chap than a decade ago, not least because of the softer grain type. The malts do come through with just enough meaning to make for a well-balanced and thoroughly enjoyable offering. *40%.*

MacQueens (89) n21.5 t22.5 f22.5 b22.5. I am long enough in the tooth now to remember blends like this found in quiet country hotels in the furthest-flung reaches of the Highlands beyond a generation ago. A wonderfully old-fashioned, traditional one might say, blend of a type that is getting harder and harder to find. *40%. Quality Spirits International.*

MacQueens of Scotland Aged 3 Years (86) n20.5 t22 f21.5 b22 Rare to find a blend revealing its age at 3 years, though of course many are that.... and a day. Enjoyable, with attractive weight and even an ulmo honey note to partner the spices which, combined, makes it distinctively a cut above for its type. *40%. Quality Spirits International.*

MacQueens of Scotland Aged 8 Years (78.5) n18 t21.5 f19 b20 A little furry and off key. *40%. Quality Spirits International.*

MacQueens of Scotland Aged 12 Years (89.5) n23 t22.5 f21.5 b22.5 Some outstanding malts have gone into this charming blend. *40%. QSI.*

Master of Malt Blended 10 Years Old 1st Edition (84.5) n21.5 t22.5 f20 b20.5. A pleasant enough, though hardly complex, blend benefitting from the lovely malty, then silky pick-up from delivery and a brief juicy barley sharpness. But unsettled elsewhere due, mainly, to using the wrong fit of grain: too firm when a little give was needed. *47.5%. ncf. WB15/353*

Master of Malt 30 Year Old Blended Scotch Whisky (86) n21.5 t23 f20 b21.5 Typical of Master of Malt blends it is the delivery which hits fever pitch in which myriad juicy notes make a mockery of the great age. Sadly, on this occasion both the nose and finish are undone by some ungainly oak interference and, latterly quite a tang. *47.5%.*

Master of Malt 40 Year Old Blended Scotch Whisky batch 1 **(93.5) n24 t23.5 f22.5 b23.5** Some outstanding oak at play here. For a blend the grains and malts appear a little isolated from the other, but the overall effect is still wonderful. *47.5%.*

Master of Malt 50 Year Old Blended Scotch Whisky (92.5) n24 t23.5 f22 b23 Hard to keep all the casks of over 50 years in line. But so much else is sublime. *47.5%.*

Master Of Malt St Isidore (84) n21 t22 f20 b21. Sweet, lightly smoked but really struggles to put together a coherent story. Something, somewhere, is not quite right. *41.4%*

Matisse Aged 12 Years (88.5) n22 t22 f22 b22.5 Creamy and pleasant, the extra tannins appear to blot out the barley which impresses so well on their standard blend, making the grain here that little bit starker. Extra spice, naturally, with the age and depth. But not quite the same elegance. *40%. Matisse Spirits Company.*

⟨⟩ **Matisse Aged 12 Years (89.5) n22 t23 f22 b22.5** A good deal of fruit can be found on both nose and delivery, though always on the light, ethereal side. Indeed the aroma has a lot of freshly cut green apple and cucumber while lime blossom honey accounts for the satisfying sweetness on delivery. Some really good spices at play, too. Light, elegant and always broadcasting an alluring charm. *40%*

Matisse Aged 21 Years (80.5) n22 t22.5 f17 b19 The sulphur rumble on the finish does a dis-service to the chocolate raisin preamble. *40%. Matisse Spirits Company.*

⟨⟩ **Matisse Aged 21 Years (88) n22 t23 f21 b22** Although toffee and grain are poking through from every direction there is enough malt to ensure depth. The highlight, though, is the resounding, thick, honey-laden delivery, bolstered by beautifully weighted spice. The slightly untidy finish is not in keeping with the excellence of the delivery, though. Bold, chewy and always on the hefty side: a substantial blend. *40%*

Matisse Old Luxury Blend (92.5) n23 t23 f23 b23.5 ONe of those very classy blends you'd rather not spit out... At 46% would probably go up a point or two. *40%. Matisse Spirits Company.*

⟨⟩ **Matisse Old Luxury Blend (86) n21.5 t23 f20.5 b21.5** All the luxuriating comes in the brilliant delivery and follow through which is sumptuous and creamy, sweet and oily like the filling in a Swiss roll. The finish is a little threadbare and tangy by comparison and the nose grain reliant. But that delivery....wow! *40%. Matisse Spirits Company.*

Matisse Royal (81) n19 t22 f20 b20. Pleasant, if a little clumsy. Extra caramel appears to have scuppered the spice. *40%. Matisse Spirits Co Ltd.*

McArthurs (89.5) n22 t22.5 f22 b23 One of the most improved blends on the market. The clever use of the peat is exceptional. *40%. Inverhouse Distillers.*

McKendrick's 3 Years Old (71) n18 t20 f16 b17 "Supple, Strong and Silky" boasts the label. Unsubtle, standard 40% abv and silky says the whisky. Cloying to a degree and with a little sulphur off note late on, presumably from the ex-sherry grain casks. Not Asda's finest. *46%. Asda*

Monarch of the Glen (81) n20 t21 f20 b20 A youthful grainfest wallowing in its fat and sweet personality. *40%. Quality Spirits International.*

Monarch of the Glen Aged 8 Years (82.5) n19 t20.5 f21.5 b21.5 The initially harsh grain takes time to settle but eventually finds a decent fudge and spiced mocha theme. *40%. QSI.*

Monarch of the Glen Aged 12 Years (88.5) n22 t22.5 f22 b22 I always enjoyed this for its unusual fruity nature. Well, the fruit has gone and been replaced by chocolate. A fair swap: it's still delicious! *40%. Quality Spirits International.*

Muirhead's Blue Seal bott code L15 138 780 21 (84.5) n21.5 t21 f21 b21 A clean, uncluttered and attractive blend with heavy emphasis on grain and no shortage of caramel and spice. A distinct wisp of malt can be located from time to time. *40%. Tullibardine Ltd.*

The Naked Grouse (76.5) n19 t21 f17.5 b19. Sweet. But reveals too many ugly sulphur tattoos. *40%.*

Nation of Scots (92.5) n23 t23 f23 b23.5 Apparently, this is a blend designed to unite Scots around the world. Well, I'm not Scottish but it's won me over. If only more blends could be as deliciously embracing as this. *52%. Annandale Distillery.*

Northern Scot (68) n16 t18 f17 b17. Heading South bigtime. *40%. Bruce and Co. for Tesco.*

Oishii Wisukii Aged 36 Years (96) n24.5 t23.5 f24 b24 Normally, I'd suggest popping in the Highlander for a pint of beer. But if they happen to have any of this stuff there...break his bloody arm off: it's magnificent! *46.2%. The Highlander Inn, Craigellachie.*

Old Masters G (93) n24 t23 f23 b23 A high quality blend with enough clarity and complexity to suggest they have not stinted on the malt. The nose, in particular, is sublime. Thankfully they have gone easy on the colouring here, as it this is so delicate it could have ruined the artistry. *40%. Lombard Scotch Whisky Ltd.*

Old McDonald (83.5) n20 t22 f20.5 b21. Attractively tart and bracing where it needs to be with lovely grain bite. Lots of toffee, though. *43%. The Last Drop Distillers. For India.*

Old Parr 12 Years Old (91.5) n21.5 t23.5 f23 b23.5 Perhaps on about the fourth of fifth mouthful, the penny drops that this is not just exceptionally good whisky: it is blending Parr excellence... *40%. Diageo.*

Old Parr Aged 15 Years (84) n19 t22 f21 b22. Absolutely massive sherry input here. Some of it is of the highest order. The nose, reveals, however, that some isn't... *43%*

Old Smuggler (85.5) n21 t22 f21 b21.5. A much sharper act than its Allied days with a new honeyed-maple syrup thread which is rather delightful. Could still do with toning down the caramel, though, to brighten the picture further. *40%. Campari, France.*

Old St. Andrews Clubhouse batch no. L2997 G2716 (87.5) n21.5 t22 f22 b22 Just a little extra grain bite to this one means the usual juiciness is down, though the slow spice build is pretty sexy. Lots of coffee-toffee tones to chew over. *40%.*

Outlaw King bott code: L19 199 PB (90) n23 t22.5 f22 b22.5 More of an Outlaw Queen with a delicate but shapely body like this. And, indeed, once upon a time blends displaying this degree of naked peatiness were outlawed. Blenders veered away from smokiness after the Second World war to concentrate on lighter, softer creations. With smoke very much back in vogue it is great to see a blend shewing so little reserve in its peaty intent. *40%. Annandale Distillery.*

Passport bott code LKBL0720 2017/02/24 **(81.5) n20 t21 f20 b20.5** Still can't get used to the brash golden colour of the whisky that shines back at me. This was once the Passport to whisky sophistication: pale and glistening on the palate rather than from the bottle with its cut glass, precision flavour-profile – First Class in every way. Now it is fat, flat, chewy, and fudged in every sense of the word. *40%. Chivas Brothers Ltd.*

Passport bott 2019/08/11 **(83.5) n20 t21.5 f21 b21** Just a fleeting moment after the delivery when Jimmy Laing old masterpiece flashes onto the scene only to be quickly eviscerated by the uncompromising caramels. *40%*

Parkers (78) n17 t22 f20 b19. The nose has regressed, disappearing into ever more caramel, yet the mouth-watering lushness on the palate remains and the finish now holds greater complexity and interest. *40%. Angus Dundee.*

Pure Scot bott code: L 08 02 17 **(87) n21.5 t22.5 f21.5 b22** The grain is both yielding and profound while the malt notes mostly are lost in a toffee swirl. Mid to late arrives spices, but complexity is at a premium and the structure perhaps a little too soft. That said, a little acacia honey goes a long way and the overall experience is very satisfying indeed, especially with the sugars always slightly ahead of the game. *40%. Bladnoch Distillery.*

Pure Scot Virgin Oak 43 virgin oak cask finish, bott code: L18/89.7 **(93) n23 23.5 f23 b23.5** A sensational little blend worth finding. Not particularly complex as to regards malt and grain layering, but the integration of the tannins for a blend is a rare joy. *43%. Bladnoch Distillery.*

Queen Margot (85.5) n21.5 t22 f21 b21. A clean, silky-textured, sweet and caramel-rich blend of disarming simplicity. *40%*

Queen Margot (86) n21 t22 f21.5 b21.5. A lovely blend which makes no effort to skimp on a spicy depth. Plenty of cocoa from the grain late on but no shortage of good whiskies put to work. *40%. Wallace and Young for Lidl.*

Queen Margot Aged 5 Years (89) n22 t22.5 f22 b22.5 A very attractive blend with a most agreeable level of chewability. The chocolate orange which bolsters the yielding grain appears to suggest some good, clean sherry influence along the way. *40%*

Queen Margot Aged 8 Years (85) n21 t22 f21 b21. Pleasant, untaxing, with a hint of oaky vanilla after the sugary crescendo. *40%*

Richardson bott L9176028 **(85) N21 t21.5 f21 b21.5** A grain heavy gentle blend which emphasis sweetness over complexity. Charmingly clean, no off notes and super-easy drinking. *40%.*

Robert Burns (85) n20 t22.5 f21 b21.5. Skeletal and juicy: very little fat and gets to the mouthwatering point pretty quickly. Genuine fun. *40%. Isle of Arran.*

The Royal & Ancient (80.5) n20 t21.5 f19 b20. Has thinned out dramatically in the last year or so. Now clean, untaxing, briefly mouth-watering and radiating young grain throughout. *40%*

Royal Park (87.5) n22 t22 f22 b21.5 A significantly improved blend which though still showing toffee appears to have cut down the amount, to the advantage of the busy vanilla, Demerara sugar and increased spices. Wholly enjoyable. Incidentally, the label helpfully informs us: "Distilled and Matured in Oak Casks." Who needs stills, eh...? *40%. Quality Spirits International.*

Royal Salute 21 Years Old bott code LKSK2858 2016/07/13 **(96) n24 t23.5 f24 b24.5** Elegant, sensual and the epitome of great blending. What else would you expect...? *40%. Chivas Brothers.*

Royal Salute 21 Year Old The Lost Blend (95.5) n24 t24 f23.5 b24 Lost Blend...? Panic over, chaps: discovered it in my Whisky Bible tasting lab....!! And well worth finding, too.... *40%.*

Royal Salute 21 Years Old The Polo Collection bott code 2017/04/25 LPNL0722 **(95) n23.5 t23.5 f24 b24** A significantly different RS21 to the last standard bottling I came across, this being much meatier – which is rather apt seeing that horses are involved. Mixes suave sophistication with a certain ruggedness: not unlike polo, I suppose. Not a dram to chukka away under any circumstances... *40%. Chivas Brothers Ltd.*

Royal Salute 21 Year Old Polo Collection 3 (92) n23 t23.5 f22.5 b23 As soft as a velvet polo jumper... *46.5%.*

Royal Salute 25 Year Old The Signature Blend (93) n24 t23.5 f22.5 b23 A curious blend which both underlines its age, yet with the lightness of touch, then proceeds to hide it, too. *40%.*

Royal Salute 32 Years Old Union of the Crowns bott code 2017/01/17 LPNL0102 **(96.5) n24 t24.5 f24 b24** I trust Nicola Sturgeon has given The Union of Crowns, this truly outstanding and worthy Scotch blend to celebrate the joining the kingdoms of England, Scotland and Ireland, her seal of approval and she will help promote it fervently as a great Scottish export... *40%.*

Royal Salute 38 Years Old Stone of Destiny bott code 2016/12/20 LPNK2479 **(93.5)** n24 t23.5 f22.5 b23.5 Knowing the blender and having a pretty educated guess at the range of stocks he would have to work from, I tried to picture in my mind's eye how this whisky would nose and taste even before I opened the bottle. In particular, I tried to pre-guess the mouthfeel, a character vital especially in older blends but often overlooked by those who eventually taste it, though it actually plays a significant role without the drinker realising it. Well, both the nose and mouthfeel were just as I had imagined, though some aspects of the finish were slightly different. An engrossing and elegant dram. 40%. Chivas Brothers Ltd.

Royal Salute 62 Gun Salute (95.5) n24.5 t24 f23 b24 How do you get a bunch of varying whiskies in style, but each obviously growing a grey beard and probably cantankerous to boot, to settle in and harmonise with the others? A kind of Old People's Home for whisky, if you like. Well, here's how...43%. Chivas.

Royal Salute The Diamond Tribute (91) n23.5 t23 f21.5 b23. Ironic that a diamond is probably the hardest natural creation, yet this whisky is one of man's softest... 40%. Chivas.

Royal Salute The Eternal Reserve (89.5) n23 t23.5 f21 b22 One of those strange whiskies where so much happens on the nose and delivery, but much less when we head to the finish 40%

Royal Silk Reserve Aged 5 Years (92.5) n23 t23 f23 b23.5 I was lucky enough to be the first person outside the tasting lab to sample this whisky when it was launched at the turn of this century. It was quite wonderful then, it still is so today though the grains aren't quite as brittle and translucent as they were back then. Still, I admire beyond words the fact that the current blenders have eschewed the craze for obscuration by ladelling in the colouring as though lives depended on it. What we can nose and taste here in this heart-gladdeningly light (both in colour and personality) blend is whisky. As an aside, very unusual for a blend to hide its age away on the back label. 40%.

Royal Warrior (86) n21 t22 f21.5 b21.5. An entirely pleasant grain-rich, young, old fashioned blend which masters the prevalent sugars well when they appear to be getting out of hand. Extremely clean and beautifully rounded. 40%

Sandy Mac (76) n18 t20 f19 b19. Basic, decent blend that's chunky and raw. 40%. Diageo.

Scots Earl (76.5) n18 t20 f19 b19.5. Its name is Earl. And it must have upset someone in a previous life. Always thrived on its engaging disharmony. But just a tad too syrupy now. 40%.

Scottish Collie (78) n18 t20 f20 b20 I thought I heard you saying it was a pity: pity I never had any good whiskies. But you're wrong. I have. Thousands of them. Thousands of them. And all drams.... 40%. Quality Spirits International.

Scottish Collie (80) n20 t21 f19 b20 A greatly improved blend with a far more vivacious delivery full of surprising juiciness and attractively controlled sweetness. Not as much toffee influence as had once been the case, so the spices cancels out the harsh finish. 43%. QSI.

Scottish Leader Aged 12 Years bott code P037533 L3 09.18 16082 **(89.5)** n22 t23 f22 b22.5 A vast improvement on the last Leader 12 I encountered, this really finding a relaxed yet intriguing style. 40%.

Scottish Leader Original bott code P03 555 L 08.35 16342 **(83)** n19 t22 f21 b21 Had this been the "original" Scottish leader I tasted 20 or so years ago we'd have a lighter coloured, less caramel heavy, more malt sparkling whisky. As it is, overcomes a cramped nose to offer some excellent complexity on delivery. 40%.

Scottish Leader Signature bott code P038914 L316256 **(90.5)** n22 t23.5 f22 b23 Thoroughly enjoyable and beautifully constructed blend in which thought has clearly gone into both weight, texture and flavour profiling: not a given for blends these days. The nose and delivery are waxy with a vague honey richness; the delivery uses that honey to full effect by offering a growing firmness and then busy interplay between light oak, spices and weightier malts. Had they gone a little easier on the dumbing-down toffee, this might have bagged an award. 40%.

Scottish Leader Supreme bott code P039255 L3 14.21 16278 **(77)** n18.5 t20 f19 b19.5 Sticky, sweet and overly simple. 40%.

Scottish Piper (80) n20 t20 f20 b20. A light, mildly- raw, sweet blend with lovely late vanilla intonation. 40%

Scottish Piper bott code L17033 **(82)** n20 t20 f21.5 b20.5 Continues its traditional toffee drone, though with a spicier finale than before. 40%. Burlington Drinks.

Scottish Piper Blended Scotch Whisky bott code: L20205 **(88)** n22 t22.5 f21.5 b22 A light smoke accompaniment drones long into the delivery like the bagpipes depicted on the quaint label. These phenols are easily detected on the nose, too, ensuring a satisfying weight and a malty countenance to balance out of the firm young grain. Might be stretching it to say this is complex, but it is still very highly satisfying... 40%

Scottish Prince (83.5) n21 t22 f20 b20.5. Muscular, but agreeably juicy. 40%

Sia Blended Scotch Whisky (87) n21 t22.5 f21.5 b22. Rare to find a blend that's so up front with its smoke. Doesn't scrimp on the salivation stakes or sheer chewiness, either. 43%

Sir Edward's Aged 12 Years bott 18-09-2018, bott code: L826170-00150 **(87.5)** n22 t22 f21.5 b22 Worth having around the house for the charming 1930s's-style label alone. They make big play of the brand having been around since 1891 – the year of my maternal grandmother's birth! – and even have 1891 included in the mould of the bottle. But an unnecessary over-reliance of caramel takes the score down. There is enough evidence on the early clarity and texture of the grain that this blend could hold its own and entertain thoroughly in its natural state. Rather lovely spices counter the sweetness impressively. Simple, but genuinely enjoyable whisky. 40%. Bardinet.

Sir Edward's Aged 12 Years Blended Whisky bott code: L104670 15/02/2021 **(88)** n22 t23 f21 b22 A slight improvement on the last bottling, mainly through a very slight injection of smoke into a blend that appears predisposed towards phenols. Again, the caramel brings the score down slightly. But when you add the light saltiness together with the heather honey on delivery, plus spice and additional smoke, you cannot but conclude that this is a more than satisfactory blend. 40%.

Sir Lawrence bott code: L17 03274 CB2 **(87)** n21 t22.5 f21.5 b22 An impressively clean blend having been matured in better quality oak. This allows you to enjoy the full-throttle delivery without fear of any tangy, off-note sub plots. The caramels do get a little too enthusiastic towards the end but before then the grain and Demerara sugars dig in for a delicious degree of mocha. 40%.

Sir Lawrence Original bott code: L2007792CB1 **(87)** n21.5 t22.5 f21.5 b21.5 A little malt has gone a long way here, perhaps reflecting the excellence of the grain at work. A little toffeed, perhaps, but the vanilla impresses mightily, as does the early jam doughnut sweetness. Clean and lip-smacking. 40%

Sir Edward's Finest Blended Whisky bott code: L027272-025111 **(83.5)** n20.5 t21.5 f20.5 b21 Doesn't quite reach the heights as their very acceptable 12-year-old either in finding its balance or narrative. Nothing wrong with the delivery, though, which makes the most of a satisfying mouth feel. 40%.

Sir Edward's Smoky Blended Whisky nbc **(93)** n23 I admit it: this is a far better nose than I expected. Very good grain means minimal interference and maximum softening of the gentle phenols that steadily build in depth; t23.5 brilliant! A near perfect match between the peat and young grain means the phenols literally melt in the mouth on arrival while the smoke is followed by the most pleasing Demerara sugars. And what a delivery! Sweet, fresh and salivating...just too rare in blended whisky these days; f23 a longer finish than it first seems: once more the grains are top notch, ensuring a lulling softness and an unrestricted view of the light oak. The slow build of spice is rather glorious and more than enough to make do with... b23.5 it is quite amazing what some judiciously added peat can do to an otherwise standard blend. I doff my hat here: the phenol levels are exactly where they need to be to maximise complexity and balance. Excellent. 40%.

Something Special bott code LPFK 1116 2016/06/30 **(90)** n22 t22.5 f23 b22.5 One of the few blends that has actually improved in recent years. Always been an attractive, interesting if non-spectacular blend which I have enjoyed when meeting it at various bars with friends around the world. Now there is personality enough to punch through the toffee and leave you wanting more. 40%. Chivas Brothers Ltd.

Something Special Legacy (92) n23 t22.5 f23 b23.5 Good, solid blender is David Boyd. And here he has married substance with subtlety. Lovely stuff. 40%

The Sovereign 45 Years Old Blended Scotch cask no. 15894, dist Dec 73, bott Mar 19 **(94.5)** n23.5 t23.5 f24 b23.5 Falls under the luxuriant heading for a blended scotch. Soft, silky and unravels at the most gentle of paces. 51%. sc. 300 bottles. Bottled for The Whisky Barrel.

Stag Hunter (79) n19 t20 f20 b20 Hard to get past the gin-type nose. Not sure if this is a bottling hall issue, or if we have a blend that celebrates a botanical-style personality. 40%.

Stag Hunter L17039 **(79)** n20.5 t20 f19 b19.5 A very basic blend which struggles to get past the grain and toffee. The bitterish finish leaves a little to be desired. 40%

Storm (94) n23 t23.5 f24 b23.5. A little gem of a blend that will take you by storm. 43%.

Teacher's Aged 25 Years batch 1 **(96.5)** n24 t24.5 f23.5 b24.5 Only 1300 bottles means they will be hard pushed to create this exact style again. Worth a go, chaps: considering this is India bound, it is the Kama Sutra of blended scotch. 46%. Beam Inc. 1300 bottles. India & Far East Travel Retail exclusive.

Teacher's Origin (92) n23 t23 f23 b23 Almost brings a tear to the eye to taste a Scotch blend that really is a blend. With a better grain input (Dumbarton, say),this perhaps would have been one of the contenders of World Whisky of the Year. Superb! 40%.

Teacher's Origin (88.5) n22 t23.5 f21 b22 A fascinating blend among the softest on the market today. That is aided and abetted by the exceptionally high malt content, 65%, which makes this something of an inverted blend, as that, for most established brands, is the average grain content. What appears to be a high level of caramel also makes for a rounding of the edges, as well as evidence of sherry butts. The bad news is that this has resulted in a duller finish than perhaps might have been intended, which is even more pronounced given the impressive speech made on delivery. Lovely whisky, yes. But something, I feel, of a work in progress. Bringing the caramel down by the percentage points of the malt would be a very positive start... *42.8%. ncf.*

Té Bheag bott code L 06 12 16 3 **(83) n19 t22 f21 b21** Reverted to its mucky nose of yore but though caramel has the loudest voice it has retained its brilliant spice bite. *40%. ncf.*

Tesco Special Reserve Minimum 3 Years Old bott code L6335 16//04171 **(83.5) n19 t22 f21.5 b21** Improved of late. Now unashamedly in the date and walnut school of blends, where before it had only dabbled; thick, uncompromisingly sweet and cloying but with enough spice and salivation to make for pleasant and characterful bit of fun. *40%.*

Ushers Green Stripe (85) n19 t22.5 f21.5 b22. Upped a notch or two in all-round quality. The juicy theme and clever weight is highly impressive and enjoyable. *43%. Diageo.*

Walton Royal Blend Deluxe Reserve (91.5) n22.5 t23 f23 b23 It's amazing what a dose of good quality peaty whisky can do to a blend. Certainly ensures it stands out as a deliciously chewy – and smoky – experience.*43%*

◈◈ **Waitrose Three-Year-Old** bott code: L1089P/015330 **(87) n21.5 t22 f21.5 b22** A very friendly whisky which is rounded in all the right places and fills the mouth with sugars and spices in a pleasing manner. Definitely too caramel dependent, but beyond the toffee – and attendant coffee – there is a delightful sweet-dry interplay. Perfectly enjoyable. *40%*

◈◈ **Waitrose 8 Years Old Aged in Bourbon Casks** bott code: L120121 **(89) n22.5** light smoke drifts above the noisy toffee; **t23** brilliant delivery with phenols upfront and giving weight to a silky, grain-led arrival which offers growing complexity as the malts arrive; **f22** the dates and walnut finish is typical of an overly darkened blend...a little in the old Whyte & MacKay style, though more smoke and spice evident on this blend; **b21.5** cut the caramel and this would be a stupendous blend. Sadly, the complexity can barely be found for toffee. Even so, still a thoroughly enjoyable dram. But so frustrating when it could so easily be on another level altogether... *40% In partnership with Ian MacLeod*

Whisky Works Quartermaster 11 Year Old Blended Scotch 2019/WV02./MX bott code: L9263 09:08 P/010456 **(89) n24 t24 f19 b22** There is malt, malt, juicy to a fault, in the blend, in the blend....there is grain, grain, that proves to be a pain, in the Quartermaster's Blend. My eyes are dim, I cannot see, I'm glad I brought my nose with me. I'm glad I brought my nose with me... *46.4%. nc ncf. 1,593 bottles.*

White Horse (90.5) n22 t23 t22.5 b23 A malt which has subtly changed shape. Not just the smoke which gives it weight, but you get the feeling that some of Diageo's less delicate malts have been sent in to pack a punch. As long as they are kept in line, as is the case here – just – we can all enjoy a very big blend. *40%. Diageo.*

White Horse (94.5) n24 t23.5 f23 b24 A masterclass in how to use peat with precision to both raise the profile and complexity of a blend giving it both weight and gravitas, but never allowing it to pompously govern or overwhelm the myriad little other battles going on in the glass. A real old school blend which, I admit, is one I am drawn to when watching old black and white British movies. A charming taste of true tradition. *40%*

White Horse Aged 12 Years (86) n21 t23 f21 b21. Enjoyable, complex if not always entirely harmonious. For instance, the apples and grapes on the nose appear on a limb from the grain and caramel and nothing like the thoroughbred of old. Lighter, more flaccid and caramel dominated. *40%. Diageo.*

White Walker bott code: L8282KS002 **(80) n19 t22.5 f19 b20.5** Pouring from the top. As you might expect, there is no nose when frozen, other than the vaguely discernible, ultra clean tip of the grain. The big surprise is that there is a decent degree of flavour on delivery – again the grains at work and carrying a presentable amount of Demerara sweetness and here's the real shock...a very thick, chewable, oily body. So, early on, much more character than I expected. But the finish is as non-specific as I had feared and trails off with a certain bitterness. OK, that was it unshaken, and pouring from the top:

◈◈◈ Now shaken: **(85.5) n19.5 t22 f22 b22** By shaking before pouring. You lose some of the early richness of the body. But there is a degree of oak on the aroma and the delivery and the sugars now last the pace, spreading more evenly over the scattered oils. There are now even spices at work late on in this much better-balance dram. *41.7%. Both tasted direct from the freezer (directly after two days at sub-zero temperatures) as instructed on the bottle.*

◈◈◈ Tasted Murray Method: bott code: L8282KS002 **(90) n22 t23 f22.5 b22.5** A surprisingly agile and entertaining blend. Untaxing, clean, pleasantly sweet and just so easy to enjoy. *41.7%.*

Whyte & Mackay bott code: P/011524 01:36 L0049 **(88.5) n22 t22.5 f21.5 b22.5** Very few things in life don't change over time. But I have to say the extraordinary lushness of character of a Whyte and MacKay is one of them. Maybe I'm imagining things, but it seems to have taken its foot off the caramel slightly, allowing the malts and grains in particular to showcase their wares with a little extra confidence. The result is a subtly sweeter dram, the date and walnut cake – the blend's signature tune – still there in all its glory, but the extra vanillas of the grain in particular, slightly extra succulence of the malt both both making their mark. Toasty and tasty at the finish, this is a blend that is moving almost imperceptibly towards sunnier ground. The dullest of sulphur notes on the finish prevents this from scoring even more highly: my guess it is from old sherry butts used to store the grain. But I refuse to let that spoil the overall enjoyment of this blend, of which there is much. 40%.

⊰⊱ **Whyte & Mackay** bott code: L1132 P/015613 **(83.5) n22 t22.5 f18 b21** Please see the notes for my last tasting, a year ago, above. Much more sulphur on the finish this time round, which is a shame as the build-up mirrors the excellence of my last experience. These disappointing finishes are a bit of a case of Russian Roulette: most probably the unforeseen consequence of aging grain in old sherry butts. No blaming the blender here. 40%

Whyte & Mackay Aged 13 Years bott code L6334 14/04116 **(89.5) n22 t23.5 f22 b22** Like the standard Whyte and Mackay...but thirteen years old and a little lighter... 40%.

Whyte & Mackay Aged 50 Years (96) n24.5 t24 f23.5 b24 Age issues from every pore of this blend like sweat from a long-distance runner. And this certainly has travelled a distance, as I get the feeling some of the whiskies here are well beyond their 50th birthday. A classy blend which give you the feeling of the great age like a sports car fills you with sensations of power and speed. 44.6%. 175th Anniversary.

Whyte & Mackay Triple Matured bott code 16/04120 L6329 **(86.5) n21 t23.5 f20.5 b21.5** The kind of blend you can not only stand your spoon up in but your knife - table or carving - and fork – table or pitch - as well. The nose suggests something furry is in the offing which, sadly, the finale confirms. But the delivery really is such wonderful fun! Thick with intense toffee, which shapes both its flavour and mouthfeel, and concentrated date and walnut cake. Roasty yet sweet thanks to the molasses this is about the chewiest blend on the market today. 40%.

William Cadenhead's 20 Year Old Blend batch no. 3 **(91.5) n23 t23.5 f22 b23** There are a depressingly withering number of us who used, each year, to head to Campbeltown not to visit the distilleries - you couldn't then gain access – but to find the Cadenhead blends which had a truly unique character and offered something no other blend could get remotely near to. Indeed, I remember driving back once not with a boot full or Springbank but blended malt that I knew would get my whisky loving friends to see this type of whisky in an entirely new light. So my heart skips a beat at the sight of Cadenhead blend in a way few others these days might – we are talking close on 40 years of memories here. The grains on this one are sublime, offering both softness and rigid backbone (a style now criminally rare) but 35 years ago there was no sulphur to worry about on the sherry butts. Here a little has crept in, visible on the finish. A shame, as biting freshness on the grape early on is a salivating joy; the determined firmness of the grain to control it, a whisky lovers delight. 46%.

William Lawson bott code: L19182ZA80 **(87) n21.5 t22 f21.5 b22** A heady, honeyed dram which puts far more emphasis on weight than most blends out there these days. The caramels do gang up momentarily, but the overall score boasts harmony...and even more honey...!! 40%.

The Woodsman freshly built oak casks & double-scorched bourbon barrels, bott code: L0118 22:04 P/011830 **(92.5) n23** highly attractive vanilla layering with a degree of covert smokiness cleverly weighing anchor. The toffee tones are restrained; **t23** the grain ensures the flavours stick around for maximum time and achieve top billing. This is lightly oiled silk making every last atom of the heather honey count for the positive. The mid-ground heads towards nuttiness with a cocoa and marzipan depth; **f23** a gorgeous chocolate toffee/butterscotch tart hybrid, all served up on those stunning grainy oils; **b23.5** one of the things so often overlooked in a whisky is the mouthfeel. The label of this blend talks much about the wood types. But the reason they work so well is because they have created a structure to the whisky which allows you to explore those flavours to their maximum. A kind of Whyte and MacKay, but with extra depth. Very impressed! 40%.

⊰⊱ **The Woodsman** L1048 **(94) n23 t23.5 f23.5 b24** This made such an impressive debut last year I wanted to check it wasn't just beginner's luck. Not a bit of it: a Woodsman certainly not deserving the axe... This still retains one of the best mouth feels of any whisky I have encountered this year. Where it scores the extra points this time is the most brilliant and discerning use of slightly extra smoke which in turn makes both the spice and cocoa notes work that little more efficiently. What an absolute treat of a blend, and one not shy to show off its malty credentials. One of those blends which if you see... just grab it!!! 40%

Irish Whiskey

Of all the whiskies in the world, it is Irish which probably causes most confusion amongst both established whisk(e)y lovers and the novices.

sk anyone to define what is unique to Irish whiskey - apart from it being made in Ireland and the water likewise coming from that isle - and the answer, if the audiences around the world at my tastings are anything to go by, are in this order: i) it is triple distilled; ii) it is never, ever, made using peat; iii) they exclusively use sherry casks; iv) it comes from the oldest distillery in the world; v) it is made from a mixture of malted and unmalted barley.

Only one of these answers is true: the fifth. Though other countries are now paying the compliment of aping this style.

And it is this type of whiskey, Irish Pot Still, which has dominated the Irish Awards in the Whisky Bible for the past 18 years, not to mention the minds and palate of whiskey lovers. I well remember in the 1990s Irish Distillers actually turning their backs on this profound and purest form of Irish, regarding it too big in style for the marketplace; and had actually withdrawn Redbreast, leaving only an old Irish wine merchant to carry the style with their Green Spot brand, which I happily championed around the world to wake people up to what they were missing. Also, I managed to get Irish Distillers to ensure Jameson restore the Pot Still character that had been lost since at least the 1960s. The irony is that now there is a range of magnificent Pot Still whiskeys that can be found, perhaps to furnish this new and grateful market, Jameson has again lost the fabulous Pot Still backbone which had made it an essential whiskey to have about the home: certainly for one reason or another, it is nowhere near as telling as it once was. My Irish eyes aren't smiling...

Jim Murray's Whisky Bible Irish Whiskey of the Year Winners

	Irish Whiskey	Irish Pot Still Whiskey	Irish Single Malt	Irish Blend
2009	Jameson 07	N/A	N/A	N/A
2010	Redbreast 12	N/A	N/A	N/A
2011	Sainsbury's Dun Leire 8	N/A	N/A	N/A
2012	Powers John's Lane	N/A	Sainsbury's Dun Leire 8	N/A
2013	Redbreast 12 Year Old	Redbreast 12 C.Strength	Bushmills Aged 21	Jameson
2014	Redbreast 12 C.Strength	Redbreast 12 C.Strength	Bushmills Aged 21	Jameson
2015	Redbreast Aged 21	Redbreast Aged 21	Bushmills Aged 21	Jameson
2016	Midleton Dair Ghaelach	Midleton Dair Ghaelach	SMWS 118.3 Cooley 1991	Powers Gold Label
2017	Redbreast Aged 21	Redbreast Aged 21	Bushmills Aged 21	Jameson
2018	Redbreast Aged 21	Redbreast Aged 21	Bushmills Aged 16	Bushmills Black Bush
2019	Redbreast 12 C.Strength	Redbreast 12 C.Strength	Bushmills Aged 12	Bushmills Black Bush
2020	Redbreast 12 C.Strength	Redbreast 12 C.Strength	Bushmills Aged 21	Jameson
2021	Midleton Barry Crockett	Midleton Barry Crockett	Bushmills Port Cask Reserve	Bushmills Black Bush
2022	Ash Tree Bushmills 30 Year Old	N/A	Ash Tree Bushmills 30 Year Old (SC)	Bushmills Black Bush

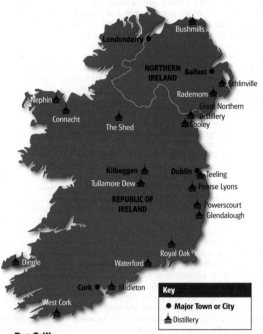

Pure Pot Still

DINGLE County Kerry. 2012. Porterhouse Group.

Dingle Pot Still Third Release db (93.5) n23.5 t23.5 f23 b23.5 This is a very impressive pot still whiskey, by which I assume they mean there is unmalted barley. Truly wonderful and can't wait to see this mature into something rather special... 46.5%. ncf. 3,400 bottles.

KILBEGGAN County Westmeath. 1757, recommended distilling 2007. Beam Suntory.

Kilbeggan Single Pot Still Irish Whiskey bott code: L19130 05/12/19 db (89.5) n23 though the cut is generous, the honeys arrive in force – heather honey leading the pack. There is even a sweetened eucalyptus note, as well as an underlying earthiness; t22.5 the oils from that cut gang-up early to giving that earthiness flavour form. Again, the heather honey makes an impact, especially with the thick oils, then a blossoming maltiness takes hold; f21.5 some caramels filter through and dampen But the oils buzz and the malt and honey duet can still be heard above the background hubbub; b22.5 the closest Pot Still to the last days of the old Jameson Distillery in Dublin I have ever tasted: this could be Redbreast from the late 1980s. 43%.

MIDLETON County Cork. 1975. Irish Distillers.

Green Spot bott code L622831252 db (95) n23.5 t23.5 f24 b24 A slightly different weight, pace and sugar emphasis to this bottling. But remains a true classic. 40%.

Green Spot bott code: L921031490 db (94) n24 t24 f23 b23 What a beautiful whiskey. If they could cut down on the pointless over-emphasis on the caramel and up the strength, they'd have a contender for World Whisky of the Year... 40%.

Green Spot Château Léoville Barton finished in Bordeaux wine casks, bott code L622331248 db (79) n20 t22 f18 b19 I'd desperately like to see this work. But, once again, far too tight and bitter for its own good. The damaging sulphur note is worthy of neither the great Green Spot or Leoville Barton names... 46%.

Green Spot Chateau Montelena Zinfandel wine cask finished, bott code: L719331280 db (88) n23 t23.5 f19.5 b22 There is something fitting that Green Spot, an Irish Pot Still whiskey brand created many generations back by Dublin's Premier wine merchants, should find itself creating new ground...in a wine cask. Any European whisk(e)ys matured in American wine casks are thin on the ground. That they should be Chateau Montelena from Napa Valley makes this all the more remarkable. Does it work? Well, yes and no. The unique style of Irish Pot Still is lost

257

somewhat under a welter of fruity blows and the fuzzy, imprecise finish is definitely off key. But there is no denying that it is a whiskey which does possess the odd magic moment. *46%*.

Green Spot Chateau Montelena finished in Zinfandel wine casks, bott code: L921931293 db **(89.5)** n23 t23.5 f21 b22 Pleasant enough, for sure. But a slight gripe that the unique Pot Still character has been over-run by the exuberance of the grape... *46%*.

Method and Madness Single Pot Still bourbon & sherry barrels, finished in Acacia wood, bott code: L91931458 db **(95)** n23.5 t23.5 f24 b24 A Pot Still creation that just gets better and better the linger you taste it. A brilliant and quite adorable exhibition of one-upmanship and profile development. *46%. ncf. Bottled exclusively for Celtic Whiskey.*

Method and Madness Single Pot Irish Whiskey bourbon barrels, finished in Virgin Hungarian oak **(94)** n23 t23.5 f23.5 b24 Now there was a nose! One that took me back almost 25 years to when I was visiting the Czech whisky distilleries soon after the fall of the communist regime. That whisky was matured in local oak, offering a near identical aroma to this Irish. *46%*.

Method and Madness Single Pot Still bourbon & sherry barrels, finished in wild cherry wood, bott code: L919831459 db **(96)** n24 the cherry wood oozes from every molecule. Significantly, though, so, too does the Pot Still. This is the type of clean nose, that could happily spend an hour with if I had the time. Or make love to, had I energy...Sexy, sexy stuff...; t24 rigid Pot Still – just like the old days!!! So wonderful when the Pot Still personality isn't slaughtered in the sacrificial slab of sherry. Barley crunches its way through the gears, as does a lovely Demerara undercurrent; f24 long, distinguished, increasingly well spiced and the cherry wood won't be outdone as here is a now telling tannin note, something quite apart from oak. Still, though the crunchy sugars and barley grains to their thing. Method. Madness. Majestic...; b24 one of the most flavoursome whiskies of the Whisky Bible 2021. A true joy to experience! Billy Leighton, I could give you a kiss! I may well have just tasted Irish Whiskey of the Year... *46%. ncf.*

Method and Madness Single Pot Still Irish Whiskey sherry & American barrels, finished in French chestnut casks db **(88)** n22 t23 f21 b22.5 Ah...memories of the late 1970s or perhaps very early '80s. Walking in the lonely winterish forests surrounding the tiny French village of Evecquemont, taking my girlfriend's soppy Alsatian for long walks, during which I would hoover up wild sweet chestnuts by the score. Never then figured it playing a part in whisky, especially Irish. Not sure it is the perfect marriage, but certainly adds to the whiskey lexicon. *46%*.

Midleton Barry Crockett Legacy American bourbon barrels, bott code L623631258 db **(95)** n23.5 t24 f23.5 b24 Thank God for my dear old friend Barry Crockett. One of the top three most knowledgeable whiskey/whisky people I have known in my lifetime, you can at least be relieved that his name is synonymous with a truly great spirit. Fittingly, his whiskey is free of sherry butts, so I can just sit back and enjoy and not be on tenterhooks waiting for the first signs of a disastrous sulphur note to take hold. Indeed, the only thing that takes hold of you here is the Pot Still's stunning beauty... *46%. ncf.*

Midleton Barry Crockett Legacy American bourbon cask, bott code: L918431409 db **(96.5)** n24 t24.5 f23.5 b24.5 It has been my privilege and honour to have known Barry Crockett slightly over 30 years now. He, 'I and the late, much missed blender Barry Walsh championed Irish Pot still at a time when it had very much gone out of favour and the higher powers within the industry did not care one way or another if it vanished altogether. These were in days when all the Irish Pot still being used came from casks entirely free from sulphur treatment and the unique grain could be seen in all its naked glory...and what a gorgeous, passion rising stunner it was. There is now a generation within the industry who have never tasted wholly clean, unspoiled Pot Still and (from conversations I have had with them around the world) think that a tangy, bitter finish is part of its natural profile. It isn't and here you can see a style not entirely unknown three decades back. Though of the many samples of Pot Still I looked at with Barry Walsh, I don't remember any coming from bourbon that had this degree of fruitiness. Murray Method style of tasting essential here to maximise sweetness, as the sugars are the key to this easily underrated Irish. *46%. ncf.*

Midleton Dair Ghaelach Grinsell's Wood Ballaghtobin Estate American bourbon barrels, finished in Irish oak hogsheads, batch no. 1, tree no. 7, bott code L504031020 db **(97.5)** n24 t25 f24 b24.5 What we have here, if I'm not very much mistaken, is a potential World Whisky of the Year. Rarely these days am I given an entirely new flavour profile to chew on. Not only do I have that, but I am struggling to find any faults at all. Ireland is not known for its mountains: well, it certainly has one now. *57.9%. ncf.*

Powers Aged 12 Years John's Lane Release bott code L623731261 **(96)** n23.5 t24.5 f23.5 b24.5 A slightly different slant on the toffee and fudge – and now has a degree of rye-recipe bourbon about it - but firmly remains the go to Pot Still of quite staggering beauty. *46%. ncf.*

Powers John's Lane Release American oak casks, bott code: L920631479 db **(83)** n21 t22 f19 b21 Ah, great!! Matured in American oak. So, for once, no sulphur then. I taste and there, on the finish (confirming what I hadn't wanted to believe on the nose), unmistakably the grim reaper of whiskey itself: sulphur notes. How come? Grabbed the bottle and read the blurb. Not just American oak. But Iberian, too. I must teach my staff to read the small print. With whiskey, like in life, there are many catches to be found... Hold on for a toffee and sulphur ride all the way. *46%. ncf.*

Powers Signature Release bott code L433231240 (**87.5**) **n21 t23 f21.5 b22** A much lazier version of this excellent Pot Still than I have become used to. Far too much fudge at play here, undermining the layering and complexity. Sexy and chewy for sure and a must for those into dried dates. But the usual Pot Still character is a little masked and the usual slightly off key sherry butt turns up at the very last moment. *46%. ncf.*

Powers Three Swallow Release bott code L617031171 (**83.5**) **n21 t21 f21.5 b20** Pleasant. No off notes. But vanishes into a sea of toffee. The fact it is pure Pot Still, apparently, is actually impossible to determine, In the last six months I have seen three swallows: a barn swallow, a Pacific and a Wire-tailed. Wherever I saw them in the world, India, The Philippines, my back garden, they all swooped and darted in joyous abandon. This Three Swallow by Powers has, by vivid contrast, had its wings clipped. *40%. ncf.*

Powers Three Swallow Release American bourbon barrels & Oloroso sherry casks, bott code: L920631483 db (**84.5**) **n22 t21.5 f20.5 b20.5** Death by chocolate? Nope: death by toffee. Slow strangulation. If that doesn't get you, the boredom will. A fanfare for the brief burst of pot still on delivery. But it is soon ruthlessly silenced. *40%. ncf.*

Redbreast Aged 12 Years bott code L634031413 db (**88.5**) **n22.5 t23 f21 b22** By far the flattest Redbreast I have tasted since...well, ever. Far too much reliance on obviously first-fill sherry, which had flattened out and virtually buried the unique personality of the Pot Still itself. Enjoyable, for sure. Beautiful, even, in its own way. But it should be so much better than this... *40%.*

Redbreast Aged 12 Years bott code: L927731644 db (**93**) **n23.5** a light smothering of orange blossom honey on deep vanilla. The oakiness possesses a little church pew dustiness...; **t23** probably the softest Redbreasts delivery of all time, a restrained fruitiness taking its time to warm up and get going. A little starchy Pot Still makes its presence felt, and spices immediately after; **f23** a Cadbury's chocolate fruit and nut finale with the grain being surprisingly reticent...; lots of toffee and vanilla late on; **b23.5** one of the most docile and pacific Redbreasts I've encountered in the last 30-odd years. Lovely, though. *40%.*

Redbreast Aged 12 Years Cask Strength batch no. B1/18 db (**96**) **n24.5 t24.5 f23 b24** Probably one very slightly sulphured cask from World Whisky of the Year. Both nose and delivery is blarney-free Irish perfection. Worth hunting this bottle down for something truly special... *56.2%. ncf.*

Redbreast Aged 12 Years Cask Strength batch no. B2/19, bott code: L921931501 db (**95.5**) **n24** so wonderful to see the grain in the ascendancy. There is a real crispness to this, a sharpness than can cut, as is the case with old-style Irish Pot Still with the muscovado and Demerara sugars having the bigger input before the peach and grape juices start to soften the feel. The slow build of the spice is fabulous; **t24** oh...heavens....!!! That is so, so beautiful. A fabulous heather honey and playful molasses blend creates just the right environment for first the pompous grapiness...and then the grains steam in as though they own the place. Which I suppose they do. Magnificently choreographed, with the weight and pace of the development beyond criticism; **f23.5** long and remains lush even though the burnt raisin and fruitcake notes are turned up a notch. A vague furriness late into the death...; **b24** just like the last time I tasted this, there is just the very faintest sulphur echo. But it is miniscule and apparent only very late into the experience...and after two or three mouthfuls. Pot still at its potiest... *55.8%.*

Redbreast Aged 15 Years bott code L624931266 db (**84**) **n21 t22 f20 b21** When you have this much sherry influence on a whiskey, it is likely that one day you will fall foul of the odd furry butt, as is the case here. *46%. ncf.*

Redbreast Aged 15 Years bott code: L930431724 db (**80**) **n19 t22 f18 b21** A few too many sulphured casks for its own good. *46%.*

Redbreast Aged 21 Years bott code L612731109 db (**97**) **n24.5 t24 f24 b24.5** The mercifully restrained fruit and absolute total 100% absence of sulphur allows the Pot Still to display its not inconsiderable beauty unmolested and to the fullest extent. One of the world's most beautiful and iconic whisk(e)ys without doubt. The fact that so many facets of this whiskey are allowed to say their piece, yet never over-run their time and that the tenets are equally divided makes this one of the truly great whiskeys of the year. *46%. ncf.*

Redbreast Aged 21 Years bott code: L918331405 db (**94**) **n24** layered fruit. A little ginger pays a surprise visit and the oak is likewise laid in distinctive strata....; **t23.5** silky and spicy for the very first moments, the grain barely recognisable by flavour but by the stiffness of spine only; the salivating qualities early on seems to run hand-in-hand with the juiciest grape; **f23** a dull toffee-vanilla-grapey fade ...where is the enlivening barley...? **b23.5** this is perennially one of the contenders for the Bible's World Whisky of the Year, and once was only a single sulphured cask away from winning it. This year sulphur isn't a problem but, ironically, the sherry is. For the grape here is a little too boisterous, meaning the balance has been compromised. Lovely whisky, for sure. But when the grape dominates – and flattens - so much greatness will elude it... 46%.

Redbreast Aged 27 Years ruby port casks, batch no. B1/19, bott code: L933633750 db **(93.5) n23.5 t25 f21.5 b23.5** If tragic can be applied to a whiskey, then it can here One minute the perfect exhibition of a wondrous whiskey type. The next, faulty obliteration... if I'm permitted a scream...... Arrrrrrggggghhhhhhh!!!!! 54.6%.

Redbreast Aged 32 Years Dream Cask db **(96.5) n24 t24.5 f23.5 b24** A fabulous pot still very comfortable in its ancient clothes. Marvellous! 46.5%.

Redbreast All Sherry Single Cask db **(73.5) n17 t23.5 f15 b18.** I mean: seriously guys....??? A single cask pure pot still whiskey and you bottle one with sulphur fingerprints all over it? I don't have the number of what cask this is from, so I hope yours will have come from clean sherry. If you have, you are in for a treat, because the sheer brilliance and magnitude of this whiskey was able to blot out the sulphur for a good seven or eight seconds as it reached heights of near perfection. A bowl of raspberries now and a 20 minute break to help cleanse my palate and relieve my tongue which is still seriously furred up. So frustrating, as I could see a clean butt of this getting Single Cask Whisky of the Year ... 59.9%. sc.

Redbreast Dream Cask Aged 28 Years ruby port casks, cask no. 400295, bott code: L933633750 db **(96) n24.5** the depth and layering of this made a liar of the label straight away – or at least the front of it. It is obvious there is more going on here than ruby port alone and an inspection of the small print reveal that oloroso and bourbon casks are at play here, too. Perhaps the cleverest, yet most easily over-looked aspect is the spice. Not just some sizzling random spice. But one that is measured and integrated. As is the fruit which varies from a cream sherry-type pillow softness to a more lusty plum pudding. There is an intrinsic toastiness, too, which mirrors the spice in its careful weight and disposition. This a 15-minute minimum Murray Method nose. And, unquestionably one of the finest in the world this year...; **t24.5** talk about cream sherry on the nose.... The marriage of oloroso and ruby port has generated the most classic cream sherry landing on the palate. But, as on the nose, is the delicate and intricate layering which sets this apart from the rest and takes this into true world class territory. There is a clever acidic touch which comes and goes, allowing the dark, salivating sugars pride and place from time to time., This is all about weight and counterweight: old-fashioned blending at is finest...; **f23** ah!...and to the Achilles heel. Toasty and an element of chocolate truffle. But that dull, bitter echo of sulphur from, presumably, the sherry butt. Not loud, but the mild furriness is indelibly there...; **b24** until the finale, this was on course for World Whisky of the Year. But that will never be won with a whiskey blemished by sulphur and, though the mark is small, it is, alas, there.... Tragic, as this is as much an art of work as it is a whiskey... 40%. 915 bottles.

Redbreast Lustau Edition sherry finish, bott code L622131242 db **(89.5) n22.5 t23.5 f22 b21.5** I somehow would have thought that, considering recent younger bottlings, going to the trouble of making a special sherry finish for a Redbreast is on a par with giving a gift of a barrel of sand to the Tuaregs... This bottling is attractive enough, with the fruit at its best on delivery when the whiskey goes through a spectacularly delicious phase. But this soon wears out, leaving a bitterness and slightly lopsided feel, especially at the death, as the balance struggles to be maintained. For those of you I know who refuse to touch anything sherry, this is entirely sulphur free I'm delighted to report. 46%. ncf.

Redbreast Lustau Edition Sherry Finish bott code: L930531725 db **(95) n23.5 t24 f23.5 b24** Faultless sherry casks at work. And the Pot Still is firm and decisive. Who can ask for more....? Well, I could ask for the toasted almonds promised on the label, being exceedingly partial to them. The fact they never turn up is compensated for by the overall excellence... and the chocolate... 46%.

Red Spot Aged 15 Years bourbon, sherry & marsala casks, bott code: L829131516 db **(83) n21 t22 f19 b21** Oh, what I'd give for the days when you could taste the actual magic of the Pot Still itself, such as in the original Green Spot, rather than some lumbering fruit casks, and slightly sulphured ones at that. 46%. ncf.

Yellow Spot Aged 12 Years bourbon barrels, sherry butts & Malaga casks, bott code L622431250 db **(87) n22 t22 f21 b22** My previous comments stand for this, too. Except here we have a persistent bitterness towards the finish which reveals a weakness with one of the butts. An exceptionally bitty whiskey that does have its moments of soaring high, especially when the varying citrus note correlate. 46%. ncf.

Yellow Spot Aged 12 Years bourbon barrels, sherry butts and Malaga casks, bott code: L929031680 db **(92.5) n24 t24 f21.5 b23** I thought the first bottlings of this were a tad out of sorts, the balance proving elusive. I backed blender Billy Leighton to crack this one eventually...and he has. This has moments of pure whiskey paradise. But the garden of Eden has a snake...and thy name is Sulphur... *46%. ncf.*

UNSPECIFIED

Glendalough Pot Still Irish Whiskey tree no. 1, batch no. 1, cask no. 3, bott code: 25519 **(87.5) n20.5 t23.5 f21.5 b22** A bold, rich Irish weakened by the feints from the over-generous cut but strengthened thanks to the brave inclusion of local oak. Not too much that is positive can be said about the nose, alas. But the same doesn't ring true for the startling delivery which first champions the barley and then, before you have time to blink, the oak which powers through with a creamy molasses attached to the stark oak. The unravelling of the myriad sugar styles is as unique as it is delicious. A bit like a mis-firing Rolls Royce, I look forward to future bottlings when they've sorted the engine out... *43%. sc.*

Hinch Single Pot Still nbc **(94.5) n23.5 t23.5 f23.5 b24** Quite a light Pot Still character with no great age. This gives the whiskey a very unusual personality, indeed one I cannot remember bottled before, as it is a style ignored by distillers as a singleton and in the lab I have used this type of Pot Still only within blends. Brilliant to see it get the airing it deserves. The only thing I can say against it: I know that, in my lab, this type of Pot Still sparkles best at about 51% abv when the sugars and oils seem to complement each other almost effortlessly. Hopefully the next bottling will be a little closer to that. *43%. The Time Collection.*

Single Malt

COOLEY County Louth. 1987. Beam Suntory.

Connemara bott code L9042 db **(88) n23 t22.5 t20.5 b22.** One of the softest smoked whiskies in the world which, though quite lovely, gives the impression it can't make its mind up about what it wants to be. *40%*

Connemara Aged 12 Years bott code L9024 db **(85.5) n23 t21.5 f20 b21.** The nose, with its beautiful orange, fruity lilt, puts the shy smoke in the shade. *40%*

Connemara Cask Strength bott code L9041 db **(90) n21.5 t23 f22 b22.5.** A juicy negative of the standard bottling: does its talking on the palate rather than nose. Maybe an absence of caramel notes might have something to do with that. *57.9%*

Connemara Peated Single Malt Irish Whiskey bott code: L19109 03/10/149 db **(89) n23** seriously sexy peat at work here, The phenols smoulder over you like the eyes possessed by an Irish redhead...; **t22.5** super-soft – perhaps too soft with the peat at first embracing then backing off as the caramels take charge; a little ulmo honey evens the sweetness; **f21.5** light spice, but even more caramel; **b22** I'm afraid I'm old and ugly enough to have been around to taste the very first ever batch of Connemara – at Cooley distillery, as it happens – after it came off the bottling line. Then the peat was rich and unhindered. Since then it has gone through a chequered career with phenols levels rising and falling like the tides at nearby Carlingford Lough. That must have been close on 30 years ago now... Pleased to say the peat is back to it old confident self..well, early on at least. But I don't remember the toffee dampening its natural spontaneity as it does here... *40%.*

Tullamore Dew Single Malt 10 Years Old db **(91.5) n23 t23 f22.5 b23.** The best whiskey I have ever encountered with a Tullamore label. Furtively complex and daringly delicate. If only they could find a way to minimise the toffee... *40%. William Grant & Sons.*

The Tyrconnell Single Malt Irish Whiskey Aged 16 Years Oloroso & Moscatel cask finish, bott code: L19020 07/02/19 db **(94) n23.5 t23.5 f23 b24** So rare to find a sherry-matured Irish whiskey that isn't benighted by sulphur. An absolute treat. *46%.*

The Tyrconnell Single Malt Double Distilled Irish Whiskey ex-bourbon casks, bott code: L18112 07/11/18 db **(87.5) n23 t22 f21 b21.5** A thoroughbred malt offers the most gorgeous freshness on the nose while lime blossom honey does the rest. But to taste it almost falls at the first jump, unable to negotiate a fence with the clearance the nose suggests. The lightness of malt has been replaced by a slightly salivating but out of sync toffee persona; a mix between Malteser candy and MacIntosh's Toffo. A thoroughbred as I say. But carrying too much weight: was always lighter and flightier than this. So much caramel! *43%.*

Tullamore Dew Aged 10 Years Four Cask Finish bourbon, oloroso, port, madeira **(89) n24 t23 f19.5 b22.5** Just a sherry butt or two away from complete brilliance. *40% (80 proof)*

⬧ **The Whisky Cask Company The Poplar Tree 2002** PX sherry cask, dist May 2002, Bott Jul 2020 **(92) n23** the trademark PX flatness is trumped by an impudent outbreak in sugars, most of that wonderful, crystallised muscovado variety sitting atop a little cloud of intense malted barley...; **t24** possibly the best delivery for a PX cask I have encountered for the last couple of years. It is different because, though making an explosive impact, it has not entirely swamped the whiskey itself, leaving room for a massive jolt of oak-induced passionfruit to cut through the grape. Truly satisfying, spicy and uncommonly intense...; **f22** spices apart, a much more lazy finish: the grape seems to be laying back with its feet up on the oak, as it drifts off to sleep as it is driven to the end of the road...; **b23** the Sherry Tree, surely. Should be "poplar" with anyone with a sweet tooth....and a taste for delicious, highly intense whiskey. *52.9% 301 bottles*

The Wild Geese Single Malt (85.5) n21.5 t21 f22 b21. Just ignore the Wild Goose chase the labels send you on and enjoy the malt, with all its failings, for what it is (and this is pretty enjoyable in an agreeably rough and ready manner, though not exactly the stuff of Irish whiskey purists): which in this case for all its malt, toffee and delicate smoke, also appears to have more than a slight touch of feints - so maybe they were right all along...!!! *43%. Cooley for Avalon.*

DINGLE County Kerry. 2012. Porterhouse Group.

Dingle Single Malt Whisky batch no. 3 db **(87) n21 t22 f22 b22** Young, much closer in personality to new make than seasoned whiskey. In fact, reminds me of the blending lab when I'd come across a barely three-year-old Dailuaine, a Scottish Speysider which, at this juncture of its development, is its closest flavour-type relative. Lovely, though, if you an looking for a taste of unspoiled, gently oiled maltiness – and a piece of Irish whiskey history. Clean and beautifully made. *46.5%. ncf. 13,000 bottles.*

Dingle Single Malt Whisky batch no. 4 db **(84) n20 t22 f21 b21** I always prefer to discover that a distillery makes gin because I have been there or been briefed about it. Not through sampling their whiskey. And I'm afraid there is juniper quite strongly on the nose here and few other odd flavours hitting the palate. Despite the mega dry finish, lots of malt on show and seemingly otherwise well made. *46.5%. ncf. 2,000 bottles.*

Dingle Single Malt Whisky batch no. 5 db **(88.5) n22 t22.5 f22 b22** Genteel malt shewing no great age but certainly celebrates an uninhibited maltiness which charms and possesses no pretentions of grandeur. Just a slight background apple cider feel to the nose, and a vague feintiness to the body. The barley is all over this, but melts towards a soft butterscotch tart finish. *46.5%. ncf.*

Dingle Single Malt Whisky Cask Strength batch no. 5 db **(92) n23 t23.5 f22.5 b23** The extra oils work a treat on this: there is a chasm between this expression and the 46.5 version, the cask strength bottling here allowing full amplification to some otherwise understated components. *59.3%. ncf.*

MIDLETON County Cork. 1975. Irish Distillers.

Method and Madness Single Malt Irish Whiskey bourbon barrels, finished in French Limousin oak casks db **(92) n22 t23.5 f23 b23.5** A very different Irish which is quietly uncompromising and seriously tasty... *46%.*

OLD BUSHMILLS County Antrim. 1784. Casa Cuervo.

Bushmills Aged 10 Years matured in two woods db **(92.5) n23 t23 f23 b23.5.** Absolutely superb whiskey showing great balance and the usual Antrim 19th century pace with its flavour development. The odd bottle of this I have come across over the last couple of years has been spoiled by the sherry involvement. But, this, as is usually the case, is absolutely spot on. *40%*

Bushmills Single Malt Aged 10 Years bourbon & Oloroso casks, bott code: L8270 IB 005 db **(92.5) n23 t23 f23 b23.5** A very consistent Irish benefitting again from faultless sherry butts. *40%.*

Bushmills Aged 12 Years Single Malt Aged in Three Woods oloroso sherry & bourbon casks, Marsala cask finished, bott code: L9102IB 001 db **(89.5) n23.5 t23 f21 b22** Slightly lumpy in style, but there are some beautiful moments in there. *40%. Exclusive to Taiwan.*

Bushmills Distillery Reserve Single Malt Aged 12 Years bott code: L8170 IB 002 db **(95) n23.5** beautiful stratum of cocoa, apricot, heather honey and the chalkiest malt in the British Isles...; **t24** very unusual for a Bushmills of any era to kick off with a sweet delivery. But that's what you are presented with here as that heather honey kicks in, followed by layers of greengages and exploding white grape. The malt and sawdusty oak form layers alongside the toffee; **f23.5** not technically perfect, but all is forgiven as this has legs despite the lack of oils. The chocolate toffee takes over, with just a slight sultana kick here and there; **b24** what a stunning example of Bushmills this is. *40%.*

Bushmills Aged 16 Years db **(71) n18 t21 f15 b17.** In my days as a consultant Irish whiskey blender, going through the Bushmills warehouses I found only one or two sulphur-treated butts. Alas, there are many more than that at play here. *40%*

Bushmills Single Malt Aged 16 Years Rare Matured in Three Woods Oloroso sherry, bourbon & port casks, bott code: L9249 IB 002 db **(90.5) n23 t23.5 f21.5 b22.5** Until the late finish barely a single off note thanks to some superb casks in use here. If only they could bring the toffee element down slight to allow a far clearer view of the excellent fruit and malt tones in play *40%.*

Bushmills Aged 21 Years db **(95.5)** n24.5 t24 f23.5 b24 An Irish journey as beautiful as the dramatic landscape which borders the distillery. Magnificent. *40%*

Bushmills Single Malt Aged 21 Years Rare Matured in Three Woods Oloroso sherry, bourbon & Madeira casks, bott 2019, bott code: L9085 IB 003 db **(82)** n21 t21.5 f19.5 b20 A very disappointing malt. Obviously the light dusting of tongue-numbing sulphur affects the nose and finale but some damage is already done behind on the palate with a stark toffee effect that keeps complexity to a minimum. The odd honey tone here and there, and a slight saltiness, too. But, from this distillery, we should be having a whiskey in the mid-90s points-wise... *40%.*

Bushmills Distillery Exclusive Acacia Wood dist 2008, bott no. L8211 IB 01S db **(83.5)** n21 t24 f18 b20.5 Not the first time I have ever tasted whiskey rounded off in acacia by a long stretch, though maybe the first after spending time – it appears – in sherry. The result for me just doesn't gel. For a start, I find the slightly imbalanced aroma a lot of hard work in getting used to, though as your nose acclimatises you can eventually pick out some half attractive buttery notes. And the finish isn't quite where it should be, with a fair bit of fuzziness at the finish. The delivery, though, is both intriguing and delicious, the acacia – as is its wont – issuing a whole batch of sugar and honey notes not normally present in whisky and never in Irish whiskey; ironically acacia honey isn't among them! Though undone by the pretty poor finish, this still represents one of the most curious and fascinating bottlings in the world over the last year. Just needs some serious tidying up before, hopefully, the next batch as the potential is great. *47%. ncf.*

Bushmills Port Cask Reserve ruby port pipes, bott code: L8170 IB 001 db **(95.5)** n24 t24 f23.5 b24 This Steamship does First Class only... *40%. The Steamship Collection.*

Bushmills Rum Cask Reserve first fill Caribbean rum casks, bott code: L9130 IB 001 db **(94)** n23.5 t23.5 f23 b24 The blender has really called this one right. Brilliant usage of rum casks to enrich the notoriously slight maltiness of Old Bushmills. A malt that is in full sail... *40%. The Steamship Collection.*

Bushmills Sherry Cask Reserve Oloroso sherry butts, bott code: L9078 IB 002 db **(90.5)** n22.5 delicate sultana and toffee. Light spices plus a buttery vanilla; t22.5 soft and middling sweet on delivery. The toastier raisins meet with a blanket of Demerara sugar and caramel; f22.5 delightfully clean, with a late malty freshness and lightly spiced chocolate fudge; b23 clean, unsullied casks make for an easy-drinking, super-rounded Irish with an untaxing complexity. Very pleasant, indeed. *40%. The Steamship Collection.*

Bushmills Single Malt The Steamship Collection #3 Bourbon Cask db **(95)** n24.5 t23.5 f23 b24 This steamship is sailing in calm seas of complexity...Take your time over this one: it is deceptively brilliant. *40%.*

The Whisky Cask Company Bushmills Capall 26 Years Old 1st fill bourbon barrel, cask no, 8391, dist 16 Oct 91, bott 26 Mar 18 **(94.5)** n22.5 t24 f24 b24 Had the nose been as sensational as the experience on the palate then some kind of award for this whisky would have been a certainty. Magnificent. *50.5%. sc. 175 bottles.*

The Whisky Cask Company Bushmills Madra 26 Years Old 1st fill bourbon barrel, cask no, 8386, dist 16 Oct 91, bott 26 Mar 18 **(94)** n23 t24 f23 b24 A little nudge to Bushmills to make the most of their older casks, methinks. *49.4%. sc. 156 bottles.*

WEST CORK DISTILLERS County Cork. 2003. West Cork Distillers.

West Cork Irish Whiskey Bog Oak Charred Cask Matured db **(88.5)** n23 t22 f21.5 b22 A little known fact: I own a 100 to 125 year-old portable Irish pot still made entirely of copper with brass handles, once owned by a Victorian or Edwardian illicit distiller. Which would explain as to why it was found in an Irish bog over 20 years ago and has been in my possession ever since. Anyway, it is extremely unlikely it ever produced a spirit which ended up quite so heavy in natural caramels... *43%. West Cork Distillers Limited.*

West Cork Irish Whiskey Glengarriff Peat Charred Cask Matured db **(90.5)** n23 t22.5 f22 b23 Well, Ireland is on the way to Kentucky from here... *43%. West Cork Distillers Limited.*

Brean Tra Single Malt Irish Whiskey db **(86.5)** n21 t22 f21.5 b22 A very safe Irish. Distinctly oily and choc-a-bloc with intense if monosyllabic malt. The tannins take time to arrive but become moderately punchy. *40%. West Cork Distillers Limited.*

Mizen Head Cask Strength Single Malt Irish Whiskey Bodega sherry casks db **(90.5)** n22.5 t23.5 f22 b22.5 Well done chaps! Until the very death, barely a sulphur atom in sight! But such is the power of this distillery's love of caramel character, it even overtakes the fruit... which takes some doing! *60%. West Cork Distillers Limited.*

UNSPECIFIED SINGLE MALTS

Artful Dodger Irish Single Malt 15 Year Old 2002 ex-bourbon hogshead, cask no. 346 **(95)** n23.5 t24 f23.5 b24 This is Irish single malt as it should be. Not vanishing behind grape thanks one type of finish or another. But out in the open, displaying its immense richness and talents – and, here, barley by the bushel-load. Clean, with intricate layering of rare intensity, the light tannins acting as the cement to the malt brick. If you ever see this bottle, just grab it. But then it might just find you, as this malt, like Irish eyes, would have a magnetic attraction. Brilliant! 57.9%. sc.

Cadenhead's Small Batch An Irish 10 Year Old bott Aug 19 **(91.5) n23** really charming layering to the greenish barley: clean and inviting; **t23** delightfully creamy maltiness sharpened by a citrus edges: some lovely salivating moments; **f22.5** a little salty, then dries with a sawdusty vanilla flourish; **b23** untaxing throughout, the malt tells a simple tale....well. 47.4%.

Currach Single Malt Irish Whiskey Atlantic Kombu Seaweed Cask ex-bourbon casks, finished in seaweed charred virgin oak casks, batch no. 1, bott Mar 20, bott code: 07220 **(83) n20.5 t22 f20.5 b20** Probably a whisky for the Swansea or Japanese market, where seaweed is held in high esteem. However, as a whisky in its own right I'm afraid this hits rough waters immediately, with the malt lurching around the palate as though in a gale. The sweet spot lasts far too briefly, a vague honey note well into the delivery but the tang on finish isn't one that is easy to savour. Salt is conspicuous by its absence, oddly enough, in the Whisky Bible 2020, I noted that Ireland had produced 29 different finishes in the previous year alone. This was not included amongst them. 46%. ncf. Origin Spirits Ireland.

The Dublin Liberties Copper Alley 10 Year Old Single Malt sherry cask finish, bott no. L16 280 W3 **(94.5) n23 t24 f23.5 b24** Well done, chaps! You have picked yourself a first class sulphur-free cask! What a rare treat that is this year! 46%.

The Dubliner 10 Year Old Single Malt bourbon casks, bott no. L17390-179 **(89) n22 t23 f21.5 b22.5** 'The real taste of Dublin" warbles the label in time-honoured Blarney tradition. Of course, the true, historic taste of Dublin is Irish Pot Still, that beguiling mix of malted and unmalted barley. But, in the meantime, this juicy little number will do no harm. 42%.

Dunville's VR Aged 12 Years Single Malt finished in ex-Pedro Ximénez sherry casks **(87) n23 t22.5 f20 b21.5** The success story here is on the nose: despite its Spanish inquisition, there is a profound Kentucky note leading the way, a sharp almost rye-like note with its fruity crispness. The delivery also has its moments, the riot of date and molasses in particular. The rest of the tale, much of it bitterly told, doesn't go quite so well, alas. 46%. ncf.

Dunville's VR Aged 17 Years Single Malt Port Mourant Estate rum cask finish, cask no. 195 **(91.5) n22.5 t22.5 f23 b22.5** Putting my blending hat on (which is the same one as I wear when writing the Whisky Bible) Port Mourant – known by us rum blenders as PM – trumps PX every day of the week when it comes to maturation. PM is a bit special in the rum world: it is a Guyanan rum that you add for its depth and powering coffee flavour: indeed, if you work in a rum warehouse in Guyana you can locate where the PMs are situated just by the change in aroma. This comes about by the fact that caramel is already into the cask before the rum spirit is added to it for maturation. It is a style symbolic with British Naval Rum. So where PX can be saccharine sweet and occasionally turn a whisky into something bland and uninteresting, PM is brilliant for lengthening out the finish, especially with rich mocha notes. Here, there are some sharp features it has to contend with from the first cask and a little extra time in PM might have ensured an extra softness to the finale. 57.1%. ncf sc.

Egan's Single Malt Fortitude Pedro Ximénez casks bott code: L18 003 264 **(79) n19 t22 f19 b19** Bitter and off-key. 42% (92 proof). ncf.

Egan's Single Malt 10 Aged Years bott code: US001 244 **(90) n22.5 t23.5 f22 b22.5** Rich, rounded and puts the "more" into this Tullamore-based bottler...47% (94 proof). ncf.

The Exclusive Malts Irish 14 Year Old refill sherry hogshead, cask no. 200503, dist 15 Dec 03, bott Jun 18 **(86.5) n22 t22 f21 b21.5** A bewildering coming together of two irremovable forces: the peat, presumably of Cooley distillery, and a superb, faultless sherry butt. But although this cask is faultless – a rare beast in the sherry world - this has been bottled before the phenols and fruits have been able to reach a compromise. So, fun whiskey. And there is much to be said about the peat and boiled candy fruitiness. But they are too individual and each out of sync with the other. Some great moments, though! 50.5%. sc. The Whisky Barrel. 264 bottles.

Glendalough Single Malt Irish Whiskey Aged 17 Years American oak bourbon cask, Japanese Mizunara cask finish **(89.5) n21.5 t23 f22 b23** Quite a cerebral whiskey, and one with a unique fingerprint. But could have done without the juniper. 46%. ncf.

Glendalough Single Malt Irish Whiskey Aged 25 Years Tree #2 Jack's Wood American white oak bourbon cask, Spanish oloroso cask & virgin Irish oak finish **(95) n23.5 t24 f23.5 b24** No discernible problems from the oloroso, other than the very faintest long-distance buzz. Which means this is one hell of a malt. 46%. ncf.

Hinch Peated Single Malt nbc **(87) n22 t22 f21.5 b21.5** So rare to find a slightly feinty note in Irish, but here it is on the peaty nose and, big delivery and quarrelsome finish. A unique character, that's for sure...and what a character! Technically not quite at the races, but the peat is taking few prisoners and the oils from that wide cut ensures that the big smoke goes nowhere in a hurry. An odd whiskey, it has to be said. Knives and forks ready for this one: tuck in to enjoy... *43%. The Time Collection.*

◈ **Hinch Single Malt Aged 18 Years Château De La Ligne Grande Reserve Finish** bott code: 0211005 **(95) n23.5** oh, oh! Just love the snap to the fruit. This is crunchy: as though cherry drop candy has been crushed into shards and mixed in with liquorice and barley. A very different take on wine-influenced whiskey...; **t24** this is a delivery that doesn't so much arrive as simply appears from nowhere alongside a big bang. The natural oils from the whiskey appear to congeal with the lusciousness of the fruit, so the mouth is filled with, at first, malt that appears flattened for the slaughter and then that eye-watering black cherry note that radiates barbed spices .... all the time drifting along on that cleverly understated tide of oil...; **f23.5** even now the mouth is shimmering. And when the chocolate arrives, we are in the realms of spiced up Fry's Turkish Delight...; **b24** pure class. Imagine a liqueur chocolate in liquid whiskey form...and here you are. A serious Covid-era bumping of elbows must go to whoever created this whiskey. Such complexity! *46%* ☙

Hyde No.1 President's Cask Aged 10 Years Single Malt sherry cask finish **(85.5) n23 t22 f20 b20.5** Pleased to report the sherry butt(s) used here offer no sulphur, so a clean malt with an outstanding fruity aroma. But it does quite literally fall flat because after the initial juicy, malty entry things go a bit quiet – especially towards the middle and finish where a dull vaguely fruity but big toffee note clings like a limpet. A wasted opportunity, one feels. *46%. ncf.*

Hyde No. 7 President's Cask Bodega sherry casks, bott code: 20518 **(69) n15 t19 f18 b17** Riddled with sulphur. The Germans will love it! *46%. ncf.*

◈ **Hyde No.7 President's Cask 1893** sherry cask, bott Jul 2019 **(83) n20 t23 f19.5 b20.5** Sweet and grapey in part, the charming delivery especially. But the nose and finish tell a contrasting sulphury tale. See it winning many friends, nonetheless. *46% ncf 5000 bottles*

◈ **Hyde No.9 Iberian Cask 1906** port cask finish, bott Jul 2020 **(92) n23** very intense malt, adorned with it ripened cherries on a tree...; **t23.5** that rarest of deliveries: an equal measure between malt and wine. Rarer still is the quagmire softness of the delivery, the malt forming a delicious swamp while the sharper grapey tones just suck you down. The spices nibble and tingle away confidently...; **f22.5** pleasant oaky waves breaking on the malty shingle...; **b23** someone managed to lay their hands on absolutely top-class port pipes here by the looks of it. Not a single quaver of a weakness in the fluting fruity note. Rich, satisfying and just amazingly friendly despite the busy spice. This is great stuff: a whiskey to create a few more converts to be sure... *43% ncf 5000 bottles*

◈ **Hyde N0.10 Banyuls Cask Finished Single Cask Singe Malt** first fill bourbon, finished first fill banyuls gran cru cask, bott Jun 2020, bott code: 31420 **(87.5) n22 t22 f21.5 b22** Beyond the citrus on the nose, there is a husky-voiced wine cask influence. A rasping, deep resonance to the fruit but slightly undone by a shortage of sugars. Dry and dusty, the bourbon cask influence appears to have been airbrushed out while the warming, pinching, white pepper spice will come as little surprise. Far from standard fare and always entertaining. *43% ncf 390 bottles*

The Irishman Aged 12 Years first fill bourbon barrels, bott 2017 **(92) n23.5 t23 f22.5 b23** Old Bushmills like you have never quite seen her before in bottle. Works a treat. *43%. ncf. 6,000 bottles.*

The Irishman 12 Years Old Florio Marsala Cask Finish cask no. 2257 **(90) n22 t23 f22.5 b22.5** A clean, unsullied cask but the grape allows the malt little room for manoeuvre. Very pleasurable though, and definitely a whisky rather than a wine..; *46%. ncf sc. 320 bottles.*

The Irishman Aged 17 Years sherry cask, cask no. 6925, dist 2000 **(95.5) n24.5 t24 f23 b24** Just a year or two after this was distilled, I was crawling around the warehouses of Old Bushmills doing some blending and sampling amazingly fine, completely un-sulphured or as near as damn it un-sulphured, sherry butts – better than any I had found in Scotland in the previous several years. This style of sherry has all the hallmarks of the Bushmills butts of that time. There is trace sulphur (so this is a as near-as damn-it butt), but unless you know exactly what you are looking for it is in such small amounts it is unlikely to be detected or trouble you. This may not be from Bushmills, but if not then someone has made a good job of hiding some gems from me. If anyone can locate half a dozen of those entirely un-sulphured butts I located, then there is an Irish Whisky of the Year (at least!) in your hands... *56%. ncf sc. 600 bottles.*

The Irishman Aged 17 Years sherry cask, cask no. 28657 **(94.5) n24 t24 f22.5 b23.5** It's the hoping that kills you. After 20-odd years of tasting sherry casks ruined in Jerez, you view every whisky from sherry butt, be it a full term maturation or partial, with suspicion. You hope... but sadly, that hope is terminated by grim disappointment. Here, though, we have a happy experience. Is it 100% perfect sherry butt? No. Does it damage the whiskey? Not really. This is a full-on sherry influenced Irish celebrating the grape with style. The finale shews the slightest of weaknesses, but in light of what is out there it is forgiveable (well, not quite forgiveable enough for it not to be robbed of an award in the Whisky Bible!) and forgettable. *56%. ncf sc. 600 bottles.*

J. J. Corry The Flintlock No. 1 16 Year Old Single Malt Autumn 2018, cask nos. 11191, 11221 & 11233 **(95.5)** n23.5 an essay in beautiful grist....; t24 such a dazzling, uncomplicated exhibition of barley. Biscuity, gristy, intense...just stunning... f24 light spices hover around. As does a thin layer of bruyere honey and molasses; b24 should Ireland ever hold a Maltfest, then this should be on the altar of worship... 46%. 650 bottles.

Jack Ryan Single Malt Irish Whisky Aged 12 Years bourbon cask **(92.5)** n23.5 t23 f22.5 b23.5 Deft, very clean malt whisky where decent bourbon wood adds all kinds of beautifully paced complexity. Not even a hint of an off note. Impressive. 46%

Kinahan's Heritage 10 Year Old Single Malt (93) n23 t23.5 f23 b23.5 A beautifully constructed whiskey where, very rare for a single malt these days, you can actually taste the malt itself... A treat of a whiskey. 46%.

 Kinahan's The Kasc Project M hybrid cask of Portuguese, American, French and Hungarian Oak and chestnut wood, batch no.01, bott code: 121001145 **(95.5)** n23.5 the sweet, strident tones of the chestnut makes a point of putting the other tannins back into their oaky box, though the Hungarian has something to say about it. The result is barley and perhaps an atom or two of fruit trying to get a word in edgeways, while the chestnut and Hungarian oaks beat their barrel chests against each other...; t24 the chestnut is again first out of the traps, or to string along, you might say, though the unique Hungarian tartness also has a confident nibble. For a moment the silky body of the malt slinks through, but soon we are back to the battle of the tannins. Thankfully, it means some varying sugars have been let loose with the not inconsiderable spices, so the middle is convoluted parade of muscovado sugars, light liquorice, and a beautiful mix of heather and manuka honeys; f23.5 spiced chocolate with light caramels....; b24.5 I thought, having a fair bit of green blood in me, that the Irish were addicted to horses and Guinness. The evidence of the last couple of years suggests that it is cask finishes, too. And here, there have gone absolutely bonkers. And conkers. Looking at the cask make up, I would predict that the chestnut influence would outrank all the other influences put together...and, my word, so it proves: it conkers all.... though the fight is absorbing. I may not be the greatest fan of the O'Finishes...but when someone has worked their fecking hard to get a whisky or whiskey to both entertain and delight with its sheer novelty and beauty, an somehow find a balance to blow you away, then I can only stand and applaud... 45% ncf

Kinahan's Special Release Project 11 Year Old Armagnac finish, cask no. 48 **(95.5)** n23 t24.5 f23.5 b24.5 This isn't good whiskey. Or even very good whiskey. It is truly great Irish whiskey. 58.9%.

Lambay Whiskey Single Malt finished in Cognac casks, bott code: L4329718 **(92.5)** n23.5 t24 f22 b23 I've always thought that Bushmills at about 7-years-old has a special esprit de coeur (as opposed to corps!) which allowed the distillery to be seen at its freshest, most fulfilling and most true to the distillery's style. There is more than a touch of this evident here as this malt, whoever made it, boasts extraordinary verve and dash. Magnificent up until the point of the late finish when things become a little too bitter for their own good. That apart, stunning. 40%. ncf.

Liquid Treasures 10th Anniversary Irish Malt 29 Year Old ex-rum barrel, dist 1989, bott 2019 **(94)** n23.5 t23.5 f23 b24 Irish whiskies of this antiquity are as rare as leprechaun's teeth. This one is gold filled. 56.5%. sc. 127 bottles.

Liquid Treasures Summer Dram 2018 Irish Malt Over 26 Years Old ex-bourbon barrel, dist 1992, bott 2018 **(90.5)** n23.5 t23 f21.5 b22.5 the oak has taken control, here but in an entirely benign manner, bringing the barley into play here, dishing out spices there, standing back and allowing the ulmo and heather honeys to do their things at other times. Complex and beautifully paced, just shewing a degree of weariness at the finale. But don't we all...? 48.3%. sc.

The Quiet Man 8 Year Old Single Malt Irish Whiskey bourbon casks **(89)** n22 t23 f21.5 b22.5 Had the finish not dulled quite so quickly this would have scored a lot higher. Nothing less than pleasant throughout. 40%

The Quiet Man 8 Year Old bourbon cask, bott code L18080088 **(88.5)** n23 t23 f20.5 b22 Forget the finale: salute, quietly, the nose and delivery! 46%. ncf sc. 385 bottles.

 The Quiet Man 8 Year Old oak bourbon cask **(88)** n21.5 t22.5 f22 b22 Sssshhhh! Keep your voices down when telling people this: but this is mouth-watering, malty cove helped along with some oaky spices. Short on complexity slightly, but big of chewy texture and creamy toffee. 40%

The Quiet Man 12 Year Old Kentucky bourbon casks **(93)** n23 t23.5 f23 b23.5 Odd, isn't it? The owner of this brand named this whisky The Quiet Man in memory of his father, John Mulgrew, who was known by that epithet. Yet, coincidentally, it was Maurice Walsh, the grandfather of one of the greatest Irish whiskey blenders of all time, Barry Walsh, who wrote the novel The Quiet Man from which the film was made. I feel another movie coming on: The Silence of the Drams. But sssshhhh: don't tell anyone... 46%. ncf.

The Quiet Man 12 Year Old Sherry Finished bourbon casks, finished in oloroso sherry casks, bott code: L17304295 db **(73) n18.5 t20 f16.6 b18** Ah. Sadly, the sulphur isn't quite as quiet as one might hope. *46%. ncf.*

⋙ **The Quiet Man "An Culchiste" 12 Year Old** Kentucky bourbon cask **(93) n23 t23.5 f23 b23.5** So incredibly similar to the last Quiet Man 12. Riveting, insanely intense malt which pricks every nerve on the palate. Find the original tasting notes from a couple of years back and be impressed by the consistency. This really puts the malt in single malt....!!! *46%*

Sansibar Irish Whiskey 1992 bott 2018 **(89.5) n23 t23 f21.5 b22.5** A honey-drenched Irish concentrating both on nose and delivery on the buttery heather-honey at the heart of its character. The finish is a little on the hot and thin side, but this forgiveable when the vanilla and honey work so beautifully together elsewhere. *49.7%.*

The Sexton Single Malt batch no. L71861F001 **(91) n23 t23.5 f22 b22.5** Unmistakably malt from The Old Bushmills Distillery, and seemingly from sherry cask, also, as that distillery probably enjoys an above average number unsullied by sulphur. *40% (80 proof).*

Teeling Whiskey Aged 30 Years Single Malt white burgundy finish **(94.5) n23.5 t24 f23 b24** A beautifully clean, faultless wine cask makes a huge difference to a whisky...as is evidenced here. The fruit has a curiously unripe chardonnay-type sharpness and vividness to it. What fun! *46%. ncf.*

Teeling Whiskey Single Malt Vol IV Revival Aged 14 Years finished in ex-muscat barrels **(95) n23.5 t23.5 f24 b24** ...Though this muscat appears to be bang on the money... indeed, this is a stunner! *46%. nc ncf.*

Teeling Whiskey Single Malt Vol V Revival Aged 12 Years cognac & brandy casks, bott code: L18 001 088 **(90.5) n23.5 t23.5 f21 b22.5** Sharper than a newly whetted knife. *46%. nc ncf.*

Tullamore D.E.W. Single Malt Aged 14 Years four cask finish: bourbon, oloroso sherry, port & Madeira, bott code: L3 5009TD 08/01/2018 **(76) n23.5 t20 f15.5 b17** Vividly reminds me of the early 1990s when I was regularly in the tasting lab of my dear old friend the late, great Barry Walsh, going through his most recent efforts to try and perfect the balance on his embryonic Bushmills 16. This works wonderfully on the nose but is immediately fragmented on delivery, a problem Barry had to battle with for a good many months, in fact the best part of a year, before things clicked into place. But, also, in those days with a malt of that age there was no such thing as a sulphur problem, either, which there is here and wrecks the finish entirely. *41.3%.*

Tullamore D.E.W. Single Malt Aged 18 Years finished for up to six months in bourbon, oloroso sherry, port & Madeira casks, bott code: L3 5089TD 11/04/2018 **(88) n23 t22.5 f20.5 b22** Drop the oloroso and this malt could really take off. *41.3%. Less than 2,500 bottles.*

⋙ **The Whisky Cask Company The Ash Tree 1989** rum barrel, dist Nov 1989, bott Jul 2020 **(96) n24** here we are in the territory of the most exotic of exotic fruit Thin lychee and guava leave barely discernible footprints. Is that trace malt...? Possibly. Think ulmo honey definitely, as well as pear and over-ripe banana; **t24.5** must be Exotic Delivery of the Year: mango and Chinese gooseberry would form a formidable partnership alone, but when the passionfruit kicks in...just surreal! The fruitiness carries appropriate acidity and as that dies down glorious chocolate mousse arrives; **f23.5** more mousse and a little custard tart, too...; **b24** Bushmills so rarely gets close to this kind of age. Most casks I have sampled have shewn an Irishman dead on his feet, riddle with tannins and the barley long vanished, eaten by oak. Here, though, we have something that celebrates elegance as only a delicate malt that has been spared can. One of the great whiskies of the year, and surely some kind of award winner... *48.1% 276 bottles* 🏆

⋙ **Whisky-Fässle Irish Single Malt 17 Years Old** barrel, dist 2002, bott 2019 **(88) n22.5 t23 f20.5 b22** Impossible not to love the delicate tangerine on the nose and the concentrated malt on delivery. Indeed, the arrival on the palate makes a nonsense of the 17 years, so fresh and salivating is it. But though the following vanilla is welcome, the late-arriving bitterness isn't. *47.6%. sc.*

The Whistler Aged 7 Years Natural Cask Strength Oloroso Finished batch no. 02-0360 **(91.5) n22.5 t23.5 f22 b23.5** If you are going to round your malt off using a sherry butt probably dripping in wine when it was filled, your best option is to make the tenancy in the second cask short and then bottle at cask strength. They may not have done the former, but certainly the latter action has helped no-end, as confirmed when tasted alongside Blue Note (below). Infinitely better structure and the spices here make a big difference. Very attractive whiskey, indeed. And helped no end by a clean, sulphur-free sherry butt of the old school. I doff my Panama in finding such (mainly) unsullied sherry butts. *59%. nc ncf.*

The Whistler Aged 7 Years The Blue Note Oloroso Finished (87) n22 t22 f21.5 b21.5 The great news: no sulphur! A clean sherry butt, which is a shock in itself. The less good news: the malt was a little too young and lacking in body to really be able to be much more than a vehicle for the grape. Enjoyable, rich sultana with attractive spice. But lacking in whisky-ish structure and complexity: just too much like a straight sweet sherry! *46%. nc ncf.*

The Whistler Aged 10 Years How The Years Whistle By Oloroso Finished (92.5) n23 t23.5 f22.5 b23.5 A fabulously clean sherry butt which is much more at home with a broader-spectrumed malt... 46%. nc ncf.

Writer's Tears Red Head Oloroso sherry butts (86) n21 t22.5 f21 b21.5 There are so many good things going on here: the gentle, salty orange-blossom honey which drifts across the nose; the voluptuous embrace of the malt on delivery, offering such a happy marriage between barley and spotted dick pudding. At times mouth-watering and alive. But, as on the nose and late on the finish, a dull ache of sulphur. A shame. But, still, the positive points are worth concentrating on... 46%. ncf.

Irish Vatted Malt

The Liberator Irish Malt Whiskey Tawny port finish, batch no. one nbc (85.5) n21.5 t22 f21 b21 A big, unwieldly malt with, I have to say, a character unmatched by any Irish whiskey I have before encountered. I can't say this is technically on the money as there appears to be a number of feinty issues bubbling around from nose to finish: not something I have often encountered with Irish malt. And at times the fruit and malt characters appear to wish to spar rather than harmonise. But.... The gristy sugars and a light molasses note does make for the odd fluting and even salivating moment and the spices give some welcome pep. Though of course, those heftier feint notes do gather, as they always tend to do, for an uncomfortable finish. A malt that certainly tells a tale... 46%. 700 bottles. Inaugural Release.

◇ **The Liberator Malt Whiskey Tawny Port Finish** ex-bourbon, batch no.2 (89) n21.5 sharp, not unattractive, but not in sync, either, with the port influence yet to entirely bond with malt and tannin; t22 the delivery is equally wayward: fresh, flighty and forceful. Only towards the midpoint does its settle into a cohesive unit...and then the fun begins. Brilliantly biting spice infiltrates the juiciness, then a flashing delivery of intense malt and milky chocolate not far behind...; f23 now we are there! Amazingly long layering with the fruit and chocolate finding the kind of rhythm the nose and delivery can only dream of. The spices offer a cool, minty bite which perfectly suits the strands of light oak; b22.5 not sure how, but a confusing, then complex whiskey which gets there in the end! At first, thought it was going the same way as their last off-beam offering, but the turn round was remarkable. 46%

Single Grain

COOLEY County Louth. 1987. Beam Suntory.

Hyde 1916 No.3 Áras Cask Aged 6 Years Single Grain bott Feb 16 (87) n22 t23 f20.5 b21.5 Cooley grain probably ranks as the best being made right now, with the loss of Dumbarton and Port Dundas in Scotland. Sadly, as deliciously rich as this is, far too much toffee on the finish rather detracts from its normal excellence. Highly enjoyable, but the flag flies nowhere near full mast. By the way: the 1916 on the label doesn't represent year of distillation or bottling. Or is there to celebrate the year of my dad's birth. No, it is something a little more political than that. 46%. ncf. 5,000 bottles.

Kilbeggan Single Grain Irish Whiskey American oak casks, bott code: L18099 24/09/18 db (85.5) n22 t22 f21 b20.5 This is one of the finest grain distilleries in the world: certainly the best in Ireland and a match for anything at the other end of the Irish Sea. The unmistakable mouthfeel and early volley of sugars confirms that this is Cooley: there is nothing quite so beautiful. But yet again, I'm tasting a Kilbeggan brand with a massive toffee footprint. I wondered at first if it was the oak. But, no, never on a grain like this. This is caramel, as in the colouring stuff. Please, kindly, will you desist from killing your own brilliant whiskey stone dead! Thank you. 43% (86 proof).

MIDLETON County Cork. 1975. Irish Distillers.

Method and Madness Single Grain Irish Whiskey bourbon barrels, finished in virgin Spanish oak casks db (89.5) n22 t22.5 f22 b23 About time they brought out another bottling, but with a little less sherry than this. 46%.

WEST CORK DISTILLERS County Cork. 2003. West Cork Distillers.

Skibbereen Eagle Single Grain Irish Whiskey Bodega sherry casks db (88.5) n21.5 t23 f22 b22 As frictionless as the post Brexit border between Britain and Ireland shall be... 43%. West Cork Distillers Limited.

UNSPECIFIED SINGLE GRAIN

Egan's Vintage Grain 10 Aged Years bourbon casks, casked 2009, bott 2017, bott code: US001 244 (92.5) n23 t23.5 f22.5 b23.5 Such a beautiful whiskey. Don't be put off by the fact this is grain: this is exceptionally high grade Irish. Very much of the Cooley style, who happen to make the best grain whisky in the British Isles. 46% (92 proof). ncf.

Glendalough 3 Year Old Irish Single Grain sherry & Madeira butts db **(91)** n22 t23.5 f22.5 b23 A much richer and more confident grain than their first, sherry-finished version. Excellent. *43%.*

Glendalough Double Barrel Irish Whiskey first aged in American bourbon casks, then Spanish oloroso casks **(88.5)** n22.5 t23 f21 b22 A very pleasant malt but rather vague and at times a little dull. *42%*

Glendalough Single Cask Irish Whiskey Grand Cru Burgundy Cask Finish cask no. 1/BY19 **(87.5)** n22.5 t24 f20 b22 Strikes me more of a grain than a malt whisky this, not least because of the gorgeous velvety mouthfeel. The honeys on delivery are sublime: predominantly ulmo honey but a little acacia slipping in, too. There is a light fruitiness getting on the act. But the finish is undone slightly by the furry tang of a naughty wine cask. A real shame, for otherwise this would have been one hell of a score... *42%. ncf sc. 366 bottles.*

Hyde No. 5 Áras Cask 1860 Single Grain burgundy cask finished, bott Jul 16 **(86)** n21 t22.5 f21 b21.5 When I first heard about this bottling I was intrigued: one of the softest yet most charismatic grain whiskies in the world rounded off in pinot noir grape casks. Would the grape add an intriguing flintiness to the proceedings, or be of a type to soften it further? Sadly, it was the latter. Yes, sulphur free and clean (itself a minor miracle) and with plenty of chewy fruit caramels and even a little spice. But the peaks have been levelled and what is left is a pleasant, easy drinking, sweet but mainly featureless malt. *46%. ncf. 5,000 bottles.*

Teeling Whiskey Single Grain wine casks, bott Mar 17, bott code: L17 004 075 **(94)** n23 t24 f23 b24 What a beautiful grain whisky this is. Thankfully the wine casks don't interrupt the already spellbinding narrative. *46%. ncf.*

Single Rye

KILBEGGAN County Westmeath. 1757, recommenced distilling 2007. Beam Suntory.

Kilbeggan Small Batch Rye Irish Whiskey bott code: L18094 20/09/18 db **(85.5)** n22.5 t22 f20.5 b20.5 Quite brilliant to see rye whiskey coming out of Ireland: long may it continue. However, for the next batch I'd like to see it up its game considerably, as this is surprisingly tame. Certainly the rye momentarily brightens up the nose like the sun peering through a cloud to unveil the rich colours of a country garden. But then it hides behind a cloud again, in this case one of unbudging caramel with no silver lining whatsoever. The fact that it feels that there is no finish to this, so anaemic has it become, means this whiskey is not yet aligned as it should be: something is blocking the glory of the rye. And we know it is there, for on delivery it shimmers like a pearl before disappearing through your fingers and into the depths. *43% (86 proof).*

Blends

Bushmills 12 Years Old Distillery Reserve db **(86)** n22.5 t22.5 f20 b21. This version has gone straight for the ultra lush feel. For those who want to take home some 40% abv fruit fudge from the distillery. *40%*

Bushmills 1608 400th Anniversary (83) n21 t21.5 f20 b20.5. Thin-bodied, hard as nails and sports a peculiarly Canadian feel. *46%. Diageo.*

Bushmills 1608 db **(87)** n22 t23 f20 b22. A blend which, through accident, evolution or design, has moved a long way in style from when first launched. More accent on fruit though, predictably, the casks aren't quite what they once were. Ignoring the furriness on the finish, there is much to enjoy on the grape-must nose and how the fruit bounces off the rigid grain on delivery. *46%*

Bushmills Black Bush (91) n23 t23 f21.5 b23.5. This famous old blend may be under new management and even blender. But still the high quality, top-notch complexity rolls around the glass and your palate. As beautiful as ever. *40%*

Bushmills Black Bush (95) n24 a teasing singing of the crisp fruit notes and far from shy and tender malt: sexy and disarming; t24 supremely rich, making the most of the rock hard grain to fully emphasis both the juicy barley and lusciousness of the grape influence; f23 dries, allowing the caramel to take a bow. But the spices up their tempo to compensate b24 a blend that just feels so right on the palate. Remains a true work of Irish art... *40%.*

Bushmills Black Bush bott code L6140IB001 **(95)** n23.5 t24 f23.5 b24 Of all the famous old blends in the British Isles, this has probably bucked the trend by being an improvement on its already excellent self. The warehouses of Bushmills distillery boast the highest quantity of quality, unsulphured sherry butts I have encountered in the last 20 years, and this is borne out by a blend which has significantly upped the wine influence in the recipe but has not paid a price for it, as has been the usual case in Scotland. Indeed, it has actually benefitted. This is a belter, even by its normal own high standards. Truly classic and should be far easier to find than is normally the case today. *40%.*

⟐ **Bushmills Black Bush Sherry Cask Reserve** bott code: L10471B **(94)** n23 t24 f23 b24 As majestic and gloriously structured as always, and vividly salivating, too. But annoyingly loses a point for the faintest furry niggle from a sherry butt on the finish. *40%.*

Bushmills Original (80) n19 t21 f20 b20. Remains one of the hardest whiskeys on the circuit with the Midleton grain at its most unflinching. There is a sweeter, faintly maltier edge to this now while the toffee and biscuits qualities remain. *40%*

❖ **Bushmills The Original** bott code: L1175IB **(92) n22.5** it has lost its trademark metal-hard aroma, which has been usurped by a much softer, kinder, sweeter greeting: a little bit of a shock. There is a firm under-currant, to be sure. But that surprise mix of butterscotch and light acacia honey transforms matters; **t23** well, that honey certainly wasn't my imagination. For it tumbles over the taste buds like the handiwork of so many bees. And where is that normal stiff girder of grain which has for so long been the backbone of this blend? It appears to have melted away as docile tannins, delicate toffee and louder spices give the palate something to think on; **f23** by now, you would normally be spitting out shattered teeth, cracked by the most uncompromising blend on the planet. Not here. Just a delicate toffee-honey fade to balance the spice **b23.5** last year, for the very first time I noticed that the steel rods which for 40 years reinforced this blend had softened. Not on the nose. But, intriguingly, on the palate. Normally it would be two years before I'd look again. But, intrigued, I couldn't wait. And yes, that transformation was not my imagination. Welcome to the new, super-soft, friendly, mouth-watering and quite delicious White Bush. Words, incidentally, I never thought I would ever write. *40%*.

Bushmills Red Bush bourbon casks, bott code: L7161IB001 db **(92) n22 t23.5 f23 b23.5** A beautifully balanced and erudite blended Irish fully deserving of discovery. And after the preponderance of wine-finished Irish from elsewhere, it was great to taste one that hadn't already set my nerves jangling in fear of what was to come. A worthy and beautiful addition to the Bushmills range. I always knew I'd be a little bit partial to a Red Bush. *40%*.

Bushmills White Bush bott code: L8185 IB 02S **(85) n21 t22 f21 b21** For decades this was the toughest blend in all Ireland, the one you not so much cut your teeth on, but broke them. The grain was hard enough to make ships from in the dockyards and you drank this not so much for the pleasantries, but the effect. In recent years it has yielded a little to finer tastes, and though the nose still gives away absolutely nothing – except toffeed grain – at least the delivery on the palate is both clean and salivating. No off notes from second rate sherry butts. Just a sweet toffee firmness that has now also done away with the old aggressive finale. Surprisingly pleasant. *40%. Known as "White Bush" due to the white label.*

Clonakilty Irish Whiskey batch no. NEBC002. bourbon cask, Imperial Stout Trooper cask finish **(88.5) n21.5 t22.5 f22.5 b22** Just love the brightness on the delivery, especially the initial burst of malt. Beer cask finishes have embittered me over the years, but pleased to report that there is no hop interference and residue here and those strikingly juicy tones on delivery carry through unmolested. Decent cocoa at the death, too. *50.2%. ncf. 1,400 bottles. Bottled for New England Brewing Co.*

Clonakilty Port Cask Finish batch no. 0012 **(90) n22 t23 f22 b23** A whiskey where you're between a rock and a soft, fruity place... *43.6%. ncf. 1,000 bottles. Cask Finish Series.*

Clonakilty Single Batch batch no. 003/2018 **(86) n21 t22 f21.5 b21.5** Clean and salivating, this is a hard as nails, simplistic Irish dependent on toffee as its principal flavour profile. *43.6%. ncf.*

Clonakilty Single Batch The Gentle Cut batch no. 012 **(86) n22 t23 f19.5 b21.5** Starts rather beautifully, with the rigid grain allowing the sugars scope to bring forward the sugars and spices out into the open. The finish, though, is dry and off balance. *43.6%. ncf. 1,500 bottles.*

The Dead Rabbit Aged 5 Years virgin American oak finished, bott no. L18001-011 **(93) n23 t23.5 f23 b23.5** The rabbit is dead: long live Dead Rabbit...! Oh, Murray Method to take this from a decent to a truly excellent Irish, by the way. *44%.*

The Dublin Liberties Oak Devil bott no. L17 048 W3 **(94) n23.5 t23.5 f23 b24** The Cooley grain at work here is of superstar status. So beautifully balanced and the word "lush" hardly does it justice... *46%.*

The Dubliner Bourbon Cask Aged batch no. 001, bott no. L0187F252 **(87.5) n21.5 t22.5 f21.5 b22** A soft, clean attractive blend which peaks on delivery with a lilting juiciness which works brilliantly with the grain which is as yielding as a feathered silk pillow. Vague spices plot a course towards the bitter lemon finish. *40%.*

The Dubliner Master Distiller's Reserve bourbon casks, bott no. L17718-320 **(91) n23.5 t23 f22 b22.5** Refreshing and tender. A bit of an understated treat. *42%.*

Dundalgan Charred Cask Irish Whiskey db **(87) n21.5 t22 f22 b21.5** This is an interesting one: you have a spirit that produces a fair chunk of oil. You then char a cask, which produces caramel. The only result possible is a thick whiskey on both nose and palate with limited scope to develop. So although the end product is the antonym of complexity, the flavours and mouthfeel are attractive and satisfying, especially if you are into malt and toffee. There are even some very late spices to stir things up a bit. *40%. West Cork Distillers Limited.*

Dundalgan Irish Whiskey db **(84) n21 t21 f21 b21.5** Pleasant, inoffensive, toffee-dominant and bland. *40%. West Cork Distillers Limited.*

Dunville's Three Crowns (80) n19 t22 f19 b20 Three casks and Three Crowns. So three cheers for the return of one of the great names in Irish whiskey! Somewhere in my warehouse I have a few original bottles of this stuff I picked up in Ireland over the years and at auction. None I opened tasted quite like this. Have to say that, despite the rich-lip-smacking delivery, certain aspects of the tangy nose and finish don't quite gel and are a little off key. The coronation remains on hold... *43.5%.*

Dunville's Three Crowns Peated (94.5) n23 t24 f23.5 b24 Even people purporting not to like peaty whisk(e)y will have a problem finding fault with this. This is a rare treat of an Irish. *43.5%.*

Egan's Centenary finished in French Limousin XO Cognac casks nbc **(94) n23 t23.5 f23.5 b24** So wonderful to find an Irish where both the spirit and the oak is in such deep harmony. A subtle Irish where the blender has carefully listened to what the casks are telling him. Superb. *46%. 5,995 bottles.*

◇ **Éiregold Irish Whisky Special Reserve** bourbon cask matured **(84.5) n20.5 t22 f21 b21** Curious that when I had whiskey a column in one of the quality Irish publications back in the 1990s, I was gently admonished for using the term Eire, for Ireland, in my copy. But here we are... The grain dominates this particular blend, in the Irish style that came to prominence in the 1960s, with toffee not far behind. Bit lost by the descriptor on the back (which I read, as always, after tasting this) as the cinnamon and cloves that they promise is always sign of great age. I get neither note either on nose or taste on this young whiskey, but the sweet toffee-vanilla theme is pleasant enough if not particularly demanding. *40%*

Feckin Irish Whiskey (81) n20 t21 f20 b20. Tastes just about exactly the feckin same as the Feckin Strangford Gold... *40%. The Feckin Drinks Co.*

Flannigans Blended Irish Whiskey (87.5) n21.5 t22.5 f21.5 b22 About as mouth-watering and easy going a blended Irish as you'll hope to find. Excellent sugars and velvety body ensure the most pleasant, if simple, of rides. Even a little spice peps up the flagging finish. *40%. Quality Spirits International.*

Great Oaks Cask Strength Irish Whiskey db **(90.5) n22 t23 f22.5 b23** A joyful whisky brimming with personality. *60%. West Cork Distillers Limited.*

Great Oaks Irish Whiskey db **(87) n22 t22 f21.5 b21.5** Easy going, full of its signature caramel chewy sweetness. Pleasant and non-threatening. *46%. West Cork Distillers Limited.*

Great Oaks New Frontiers Irish Whiskey db **(94) n23.5 t24 f23 b23.5** Very high class and inventive Irish. West Cork have seriously raised their game here and have entered a new quality dimension. *59%. West Cork Distillers Limited.*

Hinch Aged 5 Years Double Wood ex bourbon casks & virgin American oak barrels, bott code: 16919 **(93) n23 t23.5 f23 b23.5** A malt which works very well indeed, and deserves to. And even more so if at a greater strength and non-filtration. Impressive and highly enjoyable Irish which gives you minimum blarney and the truest flavour profile. *43%. The Time Collection.*

Hinch Aged 10 Years Sherry Cask Finish bott code: 23519 **(89) n21.5 t23 f22 b22.5** An, at first confused and later more relaxed, Irish that offers plenty of enjoyment. So many memorable moments, but a little more care with these casks would have brought a lot more. Still, that's my blender's perfectionist hat on. Just enjoy it! *43%. The Time Collection.*

Hinch Small Batch Bourbon Cask bott code: 16919 **(93) n23 t23.5 f23 b23.5** The bourbon casks make such a difference here. A blend which is allowed to shew both its sweeter and richer nature. *43%. The Time Collection.*

◇ **Hinch Craft & Casks Irish Whisky Imperial Stout Finish** bott code: L1098H001 **(86) n20 t23 f21 b22** I know that beer cask finishes are all the rage but forgive me if I don't become a fully paid-up member of the Supporters' Club. When the nose smells something a lot closer to an empty glass of Guinness that has been left standing on the bar-room table for an hour two than actual whiskey, you start to lose me. I agree, without the use of thumb screws, that after the tap room delivery the middle is brilliant: the texture is attractive, the creaminess to a vague, sweet chocolatey maltiness is a tasty flavour combination in particular; and there are even the odd bursts of honey. But the finish wanders off course again...though I'm pleased to report there are no technical off notes with the casks themselves. I suspect those, the stout-hearted, who have a penchant for this kind of whiskey will be in paroxysms of hoppy delight...and power to your elbow. Yes, there are aspects of this I seriously enjoy, but others...I just have to grin and beer it. *43%*

Hyde No. 6 President's Reserve 1938 Commemorative Edition sherry cask finish, bott May 17 **(77) n18 t22 f18 b19** Lush grape for sure. But the very last thing I'd commemorate anything in would be a sherry cask: unless you want sulphur to give you a good Hyding.... *46%. ncf.*

◇ **Hyde No.8 Heritage Cask 1640** stout cask finish, bott Nov 2020 **(92.5) n22** sweet, with surprising heather-honey rather than hops making an appearance; **t23** gorgeously creamy textured and salivating. The midpoint sees spices gushing like oil from a new struck geyser. But it is the Malteser candy intensity to the barley which blows you away; **f24** I'm not sure those peppery spices could be better controlled. Still the malt fills every segment of the palate with a little milk chocolate to compliment. This is amazing...; **b23.5** I admit it: I feared the worst, as is always the case when beer barrels are involved. But, in truth, the cask adds no hoppy transgression to this while the texture does at least give a nod towards oatmeal stout. An absolute surprise package: I am shocked...for all the right reasons. Far better than I could possibly imagine. *43% ncf 5000 bottles*

The Irishman Founder's Reserve Caribbean Cask Finish rum cask, cask no. 9657 **(93) n23 t23.5 f23 b23.5** This brings to an end a run of tasting six consecutive Irish whiskies, each tainted by sulphur. This, naturally, has not an atom of sulphur as, sensibly, no sherry cask was used anywhere in the maturation (three hearty cheers!). Frankly, I don't know whether to drink it, or kiss it.... *46%. ncf sc. 318 bottles.*

The Irishman Founder's Reserve Florio Marsala Cask Finish cask no. 2786 **(82.5) n21 t23.5 f17.5 b20** A nipping, acidic, biting nose: borderline aggressive. But, momentarily, all is forgiven! The fruit is as lush as any delivery in the world this year, helped along by a thin maple syrup sweetness and balancing vanillas. Shame, then, about the very late sulphur tang. Whoever put the sulphur candle in this cask wants shooting: this would otherwise have been real stunner. *46%. ncf sc. 204 bottles.*

The Irishman Superior Irish Whiskey bott code L6299L059 **(93) n23 t23 f23 b24.** What a quite wonderful blend: not of the norm for those that have recently come onto the market and there is much more of the Irish Distillers about this than most. Forget about the smoke promised in the tasting notes on the label...it gives you everything else but. *40%.*

Jameson (95) n24.5 24 f22.5 b24 I thought I had detected in bottlings I had found around the world a very slight reduction in the Pot Still character that defines this truly classic whiskey. So I sat down with a fresh bottle in more controlled conditions...and was blown away as usual. The sharpness of the PS is vivid and unique; the supporting grain of the required crispness. Fear not: this very special whiskey remains in stunning, truly wondrous form. *40%*

Jameson bott code L701012030 **(87) n22 t22.5 f21 b21.5** Now, isn't that the way it always happens! Having tasted crisp, characterful true-to-form Jamesons around the globe for the last year or so, the one I get here for a re-taste is the "other" version. Suddenly the sexiest Irish on the market has become a dullard. Where it should be soaring with Pot Still it is laden with toffee. And a little sulphur nagging on the finish doesn't help, either. Does tick the other boxes, though. But hardly representative. *40%.*

◇ **Jameson** bott code: L108512 **(86.5) n22 t22.5 f21 b21** Oh dear. For another year the once great Jameson has slipped back from a master of complexity to a decent but ultimately toffee-riddled blend. I had hoped that last year's fall from grace was temporary. But the pot still character I had managed to instal into the blend back in the 1990s appears to have been stripped away. Not entirely, as the delivery shews a little pot still at work. And there is some lovely spice-centred complexity through the middle, though this is a brief burst compared to of old. This finish, though, is deadly dull as caramel exclusively takes hold. *40%*

Jameson 18 Years Old bott code L629231345 **(91) n22 t23 f23 b23** Definitely a change in direction from the last Jameson 18 I analysed. Much more grain focussed and paying less heed to the oak. *40%.*

Jameson Black Barrel bott code L700431433 **(93) n23 t23.5 f23 b23.5** An improved, more sugar-laden and spicy whiskey. *40%.*

Jameson Black Barrel double charred bourbon barrels, bott code: L932431768 **(93) n23 t23 f23.5 b23.5** Probably the softest Irish whisky I have encountered in over 40 years. But the complex sexing up by the spice raises the standard to another level. *40%.*

Jameson The Blender's Dog bott code L608231059 **(91.5) n22.5 t23 f23 b23** A very slight variance on the previous sample (above) with the grain whiskey a little more dominant here despite the softer mouthfeel. All the usual tricks and intrigues though a little less orange blossom honey a tad more maple syrup, which helps lengthen the finale. *43%.*

Jameson Bold bott code L617431172 **(93) n24 t23.5 f22.5 b23** Absolutely spot on with the tasting notes above. Only changes are slightly more fudge through the centre ground and a degree less bitterness on the finish, though still there. Crucially, however, the honey has a bigger late say. *40%. The Deconstructed Series.*

Jameson Caskmates (91.5) n23.5 t23 f22 b23 Some serious elements of Jameson Gold involved in this, especially the acacia honey thread. Delightful. *40%*

Jameson Caskmates Stout Edition bott code L629315085 **(93) n22 t23.5 f24 b23.5** A very different experience to the Teeling equivalent. Here, the beer is far less prevalent on nose and taste, but makes a significant, highly positive, contribution to the mouthfeel. A super lush experience. *40%.*

Jameson The Cooper's Croze bott code L608231057 **(94.5)** n23.5 t24 f22.5 b24 Huh! Near enough same final score as last time, though a gentle change in emphasis and shape means the scoring itself was slightly different. Remains the most astonishingly lush and richly-flavoured of whiskeys, except on this bottling there is a bigger toffee surge, especially towards the finish and a gentle bitter tail off which has cost a half mark. Just remember: whatever anyone ever tells you, no two bottlings are identical: it is impossible. *43%. The Whiskey Makers Series.*

Jameson The Cooper's Croze bott code: L929031684 **(94.5)** n23.5 t24 f23 b24 After a spate of pretty soul-destroying sulphur-riddled and spoiled Irish whiskeys, I could almost weep for coming across a bottling that is just as beautiful as when I tasted it last. Magnificent whiskey. *43%. ncf.*

Jameson Crested bott code L635731441 **(91)** n23 t23.5 f22 b22.5 That's curious. A slight upping of the caramels here has slightly reduced the overall complexity, and the depth of the fruit. However, the bitter, off-key finish from my last sample is missing here making, when all is said and done, a slightly more satisfying all round experience. Swings and roundabouts... *40%.*

Jameson Crested bott code: L933631800 **(85.5)** n22 t22 f20 b21.5 Unquestionably dulled since its release – or re-release, if you count the classic old Crested 10 brand. A little barley sneaks through on the nose but the degree of toffee seems to have increased exponentially. A slightly furry grape kick towards the finale, but not too untoward. Incredibly far removed from the Crested 10 I used to regularly drink over 30 years ago. Unrecognisable, in fact. *40%.*

Jameson The Distiller's Safe bott code L60331023 **(93)** n24 t24 f22 b23 This brand's safe, too...at least for another bottling! As near as damn it a re-run of the last bottle I tasted, though here the butteryness kicks in sooner and there is a vague bitterness on the now chocolate-flaked finish. Still a stunner. *43%. The Whiskey Makers Series.*

Jameson Gold Reserve (88) n22 t23 f20 b22. Enjoyable, but so very different: an absolute re-working with all the lighter, more definitively sweeter elements shaved mercilessly while the thicker oak is on a roll. Some distance from the masterpiece it once was. *40%*

Jameson Round bott code L625831239 **(93.5)** n22.5 t24 f23.5 b23.5 Just such a sensual whiskey... *40%. The Deconstructed Series.*

Jameson Signature bott code L617531177 **(93)** n24 t23.5 f22.5 b23 No longer Signature Reserve, though every bit as good. This, though, like some other Jamesons of late appears to have an extra dose of caramel. Bring the colouring down and whiskey – and the scores here - will really fly! *40%.*

Jameson Signature Reserve (93) n23.5 t23.5 f22.5 b23.5. Be assured that Signature, with its clever structuring of delicate and inter-weaving flavours, says far more about the blender, Billy Leighton, than it does John Jameson. *40%. Irish Distillers.*

Kilbeggan bott code L7091 db **(86)** n21 t22 f21.5 b21.5. A much more confident blend by comparison with that faltering one of the last few years. Here, the malts make a significant drive towards increasing the overall complexity and gentle citrus style. *40%. Cooley.*

Kilbeggan Traditional Irish Whiskey bott code: L19113 16/10/19 db **(88)** n22 t22.5 f21.5 b22 A really lovely Irish blend, making best use of some prime grain whisky which allows the barley present to ramp up the complexity and oak likewise with the spices. Just a shade too much toffee at the death. *40% (80 proof).*

Kilbeggan 15 Years Old bott code L7048 db **(85.5)** n21.5 t22 f21 b21. My word! 15 years, eh? How time flies! And on the subject of flying, surely I have winged my way back to Canada and am tasting a native blend. No, this is Irish albeit in sweet, deliciously rounded form. However, one cannot help feeling that the dark arts have been performed, as in an injection of caramel, which, as well as giving that Canadian feel has also probably shaved off some of the more complex notes to middle and finish. Even so, a sweet, silky experience. *40%. Cooley.*

Kilbeggan 18 Year Old db **(89)** n23 t21.5 f22.5 b22. Although the impressive bottle lavishly claims "From the World's Oldest Distillery" I think one can take this as so much Blarney. It certainly had my researcher going, who lined this up for me under the Old Kilbeggan distillery, a forgiveable mistake and one I think he will not be alone in making. This, so it appears on the palate, is a blend. From the quite excellent Cooley distillery, and it could be that whiskey used in this matured at Kilbeggan... which is another thing entirely. As for the whiskey: apart from some heavy handedness on the toffee, it really is quite a beautiful and delicate thing. *40%*

Kinahan's Heritage Small Batch Blend (87.5) n22 t23 f21 b21.5 All aboard for the plush delivery, a gorgeous mix of briefly intense malt but overwhelmingly soft, sweet and embracing grain. The weak link is the tart and rough-edged finale, undermined further by a slight bitter note. But earlier there is plenty of fun to be had with the vanilla and spices. *46%.*

Kinahan's KASC Project B. 001 hybrid cask (Portuguese, American, French, Hungarian & chestnut) **(86)** n20 t22 f22 b22 Well, that is different. The wood has the biggest say here, especially on the nose where the spirit is left bullied, quivering and unnoticed in some inaccessible corner. While the flavour profile is very pleasant, it certainly didn't ring true and when I later spotted the chestnut inclusion, the sensations immediately made sense. Intriguing, though. *43%.*

Lambay Whiskey Small Batch Blend finished in Cognac casks, bott code: L4732519 21/11/19 **(92) n23 t23 f22.5 b23.5** The uncomfortable landing on the finish apart, this is a blend to savour with high quality malt making the most of a very sympathetic grain. Some really beautiful moments... *40%. ncf.*

⬧⬧⬧ **The Liberator Storehouse Special Small Batch Double Port** batch no.3 **(92.5) n23** the clean, understated grape is no more than a kiss. The elegance and abundance of malt for a blend is a pleasant surprise; **t23.5** not sure you can ask much more from a Port cask influenced blend: the mouthfeel is tender as your lover's embrace while the grape is sweeter than your first love. The grain is yielding and does a marvellous job of melding the clean fruit and intense barley together...; big spice kick, but so sumptuous and salivating is the mouth feel, you hardly notice it...! **f22.5** a gorgeous fade of toffee and raisin; **b23.5** if you don't feel Liberated after this, you never will. A triumph of a blend. *62.1%*

Midleton Very Rare 30th Anniversary Pearl Edition db **(91) n23.5 t24 f21 b22.5** The nose and delivery will go down in Irish whiskey folklore... *53.1%*

Midleton Very Rare 1984 (70) n19 t18 f17 b16. Disappointing with little backbone or balance. *40%. Irish Distillers.*

Midleton Very Rare 1985 (77) n20 t20 f18 b19. Medium-bodied and oily, this is a big improvement on the initial vintage. *40%. Irish Distillers.*

Midleton Very Rare 1986 (79) n21 t20 f18 b20. A very malty Midleton richer in character than previous vintages. *40%. Irish Distillers.*

Midleton Very Rare 1987 (77) n20 t19 f19 b19. Quite oaky at first until a late surge of excellent pot still. *40%. Irish Distillers.*

Midleton Very Rare 1988 (86) n23 t21 f21 b21. A landmark MVR as it is the first vintage to celebrate the Irish pot-still style. *40%. Irish Distillers.*

Midleton Very Rare 1989 (87) n22 t22 f22 b21. A real mouthful but has lost balance to achieve the effect. *40%. Irish Distillers.*

Midleton Very Rare 1990 (93) n23 t23 f24 b23. Astounding whiskey: one of the vintages every true Irish whiskey lover should hunt for. *40%. Irish Distillers.*

Midleton Very Rare 1991 (76) n19 t20 f19 b18. After the Lord Mayor's Show, relatively dull and uninspiring. *40%. Irish Distillers.*

Midleton Very Rare 1992 (84) n20 t20 f23 b21. Superb finish with outstanding use of feisty grain. *40%. Irish Distillers.*

Midleton Very Rare 1993 (88) n21 t22 f23 b22. Big, brash and beautiful – the perfect way to celebrate the 10th-ever bottling of MVR. *40%. Irish Distillers.*

Midleton Very Rare 1994 (87) n22 t22 f21 b22. Another different style of MVR, one of amazing lushness. *40%. Irish Distillers.*

Midleton Very Rare 1995 (90) n23 t24 b21 b22. They don't come much bigger than this. Prepare a knife and fork to battle through this one. Fabulous. *40%. Irish Distillers.*

Midleton Very Rare 1996 (82) n21 t22 f19 b20. The grains lead a soft course, hardened by subtle pot still. Just missing a beat on the finish, though. *40%. Irish Distillers.*

Midleton Very Rare 1997 (83) n22 t21 f19 b21. The piercing pot still fruitiness of the nose is met by a countering grain of rare softness on the palate. Just dies on the finish when you want it to make a little speech. Very drinkable. *40%. Irish Distillers.*

Midleton Very Rare 1999 (89) n21 t23 f22 b23. One of the maltiest Midletons of all time: a superb blend. *40%. Irish Distillers.*

Midleton Very Rare 2000 (85) n22 t21 f21 b21. An extraordinary departure even by Midleton's eclectic standards. The pot still is like a distant church spire in an hypnotic Fen landscape. *40%. Irish Distillers.*

Midleton Very Rare 2001 (79) n21 t20 f18 b20. Extremely light but the finish is slightly on the bitter side. *40%. Irish Distillers.*

Midleton Very Rare 2002 (79) n20 t22 f18 b19. The nose is rather subdued and the finish is likewise toffee-quiet and shy. There are some fabulous middle moments, some of flashing genius, when the pot still and grain combine for a spicy kick, but the finish really is lacklustre and disappointing. *40%. Irish Distillers.*

Midleton Very Rare 2003 (84) n22 t22 f19 b21. Beautifully fruity on both nose and palate (even some orange blossom on aroma). But the delicious spicy richness that is in mid launch on the tastebuds is cut short by caramel on the middle and finish. A crying shame, but the best Midleton for a year or two. *40%. Irish Distillers.*

Midleton Very Rare 2004 (82) n21 t21 f19 b21. Yet again caramel is the dominant feature, though some quite wonderful citrus and spice escape the toffeed blitz. *40%.*

Midleton Very Rare 2005 (92) n23 t24 f22 b23. OK, you can take this one only as a rough translation. The sample I have worked from here is from the Irish Distillers blending lab, reduced to 40% in mine but without caramel added. And, as Midleton Very Rares always are at this stage, it's an absolute treat. Never has such a great blend suffered so in the hands of colouring and here the chirpiness of the pot still and élan of the honey (very Jameson Gold Label in part) show just what could be on offer given half the chance. Has wonderful natural colour and surely it is a matter of time before we see this great whiskey in its natural state. *40%*

Midleton Very Rare 2006 (92) n22 t24 f23 b23. As raw as a Dublin rough-house and for once not overly swamped with caramel. An uncut diamond. *40%*

Midleton Very Rare 2007 (83) n20 t22 f20 b21. Annoyingly buffeted from nose to finish by powering caramel. Some sweeter wisps do escape but the aroma suggests Canadian and insufficient Pot Still gets through to make this a Midleton of distinction. *40%. Irish Distillers*

Midleton Very Rare 2008 (88.5) n22 t23 f21.5 b22. A dense bottling which offers considerably more than the 2007 Vintage. Attractive, very drinkable and without the caramel it might really have hit the heights. *40%. Irish Distillers.*

Midleton Very Rare 2009 (95) n24 t24 f23 b24. I've been waiting a few years for one like this to come along. One of the most complex, cleanest and least caramel-spoiled bottlings for a good few years and one which makes the pot still character its centre piece. A genuine celebration of all things Midleton and Barry Crockett's excellence as a distiller in particular. *40%.*

Midleton Very Rare 2010 (84) n21 t22 f20 b21. A case of after the Lord Mayor's Show. Chewy and some decent sugars. But hard to make out detail through the fog of caramel. *40%*

Midleton Very Rare 2011 (81.5) n22.5 t20 f19 b20 Another disappointing version where the colour of its personality has been compromised for the sake of the colour in the bottle. A dullard of a whiskey, especially after the promising nose. *40%. Irish Distillers.*

Midleton Very Rare Irish Whisky 2012 db **(89.5) n22 t23 f22 b22.5.** Much more like it! After a couple of dud vintages, here we have a bottling worthy of its great name & heritage. *40%.*

Midleton Very Rare Irish Whisky 2014 db **(78.5) n20.5 t22 f17 b19.** Must say how odd it looks to see Brian Nation's signature scrawled across the label and not Barry Crockett's. Also, I was a bit worried by this one when I saw the depth of orange hue to this whiskey. Sadly, my fears were pretty well founded. Toffee creaks from every corner making for a mainly flat encounter with what should be an uplifting Irish. Some lift at about the midway point when something, probably pot still, throws off the shackles of its jailer and emerges briefly with spice. But all rather too little, especially in the face of a dull, disappointingly flawed, fuzzy finale. Midleton Very Rare should be, as the name implies, a lot, lot better than this safe but flabby, personality bypassed offering. The most frustrating aspect of this is that twice I have tasted MVR in lab form just prior to bottling. And both were quite stunning whiskeys. That was until the colouring was added in the bottling hall. *40% WB15/416*

Midleton Very Rare 2016 (87.5) n22 t22.5 f21.5 b21.5 The grain, not exactly the most yielding, has the clearest mandate to show its uncompromising personality A huge caramel presence softens the impact and leads to a big show of coffee towards the finish. But between these two OTT beasts the Pot Still is lost completely soon after its initial delicious impact on delivery. *40%.*

Midleton Very Rare 2017 (90.5) n22 t23.5 f22 b23 Slightly less toffee than there has been, but still a fraction too much. But superb complexity levels nonetheless and one of the most attractively sweet MVRs for a little while. *40%.*

Midleton Very Rare 2018 bott code: L826431444 **(88.5) n22.5 t23 f21 b22** All about understatement. But like many an Irish at the moment, just weakens towards the finish. *40%.*

Midleton Very Rare 2019 bott code: L925431568 db **(92) n23 t23.5 f22 b23.5** One of the better Midletons for a while and really going full out for maximum meltdown effect. Classy, if slightly flawed. *40%.*

Mizen Head Original Irish Whiskey Bodega sherry casks db **(87.5) n21.5 t22.5 f21.5 b22** Maybe this was a bit unlucky, in that I have just come from tasting Glenfarclas sherry casks of the 1980s to this. No damaging sulphur (though a little forms late on the finale), so some Brownie points there. But the lack of body to the spirit and shortage of complexity on the grape, beyond a delicious cinnamon spice, doesn't help the cause. Enjoyable, but thinner than you might expect or desire. *40%. West Cork Distillers Limited.*

Natterjack Irish Whiskey Blend No. 1 virgin American oak finish, bott code: L19/001 044 **(92) n22 t23.5 f23 b23.5** A delicious whiskey and looking forward to seeing Blend No 2. But I find the label confusing: a "mash bill or malted barley and corn". Does this mean that is the distillation from a mash recipe of malt and corn? Hence the mash bill comment. Or, as I don't think they actually distilled this themselves, a blend of malt and corn whiskey? Which means that it isn't a mash bill of corn and barley. Far too vague for the consumer. Very enjoyable, nonetheless. *40%. Gortinore Distillers & Co.*

Natterjack Irish Whiskey Cask Strength virgin American oak finish **(89) n22.5 t22.5 f22 b22** At around 40% I thought this was pretty strange whiskey: this is 50% weirder still. Enjoyable, if head-scratching stuff – though you might end up with splinters in your fingers as it seems to be the oak which causes the extra confusion... 63%. Gortinore Distillers & Co.

Paddy (74) n18.5 t20 f17.5 b18. Cleaned its act up a little. Even a touch of attractive citrus on the nose and delivery. But where does that cloying sweetness come from? As bland as an Irish peat bog but, sadly, nothing like so potentially tasty. 40%. Irish Distillers.

⬩⬩⬩ **Paddy** bott code: 20/04/21 **(76) n20 t19 f18 b18** A blend I have never much cared for... and still don't. Hard, uncompromising, bitter and lacking balance. A kind of Hillman Imp but without the trimmings. You'll probably find the landlord serving it you at some remote Irish village inn a whole lot friendlier and better company. Even the blasted cap doesn't screw back on...! 40%

Powers (91) n23 t24 f22 b22. Is it any coincidence that in this bottling the influence of the caramel has been significantly reduced and the whiskey is getting back to its old, brilliant self? I think not. Classic stuff. 40%. Irish Distillers.

Powers Gold Label American oak casks, bott code: L927315375 db **(83) n21.5 t21.5 f19 b21** Three decades ago, this was always my preferred choice when drinking in Ireland. Not least because of all the blends this was the one that had by far the healthiest Pot Still involvement, and its sturdy magic was there to be savoured despite the outrageous amount of caramel that was added, making the whiskey a lot darker than its present incarnation. Today, it is virtually unrecognisable from what was the Irishman's most popular blend. The Pot Still has virtually no input whatsoever, while the sulphur attached to the sherry butts give an unfortunate, nagging, furry finale. Elsewhere the delicate heather honey notes do well. But for those of us who have loved this whiskey for almost a lifetime, it's all a bit of a disappointment... 40%. ncf.

Powers Gold Label (96) n23 t24.5 f24 b24.5 A slightly different breed. This is not all about minute difference in strength...this is also about weight distribution and flavour pace. It is a subtly different blend...and all the better for it...Make no mistake: this is a truly classic finish. 43.2%

The Quiet Man Traditional Irish Whiskey bourbon casks **(88.5) n22 t22 f22.5 b22** A gentle and genteel whiskey without an unfriendly voice. And with it I toast the memory of John Mulgrew. 40%

⬩⬩⬩ **The Quiet Man Superior Irish Whiskey Blend** bourbon cask matured **(86.5) n21.5 t22 f21 b22** A very quiet whiskey: beyond the charming, delicately sweet cream toffee it has little else to say. Though, to many, it will be quite enough... 40%

Roe & Co bourbon casks, bott code: L9227NB001 **(90.5) n22 t23.5 f22.5 b22.5** A silky, sexy massively-flavoured blend where the complexity is not only given room to thrive but the bourbon casks ensure an extra degree of rich, honey depth, too. If they could just kill the un-needed caramel, this would be such a big scorer. 45%. ncf.

⬩⬩⬩ **Samuel Gelston's** bott code: 05/07/2021 **(86.5) n21 t22.5 f21 b22** This appears to have taken over from White Bush as the quintessential hard-nosed, unyielding blend with a grain solid enough to demolish houses. A welcome lack of caramel does ensure that the malt positively explodes on delivery, bringing with it an excellent juiciness. A little icing sugar and spice for a lovely vanilla-rich midpoint, especially with those spices buzzing noisily. The finish returns to its rock-solid self. Kind of old school White Bush but with a sweeter, almost marshmallow-style flourish. 40%.

Slane Irish Whiskey Triple Casked bott code: L34638 **(86.5) n22 t22.5 f20.5 b21.5** Soft and supine, this whisky is all about softness and mouthfeel: that feeling of a soothing friend by your side. Could do with a bit more personality on the flavour front so the simple sugars don't over dominate as they have a tendency to do here. Excellent spices slowly grow at the finish to offset the furry bitterness of, presumably, a sherry butt or two at work here. Pleasant and promising whiskey. 40%.

Teeling Whiskey Barleywine Small Batch Barleywine finish, bott Sept 18, bott code: L18 016 270 **(84.5) n21 t21.5 f21 b21** Well, that's a new flavour profile after all these decades in the business! Am I big fan? Well, not really. Love the cream soda texture, I admit. And the suffused sweetness But there is a lurking semi-bitterness which seems to tighten everything about it. I'm sure there are those out there, though, that will worship it. Just not me. 46%. ncf.

Teeling Whiskey Small Batch rum casks, bott Apr 19, bott code: L19 014 093 **(86) n21.5 t22.5 f21 b21** A whiskey I just can't like as much as I'd like to. Certainly the delivery ticks all the boxes and offers an innate light treacle sweetness, just as one might hope. But there is an intruding bitterness – almost like hop – which interrupts the nose and finish and spoils the party a bit. Odd. 46%. ncf.

Teeling Whiskey Trois Rivieres Small Batch rhum agricole finish, bott Jul 18, bott code: L18 001 186 **(91) n22.5 t23 f22.5 b23** The most even and relaxed of the three Teeling rum expressions. What it lacks in complexity it makes up for with simple charm. 46%. ncf.

Tullamore D.E.W. bott code: L1 5297TD 30/11/2018 **(81.5) n21.5 t21 f19 b20** When you are using a grain as hard as this you have to be careful of the caramel as it amplifies its effects. Lots of toffee followed by a dull buzz. Still a very dull Irish. *40%. William Grant & Sons.*

Tullamore D.E.W. Aged 12 Years bourbon & oloroso sherry casks, bott code: L3 5294TD 22/11/2018 **(91.5) n23 t23 f22 b23.5** When a whiskey is this good, you wonder what the other two Tullamore blends are all about. *40%. William Grant & Sons.*

Tullamore D.E.W. Caribbean Rum Cask Finish bott code: L1 5184TD 23/07/2018 **(80) n21 t20 f20 b19** Sweet, soft and a dullard of the very first order. Far more effect from the caramel than the rum casks. There may have been exotic fruit in the tasting lab. But it vanished once it entered the bottling hall. So massively disappointing. *43%. William Grant & Sons.*

Uisce Beatha Real Irish Whiskey ex-Bourbon cask **(81) n21 t20.5 f19.5 b20.** The label blurb claims this is soft and subtle. That is, about as soft and subtle as if distilled from granite. Hard as nails with dominant grains; takes no prisoners at the death. *40%*

West Cork Black Cask Char #5 Level bott code: L17297 db **(89) n22 t23 f22 b22** Good grief! This must be one of the most oil-rich, heavy duty blends I have encountered in my near 30 year whisky career. Either very little grain, or it is a grain distilled to a relatively low strength. Either way...good grief! *40%. West Cork Distillers Limited.*

West Cork Bourbon Cask db **(87.5) n22 t22.5 f21 b22** No-one does caramel like West Cork, and even in their blend – in which their own grain has attractively thinned their hefty malt, it comes through loud and clear. Indeed, had I not known the distillery, I would have marked this down as a Canadian or a young, unfulfilled bourbon. Wonderfully soft and proffers some seriously lovely moments. *40%. West Cork Distillers Limited.*

West Cork Cask Strength bott code: L17293 db **(87) n21 t23.5 f20.5 b22** Just love the power of this malt on the delivery, relentlessly, mercilessly driving home the barley, a little ulmo honey and vanilla offering a controlled sweetness. Neither the nose or finish work so well, but worth finding just for that beautiful launch. *62%. West Cork Distillers Limited.*

The Whistler Oloroso Sherry Cask Finish bott code: L19/34018 141 **(83.5) n20 t22 f20 b21.5** Too much sulphur on the sherry kicks it out of tune. A shame, as some outstanding heather honey and raisin notes deserved better. *43%. nc ncf.*

The Wild Geese Classic Blend Untamed (90) n22.5 t23 f22 b22.5 Appears to shew high grain content, but when that happens to be excellent then there are no moans from me. *43%.*

The Wild Geese Fourth Centennial Untamed (87) n21.5 t22.5 f21.5 b21.5 A very firm malt, brittle almost, which crashes onto the palate in slightly ungainly style. Only in the third to sixth flavour waves does it hit some kind of rhythmic harmony, a searingly salivating experience. But the roughouse grain makes for an uncompromising finish with bite and a little attitude, which would be brilliant but for an off-key fade. *43%.*

The Wild Geese Rare Irish (89.5) n22 t23 f22 b22.5 Just love this. The Cooley grain is working sublimely and dovetails with the malt in the same effortless way wild geese fly in perfect formation. A treat. *43%. Cooley for Avalon.*

Writers Tears (93) n23.5 t24 f22 b23.5 Now that really was different. The first mix of pure Pot Still and single malt I have knowingly come across in a commercial bottling, but only because I wasn't aware of the make up of last year's Irishman Blend. The malt, like the Pot Still, is, I understand from proprietor Bernard Walsh, from Midleton, but the two styles mixed shows a remarkably similar character to when I carried out an identical experiment with pure pot still and Bushmills the best part of a decade ago. A success and hopefully not a one off. *40%. Writers Tears Whiskey Co.*

Writers' Tears Copper Pot Florio Marsala Cask Finish Marsala hogshead, cask no. 3150 **(84.5) n22.5 t22 f20 b20** Starts brilliantly, promising so much... but then falls away dramatically at the end...And how ironic and fitting is that? I decided to taste Irish whiskeys today as it looked very likely that Ireland would beat England at Lords in their very first Test Match against them, and here was a chance to toast their historic victory. And, after skittling England out for an embarrassing 85 on the opening, incredible morning an extraordinary victory looked on the horizon. But while tasting this, Ireland themselves were blasted off the pitch and comprehensively routed, when they were all out for just 38 – the seventh lowest score in Test history. Irish writers' tears, indeed... *45%. ncf sc. 336 bottles.*

Writers' Tears Double Oak American oak barrels from Kentucky & French oak Cognac casks, bott code: L9106L2273 **(89.5) n23.5 t23 f21 b22** Does really well until the last leg. *45%.*

Poitín

Mad March Hare Irish Poitín bott code: L16 001 021 **(86) n20 t22.5 f21.5 b22** Full flavoured, oily and sweet there is plenty of icing sugar here to help make for an easy experience: perhaps too easy for a poitin! The nose suggests a bit more copper might not go amiss, though. And, seeing as It's poitin, why not go for a full strength version while you are at it.. *40%.*

Japanese Whisky

How fitting that in the age when the sun never sets on where whisky is produced it is from the land of the Rising Sun that the finest can now be found.

Recently Japan, for the first time ever, won Jim Murray's World Whisky of the Year with its insanely deep and satisfying Yamazaki Sherry Cask(s) 2013, a result which caused predictable consternation among more than a few. And a degree of surprise in Japan itself. The industry followed that up by commanding 5th spot with a very different but truly majestic specimen of a malt showing a style unique to Japan. How impressive.

It reminded me of when, some 25 years ago, I took my old mate Michael Jackson and a smattering of non-friends on a tour of this year's Whisky Bible's Japanese Champions Yoichi distillery on Hokkaido, pointing out to them that here was a place where a malt could be made to mount a serious challenge to the best being made anywhere in the world. While there, a local journalist asked me what Japanese distillers could learn from Scotland. I caused a bit of a sharp intake of breath – and a pathetically gutless but entirely characteristic denial of association by some whisky periodical executive or other who had a clear idea which side his bread was buttered – when I said it was the other way round: it was more what the Scots could learn from the Japanese.

The reason for that comment was simple: the extraordinary attention to detail and tradition that was paid by Japanese distillers, those at Yoichi in particular, and the touching refusal to cut costs and corners. It meant that it was the most expensive whisky in the world per unit of alcohol to produce. But the quality was astonishingly high – and that would, surely, eventually reap its rewards as the world learned to embrace malt whisky made away from the Highlands and Islands of Scotland which, then, was still to happen. Ironically, it was the Japanese distillers' habit to ape most things Scottish – the reason why there is a near century-old whisky distilling heritage there in the first place - that has meant that Yoichi, or the magnificent Hakushu, has yet to pick up the Bible's World Whisky of the Year award I expected for them. Because, sadly, there have been too many bottlings over the last decade tainted by sherry butts brought from Spain after having been sulphur treated. So I was also pleasantly surprised when I first nosed – then nosed again in near disbelief – then tasted the Yamazaki 2013 sherry offering. There was not even the vaguest hint that a single one of the casks used in the bottling had been anywhere near a sulphur candle. The result: something as close to single malt perfection as you will have found in a good many years. A single malt which no Scotch can at the moment get anywhere near and, oddly, takes me back to the Macallans of 30 years ago.

A Japanese custom of refusing to trade with their rivals has not helped expand their export market. Therefore a Japanese whisky, if not made completely from home-distilled spirit, will instead contain a percentage of Scotch rather than whisky from fellow Japanese distillers. This, ultimately, is doing the industry no favours at all. The practice is partly down to the traditional work ethics of company loyalty an inherent, and these days false, belief, that Scotch whisky is automatically better than Japanese. Back in the late 1990s I planted the first seeds in trying to get rival distillers to discuss with each other the possibility of exchanging whiskies to ensure that their distilleries worked economically. So it can only

White Oak ▲ Yamazaki ▲ Chita ▲

Togouchi ▲ ●Osaka

●Fukuoka

Key
● Major Town or City
▲ Distillery

Map locations

Akkeshi

Yoichi ● Sapporo

Sendai

Shirakawa

Saburomaru
Karuizawa

Hakushu
Hanyu

Mars Shinshu
● Tokyo

Gotemba

Jim Murray's Whisky Bible Japanese Whisky of the Year Winners	
2004	Pure Malt Black
2005	Nikka Coffey Grain Whisky 1991
2006	The Cask of Hakusha 1989
2007	Nikka Coffey Grain Whisky 1992
2008	Hanyu King of Diamonds
2009	Nikka Coffey Grain Whisky 1992
2010	SMWS 116.4
2011	Karuizawa 1967 Vintage
2012	Hibiki Aged 21 Years
2013	Hanyu Final Vintage 2000
2014	SMWS Cask 116.17 (Yoichi) 25
2015	Yamazaki Sherry 2013
2016	Yamazaki Mizunara
2017	Yamazaki Sherry 2016
2018	Nikka Coffey Malt Whisky
2019	The Hakushu Paul Rusch
2020	Nikka Taketsuru Pure Malt
2021	Nikka Single Malt Yoichi Apple Brandy Wood Finish
2022	The Kurayoshi 18 Pure Malt

be hoped that the deserved lifting of the 2015 Jim Murray's Whisky Bible World Whisky of the Year crown, and the hitherto unprecedented international press it received has helped put the spotlight back on the great whiskies coming from the east. Because unless you live in Japan, you are likely to see only a fraction of the fabulous whisky produced there. The Scotch Malt Whisky Society should have a special medal struck as they have helped in recent years with some memorable bottlings from Japan, single cask snapshots of the greatness that is still to be fully explored and mapped.

Yet Jim Murray's Whisky Bible has provided a double-edged sword for the Japanese whisky industry. The amazing news for them was their World Whisky of the Year award precipitated sales worth billions of yen. And, consequently, a near exhaustion of stocks. The Hibiki 17 and Hakushu 12 have now vanished as brands altogether. But it means that, at long last and deservedly, whisky drinkers around the globe finally recognise that Japanese single malt can be second to no other. Their problem is how to satisfy the thirst for Japanese whisky and knowledge on what it has to offer: at the moment they cannot. But Forsyths, the Speyside-based Scottish still manufacturers, are working overtime to supply more distilling equipment for the Land of the Rising Sun.

Single Malts

AKKESHI 2016. Kenten Co., Ltd.

The Akkeshi New Born 2019 Foundations 3 Single Malt Spirit Non-Peated Hokkaido-Mizunara cask, bott Jan 2019 db (**93**) **n23 t23.5 f23 b23.5** Can't wait for this beauty to become fully-fledged whisky. The freshness of the maturing new make is particularly evident on the finish. But until then the delicately tart tannin of the Mizunarna cask works its usual wonders and combines with the outstanding grist with commendable elegance. 55%.

The Akkeshi New Born 2019 Foundations 4 Malt and Grain Spirit bott Jul 19, bott code: IGZHS (**83.5**) **n21.5 t21.5 f20 b20.5** The rawness to this transgresses new make alone and enters into territory where not enough copper has been leached into the system to give this the required depth and roundness. Plenty of slightly oily malt doing the rounds but balance is at a premium. 48%.

⬙ **The Akkeshi Single Malt Whisky Peated** bott 2020, bott code: AJOJUJD (**90.5**) **n22** though more heavily peated, a flatter nose than the Lightly-Peated version (below); **t23** fat and intense, the spices waste no time getting to work on the tongue and roof of mouth. This isn't too bothered about subtlety: its single-minded purpose is to ram young, juicy peaty barley at you and see if you can cope...... A little lemon does soften some of the aggression; **f22.5** just slightly out of alignment with the delivery, a few odd notes start filtering through. But the peat-vanilla combination still does a job; **b23** a malt with a distinctive bite, this whisky has teeth! It's at times like this you'll learn to appreciate the Murray Method. 55%.

The Akkeshi Single Malt Whisky Sarorunkamuy Lightly-Peated bott Jan 20, bott code: JAXHS (**88.5**) **n22 t22.5 f21.5 b22.5** Not quite what I was expecting following some more rounded bottlings from this distillery in the past. Much thinner in body than anticipated, the smoke playing a graceful game and attractively flirting with the busy, peppery spices. A little molasses and cocoa towards the end, but you feel a spine is missing for the gutsier notes to attack. A slightly strange but enjoyable malt nonetheless. 55%.

⬙ **The Akkeshi Single Malt Whisky Sarorunkamuy Lightly-Peated** bott Jun 20, bott code: AFMQV (**93**) **n22.5** young it may be, but the shy phenols offer a unique fingerprint. Slightly astringent, as though a little CO_2 is in the air, the sweetness is strictly grist-based; **t23.5** brilliant delivery! The subtlest but most telling of oils ensures both the softest of deliveries and maximum length, too. Doesn't do the intensity much harm, either, which is formidable for the first five or six flavour waves. The main theme is chocolate, but first there is a fizzing mouth-watering quality which rocks you back in your seat...; **f23.5** chocolate pudding with smoke and spices at the very edges. Long, complex "bitty" notes quite similar to the finish of younger 1792 bourbon whiskies; **b23.5** one of the most exciting things about my job is when you locate a new distillery whose whisky offers something different. Akkeshi is one such distillery, and in this form generates a sharpness to its malt which guarantees lashings of intensity and personality. 55%.

⬙ **BS Fuji X The Akkeshi Single Malt Whisky** cask no. 465, dist 2017, bott 2020 (**94**) **n23** the distiller has done a cracking job here: the cut is right on the bullseye, allowing the barley to show both a green fruitiness and green grassiness in its gloriously fresh delivery; **t24** the genteel smattering of peat emboldens the barley further. Now we have weight to complement the flightier fresh tones of succulent grass. The sugars a succession of melting grist notes...; **f23.5** long, poutingly spiced, and clean enough to allow both the smoke and vanillas to come through at their own pace...**b23.5** beautifully distilled, this is malt on maximum revs. No great age, but sensuous and classy. Note to self: once Covid is contained, an overdue visit to this distillery is essential...! 58%. sc. 800 bottles.

BENIOTOME

⬙ **FUK Single Grain Whisky Aged 3 Years** bott 2020 (**85**) **n21.5 t22 f20 b21.5** Oh well. Another whisky name to get me into trouble. Doubtless by including this whisky in here, I'm even more of a sexist than some warped idiots claim I am. The nose is thin, clean, and offering a little sliced cucumber. Perhaps there is a hint of a lack of copper, too, and this is later confirmed by the tangy finale. But I do love the salivating freshness of the delivery which generates a series of lemon sherbet and light acacia honey notes. 40%.

⬙ **Miyabi Single Grain Whisky Aged 3 Years** bott 2020 (**88**) **n22 t22.5 f21.5 f22** A fatter, more robust grain that the FUK with far greater confidence in its handing of its sugars, perhaps thanks to an attractive spiced counterweight. Again, the finish lacks firmness and structure, but the marshmallow and spice theme, accompanied by some outstanding vanilla tones is exceptionally pleasant. 40%.

CHICHIBU 2004. Venture Whisky.

Chichibu 2012 Vintage refill hogshead, cask no. 2089 db (**96**) **n24 t24.5 f23.5 b24** Is there anything more likely to make you sigh in delight that a beautifully made peated cask-strength malt that has spent sufficient years in non-wine casks for the light tannin and sensible phenols to marry, live happily in each other's company and have begotten myriad little flavour babies? Well, that is what has happened here with the malt even having its own little room for quiet as the smoke drifts contently about elsewhere. Simplicity and excellence. Some other distillers around the world should try this sometime. They'd be surprised just what a mind-blowing treat that can be. Only a light bitterness towards the end prevents this from picking up a major Whisky Bible award. Because the delivery and first half dozen layers of follow-through has to be nigh on perfection. *60.8%. 349 bottles. Exclusive to The Whisky Exchange.*

➢ **Cadenhead's World Whiskies Chichibu Aged 6 Years** peated, bourbon barrel **(93)** **n24** one of the best noses I have encountered for quite a few days: this is less a malt and more a mosaic. A shy smokiness hides as though behind a fan while a series of teasing tesserae, ranging from freshly diced apple to allspice drop hints of their whereabouts; **t24** just too good! The cleanest, then milkiest malt – a little like porridge with a healthy (or unhealthy) sprinkling of muscovado sugar melting in top – quickly backed by busy but never over aggressive spices. Those three intense sensations simply blow you away and making it more complex still is the light cloud of smoke which descends; **f22** much quieter. As though a much older whisky which was feeling the strain of keeping up appearances after all these years. No faults, save perhaps some later bitterness, just so much more reserved than the delivery...; **b23** another great whisky from Japan. If there was an award for delivery alone, this would probably be somewhere around the winner's rostrum. *59.0% 180 bottles*

EIGASHIMA 1919. Eigashima Shuzo co. ltd.
Dekanta Eigashima The Kikou Port Ellen cask, cask no. 11055, dist 2011, bott 2018 **(92)** **n22.5 t23 f23.5 b23** Forget the Port Ellen cask. That is just a red herring – or, rather, a smoked herring. This is all about the barley which is thick and intense, the extra depth coming late on from the tannins and, very belatedly, from very light peat. Beyond that, the phenols barely register – which is just as well, as you don't want anything to take away from the dense purity of the malt itself. *58.4%. sc.*

FUJI GOTEMBA 1973. Kirin Distillers.
The Fuji Gotemba 15 Years Old db **(92) n21 t23 f24 b24.** Quality malt of great poise. *43%.*

HAKUSHU 1973. Suntory.
The Hakushu Single Malt Whisky Aged 25 Years db **(93) n23 t24 f23 b23.** A malt which is impossible not to be blown away by. *43%*

HANYU 1941. Toa Shuzo Co. Ltd.
Ichiro's Malt Aged 23 Years (92.5) n23 t23.5 f23 b23. A fabulous malt you take your time over. *58%*

KARUIZAWA 1955. Mercian.
Karuizawa Pure Malt Aged 17 Years db **(90) n20 t24 f23 b23.** Brilliant whisky beautifully made and majestically matured. Neither sweetness nor dryness dominates, always the mark of a quality dram. *40%*

KURAYOSHI DISTILLERY 2015. Matsui Shuzo.
➢ **The Matsui Single Malt Mizunara Cask** nbc db **(95) n24** a saltier, seaweedy, coastal character to this than is normally found; then settles back into its unique Mizunara style with a charming fragility that emphasises both the effect of barley and oak working in tandem. This is young whisky, make no mistake, but the sugars seem almost perfectly weighted, every bit as brittle as the barley as well as a lemon drop boiled candy character. Everything about this aroma, even the most delicate of phenol notes, seems to be set ready to collapse if not handled with care...just amazing...! **t24** one can barely needs to do anything here: the young distillate melts in the mouth and slowly the fresh barley dissolves over the taste buds: just so sexy and salivating. In slow motion those tart tannins notes begin to form and spread - truly one-off sensation deployed by the local oak. And with no greater haste the spices spread and intensify...; **f23** just more charm in slow motion, though the sugars are not quite as well represented. The tannins are clear and gentle the spices no more than an echo...; **b24** I cannot emphasise enough the brilliance and bravery of this distillery. The Asian market puts a high price on dark whisky. Yet here is a unique malt: young, entirely naked with no caramel work to hide any fat or blemishes. This is as natural and purely Japanese as Onsen. Except this is to be taken without water... *48% nc ncf*

➢ **The Matsui Single Malt The Peated** nbc db **(89.5) n22** a degree of sharpness suggests young, as does the pungency of the phenols which possesses an attractive smoked bacon character; **t23** again, youth is the over-riding sensation on delivery. Then a burst of malt before the smoky covering comes down. The sugars are eye-watering, as is the barley: a curious cross between smoked barley sugar and lemon drops; **f22** a little smoked cocoa amid the spice and light bitterness; **b22.5** a typically idiosyncratic style of peating from this distillery, though the smoke often battles with the sugars as well as the tannin. Not quite as well balanced and rewarding as their extraordinary Sakura and Mizunara cask bottlings. Incidentally, I have just spent half an hour playing around with vatting the three styles together using instinct as my guiding light: some of the results were spectacular... 48% nc ncf

◇◇ **The Matsui Single Malt Sakura Cask** nbc db **(95.5)** n23.5 freshly peeled grapefruit blends effortlessly with vanilla-led oak. A young malty character keeps an aloof distance. The sugars are a subtle mix of grist and icing sugar. Is it the cherry wood giving delicate phenolic note...? **t24.5** the surprising oiliness works wonders in holding together and then extending the complexity. You half fancy that there is a light phenol note on the loose here. And you are convinced that there is barley concentrate at work. Also you are pretty sure the sugars range from delicate muscovado to thin orange-blossom honey. But there are no statements. Just teasing hints and whispers...; **f23.5** those brilliant oils just keep on going. And the spices rise like the moon and glows above all. The fade is one of a tannin-barley combination; **b24** forget about discreet sips. Take healthy mouthfuls and chew and allow the splendour of the complexity, complete with those mysterious hints of phenol, to unravel on your tantalised taste buds. So gentle. So genteel... Yet so understatedly enormous...yet so sprightly. A treat and a paradox of a whisky. 48% nc ncf 🏆

KIRIN 1969. Kirin Group.
Kirin 18 Years Old db **(86.5)** n22 t22 f21.5 b21. Unquestionably over-aged. Even so, still puts up a decent show with juicy citrus trying to add a lighter touch to the uncompromising, ultra dense oak. As entertaining as it is challenging. 43%. Suntory.

MIYAGIKYO (formerly Sendai). 1969. Nikka.
Nikka Coffey Malt Whisky db **(96)** n23.5 t25 f23.5 b24 Not quite the genius of the 12-year-old. But still one of the most tactile and sensual whiskies on the world whisky stage today. 45%.

◇◇ **Nikka Single Malt Miyagikyo** bott code: 6/04A041143 **(91.5)** n22.5 a very simplistic march of malt and vanilla makes for an attractive, untaxing nose; **t23.5** a little caramel flickers about the nose slightly and then bursts into action as the second major flavour-wave on delivery. The first is juicy, initially unrestrained malt; **f22.5** the spices arrive as a dull buzz. But the caramel now is perhaps a little too monosyllabic...; **b23** will I ever taste a particularly bad Japanese again? Not in a month of Sendais, it seems. Only a little too much caramel prevents this from a much higher score. So effortlessly delicious, though.... 45%

Nikka Whisky Single Malt Miyagikyo Apple Brandy Wood Finish bott 2020, bott code: 6/02J161349 db **(88.5)** n22 t23 f21.5 b22 So fascinating to compare this with the Yoichi matured in the same cask type. The Hokkaido distillery's far greater quality and versatility shines through at every level. Indeed, how can you compare against genius? It is not a fair match. This, oddly enough, struggles to make the most of the apple while the cask appears to give this malt a particular firmness which towards the end is a little wearing. That said, I really adore the delivery on this which allows the malt to let rip and pulse out some startlingly intense barley notes. But beyond the midway point it becomes a little glassy, simple and even a tad metallic. But there's no denying that big barley statement. 47%.

SENDAI 1969. Nikka.
Scotch Malt Whisky Society Cask 124.4 Aged 17 Years 1st fill butt, dist 22 Aug 96 **(94)** n24 t24 f23 b23 If there is a complaint to be made, it is that, at times, one might forget that this is a whisky at all, resembling instead a glass of highest quality oloroso.60%. sc.

SHINSHU MARS 1985. Hombo Shuzo Ltd
◇◇ **Mars Komagatake Single Malt Limited Edition 2019** nbc db **(83)** n21 t21.5 f20 b20.5 The nose lifts the red flag to warn of problems ahead and they don't hang about arriving. The malt manfully battles for its usual place transferring from taste buds to heart, but the tang of the oak is a loud, continuous nagging. And the finish, sadly, is bang off key. 48% ncf

◇◇ **Mars Komagatake Single Malt Limited Edition 2020** nbc db **(95.5)** n23.5 the layering between the oak vanilla and the delicate nature of the malt is as clever and intricate as you are likely to find. A little gristy despite the weight. Just a little gooseberry juice at play, too; **t24** the second flavour wave is almost too wonderful to be able to concentrate on writing the tasting notes...! Just like the nose, it is the fragile quality of the malt which so delights, and the delicate spectrum of sugar tones that this brings about. That and the near perfect texture: lightly oily for maximum depth but not too oily to allow the gentlest favour breeze to blow. On a deeper, rumbling level comes the vanilla and the first spices notes. But it is like watching clouds moving about the sky: shapes slowly being formed slowly, almost imperceptibly....; **f23.5** just more of the same...though with the spices now a little clearer and warmer; **b24** I have tasted some great whiskies from this distillery over the years, though this is their first batch to reach me for a little while. Has their quality in any way diminished? Not remotely! The delivery and follow-through is almost bewildering in its beauty, though the Murray Method of tasting is essential for maximum effect. Having been to Japan many times and someone who has birded there in some if its remote mountains, I am more than aware that this country is capable of natural drama and beauty. And few whiskies come more naturally beautiful than this... *50% ncf*

⬩ **Mars Komagatake Single Malt Double Cellars Bottled 2019** nbc db **(94)** n23 an unusual slight saltiness the thick malt; **t23.5** amazing how the first moments on delivery seem slightly thin...then malt concentrate crashes down on the taste buds with remarkable power. Some superb light heather honey just gives a momentary extra sweetness; **f24** now we are back to a far softer, more even fade of that unique malt this distillery dispenses....and it never seems to end...; **b23.5** there is a good case for calling this single cellars Double Malt. Once again, the maltiness is deliciously profound. *47%*

⬩ **Mars Komagatake Single Malt Tsunuki Aging Bottled 2018** nbc db **(92.5)** n22.5 young, nutty and markedly clean. A touch of the Murray Method ramps the malt up massively; **t23.5** such is the incredible effect of the malt, you actually find yourself laughing as the intensity grabs every nerve ending on your taste buds, gives them a good shaking and then overwhelms them with tender kisses; **f23** keen malt works through to the end. The sugars are perfectly dispositioned to maximise the malty intensity. But a sub plot of dry cocoa powder acts as the perfect foil; **b23.5** youthful it may be, but the beauty of the malt leaves you gobsmacked. Like most Mars bottlings... *57% ncf*

⬩ **Mars Komagatake Single Malt Tsunuki Aging Bottled 2019** nbc db **(91)** n21.5 slightly more austere on the nose: a crisper tone to the sugars, while the outline of a butyric nose just hampers the complexity slightly; **t23.5** completely back on track on delivery with a breathtaking and eyewatering explosion of intense barley, fortified by citrus, hammers with peppery spice into the taste buds. The usual outstanding delicate oils enhances the mouth feel. Once again, the intense tones of the malt – something like concentrated Maltesers candy – just leaves you purring with delight; **f23** still spicy and relentlessly malty; **b23** this distillery appears to specialise in three-dimensional malt. *56% ncf*

⬩ **Mars Komagatake Single Malt Yakushima Aging Bottled 2020** nbc db **(94)** n23.5 the driest of Mars noses. The tannin offers dusty leather and hickory, the malt is but a squeak...; **t23** first it is the mouth feel that grabs you. The oils, intense – sort of. But does the job of adhesive sticking the liquorice and toasty tannins to the mouth. Slowly the malt moves from back seat to front...and the spices begin their erotic dance; **f24** the malt, having found its voice, sings now as beautifully as it has ever done, harmonising with the cut glass tannin. This is some duet...; **b23.5** usually: think Mars, think Malt... Not this time. Where normally the tannin is little more than a helpful bystander, here it grabs the steering wheel and drives the experience. The malt is for the earliest stages a hapless passenger. But not for long. Pretty good, though. In fact, just brilliant! *53% ncf*

WHITE OAK DISTILLERY 1984. Eigashima Shuzo.

White Oak Akashi Single Malt Whisky Aged 8 Years bott 2007 db **(74.5)** n18.5 t19.5 f17.5 b19. There is certainly something distinctly small still about his one, with butyric and feintiness causing damage to nose and finish. For all the early malty presence on delivery, some of the off notes are a little on the uncomfortable side. *40%*

YAMAZAKI 1923. Suntory.

The Yamazaki Single Malt Aged 18 Years db **(96)** n23 t24.5 f24 b24.5 for its strength, probably one of the best whiskies in the world. And one of the most brilliantly and sexily balanced, too... All told, one glass is equal to about 45 minutes of sulphur-free satisfaction... *43%*

The Essence of Suntory Whisky Yamazaki Distillery refill sherry cask, dist 2008, bott 2019, bott code: LL9BNH db **(95)** n24 t24 f23 b24 I'm not sure anyone in the world is doing sherry whisky better than Yamazaki right now. Here's another unreconstructed masterpiece from them. *53%.*

The Essence of Suntory Whisky Yamazaki Distillery Spanish oak, dist 2009, bott 2019, bott code: LM9BLO db **(92.5)** n23.5 t23.5 f22 b23.5 take the finish out of the equation and this is a snorter. *56%.*

TSUNUKI MARS 2016. Hombo Shuzo Ltd

◈ **Mars Tsunuki The First** dist 2016/17, bott 2020, nbc db (**95**) n23.5 the layering between the barley, the vanillas and natural caramels are impressive enough. When the walnut cake sweetness begins to show and entwine with the sturdier notes, then we are getting into something very serious, indeed...; t24 if I could purr, I would. Just a brilliant delivery which is dependent on the complexity of character rather than oils to carry the day. And instead of soothing oils, cleverly the sugars lay the foundation: a wonderful, crystalline Demerara sweetness perfectly entangled with the gristy malts. On their own they would be too simple. So along comes the oak, the tannins imparting a salivating sharpness and a slightly beefier body. As the oak gets the salivation levels up, the malt increases in intensity in formidable style, also adding to the juiciness. All the while a deeper caramel note from the oak adds ballast; f23.5 undone slightly by the lack of oil; the finish has a more austere persona. Even with most of the sugars spent, there is still a gloriously complex vanilla fade, the elegance of which is totally in keeping with all the earlier charms; b24 when it comes to Japanese whisky, you expect thoroughness and attention to detail. Had they bottled their first-ever whisky scoring less than 89 points, I would have been both disappointed and surprised. What I certainly didn't expect was a malt of such depth and opulence Not to mention complexity and charm. This is a ridiculously good malt where the cuts from the still and cask usage just about embrace perfection. They have set themselves a very high bar from their very first bottling. Incidentally, the Murray Method is vital if you want to see what all this distillery has to offer. 59%

YOICHI 1934. Nikka.

Nikka Whisky Single Malt Yoichi Apple Brandy Wood Finish bott 2020, bott code: 6/02J181347 db (**96.5**) n24.5 t24 f24 b24 Takes me vividly back to the day I got stuck on a warehouse roof at Yoichi distillery when filming for television many years ago. Earlier in the day I had been to a nearby farm and sampled the biggest apple off a tree I have ever seen in all my life. It was also one of the juiciness and finest-flavoured outside Somerset I had encountered. The nose, with its teasing apple edge, took me right back to that uniquely eventful moment...though thankfully I made it downstairs afterwards with no rescue necessary. By the way, great to see Yoichi still offering a malt of extraordinary finesse, even when shrouded in a cask so different to normal. Indeed, this is one of the world's great distilleries here wearing a very different costume...and still looking quite stunning. 47%.

◈ **Nikka Single Malt Yoichi** bott code: 6/60A061414 (**93**) n23 such a young yet erudite nose. The old tannins one once associated with this malt are spread a little thinner and instead, we have youthful barley enabling a zesty deliverance. Playful grist notes emphasise the clarity of the cut; t23.5 the sweetness from the melt-in-the-mouth grist was wholly expected after encountering the nose. This underlines the relatively younger age of the malt, and the succulence is met full on by the budding spices; f23 some excellent light oils fill out and lengthen the experience. Some delicate chocolate on the fade fits in beautifully...; b23.5 well, I suppose you can blame me for this. I make no apology for helping the world fall in love with Japanese malt, though the consequences are, as we see here, younger malts used than a few years back. No matter: this is top quality distillate and gives the whisky lover a chance to see just how brilliantly constructed Japanese whisky is. Especially a distillery like Yoichi, which I have, for the last 25 years, been banging a gong for as one of the world's top distilleries. This shews exactly why. 45%

Vatted Malts

◈ **Kamiki Blended Malt Whisky Sakura Wood** finished in Japanese cedar casks, bott code: 2020 11 (**93**) n22.5 even more cedary than the last bottling I encountered...! t23.5 has throttled back on the chocolate I was expecting and gone gung-ho with cherry cake. This rounded with a coffee cream. Throughout, though, the barley provides an outstanding intensity, while at all times keeping the juiciness alive; f23 wonderful demerara sugars and spices thread their way through the persistent crème coffee; b24 this is strikingly brilliant! I thorough enjoyed their last bottling. This has gone up several notches and just explodes about the palate with the most magnificently balanced flavours. What a real eye-opener! And one of the most dangerous whiskies on the market today: one glass will never be enough of this... 48%.

◈ **The Kurayoshi Pure Malt Whisky** nbc (**86**) n21 t21.5 f21.5 b22 If you like your whisky young, here's your dram. The toffee notes don't quite allow the flavours to develop as they might, but the intermittent surge of barley and spice ensures there is still much to enjoy. 43% ncf

◈ **The Kurayoshi Pure Malt Whisky Aged 8 Years** nbc (**87.5**) n21.5 t22.5 f21.5 b22 Massively malty and tender on the palate. But a little too much toffee interferes with the more delicate tones. The weight of the spices are superb, though. Just a shame about the relative flatness of both the nose and finish. 43% ncf

The Kurayoshi Pure Malt Whisky Aged 12 Years nbc (89.5) n22 good bourbon cask lead but slightly over toffee reliant...; t22.5 ridiculously soft and supine. The toffee and muscovado sugars gang together but allow the barley to pass unhindered. Spices grows with the confidence of the malt itself; f22 toasty, even a hint of burnt raisin; b23 thick and endearing malt. The spices play a clever game. 43% ncf

The Kurayoshi Pure Malt Whisky Aged 18 Years nbc (95.5) n23.5 such a delicate nose: rice paper infused with the lightest heather-honey and the most apologetic nuance of smoke...; t24 just brilliant...! Though the heather-honey is little more than a coded message on the nose, it arrives on the palate like an Emperor upon a throne. And although salivating, there is a depth beyond the simple broadcast of sugar and grist. Sugars are extracted from the tannins, also and these have a spicy hue. This is all about layering and subtlety, and it is hard to imagine that they could have got it better than this...; f24 the spices buzz on. A little cocoa bitterness now as the honey tones have receded. A little molasses compensates excellently; b24 a malt which celebrates its great age in style and considerable complexity. Indeed, so complex, so mouthful brings you a little stand and nuance you are sure wasn't there before. Definitely knocking on the door as Japanese Whisky of the Year. 50% ncf ♈

The Kurayoshi Pure Malt Whisky Sherry Cask nbc (90.5) n22 a plodding nose, but safe and secure with light grape and toffee on nodding terms; t23 very young barley and toffee hold court until spice and dried plums notes begin to find their home; f22.5 an unusual finale with an intense dryness at odds with the chest-beating muscovado sugars; b23 chewy and sticky, the youthfulness of this vatted malt is overcome by the intensity an richness of the malt and dark sugars. A complex, pleasing experience. 43% ncf

The Kyoto Murasaki-Obi purple belt nbc (79) n18.5 t22 f18.5 b20 an incredibly gentle and soft experience on the palate. However, a vague but telling butyric note on the nose – nearly but not quite overcome by the delicate peat – leaves ground that is never quite made up. The weakness is also evident on the finish. The only whisky I have found from this company with technical faultline. A shame. 43%

Nikka Taketsuru Pure Malt bott no. 6/22H10 1540 (95.5) n23.5 t24 f24 b24 Classy. 43%.

Nikka Taketsuru Pure Malt bott code: 6/06J341519 (94) n24 it would probably be impossible to find a malt with a more subtle but important phenol note as this. Indeed, if any whisky you find this year hides a telling peatiness so well, please let me know...; t23.5 the youth of the whisky is disguised on the nose but laid bare on delivery. However, the malts are in such pristine condition, so beautifully made, that this is hardly an admonishment....; the phenols lead the way, though quietly. The chalky vanillas are not far behind; f23 light oils gather and the vanillas forge something that borders intensity. A cream soda sweetness plays out late on...; b23.5 such an elegant malt. 43%

The Shiki Malt Whisky (86) n22 t22.5 f20 b21.5 This is as exceptionally young as it is malty. Virtually no tannins can be detected on the nose but we are compensated by the youthful, citrussy call of undisturbed barley. Just how juicy and intense this barley is, is witnessed on delivery where, at the midpoint, some tannins do move in to add a drying balance. The Achilles heel is the finish which appears to lack a coppery depth and, with little oaky resistance, becomes tangy. A real curate's egg. And one that was hatched a little too early... 43%.

Japanese Single Grain
CHITA 1972. Suntory.
The Chita Single Grain bott code L1610R db (91.5) n23 t23 f22.5 b23 Spot on Corn Whiskey-type grain: could almost be a blueprint. Simple, but deliciously soft and effective. 43%.

KUMESEN 1952.
Makoto Single Grain Whisky Aged 23 Years bourbon cask, bott 2019 (95.5) n24 t24 f23.5 b24 The more I taste of this grain distillery, the greater I am impressed. What a thoroughly charming, beautifully integrated whisky. Not a single false step or off note. Unquestionably one of the friendliest and most genteel whiskies of the year. Ignore this one at your peril...it is an absolute gem. 42%. Bushido Series.

TOYONAGA 1894.
Kangakoi Single Grain Whisky Aged 7 Years oak sherry casks (86.5) n23 t22 f20 b21.5 The nose is exceptionally fine, full of delicate charm. Indeed, the aroma of succulent fruit carries a lightly honeyed sweetness, too. The complexity is nowhere near so abundant on delivery and the thin body may offer an attractive fragility, but means it does not have weight enough to counter the growing bitterness on the finish. 40%.

MIYAGIKYO 1969. Nikka.

◇ **Nikka Coffey Grain Whisky** bott code: 6/16J101111 db **(95.5) n23.5** coffee from the Coffey still: milky medium roast Brazilian/Java mix, sweetened with a little molasses and brightened by delicate black pepper. Yet, everything done in a super-soft way...; **t24** there you go! That unique Nikka Coffey delivery: no other whisky on the planet matches this. We are talking the kind of yielding silkiness known only by the Debs of the 1920s, so the oils frictionlessly follow every contour of the mouth. As it does so, the sugars melt and the tannins tease with a spicy prickle; **f24** this is the point where you slump into your chair with your brain aching trying to work out the myriad complexities at work. Everything is a hint. A hint of spice. A hint of honey. A hint of barley. A hint of oak. A hint of oil.... All mixed together for a final, very long exotic, frankly erotic, caress...; **b24** this remains, without any fear of contradiction, the finest grain whisky made anywhere in the world. Marginally not quite the force of a few years back, presumably due to less stock to draw upon. But still a very special experience in anyone's whisky life... 45% 🍷

Blends

◇ **The Akkeshi Blended Whisky** bott 2021, bott code: BAONURE **(86.5) n22 t22.5 f20.5 b21.5** I long remember the days of walking into a Scotch malt whisky distillery and being fascinated, perhaps above all, by the different smells that emanated from one part of a distillery to another. Most of those distinct aromas have gone now, thanks to the Health and Safety outbreak which has neutralised the fun and unique character of so many distilleries. So, I hardly expected to be thrown back some 45 years to when I first started exploring Scotland's distilleries by a Japanese blend, for the aroma of this whisky is a throwback. Not to the whiskies of that era. But the distilleries themselves. I cannot say that that oily, gristy, dank, vaguely peaty aroma is perfect for a blend, even if it does leave you transfixed. The palate is busy to the point of borderline feistiness, light phenol ensuring depth and extra chewability. Once the smoke is done the finish is a little raw, thin and ungainly. Technically, perhaps not the best. But I'll tell you what: when I'm back flying again and I have driven home from the airport after a 12-hour flight, this might just be the whisky I need to batter my senses back into working order... 48%.

The Essence of Suntory Whisky Clean Type bott 2019, bott code: LD9JKO db **(88) n22 t22.5 f21.5 b22** Not often I come across aroma and flavour profiles entirely alien to any whisky I have before sampled – and remember last year I completed 20,000 different whiskies for the Whisky Bible alone. But different this is. The aroma – has a mix between old-fashioned Dentyne gum, new pine furniture and sweetened eucalyptus. The apparent barley sparkle on delivery is short-lived, the fade is long and drying, But all the time those unique notes on the nose cruise quietly around the palate, too. Clean...and very different! 48%.

The Essence of Suntory Whisky Rich Type bott 2019, bott code: LG9JPE db **(93) n23.5 t23.5 f22.5 b23.5** Such a sensual texture. And such elegance as the fruit unfurls. Quite stunning. 48%.

◇ **The Kyoto Aka-Obi** red belt nbc **(86.5) n21.5 t22.5 f20.5 b22** A near miss of a whisky: a blend that is so close to being a cracker, but the odd out of sync note takes it away from where it might have been – especially on the bitter finish. The timbre of the vanillas are a delight...but the bittering out was avoidable. It is at times like this I miss the fact I can't get on a plane with my blending hat on and sort out an easily avoidable problem... 40%

◇ **The Kyoto Kuro-Obi Black Belt** nbc **(94.5) n23.5** the bourbon barrels in use here have gone into overdrive: black liquorice mingles with delicate phenols, manuka honey....and even a touch of vegetable biryani...; **t24** the succulent delivery was a given. I wasn't sure how the bourbon oakiness might come through...but it does so with muscovado sugars and molasses at the ready. The spices take their time...but make their mark...; **f23** now it is warming, tingling spice all the way...; **b24** like the Red Belt, this appears to have a textile label: superb...and unique so far as I can remember in 45 years of whisky tasting. And as for the whisky...? Worthy of the label. The mouth feel, texture and bourbon and spice combination work a treat, as does the toastiness of the sugars. Perhaps the greatest compliment is that, mouth feel apart, the grains are barely discernible. It is the malt and oak which create the storyline and structure. And beauty. 46%

Master's Blend Aged 10 Years (87) n21 t23 f22 b21. Chewy, big and satisfying. 40%.

Nikka Days bott no. 6222H261103 **(89) n22.5 t22 f22 b22.5** Unquestionably the softest, least aggressive whisky I have tasted for the 2020 Whisky Bible. 40%.

Nikka Whisky From The Barrel db **(91) n22.5 t23 f22.5 b23** I have been drinking this for a very long time – and still can't remember a bottle that's ever let me down. 51.4%.

The Nikka Tailored bott code: 6/04J141353 **(88.5) n23 t24 f19.5 b22** This was on course for super stardom...then that finish happened. The odd cask here with a sulphurous taint. Clean wine casks and this might have been on course for a very major award... 43%.

⬞ **The San-In Blended Japanese Whisky** nbc **(89)** n22 big emphasis on grain. But the molten muscovado sugars work well with the custard powder...; **t23** silky and fat, those sugars on the nose shine wonderfully once they hit the palate. There is a surprising surge of warming spice and a slow build of vanilla; **f21.5** tends slightly towards the dry and mildly bitter side, though the spice glow delightfully; **b22.5** a silky, grain-rich blend which is quite beautifully-made and shows its sugar-spice charms to its fullest extent. *40%*

⬞ **The San-In Blended Japanese Whisky** ex-Bourbon Barrel nbc **(94.5)** n23.5 Japan goes to Kentucky: the liquorice and tannin would be recognised and appreciated by distillers east of the Blue Ridge Mountains...; **t24** for a blend, the mouth-feel is lush and lingering. The Kentucky-style tannins arrive early and then we are thrown into series of intense "Love Hearts" candy notes – the purple ones in particular. There is a fizzing liveliness to the sugars, but the blend of black and red liquorice really tops the bill...; **f23** massive tannin. A little sweetened hickory just to round it off; **b24** this is truly magnificent. The label promises fruit that doesn't arrive. But it doesn't need it. It's a show-stopper in its own right. *43%*

⬞ **The Shiki Blended Whisky (83)** n21.5 t22 f19 b20.5 For a while a degree of malt and toffee entertains. That tangy, untidy finish found on the malt is here, too, and bitters a bit on top. Attractive chewy mouth feel and early sugars but, overall, needs a bit of work. *43%*

⬞ **Suntory Toki** bott code: LEX1DEY **(95)** n23.5 so gentle. Wisps of citrus play with softening vanilla and salivating echoes of barley untroubled by time. The tannins match the citrus in its fragility; **t24** you find yourself smiling at this delivery and follow-through: it is like the blueprint to a classic Japanese blend. Salivating: check! Delicate: check! Multi-layered: check! Melts-in-the-mouth: check. This has all the hallmarks of the finer younger blends I used to work my way through in Japan back in the early 1990s. The high point is a stunning plateau of malt and oak slowly spinning together in suspension, like butterflies with their mate; **f23.5** as the midpoint finish some gorgeous spices strike up alongside vanilla and butterscotch, the oils keeping the acacia honey going as long as possible; **b24** when I first visited Japan some 30 years ago, I lamented how Japanese blends were more or less exclusively confined to the borders of their islands. The industry was convinced that these blends were inferior to Scotch, which they treated as a liquid god, and therefore not worthy of marketing anywhere other than in their own home markets. I strongly disagreed. Since I awarded World Whisky of the Year to a Japanese malt – also from Suntory – the world perception of Japanese has markedly changed and supermarket buyers are now looking to include Japanese on their shelves where once they were far more reserved and if they did, it would normally be a single malt. So, it is heart-warming to see Toki gain a wide market. And even more wonderful that this blend shews the singular finesse and lightness of touch which enabled me to fall in love with this style some three decades ago. *43%.* ♀

⬞ **The Tottori Blended Japanese Whisky** nbc **(91.5)** n23 the grains preen and shew off their clarity and versatility; the tannins refuse to either confront or dominate; the sugars stick to a low-key lemon zestiness...Young, green...and deeply attractive; **t23** the grains deployed by Matsui really do have outstandingly beautifully weight and the vital ability to allow the malts to have their say. The sharpness of the barley ensures the salivation levels are high; **f22.5** delicate vanillas and spice; **b23** elegant, light, and sophisticated, this blend would be the perfect welcome home moment for when we are finally able to return from a day in the office.... *43%*

⬞ **The Tottori Blended Japanese Whisky** aged in bourbon barrel, nbc **(89.5)** n22.5 the tannins buzz with a Kentucky burr.... Astonishingly and intriguingly, there is also a theme of every soft drink in the State other than Ale 8....; **t23** big, fat and maxes out on the chocolate and liquorice lead. The spices are lazy and instead make way for a buttery sub-plot...; **f22** a very curious fade of sarsaparilla and root beer mix. The chocolate holds its ground; **b22** well, it certainly goes Kentucky, but for the finish not in the way you'd expect. That said...what a great entertainer this whisky is... *43%*

Other Japanese Whisky

⬞ **Umiki Ocean Fused Whisky** finished in pine barrels, bott code: 2020.09.24 **(87)** n21.5 t23 f20.5 b22 The Japanese seem to love stretching the taste buds and leading them into places they had not before been. The entire structure of this whisky again meanders into unknown territory: the mix of saltiness and unmistakable pine resin is a first in the 20,000-plus whiskies I have tasted for The Whisky Bible over the years. As with most experimental whiskies, there are hits and misses to be found. The combination of salt and ulmo honey creates a sensational delivery and one that just makes the taste buds drip with salivation. The finish, as so often can be the case, is another matter as the bitterness of the resin finds nothing it can naturally balance itself against. Worth experiencing, though, just for that never to be forgotten delivery! *46%. ncf.*

English & Welsh Whisky

When, exactly, do you decide that a new whisky region is born? Is it like the planets forming after the Big Bang, cosmic dust gathering together to form a solid, recognisable whole?

That is the question I have had to ask myself for a long time and, since the Whisky Bible began 18 years ago, look for an answer that is beyond the hypothetical. At last I have come to a conclusion: it is, surely, when a country or region produces sufficient whisky of high enough consistency and character that its contribution to the lexicon of the world's greatest whiskies cannot be ignored. Or should that whisky be lost for any reason its effects would be greatly felt. There is no denying that this is now the case in the varied and often glorious lands to be found south of the Scottish Border.

When in 2003, on the cusp of world whisky's very own Big Bang, I sat down and tasted the whiskies for the inaugural 2004 edition of Jim Murray's Whisky Bible, Ireland boasted just three distilleries, four if you included Cooley's grain plant. Today, England and Wales provide us with three distilleries producing exceptionally high class whiskies: Penderyn, St George's and The Cotswolds. The latter is still very much in its infancy, but the quality is already beyond doubt. The English Whisky Co's remarkably consistent St George's have won numerous awards in the Whisky Bible, including this year's European Whisky of the Year.

These three distilleries are not micro distilleries. They are set up to make whisky on an industrial scale and have forged markets all over the world. On their skirt tails comes The Lakes in the beautiful Lake District while dotted around the region comes a plethora of other distilleries of varying shapes and sizes, not least the Spirit of Yorkshire Distillery in the North Yorkshire Wolds and whose maturing spirit seems as graceful as its emblem, the gannet. Bimber, in East London, have also made their mark with some fine early malts.

Over the last years I have been busy actively encouraging the larger English and Welsh distillers to create their own Whisky Association, especially as Britain has now at last left the EU. Why not? They are now their own region: they demand respect as their very own entity.

Key
- ● **Major Town or City**
- ⬈ **Distillery**

Durham

The Lakes Distillery

Spirit of Yorkshire Distillery

Cooper King Distillery

Liverpool ● ● Manchester

Aber Falls

White Peak

Henstone

● Birmingham   St George's

Adnams

Chase   The Cotswolds Distillery

Dà Mhile Distillery

Penderyn

Swansea   The Oxford Artisan Distillery

Cardiff ●   London ●   Copper Rivet
Millwall
Merstham

Isle of Wight Distillery

Exeter

Dartmoor Distillery

Hicks & Healey

London
Bimber Distillery
East London Liquor Co.
London Distillery Co.

ENGLAND

ADNAMS Southwold, Suffolk. 2010. Working.

Adnams Rye Malt Whisky French oak casks, bott code: L17269 db **(90.5) n**22.5 t23.5 f21.5 b23 Almost an immeasurable improvement on this distillery's early offerings. This has some serious charisma and amplifies the home-grown rye rather beautifully. *47%. ncf.*

Adnams Single Malt Whisky French oak casks, bott code: L18039 db **(85.5) n**22 t22 f20; b21.5 Technically not quite the ticket. But there is no faulting the big malt. *40%.*

Adnams Triple Malt Whisky American oak casks, bott code: L18103 db **(91) n**22.5 t23.5 f22 b23 Considering malted barley, wheat and oats have all gone into the mash, there is hardly any surprise that the nose and flavour profile is starchy and busy. Indeed, the oats have the biggest say here (a little bit of oat can go a long way in whisky!) in both aroma and on the palate; and the added sweetness from the cask gives a distinctive porridge-like feel to the delivery. But the cut is a tad wide, so the oils are a bit on the tangy side. Even so, a stylised and stylish whisky well worth experiencing, not least for that fabulous porridge delivery. A whisky to start the day with... *47%. ncf.*

BIMBER DISTILLERY London. 2015. Working.

Bimber Distillery Single Malt London Whisky re-charred American oak casks, batch no. 01/2019 db **(95.5) n**23.5 t24.5 f23.5 b24 It almost defies belief that a distillery seemingly operating for little over five minutes can come up with a whisky of such depth, magnitude, balance and all-round stunning beauty. The distillate here was of better quality than for their first bottling, and from that all else blossomed. Yet another brilliant whisky distillery is added to the already impressive English catalogue. The good people of Bimber have every right to be proud of such a malt whisky. *51.9%. nc ncf. 5,000 bottles.*

Bimber Distillery Single Malt London Whisky The 1st Release db **(90.5) n**21 t24 f22.5 b23 A superb first bottling from a new distillery. Historic stuff. And though technically not quite on the money, this has so much charm, personality and sheer presence it is impossible not to fully enjoy. Here on St George's Day, congratulations with your astonishing entry into the whisky world, planting another English flag in the process! *54.2%. nc ncf. 1,000 bottles.*

Bimber Single Malt Test Batch Sample ex-sherry cask, cask no. 38, bott 22 May 19 db **(94.5) n**23 t24 f23.5 b24 Well done, Bimber! You've only gone and found yourself an absolutely flawless ex-sherry butt with not a single of atom of sulphur to be found: possibly the cleanest I have tasted this year. The mixture of ripe plummy fruit and nuttiness is a wonder to behold, as is the clarity of the grape on the palate which allows the barley to filter through at the very death. If they have set out to astound and impress, then they have succeeded. Give this another ten years for the oak to integrate and...oh, my word...! *57.8%. sc.*

Bimber Single Malt Test Batch Sample re-charred cask, bott 3 Jun 19 db **(95) n**23.5 t24 f23.5 b24 When I taste samples like these, it is hard not to get excited about what is to come in forthcoming years. To get something this beautiful and then stick it into a PX cask or suchlike would be something akin to industrial sabotage. Brilliantly distilled, the spirit is a perfect foil for the myriad dark sugars extracted from the oak. Malty, too. *55.6%. sc.*

Bimber Single Malt Test Batch Sample virgin cask, cask no. 7, bott 22 May 19 db **(94) n**24 t23.5 f23 b23.5 What a stunning natural caramel-lashed young Canadian this is. Hang on: with that heather honey and light liquorice mix with spice a bourbon, surely...no, wait a minute.... *57.7%. sc.*

Artful Dodger Bimber New Make (92) n22.5 t23 f23.5 b23 An intense and creamy new make, shewing some bubblegum characteristics on the nose, but goes full throttle barley on delivery. On the sweeter end of the spectrum. *63.5%.*

COPPER RIVET DISTILLERY Chatham, Kent. 2016. Working.

❖ **Dockyard Distilled Masthouse Column Malt** ex-bourbon ASB 1st & 2nd fill vintage 2018, db **(90) n**22.5 lime blossom honey propped up by slightly drier vanilla wafer; t23 the malt takes on all kinds of incarnations in a relatively short time. Mainly it is biscuit – thankfully not ship's biscuit – with a mix of sweet, buttery Lincoln variety to Malted Milk. All the time a light lemon blossom honey continues to infiltrate and guarantee against any overexuberance from the cask; f22 a little more limited on the finish, though the maltiness carries though with something to spare; b22.5 beautifully refreshing malt whisky with a delightful lime sharpness to it from beginning to end. Obviously to reduce scurvy.... *45%. nc ncf.*

❖ **Dockyard Distilled Masthouse Single Malt Vintage 2017** cask nos.2017/07-08-09-10-18-19-20-21, dist 2017, bott Dec 20 db **(88.5) n**23 this, unquestionably is the most impressive part of the Masthouse experience. This is young whisky, yet the malt maintains a beautifully straight course with calm seas and very little wake. Most unusually, there is a delicate exotic fruit subcurrent, usually found in aged malts, not youngsters like this. Pineapple leads the way

– rather like pineapple cube sugar candy – with a vague passionfruit nip clinging on to the barley. Even, enticing and elegant...; **t22** the youth is apparent from the moment it connects with your tongue: gristy barley melts; **f21.5** here things run aground slightly as a degree of bitterness makes the malt list slightly, though a little chocolate does arrive to add ballast...; **b22** a very promising start from a fascinating distillery found in one of the most historical parts of England. Just need, I think, to carefully weed out the odd cask or two to try and bring the finale back into line when they bottle next. With the right casks there is no doubt that they will produce a fulfilling malt – and increasingly so with older whisky used - with their own unique and intriguing stamp. Meanwhile, in a little under five hours' time England will be taking part in their first football cup final since 1966. So, I thought it was only right that today I should taste both English and Italian whisky, Italy, of course, standing in the way of the European Champion trophy. I chose Chatham to represent England for two reasons today: firstly, because it is a town linked with the very earliest known competitive football in southern England, their club even being founder members of the Southern League in 1894 – which had been formed to run as a counter League to the all-powerful Midlands and Northern-based Football League. The second was more personal: my mother's father was stationed and trained at Chatham during World War 1 (I still have all his papers), serving the British navy until 1918. He survived. Three of my maternal grandmother's brothers didn't: they were also trained at Chatham but were lost in the Battle of Jutland. Which rather puts today's football final into perspective. And also makes one wonder why, when you consider the hardships and sacrifices our forefathers went through all those years ago, not least those who passed through Chatham Dockyards, why so many idiotic, tiny-minded people today deliberately want to make western society such a bloody intolerant and nasty place in which to live. *45%. nc ncf.*

   Son of a Gun Cask Finished English Grain Spirit batch. 02 db **(87) n22 t22 f21 b22** A much sweeter cove than their first bottling. Richer and more intense, too. Still the odd hint of copper starvation but well made and a juicier, fatter all round experience. *47.4%.*

   ◇ **Son of the Sea Cask Finished English Malt Spirit** ASB first fill, cask no. 144, harvest date: 21/07/2018, batch no. 01 db **(90) n22 t23 f22 b23** Remember, I mark this as a malt spirit rather than a whisky. And I have to say it is quite beautiful. Maybe a little copper is missing from the line-up. But as that can sometimes be case – such as in certain rums from Guyana or Fiji – it can massively add to complexity, and it appears to have worked here. The sugars from the grist melt in the mouth and the citrus notes are forthright and delight. Perhaps a hint of tobacco from the cut apparent on the finish, but this is going through a transformation in its life when many strange things happen. I have to say this distillery has the rare ability to remind me of my own family history. Elsewhere I mention the link betwen Chatham, my grandfather on my mother's side and the First World War. Well, this is a spirit I toast my great grandfather on my father's side. My great-great grandfather, a Dubliner called John Murray was British solder married to a girl from the insanely remote village of Patrington in the East Riding, where I now stay when birdwatching at Spurn Head. After they married, he was posted to the Crimea, where he fought...and survived. And on the British naval ship that took soldier and wife from the Crimea to the British garrison at Corfu, the first James Murray in a line of five (I'm the 4th) was born aboard. This infant, born in 1857 (exactly 100 years before me) on sturdy British oak perhaps out of Chatham floating above the Mediterranean was given the proud seafaring name of James Columbus Murray: a Son of the Sea, indeed... *47.4%.*

COTSWOLDS DISTILLERY Shipton-on-Stour, Warwickshire. 2014. Working.

   ◇ **Cotswolds Bourbon Cask Single Malt** db **(92) n23** the malt gangs together and makes a light oily statement. The vanillas throb their presence. Brilliant balance on the sweetness front: I defy you to tell me, conclusively, if it is sweet or dry. Impossible: it is both...; **t23.5** not sure what impresses me most: the slow by inexorable built of manuka honey and icing sugar or the creamy butter toffee. As for the spice: you could hardly ask for a more fitting intensity if they could be added in by hand...; **f22.5** duller now and more vanilla centric. Just a slight bitterness on the fade; **b23** after England last night getting through to their first-ever Final in 55-years – and yes, I do remember watching England winning the World Cup in 1966 – I really had no option but to celebrate tasting the great whiskies of England. One thing England and vanquished Denmark have in common are magnificent casks of maturing whisky in their new wave distilleries. Few, though, are as creamy as this. *60.4%*

   ◇ **Cotswolds Founder's Choice Single Malt** db **(89.5) n22** busy, sharp, grapey...just a little musty; **t23.5** salivating, with an eye-watering volley of grape (grapeshot?) that peppers the tastebuds with immediate relief from a light ulmo honey and butterscotch sweetness; **f21.5** a fruitcake with no shortage of burnt raisin. A tad off key towards the finish...; **b22.5** quite a rugged little number, despite the best effort of some, presumably, wine casks to add a fruity lustre. *60.5%*

⟨⟩ **Cotswolds Hearts & Crafts Pineau de Charentes Single Malt** db (93.5) n22.5 a slightly confused nose. Some elements of bourbon at work here alongside the cake counter at Fortnum and Mason; t23.5 youthful but never less than luscious. The malt appears to be on steroids, the fruit a mix of glacé cherry, barely sweetened rhubarb, and butterscotch tart; f23.5 the natural oils and strength guarantee a very long finish. Amid the still teeming malt comes a wonderfully sharp and sweet citrus kick, not unlike a soft-centre chocolate...; b24 just love it!!! This beautiful malt appears to be the pinnacle of the Hearts and Crafts movement... 55.2%

⟨⟩ **Cotswolds Hearts & Crafts Sauternes Cask Single Malt** db (85.5) n21 t22 f21 b21.5 Malty at times. But precious little sparkle in the normal Cotswolds manner. An inoffensive but dull whisky with the kind if character that, were he or she sitting next to you at a dinner table, you'd be looking longingly at the seats from which laughter was emanating. 55.2%

Cotswolds New Make Spirit White Pheasant db (92) n23 t23 f22.5 b23.5 Sweet, massively malty, moderately well-oiled and fabulously made. Has that late trace of cocoa which all excellent new make malts possess. Decided to taste this today as it is April 23rd: St George's Day, the day we celebrate the patron saint of England. Mind you, had you checked the BBC news website you would never know as it wasn't mentioned anywhere: but then BBC news long gave up trying to pretend to be interested in covering traditional British interests, English ones in particular. So here I sit, this time in my garden in this green and pleasant land, just a few miles from the Cotswolds itself, with barely a breath of wind and the late Spring birdsong filling the delightfully warm air. So: to St George and England, a toast. And to the disgraceful BBC: I look forward to the day when they have the licence fee ripped off them and their newsroom, preferably under new management and at long last populated with real journalists, actually starts covering relevant news and not that set to a woke agenda as, unlike this beautiful new make, they are not fit for purpose. God, I fell better for that... 63.5%. nc ncf.

⟨⟩ **Cotswolds Peated Cask Single Malt** db (95) n23.5 just ridiculously handsome. The brushing of slightly minty peat over the delicate barley is a masterstroke. The elegance and balance to this is off the scale....; t24 the malt is obviously still of no great age. Yet somehow it works in its favour as there is a controlled vibrancy which ensures the malt has maximum juiciness and keeps the smoke as no more than gentle weights to ensure the barley doesn't fly off. Measured spice and truly perfect layering thanks to the confident, creamy oils. The lightly phenolic ulmo honey is to die for; f23.5 again, defies its age with another amazingly complex finale, the delicate structure never for a moment bowing under the increasing weight...; b24 if I had the time, I think I could nose and taste this all day: an essay in understatement. And a malt, despite the peat influence, that lets the true character of the distillery filter through... 59.3%

⟨⟩ **Cotswolds Private STR Cask 140 Single Malt** db (94.5) n23 burnt toast with all its acrid bite, but gorgeously softened by blood orange marmalade and heather honey sub plot; t24 just massive! Both the fruit and the concentrated barley combine to make this a slobbering mouthful, the juiciness further sharpened by a delightful buzz of spice. Missing most of the usual oiliness, this is jagged and sharp-featured; f23.5 plum jam, butterscotch and light molasses: that is some dessert....! b24 essence of Jim Swan. His cask preference is here thumping out its juicy, jammy, toasty qualities at full blast. 62.3%

⟨⟩ **Cotswolds Reserve Single Malt** db (88.5) n22 t22.5 f22 b22 Malty and very low key. Love the nibbling citrus on the pure barley on the nose, while at the other end how the spices finally come out into the open. Elsewhere, good young malt stock taking on the character of a gentle cask. 46%

⟨⟩ **Cotswolds Sherry Cask Single Malt** db (94.5) n23 mildly peppery, but even though the sultana has a slightly cooked feel there is still enough barley poking through to guarantee the requisite sweetness...; t24 one of the best sherry deliveries I have tasted this year. Layers of sultana and raisin, bound together by a blend of heather honey and muscovado sugars, then a firm striking of a malty bell and a peel of busy spice. Everything in magnificent order and elegance, helped all along the line by the softest oils...Take ten minutes minimum to chew and study this, please...; f23.5 Cadbury's fruit and nut....; b24 a faultless sherry butt meats faultless distillate. Guess the outcome... 574%

⟨⟩ **Cotswolds Signature Single Malt** db (94) n23.5 the sexiest marzipan mingles with milk chocolate and malt of rare clarity. Freshly diced Cape Gooseberry also lends a fruity hand; t24 I quite literally groaned with pleasure as this sploshed around my palate. The barley is sharp, but the edges all the time are softened with increasing muscovado sugars; creamy vanilla hits the midpoint with a sprinkling of red liquorice; f23 just a little shorter than one might hope for, but still long enough! Still those vanillas and sugars work their magic. The oils have vanished now, and a spice tingle just begins to crown...; b23.5 there is always the fear than when you reduce a malt, even as one as good as Cotswolds, you break up the oils and length is lost. Well, maybe a little has been shaved off here, but the malt keeps its structure so well you can only sit here and be pleasantly amazed. 46%

Cotswolds Single Malt Whisky 2015 Odyssey Barley Batch No. 05/2019 first fill oak barrels db **(91.5) n23 t23 f22.5 b23** One of those understated malts that can be too easily overlooked. Worth time and a compass... 46%. nc ncf.

Cotswolds Single Malt Whisky Blenheim Palace Single Cask cask no. 901, STR cask db **(94.5) n23.5 t23.5 f23.5 b24** How could I taste this whisky at another time other than VE day: the 75th anniversary of victory in Europe for Britain and its allies against Hitler? The family home of the Churchills is Blenheim Palace – not that far from where I sample this whisky now on a stunning late Spring day. I have escaped my tasting room, my usual dungeon, to sit outside amid the orange-tipped butterflies and with a whitethroat dancing and singing its scratchy mating call; blackbirds feeding their young, while chaffinches, greenfinches, goldfinches trill and dunnocks chatter in a glorious, quintessential English setting. Even a resplendent cock pheasant (ironically the emblem of the distillery) has wandered into my garden to enjoy the moment. Doesn't he know there's a Lockdown...? 46%. nc ncf sc. 375 bottles.

Cotswolds Single Malt Whisky Founder's Choice STR American oak red wine casks db **(95.5) n23.5 t24 f24 b24** How can one not be truly won over by the way this flits from enormity to refined elegance...? 60.5%. nc ncf.

Cotswolds Single Malt Whisky Peated Cask Batch No. 01/2019 ex-peated Quarter casks db **(96) n24.5 t23.5 f24 b24** Unlikely you'll find a more perfectly balanced and complex peat cask malt than this, this year. First it is a tease. And then a complete seduction... On St. George's Day an English Whisky that is unquestionably among the world's elite this year. Amazing. 59.3%. 2,950 bottles.

Cotswolds Single Malt Whisky Sauternes Cask Batch 01/2020 db **(86.5) n22 t22.5 f20.5 b21.5** Just a little duller than you'd like to see from a Sauternes cask. A brief Cape Gooseberry moment, but mainly we are talking a dry, biscuity vanilla and just a light furry niggle on the finish. 55.2%. nc ncf. 2020 bottles. Hearts & Crafts Range.

Cotswolds Single Malt Whisky Sherry Release db **(90) n22 t23 f22 b23** A complex malt where the fruit appears to wish to play games. Very easy to join in... 50.2%. nc ncf.

Fortnum & Mason English Single Malt cask no. 532, bott Mar 19 db **(94) n24 t23.5 f23 b23.5** So delicate...yet so big, too...! 46%. nc ncf sc.

Fortnum & Mason English Single Malt cask no. 503, bott Jan 19 db **(90.5) n22.5 t23.5 f22.5 b22.5** Although it is obvious there is no great age to this malt, the pounding waves of tannin and the quiet elegance to the malt would have you thinking otherwise. 46%. nc ncf sc.

Fortnum & Mason English Single Malt cask no. 527, bott Mar 19 db **(92.5) n23 t23.5 f23 b23** For a whisky of no great age, the degree of balance is both startling and wonderful. A real English treat awaits you in St. James'... 46%. nc ncf sc.

The Boutique-y Whisky Company Cotswolds Single Malt English Whisky Aged 3 Years batch no. 1 **(92.5) n23 t23.5 f23 b23** A beautifully distilled malt which makes brilliant use of the oak's generous sugars. 50.4%. 1,783 bottles.

EAST LONDON LIQUOR COMPANY Bow Wharf, London. 2014. Working.

East London Liquor Company Whisky London Rye new French oak, ex-bourbon & PX finish db **(88.5) n22.5 t22.5 f21.5 b22** A bewildering first bottling from this new distillery. As gingery as ginger liqueur, as dry as a gin, as confusing as a rye whisky matured in French, American and Spanish oak, one of which carried PX. It is almost impossible to say under all that what the actual spirit itself is like, though pleased to report not a single off note on both nose and finish. I really do hope they also bottle some whisky which gives us a chance to savour the grain. And remember that, in whisky, a little less can give you so much more. 46.8%. 269 bottles. Inaugural release.

LAKES DISTILLERY Cockermouth, Cumbria. 2014. Working.

❖ **The Lakes Single Malt The Whiskymaker's Editions Colheita** Colheita port casks and bourbon barrels, bott code: L 01 06 20 db **(94) n23** this is an interesting nose for those looking to understand whisky. On one hand there are few cleverly concealed signs of youth: a certain firmness to the malt being a little clue, as it has not yet blended in with oak, which happens over time. And the way the wine, though seemingly soft and embracing, also reveals an angular feel. What I love about this as that it has been disguised by clever balancing, the trick not allowing the Port to overly dominate but still get plenty of its peppery personality into the frame. Even though there is a certain sludginess to the oils – again wonderfully masked - this is joy...; **t24** brilliant! The joins are equally well concealed on the intense delivery also. So, first you get a light almost glossy fruit involvement on delivery and slowly, like a flower blooming on time lapse film, the oaks arrive with a growing degree of gentle chocolate, which is then sweetened with fruit. Rich and chewy fare...; **f23** just a half mark or so coming off as the finale reveals, in the departing tide, a little overweight and untidiness on the oils from the cut. The lingering cocoa and fruit does help to make this a very minor, barely noticable blemish; **b24** now this is very serious, and breathtakingly beautiful whisky. The cask choice is more than impressive. Anyone who remembers Old Jamaica chocolate bar from the 1970s will delighted with this one. A very clever whisky, indeed. *52%.*

The Lakes Single Malt Whiskymaker's Reserve No. 1 bott 25 Sept 19 db **(86.5) n21.5 t23 f20.5 b21.5** So, now The Lakes are off and running, too. They are now a whisky distillery for real. To be honest, I was expecting a slightly greater fanfare for a first bottling. Not the greatest distillate at work here, slightly at odds with the oak, especially at the finish. But this is a first effort and they have yet to get to understand their whisky fully. The nose struggles for identity, the barley having to overcome the grumbles of the wide-ish cut. But just love the delivery, a thickset piece full of intense barley, milk chocolate praline and even a brush with marmalade. Quite a juicy introduction. But the finish and overall balance is lacking somewhat. Early days. *60.6%.*

The Lakes Single Malt Whiskymaker's Reserve No. 2 Cask Strength PX, red wine and bourbon casks, bott code: 31 Jul 19 db **(91.5) n23 t23 f22 b23.5** A much more forthright and altogether happier bottling than their inaugural one. Seems as though there is marginally better distillate at play here and, if not, the PX cask has been used to act as an attractive bind for all the elements at play here, rather than dominating and boring us into submission, as can so often happen with that type of butt. Very impressed and suitably entertained... *60.9%.*

SPIRIT OF YORKSHIRE DISTILLERY Hunmanby, Filey. 2016. Working.

Filey Bay Yorkshire Single Malt Whisky First Release db **(95) n23.5 t24 f23.5 b24** I know it seems like an inappropriate thing to do when tasting the first-ever whisky bottled by a distillery, but I feel I have no option but to compare it with a distillery elsewhere. However, the Whisky Bible lives by its honesty. And I have to say that the first thing that flashed through my mind on tasting my first mouthful was: Glenfiddich! And that same thought kept recurring throughout this delightful experience. None of the whiskies you can find from that celebrated Speyside distillery today. No, I'm talking about the classic non-age statement version, for years its trademark brand, that was sadly lost a great many years ago to make way for the 12-Year-Old, one of two drams I miss most from the early days of the Malt Whisky Revolution. When you taste this, you'll see why. It is the sheer élan, the fabulous brightness of this whisky that both wins your heart and takes you back the best part of a couple of decades: youthful, fun, stunningly well made, the malt coming at you in varying intensities, never for a moment sitting still on the palate – always somewhere to go, something to do: fresh and massively satisfying. For a first-ever bottling this is right up there with the very best I have encountered. Of course it is youthful, but the tannins have presence and complexity enough to make that no issue at all. If it does, it is to make it to its own advantage. Why, this newby even has the temerity to be an identical colour to the famed old Glenfiddich. *46%. nc ncf.*

Filey Bay Yorkshire Single Malt Whisky Second Release db **(93) n23 t23.5 f23 b23.5** Another quite beautiful malt, but just lacking that priceless, enigmatic sparkle of the first bottling... *46%. nc ncf.*

Filey Bay Yorkshire Single Malt Whisky Moscatel Finish bourbon casks, finished in ex-Moscatel barrels db **(94.5) n24 t23.5 f23 b24** A gorgeously weighted, charismatic malt with a sublime usage of fruit which does not – and this is so rare these days - overburden. As this is called Filey Bay, for a second I'd like to make this very personal. It has since 1985 had an extraordinary special place in my heart, for professional reasons, too, and here I toast the memory of both Graham Jones the one time landlord of the Belle View at Filey, whom I never met and whose life was so tragically cut short, and his lovely mother, whom I did, who happened to be the daughter of Huddersfield Town and England legend George "Bomber" Brown. I trust you have both now found peace. *46%. nc ncf.*

ST. GEORGE'S Rowdham, Norfolk. 2006. Working.

The English Single Malt Whisky Aged 11 Years nbc db **(96.5) n23.5 t24.5 f24.5** The oldest whisky bottled by St George I have yet encountered, I think. But they wear the age as a princess might a tiara. Not for a moment is the freshness and clarity of the whisky lost or even compromised. Like so many of their whiskies, this malt unfurls in the glass to reveal a whisky exactly as it should be: natural, relaxed and able to display all its tricks and charms without hindrance. Excellent. *46% .*

◈ **The English Single Malt Whisky Aged 11 Years** 2nd Batch, bott code: L00121, nbc, db, **(94.5) n23.5** a delightfully metallic feel to this as the copper reacts favourably with the malt in particular. The oak contributes a buttery burr to this Norfolk booty, though less honey to be had than last time round. A little saltiness had even mysteriously crept into play...and does no harm whatsoever..... **t24** as sumptuous as it scrumptious. A coppery kick arrives early and almost with a degree of arrogance. The malts attack back and increase the salivation levels further; **f23.5** just a little tang, but the malt is disinclined to reduce its intensity. At last, the oak softens matters with some gentle chocolate...; **b23.5** fascinating going back to some of the earliest days from this distillery, how the malt has changed slightly to now. On this second batch of the 11-year-old, that difference is slightly easier to spot because here we see much more copper at work and having a say in the overall character. *46%*

The English Single Malt Whisky 'Lest We Forget' 1914 - 1918 nbc db **(95.5) n24 t23.5 f24 b24** Probably the most touching of any whisky label I have ever encountered, it is a British Tommy silhouetted against the flag of St George. "Lest We Forget" are, of course the words used to remember those who died during the 'Great War'. Rather than taste this in my lab, I am outside in my garden to sample this, late on a warm summer's evening. At the going down of the sun I tasted....and remembered...and it gives me the chance to pay my respects to my Grandmother's three brothers who were lost in the Battle of Jutland in May 1917 (just two months after the birth of my father). A whisky worthy of their memories... *43%. 1,499 bottles.*

The English Whisky Co. Original batch no.003 18, bourbon casks db **(94.5) n24 t23.5 f23 b24** Annoyingly, I appear to have missed out on batch 2, but I remember the original version of this – batch 1 – was a little undercooked. What you have here, I am delighted to report, is the Full English....thoroughly recommend for breakfast. *43%. ncf.*

The English Single Malt Whisky Original bourbon casks, batch no. 001 19, nbc db **(90.5) n22.5 t23 f22 b23** The idea was to taste the remaining of my Australian and English whiskies during the semi-final of the cricket World Cup, as the two countries did battle. But I have had to bring the English tasting forward slightly as Surrey opener Jason Roy has made short work of the Australian bowlers. So this whisky is dedicated to another Surrey opener, John Edrich, my boyhood hero who played not just for England, but Norfolk as well... the home of this distillery. And as for this whisky: as gentle and as easy to put away as a Mitchell Starc bouncer.... *43%. ncf.*

The English Single Malt Whisky Original bourbon casks, batch no. L00120, nbc db **(89.5) n21.5 t22.5 f23 b22.5** A real youngster with the fresh, citrusy barley adorned with a surprising degree of oil. Beautifully distilled and matured in, I guess, 2nd or 3rd fill casks which allows the full magnitude of the malt to do battle with the significant oils. The late chocolate flourish rounds off the experience beautifully. One of the most refreshing malts you'll find this year without a single technical blemish. *43%. ncf.*

The English Single Malt Whisky Small Batch Release Rum Cask Matured dist Mar 14, bott Mar 20, batch no. 01/2020, nbc db **(94) n23 t23.5 f23.5 b24** So simple. Yet so complex. Just fiendishly brilliant. *46%. 1,985 bottles.*

The English Whisky Co. Smokey batch no.002 18, bourbon casks db **(94) n24 t23.5 f22.5 b24** This has to be one of the most relaxed peaty whiskies on the planet: the way it gets its smokiness across borders on the indolent. But, my word, it is so lovely... *43%. ncf.*

The English Single Malt Whisky Smokey bourbon casks, batch no. 001 19, nbc db **(92) n23.5 t23.5 f22 b23** One of those, warm sultry malts, where the peat acts as a pillow and blanket you can snuggle into. *43%. ncf.*

The English Single Malt Whisky Smokey bourbon casks, batch no. L00419, nbc db **(92.5) n23.5 t23 f22.5 b23.5** A far more complex and confident version of the last Smokey I tasted from St George. At 46% this could be a revelation... *43%. ncf.*

⬦ **The English Single Malt Whisky Small Batch Release** 1st fill American oak, bourbon cask matured, batch no: 03/2021, bott: May 2021, nbc db **(92.5) n23** the first fill bourbon casks have not hung around. The intense but clean malt is, literally, peppered with tannins. But the fun is in the variations: from walnut to dank leather with delicate vanillas and red liquorice in between. Most curious, though, is the sugar deployment: a little residual grist has to do the trick...; **t23.5** just adorable...truly wonderful. Only five, yet the layering almost bewilders. Where sweetness had been rationed on the nose, there are no such restrictions on the palate. There is the softest ulmo honey coating, delicate enough for the gristy sugars of the malt to also make their mark. With the table set, the main course of oak is served...so tenderly done you are as likely to pick up gentle citrus notes as you are more intense, toastier tannins; **f22.5** the spices are less accompanied and given more room to buzz...; **b23.5** you know when a magician pulls off a trick and you can't help smiling or laughing to yourself. That's the effect this whisky had on me: five years old, matured in England – hardly up there with Kentucky or India in the hot summers league. And yet there it was: a malt absolutely spilling over with mouth-watering charm and personality. *46%, 1806 bottles*

⬦ **The English Single Malt Whisky Small Batch Release Heavily Smoked Vintage 2010** batch no: 02/202, bott: Apr 2021, nbc db **(96) n24** one of those peaty aromas which makes you melt in your seat: a truly magnificent mix of milky chocolate and intensifying peat, gentle for the most part. Everything understated, though occasionally the odd phenolic note or three combine to give that intense – and wonderful - cattle byre kick. Fitting, when you consider it is a distillery owned by a farmer...; **t24.5** ridiculous! The silkiest delivery to a peaty whisky I have tasted this year. And he marriage between the sugars of the gristy malt, the wonderfully ethereal smoke and the elegance of the oak is truly faultless: overall, a peat lover's wet dream...; **f23.5** long, with the spices hanging on to the limited – but just about perfect – oils. Smoke continues to gently billow, while th vanillas wrap up the tannins...; **b24** mountainous Norfolk: England's Isle of Islay.... This is, incidentally, magnificent: pure peated whisky heaven. Nothing less. *46%, 1776 bottles* 🏆

The English Single Malt Whisky Small Batch Release Smokey Virgin peated virgin oak cask, dist Oct 12, bott Aug 19, batch no. 01/2019, nbc db **(93.5) n23.5 t23 f23.5 b23.5** The nose apart, the virgin casks don't have quite the impact I expected. But there is no quarrel with the overall quality or complexity levels which are outstanding. Superb! *46%. 2,652 bottles.*

◈ **The English Single Malt Whisky Small Batch Release Triple Distilled** batch no: 01/2021, filled: Dec 2013 bott: Mar 2021, nbc db **(95) n23.5** being triple distilled you'd expect delicacy. And that's exactly what you get: one of the most fragile noses of the year with the lemon blossom honey and pristine barley forming a nose of almost glass-like clarity...; **t24** if you think the nose is fragile, wait until this greets your tastebuds. The barley is, literally, crisp on the palate and has a unique mouth feel, too, as it seems to glide around your palate, frictionless. The sugars appear to crystalise, a glorious citrussy maltiness which sometimes even deepens in flavour to something as outrageous deep as butterscotch...! **f23.5** the relentless charm continues. Now with a little posturing spice fronting the malt and vanillas; **b24** when you taste a malt like this, the days when the Scots and Irish could lord it over the English because of their whisky are now well and truly over. A malt of singular beauty... *46% 1532 bottles*

The English Single Malt Whisky Triple Distilled batch no. 01/2019, dist Jun 11, bott Jun 19 db **(96) n24 t24 f23.5 b24.5** Malt whisky of this super-delicate type are rarely found better than this. *46%. 1,462 bottles.*

The English Single Malt Whisky Virgin Oak batch no. 01/2019, dist Jul 13, bott Mar 19, nbc db **(95) n23.5 t24 f23.5 b24** For those who like some whisky in their honey... This was my 500th whisky for the 2020 Bible, and it certainly lived up to the billing... Sublime. *46%. 2,689 bottles.*

The Norfolk Farmers Single Grain Whisky batch no. 02/2018, bourbon cask, bott 28 Feb 18 db **(96.5) n23.5 t24.5 f24 b24.5** Some people might be a little confused by the labelling of this whisky, and you have my sympathy. It is called a "single grain whisky" which kind of suggests that only one grain type has been used. Well, no, there are four: in no particular order, rye, wheat, oats and several styles of malted barley. In fact, all the grains are malted, but they didn't want to call it a "Malt Whisky" in case people automatically assumed it was a single malt like Scotch, made from 100% barley. While the "single" term reflects it is from just the one distillery, St George's in Norfolk. Complicated? Well, not half as complex as this truly beautiful and gloriously idiosyncratic malt whisky. *45%. ncf sc. 392 bottles.*

The Norfolk Single Grain Parched db **(96.5) n24.5 t24 f23.5 b24.5** A classic Irish "mod pot" style Irish pot still whiskey...from Norfolk! Nosed this when it was just a few months old...and it has moved on magnificently; indeed, beyond hope and expectation. Only the cat's bowler on the label and a green bottle seems to give the faintest hint towards anything Irish... For the record, by far the best Pot Still I have ever encountered made outside Ireland's shores... *45%. nc ncf sc.*

◈ **M & S Norfolk Distilled English Whisky (94) n23.5** clean, grassy, fresh and profoundly malty. No great age, but old enough to stand tall and proud with the spices balanced excellently against the teaming gristy malt; **t23.5** from the nose, you know this can be only intensely salivating...and my word, it most certainly is. The light oils comes as a pleasant surprise, and this helps spread the sugars and natural caramels off the oak over a wide area. Lemon blossom honey works alongside the rich but relaxed malt to keep the spices in place; **f23** those light oils ensures this malt travels far. It dries as the tannins from the bourbon casks make their chalky mark. But, always, you can never quite escape the malt and spice tandem...; **b24** this is a straw-coloured classic. Not often can you walk into a supermarket – in this case M&S in the UK – and pick up from the shelf such a technically outstanding and beautifully made whisky which simply aches of gloriously uncluttered gristy barley. For those of you who still don't trust English – which is a shame, because much of it is every bit as good as Scotch and, in the case of this distillery, usually very much better - think in this instance high class elegant and charmingly fragile Speyside. Youthful, but understatedly glorious. And just about the perfect pre-prandial whisky. *43% nc*

THE OXFORD ARTISAN DISTILLERY Headington, Oxford. 2017. Working.

Exploratory Flask Series Rye batch. 1, English oak medium char db **(89.5) n21** t23 f22.5 **b23** Now this is much more like it! Still not quite technically on the money, but the happy marriage of rye and cocoa – presumably courtesy of the English oak. For all its faults I adore this. And I suspect future bottlings could get a lot better yet, if they can iron out the wrinkles. *40.5%.*

Oxford Pure Rye Spirit batch. 5, new American oak casks db **(83) n20 t22.5 f20 b20.5** The tobacco notes radiating from this shows that they are still a long way from really having where they want this still to be for a high-class malt of the general English style. We have something far more of the central European mould, which is briefly attractive – especially on the third and fourth waves when the rye has shaken off its oily marker to make an intense appearance. But those unwanted oils stick to the dry and untidy finish. *40%.*

Oxford Rye Distiller's Edition new American oak cask, cask no. 101 db **(76.5) n18 t20.5 f19 b19** It is very hard to get past the unhappy, butyric-type note – both on nose and palate. It is my nature to be kind to new distilleries, if always honest. But a lot is being asked of me here... I will say, though, that just after the delivery there is a very attractive ultra-malty-nutty note which is enjoyable. But it is constantly under pressure. *45%. sc. 388 bottles.*

Oxford Rye Very Special Inaugural Edition new American oak cask, cask no. 3, dist Nov 17 db **(88) n22 t22.5 f21.5 b22** Full-flavoured and chewy, this is a rye that has decidedly nougat tendencies. But it also veers at odd times towards kumquat and molasses. There is no rhyme nor rhythm to this spirit but, for all its anarchy, it certainly deals a few aces on the flavour profile. The rich chocolate as the oak gets more involved is also to be celebrated. Technically, not one for the purist. But for the flavour junkie, this has to be a big hit... *53.4%. ncf sc.*

WHITE PEAK DISTILLERY Ambergate, Derbyshire. 2016. Working.

White Peak Single Malt Spirit 24 Months Old STR cask, bott 26 May 20 db **(92) n23.5 t23 f22.5 b23** Ah, a distillery not 75 miles away from where the non-American section of the Whisky Bible is written each year and in one of my favourite areas of England. And, indeed, very close to where I would visit a girlfriend back in the late 1970s. It is a dramatic area and just a few miles from this distillery the car I was driving was once hit by lighting during a ferocious summer storm I was battling through in that part of the Peak District. Well, there's some pyrotechnics here, too, with all kinds of huge aromas and flavours meeting head on. Not least a delicate smokiness drifts across the nose, wrong-footing the chest-thumping fruit and tannins notes from the STRs. The delivery is muddled, as well it might be for a malt of this immaturity. But it is amazingly juicy, too, and the chocolate, dark cherry and grumbling smoke and spice work well from late delivery to finish. Beautifully distilled and they have invested in good wood, though I'd like to see this working in top ex-bourbon, too. When it is safe, I might just take a drive Matlock way and into the lands of my comparative youth to see what they are getting up to here. On this evidence it is looking very promising. Though, for safety's sake, I might drive with the hood of my Jag up.... *62.9%. sc.*

WALES

DA MHILE DISTILLERY Glynhynod Farm, Llandysul. 2012. Working.

Dà Mhile Tarian Organic Single Malt Welsh Whisky barrel no. MS1511 db **(86.5) n21.5 t22 f21.5 b21.5** Every aspect of this malt screams "small still" at you. Or, to be precise, "new small still" as the depth of the copper on this is significant. Also, it looks as though great efforts have been made to keep the cut narrow, though still some feints have made it through – with a degree of inevitability, I must say. That smoky tobacco note on the nose, not unknown with certain German malts, is a bit of a giveaway there, and it is confirmed on the finish. But there is a rich seam of barley to be mined on the palate, for a moment or two even becoming very sweet – some intense barley sugar and maple syrup do make it into the mix. A typical new distillery first release in its occasional confusion. But if those beautifully intense moments can be harnessed and the tobacco notes eradicated, then this will become a delightfully singular malt produced by a truly singular individual. *46%. nc ncf sc.*

🔹 **Dà Mhile Organic Single Malt Port Cask** cask no: MP1609, db **(91) n23** from a Port cask you expect the grape to, if not dominate, certainly have a considerable say. Not here: this is a celebration of youthful but not young barley as fresh as an easterly wind on the Brecon Beacons. The grape is little more than a gentle counterweight, seemingly helping to parcel up the barley; **t23.5** what a fabulous delivery. A celebration of malted barley: a controlled explosion of sweet grist from the very heart of the heart of the cut. The barley sugar absorbs enough oak to branch out into a more heather-honey and treacle mix; **f22** just a light bitterness attaches to the delicate vanilla and butterscotch.... kind of bitterscotch...; **b22.5** I have to say that a past weakness of Da Mhile – even when the first-ever run was produced at Springbank back in about 1992 – was that there was always a hint of feint to be found. Not this time: this is as pure as the driven Welsh snow: quite beautifully made and despite the Port Cask influence, always shews the malt to maximum advantage. Absolutely delicious, look you... 46% sc

PENDERYN Penderyn, Aberdare. 2004. Working.

Penderyn Celt bott code 200503 db **(95.5)** n24 t24 f23.5 b24 If this was a woman, I'd want to make love to it every night. And in the morning. And afternoon, if I could find the time...and energy... 43% (89 proof). nc ncf. USA Market.

⟨⟩ **Penderyn Celt** bott code 201422 db **(89.5)** n22.5 a sexy combination of apologetic peat and shy citrus. Very alluring...; t22.5 fresh, malty but with slightly more tannin than peat... remains joyously zesty; f22 just bitters out very slightly from the oak; b22.5 a relatively simplistic Celt compared to, say, the 503 bottling. One of the lightest peated malts you'll ever encounter. 41% nc ncf

⟨⟩ **Penderyn Celt** bott code 202966 db **(81)** n21 t22.5 f18 b19.5 A slightly off kilter cask can do some damage to a delicate malt, and it has here. Some pleasant early smoky moments, but the bitterness at the end undoes a lot of the good... 41% nc ncf

⟨⟩ **Penderyn Celt** bott code 202466 db **(91.5)** n22.5 the peak-a-boo peat (or is that peat-a-boo peak?) is more peak than boo...; t23 the most beautiful stroll over the taste buds by wonderfully intense and clear barley just slightly infiltrated by gently spiced oak. The peat is still hiding...; f23 wonderful: light malt hobnobbing with increasingly spicy tannins; b23 think they should re-label this one and call it Spot The Peat. It is there...but your senses have to be on full alert to find it. Even so, it is gorgeous whisky with lashings of delicious malt to savour. 41% nc ncf

⟨⟩ **Penderyn Celt** bott code 200503 db **(94)** n23 even by Celt standards, the smoky fingerprints on this are faint. But the overall piece is delicate and light enough to allow the phenols to impose a presence...even if a ghostly one...; t23.5 the smoke is now in no doubt and it steps out from the shadows with no little confidence. Meanwhile the barley goes on a salivation rampage, but the smoke and spices are always on its tail; f23.5 pleasingly long. Certainly long enough for the chocolate to embed with the barley. The spices carry on indefinitely...; b24 this probably has to be the most malty of all Penderyn's output. The smoke works on a different level to the barley, giving it a double identity. This is a particularly fine example. Truly satisfying Welsh. 43% (86 proof) nc ncf Exclusively imported by ImpEx Beverages, Inc.

Penderyn Celt bott code 90165 db **(91)** n22.5 t23 f22.5 b23 A little miserly on the phenol front. But the interplay with the fruit is a joy! 41%. nc ncf.

Penderyn Celt bott code 92201 db **(91.5)** n23 t22.5 f23 b23 Just love this as you are never quite sure where it will take you next. A charmer, and a mystery one at that...!! 41%. nc ncf.

Penderyn Club rich Madeira finish, bott code 93101 db **(93.5)** n23.5 t24.5 f22 b23.5 It noses with the elegance of Swansea City (in its Premier League days). 50%. nc ncf.

Penderyn Legend db **(93)** n23.5 t23.5 f22.5 b23.5 An exhibition in how to allow the fruit to tease, but never dominate. 43% (86 proof). nc ncf. Exclusively imported by ImpEx Beverages, Inc.

⟨⟩ **Penderyn Legend** bott code 200421 db **(90.5)** n22.5 you know when you have a light one on your hands when the main thrust are black peppers generated by the oak; t22.5 the soft mouth feel helps the juicy barley and lemon blossom honey to make their mark; f22.5 a layer of praline comes second to the peppers; b23 Legend at its lightest and most delicate, though never for a moment taking its foot off the gas flavour-wise.. Such joyful fragility...! 41% nc ncf

⟨⟩ **Penderyn Legend** bott code 201213 db **(86.5)** n22 t22 f21 b21.5 Although it starts brightly with refreshing citrus on the nose, the marriage of oak and barley never quite comes off in usual Legend style. The result is a relatively monotoned malty effort, juicy at times, but with an annoying bitterness at the death. Have to say the mouth feel is impressive, though. 41% nc ncf

⟨⟩ **Penderyn Legend** bott code 202741 db **(91.5)** n21 malty, though the oak note is slightly quarrelsome...; t23.5 succulent barley with an early release of controlled spice. Elegant fruit tones – mainly sultana and pear – mixed beautifully with clean vanilla and encroaching milky chocolate; f23.5 long with those spices hanging on for dear life. Has the feel of brand new Jag at the end of its journey and being parked up: quiet, frictionless and giving the sensatoin of effortless class...; b23.5 the nose isn't much to write home about and I feared the worst. But I had been hoodwinked: this is an essay in understated complexity. 41% nc ncf

⟨⟩ **Penderyn Legend** bott code 203301 db **(94.5)** n23.5 not sure you can do much better with a light grape juice sweetness, clean barley and weighty tannins working together. Excellent poise...; t24 I could almost swoon! Someone seems to have made the barley into ridiculously concentrated form but added just the right muscovado sugars to balance out the chunky, spicy oak. So many layers...so ridiculously lip-smacking. And not a false note...; **f23** long: a kind of Welsh Malt Fest...just a late hint of bitterness of the barrel but disguised by cocoa; **b24** here we go! Legend back to being a Legend again. Superb! *41% nc ncf*

◈ **Penderyn Legend** bott code 202606 db **(92.5) n23** the lightest lemon blossom honey infiltrated the barley...; **t23** superb delivery and follow-through. No off notes; spices apart no major tannin presence – virtually an oily massaging of the malt and spice into the palate is a simplistic treat; no major tannin presence. But look out of the delicious bourbon outlines with the intensifying of honey and red liquorice.... **f23** ....is completed on the elegant finish; **b23.5** this one really ramps up the malt. But the slow flowering of the honey is equally impressive. *41% nc ncf*

◈ **Penderyn Legend** bott code 931010 db **(95) n23.5** some wonderful grapefruit mingles with the fresh barley; **t24** it is as though your taste buds are being cleaned, such is the clarity of the spirit. The barley is in aspic with acacia honey generating a delicate sweetness. The oak thickens the cream soda; **f23.5** sultanas and now impressive spice making a surprisingly warm finale. A little cocoa power is tipped in to counter the heather homey; **b24** Legend at its most chewy and succulent. And complex. Rarely do you find a whisky where its constituent parts are so brilliantly calibrated: "delicious" doesn't quite do it justice... *43% (86 proof) nc ncf Exclusively imported by ImpEx Beverages, Inc.*

◈ **Penderyn Madeira Finish** bott code 200219 db **(89) n23** seriously chunky by Penderyn standards: the tannins don't float across the nostrils as thud into them, thankfully a lighter citrus note eventually hovers into view. There are rapier thrusts from the fruit, most rebuffed by the wooden shield. For a Penderyn, it is certainly different; **t23** surprisingly voluptuous to begin with, the oils coating the palate and making the most of the early sugars. By the midpoint the drying process is not only in full swing but gathering pace...; **f21** incredibly dry: even a hint of juniper it seems. Unusually for this distillery, the sugars have burned out early; **b22** a very different, dark-coloured Penderyn, heading towards full amber. The dryness of the oak is vaguely severe at the finish, but still a malt that is fascinating in its layering. *46%. ncf.*

◈ **Penderyn Madeira Finish** bott code 203085 db **(94) n23.5** adorable subtlety to this one: it is a tease of an aroma, with playful caresses where in the previous bottling there had been a muscular massage. The delicate acacia honey attaching to the outline of grape delights...; **t23** one of those rare whiskies which is both salivating and quite weighty on delivery. However, it lightens up as the vanillas and spices come to the fore. Outstanding oils of almost perfect viscosity does enough but not too much in the lingering department...; **f23** so long, beautifully spiced and a little demerara sugar on the coco, too; **b24** lighter in both colour and in its footstep than the 219. The complexity levels seem to rise dramatically as a consequence. And although seemingly easy going both depth and length are magnificent... Talk about less being more....! *46%. ncf.*

◈ **Penderyn Madeira Finish** bott code 203383 db **(91) n23** a distinct doughiness, the spices and raisins pointing towards a fruitcake mix; **t23** aaah, that malty juiciness....!!! Wow! Excellent barley sugars in the background, too, lingering on the oils. The fruit has a much more fragile role than normal. Outstanding spices, too...; **f22** the spices dominate an otherwise simplified finale...the vanilla and barley still easy to identify and enjoy **b23** even lighter in colour and character than the 085. But doesn't boast the same mesmerising proportions, for all its considerable charm. Very high-quality fare. *46%. ncf.*

◈ **Penderyn Madeira Finish** bott code 202684 db **(94.5) n23.5** here we go: this is much nearer in style to traditional Penderyn, the chalkiness and pithy grape harmonising in that unique Welsh way; **t23.5** and the same goes for the flavour profile and mouth feel on delivery: pure, unalloyed Penderyn. Also beautifully warmed with the busiest of spices. Oh, but that malt-vanilla-grape harmony.... unmistakable; **f23.5** long, lush thanks to superb oils, controlled spice, a sprinkling of cocoa and even some late orange blossom honey...gosh! **b24** vaguely youthful, yet still Penderyn at its Penderynist. *46%. ncf.*

◈ **Penderyn Madeira Finish** bott code 2003312 db **(91.5) n23** a spiced, sugar-coated fruitiness is etched into a disarming bourbon backdrop. Genteel and soft...; **t23** every bit as crisp and salivating as the nose promise, but now with a serious blast of barley to add to the intensity and completeness; **f22.5** superb spice working in tandem with a distinct Kentucky kick. The hallmarks of very high-quality wood at work in this improbably long finish; **b23** what a ridiculously satisfying whisky. On a slightly different level to the very earliest Penderyns with an estery residue that makes this particular bottling seem never-ending... *46% ncf.*

◈ **Penderyn Madeira Finish** bott code 200581 db **(94) n23.5** the lightest touch of peach is the only nod towards sweetness. All else is a subtle, dry chalkiness, delicate tannin, and teasing spice. It is as though the grist has no sugars. Peculiar...but also mesmerising; **t23.5** a wonderful interplay between much drier tannins and almost enigmatic sweetness: you pick up on its barley sugar outline, but when you look for more...it vanishes. The tannins dance with a vague roastiness – not quite the usual Penderyn style, but this fits in with its surroundings perfectly; **f23** such a distinguished finale: a little barley has glided its way through and joins forces with drier grape skin and a light rumbling spice; **b24** a typically multi-layered offering from Penderyn, though with the fruit element a little quieter than usual. Less silky, estery and soft as their last bottling, this is far more complex and relentlessly elegant. A great whisky deserving of time and exploration. *46% (92 proof) ncf. Exclusively imported by ImpEx Beverages, Inc.*

Penderyn Madeira Finish bott code 83273 db **(95.5) n24 t24 f23.5 b24** If you think that Penderyn has upped its game in subtlety and complexity in recent years, then get a glass-full of this. 'Tis a thing of Welsh beauty *46%. ncf.*

⬩ **Penderyn Myth** bott code 200292 db **(95.5) n24** super complex malt: multi-layering at the highest level. The malt and vanilla appear to be in cahoots and almost indistinguishable; gentle phenol notes hangs around like a ghost while the sugars just hint their presence and no more...; **t24** I am purring with delight: a light saltiness has raised the voices of the malt and tannins above a whisper. The thinned ulmo honey hangs on the surprisingly oily body...and, as though in slow motion, the alt not only comes into view but intensifies majestically; **f23.5** malt---cocoa...spice...all in hushed tones. And forever and a day...; **b24** a malt beautifully weighted and complex lends one to think that we have encountered here a distillery that has mastered the whisky in its charge. This is cask selection at the highest level. And a contender for British Whisky of the Year. Not for its drama and noise.... for quite the opposite. Even if not the best, it will almost certainly be among the most elegant. *41%. nc ncf.*

⬩ **Penderyn Myth** bott code 90644 db **(94) n23** the malt leaves a trail of smoke as light tannin and spices loop the loop; **t23.5** mouth-watering and tart, this is thinner than most Penderyns these days. This means the barley and light biscuit and honey ones thump against the taste buds with more dramatic impact. About halfway in ulmo honey starts to make its mark, quietly, but with great effect; **f23.5** drier now, but with more light smoke and spice; **b24** a very different Myth to the previous bottling, this is using its meagre smoke resources to full effect thanks to the drier make up. Another malt for those who prefer their whisky complex and sophisticated rather than being a drama queen. But if you want to know how to maximise low-level smoke, rich barley and delicate honey, here is your go-to whisky. Even more beautiful than a leg of Welsh lamb...and that, believe me, is saying something... *43% (86 proof) nc ncf. Exclusively imported by ImpEx Beverages, Inc.*

Penderyn Myth bott code 90647 db **(91.5) n22.5 t23 f23 b23** It is like a Penderyn legend being whispered, though with more emphasis on grist while the fruitiness has a definite zinginess... *41%. nc ncf.*

Penderyn Myth bott code 92883 db **(88.5) n22 t22.5 f22 b22** The little extra vanilla here reduces the sharpness of the fruit. Lots of flavours still working the palate, but significantly duller than most Myths. *41%. nc ncf.*

Penderyn Oloroso Sherry Finish bott code 91911 db **(89) n23 t23.5 f20.5 b22** If it's sherry you'll be liking...come and get it! Just the slightest hint of furriness around the edges, though. *59.6%. ncf. 1,349 bottles. Released August 2019.*

⬩ **Penderyn Peated** bott code 200421 db **(91) n22.5** even on full volume the smoke is sparse, teasing almost. A light lemon zestiness biffs up the complexity; **t23** the adorable mouth feel is equalled by the sublime heather honey. Even now the smoke feels no more than chewing on the fumes of a distant haystack fire; **f22.5** a tad thin but the apologetically smoked mocha works well to maximise the finish; **b23** with the Murray Method the peat comes through loud and clear. Without it...happy hunting! *46% (92 proof) nc ncf. Exclusively imported by ImpEx Beverages, Inc.*

Penderyn Peated bott code 90162 db **(93) n23 t23.5 f23 b23.5** Youthful, exuberant and among the most teasingly-weighed peated Penderyns... *46%. ncf.*

Penderyn Peated bott code 90821 db **(94) n23.5 t23.5 f23 b24** Penderyn at its weightiest. But where it wins the heart comprehensively is that it never throws that weight around. So sexy! *46% (92 proof). ncf. Exclusively imported by ImpEx Beverages, Inc.*

Penderyn Peated bott code 91541 db **(92.5) n22.5 t23 f23.5 b23.5** Penderyn Peated coming at you from a very different, but still very delicious, angle... *46%. ncf.*

⬩ **Penderyn Portwood** bott code 203071 db **(84.5) n21 t22 f20 b21.5** The tightness on the nose signals trouble ahead, and it doesn't lie. Sulphur, sadly, has leaked into this one – though those lucky ones who can't pick that up can enjoy a feast of muscular fruit and black pepper instead. *46%. ncf.*

⬩ **Penderyn Portwood** bott code 203371 db **(84) n21 t22 f20 b21** Another Port in a storm. Again, this is a tight cask with a vaguely sulphury edge. Big fruit through the middle, but the sweetness is nipped in the bud and balance compromised. *46%. ncf.*

Penderyn Portwood bott code 91284 db **(86.5)** n22 t22 f21 b21.5 Dull is not a word I normally link with Penderyn. But I have no problems applying it here. You know those satellite things that travel, relentlessly and without err and aberration across the night sky. But so dim you need your binoculars to make them out clearly, briefly, before they vanish into the void.... Well, this is such a whisky...Pleasant. But so bloody dull.... *46%. ncf.*

Penderyn Portwood Grand Slam Edition 2019 bott code 91051 db **(93)** n23.5 t23.5 f23 **b23** Moments of this whisky, especially on delivery, are as tightly packed and exert as much power as your average scrum. As dry as a Ken Gorman one liner. *46%. ncf.*

Penderyn Portwood Single Cask 12 Year Old cask no. PT1113 db **(96)** n23.5 t24 f24 **b24.5** The odd thing about his fellow is that the oak plays a surprisingly low-key role for a 12-years-old. Instead it is the fruit which calls the shots – literally! – first with its airy dried date aroma and then mouth-watering, eye-squinting delivery which always seems to have Venezuelan chocolate drifting around the scene. I think we have to accept that Penderyn are moving into a higher sphere than most other distilleries and the controlled enormity of some of their whiskies take a good half hour to fathom. Minimum. This is one such beast. Selecting British whisky of the year - and world whisky of the year – has just become a whole lot more interesting... *60.4%. ncf sc. Selected & imported by ImpEx Beverages, Inc.*

Penderyn Rhiannon sherrywood Grand Cru finish, bott code 91852 db **(96.5)** n23.5 t24 f24.5 b24.5 A cerebral whisky playing games and tricks. Near enough perfectly balanced and different enough to set this apart from any whisky before. Few whiskies ever reach this level of complexity... *46%. Icons of Wales No. 7.*

◈ **Penderyn Rich Oak** bott code 200561 db **(93)** n23 in simplistic mode today, a light nuttiness clinging to the leading vanillas. Just a gentle pull of ulmo honey...; t23.5 the mouth feel is relaxing and soft, the sugars crisper and happy to help dredge up the weightier, toastier notes for an intense middle. Spices start on slow burn...then warm up busily; f23 superb oils conjure up heather honeycomb and chocolate. Devotees of Crunchie bars will be in their element here...; b23.5 such a lot of understated whisky in one small glass... *46% (92 Proof). nc ncf. Exclusively imported by ImpEx Beverages, Inc. 1 (250) 634 2276*

◈ **Penderyn Rich Oak** bott code 200563 db **(95.5)** n23.5 busy, busy, busy: tune in properly and the influence of the oak is mesmerising. The perfect little malt interludes impresses no less; t24.5 busy, busy, busy: intriguing and mind-blowingly complex. The early arrival of the spices – a bit like the small grains on a bourbon – keep the taste buds bombarded and seems to shift the mood and intensity of the malt from one moment to the next. The overall feel is a whisky of amazing substance and depth. The stunning heather and ulmo honey mix is something beekeepers should keep in mind...; f23.5 fabulous length to this. Toasted honeycomb (with the emphasis on the toast), excellent light oils and still those spices; b24 this at times strays into high class Bourbon territory, while always keeping its malty credentials. Simply brilliant! One of the great whiskies of the year. *46%. nc ncf.*

◈ **Penderyn Rich Oak** bott code 202812 db **(89)** n22 dull though decent t23 here's the best bit by far: the delivery! Wow, it is like a warm embrace of manuka honey and molasses, though the sweeter tones keep on the right side of decency. The follow up is a little one-dimensional with the vanilla; f22 a little shorter than expected but some residual honey; b22 very pleasant fayre, there is no doubt and rich. But lacking the complexity which normally wins the heart. *46%. ncf.*

Penderyn Rich Oak bott code 82504 db **(94)** n23 t23.5 f23.5 b24 Jack Daniels was of Welsh descent. The layered tannins here, not entirely dissimilar to some Kentucky and Tennessee whiskey, would make him feel very much at home. Superb. *46%. ncf.*

Penderyn Rich Oak bott code 90742 db **(91)** n23 t24 f21 b23 When they say "Rich" they mean rich... Penderyn at its most muscular. Probably ever.... *46%. nc ncf.*

Penderyn Rich Oak bott code 91222 db **(95.5)** n24 t24 f23.5 b24 As is the Penderyn way, this cleverly reveals the other side of the coin. Quietly intense and far less domineering, this is an easily overlooked gem of a whisky! *46% (92 Proof). nc ncf. Exclusively imported by ImpEx Beverages, Inc.*

Penderyn Royal Welsh Whisky bott code 90532 db **(86)** n22 t23 f20 b21 One of the softest deliveries of the Penderyn range, briefly enjoying a salivating grape and grain combination which for several excellent moments hit wonderful fruit and chocolate heights. But the finish is untidy and the furry buzz reveals a rogue cask in the mix. The delivery, though, is something a little special. *43%. ncf. Icons of Wales No. 6.*

◈ **Penderyn Sherrywood** bott code 200932 db **(93)** n23 light fruit softens, decent oak firms...; t23 a very different delivery to 221 (below), the oak having a much more telling input while the fruit is along the lines of fruit pastels. However, it is the marriage of spice and ulmo honey which captivates; f23.5 long, increasingly chocolatey with a perfect escort of pinging spice. Ridiculously long thanks to the decent oils; b23.5 a blemish-free sherry butt at work here allowing the full scope of this complex and superbly weighted whisky to be enjoyed unhindered. *46%. ncf.*

⟡ **Penderyn Sherrywood** bott code 203221 db **(89.5) n22.5** just a little cherry protrudes from the oak; **t23.5** spot on delivery: the weight, pace of flavour evolvement and intensity all score top marks making this uncommonly complex and satisfying. The grape has a rich texture and lighter lemon blossom honey weaves through it on behalf of the barley; **f21** long, residue muscovado sugars and increasing milky chocolate along with the warming spice. Loses a mark and a half for a late tang...; **b22.5** maybe a semi-feeble blemish at the end, but at least the journey was panoramic. *46%. ncf.*

Penderyn Sherrywood bott code 82111 db **(94) n23 t23.5 f24 b23.5** Quite simple, but goes out of its way to do the simple things very well – and deliciously - indeed... *46%. ncf.*

Penderyn Sherrywood bott code 90113 db **(86) n22.5 t22 f20.5 b21** The nose is interesting enough, but otherwise this lies flat on the palate and steadfastly refuses to sparkle. A disappointing dullard by Penderyn's high standards. *46%. ncf.*

Penderyn Sherrywood bott code 91331 db **(91.5) n23 t23 f22.5 b23** Elegant and even: a portrait of charm itself. *46%. ncf.*

Penderyn Sherrywood bott code 92392 db **(95) n23.5 t24 f23.5 b24** Boasting a balance and complexity which borders belief, this is one very sophisticated whisky... *46%. ncf.*

Penderyn Single Cask bourbon cask, cask no. 182/2006, bott 11 Jul 19 db **(96.5) n24.5 t24.5 f23.5 b24** This is one of those rare, magical whiskies that is not about tasting notes but the shape, depth and overall experience. Which, has to be said, is pretty close to as good as it gets... *62%. ncf sc. Selected by Harrods.*

Penderyn Single Cask bourbon cask, cask no. 2/2006 db **(95.5) n23.5 t23.5 f24.5 b24** Massively tasty, but a curious Penderyn, all the same. The precise and eye-wateringly sharp grapefruit acts as a juicy diversion away from the barley, which slowly composes itself to mount to compelling challenge. This celebrates maltiness in the same way a sex addict revels in a threesome. A malt which simply refuses to leave the taste buds alone until they finally submit. *56.8%. ncf sc.*

Penderyn Single Cask ex-bourbon cask, cask no. 71/2007, dist Feb 07, bott Aug 19 db **(95) n24 t24 f23 b24** On this evidence, Penderyn is ready for a run of bourbon cask bottlings. The enormity and purity of the malt takes some believing... *58.6%. ncf sc. 196 bottles. Selected by La Maison du Whisky.*

⟡ **Penderyn Single Cask Ex-Bourbon** cask no. 195/2007, dist Apr 2007, bott Jul 2020 db **(96) n24** technically just about perfect: the clarity of the barley is faultless, the injection of delicate citrus exquisite. The depth to the vanilla is considerable. Another malt which benefits from the Murray Method as the layering at different temperatures is astonishing. But there is never less than crystal clarity and the tumbling around of delicate fruit tones, mainly grapefruit, with the sawdust is magnificent; **t24.5** just blown away. Like the nose faultless...but this is even more faultless (if you get what I mean) ...! The vibrant grassy barley kick on delivery is... well, faultless. The barley-tannin weight and balance is perfect. The degree of dark sugars mixing with the more even, softer ulmo honey is perfect. The midground cocoa mixed with vanilla is faultless....; **f23.5** the finish retains the graceful demeanour of the nose and delivery, though now with added peppers and cocoa. Long and very slightly lush...which is another surprise; **b24** simply majestic. A John Charles of a single malt...If there wasn't such a thing as a Welsh heaven before, there is now... *60.8% sc. Exclusively bottled for France*

Penderyn Ex-Madeira Single Cask cask no. M524, dist Nov 13, bott Jan 20 db **(95.5) n23.5 t24 f23.5 b24.5** Another Penderyn it is really hard to find fault with. The most astonishing thing, perhaps, is its strength. The luxurious, creamy softness of this malt means the alcohol is barely noticeable at all..This is one very substantial whisky. *60.4%. ncf sc. Franconian Edition 2016.*

⟡ **Penderyn Single Cask Ex-Olorosos Cask** cask no. S76, dist Feb 2012, bott Aug 2020 db **(94.5) n23.5** just gorgeous, soft, moist yielding fruitcake, the Welsh equivalent of a Dundee cake, perhaps...; **t23** works magnificently on two levels: both fresh, juicy, clean and salivation as well as malty but displaying an unlikely, yet unmistakable, fragile maltiness; **f24** as it settles and the demerara sugars ramp up, the complexity levels rise wonderfully. Now moist dates...even with some late walnut thrown in. Again, the mouth feel is calming and gentle, despite the best efforts of the spice, late interlacing mocha and praline rounds matters off exquisitely; **b24** a nutty cask that has cracked it. Not a single off note and not so powerful as to dominate ruthlessly. More sorcery from the Welsh mountains: magic and majestic... *60.7% sc. German selection by Schlumberger.*

Penderyn Single Cask purple moscatel finish, cask no. W23 db **(88) n22 t22.5 f21.5 b22** A tart and mildly aggressive malt. Just a little too heavy of the sharper fruit notes with the malt vanishing under a near brutal regime of murderous spices. Amazing flavour profile, I admit. But a little too vicious and blood curdling for me... 61%. ncf sc.

Penderyn Single Cask PX sherry finish, cask no. S74 db **(87) n23 t23 f20 b21** While the nose displays a highly unusual salty edge to a Penderyn, the direction of the PX involvement is predictable, though not before a superb volley of spices gather your attention early on. After a salivating entry it becomes syrupy and sticky, though the fruit does have an attractive date and walnut touch when at its best; a molassed noble rot when at its most basic. The finish, however, is furry and dull. 59.1%. ncf sc.

Penderyn Single Cask rum finished, cask no. R13 db **(93.5) n23 t24 f23 b23.5** A very different whisky from Penderyn that at times shews just a little bit of youth, but some outstanding yumminess. Oh, and really profits under the Murray Method. 50%. ncf sc. Bottled for Schlumberger.

Penderyn Single Cask purple moscatel finish, cask no. W28 db **(88.5) n22.5 t22 f22 b22** Like Cask W23, the malt is buried under a tsunami of unforgiving grape. Certainly captures the attention but, again, the spices have little compassion and the oak is its accomplice. But providing you are tucked into your seatbelt this is an enjoyable ride, the outrageous plums offering astonishing chewiness and depth. But the corners are taken just a little too sharply. 59.8%. ncf sc.

◈ **Penderyn Single Cask Ex-Purple Moscatel Cask**, cask no. W21, dist Feb 2021, Aug 20 db **(93.5) n23.5** while some Penderyn noses are dry enough to make your nose bleed, this might also, but only because it is so sharp. The kind of fruitiness normally experienced after opening the jam jar...; **t23** yikes! The nose doesn't lie! Eyewatering tartness to the delivery and just to ensure you get the message the spices come blundering in like the Keystone Cops...The fruit appears to centre around freshly diced passionfruit; **f23.5** settles down into some kind of sanity, especially when chocolate liqueur mode arrives; **b23.5** what a fun whisky! One of those malts that refuses to give your taste buds a moment's respite. 58.7% sc. German selection by Schlumberger

Penderyn Single Cask ex-Tawny port cask, cask no. PT267, dist Jun 13, bott Nov 19 db **(94.5) n23.5 t23.5 f23.5 b24** With its distinct pink hue, this is the most porty-looking malt of all time. But like the Tawny owl which frequents my garden, it has a certain gravitas to it too, as well as ageless elegance. 59.6%. ncf sc. Exclusive bottling for Whisky Live Manila 2020.

◈ **Penderyn Single Cask Ex-Tawny Port Cask**, cask no. PT266, dist Jun 2013, bott Jul 2019 db **(95) n24** wonderfully dry and sophisticated with the grape skin as close to concentrated form you'll ever find; **t24** such precision to the cask, such concentration needed to work out the spellbinding layering, you'll need someone to mop your brow as you concentrate. Most amazing is how the malt forms thin, delicate stratum among the much more intense fruit tones. The sugars, after their initial burst of acacia honey, are on ration and it is the spiced dryness of the fruit which dominates...though that fragile malt ensures the salty plum and grape skins don't get all their own way; **f23** I'd say the spice fade on this must be nudging perfection. The fruits fatten at last, briefly, before gong back into their skinny shell.....; **b24** if James Bond wants his dry Martinis made with whisky, I suspect this would be his choice.... 60.5% sc. 724 bottles

Penderyn Single Cask Terrantez cask finish from Blandy's Madeira Wine Lodge, cask no. 078-2, bott 6 Aug 19 db **(94.5) n24** now, that is one very proud nose! The fruit boasts a solidity, an uncompromising depth and almost regal stature. Not an atom out of place, but an almost regimented procession thick then deft grapey tones, each taking turn to hold the attention. The sugars are likewise fulsome, a mix of muscovado and molassed variety but also with a tantalising sliver of kumquat peel. Superb...; **t23.5** curiously, the delivery does not have the same initial gravitas revealed on the nose. But the fruit does soon build up into a dizzy, busy spiced concoction holding vanilla and butterscotch in major quantities; **f23** a slightly duller finish as the oak reveals its toasty nature, though the fruit does retain a creamy presence; **b24** a formidable malt where the whisky has just enough body to hold the weight of the grape without trembling. A unique assemblage of personality traits. 57.4%. ncf sc. Selected by Harrods.

◈ **Penderyn Single Cask 2010 Ex-Bourbon Cask** cask no. B331 db **(91.5) n22.5** a light, creamy cream soda sweetness with a pleasant chocolate vanilla wafer undertone; **t23.5** soothing and sensual, this is malt which caresses the taste buds with a series of sweet tones of varying intensity. Ulmo honey leads the profile (as is so often the case with bourbon cask Penderyn) with light molasses and mocha strands trailing in all directions. All the time, though, the malt is knocking on the door; **f22.5** a much quieter finish than usual with a medium length malt and vanilla fade and delicate spice for accompaniment; **b23** a distinctly fatter version of their other bourbon cask vintage bottlings played out on far more simplistic lines. Effectively delicious, though. 59.7% sc. Specially selected for Taiwan exclusive bottling

⟜ **Penderyn Single Cask 8-year-Old Ex-Moscatel Cask** cask no. M2 db **(95.5)** n23.5 pre-Murray Method: dry enough to make your nose blead. During/post Murray Method... some beautiful Chinese gooseberry notes mingle with the barley to sweeten the dry grape; **t24** Murray Method or not, the delivery is one of intense fruit, sharp and dry enough to make your tongue shrink. But, slowly, your palate acclimatises to the salty onslaught of tannin and the frighteningly clever layering of at first dry and then increasingly juicy fruit. A highly unusual – and wonderfully delicious – and not a miss of a beat of an off note to be found...; **f24** to make this near perfect, your needed high-quality cocoa to leach into the fruit...and guess what. Salty and perfectly spiced, too...; **b24** it is as though Penderyn are sewing up the world market in dry, sophisticated single malt.... this is so good it is nearly silly. *60.09% sc. Specially selected by The Wine & Spirit Co. of Greenville and Tim's liquors*

⟜ **Penderyn Single Cask 9-Year-old Ex-Oloroso Sherry Cask** cask no. 575 db **(89)** n22 no escaping the curious juniper clinging to the grape; **t23.5** lush and sugar-laden on delivery, there is almost a dessert feel before a secondary wave of rushing, pinging peppers; **f21** a fraction tight and bitterness in the finish is a tad short; **b22.5** a bit of a schizophrenic malt, for sure. The delivery and follow-through though is a bit special. *59.98% sc. Specially selected by Jack Rose Dining Salon*

⟜ **Penderyn Single Cask 12-Year-Old Ex-Ruby Port Cask** cask no. PT136 db **(93)** n23.5 didn't expect the marzipan and most discreet of sweet chestnut to be found almost concealed amid the grape; **t23.5** the usual dry wine delivery Penderyn appear to be specialising in now, but slowly boosted by the united front of toasty tannin and molasses; **f23** lime jam on toast; **b23** another excellent bottling from Wales. This one is slightly different from the rest in the way it mixes broad and thin brush strokes together, so the more complex moments are found right in the middle of a seemingly simplistic phase. *60.38% sc. Specially selected and imported by ImpEx Beverages, Inc.*

⟜ **Penderyn Single Cask 13 Year Old Rich Oak Cask** cask no. D1062 db **(95.5)** n23.5 the depth of fruit is almost incalculable. The clarity of the concentrated raisin defies reason. The dried dates.... the prunes. The dried orange peel. The precision of both timing and intensity of the spices defies belief. Then, to cap it all...there is that chocolate, turning the whole thing into a Mayfair-quality Old Jamaica candy bar.... Oh, and the tannins suggesting an impressive number of passed summers...; **t24.5** salivating, though thick enough on the palate to have been mashed in a cauldron. The fruit has no aggression, but the intensity has your taste buds up against the wall: this is full on and non-compromising.... yet gentle at the very same time. The malt seams to flicker here and there. But it is the lush grape, still with those dates and intense grape skin – though now helped along by a no less intense molasses (makes a very early appearance) – which hold sway...; **f22.5** spicy, complex, and satisfying, the vanilla helps make for a much less demanding finale; **b24** this was the last of the full range of Penderyn I tasted this year. And did I, through mixture of luck and instinct, leave the very best to last? *58.1% sc. Specially selected and imported by ImpEx Beverages, Inc.*

⟜ **Penderyn Single Cask 15-Year-Old Bourbon Cask** cask no. B105/2005 db **(96.5)** n24 a decade and half of complexity has built up like silt in an estuary: layer upon layer of charm. A mix of salt and barley gives this a rare sharpness. But the tannins play out in varying strata vanilla the first tentacles of hickory as it moves towards the most delicate of bourbon character. The sugars are provided by gentle waves of ulmo honey. There is an unmistakable nip of copper in the air, too, re-igniting that sharpness; **t24** the first five or six layers of maltiness combined with vanilla is a style I have seen only once before in my 30-year professional tasting and blending career, which I will explain anon. This is top quality malt, surprising in its malty intensity and delightful in the coppery sheen attached to the ethereal honey. The playful hickory on the nose has a firmer presence here moving towards malty mocha and further delicate bourbon tones towards the middle; **f24.5** you suspect earlier that a little exotic fruit has made its mark but vanishes. However, as the rich chocolate descends, those exotic fruit notes return, giving the effect of a high-class chocolate liqueur...; **b24** how fascinating to see a 15-year-old Welsh whisky. Curiously, in style it reminds one of a 12 or 13-year-old top-rank Bushmills filled into first fill bourbon. As much as I hate to compare distilleries from different countries, there is no getting away from it....it is uncanny. And while we are at it.... What about the Glen Grant strains from the midpoint to the finish. Indeed, from midpoint onwards we are in entirely unrecognisable ground so far as Welsh whisky is concerned: the barley has retreated behind a gorgeous coppery vanilla/honey mix, and we are luxuriating in the chocolate liqueur of the finish. What an absolutely cracking cask, doubtless set aside for this special day. And if anyone now doesn't recognise Welsh as being among the Grand Cru of the world's whiskies, then let's see what they have to say after spending half an hour with this masterpiece *59% sc. Specially selected and imported by ImpEx Beverages, Inc.* 🍸

Australian Whisky

It is not surprising that Australia, cast adrift it seems from the rest of the world until Captain James Cook thrust his triangulation apparatus at it some 240 years ago, has many indigenous species. The result of biodiversity having to get on with it alone, often bravely and against the odds.

From the kangaroo to the koala, the wombat to the platypus, the kookaburra to the bearded Lark. Now it is the Bearded Lark (Billius Distillus) in its native Tasmanian habitat, a small creature found mainly flying around darkened buildings in the vicinity of Hobart, that has had the greatest impact on Australian whisky, and without whom there would be no chapter given only to that singular scion of the world's malt distillation family.

Bill Lark is a one-man force majeure who took a country out of a starch-knickered Victorian reactionism, so far as distilling was concerned, into one that now proudly boasts over 25 distilleries either operating or in the process of being built. And a standard achieved by many so far that is way above the norm.

We must go back to 1992, seemingly recent in the grand scheme of whisky matters but a year before many of the people I met attending a recent (though just pre-Covid) Chengdu, China, whisky festival were actually born. It was the year I gave up my work as a national newspaper journalist to become the world's first full-time whisky writer. And was the year Bill Lark began taking on the Australian government to change a law that forbade private distilling in Australia. Having got sympathetic politicians on board – always a wise move – he found his battle shorter and less bloody than expected and it was not long before he and his wife Lyn were hard at work distilling an unhopped mash made at the local – and historic – Cascade brewery. Soon their daughter, Kristy, was on board shewing exceptional skill as a distiller. And next a family affair became a national one, as, inspired by the Larks, small distilleries began rising around the country. First Dave Baker, whose Bakery Hill malt scooped the Whisky Bible 2020's Southern Hemisphere Whisky of the Year, across the Tasman Straight in Melbourne and then onwards along and up the coast. A new whisky nation was born. And is growing prodigiously. Now I have given Australia its own section in Jim Murray's Whisky Bible, perhaps not before time. It is a form of award well merited, because Australian malt has constantly proved to be something worth finding: often as bold and brave as Bill Lark's vision. And, like the great man and dear friend himself, you always feel better for its company.

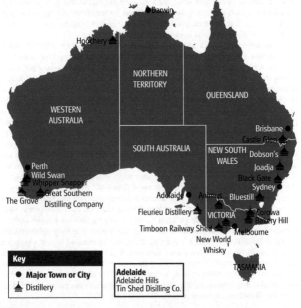

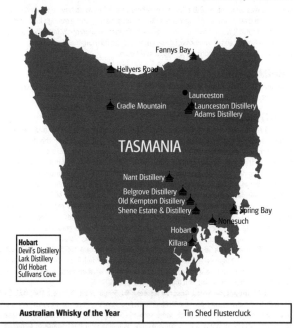

Australian Whisky of the Year	Tin Shed Flustercluck

AUSTRALIA
ADAMS DISTILLERY Perth, Tasmania. 2012. Working.

Adams Distillery Tasmanian Single Malt Whisky Cask Strength peated - slosh 200L Pinot Noir cask, cask no. AD 0128 db **(91) n23 t23 f22.5 b22.5** Too often wine casks and peat hit the buffers. This stays on track, even if there isn't quite enough smoke to keep this one going at full speed.. *61.2%. ncf sc. 132 bottles.*

Adams Distillery Tasmanian Single Malt Whisky Cask Strength peated - slosh 300L port cask, cask no. AD 0113 db **(96) n24 t23.5 f24.5 b24** You've got to Hand it to them: simply brilliant! A Munster, sorry a mean monster, whisky...(I've been in Lockdown too long...) *59.5%. ncf sc. 130 bottles.*

ADELAIDE HILLS DISTILLERY Nairne, South Australia. 2014. Working.

◈ **78 Degrees Australian Whiskey** ex-wine American & French oak, batch no.002, db **(86) n20.5 t22.5 f22 b21** It is just as well that the delivery and mouth development is bursting at the seams with character. Because the nose is a tough one to negotiate, all sharp, angular and out of sync. The delivery, though, is an intriguing mix if acacia honey and fruit which thanks to the spices and attractive layers of tannin, grows on you. *44% 2000 bottles*

◈ **78 Degrees Muscat Finish Whiskey** ex-wine American oak, ex-bourbon, ex-Muscat, db **(89) n21** extremely pithy and sharp. Just a little away from finding its natural balance; **t23** succulent delivery with an increasing feel of dark cherry and darker chocolate; **f23** simply more of the same, though with a little spice now to add confusion to the cocoa; **b22** technically not quite tickety-boo. But all is forgiven for the intensity of the chocolate cherry treat. *44%*

◈ **78 Degrees Native Grain Whiskey** ex-cabernet French oak, batch no.003 db **(93) n22.5** the wine gives the impression of a dried old cork; **t24** although obviously pretty young, the mouth feel is astonishing. Enough weight on the cut has combined with the thickening fruitcake. But then this shifts into overdrive as the grains become more varied in texture and busier in their degree of flavour output. The result is a tongue constantly searching around the palate and smacking the roof of the mouth trying to work out just what the hell is going on! A few bourbon-style liquorice notes, to while the spices at time sooth, at times bristle...; **f23** I think I remember a vague bitterness at this point last year. There is a slight one here, too. But it fits in perfectly with the countering manuka honey and spice. Dark cherries circle, also...; **b23.5** when I set out on writing the Whisky Bible back in 2003, my wonderful old budgie, Borat, kept me company through the long tasting days, right until the summer I was writing the 2010 edition. Somehow, I think he would have approved of these native Australian grains, and fought me for them. Because they come through loud and clear about the fourth flavour-wave in and entertain with gusto and uniquely from then onwards. Would still like to see the wine cask being a more respectful though and stop trying to drown these fascinating flavour tones out. *46.2% 400 bottles*

ANIMUS DISTILLERY Kyneton, Victoria. 2012. Working.
Animus Distillery Alpha Whisky db **(90.5) n23 t23.5 f22 b22.5** Impressively forceful and confident it is helped by the clean, unsullied spirit. *54.5%.*

ANTHROPOCENE
⬦ **VI Anthropocene First Release Single Malt** Port/bourbon cask **(91) n23** a muscular, jammy character – mainly plum and gooseberry – says "goodday" from the distillery. The layer of malt is discernible, as are several roasty tannin notes. All-in-all, a full on signature sharpened, it seems, by a coppery metallic vibe; **t23** simultaneously fat and tart. The fruit really is dripping, but a peculiar nip gathers your attention; **f22** a bipolar personality that is as confusing as it is entertaining. There is a hot sub-plot which is baffling me slightly: the still run a little faster than is best for the stills? Settles for a malty fade; **b23** cheers to a new Ozzie distillery, and I toast its success with its first bottling. Like so many other whiskies from Australia, it is not exactly shy and just bursts onto the palate with a melee of intense – sometimes slightly too intense – flavours. Certainly knows how to grab your attention. But this is one bucking bronco of a dram. Fasten your seat belts, folks... *54.4%*

⬦ **VI Anthropocene Second Release Single Malt** sherry cask **(85.5) n21 t22 f21 b21.5** The cuts just aren't right on this fellow, allowing too many underlying feints to get a foothold. The grape itself is intense and means business. And for a while there is so much fruit to conjure with. Pleasant in part, but too many fault lines. *50.45%*

⬦ **VI Anthropocene Small Reserve Release 01 Single Malt** Port cask **(86) n21.5 t22 f21 b21.5** Attractively succulent thanks to another outstanding Port cask this distillery seems to be able call upon at will, though some stewed cabbage can be detected on the nose. A charming pastiche of plum and cherry jams intertwanging with the bedrock of firm malt. A little hot late on as per the house style. But perhaps a little too much vegetable where sugars should be. *46.2%*

⬦ **VI Anthropocene Small Reserve Release 02 Single Malt** Port cask **(83.5) n21.5 t21 f20 b21** The wide cut on this gives the grape very little leeway. Never quite finds its rhythm or purpose. *46.2%*

⬦ **VI Anthropocene Small Reserve Release 03 Single Malt** bourbon cask **(91.5) n22.5** a wide cut, but just on the right side of decency. A hint of nougat, delicate hickory and ginger, but malt and heather honey are well represented, also; **t23** that fatness on arrival comes as absolutely no surprise, as the cut has lassoed some oils into the frame. It is the honey, however, which holds court...a kind of moist honey-laden ginger cake; **f22.5** after the sweetness invariably on wide cuts, comes the bitterness, though more of a contrarian moan rather than anything negative or aggressive; **b23.5** if the cut is slightly generous, then the honey to be found on this is positively philanthropic... *47.2%*

⬦ **VI Anthropocene Small Reserve Release 04 Single Malt** Port cask **(94) n23.5** the last time I received a blast of Port this intense was from opening a 1970 vintage about three years ago. Not, of course, in that league, but there is a unique intensity to the grape, followed by mesmerising laying, which comes through here loud and clear; **t23.5** so impressive! I adore the marriage of sweet and dry on arrival, bound together by a firm oaky content and succulent grapiness; **f23** the spices and chocolate adorn the fruity remnants; **b24** top of the range Australian single malt using magnificent oak throughout. *43.8%*

⬦ **VI Anthropocene Small Reserve Release 05 Single Malt** bourbon cask/Canadian maple finish **(88.) n21.5 t22.5 f22 b22** Not the first Canadian maple influenced whisky I've ever encountered. But certainly, the most mouth-puckering and intense. A very brave bottling for a new distillery. The maturation properties of maple is barely understood as little work has been done with controlled variants. Add in a new distillery, too, still coming to terms with their own output and you get something way off the charts. The nose, though subtly spiced, is rewarding and quite agile in both its tannins and malt. Works on many levels, with the sugars always in harmony with th spices. But perhaps the oils which form the cut makes for a heavier dram than it intends to be, *47.2%*

⬦ **VI Anthropocene Small Reserve Release 06 Single Malt** Port cask **(91) n22** green grape. Fresh and attractive; **t23** salivating and fruity, the malt comes a distinct second to the grape. Spices begin to bite with surprising intensity from the midpoint...; **f23** spiced chocolate raisin. The vanillas boast a surprisingly dry, sawdusty oakiness considering the earlier juices on tap...; **b23** a loose-fitting malt where the grape sloshes around the palate with a salivating abundance. *45.3%*

BAKERY HILL North Bayswater, Victoria. 1999. Working.
Bakery Hill Classic Malt Single Malt Whisky db (88) n22 t22 f22 b22 A straight as a die malt which makes little attempt to veer away from its cream toffee theme. *46%. ncf.*

Bakery Hill Classic Malt Cask Strength Single Malt Whisky db (94) n23 t23.5 f23.5 b24 Because of the lack of oils present on Baker Hill malt, it can suffer slightly when reduced. Here the whisky, oils and all, is intact we get the malt in full glory. "Classic Malt" says the label. You hear no quibbles from me... *60.5%. ncf.*

Bakery Hill Death or Glory (94) n23 t23.5 f23.5 b24 Oh, my! Get the complexity on this fella! As minty as it is malty, on the nose especially, this has a colossal amount of development between the sweeter tones, mint included, and the drier oaks which act as anchor. Right in the middle of all this is sublime malt, salivating and sharp on one level, and almost biscuity and salty on another. One of those 15 minutes malts using the Murray Method to unlock a true beauty. When a malt is this on song, surely it should be called "Tunes of Glory"... *48%.*

Bakery Hill Double Wood Single Malt Whisky db (90) n22 t23 f22.5 b23 A busy, attractive and quite full bodied Bakery Hill. *46%. ncf.*

Bakery Hill Peated Malt Cask Strength Single Malt Whisky db (95.5) n24 t24 f23 b24 Doing the Australian whiskies today (well, some of them) as England and the Aussies are battling it out in the semi-final of the cricket World Cup. Duty over pleasure means I am here tasting instead of at Edgbaston. And it is so wonderful to find David Baker's malt still very much up in smoke, a bit like Australia who have slipped to 175-7 – which doubtless means the Aussies will win.... A malt as glorious as England's bowling... *60%. ncf.*

BELGROVE DISTILLERY Kempton, Tasmania. 2010. Working.
Belgrove Distillery Rye Whisky 100% Rye bott 11 Apr 19 db (93) n22.5 t24 f23 b23.5 Belgrove back to its bristling self. Full set of cutlery required for this three-course rye. *62.5%. ncf sc.*

BLACK GATE DISTILLERY Mendooran NSW. 2012. Working.
Black Gate Distillery Peated Cask cask no. BG068, dist Apr 17, bott Dec 19 db (91.5) n23 t23 f22.5 b23 The caramels dampen the peat fire a little, but no mistaking a superb whisky when you see one. *58.7%. sc.*

Black Gate Distillery Port Cask Solera Batch No. 3 db (87) n21.5 t22.5 f21 b22 A neat and comfortable malt, if not technically in the same league as their peated cask bottling, that seems as though it doesn't want to ruffle too many feathers. The port acts as a silky base but also ensures development and complexity is limited. *46.8%.*

CHIEF'S SON DISTILLERY Somerville, Victoria. 2014. Working.
◇ **Chief's Son 900 Pure Malt** db (88) n22.5 t23 f20.5 b22 Much more to celebrate on the nose now with the vanilla and muscovado sugars at full throttle. This directly translates to a rich malt and honey delivery with the sugars working overtime to enhance complexity. Sadly, the tangy finish lets the side down. *45%*

◇ **Chief's Son 900 Pure Malt** db (89) n23.5 more than a hint of Bourbon on here! The tannins pulse out all the right Kentuckian tunes, with the muscovado sugars moving increasingly towards liquorice and Manuka honey; **t23** the intensity is captivating, the honeyed sugars working hard with the toastier notes. Unlike on the 45% version, here the Murray Method can unravel the malt itself. Some superb spices, too, with perfect intensity; **f20.5** again, the finish comes abruptly with a semi-metallic tang; **b22** pity about the finish. But the extra strength helps bring out the star quality of the bourbon-style sweetness. At times absolutely delicious. *60%*

Chief's Son Single Malt Whisky 900 Standard db (91) n22.5 t23 f22.5 b23 Wonderful to find an Australian that is not depending on power and/or muscular fruit. Complex and fabulously malty. *45%. nc ncf.*

◇ **Chief's Son 900 Standard** db (92) n22.5 the fruitiness, almost a delicate Sauternes, works charmingly with the vanilla and tannin happy to bolster the complexity; **t23** succulent delivery with excellent sweet-dry balance. The vanilla seeps in almost unnoticed; **f23** excellent raise fruit cake toastiness, sprinkled with muscovado sugars. A good dollop of vanilla custard, too...; **b23.5** a beautiful malt which from the first moment appears to put balance before all else. Excellent length on the finale rounds this off wonderfully, too. *45%*

Chief's Son Single Malt Whisky 900 Standard db (95) n23 t23.5 f24.5 b24 It is as though someone has put the 45% version up another gear or two...It is like taking your taste buds to the gym where they are fully worked over. And, just like a good work out, you feel so bloody good afterwards... Oh, and as this stunning malt was made at Mornington Peninsula, a warm toast to the memory of British comic legend Tim Brook-Taylor, forever associated with Mornington Crescent, who was stolen from us by Covid-19 as I wrote this Bible... 60%. nc ncf.

⬥ **Chief's Son 900 Standard** db (94) n23 a much drier version than the 45%, the nose having to work hard to find the sugars. They are there, though and a little spice prickle thanks you for the search...; t23.5 the fruit first glides in, then explodes on impact spraying spices in all direction. The next waves are ones of pure bourbon intensity, the magnificent toastiness intertwangling with delicate liquorice and ever-thickening vanillas; f23.5 the finish is long, studied and hell-bent on getting the drier vanillas; sweet muscovado sugars and other light fruit notes in harmony. Good light oils, too...; b24 just one of those annoying drams that it would be far too easy spending too much time drinking. Big...and beautiful. 45%

Chief's Son Single Malt Whisky 900 Sweet Peat db (88) n22 t22 f22 b22 The peat is little more than a gentle breeze. And even that is lost in the moderate winds of the fruit. Just a little too even and, though pleasant, you get the feeling differing forces are as much cancelling the other out as they are making for a complex malt. Even so, sweet, attractive and easy going. 45%. nc ncf.

⬥ **Chief's Son 900 Sweet Peat** db (88.5) n22.5 t22.5 f21.5 b22 A little extra zip on both nose and delivery – certainly more than I remember it. But still flattens out a little too easily as smoke and a sweet fruitiness mingle themselves to death. Just love that delivery, though! 45%

⬥ **Chief's Son 900 Sweet Peat** db (92.5) n22.5 t23.5 at this strength – and aided and abetted by the Murray Method - you can see why this is called Sweet Peat. In this form the heather honey tumbles over the taste buds on delivery, the extra oils thickening them and ensuring their durability. The smoke huffs, but never quite puffs...; f23 long with a beautiful vanilla touch to the lazy peat and relaxed sugars; b23.5 this has unquestionably gone up a gear. Here's a poser, though: the stronger a spirit, the tighter the bubbles formed when shaken and the longer they remain. Yet do this trick with this whisky, the stronger version's bubbles disappear long before the weaker ones. But the intensity of the whisky experience confirms and underlines the difference in strength. Like water disappearing anti-clockwise down the plug hole, things are the opposite in Australia.... 60%

Chief's Son Single Malt Whisky Cask Expression db (93) n23 t23 f23.5 b23.5 My very old friend, the late distillery consultant Jim Swan, would probably have cut your arm off to get a bottle of this. This was one of his preferred styles of whisky, and here it has been executed almost faultlessly. Most impressive is the way this malt just kept getting better as it went along. 47.85%. nc ncf.

⬥ **Chief's Son Cask Expression** Imperial Stout cask, db (85) n20 t22.5 f21 b21.5 Must admit that the hoppy nose makes this hard going from the start: I'm no fan of whisky fashioned by hop. I adore great whisky. And I adore great beer (the ancient real ales of the UK in particular). but you'll never find me putting my beer in my whisky, or my whisky in my beer: I feel the bittering quality of the hop throws out of kilter the balance. Others, I know, love this style...so I'm afraid you'll just have to accept my purist stance, if not agree with it. Still, having said that.... I think the rich texture is first class and the mix of molasses and vanilla a delight and the cocoa notes don't hurt, either. But along comes that hop again to tarnish the gold. 47.85%

⬥ **Chief's Son The Tanist** db (84) n21.5 t22.5 f20 b20 Unbelievably fat in texture. The delivery wallows in a muted cream soda sweetness with barley and marshmallow through the middle. The finish though is a tad bitter despite a chocolatey intervention. A pretty idiosyncratic offering, but feels it loses its balance at about the halfway point as the bitterness creeps in. 43%

CORRA LINN DISTILLERY Relbia, Tasmania. 2015. Working.

Corra Linn Fumosus Aqua Vitae Single Malt Whisky db (87) n21.5 t22.5 f21.5 b21.5 A particularly dry malt with a busy cross section of seasoning. The tannins bite a bit while a strange, meandering semi-fruitiness pitches up here and there, as does a lagging phenolic tone. An oddball malt which never quite settles on the direction it wants to take. Plenty of flavour and certainly intriguing. 56.2%.

CRADLE MOUNTAIN WHISKY PTY LTD Ulverstone, Tasmania. Closed.

⬥ **Cradle Mountain The Alpine Trail** batch no: 20007 db (89.5) n23.5 a tingling aroma, the peppers light yet playful. Lovely marriage between a bourbon-style leathery tannin and a fruitier muscovado sugar and marmalade. So attractive...; t22.5 slightly creamy textured and buttery on arrival. However, the big dollop of honey I was expecting from the nose had obviously missed the bus. Certainly, a packet of muscovado sugar is on hand early on, but it soon vanishes behind a tight, dry toastiness; f21.5 if you think the middle was dry, get a load of this...; **b22** such a curious whisky which decides to take a separate path from where the nose is pointing. The aroma really is the peak of this Alpine Trail, the charm of the early bourbon sweetness is quite irresistible... 48.7% ncf

Cradle Mountain Whisky Single Malt The Long Trek batch no. 20005 db **(95) n23.5 t24 f23.5 b24** I love a whisky with not just personality but one that's all its own. And this has it in spades. Superb! Happy anniversary! 57%. 240 bottles. 30 Year Anniversary.

⬧ **Cadenhead's World Whiskies Cradle Mountain Aged 24 Years** cabernet sauvignon cask **(95.5) n24** there is something of an old Guyanese rum about this nose: the oak influence is magnificently structured, happy to show great age but ensuring that nowhere have the tannins begin to take on an overly toasted, tired feel. Old, yes. Dead, no. This not only has wonderful life but manages to dovetail the manuka honey into the quietly dominant, rum-like esters; **t23.5** we are back to a slight rum feel, though this gives way, slowly to barley, and fruit chocolate. The texture is near perfect and again the tannins refuse to make a fuss, while always underlining their antiquity. Amazingly, though, early on there is some serious juiciness, again with a barley slant..; **f24** the modest oils keep that fruit and chocolate in a hold; **b24** a 24-year-old Australian...the first one I have ever found that wasn't either backpacking, playing professional cricket or working in a bar... Actually, this one is far too good for a bar: this needs to be given a good half hour somewhere quiet and free from aroma. This is going into territories that no Australian whisky I have ever tasted has before travelled. And it is doing it in style... By the way: such is the complexity of this whisky, it took me over an hour to satisfactorily analyse. Believe me when I say we are talking complex... 52.7% 180 bottles

DEVIANT DISTILLERY Sandy Bay, Tasmania. 2017. Working.
Deviant Distillery Anthology 16 Single Malt Spirit Pinot Noir F.O. cask, finished in a coffee cask db **(91.5) n22.5 t23 f23 b23** For those of you looking for a spirit to wake you up first thing in the morning, here it is. You can even dip biscuits in it. Actually, the coffee isn't quite as profound as you might think...but it is there and its subtlety makes it all the more attractive. 43.7%.

DEVIL'S DISTILLERY Hobart, Tasmania. 2015. Working.
Hobart Whisky Tasmanian Dark Mofo 2019 Winter Feast Exclusive ex-bourbon cask, rum maple finish, bott 25 Apr 19 db **(82.5) n20 t22 f20.5 b20** Not sure what to say about this. Far more a liqueur than a whisky in character with the maple dominating the aroma to the cost of all else and the muscular sugars, though attractive, decidedly OTT. 59.1%.

Hobart Whisky Tasmanian Single Malt Batch 19-002 ex-bourbon cask, pinot noir finish, bott 25 Apr 19 db **(94) n23 t24 f23.5 b23.5** Like being hit by the waves of a tropical storm, one flavour smashing into you after another. Just brilliant...! 57.5%.

Hobart Whisky Tasmanian Single Malt Batch 19-003 French oak port cask finish, bott 25 Apr 19 db **(93.5) n23 t23.5 f23.5 b23.5** More beautifully intense than a harem... 46.4%.

Hobart Whisky Tasmanian Single Malt Batch 19-004 bott 25 Apr 19 db **(93) n23 t23.5 f23 b23.5** How the Devil do they make their bourbon matured malt so buttery...? 55.5%.

Tasmanian Moonshine Company Tasmanian Malt Barrel Aged New Make port cask db **(91.5) n23 t23 f22.5 b23** Big almost jammy fruit. But that is only half of it: a huge injection of hefty tannin has ensured backbone to the plummy muscle. And as for the spices....? Wow! A huge dose of flavours: this youngster isn't mucking about! 50%.

FANNYS BAY DISTILLERY Lulworth, Tasmania. 2014. Working.
Fannys Bay Single Malt Tasmanian Whisky bourbon barrel, cask no. 33 db **(89.5) n22.5 t23 f22 b22** A brusque malt which certainly doesn't lack confidence. Just a little bitterness here and there weakens it slightly, though the intensity of the malt will win many friends. 63%. sc.

Fannys Bay Single Malt Tasmanian Whisky sherry cask, cask no. 76 db **(91.5) n23 t23.5 f22 b23** A more rounded and less fractious wine influenced malt than their Shiraz. Polite... and not half the fun. 64%. sc.

Fannys Bay Single Malt Tasmanian Whisky Shiraz cask, cask no. 61 db **(93) n22 t24 f23 b24** The nose may be surprisingly non-commital. But the same can't be said once it hits the taste buds. Wow! This malt packs a fruity punch! 63%. sc.

FLEURIEU DISTILLERY Goolwa, South Australia. 2004. Working.
Fleurieu Distillery The Rubicon ex-Seppeltsfield Port barrels db **(89) n22.5 t22.5 f22 b22** A muscular whisky with some big flavour egos at work. When they gel, there are some magical moments. 55%. 500 bottles.

Tasmania Independent Bottlers Fleurieu Release 2 sherry cask, cask no. TIB FL 0011, bott Apr 19 db **(86.5) n22 t22 f21 b21.5** Not sure the wine cask has been as kind to the distillate as it might have been. Clipped to the point of being austere at times, the grape has its odd tart and lucid moment, but seems far too happy to paint a forlorn figure. The finale is just a little too dry and slightly off tune. *49.2%. sc.*

HELLYERS ROAD Havenview, Tasmania. 1999. Working.

Hellyers Road Aged 8 Years Pinot Noir Finish db **(86.5)** n22 t22 f21 b21.5 It may sound a little strange, but the Pinot Noir cask was a little too much for the whisky itself, refusing to let the malt have a meaningful presence. The result was an attractive but lop-sided feel. *61.6%.*

Hellyers Road Henry's Legacy Wey River American oak casks, Pinot Noir finish db **(88.5)** n22.5 t23 f21 b22 Wey River...? Thought for a moment we had our first whisky from my native county of Surrey...! Mouth-watering and entirely presentable single malt enlivened and enriched by an exceptionally healthy wine cask which has imparted just the right degree of sharpness and weight. Good spices, also. *60.8%.*

Hellyers Road Single Malt Whisky 12 Year Old Original db **(84.5)** n19 t22 f21.5 b22. Forget the nose and get stuck into the massive malt. *46.2%.*

Hellyers Road Original Aged 15 Years db **(92.5)** n23.5 t23.5 f22.5 b23 Almost, literally, a peach of a whisky from Hellyers...the most deft whisky ever from this distillery. *46.2%.*

Hellyers Road Original Aged 16 Years db **(90.5)** n22 t23 f22.5 b23 Put on your tin hats for this one – there is shrapnel everywhere... Carnage...and it's delicious..! *66.8%. Master Series.*

Hellyers Road Peated db **(91)** n22.5 t23.5 f22 b23 Hellyers offers a unique character in its own right. Put some pretty full-on peat into the mix and you are left with one of the most idiosyncratic whiskies in the world. And a sheer, if at times perplexing, delight...! *46.2%.*

Hellyers Road Peated Aged 14 Years db **(87.5)** n22 t23.5 f21 b21 Despite the enormity of the peat, the sheer chutzpa of the strength and sweetness for a brief few moments have you at a point of near ecstasy, the technical gremlins are still there and make themselves heard at the finish. But, my word! What a ride!!! *63%. Master Series.*

Hellyers Road Slightly Peated Aged 10 Years db **(91.5)** n23 t23 f22.5 b23 Hellyers Road has come of age in every sense: the lack of copper in their system that held them back for so long has now been mostly overcome by a mix of peat and extremely high quality oak. This is a quietly spoken little beaut. Congratulations all round: it has been a long journey... *46.2%.*

Hellyers Road Single Malt Whisky Slightly Peated Aged 15 Years db **(92)** n23 t23.5 f22.5 b23 Hell, yes! *46.2%.*

HUNNINGTON DISTILLERY

⬥ **Hunnington Tasmanian Single Malt** cask no. 001, origin Aust, 20 litre sherry cask, dist 12 Apr 18, bott 17 Jul 20 db **(91)** n23 what a confident and competent nose. No off notes from the still, allowing the malt to have a say despite the muscular presence of the sherry. The fruit is borderline lush and marries sweet and dry with little effort, showing a dry, green plummy side, not unlike sloes; t24 no new whisky has a right to be this good on delivery! Not only is the mouth feel just about spot on, but the intensity of the fruit can hardly be bettered. The star turn, though, is the slow build of chocolate which gives a certain fruit and chocolate feel to this, aided by a little heather honey; f21.5 just loses its bearings slightly as a degree of bitterness creps in; b22.5 welcome to the Whisky World, Hunnington. This is a statement of a first bottling! I knew that some distillers put their early whiskies into sherry to hide any mistakes in their distillate. Well, that was certainly not the case here: technically this is top grade whisky and if a weakness can be found it is from the cask itself. A standing ovation for this first-ever cask! *45.3%. 46 bottles.*

KILLARA Kingston, Tasmania. 2016. Working.

Killara Distillery KD01 Cask Strength ex-port barrel db **(94)** n24 t24 f22.5 b23.5 Now, that is impressive! And that's what I call a whisky! *64.5%. 1st Release.*

Killara Distillery KD02 ex-port barrel db **(94.5)** n23 t24 f23.5 b24 A very chewable and entertaining malt just dripping with flavour. *50%.*

Killara Distillery KD03 ex-sherry barrel db **(90.5)** n23 t23 f22 b22.5 A genteel and understated whisky. *46%.*

LARK DISTILLERY Hobart, Tasmania. 1992. Working.

Lark Single Malt Whisky Cask Strength db **(94)** n23 t24 f23.5 b23.5 Sweet, profound and with jaw-aching chewability. *58%.*

Lark Single Malt Whisky Classic Cask db **(89)** n22 t23 f21.5 b22.5 Another slightly more full-bodied version. *43%.*

Lark Distillery Muscat Cask Finish db **(91.5)** n23 t23 f22.5 b23 The one thing you can say about Lark whisky: when they decide to ramp up the flavours, they don't do things by halves... *46%.*

Lark Distillery Sherry Matured & Sherry Finished db **(95)** n24 t23.5 f23.5 b24 I know Bill Lark abhors sulphur-treated sherry butts as vehemently as me. Which is why this is the only double sherry-matured whisky I picked up this year without fear that it would fail...And, of course, it didn't. It's a beaut! *50.8%.*

Lark Distillery Single Malt Shiraz Cask Release 2020 ex-Shiraz casks db **(92.5)** n24 t23 f22.5 b23 Have to say this is a nose and flavour profile I have never quite encountered before. Keeps just the right side of being a liqueur. Love it! *42%. 300 bottles.*

Lark Distillery Symphony No. 1 db **(93)** n23.5 t23 f23 b23.5 Less a symphony and more tone poem or, to be even closer to the mark, a heart-stopping Olivia Newton-John from circa 1972... *40.2%.*

LAUNCESTON DISTILLERY Western Junction, Tasmania. 2013. Working.

Launceston Distillery Apera Cask Tasmanian Single Malt Whisky batch no. H17:11 db **(89.5)** n23 t22 f22 b22.5 About as subtle as a knee in the groin and no less eye-watering. Thankfully nothing like so unpleasant and, in fact, grows on you with time. Quite a statement whisky! *46%.*

Launceston Distillery Bourbon Cask Tasmanian Single Malt Whisky batch no. H17-14 db **(89)** n22.5 t22 f22.5 b22 Well, if you are looking for something malty, tasty and little different here's your chap. *46%.*

◈ **Launceston Distillery Cask Strength Bourbon Cask Tasmanian Single Malt** batch no. H17:18, db **(96)** n23.5 the light fruitiness which dominated before now has company and dominates no longer... The barley appears to have been polished and kissed while the oak comes onboard to offer the most delicate hints of bourbon – mainly a light polished liquorice, with the first signs of vanilla and hickory arriving.... beautifully weighted and complex; t24 that is sensational. I'm not sure you can ask for much more than this: the barley is supremely intense. But such is high calibre of the oak, it refuses to either cower or attack. Instead, it somehow threads its way through the grain to form a rich malleable structure which caresses the palate with erotic delicacy; f24 the longest trail of vanilla and barley imaginable. Simple, but so effective... especially with the light ulmo honey and spices playing their part; b24.5 for a long time I have been pleading with distilleries to cut out the fancy stuff and bottle from ex-bourbon, so the true personality of the distillery is there to be seen. Well, this shews Launceston in a light I hoped but dare not believe they'd reach. Their last bottling from Bourbon cask I sampled was a bit undercooked. This is what happens when great spirit and great oak combine. Sublime: the richer textured Glen Grant of Oz. I think I've just tasted the Australian Whisky of the Year *61% 242 bottles*

Launceston Distillery Cask Strength Tawny Cask Matured Tasmanian Single Malt Whisky batch no. H17-12 db **(94)** n23.5 t23.5 f23 b24 A whisky matured in a faultless cask. No off notes and not so much fruit we are talking a one trick pony. A fruity but beautifully measured delight. *63%.*

◈ **Launceston Distillery Tawny Cask Tasmanian Single Malt** batch no. H17:19, db **(87)** n21.5 t22.5 f21 b22 For its strength, this has a surprisingly sticky quality on the taste buds. But the nose is nowhere near as composed and happy as the full-strength version and has a slightly more vegetable than fruit in its make-up. These niggardly notes play out on the slightly bitter finish, also. Not too many complaints, though, about the eye-watering delivery, a little salty and forceful with both grape and spice. *46% 702 bottles*

◈ **Launceston Distillery Cask Strength Tawny Cask Tasmanian Single Malt** batch no. H17:20, db **(94)** n24 n23 any sharper and you could cut your nose on this. The fruit is precise, intense, grapey. Something about the boiled sweet with this also; t23.5 well...if you think it sharp on the nose... Not quite puckering a black of lemon blossom honey sees to that. But there is some sharp marmalade at work, also before the spices start to throw their weight about; a little chocolate and raisin comes into play; f23.5 in the majority of casks of this style, the malt would start to get bitter about...now. But this does. The sugars keep their intensity long enough to allow the dried grape skin and growing vanilla to have only so much effect; b24 for those who refer their whisky, fruity, clean, powerful, sharp, and entirely free of off notes. Another example of very highly skilled distillation and maturation. *63% 204 bottles*

Launceston Distillery Tawny Cask Tasmanian Single Malt Whisky batch no. H17-13 db **(88.5)** n22 t23.5 f21 b22 Yes, enjoyable and beautifully made. But the lack of oils, presumably by strength reduction, has left the drier aspects of the cask open to scrutiny, especially on the vaguely bitter finish. However, the late delivery and midground is a treat thanks to the light marbling of the fruit against the fabulous malt and vanilla interlay which dominates. *46%.*

◈ **Tasmanian Heartwood The Angel of Darkness Cask Strength** Apera, Oloroso casks **(96)** n24 of all the distilleries in Australia, only Launceston seems able to kick out this much salt on the nose. It ensures the house-style piquancy to the fruit which dangles off the nose like so many grapes on a vine. If the salt isn't enough, pepper makes a matching pair.

But the real complexity arrives when the oak makes itself heard with a series of underlying drier strands of varying intensity; t24 a profound delivery, which comes as no great surprise: the fruit cascades onto the palate meaning business. But the back-up heather and manuka honey mix just softens the more acidic elements of the fruit. Together they make for a surprisingly soft and salivating entrance and follow through and ensure the most luxurious, vaguely waxy mouthfeel. And, just as on the nose, the oak finally arrives to create complexity levels which quietly go through the roof; f24 just a little spice keeps those salivation levels high enough to counter the growing and growling oaky influence. But late on, too, there is a wonderful grape skin intensity which breaks down only as the chocolate begins to build; b24 my word. What a wonderful whisky. This was a last minute arrival which now goes straight into the taste-off Final for Australian Whisky of the Year. It has to beat two others, one of which also comes from the outstanding Launceston distillery. It has every chance. Talk about better late than never... *56.8% Distilled at Launceston*

LIMEBURNERS Albany, Western Australia. 2014. Working.

Limeburners Western Australia Single Malt Whisky American Oak bott code: 219 db **(88.5) n22 t22.5 f22 b22** Just a little on the light and flighty side. Enjoyable, but if there is a problem this has been reduced to a strength the malt is not naturally happy with, the oils breaking up leaving a slightly chalky dryness. Even so, after the initial intense barley some lovely vanilla and custard notes. But up the strength by anything between three and seven per cent, and the structure and quality will be a sounder. *43%. ncf.*

Limeburners Western Australia Single Malt Whisky Darkest Winter Cask Strength cask no. M492 db **(94) n23.5 t24 f23 b23.5** Delighted to report that now is not the darkest winter of our discontent. In fact, I'm very contented with this, indeed... *65.2%. ncf sc. 201 bottles.*

Limeburners Western Australia Single Malt Whisky Heavy Peat Cask Strength cask no. M221 db **(90) n22 t23 f22 b23** Sherlock Holmes. Miss Marple. Inspector Morse. Father Brown. Philip Marlow. Hercule Peroit. Maigret. Sam Spade. Paul Temple. Inspector Clouseau. Don't think any of those are Australian. But we need to call the whole lot in to find out who the fuck made off with all the peat... *61%. ncf sc. 205 bottles.*

Limeburners Western Australia Single Malt Whisky Port Cask Cask Strength cask no. M512 db **(95.5) n23.5 t24.5 f23.5 b24** This one rolls its sleeves up and doesn't muck around. On the muscular side, but a bit of a softy, too... God, I love this distillery! *61%. ncf sc. 214 bottles.*

McHENRY DISTILLERY Port Arthur, Tasmania. 2010. Working.

McHenry Singe Malt Whisky 100L Makers Mark American oak cask, barrel no. 17, dist 10 Sept 14, bott 14 Jul 19 db **(88.5) n22 t22.5 f22 b22** Very pleasant but the grape makes things just a little too one-dimensional for its own good. *44%. nc sc. 250 bottles.*

⬦ **McHenry Singe Malt Whisky** 200L ex-bourbon American oak cask, barrel no. MD55, dist 23 Sept 15, bott 26 Jan 21 db **(94) n23.5** truly adorable. The elegance and quiet intensity to the barley may be textbook, but it is also very rare to find these days. A couple of sniffs and you are also more than aware that the cut is just about perfect: clean but characterful....; **t23.5** delightful oils form early and allow the gorgeous maltiness to grow, thicken and stick. The tannins do exactly what is asked of them: form a gentle base, which when mingling with barley creates a digestive biscuit feel. The spices start from about the midpoint and stay constant, offering no more than a background buzz. Meanwhile the sweetness is provided by almost apologetic ulmo honey mingling with the grist; **f23** no off-notes, no bitterness from a spent cask. Just a gentle meander of vanilla, spice and barley passing over the taste buds like a gentle breeze ruffling the leaves on a tree...; **b24** now that is what I call a single malt whisky! Their last offering, though matured on bourbon, had a peculiar grapey quality which confused and distracted. No such problem here. This is first class distillate matured in high quality American oak and plucked from the warehouse at a very interesting period in its development. Hearty congratulations all at McHenry. Now let's just hope that some idiot doesn't complain that it sounds too much like a Scotch. *50%. sc.*

MT. UNCLE DISTILLERY Walkamin, Queensland. 2001. Working.

Watkins Whisky Co. Single Malt Whisky nbc db **(87.5) n22.5 t22.5 f20.5 b22** A distinctive malt, though one with a bit of multiple personality disorder. The nose certainly owes far more to a rum style than malt, as the esters are belted out. And there is even a hint of rye on the crisp and chipper fruitiness o the early flavour waves that follows the delivery. All this, of course, is down to an over the top cut which certainly glues up the finale. But after a number of pretty run of the mill whiskies today, this one has certainly got my nerve endings fired up. Lots of heather honey at work, too, though some of that comes from the wide-ish cut. All this care of Mark Watkins, head distiller: The Man From Uncle. And this is a very solo whisky... *43%.*

NANT DISTILLERY Bothwell, Tasmania. 2008. Working.

Nant Distillery Single Malt Whisky White Oak Cask cask no. 951 db **(94.5) n23 t24.5 f23 b24** Some of the passages in this malt as good as any Australian malt you are likely to taste. Just brilliantly distilled. 43%. sc.

NEW WORLD WHISKY DISTILLERY Melbourne, Victoria. 2007. Working.

⬧ **Starward Left-Field Single Malt** bott code: 200824 **(94) n23** very clean distillate in the hands of some macho casks. The casks win and tattoo all kinds of shades of tannin over the malt. Indeed, it is hard to find the barley as fruit has usurped it: spicey figs and dates are making their mark; **t23.5** not often I pick out blackcurrant jam as the first thing to hit the palate, but I certainly do here. Then what's next? Spiced greengages in full bloom, juicy and sweet. But always there is the background tannin, creating almost a thick paste to ensure weight and gravitas. And, if that wasn't enough, look out for the honeydew melon and ulmo honey...bloody hell, fellas! What have you done to this whisky...? **f23.5** usually 40%abv whiskies have a limited finish. By some Ozzie standards this does too. But what it lacks in length it makes up for with quality. The intertwangling between malt, chalky vanilla, sweet and dry fruit is well worth anyone's time studying; **b24** how wonderful to find an Australian whisky which has escaped the considerable gravitational pull of its own country. Nothing like as beefy or chunky as many of its fellow Australians...and a bit of a rarity to find one at 40%abv, too! But what it lacks in traditional Ozzie Ooomph it makes up for with an attractive, oaky complexity. This is a considerable step up in quality from earlier bottlings I have had from this distillery. Indeed, not just a step up, but a journey to another world. This quite brilliant and a softer side of Australian whisky we have never quite seen before. 40%

NONESUCH DISTILLERY Hobart, Tasmania. 2007. Working.

Nonesuch Single Grain 20 litre ex-bourbon cask, cask no. 25 db **(90.5) n22 t23.5 f22.5 b22.5** Reminds me of some millet whisky I have tasted in the past with its intense flavour profile: a bottling for budgies. 48%. sc.

Nonesuch Single Grain 20 litre new French oak no. 17 db **(93.5) n23.5 t23.5 f23 b23.5** The French oak not only stands up to the muscularity of the grain, but gives it a leg-up, too... 45%. sc.

Nonesuch Single Malt 20 litre ex-bourbon cask, cask no. 22 db **(86) n22 t22.5 f20.5 b21** A splendidly malty fellow, this making good use of some light acacia honey to accompany the barley. Just loses direction a bit on the slightly bitter finish. 45.3%. sc.

Nonesuch Single Malt 20 litre Pinot cask, cask no. 13 db **(85.5) n22 t22.5 f20 b21** Pleasant enough, but pretty flat by Nonesuch's peculiarly complex standards. Lots of fruit and at times salivatingly enjoyable. But a little too one-dimensional after tasting their previous whiskies and not helped by the tight finale. 48%. sc.

OLD HOBART DISTILLERY Hobart, Tasmania. 2007. Working.

Overeem Single Malt Whisky Port Cask cask no. OHD-178 db **(94.5) n23.5 t24 f23 b24** one of those rare malts where a lot happens, but does so organically and with every shift in the gears getting the taste buds revving. 60%. sc.

OLD KEMPTON DISTILLERY Redlands, Tasmania. 2013. Working.

Old Kempton Distillery Single Malt Tokay cask, cask no. RD023 db **(91) n22.5 t23 f22.5 b23** So many Tokay casks through the years have been wasted in the whisky world through being sulphur treated. No such worry here as the fruit gets a free hand to weave its intense, almost citrusy, magic on this malt. Just love the creaminess to this whisky and the busy, prattling spices which prevent things becoming a little too comfortable. A very satisfying experience. 46%. sc.

Tasmania Independent Bottlers Old Kempton Redlands Release 9 sherry cask, cask no. TIB RD 0010, bott Jul 19 **(90) n23 t23.5 f21.5 b22** Fantastically clean throughout, the finish may be short and lacking depth. But the delivery...? Wow! 49.2%. sc. 181 bottles.

Tasmania Independent Bottlers Old Kempton Redlands Release 10 sherry cask, cask no. TIB RD 0027, bott Oct 19 **(87) n22 t22.5 f21 b21.5** Rotund and fruity, there is a surprising light nougat touch to this one. The fruit is of the sweet shop variety but there is a dullness to this bottling very unlike what I was expecting. 47.9%. sc. 171 bottles.

SHENE ESTATE DISTILLERY Pontville, Tasmania. 2014. Working.

⬧ **Shene Cognac Release Tasmanian Single Malt** nbc db **(94.5) n24** right. I might as well take my watch off: time is going to stand still. Even the layers appear to have layers... Yes, it fruity...but just not that simple. There is even a layering of the barely discernible malty structure while fruit is both sharp enough to chisel its mark on the nose buds, there is a cherry and dark grape jam softness to caress and kiss better. The spices are restrained, but there. The tannin is an underlying throb...; **t23.5** just laughed to myself. The inflection of the fruit is just about identical to the nose. And my word! That sharpness really does bite! The softer tones are then underwritten by a healthy layer of ulmo honey which gives the oak every chance get on the scoreboard...; **f23** a slightly tart fruitiness clings to the burgeoning vanilla; **b24** just so complex and beautiful. Been playing around blending percentages of both the Cognac and Trinity bottlings, seeing if I could unleash the chocolate notes which I found bubbling just below the surface. I managed, and a few more hidden characteristics besides. Wow...this distillery has scary potential! 49% nc ncf

⬦ **Shene Mackey Trinity Tasmanian Single Malt** nbc db **(90.5) n23** much more astringent than the Cognac Release, though the vaguely bourbon-stye tannins are not frightened to give your nose a good clonk. Quite salty and coastal, too...; **t24** eye-watering... but it would have been foolish to expect anything else. Some buttery elements to the midlife vanilla. But your mind is fully focussed on the delivery and aftermath. Not least because it unlikely you'll find another whisky this year with such an immediate fruit kick. The manuka and ulmo honey blend both sweeten and aid the texture; **f21** relatively quiet and tamed, though some bitterness and a slight tang is detectable; **b22.5** if you are not seduced by this full-on delivery, nothing will win your heart! 49% ncf

SOUTHERN COAST DISTILLERS Adelaide, South Australia. 2014. Closed.
Southern Coast Single Malt Batch 007 db **(94.5) n24 t23 f23.5 b24** This has to be the most rum oriented whisky on the planet. I thought their previous bottlings had to be slightly freakish: nothing could be that Guyana-Demerara style on purpose. But here we go again, with its massive esters. Stunning bruyere honey on both nose and delivery and light red liquorice for back up. But then those unmistakable rum notes strike, metallic almost. Superb. 46%. ncf.

SPRING BAY DISTILLERY Spring Beach, Tasmania. 2015. Working.
Spring Bay Tasmanian Single Malt Whisky Rare Release Mystery Bourbon dist 2017 db **(90.5) n23 t23 f22.5 b22** A malt which improves tremendously using the Murray Method. Refreshing, juicy and magnificently malty. 58%. sc.

SULLIVANS COVE DISTILLERY Cambridge, Tasmania. 1995. Working.
Sullivans Cove American Oak bourbon cask, cask no. TD0267, filled 11 Apr 08, bott 26 Oct 19 db **(86.5) n21.5 t22 f21.5 b21.5** A big malty fellow. But the bitterness at the death confirms the over exuberant cut one detects on the nose. 47.5%. sc.

Sullivans Cove American Oak Tawny cask, cask no. TD0283, filled 16 May 08, bott 26 Jun 19 db **(94.5) n24 t24 f22.5 b23.5** I have crawled around warehouses in Guyana and opened 18-year-old casks with less than an aged rum feel than this little beauty. A classy malt whisky which will get the rum cognoscenti flocking... 47.3%. sc.

Sullivans Cove American Oak Tawny cask, cask no. TD0324, filled 27 Oct 08, bott 1 Jun 19 db **(86.5) n22 t22 f21 b21.5** A much tighter whisky than cask TC0267 with none of the expansive and beguiling Demerara rum notes. Has a much younger feel all round though the mix of prunes and vanilla does impress at the midpoint. Bitters slightly and dries considerably as the spices make up ground. 47.5%. sc.

Sullivans Cove French Oak Tawny cask, cask no. TD0268, filled 17 Apr 08, bott 13 Mar 19 db **(95) n23.5 t24 f23.5 b24** Much more along the excellent lines of the TD0283, except the more active tannins restricts the rum element in tangible degrees, but let loose the sugars. Quite beautiful, though. 47.5%. sc.

Sullivans Cove Old & Rare American Oak cask no. HH0296, filled 9 May 00, bott 10 Sept 19 db **(93.5) n23 t24 f23 b23.5** A delightful and unusual whisky which concentrates solely on the intensity of the barley. The delivery is something to savour. 49.2%. sc.

Sullivans Cove Special American Oak Apera cask, cask no. TD0214, filled 7 Nov 07, bott 15 Oct 19 db **(92) n22.5 t24 f22.5 b23** Can't get enough of that ultra-delicious delivery! 45.8%. sc.

TIMBOON RAILWAY SHED DISTILLERY Timboon, Victoria. 2007. Working.
Timboon Single Malt Whisky Bailey Street dist 23 Apr 16, bott 13 Feb 20 db **(89) n22 t22 f23 b22** When the nose comes across as freshly cut and salted celery, you know you are in the presence of something very different... 63.9%.

Timboon Single Malt Whisky Bourbon Expression dist 14 Feb 14, bott 13 Feb 20 db **(92) n23 t22 f24.5 b22.5** Takes its time to get there, but one of the best finishes of the year – anywhere on the planet! 71.1%.

Timboon Single Malt Whisky Christie's Cut dist 30 Oct 14, bott 29 Jan 20 db **(88.5) n23 t23.5 f20 b22** Not quite the same seamless experience enjoyed with their last Christie's cut: far too much tangy bitterness on the finish here for its own good. But as for the delivery...

wow! An improbable mix of jammy fruit notes and honey mixed almost into a thick paste. That is such a delicious and huge combination. *60%*.

TIN SHED DISTILLING COMPANY Adelaide, South Australia. 2013. Working.

◈ **Iniquity Anomaly Series Flustercluck Single Malt** db (96) n24.5 this is, unquestionably, one of the most complex peated noses of the year. The smoke both drifts and plummets, plays anchor and the ethereal. Add to that the nibbling spice and the layering of acacia honey against the most sooty of the drier phenols and we are beginning to swoon... and it has nothing to do with the alcohol. Like peated diazepam, it just sends you off on a pain-free trip...; t24 sumptuous, with the malt sticking to the rich, clean oils: this is masterful work at the still to create this degree of entirely feint-free richness. But, even better, is the incredible intensity of the malt: basically, malt concentrate. With heather honey adding to the intense grist...; f23 milk chocolate and later praline. But still the malt lingers and the smoke massages; b24.5 this may sound like a whisky for my daily breakfast-producing hen, Henrietta. But, in fact, this is an outstanding malt for the most serious whisky lover. One of the most complex whiskies I have come across from south of the equator ever, the use of both the peat and malt will, in time, become the stuff of legend. I've just broken off, as I have just found a note from Tin Shed's Ian Schmidt about this whisky sent to me. Well, Tim, I entirely take your point (which makes sense). And informing me the peat is pure Ozzie, which I would not have guessed, but possibly accounts for the unique fingerprint and complexity. I am doffing my hat. And in the meantime, well done on distilling, maturing, and, presumably, vatting and then bottling a malt which is, indubitably, world class. And, very unusually for an Australian whisky, incredibly delicate, despite the peat. *49.1%* ☙

◈ **Iniquity Anomaly Series The Merlot Single Malt** db (91.5) n22 youth. A little stringent. Actually, a lot stringent...; t23.5 strap yourself in: seatbelt required for one hell of a take-off. The grape is terrifying intense and tart at first, but settles as the sugars are tapped into combine. Again, the malt has been cowed into semi-obscurity...; f22.5 as the honey burns of, the more aggressive fruit returns. The spices up their game accordingly; b23.5 the grape has it...and how! The malt is blown away by the vibrancy of the fruit which presents a superbly mouth-watering creation. Appears to be quite young, but this is all about energy and vitality. And with the spice and honey on delivery, it is worth ignoring the slightly tart nose and finish just to concentrate on the pure, naked beauty of the delivery. Incidentally, not an atom of sulphur: not something I've often been able to say about merlot casks... *51%*

Iniquity Gold Label Single Malt Batch 005 db (95) n23.5 t24 f23.5 b24 This is knife, fork and spoon whisky, as thickset on the palate as any malt comes. Slightly different yet slightly the same as their marvellous Batch 004, this time a little extra wide cut being apparent and confirming the glutinous quality of the whisky. At lower temperatures has something of a top-rate Fijian rum about it – a definite compliment! – with a spice and busy-ness which leaves you spellbound. All kinds of manuka and heather honey tones combined here with a dash of molasses to keep that sticky feeling going. And also ensures a distinctive dry toastiness to the controlled sweetness. A five-course meal of a malt, again shewing the distillery in its most favourable light. For those who love their whiskies uncompromising and muscular, yet with a consistent honey sweetness, this might be your whisky of the year. *60%. ncf.*

◈ **Iniquity Gold Label Batch 006 Single Malt** db (92.5) n22.5 nothing like as abrasive as it might be, although the fruit tones do have a side to them. The pithy fruit is almost, though not quite, matched by the game barley; t23.5 superb! Both the fruit and malt combine for an intense meeting on the palate with a blanket of ulmo honey and butterscotch ensuring things don't get out of hand...; f23 ah...at last some oaky offerings. Nothing too intense, but settles on an increasingly rich vanilla note, though the maltier side slowly gains back control. Good, understated spice, too...; b23.5 seriously good whisky this. Having a malt at this strength, yet still being able to see every nuance of its shape and personality is like driving a sports Jag at high revs around the back lanes of the countryside and never once losing your line. Excellently constructed. And driven. *60.1%*

Iniquity Single Malt Batch 016 db (83.5) n21 t21 t20.5 b21 Carried on where Batch 015 left off: a bit of a Feint Fest. Has its attractive nutty moments, though. *46%. ncf.*

Iniquity Single Malt Batch 017 The Den's Dram db (91) n22 t22.5 f23 b23.5 The Den, of course is where my beloved Millwall FC play, and over the years I have watched an above average number of Australians represent the side; or even Englishmen who on retirement emigrated to the land of Oz. So maybe a dram from Tim Cahill, Kevin Muscat and others, including the one and only Keith "Rhino" Stevens, whom, with my late Dad, I saw make his Lions debut at 16, and the following season I actually sponsored. A sound choice: he later helped take Millwall to the top flight for the one and only time in their history, and even went on to manage them. Now living in Australia he was, like Muscat and Cahill, a player who in each and every game gave 100% and never flinched, never compromised. Even for a 46 percenter, I think the same can be said for this malt. There is a robust, raw element at times – especially at the beginning - but as it progresses there is no little quality, too: again, a fair way of describing those Lions players during their days at The Den. That marriage of spicy steel and the deftest interplay between malt and ulmo honey makes for excellent entertainment. A dram for those looking for a full bodied but deceptive malt; and one for Antipodean Millwall legends, too... 46%. ncf.

Iniquity Single Malt Batch 018 db (93) n22.5 t23 f23.5 b24 Great to see that Tin Shed have got out of the little rut their malt batches lapsed into and are now back to being full of personality - and well-distilled malt all but free from feints. Or gorgeous peppery quality to the plummy nose is handsomely matched by the lush delivery where a mix of exploding greengage and toasty raisin gives the palate much to cogitate on. The late chocolate is a masterstroke. Better still, the spices never seem to run out of steam. Beautiful! 46%. ncf.

◇ **Iniquity Silver Label Batch 019 Single Malt** db (87) n21 t22.5 f21.5 b22 A decent enough whisky, but somehow not up to snuff so far as the great Tin Shed distillery is concerned. The nose sends out the message that things are a little below par with some non-committal malt against hesitant tannin. A youthful, muddled delivery confirms that, for all the later buttery richness and dark sugar involvement, this doesn't entirely click. 46%

◇ **Iniquity Silver Label Batch 021 Single Malt** db (90) n22 almost a blast of bourbon here, with a little hickory finding itself unexpectedly leading the way...; t22.5 the mouthfeel is gorgeous: creamy with a malty sub-strata. But it is the launch of the spices and the countering ulmo honey which really gets the taste buds excited. Both on the delivery and about three quarters in there is a distinctive fruit kick; f22.5 long, well spiced and surprisingly malty so late in the day. A little chocolate and sultana rounds matters off with charm; b23 that's more like it. An excellent malt with great depth and massive chewability. 46%

◇ **Iniquity Solera Peated Shiraz Single** Malt db (82) n20 t22.5 f19.5 b20 No fan of the nose and from that moment onwards I am struggling. Some good sugars on delivery and even some attractive hickory amid the smoke. But the grape and peat are simply not happy together, and I'm not too sure about the shiraz cask, either. The weak strength disrupting the oils helps not a jot. 43%

TRIA PRIMA Mount Barker, South Australia. 2018. Working

◇ **Tria Prima Single Malt Traditional Release** Bruxa tawny cask, batch no.1, db (86.5) n22 t23 f20 b21.5 One of those big, dense whiskies which allows the cask type the predominant say. Love the nuttiness to this and the slow build on delivery of the marzipan and vanilla. Just a shade too dry on the finish, perhaps. 46%

◇ **Tria Prima Single Malt Traditional Release Enchantress** Apera cask, batch no.1, db (90.5) n22.5 had I a spoon here, I have no doubt it could be stood up in this grapy nose, alone. A slightly wide cut but the fruit and tannin has it under control...; t22 the very thick first moments on delivery give little away. But slowly the malt relaxes to releases countless mini-waves of muscovado sugars and spice; f23 excellent finish. Both the oils from the cut and from the cask make this an elongated finale. The sugars now take a more liquorice form, the grape something along the lines of a Dundee cake...; b23 another where the cask type has a huge say. However, this time we have a better cask and more sugars to ensure better balance throughout. Impressive. 46%

WHIPPER SNAPPER DISTILLERY Perth, Western Australia. 2012. Working

Upshot Australian Whiskey Cask Strength Single Barrel batch no. 1 db (94.5) n23.5 t24 f23 b24 It has long been the tradition of the Whisky Bible to taste Australian whisky – or whiskey – on the first morning of an Ashes series. And here I am doing this again with the Aussies at 35-3. An interesting series with barely a batting side between the two teams, I won't be taking that early devastation of the Baggy Greens' top order to mean anything just yet. But I will say that if Australia need to discover how to put together something big and meaningful, with a fabulous start and carrying on from there, they could do worse than study this beaut. Western Australia now, by the way, appears to be in Kentucky... 64%. sc.

UNSPECIFIED SINGLE MALT

Heartwood Market Correction Tasmanian Single Malt Whisky port, muscat, sherry, sherry cask, cask no. TD 0053, dist Oct 05, bott Jun 19 (94) n23.5 t23.5 f23 b24 A typical Heartwood free-for-all of rich, unblemished fruits. 64.6%. sc. 280 bottles.

Heartwood Witch's Cauldron Tasmanian Malt Whisky all sherry casks, cask nos. LD766, RD166 & PB121, bott 11 Dec 19 (93.5) n23 t24 f23 b23.5 A typical Heartwood whisky which leaves not a single taste bud in your head unexhausted... 61.2%. 358 bottles.

Heartwood Wizard's Sceptre Tasmanian Malt Whisky all sherry casks, cask nos. LD766, RD189 & PB121 (0.0015%), bott 12 Mar 20 **(92.5) n23.5 t23 b23** Like the Witch's Cauldron it doesn't have to tell you this is all-sherry cask: the wine comes at you from every angle and enters every pore. But so clean and beautifully appointed, it is impossible to escape its spell. *60.7%. 332 bottles.*

UNSPECIFIED SINGLE MALT

⟐ **Heartwood A Serious Whisky** Adams peated second fill sherry AD295 & Launceston sherry C-001, bott Oct 20 **(89.5) n23** it's a serious nose and make no mistake: the smoke makes a comforting bed on which the sherry can lie. Or is it the other way round? There's so much tumbling around it is hard to know. A youthful bite, too...; **t23.5** someone has done a cracking job marrying these casks together. The tartness of the grape is matched by the acidity of the smoke. The result is a delicately sweet mouth explosion in which light oils cling to the taste buds; **f21** maybe just a little tang off the sherry, alas; **b22** if it is supine or frivolous malt you are after, look elsewhere: this is serious whisky. *60.5%. 290 bottles.*

⟐ **Heartwood Don't @#$%&* It Up, Son** LD965 + TIB0016 + AD295, Tokay, sherry and peat 2nd fill casks **(95) n23.5** beautifully two toned...and weighted. At once delicate and chunky; at once smoky and fruity. Impressively, there is that rather wonderful smell of a 2nd Growth cork extracted an hour before drifting in and out of the otherwise youngish piece...; **t24** no two ways of describing the delivery: brilliant! Everything works – the weight, structure, degree of sugar, fruit, and spice. An element of youthful malt also appears to kick off the salivation levels. As we head towards the middle the blood orange tuns to chocolate orange....; **f23.5** ...which in turn melts into chocolate raisin.... with spice accompaniment... and always the gentle smoke...; **b24** too often whiskies with a Tokay cask involvement has ended in tears: not so this time As beautifully measured a fruit chocolate statement as you'll ever find. He certainly didn't @#$%&* this one up.... In fact, he created a Classic. *59.65%. 278 bottles.*

⟐ **Heartwood The Beagle 9** bott Nov 2020 **(89) n22** a real soup of a nose: as expected there is a lot of Cancel Culture: one cask type cancelling out the effects of another. Strangely flat and quiet, with vague hints of smoke drifting with limited intermingling. Sharp and naively charming...and ostensibly young; **t23** ahhh...that's much better. There is a statement of happy union as a wonderful, silky fruitiness, with sultanas and dates at the centre is bookended by molasses and liquorice. Still quite young, but the complexity is compelling; **f21** the house fruit chocolate style enjoys an extra dose of date, walnut, and dried molasses; some nagging sulphur grows at the end; **b23** get this: this malt from the combined output of FIVE Tasmanian distilleries and two sherry casks, two peat ones and one each of Bourbon, Tokay, Muscat, and Port. When you get something this diverse, experience has taught me that it is best not to hold out too much hope for balance. Well, it exceeded all my expectations, mainly thanks to the faultlessness of the casks. The nose doesn't quite shape up as a little youthfulness interferes perhaps. But it is far more relaxed on delivery and the harmony achieved for such an obviously young malt is way above the norm for such a wide diaspora of casks. OK, one of them offers some late sulphur, which is always a possibility. But, otherwise, so impressed! *58.5%. 160 bottles.*

⟐ **Tasmanian Independent Bottlers The Blend Malt and Oat Sherry x 3 Virgin Oak** **(94.5) n23.5** something very different: look beyond that sticky acacia honey note for an oily sweetness: unmistakable oats. All encompassed in a fruit candy wrap which juices up the warmer it gets; **t24** as with the nose, the delivery is unique. The sharpness is magnificent, all the better for being controlled. The exploding fruit follows the aroma's lead by being of the candy variety: where the nose was more like a fruit chew, here we are much closer to boiled cherry fruit. But the oaty oils make their mark, too, about halfway in, followed by a bright glow of delicate tannin and spice. The honey is more subdued, but hangs on in there...; **f23** the oils, both from the oat and distillate, help lengthen the finish an stretched the tannins towards drier ground. This makes for a more nuanced finale, a slightly confusing mishmash of whisky notes I have never before seen linked together. The dying embers are a little untidy, but little wonder because whoever blended was entering an area where there is no map...; **b24** one of the favourite parts of my job is to identify unique whiskies, flavour profiles previously unknown. And here is one of the most memorable for this year. Oat has the second most impactful flavour style after rye. And because of the oiliness of oat whisky, it can pop up and linger in unexpected places. A very slight tang on the finish costs it a point or so, but that is a minor and understandable weakness. For what had gone on before is both formidable and uncompromisingly delicious. A new star has been spotted in the whisky galaxy, one that is a little different from the rest. *50.4% Whiskies from Launceston, Old Kempton, Belgrove and Adams Distilleries. 207 bottles.*

European Whisky

Jim Murray's Whisky Bible 2022 European Whiskies of the Year	
ALL EUROPEAN WHISKY (Inc England & Wales	Penderyn 15 Year Old
European Mainland Whisky of the Year MC	Kornog St Erwan
European Mainland Whisky of the Year MC	Belgium Owl 15 Year Old
English Whisky of the Year	The English Vintage 2010
Welsh Whisky of the Year	Penderyn 15 Year Old

Jim Murray's Whisky Bible European Whisky of the Year Winners		
	European Whisky Multiple Casks	**European Whisky Single Cask**
2004	**Waldviester Hafer Whisky 2000**	N/A
2005	**Hessicher Whisky**	N/A
2006	**Swissky Exklusiv Abfullung**	N/A
2007	**Mackmyra Preludium 03 Svensk**	N/A
2008	**Mackmyra Privus 03 Svensk**	N/A
2009	**Old Buck 2nd Release (Finland)**	N/A
2010	Santis Malt Highlander Dreifaltaigheit	**Penderyn Port Wood Single Cask**
2011	**Mackmyra Brukswhisky**	The Belgian Owl Aged 44 Months
2012	Mackmyra Moment "Urberg"	**Penderyn Bourbon Matured SC**
2013	**Penderyn Portwood Swansea**	Hicks & Healey 2004
2014	**Mackmyra "Glod" (Glow)**	Santis Malt Swiss Highlander
2015	**English Whisky Co. Chapter 14 N.P**	The Belgian Owl '64 Months'
2016	English Whisky Co. Chapter 16	**Kornog Chwee'hved 14 BC**
2017	**English Whisky Co. Chapter 14**	Langatun 6YO Pinot Noir Cask
2018	Penderyn Bryn Terfel	**The Norfolk Parched**
2019	Nestville Master Blender 8YO	**The Norfolk Farmers**
2020	Thy Whisky No. 9 Bøg Single Malt	**Penderyn Single Cask no. M75-32**
2021	**PUNI Aura Italian Single Malt**	Braeckman Single Grain Aged 12 Years
2022	Kornog St Erwan	Belgium Owl 15 Year Old

AUSTRIA
ALPEN WHISKY DISTILLERIE Franstanz. Working.

Alpenwhisky Single Malt Whisky refill port cask, dist Oct 15, bott 10 Nov 18 db **(87.5) n19.5 t24 f22 b22** This distillery should get a degree in producing monumentally huge whisky. And when it comes in at this strength, perhaps a doctorate for good measure. As usual, their whisky tends towards the feinty side. And that means something that starts out as big suddenly becomes truly massive. Yet, despite its faults, how can you not just love that mental intensity to the barley? In fact, if there is a bigger malt kick from any whisky on the planet this year, then I haven't seen it. Naturally, the finish is a delicious chocolate nougat, the Port being a bit of a bystander here, adding only a chirruping cherry sweetness. Flawed, but fabulously fulsome. *67%.*

BROGER PRIVATBRENNEREI Klaus. Working.

Broger 25 Jahre Brennerei 10 Jahre Whisky Jubiläums Edition bott code: LJU-11 db **(82.5) n21.5 t22 f19 b20** This distillery hits the heights when bottling their smokier output. This doesn't carry phenols, but has plenty of nougat to chew on, instead. Sadly, there appears to be a sherry influence here as well which is not entirely sulphur free. *46%.*

Broger Distiller's Edition Whisky Malaga Cask bott code: L DE-18 db **(93) n22.5 t23.5 f23 b24** Technically, it's all a bit of a nightmare with discipline at a premium. But this whisky has personality in spades and takes every opportunity to show just how much. Love it! This is pure entertainment.... *59.3%.*

Broger Hoamat Gerste bott code: L GE-15 db **(83.5) n20.5 t22 f20 b21** Nowhere near this distillery's usual high standards. There is a wonderful barley-packed delivery which makers you think you are back on track after the iffy nose, but it is not to be: the feints are a little too all consuming. *42%.*

DACHSTEIN DESTILLERIE Radstadt. Working

Mandlberggut Rock Whisky 5 Years bott code LWh15 db **(87) n22 t22 f21 b22** Have to say that this is one of the most consistent whiskies in Europe. A light smattering of toffee and nougat amid the big malt. Makes for an enjoyable dram thanks to the delicate heather honey ensuring a gentle juiciness. But always with that touch of nagging feint in the background. *41%.*

DESTILLERIE FARTHOFER Öhling. Working.

Farthofer Bio-Nackthafer 2016 Fassprobe Single Grain Whisky Fässstarke reifung: mostellofass, jahr: 2016, abgefüllt Oct 19, bott code: LbNHW116 db **(87) n21 t22.5 f21.5 b22** A slight butyric note on the nose, which struggles alongside a sharper stonefruit tone, gets the whisky off on the wrong footing, but it then redeems itself somewhat by producing a pleasant intensity to the marzipan middle and milky chocolate finish. Good depth in just the right places. *44.6%. nc ncf sc. 224 bottles.*

⬥ **Farthofer Bio-Nackthafer 2016 Fassprobe Single Grain Fassstärke** 3 years in mostellofass, cask no: LbNHW116, bott Nov 2019 db **(87) n20 t23 f22 b22** Retains the butyric note the distillery produces for this particular whisky style. And while the nose might be a dud, what follows is shockingly beautiful. Magnificently intense yet silky heather honey is aided by a buttery charm and slow build of spiced chocolate. Forget the nose. Just swim in that big, characterful lake of a delivery.... *44.6% ncf sc 300 bottles*

⬥ **Farthofer Braugerste 2014** aged in mostellofass, finished in Dubbel starkbierfass, cask no: LBGWd120, bott Jul 2020, db **(92) n22.5** when I was a kid, we used to get a strawberry lolly with an interior of ice cream. What did it smell like...? This...; **t23** the delivery is one of pure silk. There is a barley-rich fanfare.... then it heads in the same direction as the nose with a mix of strawberry and vanilla ice cream... **f23.5** some gorgeous chocolate spice just rounds off the vanilla superbly; **b23** distilled from ice cream? This is extraordinary....and so lovely! Unlikely to win a prize, yet one of my favourite and most memorable whiskies of the year. Unique. *40% ncf sc 560 bottles*

Farthofer Braugerste & Schlägler Roggen Whisky Fässstarke reifung: mostellofass, jahr: 2014/15, abgefüllt Oct 19, bott code: LGSRW0915 db **(86) n21 t21.5 f22 b21.5** There is some hugely concentrated rye just screaming to get out, here. But a tobacco-nougat kick points towards a too generous cut. A real shame about those feints. *40%. nc ncf sc. 189 bottles.*

⬥ **Farthofer Emmer 2015 Single Grain** aged in mostellofass, cask no: LEW115, db **(87.5) n21 t22 f22.5 b22** While the nose may not be the most promising, you'll encounter, getting itself into a right old fruity tangle, the sheer force and personality of this rare wheat type on the palate certainly sets the taste buds jangling. The first four or five mouthfuls of this and you can see the question-marks forming on your palate. Then, slowly, you begin to work out its rhythms and patterns of play and understand the flavour sequencing; a kind of alternating dance between fruit and oily, vaguely peppered grain. Trying to work out exactly what the oak is up to is much harder. A genuinely intriguing whisky and one guaranteed to grow on you. 41.4% ncf sc

DESTILLERIE WEIDENAUER Kottes. Working

Waldviertler Haferwhisky Classic bott code L11 db (**91**) n22.5 t23 f22.5 b23 As ever, a pleasure to get my oats. 42%.

Waldviertler Hafer Whisky Unit 2/3 Hafermalz bott code L10 db (**92.5**) n22.5 t23.5 f23 b23.5 Like a sensuous massage in oaty oils... 42%.

DISTILLERY ZWEIGER Mooskirchen. Working.

Zweiger Smoked Prisoner bott code SH/L0601/17 db (**89**) n22 t22 f22.5 b22.5 Probably not the whisky of choice for officials of the European Court of Human Rights. 44%.

EDELBRENNEREI FRANZ KOSTENZER Maurach, Working.

⬦ **Selektion Franz Single Malt 6-Year-Old** batch no. L2/2013, db (**90**) n23 here comes that powder-dry, sooty peat reek...like the ash from a crofter's fire being emptied into a bin. Attractively acidic and charmingly punctuated by delicate heather honey; t23 you know when you are sitting outside on a day where there isn't breath of wind, everything thing is still save the birds flitting about you. Then you notice in the distance a dark cloud and soon after a dull rumbling noise, getting louder and louder and heading towards you. Finally, the stillness is ended by the wagging of branches and leaves, then all of a sudden a powerful wind hits you as the cold front ahead of the cloud pushes its way through... Well, that kind of describes how the peat hits you here. Because the delivery at first is still, honeyed affair. Then slowly the peat drifts in before boom! The phenols are upon you...; f21.5 spicy, with just a late tang; b22.5 wonderful to have a glass of whisky from a distillery I haven't tasted for a year or two. I've missed their wonderfully distinctive style. Though I have to say the distillate now is of higher quality than it once was, with the cuts doing far more favours. 52.2%

LAVA BRÄU Feldbach. Working.

⬦ **Bio Brisky Lava Bräu Single Malt Eiche Rum Fass Jg 2015** bott code: H 4 15 db (**91.5**) n22.5 rum casks usually gift a whisky a sugary nose hard enough you have to break with nut crackers. This is much softer and fruitier...; t23 softer than laying on a quilt of feathers the mouth feel is ridiculously yielding with muscovado sugars in molten rather than rigid state. The fruit nosed mingle with the gristy barley...; f23 a melting of gristy sugars so delicate you feel that it could lull you to sleep; b23 so unusual for a rum cask. None of the firmness and cult de sacs a rum cask can often bring you. But lots of fruit and gentle grist. What a joy of a dram... 40.8%.

⬦ **Brisky Lava Bräu Single Malt Eiche JG 2007** bott code: B 04 07 db (**87**) n21.5 t22.5 f21.5 b22 the wide cut has generated a moist gingerbread persona to this – slightly so on the spiced nose but especially to the finish. Thick, weighty, chewy and salivating and not afraid to get the oils working, too. 40.1%.

Bio-Whisky Smokie dist 2015, bott code: L S 05/16 db (**92.5**) n22.5 t23.5 f23 b23.5 A peaty whisky which has its own unique take on things. One of the most compressed peaty whiskies I have encountered... 41.2%.

⬦ **Genesis Rare Cask Single Malt JG 2012** bott code: H 3 12 db (**90.5**) n23.5 nosed blind you could mistake this for bourbon. Layers of blood orange peel mingling with light liquorice and, toasted mallows and thinned molasses. As for finding the malt...good luck with that...! t23 thick oils and vanilla say howdy before a less friendly crowd rolls onto the palate, hands above holsters then drawing to fire off rounds of toasty, tasty, triumphant tannins which quickly gain control. The sub lead is one of lightly honeyed vanilla; just a tad salty, too...; f21.5 just a little wobble of the late spicy warble...; a light coffee note tries to make amends; b22.5 I have met many a distiller in Kentucky who comes from German stock. This single malt appears someone has decided to take the return ticket. 47.2%.

Mehr Leben Brisky Single Malt Eiche dist 2013, bott code H 02|13 db (**88**) n22 t22.5 f21.5 b22 "Brisky". Thought this was the first whisky made in Britain after the people had decided to get the hell out of Europe. But apparently not... A very well made malt with some serious loganberry on the nose – not exactly the most usual of aromas. But eventually disappears under its own weight of caramel on the palate. 40.8%.

LEBE & GENIESSE Lagenrohr. Working

Bodding Lokn Blended Malt Nr. 3 French oak, refilled oloroso & Pedro Ximenez casks, flaschennr. 100, dist 2012 db (**90**) n21.5 t23 f22.5 b23 These chaps do believe in giving their fans lots of flavour... 45%. ncf.

Bodding Lokn Double Cask PX Master American white oak & Pedro Ximinez sherry casks, fassnr. 11/18, flaschennr. 48, dist 2012, bott Jan 19 db **(92) n22.5 t23 f23 b23.5** This unlocks at least a couple of the secrets of an enjoyable PX whisky: firstly the spirit has to have bristle and character enough to punch through the enveloping grape. And, secondly, the PX cask must be entirely free of sulphur, which this is. So, a rare treat! 55%. ncf.

Bodding Lokn Golden Wheat Single Malt Lagerung Double Cask fass nr. 1120 & 111, gebrannt 2008 db **(91.5) n22.5 t23 f23 b23** Though perhaps a little too sweet for some, this is truly one of a kind. Almost too beautiful and demure to drink... 45%. ncf.

Bodding Lokn Single Cask Classic American white oak cask, fassnr. 17, flaschennr. 70, dist 2013 db **(94) n23.5 t24 f23 b23.5** A delicious, beautifully made malt bursting with personality, vitality...and chocolate! 43%. ncf sc.

Bodding Lokn Single Malt Blended Malt Nr. 2 refilled bourbon & sherry casks, dist 2011, bott 2018 db **(94) n23 t23.5 f23.5 b24** Confusingly, the label describes itself as both a single malt and a blended malt. I presume they mean it is from a single distillery but from more than one barley or perhaps cask type...though I could be wrong. Whatever it is, there is no doubting its high quality. 43%. ncf.

Bodding Lokn Single Malt Double Cask American white oak & a 50 Litre Oloroso sherry cask, dist 2010, bott 2018 db **(88) n22 t22.5 f21.5 b22** A generous cut gives the big grape something to work on. 49.5%. ncf.

Bodding Lokn Single Malt Double Cask Classic French Limousine oak & American white oak casks, dist 2012, bott 2018 db **(92) n22.5 t23.5 f22.5 b23.5** The limousine takes you on a very pretty journey... 43%. ncf.

◈ **Bodding Lokn Single Malt Whisky Lagerung Double Cask Sherry Finish** Amerikanischen weisseichenfass, finish in Pedro Ximénez sherry fass, fass nr. 18, dest 2014, bott 2020 db **(82.5) n22 t22.5 f18 b20** An eye-watering sharp production in contrast to the cream sherry nose on delivery which has you puckering from the get-go. The early crystalline sugars give way to a bitter and uncomfortable finale. A shame. 45%. ncf sc.

◈ **Bodding Lokn Single Malt Whisky Lagerung Single Cask Classic** Amerikanischen weisseichenfass char #3 toast, fass nr. 19, dest 2014, bott 2020 db **(89.5) n22.5** almost a Kentucky flourish to this on the nose with as the tannins pulse out a light liquorice lead with a delightful spice and toasted demerara sub-plot; **t23** superb weight and early offering of almost bready sugars before the cask rasps out its rich tannins. The sugars are restrained but essential; **f22** just a little on the simplistic side, but the oils are impressive; **b22.5** the mouth feel to this is remarkably similar to their smoky version (below). This distillery has upped its game on the distilling front, for sure: this a high-quality malt spirit entering the cask here. 44%. ncf sc.

◈ **Bodding Lokn Single Malt Whisky Smoky Lagerung Single Cask** Amerikanischen weisseichenfass char #3 toast, fass nr. 20, dest 2014, bott 2020 db **(91) n22.5** an attractive sweet nuttiness mingles delightfully with the distant bacon smokiness; **t23** perhaps the best mouth feel on delivery from this distillery in recent years. Beautifully made, there is still enough oil on this to give a singular weightiness to the malt which grows in smoke and spice by the moment. The subtlety of the delicate sugars is a joy; **f22.5** impressively long finish. All the more impressive as there is not a single fault noticeable from either cask or distillate. That allows the spices to buzz unspoiled. The tannins and delicate smoke offer just the right weight; **b23** superb cask at work and very competent distillate. Their marriage is a very happy one. Bodding at its best! 45%. ncf sc.

MARILLENHOF DESTILLERIE KAUSL Mühldorf. Working.

Wachauer Whisky M43 Double Oak bott code L:WD01 db **(80.5) n21 t21.5 f19 b19** This is the 1,137th whisky I have tasted for the 2020 Bible, but none of the previous 1,136 have given me quite the shock this has done. I cannot say exactly what kind of oak this has been in, other than to admit that I would not be surprised if one was a vat of cough syrup. Well, it certainly made me cough... There appears to be a huge, bitter, tannin kick, as well as sweet cherry juice. But you just can't get away from the cough mixture. A whisky to be taken three times a day after meals... 43%.

Wachauer Whisky M48 Triple Cask bott code L:WTC1 db **(77) n19 t20 f19 b19** I have in the past greatly enjoyed whisky from this distillery. But the three offerings that have come my way this year have left me scratching my head. This begins life far closer to being a liqueur than a whisky. And though a light ginger note on the mid-point distracts you from the bizarre goings on of before, it isn't close to being enough to save it. 48%.

Wachauer Whisky Multicorn bott code L:13WE db **(87.5) n21 t23 f21.5 b22** You get the distinct feeling that oats lay at the heart here as the mid-point give you a delightful, sticky porridge, complete with dollop of honey. But both the nose and finish are a little untidy from the barrels, the latter heading out towards a bitter tannin kick. 40%.

PETER AFFENZELLER Alberndorf in der Riedmark. Working.

Peter Affenzeller Blend dist 2011, bott code: L-1117105 db (**89.5**) n21.5 t22 f23 b23 A whisky with no backbone whatsoever. Softer than any bathroom essential that people have been fighting for all over the world. While there might be a slight vegetable note on the nose, the array of syrupy sugars on delivery and beyond make the aroma an irrelevance. 42%.

Peter Affenzeller Grain dist 2011, bott code: L-1018306 db (**89**) n22 t23 f22 b22 Any sweeter and this might qualify for a liqueur. Just stays within the boundaries of whisky, not least due to some excellent tannins planting their flag. 42%.

Peter Affenzeller Single Malt 6 Years Old bott code: L-1903207 db (**92**) n22 t23.5 f23 b23.5 One of those unusual whiskies where the nose puts you on your guard, but the overall performance simply seduces you. 42%.

PFANNER Vorarlberg. Working.

Pfanner Single Malt Single Barrel 2011 first fill sherry oak cask, cask no. 5, dist 16 Jun 11, bott 09 Oct 17 db (**93.5**) n23 t23.5 f23 b23.5 Delightful whisky benefitting from an entirely clean sherry cask. 56.2%. sc. 412 bottles.

REISETBAUER Axberg, Thening. Working.

Reisetbauer 12 Year Old Single Malt Whisky Chardonnay & Trockenbeerenauslese casks, bott code. 180120 db (**80**) n19 t20.5 f20 b20 Despite the cask yet, hard to get away from the feinty nose revealing a weakness in the distillate. No amount of patience sees the TBA improve matters. 48%. 1,253 bottles.

Reisetbauer 15 Year Old Single Cask Single Malt Whisky dist 2001 db (**86.5**) n20 t21.5 f23 b22 From the earliest days of this distillery, the technical flaws of the distillate are obvious. However, the malt has reacted favourably with some high class oak. The result is a whisky that grows in confidence as it goes along, like the girl who thought she was too plain to go to the ball, only to find she was as pretty as many. Late on the mix of chocolate nougat and treacle tart is rather compelling and worthy of drinking from a glass shoe.... 48%. sc. 500 bottles.

WALD4TLER GRANIT-DESTILLLERIE Hollenbach. Working.

Mayer Granit Grain-Whisky Waldstaude Waldviertler Ur-Roggen bott code: L/14 db (**83.5**) n21 t21 f21 b20.5 The oils don't know whether to twist or bust on this one, the clunking awkwardness of the over-indulgent cut making its mark on both nose and body. And though the rye bares its chest here and there, there is far too much of a gin-style flavour profile to this. Not a usual Waldviertler as I know it. 44%.

Mayer Granit Moar Whisky Gluatnest Torfrauh-Gerstenmalz bott code: L/15 db (**88.5**) n22 t22 f22.5 b22 One of those typically central European tight peated malt whiskies. Absolutely no give on this one, either on the nose or the palate: this is rock hard and rather than gently spreading the smoke around seems intent on giving you a prescribed dose of it. That said, impossible not to enjoy, especially when the molasses melt and feel it safe to come out and play. 44%.

Mayer Granit Whisky Edelprinz Mais-Roggenmalz bott code: L/09 db (**86.5**) n21 t23 f21 b21.5 Unquestionably flavoursome and full bodied with a sublime and full throttle impact from the grains on delivery. Just needs to be slightly more well controlled on the cut, though. 44%.

Mayer Granit Whisky Goldader Dinkelmalz bott code: L/13 db (**92**) n22 the slight vegetable note on here is hardly sulphurous, but infused with black peppers; t23.5 now that is impressive! The delivery is first a wonderful announcement of the dinkel – spelt – grain at its most delicate, then a gentle wave of Demerara sugar locked in with ulmo honey; f23 the peppers return alongside the growing vanilla and tannin; b23.5 you are left nodding your head with approval at this one. A real touch of Austrian aristocracy at play. 44%.

Mayer Granit Whisky W4 Blended bott code: L/15 db (**88**) n21.5 t22.5 f22 b22 Light and fully entertaining, the cut is cleaner and its personality relaxed, allowing a gentle meandering of acacia honey and ginger to add sweetness and warmth in just-so quantities. Enjoyable. 42%.

WHISKY-DESTILLERIE J. HAIDER Roggenreith. Working.

J.H. Dark Rye Malt 6 Jahre Gelagert 100% Roggenmalz dunkel geröstet, bott code L2 10 db (**89**) n21 t23 f22 b23 Far less butyric (though still there) and far more nougat, this offers a much more pleasing aspect from the moment it hits the palate until the last considerable spices fade away. Some lovely roast chestnut and chocolate notes also perk this rye up considerably. Takes time to understand, but worth the effort. 41%.

J.H. Dark Rye Malt Peated 7 Jahre Gelagert 100% Roggenmalz, dunkel geröstet & mit Torf geräuchert, bott code L2 P12 db (**86**) n19.5 t23 f21.5 b22 The butyric nose I spotted on this style last year is present in this bottling in even greater force. However, the double fruit delivery of intense lime and rye does its best to make amends. As fresh and citrussy as you'll ever find, with the coming through in secondary waves. But, overall, not quite at the races. *46%.*

J.H. Dark Single Malt 6 Jahre Gelagert 100% Gerstenmalz dunkel geröstet, bott code L5 11 db **(87.5) n21.5 t23 f21 b22** The over enthusiastically wide cut generates a spicy oiliness where it is not always wanted. Big and chewy, but a really awkward customer that seems to keep tripping over itself. *41%.*

J.H. Single Malt 6 Jahre Gelagert 100% Gerstenmalz hell geröstet, bott code L4 11 db **(91) n22** just a little bit on the chocolate-nougat side; **t23.5** outrageous malt concentrate; **f22.5** a very simplistic chocolate malt effect; **b23** if anyone likes their malt malty, then they had better go no further than this: like an alcoholic version of Horlicks. *41%.*

J.H. Original Rye Whisky 6 Jahre Gelagert 60% Roggen, 40% Gerstenmalz, bott code L3 12 db **(95.5) n23 t24 f23.5 b24** There are few whiskies in the world that pack more flavour into a glass than Haider. Here it has gone into overdrive with the rye-barley mix offering just the right degree of thrust and juiciness. What a classic this is...! *41%.*

J.H. Rye Malt 6 Jahre Gelagert 100% Roggenmalz hell geröstet, bott code L1 12 db **(88) n22 t23 f21 b22** Overdoses very slightly on the feints. Not enough to spoil the whisky, but enough to reduce it from its normally outstanding status to just very good. Those feints are first to the nose and the delivery − and last to leave the building. But in the meantime, the rye puts up some show. *41%.*

BELGIUM
THE BELGIAN OWL Grâce-Hollogne. Working.

◈ **Belgian Owl Evolution Single Malt 48 Months** first fill bourbon cask, bott code: LH043143, db **(89) n22.5** slightly unusual malty bubble gum for this distillery...; **t23** a confident strike of malt and muscovado sugar. Friendly tannins link delightfully with the full-on malt; **f21.5** just a slight bitterness from the cask gives ait a jaded fade; **b22** not exactly faultless − but blame the cask rather than the stills! *46% nc ncf*

◈ **Belgian Owl Evolution Single Malt 48 Months** first fill bourbon cask, bott code: LH048089, db **(92.5) n22.5** the odd collectors' item BO shews a little citrus on the nose, and here is one of them. Splendidly combines with the malt to give an ethereal feel despite the weightier work of the oak; **t23.5** fatter than the norm, the oils do a job in making this into a sumptuous combination of simplistic malt and elegant tannins, the layering and build of the spice shewing almost textbook complexity. All the sweetness is provided by the barley which steers a course between gristiness and orange blossom honey; **f23** still the spices buzz and warm. Still the barley offers a gentle, soothing and satisfying layer. Still the tannins link and waver between sweeter red liquorice and a drier chalky note; **b23.5** complex and just ridiculously in tune... *46% nc ncf Imported by Lion Imports LLC, Oklahoma City*

◈ **Belgian Owl Identité Single Malt 36 Months** first fill bourbon cask, bott code: LH036153, db **(91.5) n23** for 36 months, this is bordering the ridiculous: this must have been one hell of a bourbon cask because the tannins are not only layered and bewilderingly complex. Lemon drizzle cake, accompanied by walnut cake and an open jar of barley sugar candy...; **t23** a lighter bodied bottling than the others I tasted today, the juicy malt working overtime to make an impact with so little oil in the equation. Not only does it succeed but the butterscotch and vanilla off the cask offers the perfect foil; the spices come through on cue; **f22.5** surprisingly dry for such a young malt. Somehow the oak dominates but does so with a gentle touch; **b23** it is almost bordering Alice In Wonderland ridiculousness that a whisky this young can be so good. Fantasy single malt in glass... *46% nc ncf*

◈ **Belgian Owl Intense Single Malt 58 Months** first fill bourbon cask, cask no: 1573553, edition 2021-01, db **(94) n23** using the Murray Method (which is essential to master this), you'd just never know that this is a full-blown, unreconstructed malt. Some 73% alcohol, this is delicate to the point of fragility...; the tannin is light and playful...showing al the tell-tale signs of a mocha follow though later...; **t24** and thar she blows...!!! Wow...and whale! This is a whale-sized malt which blasts out barley like Casey Jones used to belch out smoke. The delivery is salivating and just brimming is green grass and the cleanest barley tones imaginable. The sugars are a complex mix of molasses and muscovado with a little concentrated dried date, too. The cask offers a light layering of vanilla which appears and disappears at regular intervals; **f23.5** even on the nose I had predicted a light mocha finish... and here it is! Accompanied on all sides by the uncorrupted barley; **b23.5** Oklahoma! OK! Are you ready for this...? *72.9% nc ncf Imported by Lion Imports, Oklahoma City*

◈ **Belgian Owl Intense Single Malt** cask no: 6188632, lot no: 2021-06, db **(95.5) n24** malt on steroids; the outstanding vanilla hanging on for dear life. The praline wafer sweet/ dryness borders on the brilliant...; **t23.5** a blend of salivating malt concentrate and light lemon blossom honey. There is an unexpected gristiness which develop halfway through gives the intense vanilla a lighter touch; **f24** praline based, the chocolate keeps its shape throughout. Somehow, from somewhere the barley filters though still intact and confident. Indeed, this will be probably only one of two or three malts I'll taste this year that is still juicy on the finish, indeed there are precious few finishes on the planet quite like this...; **b24** I really do think that Belgian Owl is responsible for the most consistently brilliant whisky in the world outside of Kentucky. Yet another absolutely faultless bottling... *73.2%*

⬧ **Belgian Owl Intense Single Malt** cask no: 6181957, lot no: 2021-07, db **(89.5) n22** a thinner nose than normal, the malt dictating, however...; **t21.5** hot as hell: the thinness of the nose matched by the body. The malt, however, stakes its claim like a mountaineer his flag atop a previously unconquered peak...; **f23** quietens down, thankfully. Now a much more easily enjoyed marriage of concentrated malt and vanilla, with a little cocoa thrown in for good measure; **b23** perhaps distilled a little faster than normal for the distillery, this is still magnificent whisky but lacking slightly in the usual weight, complexity, and finesse. *73.5%*

⬧ **Belgian Owl Intense Single Malt** cask no: 6188631, lot no: 2021-08, db **(94) n23** such a sexy mix between gristy malt and sherbet lemon: adorable! **t23.5** unbelievable! The delivery is exactly as the nose: sherbet and grist. Except now it has been beefed up to barely recognisable oak **f24** concentrated malt. Layered with concentrated malt. Backed-up by malt concentrate; **b23.5** that's much more like it...! *73.2%*

⬧ **Belgian Owl Intense Single Malt** cask no: 6188633, lot no: 2021-09, db, **(93) n23** the oak has taken control here. There is a certain nibble to the citrus which suggests something rather remarkable further down the line. I'm just strapping myself down in my seat before tasting this: I'm expecting a spice-riddled extravaganza. Right.... here we go...; **t23** Jesus...H ... Christ! OK, I had mentally prepared for the mother of all spice attacks. What I didn't expect was an all-out, unrelenting blitzkrieg on my tastebuds. I sit here exhausted having ridden this bucking bronco without dismounting. Actually, I can boast from all my riding days that I was never thrown by a horse. But then I never rode anything four-legged that was the equivalent of this...; **f23.5** well, I'm over that fence and still attached to this malty nag. Don't ask me how. But at least it calms down enough for the citrus notes to filter through and make a sublime partnership with the clarified barley. The vanilla wanders through, dry and increasingly shewing signs of praline charm...; **b23.5** well, I certainly chose the most volcanic of all the Belgian Owls to finish their extraordinary portfolio for this year's Intense... In tents. In igloos. In cottages. In apartments. It doesn't matter where you taste this. It will provide you with one of the most extraordinary and memorable whisky experiences you'll ever have... *73.5%*

⬧ **Belgian Owl Passion Single Malt 40 Months** first fill bourbon cask, cask no: 1538337, edition 2020-002 db **(87) n22 t22.5 f21 b21.5** Just a slight tanginess to the cask undermines the usual peppery honey theme. The malt is astonishingly intense. Quite a mouthful, but by BO standards relatively simplistic. *46% nc ncf*

⬧ **Belgian Owl Passion Single Malt 40 Months** first fill bourbon cask, cask no: 5564242 , edition 2020-006, db **(90.5) n22.5** an usual citrus note for this distillery accompanies the rich malt; **t22.5** young and impressively gristy. The spices are stark but in tune with the barley; **f22.5** much more complexity as the oils begin to mix the simple but impressive elements up slightly; **b23** untaxing, but just ridiculously delicious! *46% nc ncf*

⬧ **Belgian Owl Passion Single Malt 40 Months** first fill bourbon cask, cask no: 6631675, edition 2020-007, db **(93) n22** new-make at first, but as it warms the malts and vanillas form an attractive bond; **t23.5** thin at normal temperature, the MM transforms this into a gloriously malty cove with ulmo honey and pepper working in tandem to ensure the vanillas have a real weight; **f24** long, light milk chocolate the demerara sugars and red liquorice combining beautifully with the barley: a magnificent structure so late in the day...; **b23.5** Perhaps I should take his around the world with me to display the magic of the Murray Method. Just at normal temperature, or with a little water added, we have something that struggles to raise itself above advanced New Make status. It scored 87. Warm gently, using the Murray Method and the transformation is astonishing: where the hell did all those honey tones come from...? Boring and nondescript at normal temperature, the MM turns it into malt to celebrate. *46% nc ncf*

⬧ **Belgian Owl Passion Single Malt 40 Months** first fill bourbon cask, cask no: 6631681, edition 2020-004, db **(91) n22.5** doesn't quite follow the usual party line: a light blancmange aroma alongside a peppery vanilla note; **t22.5** it is the mouth feel which wins the heart here: surprisingly rich early on with decent oils coating the palate. So, although a New Make quality is never far away, the honeycomb chocolate, and heather honey sticks; **f23** long, lush and layered. The honey keeps pace while the barley grows...; **b23** thoroughbred malt doing as much as it can below the radar... *46% nc ncf*

⬧ **Belgian Owl Passion Single Malt 40 Months** first fill bourbon cask, cask no: 6631692, edition 2020-005, db **(95) n23.5** when you get nougat, it usually the sign of a poor choice of cut for the spirit. Not here. The lightest nougat note fits rather beautifully with the clean malt and multi-layered tannin. Delicate rapeseed honey flits in and out like pollen tossed about the breeze...; **t24** the succulence of the barley combined with deftness of the oil, the exactitude of the salt and the quiet intensity of the oak makes for something rather special for any whisky on the planet at this age. The fact the quiet gaps are filed in by ulmo honey and the lightest molasses just adds to the almost ridiculous complexity; **f23.5** how can a whisky this age have such a long and spellbinding finish. The mocha tones arrive quite late but also manages to underscore the depth of the vanilla-honey mix. Just glorious... **b24** if I was the distiller, I really wouldn't know what more I could possibly get out whisky from those stills, in these casks at this age. Had Belgium performed as well against Italy as this malt does in my glass, I wouldn't be tasting this whisky today... *46% nc ncf*

⟫ **Belgian Owl Passion Single Malt 40 Months** first fill bourbon cask, cask no: 6632090, edition 2020-003, db **(91) n22.5** don't know about "Passion Single Malt" ... Definitely a hint of passionfruit... **t23** wow! One of the mouth explosive, mouth-watering BOs yet. The barley erupts all over the palate, with pretty crude – but no less delicious – spices adding to the pyrotechnics; **f22.5** settles down to a deliciously malty finish, the spices, and tannins now under control...; **b23** a markedly different going for the spectacular over the subtle... BO *46% nc ncf*

Belgian Owl Single Malt 36 Months First Fill Bourbon Cask db **(91) n22.5 t23.5 f22 b23** Such an improbably good whisky for something so young. This has been so beautifully distilled! *46%*

Belgian Owl Single Malt 40 Months First Fill Bourbon Single Cask No 1538333 db **(92) n23 t23.5 f22 b23.5** This is so young, so delicate. Beautifully distilled malt and either because or despite its age just so juicily entertaining. That vague now-you-see it, now you don't smokiness is a wonderful tease... *46%*

Belgian Owl Single Malt 40 Months First Fill Bourbon Single Cask No 66381680 db **(90.5) n22 t22.5 f23 b23** One of those rare malts which just gets better towards the end. Not an atom of the intricate smoke as on cask 1538333. *46%*

Belgian Owl Single Malt 40 Months First Fill Bourbon Single Cask No 6631688 db **(94.5) n23.5 t23.5 f23.5 b24** Though a sister cask to the one above, their performances are fascinatingly different. Here the oils and weight forms early on, coating the mouth immediately for a much bigger, more chewy and better-balanced experience. It is hard to believe this malt is a mere three years old. Coming from the sister stills of the great Glen Grant distillery, Belgian Owl has planted its flag – or is that feathers? – firmly in the camp of ultra-elegant single malt. At the moment, no-one on mainland Europe can match their élan. This is really lovely stuff. *46%*

⟫ **Belgian Owl Single Malt Aged 5 Years** bott code: LH060177, db **(91) n22.5** sublime barley with a surprise saltiness to add piquancy **t22.5** initially, the most simplistic of intense malty tones. But as they are layering the oak grows, so does the complexity. The midground is a light warble as (or should that be hoot?) of heather honey and delicate spice; **f23** surprisingly long with a late oily development. The spices and malt are top notch; **b23** and there I was, preparing to taste all the Belgian Owl whiskies on the day of the European Championship Finals, where I fully expected them to be performing. Then, last night.... Italy.... Oh well: at least the compensation is for me of being treated to this excellent distillery's wares – which are normally banging hard on the door of the Bible's European Whisky of the Year a little earlier than expected. This is a real departure from the usual BO narrative: not only young for these stills but reduced to 46%. Here you can see the lightness of the old Speyside stills in full play. A malt that really does know where the heart of the cut is, but still light enough for the oak to have a telling say. The result is a big malt and toffee interplay with some rather lovely spices performing, too. *46%*

⟫ **Belgian Owl Single Malt Aged 6 Years** bott code: LH072177, db **(89) n22** quite a muddled nose with the malt less dominant, yet the oak not quite as well defined as it might be, either. Even so, the heather honey and spice is a pleasant marriage; **t23** a thin, slovenly arrival. But this soon picks up and a cascade of spiced honey and sugars rise as though from a spring, tumbling down a malty hillside; **f22** pleasant malt but a casual bitterness from the cask; **b22** fascinating. A year older, but a very different structure. Which, oddly, doesn't work as well as the 5-year-old, though the cask is not of such a high standard. *46%*

⟫ **Belgian Owl Single Malt Aged 7 Years** bott code: LH084177, db **(95) n23.5** for those of you into clean yet characterful, malt, spiced malt with countless rungs of understated oak: wonderful **t24** just fantastic! One if the best deliveries this year. So rare that the actual arrival on the palate is already a complex array of acacia and ulmo honey, red liquorice, thinned hickory and stand your spoon up in malt. And of course, the delicate rumble of peppers... plus a little salt, too, to ensure everything comes through that little bit sharper; **f23.5** whoever distilled this successfully carried out one of the hardest tricks in the book: to ensure the heart of the run was captured without losing essential oils to help extend the finish. Just a late addition of mocha is added to a lighter version of the delivery; b24 a truly classy act. If anyone from a blind tasting can tell the difference between this and the highest-grade Speyside malt, then you are a better man – or woman – than me... 46%

◆ **Belgian Owl Single Malt Aged 8 Years** bott code: LH096177, db **(93) n23** light acacia honey and spice has a slightly bigger say than the malt; **t23** hang on to your hat! A volley of spice is not far behind the seemingly docile malty delivery. An array of delicate honey notes fans out from there; **f23.5** long, oily, unremittingly spicy with a lovey malted milk biscuit dunked in coffee finale; **b23.5** though a year older, possesses only fraction of the complexity of the 7-year-old. That said, typically of this distillery, there are no failures in the distillate as hard as, you might look. Until the very last malty fade, the spices, though, refuse to take second place to anything. 46%

Belgian Owl Single Malt 12 Years Vintage No 5 Single First Fill Bourbon Cask No 4279860 db **(94.5) n23.5 t23.5 f23.5 b24** Old school Belgian Owl from their original stills. Even at the modest (by their standards) 46% abv, the intensity to the nuttiness is something to savour. 46%

Belgian Owl Single Malt 12 Years Vintage No 6 Single First Fill Bourbon Cask No 4018737 db **(96) n23.5 t24.5 f24 b24** Heading towards Bourbonland here. Fabulous. Just fabulous. If there is a better European whisky this year, it will have to go some... 46%

Belgian Owl 12 Years Vintage No. 07 First Fill Bourbon Single Cask No 4275925 db **(96.5) n24 t24.5 f24 b24** Dark Belgium chocolate at nearly 80%. Not cocoa solids, but alcohol by volume. An astonishing and absolutely delectable experience. 78.9%. nc ncf sc. 93 bottles.

Belgian Owl Single Malt 12 Years Single Cask No 14018725 db **(96) n23.5 t24.5 f24 b24** Anyone who doesn't experience this whisky is missing out on something truly unique and beautiful. It's like going on a roller-coaster ride – in a top-of-the-range Aston Martin.... 78%.

◆ **Belgian Owl Single Malt Aged 13 Years First Fill Champagne 6** cépages cask cask no: 401 87 20, edition: 2008-001, db **(95) n23** minty. Even more than a trace of eucalyptus: were this a Scotch single malt these are indicators of a whisky way into its third decade or beyond. It simply creaks with age. But a wonderful blend of heather honey and lemon blossom honey makes a huge difference to the overall balance...and happiness; **t24** it is perhaps surprising that of all the massive personalities at play on the nose, the one that comes through most lucidly on the palate is the lemon blossom honey which is almost rudely salivating. Though the way it shapes, this soon becomes the silky soft centre of a lime pastel...The malt remains intact and intense – and has to successfully negotiate the sheer brio of the tannins which propagate a series of chocolatey treats, usually fruit involved but also with the odd hint of mocha and praline...; **f24** long with that languid oiliness ensuring all the flavours found on the delivery linger and merge together, sometimes amalgamating, sometimes crossing through to the other side unchanged and unchallenged; **b24** there is more than a passing resemblance here to a box of Belgium soft-centre chocolates: indeed, it is uncanny. The beauty is, you pop a reasonable sip of this mouth, and you are slowly but delightfully introduced to the entire contents. This is a truly special whisky boasting a joint style and complexity previously unknown to the whisky world, truly world class, this will be having a battle with its sister 15-year-old when it comes to the major awards this year. The two, I have to say, have only ever been matched by Buffalo Trace and Glen Grant in producing two whiskies of such extraordinary quality, exhibiting true genius and brilliance, within the same year. 75.1%, nc, ncf, sc

◆ **Belgian Owl Single Malt Aged 15 Years First Fill Bourbon cask** cask no: 4 275 954, edition: 2006-003, db **(96) n23.5** almost hard to believe this is first fill: it could almost be virgin oak, except the preliminary sugars are missing. Instead, we are treated to a warbling red liquorice and spiced butterscotch. But there is layered malt, too, which settles in with the crisper Demerara notes. Very, very good, indeed...; **t24.5** truly sensational. Yes, super-high strength, but that works so much in its flavour as the vanillas erupt with an intensity which only does justice to the sublime bourbon-style black liquorice and molasses. Most sensational, though, is the control of the spice which engineers the growth and intensity of the malt; **f24** in classic Belgium Owl style, there are sufficient oils to paste the personality of this malt around the palate and into every crevice. We are left with a slow-burning, intense yet controlled Blue Mountain/Java (60/40) mix at medium to high roast, frothed up and creamy, with just a little countering molasses. The buzz of the spice is never more than that and refuses, even late on, to outflank the lingering malt. And like all truly great whiskies, not only is it free of a single off or tiring note, but almost refuses point blank to finish...; **b24** is it an Eagle owl? Or a Blakiston's Fish Owl. No, neither of those lightweights. This is a Belgian Owl... the biggest in the world. If you don't implement the Murray Method, you will never be able to master this whisky which is to malt what George T Stagg is to bourbon. With the 13-year-old these are, unquestionably the finest whiskies ever to come from mainland Europe. 79%, nc, ncf, sc ♈

BRAECKMAN GRAANSTOKERIJ Oudenaarde. Working

⬧ **Braeckman Belgian Single Grain Whisky Oloroso Sherry Aged 13 Years** first fill bourbon barrel, finished oloroso sherry butt, cask no. 284, dist 2007 db **(90.5) n22.5** spiced grape. Dry oloroso at its most buttock-clenching parched! Almost like a salted fruitcake...; **t23.5** all the sugars hiding away on the nose suddenly jump out and make their presence felt on delivery. A little golden syrup mixed in with the plum pudding. There are other forces at work, and they are determined to restrict any further sugary development. So, the fruits become sharp, tart with a rhubarb kick to the midground. That's if you use the Murray Method. Just take at room temperature and you'll struggle to find those sugars and be blasted back ten feet by the eye-watering fruit...; **f22** the oloroso leaves another mark: a charming silkiness which makes the dry, tart finish quite comfortable. Some decent chocolate at the death turns it late on into bar of chocolate fruit and nut...; **b22.5** this must have been finished in a first fill sherry butt...because this is just dripping in the stuff! For those who like a little whisky with their sherry..Oh, and this orgy, this white-knuckle ride of under-ripe fruit is about as far removed from their previous bottlings as could possibly be...! *60.2%. nc ncf sc. 796 bottles.*

Braeckman Belgian Single Grain Whiskey Single Barrel Aged 10 Years first fill bourbon barrel, cask no. 106, dist 2008 db **(94) n23.5 t24 f23 b23.5** Beautifully made, excellently matured and delivers impressively on the palate. Not much more you can ask. Well, less confusion on the label, perhaps. When it says single grain, I was thinking: "oh, I wonder which grain this will be" and tasted it before consulting the label. And I was immediately confused. As I was getting both rye and, slightly less prominently, unmistakable barley. And, indeed, that is the mash bill: they mean single grain as in it coming from a single distillery. Puzzle solved. Though this high grade whisky itself is more than enigmatic. Wonderful. *46%. nc ncf sc.*

Braeckman Belgian Single Grain Whiskey Single Barrel Aged 10 Years Oloroso Sherry Cask Finish first fill bourbon barrel, cask no. 218, dist 2008 db **(91) n23 t23 f22.5 b22.5** First of all: standing ovation on finding such a great oloroso butt. Such a rarity to find one of this clarity. On the slightly negative side, the fruit does a good job of wiping out the usually fascinating interplay of the rye and barley grains. But I'm being hypercritical: the overall picture is a very pretty one. *60.5%. nc ncf sc. 916 bottles.*

Braeckman Belgian Single Grain Whiskey Single Barrel Aged 12 Years first fill bourbon barrel, cask no. 83, dist 2007 db **(96.5) n23.5 t24.5 f24 b24.5** There are times when you want to stop spitting, close down the computer and just drink the whisky: this is one of them... *66.1%. nc ncf sc. 242 bottles.*

⬧ **Braeckman Belgian Single Grain Whisky Single Barrel Aged 12 Years** first fill bourbon barrel, cask no. 97, dist 2007 db **(95.5) n23** though from first fill, this never attempts to be anything other than a light aroma with a fusion of varied tannin notes, the sugar never straying far from the firm, boiled sweet variety; **t24** here we go....it is happening again... A Twin Peak of sugar and tannin one hitting after the other, vanishing and then reappearing. While the spices buzz, the texture never shifts from soft and enveloping...; **f24.5** of all the world's distilleries, Braeckman have few peers when it comes to the finish of their whiskies. This is as long as the sunset I have just witnessed here: slow but subtle changes in colouring, texture and intensity of glow. All predominantly around a chocolate and butterscotch theme... but that is oversimplifying it. A particular trait that develops early on, but you're not quite able to pinpoint or identify, now settles into rich vanilla. The sugars never quite lose that butterscotch hue. But it peaks when we reach Malteser Max...a heady mix of concentrated, melt-in-the-mouth malt and milky chocolate...; **b24** the equivalent bottling was last year's European Single cask Whisky of the Year, and deservedly so. This one is also superstar status. Not quite up to the overall near perfection of last year's offering, due mainly to a slightly shy or lazy nose. But it certainly confirms that last year's winner was no fluke: this is quite brilliant in its own right. What a treat... *62.9%. nc ncf sc. 215 bottles.*

⬧ **Braeckman Belgian Single Grain Whisky Single Barrel Aged 13 Years** first fill bourbon barrel, cask no. 101, dist 2007 db **(92) n23** you'd expect a whisky of this strength to nip or show a bit of aggro. Nothing. Keeps on a vanilla-rich course and refuses to stray too far into the sugars like other first fill bourbon bottlings from Braeckman...except for hitting a decidedly bourbon-style note with an array of soft liquorice tones; **t23.5** now we are back on track with a texture that must come from the manual of seductive whiskies. Again, as on the nose, this is far more restrained, like the nose keeping on the track of the rich vanilla. However, there is a muscovado sugar and spice bite which induces some serious mid-term salivation; **f22.5** much more restrained than previous bottlings, you'll not be surprised that vanilla champions the cause...; **b23** another beautiful whisky from Braeckman. Doesn't have the heart-stopping drama of their bottling which won the awards in last year's Bible...and there appears to have the handbrake – or do I mean handbraeck? – on. But, as you'd expect from this distillery, the charm offensive works. *64.9%. nc ncf sc. 218 bottles.*

BROUWERIJ PIRLOT Zandhoven. Working.

Kempich Vuur Single Malt Aged 3 Years Laphroaig quarter casks, cask no. L5, bott 24 Jan 17 db **(91) n22 t23 f23 b23** Well, those quarter casks weren't wasted! What a joy of a malt! 46%. sc.

DISTILLERIE WILDEREN. Wilderen. Working.

Wild Weasel Finest Blend Whisky cask no. 21, dist 2013 db **(82) n21 t21 f20 b20** Even by a weasel's standard, this is a particularly thin one. Over tame, Needs feeding and fattening. 40%.

Wild Weasel Single Cask Single Malt Whisky cask no. 23, dist 2013, bott 6 Dec 18 db **(88.5) n21.5 t22.5 f22.5 b22** An unusually sweet whisky: in fact an unusual single malt all round. The signature on the nose is unique, with its strangely scented softness: a kind of mix orange blossom and smothering flowers in full bloom on a very warm summer's evening. There is also a rare softness to the mouthfeel which deserves applauding, and a thick barley intensity, too. But there is something else besides, something unfathomable along the lines of those flowers on the nose, before it trails off with a burnt fudge kiss to the tannin. Rich, scented, uncommonly sweet whisky very much of its own type. 46%. nc ncf sc. 349 bottles.

◈ **Wild Weasel Single Cask Single Malt** cask no. 37, bott 9/11/20 db **(87.5) n21.5 t22.5 f21.5 b22** from the very first sniff the house style kicks in with its truly unique fruity, scented aroma. The brain is in a whirr trying to work out exactly what that aroma may be...and you come to the conclusion the one and only time you have ever found it before was when nosing a Wild Weasel. Whisky, that is – not the furry alternative. Maybe there is another time I have spotted this nose – back to my childhood Christmases and dipping into the tin of Roses chocolates. There is a soft centre on the ultra-malty middle once on the palate, too... 46%. nc ncf sc. 337 bottles.

◈ **Wild Weasel Single Malt Red Port Cask Finish** dist May 2014, bott 9/11/20, cask no. 36 db **(88) n21.5 t22.5 f22 b22** Big and spicey with some mean tannin at work here. But doesn't quite work as well as the White Port Cask bottling (below). The fruit is more game here, fuller and fatter while the sugars and spices are more random and less controlled. Makes a point of being as rich and full on as possible. Not a Wild Weasel to lay down and be tickled 46% nc ncf sc

Wild Weasel Single Malt Whisky Sherry Cask Finish cask no. 26, dist 16 Oct 13, bott 4 Dec 18 db **(88.5) n21.5 t22.5 f22 b22.5** There is something very different about the whiskies from this distillery: both fascinating and confusing. No other distillery offers a nose quite so scented, sherry finish or no. One could say, with some assurance, that this is a very feminine style of whisky, all curves, softness and scents. There is a sting in the tail, too, with the spices being quite so on the warpath towards the end, accentuated by the all-round lightness of the malt itself. No off notes, as the sherry cask is safe and sound. It is hard not to like this very singular distillery. 46%. nc ncf sc.

◈ **Wild Weasel Single Malt Sherry Cask Finish** dist Apr 2015, bott 9/11/20, cask no. 33 db **(88) n22 t22.5 f21.5 b22** Easily the most simplistic Weasel I've encountered yet. A safe sherry butt essentially fee from taint. But, equally, the least complex of this year's bottlings I've sampled, happy as it is to pulse a friendly, mildly fruity, lightly honeyed message. A very safe whisky. 46% nc ncf sc

◈ **Wild Weasel Single Malt White Port Cask Finish** dist May 2014, bott 9/11/20, cask no. 35 db **(92.5) n22.5 t23.5 f23 b23.5** Good Lord! This whisky makes some statement. And the grammar and diction are superb. Not so much silky as pure ermine. Oh, and a word of warning: these peculiarly shaped, interesting and explosive bottles are not to be opened anywhere near a computer, trust me... 46% nc ncf sc

IF GOULDYS FILLIERS DISTILLERY Deinze. Working.

Goldys Distillers Range 14 Years Old Belgian Single Grain Whisky Madeira cask finish, bott code: L16240900 db **(90.5) n22.5 t23 f22.5 b22.5** A whisky, but one without muscle or threat. The Madeira cask is a little too rich to allow this whisky to move up into the next level of excellence: in whisky less is often more... 43%.

STOKERIJ DE MOLENBERG Willebroek. Working.

Golden Carolus Single Malt first fill bourbon cask, Het Anker cask finish db **(88) n22 t22.5 f21.5 b22** Cream toffee, anyone? 46%. nc ncf.

CORSICA
DOMAINE MAVELA Aléria. Working.

P & M Red Oak Corsican Single Malt Whisky bott code L1783 db **(91.5) n22.5 t23.5 f22.5 b23** A wonderfully understated, complex malt, despite the voluptuousness of the fruit. 42%. nc ncf. 567 bottles.

P & M Signature Corsican Single Malt Whisky bott code L1684 db **(89.5) n21.5 t23 f22 b23** A very charming malt which at its peak sings like a Corsican Finch. 42%. nc ncf. 6,600 bottles.

P & M Tourbé Corsican Single Malt Whisky bott code L1682 db **(92) n22.5 t23 f23 b23.5** A beautifully paced, gentle malt which always carries a threat on the peaty wind. 42%. nc ncf.

P & M Aged 13 Years Corsican Single Malt Whisky bott code L2984 db **(95.5) n23.5 t24 f24 b24** Enough oak to make a Corsican nuthatch sing with happiness. This has swallowed up the years with ease and maximised complexity. World class whisky. 42%. nc ncf. 217 bottles.

CZECH REPUBLIC
Single Malt
RUDOLF JELÍNEK DISTILLERY Vizovice. Working.
Gold Cock Single Malt Whisky 2008 Virgin Oak Czech oak barrels, dist Feb 08, bott Mar 17 db **(96) n24 t24 f24 b24** Not often you get gold cocks and virgins mentioned in the same sentence in a drinks guide. Or anywhere else, come to that. Equally few rampant cocks can crow so loudly; no virgin give so passionately. A consummate whisky consummated... 61.5%. nc ncf sc. 270 bottles.

SVACH DISTILLERY Mirkovice. Working.
⬗ **Svach's Old Well Single Malt Bohemian Whisky Peated** aged in Laphroaig barrel, 2nd release, db **(90) n23** more than a hint of south-east Islay, as you might expect. But the malt is accommodating: firm enough for the phenols to land and also project a degree of attractive spice. There is some growing oiliness, to; **t22.5** not quite as beautifully constructed as the nose. Thicker bodied and less delicate than the nose hints at, the marks of a wider cut present; **f22** yep, definite tang of light feints. But the buttery peat still has more than enough charm to be getting on with. Like the middle, offers a persistent dryness; **b22.5** would struggle to call this complex, but what it does, it does rather well the use of the phenols is rather lovely. 46.3% nc ncf sc

⬗ **Svach's Old Well Single Malt Bohemian Whisky Peated** aged in Bourbon and Porto barrels, 2nd release, db **(87.5) n22.5 t22 f21.5 b21.5** A slightly muddled malt. Hefty and smoky, the fruit grapples with both the phenols and tannins rather than plays along with them. Again, as is the house style, very dry and missing some much-needed honey, especially on the finish. have to say I do love the sooty dryness of the peat on the nose. Classy. 46.3% nc ncf sc

⬗ **Svach's Old Well Single Bohemian Whisky Malt Unpeated** aged in Bourbon and Pineau Des Charentes barrels, 2nd release, db **(94) n23.5** there may be a lack of peat to this one, but it certainly makes up for it in spice, which complements the dried orange peel rather well. The gristy sweetness is rounded off by subtle Lubec marzipan; **t23.5** a beautiful arrival of intense yet subtle buttery grist, the sugars pulsing quietly with a gentle breeze and no more of a blend of heather and ulmo honeys. Light cherry cake drifts around the palate; **f23** you would swear there was a touch of peat to this. Light cocoa mingles with the persistent buttery barley which is much oiler now **b24** was it the peat in the other bottlings which was hiding he sugars? Elegant, oily and complex, a malt which is complimented by the higher strength. A true delight to sample and the gently burning beacon to illuminate this distillery... 51.9% nc ncf sc

⬗ **Svach's Old Well Single Bohemian Whisky Malt Me and Whisky** Gang Peated bourbon and Sauternes barrels, dist 2017, db **(89) n23** that is one fabulous peat nose: soft, friendly and not scared of shewing its butterscotch and vanilla side, too...; **t23.5** so much flavour on delivery....just wow! There are so many layers of phenol at work here; the complexity is increased further by layering of ulmo honey and intense malt. The first half dozen flavour waves should be in a frame and hung in a gallery; **f20.5** overly bitter and tar, it loses its way by comparison; **b22** worth an extra 5 points just for being the first whisky label in the world to state: "fuck covid". I'll drink to that.... 50.8% 465 bottles

Svach's Old Well Whisky Peated bourbon & Porto barrels, bott 2019 db **(86) n21.5 t22 f21 b21.5** While the smoke, on the nose especially, draws you in, the overall experience is one of a whisky with a body not quite strong enough to carry the weight of the phenols. Some decent ulmo honey early on. But this clunks around ungainly like a slim 12-year-old lush in a massive suit of armour. You know that at some stage this is going to collapse...and it does. 46.3%. sc.

Svach's Old Well Whisky Peated Laphroaig barrel, bott 2019 db **(89) n23 t22.5 f21 b22.5** Well, well: if this ain't Laphroaig influenced...well, then I don't know what is. Perhaps a bit of a one trick pony, but what a trick! 42.4%. sc.

Svach's Old Well Whisky Peated virgin oak, first fill Bohemian barrel, bott 2019 db **(90) n22.5 t23 f22 b22.5** Very unusual...and works a treat. Superb balance and complexity: a real surprise package. 54.8%. sc.

Svach's Old Well Whisky Unpeated bourbon & Pineau Des Charentes barrels, bott 2019 db **(91) n22** a nose nipper: there is a tightness to the spirit and a sharpness to the fruit; **t23** now, that's very much better. Fatter than anything from this distillery before, allowing the vanilla and grape to forge a charming, almost pudding-style duet; **f23** superb spices and lovely butterscotch fade; **b23** the higher strength suits this distillery as it ramps up the oils to ensure better weight, body and structure. A good, very clean, chewing whisky. *51.9%. sc.*

Svach's Old Well Whisky Unpeated bourbon & sherry barrels, bott 2019 db **(88.5) n22 t23 f21.5 b22** You have to take your hats off. This is an exceptionally clean distillate – as are all this distillery's expressions – and here finding itself in no less unblemished sherry casks. That is some achievement. The grape is quite flighty, to the extent of a vague under-ripe strawberry note to the fruit on the nose. The body revels in its ultra thin style, but now helped along by a chewy candy fruitiness. Sadly, all this quickly evaporates on the unusually brief finale. *46.3%. sc.*

DENMARK
BRAENDERIET LIMFJORDEN Øster Assels. Working.
Lindorm Danish Single Malt Whisky 2nd Edition db **(94) n23.5 t23.5 f23 b24** An incredibly sure-footed and complex whisky for a distillery so young. Wonderful stuff! *46%. ncf. 537 bottles.*

Lindorm Danish Single Malt Whisky 3rd Edition db **(89.5) n23 t22.5 f22 b22** Not so well distilled this time and though this means huge flavours, the complexity and nimble-footedness of the 2nd edition is not quite there. A real knife, fork and spoon job... *46%. ncf. 500 bottles.*

BRAUNSTEIN DISTILLERY Køge. Working.
Braunstein Danish Single Malt Cask Edition no. 2 db **(94) n23.5 t23.5 f23 b24** Seriously high quality distillate that has been faithfully supported by good grade oak. Complex, satisfying, and for its obviously tender years, truly excellent malt. A welcome addition to the Scandinavian – and world! – whisky lexicon. *62.4%*

COPENHAGEN DISTILLERY Copenhagen. Working.
Copenhagen Single Malt Emmer Whisky cask no. B001, bott 2020 db **(93.5) n23 t24 f22.5 b24** If it were possible to go back in time, say 10,000 years and find that early man had somehow happened upon distillation, then the chances are it would have been Emmer, a form of wheat crop, that would have been used as the basic ingredient for fermentation. Ironic – and wholly fitting – that Scandinavia's newest distillery should also make one of their first whiskies from this rare, full-flavoured grain. And when I say full-flavoured...this was my first whisky of the day and rarely have my taste buds been awakened so stirringly and to such a rich and resounding stimulation. My 1,218th whisky for the 2021 edition (though I had encountered this at their wonderful distillery), and it is such a joy to have my nose and taste buds taken in a direction the previous 1,217 whiskies had failed to do. A superb malt which just oozes personality. *53.1%. sc. 36 bottles.*

Copenhagen Single Malt Whisky First Edition db **(96) n24 t24.5 f23.5 b24** The first-ever whisky bottled by this outstanding new distillery. I had the honour of being here when this first bottling was launched though, as is my custom, I always taste for the Bible away from the place of distillation – and I have the sample here back in my UK tasting room. But even away from the history and romance, the excellence of this whisky breezes through just as it did that day. The Danes were once known for their pork, potatoes and marzipan. Now with Copenhagen adding to the country's ever-growing fine whisky production, I think you can safely include Malt amongst their most excellent exports. *56%. 100 bottles.*

Copenhagen Single Malt Whisky Second Edition db **(89) n21 t23.5 f22 b22.5** One of the most barley-intense malts to be produced not just in Scandinavia, but the whole world this year. The cut is a little too wide and undoes the nose slightly and makes an early mark on delivery. But, that said, this is the maltiest of malts with enough barley to blow your socks off... Strap yourself in for a glorious ride! Incidentally, I carefully used a little of this in a blend of all three Copenhagen bottlings. The result was the richest single malt from any distillery I have tasted in the world this year, and something around the 95 mark in points. This distillery will have to be watched closely. *574%.*

◈ **Whisky Raw Edition Single Malt 2020** batch no.1, db **(91.5) n21.5** the youthfulness of this malt is never far away on this aroma. A slightly wider cut than their previous bottlings, it seems with a light vegetable note mixing in with malt and lightly molassed spices; **t24** just... sensational...! An all-engulfing mouth feel with those extra oils making for an all-enveloping intensity, but one which appears controlled to the point of being manicured. The thinned heather honey thickens once the malts get involved. Indeed, it isn't just the flavours that catch the eye, but the mouth feel, too, as there appears to be two different strands of intensity to the malt, one light, the other more chewable. Very unusual...and rather delightful. The best point comes about 12-15 flavour waves in near the midpoint when the tannins really do make a stand. Curiously, part of the delivery's most charming feature is a brief burst of almost sheer bourbon, which vanishes as quickly as it appears. But then resurfaces in those later favour waves, alongside some chocolate; **f22.5** stubbornly long. And still allows the vanilla and chocolate an uninterrupted performance. Just a little tang of that vaguely wide cut at the very death...; **b23.5** a compellingly delicious malt. While the nose never quite gets going, things certainly do once the whisky has crossed the lips. And then you are in for a five-course malt. Another memorable bottling from this new distillery. *61.1% 300 bottles*

⬦ **Whisky Rare Edition Single Malt 2021** batch no.2, db **(91) n21.5** soothing oaky caramels offer a floaty softness. Just the vaguest hint of juniper – a caress and no more – but this helps concentrate the mind on the lurking spices. Again, just a little vegetable; **t23** not sure any European whisky this year betters this for sheer mouth feel. The fact that first notes on delivery are a bit confused hardly matters. The fact is, they glided there without frictin and as soon as the sugars, tannins, malt, spices, natural caramels, and vegetables have sorted themselves out we are then subject to a wonderful treat. The delicate butterscotch and heather notes mix and mingle with the malt and hold your thoughts until the spices re-emerge; **f23** a rather glorious procession of malt, toffee-mocha notes with buzzing – almost German-style - spices for company...; **b23.5** Denmark is rightly famous for its pork, its marzipan, its divorce rate, its beards, and its goalkeepers. But not until now, silk. On this evidence it soon will be. I have to admit that I feared the worst when I learned that aged gin casks had been used here. But I shouldn't have worried. After from a brief salute on the nose, the juniper vanishes. Still would like to see the distillate just a little finer in the cut. Must say, though, that the oils have been put to jolly good use. *49% 100 bottles*

FARY LOCHAN DESTILLERI Give. Working.

Fary Lochan Efterår #03 cask no. 2013-16 (sherry cask), dist 19 Nov 13, bott 19 Nov 19 db **(85.5) n20 t22.5 f21.5 b21.5** This is almost like a distillation of the distillery style itself. The less than attractive nose reminds you the cuts aren't always precise here. Then the delivery itself blasts your taste buds into orbit with one of the most joyful celebrations of the grain around, yet always kept in check by a slight tobacco note. All this backed by a light dribble of acacia honey. A Fary which alternates between beauty and the beast... *48.3%. sc. 500 bottles.*

Fary Lochan Jubilæumsaftapning #01 cask no. 2012-07 (sherry cask no. 2), dist 23 Jun 12, bott 3 Dec 19 db **(92.5) n23.5 t23.5 f22 b23.5** We should get down on our hands and knees and worship Sherry Cask No 2. An air punching deliciousness. *51.3%. sc. 500 bottles.*

MOSGAARD DISTILLERY Oure. Working.

Mosgaard Organic Single Malt Whisky Oloroso cask, batch no. 6, bott 10 Jan 20 db **(87) n21.5 t22 f21.5 b22** Not a perfect cask, but not the worst, either. An ultra-simple tale of grape and malt that would make a good bedtime story, especially if you have had problems sleeping of late. The thickish cut ensures extra weight. I think this distillery would be better served concentrating on ex-bourbon to allow the distillery character to shine through. *46.2%.*

Mosgaard Organic Single Malt Whisky peated/bourbon cask, batch no. 1, bott 14 Oct 19 db **(94) n23 t23.5 f23.5 b24** Wonderfully distilled and it has blossomed in the cask. Could probably have done with a few more years for peak complexity, as this malt had a long way still to travel. Quite beautiful. *48.4%.*

Mosgaard Organic Single Malt Whisky Pedro Ximenes cask, batch no. 3, bott 4 Jun 19 db **(87) n21.5 t22.5 f21.5 b21.5** This distillery genuinely knows how to distil malt whisky. This is technically ship shape, but the Bristol fashion of PX cask, though clean and clear of sulphur interference, has again ill-served the malt. After a momentary attractive spasm of spice and toasty muscovado sugars, this malt flatlines into a toffee-riddled fade. Pleasant, but ultimately duller than a speech by "Just Call Me Kier" Starmer, which is seriously going some. Once more a PX cask claims an innocent victim. *46.3%.*

Mosgaard Organic Single Malt Whisky Pedro Ximenez cask, batch no. 6, bott 13 Feb 20 db **(86.5) n21.5 t22 f21.5 b21.5** I could have written this just from the nose alone: the taste is equally one-dimensional is so often the case from PX. It is like putting the malt into a sugary straight jacket. Just the slightest degree of feint to make it a little more interesting. *46.3%.*

Mosgaard Organic Single Malt Whisky Port Wine cask, batch no. 1, bott 20 May 20 db **(72.5) n18 t21.5 f16 b17** Sulphur massacred. Organic sulphur, presumably. *48.3%.*

NYBORG DESTILLERI Nyborg. Working.

Nyborg Destilleri Danish Oak Isle of Fiona batch no. 167 db **(93) n23 t23.5 f23 b23.5** Denmark is by far and away the least forested of all Scandinavian countries. So finding an oak tree to make a barrel from must have been a major achievement in itself. It was well worth the effort, because this is a stunner and the impact of the tannin is the least assertive of any European oak I have encountered outside of Spain. The balance of the nose is spot on with lazy harmony between grain and light toasty tannin with a little orange blossom honey as the buffer. The grist is on overdrive on the palate, the oak providing a slightly salty back up. With its Jaffa Cake sub-strata, there is much to celebrate here. *46%. nc ncf.*

SMALL BATCH DISTILLERS Holstebro. Working

Small Batch Distillers Edition 2017 Whisky One Peated Single Malt db **(91) n23 t22 f23.5 b22.5** Takes time for the brakes to be disengaged, but a malt which travels well when they do. A dram to persevere with as the first mouthful or two hardly do it justice. *52%. sc. 61 bottles.*

Small Batch Distillers Hjerl Hede Nr. 1 Dansk Produceret Single Malt 2019 db **(88.5) n22 t23 f22 b21.5** Young and bristling with malty tendencies. Eye-watering in its salivating properties, a gristy sweetness is never far away. *59%. nc ncf*

Small Batch Distillers Peatman Dansk Produceret Single Malt 2018 db **(92) n23.5 t23 f22.5 b23** It has been a little while since I last tasted this distillery and the first thing to strike me was the clarity of the distillate compared to previously. Beautifully run stills with now a more refined middle cut. A thoroughly enjoyable, mildly charismatic malt that sets out to stimulate both nose and palate...and succeeds handsomely. *59%. sc nc ncf.*

Small Batch Distillers RugBy Double Cask Dansk Produceret Selected Malt Edition 2019 db **(86) n21.5 t22.5 f21 b21** A bit of a bucking bronco, this, with both the nose and palate having problems coping with the youthful rye. Or perhaps it was the casks which failed to find a formula to get the best out f the grain, especially after the attractively intense delivery starts unravelling. Flavoursome and rugged, especially when the oak kicks in, harmony is always the one thing that eludes it. *46% ncf.*

STAUNING WHISKEY Skjern. Working.

Stauning Bastard Rye Whisky Mezcal cask finish, dist 2016, bott Nov 19 db **(84.5) n22.5 t22 f19 b21** With the lemon and cherry drops fizzing around with the rye on the nose, I hoped for the best. But the delivery, with the tannins taught, the rye recalcitrant and tannins testing, was something else again. The finish, though, fell prey to the wine cask. There is a word for that kind of cask... *46.3%.*

Stauning Heather 1st fill Maker's Mark bourbon casks, dist 2013-14, bott May 19 db **(86) n22.5 t22 f20 b21.5** Last time I tasted this I felt things didn't pan out as I'd have like due to a little niggling feintiness. This time the feints have gone, replaced by a nagging sulphur note on the finish. I prefer the feints! *48.7%. ncf.*

Stauning Kaos 1st fill Maker's Mark bourbon casks & virgin Missouri white oak casks, dist 2015/16, bott Apr 19 db **(96) n24 t23.5 f24 b24.5** As I taste for the Whisky Bible 2021, I needed to choose which whisky would be perfect for the 500th - set right in the middle of the Covid-19 Pandemic. Well, it just had to be this: Kaos...!!! And it was the perfect choice as it is a reminder that amid all the suffering and unhappiness, there's beauty, too. And, my word: this is a very beautiful whisky... *47.1%. ncf.*

Stauning Kaos new American oak & Maker's Mark bourbon casks, dist 2015/17, bott Feb 20 db **(89) n23 t23 f21 b22** Well, this is certainly more chaotic than the Kaos above. Which, sadly, means it doesn't work anything like so well... *47.1%. ncf.*

◈◈◈ **Stauning Kaos Triple Malt Whisky** batch no. 1-2020 db **(86) n22.5 t22.5 f19.5 b21.5** The thing about Kaos, is that you never quite know – as the name implies - what you are going to get. Sometimes it works magnificently. Other times it stumbles over itself, never quite able to find a rhythm or even a reason. Here we have a bottling which appear to be a succession of dead ends; at times intriguing, others you find yourself in dark alleyways. The slight feint kick doesn't work too much to its advantage here as it lets in a slightly over-bittered finish. Soupy honey notes liven things with rye but is then shut off. Some short bursts of excellence. But too short. Taking the nature of the beast into account, the next Kaos will be brilliantly chaotic...you just never know *46%.*

Stauning Peat 1st fill Maker's Mark bourbon, 1st fill ex-oloroso sherry & virgin American white oak casks, dist 2012-14, bott Jul 19 db **(90) n23 t23 f21 b23** Not sure this whisky needs the sherry butt inclusion with its capricious tendencies, as the youth of the malt and the boldness of the peat were already very happy with the bourbon cask lead *48.4%. ncf.*

◈◈◈ **Stauning Peat Single Malt Whisky** batch no. 1-2020 db **(88.5) n22 t22 f22 b22.5** Very young grains at work here. Which means the phenols still have an edge to them. A wide, oily cut at work here. But that slight error is forgivable as it helps stoke up the thick intensity of the barley sugar and smoked honey. Never quite manages to disrobe from its cloak of youth. But just sweetly charms you to death... *47%.*

Stauning Port Smoke Calheiros Cruz tawny port casks, nos. 357, 364, 365, 369, 381 & 394, dist 2015, bott Apr 19 db **(91) n22.5 t23 f22.5 b23** Attractive, yet strangely austere – enlivened by a brief puckering fruitiness. *51.5%. ncf.*

Stauning Rye new American oak casks, dist 2015/16, bott Jun 19 db **(88.5) n22 t23 f21.5 b22** Raucous rye...,but a shade too much feint. Had the cut been that little tighter, this would have been something special. The rye and ulmo honey tango is gorgeous, though. *50%.*

Stauning Rye new American oak casks, dist 2016, bott Jan 20 db **(94.5) n23 t24 f23.5 b24** Of all the grains in the world, only malted rye can churn out such intense flavour. Technically, not quite perfect, having this tone poem at nearly full volume more than compensates. What an experience! *50%. ncf.*

◇ **Stauning Rye Whisky** New American oak barrels, batch no. 1-2020 db **(94.5) n23.5** love this nose: quite unique in that there is a flintiness to grain not always found when rye has been malted: the Demerara sugars are positively crunchy while lazy honeys offer some softening. A green-ness pervades, too, carefree youth amid earnest oak, sweetened further by a sprig of mint. Pure intrigue and entertainment; **t24** the delivery has that rare talent to parade honey and darker sugars around with abandon but pull back from ever being overly sweet. A momentary fear we are heading towards a liquor, as thick honey is the dominating factor early on. But the tannins bite, and with them comes the spices: busy, warming, and proud; **f23** so much heather honey on the finish: indeed, one of its most honey-rich fades I have enjoyed in years; **b24** probably no grain on the planet offers a flavour kick like malted rye. It has an intensity and richness all its own, though the results can vary wildly from distillery to distillery. The best I have ever encountered is found at Alberta. Stauning has a different persona, retaining some of the sharper elements of unmalted rye, too. And from this evidence it is taking a quite unique and now magnificent shape. As it was I who suggested they produce rye whisky when Stauning was still but dream in its founders' eyes, I always take proud interest in their rye bottlings. This isn't a mile off what I had in mind... *48%. ncf.*

Stauning Rye Rum Cask Finish virgin-heavy charred American white-oak casks, dist 2016, bott Jul 19 db **(87) n22 t22.5 f21 b21.5** Thickset and hefty, a little too much tannin here has negated the effect of the rye. Struggles to find quite the right kind of balance, though the initial disgorge of complex, juicy, lightly sugared tones on delivery had at first bode well. *46.5%. nc ncf.*

Stauning Rye Rum Cask Finish virgin-heavy charred American white-oak casks, dist 2016, bott Sept 19 db **(94.5) n23 t24 f23.5 b24** Struts around knowing that this is what their July bottling wanted to be. Some fabulous rye sharpness and just an all-round high-class whisky. *46.5%. nc ncf.*

THY WHISKY Snedsted. Working.

◇ **Thy Danish Whisky Distillery Edition Aged 4 Years** ex-oloroso, cask no: 61-62, dist 2016, bott 2020 db **(93) n23.5** very, very young: despite the colour. The barley is still in its baby clothes offering a real eye-watering sharpness; **t23** on deliver, the mout hfeel is more impressive than the original flavour scheme. But then on the fifth and sixth waves the sherry powers through in highly impressive fashion: faultless grape offering a spiced succulence that delights; **f23** excellent oils keeps the oils and barley in play while the spices grow...and grow...; **b23.5** the difference to a whisky a faultless sherry butt can make. Oddly enough, although 4-years-old, the youthfulness is more pronounced here than most of their 3-y-o bottlings. A treat of a bottling from one of the best exponents of young malt whisky in the world. *61.7% ncf*

◇ **Thy Danish Whisky No. 10 Fjordboen Aged 3 Years** ex-Oloroso cask, dist Jan 16, bott May 19 db **(91) n23** an intriguingly different aroma to the glorious bottling 9: as well as a peppery grape edge, there is also a far more mossy, vegetable-inclined earthiness, too. New territory for Thy...; **t23** like the nose, distinctly to-toned, even on the split delivery. The oloroso influence is obvious...and not at all bad. The malt/cask influence has its own unique story. Young, not quite hitting it off between the contrasting styles, but when the intensity mounts a delicious balance is found, the delicate sugars now at full stretch; **f22.5** the nose broadcasts the dryness of the finale well in advance, though tannin attaches to the grape skin; **b22.5** should you ever need to discover what is meant by a dry oloroso finish to a whisky, here's your bottle! Youthful, but elegant. *49.9%. 1,005 bottles.*

◇ **Thy Danish Whisky No. 11 Stovt Aged 3 Years** ex-port, ex-bourbon, ex-stout casks, dist May 16, bott Oct 19 db **(87) n21.5 t22.5 f21 b22** I hadn't looked at the cask make up of this bottling before I nosed it. But I certainly did once I took my first sniff: hops! Now, the one thing I am no fan of is hops and whisky together. Rarely a comfortable combination, as the hop is a natural bittering agent and that plays havoc with the balance of a whisky. However, here an old Port cask has come to the rescue by offering a silky, fruity sheen to the heather-honey of the malt and bourbon cask. However, the heads and tails of short hop give a strange persona. The middle, though, is a beautiful, creamy experience. *48%. 831 bottles.*

◇ **Thy Danish Whisky No. 12 Kornmod Aged 3 Years** ex-Oloroso and ex-bourbon casks, dist Mar 17, bott Apr 20 db **(96) n24** here we go: shades of bottling 9. Glorious oloroso harmonising with sweet barley. The oak injection seems to neutralise the youthfulness of the malt, while the barley gives it such life. Delicate peach mingles with spiced lemon drops; **t24** that....is...just...brilliant! Is this really only three-years-old...?!?!? The voluptuousness of the intense, silky sherry is matched only by the near perfect weight to the controlled explosion of spice. Initially the barley has confidence enough to set off with maximum juiciness. It's the slow, calculated, increasingly oily infusion of the fruit which wins your heart...and the slower build of the spice is almost showing off; **f23.5** a textbook fade: almost a reversing of the build up with the barley and fruit lingering longest, not the spice; **b24.5** such magnificence for a whisky so young: the complexity and the layering are almost off the charts. Beautifully distilled and, for its age, just about perfectly matured. What a thrill to encounter oloroso influence this faultless. When this distillery gets it right, they get it very right. Simply wonderful whisky, irrespective of its age. *52.5%. 1,486 bottles.*

⬦ **Thy Danish Whisky No. 13 Stovt Aged 3 Years** bourbon, oloroso, PX and stout casks, dist Jan-Oct 2017, bott Nov 2020 db **(80)** n21 t21.5 f19.5 b18 What it is they say about too many cooks...? Ditto casks styles, sometimes. Had to smile when I saw they had pitted the ultimate sweetener, PX casks, against the ultimate bitterer... beer. The hops win in the pretty unattractive nose, then the PX kicks in to act as a kind of eraser. But instead, everything is flattened, except some uncontrolled spice and the late hop bitterness. Hopefully an experiment not to be repeated from this great distillery. *51.0% ncf 1825 bottles*

⬦ **Thy Danish Whisky No. 14 Bøg Aged 3 Years** oloroso cask,dist Apr-Dec 2017, bott Mar 2021 db **(94)** n23 distinctively sharp phenols. Nips at the nose with a Demerara sugar accompaniment. The softness is provided by the clean grape; **t23.5** no matter the cask, there is no disguising young peat – the intensity and structure of phenol on delivery is usually a giveaway – here we doubtless have young malt restrained only by juicy fruit; **f23.5** the spices warm relentlessly. Vanillas slowly make an entry, so a lightly smoked chocolate toffee complexity develops. Absolutely no sign of tiredness...; **b24** a prickly smokiness reminds me a little of the bacon Denmark is so rightly famed for. Not for stuffy Islay-style peat purists. But certainly, one for those who love it when high-class peat racks up the weight and complexity and a faultless sherry butt is on hand to soothe! *57.4% ncf 1627 bottles*

TROLDEN DISTILLERY Kolding. Working.

Trolden Nimbus Danish Single Malt cask no. 6 db **(92.5)** n22.5 t23.5 f23 b23.5 Avery understated whisky and it's the oils that do it. Huge weight and body, but so evenly distributed. *46%. nc ncf sc.*

Trolden Nimbus Peated Single Malt cask no. PX db **(86.5)** n22 t21.5 f22 b21 This isn't the first peat and PX fallout and it won't be the last. Only towards the very death do the two bruising elements find common ground. Until then it is an unbalanced stand-off, especially on the delivery, where they both appear to back off to create a very odd void. Peat and PX are rarely happy bedfellows and though you might find the odd charming moment – I did here briefly on the nose and certainly with the massive spices at the death – the gears grind a little too noisily. Still, I guarantee some peatophiles will find this one of the greatest experiences of their lives... *56%. nc ncf sc. 177 bottles.*

ESTONIA
MOE DISTILLERY Moe. Working.

Tamm & Rukis 100% Rye Malt Whisky virgin American oak for 3 years, distilled from Sangaste winter rye, batch no. 1, bott 2019 db **(89)** n23 t21.5 f22.5 b22 Seeing as Estonians helped colonise America as far back as the very early 17th century, perhaps it should be no surprise Moe have decided to give this whisky a very Kentuckian slant, evident on both nose and palate. And very attractive it is, too. A fascinating and entertaining introduction by a new country to whisky. Or do I mean whiskey....? *44%.*

FAROE ISLAND
EINAR'S DISTILLERY Working.

⬦ **Einar's Distillery Single Malt Whisky Inaugural Release** sherry & bourbon casks db **(88.5)** n22 t22 f22.5 b22 Despite some fragrant fruitiness on the nose, there is no escaping the undercooked nature of the spirit itself, the barley seemingly unhappy with the lack of tannin against the sultanas. This gives the nose a skewed aroma, not entirely happy in itself and needing a little extra time for the warring factions to find common ground. The mouth feel in delivery is much better. But again, this is distinctly two-toned. On one hand we have the silky fruit gliding along like a swan, while below it the too youthful grains nibble and attack with nothing like the same grace. Altogether, though, this possesses huge flavour. Peppery spices arrive early on and last the course, ramping up its intensity as it travels –

and this assists the finish which has increased in oil significantly and revels in a playful bitter-sweet persona, the sweetness coming from some understated demerara sugar. This is hugely characterful whisky, well-made and even in this form abounding with excellent personality. But at the moment there is a little too much youth for it to be as confident as it should be, something which mildly distorts both the nose, complexity and, ultimately, the balance. Make no mistake: this whisky, had it been left alone in the warehouse, was on course for something rather grand. Because time will be this new distillery's friend. Love it. Congratulations to all at Einar: we have a Fair Ol' distillery on our hands.... *51%. 861 bottles.*

⬧⬧ **Einar's Distillery Single Malt Whisky** oloroso sherry casks db **(88.5) n22 t22.5 f21.5 b22.5** Firstly, this is much closer in style to the Inaugural Release, especially on its playfully youthful nose. However, the once gaunt features have fattened out slowly. A spirit that was characterful if in art linear, is now taking a distinct shape. What is quite fascinating here is that although it obvious that the whisky has matured slightly and moved on, it is no better entertainment than the younger spirit. This is caused by the early years wobbles of all casks which shoot up and down in quality, sometimes dramatically so, until it reaches an age where it levels out and the changes can be more or less plotted and forecast. Einar's Whisky has not reached that stage yet: we are still very much in a fascinating, experimental mode of discovery *51% 664 bottles*

⬧⬧ **Einar's Distillery Single Malt Whisky Single Cask** oloroso sherry cask db **(87) n22 t22.5 f20.5 b22** Wow! Well, this whisky certainly makes a statement. This is a malt style I will regularly find when checking through malt spirit in Scotland with still a little way to go before it can legally be called Scotch. We still have a whisky in its most malleable stages: for quite a while the balance between malt and grape will jump up and down and only after time (in your case you are still discovering when) does it settle into a happy marriage. This malt hasn't quite met this stage yet, as the bitter finish testifies, with the sherry influence is still a little on the aggressive side. Happily, this is well-distilled distillate and that has helped enormously in controlling the excesses of the cask. But always a work, as they say, in progress. *57.1% nc ncf sc 448 bottles*

⬧⬧ **Einar's Distillery Single Malt Cask Strength Batch 5** Oloroso casks, ex-Laphroaig casks, bott code: **(94) n23** the underpinning of the smoke from the Laphroaig cask is a masterstroke. It gives the nose not just charm and attractiveness but a serious degree of depth, too, to compensate for the new makey feel which is still to be found, especially before the Murray Method kicks in. A light layer of clean, attractive fruit is found somewhere between the malt and the smoke; **t24** easily this distillery's most accomplished arrival on the palate. To be honest, it is hard to see how, at this age, it can be improved upon. The youthfulness and strength ensures salivation levels are already through the roof before an extra dollop of grape juice makes it juicier still. The peat compensates for the lack of oak marvellously, offering just the right amount of gravitas without the smoke in any way dominating; **f23** superb chocolate raisin towards the oily and still persistently malty finish. Chewy and lightly spiced, too...; **b24** OK. So this is precociously young, unquestionably. But, then so was Mozart when the composed his first symphony. This is the first whisky from this distillery where I have felt that they have got the essential balance absolutely spot on, allowing the malt to spring at you with astonishing agility but then smother you with a degree of complexity you might consider improbable at this age. Evidence here that Einar's will be producing some first rate whisky for years to come. Because, and this cannot be overstated, the distillate is excellent with not a fault or blemish. And the cask usage is of no less high class. A giant, and quite delicious, step forward. *59.8%. 471 bottles*

FINLAND
THE HELSINKI DISTILLING COMPANY Helsinki. Working.

The Helsinki Distilling Co Small Batch Helsinki Whiskey Rye Malt 6th Anniversary Bottling for Viskin Ystävien Seura new American oak, rum cask finish db **(90) n22 t23 f22 b23** Until I encountered this, I associated Helsinki whisky with a feinty, unbalanced whisky. Not anymore. Still a tad generous on the cut, but a massive improvement and the rye is to be found in all its most juicy glory. *59.3%. 680 bottles. Release VYS#8.*

The Helsinki Distilling Co Small Batch Helsinki Whiskey Rye Malt Finnish Summer Edition 2019 American virgin oak db **(85) n21 t23 f20 b21** Eye-watering rye intensity. But too much of a feints storm. *47.5%. 700 bottles. Release #15.*

The Helsinki Distilling Co Small Batch Helsinki Whiskey Rye Malt Special Fall Release American virgin oak, rum cask finish db **(88) n21.5 t22.5 f22 b22** Sweet, even slightly syrupy in part a little bit of extra feint doesn't help on the complexity front. That said, the sugar-pepper ratio is impressive as is the rye crescendo about five or six flavour waves in. *47.5%. Release #14.*

The Helsinki Distilling Co Small Batch Helsinki Whiskey Single Malt 4 Years Old American virgin oak, Pedro Ximénez finish db **(93) n23.5 t23 f23 b23.5** Right. How can we give our unpeated malt whisky the most massive flavour injection? Shove it into American virgin oak for maximum tannins. OK, that's done. What can we do next for a bit of dramatic overkill? PX, anyone? Right, we'll do that! I have seen similar attempts around the world come to grief. This one works, helped by this being the best quality distillate I've encountered from them yet. *47.5%. ncf. 80 bottles. Release #16.*

The Helsinki Distilling Co Small Batch Helsinki Whiskey Single Malt 4 Years Old small new French oak db **(92) n22.5 t23.5 f23 b23** Don't expect compromises: this malt fair belts it out! *56.6%. ncf. 240 bottles. Release #11.*

KYRÖ DISTILLERY COMPANY Isokyrö. Working.

Kyrö Single Malt Rye Whisky No. 6 bott code: L 30/01/19/A db **(88.5) n22 t22.5 f21.5 b22.5** Feinty to a fault, there is no criticism of the extraordinary intensity of the grain itself. If Superman drank rye whisky, it would probably be this, as the enormity of the fruity personality – so much richer from being malted (a very wise choice). Heather honey bobs in and out of this, as do some black peppers but it is the crisp sharpness of the grain which makes this malt. When they have mastered their stills to reign in the feints, this is going to be one hell of a rye whisky. Watch this space. *47.2%.*

Kyrö Single Malt Rye Whisky No. 8 bott code: L 25/07/19/A db **(88) n21.5 t22 f22.5 b22** Very interesting. Much better distillate. Not quite the bee's knees. But the feints have been reduced (if not yet eradicated), though the intensity of the rye has likewise diminished, making for a more soporific experience. Here, though, the finish picks up as the rye tones congregate, the spices tumbling into the mix, too. *47.2%.*

PANIMORAVINTOLA KOULU Turku. Working.

Sgoil Sherry Cask db **(90) n23 t23.5 f21.5 b22.5** Sherry...and clean as a whistle! A sulphur-free dram from Finland. *59%. sc. 80 bottles.*

TEERENPELI Lahti. Working.

⁂ **Teerenpeli Aged 10 Years** matured sherry & bourbon cask, batch no. 1/20, db **(91) n23** Chelsea bun. Apple strudel. This nosing lark is a piece of cake...; mind you, there also appears to be some intense malty residue complete with phantom phenols...one minute you can nose then...next you can't...; **t23** while the nose kicks off with a fruity theme before the malt takes control, the flavour profile is the exact opposite. In fact, the early barley is not only massive but gloriously well defined, benefitting from a clean, gristy sweetness. Slowly a few raisins hove into view giving a much toastier feel; **f22.5** carries on with the raisin, toasty theme; **b22.5** a well-balanced, essentially malty whisky which, like other Teerenpeli, is not done any favour by the relatively low bottling strength. *43% nc ncf*

Teerenpeli Kaski Single Malt Whisky sherry cask, bott code: 1-19 db **(95) n23.5 t23.5 f24 b24** What a stunning piece of whisky artwork. A sherry butt revelling in a glory common 30 years ago but rarer than hen's teeth today. Pure joy. *43%. nc ncf.*

⁂ **Teerenpeli Kaski Single Malt** aged in sherry cask, batch no. 3/20, db **(94.5) n23.5 t24 f23 b24** It is though one is tasting this remarkable whisky through a prism, with all its pure colours of flavour split into sharp, deeply attractive tone poems. Clarity on the palate rarely happens along by chance: someone has done some outstanding distilling and used to-die-for casks. *43% nc ncf*

⁂ **Teerenpeli Kulo Single Malt** aged in sherry cask, batch no. 2/20, db **(86) n23 t23 f19 b21** As modern classic sherry casks go, it's pretty classic...even to the extent of the distinct weakness on the finish... A shame as the nose has many of the grapey traits that once made sherry cask whisky so seductive. *50.7% nc ncf*

Teerenpeli Lemmon Lintu Double Wood bourbon & rum casks db **(91) n22.5 t23 f22.5 b23** Certainly benefits from the Murray Method. The rum casks have cordoned off much of the more complex personality, which are fully released on being warmed. Deceptively distinguished. *43%. nc ncf. Rum Cask Whisky Trilogy.*

Teerenpeli Porti Single Malt Whisky port wine cask finish, bott code: 1-19 db **(89) n21.5 t22.5 f22.5 b22.5** All a bit gung-ho and overly sharp. What it lacks in structure, it certainly makes up for in personality! *43%. nc ncf.*

Teerenpeli Savu Single Malt Whisky bott code: 1-19 db **(94) n23 t23.5 f23.5 b24** The last time I tasted this, it was a classic case of the blender not having taken into account the change in structure of a whisky when reduced down to this relatively low strength. Lessons, it appears have been learned. This is better balanced and entirely whole: a whisky much more at home with itself than had previously been the case. Someone has been to Finishing School... *43%. nc ncf.*

⁂ **Teerenpeli Savu Single Malt** peated, batch no. 1/21, db **(89) n23** exemplary. Shews off both the excellence of the actual spirit and just how cleverly this has been malted. No acrid burnt shirts from the iron here: this is of the subtlest, teasingly minty variety; **t21.5** a thinner body than the nose hints at comes as a bit of a surprise, then the smoked barley lands and the world seems a better place; **f22.5** too brief by half! However, before the flavours make their hasty exit, we get to the best bit: and excellent layering of juicy barley, chocolate mint phenols and delicate vanillas. Then, though, this basically oil-less trinity are gone leaving behind only the dull ache of spice; **b22** what a nose! A gently peated whisky even more gently delivered. Again, lapsed into a style, unlike its last bottling, that could do with upping the strength to at least 46% (preferably 50%) because in this guise the oils are slightly too broken up to give both the fuller body and length of finish it deserves. There are fine margins in getting this whisky at its best at this strength. *43% nc ncf*

Teerenpeli Single Malt Whisky Aged 10 Years db (**91**) **n23 t23.5 f21.5 b23** The last time I tasted this whisky the poor sherry casks did no favours at all. Here, if there is a sherry influence, it comes into play only at the disappointing finish: the malt and oak have by far the most important lines. A massive improvement. *43%.*

FRANCE
Single Malt
DESTILLERIE MOUTARD

⬦ **M Whisky Larché 3 Years Old** lot: WML1*18320, bott 1 Jul 17 db (**87.5**) **n21.5 t22 f22 b22** The Ark is a Triumph of tannins on both nose and finish, as they never quite dominate despite making a massive contribution. The mouth feel – indeed, the entire persona – is slightly different to any whisky I have tasted for quite a little while, boasting a milky style both at once buttery and nutty. But there are infused sugars, too, and these have probably the greatest say, of a muscovado bent. Technically questionable. But its effect, once you acclimatise, is very pleasant. *45%. sc.*

⬦ **M Whisky La Roof 3 Years Old** lot: WRO1*01821, bott 18 Jan 21 db (**84**) **n19.5 t22.5 f20.5 b21.5** Another which is, technically, all over the shop with more than the odd personality disorder. But, again, there is something strangely attractive to this whisky, mainly in the way that the sugars in an oaty-porridge way makes for a salivating and inviting chewy pleasantness, except perhaps for the butyric at the death. Whether you like this whisky or not, I'll say this for it: it is truly unique. *45%. sc.*

DISTILLERIE ARTISANALE LEHMANN Obernai. Working.
Elsass Whisky Single Malt Whisky Alsacien Premium db (**86**) **n20.5 t21.5 f22 b22.** This is about as close as you'll get to an abstract single malt. The early discordant notes of the distillate are thrown against the canvas of the malt, and then fruit is randomly hurled at it, making a juicy, then spicy, splash. The overall picture when you stand back is not at all bad. But getting there is a bit messy. *50%. ncf.*

DISTILLERIE CASTAN Villeneuve-sur-Vère. Working.
Vilanova Terrocita db (**91.5**) **n23 t23.5 f22 b23** Have to admit that this is a nose and flavour profile I have never quite encountered before. What a shame it wasn't at about 55% abv, I think we might have been heading off the planet from terra firma to terro cita... *43%. ncf.*

DISTILLERIE DE LAGUIOLE Laguiole. Working.
Esprit De Twelve Malt Spirit Like a Cognac Pineau cask db (**86**) **n21.5 t22 f21 b21.5** Malty, very clean very green – as it should be. Travelling through a relatively tame period of its development, here, where the cask is redacting rather than adding to the story. *65%. sc.*

Esprit De Twelve Malt Spirit Peat Project port cask db (**92.5**) **n23 t23.5 f23 b23** Beautifully distilled and massively impressive, at times having a touch of the Islays about it. Very youthful, of course, but where it is impresses most is the way the high phenol content appears controlled without losing any of its impact. And the clever way the sugars emerge from the smoke. The wine causes a slight wobble on the balance front, especially on immediate impact. But this beast has time in its favour. A great way to start the tasting day. *65%. sc.*

Esprit De Twelve Single Malt Whisky First Release db (**89**) **n22 t22.5 f22 b22.5** It is always such a pleasure to find a new distillery which is immediately feint-free. Still pretty much on the kindergarten side of things. But there is a joy to the free-handedness of the barley and the openness of the sugars against the weightier oak. When aged slightly longer this malt has the ability to move on to greater things. *47%.*

DISTILLERIE DE PARIS Paris. Working.
Distillerie De Paris Whisky Paris Single Malt db (**89**) **n21 t23 f22 b23** Usually distilleries are named after remote hamlets or villages, located as they are in the countryside where modest streams provide the cooling water and just enough people live roundabout to be

employed there. Calling yourself Paris Distillery is another way of doing it....if you want to make a statement! And the whisky seems to reflect this mode of thought as this is big, earthy stuff which pumps its chest out early and is determined to make its way in the whisky world. A distillery to keep a watchful gaze upon... 43%.

DISTILLERIE DES MENHIRS Bretagne. Working.

Eddu Brocéliande pure buckwheat aged for 5 years in French oak, bott code: L2052, db (86) n21 t22 f21.5 b21.5 As clankingly heavy and ungainly as their Ed Gwenn is as clean, delicate, and fragile: the opposite end of this distillery's spectrum. The wide cut gives nutty and chewy personality to this, as does the unwieldly molasses 43%

Eddu Gold db (93) n22 t23 f24 b24. Rarely do whiskies turn up in the glass so rich in character to the point of idiosyncrasy. Some purists will recoil from the more assertive elements. I simply rejoice. This is so proud to be different. And exceptionally good, to boot!! 43%

Eddu Gold pure buckwheat aged for 10 years in French oak, db (95.5) n24 brilliant, quite brilliant! Such complexity! Somehow, this whisky imparts very good age, but at the same time a fragility you wouldn't believe possible. Sniff too hard and the light gooseberry note might snap in two, drawn too hard on sugars and the gristiness might crumble to bits. A little muscovado sugars aid the tannins....; t24 perfectly weighted distillate boasting just the right oils to form both a platform for maximum length. Ulmo and acacia honey combine, then a shock of lemon bon bon. Towards the middle the grain and the tannins combine for a wave of spiced butterscotch tart; f23.5 much drier now, though a delicate minty chocolate note persists. The sawdusty late vanillas, still bring a citrussy imprint, excel...; b24 and when they say Gold, they aren't joking. The whole structure of this whisky, from nose to finish is like a house of cards... Magnifique! 43%

Eddu Grey Rock db (87.5) n21.5 t22 f22 b22. A docile whisky reliant on friendly muscovado sugars which match the vanilla-oak very attractively.40%

Eddu Grey Rock Affinage Porto db (83) n19 t21 f22 b21 Tasting whisky from this distillery is like taking part in a lucky dip: no idea if you'll pick a winner or the booby prize. This has the uncontrollable nose of a dud, as does the fruit helps it pick up on the palate to an acceptable level. Good late spices, too. 40%.

Eddu Grey Rock Brocéliande db (86.5) n22 t22.5 f20.5 b21.5. Dense whisky which enjoys an enjoyable molassed fruitcake theme. A bit thin and wonky towards the finish.40%

Ed Gwenn Whisky D'orge distilled from pure barley aged for 4 years in French and American oak casks, bott code: L2121, db (91.5) n23 gooseberry and grist.... wonderful! t23.5 supremely clean, salivating grist melts on the tongue with light muscovado sugar and ulmo honey for company; f22.5 this is where such a clean malt from old casks so often goes wrong as the spirit leaches into the more bitter elements. Not this time! Remains sweet as a nut...indeed, with the grist going the distance, a lot sweeter. Some lovely spices buzz in for good measure b22.5 the colour of Riesling, this promises a juicy barleyfest...and there are no disappointments. The cleanest, juiciest French whisky of the year. Beautifully made...and bravely matured! 45%

Eddu Silver pure buckwheat aged for 5 years in cognac casks, bott code: L2113, db (89.5) n21.5 doesn't hit the normal harmony I expect from Silver: untidy, nougat-rich and heady; t22.5 recovers beautifully not just from the nose, but the very first tangy notes on delivery. The grain kicks in with a bread pudding spiciness and gristy sweetness. The vanilla of the oak adds control...; f22.5 long with more generous honey to balance the spices; b23 not the great Edu Silvers I have enjoyed in times past. But still, plenty of entertainment value, if a little clumsy in its execution. 43%

Eddu Silver Broceliande db (92.5) n23 t23 f23 b23.5 Pure silk. A beautiful and engaging experience. 40%.

Eddu Silver The Original db (92.5) n23 t23 f23.5 b23 J'adore! 40%.

DISTILLERIE DU PÉRIGOLD Sarlat. Working.

Lascaw Blended Malt Whisky Aged 12 Years finished in Perigord truffle flavoured speciality oak barrels, bott 10/12/2019, bott code: L 65752/05/00 db (91.5) n23.5 t22 f23 b23 Usually I get my truffles when breakfasting at Claridge's in London, their delicate tones emanating from my stupendous Eggs Benedict. I have to confess that I cannot be certain if what I get on the nose is that rare and celebrated fungus. But what I cannot deny is that this malt does have a certain je ne sais quoi, ensuring far above average complexity and grace. Mind you, at 46% this would be so much better... 40%.

Lascaw Blended Malt Whisky Aged 15 Years finished in Perigord truffle flavoured speciality oak barrels, bott 04/11/2019, bott code: L 63865/05/00 db (86) n22.5 t22.5 f20 b21 Nowhere near as finely structured as their 12-year-old and a bit of a slave to the bitterness which seems to be a threat throughout but arrives late and decisively. There is a lovely praline moment, though, as the malt peaks. *40%.*

DISTILLERIE ERGASTER Passel. Working.
ER 2015 Single Malt Whisky Tourbé No. 001 db **(94)** n23.5 t23.5 f23 b24 Magnifique! A stunning first bottling from Ergaster. Very much their own style of peatiness...and what style! Encore! *45%. 1,900 bottles.*

DISTILLERIE GILBERT HOLL Ribeauvillé. Working.
Lac'Holl Vieil Or 10 Years Old Single Malt Whisky db **(92.5)** n22.5 t23.5 f23 b23.5 A malt which gives one's taste buds a real working over. Superb balance. *42%*

Lac'Holl 15 Years Old Single Malt Whisky db **(90.5)** n23.5 t22.5 f22 b22.5 Such a rare display of barley and gristy sugars. Very impressive malt. And fabulously refreshing. *42%*

DISTILLERIE GLANN AR MOR Larmor-Pleubian. Working.
◇ **Glann ar Mor Single Malt Bourbon Barrel** bott 2021, db **(87)** n22 t22.5 f21 b21.5 Still a long way from the honeyed greatness that this brand for so long exhibited. The extra width on the cut has ensured a little toffee-nougat is mixed in with the massive malt. Much more chewy, cumbersome and, finally, bitter than had long been its trademark, but at least doesn't stint on the malt. *46%*

◇ **Glann ar Mor Single Malt Pedro Ximenez Finish 2021** bourbon barrel, PX cask finish, bott 2021, db **(92.5)** n23 moist sultana-rich fruitcake; t23.5 succulent and sweet, as you might imagine, but the early arrival of perfectly weighted spices is a surprise. The malt protrudes through like bedrock through a vineyard...; f23 one of the most subtle and sophisticated finishes to a PX cask I have come across for a good while. The malt really is in full song now...; b23 once more, this distillery has managed to find an absolutely top quality PX cask – vitally, without even the faintest hint of sulphur. It is absolutely taint free...so rare! Being a finish, the malt itself has had time to build up enough weight and body to carry the grape without being crushed by it. Silky, fruity, and always thoroughly enjoyable. Massively impressed by this. *56.3% sc*

◇ **Kornog Single Malt Oloroso Finish 2019** peated, bourbon barrel, sherry oloroso butt finish, bott 2019, db **(96)** n23 a little peat, a little anthracite, a little grape....and a whole lot of elegance and complexity; t24 astonishingly salivating. At first, we have the unlikely arrival of Malteser candy, the milky chocolate the perfect foil for both the layered smoke and the sultana. The required oils to make this mingle with minimum traction are near perfect; f24.5 one of the best finishes of the year from any distillery on the planet. It is like a rainbow suddenly appearing, its colours getting more vivid and then reluctantly fading. In no particular order you will find light peach juice, smoked of course; both praline and chocolate nut and raisin b24.5 at normal temperature, by this distillery's exacting and demanding standards, a malt ordinaire. The nose, while smoky, is flat. The palate, while silky and sweet, simply too one dimensional. But the Murray Method changes that dramatically and now we can see the finish alone is worthy of a place in the Louvre, rather than your glass... Improves as it goes along, especially on the peaty fruitcake finish and is so magnificently layered. And, delighted to report yet again, not a single atom of sulphur to be found: this is top rate sherry cask added to the mix. Reveals with growing confidence that unique Kornog brilliance. So much so, that this is not only their best whisky for quite a while, it is undoubtedly one of the greatest whiskies I have tasted this year. *46%* ☗

◇ **Kornog Single Malt Pedro Ximenez 2020** peated, sherry PX butt, bott 2020, db **(95)** n23.5 sharp, acidic, fascinating, and threatening. The smoke really is loath to give any ground to the fat grape; t23.5 a sumptuous oil slick of a delivery. Fat, lush and stand-your-spoon-in grape, though the sugars are refined. Or perhaps I mean unrefined, for there is certainly some molasses at work. While from the very first moment the smoke puffs, bellows an encircles...; f24 only towards the finish does the peat actually take control. A subtext of toffee and vanilla melts into praline...; b24 PX and peat. Nearly always less a tale of harmony as one of open warfare. And though it may be on the nose, against the mid-arrival weapons have been down and compromise has been reached. So rare do I find a PX cask which is involved with complexity. And yet here one is. For this is very, very complex, indeed... *56.2% sc*

◇ **Kornog Single Malt Roc'h Hir 2021** peated, bourbon barrel, bott 2021, db **(94)** n24 glorious: it is like dozing by a peat fire, the reek offering a comforting blanket of warmth. Salty and even very slightly honeyed, this is a brilliant blend of confidence and subtlety; t23.5 sweet grist melts in the mouth and though the delicate barley sugars never fade, the smoke, gentler than you might expect from the nose, grows; f23 dries as a late saltiness also arrives. A little mocha mixes with the phenols; b23.5 under new ownership this distillery may be –

and even found now with a change of name – but the exceptionally high quality of the Glann Ar Mor it was distilled as has not been remotely compromised. Excellent. *46%*

⬩ **Kornog Single Malt Roc'h Hir 2019** peated, bourbon barrel, bott 2019, db **(95)** n23.5 the amalgamation of citrus and peat charms and delights in equal measures; t24 much more peaty punch on delivery than on the nose. This is magnificently intense, which chocolate arriving early and in no hurry to depart. The saltiness intensifies the malt dramatically and has a similar effect on the tannins as it slowly makes its entrance; f23.5 long, layered, spicy, cocoa-rich and, for all the peat, malty to the last....; b24 another world class malt from this world class French distillery... *63.1% sc*

⬩ **Kornog Single Malt Sant Erwan 2021** peated, bourbon barrel, bott 2021, db **(95.5)** n24 as coastal in style as any home-matured Islay, the spread of the saline sharpness amid the ulmo honey, grist and breezy peat reek is such a treat; t24 just about a perfect mouth feel. Just the right amount of light oils to give length and weight. A little citrus on the gristy malt moves towards smoked mocha; f23.5 more lightly peated mocha on the beautifully smoked grist...; b24 a growling, heavyweight of a malt which shows the peat in full muscular fashion. And with no shortage of hairs for good measure. However, it is the clever control of the honey that sets this one apart and ensure that this is a heavyweight with a gentle touch. Just brilliant. *50% sc*

DISTILLERIE GRALLET-DUPIC Rozelieures. Working.

G.Rozelieures Whisky De Lorraine Single Malt Whisky bott code: L446 db **(87)** n21.5 t22.5 f21 b22. Exceptionally nutty. The blossoming of the sugars on delivery is always attractive, as are the complex nougat/caramel/cocoa tones. Though the feints are always a threat, the genteel pace and softness of the malt makes it well worth a look. *40%*

DISTILLERIE HEPP VUM MODERTAL Uberach. Working.

Authentic Whisky D'Alsace Whisky Single Malt Doble Fût No. 7 db **(87)** n21 t23 f21 b22 A much more complete malt than their No.6. The nose is a tad austere and, again, the finale requires a fire extinguisher as the degree of burn increases. But there is no doubting the beauty and integrity of the delivery, a kind of malt and chocolate bonbon, even with a Milky Way element. My word it's hot, though. *40%. ncf.*

DISTILLERIE J.ET M. LEHMANN Obernai. Working.

Elsass Single Malt Whisky Gold Aged 7 Years Bordeaux Blanc finition db **(90)** n23 t22.5 f22 b22.5 Deceptive and delicious. *40%.*

Elsass Single Malt Whisky Origine Aged 7 Years Bordeaux Blanc barrel db **(90.5)** n23 t23 f22b22.5 A picture of understated elegance. *40%.*

Elsass Single Malt Whisky Premium Aged 8 Years Sauternes barrel db **(94.5)** n23 t24 f23.5 b24 There is no finer wine cask in which to mature whisky than a clean Sauternes one. This does nothing to undermine my argument. Truly superb. *50%.*

DISTILLERIE MEYER Hohwarth. Working.

⬩ **Meyer's Le Whisky Artisanal Hohwarth Blend Superieur (91.5)** n22.5 delicate with a light, spiced sultana fruitcake sweetness; t23 a genteel delivery, full of finesse and good manners. The muscovado sugars melt in the mouth which a slightly weightier vanilla sub-strata makes the oak easier to identify; f23 the lightest ulmo honey, vanilla, and spice... so soothing...; b23 clean, silky and beautifully structured, this allows the cask to relax. The sweetness ensures a charm that hints at rather than states a fruity persona. *40%*

⬩ **Meyer's Le Whisky Artisanal Affinage En Fût De Sauternes Finition En Fût Bourgogne** db **(88)** n21 t22 f23 b22 Has more fruit pastel characteristics than a fruit pastel. The nose is gorily off key thanks to a broad cut off the stills. But it recovers as the concentrated malt begins to find its range with the fruit. Slowly, though, those fruit notes take control – save a little spice off the cask – as the whisky recovers beautifully. *40%*

⬩ **Meyer's Le Whisky Artisanal Hohwarth Blend Affinage En Fût De Sauternes Superieur Finition Pinot Noir** db **(89)** n22.5 this has been re-shaped by a beautifully bold Pinot cask which has dried and hardened the grapey outline: wonderfully attractive; t23 mouth-filling and rich on deliver, the Sauternes springs into action immediately with an unmistakable sweetness which is further by ulmo honey and grist. That starker grape note on the nose arrives a little later to firm things up. Good spice, too...; f21 just a little tang from the cask towards the end counts as a blemish, but the fruit from the Pinot persists; b22.5 shame about the late S note late on. However, it is relatively light and, on this occasion, doesn't entirely undo the great work by the two cask combination. Rather enjoyable. *40%*

⬩ **Meyer's Le Whisky Alsacien Pur Malt No 05297** db **(85)** n21.5 t22.5 f20 b21 I was hoping Percy, my Meyer's parrot, would be happier with this bottling than in previous years.

But he's a bit of perfectionist is my Percy, and he certainly doesn't regard this malt as a pretty boy. He's big into seeds, grain and fruit so rather loves the delivery, with its intense citrus-lightened maltiness. But he is still turning his beak up at the nose and finish due to a far too generous cut from the still leaving quite a bitter aftertaste. 40%

⬧ **Meyer's Le Whisky Alsacien Pur Malt Affinage En Fût De Sauternes Finition En Fût Bourgogne No1291** bott code: L1922596 67430A db (**88.5**) n22 t22.5 f22 b22 As soft an even a whisky as you are likely to find. Curiously, this has a far lighter body than other similar bottlings which means it struggles to get up a head of steam. But there is something very attractive about the sugar candy fruitiness of this blend. Cleansing the palate as it does, it is almost the perfect aperitif. 40%.

Meyer's Le Whisky Artisanal Pur Malt No. 08720 bott code: L1931996 67430A db (**85.5**) n21 t22.5 f20.5 b21.5 Definitely an improvement on their last similar bottling. But still those feints bite deep, though now at least the barley has far more thrust than before, giving the odd delightful moment on delivery. Frustrating, as you get the feeling they could have a really top class malt here. 40%.

UNSPECIFIED

Évadé Whisky Français Peated Single Malt db (**87.5**) n21.5 t23 f21 b22 A distinct trace of bittering tobacco running through this as the extra oils make their mark: indeed the smoke, to a non-smoker like me, has a little more to do with Gauloises than peat. But there is no denying the beauty of the delivery where the barley has been expanded for maximum flavour and the sub-plot of phenol carries delicate Demerara sugars. The bitter finish, though, is a tad tardy by comparison. 43%. *Whiskies du Monde.*

Évadé Whisky Français Single Malt bott code: 1945WDMNT db (**89**) n22 t22.5 f22 b22.5 Even at 40%, this has a robust quality which matches the intensity of the barley. Attractive. And certainly not a malt to evade. 40%. *Whiskies du Monde.*

Maison Benjamin Kuentz Aux Particules Vines Single Malt Whisky Edition 2 finished in a Grand vin de Bordeaux rouge barrel for 18 months (**84.5**) n20.5 t20.5 f22 b21.5 Struggles initially to find its feet. A light feint note on the nose, though a vague hickory note steadies it slightly; and it is no more precise or happy on delivery. But from the midpoint matters take an upturn as vanilla and grape melt together attractively while the oils keep the sugars on a long lead. 579%. sc.

Maison Benjamin Kuentz Aux Particules Vines Single Malt Whisky Edition 3 Macvin barrel, finished in a Grand vin de Bordeaux rouge barrel for 8 months (**87**) n22 t21.5 f21.5 b22 The Bordeaux barrel has a far more significant impact after eight months than Edition 2 managed in more than twice that time. Grinds around the palate in the house style, but cannot but enjoy the Turkish Delight/Chocolate Liqueur feel to the midpoint and finish on this one. Tasty! 46%. sc.

⬧ **Maison Benjamin Kuentz Aux Particules Vines Edition 5 Blended Whisky** finished in Lafon-Rochet barrels (**89**) n22 malt and butterscotch combine quite sensually; t22.5 super-soft delivery. Young, a little aimless at first but settles on exactly the same path as the nose with a some cocoa thrown in for good measure; f22 warming with a late jammy flourish; b22.5 pleasant and salivating, the spices are just kept in check by the fresh fruitiness. 46%

⬧ **Maison Benjamin Kuentz Aux Particules Vines Edition 6 Single Malt** finished in red wine barrels (**86.5**) n22.5 t22 f20.5 b21.5 On the nose the grape takes advantage of the light clean body. While on delivery there is sweet, succulent boiled fruit candy. Light tannins add a backbone and weight, The midpoint is not unlike the old sherry trifles of long ago; Finishes with aggressive spices and cherry. These whiskies have their own very unusual foibles. So many enjoyable outlines, but never seems to connect up to a main body. Great fun, though. 52%

⬧ **Maison Benjamin Kuentz Aveux Gourmands Single Malt** finished in Rayne-Vigneau barrels (**88**) n22 t21 f23 b22 Sometimes, as seriously as I take my work, you sometimes just have to laugh. Just recovering from the ploughing my tastebuds had received from the fish on their Cognac cask version, we now travel 180 degrees to a whisky which struggles on delivery, but positively massages your taste buds at the finish into whimpering, ecstatic submission. When I say, "struggles on delivery", what I mean is that the mouth feel on arrival is so uniquely slick and oily, that the mouth is momentarily thrown into confusion, and you have problems registering the actual taste. The nose is a little different, too: a vague maltiness mixed with an earthy-vegetable note. After the confusion of the delivery, the malt stakes its claim and builds up with a deliciously concentrated gristiness. You can certainly depend on Maison Benjamin for broadening your whisky horizons... 46%

⬧ **Maison Benjamin Kuentz Fin de Partie Single Malt** ex cognac, bourbon, PX, oloroso and new oak barrels (**94**) n23 t24 f23 b24 Someone has done a truly exceptional job in bringing all these cask types together and creating a malt as exceptionally balanced as this. Usually, such ventures are more likely to end in tears of disappointment than delight. Not this time. The nose has great fund bowling out various grapey sugars in tandem with a pasty, thick maltiness. At times you wonder, even, if some phenol has crept in from somewhere or whether it is a freak by-product of mixed tannins. But it is the delivery and follow-through which stuns: woven silk of salivating grape and malt purring through with varying levels of intensity. There is a hotness which reflects not so well on the distillate itself. But still the tastebuds are worked over by a chocolate milkshake of the British school and then a maltshake of the American, which fruitier sugars ping around like a British NHS ap. Wonderfully flawed. But the price to pray for such brilliant balance. *46%*

⬦ **Maison Benjamin Kuentz Inouïe Mélodie Single Malt** finished in red wine barrels **(87.5) n22.5 t22.5 f21 b21.5** Despite the house hotness and bite on delivery, the remainder of the story lacks many thrills and spills. Very warm whisky which is worth a go just for that astonishingly tart fruit explosion on delivery. Have a hanky on hand to dab away a tear. *46% sc*

⬦ **Maison Benjamin Kuentz Vegetal Musette 3 Year Old Single Malt** aged in cognac barrels **(87.5) n22.5 t22 f21 b22** An outline feintiness gets the oils all in a dither. These work better on the nose, where a sticky gently spiced kumquat note quite impresses, than on the ultimately austere palate. Once past the chewy and intense malt on delivery – which appears to have a monopoly on the sugars - we are into slightly roughhouse territory. Still, the one thing that can't be levelled at this malt is dullness. Nor technical perfection. *45%*

Vatted Malts
Bellevoye Bleu Whisky Triple Malt Finition Grain Fin bott code: A18184A **(87.5) n21.5 t22 f22 b22** Goes pretty hefty on the tobacco note on both nose and delivery. But the wide cut delivers impressively on the chocolate nougat and even, surprisingly, a degree of chewy date alongside the malt. *40%*.

Bellevoye Blanc Whisky Triple Malt Finition Sauternes bott code: A18199A **(82.5) n20 t21.5 f21 b20** I am tasting in the near dark here for maximum sensory effect – and this one nearly knocked me off my chair. Certainly one of the strangest malts I have tasted this year with the most vividly citrusy nose on a Sauternes finish I have ever encountered – almost like washing up liquid. To say this whisky has a clean nose would be an understatement... Malty on the palate, but never quite feels right.*40%*.

Bellevoye Rouge Whisky Triple Malt Finition Grand Cru bott code: A18200A **(83) n21.5 t22 f19.5 b20** Despite the Grand Cru, there Smoke Blue as a tobacco element makes an undesired contribution. The fruit is sweet and intense, though. The finish a bit of a mess. *43%*

Bellevoye Noir Whisky Triple Malt Édition Tourbée bott code: A18232A **(87) n22.5 t22 f21 b21.5** There is a certain primitive quality to the peatiness which, for all its simplistic naivety, packs no end of charm. Lots of toffee kicks in, reducing the complexity somewhat. But that peat, flighty on the nose and warming on the palate, has a distinctly more-ish quality. *43%*.

GERMANY
ALTE HAUSBRENNEREI A. WECKLEIN Arnstein. Working.
Wecklain A.54 Rushburn Frankonian Single Malt barrels 8 & 19, bott code LN 1005-17 db **(90) n23.5 t23 f21.5 b23** A very different, highly evocative whisky. *43%. 650 bottles.*

BIRGITTA RUST PIEKFEINE BRÄNDE Bremen. Working.
Van Loon 5 Year Old Single Malt Whisky batch 2012 db **(85) n21.5 t22 f20 b21.5** Usually, a little extra strength will greatly enhance a complex whisky - if given time in the glass. The exception is when the cut is already a little too wide, resulting in a lumpy, ultimately bitter effort. Where this does benefit is in the richness of the fruit and the light mocha effect. *55%*.

BLACK FOREST WHISKEY Neubulach. Working
⬦ **Doinich Daal Blackforest Single Malt Erbenwald** aged in ex wine, whisky & bourbon casks, finished in virgin casks, batch no.05, db **(94) n23.5** adorably attractive, clean grape intertwangling with effortless grace with crisp barley and light vanillas. Complex with much going on below surface...; **t23.5** the nose promised this would be a mouth-watering whisky, and so it proves. Just as on the nose both the grape and grain are in seamless cahoots. The lightest thread of heather honey works in beautiful tandem with the fragile tannins. Excellent spices are on cue...; **f23** medium length, free from an oils or bitterness the gentlest mocha joins the fade...; **b24** keeps a decent weight thorough out yet is never less than elegant. Wonderfully complex with refined layering. Genuinely impressive and beautiful whisky. *46% ncf 200 bottles*

⬦ **Doinich Daal Blackforest Single Malt Krabbawäldle** fine smoked malt from traditional Black Forest smoking, batch no.05, db **(88) n21.5 t22 f22.5 b22** It is too easy to equate the Blackforest with chocolate, but here you have no option. The cut is a little generous, which in itself lets in not just extra oils and spices but a hint of nougat. It is towards the middle light praline and vague heather honey combine for a delightful finale with an excellently weighted sweetness. The smoke, incidentally, is enigmatic. *43.5% ncf 120 bottles*

◇ **Doinich Daal Blackforest Single Malt Moosäcker** aged in ex wine, cognac & bourbon casks, finished in apple aperitif casks, batch no.05, db **(91.5) n23** this distillery loves playing games with the nose. Another teasing offering with the nose buds are gently kissed by grape and barley, the wine casks being the more passionate; **t23.5** full throttle juiciness at work here. The wine cask appears to have a huge say in this one and though the malt has a presence, it is the tartness of the grape which ultimately shapes the story; **f22** just a slight overenthusiastic tang from the wine cask, though nothing damaging. For once the late chocolate style is foresaken; **b23** usually, casks involved with apples either from their wood or content, impart a certain personality on the whisky. Not so much from this distillery, save a light brushing of delicate, fruity sugars. It is present here, as is with their Erbenwald...but you have to work very hard to find it. *40% ncf 950 bottles*

◇ **Doinich Daal Blackforest Single Malt Tannenrein** aged in ex wine, whisky & bourbon casks, finished in apple aperitif casks, batch no.05, db **(92) n23** apple blossom honey and spiced butterscotch. Just a pinch of salt sharpens it very slightly. So elegant...; **t23.5** a fabulous cut gives ulmo honey and grist a very impressive head start. The spices are not massive, but don't have to be to make an impression against such a quiet backdrop...; **f22.5** back to vanilla and light apple; **b23** you have to laugh: having on my previous tasting noted how the apple aperitif casks have played little part in the whiskies I had so far tasted from this distillery, the last one is just awash with the stuff...My word, I am so very impressed with this distillery! *42.5% ncf 250 bottles*

BRENNEREI AM FEUERGRABEN Achern. Working.

◇ **Salamansar Germanica Single Malt 8 Years Old** double wood vintage Port finish, db **(91.5) n22.5** attractive chocolate fruitcake...with no shortage of burnt raisins; **t23** there appeared to a hidden phenolic note on the nose, and there appears to be a faux one here, also. But the brain is guided principally to the industrial scale salivating properties of the malt itself, aided and abetted by intense cake-like spices; **f23** a little golden syrup with the malt, chocolate and spice...; **b23** on its day, this distillery is capable of excellence. Pretty much on its day here... *45.5%*

◇ **Salamansar Orion Single Malt 6 Years Old** port finish, db **(93) n23.5** incredibly intense fruit: salted gooseberries with a little custard on the side...; **t23.5** the salt on the nose prewarns of sharpness to come. And this malt tells no lies: this is a clean delivery. There is a brief puff of barley which perfectly matches the clean, precision bombing of the taste buds; **f23** a lovely salty, fruity, spicy fade....; **b23** the saltiness on this at times suggests it was finished in a port, rather than Port finished. A very bright, complex and satisfying whisky. *42%*

◇ **Salamanser Single Malt 5 Years Old** 2 years new barrel, 18-month PX barrel, 18 months oloroso barrel, sherry finish, db **(89) n21.5** for five year old malt which has spent a couple of years in virgin oak, this is surprisingly flat; **t22** the sugary incantation of the silky grape has PX stamped all over it. The spicier, lighter raisins, suggests oloroso; **f23** at last the tannins battle through the grapey shield. Much more layering and structure here: an entertaining finale...; **b22.5** can't help getting the feeling that although the PX cask has given this both length and sweetness – and a very yielding body – it has possibly taken away the very best and most complex contribution by the new oak, also. Pleasant, but over graped. *40%*

Salamansar Septem Ignis Single Malt Whisky bott code: L99 db **(86) n21.5 t22.5 f20.5 b21.5** A little kink in the distillation is revealed on both nose and finish. But no quibbles about the barley intensity which rises like mercury in the Sahara... *45%.*

Salamansar Single Cask Whisky Batch no. 1 triple wood Jamaican rum finish, bott code: L19/22 db **(94.5) n23.5 t24 f23 b24** Most whiskies which claim "rum finish" or "Jamaican Rum finish" rarely show little more than a firm, sugary coating. This reminds me of the days in the early '90s when I was in Jamaica putting rum together. This has a kind of Longpond feel to it, with its elongated sweetness and gentle esters. Adorable whisky, which was very well distilled, incidentally. *42%. sc.*

Salamansar Single Malt Whisky Batch no. 3 triple wood, bott code: L19/24 db **(85.5) n22 t23 f19 b21.5** If they didn't know in Germany what a British "Jammy Dodger" smells like, then they do now. Fat, mildly unctuous and makes excellent play between the barley, grape and vanillas. Until the finale this is creamy, jammy and entertaining. Such a shame about the late sulphurous intervention. *43.7%. sc.*

BERGHOF RABEL Owen-Teck. Working.

Whisky Stube Spirit of the Cask OWEN Albdinkel Jamaika rum fass finish, destillert am 01/2012, abgefüllt am 11/2017 **(90) n21.5 t23 f22.5 b23** The spirit is not exactly faultless. But a stupendous rum cask has generated a treasure chest of untold honeyed riches. *46%.*

BOSCH-EDELBRAND Unterlenningen. Working

◈ **Whisky Stube Spirit Of The Cask Gelber Fels Whisky** French limousin oak, dist Oct 2014, bott Nov 2020, bott code: L01B11R20 (85.5) n20.5 t22.5 f21 b21.5 Not the first and won't be the last European whisky to fail slightly on the nose due to an over-exaggerated cut...and then blow you away with the enormity on the palate. The grain is not only intense, it appears to double up and come back at you again, this time bringing with it a light dose of acacia honey. With a wide cut comes the inevitable untidy finish. But a shrinking violet this is not... 60.9%

BRENNEREI FELLER Dietenheim-Regglisweiler. Working

Feller Valerie Amarome Cask Single Malt db (91) n23 t23 f22 b23 This is one spicy Feller! 59%. nc ncf.

◈ **Feller Single Malt Torf** bourbon cask, dist Aug 2017, db (95) n24 just amazing... dry enough to make you nose bleed. The nip has nothing to do with the alcohol: this is about the acidity of the anthracite and peat mix. Another example of its excellence is the slow, deft arrival of sugars. Impossible to spot unless you are able to park the smoke to one side...; t23.5 the deployment of heather honey to pave the way for the peat is a masterstroke...; salivating and more layers than you can shake a peat cutter at...; f23.5 long...meandering... even slightly creamy despite the best drying intention of the peat. Just a little saltiness late on as the vanilla at last turns up; b24 if anyone is tasting this and disliking it because it is not like an Islay, then may I have a short word with you: this is not an Islay. It is from Germany. And, therefore, has a style all its own. Of that European type of highly acidic, dryly smoked whiskies this is – again – an exceptional example. It is worth spending time to get to know the unique idiosyncrasies of these types of whisky, rather than comparing it to Scotch. Another true classic of its type. 65.8% nc ncf

Feller Torf Single Malt bourbon cask, bott code los 2911 db (94) n24 t23.5 f23 b23.5 What a gorgeous whisky! Adorable because it is as deft as it is enormous. 48%. nc ncf.

◈ **Feller Single Malt Valerie Madeira** Cask 2 years bourbon cask, 5 years madeira cask finish, dist Mar 2014, db (96) n23.5 good grief: they have struck gold with this cask: not an off note and so much spice to accompany the honeyed grape. The spirit itself battles through, though its signature is weak; t24.5 a kind of cross between a glass of high-class madeira and madeira trifle (as opposed to sherry). Strands of salt, ulmo honey, the lightest red liquorice and molasses can be detected; f24 more dark liquorice now, manuka honey....and the most elegant grape; b24 no matter how long this distillery produces whisky, it will never find a better madeira cask than this. It is faultless. Rich enough to impart the very highest wine influence while just light enough to allow some aspect of the distillery to break through to increase complexity. It took me over half an hour to taste this one. The tasting notes were originally three times the length of this, but I pruned it back for space. Whoever chose this Madeira cask, please take a bow...! 65.4% nc ncf

◈ **Feller Single Malt Valerie Rye Malt** 6 years bourbon cask, dist Jan 2015, db (91) n22 surprisingly hesitant aroma: the rye not sure whether to stick or bust against the solid tannin; t23 wonderfully lush, thus allowing the enormous, malted rye flavour maximum contact with the palate, as it sticks to every crevice. A little salt and vanilla sharpens the effect further, though it is the manuka honey with the biggest say. The rye tones never for a moment let up...; f23 toasted honeycomb and muscovado sugars; b23 a notch up on their last bottling with their grain and honey ramping up the flavour profile. But it's unwavering confidence of the grains which really catch the eye...and palate. 64.9% nc ncf

◈ **Feller Single Malt Valerie Sherry Cask** 2 years bourbon cask, 3 years sherry cask finish, dist Jan 2016, db (92.5) n22.5 a classic cream sherry lilt; t23 such a soft touch to the sweetness, such a delicate flourish to the sherried signature; such polite intervention from the oak....; f23.5 long, and here it stars as the malt is at its maximum intensity despite the close attention of the first-rate grape. A rare treat of a finish...beautifully even, two...; b23.5 a few years back, seeing the finish of a sherry cask finish highest than the delivery would have been just about unheard of, such was the dire state of the sulphur situation. Not today. Here's another distillery that has gone to pains to locate a clean, untainted sherry cask....and the excellence of this malt is the reward. 62.7% nc ncf

BRENNEREI HENRICH Kriftel, Hessia. Working.

◈ **Gilors Single Malt Islay Cask Finish** ex Islay fass, dist Jul 2013, bott Oct 2019, db (86) n21 t21.5 f22 b21.5 Pleasantly malty. But the disjointed nose and slightly over enthusiastic oils limits promise and growth. 45%

◈ **Gilors Single Malt Peated Fassstärke** bourbon fass, dist 2012 & 2013, bot May 2021, db (88.5) n22 t22.5 f22 b22 There is no doubting the singular style of the peat to this distillery's whisky: not the kind of phenol to lull you into a smoky comfort zone; more one bite acidly into both the nose and palate. This is especially true on the stark aroma, though the eye-watering delivery leaves you in no doubt that you are in the presence of malt with little inclination to take prisoners. A butterscotch-barley note – perhaps sweetened by thin ulmo honey - settles down the fuss somewhat. 54.9%

◇ **Gilors Single Malt Peated Madeira** Madeira fass, Dist Dec 2016, bott May 2021, db **(90) n22.5** punchy and acidic, the peat has an extraordinary dry and biting quality. The fruit at this stage hardly gets a look in; **t23** brilliant! The barley sugar is absolutely in sync with the phenols to give a friendly side to the otherwise storming peat. Butterscotch leads, apologetically, to light sultana; **f22** vanilla and spiced peat dries; **b22.5** a better distillate than in previous years takes this malt up another gear. Most enjoyable – and not a gremlin to be found. 45.3%

◇ **Gilors Single Malt Portwein Fass** dist Nov 2015, bott Jan 2021, db **(86.5) n20 t23 f21.5 b22** Once you get past the nose it is plane sailing. The aroma simply doesn't work, but the malt rallies charmingly on delivery which enjoys a lovely cherry candy fruitiness. A little Jekyll and Hide it might be. But the good moments are very good... 43%

◇ **Gilors Single Malt Sherry Duett** PX fass & olorosso fass, dist 2013 & 2014, bott May 2021, db **(89) n21.5 t23 f21.5 b23** I have often been asked if I'd like some nuts with my sherry. And here I been presented with it as a fete accompli. The nose isn't the easier work. And there is a slight niggle to the finale, too. Nut such is the thoroughness of the barley, such is the understatement of the molasses, such is the purity of the strands of fruit...it all works rather well. And it looks like it was that nuttiness that cracked it... 46.4%

BRENNEREI ZIEGLER Freudenberg, North Württemberg. Working.

Aureum Single Malt Whisky 6 Year Old Chestnut Cask db **(91.5) n23 t23 f22.5 b23** I have long been an admirer of chestnut matured whisky, having first come across it at a remote and little-known distillery in Austria nearly 25 years ago. After all this time, this gorgeous malt reaffirms my attraction to these casks. The house creamy style is maintained as a constant. But the configuration of malt and sugars now takes on a very different shape; even the sweetness has a very tone and one, not surprisingly, unique to cask. Here the sugars boast a light lemon blossom honey tone before natural caramels intermingle... and then the malty essence of grist. No off notes from spirit of cask and despite the unique tannin character the malt is allowed to fly its flag without interference. Charming and a chestnut cask bottling that conkers many others... 48%.

Aureum Single Malt Whisky 6 Year Old Peated db **(90.5) n22.5 t22.5 f22.5 b23** It's the creaminess on the palate which provides the surprise package here. And probably the shyness of the peat, too. Despite its relatively tenders years, the tannins have impacted with a degree of force but have brought with the extra sugars to prop up the gristier notes. Beautifully made and fascinating cask integration of black peppers and brown sugars. The late arrival of vanilla and butterscotch tart underlines the point. A lovely cask, but the wine does take away very slightly from the malty charm of their standard bottlings. 48%.

Aureum Single Malt Whisky 8 Year Old Portwine Cask db **(89) n22.5 t23 f21 b22.5** To get to the vital things first: a sound cask with no off notes. That established we can thoroughly enjoy this lively malt where the Port at times threatens overkill, but a fightback of intense barley alongside the big spice and molasses means complexity always remains the leading light. A little bitterness on the finish, though thankfully it isn't sulphur. 59.2%.

Aureum Single Malt Whisky 10 Year Old Cask Strength db **(94) n23 t24 f23 b24** Quite often a malt which shews as much natural caramel early on as this does ends up swamped by it, lifeless and uninteresting even during the post mortem. Not this time. It is as though the malt sensed when enough was enough and instead moved on to far more interesting matters: in this case how far towards being a beautiful bourbon in character it could sail? The answer is: so close that once or twice it crosses the border and for a few moments takes on a distinctly Kentuckian hue, all liquorice and molasses in full spate. Certainly the delivery is the sweetest in Europe this year though, miraculously, never for a moment takes the cloying route and embraces pugilistic spices which come out jabbing away looking to make short work of your taste buds. Only a little gnawing bitterness – tiredness from the oak maybe – prevents a higher score, though those warming cocoa tones still offer up much to enjoy. A malt with massive character to go the distance with. 58.3%.

Aureum Single Malt Peated New Make db **(92) n23 t23 f22.5 b23.5** A sound and confidently made new make, free from feints of any variety and homing in deliciously on the malt. Just the right degree of gristy sweetness and oil, too. An excellent base on which to begin any malt whisky. The peat, which is far from demonstrative, is kept on a manageable and even keel. 68.5%.

DESTILLERIE ARMIN JOBST E.K. Hammelburg. Working.

Jobst Grain Whisky 9 Jahre Madeira Cask A7 6 Jahre Barrique fass, 3 Jahre Madeira fass db **(92.5) n22.5 t23.5 f23 b23.5** At last! An indisputably excellent bottling from Jobst after so many attempts that one way or another fell at one of the hurdles. Here it clears all the fences with something to spare (well, maybe on the nose the back hooves clip something). But off this one trots to the winners' enclosure, unquestionably a thoroughbred. How can you not applaud the measured resonance of the fruit and the way the tannins interlink with almost effortless grace. The house nutty style is there in force, but this time isn't cracked with a sledgehammer cut and even allows the grains to have some kind of say in the matter. What superb balance and character this filly has. Definitely worth a flutter on.... 50%. sc.

Jobst Single Malt Whisky 3 Jahre Cognac-Fass No. 26 db **(81)** n17 t21 f22 b21 I think this is the distillery I once famously called a pfennig short of a Deutschmark. Never before have I made such great cents. Malty, in its very own peculiarly odd way. By the way: anyone who ever tasted the first-ever efforts of the Old Hobart distillery in Australia will be taken back 20 years or so by this nose... 58.4%. sc.

Jobst Single Malt Whisky 4 Jahre Bourbon-Fass B4 3 Jahre Rotwein Barrique, 1 Jahre Kentucky bourbon barrel db **(83)** n20 t23.5 f19 b20.5 There are moments when this malt is a winner. Especially when the crème chocolate is in full flow, that then moves into more praline mode. Make no mistake: that later delivery and middle is truly beautiful. The nose and finish, typical of this distillery, are best forgotten – though, sadly, the late tang ensures you can't. 43.7%. sc.

Jobst Single Malt Whisky 4 Jahre Portweinfass No. 44 db **(84)** n19 t21 f22 b22 The nose is the usual technical horror show. But a subtle, untarnished grapey fruitiness offers the sexy love interest that needs saving. 43%. sc.

Jobst Single Malt Whisky 4 Jahre Portweinfass No. 44 db **(87)** n20 t22.5 f22 b22.5 If you ever want to see why cask strength outranks a diluted version, you could do no better than sample this against their 43% version. Here the natural oils hold together the integrity of both the malt and the fruit, allowing it to fuse with the rich natural oils and overcome the weakness of the cut. Beautifully chewy and intense, the spices play out like a demented fruit cake, sweetingly warm but still in league with the intensity of the earlier sugars. Hang on and just go for the ride: it's fun! 58.8%. sc.

Jobst Single Malt Whisky 6 Jahre Kastanien-Fass R1 db **(86.5) n20 t22.5 f21.5 b22.5** It takes something as profound as a top-quality chestnut barrel to first control and then obliterate the edginess to the distillate. This offers a really enjoyable experience once you are past the nose and, indeed, a rich nuttiness makes the most of the silky oils and light Demerara sugars to ensure there is sublime layering to complement the mouthfeel. The spices have teeth and ensure extra depth. Pinch your nose...then enjoy...!!! 50.4%. sc.

DESTILLERIE & BRENNEREI MICHAEL HABBEL Sprockhövel. Working

Hillock 8 Year Old Single Malt Whisky 82 monate in ex bourbon fässern, 14 monate zum finish in ex Recioto fässern, bott code: L-2118 db **(87) n22 t22 f21.5 b21.5** A soft, friendly malt determined not to upset any apple carts, but in so doing rather lays too supinely at the feet of the dominant toffee. Malt and spices apparent and, overall, quite pleasant in the German style. 45.3%.

DESTILLERIE RALF HAUER Bad Dürkheim. Working.

Saillt Mór Bad Dürkheim Whisky Oloroso sherry peated cask, los no. 0319, fassreifung 3/16, gefüllt am 08/19 db **(93) n23.5 t23 f23 b23.5** The majority of distilleries have the alarming, and frankly depressing, habit of falling flat on their face when they combine the big two: peat and wine cask. Pleased to say, this fares far better than most. 55.6%. nc ncf.

Saillt Mór Bad Dürkheim Whisky Pfälzer oak, los no. 0219, fass-nr. 23 & 24, jahrgang 3/14, gefüllt am 08/19 db **(91.5) n22 t24 f22.5 b23** If you are looking for a whisky which launches stunning flavours around your palate, then you've now found it. What a delivery... easily one of the most memorable in Europe this year! 46%. ncf.

◈ Saillt Mór Geraint In Woodford Reserve Bourbon Cask lightly peated, dist Mar 2015, bott May 2021, barrel no.60, db **(90) n23** flits between smoky bacon and smoky bourbon.... highly attractive, but a little disconcerting! **t23** it is as though the mouth is kissed by a corn oil succulence before a repertoire of bourbon-style liquorice and heather honey kicks in. Amid the rumbling vanillas and spices comes the smoke...; **f21.5** loses its earlier surety and bitters out slightly; **b22.5** a truly full blooded but bewildering whisky whose opening movement on the palate feels a though it was composed in Kentucky. 57.7% sc

◈ Saillt Mór PX Sherry dist Mar 2014, bott Aug 2020, barrel no. 27, db **(85.5) n21.5 t21 f22 b21** No sulphur notes: a healthy and trustworthy cask. But a classic example of the whisky being swamped, fatally, by PX. No balance, save some late spices against the earlier overwhelming sugars. In whisky, as often as not less means more. And this needs a lot less... 57.2% sc

◇◇ **Saillt Mór PX Sherry & Bourbon Finish** dist Mar 2015, bott May 2021, barrel no.51+65, db **(93) n22.5** eye-opening! This has a saline sharpness that seems to extract every last atom of fruit and attacks the nose like a pointy stick.... Talk about fresh fruit...! **t23.5** an incredibly rare opening fingerprint. Yes, the fruit is vivid, especially when the spices give it a big nudge...but take your mind off that for a moment and just look at that vanilla...I mean: just look at it...!!! **f23.5** that spice keeps its path straight and unwavering to the end. The vanilla now moves, very unusually towards delicate ulmo honey; **b23.5** yikes! This is like some kind of flavour stampede. I have spent the day tasting genteel fruity whiskies. This has come along like a bull in a china shop, clattering into my taste buds and springing surprises left, right and centre. One of the least boring PX cask whiskies I have ever encountered. Just love it...! Correction: adore it...!!! 576% sc

DESTILLERIE RIEGER & HOFMEISTER Fellbach. Working.

◇◇ **Destillerie Rieger & Hofmeister Schwäbischer Malt & Grain** bott code: L-MG-140421 db **(83) n21.5 t21.5 f19 b21** Certainly flavoursome with a big dose of malt and heather honey in the foreground. But strangled a little too tightly by the increasingly bittering feints from the generous cut. 42%

◇◇ **Destillerie Rieger & Hofmeister Schwäbischer Single Malt** portweinfass finish bott code: L-SM-221020 db **(85) n22 t22 f20 b21** A whisky greatly boosted by the Murray Method. Nose and tasted at room temperature the feints have far too big a say. But the MM fires up the fruit and sugars to at least give the nose and delivery a sporting chance which it takes with both hands. Sadly, less can be done for the hot finish. 40%

◇◇ **Destillerie Rieger & Hofmeister Schwäbischer Roggenmalz Rye** bott code: L-RW-141220 db **(88) n22 t23 f21 b22** Absolutely no doubting the starring grain here whatsoever: the rye is positively sparkling. All polished, crisp Demerara and spice on the delivery, which is an absolute joy. Again, the wide cut catches up with this at the finish which loses its lustre. But that nose and delivery....! What a treat! 42%

◇◇ **Destillerie Rieger & Hofmeister Schwäbischer Whisky No.4** sherryfass finished L-W04-050321 db **(86) n20 t23 f21 b22** The fruit is profound from the delivery onwards, offering a delightful sugar candy juiciness throughout. The spices also fit the bill, too. Only the wider cut, which causes a bit of chaos on the nose and bobbles at the finish makes this down slightly. A shame, as there really is a delicious middle section worth investigating. 42%

◇◇ **Destillerie Rieger & Hofmeister Schwäbischer Malt** smoky malt 2012/2020 L-RM-141220 db **(90.5) n23** oh, what harmony! The gentleness of peat perfectly accords with the tune if the lightly honeyed tannin. The phenols flit rather than rumble, but you are always aware of its elegant presence; **t22.5** on the nose you get the feeling, that for all its charm and joy, the cut wasn't quite perfect. And soon this becomes apparent as a little nougat feintiness appears in the background. But this hardly matters as it seems to blend in seamlessly with the sweet peat which dances nymphlike across the palate; **f22** there is still a mildly uncomfortable tongue from that slightly wide cut. But the pretty sugars have already gone on ahead to reduce any possible damage. Lightly spiced and still rather lovely...; **b23** the harmony of this beautiful whisky reminded me of a Sunday morning in a German village, the ancient church bells calling. To an English ear, it strikes slightly out of tune. But possesses a charm which captures the country with a disarming vibrancy. 45%

Rye Schwäbischer Roggenmalz-Whisky bott code: L-RW-150819 db **(94.5) n23.5 t24 f23.5 b23.5** A style of whisky this distillery does wonderfully well. A real handful of a rye, bustling and muscular, allowing the earthier element of this grain full scope. 42%.

Whisky No.4 Sherryfass Finished Schwäbischer Whisky bott code: L-W04-010220 db **(89) n22 t22.5 f22 b22.5** An excellent sherry cask does a very good job here. At times a delicious whisky, if inconsistent. 42%.

DESTILLERIE THOMAS SIPPEL Weisenheim am Berg. Working.

Palatinatus Single Malt Whisky American Oak Peated 2014 db **(91) n23.5 t23 f22 b22.5** A distillery that does peat so well. Slightly more of a tanginess on the finish this time out, though. 45%.

Palatinatus Single Malt Whisky Bordeaux Single Cask Strength 6 Jahre db **(89) n22 t23 f22 b22** Far from technically on the money, but the flavours are huge. I should be marking this down, but find myself entranced and at its mercy! Prepare yourself for a chewathon. 54.5%. sc.

Palatinatus Single Malt Whisky French Limousin Oak Spätburgunder Singel Cask 2014 db **(81) n21.5 t21.5 f18.5 b19.5** Interesting tasting this after their sublime German oak bottling. That works on so many levels that this just doesn't. Bitter and unbalanced. 45%. sc.

Palatinatus Single Malt Whisky Single Cask German Oak 2014 db **(94) n23.5 t23.5 f23 b24** Profound whisky so beautifully distilled (not something I have always said about Palatinatus). It appears that German oak bests suits this German malt. Neat! 45%. sc.

Palatinatus Single Malt Whisky Ruby Port Single Cask First Fill 2014 db (85.5) n22 t21.5 f21 b21 I'm a little surprised that a first fill Port pipe didn't generate more intense fruit than is seen here. No shortage of busy flavours many of them malty. But has real problems getting them to assemble in attractive order. 45%. sc.

EDELBRÄENDE-SENFT Salem-Rickenbach. Working.

Senft Whisky Edition Herbert dist 2014, bott code: L-WE551 db (87) n21 t23 f21.5 b21.5 No faulting the mouthfeel which benefits from the extra oils from the wide-ish cut. Not just from the nougat school of European whisky, but at around the midpoint hits the most glorious chord of intense sweet malt, chocolate and oak-induced dry vanilla. For five or six glorious seconds as those notes align, this is stunning! 45%. nc.

EDELBRENNEREI BISCHOF Wartmannsroth. Working.

Bischof's Rhöner Whisky Grain Whisky Aus Rhöner Weizen Single Cask bott code: L-9 db (85) n21 t22.5 f20.5 b21 Not as neat and tidy as the last bottling I enjoyed from them, the feints knocking things askew here. That said, it does have its tender moments especially when the particularly nutty character softens and moves towards a light praline, even vaguely coconut hue. Spices gather, but the balance dissipates. 40%. sc.

EDELBRÄNDE PREISER Stuehlingen. Working

◇ **Whisky Stube Sulmgau Whisky Single Malt** acacia & chestnut wood, dist Dec 2016, bott Jan 2021 bott code: L0121 (88.5) n20.5 t23.5 f22 b22.5 For fun, I often nose a whisky from pouring blind just to try and guess what is coming next. And as I sniffed at this I said under my breath: "chestnut!" Which was, indeed, the case, though a degree of feints tries to disguise the wood type...and much else. And here's a question: does acacia wood help instal a degree of acacia honey into a malt. Well, if this is anything to go by, the answer is "yes". Because as uncomfortable the nose might be, the delivery is pure barley stirred into a honey pot. Another thing I expected was bitterness on the finish. And though it arrives it is nothing like so destructive as I feared. So with spices joining the fading remnants of the barley-honey mix there is so wonderful many layers to get through. Different. And truly delicious. 47%

EDELBRENNEREI DIRKER Mömbris. Working.

Dirker Whisky Aged 4 Years Sassicaia cask, bott code L A 16 db (80.5) n18.5 t22.5 f19 b20.5. A deeply frustrating whisky. This is one exceptionally beautiful cask at work here and - in the mid ground - offers all kinds of toffee apple and muscovado-sweetened mocha. Sadly, the initial spirit wasn't up to the barrel's standard. This really needs some cleaning up. 53%

EIFEL DESTILLATE Koblenz. Working.

◇ **Eifel Whisky 746.9 Single Malt 10 Jahre Alt** Amontillado cask db (89.5) n22.5 so many nuts with the fruit this could be a high end Amontillado...oh, hang on a minute....; t22.5 a barrage of muscovado sugar and grape...and eventually hazelnut...; f23 ah, some layering at last as the oak digs deep. Spices too...; b21.5 I'm sure there some whisky in there somewhere. The malt has disappeared under a mountain of sherry. The good and bad side of this, is that balance has been compromised yet we are treated to exceptionally high class Amontillado with the nuttiness of one of the better houses shining through as the dominant feature. The Murray Method does help in bringing some of the whisky back into play, though it is the finer vanillas of the oak which does set about ensuring rung of complexity....and spice. 46% nc ncf

◇ **Eifel Whisky 746.9 Single Malt 12 Jahre Alt** Madeira cask db (91) n23 the spice is playful but needed; the oak is dry but restrained; the fruit is dense, but sharp and controlled in its sweetness: an attractive combination...; t23.5 just the right side of dense fruit: close to being too dominant in grape, but holds back sufficiently for attractive smattering of malt and salt to up the salivations levels. Strands of tannin through the idle...; f22 drier now as the oak grows in confidence and spices tingle; b22.5 an irregular malt with the wine appearing to want to control every aspect on the delivery onwards, then thinking better of it and holding off. Thoroughly enjoyable and at times classy... 46% nc ncf

◇ **Eifel Whisky 746.9 Single Peated Malt 9 Jahre Alt** moscatel cask db (89.5) n22 pretty decent oak giving extra substance to the untainted, young plummy fruit; a little smoke swirls about the composition; t22.5 the first moment or two is dry...then a cascade of fruit liquor bursts around the palate. The thickening agent appears to have a little phenol, too...; f22.5 the oak returns and now we can enjoy some serious structure. Still the fruity sweetness persists, not unlike a soft-centre bon-bon; b22.5 eccentrically sweet and fruitier than a plum orchard...; 46% nc ncf

◇ **Eifel Whisky 746.9 Single Peated Malt 10 Jahre Alt** moscatel cask db (88) n22 t22.5 f21.5 b22 Although a year older than their other Muscatel bottling, it lacks the complexity with the oak involvement being virtually eradicated by the syrupy sweetness of the grape and denser background of the phenol. Very enjoyable simply as a sensation, but this will appeal to liqueur lovers far more than whisky aficionados *46% nc ncf*

Eifel Whisky 746.9 Single Rye 10 Jahre Alt Malaga cask db **(91.5) n22.5** the firmness of the grain is matched only by the softness of the fruit. Delicate and pleasing...; **t23** salivating with a magnificent array of light honey tones, acacia honey mainly, perhaps with a smattering of rape seed. Against the firm backbone some plummy fruits develop; **f23** liquorice and chocolate with a fruity topping: very unusual for a finish; **b23** I have no idea where this distillery is sourcing its casks. But I can only applaud...very loudly..!!! *46% nc ncf*

Eifel Whisky 746.9 Single Rye 12 Jahre Alt Malaga cask db **(94) n23.5** sometimes with rye you get a certain type of spice off the grain. But this is different: it is from the cask, giving a bourbony dimension. The fruit has a distinctly roasty raisin style...; **t23** plum pudding meets chocolate cake. With a crusty Demerara sugar topping for good measure. Someone has sprinkled in some livid spice...; **f23** long, still tangy from the sharpness of the grain. And still plummy...; **b24** the extra two years in the Malaga cask has been converted into spices – none of which were apparent on the 10-year-old. A towering Eifel and quite glorious! *46% nc ncf*

Eifel Malz Whisky Duo Malt & Peat Reserve Pedro Ximenes cask db **(87.5) n21.5 t22 f22.5 b21.5** While the nose is a little rough and glutinous, the story on palate is something else beside. Here the cask goes into overdrive, dispensing its sugar fruitiness like Lord Bountiful. Preposterously OTT, but th slight spiciness to th cough syrup sweetness does make this ultimately quite attractive. *46% nc ncf*

Eifel Malz Whisky Single Malt Einzelfass Port cask db **(92.5) n22.5** clean grape, but a fascinating spicy sub plot. A little butterscotch and malt flickers around the nose now and again...; **t23.5** a mouth feel to die for. Fruit dominates but is a relatively subtle way thanks to the spices and early liquorice. Manuka and heather honey arrive, but are a side dish rather than the mains...; **f23** long, still fruity...but remains spicy and surprisingly dry very late on; **b23.5** this is a distillery which appears to know how to procure some exceptionally good casks. Again, it is almost too good with the Port having the lion's share of the of the influence. But here the vital bit: this has no pretensions of being a sugar-laden liqueur: the wine is just light enough to allow other factors to come into play. Complex, but only if you're prepared t give it time and investigate... *46% nc ncf*

Eifel Roggen Whisky Ahrtaler Reserve Pinot Noir cask db **(94) n23.5** you'd think the richness of the grape would dominate here. But no: it is clean, light and more than happy for the rye to poke its way through with a sharp, sugary countenance; **t23.5** this is such high grade rye. Rye is fruity at the best of times, but with a pinot cask this fresh...just wow...!!! **f23** you know the spices will be along soon....and here they are. How can a finish be this salivating...this lively...? Even the undertone is one of chocolate toffee as the tannins take up their position...; **b24** brilliant distillate, magnificent cask...then end product is a super complex whisky. Unlike any rye whisky I have tasted for several years, this is the rarest of experiences where both the grain and the wine cask both have equally starring roles. Clean, complex and commanding. *46% nc ncf*

Eifel Roggen Whisky Single Rye Einzelfass Malaga cask db **(81.5) n22 t22.5 f17 b20** Sometimes the fruit can been too overbearing from a wine cask, and that appears to be the case here. Also, some undesired tang on the finish confirms this to be not in the same league as their other Malaga cask bottlings. *46% nc ncf*

Eifel Roggen Whisky Vintage Reserve Pinot Noir cask db **(88) n21.5 t22 f22.5 b22** Pleasant enough, but leaden by comparison to Eiffel's extraordinary Ahrtaler Reserve. Here the Pinot barrel lands too much grape on its target, obliterating most of the rye's complexity and character. Still, fat and fabulously fruity. *46% nc ncf*

ELCH WHISKY Gräfenberg. Working.

Elch Torf vom Dorf losnr.: 19/05 db **(95) n23.5 t24 f23.5 b24** When you get a whisky that combines a fascinating narrative with clever and subtle understatement yet fortified by occasional boldness, it is hard not to be won over and seduced. Fantastic. *51%.*

FESSLERMILL 1396 DESTILLERIE Sersheim. Working.

Mettermalt American Style Whisky new American bourbon barrel db **(85) n21 t21.5 f21 b21.5** American style it may be, but the closest I can think of to this is American blend. Light and lacking direction, this goes down as pleasant but far from memorable whisky. *40%. nc sc.*

Mettermalt Single Malt Whisky new American white oak barrel db **(86.5) n21.5 t22 f21.5 b21.5** Dines out on the toasted honeycomb notes and spices which slalom in and out of this malt. The wide cut is equally responsible for a little extra bitterness, too. *46%. nc sc.*

Mettermalt Single Rye Whiskey db **(82.5) n21 t21.5 f19.5 b20.5** The rye's fulsomeness is not in doubt. Sadly the quality of the distillate is. Far too much feint, I'm afraid. *55.5%. nc sc.*

Mettermalt Smoky Single Rye Whiskey ex-Laphroaig barrel db **(93)** n23 t23.5 f23 b23.5 Fabulously distilled, this is clean rye offering a crisp, fruity and salivating backdrop to the loitering phenols. The sugars are sharp and act with rare purity. Big, though it takes one a little while to realise just how...! *55.5%. nc sc.*

FINCH WHISKYDESTILLERIE Nellingen, Alb-Donau. Working.

Finch Schwäbischer Hochland Whisky Barrel Proof 19 bott code: L19056 db **(90.5)** n22.5 t23 f22 b23 As I taste this, a greenfinch calls gutterally, wheezily, to its prospective mate, while nearby a goldfinch is more than happy to use its metallic red face to dazzle, topping it off with its jaunty, equally metallic trill for good measure. Meanwhile, in the glass, this Finch entices you with its song of alluring ulmo honey and caramels. *54%.*

Finch Schwäbischer Hochland Whisky Barrique R 19 bott code: L19130 db **(92)** n23 t23 f22.5 b23.5 The model of a beautifully balanced whisky able to contain any minor lurking feints. *42%.*

Finch Schwäbischer Hochland Whisky Private Edition Single Malt Madeira 19-1 flasche nr. 1093 von 1416, bott code: L19230 db **(93)** n23 t23 f23.5 b23.5 It's like unwrapping a raisin toffee. An elegant Finch with much greater complexity than first seems possible.. *45%. sc.*

GUTSBRENNEREI JOH. B. GEUTING Bocholt. Working.

◇ **J.B.G Münsterländer Single Malt Aged 6 Years** bourbon barrels, cask no. 101&102, dist Dec2014, bott Dec 2020, db **(90.5)** n22.5 slightly unusual raw carrot mixes with the heather honey and red liquorice. Attractively earthy....; t22.5 spiced silk. The malt carries a mocha and biscuit middle; f22.5 for a malt matured only in a bourbon, there is a distinctly fruity flush to the finish. A lovely light chocolate touch, too, to complement the buzzing, busy spice...; b23 like so many German distilleries, the quality is improving year on year with the cuts becoming increasingly more complex and enjoyable. This one is no exception, boasting delightful depth. *43% 520 bottles*

HAMMERSCHMIEDE Zorge. Working.

The Glen Els The Journey Distiller's Cut 2019 Single Malt bott code: L1879 db **(90)** n22 t23 f22 b23 When the Coronavirus epidemic is finally over, there will be worse things to do than nip over to Glen Els to track down a bottle of this Distillery Exclusive. Rich and rewarding. *48%. nc ncf. 2,000 bottles.*

The Glen Els Willowburn Grand Cru Claret Casks Single Malt batch no. 1, bott code: L1893 db **(68)** n17 t18 f16 b17 Some Glen Els fail spectacularly. Here is one such example. Doesn't work on a single level. *46%. nc ncf. 1,000 bottles.*

The Glen Els Willowburn Malaga Casks Single Malt batch no. 1, bott code: L1890 db **(88.5)** n21.5 t22 f22.5 b22.5 An enjoyable, almost flippant, whisky which is about as relaxed as they come. The grape has no sharpness or shape but prefers to smother the malt with juicy, lightly spices Demerara-style notes. Positively grows and - glows - into its task. *46%. nc ncf.*

The Glen Els Willowburn Marsala Casks Single Malt batch no. 1, bott code: L1887 db **(75)** n18 t19 f19 b19 Some whiskies work beautifully. This doesn't. The original distillate offered a challenge the Marsala was unable to surmount. *46%. nc ncf. 1,000 bottles.*

The Glen Els Willowburn Moscatel Casks Single Malt batch no. 1, bott code: L1892 db **(90.5)** n23 t22.5 f22 b23 Technically a bit hit and miss. But some breathtakingly high class casks has worked wonders. *46%. nc ncf. 1,000 bottles.*

The Glen Els Willowburn Ruby & Tawny Port Casks Single Malt batch no. 1, bott code: L1886 db **(87)** n22.5 t23 f20 b21.5 The influence of the Port casks is truly fabulous: this is very high-class barrels they have put into use here. The influence of the basic distillate isn't quite of the same calibre, so as it spends longer on the palate, the less magic the wine can spread. Ruby on a Train to Nowhere, one might say... *46%. nc ncf. 1,000 bottles.*

Hercynian Willowburn Cask Strength 2019 batch no. 1, bott code: L1889 db **(91.5)** n23 t23.5 f23 b22 Well-made whisky. Fruity to a fault and peppered with spice. But just a little too one dimensional for greatness. *54.8%. nc ncf. 1,000 bottles.*

Hercynian Willowburn Exceptional Collection Aged 5 Years Single Malt bourbon firkin cask no. V14-10, dist 2014, bott 15 Jun 19, bott code: L1902 db **(96)** n24 t24 f23.5 b24.5 Firkin brilliant!!! A potential European Whisky of the Year. *61.9%. nc ncf sc. 36 bottles.*

HARDENBERG DISTILLERY Nörten-Hardenberg. Working

◇ **Beverbach Double Oak Aged Single Malt Whiskey** aged in American & French oak casks, bott code: L08320073 db **(90)** n21.5 lots of buttery malt. But slightly out of tune...; t22.5 ahhh...!! That's much better. Has discarded the unbalanced wobble on the nose to concentrate fully on the amazing density of the gristy barley. The ulmo honey is to die for;

f23 how the malt manages to keep up its intensity right to the death, God only knows. There is a stunning Malteser candy touch to this, then a late latte coffee note. Meanwhile the excellent spices nibble away...; **b23** ignore the nose. I was fearing the worst – and shouldn't have bothered. This is one of the most intensely malty whiskies from the whole of mainland Europe to be found this year... So impressed! *43%*

HAUSBRAUEREI ALTSTADTHOF Nürnberg. Working.
Ayrer's PX Sherry Cask Finished Organic Single Malt dist 2009 db **(90)** n22 t22.5 f23 **b22.5** Always brave to use PX, as the intensity of the sugars can sometimes put the malt into the tightest of straight-jackets. However, this is fine, sulphur-free butt and is eventually relaxed enough for the malt to share equal billing once it finds its rhythm. *56%*

HINRICHSEN'S FARM DISTILLERY Dunsum. Working.
Hinrichsen's Farm Distillery New Virgin Malt Spirituose Aus Gerstenmalz lot no. 400 db **(92.5)** n24 t23.5 f22 b23 The nose is of the Spirit Safe when the middle cut is running: possibly the sexiest aroma of any part of the distillery. A feint-free spirit radiating beautifully composed barley: who could ask for more? The delivery is satisfyingly intense malt aided by the lightest of oils, though the finish perhaps suggests a little more copper could do with attaching itself. But this is a very promising base for any malt whisky and true delight to sample in its own right. *42%. ncf.*

KLEINBRENNEREI FITZKE Herbolzheim-Broggingen. Working.
Derrina Dinkelmalz Schwarzwälder Single Malt Whisky bott code L 5513 db **(87)** n21 t21 f23 b22 Neither the nose nor delivery instil much confidence, as both are on the earthy, feinty side. However, no complaints about the finish which offers more praline than any other whisky I have tasted this year. Talk about clouds and silver linings... *43%.*

Derrina Gerstenmalz Schwarzwälder Single Malt Whisky bott code L 5413 db **(84)** n19 t21.5 f22 b21.5 No doubting the enormous intensity of the barley on delivery, or its richness on follow through. But the nose leaves no doubt the cut wasn't the best and its problems stem from there. *43%.*

Derrina Granat Rotkorn Ur-Weizen Schwarzwälder Single Grain Whisky bott code L 13912 db **(93)** n22.5 t24 f23 b23.5 A sensational whisky that attacks you from the first second to the last with a plethora of unique and unorthodox flavour profiles which leave you wondering what's around the corner. The nose may be slightly caramel centric but the delivery and follow-through are a different proposition thanks to the marriage of the rich oils and the teasing, bitty grain. If you insist on identifiable landmarks, then you'll uncover butterscotch and light cream toffee, but the brilliance of this whisky is that the favours are...well...like nothing else! *43%.*

Derrina Grünkern Schwarzwälder Single Grain Whisky bott code L 11013 db **(88)** n21.5 t22.5 f22 b22 A typical Derrina full bloodied whisky bursting at the seams with flavour. Oily, chewy the grain has a great ally in the heather honey. *43%.*

Derrina Hafer Schwarzwälder Single Grain Whisky bott code L 6212 db **(91)** n22 t23.5 f22.5 b23 I started today's tasting with an oat whisky and now, nearly ten hours on, I taste my 25th and final whisky of the day with another one. This is far the superior of the two, more cleanly distilled and the grain far more prominent in its rich and sweet character. The blend of ulmo honey and mocha is irresistible. *43%.*

Derrina Hafermalz Schwarzwälder Single Malt Whisky bott code L 6713 db **(94.5)** n23.5 t24 f23 b24 Oat whisky, when made well, is unquestionably one of the most flavoursome spirits on the planet. Here is a rare example of Hafermalz at Bundesliga standard... *43%.*

Derrina Müsli Schwarzwälder Single Grain Whisky bott code L 7112 db **(94.5)** n23.5 t24 f22.5 b23.5 I wasn't sure if I was supposed to add milk to this and throw in a few fresh raspberries and strawberries for good measure. In the end, I tasted it using the Murray Method, which requires none of those props. And just as well, for the complexity on this is the stuff of dreams and legends. Big enough to make a film about. Indeed, it should become a cereal...(don't think the Germans will get that one!). Anyway, definitely up there as a possible award winner! *43%.*

Derrina Oberkulmer Rotkorn Ur-Dinkel Schwarzwälder Single Grain Whisky bott code L 13712 db **(92.5)** n23 t23.5 f23 b23 Impossible not to be delighted by the gentle elegance of this whisky, the welcoming ulmo honey on the nose matched by the light touch of Lubek marzipan and ulmo honey on delivery. To maximise this, it needs a lightness of touch from the oils...and that's exactly what it gets. *43%.*

Derrina Weizenmalz Schwarzwälder Single Malt Whisky bott code L 5713 db **(93)** n23.5 t23 f23 b23.5 A proudly singular style here with the distillery going great guns, as ever, with their wheated version. The odd stray feint note here and there, but this seems to ensure that the grain gains even greater weight and a more fizzy intensity to its mix of spice and light Demerara sugars. Few German whiskies can hold their salivation levels for so long and at such a high pitch. Expect your jaw to ache by the end of all the chewing. But it is a pain well worth bearing... *43%.*

KORNBRENNEREI J.J. KEMPER Olpe. Working.

⬧ **Whisky Stube Spirit Of The Cask Roggen Whisky** American white oak barrel, dist Jun 2015, bott Nov 2020, bott code: L01B11R18 **(94) n23.5** just love that nose. So much creamy vanilla at work and some really fascinating tannins at play, too, with a subtle blend of roast chestnut and traditional bourbon. Light ulmo honey and spices form an excellent sub-strata; **t23.5** plays in reverse: the ulmo honey and spice tumble over the taste buds ahead of the complex tannins. Justos on the nose, a creaminess is apparent. At the midpoint the oak has the upper hand, but it is floating in a sea of honey and spice; **f23** long, and still not the vaguest sign of a weak spot. A little praline seeps into the mix but this is now mainly about the multi-layered tannins, though Demerara sugars also have a heathy presence giving the fade a distinctly Kentuckian feel...; **b24** absolutely top rate. The intensity is matched only by the delights of the semi-bourbon kick. No feints to worry about here: beautifully made and distilled. A triumph of a whisky... *61.23%*

KYMSEE WHISKY Grabenstätt. Working.

Kymsee Single Malt Moran Cask Strength db **(89) n22 t23 f21.5 b22.5** Were I in a Scottish blending lab, putting a young blend together, I wouldn't bat an eyelid if this was one of the standard Islay whiskies I had to work from. Perhaps a little thin on structure but otherwise presses all the right buttons. *58.6%.*

MARDER EDELBRÄNDE Albbruck-Unteralpfen. Working.

⬧ **Marder Single Malt Finest Black Forest Limited Edition** batch L 2021 dist: 03.2015, bott: 01.2021, db **(89.5) n22.5** magnificently nutty; **t22.5** chewy wth a busy interplay between straightforward malt and busy, lightly spiced tannins; **f22** a simplistic but attractive praline and spice fade; **b22.5** a real knife and fork malt, this. Hardly abounding with complexity, but concentrates instead with the massive intensity of the malt and the delicate spices and oaky vanillas which play off it. A very satisfying whisky. *43%*

⬧ **Marder Single Malt Black Forest Reserve Aged 5 Years** Amarone cask db **(93) n23** excellent fresh grape and plum galvanised by heady spices; **t23.5** the grape ensures a wonderful crispness to this malt, the burnt raisins crystalline. The spices buzz and nip playfully while the gristy malt is still loud enough to be heard. The salivating properties to this are second to none; **f23** still a little spicey crackle to the crisp fruit; **b23.5** another beautifully made malt, technically worth a congratulatory handshake. Another pat on the back is deserved for the selection of a cask which appears to perfectly fit the house style, giving it a pleasingly fresh yet allows the age to show appropriately. Fantastic fun! *46.2% sc 197 bottles*

⬧ **Marder Single Malt Black Forest Reserve Aged 10 Years** Islay cask with a hint of peat, bott: 07.2021, db **(95) n23.5** talk about an understated nose. Talk about a tease. The lightness of the smoke is just as telling as had it been a 50ppm phenol explosion. Glorious...; **t23.5** much fuller on the palate than on the nose. Surprisingly oily and malty, the smoke taking its time to gather up enough strength to interfere. The sweetness filters through from the grist; quite warming, too...; **f24** ahhh...just love the re-emergence of the smoke. The oils have thinned and now the spices are in perfect sync with the peat. The weight and pace can barely be improved upon: this is very special. And so elegant...; **b24** there are those, whose minds are as closed as their palates who will tell you, apparently with a moral authority which is higher than yours or mine, that I cannot call this whisky sexy. Apparently, these humourless, puritan imbeciles regard this as a sexist comment. Well, when a whisky is this elegant and teasing, from first nose to last fading smoky pulse, then it is sexy. *48.3% sc 296 bottles*

MÄRKISCHE SPEZIALITÄTEN BRENNEREI Hagen. Working.

DeCavo Single Malt Höhlenwhisky 3 Jahre fass-nr. L55 db **(84.5) n21.5 t21.5 f20.5 b21** Thin, young and the striking bitter lemon note makes the whisky wobble off its malty course. *47.3%. sc.*

DeCavo Single Malt Höhlenwhisky 5 Jahre fass-nr. L19 db **(93.5) n23 t23.5 f23 b24** The best whisky I have encountered from this distillery, by far. Few German whiskies come maltier than this! *58.3%. sc.*

NORDPFALZ BRENNEREI Höning. Working.

⬧ **Eagle Bow Pfälzer Börben Aged 6 Years** matured American oak, finished chestnut barrel, bott code: L1836-1, db **(89.5) n22** forget about the bourbon casks...the chestnut is not allowing the oak a word in edgeways....delicately sweet...and very dense. The grains (is that a little rye...?) is practically lost in the distinctive tannins; **t22.5** as the nose foretells, this is a pea-souper of a body. Thick enough to stand a spoon in, a gorgeous heather honey sweetness mingles with the livewire chestnut while the grains – can't work out if this is a rye or wheat whisky - offer both a sharp and vaguely spicey subtext. The cut is a little on the wide side, but it gets away with it...; **f22.5** just love that chocolate-orange fade...; **b22.5** for the second day in a row, one sniff told me we were looking at chestnut casks – one of the most distinctive aromas in whisky – and by no means least attractive. *42.7%*

⟫ **Paltarmor 5 Years Old Blended Malt** aged in American oak, oloroso sherry and Old Forester peated casks, bott code: L-SHH-666 **(91) n23** teasing with peat like this should be made illegal: light acacia honey and rich barley is no less playful...; **t23** very profound barley, somewhere between concentrated grist and Glen Moray-style malt intensity. A little ulmo honey attracts the lightest phenols...; **f22** refuses to be diverted from its malty course, even when the spices arrive; **b23** best quality distillate I have yet encountered from this distillery. To achieve such an intensity of malt takes some doing. A highly pleasurable whisky experience. *47.7% distilled by Thomas Sippel, Bernhard Höning & Ralf Hauer*

⟫ **Taranis Pfälzer Single Malt Never Surrender Edition 2020** port cask finished, dist Seot 2013, bott code: L-1836-8, db **(88) n22** dry and elegant. It is as though all the sugars were extracted from the plum cake...; **t23** gorgeously silky on delivery – and bit of a shock as a sweetness slowly unfolds. The base is not unlike a caramel biscuit with a developing fruity juiciness and spices to ensure depth; **f21** just a little on the dry and tart side of things; **b22** a niggardly Port cask, spoiling for a fight. Doesn't appear to want the sugars to thrive...but the barley and tannins ensure otherwise. Complex. *46.5% 229 bottles*

⟫ **Taranis Pfälzer Single Malt Never Surrender Edition 2021** oloroso sherry cask and bourbon barrel, dist Dec 2014, bott code: L-1836-9, db **(93) n23** oloroso at its cleanest and most erudite. The dark sugars off the grape virtually sing from the glass...; **t23.5** the nose quietly suggested a slightly thick cut. The delivery confirms it. Yet, despite the oils, the outstanding quality of both the malt and grape influence simply bowls you over. The midpoint offers a splendid harmony of cocoa powder, muscovado sugar and white pepper...; **f23** just a slight tang off the still. But that weakness is easily overcome by the residual complexity from the midpoint which fades in slow motion..; **b23.5** a whisky of great confidence and character. What a great oloroso cask on show here. *52.7%*

NUMBER NINE SPIRITUOSENMANUFAKTUR Leinefelde-Worbis, Working.

⟫ **The Nine Springs Single Malt Peated Breeze Edition** finished in oloroso sherry cask db **(94) n23.5** so rare to report the high quality phenols able to breath and expand with oloroso on the scene. But the grape is happy to take a back seat while the peat drives around all kinds of malty lanes...; **t23.5** sublime mouthfeel. And - I'll not be writing this many times this year – a fabulous intertwangling between robust grape and no less enormous peat. But, and here's the rub, this just isn't about peat: there is also a huge wave of intense barley, too; **f23** a kind of garibaldi biscuit dunked in peaty coffee. The spices rattle to the end...; **b24** this is faultless oloroso. Not even a hint of a hint of the dreaded S word. And grape which refuses dominate, just add and embellish. Seeing as this is already a quite excellently made malt, you really could hardly ask for more... *50% nc ncf*

⟫ **The Nine Springs Single Malt Single Cask Selection Pedro Ximénez** db **(87) n21 t22.5 f22 b21.5** Undermined by a slightly less impressive distillate than normal, the malt still has enough muscle to take on the PX. Of course, as is the usual case for this type of sherry, it thickens and nullifies complexity. But it doesn't seem to do anything about the spices which glow amid the grape... *50% sc*

⟫ **The Nine Springs Single Malt Single Cask Selection Rioja Aged 7 years** cask no. 464 db **(89) n22** slightly punchy thanks to the spices. The fruit sits elegantly within the oaky frame sharing top billing with the malt; **t23.5** outstandingly sumptuous and sexy mouth feel. These are teasing caresses of varying intensity. Both the malt and the fruitcake expand and contact in intensity in tandem...; **f21** bitters slightly, losing its rhythm; **b22.5** excellently constructed malt which, though bittering at the finish, boasts enormous charm and complexity throughout. *50.7% nc ncf sc*

SAUERLÄNDER EDELBRENNEREI Ruthen-Kallenhardt. Working.

⟫ **Thousand Mountains McRaven Single Malt Fassstärke** db **(89.5) n22.5** ah...! Relatively clean and leaving no doubt about the type of grain in use here. The malt is crystal clear as though reverberating around a thousand mountains....; **t22.5** again, the malt is not only first out of the traps, but second, third and fourth, too. The vanillas are good company but try not to intrude too far. Some fruitier notes linger; **f22** still malty, but a little nutty, too, even though it bitters slightly. Remarkably salivating so late on, and till those now spiced dates have something to say; **b22.5** remembering what a Feintfest this was when I first encountered this distillery, absolutely delighted how this has progressed. Not even a hint of feint now: the intense, unsullied malt dominates quite beautifully. *59.8%*

⟨⟩ **Thousand Mountains McRaven Single Malt** db (86.5) n22 t22 f21 b21.5 A simple, malty, pleasing whisky. A degree of vegetable – detectable on the fuller strength model - tries to interfere and in so doing appears to up the spiciness considerably and increase the bitterness on the finish. The compensating dark sugars late on are impressive. Attractive, though not exactly flawless. *46.2%*

SCHRAML - DIE STEINWALD - BRENNEREI E.K. Erbendorf. Working.

Stonewood 1818 Bavarian Single Grain Whisky 10 Jahre Alt bott code: L40120 db (89.5) n22 t22.5 f22.5 b22.5 Never let it be said tht this distillery doesn't perpetuate its own character. I was expecting a little feint on this...and got it. I was expecting a grassy freshness to this despite the extra weight. And got it. Really salivating and palate cleansing...and it is not often you can say that about a whisky carrying a little feint. Lovely stuff. *45%.*

Stonewood Woaz Bavarian Single Wheat Whisky 7 Jahre Alt bott code: L-120119 db (91) n22.5 t23 f22.5 b23 Ah, I remember this one! The wheat whisky that's like a new loaf straight out of the oven. Well it reminded me of that because that is exactly what comes across here, the steam filling the nostrils as you cut through the crusts. There is, as is this distillery's trait, a little feint turning up here and there, but the wheat is spurred on by crispy Demerara sugar so at times it has the feel of a of a British Hot Cross Bun. Not sure if you are meant to drink this or have it with your 11 O'clock coffee... *43%.*

SINGOLD DESTILLERIE Wehringen. Working.

SinGold 7 Year Old dist 19 Apr 12, bott Dec 19 db (92) n22.5 t23 f23.5 b23 After battling my way through a series of very average and not particularly well distilled European whiskies, I can't say what kind of relief it was to find this one. Impressively manufactured, it has also spent time in an appropriate cask, thus allowing the natural sugars to flourish and sparkle while the oak criss-crosses the piece with some excellent anchoring vanilla notes. A joy. *59.8%. sc. 249 bottles. Whisky Tasting Club Bottling.*

SLYRS Schliersee-Neuhaus. Working.

⟨⟩ **Slyrs Bavarian Rye Whisky** bott code: A 08140 db (88.5) n22 t22 f22 b22.5 A well-made rye where the grain is allowed a free hand at dictating the character throughout. Curiously, the nose has a bready spiciness more akin to a wheat whiskey. But the rye, mingling with the tannins battle through. However, the grain is far more prominent on delivery, sitting prettily with a slightly viscous honey and Demerara combination which soon slides beneath the tannin and spice. Big, confident but never over Bolshie. *41%.*

Slyrs Bavarian Single Malt Whisky Aged 12 Years American oak casks, bott code: A 3875 db (88.5) n22 t23 f21.5 b22 A typical Slyrsian bottling, this, with the intensity of the barley practically launching itself into orbit, despite the close attentions of vanilla-riddled oak. But also bitterness on the finish which subtracts enough to rob it of greatness. *43%.*

Slyrs Bavarian Single Malt Whisky Classic American oak casks, bott code: D09951 db (85) n21 t21.5 f21 21.5 Malty, rich and even minty. But by no means, alas, technically one of their better bottlings. *43%.*

⟨⟩ **Slyrs Bavarian Single Malt Madeira Cask Finishing** bott code: B 22380 db (94.5) n24 this must have come from some cask: almost perfect in its bitter-sweet charm, especially the marriage of blood orange and lime. Just a little liquorice - vaguely bourbony in style - on the spice is an act of rare genius; t23.5 just so beautifully textured. Though the initial mouth feel doesn't suggest great age, it's been around long enough for the malt and fruit to form a fabulous partnership. Initially salivating, dries with aplomb yet with excellent little fruit notes darting out here and there; f23 the slow build of spice keeps pace with the growth of cocoa... and always lightened by residual citrus: a delight... b24 if this was a fencing opponent, you would finish with a nod of appreciative recognition towards his agility and excellence of balance, plus its ability to thrust at you when least expected. One of the best Bavarian malts I have tasted for a very long time: a minor classic mong German malts. And from a distillery whose greatly improved whiskies appear to have reached a zenith: along with their "51" and oloroso single cask, it is hard to imagine malts of this age being much better. *46%.*

⟨⟩ **Slyrs Bavarian Single Malt Finished in Marsala Faß** bott code: AL0666 db (89) n23 a nose that makes some statement: though good luck in trying to read it. Fruit pastels, peppery spices, bourbon, rum and tequila...all those notes can be found at some stage or other. A genuine bombardment of the senses...; t22.5 rounded and juicy from the off, the spices pile in quickly. The fruit first gushes, then puckers. The early sweetness soon makes way for the drier tones; f21 just a slight tang on the finale weakens things slightly. Remains unremittingly spicy, though; **b22.5** maybe not quite the perfect cask. But the good bits are very good. And the complexity levels, when in full flow, are astounding. 46%.

◇ **Slyrs Bavarian Single Malt Finished in Oloroso Faß** bott code: A0731 db **(85.5) n21.5 t22 f20.5 b21.5** A hefty dram with a little nougat to accompany the malt. An interesting salty/honey/spicy delivery. But the remainder, though pleasant, fails to entertain or intrigue quite like most other Slyrs bottlings. The finish does buzz a little... 46%.

◇ **Slyrs Bavarian Single Malt Pedro Ximénez Cask Finishing** bott code: A L2373 db **(85) n22 t21.5 f20.5 b21** In recent years Slyrs has grown from a light-middleweight malt to a heavyweight...sporting a jab and uppercut which, if not in better hands, could easily floor you. However, putting such a big whisky into a PX cask is unquestionably looking for trouble. And it finds it. Certainly, an enjoyable malt if you like your taste buds to have a good biffing. But of subtlety, there is none. Still the house chocolate praline can be located, but the thick sugary grape ensures an intense, unremitting buzzing rumble throughout rather than nuance. 46%.

◇ **Slyrs Bavarian Single Malt Finished in Port Faß** bott code: A1780 db **(89) n22.5** a chunky nose, the fruit coming at you thickly. The barley has a youngish air, bolstered by a peppery sub-plot; **t22** fat, chewy, lip-smacking delivery, but as the malt filters through, again the age comes across as very youthful. Even so, the middle is as dense as the nose with weighty fruit meeting a sudden rush of tannin; **f22** exceptionally dry with an attractive cocoa lilt; **b22.5** one cannot help feeling this was pulled from the warehouse many years too early: a solid, faultless cask at work. But plenty to enjoy as it is. 46%.

◇ **Slyrs Bavarian Single Malt Finished in Sauternes Faß** bott code: L4028 db **(92.5) n24** one of the best Slyrs noses I have ever encountered. A blender can only pray for casks to offer such shimmering delights....and here we have a ten minute nose, no less, which lures you into its gorgeous chalk and fruit pastel interplay. Weight and balance are quite perfect....; **t22.5** the immediate buzz on delivery is like a Slyrsian signature. Spices abounding from the first seconds followed by intense fruit layering – again, like the nose, of a fruit pastel type. Most surprising is the early arrival of the drier tannins; **f23** much drier now with the oak taking on a pithy countenance. This could go too far too early. But subtle oils and spices arrive late to ensure balance and length are maintained; **b23** this effete charmer is the antidote to the macho PX finish. Where that groans, rumbles and bullies, this kisses, teases and cajoles. Sauternes offers the best wine finishes in the whisky world, and such is the elegant complexity here you can see exactly why. Superb. 46%.

◇ **Slyrs Mountain Edition Single Malt** bott code: B 2901 db **(90) n23** well, this mountain has no shortage of oak forest growing on its slopes. The degree of tannin is almost dizzying. Here, though, the Murray Method comes into its own. Because ay the foot of each trunk can be found the most delicate of honeyed fingerprints (rape seed is probably the closest match), which becomes clearer as the nose adjusts. At normal temperature this is not apparent...nor is it when water is added. But warmed slightly this sweeter third dimension is not only there, but makes the absolute perfect counter to those oak notes, which re now also offering the first delicate spices. Adorable...; **t22.5** again, a whisky where the mouth-feel plays just as an important part as the flavour profile itself. A wonderful midweight of light oils enmeshed into a confident and firm oak and barley body armour, making for a firm and crunchy experience. The midpoint of rising spices and barley sugar is sublime. Never quite casts off its youthful persona, but the oak does a great job of putting a few hairs on it...; **f22** just a little short, though some barley scrambles through to balance the persistent spiced oak; **b22.5** no wonder they call this the Mountain Edition: it is reaches impressive heights, gives amazing views and is as solid as a rock. Nothing like as simplistic as it first seems. Well worth the climb. 45%.

◇ **Slyrs Single Malt Whisky Classic** new American oak bott code: F 36029 db **(88) n22 t22.5 f21.5 b22** The generosity of the cut ensures a chunky weightiness from nose to finish. And excellent oak also galvanises the spices. But at times this is austerely dry – excellent for creating a sense of elegance. But also compresses the sugars into the front compartments of the experience, rather than allowing them to filter through. Lots of malt to chew over, though. 43%.

Slyrs Bavarian Single Malt Whisky Fifty One bott code: A L18932 db **(91.5) n22.5 t23.5 f22.5 b23** Slyrs in tip-top form adding creamy dark sugars to their usual concentrated malt. Delicious! 51%.

◇ **Slyrs Single Malt Whisky Fifty One** bott code: B 4205 db **(94) n23.5** such a rich, enticing nose: draws you in with a lightly oiled, praline touch but as the spices gather, so does the red liquorice...; **t24** probably the best Slyrs delivery of all time...well, in bottle form, as I have tasted some crackers in their warehouse. This really is a controlled explosion with the still juicy barley generating just the right degree of sweetness to allow the expanding spices to fizz without burning. Feels...just so right..! **f23** a much more relaxed finale with the spices settling down and the presence of ever-intensifying tannins offering a wonderful cocoa-toastiness with a little hickory for good measure; **b23.5** the Bavarian malt with an American strength and distinctive Kentucky accent. 51%.

Slyrs Single Malt Whisky Oroloso Cask Finish cask no. OR15/29, dist 2012, bott 2018 db **(94) n24** truly classic oroloso: more dry than sweet and the grape alternating between almost a freshly pulled cork from a vintage oroloso bottle and a more solidified, pastel style fruitiness. Spices hint at a tingle and no more while the tannins form their own layer sturdier, drier tones. Majestic...; **t23.5** just love the fact that there is still youth and vitality to the malt itself, which in turn give the grape a more malleable quality. But the intensity encompasses a magnification of both the base malt and the rich tannin. Together, they are a dream; **f23** Garibaldi biscuits in concentrated form...; **b23.5** someone has done a brilliant job of picking a sublime sherry butt: sulphur free, powering yet, essentially, not-over dominant. Take a bow! This is a corker! 55.6% sc 613 bottles

Slyrs Single Malt Whisky Pedro Ximénez Cask Finish bott code: L4414 db **(83) n21 t22 f19 b21** Slyrs' whiskies have noticeably upped in quality in recent years and are now a force to be reckoned with on an international stage. Sadly, this PX version is a one-dimensional dullard with a monotonous flat pitch. A little spice tries to breathe life into matters, but fails. 46%.

Slyrs Bavarian Single Malt Whisky Rum Cask Finishing bott code: C2941 db **(90.5) n23 t23 f22 b22.5** Forget the rum: this is all about the malt! 46%.

Slyrs Single Malt Whisky Sauternes Cask Finish bott code: A 1527 db **(93) n23** pulsing oak and blood orange; **t23.5** a knife and fork malt: a three course meal of tannin and marmalade. The oils are exquisite; **f23** so oaky, you feel there maybe splinters on your tongue But the oils sooth, as does the residual fruit and spice the fruit is there on every level... but, cunningly, so well integrated you have to look for it...; **b23.5** so enjoyable! The extra oak generates a huge colour difference to batch 4028. And greater overall intensity. This is powerful medicine, lacking the overall finesse of its sister bottling but making up for it with a glorious white-knuckle ride of ever-increasing intensity. Two very different variations on a theme. 46%.

Sild Crannog Single Malt Whisky 2019 bott code: 3207 db **(94) n23 t24 f23 b24** Sometimes it can be the texture of a whisky that wins your heart and makes you swoon. Here is one such malt. No feints: whisky as it should be. It is not unknown for me to have sild sandwiches, sild being a type of oily fish: young herring. I'd make a sandwich of this whisky any day.... 48%.

SPREEWOOD DISTILLERS GMBH Schlepzig. Working.

Stork Club 100% Rye New Make bott 26 Mar 19 db **(90) n22 t24 f22 b22** Surprisingly tight and quiet on both nose and finish. But the delivery is another matter entirely with explosive grain followed by exemplary new make chocolate mousse follow through. 72.01%. ncf.

Stork Club 100% Rye Still Young Aged 2 Years medium toasted virgin German Napoleon oak casks, bott 26 Mar 19 db **(91.5) n23 t23 f22.5 b23** On this evidence the Germans should have an annual celebration of local whisky matured in native wood: Oaktoberfest.... 59.7%. ncf.

Stork Club Full Proof Rye Whiskey American & German oak, bott code: 10-19 db **(91) n23 t23 f22 b23** One of Germany's most consistently high-class distillers has struck again! Delightfully crafted rye. 55%.

Stork Club Single Malt Whiskey ex-bourbon, ex-sherry & ex-Weißwein casks, lot no. 008543 L002 db **(88.5) n22.5 t22.5 f21 b22.5** Not a faultless sherry butt. But one that offers more ticks than crosses. 47%. ncf.

ST. KILIAN DISTILLERS GMBH Rüdenau. Working.

St. Kilian Single Malt Whisky Signature Edition One chestnut (5%), ex bourbon (37%), ex PX sherry (18%), ex bourbon quarter casks (3%) & ex Martinique (37%) casks, dist 2016, bott 2019, los nr. 190508 db **(88) n22.5 t23 f21.5 b21** Such is the singular shape of the tannins, a kind of nondescript nuttiness, you know there is chestnut cask involvement even before you look on the label for confirmation. The only surprise is that it is a mere 5%, because it comes through a lot louder and clearer than that here, both on nose and palate. There is a mouth-filling maltiness to this, but it is constantly mithered by tannin tones that refuse to settle or agree up on their strategy and end up a little too bitter for their own good. The result is a full-flavoured but slightly incoherent whisky which sparkles best when the acacia honey gets a few clear punches in... 45%. nc ncf.

St. Kilian Single Malt Whisky Signature Edition Two ex Amarone 50L (3%), ex Amarone 325L (61%), & ex Amarone 225L (36%) casks, dist 2016, bott 2019, los nr. 190717 db **(75.5) n18 t21.5 f17 b19** Creamy textured but tight, bitter and very limited in development. Sometimes these casks work. Sometimes, like here, they are not a success. 54.2%. nc ncf.

St. Kilian Single Malt Whisky Signature Edition Three peated 38 ppm, ex bourbon quarter casks (6%) & ex Tennessee Whiskey (94%) casks, dist 2016, bott 2019, los nr. 191113 db **(94.5) n23.5 t23.5 f23.5 b24** A distillery which can carry off subtlety even with a thumpingly well-peated malt. When St. Kilian are on form, they really do make first-class whisky! 50%. nc ncf.

St. Kilian Single Malt Whisky Signature Edition Four peated 54 ppm, PX sherry (51%) & Oloroso (49%) casks, dist 2016, bott 2020, los nr. 200115 db **(84) n23 t23 f17.5 b20.5** I cannot say that the teaming of PX cask and high peat is one of my favourite combinations, not least because even if there isn't sulphur being hidden away, the battle between these two super egos rarely ends in harmony – and harmony and balance is always the key to good, let alone great, whisky. There is, as it happens, some nagging bitter sulphur lurking around on this, which rather does for the finish. But I have to say that I am uncommonly impressed by both the nose and delivery where the muscular peat is allowed to battle through the grape and heroically plant its flag. A decent experience...until the sulphur kicks in... 48%. nc ncf.

STEINHAUSER GMBH Kressbronn. Working.

◈ **Brigantia Aged 8 Years** db **(88.5) n21.5 t22.5 f22 b22.5** The cut is wide, meaning a little heavyweight oils leaks into an otherwise delicate malt. The delivery is s celebration of stone fruit, wild plums in particular. These work rather well with the chocolate and spices which eventually make their presence felt. Rather enjoyable whisky which would benefit with slightly more precision on the cut itself, thus denying the more tangy notes entry into would could be something rather excellent. 44%

Brigantia Aged 8 Years Single Malt db **(89) n22 t22 f22.5 b22.5** Not sure if this has been matured in a warehouse housing apple brandy, because there is an essence of apfel from the first sniff to the last fruity dying note. Throughout the barley is shadowed by a light fruitiness. Even when it turns spicy, there is still a fruit and nut character lurking...and that fruit is, of course, apple.... 44%.

◈ **Brigantia Classic** db **(89) n21** the usual untidy nose; **t23** but nothing untidy about the sweeping malt which kicks in after the hesitant delivery. Malt intensity like this – full of gristy sugars and bready chewiness – is a find to be savoured; **f22.5** allows the spices to intertwangle with the malt and increasing oaky vanilla without any drama. Long and very attractive; **b22.5** after the stop-start nose and delivery, we enter another world altogether, one where the malts reigns supreme. Love those spices, too. 43%

Brigantia Classic Single Malt db **(90) n22 t22.5 f23 b22.5** I'm massively impressed with this. Possibly the most beautifully distilled of all the German whiskies, the malt positively shimmers on both nose and palate. I do hope, though, that they allow their malts to mature further than this, as there is no great age on display here and you get the feeling that this was just setting out on the road, rather than completing the journey. 43%.

◈ **Brigantia Cognac Single Cask** db **(91) n22.5** stern tannin and a rigid fruit note seems to hold the barley in thrall; **t23.5** gushing barley is further primed by a fruitiness usual for a Cognac cask. This is just a brilliant delivery, designed to send malty shockwaves through first the taste buds then brain. How many layers of malt...? I lost count after about the tenth...; **f22** just a little bitterness has crept in, but the malt still reigns, though with a little (green) fruit pastel in the background; **b23** forget about having this for a nightcap. So vivid is this on the palate, it'll wake you up completely. 57% sc

◈ **Brigantia Gin Cask Finish** db **(80) n21 t20 f19 b20** Gin is gin. And whisky is whisky. And never should the two twains meet. Grim. 46%

Brigantia Rum Cask Finish Single Malt db **(88) n21 t23 f22 b22** Like many rum casks before, a crisp and firm embrace allows the malt to expand in personality only so far. What it can't control is the delivery which is full-bodied and sees the malt exploding in all directions, though in a controlled manner. Light chocolate tones also please. 46%.

◈ **Brigantia Single Malt Rum Cask Finish** db **(91) n22.5** spells out r-u-m. Not so much from having a nose like a standard rum, but the clipped malt and sugars on show; **t23** wow! That mouth feel could hardly be silkier if it tried, which is not the usual delivery for a rum. However, the follow-up crispness is. The blend of warming spices, sugars and tannins at the midpoint quite wonderfully bursts with character; **f22.5** we still have those glistening sugars at the death, again with that angular crispness unique to rum casks. The spices have taken on a little more hostile nature...; **b23** a sweeter, oilier version than their last bottling. Such is the ruminess of this, I poured what I thought was the Cognac cask version, nosed it and instantly realised I had the wrong sample! It doesn't come much rummier than that! A tad bitter at the death, though spices compensate. 46%

◈ **Brigantia Schwaben Single Malt** db **(89.5) n22** this distillery doesn't specialise in noses: they certainly are never a pointer to what will be happening next. Some pleasant apple notes; **t23** impressive malt coming through with light apple and pear just giving a gentler air; **f22** lovely vanilla; **b22.5** comprehensively malty and clean... *45%*

Brigantia Schwaben Single Malt db **(85)** n20.5 t22 f21 b21.5 Never quite seems to find its stride or narrative. The nose and finish are not particularly attractive, though the creamy vanillas and light butterscotch on delivery is more than agreeable. *45%.*

Brigantia Sherry Cask Finish Single Malt db **(82)** n21.5 t21 f19.5 b20 No sulphur on the sherry....hurrah! But that' the only really good news as this never quite finds the meaning of life with too many tangy, untidy and slightly bitter threads are left untied. Some petulant and nagging spices do ensure some entertainment. *46%.*

◈ **Brigantia Sherry Cask Finish** db **(89)** n21.5 a little feint undermines what appears to be a booming wine presence; **t23** rarely does the sherry butt offer quite such acidic sharpness on the palate: almost like underripe gooseberry attacking head on with a little muscovado sugar...and then jam tart to sooth the furrowed brow. Rather delicious, I have to say...; **f22** the feints were bound to return, and they have done here. The boldness of the fruit, though, acts as a wonderful diversion; **b22.5** a bold, assertive fruitiness to this malt sets it apart. Far from technically faultless, but highly enjoyable, nonetheless. *46%*

WHISKY-DESTILLERIE DREXLER Arrach. Working.

Bayerwold Pure Rye Malt Whisky los no. L19, destilliert 2/13, abgefüllt 5/19 db **(82.5)** **n19.5 t22 f20 b21** Well, they are nothing if not consistent these Dexler chaps. Just like the last bottling of their rye I encountered, some tasty and promising rye bound and gagged by thudding feints. *42%. 186 bottles.*

Bayerwold Single Malt Whisky los no. L29, destilliert 8/20/14, abgefüllt 9/20/19 db **(86)** **n19 t23 f22 b22** As kind as you'd like to be, not too much positive can be said about the feinty, vaguely butyric nose. However, the delivery: now that's a different matter! Barley on steroids, slightly of the grassy type but the Demerara sugars inject a further succulence that boasts weight, too. The finish is patchy, but still boasts a big maltiness which overcomes many of the obvious faults. *42%. 240 bottles.*

Drexler Arrach No. 1 Bayerwald Single Cask Malt Whisky Bourbonfass, fass no. H36, los no. L19, destilliert Dec 15, abgefüllt Sept 19 db **(87.5)** n21 t22 f22 b22.5 Ah, the Drexler character all over the nose: unmistakable! Theirs is a unique style, the extra feints here drumming up a fascinating combination of chestnut and cherries – even in a bourbon cask. Dry in part and always making you wonder where it is going next. Malty late on and entertaining. *46%. nc ncf sc. 72 bottles.*

Drexler Arrach No. 1 Bayerwald Single Cask Malt Whisky Cognacfass, fass no. H86, los no. L19, destilliert Aug 14, abgefüllt Sept 19 db **(86.5)** n20 t22.5 f22 b22 While the curiously salty nose never quite works, the gathering together of the more intense flavours for the main thrust of the delivery certainly get the juices running. Again, there is a deep saline content with spices matching the candied fruit punch for punch. Light cocoa notes at the death. *46%. nc ncf sc. 192 bottles.*

Drexler Arrach No. 1 Bayerwald Single Cask Malt Whisky portweinfass, fass no. H110, los no. L29, destilliert Nov 14, abgefüllt Sept 19 db **(89)** n21 t23.5 f21.5 b23 Yes, it balances, but probably more by luck than judgement. As a piece of art, this whisky comes under the Abstract movement... *46%. nc ncf sc. 85 bottles.*

Drexler Arrach No. 1 Bayerwald Single Cask Malt Whisky sherryfass, fass no. H48, los no. L19, destilliert Aug 11, abgefüllt Sept 19 db **(92)** n22.5 t23 f23 b23.5 So often I leave the sherry-matured whisky to the last of the pack as, more often than not, it will be the weak link of a distillery's output. I have left this to last and...struck gold! No sulphur! And, unusually for a Drexler, no weakening feints. Just lyrical malt without a bum note... *46%. nc ncf sc. 205 bottles.*

WHISKY-DESTILLERIE GRUEL Owen/Teck. Working.

Tecker Single Grain Whisky Aged 10 Years Chardonnay casks db **(93)** n23.5 t23 f23 b23.5 Now, that is all rather beautiful... *53.2%. ncf.*

WHISKY DESTILLERIE LIEBL Bad Kötzting. Working.

Coillmór Single Malt Whisky Bavaria x Toscana II Caberlot Rotwein Cask Finish cask no. 687, destilliert 08 Jun 10, abgefüllt 13 Feb 19 db **(80.5)** n18.5 t23 f19 b20 A fantastic cask which radiates high quality grape from the moment it hits the palate. But even that struggles against the feints from the distillate. *46%. sc. 364 bottles.*

WHISKY DESTILLERIE BLAUE MAUS Eggolsheim. Working.

Blaue Maus New Make dest Sept 18, los nr. 0918 db **(95)** n24 t24 f23 b24 The last time I tasted their new make it was a mind-blowing 87%abv: this is a watered down and pathetic

81%, though have to say it really does seem a lot less. Beautifully smoked and garnished in cocoa, there is so much to enjoy here. *81%. sc.*

Blaue Maus Single Cask Malt Whisky German oak cask, fass/los nr. 1, destilliert Jun 13 db **(88.5) n22 t23 f21.5 b22** Reminds me, this, of when I eat authentic local food in India, so busy and slowly warming are the spices. Not quite so buttery and malty as usual but the heather honey pinnacle on delivery is superb. *40%. sc.*

◈ **Blaue Maus Single Cask Malt Whisky** German oak cask, fass/los no.2, dist Jul 2012, db **(84.5) n21 t22.5 f20 b21** The uncommonly bitter finish confirms not all is right with the world here; the first clue given on the nagging nose. Such is the sweet and silky embrace on delivery – a kind of plum juice and molasses blend – that you feel this is going to be an unusually calm sailing for a Blaue Maus whisky. But the early impressions prove correct. *40% sc*

Blaue Maus Single Cask Malt Whisky Fassstärke German oak cask, fass/los nr. 1, destilliert Mar 02 db **(86.5) n20.5 t22 f22 b22** Feinty and chewy, the nose might be a bit of a mause trap but the extra oils on the body certainly make the most of maple syrup and delicate spices. *48.1%. sc.*

Elbe 1 Single Cask Malt Whisky German oak casks, fass/los nr. 5, destilliert Apr 08 db **(90) n21.5 t23 f22.5 b23** Gentle and elegant. *40%. sc.*

Elbe 1 Single Cask Malt Whisky Fassstärke German oak casks, fass/los nr. 1, destilliert Apr 06 db **(88) n21 t22 f22.5 b22.5** Maybe a bit wonky on the nose. But the salivating delivery is the prelude to a beautifully honeyed slow burn as the flavours build up like tributaries feeding a stream. The heather honey and light spice at the death charms. *45%. sc.*

Grüner Hund Single Cask Malt Whisky German oak casks, fass/los nr. 1, destilliert Jun 08 db **(88.5) n22.5 t22.5 f21.5 b22.** Another whisky which has suffered by the drastic weakening of strength. Some gorgeous acacia and ulmo honey notes gel well with the salt and vanilla. But dries out massively toward the end as there isn't quite muscle enough to support the structure. *40%. sc.*

Mary Read Single Cask Malt Whisky German oak cask, fass/los nr. 4, destilliert Apr 09 db **(90) n22 t23 f22.5 b22.5** Always regard this as the closest thing they produce to a bourbon-style whisky. The tannins have a sweet and significant input. *40%. sc.*

◈ **Mary Read Single Cask Malt Whisky Fassstärke 20 Years Old** German oak cask,fass/los nr.1, dist Apr 1998, db **(94.5) n23.5** what a nose! Sexy caresses of black cherry over muscovado sugars and firm, confident malt. There is even the vaguest hint of something phenolic drifting about. The oak bares that slightly astringent bite of Germen tannin. Together, this makes a very pretty – and magnificently complex - picture...; **t23.5** what a texture on the palate. If you wanted to create something so silky and absorbing, you'd be hard pushed. First comes a cherry juice arrival, backed by creamy pears. The intensity of the chocolate in the midground, perfectly matching the sultana, can hardly be bettered; **f23.5** you're wondering if this is some kind of illusion. But the beauty of the chocolate dispels that theory....; **b24** I'm not sure what is going on at this distillery, but this is the third bottling in a row which is a marked in improvement on their last and moved away from the bizarre spiciness which was undoing some of the brilliance of their early days. Here we have a bottling which comfortably embraces the fruitier aspects of malt whisky. And with a unique German oak tang as extra *46.8% sc*

Old Fahr Single Cask Malt Whisky German oak cask, fass/los nr. 2, destilliert Jun 10 db **(82) n20 t21 f20 b21** Not the old charmer I was expecting. Fahr too feinty... *40%. sc.*

Old Fahr Single Cask Malt Whisky Fassstärke German oak cask, fass/los nr. 1, destilliert May 05 db **(86) n20 t22.5 f21.5 b22** Once past the messy, butyric nose the flavours explode on the palate in salivating fashion, making a big play with the spiced orange blossom honey, moving them into eye-watering citruses. Technically incoherent, this certainly packs a punch. Not sure whether to love or hate it: even by Blaue Maus standards this is pretty outrageous. *52.1%. sc.*

◈ **Old Fahr Single Cask Malt Whisky** German oak cask, fass/los nr.4, dist Jun 2010, db **(91) n22** concentrated Malteser candy mixing it it that slightly unusual, dense German tannin...; **t23** excellent oils welcome the malt promised on the nose and appears to be able to wrap it up and deliver it in even more concentrated form. Meanwhile a slightly unusual tannin note – a little more astringent but vanilla flanked – proves a fascinating and effecting counterpoint...; **f23** wonderful, soft, oily malty chocolate with the lightest ulmo honey accompaniment; **b23** not the feinty failure f last year: this is Fahr too good, his time round. Seriously malty! And just so adorable! *40% sc*

◈ **Otto's Uisge Beatha Single Cask Malt Fassstärke** German oak cask, fass/los nr.2, dist Sep 2007, db **(94) n23.5** that unique acidic tannin from the German oak burns through. But the peat acts only as a fire retardant to offer light smoke rather than flame. It must be said: this is rather beautiful...; **t23.5** instead of billowing smoke, we get a delivery of thick molasses, muscovado sugars and then a far more serious layering of tart tannin which sets off the taste buds. Miraculously, after all that, the malt comes through loud and clear...with a light smokiness in its wake...; **f23** Black Forest Gateaux...lightly smoked, of course...; **b24** peat and German oak. In this form, something to celebrate. One of the best whiskies from Blaue Maus for quite some time... *55.6% sc*

Schwarzer Pirat Single Cask Malt Whisky German oak cask, fass/los nr. 1, destilliert Jul 06 db **(77) n22 t21 f16 b18** Starts so well with nuts and citrus on the nose followed by a vague bourbon, sugary delivery...then it all goes horribly wrong as the far too bitter as spices dig in. What the hell happened there...? *40%. sc.*

◈ **Schwarzer Pirat Single Cask Malt Whisky** German oak cask, fas/los nr.3, dist Jul 2006, db **(93) n23** complex and salty. Delightful strands of heather honey tie in very comfortably with the malt. Some excellently marshalled age here, too...; **t23.5** the heather honey needs no second invitation to set out its position. Light ulmo honey and malt are not very far behind. The coastal feel is like the sea spray washing over the skull and crossbones....; **f23** perfect oils keep the honey sweet...literally. The tannins, along with light chocolate, lap serenely at the death...; **b23.5** magnificent honey buzzing away with an intensity in keeping with the overall piece. Charming. *40% sc*

Spinnaker Single Cask Malt Whisky German oak cask, fass/los nr. 1, destilliert Apr 09 db **(78) n19 t20 f19 b20** My least favourite of the Blaue Maus cannon and it hasn't let me down again – or has, depending how you look at it. The reduction in strength has done it few favours as the butyric is still there, but the lowering in strength has upped the dry chalkiness and lowered the sugars. *40%. sc.*

◈ **Sylter Tide Single Cask Malt Whisky** fass/los nr.1, dist Mar 2012, bott Nov 2020, db **(91.5) n22** malt and salty coconut water is thickened by a near bourbonesque dose of liquorice...; **t23.5** as on the nose, the salt shows quickly, but the accompanying sugars ensure there is no sharpness. Salivating malt and acacia honey is thickened by light ulmo honey and vanilla; **f23** increasingly tang as the toastiness of the oak begins to creak and bite....; **b23** yet again, the ocean charts have been brought out, the sextant and compass deployed and now they have plotted a course in very different direction from the last Sylter I experienced. This one is for calmer seas, most interesting coastlines and a sweater breeze. No-one needs walk the plank for this idiosyncratic little beauty... *40% sc*

WHISKY-DESTILLERIE MEW Neuried. Working.

MEW Single Malt Whisky 8 Years Old Jamika rum finish, fass no. 1, bott 14 Apr 19, bott code: L2011 db **(91.5) n23 t23.5 f22.5 b22.5** Far less esters than the Salamansar Jamaica rum bottling, which means less depth. A very gentle journey, and never less than delicious, but might benefit further from upping the strength slightly *42%. nc sc.*

MEW Single Malt Whisky Single Cask Collection 8 Years Old Pedro Ximénez sherry finish, PX-fass no. 1, bott 8 Apr 19, bott code: L111 db **(86.5) n22 t23 f20 b21.5** A well-made, clean malt tipped into an excellent but not quite unspoiled PX cask. Very attractive and much to commend it. However, the one-dimensional style of the PX rather means the flavour course is unwavering and as beautiful as this whisky may be, it lacks rather in personality. *40%. nc sc.*

MEW Single Malt Whisky Single Cask Collection 8 Years Old Oloroso sherry finish, Oloroso-fass no. 1, bott 25 Apr 19, bott code: L222 db **(86) n22.5 t21.5 f21 b21.5** Unerringly sherry dominated. But just a little too bitter, if you bitte... *40%. nc sc.*

UNSPECIFIED

Trader Sylter Single Malt Whisky PX cask, cask no. 1018, dest Dec 14, bott Nov 18 **(90.5) n22.5 t23 f22 b23** A much better PX cask here with the malt actually getting some air- time despite thickness of the grape. Superb heather honey in the mix. *56.5%. sc.*

ICELAND
EIMVERK DISTILLERY Gardabaer. Working.

Flóki Icelandic Single Malt Whisky 3 Year Old Single Cask ex-Flóki Young Malt casks, cask no. 21, bott 2019 db **(85.5) n21 t22 f21 b21.5** Big and malty but a vague tobacco note hangs around, starting at the nose and holding a presence through to the very finish, which turns a tad bitter. The barley is big though at times glacial in its quality and is at its height moments after the delivery. Attractive, if a little untidy. *47%. sc.*

◈ **Flóki Icelandic Single Malt Whisky 3 Year Old Single Cask** ex-Flóki Young Malt casks, cask no. 21, bott 2020 db **(83.5) n20.5 t20.5 f22 b20.5** I had hoped that having got the bitterness and tobacco tones lightly out of sync last time, they might have tweaked it in the right direction for their next bottling. Sadly not. The sugars which build slowly from the intense malt augers well for the future and you feel the whisky should be better than its final product. The wide cut needs addressing as a tobacco note is never good. But there is also a kind hop-style bitterness in play, too, now and with the sugars so delicate balance is immediately compromised. About as frustrating as having Jon Dadi Bodvarsson playing up front for your football team... 47%. sc.

◈ **Flóki Icelandic Single Malt Whisky Beer Barrel Finish** American oak, finished in stout barrel, cask no. 1, bott 2019 db **(88) n21.5 t22 f22.5 b22** My experience with beer-finished whiskies over the years has not been the highlight of my career, I must admit. And I feared the worst here. Certainly, tasted cold there is little too positive to say about this whisky. But once gently warmed using the Murray Method we have an entirely different proposition. The entire mood and mouth feel changes – from a little harsh and bitter to something as warm and accommodating as an ancient inn. The growing sugars on the nose can't entirely eradicate the tobacco but the texture on the palate is silky and luxurious, allowing the heather honey to play up to full volume. The best, though, is saved until the last when a delightful chocolate paste mingles with the honey and intense malt: very, very impressive. My local brewery, Hook Norton, make a pretty wicked Double Stout, of which at least half a dozen bottles occupy the 60-year-old wooden brewery crate in my kitchen at any given time (and yes: I do buy them!). The finish reminds me of that; the texture a little closer to Sam Smith's Oatmeal Stout. If they could eliminate the tobacco note this would score pretty highly indeed. 47%. sc.

◈ **Flóki Icelandic Single Malt Whisky Double Wood Reserve 3 Year Old** primary cask smoke no.171, secondary cask meed no.2, bott 2020 db **(86.5) n21 t21 f23 b21.5** You know how frustrating it can be when a corner kicks fails to clear the first defender. Well, this whisky is a bit like that with the peat. You get all ready for the phenols to come floating in, but it doesn't clear the slightly hefty feints, first on the nose and then the delivery. However, there is a delicious frothiness to this once established on the palate. And from this light honey and chocolate tones emerge. Just about finds some kind of balance. I can't wait to see how this malt develops when they've sorted those cut points out. It is obvious from the complexity on the finish that his distillery has the capability to progress. 45%. sc.

Flóki Icelandic Single Malt Whisky Icelandic Birch Finish American oak, finished in Icelandic birchwood, cask no. 3, bott 2020 db **(90.5) n22 t23 f22.5 b23** Birch wood...? They should have no problem flogging this... Beautifully idiosyncratic. And though the first two or three mouthfuls are a shock, once you acclimatise, so many things suddenly become visible...; 47%. sc.

Flóki Icelandic Single Malt Whisky Sheep Dung Smoked Reserve 3 Year Old ex-Flóki Young Malt casks, cask no. 8, bott 2020 db **(91.5) n22.5 t23.5 f22.5 b23** And I remember the ancient days when Sheep Dip was supposed to be the avant-garde whisky... Should do well in baaaahhhs the world over... I suggest this whisky's taken neat, with neither water... nor mint sauce... 47%. sc.

◈ **Flóki Icelandic Single Malt Whisky Sheep Dung Smoked Reserve 3 Year Old** ex-Flóki Young Malt casks, cask no. 10 bott 2020 db **(87.5) n20 t23 f22 b22.5** Again badly needs the Murray Method to make it sing and bring out the considerable honey on tap. Very much a mood whisky and distinctly in the Marmite category. But the tobacco/hoppy/dungy kick may at times prove a little too much. A whisky that takes time to warm to but, once you become accustomed and the honeys start having their say, there is no denying this is not only huge, but hugely complex. 47%. sc.

◈ **Flóki Icelandic Single Malt Whisky Sherry Cask Finish** American oak, finished in first fill Oloroso sherry cask, cask no.2, bott 2019 db **(83.5) n20 t21.5 f21 b21** Just a huge hay/ tobacco kick on this, on both nose and delivery. The sherry doesn't even come in the runners-up spot. Whichever, should be matured in a barn rather than a warehouse. Just now and then a crisp fruitiness breaks free....but it is fleeting... 47%. sc.

ISRAEL
THE MILK & HONEY DISTILLERY Tel Aviv-Yafo. Working.

Milk & Honey Classic Single Malt Whisky db **(92) n22 t23.5 f23.5 b23** A dry malt which keeps the sugars under control at all times. The result is a complex dram where the barley plays an ever-increasing part in the overall flavour structure, especially when it finds it has muscle enough to accept the growing oak without for a moment losing its poise. Reminds me of some old malt whiskies from Scotland that could be found in the early 1980s where intense malt met equally full-on oak but had personality enough to ride the storm. Loses a mark for a hint of juniper on the nose: I didn't know they made gin at this distillery. I'd bet any money now that they do. Chaps, please be more careful in your bottling hall. Otherwise, absolutely delicious. 46%.

Milk & Honey Elements Single Malt Whisky Israeli Red Wine db **(92.5) n22.5 t23.5 f23 b23.5** Whichever red wine they used, you get the distinct feeling that it was pretty full bodied and dry: indeed, the kind of chalky middle-eastern wines I adored with lamb. Certainly this is a fat beast on the delivery both the oils from the malt and the richer elements of the fruit combining to give the deep oaky tones a run for their money. A malt which handsomely repays time and perseverance as the Murray Method certainly unlocks far more complexity than at first seems apparent. The growth of the spices is also a feature and curiously increases its presence as the malt begins to flourish. Complex and superbly well-weighted. *46%*.

Milk & Honey Elements Single Malt Whisky Peated db (84.5) n21.5 t22 f20.5 b20.5 A bit of a mess, this. Well distilled, though the half-hearted peat is never entirely convincing. But there seems to be something else at play here...gin, again, perhaps. Maybe, maybe not. Whatever, the flavour profile is confused and a little odd, the finish in particular. *46%*.

Milk & Honey Elements Single Malt Whisky Sherry db (87) n21 t22.5 f21.5 b22 About a year ago I was at my home in Kentucky and had been invited to a plush event that required a tuxedo. Discovering I presently didn't have one in the USA, I went to the tailor who had faithfully served me for the last 20 years and bought from him a "brand new" penguin suit. On the evening I dressed into it for the very first time, I found that I could not get my glasses to fit into the inside jacket pocket. Which was a bit strange. Something was preventing them from going in. So I investigated and found that my brand new dinner jacket contained a silk-claret kippah. And three single one dollar bills. The kippah had been presented for the wedding of Naava and Michael Schottenstein on 12th January 2019. Mazel tov, Naava and Michael...! I wasn't quite sure what to do with this skullcap, (since when have I been Jewish? What do I want with a kippah? I have hats already!), until it was time to taste the Israeli whiskies. Then I for once removed my famous Panama and replaced it with my kippah which, as a respectful Gentile, I wear as I write this. Now everything seems right in the world. Well, almost. Seeing that this was an Israeli whisky from a sherry cask I must admit confused me. I was present – ooh, maybe 25 years ago now – when the first-ever kosher Scotch single malt was bottled. I had a good chat with the Rabbi who was present to give the whisky his thumbs up and blessing; and I distinctly remember him telling me that providing the whisky was not matured in sherry, there was no problem. Bourbon casks kosha. Sherry casks unkosher. So what's this then....? Actually, I'm scratching my non-covered bit of head to work it out. Like the peated malt, you get the feeling that there is some type of alien intervention that is playing games with the grape and sending confusing messages. The one thing that escapes the mélee is the malt itself, which certainly manages to stand up for itself, and proudly. You know this is well made: the lusciousness of the mouthfeel confirms that. But... *46%*.

ITALY
L. PSENNER GMBH Tramin an der Weinstrasse. Working.
◈ **eRètico Single Malt** aged in grappa & sherry casks, serie CVP, no. 313908. bott code: L21084, db (85) n22 t21.5 f20.5 b21 A sherry-induced bitterness pervades too many areas of this malt for it ever to be a particularly comfortable whisky. I would really love to see what this was like in grappa and bourbon casks, as the distillate itself appears to be pretty well made. Must say I do love the sweet, gristy thrust of the barley soon after delivery. But a little too short, due to cask influence. Anyway, I felt compelled to taste the whisky today because in slightly more than two hours Italy will be at Wembley to face England and attempt to break English hearts. I once sat next to Italy manager Roberto Mancini at another international at Wembley stadium, during his days at Manchester City. And I have to say that, despite being proudly English and my heart telling me we'll win 1-0, my cold footballing brain is warning me of a 2-0 victory to Italy...as I have now told my friends. Italy's crisp passing and moving, plus ability to infiltrate almost unnoticed between the lines, has helped them become the most clever team in the tournament, and they are under less pressure. And I suspect their finishing will be better than this whisky's. Just hope I am wrong... Whichever, as a sportsman I sincerely hope the better team wins. *43%*

PUNI WHISKY DISTILLERY Glurns, Bozen. Working.
PUNI Arte I Italian Single Malt db (92) n23.5 t23 f22.5 b23 Just loses something in translation by dropping to 43%. The oils aren't quite abundant enough to take this to the next level of excellence. Even so, quite beautiful, unfailingly elegant and a lovely exhibition of honey. *43%. nc ncf.*

PUNI Aura Italian Single Malt 2 years in bourbon barrels & 4 years in peated Scotch whisky casks from Islay, dist 2012, bott 2019 db (96.5) n24 t24.5 f23.5 b24.5 This distillery is beginning to seriously impress me: the high scores from last year were obviously no flash in the pan. Make no mistake: this is beautifully constructed malt whisky: I doubt if Michelangelo could have done better. A European Whisky of the Year contender for certain. *56.2%, nc ncf.*

PUNI Sole 4 Year Old Italian Single Malt batch no. 04, bourbon barrels & Pedro Ximénez sherry casks db (90.5) n22.5 t23.5 f21.5b23 Now this is where I take my hat off and bow. Normally I face a PX cask much in the same way a revolutionary might face a firing squad. Is the PX cask 100% uncontaminated with sulphur? Actually, no it isn't. But the taint is minimal and this is a brilliant example of how to bring PX into the mix without it dominating to the deficit of all else. *46%. nc ncf.*

LIECHTENSTEIN
TELSER DISTILLERY Triesen. Closed.
Telser Liechtenstein Annual Release No. 1 Double Grain triple cask db (**92**) n22.5 t24 f22 b23.5 Just incredible mouthfeel to this. And to add to the joy, the sugar profile is just about unique, the lion's share of the flavour profile dedicated to a beautifully lush malt concentrate. Liquid ulmo honey fills in the gaps. Something very different and simply brilliant. *44.6%. sc.*

THE NETHERLANDS
ZUIDAM BAARLE Nassau. Working.
Millstone Dutch Single Malt Whisky Aged 10 Years American Oak bott code: 0378ZU db (**92.5**) n24 t23 f22.5 b23 Bang on the money with the honey and the malt. Love it!! *43%.*

Millstone Dutch Single Malt Whisky Aged 10 Years French Oak bott code: 2927 ZU db (**88.5**) n22 t22 f22.5 b22 A surprise malt, this. French oak normally belts out a bit more bite and tannic pungency. Here it seems to be happy to go with the malty flow. *40%.*

Millstone Dutch Single Malt Whisky Aged 12 Years Sherry Cask nbc db (**86**) n22 t21.5 f21 b21.5 A clean sherry butt, but there are buts. There is a tang from the spirit itself which gives a slight feinty buzz. Characterful, but there is a dark side. *46%.*

Millstone 2010 Dutch Single Malt Whisky Double Sherry Cask Oloroso & PX nbc db (**88**) n22.5 t22 f21.5 b22 Like most PX involved whiskies, don't bother looking too hard for complexity. *46%. Special #16.*

Millstone Dutch Single Malt Whisky Oloroso Sherry bott code: 0328ZU db (**81**) n19 t23 f18 b21 Make no mistake: this is a fabulous, faultless sherry butt at work here. And the delivery offers grapey bliss. But, sadly, the underlying structure of the spirit itself throws up a few question marks. *46%.*

Millstone Dutch Single Malt Whisky Oloroso Sherry bott code: 0580ZU db (**84.5**) n21 t21.5 f21 b21 Eye-wateringly tart. *46%.*

Millstone Dutch Single Malt Whisky Peated Double Maturation American oak, Moscatel cask finish, dist 2013, nbc db (**89**) n22 t22.5 f22 b22.5 An oily and deceptively full bodied whisky. Full entertainment value here. *46%. Special #14.*

Millstone Dutch Single Malt Whisky Peated Pedro Ximenez bott code: 0659ZU db (**89.5**) n22.5 t22 f22.5 b22.5 One of the combinations which most consistently fails around the world is peat and PX, one seemingly always cancelling out the other. Here, though, it somehow works and though complexity and elegance are at a premium, it is not short on personality. *46%.*

Millstone Dutch Single Malt Whisky Peated Pedro Ximenez bott code: 0590ZU db (**91**) n22.5 t23 f22.5 b23 I still remain no great fan of the unholy trinity of PX, peat and barley. But. have to say that this one does have enough character, on the delivery especially, to win a few friends...me included! *46%.*

Millstone Dutch Single Rye 92 Rye Whisky 100% new American oak casks, nbc db (**94**) n23.5 t23.5 f23 b24 Everything I was hoping from their 100 Rye, but never got. A European mainland classic! And less of a Millstone: more of a milestone... *46%.*

Millstone Mill am oak 10 Year Old db (**87**) n21.5 t22.5 f21 b22 Bit of a curiosity this one: the crunchiness of the barley on this is as hard as the millstone which crushed the malt. Out of sync on both nose and finish – there is a distinct tang to the finish of the latter – this is all about the gorgeous sugars that meld with the barley for the bright and chewy delivery. *46%.*

Single Barrel Oloroso Sherry 23 Year Old db (**93.5**) n23.5 t23.5 f23.5 b23 A faultless sherry butt paints a very pretty picture of oloroso at its most luxuriant: delicious! The whisky, though, appears to have been lost somewhere along the line... *46%. sc. Special #18.*

NORWAY
AURORA SPIRIT DISTILLERY AS Lyngseidet. Working.
Bivrost Niflheim Artic Single Malt Whisky triple cask matured db (**88.5**) n22 t23 f21 b22.5 So Norway proudly joins the roll call of world whisky nations, and with this first-ever bottling also completes the Scandinavian set. It is certainly a creature hewn from its land, as this is a malt that matches the country's rugged geology with an awe-inspiring delivery, full of peaks and valleys, inlets and fjords: it is not an easy whisky to navigate. The nose is far from perfect, revealing a feinty nature which you know will return on the finish. The Murray Method will help you burn some of those oils off and release more of the lime blossom honey that is dying to escape and reveal something a lot more enticing, sexy even. The delivery, though, is about as rugged as it comes thanks again to those big oils, but also the

malt which is fighting its corner frantically. Again the honey comes up for air, but it's frantic stuff - especially when the feints make their predictable return. So, a wonderful choice for my 1,000th sample for the Whisky Bible 2021. A King amongst Scandinavian malts and an experience you can't afjord to miss... 46%. 1,622 bottles.

MYKEN DESTILLERI AS Nordland. Working.

Myken Artic Single Malt Whisky Hungarian Touch 2019 3 Years 10 Months db (93) n23 t23.5 f23 b23.5 Is a Hungarian touch salty...? Beautifully made and matured whisky that keeps things simple. 47%.

Myken Artic Single Malt Whisky Octave Symphony 2020 4 Year Old db (95) n23.5 t24 f23.5 b24 this is actually far better than the last eight scotch single malts I tasted: not a sulphur molecule in sight. "Robert Louis Stevenson, Robbie Burns, Robert The Bruce, Bonnie Prince Charlie, Alec Salmond, Sean Connery, The Loch Ness Monster vi har slått dem alle sammen, vi har slått dem alle sammen! Nicola Thatcher can you hear me? Margaret Sturgeon... your distilleries took a hell of a beating! Your distilleries took a hell of a beating!" 47%.

Myken Artic Single Malt Whisky Peated Sherry 2019 3 Year Old db (94.5) n23.5 t24 f23 b24 I think they mean sherried peat... Some great complexity here. And they have been judicious in their choice of cask, which is 100% sulphur free. 47%.

Myken Artic Single Malt Whisky Solo PX 2020 4 Year Old db (88.5) n22 t22.5 f22 b22 A perfectly sound, sulphur-free sherry cask. That's the good news. The not so good news is that this PX cask does what PX casks do: they wipe out any trace of the malt or the distillery identity. Except in this case for the salt, which fair rattles about the nose and palate. So, yes, very enjoyable, if at times overly sweet and sticky in a cloying, old date kind of way. But hearty congrats on them obviously going out of their way to secure a pure and clean butt. 59.7%. sc.

PORTUGAL
VENAKKI DISTILLERY Alpiarça. Working.

◇ **Venakki Moonshine Single Cask** Cask No 6 (93) n23.5 t23.5 f23 b23 When is a whisky not a whisky? When it is just weeks away from being three years old and tastes as good as this. The nose alone can have you in a trance as you try to work out its distinctive but fabulously attractive mix of mallow, marzipan and a kind of soft, creamy cedarwood: a truly unique aroma in the whisky world. Very unusually, the delivery is the nose now in taste form, those semi-pungent tannins becoming, immediately, the source of the spice. But it is the soothing oils, spreading both warmth and an almost orangey sweetness across the roof of the mouth, making a fool of the spirit's non-whisky status. Precocious? Not half!!! And how I'd love to see the aroma of this Moonshine as a soap... 50% Moonshine Ltd

Woodwork Batch No. 1 Cask Strength Blended Whisky ex-bourbon barrels with first fill barrique of ex-Douro wine and ex-Madeira wine, bott Apr 20 db (87.5) n21.5 t22 f22 b22 Simutaneously light and aggressive. That said, juicy, sweet and easy drinking despite the strength, but never quite achieves the depth of layering you feel it is capable of. Enjoyable. 60.5%. nc ncf.

Woodwork Cask Strength Single Malt Whisky matured in a 20 year old vintage port Tawny cask, first maturation in a bourbon barrel with extra maturation in a single cask first fill 500l, cask no. 1, bott Apr 20 db (93) n23 t23.5 f23 b23.5 This is the first cask from a brand new distillery? Astonishing. I chose this as whisky number 999 sfor the Whisky Bible 2021. And so glad I did for this is top- flight quality, clean enough not to interrupt the intricate flow of the barrel influence; hefty enough to allow a little malty breeze to ruffle fruit leaves. For a first bottling...amazing. And for an entire nation...? They have done Portugal proud... 63.8%. nc ncf sc.

Woodwork Duoro STR Cask Strength Single Malt Whisky first maturation in a bourbon barrel with extra maturation in a single cask first fill 225l, cask no. 8, bott Apr 20 db (94) n23 t23.5 f23.5 b24 You can certainly count on STR casks to kick up the piercing juiciness and it doesn't let you down here! Some statement being made here, believe me! 64.6%. nc ncf sc.

Woodwork Duoro STR Cask Strength Single Malt Whisky first maturation in a bourbon barrel with extra maturation in a single cask first fill 225l, cask no. 9, bott Apr 20 db (91) n22 t23.5 f22.5 b23 A drier, more spiced-up version of Cask 8, with a load more caramel to boot...! Another gorgeous Portuguese single malt whisky. I wonder if that is the first time that last sentence has ever been written... 64.8%. nc ncf sc.

Woodwork Madeira Cask Strength Single Malt Whisky first maturation in a bourbon barrel with extra maturation in a single cask first fill 225l, cask no. 10, bott Apr 20 db (91.5) n23 t23 f22.5 b23 Well, that's made a statement. Venakki are not scared of going gung-ho on the flavour front and providing edge of seat, gripping entertainment. A few little changes will be required to be made if refinement ever becomes part of their plans. But, in the meantime, sit down, fasten your seatbelt...and hold on for dear life! 63.5%. nc ncf sc.

❖ **Venakki Woodwork Mature Brandy Cask** Cask No 3 **(90.5) n22.5 t23 f22.5 b23** Such a different animal to the Moonshine Cask no 6... That is a voluptuous, sexily scented, tease of a spirit. This is an altogether more straightforward experience, much more dependent on the barley which broadcasts the malt with all the confidence of the blemish-free, cask strength bottling it is. And grape, which despite a chalky haze on the nose, offers a firmness to match the malt. Salivating and succinct in delivery, the fruit grows in confidence and stature. Crisp, no-nonsense and as refreshing as a spirit on the threshold of whiskyhood should be. *64.7% Moonshine Ltd*

SLOVENIA
DISTILERIO MOLINO DEL ARCO Segovia. Working.
❖ **Broken Bones Single Malt Aged 3 Years** barrel no. 1/20 db **(91) n22.5** a satisfying, soft maltiness does battle with the rather unusual tannin which sparks the spices into this, the likes of which I have never before encountered. A light cedarwood kick, too, which veers off towards something semi-bourbony: unique ...; **t23** when malt is this intense, the salivation qualities go through the roof. It is as though the grist has grist and the accompanying sugars ensure those salivating notes last. The midpoint is a fascinating interplay between pure, solid malt and a tannin-led vanilla which, like on the nose, has a unique signature...a kind of grizzled bite; **f22.5** now that oak note really kicks in deep...and dries the palate towards a degree of slightly nutty, at times mocha, sophistication; **b23** a distillery I have never visited – and I must put this right as soon as the Covid insanity has died down. One of the most fascinating malts of the year as there is a tannin note here which reminds me very slightly of Hungarian oak but with a little more of a dry snarl about it. That said, it complements the fresh gristiness superbly. What an unexpected treat! With Broken Bones this delicious, it would be all too easy to get plastered. So remember to spit... *46%. sc.*

SPAIN
DISTILERIO MOLINO DEL ARCO Segovia. Working.
DYC Aged 8 Years (90) n22 t23 f22.5 b22.5. I really am a sucker for clean, cleverly constructed blends like this. Just so enjoyable! *40%*

DYC Single Malt Whisky Aged 10 Years (91) n22 t23 f23 b23 Far more complex than it first seems. Like Segovia, where the distillery is based, worth exploring...*40%*

DESTILERÍAS LIBER Granada. Working.
❖ **Whisky Pura Malta Embrujo De Granada** bott code: Lote 21/049 db **(92.5) n23.5** as Eliza Doolittle might have said: "the Spanish malt falls mainly for the salt..." Light ozone kicks in to give a remarkable rockpool feel to this...; **t23.5** exceptional silk on delivery, the malt doesn't as much arrive as ooze on to the palate. Salt and grape form a somewhat tangy, invigorating unison to the midpoint. It then dries as the vanillas kick in...and kick in hard...; the grape meanwhile had something angular and sharp to say early on, and in a more rounded way later...; **f22.5** duller and drier, with chalk now for salt...; **b23** a dramatic variation from their last bottling with a highly attractive degree of salt giving this malt a distinctly coastal air, despite it being somewhat inland from the southern coast of Spain. My Fair Whisky...(Incidentally, the Murray Method lifts this whisky onto a far higher level than when served cool or chilled.) *40%*

Whisky Puro Malta de Granada bott code: LOTE 19-014 db **(88) n22 t22.5 f21.5 b22** An hospitable and friendly malt throughout. Cream toffee and raison in abundance both on nose and delivery. The finish does dry with a little quaver to the previously clear tone but the sweetness levels are well tuned and seem to act as a perfect foil to healthy tannins. Enjoyable and at higher strength could certainly make a mark. *40%.*

UNSPECIFIED
❖ **Airem Single Malt Aged 14 Years** matured in PX casks bott code 21\072 **(89) n22.5** a singular nose, wrapped in sultana fruitiness the kind of aroma you might find in a barley as spices are mixed in with the sultana and raisin: almost a breakfast whiskey nose, you might say....; **t23** the silky denseness of the grape says two letters: P and X. The malt has broken up the complete lushness you've find from, say a 15 year old PX sherry in bottle, but not by much on delivery. The sherry sweetness contains all those biting spices you'd expect. The main interference to the grapey charge comes from the backdrop of layered tannins, This is some chewy experience; **f21** just as when drinking PX, the sugars feel a little spent and spicy at the death. The tannins also duck and dive, weave and bob, and a little bitterness ensues, which may or may not be of the sulphur variety....; **b22.5** not entirely sure I have ever encountered a whisky which appeared to have been so solidly carved from grape. Forget your Macallans. This is something else entirely. Of course PX are on a different plane to any other

sherry butt. There is no forgiving, no relenting. They take a whisky and make it bow to its sugary command. Somewhere beneath this tumult of grape lies some 14-year-old whiskey. However, it was clear to the palate as an airfield is to the pilot of a bi-plane as he tries to land in thick fog. But this is Spanish whiskey, presumably, maturing in the most Spanish of sherry butts. So, you have to shift your thinking and get into the mood. A bit like getting your shoulders under the waves, you have to take the plunge to enjoy the moment. And I admit, though despite some early reservations about the finish, once I dived in this was a whiskey I thoroughly enjoyed... *43% 5,000 bottle*

SWEDEN
HIGH COAST DISTILLERY Bjärtrå. Working.
High Coast Distillery Archipelago Baltic Sea 2019 bott Dec 2018 db (95) n24 t23 f23 b24 Nautical...but nice! A deep whisky...and deeply impressive. *54.5%. nc ncf. 1,000 bottles.*

High Coast Distillery Visitor Center Cask batch no. 5 db (95.5) n24 t24 f23.5 b24 That's their best use of bourbon casks yet. Superb. There are many great reasons to visit Sweden. Here's another one...Hang on a minute, I'm on my way... *50%. nc ncf.*

MACKMYRA Gästrikland. Working.
Mackmyra 10 Years Single Malt art. nr. MC-008 db (89) n22.5 t23 f21.5 b22 Taking into account the use of the number on this bottling, not sure if I should be tasting this to Ravel's Balero... *46.1%.*

Mackmyra Brukswhisky art. nr. MB-004 db (95.5) n24 t23.5 f24 b24 Having just tasted a succession of Scotch whisky brands each spoiled at the end by the unmistakable and unforgiving pollutant of sulphur; and after giving my poor, duffed-up taste buds a rest of over an hour during which time strawberries and crisps were consumed to try and neutralise the deadening effect on my palate, I have deliberately re-started my tasting day with a whisky I know to be as clean yet entertaining as can possibly be found. Was this a wise choice? You bet! Carrying a little more weight than some previous bottlings but still a real Scandinavian beauty... *41.4%.*

Mackmyra Grönt art. nr. MC-014 db (91) n23.5 t23.5 f22 b22.5 Begins life bold and with a roar and finishes with a bit of a whimper. Bloody tasty and complex, though! *46.1%.*

Mackmyra Jaktlycka db (87.5) n23.5 t23.5 f19 b21.5 Concentrates on the grain and associated vanillas on delivery, which is some distance away from the sexy, passion fruit nose. The finish, though, is a little off beam thanks to the casks. *46.1%.*

Mackmyra Moment Lava db (95) n24 t24 f23 b24 Maybe this should be called Momint, for the mintiness on the delivery is amazing! Usually this note can be achieved only by long aging in cask, in the same way diamonds can only come about through volcanic activity. And this really is a gem of a whisky combining an adroit usage of smoke with the vaguest undertones of clean raisins. But it is all there to be found with the Murray Method and time, unlocking some closely guarded secrets. Even the finish has that wonderful chocolate mint fade. This is blending at its very finest and European whisky that will be among the best to be found this year. *44.4%.*

Mackmyra Single Cask 2nd Fill ex-Bourbon Cask Fat Nr 11638 dist 26 Feb 14 db (95.5) n24 t24 f23.5 b24 One of those brain-busting bottlings where the dryness if so intrinsic, yet the sweetness so confident, astonishing complexity pulses from every single atom. The smokiness is of the driest, most acidic and sooty kind, and obviously makes a point of being. The sweetness is of the heather-honey variety. Surely when those two meet the result will be a mess. Not a bit of it. Instead, the sugars melt down into a more marzipan nuttiness, the smoke oils up very slightly and embraces the honey. I have no doubt that when my much-loved friend Angela opened this cask for the first time and sampled its wares a few Swedish-Italian expletives of semi-orgasmic delight issued from her lips. And with every good reason! *51.4%. sc.*

Mackmyra Single Cask 2nd Fill ex-Bourbon Cask Fat Nr 11641 dist 26 Feb 14 db (94.5) n24 t23.5 f23 b24 A close relation to cask 11638, but with some subtle but telling differences. Here both the dryness and sweetness are both just a notch below optimum intensity: no bad thing. The result is a drizzle of aromas and flavours rather than a downpour. But then that is the beauty of second fill bourbon cask, as a blender my preferred choice of cask to make memorable things happen. Here, though, the natural caramels have a bitter say, which means there was a little less left in the tank of this cask than the last one, thereby dumbing down slightly more the more intricate nature of the sugars and tannins combined. Even so...just so lovely! *50.8%. sc.*

Mackmyra Single Cask 1st Fill Gravity Amarone Wine Cask Fat Nr 34618 db (95) n23.5 t23.5 f23 b23.5 The gooseberry jam on buttered toast nose has to be one of the best aromas of the day for me – certainly the most stomach rumbling. Likewise the delivery of warming cherry fruitcake with a light cocoa powder topping is ramping my appetite up further. This must be the ultimate pre-prandial whisky. It's certainly one good enough to eat.... *50.3%. sc.*

Mackmyra Single Cask 1st Fill Gravity Amarone Wine Cask Fat Nr 36558 db (**90**) **n23 t23 f21.5 b22.5** A marginally drier version of the Amorone above though sharper, too. And with far more of a niggle on the finish. But then when fruit is on song, it certainly hits the high notes. 50.3%. sc.

Mackmyra Single Cask 1st Fill Gravity Port Wine Cask Fat Nr 37574 db (**88.5**) **n23 t22 f21.5 b22** Peppery on the nose – almost to sneezing point. But the fruit is a little too broad, yet intense and plummy, for top vibes even though a little custard too does make it into the mix. Untidy finale. 49.6%. sc.

Mackmyra Single Cask 1st Fill Gravity Port Wine Cask Fat Nr 38624 db (**91.5**) **n23 t23 f22.5 b23** A slightly more jammy personality to the grape aligned with a better integrated spiciness makes for a much more comfortable ride here. Indeed, some of the phases on this are a joy, the custard making way for a slightly drier vanilla and even a wave or two of bourbon-style liquorice. Still the finish is not quite in tune with nose and delivery. The differences between this and cask 37574 are only minor, but when they add up there is a real feel of class to this one. 49.6%. sc.

Mackmyra Single Cask 1st Fill ex-Bourbon Calvados Cask Fat Nr 40233 dist 10 Jun 17 db (**85.5**) **n22 t22 f20.5 b21** Just a little too aggressive with the tannins. Austere in all the wrong places, especially the transitional ones where some deft sweetness is required but doesn't quite materialise. 49.4%. sc.

Mackmyra Single Cask 1st Fill ex-Bourbon Calvados Cask Fat Nr 40234 dist 10 Jun 17 db (**93.5**) **n23 t23.5 f23 b24** Ah, that's more like it! Shews none of the aggressive intransigence of its sister cask and even a delicate degree of apple flits across both the nose and palate with something approaching elegance. Much creamier and fuller-bodied with the delicate ulmo honey and more boisterous molasses forming a beautiful counter to the drier vanillas. But the malt never stops singing, the spices accompanying and the apple teasing. Everything that cask 40233 wants to be...but isn't... 49.2%. sc.

Mackmyra Svensk Moment 22 Swedish oak, warehouse: Bodås mine db (**95.5**) **n24 t24 f23.5 b24** A very beautiful, lightly smoked moment. In fact a great many moments: enough to put this into the taste off for European whisky of the year. Utterly adorable and puts to shame the sulphur-spattered Scotch single malt I was tasting earlier. 42.4%. 1,100 bottles.

Mackmyra Svensk Single Cask Whisky Reserve The Dude of Fucking Everything fatnr. 14-0304, fattyp: refill bourbon, lager: Smögen, flasknr: 30, fatfyllmning: 2014-10-06, buteljering: 2019-09-12 db (**96**) **n24.5 t24 f23.5 b24** Just one of those astonishing, almost hypnotic whiskies, the nose in particular, which you find you can't tear yourself from: a bit like Agnetha Fältskog's part pure, part faltering, part fragile, part vulnerable but always haunting singing in The Day Before You Came, operating well within itself, but occasionally letting rip with a stunning, faultless, soul-piercing note to leave you in no doubt that you are in the presence of something uniquely special. And beautiful. As I taste and write this it is someone's birthday today: Happy 70th Agnetha Fältskog. 49.9%. sc.

Mackmyra Vintersol art. nr. MC-013, ex-port wine casks db (**74**) **n22 t20 f15 b17** Nope! After the promising (and threatening nose) becomes flat as a witch's tit and casts a less than pleasant spell on the finish. Poor casks like these are so un-Mackmyra-ish. 46.1%.

NORRTELJE BRENNERI Norrtälje. Working.

Roslagswhisky Eko No. 1 Single Cask batch: Bourbonfat 23-200/No3, dest Nov 13, bott 5 Feb 20 db (**86**) **n21 t22.5 f21 b21.5** Exceptionally malty, making great use of the heather-honey which runs through it. A slightly unconvincing cut ensures big oils which dull and bitter just a little too much late on. 61.6%. nc ncf sc. Bottled for Cinderella Whisky Fair 2020.

Roslagswhisky Eko Single Cask batch: Sherry olorosfat 28-30, dest Jun 13, bott 31 Jan 20 db (**86.5**) **n21.5 t21.5 f22 b21.5** A curious whisky where the distillery's thick-set style is again evident bolstered further by a chubby fruitiness. A bit untidy as the feints kick in, though now some extra cocoa and hickory tones up the complexity. 46.2%. nc ncf sc.

Roslagswhisky Eko Single Cask batch: Sherry olorosfat 43-250, dest Apr 16, bott 31 Jan 20 db (**91**) **n22.5 t23 f22.5 b23** Oh, so much better! A cleaner, more precise distillate ensures there are no luring feints around to take the edge of the charm and complexity which abounds here. An excellent sherry cask offers a grapey gloss on the intense vanilla and muscovado sugar mix. Layered, relaxed and the slow build of the spice and its salivating consequences cannot be faulted. Now they have found the right path, I hope they can stick to it. 48.7%. nc ncf sc.

SMÖGEN WHISKY Hunnebostrand. Working.

◇ **Smögen 100 Proof Single Malt Whisky** (**96**) **n24.5** faultless. The distillate is feint free and from the heart; the oils assist rather than hinder and hide; the phenols are thick with intent and boast a vague anthracite acidity, too. The sugars head in the direction of lighter molasses. There is even a hint of the cattle byre. All in all, it would be churlish and impolite to ask for more; **t24** those sugar notes mix in with flaked chocolate and barley grist and thickened with the creamy oils....; **f23.5** long, long, long...all that was going on before except now the chocolate is taking control and adding extra vanilla; **b24** I'm almost certain that if I slipped this into one of my tastings anywhere around the world and told people this was a south coast Islay, not a single person would dispute my word. However, few casks even from Islay are as faultless and so magnificently weighted as this. A landmark malt. *57.1%. Highfern*

Smögen Primör Revisited Single Malt 2019 cask no. 46-53, dist 2013 db **(95.5) n23.5 t24.5 f23.5 b24** Yet another brutally beautiful no holds barred peat orgy from this distillery where the lush mouthfeel is matched only by the uncompromising smokiness. Young and lusty, just one mouthful battles with your taste buds for a good six or seven minutes without letting go. Superbly distilled, this is a five-course malt that is neither for the faint or feint hearted. Indeed, smogen by name and nature. *68.2%. nc ncf. 1,616 bottles.*

SPIRIT OF HVEN DISTILLERY Sankt Ibb. Working.

Spirit of Hven Charlies Wagon Single Malt Whisky bott code: 82T015 1333 db **(79) n20 t22 f18 b19** I have to say that I am a big fan of this distillery, and it usually scores exceptionally well in the Bible: it has set its own bar very highly. But this malt is far from Hvenly, being off balance, at times too sweet at others too bitter and, overall, off key – especially towards the end. Very disappointing. *47.1%.*

SWITZERLAND
BAUERNHOF BRENNEREI LÜTHY Muhen. Working.

Herr Lüthy Pure Swiss Corn Bööron cask no. 554, dest 2014, abge 2018 db **(91) n23 t23 f22 b23** A surprising Swiss bourbon offering a chance to draw delicious flavour map of previously uncharted territory. *43%. sc.*

DISTILLERIE BRAUEREI Locher Appenzell. Working

◈ **Säntis Malt Single Malt Edition Alpstein** edition no. XVII, aged 7 years, rum cask, bott 18/03/2021, db **(88.5) n22 t22.5 f22 b22** Rum casks can sometimes have a tendency to put a hard outer shell round both the nose and mouth experience. That is exactly what has happened here: the sugars are captured and unable to move around freely. That leaves the delicate hop and spice to have a bigger say than they otherwise might. The result is a genuinely unique DNA, at its best early in delivery when the lemon blossom honey is in full bloom. *48% nc ncf 2421 bottles*

◈ **Säntis Malt Single Malt Edition Genesis No.2** aged 7 years, matured in beer & bourbon barrels, finished acolon wine cask, bott 4/6/2020, db **(89) n23.5** a complex array of sugars settles for moist Melton Hunt cake with an extra dollop of molasses. A pint of Ruddles County sits warming in the summer sun on the other side of the table: a nose to take some of us back 40 years....; **t22.5** sensual and oily, the malt says a brief how-do before the sugars on the nose cascade down in raisin-rich fashion...; **f21** the late slight hoppy bitterness was expected; **b22** the amazing nose means the delivery has much to live up to. Give it a dose of the Murray Method, release the sugars and oils...and makes a pretty good fist of it. *48.5% nc ncf 1088 bottles*

◈ **Säntis Malt Single Malt Edition Liechtenstein** edition no. VIII, aged 7 years, matured in old beer cask, pinot noir finish, db **(90.5) n23** steaming Staffordshire oatcakes next to a freshly opened jar of plum jam...; **t24** one of the best European deliveries of the year. Such beauty cannot be attained by taste alone: there is, vitally, the mouth feel. This is midweight with a hint (and no more) of stickiness. But the complex berry fruit helps including, wondrously, a fair punnet of loganberry aided by an alchemist's measure of manuka honey and spiced molasses...; **f21** the finish is as entangled, tangy and uncomfortable as the delivery loiters around perfection...; **b22.5** if only they could bottle the intensity of those concentrated fruits, spices and sugars on delivery....oh, hang on: they have...! *53% 500 bottles*

◈ **Säntis Malt Single Malt Golfer's Birdie Water** aged 6 years, matured old oak beer casks, finished sherry casks, db **(88.5) n22 t23 f21.5 b22** Those who are rather fond of German Christmas markets and biting into their seasonal cakes and biscuits will probably need a bottle of this around the house come December. This is virtually a liqueur masquerading as a whisky and bursting at the seams with intense spices as well as golden syrup and molasses. Thankfully the hops have vanished and you don't have to fear the beer... well. Maybe not until the very end. The malt has vanished and fruit and spices enjoy some kind of wild Thelma and Louise spree before going over the slightly bitter hoppy cliff at the end. Too sweet for greatness. Too much fun to be ignored... *46% nc ncf 2000 bottles*

◈ **Säntis Malt Single Malt Snow White No.8** aged 6 years, Pineau finish, db **(87.5) n23 t22.5 f20.5 b21.5** Another Santis which gives the taste buds a thorough, back-of-hand-slapping working over: nothing is straightforward with this distillery. Toffee and grape appear to be working in close harmony so far as the nose and delivery is concerned. As soon as the salt kicks in – to armchair gripping, eye-watering effect – a bitterness (hops?) wanders into view, slightly destabilising the balance. *48%*

DISTILLERIE ETTER Zug. Working.

⬧ **Johnett Single Malt single Cask no 127** 7 year Pinot Noir barrel, 5 year Merlot finish, dist May 2008, bott Sep 2020, db **(90) n22** a soft, soupy fruitiness that gives lie to the strength of the malt. Instead we get stewed plums and light molasses; **t23.5** the silk delivery is the lull before the storm of intense raisin and red liquorice. Chewy, toasty and some excellent balancing tannin. Gosh...! **f21.5** just bitters out very slightly. The vanilla controls the fruit with ease, but the late tang is slightly off-key; **b23** however you look at this, this is a remarkable malt. With those two casks types so many things could go wrong, and creating harmony is by no means a straightforward task. Yet the delivery and follow-through is nothing less than something to marvel at. *50.1% sc*

DESTILLERIE MACARDO Strohwilen. Working.

Macardo Single Malt dist 2010, bott code 7002 db **(92.5) n22.5 t23.5 f22.5 b23.5** An honest and attractive, beautifully distilled, single malt squeezing out every last barley note. *42%.*

LANGATUN DISTILLERY Langenthal, Kanton Bern. Working.

Langatun 10 Year Old Second Edition Single Malt dist 18 Sept 10 db **(95) n24 t24 f23 b24** When it comes to balance and structure of a European mainland single malt whisky, I doubt if anyone has been more consistent over the last decade than Langatun. Indeed, I always leave their whiskies to the very end of my annual European sojourn as a kind of reward to myself... and also to see if they are still worth waiting for. They are.... *61.1%.*

Langatun Founder's Reserve 10 Year Old Single Malt cask no. 135, dist 10 Oct 10 db **(94.5) n23.5 t23.5 f23.5 b24** Another Swiss to watch... *60.7%. sc*

⬧ **Langatun Marsala Cask Finish Single Malt** dist Aug 2012, Mar 2021, Lot no. B01/03/21, db **(87.5) n22.5 t22 f21 b22** To nose, the wine is in concentrated concentrate form: tight, almost earthy, acidic. Can fair take the breath away...; a youthful malt punches out from beyond the fruit. To taste, the new make cocks a malty snook at the fruit, which then retaliates by landing a series of intense fruity blows on the taste buds. Irritatingly, the finish is quite bitter and tingly; this doesn't go quite according to plan by Langatun standards. An unusual minty cool finale. So despite the eight years in the cask this still boasts a very young persona on both nose and delivery. The Marsala cask, meanwhile, works like the devil to make amends... *49.12% nc 495 bottles*

⬧ **Langatun Old Bear (89.5) n22.5** no tricks or thrills: just stand up malt and vanilla with a modest hint of nutmeg; **t23** now the complexity kicks in. Langatun appear to have mastered the difficult task of layering varying sugar and honey tones: not just in intensity of sweetness but density on the palate, also. Some skill, that! Ulmo honey and rapeseed honey combine with a strata of Demerara. Elsewhere the vanilla and barley refuse to be mere bystanders, the latter combining with the sugars to offer a welcome juiciness; **f21.5** dries with a slight wobble; **b22.5** definitely a different direction here for this distillery. *46%. Highfern*

⬧ **Langatun Old Deer (93.5) n22.5** The malt has been placed on a dais here. No big age, but the intensity...wow! **t24** Chelsea bun! Sticky, sweet and a light muscovado sugar fruitiness combine beautifully. Like the nose the age doesn't seem great, but the layering and concentration of the malt is astonishing. Demerara sugars cascade over the taste buds; **f23.5** long, remains lush with excellent oils and a coppery sharpness amid the chocolate fudge-like tannins; **b23.5** Old Deer? This is a 16 point stag of a malt.... *46%. Highfern*

⬧ **Langatun Rioja Cask Finish Single Malt** dist 2014, bott 17/11/2020, cask no. 433, db **(92.5) n23.5** a ten to fifteen-minute nose: the interplay between malt, marmalade and orange-blossom honey is something to savour. The bottom, weightier note is pure tannin....; **t23.5** few distilleries in mainland Europe so often comes up with such a succulent and satisfying mouth feel as Langatun. The weight is sublime, compelling you to chew...and as you'd more honey notes become apparent, spanning from heather honey to a dimmer rapeseed honey which allows the light peppers to slowly establish itself...; **f22.5** very light honey and tannin residue; **b23** never sure why unsulphur-treated Rioja casks like this aren't more widely used. I have encountered only a handful over the years, and they have usually been above average. This probably boasts the best nose of them all.. *49.12% nc sc 467 bottles*

⬧ **Langatun Single Malt Old Crow** peated, batch no. 309/10/20, db **(95.5) n23** peated it most certainly is. But adore the way that the phenols simply add a weighty roundness to the aroma, rather than a dominating smokiness. This is big, but never less than subtle;

t24 marvellous delivery obtainable only from top quality distillate. The cut from the still has allowed maximum oils but zero feints: perfect distillation for character and complexity. The smoke is laid back on the nose, but much more muscular here as it slowly builds into a chewy, chocolatey mass, the smoke working beautifully with the manuka honey; **f24.5** that smoke and chocolate combination is in itself a reason to live. Heavenly....! **b24** well, I've tasted a few Old Crows in my time, but nothing like this new edition from Langatun. No traditional bourbon here. This is a whisky which stretches its malty, peaty muscles like a crow extends its wings in flight. If there was an award for the intense smoky chocolate malt of the year, no other whisky would get close. Caw! *59.7% nc*

 Langatun Swiss Single Malt Whisky Aged 10 Years 2nd Release, Pinot Noir cask, cask no. 132, dist 2010 **(84.5) n21.5 t22.5 f20 b20.5** Pleasant enough. But a rare misfire by Langatun standards, the Pinot Cask not being up to the quality of the distillate. A little untidy sulphur at the end (and nose), but no problem as it slips though the honey-laden gears on delivery. *49.12% sc. Highfern*

SEVEN SEALS DISTILLERY AG Schweiz, working.

 Seven Seals Peated Double Wood (95) n23.5 phenomenally as well as phenomenally acidic to the point of being almost acerbic! There is a real niggle to this peat, which in turn lessens the impact of any fruit. A peat-freak's paradise...; **t24** stunning! The delivery is an astonishing eruption of highly charged malt, Already thick with oils off the still, it becomes positively gooey as the peat lands and embellishes. The sugars are beautifully represented by light muscovado sugar and a thicker dose of golden syrup; **f23.5** the smoke is still in control, powdery and handsome. A little butter on the malt, too, as well as spice. But those phenols notes are sublime...; **b24** massively impressive whisky, and manner from heaven for the peat freaks. So rare to find a peat as heady as this which seems to instinctively know when and when not to strike. Probably the best whisky I have ever encountered from this distillery...

 Seven Seals Port Wood (86) n21.5 t22 f21 b21.5 A pleasant enough malt, but one which shows up a few weaknesses on the distilling side with feints being spotted from nose to finish. Lots of light butterscotch and vanilla, though.

 Seven Seals Peated Port Wood Finish (88.5) n21.5 t22.5 f21.5 b22 The laid-back oak on the nose doesn't quite see eye to eye with the fruit: relaxed but out of sync, too. While on delivery a quite extraordinary exhibition of vanilla grips your attention. You expect fruit...but, no...it's vanilla. And lashings of it, to the extent that when that expires we are back to a malty outline but also an off-kilter finish as a weakness from the distillate is exposed.

 Seven Seals Peated Sherry Wood Finish (93) n23 the smoke offers little more than a softening pillow for the most genteel grape to sink into. Elegant and balanced, this is all about understatement...; **t23.5** malt melts on the palate upon arrival, leaving a sharper fruitiness behind. The smoke, like on the nose, is super-delicate and offers a limited degree of weight and strictly no more. Instead, it is the oak which offers the extra weight as the midground sinks into a juicy sherry trifle countenance....; **f23** the sugars and fruit soon tail off, though the vanillas which replace them offer a soothing postscript; **b23.5** a faultless sherry cask has been deployed here to compliment rather than obliterate or do battle with the most delicate of peat influences. This works rather beautifully...

Seven Seals Age of Aquarius Single Malt Whisky Double Wood Finish db **(81) n21 t22 f18 b20** Big, full-bodied, smoked fish. But the sulphur on the finish means it's a malt that gets away from you... *58.7%.*

Seven Seals Age of Aries Single Malt Whisky Triple Wood Sherry Finish db **(86) n23 t23 f19 b21** It is a rare thing when the peat has such a bristling countenance it is able to take on such rich fruit and come through so loud and clear. At least on the nose. And the delivery, too, where the second wave is a gorgeous heather honey thread. Sadly, the finish has a distinct and lingering sulphur kick. But even then, the sugars and smoke are still working flat out. *58.7%.*

 Seven Seals The Age of Aquarius Single Malt (87) n21.5 t23 f21 b21.5 Age of Aquarius must mean smoked fish... Better than last year's offering, though the finish still has a little bumbling sulphur hanging round, unfortunately, though nothing too devastating. Equally, the nose also offers a curious juniper kick. Where there is no problem whatsoever is the delivery which is a complex and busy array of smoked honey tones and salt which is quite aloof from the nose and finish. A curious shoal of sensations, indeed. *49.7%. Highfern*

Seven Seals Age of the Gemini Single Malt Whisky Triple Wood Sherry Finish db **(87.5) n22 t23 f20.5 b22** A big, blustering, anarchic malt seemingly set on not following any particular shape or path. The nose is like kippers cooked in a plum pudding; the delivery lurches around the palate, picking up molasses here, depositing spice there, skidding and crash landing on juicy grape skins all over the place. A light vanilla touch creates some tangible sanity to the finish, though a light sulphur note is also detectable in extra time. Fun, if slightly insane... *58.7%.*

Seven Seals Age of The Lion Single Malt Whisky Triple Wood Sherry Finish db **(90) n22.5 t23 f22 b22.5** Seeing I'm a lifelong supporter of The Lions – Millwall FC – it was important they got this one right! No sulphur on display here – and that makes a huge difference to the experience, even though this is one crazy, mixed up malt. A fat cut, huge tannins mined from the oak, a vague, indecipherable phenol note and untamed fruit means there is precious little structure to this...just effect. But my word! Your taste buds get the working over of their lives and if you can't enjoy something as singular as this, what's the point? *58.7%.*

Seven Seals Age of Sagittarius Single Malt Whisky Double Wood Sherry Finish db **(85) n22 t23 f19 b20** A young whisky with lots of hurried tannin extraction, giving this real oaky pep. Sulphur on the finish, alas. The star turn is on delivery and just after when the sugars ripped from the cask are on full, luscious display. *58.7%.*

◇◇ **Seven Seals The Age of Scorpio Single Malt (90.5) n22** fascinating mix between blood orange and melted praline; malt discernible, too...; **t23** wow...so sweet! Honeycomb leads the way before a rich, biscuity volley of malt hurtles into the centre of attention; **f22** thinner, mildly metallic but still malty; **b23** I well remember last year's bottling, which was serious rough-house whisky determined to battle out World War 3 on your palate. This is an altogether more timid affair where your taste buds are at least given a sporting chance to work out what is happening on your palate. The answer is some surprisingly sweet and genteel, the delivery in particular likely to win your heart ... *49.7%. Highfern*

Seven Seals Lucerne Whisky Ship Single Malt Whisky Double Wood Sherry Finish db **(94) n23.5 t23.5 f23 b24** Beautifully made, superbly matured and delighted to say the sherry casks are not only clean, but do as little as possible to stand in the way of the beautiful phenols that drift over both nose and palate. Spices and molasses in all the right places at the right times and ticking all the right boxes. By far their best bottling of the year: in fact in a different class altogether... *58.7%.*

Seven Seals Single Malt Port Wood Finish db **(87) n21 t22.5 f21.5 b22** A lush frenzy of fruit. A little cloying, but the spices are a treat. *58.7%.*

Seven Seals Single Malt Whisky Sherry Wood Finish db **(88) n21.5 t23 f21.5 b22** Big on the grape and even bigger on the spice and maple syrup. A bit of an untidy mishmash. But when it is good, it is very good. *58.7%.*

WHISKY CASTLE Elfingen. Working

◇◇ **Whisky Castle Single Malt Doublewood** cask no.508, db **(86.5) n20 t23 f21.5 b22** Plenty of toffee and malt on display, and there follow through on delivery pits spice against sweetened liquorice is a rather delicious way. But the wonky nose and slightly skewed finale takes this away from the distillery's usual assured excellence. *43% sc*

◇◇ **Whisky Castle Edition Käser** cask no.504, db **(91.5) n22.5** thick, pasty sultana stiffened by giant oaky splints...; **t23.5** though there may be an explosion of youthful malty grist, that soon quietens down as both the tannins and concentrated raisins have much to say...and say it loudly; **f22.5** some very high roast Java coffee rounds things off impressively; **b23** once upon a time, castles - or the fortress settlements that stood as castles - were built with wood, often sturdy oak, before they got round to stone fortifications. This is as though one of those great wooden structures has been distilled down: the tannin almost outmuscles the fruit. Youthful, strapping stuff. *62% sc*

◇◇ **Whisky Castle Single Malt Family Reserve** cask no.17, db **(92.5) n23** distinctly estery and rummy in style, of the Guyanese kind. Rich and massively rewarding on the nose with a light layering of golden syrup balancing the saltier, dryer edge; **t23** wow....just get a load of this complexity! A slight metallic lilt at first, but this gives way to a light heather honey/muscovado sugar combination. There is the vaguest touch of feint on the delivery, which translates to the lightest nougat through the late middle; **f23** long, back to an attractive metallic tang and – and this is really impressive – intense malt at the very death...; **b23.5** an altogether different style to their other bottlings. Much more copper noticeable on the finish, which suggests the stills were either younger or had just undergone some work. This is all about layering and complexity: a malt which takes you on long and convoluted journey. Though the journey seems mostly to be back in time...to the distillery's early days. Delicious! *43% sc*

◇◇ **Whisky Castle Single Malt Smoke Barley** cask no.502, db **(90) n22.5** very youthful it may be, but the smoke caresses the nose rather than attacks. There is a sweet beechwood style smokiness to this as well as peat – but the overwhelming sensation is one of fresh smoked grist; **t23** the sugars tumble over the palate to give the friendliest of deliveries, the smoke slowly welling up as the dryness gathers; **f22** a little molasses balances with the vanilla nimbly; **b22.5** made with Whisky Castle's usual attention to detail, this is excellently distilled malt, though still on the young side. The peat is halfway between being within its bricks and mortar and an adornment *43% sc*

Deciphered and Distilled. The Bible's European Guide to Whisky Labels

English	German	French
Malt	Malz	Malt
Grain	Getreide	céréales
Wheat	Weizen	blé
Barley	Gerste	orge
Rye	Roggen	seigle
Spelt	Dinkel	épeautre
Corn	Mais	maïs
Oat	Hafer	avoine
Peated	getorft	tourbé
Smoked	geraucht	fumé
Organic	biologisch	biologique
Cask	Fass	fût
Matured in/Aged in	gereift in	vieilli en
Finish	Nachreifung	déverdissage
Double Maturation	Zweitreifung	deuxième maturation
Oak	Eiche	chêne
Toasted	wärmebehandelt	grillé
Charred	ausgeflammt, verkohlt	carbonisé
Years	Jahre	ans
Months	Monate	mois
Days	Tage	journées
Chill Filtration	Kühlfiltration	filtration à froid
Non Chill Filtered	nicht kühlgefiltert	non filtré à froid
No Colouring	nicht gefärbt	non coloré
Cask Strength	Fassstärke	brut du fût
Single Cask	Einzelfass	single cask
Cask No.	Fass-Nummer	numéro du fût
Batch	Charge	Lot/charge
Distillation Date	Destillations-Datum	date de distillation
Bottling Date	Abfüll-Datum	date de mise en bouteille
Alcohol by Volume/abv	Volumenprozente/% vol.	teneur en alcool/abv
Proof (American)	amerikanische Einheit für % vol.	unité américaine

Danish	Dutch	Swedish
Malt	Gerst	Malt
Korn	graan	säd
hvede	tarwe	vete
byg	gerst	korn
rug	rogge	råg
spelt	spelt	speltvete
majs	mais	majs
havre	haver	havre
tørv	geturfd	torvrökt
røget	gerookt	rökt
organisk	biologisch/organisch	ekologisk
fad	vat	fat
modning i	gerijpt in	mognad på/lagrad på
finish	narijping/finish	slutlagrat
dobbelt modning	dubbele rijping	dubbellagrat
egetræ	eik	ek
ristet	getoast	rostad
forkullet	gebrand	kolad
år	jaren	år
måned	maanden	månader
dage	dagen	dagar
kold filtrering	koude-filtratie	kylfiltrering
ikke kold filtreret	niet koud gefilterd	ej kylfiltrerad
ikke farvet	niet bijgekleurd	inga färgämnen
fadstyrke	vatsterkte	fatstyrka
enkelt fad	enkel vat	enkelfat
fad nr.	vat nummer	fatnummer
parti/batch	serie/batch	batch
destillations dato	distillatie datum	destilleringsdatum
aftapnings dato	bottel datum	buteljeringsdatum
volumenprocent	alcoholpercentage/% vol	volymprocent/% vol.
Proof	amerikaanse aanduiding voor % vol	Amerikanska proof

World Whiskies

I have long said that whisky can be made just about anywhere in the world; that it is not writ large in stone that it is the inalienable right for just Scotland, Ireland, Kentucky and Canada to have it all to themselves. And so, it seems, it is increasingly being proved. Perhaps only sandy deserts and fields of ironstone can prevent its make physically and Islam culturally, though even that has not been a barrier to malt whisky being distilled in both Pakistan and Turkey. Whilst not even the world's highest mountains or jungle can prevent the spread of barley and copper pot.

Outside of North America and Europe, whisky's traditional nesting sites, you can head in any direction and find it being made. Australia, in particular, has gained a deserved reputation for magnificent malt though, like its finest wines, it can be hard to locate outside its own country. Indeed, Australian whiskies are of such high quality and relatively abundant that it has, like England and Wales now been rewarded with its own section in the Whisky Bible, though Australian whisky will still be found in the World Whisky awards section. World class whisky can be found in other surprisingly lush and tropical climes with Taiwan leading the way thanks to the wonderful Kavalan distillery, no stranger to the Whisky Bible awards.

Japan has long represented Asia with distinction and whisky-making there is in such an advanced state and at a high standard Jim Murray's Whisky Bible has given it its own section - and World Whisky of the Year for 2015! But while neighbouring South Korea has ended its malt distilling venture, further east, and at a very unlikely altitude, Nepal has forged a small industry to team up, geographically, with fellow malt distillers India and Pakistan. The main malt whisky from this region making inroads in world markets is India's Amrut single malt, though Paul John is also now beginning to forge a deserved following of fans. 'Inroads' is hardly doing Indian whisky justice. Full-bloodied trailblazing, more like. So good was Amrut's fantastically complex brand, Fusion, it was awarded Jim Murray's Whisky Bible 2010 Third Finest Whisky in the World. A top award repeated last year by Paul John with their astonishing Mithuna, a single malt comprising some of their oldest casks giving one of the most complete finishes of any whisky I have ever tasted. If Indian whisky wasn't on the map before, it certainly is now...

Jim Murray's Whisky Bible World Whisky of the Year Winners

	Asian Whisky	Southern Hemisphere Whisky
2010	**Amrut Fusion**	N/A
2011	**Amrut Intermediate Sherry Matured**	N/A
2012	Amrut Two Continents 2nd Edition	**Kavalan Solist Fino Single Cask**
2013	N/A	**Sullivan's Cove Single Cask HH0509**
2014	Kavalan Podium Single Malt	**Timboon Single Malt Whisky**
2015	Kavalan Single Malt Whisky	**NZ Willowbank 1988 25 years Old**
2016	**Amrut Greedy Angels 46%**	Heartwood Port 71.3%
2017	**Kavalan Solist Moscatel**	Heartwood Any Port in a Storm
2018	Paul John Kanya	**Limeburner's Dark Winter**
2019	Amrut Greedy Angels 8 Years Old	**Belgrove Peated Rye**
2020	**Nantou Distillery Omar Bourbon Cask**	Bakery Hill Peated Malt
2021	**Paul John Mithuna**	Adams Distillery Tasmanian Single Malt
2022	**Cyprus WA Paul John**	Tin Shed Flustercluck

BRAZIL
LAMAS DESTILARIA

◈ **Lamas Caledônia Single Malt Whisky** smoked barley/double wood, ex bourbon, ex-Port, lot no: 90421 db **(93) n23** the nose may be young, but there is a very attractive cross between the house smoky bacon-style phenol and a more Islay-oriented smokiness to enjoy. Sharp and acrid, the sugar and salt are a battle for supremacy; **t23.5** just love the authentic, rough-around the edges smokiness to this. This is a whisky which means business and sets to work with a few blistering spices, but sooths with some outstanding heather-honey. The phenols are bitty and battling...wonderful! **f23** never for a moment complex, it is, however, persistent and the smoke and spice combine to ensure a very long finish. At last oak plays a telling part, helping to staunch those sweeter honeyed notes with growing vanillas; **b23.5** technically, this is beautifully made and matured whisky. No off notes either from the distillate or the barrels. There appear to be two styles batting away at first which, though never uncomfortable, makes it difficult to settle into any rhythm. However, the slight awkwardness, plus the youth, begins to grow on you...this is a whisky with personality and depth and the lashings of honey the perfect counterweight to the phenol. Very highly enjoyable whisky considerable its apparent youth. *50%*

◈ **Lamas Canem Blended Whisky** 1/3 malt 2/3 grain, American oak cask, lot no: 150515 db **(88) n21.5 t22.5 f22 b22** No great age, a little bit of extra width on the cut of the malt. But, all-in-all, a satisfying blend with a distinct development on the palate and plenty of toffee to chew on. The sweetness level is excellent: not too much, but enough to ensure a friendly experience. *40%*

◈ **Lamas Plenus Single Malt Whisky** ex-bourbon cask, cask no. 010R, lot no: 301015 db **(86.6) n21.5 t21.5 f22 b21.5** A slightly wide cut gives this big weight. Well layered at times but caramel is keeping the complexity levels down slightly. Love the smokey-bacon element to the nose. *43% sc*

◈ **Lamas Verus Single Malt Whisky** ex -bourbon cask, ex-port cask, lot no: 230115 db **(88.5) n22 t22.5 f21.5 b22.5** Though the complexity peters out at finish, the voluptuous intensity of the malt and toffee, not to mention the liveliness of the spice makes for pure entertainment. Big, a tad feinty, but always showing control. *43%*

◈ **Lamas Smoked Single Malt Whisky** ex-bourbon, ex-imperial stout cask, lot no: 100521 db **(94) n23** there is a wonderful cross fertilization of the distillery's now famous bacon-style smokiness, salted porridge and light barley sugar. The spice is tight and warming while roasted nuts hangs in the air with the phenols; **t23.5** the delivery is an orgy between the smoked mollassed sugars and confident, resounding spices which raises the temperature magnificently. Astonishingly, there is a clear vein of barley running though this, despite the phenols quietly occupying as much space on the palate as possible; **f23** there is a creamy milk stout finish to this – sweet, hop free but toasty. Anyone who remembers Mackeson at its best will be in for a shock here. The spices tingle while the vanillas sooth; **b24** it was a brave move to go do the stout cask route: I have seen more whiskies spoiled this way than improved. Fortunately, the cask has imparted roastiness rather than hops. The moment hops get into a whisky balance is seriously compromised by the bitterness reducing the sweetness. So this is Russian Roulette maturation. Having said all that, this is a roaring success of a whisky, forever keeping the taste buds on full alert and trying to work out in which direction they will be taken next. Also very unusual for the fact that appears to be two types of spices at work simultaneously, working at different frequencies and intensities. The sugars might be over the top, except the smoke and vanilla balances things out beautifully. What a beautiful, beautiful whisky. Fiery. Fascinating. Unpredictable. But very, very beautiful. And, in this mood, so easy to love. Kind of reminds me of someone... *51%*

Nimbus Smoked Single Malte Whisky Puro Malte lote 5, barril 10 nbc db **(93) n23 t23.5 f23 b23.5** A truly unique style in all the world's whiskies: a strange but delicious mesquite/peat hybrid. So different and so delicious, it had me pouring another one – this time for fun rather than work... *40%. sc.*

Plenus Whisky Single Malt Puro Malte lote 21, barril 62/64 nbc db **(85.5) n21.5 t21 f21.5 b21.5** Pleasant enough but, despite the barley juiciness which pops up here and there on the nose and delivery, overall a dull whisky, the buzzing spices apart. Seemingly well made, but otherwise flat and lacking much in the way of personality. Just a little too dry, as well. *40%.*

Verus Whisky Single Malt Puro Malte lote 19, barril 77/84 nbc db **(87) n21.5 t22 f21.5 b22** An unusual whisky but one that shews some of the hallmarks of a European-style distillation. Big in malt, but feints also. Well coloured up, as much with dry tannins as toffee. This is a lively whisky, with a surprisingly delicious turn of malty phrase at the midway point, and spices, too. Though, because of the strength, the finish lacks great length and depth. *40%*

TRÊS LOBOS DISTILLERY

3 Lobos Whiskey Artesanal Experience Single Malt Puro Malte 6 Anos batch no. 2-0715, dist 17 Jul 13, bott 17 Jul 19 db **(91.5) n23 t23 f22.5 b23** Distilled gingerbread. A delicious malt, but one of the most ginger-infested whiskies I have encountered in a very long time. A malt with fabulous personality and joie de vivre: how Brazilian! 40%.

INDIA
AMRUT DISTILLERY

Amrut Fusion batch no. 82, bott Jun 19 db **(90.5) n22 t23.5 f22 b23** slightly more Confusion than Fusion. Again, there is a strange finish to this after a really gorgeous take off. Seems to land without any wheels or fuel everything having run out. Enjoyed this malt, but in a very different way to the Fusions of old where the layering, pace and balance were exemplary from the first moment to the last. The delivery apart, this is much more anarchic. 50%.

Amrut Greedy Angels 10 Years Old Chairman's Reserve ex bourbon cask, batch no. 01, bott 25 Jun 19 db **(94.5) n23 t24 f23.5 b24** High quality whisky. And a must find for honey lovers... 55%. 900 bottles.

Amrut Greedy Angels Peated Rum Finish Chairman's Reserve 10 Years Old batch no. 01, bott Oct 19 db **(95.5) n23.5 t24 f23.5 b24.5** Keeps shewing more depth and intensity each time you taste it. Astoundingly beautiful malt of the true Amrut tradition. Sensual beyond measure and one to take your time with and cherish every erotic moment... 57.1%. 450 bottles.

Amrut Greedy Angels Peated Sherry Finish Chairman's Reserve 10 Years Old batch no. 01, bott Feb 19 db **(94) n23.5 t24 f23 b23.5** A faultless sherry cask at work here: the rarest of the rare! So powerful the peat at times has problems making itself heard and has to content itself as being the backing group. Elegant, intense and very high quality. 60%. 324 bottles.

Amrut Indian Single Malt Whisky batch no. 141, bott Feb 19 db **(89) n22** lighter in body and more simplistic than earlier bottlings, a thin citrus sweetness hangs over this; **t23.5** uncomplicated barley which gather and grows in intensity in almost linear fashion. At the brow of the climb it really is massively enjoyable...; **f21.5** hmmm...that thinner quality in the finish which is just so un-Amrut! Slightly bitter...; **b22** another puzzling bottling which at its very best is a treat, but the decline in the pleasure graph is pretty steep. 46%. nc ncf.

Amrut Kadhambham 2019 Release bott 20 Jun 19 db **(93) n23 t23 f23 b23.5** A beautifully rich Amrut; a much heavier, maltier style than normal. 50%. 7,200 bottles.

Amrut Peated Indian Single Malt Whisky batch no. 89, bott Feb 19 db **(86) n22 t22.5 f20.5 b21** It is as though this whisky has had a personality transplant. The peat is thrusting and pretty confident with its sooty dryness. But the malt shews remarkable youth which probably accounts for the imbalance in the thin finish. Some good moments, but not as many as usual. 46%. nc ncf.

Amrut Peated Port Pipe Single Cask batch no. 01, bott 12 Feb 19 db **(95.5) n24 t24.5 f23 b24** Very often a well peated malt and wine cask don't work particularly well together, one element cancelling out the other. This, it must be recorded, works a treat. It is so good, in fact, I raise this glass to the memory of Amrut's founding father, whisky visionary Neelakanta Rao Jagdale...and friend. 48%. nc ncf. The Vault Biennale Edition

Amrut Raj Igala Indian Single Malt Whisky batch no. 20, bott Oct 19 db **(86) n22.5 t22 f20.5 b21.5** A distinctly Speyside-style malt focussing on gentleness of touch and light caramels. As is the present Amrut style, the finish is a little feeble and bitter. But there is much to enjoy with is early grassy quality both nose and delivery. 40%.

DEVANS

◇ **DeVans Gianchand Single Malt** db **(91.5) n23.5** unquestionably the most delicate Indian malt I have nosed in the near 30 years I have spent travelling to sub-continental distilleries. The lightness of touch is underlined by the pineapple drop candy sweetness which is carried hand-in-hand by the barley; **t23** malt strikes early, but there is a firm vanilla backbone softened by thin, helpful oils which ensure the intensity of the tannin builds and lingers...but not in the way you would normally expect from an Indian pot still malt. This is far more delicate and refined, with soft barley and spice taking different but vital paths as the complexity increases; **f22** warming and lingers for a while on a malty theme before those polite tannins move towards a drier, more chalky finish; **b23** this was one of the most fascinating whiskies I came across this year: unlike any other Indian malt I have before encountered. Being located 900 feet up in foothills close to the northern Pakistan border, the distillery is as remote as it is unique. Although the casks have matured for several years in high heat, the oak involvement is gloriously restrained, allowing the fragile malt and exotic fruit notes space to perform. And ensure the whisky retains its charmingly light touch. 42.8%

JOHN DISTILLERIES

Paul John Brilliance db (94.5) n23.5 t24 f23.5 b23.5 Yet another astonishing malt from India. *46%*

Paul John Chairman's Reserve db (89) n22 t23 f22 b22 I cannot say I am much of a fan of the mixing of PX and peat. Sometimes it works, usually it doesn't: often it is a case of two heavyweight fighters landing punches simultaneously, each knocking the other out. Well, both contestants hit the deck here but, thankfully, got up again briefly for a becalmed finish. Oh, and the really good news: 100% sulphur free...! *59.7%. ncf.*

Paul John Christmas Edition batch no. 02, mfg. date 16-nov-18 db (95.5) n24 t24 f23.5 b24 Question: when is a big whisky not a big whisky? Answer: when it is as well balanced as this... *46%. ncf.*

Paul John Classic Select Cask db (94.5) n23 t24 f23.5 b24 One of those whiskies which just overflows with flavour. Delicious! *55.2%. nc ncf.*

Paul John Distillery Edition db (94.5) n23.5 t23.5 f23.5 b24 Compared to the enormity of the other Paul Johns I have tasted today, this is but a mere child. But what a charming one... *46%. ncf.*

Paul John Exceptional db (95) n23 t24 f24 b24 The sheer élan of the controlled intensity is something to behold: Indian malt at its maltiest and most charmingly expressed. *47%. ncf.*

Paul John Kanya db (96) n23.5 t24 f24 b24.5 When a distillery can find honey at the very end of the its flavour range and profile, you know they have cracked it. Superb! *50%. ncf.*

Paul John Mithuna db (97) n23.5 rarely am I lost for words. But so rich and complexly entangled are these chocolates, molasses, dates, ultra-delicate spices – oh, and all slightly leavened by passion fruit – that it is only the absolute perfectionist in me that is docking the marks. Murray Method. Half an hour...whisky perception changing...; t24 oh, my word! Goodness gracious me! Mouthfeel...perfect. Sweetness levels...perfect. Volume of intensity... perfect. The main theme is a chocolate liqueur, with high volumes of the very finest cocoa to chew on, always oily, always able to enhance itself with a molasses sub culture and the very finest vanilla pods. But the mouthfeel...it is oily but at the same time embracing and moulded like no other whisky I have ever encountered; f25 so long, with the vanillas now holding sway and just the politest hint of spice. But the earlier chocolate theme still echoes around... seemingly forever... and gloriously; b24.5 the end of the experience is like after you have just made love...and you are unable to speak or move while your senses get back into some kind of normality. If Mithuna means "Ultimate", then it is the perfect name. Or maybe Mithuna means "Perfect", then it is pretty close. Whichever, this is a kind of Indian version of a William Larue Weller, shewing that same extraordinary intensity, complexity and beauty. It is that very rarest of things. And, if nothing else, announces Paul John distillery on the world stage of truly great distilleries. This is a whisky to devour...while it devours you. Almost certainly destined for a top three spot in the Whisky Bible 2021. *58%. ncf.*

Paul John Nirvana Unpeated Single Malt batch no. 01, mfg. date 12-nov-18 db (94) n24 t23.5 f23 b23.5 While writing these notes a wasp decided to fly into my tasting glass, fall into the whisky called Nirvana...and die. Ironic, or what? But wasps have a sweet tooth, so tells you all you need to know. That and the fact it climbed back in three times before it finally succumbed... *40%. ncf.*

Paul John PX db (90.5) n22.5 t23.5 f21.5 b23 The plan was to write these tasting notes while England were playing India during the first Test match in Birmingham. England, as usual, collapsed after previously having their foot on India's throat and potentially all out for a very low score...but then blew it. So with India now favourites to win, thought I'd better get these tasted today, rather than tomorrow, while there is still a Test match. For the cricket: why do England have only one Surrey player, Sam Curran? And not surprisingly the only one to show any resistance. And as for the whisky: enjoyable with a truly brilliant delivery. But not showing the true subtlety and colours of PJ's excellent malt. *48%. ncf.*

Paul John Single Cask Non Peated #4127 db (96.5) n24 t24.5 f24 b24 I think we can safely say that Paul John has now reached a stage in its development as a relatively new distillery where it can step into its warehouses and pluck out single casks of bewildering and unforgettable beauty and near perfect maturity. Here is one such cask. There are others listed in this Whisky Bible 2021, too... *58.6%. sc.*

Paul John Single Cask Non Peated #6758 db (96) n23.5 t24.5 f24 b24 Simplistic...in a complex kind of way! One of those rare malts where if you could give marks for mouthfeel alone, it would top score. A very sensuous experience...a whisky to be shared with your partner, but without a glass... *59.3%. sc.*

Paul John Single Cask Peated #6086 db (95) n24 t23.5 f23.5 b24 A stunning display of controlled peat seemingly revelling in the accompaniment of well-aged oak. Beautifully structured and paced. And a serious step up from their last Peated single cask. *58.9%. sc.*

Paul John Single Cask Peated #6355 db (96) n24 t24 f24 b24 If you imagine cask 6086 as top of the range Paul John single cask, then this is the turbo-charged all-leather edition. The sheer élan for a single cask is jaw-dropping. 59.1%. sc.

Paul John Select Cask Peated (96) n24 t24 f24 b24 A peated malt whisky which will make a few people sit up and take even further notice of Indian whisky. World class... 46%

Paul John Tula (96) n23.5 over-ripe plums and liquorice form a soft but rich backdrop to the startling spices. The more distant background noise is a lovely manuka honey and molasses mix...all this leavened by the most insouciant of orange blossom honey notes; t24.5 after such a soft make-up on the nose, the crispness on delivery comes as a surprise. But crunchy Demerara sugars arrive in double quick time as the tannins make their mark early. The sheer power is matched only by the élan as the deep chocolate tones melt with ginger and liquorice. One crashing layer after another is a joy to behold; f24 just more of the same with a slow rising of the vanilla and spice; the notes to the original bottling hold firm; b24 a delightful second batch of Tula with all the same stars, just the odd one or two shifting constellations. Seemingly effortless magnificence. 58%. ncf.

◈ **The Cyprus Whisky Association Paul John Single Malt** cask no. 8566, dist Sept 15, bott Nov 20 (95.5) n23.5 a succession of varied coffee notes – from crushed unroasted to high roast – sits very comfortably with the light liquorice, bourbon-style tannins. Despite the gentle enormity surrounding it, the malt itself gets a telling word in, too, forming a significant sub-strata which softens and sweetens. Decent spices don't exactly have their hands in their pockets during this time, either; t24.5 pure Paul John! A cascade of dark sugars and vanilla presents the opening shots before the lusty spices home in and hit bullseye. To make this even more engulfing is the ulmo honey which thickens with the existing oils. The mid-ground is far less dramatic, but certainly no less delicious. The malt had re-emerged, obviously judging the situation safe, and flutes some charming barley-sugar and heather honey notes at the calming waters; f23.5 residual - and resident - oils lay a big part here in keeping the flame burning as long as possible. The spices provide the heat, the sticky vanilla and honey the light...; b24 there are few distilleries on this planet that makes this kind of gasp-out-loud impact on the palate as Paul John does. But there are far more to this than its spine-tingling attack. The nuances are so easily overlooked in a whisky of this weight. But take your time. Also, let the oils and spices to do their job. And regard what fine a tapestry has been woven from seemingly so course a cloth... 59.5%. sc. 234 bottles. ☙

RAMPUR DISTILLERY

◈ **Rampur Single Malt Asava Cabernet Sauvignon** American bourbon barrels and Indian red wine casks, batch 08/20, batch no.855, db (92.5) n22.5 a dry nose: like a poker player holding his cards close to his chest, this is refusing to say which way it will go on the palate: most inscrutable...; t23.5 ahhh, now that is rather lovely. The malt is confident to hit the taste buds in blocks. But the spiced-up concentrated grape counters with its own layered intensity; f23 dry grape skin and a slow dissolving of the remaining sugars. The spice still has much to say, though the chalky vanillas are louder still...; b23.5 this is a distillery I first visited over 25 years ago and have held them in high esteem for that amount of time. Here they have worked exceptionally hard to get the balance between the fruit and malt into as complex a form as possible – and have largely pulled it off. The fifth to tenth flavour waves are borderline perfect. Anyone who doesn't give this malt 20 minutes – and the full Murray Method – are doing both the distillery and themselves a grave disservice. 45% ncf

◈ **Rampur Single Malt Double Cask** American oak barrels and European oak sherry casks, bott 07/20, batch no.924, db (91) n22 the sherry casks act as a brake on the malt, tightening the sugars until they can barely breath; t22.5 and in goes the sherry again: this is dry sherry at work, fine in character but slightly dominant and forbidding. Slowly, however, first spices and then some excellent rich, malty tones escape the grapey grip; f23 now we have full throttle complexity, including some outstanding cocoa notes which work rather well with the burnt raisin. Just a slight untidy growl at the death whips of a half point...; b23.5 highly unusual for a sherry cask influenced whisky to be remembered for its big chocolate personality. But there you go...! Rampur are upping their game considerably. Still a little way to go before they hit the dizzy heights reached by Paul John and Amrut, but they are certainly moving in the right direction. I suspect, however, that the use of Spanish sherry butts will not take them to the road of Shangri-La... 45% ncf

Rampur Indian Single Malt Whisky Sherry PX Finish American oak barrels, finished in Spanish sherry PX butts db (86) n22 t22.5 f20 b21.5 A real shame this. It is obvious that the underlying malt is very attractive. But the PX has intervened to slightly flatten and dull and then leave a sulphurous deposit on the finish. Indian distilleries have to learn, like some in Scotland and Ireland refuse to, that using Spanish oak can be a very dangerous game. 45%. ncf.

NEW ZEALAND
WILSON DISTILLERY

The New Zealand Whisky Collection The Oamaruvian 18 Year Old aged 6 years in American oak, ex-bourbon casks and transferred into French oak, ex-New Zealand red wine casks for 12 years **(94) n23 t23.5 f23.5 b24** For my 750th whisky for the Jim Murray's Whisky Bible 2021, I thought I'd travel as far as possible from my home in England which, as beautiful as it is, for the last two months has been my gaol. Way back in 1994 I travelled to the Wilson's Distillery in Dunedin to clamber through the warehouses to taste probably over 100 samples of a whisky which, then tragically unloved, has now assumed, rightfully, legendary status. Then the unique part copper part stainless steel stills were running, so I was able one minute to taste the new make, and the next sample their oldest stock and everything in between. And later in the day, travel just a couple of miles to spend time among the penguins as they dipped in and out of the sea. With my now being in my second solid month of Covid-19 lockdown, this journey back to one of the most remarkable distilleries (and now sadly lost to us) it has ever been my privilege and pleasure to visit and inspect is something I need to do once more...if in my mind's eye, only... 50%.

UNSPECIFIED SINGLE MALT

The New Zealand Whisky Collection Dunedin Double Cask Single Malt Whisky small American oak, ex-bourbon casks and French oak, ex-New Zealand red wine casks **(87) n21.5 t22.5 f21.5 b21.5** A malty cove despite the intervention of wine casks and French oak. However, there is a slight discordant note that is hinted at on the nose and certainly makes its mark towards the cotton wool end. The malt, though, ploughs on regardless and finds a little milk chocolate to team up with. 40%.

The New Zealand Whisky Collection Oamaruvian Revolution Single Malt small American oak, ex-bourbon casks and French oak, ex-New Zealand red wine casks **(90.5) n22.5 t23 f22.5 b22.5** Fulsome, forceful and rich, this malt doesn't pander to sophistication. Well distilled and matured. 46%.

SOUTH AFRICA
JAMES SEDGWICK DISTILLERY

Bain's Capetown Mountain Single Grain Whisky bott code: 1869721 L5 18260 db **(87.5) n22 t22 f21.5 b22** Even though the strength of Capetown Mountain has been reduced slightly, it offers a marginally better whisky than of old with far better balance and far greater presence to ensure a more satisfying finale. Its weakness, still, is simplicity though the nip of the spice has been enhanced and fares well against the rich cream toffee. 40%.

Bain's Cape Mountain Whisky Single Grain bott code: L611 28 E 19 db **(87) n21.5 t22 f21.5 b22** Well, the year of tasting this, 2020, is the year of the toilet tissue, as that is what everyone around the world has been busy collecting. But none will be as gentle and super-soft as this South African grain which appears to be distilled from MacIntosh's Cream Toffee. 43%.

Bain's Cape Mountain Whisky Aged 15 Years Single Grain bott code: LA64 27K 18 db **(90.5) n23 t23 f22 b22.5** At times, especially on the nose, there is the unmistakable feel of antique shop here. Must make this a very collectable whisky... 52.5%.

Bain's Founder's Collection Aged 18 Years Single Grain Whisky Fino Cask Finish bott code: LA64 10 D 19 db **(92) n24 t23 f22 b23** Works far better than the PX as this has guile and complexity. And is less sulphur challenged to boot. Charming South African whisky. 50.5%.

Bain's Founder's Collection Aged 18 Years Single Grain Whisky Oloroso Cask Finish bott code: LA64 15 D 19 db **(92) n23.5** incredibly soft grape juice backed up by moist fruit cake; **t23** the fruit dominates with a voluptuous embrace and, after starting sweetly, veers off directly towards slightly burnt Christmas pudding. For a good ten seconds after initial delivery there is enough spice prickle and honey to ensure an attractive balance and depth; **f22.5** despite the obvious lack of body, the fruit has enough toasted weight to lengthen the finale out – staying a complete softy all the way...; **b23** a plump whisky boasting a yielding softness rare among any whisky. And not a single sulphur note to be found! Delicious! 50.5%. 1,900 bottles.

Bain's Founder's Collection Aged 18 Years Single Grain Whisky PX Cask Finish bott code: LA64 17 D 19 db **(88.5) n23 t23 f20.5 b22** A clean, light, delicate grain as produced at James Sedgwick versus PX Casks. Well, there can be only one winner. As you might expect, this is all about the grape. And being PX, there is a transition to the mouthfeel, ensuring that this is maximum stickiness to the already silky undercoat. The finish, I have to say, is no great shakes. But it is impossible not to be blown away by the first three or four shockwaves on delivery: concentrated dates, molasses and spice. Kind of withers on the vine after that... 50.5%. 1,900 bottles.

TAIWAN
KAVALAN DISTILLERY

Kavalan 40th Anniversary Limited Edition Single Malt Selected Wine Cask Matured Single Cask cask no. LF121122043A, bott code: 2019.11.19 db **(96) n24 t24.5 f23.5 b24** One huge and shapely bottle for one huge and shapely whisky. I think the cask was still dripping with wine when this was filled because the voluptuousness of the grape out-voluptuates anything I have encountered so far this year *56.3%. sc. 85 bottles. 40th Anniversary King Car Group.*

Kavalan Single Malt Whisky 10th Anniversary Bordeaux Margaux Wine Cask Matured bott code: 2018.12.26 db **(95) n23.5 t24 f23.5 b24** A very quiet, understated complexity and confidence that just exudes class. Much more here than originally meets the eye...and nose. *57.8%. nc ncf sc.*

Kavalan Single Malt Whisky ex-Bourbon Oak bott code: 2018.06.27 db **(93.5) n23 t23 f23.5 b24** Something for everyone with a malt with early attitude but reveals some class late on, too. *46%.*

Kavalan Single Malt Whisky Kavalan Distillery Select bott code: 2018.07.17 db **(87.5) n22 t22 f22 b21.5** Must have been distilled on the silk road. As this is exceptionally soft but much simplified from the Distillery Selects of old. Very good spice fruity spice. *40%.*

⬩ **Kavalan Single Malt Whisky Madeira Cask Solist** cask no. D150507044A, bott code: 2020.10.06 db **(94.5) n23.5** if the fruit coming off this nose was any thicker, you'd be able to pick it. The controlled intensity is sublime, because beneath the fruit comes some unmistakable layering of malt, which ramps up the balance and complexity several rungs; **t23.5** a jammy delivery – damsons and greengages are all in full swing here – is met by a couple of lovely layers of Jaffa Cake and barley sugar. That makes the salivation levels pretty high, especially as the malt battles through in spectacularly crispy fashion; **f23.5** this must have been an exceptional cask at work. No bitterness or tiredness. Still more of that fruit and malt interplay. Such silky elegance...; **b24** when Madeira casks are this good, the memory of my old friend and colleague Jim Swan lives on. In the early days of the distillery they were looking for a style which left no doubt to the high quality of the whisky-making art that was being carried out in Taiwan. This bottling, despite the full-throated roar of the fruit, does that rather well. *56.3%. nc ncf sc. 241 bottles.*

Kavalan Single Malt Whisky Port Cask Finish Concertmaster bott code: 2018.06.30 db **(92.5) n23 t23 f23 b23.5** Kavalan at this strength always seems a little underpowered, as if the woodwind haven't turned up for a Bruckner concert. But the elegant restraint of this whisky should certainly be admired. *40%.*

Kavalan Single Malt Whisky Podium bott code: 2018.04.20 db **(88) n22 t23 f21 b22** A very fat malt but not quite shewing the usual Kavalan character. *46%.*

Kavalan Distillery Reserve Single Cask Strength Rum Cask cask no. M111104056A, bott code: 2018.01.04 db **(90.5) n22.5 t23 f22 b23** On the nose it seems innocuous enough, but turns into being a huge whisky. *59.4%. sc. 401 bottles.*

Kavalan Single Malt Whisky Sherry Oak bott code: 2018.06.27 db **(87.5) n22.5 t22 f21.5 b21.5** The nose leaves little doubt about the keen sherry influence but beyond the delivery the malt has surprisingly little to say. Pleasant, but hardly stirs your blood or makes you gird your loins *46%.*

Kavalan Single Malt Whisky Sherry Cask Finish Concertmaster bott code: 2019.11.15 db **(81) n21 t21 f19 b20** The driest sherry on any Kavalan I have yet encountered. Also the most uncompromisingly tight and most bitter. It could have done without that sherry finish. *40%.*

Kavalan Solist Single Cask Strength Moscatel Sherry Cask cask no. MO110321014A, bott code: 2017.03.14 db **(84.5) n20 t22 f21 b21.5** Fruity for sure. But the oily, disconcerting tang is usually the result of a wide cut, not the barrel. *56.3%. nc ncf sc. 518 bottles.*

Kavalan Solist Single Cask Strength Pedro Ximenez Sherry Cask cask no. PX100630027A, bott code: 2018.03.12 db **(89) n22 t23.5 f21.5 b22** Sticky and full-bodied. *56.3%. nc ncf sc.*

Kavalan Solist ex-Bourbon Cask cask no. B101214030A, bott code: 2018.06.13 db **(94) n23.5 t23.5 f23 b24** A beautifully relaxed malt which shows the distillery off in a golden glow. Such class! *56.3%. nc ncf sc. 169 bottles.*

Kavalan Solist Fino Sherry Cask cask no. FI00714038A, bott code: 2018.07.26 db **(94.5) n23 t24 f23.5 b24** An essay in subtlety and understatement despite the apparent bigness. *57.1%. nc ncf sc. 489 bottles.*

Kavalan Solist Oloroso Sherry Cask cask no. S090102047, bott code: 2018.02.03 db **(87) n22.5 t21.5 f22 b21** Nearly three decades ago I was criticising these kind of sherry butts, then, unlike now, found exclusively in Scotland, as they were simply too heavy and cumbersome for the malt they had conjoined: rather than integrate, it had conquered. The opaque colour of the malt – almost blackcurrant juice in its darkness – offers a fair warning.

The nose is attractive, especially if you happen to love oloroso sherry. But that is the problem: the whisky has vanished with barely a trace beneath it. Nonetheless, enjoyable for sure with all the spices present and correct. *57.1%. nc ncf sc. 470 bottles.*

Kavalan Solist Port Cask cask no. 0090619059A, bott code: 2018.08.10 db **(95) n23.5 t24 f23.5 b24** Very much in the Kavalan house style of rich and substantially spiced - but never hot - single malt. Superb whisky from a faultless cask. *59.4%. nc ncf sc. 183 bottles.*

Kavalan Vinho Barrique Cask cask no. W120614024, bott code: 2018.02.21 db **(94.5) n24 t23.5 f23 b24** Kavalan has that very rare talent for brilliance without apparent effort... *54.8%.*

King Car Whisky Conductor Single Malt bott code: 2018.03.26 db **(89) n22.5 t22.5 f22 b22** Hefty malt with a rare but disarming honey thread. *46%.*

Golden Gate Sunset Kavalan Single Malt Whisky Sherry Cask cask no. S060710001 db **(94) n23.5 t24 f23 b23.5** Absolutely delicious. But needed the malt to stand its ground just a little more firmly. What this whisky can do with is a bridge between the malt and grape... *58.6%. sc. 479 bottles. Bottled for WhiskySifu & SF Whisky, Bourbon and Scotch Society.*

NANTOU DISTILLERY

Nantou Distillery Omar Cask Strength Bourbon Cask cask no. 11110613 **(93) n23 t23.5 f23 b23.5** A beautifully made malt where subtlety is the key – even at 58% abv. There are as many quiet moments as crescendos, one emphasising the other, but this is a roller-coaster ride in subtlety. *58%*

Nantou Distillery Omar Cask Strength Bourbon Cask cask no. 11140804, dist May 14, bott 25 May 17 db **(96.5) n24 t24.5 f23.5 b24.5** Beautifully distilled; beautifully matured. Simply stunning! One of the single casks of the year, not least for its unique and almost exhaustingly delicious style. *56%. sc. 248 bottles.*

Nantou Distillery Omar Cask Strength Lychee Liqueur Barrel Finished bott 28 Sept 17 db **(94) n23 t23.5 f23.5 b24** This whisky astounds me as much as it delights me! Curiously, lychee is a flavour sometimes picked up in well-aged Speyside-style light single malts. However, this is the first time I have ever encountered a malt matured in a lychee barrel. And it offers nothing like the cloying sweetness of say, PX. Thank god! A charming, classy malt. Oh, and the first whisky ever to include the stunning black-naped oriole (for those wondering what it is) on its label! *55%. 887 bottles.*

Nantou Distillery Omar Cask Strength Plum Liqueur Barrel Finished bott 28 Sept 17 db **(93) n23 t23.5 f23 b23.5** Another new flavour profile kindly brought to me by Nantou Distillery. And another that is absolutely impossible not to like. *53%. 795 bottles.*

Nantou Distillery Omar Cask Strength Sherry Cask cask no. 21130120, dist Jun 13, bott 1 Mar 18 db **(87.5) n22 t22.5 f22 b21** A good clean sherry cask – entirely sulphur free – but the balance between the oak and grape isn't quite there yet as the fruit is far too pugnacious. Still, the spiced-up delivery is a delight and the intensity of grape something to grapple with. *59%. sc. 246 bottles.*

Nantou Distillery Omar Cask Strength Sherry Cask cask no. 21130121 **(91.5) n23 t23 f22.5 b23** Not a single off note to be had. Beautifully distilled and matured, this is a malt with many years life left in it...one to lay down and forget about for two or three years...Or you can bottle now for a very fresh and clean (if underdeveloped) sherry bottling. *59.3%*

Nantou Distillery Omar Single Malt Whisky PX Solera Sherry Cask cask no. 22160006, dist Jun 08, bott Nov 18 db **(84) n22 t22 f20 b20** First things thirst. No sulphur: hurrah! The not such great news: the single malt whisky which was filled into this PX cask has vanished without trace. It will probably take archaeologists and sonar equipment to find. And this is the problem with PX, it is so all-consuming that if you are not careful you're left with massive grape. But not a single hint of an outline of the whisky itself. *52.1%. sc. 251 bottles.*

Nantou Distillery Omar Cask Strength Black Queen Wine Barrel Finished bott 29 Sept 17 db **(91) n23 t23.5 f22 b23** The sheer redness of this whisky means that you stare at it in near disbelief for a while before you even get round to tasting it. But when you do, you are well rewarded. Another very different whisky – and delicious, too! *56%. 863 bottles.*

MISCELLANEOUS

Sir John Moore Blended Whisky bott code: L-1805 **(71) n17 t19 f17 b18** It is as though their Galacian water source comes directly from the Pump Room at Bath. Or, more likely, it's the sherry butts at play. *40%. Sansutex Alimentacion. Scotch blended with Galacian water.*

Sir John Moore Blended Whisky Malta bott code: L-1812 **(73) n18 t20 f17 b18** Riddled with sulphur. Ironic when you think about it.... *40%. Sansutex Alimentacion. Scotch blended with Galacian water*

Sir John Moore Blended Whisky Malta 10 Años bott code: L-1814 **(87.5) n21.5 t22.5 f21.5 b22** Well, after the last two bottlings I was fearing the worst. But no sulphur here and instead we have an amazingly salty malt, especially on the nose, which offers up a sweet and juicy light fruitiness on the palate. The finish, like the nose, has a certain peculiarity, but when hitting the heights the sugar-tannin combination works attractively. *40%. Sansutex Alimentacion. Scotch blended with Galacian water.*

CROSS-COUNTRY VATTED WHISKIES

All Seasons Connisseur's Collection Reserve Whisky batch no. 092, mfg. date JUL-19 **(87)** n21 t22 f22 b22 Charmingly soft. Relaxed on both nose and delivery, it is happy to wallow in a toffee-rich sweetness. Sensual, not without weight and even the mildest smokiness and wraps up with a disarming degree of spice. *42.8%.*

Amrut Amalgam Malt Whisky db **(86.5)** n22 t22.5 f20 b22 Bright and juicy, the youthfulness of this malt is masked somewhat by the not inconsiderable amount of peat flowing through this. While the finish may be a bit bitter and out of sorts, the nose, delivery and early follow through have no shortage of charm. *42.8%.*

Amrut Amalgam Peated Malt Whisky db **(81)** n20 t21 f20 b20 Not remotely in the same class as their Amalgam Malt which, ironically, shews how to incorporate peat into a whisky with far greater elegance. This is an untidy malt, with harmony at a premium. Both the nose and finish are a bit on the dirty side while the delivery struggles to make sense of the apparently competing rather than unifying malts. *42.8%.*

High West Whiskey Campfire batch no. 19K12 **(91)** n23.5 t22 f22.5 b23 This style of whisky, which I used to make as a party trick for my friends (and my now ex-wife in particular, and using single malt Scotch rather than blend) some 30 years ago, has a horrible habit of going wrong if you get the proportions off balance. Here it is not always quite where it wants to be, but delighted to say that eventually harmony is reached. All the elements are present and correct (if not in ideal proportions) and crank up the complexity levels….as they should. Ultimately, lovely stuff. *46% (92 proof). nc ncf. Made with straight rye whiskey, straight bourbon whiskey & blended malt Scotch whisky.*

The Lakes Distillery The One Port Cask Finished finished in first-fill Tawny Port hogsheads, bott code: L 30 04 19 **(84.5)** n22.5 t22 f19 b21 A better effort than their signature blend. But again fails ultimately because of the unwieldly, off-key finale. The nose perhaps yields a little too much to youth, but gets away with it thanks to the gristy sugars and fruits combining to make a beautifully fresh combination, though there is a weakness which may threaten later on. Likewise, the delivery is salivating, fat, malty and chewy…but tempered with a grumbling furriness at the midpoint. And this furriness goes slightly out of control at the dry finale. So much here to enjoy for sure, but… I have no idea if this is blended by an individual new to whisky or by an amateur but enthusiastic committee. Either way, for a fledgling distillery, they have to learn how important a finish is to a whisky and the amount of attention that has to be paid to it….and the quality of the casks…. Which, again, hasn't happened here. Like the Signature Blend, a naïve and ill-disciplined malt, though the early stages are just about worth the later pain, for this does at least have a delightful moment or two early on. Worth trying, though for the early moments only…. *46.6%. The Lakes (English) single malt blended with Scotch grain and malt. nc ncf.*

The Lakes Distillery The One Signature Blend bott code: L 04 09 19 **(83.5)** n22.5 t23 f18 b20 Love the marriage between the gentle phenols and natural caramels which gives the unusual aspect of the tannins outranking the peat, certainly so far as the delivery is concerned. But for all its excellent flavour development here the finish is hugely disappointing with a drying, bittering furry off-note which lets the side down. *46.6%. The Lakes (English) single malt blended with Scotch grain and malt. nc ncf.*

Lucifer's Gold bott code: L8257 **(85.5)** n22 t22 f20.5 b21 A thin but pleasant blend which starts at a gallop on the palate but soon flags and bitters out slightly. Still, a delightful mouthfeel early on and the odd kick and sparkle for entertainment. *40%. A blend of bourbon and three year old grain Scotch whisky. Charter Brands.*

Mister Sam Tribute Whiskey bott code: L19011331914E db **(94.5)** n24 t23.5 t23.5 b24 Big, brash…absolutely love it! What a fantastic tribute to the great whiskies of North America. I was going to say this is without parallel…but then I remembered the 49th one…*66.9% (133.8 Proof).*

The One British Blended Whisky Sherry Expression finished in Spanish sherry casks, bott code: L 01 10 18 **(94)** n22.5 t23.5 f24 b24 Can't be any backstop agreement here as things are working really well between the UK, Ireland and mainland Europe with its sherry influence. Shewing all the elegance and refinement of a Jacob Rees-Mogg this, surely, should be known as the Boris Blend… *46.6%. nc ncf. 5,500 bottles.*

That Boutique-y Whisky Company World Whisky Blend (68) n18 t18 f16 b16 Maybe it was the juniper on the nose or the grapefruit at the midpoint. But as a whisky, if that is what this indeed is, I'm sorry to say is just awful. *41.6%.*

Star Walker Ultra Premium Blended Whisky Old Cask Collection batch no. 001, mfg. date AUG.19 **(85.5)** n22 t21.5 f20.5 b21.5 A satin-lined blend offering a sleek, sweet delivery. The balance is disturbed, though, by a slightly bitter intrusion. *42.8%.*

Slàinte

This, as we all know, has been an amazingly testing time for the Whiskey Bible. And here we are, with the 19th edition. So, rather than thanking people individually by name as is normally the case, I'd like to, instead, use this platform to personally thank the countless number of people, from my battle-fatigued staff and family, to my wider circle of intimate friends, to myriad individuals in whisky companies across the globe and an improbable number of readers and general whisky lovers who have sent their messages of love and support (and whisky!) to me. And asked me never to lose my sense of humour or purpose. To you all, I can assure you I have lost neither. My work continues.

Nor will I ever forget the humbling and touching warmth of you all that has been the constant rising sun set against the darkness of the worst of human nature. I am forever in your debt.

Thank you.

Looking to Book Jim Murray?

Jim Murray hosts a wide range of private, corporate and training events around the globe.

To speak to us about booking Jim Murray for your event, please contact:

info@whiskybible.com

Tel: *+44 117 317 9777*